Seventh Canadian Edition

ACCOUNTING:
The Basis for Business Decisions

Volume 3

Managerial Accounting

8 A-2	(a) Estimated uncollectible accounts, $38,880	11-4	(b) Interest expense on Western Bank note, $3,200
8 A-3	(a) Estimated uncollectible accounts, $11,540	11-5	(b) Interest expense on National Bank note, $4,704
8 A-4	(b) Total estimated uncollectible accounts, $52,500	11-6	(c) Total current liabilities, $337,186.50
8 A-5	(a) Feb. 2, cash collected from note, $42,653	11-7	(c) Unpaid balance, $8,331
8 A-6	(c) Total current assets, $373,195	11-8	(c) Jan. 1, 1997, unpaid balance, $539,370
8 A-7	(c) One-year interest charge originally included in face amount, $25,500	11-9	(b) Total payroll cost, $27,538
		11-10	(b) (4) Employer's total payroll costs, $251,854
8 B-1	(a) (2) Number of days' sales uncollected, Advantec, 81	11-11	(c) Total payroll cost, $15,089
8 B-2	(a) Estimated uncollectible accounts, $27,180	12-1	No key figure
8 B-3	(b) Net accounts receivable, Jan. 31, $461,280	12-2	No key figure
8 B-4	(a) Estimated uncollectible accounts, $6,740	12-3	No key figure
8 B-5	(a) Feb. 2, cash collected from note, $30,688	12-4	No key figure
8 B-6	(c) Total current assets, $741,232	12-5	No key figure
8 B-7	(c) One-year interest charge originally included in face amount, $13,200	12-6	(a) Profit under percentage-of-completion, 1995, $3,000,000
		12-7	(a) (1) Gross profit, $184,000
9-1	No key figure	12-8	No key figure
9-2	(a) May 31 inventory, $280	12-9	No key figure
9-3	(a) Sept. 30 inventory balance, $3,450		
9-4	(b) (4) Jan. 15 LIFO inventory, $18,500	13 A-1	(b) Total assets, $220,800
9-5	(a) (2) FIFO cost of goods sold, $18,100	13 A-2	(a) Net income, $54,000; (c) total assets, $217,720
9-6	(a) (3) LIFO cost of goods sold, $18,700	13 A-3	(a) (4) Pascal's share, $28,000
9-7	(a) (1) Average cost shrinkage loss, $567	13 A-4	(c) Stein's share, $26,100
9-8	(a) (2) LIFO cost of goods sold, $303,480	13 A-5	(c) Bonus to Ritter, $30,000
9-9	(b) (3) LIFO cost of goods sold, $7,420	13 A-6	(c) Bonus to Kim, $60,000
9-10	(a) Gross profit rate, 1995, 43%	13 A-7	(a) Cash to Nix, $11,600
9-11	(b) (3) Gross profit, $264,144		
9-12	(b) (1) Turnover rate, FIFO, 2.4 times	13 B-1	(b) Total assets, $277,800
		13 B-2	(a) Net income, $54,500; (c) total assets, $175,500
10 A-1	(c) Total cost of equipment, $91,200	13 B-3	(a) (2) Martin's share, $58,000
10 A-2	Depreciation for 1997, (b) $36,000; (c) $33,750	13 B-4	(a) Conrad's share, $102,600
10 A-3	(a) Depreciation for 1998, (3) $15,000	13 B-5	(c) Bonus to Lee, $70,000
10 A-4	(c) Depreciation expense for 1996, $134,175	13 B-6	(d) Debit to Spence, Capital, $22,500
10 A-5	Gain on disposal of moving van, $4,000	13 B-7	(b) Cash payment by Merit, $18,000
10 A-6	No key figure		
10 A-7	No key figure	14 A-1	(b) Dec. 31, 1996, retained earnings, $1,937,000
10 A-8	(b) (1) Book value, $17,000	14 A-2	(a) Total shareholders' equity, $15,370,000
		14 A-3	Total shareholders' equity, $2,063,000
10 B-1	(a) Total cost of equipment, $220,720	14 A-4	(b) Total shareholders' equity, $1,150,960
10 B-2	Depreciation for 1997, (b) $65,600; (c) $64,800	14 A-5	(b) Total assets, $1,512,100
10 B-3	Depreciation for 1995, (b) $15,000	14 A-6	(e) Total contributed capital, $11,800,000
10 B-4	(a) Accumulated depreciation: Machine C, $36,000		
10 B-5	Gain on disposal of truck, $1,000	14 B-1	(b) Dec. 31, 1996, retained earnings, $1,490,000
10 B-6	No key figure	14 B-2	(a) Total shareholders' equity, $3,405,000
10 B-7	No key figure	14 B-3	Total shareholders' equity, $2,112,000
10 B-8	(b) (1) Book value, $6,800	14 B-4	(d) Total shareholders' equity, $890,200
		14 B-5	(b) Total assets, $1,352,950
CP-3	(a) Total assets: Alpine, $494,400; Nordic, $496,200; (b) revised net income: Alpine, $225,000	14 B-6	(f) Total contributed capital, $9,660,000
		15 A-1	(a) Income before extraordinary items, $13,620,000
11-1	No key figure	15 A-2	(a) Cumulative effect, $91,000
11-2	No key figure		
11-3	(a) Total current liabilities, $375,403		

(continued on inside back cover)

EX LIBRIS

Name

Seventh Canadian Edition

ACCOUNTING:
The Basis for Business Decisions

Volume 3

Managerial Accounting

ROBERT F. MEIGS, D.B.A.
San Diego State University

WALTER B. MEIGS, Ph.D., C.P.A.
University of Southern California

WAI P. LAM, Ph.D., F.C.A.
University of Windsor

McGraw-Hill Ryerson Limited

Toronto Montreal New York Auckland Bogotá
Caracas Lisbon London Madrid Mexico Milan
New Delhi Paris San Juan Singapore Sydney Tokyo

ACCOUNTING: THE BASIS FOR BUSINESS DECISIONS
Seventh Canadian Edition
Volume 3 / Managerial Accounting

ISBN: 0-07-551659-4

1 2 3 4 5 6 7 8 9 0 BBM 4 3 2 1 0 9 8 7 6 5

Printed and bound in Canada by BBM

Sponsoring Editor: Kelly Smyth

Production Editor: Gail Marsden

Cover Design: Dianna Little

Cover Photograph: © G. K. and Vikki Hart/The Image Bank

Canadian Cataloguing in Publication Data

Meigs, Robert F.
    Accounting: the basis for business decisions

7th Canadian ed.
Includes index.
Contents: v. 1–2. Financial accounting—v. 3.
Managerial accounting.
ISBN 0-07-551660-8 (v. 1) ISBN 0-07-551795-7 (v. 2)
ISBN 0-07-551659-4 (v. 3)

1. Accounting. I. Meigs, Walter B., date–   .
II. Lam, Wai P., date–   .   III. Title.

HF5635.M45   1994   657′.044   C94-932029-3

Contents

Preface

These texts, Volumes 1, 2, and 3, are an introduction to the field of accounting and to the use of accounting information as a basis for business decisions. They are intended for use in the first university-level accounting course, which usually spans two semesters.

OUR GOALS IN THIS SEVENTH CANADIAN EDITION

We have tried to accomplish many things in this edition. Among our most important goals have been to:

1. Provide students with a better understanding of the environment in which accounting information is developed and used.
2. Shift emphasis from the preparation of accounting information to its interpretation and use.
3. Retain a course structure that meets the specific content requirements of most universities and colleges.

Providing Students with a Better Background

If students are to appreciate the nature of accounting, they first should have a basic understanding of the business environment. We find, however, that many introductory students lack this background. Often the introductory accounting course is also the students' first course in the business curriculum.

We give increased attention to explaining business practices before discussing accounting issues. Our focus is upon *current* business and accounting practices, not those of the past. For example, virtually every business with external reporting obligations now uses a perpetual inventory system. Yet many accounting textbooks continue to emphasize periodic systems. We emphasize *perpetual* inventory systems.

For purposes of illustration, textbooks traditionally assume the use of simple, manually maintained accounting records. Such records do not meet the needs of most modern businesses. We, too, find it convenient to use simple accounting records as the basis for many illustrations. However, we also explain how the information is processed in a computer-based environment.

Attention is given throughout the text to the role of *professional judgment* in both the development and interpretation of accounting information. We explain in some depth professional ethics for accountants in the field of public and private accounting. We also discuss audits, reviews, and the independent auditors' potential liability to the users of financial statements. Furthermore, we delineate the development and importance of international accounting standards in today's global business environment.

Shifting to a "User Orientation"

Today, relatively few introductory students will become professional preparers of accounting information. All, however, will become life-long information **users.** For this reason, we have shifted our emphasis significantly from the preparation of accounting information to its interpretation and use.

This shift in emphasis affects the text in several ways. For example, we have added new assignment material designed specifically to develop students' analytical, decision-making, and communication skills. Accordingly, a substantial number of stimulating and challenging problems/cases requiring the application of these critical skills have been incorporated in the final section of the assignment material entitled "Analytical and Decision Problems and Cases."

A user-oriented approach also affects topical content and emphasis. Topics relevant to basic business decisions now are addressed, even if these topics traditionally have been deferred to later accounting courses. Examples of such topics include accounting for postretirement costs, audits and reviews, "window dressing," and many of the disclosures that accompany financial statements.

Throughout the text, attention is given to analytical ratios and financial relationships. The chapter on analysis of financial statements now serves primarily as a review.

Increased attention also is given to the use of accounting information **by management.** No longer is this topic addressed only in a group of "managerial" chapters; it now is integrated throughout the text.

Some "traditional" accounting topics relate primarily to the preparation of accounting information and are of little significance to the information user. Examples include reversing entries, manual special journals, and alternative methods of recording accruals and deferrals. In our user-oriented approach, such topics are given less emphasis. Often they are presented in Supplemental Topic sections.

Preserving a Proven Course Structure

Some universities are experimenting with radically different approaches to the introductory accounting course. We have **not** embarked upon such a path. We have great respect for the existing structure of the introductory course, which has evolved from decades of experience and research. We recognize that many students transfer credit for this course from one institution to another. Some standardization of the curriculum is therefore essential.

We regard our changes in this seventh Canadian edition as **evolutionary,** not **revolutionary.** Faculty acquainted with our past editions will find much that is familiar.

ELEMENTS OF THE TEXTBOOK

This seventh Canadian edition introduces many new features and retains all of the time-honoured materials. Such a well-balanced blending makes this text uniquely suitable for today's business environment.

Chapter Introductions and Learning Objectives

Each chapter begins with a brief overview and a set of basic learning objectives. These learning objectives then are integrated with the text discussions.

Cases in Point

A distinctive feature of past editions has been the use of short **Cases in Point,** which are based upon actual events. Many new Cases in Point have been created for this edition as part of our increased focus on the contemporary business environment.

Supplemental Topics and Appendixes

A new feature in the structure of this edition is the inclusion of short **Supplemental Topic** sections at the end of several chapters. These Supplemental Topics are closely related to the content of the chapters in which they appear.

Students always should read the Supplemental Topic sections, as these discussions will enhance their overall understanding of the chapter. Instructors, however, may decide whether these topics are of sufficient general interest for inclusion in class discussions, homework assignments, and examinations. [Assignment material relating to Supplemental Topics are preceded by an asterisk (*).]

Chapter Reviews

Each chapter is followed by such learning aids as a **Glossary of Key Terms** and, in most chapters, a **Demonstration Problem** with a complete solution.

Assignment Material

One of the distinctive features of this seventh Canadian edition is the increase in the quantity and variety of the assignment material. Increased emphasis is placed upon the development of students' analytical abilities, decision-making skills, and communication skills. Much of the new assignment material is based upon the operations of well-known companies.

Six categories of assignments accompany the text. These are (1) Discussion Questions, (2) Multiple Choice Questions, (3) Exercises, (4) Problems, (5) Analytical and Decision Problems and Cases, and (6) Comprehensive Problems.

Discussion Questions are short and usually call for expository answers. In addition to developing writing and communication skills, these questions explore students' conceptual understanding of accounting.

Multiple Choice Questions focus on many of the most important concepts in the chapter. These questions are very useful in testing students' understanding of key aspects of the chapter material. They are both stimulating and challenging.

Exercises are short assignments, usually focusing upon a single concept. We have greatly increased the number and the variety of Exercises. By enabling instructors to cover basic concepts quickly, we hope to allow more time for discussing in class such assignments as our Analytical and Decision Problems and Cases.

Problems are longer than the Exercises and address several concepts at one time. Most chapters contain both an *A* and *B* problem series, each providing thorough coverage of the chapter. A few chapters contain a single—but longer—series of problems. The single series accommodates a greater variety of assignments.

Analytical and Decision Problems and Cases emphasize the development of analytical, decision-making, and communication skills. They also provide a wealth of assignment material well suited to in-class discussions.

To encourage the use of these assignments, we have developed a large number of Analytical and Decision Problems and Cases that cover a wide range of time requirements and difficulty levels. Many of our Exercises and Problems also call for analysis and the use of judgment.

We consider our six *Comprehensive Problems* to be among the most useful assignments in the text. Each of these problems ties together concepts presented over a span of chapters. Two of the Comprehensive Problems are similar in scope to a "practice set," and another involves the analysis of an actual annual report.

A *Checklist of Key Figures* for Problems and Comprehensive Problems appears on the front and back inside covers of the text. The purpose of these check figures is to aid students in verifying their problem solutions and in discovering their own errors.

The Flexibility of PRIMIS

The U.S. text, *Accounting: The Basis for Business Decisions,* Ninth Edition, by Meigs and Meigs, and selected supplementary materials are available on the McGraw-Hill/Primis custom publishing database. Any materials on the database can be configured and created to your specifications. The Primis database includes several McGraw-Hill accounting texts, selected Harvard business cases, and articles from various journals.

NEW AND EXTENSIVELY REVISED CHAPTERS

Many chapters in this seventh Canadian edition have been revised significantly. Almost every chapter contains greater emphasis upon the use of accounting information and more assignment material than ever before. Among the changes in topical content that will be noticed most readily are:

Chapter 1, "Accounting: The Language of Business," has been rewritten to provide a more comprehensive introduction to the process of financial reporting. We have added discussions of such topics as reporting requirements of publicly owned companies, auditing, and professional ethics. Also included is a new discussion of the nature and sources of generally accepted accounting principles. Moreover, the importance of a background in accounting as a "stepping stone" to positions in top management is illustrated. Career opportunities in accounting are discussed in a Supplemental Topic section at the end of the chapter.

In *Chapter 4,* we have revised the format of the work sheet. Our goal is to focus upon the *accounting processes* illustrated within the work sheet, not to present the document itself as a component of the accounting cycle.

Chapter 5, now entitled "Accounting for Merchandising Activities; Classified Financial Statements," exemplifies many of the changes in this edition. The opening pages of this chapter illustrate our concerted effort to explain business practices before discussing the accounting treatments accorded those practices.

In keeping with contemporary business practices, this chapter now emphasizes *perpetual inventory systems*—the type of system used in every large business organization. Periodic systems still receive thorough coverage; in fact, we have added an explanation of a "shortcut" periodic system that is used by many small businesses. Also, additional coverage on periodic inventory system is presented in a Supplemental Topic section at the end of the chapter.

The final portion of Chapter 5, "Introduction to Classified Financial Statements," typifies our increased emphasis upon the *use* of accounting information.

Chapter 6, "Accounting Systems, Internal Control, and Audits," emphasizes the capabilities of computer-based accounting systems, rather than the use of manual special journals. Among the new features of this chapter are examples of how data bases tailor information to meet the needs of different decision makers. New elements of this chapter also include discussions of financial and operational audits, and the related topics of employee fraud and management fraud. However, the coverage of manual special journals is not neglected; it is presented in a Supplemental Topic section at the end of the chapter.

Chapter 8, "Accounts Receivable and Notes Receivable," now includes discussions of the goals of credit management, accounts receivable turnover rates, strategies for quickly converting receivables into cash, and disclosure of concentrations of credit risk. These additions illustrate our increased emphasis on the use of accounting information by management, as well as by persons outside of the business organization.

Our coverage of notes receivable with interest included in the face amount has been moved to a Supplemental Topic section, as such notes are held primarily by financial institutions.

Chapter 9, "Inventories and the Cost of Goods Sold," has been revised extensively in light of our emphasis upon perpetual inventory systems. Also included are discussions of the just-in-time concept, inventory turnover rates, and the objectives of efficient inventory management.

Chapter 10, dealing with capital assets such as plant and equipment, includes extensively revised coverage of trade-ins.

Our coverage of liabilities, contained in **Chapters 11** and **16,** has been revised extensively. **Chapter 11** now focuses upon the types of liabilities **common to most business entities,** including long-term instalment debt. **Chapter 16,** in contrast, addresses those types of liabilities found primarily in the financial statements of large, publicly owned corporations. This format completes our coverage of accounting for the sole proprietorship type of unincorporated businesses in the first semester. It also heightens students' awareness of the differences in the business environments of small businesses and of large corporations.

Our coverage of liabilities also has been expanded in terms of topical content. Chapter 11 now includes long-term instalment debt, disclosure requirements relating to long-term debts, and increased emphasis on contingent losses and commitments. Extensively revised coverage of payroll liabilities now appears as a Supplemental Topic.

In Chapter 16, new or expanded coverage is given to topics that, because of their materiality, are relevant to the users of corporate financial statements. Examples include deferred income taxes and an employer's obligation for postretirement benefits.

Chapter 12, "Accounting Concepts, Professional Judgment, and Ethical Conduct," is new to this edition. One objective of this chapter is to review at one time many of the generally accepted accounting principles discussed throughout the text. Another objective is to look in some depth at key elements of a code of professional ethics.

Chapter 18, "Income Taxes and Business Decisions," has been substantially updated to include the most recent changes in tax legislation.

Chapter 20, "Analysis and Interpretation of Financial Statements," has been revised to reflect our emphasis of this topic throughout the textbook.

Chapter 22, "Cost Accounting Systems," contains new coverage of activity-based costing, just-in-time inventory systems, and total quality management.

SUPPLEMENTARY MATERIALS

This text is accompanied by a large number of supplementary learning and teaching aids. These supplements are listed below. A complete description of these materials is contained in the **Instructor's Guide.** If you would like information and costs on the supplemental materials, please contact your local McGraw-Hill Ryerson representative. We value both your interest and our supplements.

For the Student:

Study Guide to accompany Volume 1 by Meigs, Meigs, Meigs, and Lam
Study Guide to accompany Volume 2 and Volume 3 by Meigs, Meigs, Meigs, and Lam
Accounting Work Sheets, Chapters 1–12 by Meigs, Meigs, and Lam
Accounting Work Sheets, Chapters 13–26 by Meigs, Meigs, and Lam
Blank Forms for Problems and Cases

Accounting Information Manager: A General Ledger Program by John W. Wanlass

Accounting Information Manager: A Spreadsheet Program by John W. Wanlass

MicroGuide Computerized Accounting Tutorial by Jean Gutmann

Manual Simulations and Applications:

    The Next Dimension: An Accounting Cycle Application by Mary A. Meigs and Wai P. Lam

    Remington Restaurant Supply: An Accounting Cycle Application

    Valley Building Materials Inc.; A Corporate Accounting Cycle Application

    Adders 'n Keyes, 2/e by Brenda Mallouk

    Deluxe Spa Products Incorporated: Using Management Accounting for Costing and Decision Making by Brenda Mallouk and Catherine Seguin

    Premium Foods Corporation: A Financial Statement Analysis Case by Christie W. Johnson

    Facts-by-FAX: An Accounting Cycle Application

    Color Copy Co.: An Accounting Cycle Application

    Echo Paint Co.: A Small Business Application with Forms by Richard A. Wright

    Executive Woodcraft: A Managerial Accounting Application by Ronald W. Hilton

    Printer Recharge, Inc.: A Corporate Practice Set by Phillip Ricci and Wanda G. Spruill

Computer-Based Simulations and Applications:

    CȲMA General Ledger Package: Shadow Mountain Hotel

    CȲMA General Ledger Package: Authenticity and Facts-by-FAX

    Echo Paint Co.: A Small Business Application with Forms, by Richard A. Wright

    Remington Restaurant Supply: A Computerized Accounting Cycle Application

    Electronic Spreadsheet Application to Accompany the Premium Foods Corporation Financial Statement Analysis Case by Christie W. Johnson

For the Instructor:

Canadian:

Instructor's Manual

Solutions Manual

Overhead Transparencies

Test Bank (Manual and Computerized Versions)

Solutions to accompany The Next Dimension

Solutions to accompany Deluxe Spa Products Incorporated

American:

Lecture Video Series

Case Study Videos for Analysis and Critical Thinking

Instructor's Manual/Critical Thinking Guide to Accompany Case Study Videotapes by Mark S. Bettner

Electronic Classroom Presentations by Glenn Owen

Interactive Solutions Software
Teaching Transparencies
Report Card: Electronic Grading Software
Financial Statement Analysis Problem Set and Software
Solutions to Applications

Acknowledgements

This seventh Canadian edition has benefited from the perceptive inputs of the instructors and students who used the preceding edition. To those instructors and students, I express my sincere appreciation.

I am especially indebted to those reviewers who provided critical and constructive suggestions and to those who bestowed me with valuable advice. The suggestions and advice contributed greatly to the improvement in the text, supplementary, and assignment materials. Accordingly, I wish to thank all of the following individuals:

Mortimer Davis, Vanier College
Bruce W. Densmore, Mount Saint Vincent University
Randy Dickson, Red Deer College
Wendy Doyle, Mount Saint Vincent University
Gary Earle, Loyalist College
Adrian Feigelsohn, Royal Trust
Leo Gallant, St. Francis Xavier University
Peter Henderson, Douglas College
Tilly Jensen, Northern Alberta Institute of Technology
Ross Johnston, University of Windsor
Chris Kellman, Northwest College
Loris Macor, Coopers & Lybrand
Jim Macri, Ernst & Young
John Mitchell, Sault College
R. C. (Bob) Nichols, British Columbia Institute of Technology
Chris O'Neill, Algonquin College
Bill Ralston, Northwest College
Catherine Seguin, University of Toronto
Glen Sikorski, Niagara College
Ralph Sweet, Durham College

I greatly appreciate the expert attention, advice and assistance given to the seventh Canadian edition by the staff of McGraw-Hill Ryerson, especially Kelly Smyth, Susan Calvert, and Betty Tustin. Also, the excellent editing by Gail Marsden is much appreciated. My special thanks go to Sandy Berlasty for her assistance in typing part of the manuscript.

Finally, heartfelt appreciation is due to my family members—Jean, Angela, Lambert, and Gloria. Their patience and understanding have made this important academic endeavour more enjoyable. As well, they have done an outstanding job in typing, editing, and proofreading the manuscript of the text, solutions, and supplements.

Wai P. Lam

7 Managerial Accounting: Cost Accounting Systems

*T*he next two chapters provide the basic foundation for our study of managerial accounting. In these chapters, we will show how accounting systems can measure the cost of manufacturing specific products and of performing specific services.

Part 7 concludes with a Comprehensive Problem providing a review of both process and job order cost accounting systems.

Introduction to Managerial Accounting; Accounting for Manufacturing Operations

Chapter 21 is the first of six chapters emphasizing the specialized use of accounting information by managers. In the opening pages, we contrast managerial accounting with financial accounting. The major purpose of this chapter, however, is to introduce accounting concepts relating to manufacturing activities. We explain the nature of manufacturing costs, with emphasis upon the idea that these are "product costs" not "period costs." Next, we illustrate the "flow" of manufacturing costs through perpetual inventory records. A distinction is drawn between direct and indirect manufacturing costs, and the use of overhead application rates is explained and illustrated. Finally, we illustrate the schedule of cost of finished goods manufactured, which summarizes the relationships between manufacturing costs and completed units of product.

Learning Objectives

After studying this chapter you should be able to:

1 *Distinguish between the fields of managerial accounting and financial accounting.*

2 *Describe the three basic types of manufacturing cost.*

3 *Distinguish between product costs and period costs and explain how product costs are offset against revenue.*

4 *Describe how manufacturing costs "flow" through perpetual inventory accounts.*

5 *Distinguish between direct and indirect manufacturing costs.*

6 *Explain the purpose of overhead application rates and the importance of basing these rates upon significant "cost drivers."*

7 *Prepare a schedule of the cost of finished goods manufactured.*

INTRODUCTION TO MANAGERIAL ACCOUNTING

OBJECTIVE 1 Distinguish between the fields of managerial accounting and financial accounting.

In preceding chapters we have emphasized the topic of financial accounting. The term *financial accounting* refers to the preparation and use of accounting information describing the financial position and operating results of a business entity. Financial accounting serves as the basis for the preparation of both financial statements and income tax returns. Because financial statements are used primarily by outsiders, such as creditors, shareholders, and potential investors, the information in these statements is presented in conformity with *generally accepted accounting principles.* Although income tax rules differ somewhat from generally accepted accounting principles, there are many similarities between these two sets of reporting standards.

Beginning with this chapter, we shall shift our emphasis toward the field of managerial accounting. *Managerial accounting* (or management accounting) involves the preparation and use of accounting information designed to assist managers in planning and controlling the operations of the business, and in decision making. In short, managerial accounting information is designed to meet the needs of *insiders,* rather than decision makers *outside* the business entity.

Since managerial accounting reports are used exclusively by management, their content is *not* governed by generally accepted accounting principles or income tax rules. Rather, managerial accounting reports should contain whatever information *best suits the needs of the decision maker.* The greatest challenge to managerial accountants is providing managers with the information that is most relevant to a particular business decision.

The diagram on the following page compares the basic characteristics of financial and managerial accounting. Notice that both types of accounting information are developed within the same accounting system. Thus, the accounting system of a business should be able to provide the special types of information needed by management, as well as to meet the company's financial reporting requirements.

Interdisciplinary Nature of Managerial Accounting

In meeting the information needs of management, managerial accountants often must obtain estimates and data from experts in fields other than accounting. For example, many managerial accounting reports are forecasts of future operating results. Forecasting the sales of a multinational corporation, however, may involve marketing research, assumptions about future economic conditions, an understanding of international trade agreements, and familiarity with numerous foreign cultures. Managerial accountants do not need personal expertise in each of these areas, but they must have a broad understanding of the company's business environment.

To encourage a professional level of training and competence for managerial accountants, the provincial societies of Certified Management Accountants offer a program leading to the CMA designation. To become a *CMA,* an individual must meet educational and experience requirements, and also pass a rigorous set of examinations, including the national final examination.

THE ACCOUNTING SYSTEM

FINANCIAL ACCOUNTING

Purpose

To provide a wide variety of decision makers with useful information about the financial position and operating results of a business entity.

Types of Reports

Financial statements, income tax returns, and special reports, such as loan applications and reports to regulatory authorities.

Standards for Presentation

In financial statements, generally accepted accounting principles. In income tax returns, tax regulations.

Reporting Entity

Usually the company viewed as a whole.

Time Periods Covered

Usually a year, quarter, or month. Most reports focus upon completed periods. Emphasis is placed on the current (latest) period, with prior periods often shown for comparison.

MANAGERIAL ACCOUNTING

Purpose

To provide managers with information useful in planning and controlling business operations, and in making managerial decisions.

Types of Reports

Many different types of reports, depending upon the nature of the business and the specific information needs of management.

Standards for Presentation

No specific rules; whatever information is most relevant to the needs of management.

Reporting Entity

Usually a subdivision of the business, such as a department, a product line, or a type of activity.

Time Periods Covered

Any period: year, quarter, month, week, day, even a work shift. Some reports are historical in nature; others focus on estimates of results expected in future periods.

Users of the Information

Outsiders as well as managers. For financial statements, these outsiders include shareholders, creditors, prospective investors, tax and regulatory authorities, and the general public. Income tax returns normally go only to tax authorities.

Users of the Information

Management (different reports to different managers). Managerial accounting reports usually are not distributed to outsiders.

Our Approach to Managerial Accounting

In this introductory textbook, we divide our discussion of managerial accounting into three broad categories: (1) *cost accounting* (with an emphasis on determining the cost of manufactured products), (2) the use of accounting information in *planning and controlling* business operations, and (3) *tailoring accounting information* for use in specific managerial decisions. These closely related topics provide an overview of the nature and use of managerial accounting information. Many topics, however, remain to be explored; the study of managerial accounting may be continued throughout a professional career.

Cost Accounting   In order to plan and control the activities of a business, management must first have information about the costs involved in performing different business operations. This information about costs will help management in determining whether specific activities are profitable and whether the various departments within the business are operating efficiently. The accounting concepts and practices for measuring the cost of performing different business activities and of manufacturing various products are called *cost accounting.*

Let us consider, for example, a company that manufactures several different products. The company's accounting system should provide information about the cost of manufacturing *each product* and the cost of conducting other business activities, such as operating the accounting, human resources, and marketing departments. We will discuss accounting for the costs of manufactured products in the remainder of this chapter and in Chapter 22. Measuring the cost of performing other business activities will be discussed in Chapter 24.

Planning and Control   The term *planning* refers to setting objectives or goals for future performance. Often, these objectives are stated in terms of dollar amounts, such as achieving "net sales of $10 million in the coming year."

Control refers to monitoring the extent to which these planned objectives are being accomplished and to taking corrective action when actual results differ from the plan. In Chapters 23, 24, and 25, we focus upon the use of accounting information in planning and controlling business operations.

Tailoring Information to Specific Decisions   Managerial accounting information often is collected and arranged to assist a particular manager in making a specific business decision. This process is explained and illustrated in Chapter 26.

Overlap of Managerial and Financial Accounting

It is useful to recognize that financial and managerial accounting are *not* two entirely separate disciplines. Financial accounting information is widely used in many managerial decisions. For example, managers daily use information about sales, expenses, and income taxes in many business decisions. However, managers also require additional information, such as revenue and expenses broken down by department or by product line. Thus, much managerial accounting information is actually financial accounting information, rearranged to suit a particular managerial purpose.

As you progress through the remaining chapters, you should encounter many familiar accounting terms and concepts. However, you will also encounter new terms and concepts, as well as new ways of interpreting familiar accounting information.

ACCOUNTING FOR MANUFACTURING OPERATIONS

One area in which managerial and financial accounting overlap is in accounting for manufacturing activities. A merchandising company buys its inventory in a ready-to-sell condition. Therefore, the cost of this merchandise is simply the purchase price. A ***manufacturing*** company, on the other hand, ***produces*** the goods that it sells. In this case, the cost of the merchandise consists of various ***manufacturing costs,*** including the cost of the direct (raw) materials used in the production process, wages earned by factory workers, and all of the other costs of operating a factory.[1]

In a manufacturing company, manufacturing costs are of vital importance both to managerial and financial accountants. Managerial accountants must supply managers with prompt and reliable information about manufacturing costs for use in such decisions as:

- What sales price must we charge for our products to earn a reasonable profit?
- Can we produce a particular type of product at a cost that will enable us to sell it at a competitive price?
- Would it be less expensive for us to buy certain parts used in our products, or to manufacture these parts in our plant?
- Should we install a more highly automated assembly line?

Financial accountants need information about manufacturing costs in order to determine the cost of a manufacturing company's inventories and its cost of goods sold.

Types of Manufacturing Costs

A typical manufacturing company buys direct (raw) materials and, through the efforts of factory workers and the use of machines, converts these materials into finished products. Manufacturing costs may be divided into three broad categories:

OBJECTIVE 2
Describe the
three basic
types of
manufactur-
ing cost.

1 **Direct materials**—the cost of the raw materials and component parts used in the manufacture of the finished products.

2 **Direct labour costs**—wages and other payroll costs relating to employees who work directly on the goods being manufactured, either by hand or with tools.

3 **Manufacturing overhead**—a "catch-all" classification, including all manufacturing costs ***other than*** the costs of direct materials and direct labour. Examples include depreciation on machinery, supervisors' salaries, factory utilities, and equipment repairs.

Manufacturing costs are ***not*** regarded as expenses of the current period; rather they are costs of ***creating inventory.*** For this reason, manufacturing costs are often called ***inventoriable costs,*** or ***product costs.***

Product Costs and Period Costs

The terms ***product costs*** and ***period costs*** are helpful in explaining the difference between manufacturing costs and expenses. ***Product costs*** are

---

[1]   Manufacturing costs are the cost of producing inventory, which is an asset. Therefore, these expenditures are termed ***costs,*** rather than ***expenses.*** Unexpired costs are assets; expired costs are expenses.

OBJECTIVE 3
Distinguish
between
product
costs and
period costs
and explain
how product
costs are off-
set against
revenue.

the costs of purchasing or manufacturing inventory. Thus, until the related goods are sold, product costs **represent inventory,** which is an asset. When the goods are sold, the product costs are deducted from revenue as the cost of goods sold.

Costs that are associated with time periods, rather than with the purchase or manufacture of inventory, are termed **period costs.** Period costs are charged directly to expense accounts on the assumption that the benefits are received in the same period as the cost is incurred. Period costs include all selling expenses, general and administrative expenses, interest expense, and income taxes expense—in short, all the items classified in an income statement as "expense."

The "flow" of product costs and of period costs through financial statements is shown in the following diagram:

Product costs become inventory

Period costs become expense

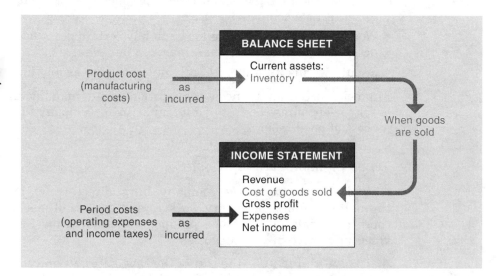

To illustrate this distinction, let us consider two costs that, on the surface, appear quite similar: depreciation on a direct materials warehouse and depreciation on a finished goods warehouse. Depreciation on the direct materials warehouse is a **product cost,** because this cost relates to the manufacturing process. Once the manufacturing process is complete and the goods are available for sale, however, storage costs are viewed as a selling expense. Thus, the depreciation on the finished goods warehouse is a **period cost.**

Product Costs and the Matching Principle The distinction between product costs and period costs may be explained by the **matching principle—** the idea that revenue should be offset by the costs incurred in generating that revenue. To illustrate, consider a real estate developer who starts construction on a tract of 10 homes in 1996. During the year, the developer spends $100,000 on each house ($1 million in total) in direct materials, construction wages, and overhead. At the end of 1996, all 10 houses are complete, but none has yet been sold. How much of the $1 million for construction costs should the developer recognize as expense in 1996?

The answer is **none.** These costs are not related to any revenue earned by the developer in 1996, but they are related to revenue that the developer will earn when the houses are sold. Therefore, at the end of 1996, the $1 million of product costs should appear in the developer's balance sheet as *inventory.* As each house is sold, $100,000 will be deducted from the sales revenue as the cost of goods sold. In this way, the developer's income statements in future periods will reflect properly both the revenue and the cost of each sale.

Inventories of a Manufacturing Business

In the preceding example, the houses all were completed by the end of 1996, so our developer's inventory consisted only of finished goods. Manufacturing companies, however, normally have *three types* of inventories:

1 **Materials inventory**—direct materials on hand and available for use in the manufacturing process.
2 **Work in process inventory**—partially completed goods upon which production activities have been started but not yet completed.
3 **Finished goods inventory**—finished products available for sale to customers.

All three of these inventories are shown in the balance sheet at the lower of cost and market and are classified as current assets. The cost of the materials inventory is based on purchase prices; the costs of the work in process inventory and of the finished goods inventory are based on the manufacturing costs incurred in producing these units.

Manufacturing companies may use either a perpetual or a periodic inventory system. Perpetual systems have many advantages, however, such as providing managers with up-to-date information about the amounts of inventory on hand and the per-unit costs of manufacturing products. For these reasons, virtually all large manufacturing companies use perpetual inventory systems. Also, the flow of manufacturing costs through the inventory accounts and into the cost of goods sold is most easily illustrated in a perpetual inventory system. Therefore, we will assume the use of a perpetual inventory system in our discussion of manufacturing activities.

Flow of Costs Parallels the Physical Flow of Goods

*OBJECTIVE 4
Describe
how manu-
facturing
costs "flow"
through
perpetual
inventory
accounts.*

When a perpetual inventory system is in use, the flow of manufacturing costs through the company's ledger accounts closely parallels the physical flow of goods through the production process. This relationship is illustrated in the diagram on page 1006. The gray shaded boxes in the bottom portion of this diagram represent the *ledger accounts* used by a manufacturing company in accounting for manufacturing costs.

Accounting for Manufacturing Costs: An Illustration

The diagram introduces six ledger accounts used in accounting for manufacturing activities: (1) Materials Inventory, (2) Direct Labour, (3) Manufacturing Overhead, (4) Work in Process Inventory, (5) Finished Goods Inventory, and (6) Cost of Goods Sold.

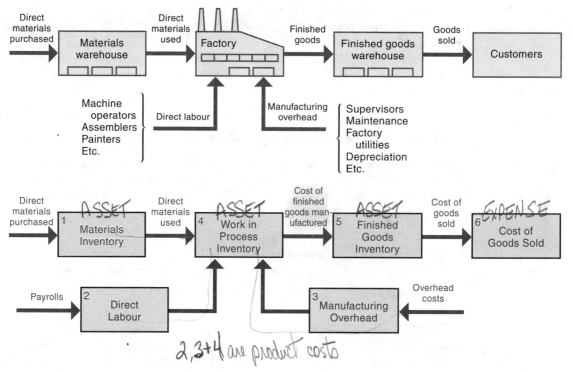

The manner in which manufacturing costs "flow through" these accounts is illustrated on page 1007. The data in this illustration represent the manufacturing costs of Allied Manufacturing Corporation during 1996. (The debit and credit entries appearing in this illustration summarize numerous transactions recorded by Allied throughout the year.)

Our use of colour in this illustration is intended to help you follow the flow of manufacturing costs through the accounts. The beginning balances in the three inventory accounts are shown in black. Manufacturing costs are shown in blue, as are the arrows showing the transfers of these costs from one account to another. Account balances at year-end, which will appear in the company's financial statements, are shown in light blue.

Let us now look more closely at the flow of manufacturing costs through these ledger accounts.

Materials Inventory

The Materials Inventory account is used to record purchases of direct materials and the use of these materials in the manufacturing process. **Direct materials** are those raw materials and component parts that become an integral part of the finished product, and that can be traced conveniently and directly into the quantity of finished goods manufactured. For example, the direct materials used by an automaker include sheet steel, glass, plastic, tires, transmissions, and batteries. The completed automobiles assembled from these components are the automaker's finished goods.

The terms **direct materials** and **finished goods** are defined from the viewpoint of each manufacturing company. For example, Ford Motor company views tires as a direct material; the Goodyear Tire & Rubber company, however, views tires as finished goods.

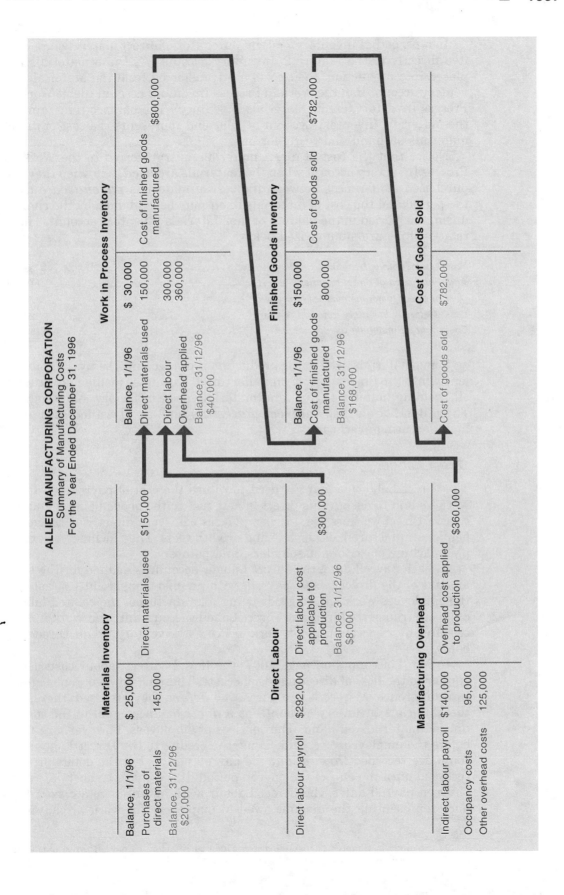

ALLIED MANUFACTURING CORPORATION
Summary of Manufacturing Costs
For the Year Ended December 31, 1996

Materials Inventory

Balance, 1/1/96	$ 25,000	Direct materials used $150,000
Purchases of direct materials	145,000	
Balance, 31/12/96 $20,000		

Work in Process Inventory

Balance, 1/1/96	$ 30,000	Cost of finished goods manufactured $800,000
Direct materials used	150,000	
Direct labour	300,000	
Overhead applied	360,000	
Balance, 31/12/96 $40,000		

Direct Labour

Direct labour payroll	$292,000	Direct labour cost applicable to production $300,000
		Balance, 31/12/96 $8,000

Finished Goods Inventory

Balance, 1/1/96	$150,000	Cost of goods sold $782,000
Cost of finished goods manufactured	800,000	
Balance, 31/12/96 $168,000		

Manufacturing Overhead

Indirect labour payroll	$140,000	Overhead cost applied to production $360,000
Occupancy costs	95,000	
Other overhead costs	125,000	

Cost of Goods Sold

Cost of goods sold	$782,000

In a perpetual inventory system, purchases of direct materials are debited directly to the Materials Inventory account. As these materials are placed into production, their costs are transferred from the Materials Inventory account into the Work in Process Inventory account (debit Work in Process Inventory, credit Materials Inventory). The balance remaining in the Materials Inventory account at year-end represents the cost of direct materials on hand and ready for use.

Notice that the cost of direct materials is transferred to the Work in Process Inventory account when the materials are **used**, not when they are purchased. Differences between the cost of materials **purchased** during the period and the cost of materials **used** may be explained by the change during the period in the balance of the Materials Inventory account. These relationships are summarized below:

Materials inventory, beginning of the year	$ 25,000
Add: Purchases of direct materials	145,000
Cost of direct materials available for use	$170,000
Less: Materials inventory, end of the year	20,000
Cost of direct materials used	$150,000

Some materials used in the production process cannot be traced conveniently into the finished goods manufactured. Examples include lubricating oil, welding materials, glue, and materials used in factory maintenance. These items are called **indirect materials** and are classified as part of manufacturing overhead.

Direct Labour

The Direct Labour account is used to record the cost of payrolls to direct workers and to assign this direct labour cost to the goods being manufactured.[2] Direct workers are those employees who work directly on the goods being manufactured, either by hand or with tools. They include, for example, machine operators, assemblers, and painters.

At each payroll date, the Direct Labour account is debited for the total amount of the direct labour payroll, with an offsetting credit to Cash. As the employees work on the goods being manufactured, the related labour costs are transferred from the Direct Labour account into the Work in Process Inventory account (debit Work in Process Inventory, credit Direct Labour).

In our T accounts on page 1007, the flow of direct labour costs looks similar to the flow of direct materials costs. There is, however, one significant difference. Materials are purchased **before** they are used; therefore, the Materials Inventory account has a **debit** balance equal to the cost of unused materials on hand. The services of employees, however, are used before the employees are paid. Thus, the credits to the Direct Labour account are recorded **throughout** the payroll period, but the debits are not recorded until the **end** of the payroll period. If the balance sheet date falls between payroll dates, the Direct Labour account will have a **credit** balance representing the amount owed to employees for work already per-

---

[2] As explained in Chapter 11, payroll costs include such factors as payroll taxes and "fringe benefits," as well as the wages earned by employees.

formed. This credit balance should be listed in the balance sheet as **wages payable,** a current liability.

Many employees in a manufacturing plant do not work directly on the goods being manufactured. Examples of these indirect workers include supervisors, timekeepers, maintenance personnel, and plant security guards. **Indirect labour** costs are considered part of manufacturing overhead rather than being included in direct labour costs.

Manufacturing Overhead

The Manufacturing Overhead account is used to record all costs classified as "overhead," and also to assign these costs to the products being manufactured. Manufacturing overhead is a broad category of manufacturing costs, representing all manufacturing costs **other than** direct materials and direct labour. Examples of manufacturing costs classified as overhead include:

1 **Indirect materials used**

   a Factory supplies that do not become an integral part of the finished goods, such as lubricating oil and parts used to maintain or repair equipment.

   b Materials that become an integral part of the finished goods, but would be traceable into the products only with great effort and expense. Examples include glue, welding materials, and staples.

2 **Indirect labour costs**

   a Supervisors' salaries

   b Salaries of factory maintenance, medical, and security personnel

3 **Plant occupancy costs**

   a Rent or depreciation on buildings

   b Insurance on buildings; property taxes on land and buildings

   c Maintenance and repairs on buildings

   d Utilities—gas, electricity, water, and telephone

4 **Machinery and equipment costs**

   a Rent or depreciation on machinery

   b Insurance and property taxes on machinery

   c Maintenance and repairs on machinery

5 **Cost of compliance with government regulations**

   a Meeting factory safety requirements

   b Disposal of hazardous waste materials

   c Control over factory emissions (meeting clean air standards)

These are only examples; because of the diverse nature of manufacturing companies, it is not possible to prepare a complete list of all types of overhead costs. As there are many different types of overhead costs, Manufacturing Overhead is a controlling account. Subsidiary records are maintained to keep track of the different types of overhead costs.

Selling expenses and general and administrative expenses do **not** relate to the manufacturing process and are **not** included in manufacturing overhead. Certain costs, such as insurance, property taxes, and utilities, may be applicable in part to manufacturing operations and in part to administrative and selling functions. In such cases, these costs should be ***apportioned*** among manufacturing overhead, general and administrative expense, and selling expense accounts.

Recording Overhead Costs The Manufacturing Overhead account is debited to record any cost classified as "overhead." Examples of costs debited to this account include purchases of indirect materials, payments of indirect labour payrolls, payments of factory utilities, and recording depreciation on machinery. The account credited may vary, depending upon the nature of the overhead cost. For example, in recording purchases of indirect materials or factory utilities, the account credited usually will be Cash or Accounts Payable. In recording depreciation on machinery, however, the account credited is Accumulated Depreciation.

As the items included in total overhead costs are "consumed" by production activities, the related costs are transferred from the Manufacturing Overhead account into the Work in Process Inventory account (debit Work in Process Inventory, credit Manufacturing Overhead). In the course of the year, all the overhead costs incurred should be assigned to units of product manufactured. Thus, at year-end, the Manufacturing Overhead account should have a zero balance.[3]

Direct and Indirect Manufacturing Costs

OBJECTIVE 5
Distinguish between direct and indirect manufacturing costs.

The costs of direct materials and direct labour may be traced conveniently and directly into specific units of product. Consider, for example, a company that manufactures many types of fine furniture. It is relatively easy to determine the cost of the wood and the cost of the direct labour that go into making a particular dining table. For this reason, accountants call these items ***direct*** manufacturing costs.

Overhead, however, is an ***indirect cost.*** Consider, for example, the types of costs that a furniture manufacturer classifies as overhead. These costs include property taxes on the factory, depreciation on tools and equipment, supervisors' salaries, and repairs to equipment. How much of these indirect costs should be assigned to the dining table?

There is no easy answer to this question. By definition, indirect costs ***cannot*** be traced easily and directly into specific units of product. These costs often relate to manufacturing operations viewed ***as a whole,*** rather than to specific units of product. However, we cannot ignore indirect manufacturing costs. In many companies, overhead is by far the largest of the three basic categories of manufacturing costs. Therefore, manufacturing companies must develop a method of allocating an appropriate portion of total manufacturing overhead to each product manufactured. The allocation of overhead costs to production is accomplished through the use of ***overhead application rates.***

Overhead Application Rates

An overhead application rate is a device used to assign appropriate amounts of manufacturing overhead to specific units of manufactured

---

[3] The disposition of over- or underapplied overhead will be discussed in Chapter 22.

OBJECTIVE 6
Explain the purpose of overhead application rates and the importance of basing these rates upon significant "cost drivers."

products. The rate expresses the expected relationship between manufacturing overhead and some *activity base* that can be traced directly to the manufactured products. Manufacturing overhead is then assigned to products *in proportion* to this activity base.

The overhead application rate is determined at the beginning of the accounting period, based upon estimated amounts. The formula is:

$$\text{Overhead Application Rate} = \frac{\text{Estimated Manufacturing Overhead Costs}}{\text{Estimated Units in the Activity Base}}$$

(handwritten: actual or)

The mechanics of computing and using an overhead application rate are quite simple. The challenging problems for accountants are (1) selecting an appropriate activity base, and (2) making reliable estimates of total overhead costs for the period and of the units in the activity base.[4] Let us first address the easy topic—mechanics.

Computation and Use of an Overhead Application Rate Assume that at the beginning of 1996, Allied Manufacturing makes the following estimates relating to its manufacturing activities for the coming year:

Estimated total manufacturing overhead costs for the year...............	$360,000
Estimated total direct labour cost for the year..........................	$300,000
Estimated machine hours for the year...................................	10,000 hours

Using this estimated data, we will illustrate the computation and use of an overhead application rate under two independent assumptions:

Assumption 1: Allied uses direct labour cost as the "activity base" in the application of overhead costs.
In this case, the overhead application rate will be *120% of direct labour cost* ($360,000 estimated overhead ÷ $300,000 estimated direct labour cost = 120%). Manufacturing overhead will be assigned to manufactured units in proportion to the direct labour cost assigned to those units. Thus, if $2,000 in direct labour is charged to specific units of product, $2,400 of overhead will be charged to these units ($2,000 direct labour cost × 120% overhead application rate = $2,400).

Assumption 2: Allied uses machine hours as the activity base.
In this case, the overhead application rate will be *$36 per machine hour* ($360,000 ÷ 10,000 hours). Using this approach, manufacturing overhead costs will be assigned to units based upon the number of machine hours used in producing the units. If 10 machine hours are needed to manufacture a particular group of units, those units will be charged with $360 in overhead costs (10 hours × $36 per hour).

(handwritten: for company more automated)

What "Drives" Overhead Costs?

For the use of an overhead application rate to provide reliable results, the activity base must be a significant "driver" of overhead costs. A *cost driver*

[4] Errors in estimating the amount of total overhead costs for the coming period or the number of units in the activity base will cause differences between the actual overhead incurred and the amounts assigned to units manufactured. These differences usually are small and are eliminated by an adjusting entry at the end of the accounting period. We will address this issue in Chapter 22.

is an activity base that is a *causal factor* in the incurrence of overhead costs.

In the past, direct labour costs (or direct labour hours) often were viewed as the primary driver of overhead costs. Products that required more direct labour often required more indirect labour (supervision), more wear and tear on machinery (maintenance and depreciation), and greater use of factory supplies and of electricity. Therefore, many manufacturing companies followed the practice of allocating all overhead costs to production in proportion to direct labour costs (or hours).

As factories have become more highly automated, direct labour has become much less of a causal factor in many overhead costs. Today, many manufacturing companies find that activity bases such as machine-hours, computer time, or the number of component parts to be assembled result in a more realistic allocation of overhead costs.

The Use of Multiple Overhead Application Rates In an effort to determine the "true" cost of manufacturing different types of products, many companies are refining the techniques used in associating overhead costs with specific units of production. These companies may use different overhead application rates in allocating different types of overhead costs. For example, supervision costs may be allocated to production based upon direct labour cost, whereas maintenance and depreciation on factory machines may be allocated on the basis of machine-hours. Different application rates also may be used in each production department and in applying overhead costs to different types of products.

The key point is that each manufactured product should be charged with the overhead costs *generated by* the manufacture of that product. If the activity base used in applying overhead costs is *not* the primary overhead cost driver, the relative production cost of different products may be *significantly distorted.* This, in turn, may lead to faulty decisions by management.

CASE IN POINT A large dairy products company allocated its overhead costs to production in proportion to the amount of butterfat used in each product. The quantity of butterfat used in producing a product had been a major driver of overhead costs until the dairy began producing dehydrated milk.

The manufacture of dehydrated milk required the use of expensive machinery and greatly increased overhead costs. However, the dehydrated milk contained almost no butterfat. Based on the "butterfat method" of allocating overhead costs, the increased overhead stemming from the manufacture of dehydrated milk was allocated primarily to ice cream and other products high in butterfat. The cost of manufacturing dehydrated milk appeared to be quite low, because almost no overhead costs were allocated to this product.

As a result of the distorted cost figures, management cut back on the production of ice cream and increased production of dehydrated milk. This strategy, however, resulted in a substantial decline in the company's profitability. Only after a business consultant pointed out the improper allocation of overhead costs did management learn that ice cream was the company's most profitable product and that dehydrated milk was being sold to customers at a price below its actual production cost.

The Increasing Importance of Proper Overhead Allocation In today's global economy, competition among manufacturing companies is greater than ever before. If a company is to determine whether it can compete effectively in this marketplace, it must first know with some precision its per-unit cost of manufacturing its products. In highly automated factories, overhead often is the largest of the three basic categories of manufacturing costs. Therefore, the proper allocation of overhead costs is one of the major challenges facing managerial accountants.

Work in Process Inventory, Finished Goods Inventory, and the Cost of Goods Sold

The Work in Process Inventory account is used (1) to accumulate the manufacturing costs relating to all units of product worked on during the period and (2) to allocate these costs between those units completed during the period and those that are only partially completed at year-end.

As materials are placed into production and manufacturing activities take place, the related manufacturing costs are debited to the Work in Process Inventory account. The flow of manufacturing costs into this inventory account is consistent with the idea that manufacturing costs are *product costs,* rather than period costs.

As specific units are completed, the cost of manufacturing them is transferred from the Work in Process Inventory account to the Finished Goods Inventory account. Thus, the balance in the Work in Process account represents only the manufacturing costs associated with units still "in process."

Notice that manufactured products are classified as finished goods only *after* all manufacturing processes have been completed. Therefore, any costs of storing, marketing, or delivering finished goods are regarded as *selling expenses,* not manufacturing costs. When units of finished goods are sold, their cost is transferred from the Finished Goods Inventory account to the Cost of Goods Sold account.

The Need for Per-Unit Cost Data Transferring the cost of specific units from one account to another requires knowledge of the *per-unit cost—* that is, the total manufacturing costs assigned to specific units. (The determination of unit cost is one of the primary goals of every *cost accounting system* and will be explained and illustrated in the following chapter.)

Unit costs are of importance to both financial and managerial accountants. Financial accountants use unit costs in recording the transfer of completed units from the Work in Process account to the Finished Goods account and also in recording the cost of goods sold. Thus, both a manufacturing company's inventory of finished goods and its costs of goods sold are based upon the *cost of manufacturing* the related units of product. Managerial accountants use unit costs in developing information to assist management in making pricing decisions, evaluating the efficiency of current operations, and planning future operations.

Schedule of the Cost of Finished Goods Manufactured

OBJECTIVE 7
Prepare a
schedule of
the cost of
finished
goods manu-
factured.

Most manufacturing companies prepare a **schedule of the cost of finished goods manufactured** to provide managers with an overview of the costs relating to manufacturing activities during the period. Using the data in our illustration on page 1007, a schedule of the cost of finished goods manufactured for Allied Manufacturing Corporation is shown below.

ALLIED MANUFACTURING CORPORATION
Schedule of the Cost of Finished Goods Manufactured
For the Year Ended December 31, 1996

Work in process inventory, beginning of the year		$ 30,000
Manufacturing cost assigned to production:		
Direct materials used	$150,000	
Direct labour	300,000	
Manufacturing overhead	360,000	
Total manufacturing costs		810,000
Total cost of all work in process during the year		$840,000
Less: Work in process inventory, end of the year		(40,000)
Cost of finished goods manufactured		$800,000

[handwritten annotation: incurred current period]

Notice that all the amounts used in this schedule may be obtained from the Work in Process Inventory account illustrated on page 1007. In short, the schedule of cost of finished goods manufactured summarizes the flow of manufacturing costs into and out of the Work in Process Inventory account.

Purpose of the Schedule   A schedule of the cost of finished goods manufactured is **not** a formal financial statement. Rather, it is intended primarily to assist managers in understanding and evaluating the overall cost of manufacturing the company's products. By comparing these schedules for successive periods, for example, managers can determine whether direct labour or manufacturing overhead is rising or falling as a percentage of total manufacturing costs. The schedule is also helpful in developing information about unit costs.

If the company manufactures only a single product, the **cost per unit** of manufactured product is equal to the **cost of finished goods manufactured** divided by the **number of units produced.**[5] For example, if Allied produced **10,000** finished units during 1996, the average cost per unit was **$80** ($800,000 ÷ 10,000 units). Knowing the manufacturing cost per unit is useful to managers in setting sales prices, in evaluating the efficiency of manufacturing operations, and in deciding whether the company should devote more or less of its resources to manufacturing this product.

---

[5]   Many companies, of course, produce more than a single product. In this case, the company's accounting records should include separate work in process inventory accounts for each type of product. A separate schedule of the cost of finished goods manufactured then may be prepared for **each product line.**

Financial Statements of a Manufacturing Company

Let us now illustrate how the data used in our example (see page 1007) will be reported in the 1996 income statement and balance sheet of Allied Manufacturing Corporation.

The company's 1996 income statement is illustrated below.

ALLIED MANUFACTURING CORPORATION
Income Statement
For the Year Ended December 31, 1996

Sales		$1,300,000
Cost of goods sold		782,000
Gross profit		$ 518,000
Operating expenses:		
Selling expenses	$135,000	
General and administrative expenses	265,000	
Total operating expenses		400,000
Income from operations		$ 118,000
Less: Interest expense		18,000
Income before income taxes		$ 100,000
Income taxes expenses		30,000
Net income		$ 70,000

Notice that no manufacturing costs appear among the company's expenses. Manufacturing costs appear in two places in a manufacturer's financial statements. The cost of manufacturing units *sold* during the period appears in the income statement as the ***cost of goods sold.*** Manufacturing costs associated with goods ***still on hand*** are classified as ***inventory*** and appear in the company's balance sheet. The balance sheet presentation of Allied's three types of inventory is illustrated below:

ALLIED MANUFACTURING CORPORATION
Partial Balance Sheet
December 31, 1996

Notice the three types of inventory

Current assets:		
Cash and cash equivalents		$ 60,000
Accounts receivable (net of allowance for doubtful accounts)		190,000
Inventories:		
Materials	$ 20,000	
Work in process	40,000	
Finished goods	168,000	228,000
Total current assets		$478,000

Allied's balance sheet also should include a current liability for wages payable, representing the $8,000 credit balance in the Direct Labour account. The credit balance in the Direct Labour account indicates that direct workers have rendered services costing $8,000 since the last payroll date.

CHAPTER REVIEW

KEY TERMS INTRODUCED OR EMPHASIZED IN CHAPTER 21

Cost accounting The accounting concepts and practices used in determining the costs of manufacturing various products or of performing different business activities.

Cost driver An activity base that can be traced directly into units produced and that serves as a causal factor in the incurrence of overhead costs. Serves as an activity base in an *overhead application rate.*

Cost of finished goods manufactured The manufacturing costs relating to units of manufactured product completed during the period.

Direct labour Payroll costs for employees who work directly on the products being manufactured, either by hand or with tools.

Direct manufacturing cost A manufacturing cost that can be traced conveniently and directly into the quantity of finished goods manufactured. Examples include *direct materials* and *direct labour.*

Direct materials Materials and component parts that become an integral part of the manufactured goods and can be traced directly into the finished products.

Financial accounting Developing and interpreting information describing the financial position and operating results of a business entity, primarily for use by decision makers outside the entity.

Finished goods inventory The completed units that have emerged from the manufacturing process and are on hand available for sale.

Indirect labour Payroll costs relating to factory employees who do not work directly upon the goods being manufactured. Examples are wages of security guards and maintenance personnel. Indirect labour costs are classified as *manufacturing overhead.*

Indirect manufacturing cost A manufacturing cost that cannot be conveniently traced into the specific products being manufactured. Examples include property taxes, depreciation on machinery, and other types of *manufacturing overhead.*

Indirect materials Materials used in the manufacturing process that cannot be traced conveniently to specific units of production. Examples include lubricating oil, maintenance supplies, and glue. Indirect materials are accounted for as part of *manufacturing overhead.*

Inventoriable costs See *product costs.*

Managerial accounting Developing and interpreting accounting information specifically suited to the needs of a company's management.

Manufacturing costs The cost of manufacturing goods that will be sold to customers. The basic types of manufacturing costs are *direct materials used, direct labour,* and *manufacturing overhead.*

Manufacturing overhead A "catch-all" category including all manufacturing costs other than the costs of *direct materials used* and *direct labour.*

Materials inventory The cost of direct materials on hand and available for use in the manufacturing process.

Overhead application rate A device used to assign overhead costs to the units being manufactured. Expresses the relationship between estimated overhead costs and some activity base that can be traced directly to manufactured units. Results in overhead costs being applied to units produced in proportion to the selected activity base.

Period costs Costs that are charged to expense accounts in the period that the costs are incurred. Includes all items classified as "expense."

Perpetual inventory system A system in which transactions increasing or decreasing inventory are recorded directly in the inventory accounts, thus creating an up-to-date record of the level of inventories and the flow of costs into and out of the inventory accounts.

Product costs The costs of purchasing or manufacturing inventory. Until the related goods are sold, these product costs represent an asset—inventory. Once the goods are sold, these costs are deducted from revenue as the cost of goods sold.

Schedule of the cost of finished goods manufactured A schedule summarizing the flow of manufacturing costs into and out of the Work in Process Inventory account. Intended to assist managers in evaluating manufacturing costs.

Work in process inventory Goods at any stage of the manufacturing process short of completion. As these units are completed, they become finished goods.

DEMONSTRATION PROBLEM FOR YOUR REVIEW

The following T accounts summarize the flow of manufacturing costs during the current year through the ledger accounts of Federal Manufacturing Corporation:

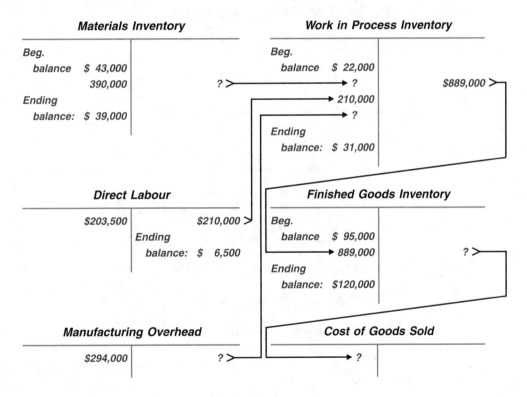

INSTRUCTIONS From the data supplied above, indicate the following amounts. Some amounts already appear in the T accounts; others require short computations.

a Purchases of direct materials

b Direct materials used during the year

c Direct labour costs assigned to production

d The year-end liability to direct workers for wages payable e   The overhead costs applied to production during the year, assuming that overhead was applied at a rate equal to 140% of direct labour costs

f   Total manufacturing costs charged to production during the year

g   The cost of finished goods manufactured

h   The cost of goods sold

i   The total costs classified as "inventory" in the year-end balance sheet

SOLUTION TO DEMONSTRATION PROBLEM

a   Purchases of direct materials **$390,000**

b   Computation of direct materials used:

Materials inventory, beginning of year	$ 43,000
Purchases of direct materials	390,000
Direct materials available for use	$433,000
Less: Materials inventory, end of year	39,000
Direct materials used	$394,000

c   Direct labour costs assigned to production **$210,000**

d   Year-end liability for direct wages payable .... **$ 6,500**

e   Overhead costs applied during the year
($210,000 direct labour costs × 140%) **$294,000**

f   Total manufacturing costs charged to production:

Direct materials used (part b)	$394,000
Direct labour costs assigned to production	210,000
Manufacturing overhead applied (part e)	294,000
Total manufacturing costs charged to production	$898,000

g   Cost of finished goods manufactured **$889,000**

h   Computation of cost of goods sold:

Beginning inventory of finished goods	$ 95,000
Cost of finished goods manufactured	889,000
Cost of goods available for sale	$984,000
Less: Ending inventory of finished goods	120,000
Cost of goods sold	$864,000

i   Total year-end inventory:

Materials	$ 39,000
Work in process	31,000
Finished goods	120,000
Total inventory	$190,000

ASSIGNMENT MATERIAL

DISCUSSION QUESTIONS

1   Briefly distinguish between managerial and financial accounting information in terms of (a) the intended users of the information and (b) the purpose of the information.

2 Briefly explain what is meant by the terms *managerial accounting* and *cost accounting.* Are the two terms related to one another? Explain.

3 Are financial accounting and managerial accounting two entirely separate disciplines? Explain.

4 Is managerial accounting information developed in conformity with generally accepted accounting principles or some other set of prescribed standards? Explain.

5 What are the three basic types of manufacturing costs?

6 A manufacturing firm has three inventory controlling accounts. Name each of the accounts, and describe briefly what the balance in each at the end of any accounting period represents.

7 Explain the distinction between *product costs* and *period costs.* Why is this distinction important?

8 Is the cost of disposing of hazardous waste materials resulting from factory operations a product cost or a period cost? Explain.

9 During the current year, Coronado Boat Yard has incurred manufacturing costs of $420,000 in building three large sailboats. At year-end, each boat is about 70% complete. How much of these manufacturing costs should be recognized as expense in Coronado Boat Yard's income statement for the current year? Explain.

10 What amounts are *debited* to the Materials Inventory account? What amounts are *credited* to this account? What type of balance (debit or credit) is this account likely to have at year-end? Explain.

11 During the current year the net cost of direct materials purchased by a manufacturing firm was $340,000, and the direct material inventory increased by $20,000. What was the cost of direct materials *used* during the year?

12 What amounts are debited to the Direct Labour account during the year? What amounts are credited to this account? What type of balance (debit or credit) is this account likely to have at year-end? Explain.

13 The illustration on page 1017 includes six ledger accounts. Which of these six accounts often have balances at year-end that appear in the company's formal financial statements? Briefly explain how these balances will be classified in the financial statements.

14 Explain the distinction between a *direct* manufacturing cost and an *indirect* manufacturing cost. Provide two examples of each type of cost.

15 Central Mfg. Ltd. uses approximately $1,200 in janitorial supplies to clean the work area and factory equipment each month. Should this $1,200 be included in the cost of direct materials used? Explain.

16 What is meant by the term *overhead application rate?*

17 What is meant by the term *overhead cost driver?* How does the cost driver enter into computation of an overhead application rate?

18 Identify two possible overhead cost drivers for a company that:

a Manufactures handmade furniture using skilled craftspersons and small hand tools.

b Manufactures microchips for computers using an assembly line of computer-driven robots.

19 What amounts are **debited** to the Work in Process Inventory account during the year? What amounts are **credited** to this account? What does the year-end balance in this account represent?

20 What amounts are **debited** to the Finished Goods Inventory account during the year? What amounts are **credited** to this account? What type of balance (debit or credit) is this account likely to have at year-end?

21 Briefly describe the computation of the cost of finished goods manufactured as it appears in a schedule of the cost of finished goods manufactured.

22 A schedule of the cost of finished goods manufactured is a helpful tool in determining the per-unit cost of manufactured products. Explain several ways in which information about per-unit manufacturing costs is used by (a) managerial accountants and (b) financial accountants.

MULTIPLE CHOICE QUESTIONS

1 Indicate which of the following statements are more descriptive of managerial accounting than of financial accounting. (More than one answer may be appropriate.)

  a Recognized standards are used for presentation.

  b Information is tailored to the needs of individual decision makers.

  c Information is more widely distributed.

  d Emphasis is on expected future results.

2 In a manufacturing company, the costs debited to the Work in Process Inventory account represent:

  a Direct materials used, direct labour, and manufacturing overhead.

  b Cost of finished goods manufactured.

  c Period costs and product costs.

  d None of the above; the types of costs debited to this account will depend upon the type of products being manufactured.

3 The Work in Process Inventory account had a beginning balance of $4,200 on February 1. During February, the cost of direct materials used was $29,000 and direct labour cost applied to production was $3,000. Overhead is applied at the rate of $20 per direct labour hour. During February, 180 direct labour hours were used in the production process. If the cost of finished goods manufactured was $34,100, compute the balance in the Work in Process Inventory account at the **end** of February.

  a $9,900   b $1,500   c $2,100   d $5,700

4 The purpose of an overhead application rate is to:

  a Assign an appropriate portion of indirect manufacturing costs to each product manufactured.

  b Determine the type and amount of costs to be debited to the Manufacturing Overhead account.

  c Charge the Work in Process Inventory account with the appropriate amount of direct manufacturing costs.

  d Allocate manufacturing overhead to expense in proportion to the number of units manufactured during the period.

5 The accounting records of Newport Mfg. Ltd. include the following information for 1996:

	Dec. 31	Jan. 1
Inventory of work in process	$ 20,000	$10,000
Inventory of finished goods	80,000	60,000
Direct materials used	200,000	
Direct labour	120,000	
Manufacturing overhead (150% of direct labour)	180,000	
Selling expenses	150,000	

Indicate which of the following are correct. (More than one answer may be correct.)

a Amount debited to the Work in Process Inventory account during 1996, $500,000

b Cost of finished goods manufactured, $490,000

c Cost of goods sold, $470,000

d Total manufacturing costs for the year, $650,000

EXERCISES

EXERCISE 21-1
Accounting
Terminology

Listed below are nine technical accounting terms introduced or emphasized in this chapter:

Work in process inventory	Period costs	Cost of finished goods manufactured
Overhead application rate	Product costs	Cost of goods sold
Manufacturing overhead	Cost accounting	Managerial accounting

Each of the following statements may (or may not) describe one of these technical terms. For each statement, indicate the accounting term described, or answer "None" if the statement does not correctly describe any of the terms.

a The preparation and use of accounting information designed to assist managers in planning and controlling the operations of a business.

b All manufacturing costs other than direct materials used and direct labour.

c A means of assigning indirect manufacturing costs to work in process during the period.

d A manufacturing cost that can be traced conveniently and directly into manufactured units of product.

e The concepts and practices used in determining the cost of manufacturing a specific product or performing a particular type of business activity.

f The account debited at the time that the Manufacturing Overhead account is credited.

g The amount transferred from the Work in Process Inventory account to the Finished Goods Inventory account.

h Costs that are debited directly to expense accounts when the costs are incurred.

EXERCISE 21-2
Basic Types of
Manufacturing
Costs

Into which of the three elements of manufacturing cost would each of the following be classified?

a Tubing used in manufacturing bicycles

b Wages paid by an automobile manufacturer to employees who test-drive completed automobiles

c Property taxes on machinery

d Gold bullion used by a jewellery manufacturer

e Wages of assembly-line workers who package frozen food

f Salary of plant superintendent

g Electricity used in factory operations

h Salary of a nurse in a factory first-aid station

**EXERCISE 21-3
Product Costs
and Period
Costs**

Indicate whether each of the following should be considered a **product cost** or a **period cost.** If you identify the item as a product cost, also indicate whether it is a **direct** or an **indirect** cost. For example, the answer to item **0** is "indirect product cost." Begin with item **a**.

0 Property taxes on factory building

a Cost of disposal of hazardous waste materials to a chemical plant

b Amounts paid by a mobile home manufacturer to a subcontractor who installs plumbing in each mobile home

c Depreciation on sales showroom fixtures

d Salaries of security guards in administrative office building

e Salaries of factory security guards

f Salaries of office workers in the credit department

g Depreciation on direct materials warehouse

h Income taxes on a profitable manufacturing company

**EXERCISE 21-4
Flow of Costs
through Manu-
facturing Ac-
counts**

The information below was taken from the accounting records of Craftsman Products for the current year:

Work in process inventory, beginning of the year	*$ 31,000*
Cost of direct materials used	*260,000*
Direct labour cost applied to production	*100,000*
Cost of finished goods manufactured	*665,000*

Overhead is applied to production at a rate of $30 per machine hour. During the current year, 10,000 machine hours were used in the production process.

Compute the amount of the work in process inventory on hand at year-end.

**EXERCISE 21-5
Computation
and Use of an
Overhead Ap-
plication Rate**

The production manager of Del Mar Manufacturing has made the following estimates for the coming year:

Estimated manufacturing overhead	*$1,200,000*
Estimated direct labour costs	*$ 500,000*
Estimated machine hours	*80,000 hours*

INSTRUCTIONS

a Compute the overhead application rate based on:

1 Direct labour cost.

2 Machine hours.

b Assume that the manufacture of a particular product requires $2,000 in direct materials, $400 in direct labour, and 62 machine hours. Determine the total cost of manufacturing this product assuming that the overhead application rate is based upon:

1 Direct labour cost.

2 Machine hours.

EXERCISE 21-6
Preparing a Schedule of the Cost of Finished Goods Manufactured

The accounting records of NuTronics, Inc., include the following information for the year ended December 31, 1996:

	Dec. 31	Jan. 1
Inventory of materials	$ 24,000	$20,000
Inventory of work in process...	8,000	12,000
Inventory of finished goods..	90,000	80,000
Direct materials used	210,000	
Direct labour	120,000	
Selling expenses	170,000	
General and administrative expenses.................................	140,000	

Overhead is applied to production at a rate of 160% of direct labour costs.

INSTRUCTIONS

a Prepare a schedule of the cost of finished goods manufactured.

b Assume that the company manufactures a single product and that 20,000 units were completed during the year. What is the average per-unit cost of manufacturing this product?

EXERCISE 21-7
Overhead Cost Drivers; Determination and Use of Unit Cost

During June, Assembly Department no. 4 of Riverside Electronics produced 10,000 Model 201 computer keyboards. Assembly of these units required 1,230 hours of direct labour at a cost of $22,000, direct materials costing $265,800, and 2,400 hours of machine time. Based upon an analysis of overhead costs at the beginning of the year, overhead is applied to keyboards using the following formula:

Overhead = 80% of Direct Labour Cost + $30 per Machine-Hour

INSTRUCTIONS

a Compute the total amount of overhead cost applied to the 10,000 keyboards.

b Compute the *per-unit cost* of manufacturing these keyboards.

c Briefly explain *why* the department might use *two separate activity bases* in applying overhead costs to one type of product.

d Identify at least two types of overhead costs that might be "driven" by each of the two cost drivers indicated in this situation.

e What appears to be the *primary* driver of overhead costs in the manufacture of keyboards?

f Compute the gross profit that will result from the sale of 2,000 of these keyboards at a sales price of $60 each.

PROBLEMS

Group A

PROBLEM 21A-1
An Introduction to Product Costs

Aqua-Craft manufactures fibreglass ski boats. The manufacturing costs incurred during the first year of operations are shown below:

Direct materials purchased	$224,500 (b)
Direct materials used	215,600
Direct labour assigned to production	180,000 (c)
Manufacturing overhead	342,000
Cost of finished goods manufactured (112 boats)	~~706,000~~
	705,600 (a)

During the year, 112 completed boats were manufactured, of which 100 were sold. (Assume that the amounts of the ending inventory of finished goods and the cost of goods sold are determined using the average per-unit cost of manufacturing a completed boat.)

INSTRUCTIONS

a Compute each of the following and show all computations:

1 The average per-unit cost of manufacturing a completed boat during the current year 6300

2 The year-end balances of the inventories of materials, work in process, and finished goods 15 600   8900   32000

3 The cost of goods sold during the year 630,000

b For the current year, the costs of direct materials purchased, direct labour assigned to production, and manufacturing overhead total $746,500. Is this the amount of the manufacturing costs deducted from revenue in the current year? Explain fully.

PROBLEM 21A-2
Flow of Manufacturing Costs through Ledger Accounts

The "flow" of manufacturing costs through the ledger accounts of Superior Locks, Inc., in the current year is illustrated below in summarized form:

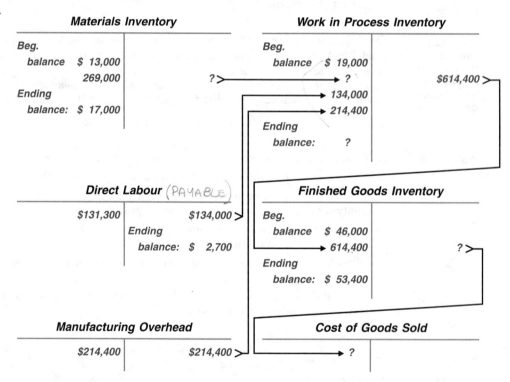

INSTRUCTIONS

Indicate the amounts requested below. Some amounts are shown in the T accounts above; others require short computations. (Show all computations.)

a Purchases of direct materials 269,000

b The cost of direct materials used 265,000

c Direct labour costs assigned to production 134,000

d The year-end liability for direct wages payable *2700*

e The overhead application rate in use throughout the year, assuming that overhead is applied as a percentage of direct labour costs *160%*

f Total manufacturing costs charged to the Work in Process Inventory account during the current year *613,400*

g The cost of finished goods manufactured *614,400*

h The year-end balance in the Work in Process Inventory account *18,000*

i The cost of goods sold *607,000*

j The total amount of "inventory" listed in the year-end balance sheet *88,400*

PROBLEM 21A-3
Flow of Manu-
facturing
Costs: A Com-
prehensive
Problem

The balances in the perpetual inventory accounts of Sunnyvale Manufacturing at the beginning and end of the current year are as follows:

	End of Year	Beginning of Year
Inventory accounts:		
Materials	$25,800	$22,000
Work in process..	8,000	5,000
Finished goods inventory......................................	24,000	38,000

The total dollar amounts debited and credited during the year to the accounts used in recording manufacturing activities are summarized below:

	Debit Entries	Credit Entries
Account:		
Materials Inventory	$410,000	$?
Direct Labour	189,000	192,000
Manufacturing Overhead..	393,600	393,600
Work in Process Inventory......................................	?	?
Finished Goods Inventory	?	?

INSTRUCTIONS **a** Using this data, state or compute for the year the amounts of:

1 Direct materials purchased

2 Direct materials used

3 Payments of direct labour payrolls

4 Direct labour cost assigned to production

5 The overhead application rate used during the year, assuming that overhead was applied as a percentage of direct labour costs

6 Total manufacturing costs charged to the Work in Process Inventory account during the year

7 The cost of finished goods manufactured

8 Cost of goods sold

9 The total amount to be classified as "inventory" in the year-end balance sheet

b Prepare a schedule of the cost of finished goods manufactured.

PROBLEM 21A-4
**Flow of
Manufacturing
Costs**

Shown below are 1996 data regarding Talking Teddy, one of the major products manufactured by St. Nicholas Toy Co. Ltd.:

Purchases of direct materials	$332,000
Direct materials used	333,600
Direct labour payrolls (paid during the year)	176,700
Direct labour costs assigned to production	180,000 —
Manufacturing overhead (incurred and applied)	288,000

During the year 60,000 units of this product were manufactured and 62,100 units were sold. Selected information concerning inventories during the year is shown below:

	Dec. 31	Jan. 1
Materials	$?	$ 12,800
Work in process..	4,700	4,100
Finished goods, Jan. 1 (3,000 units @ $13)	?	39,000

INSTRUCTIONS   a   Prepare a schedule of the cost of finished goods manufactured for this product in 1996.

13.35   b   Compute the average unit cost of Talking Teddies completed in 1996.

c   Compute the cost of Talking Teddies goods sold during the year. Assume that there is a first-in, first-out (FIFO) flow through the Finished Goods Inventory account and that all units completed in 1996 are assigned the per-unit cost determined in part **b**.

d   Compute the amount of "inventory" relating to this product that will be listed in the company's balance sheet at December 31, 1996. (Show supporting computations for the year-end amounts of materials inventory and finished goods inventory.)

e   Explain how the $180,000 in direct labour costs assigned to production in 1996 affect the company's 1996 income statement and balance sheet.

PROBLEM 21A-5
**"I Don't Need
an Accountant
. . . ."**

Early in the year, John Raymond founded Raymond Engineering Ltd. for the purpose of manufacturing a special flow control valve that he had designed. Shortly after year-end, the company's accountant was injured in a skiing accident, and no year-end financial statements have been prepared. However, the accountant had correctly determined the year-end inventories at the following amounts:

Materials	$46,000
Work in process..	31,500
Finished goods (3,000 units)	88,500

As this was the first year of operations, there were no beginning inventories.

While the accountant was in the hospital, Raymond improperly prepared the following income statement from the company's accounting records:

Net sales..		$610,600
Cost of goods sold:		
Purchases of direct materials	$181,000	
Direct labour costs assigned to production.....................	110,000	
Manufacturing overhead applied to production..................	170,000	
Selling expenses	70,600	
Administrative expenses...	132,000	
Total costs...		663,600
Net loss for year		$ (53,000)

Raymond was very disappointed in these operating results. He states, "Not only did we lose more than $50,000 this year, but look at our unit production costs. We sold 10,000 units this year at a cost of $663,600; that amounts to a cost of $66.36 per unit. I know some of our competitors are able to manufacture similar valves for about $35 per unit. I don't need an accountant to know that this business is a failure."

INSTRUCTIONS
a Prepare a schedule of the cost of finished goods manufactured for the year. Show a supporting computation for the cost of direct materials used during the year.

b. Compute the average cost per unit manufactured.

c Prepare a corrected income statement for the year, using the multiple-step format. If the company has earned any operating income, assume an income tax rate of 30%. (Omit earnings per share figures.)

d Explain whether you agree or disagree with Raymond's remarks that the business is unprofitable and that its unit cost of production ($66.36, according to Raymond) is much higher than that of competitors (around $35). If you disagree with Raymond, explain any errors or shortcomings in his analysis.

Group B

PROBLEM 21B-1
An Introduction to Product Costs

Explorer, Inc., began operations early in the current year building luxury motor homes. During the year the company started and completed 50 motor homes at a cost of $52,000 per unit. Forty-eight of these completed motor homes were sold for $80,000 each. In addition, the company had 5 partially completed motor homes in its factory at year-end. Total costs incurred during the year (summarized alphabetically) were as follows:

Direct materials used	$ 700,000
Direct labour applied to production	800,000
General and administrative expenses...	480,000
Income taxes expense	105,000
Manufacturing overhead	1,280,000
Selling expenses	550,000

INSTRUCTIONS
Compute for the current year:

a Total manufacturing costs assigned to work in process during the period

b Cost of finished goods manufactured

c Cost of goods sold

d Gross profit on sales

e Ending inventories of (1) work in process and (2) finished goods

PROBLEM 21B-2
Flow of Manufacturing Costs through Perpetual Inventory Records

The following T accounts summarize the flow of manufacturing costs during the current year through the ledger accounts of Intruder Alert, Inc.

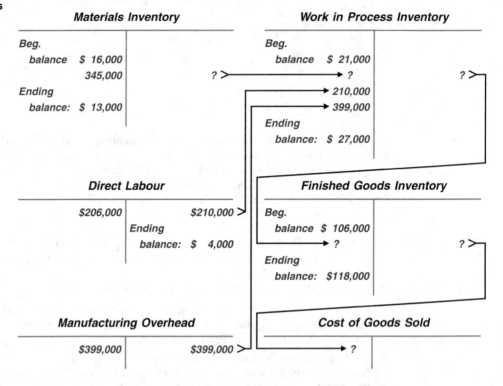

Materials Inventory	
Beg.	
balance $ 16,000	
345,000	
Ending	
balance: $ 13,000	

Work in Process Inventory	
Beg.	
balance $ 21,000	
?	
210,000	
399,000	
Ending	
balance: $ 27,000	

Direct Labour	
$206,000	$210,000
Ending	
balance: $ 4,000	

Finished Goods Inventory	
Beg.	
balance $ 106,000	
?	
Ending	
balance: $118,000	

Manufacturing Overhead	
$399,000	$399,000

Cost of Goods Sold	
?	

INSTRUCTIONS

From the data supplied above, indicate the following amounts. Some amounts are shown in the T accounts; others require short computations. (Show all computations.)

a Purchases during the year of direct materials

b The cost of direct materials used

c Direct labour payrolls paid during the year

d Direct labour costs assigned to production

e The overhead application rate in use during the year, assuming that overhead is applied as a percentage of direct labour costs

f Total manufacturing costs charged to the Work in Process Inventory account during the year

g The cost of finished goods manufactured

h The cost of goods sold

i The total costs to be classified as "inventory" in the year-end balance sheet

PROBLEM 21B-3
Schedule of the Cost of Finished Goods Manufactured; Use of Unit Costs in Financial Statements

The accounting records of Scott Mfg. Co. include the following information relating to the current year:

	Dec. 31	Jan. 1
Materials inventory	$ 20,000	$ 25,000
Work in process inventory	37,500	40,000
Finished goods inventory, Jan. 1 (10,000 units @ $21 per unit)	?	210,000
Purchases of direct materials during year	285,000	
Direct labour costs assigned to production	240,000	
Manufacturing overhead applied to production........................	457,500	

The company manufactures a single product; during the current year, **45,000** units were manufactured and **40,000** units were sold.

INSTRUCTIONS   a   Prepare a schedule of the cost of finished goods manufactured for the current year.

b   Compute the average per-unit cost of production during the current year.

c   Compute the cost of goods sold during the year, assuming that the FIFO (first-in, first-out) method of inventory costing is used.

d   Compute the cost of the inventory of finished goods at December 31 of the current year, assuming that the FIFO (first-in, first-out) method of inventory costing is used.

PROBLEM 21B-4
Flow of Manu-facturing Costs: A Comprehensive Problem

Shown below are the beginning and ending balances in the inventory accounts of ProTools, Inc., for 1997:

Inventory accounts:	End of Year	Beginning of Year
Materials	$52,000	$47,000
Work in process...	24,000	26,000
Finished goods inventory.......................................	?	98,000

The amounts debited and credited during the year to the accounts used in recording manufacturing costs are summarized below:

Account:	Debit Entries	Credit Entries
Materials Inventory	$ 690,000	$?
Direct Labour	395,000	400,000
Manufacturing Overhead.......................................	880,000	880,000
Cost of Goods Sold	1,975,000	-0-
Work in Process Inventory.....................................	?	?
Finished Goods Inventory	?	?

INSTRUCTIONS   a   Using the above information, state (or compute) for 1997 the amounts of:

1 Direct materials purchased

2 Direct materials used

3 Direct labour payrolls paid during the year

4 Direct labour costs assigned to units being manufactured

5 The year-end liability for direct wages payable

6 The overhead application rate, assuming that overhead costs are applied to units being manufactured in proportion to direct labour costs

7 Total manufacturing costs debited to the Work in Process Inventory account

8 Cost of finished goods manufactured

9 Ending inventory of finished goods

b   Prepare a schedule of the cost of finished goods manufactured for the year.

PROBLEM 21B-5
Effect on Income Statement of Errors in Handling Manufacturing Costs

William Nelson, the chief accountant of London Corporation, was injured in an automobile accident shortly before the end of the company's first year of operations. At year-end, a clerk with a very limited understanding of accounting prepared the following income statement.

LONDON CORPORATION
Income Statement
For the Year Ended December 31, 19__

Net sales...		$1,300,000
Cost of goods sold:		
Purchases of direct materials	$ 460,000	
Direct labour	225,000	
Indirect labour	90,000	
Depreciation on machinery—factory...........................	50,000	
Rent	144,000	
Insurance	16,000	
Utilities	28,000	
Miscellaneous manufacturing overhead........................	34,600	
Other operating expenses	273,800	
Dividends declared on common stock..........................	46,000	
Cost of goods sold...		(1,367,400)
Loss for year..		$ (67,400)

You are asked to help management prepare a corrected income statement for the first year of operations. Management informs you that 60% of the rent, insurance, and utilities apply to factory operations, and that the remaining 40% should be classified as operating expense. Also, the correct ending inventories are as follows:

Material		$ 38,000
Work in process..		10,000
Finished goods..		110,400

As this is the first year of operations, there were no beginning inventories.

INSTRUCTIONS

a Identify the shortcomings and errors in the above income statement. Based upon the shortcomings you have identified, explain whether you would expect the company's actual net income for the first year of operations to be higher or lower than the amount shown.

b Prepare schedules to determine:

   1 The cost of direct materials used.

   2 Total manufacturing overhead.

c Prepare a schedule of cost of finished goods manufactured during the year.

d Prepare a corrected income statement for the year, using a multiple-step format. Assume that income taxes expense amounts to 30% of income before income taxes.

ANALYTICAL AND DECISION PROBLEMS AND CASES

A&D 21-1
Poor Drivers
Are Cost Drivers

Ye Olde Bump & Grind, Inc., is an automobile body and fender repair shop. Repair work is done by hand and with the use of small tools. Customers are billed based on time (direct labour hours) and materials used in each repair job.

The shop's overhead costs consist primarily of indirect materials (welding materials, metal putty, and sandpaper), rent, indirect labour, and utilities. Rent is equal to a percentage of the shop's gross revenue for each month. The indirect labour relates primarily to ordering parts and processing insurance claims. The amount of indirect labour, therefore, tends to vary with the size of each job.

Henry Lee, manager of the business, is considering using either direct labour hours or number of repair jobs as the basis for allocating overhead costs. He has estimated the following amounts for the coming year:

Estimated total overhead	123,000
Estimated direct labour hours..	10,000
Estimated number of repair jobs	300

INSTRUCTIONS

a Compute the overhead application rate based on:

1 Direct labour hours.

2 Number of repair jobs.

b Shown below is information for two repair jobs:
Job 1 Repair a dented fender. Direct material used, $25; direct labour hours, 5; direct labour cost, $125.
Job 2 Repair an automobile involved in a serious collision. Direct materials used, $3,800; direct labour hours, 200; direct labour cost, $5,000.
Determine the **total cost** of each repair job, assuming that overhead costs are applied to each job based upon:

1 Direct labour hours.

2 Number of repair jobs.

c Discuss the results obtained in part **b**. Which overhead application method appears to provide the more realistic results. Explain the reasoning behind your answer, addressing the issue of what "drives" overhead costs in this business.

A&D 21-2
The
Meadowbrooke
Miracle

Prescott Manufacturing operates several plants, each of which produces a different product. Early in the current year, John Walker was hired as the new manager of the Meadowbrooke Plant. At year-end, all the plant managers are asked to summarize the operations of their plants at a meeting of the company's board of directors. John Walker displayed the following information on a chart as he made his presentation:

	Current Year	Last Year
Inventories of finished goods:		
Beginning of the year (30,000 units in the current year and 10,000 units last year)	$ 255,000	$ 85,000
End of the year (20,000 units in the current year and 30,000 last year).................................	202,000	255,000
Cost of finished goods manufactured	909,000	1,020,000

Walker made the following statements to the board: "As you know, sales volume has remained constant for the Meadowbrooke Plant. Both this year and last, our sales amounted to 100,000 units. We have made real gains, however, in controlling our manufacturing costs. Through efficient plant operations, we have reduced our cost of finished goods manufactured by over $100,000 from last year's levels. These economies are reflected in a reduction of the manufacturing cost per unit sold from $10.20 last year ($1,020,000 ÷ 100,000 units) to $9.09 in the current year ($909,000 ÷ 100,000 units)."

Father Alan Carter is president of St. Mary's University and is a member of Prescott Manufacturing's board of directors. However, Father Carter has little background in the accounting practices of manufacturing companies, and he asks you for assistance in evaluating Walker's statements.

INSTRUCTIONS **a** As a preliminary step to your analysis, compute the following for the Meadowbrooke Plant in each of the two years:

1 Cost of goods sold

2 Number of finished units manufactured

3 Average cost per unit manufactured

4 Average cost per unit sold

b Evaluate the statements made by Walker. Comment specifically upon Walker's computation of the manufacturing cost of units sold and upon whether it appears that the reduction in the cost of finished goods sold was achieved through more efficient operations.

22 Cost Accounting Systems

How much does it cost IBM to manufacture each IBM ThinkPad (a portable P.C.)? If you are a manager at IBM, you need this information. You need it to set selling prices, to determine the cost of goods sold, to evaluate the efficiency of the company's manufacturing operations, and to plan for the future. In this chapter, we show how manufacturing companies use cost accounting systems to determine on a timely basis the per-unit cost of each product manufactured. Both job order and process cost systems are illustrated and explained.

Several recent developments in the field of cost accounting, including activity-based costing and just-in-time (JIT) systems, are discussed in the Supplemental Topic section at the end of the chapter.

Learning Objectives

After studying this chapter, you should be able to:

1   Explain the purpose of a cost accounting system.
2   Explain the characteristics of a job order cost accounting system.
3   Describe the purpose and the content of a job cost sheet.
4   Explain the characteristics of a process cost accounting system.
5   Define and compute "equivalent full units" of production.
6   Prepare a process cost summary for a production department using a process cost system.
*7   Distinguish between "value-adding" activities and "non-value-adding" activities in a manufacturing business.
*8   Describe activity-based costing and explain the potential benefits of this technique.
*9   Explain the nature and goals of a JIT manufacturing system.

---

*   Supplemental Topic, "The New Manufacturing Environment"

Assume that during the current month, Kaitak Manufacturing Corporation incurs manufacturing costs of $10 million. At month-end, how much of this $10 million represents the cost of finished goods manufactured, and how much is applicable to goods still in process at month-end? If the company produces 20 different types of products, how should the manufacturing costs be allocated among these products? Answers to these questions can only be provided by the company's *cost accounting system.*

What Is a Cost Accounting System?

*OBJECTIVE 1
Explain the
purpose of a
cost ac-
counting
system.*

A cost accounting system consists of the techniques, forms, and accounting records used to develop timely information about the cost of manufacturing specific products and of performing specific functions. Because cost accounting systems are most widely used in manufacturing companies, we will focus upon the use of these systems to determine the cost of manufactured products. However, the concepts of cost accounting are applicable to a wide range of business situations. For example, banks, accounting firms, and governmental agencies all use cost accounting systems to determine the cost of performing various service functions.

In a manufacturing company, cost accounting serves two important managerial objectives: (1) to determine the per-unit cost of each manufactured product and (2) to provide management with information that will be useful in planning future business operations and in controlling costs. *Unit costs* are determined by relating manufacturing costs—the costs of direct materials used, direct labour, and manufacturing overhead—to the number of units manufactured.

A "unit" of product is defined differently in different industries. We tend to think of "units" as individual physical products, such as automobiles or television sets. In other industries, however, the number of units manufactured may be stated as a number of tonnes, litres, cubic metres, or other appropriate unit of measure.[1]

Unit costs provide the basis for inventory valuation and measurement of the cost of goods sold. They also provide managers with information useful in setting selling prices, deciding what products to manufacture, and evaluating the efficiency of operations.

Controlling costs refers to keeping costs down to reasonable levels. When a cost accounting system provides timely information about unit costs, managers are able to react quickly should costs begin to rise to unacceptable levels. By comparing current unit costs with budgets, past performance, and other yardsticks, managers are able to identify those areas in which corrective actions are most needed.

Two Basic Types of Cost Accounting Systems

There are two distinct types of cost accounting systems: job order cost systems and process cost systems. Both systems produce the same end results: timely information about manufacturing costs, inventories on hand, and unit costs.

---

[1]   Some service industries also express their operating costs on a per-unit basis. The "units of product" used in the airline industry, for example, are *passenger-kilometres* flown.

Job order cost systems are used by companies that manufacture "one-of-a-kind" products or that tailor products to the specifications of individual customers. In a job order cost system, the costs of direct materials used, direct labour, and manufacturing overhead are accumulated separately for each job. A "job" represents the goods manufactured at one time to fill a particular order. If the job contains more than one unit of product, unit costs are determined by dividing the total costs charged to the job by the number of units manufactured.

Construction companies use job order cost systems because each construction project has unique characteristics that affect its cost. Job order cost systems also are used by shipbuilders, motion picture studios, defence contractors, print shops, and furniture makers. In addition, these systems are widely used in service-type businesses, including repair shops, hospitals, accounting firms, and law firms.

Process cost systems are used by companies that produce a "steady stream" of nearly identical products over a long period of time. In a process cost system, the focal points in accumulating manufacturing costs are the individual **production departments** (or **processes**) involved in the production cycle. As a first step, the costs of direct materials used, direct labour, and overhead applicable to each production department are compiled for a given period of time (usually one month). The average cost of running a unit of product through each production department then is determined by dividing the departmental costs by the number of units processed during the period. If a product passes through two or more processing departments, the unit costs of performing each process are combined to determine the unit cost of the finished good.

Companies that use process cost systems include oil refineries, power plants, soft-drink bottlers, breweries, flour mills, and most "assembly-line" or "mass-production" manufacturing operations.

The type of cost accounting system best suited to a particular company **depends upon the nature of the company's manufacturing operations.** Both job order and process cost systems are widely used. In fact, a given company may use a job order cost system to account for some of its production activities, and a process cost system to account for others. In the following sections of this chapter, we will illustrate and explain each of these cost accounting systems.

JOB ORDER COST SYSTEMS

OBJECTIVE 2
Explain the characteristics of a job order cost accounting system.

The distinguishing characteristic of a job order cost system is that manufacturing costs are accumulated **separately for each job.** As explained in Chapter 21, manufacturing costs are charged (debited) to the Work in Process Inventory account. In a job cost system, Work in Process Inventory is a controlling account, supported by a subsidiary ledger showing the manufacturing costs charged to each job. The accounts in this subsidiary ledger are called **job cost sheets.**

The Job Cost Sheet

Job cost sheets are the heart of a job order cost system. A separate job cost sheet is prepared for each job and is used to accumulate a record of all

OBJECTIVE 3
Describe the
purpose and
the content
of a job cost
sheet.

manufacturing costs charged to the job. Once the job is finished, the job cost sheet indicates the cost of the finished goods manufactured and provides the information necessary to compute the unit costs of production.

Direct manufacturing costs (direct materials used and direct labour) are recorded on the job cost sheet as quickly as these costs can be traced to the job. Once the job is complete, overhead costs are applied using an overhead application rate. Shown below is a completed job cost sheet of the Oak & Glass Furniture Co. This "job" involved the manufacture of 100 dining tables of a particular style.

OAK & GLASS FURNITURE CO.
JOB COST SHEET
831

Product French Court dining tables   Date started Jan. 3, 1996

Number of units manufactured 100   Date completed Jan. 21, 1996

Costs Charged to This Job

Manufacturing Department	Direct Materials	Direct Labour		Manufacturing Overhead	
		Hours	Cost	Rate	Cost Applied
Milling & Carving	$10,000	700	$14,000	150%	$21,000
Finishing	15,000	300	6,000	150%	9,000

Cost Summary and Unit Costs

	Total Costs	Unit Costs
Direct materials used	$25,000	$250
Direct labour	20,000	200
Manufacturing overhead applied	30,000	300
Cost of finished goods manufactured (100 tables)	$75,000	$750

Throughout the production process, manufacturing costs traceable to the job are accumulated in the "Costs charged to this job" section of the job cost sheet. The "Cost summary" section is filled in when the job is completed.

The total cost of completing job no. 831 is **$75,000.** Upon completion of the job, this amount should be transferred from the Work in Process Inventory account to the Finished Goods Inventory account. The unit cost figures shown in the job cost sheet are determined by dividing the total manufacturing costs by the 100 units manufactured.

Flow of Costs in a Job Cost System: An Illustration

On pages 1038 and 1039, we expand our example of Oak & Glass Furniture Co. to illustrate the flow of costs through a complete but simple job cost accounting system.

This flowchart summarizes the company's manufacturing operations during the month of January. Notice that each of the inventory controlling accounts (Materials, Work in Process, and Finished Goods) is supported by a subsidiary ledger.

In our flowchart, all subsidiary ledger accounts are shown in T account form to conserve space. In practice, the individual job cost sheets serve as the subsidiary ledger for the Work in Process Inventory controlling account. Also, the subsidiary ledger accounts for direct materials and finished goods would have additional columns providing detailed information as to quantities on hand and unit costs.

We will now use our example of Oak & Glass Furniture Co. to explain the flow of manufacturing costs through a job order cost accounting system.

Accounting for Direct Materials

In a perpetual inventory system, purchases of direct materials are posted from the purchases journal to the accounts in the materials subsidiary ledger. The entries in the subsidiary ledger indicate the type, quantity, and cost of the material purchased. At the end of each month, a summary entry is made debiting the Materials Inventory controlling account for the total cost of direct materials purchased during the period. (The offsetting credit normally is to Accounts Payable.)

To obtain materials for use in the production process, the production department must issue a *materials requisition* form to the materials warehouse. This requisition shows the quantity of materials needed and the job on which these materials will be used.

Copies of these requisitions are sent to the accounting department, where the cost of the materials placed into production is determined from the materials subsidiary ledger. The cost of the requisitioned materials is entered on the requisition form and in the subsidiary ledger accounts. In the subsidiary ledgers, usage of direct materials is recorded by (1) entering the cost of the materials used on the appropriate job cost sheet and (2) crediting the materials subsidiary ledger.

At month-end, all the materials requisitions issued during the month are totalled, and the following summary entry is made in the controlling accounts:

Recording materials used during the month	*Work in Process Inventory*	*50,000*
	Materials Inventory	*50,000*
	To record the cost of all direct materials placed into production during January.	

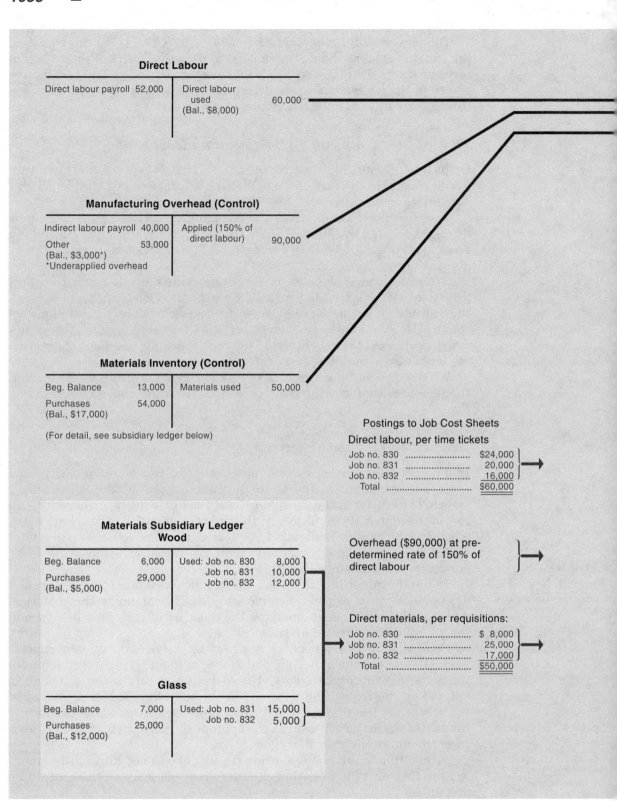

Direct Labour

Direct labour payroll 52,000	Direct labour used (Bal., $8,000)	60,000

Manufacturing Overhead (Control)

Indirect labour payroll 40,000	Applied (150% of direct labour)	90,000
Other 53,000		
(Bal., $3,000*)		
*Underapplied overhead		

Materials Inventory (Control)

Beg. Balance 13,000	Materials used	50,000
Purchases 54,000		
(Bal., $17,000)		

(For detail, see subsidiary ledger below)

Materials Subsidiary Ledger
Wood

Beg. Balance	6,000	Used: Job no. 830	8,000
Purchases	29,000	Job no. 831	10,000
(Bal., $5,000)		Job no. 832	12,000

Glass

Beg. Balance	7,000	Used: Job no. 831	15,000
Purchases	25,000	Job no. 832	5,000
(Bal., $12,000)			

Postings to Job Cost Sheets

Direct labour, per time tickets

Job no. 830	$24,000
Job no. 831	20,000
Job no. 832	16,000
Total	$60,000

Overhead ($90,000) at pre-determined rate of 150% of direct labour

Direct materials, per requisitions:

Job no. 830	$ 8,000
Job no. 831	25,000
Job no. 832	17,000
Total	$50,000

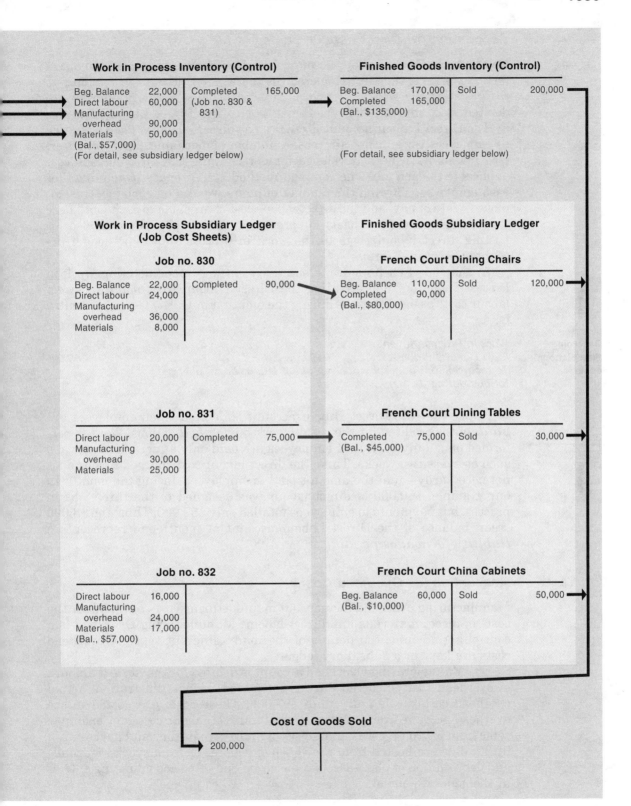

Accounting for Direct Labour Costs

Debits to the Direct Labour account arise from making payments to direct factory workers; the offsetting credit is to the Cash account.[2] Payments to *indirect* factory workers (such as supervisors and security guards) are debited to Manufacturing Overhead, not to the Direct Labour account.

The Direct Labour account is credited as direct labour is *used*—that is, as employees work on specific jobs. A number of mechanical and computerized means have been developed for determining the direct labour cost applicable to each job. One common method is to prepare *time cards* for each employee, showing the number of hours worked on each job, the employee's rate of pay, and the direct labour cost chargeable to each job. These time cards become the basis for preparing factory payrolls and also for posting direct labour costs to the work in process subsidiary ledger accounts (job cost sheets).

At the end of each month, a summary entry is made debiting Work in Process Inventory and crediting the Direct Labour account for all direct labour costs assigned to jobs during the month. For Oak & Glass, this entry is:

Recording direct labour costs	*Work in Process Inventory* *60,000*	
	Direct Labour	*60,000*
	To record in the general ledger all direct labour costs charged to jobs during January.	

Notice that the Direct Labour account is debited when employees are *paid,* but is credited for the cost of work *performed* on jobs. Work is performed on a daily basis, but employees are paid only at periodic intervals, such as every two weeks. Thus, the direct labour cost charged to jobs does not necessarily equal the amount paid to employees during the month. In our example, $60,000 of direct labour was assigned to the three jobs in process, but payments to employees totalled only $52,000. Thus, the $8,000 credit balance of the Direct Labour account at month-end represents a *liability for wages payable.*

Accounting for Overhead Costs

Manufacturing overhead includes all manufacturing costs *other than* the costs of direct materials and direct labour. Manufacturing Overhead is a controlling account; the details of the many different types of overhead costs are kept in a subsidiary ledger.

The Manufacturing Overhead account is debited for the *actual* amount of overhead costs incurred during the period. In our illustration, actual overhead costs in January total $93,000. These costs are posted to the overhead account from several sources. Indirect labour costs, for example, come from payroll records; purchases of indirect materials and payments of utility bills are posted from the voucher register or from special journals, and depreciation of plant assets comes from end-of-period adjusting entries in the general journal.

---

[2] To the extent that amounts are withheld from employees' pay for such purposes as income taxes and other deductions, the offsetting credits are to various current liability accounts. Accounting for payrolls was discussed in Chapter 11.

Application of Overhead Costs to Jobs As explained in Chapter 21, overhead is an ***indirect*** cost and cannot be traced conveniently into specific jobs or units. Therefore, a predetermined ***overhead application rate*** often is used to assign appropriate amounts of overhead costs to work in process. (An alternative approach to the application of overhead costs, called ***activity-based costing,*** is discussed in a Supplemental Topic section at the end of this chapter.) Oak & Glass uses an overhead application rate equal to ***150% of direct labour cost.*** Therefore, each job cost sheet is charged with overhead costs equal to 150% of the direct labour cost relating to the job.

The entry to apply overhead costs to the job cost sheet usually is made when the job is completed. However, overhead costs also should be applied to any jobs that are still in process at the end of the accounting period. At the end of each month, a summary entry is made in the general ledger to record all overhead costs applied to jobs during the period, as follows:

Entry to "apply" over- head costs to production	*Work in Process Inventory*	*90,000*	
	Manufacturing Overhead		*90,000*

To charge the Work in Process controlling account with overhead costs applied to jobs during the month (150% of direct labour costs for the month; $60,000 × 150% = $90,000).

Over- or Underapplied Overhead In our example, actual overhead costs incurred during January amounted to $93,000, while the overhead applied to jobs using the overhead application rate totalled only $90,000. We should not expect that applied overhead will exactly equal actual overhead because the predetermined overhead application rate is based on estimates.

A debit balance in the Manufacturing Overhead account at month-end indicates that overhead applied to jobs was ***less*** than the actual overhead costs incurred during the month. Therefore, a debit balance remaining in the Manufacturing Overhead account is called ***underapplied overhead.*** A credit balance remaining in the amount indicates that overhead applied to jobs ***exceeded*** actual overhead costs; thus, a credit balance is termed ***overapplied overhead.***

The month-end balances remaining in the Manufacturing Overhead account normally are allowed to accumulate throughout the year. These amounts tend to "balance out" from month to month, and the amount of overapplied or underapplied overhead at year-end usually ***is not material*** in dollar amount. In this case, the year-end balance in the Manufacturing Overhead account may be closed ***directly into the Cost of Goods Sold,*** on the grounds that most of the error is applicable to goods sold during the year. If the year-end balance in the overhead account ***is material*** in dollar amount, it should be apportioned among the Work in Process Inventory, Finished Goods Inventory, and Cost of Goods Sold accounts.

Accounting for Completed Jobs

We have now explained how manufacturing costs are charged (debited) to the Work in Process Inventory account, and also how the costs of specific jobs are separately accumulated on job cost sheets.

As each job is completed, the job cost sheet is removed from the work in process subsidiary ledger and the manufacturing costs on the sheet are totalled to determine the cost of finished goods manufactured. This cost then is transferred from the Work in Process Inventory account to the Finished Goods Inventory account.

During January, Oak & Glass completed work on job nos. 830 and 831. The entries to record completion of these jobs are illustrated below:

Entries to record completed jobs

Finished Goods Inventory	*90,000*	
Work in Process Inventory		*90,000*
To record completion of job no. 830, consisting of 600		
French Court dining chairs (unit cost, $150).		
Finished Goods Inventory	*75,000*	
Work in Process Inventory		*75,000*
To record completion of job no. 831, consisting of 100		
French Court dining tables (unit cost, $750).		

As sales of these units occur, the unit cost figure will be used in determining the cost of goods sold. For example, the sale of 40 of the French Court dining tables at a total sales price of $48,000 is recorded below:

Accounts Receivable (Anthony's Fine Furniture)	*48,000*	
Sales		*48,000*
Sold 40 French Court dining tables on account, terms		
2/10, n/30.		
Cost of Goods Sold	*30,000*	
Finished Goods Inventory		*30,000*
To record the cost of the 40 French Court dining tables sold to		
Anthony's Fine Furniture (40 × $750 cost per unit = $30,000).		

Job Order Cost Systems in Service Industries

In the preceding discussion, we have emphasized the use of job order cost systems in manufacturing companies. However, many service industries also use these systems to accumulate the costs of servicing a particular customer.

In a hospital, for example, each patient represents a separate "job," and the costs of caring for the patient are accumulated on a job cost sheet. Costs of such items as medicine, blood transfusions, and x-rays represent the usage of direct materials; services rendered by doctors are direct labour. The costs of nursing, meals, linen service, and depreciation of the hospital building and equipment all are part of the hospital's overhead. In a hospital, overhead usually is applied to each patient's account at a daily rate.

PROCESS COST SYSTEMS

As emphasized in the preceding section, job order cost systems are appropriate when each unit of product, or each "batch" of production, is manufactured to different specifications. In order to operate a job order system, it is necessary to be able to *identify the units* included in each job at every stage of the production process. What happens, then, when a company produces a continuous stream of identical products, such as bottles of beer or kilowatts of electricity? The answer is that these companies use ***process cost systems,*** rather than job order systems.

Characteristics of a Process Cost System

OBJECTIVE 4
Explain the characteristics of a process cost accounting system.

The manufacture of any product usually involves several specific steps, or manufacturing ***processes.*** For accounting purposes, each manufacturing process is viewed as a separate processing department. A separate Work in Process Inventory account is maintained for each processing department; this account is charged (debited) with all manufacturing costs incurred in performing the process during the current accounting period.[3] At the end of the period, the per-unit cost of performing the process is determined by dividing the costs charged to the departmental work in process account by the number of units processed during the period. The cost of a finished unit is determined by combining the per-unit cost of performing each process involved in the unit's manufacture.

Flow of Costs in a Process Cost System

To illustrate the basic features of a process cost system, assume that Baker Labs manufactures a nonprescription cold remedy called Conquest. Two processing departments are involved in the manufacture of Conquest: the Mixing Department and the Packaging Department. In the Mixing Department, the various chemicals used to make the cold remedy are blended together. The product is then transferred to the Packaging Department, where it is sealed in small "tamper-proof" packages. Packages of Conquest are the company's finished product; these packages are stored in a warehouse and shipped to customers (drug stores and grocery stores) as orders are received.

The flow of manufacturing costs through the process cost system of Baker Labs during the month of July is summarized on the next page. Notice that a separate Work in Process Inventory account is used for ***each production process,*** enabling accountants to accumulate separately the manufacturing costs relating to each process. As the Mixing Department completes work on specific units, the cost of these units is transferred into the Work in Process Inventory account for the Packaging Department. Only when units emerge from the Packaging Department are they regarded as finished goods.

The cost flows summarized in this illustration will now be used to explain the operation of a process cost accounting system. Our illustration is based on the assumption that Baker Labs uses the ***first-in, first-out*** (FIFO) method of inventory valuation. (Other inventory valuation methods, such as average cost, will be discussed in the cost accounting course.)

Direct Materials   Purchases of direct materials are debited to the Materials Inventory controlling account, and a subsidiary ledger is maintained

---

[3]   One objective of a cost accounting system is to provide managers with ***timely*** information as to manufacturing costs. Therefore, the time period used in a process cost system usually is one month or less.

Cost flow diagram for process costing—notice the departmental Work in Process accounts

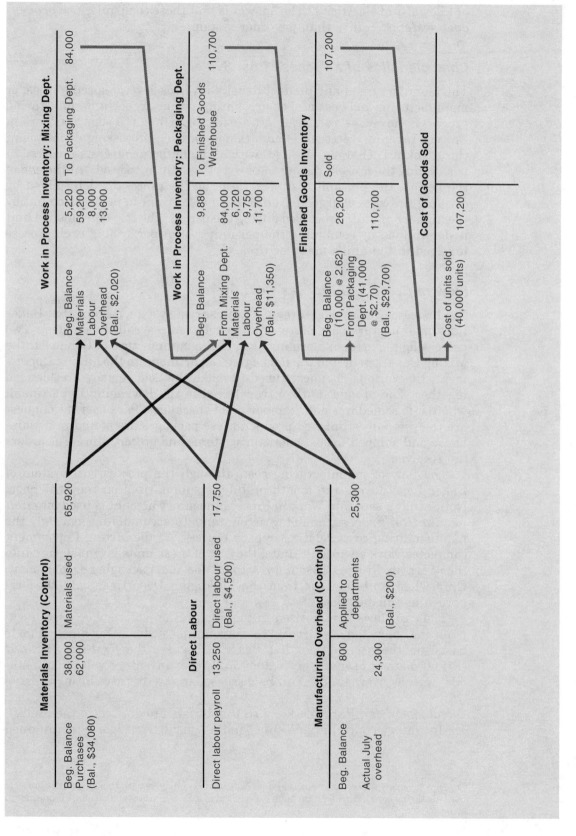

showing the unit cost and quantity on hand for each type of direct materials.

To obtain direct materials for use in production, the Processing Departments must issue materials requisition forms, and copies of these forms are sent to the Accounting Department. (Direct materials used in the Mixing Department include various chemicals; direct materials used in the Packaging Department are the "tamper-proof" containers.) The Accounting Department immediately updates the materials subsidiary ledger and, at the end of the month, makes a summary entry to charge the departmental work in process accounts for all direct materials requisitioned during the month. The summary entry for July appears below.

Work in Process Inventory: Mixing Department	59,200	
Work in Process Inventory: Packaging Department	6,720	
Materials Inventory		65,920

To record the cost of direct materials requisitioned for use in production during July.

Direct Labour   During July, payments to direct workers totalled $13,250, and this amount was debited to the Direct Labour account. The direct labour cost used within each processing department during July is determined from employees' time cards. The month-end entry to record the direct labour costs chargeable to each department is:

Work in Process Inventory: Mixing Department	8,000	
Work in Process Inventory: Packaging Department	9,750	
Direct Labour		17,750

To record the cost of direct labour used in July.

Manufacturing Overhead   During July, actual overhead costs of $24,300 were charged to the Manufacturing Overhead account. Baker Labs follows a policy of applying overhead costs to production **as a percentage of direct labour costs.** (Later in this chapter, we will discuss the alternative of charging actual overhead costs to production.) At the beginning of the year, the company developed the following overhead application rates, based upon the budgeted amounts of overhead and direct labour costs for each processing department:

Mixing Department	*170% of direct labour cost*
Packaging Department.......................................	*120% of direct labour cost*

At the end of July, the following entry is made to apply overhead to the departmental Work in Process Inventory accounts:

Work in Process Inventory: Mixing Department	13,600	
Work in Process Inventory: Packaging Department	11,700	
Manufacturing Overhead.................................		25,300

To apply overhead costs to departments, based on direct labour costs (Mixing Dept., $8,000 × 170% = $13,600; Packaging Dept., $9,750 × 120% = $11,700).

Notice that the Manufacturing Overhead controlling account had a debit balance of $800 at the beginning of July. This debit balance represented a small amount of **underapplied overhead** that had accumulated over the first half of the year. In July, however, applied overhead exceeds actual overhead costs by $1,000. Thus, at the end of July, the overhead account has a credit balance of $200, representing a small amount of **overapplied overhead.** Throughout the year, the balances in the overhead account are allowed to carry forward from month to month. At year-end, any remaining balance normally is closed out to the Cost of Goods Sold account.[4]

Equivalent Full Units—The Key to Determining Unit Cost

A basic objective of a process cost system is to determine the unit cost of direct materials, direct labour, and overhead for each manufacturing process or department. These unit costs become the basis for valuing inventories and for tracing the flow of costs through the departmental work in process accounts and finally to Finished Goods Inventory and to Cost of Goods Sold.

If all units of product in a given department are **completely processed** (started and completed) during the period, computing unit costs is a simple matter of dividing the departmental costs by the number of units processed. In most cases, however, there are unfinished units of product on hand at the beginning as well as at the end of the accounting period. When some of the units on hand are unfinished, we cannot compute unit costs merely by dividing total costs by the number of units worked on, for this would assign the same unit cost to finished and unfinished goods. If completed and partially completed units of product are expressed in **equivalent full units** of completed product, however, this difficulty is overcome. Meaningful unit costs can then be determined by dividing the total cost by the equivalent full units produced. This computation is illustrated below for direct materials:

Units Costs Based on Equivalent Full Units

$$\text{Materials Cost per Unit} = \frac{\text{Total Cost of Direct Materials Used During Month}}{\text{Equivalent Full Units Produced During Month}}$$

OBJECTIVE 5 Define and compute "equivalent full units" of production.

What Are "Equivalent Full Units"?   Equivalent full units are a measure of the **work done** in a given accounting period. The concept of an equivalent full unit is based on the assumption that creating two units, each of which is 50% complete, represents the **same amount of work** as does producing one finished unit. Similarly, producing 1,000 units that are 25% complete is viewed as equivalent to 250 full units of production.

The work accomplished by a manufacturing department during a given accounting period may include (1) completing units that were already in process at the beginning of the period, (2) working on units started and completed during the current period, and (3) working on units that are still in process at the end of the current period. If we are to measure the work accomplished by the department, we must determine the equivalent full units of production represented **by each of these three types of work effort.**

---

[4]   As explained earlier in this chapter, if the year-end balance in the overhead account is material in dollar amount, it should be apportioned among the Cost of Goods Sold, Finished Goods Inventory, and Work in Process Inventory accounts, based on the relative balances in each account. This allocation procedure is seldom necessary.

To illustrate this concept, we will use the production activities of Baker Labs during the month of July. Assume that the production managers of the company's two processing departments provide the following summary of the *numbers of units* processed within their departments during July. (Notice that the following schedule describes the *extent of completion* of units in process at the beginning and end of the month.)

Production Summary—in Units
for the Month Ended July 31, 1996

	Mixing Department	Packaging Department
Units in process, July 1	5,000[a]	4,000[c]
Units started and completed in July	37,000	37,000
Units completed and transferred to next department or to finished goods in July..................................	42,000	41,000
Units in process, July 31	4,000[b]	5,000[d]

[a] 60% complete as to materials and conversion costs on July 1.
[b] 25% complete as to materials and conversion costs on July 31.
[c] 100% complete as to materials and 75% complete as to conversion costs on July 1.
[d] 100% complete as to materials and 20% complete as to conversion costs on July 31.

In describing the extent of completion of the units in process, notice the use of the term *conversion costs.* This term is used to describe the costs of both direct labour *and* manufacturing overhead, as these are the costs of converting direct materials into finished goods.

The number of equivalent full units of production processed by the Mixing Department during July is determined as follows:

Computation of Equivalent Full Units—Mixing Department
(Direct Materials and Conversion Costs)

	Units ×	Portion Completed = in July	Equivalent Full Units Produced
Units in process at the beginning of July (60% completed in June as to materials and conversion costs)...	5,000	40%	2,000
Units started and completed in July	37,000	100%	37,000
Units completed and transferred to Packaging Dept. in July	42,000		
Units in process at the end of July (25% complete as to materials and conversion costs)............	4,000	25%	1,000
Equivalent full units of production during July.............................			40,000

Although 42,000 units of product were completed and transferred to the Packaging Department, the actual amount of work accomplished in the Mixing Department during July was equivalent to producing only *40,000 "full" units.* The work performed in July consists of 2,000 equivalent full units of work (40% of 5,000) to complete the beginning inventory of work in process, 37,000 equivalent full units of work to start and complete additional units during July, and 1,000 equivalent full units (25% of 4,000) on the units still in process at month-end.

Conversion costs normally are added to units of product at a uniform rate throughout the production process. Thus, units that are 25% complete are assigned 25% of the per-unit conversion costs. In the Mixing Department, direct materials also are added to units at a uniform rate. Therefore, the equivalent number of full units produced in the department is *the same* with respect to materials used and conversion costs.

Materials and Conversion Costs Added at Different Rates It is not unusual for materials and conversion costs to be added to units of product at *different* rates. For example, 100% of the materials needed to produce finished goods may be placed into production at the beginning of the production process. In these situations, the number of equivalent full units produced during the period must be *computed separately* for materials and for conversion costs.

To illustrate, assume that in the Packaging Department of Baker Labs, all direct materials are placed into production at the *beginning* of the production process, but that conversion costs are applied at a *uniform rate* throughout the process. The equivalent number of full units produced is computed separately for materials used and for conversion costs, as illustrated below.

Computation of Equivalent Full Units—Packaging Department

	Units ×	Portion Completed = in July	Equivalent Full Units Produced
Direct Materials:			
Units in process at the beginning of July (100% completed in June as to materials)	4,000	-0-	-0-
Units started and completed in July	37,000	100%	37,000
Units completed and transferred to Finished Goods Warehouse in July	41,000		
Units in process at the end of July (100% complete as to materials)	5,000	100%	5,000
Equivalent full units of production during July— direct materials			42,000
Conversion Costs:			
Units in process at the beginning of July (75% completed in June as to conversion costs)	4,000	25%	1,000
Units started and completed in July	37,000	100%	37,000
Units completed and transferred to Finished Goods Warehouse in July	41,000		
Units in process at the end of July (20% complete as to conversion costs)	5,000	20%	1,000
Equivalent full units of production during July— conversion costs			39,000

In the Packaging Department, enough direct materials were placed into production to produce 42,000 units of product. However, the amount of direct labour and manufacturing overhead used was sufficient to produce only 39,000 equivalent full units. Thus, the equivalent full units of production by the department during July **differ** with respect to direct materials and to conversion costs.

Determining Unit Costs

At the end of each month, the Accounting Department prepares a **process cost summary** for each production department. These cost summaries are specially designed working papers, upon which accountants (1) summarize the manufacturing costs charged to each department, (2) determine the departmental unit costs of production, and (3) allocate the departmental manufacturing costs between completed units and work still in process at month-end.

Process Cost Summary for the Mixing Department

The process cost summary for the Mixing Department is illustrated below:

BAKER LABS
Process Cost Summary—Mixing Department
For the Month Ended July 31, 1996

	Total Costs ÷	Equivalent Full Units =	Unit Cost
Costs charged to the department and unit costs:			
Work in process inventory, beginning of July	$ 5,220		
Manufacturing costs charged to the department during July:			
Direct materials used	59,200	40,000	$1.48
Direct labour	8,000	40,000	0.20
Manufacturing overhead	13,600	40,000	0.34
Unit cost per equivalent full unit processed during July . . .			$2.02
Total costs to be accounted for	$86,020		
Allocation of costs charged to the department:			
*Work in process inventory, end of July (4,000 units, 25% complete as to all costs; 4,000 units × **$2.02** per full unit × 25%)*	$ 2,020		
Cost of units completed and transferred to Packaging Department (42,000 units):			
*Total cost (86,020 − **$2,020**)*	84,000		
Unit cost ($84,000 ÷ 42,000 completed units)			$2.00
Total costs accounted for	$86,020		

Notice all costs are allocated

Notice two unit costs

We will now explain the steps in the preparation of this working paper.

Step 1: Summarize the Manufacturing Costs Charged to the Department
The top portion of the process cost summary begins with a list of all manufacturing costs applicable to units worked during July. These costs include the beginning inventory of work in process and all manufacturing costs charged to the department during July. Notice that the sum of these costs,

*OBJECTIVE 6
Prepare a
process cost
summary for
a production
department
using a pro-
cess cost sys-
tem.*

$86,020, is labelled "Total costs to be accounted for." As we shall see, "accounting for" these costs means assigning them either to units completed during July, or to units still in process at July 31. The information needed to complete the "Total costs" column is found in the debit side of the departmental work in process account (page 1044).

Step 2: Determine Unit Costs   The second step in preparing a process cost summary is to determine the per-unit cost of the manufacturing activities performed by the department during the month. This is accomplished by dividing each of the three categories of manufacturing costs incurred during July by the **equivalent full units** of production for the month.

For example, during July the Mixing Department used direct materials costing $59,200. Our computations above show that the department produced the equivalent of 40,000 full units. Therefore, each equivalent full unit produced by the Mixing Department during July required an average of **$1.48** in direct materials costs ($59,200 ÷ 40,000 units = $1.48 per unit). Similar computations are made to compute the per-unit costs of direct labour and manufacturing overhead.[5] These three unit costs then are combined, indicating an average cost of **$2.02** for each **equivalent full unit** produced by the Mixing Department during July.

Step 3: Allocate the Costs Charged to the Department between Completed Units and Units Still in Process   Once the per-unit manufacturing costs have been determined, we may allocate our $86,020 in "Total costs to be accounted for" between the two types of departmental output—units completed and transferred to the Packaging Department, and units still in process in the Mixing Department at month-end. This allocation of costs is illustrated in the bottom section of the process cost summary.

We could use the unit cost figures from the top section of our cost summary to compute separately the cost of the ending inventory of work in process and the cost of units completed during the period. However, it is **not necessary** to compute both of these amounts in this manner. It is quicker and easier to use unit costs to compute only the value of the ending inventory of work in process. We may then simply **assign the remainder** of the $86,020 total costs to the units completed during July.

Baker Labs uses the first-in, first-out (FIFO) method of inventory valuation; therefore, the ending inventory of work in process is valued using the **most recent** unit costs—namely, those incurred during July. Work in process in the Mixing Department at July 31 amounts to 4,000 units, each of which is 25% complete with respect to all manufacturing costs. Therefore, the cost of this ending inventory is **$2,020** (4,000 units × $2.02 × 25%).

Deducting this $2,020 from the $86,020 total costs to be accounted for leaves a remainder of **$84,000,** representing the cost of units completed by

---

[5]   In determining the unit cost of work done in July, we do not express the $5,220 beginning inventory of work in process on a per-unit basis, as these manufacturing costs were incurred in June.

the Mixing Department during July.[6] The $2.00 unit cost of these completed goods is determined by dividing their total cost ($84,000) by the number of completed units (42,000).

Upon completion of the process cost summary, the following journal entry is made to summarize the cost of units completed by the Mixing Department during the month:[7]

Cost of units transferred from one processing department to the next.	**Work in Process Inventory: Packaging Department**	**84,000**
	Work in Process Inventory: Mixing Department	**84,000**
	To record the cost of 42,000 units transferred from the Mixing Department to the Packaging Department during July. (Unit cost, $84,000 ÷ 42,000 units = $2.00.)	

Unit Cost of Completed Products Notice that the average cost of units *completed* during July ($2.00) differs slightly from the average cost of manufacturing an ***equivalent full unit*** of product during the month ($2.02). The reason for this small difference is that the cost of producing an equivalent full unit is based ***entirely upon manufacturing costs incurred during July.*** Some of the units completed during July, however, received part of their processing during June.[8]

Each of these two unit costs is important and serves a separate purpose. The $2.02 per unit is the ***most current*** unit cost figure; therefore, this amount is helpful in evaluating the efficiency of the Mixing Department during July. Also, this current unit cost is used in valuing the ending inventory of work in process under the FIFO method.

The $2.00 unit cost, on the other hand, is the average cost incurred in manufacturing the 42,000 units ***completed*** during July. This is the unit cost that will be carried forward into the process cost summary of the Packaging Department and, eventually, into the Finished Goods Inventory and Cost of Goods Sold accounts.

---

[6] The $84,000 cost of the 42,000 units completed by the Mixing Department during July may be verified as follows:

Work in process inventory, July 1 (5,000 units, 60% complete)		$ 5,220
Costs added in July to complete these 5,000 units:		
Direct materials used (5,000 units × $1.48 × 40%)	$ 2,960	
Direct labour (5,000 units × $0.20 × 40%)	400	
Manufacturing overhead (5,000 units × $0.34 × 40%)	680	4,040
Total cost of first 5,000 units completed in July		$ 9,260
Cost of 37,000 units started and completed during July:		
Direct materials used (37,000 units × $1.48)	$54,760	
Direct labour (37,000 units × $0.20)	7,400	
Manufacturing overhead (37,000 units × $0.34)	12,580	
Total cost of next 37,000 units completed during July		74,740
Cost of 42,000 units completed and transferred to Packaging		
Department during July		$84,000

[7] In practice, it is not necessary to wait until a monthly process cost summary is completed to record transfers of completed units from production departments. These transfers may be recorded at any time using ***standard costs*** (estimated amounts). Standard cost systems are discussed in Chapter 25.

[8] In our illustration, 5,000 of the units completed in July received 60% of their processing in June.

Process Cost Summary for the Packaging Department

The process cost summary for the Packaging Department is illustrated below. In most respects, this schedule parallels that prepared for the Mixing Department. There are, however, several new features that deserve attention.

BAKER LABS
Process Cost Summary—Packaging Department
For the Month Ended July 31, 1996

	Total Costs	÷ Equivalent Full Units	= Unit Cost
Costs charged to the department and unit costs:			
Work in process inventory, beginning of July.........	$ 9,880		
Cost of 42,000 units transferred in from Mixing Department during July.............................	84,000		$2.00
Manufacturing costs added by Packaging Department during July:			
Direct materials used	6,720	42,000	.16
Direct labour	9,750	39,000	.25
Manufacturing overhead	11,700	39,000	.30
Unit cost per equivalent unit processed during July ...			$2.71
Total costs to be accounted for	$122,050		
Allocation of costs charged to the department:			
Work in process inventory, end of July (5,000 units, 100% complete as to materials, 20% as to conversion costs):			
Cost of units transferred in from the Mixing Department (5,000 units × $2.00)	$ 10,000		
Direct materials added (5,000 units × $.16 × 100%)...	800		
Direct labour (5,000 units × $.25 × 20%)	250		
Manufacturing overhead (5,000 units × $.30 × 20%) ..	300		
Total cost of work in process inventory at July 31 .	$ 11,350		
Cost of units completed and transferred to Finished Goods Warehouse (41,000 units):			
Total cost ($122,050 − $11,350)...................	110,700		
Unit cost ($110,700 ÷ 41,000 finished units)...........			$2.70
Total costs accounted for............................	$122,050		

First, notice that the manufacturing costs charged to the Packaging Department include the ***cost of units transferred in from the Mixing Department*** during the month. The $84,000 cost of these units, and also the $2.00 unit cost, were computed in the process cost summary of the Mixing Department (page 1049). From the viewpoint of the Packaging Department, the units transferred in from the Mixing Department are a form of direct material to be used in the packaging process.

Second, notice that ***different amounts*** of equivalent full units of production are used in computing the unit costs of direct materials and conversion costs (direct labour and manufacturing overhead). We explained earlier in this chapter that in the Packaging Department, 100% of the direct materials are placed into production at the start of the production process, while conversion costs are applied uniformly throughout the process. As a result, the equivalent full units of production turned out by the department may *differ* with respect to materials and to conversion costs. (The equivalent full units of production for the Packaging Department in July were computed in the schedule on page 1048.)

A third new feature in the process cost summary of the Packaging Department is the itemizing of the various cost elements included in the ending inventory of work in process. Since these units are 100% complete as to direct materials, but only 20% complete as to conversion costs, the amount of each manufacturing cost to be included in these units must be computed separately. Also note that the costs transferred in from the Mixing Department, amounting to $2.00 per unit, are included in the cost of the 5,000 units in process at July 31.

All of the $122,050 in costs charged to the Packaging Department during July are applicable either to units still in process at July 31 or to units completed during the month. Since we have assigned $11,350 of these costs to the ending inventory of work in process, the remaining $110,700 ($122,050 − $11,350) represents the cost of the 41,000 units completed during July. The entry to transfer the cost of goods completed by the Packaging Department during July to the Finished Goods Inventory account is:

Finished Goods Inventory..................................	**110,700**	
Work in Process Inventory: Packaging Department		**110,700**
To record the cost of 41,000 units of finished goods		
completing the production process during July. (Unit		
cost, $110,700 ÷ 41,000 units = $2.70.)		

As these finished units are sold, their cost will be transferred from the Finished Goods Inventory account to the Cost of Goods Sold at a rate of $2.70 per unit.

Process Cost Systems: Actual Overhead or Applied Overhead?

In our example of a process cost system, we used an *overhead application rate* to charge an appropriate amount of manufacturing overhead to the departmental work in process accounts each month. We mentioned, however, that the possibility of using *actual overhead costs* would be discussed later in the chapter.

In a process cost system, overhead is not charged to the departmental work in process accounts until the end of the accounting period. Therefore, it is possible to charge these accounts with the actual overhead costs incurred during the month, rather than with the amount of overhead indicated by using an overhead application rate.[9] In fact, many manufacturing companies *do* charge production departments with actual overhead costs on a monthly basis.

---

[9]   Actual overhead *cannot* be applied to specific jobs in a job order cost system, because actual overhead costs for the month are *not known* at the time that specific jobs are completed. Therefore, all companies with job order cost systems use overhead application rates.

At first glance, charging the actual overhead costs to production departments has great appeal. For one thing, this approach eliminates the problem of accounting for overapplied or underapplied overhead. However, the use of an overhead application rate often provides *more useful* unit cost information, especially if (1) some major overhead costs occur at infrequent intervals or (2) the volume of production varies from month to month.

Costs Occurring at Infrequent Intervals Some overhead costs occur at infrequent intervals, rather than uniformly from month to month. Examples include repairs and refurbishing projects. If actual overhead costs are assigned to production on a monthly basis, the entire amount of these infrequent costs is assigned to the units produced during the month in which the cost happens to occur; none of the cost is borne by units produced in other months.

To illustrate, assume that Baker Labs shuts down its factory for two weeks every August to repair equipment and repaint the building. It is not reasonable to say that these actions relate only to the limited number of units produced during the remainder of August. Obviously, these annual costs relate to production throughout the year.

An overhead application rate avoids the "infrequent cost" problem, because the rate is based upon the estimated cost for the *entire year.* Thus, the costs of infrequent events, such as repairs, are spread uniformly over units produced throughout the year.

Fluctuations in the Level of Production A second problem in the use of actual overhead costs may arise if the number of units produced fluctuates from month to month. This problem stems from the fact that many elements of manufacturing overhead are fixed costs, rather than variable costs.

Fixed costs are those that tend to remain relatively fixed (constant) from month to month. Examples of fixed overhead costs include the monthly salary paid to the plant manager, and the depreciation, property taxes, and insurance on plant assets. ***Variable costs,*** in contrast, are those that ***change in approximate proportion to the level of production.*** Examples of variable overhead costs include factory utilities and the costs of some indirect materials used in the manufacturing process.[10]

Because many overhead costs are fixed, total monthly overhead ***does not*** vary in direct proportion to the number of units produced. Thus, if we allocate actual overhead costs incurred each month to output for that month, the unit cost of production may vary widely from month to month. In months of high output, per-unit overhead costs would be relatively low; in months of low output, per-unit overhead costs would be relatively high.

To illustrate, assume that Drew Corporation has the capacity to produce 10,000 units per month. Fixed overhead costs are ***$120,000 per month,*** and variable overhead amounts to ***$2 per unit*** manufactured. The overhead costs per unit at different levels of output are as follows:

---

[10] The concepts of fixed and variable costs extend to many costs and expenses other than manufacturing overhead. The costs of direct materials and direct labour, for example, are variable costs. These concepts are explored further in Chapter 23.

Overhead Costs per Unit at Different Levels of Output

	Level of Output		
	10,000 Units	*8,000 Units*	*6,000 Units*
Fixed overhead costs......................................	$120,000	$120,000	$120,000
Variable overhead costs ($2 per unit)....................	20,000	16,000	12,000
Total overhead costs (a)	$140,000	$136,000	$132,000
Units produced (b)	10,000	8,000	6,000
Overhead cost per unit (a) ÷ (b)........................	$14	$17	$22

For most business purposes, management needs to know the "normal" unit cost of producing a product, not monthly costs that vary significantly depending upon the volume of production. Again, this problem is solved by using an overhead application rate. As the application rate is based upon budgeted overhead for the entire year, the fixed overhead costs are "averaged out" over all units, regardless of whether the units are produced in a high-volume month or a low-volume month.

Using Actual Overhead May Work Well in Large Companies The problems that we have described above are far more likely to arise in small companies than in large ones. In large companies, such costs as maintenance and repairs do not vary much from month to month. Also, most large companies are able to schedule their production so as to produce approximately the same number of units each month. Thus, for a large company using a process cost system, charging the work in process accounts with the actual amount of monthly overhead costs may work just as well as using an overhead application rate.

■ ■ ■ * *Supplemental Topic*
The New Manufacturing Environment

In recent years, the competition among manufacturing companies has become international in scope. If Canadian companies cannot produce quality products at competitive prices, the market soon is lost to efficient foreign producers.

To compete effectively in today's global economy, Canadian manufacturing companies must strive constantly to improve the efficiency of their manufacturing processes and the quality of their products. Cost accounting systems can aid managers in achieving these goals by providing more detailed and more accurate information about unit costs, and by developing useful measurements of product quality.

THE USEFULNESS OF DETAILED INFORMATION

In this chapter, we have illustrated how a cost accounting system determines separately the cost of performing various manufacturing processes.

Our Baker Labs example included two major processes—mixing and packaging. Such broad definitions of "processes" are satisfactory for developing information for financial statements, but not for use by management in evaluating the *efficiency* of business operations.

To enable managers to evaluate the efficiency of business operations, a cost accounting system ideally should measure separately the cost of each step, activity, and use of materials in the manufacturing process. Accounting systems also should be *cost-effective,* however; meaning that the cost of developing information should not exceed its value to the intended users.

With the aid of computers, managerial accountants are finding that they economically can develop more detailed unit cost information than they previously thought possible. This detailed information often highlights opportunities for significant cost savings.

CASE IN POINT If you fly first class on American Airlines, your dinner salad probably will contain only one black olive. The company's cost accounting system revealed that reducing the number of olives in these salads from 2 to 1 would reduce operating costs by more than $40,000 per year.

H. J. Heinz made a similar discovery. By placing one label on its large catsup bottles instead of two, the company reduced its annual manufacturing costs by several hundred thousand dollars.

"Value-Adding" and "Non-Value-Adding" Activities As stated previously, cost considerations may limit the extent of detailed information that is developed. Of particular importance however, is measuring separately the costs of performing *non-value-adding activities.*

OBJECTIVE 7 Distinguish between "value-adding" activities and "non-value-adding" activities in a manufacturing business.

An *activity* is any repetitive action performed in the conduct of business operations. Activities that increase the worth of a product (or service) *to the customer* are said to be "value-adding" activities. Non-value-adding activities are those functions that *do not* directly increase the worth of the product to the consumer. Therefore, cost savings achieved through the reduction or elimination of non-value-adding activities usually *do not lessen customer satisfaction.*

A few examples of activities often classified as value-adding or as non-value-adding activities are as follows:

Value-Adding Activities	Non-Value-Adding Activities
Product design	Inventory storage and handling
Manufacture and assembly	Machinery setup and idle time
Packaging	Storing work in process awaiting further processing
Delivery	
Technical support services after sale	Production of excess quantities of finished goods
Extension of credit	Quality control inspections and rework of defective units
	Spoilage, breakage, and scrapping of defective output

Our classification of quality control inspections and the rework of defective units as non-value-adding activities requires additional explanation. Quality, of course, adds value to the product. However, inspections and rework would ***not be necessary*** if the manufacturing process ***had been performed properly in the first place.*** Therefore, these activities may be viewed as the "cost" of errors or inefficiencies in the production process. Mistakes and inefficiencies do not add value.

Whether or not a specific activity "adds value" to the product may vary from one situation to the next. For example, most customers probably regard quality control inspections of newly manufactured aircraft engines as a value-adding activity.

In summary, non-value-adding activities are ***unnecessary,*** and the costs relating to these activities ***should be minimized.*** The concepts of value-adding and non-value-adding activities are applicable to ***all aspects*** of business operations, not merely to manufacturing activities.

ACTIVITY-BASED COSTING (ABC)

OBJECTIVE 8
Describe activity-based costing and explain the potential benefits of this technique.

Activity-based costing is a technique of allocating overhead costs among different types of manufactured products using a wide variety of cost drivers.[11] Activity-based costing serves two basic purposes. First, it forces careful consideration of the factors that drive specific overhead costs. This analysis may bring to light means of reducing these costs. Second, activity-based costing results in a more accurate measurement of unit cost than is achieved through the use of a single overhead application rate. A realistic knowledge of unit cost is a prerequisite to setting sales prices at levels that are both profitable and competitive.

The allocation of overhead costs through activity-based costing involves the following steps:

1 Subdivide total overhead costs into specific activities, and determine the cost driver(s) for each activity.

2 Forecast for the coming year (a) the cost of each overhead activity, (b) the level of cost driver activity, (c) the number of units of each type of product to be manufactured, and (d) the percentage of cost driver activity relating to each type of product manufactured.

3 Using the relative percentages of cost driver activity, allocate each type of overhead cost among the product lines.

4 Express the estimated overhead costs applicable to each type of product as a per-unit dollar amount.

5 Apply overhead costs to units of production using the estimated per-unit amounts.

An Illustration of Activity-Based Costing

To illustrate the basic concept of activity-based costing, we will use this approach to determine how selected overhead costs might be allocated among three products.

---

[11] Activity-based-costing procedures also may be applied to activities ***other than*** overhead. Examples include marketing and distribution activities, billing, and providing services either within the organization or to customers. Our discussion of ABC, however, is limited to activities classified as manufacturing overhead.

Assume that Arc Electronics manufactures three products, which we will call A, B, and C. The schedule on page 1059 summarizes the determination of the overhead costs relating to the ordering, storage, and handling of direct materials that will be charged to each unit of production during the year.

Arc's managerial accountants began this process by identifying the major overhead activities involved in the ordering, storage, and handling of direct materials—and also identifying the related cost drivers. Next, they forecast the cost of each overhead activity, the activity base (cost driver), and the percentage of this activity base applicable to each product line.

Often, the percentage of cost driver activity applicable to each product line is based upon the estimated **number of transactions** involving that product. (With respect to ordering materials, for example, each issuance of a purchase order may be viewed as one "transaction.") For this reason, activity-based costing sometimes is called **transaction-based costing.**

The dollar amount of each overhead activity charged to a specific product line is determined by applying the percentage of cost driver activity for that product line to the estimated annual cost of the overhead activity. Finally, a **per-unit application rate** is determined by dividing the total cost applicable to that product line by the estimated number of units to be produced. As units are produced, they will be charged with materials-handling costs based upon this per-unit application rate. (Of course, per-unit application rates also are developed for the other elements of manufacturing overhead.)

Benefits of Activity-Based Costing

Let us briefly discuss two benefits of activity-based costing.

First, management is made aware of the various factors comprising overhead costs. This may direct managers' attention to areas in which costs may be reduced. For example, the cost of inspecting materials ordered for product C is expected to total $40,000 in the coming year. Perhaps this cost could be reduced or eliminated if these materials were ordered from a more quality-oriented supplier. Also the costs of storing materials used in the manufacture of product A are expected to total $54,000 this year. Perhaps these storage costs could be reduced by ordering smaller quantities of these materials and having shipments delivered more frequently.

Second, notice the use of **four different cost drivers** in allocating only these few types of overhead costs. The purpose of this detailed allocation is to associate overhead costs **as closely as possible** with the units generating these costs.

JUST-IN-TIME MANUFACTURING SYSTEMS

Much attention recently has been given to just-in-time *(JIT)* manufacturing systems. The phrase "just in time" refers to acquiring materials and manufacturing goods only as needed to fill customers' orders. JIT systems sometimes are described as "demand pull" manufacturing, because production occurs only in response to customer demand. This contrasts with the more traditional "supply push" systems, in which the manufacturer simply produces as many goods as possible.

OBJECTIVE 9
Explain the nature and goals of a JIT manufacturing system.

A JIT system is characterized by extremely small or nonexistent inven-

ARC ELECTRONICS
Determination of Certain Overhead Costs per Unit
Using Activity-Based Costing Procedures
for the Year Ended December 31, 19___

Overhead Activities (Relating to Materials)	Estimated Annual Cost	Cost Driver	Cost Driver Activity Applicable to Each Product					
			Percentage			Dollars		
			A	B	C	A	B	C
Ordering materials and stocking incoming shipments	$170,000	Number of purchase orders	20%	30%	50%	$34,000	$51,000	$ 85,000
Inspecting incoming shipments	40,000	Inspection hours	0%	0%	100%	-0-	-0-	40,000
Storage of materials	90,000	Square metres of storage space	60%	10%	30%	54,000	9,000	27,000
Moving materials into production	10,000	Number of production runs	20%	50%	30%	2,000	5,000	3,000
Total	$310,000					$90,000	$65,000	$155,000
Scheduled number of units to be manufactured during the year						45,000	100,000	50,000
Materials handling overhead costs to be applied per unit						$2.00	$0.65	$3.10

tories of materials, work in process, and finished goods. Materials arrive only as needed by the production departments—sometimes within a few hours of their scheduled use. Work in process flows quickly from one production process to the next, without moving temporarily into storage facilities. Finished goods are not produced in excess of existing customer orders.

Storing large amounts of inventory can be costly. Among the costs generated by the storage function are the acquisition and operation of storage facilities, insurance, the cost of money "tied-up" in the inventory, and potential losses that may be incurred from spoilage or obsolescence. One goal of a JIT system is the reduction or elimination of storage costs, because these costs *do not add value* to the product.[12]

JIT is much more, however, than an approach to inventory management. It is the philosophy of *eliminating non-value-adding activities* and *increasing product quality* throughout the manufacturing process.[13]

CASE IN POINT   Chrysler's two van plants (which manufacture Chrysler's popular minivans) in Windsor acquire the paint and other topcoat products for their vans on a daily just-in-time basis. The supplier operates a new plant in Windsor solely for the purpose of providing its products for Chrysler.

The most important objective of implementing the daily just-in-time system is to improve Chrysler's minivan product quality; for this purpose, the paint and other topcoat products are delivered at the right temperature and viscosity. Since the supplier is located in the same city, the supplier can fix any unexpected problems right on the assembly line. Moreover, this system will minimize such non-value-adding costs as storage, insurance, and inventory investment.

JIT Systems and Product Quality

Perhaps the most significant benefit of a successful JIT system is the overall contribution that the system can make to product quality.

If materials are purchased and goods are produced "just in time," the production process must be performed "just right." No inventories of spare materials or of finished goods are available to "take up the slack" if defective materials must be returned to the supplier or if finished goods must be reworked. Therefore, *everyone involved in the manufacturing process must strive toward a "zero defects" level of performance.*

At first glance, it may appear that the JIT concept involves great risk that quality goods will not be completed on schedule. If materials do not arrive on time, or if they are defective, the entire manufacturing process may be forced to shut down until more materials can be obtained. Similarly, if some of the finished goods are defective, sales opportunities—and customers—may be lost.

[12]   Factors to be considered in determining the optimal size of inventories are discussed in Chapter 9.

[13]   JIT refers to the movement of goods and, therefore, to manufacturing processes. However, the goals of eliminating inefficiency and improving quality can be extended to many other types of organizational activities. The extension of the JIT philosophy *throughout the organization* is called *total quality management (TQM).*

Interestingly, however, many manufacturing companies have found that a nearly zero-defects level of production *can be achieved* when this goal becomes a priority recognized and enforced throughout the organization.

Zero Defects Starts with Reliable Suppliers As previously stated, defective materials can force the entire production process in a JIT system to shut down. Therefore, the purchasing department of a JIT manufacturer seeks suppliers that can provide *quality materials on a reliable schedule.* Once specific suppliers have proven their reliability, the JIT manufacturer can dispense with quality inspections of incoming materials, thus eliminating another non-value-adding activity.

Product Design Plays a Critical Role In a JIT system, product quality is "designed-in" and "manufactured-in," rather than being achieved through "inspecting-out" of defective units at the end of the manufacturing process. When zero defects becomes the goal, products are *designed in a manner that simplifies the manufacturing process and reduces the risk of defects.*

The Need for a Multiskilled Work Force In a JIT system, goods are produced only as needed. Therefore, workers and machinery must be versatile—that is, able to shift quickly from the manufacture of one product to another. Workers must learn to perform various tasks and to operate different machines. Many companies have found that this concept of *flexible manufacturing* increases employees' morale, skill, and productivity.

Workers are trained to *recognize and correct defects as they occur,* rather than allowing defective products to continue down the assembly line. This approach eliminates (or greatly reduces) the need for inspecting finished units and for scrapping or reworking defective finished goods.

Machinery, Too, Plays a Vital Role In a JIT system, machines used in sequential manufacturing processes are located next to one another in order to achieve a smooth and rapid flow of work in process. This factory arrangement minimizes the movement of work in process and "wait-time."

Machinery downtime can interrupt the entire production process. Therefore *equipment reliability* is a vital consideration in machinery-acquisition decisions. Also, maintenance is performed on a *preventive basis,* rather than only when a breakdown occurs. Production workers are trained to maintain the machinery and to make routine repairs themselves.

Accounting Implications of a JIT System

A JIT cost accounting system possesses characteristics of *both* job order and process cost accounting systems. The concept of flexible manufacturing—producing different products as they are needed—means that units are produced in batches, or "jobs." However, a basic goal of a JIT system is to eliminate or minimize non-value-adding activities. Therefore, the accounting system must measure separately the costs of many specific processes performed in the course of each job—especially the costs associated with non-value-adding activities.

In order to bring to management's attention the costs and cost drivers associated with non-value-adding activities, JIT systems normally utilize activity-based costing.

The Need for Time Measurements Timing is all-important in a JIT system. Therefore, a JIT cost accounting system measures the ***time*** required for each manufacturing process. These time measurements are essential for scheduling production activities in a manner that avoids "bottlenecks" and ensures that jobs are completed "just in time."

Measures of Efficiency in a JIT System The length of time required for a product to pass completely through a manufacturing process is called ***cycle time.*** Cycle time often is viewed as containing four separate elements: (1) processing time, (2) storage and waiting time, (3) movement-time, and (4) inspection-time. ***Only during processing time, however, is value added to the product.*** Ideally, the other elements of cycle time should be reduced as much as possible.

A widely used measure of the efficiency of a JIT system is the ***manufacturing efficiency ratio*** (or throughput ratio). This measure expresses the time spent in value-adding activities (such as processing) as a percentage of total cycle time, as follows:

$$\text{Manufacturing Efficiency Ratio} = \frac{\text{Value-Adding Time}}{\text{Cycle Time}}$$

The manufacturing efficiency ratio may be applied to specific production processes or to the manufacturing process viewed as a whole. (When the manufacturing process is viewed as a whole, cycle time begins with the arrival of direct materials and ends with the shipment of the finished goods.)

The basic purpose of the manufacturing efficiency ratio is to highlight the percentage of time spent in non-value-adding activities. The optimal efficiency ratio is ***100%,*** which indicates that ***no*** time is being spent on non-value-adding activities. In practice, however, this ratio is always less than 100%. If a manufacturing company has not made a concerted effort to reduce all its non-value-adding activities, its manufacturing efficiency ratio often is substantially less than 100%.

Accounting for Scrap and Spoilage Prior to the recent emphasis on better efficiency and tighter control of costs, most manufacturing companies considered some amount of scrap, waste, and defective units as "normal spoilage." As long as spoilage costs remained within an "acceptable" range, they were not accounted for separately. Thus, spoilage simply became part of the total manufacturing cost assigned to completed units.

When a company is striving to achieve a zero-defects level of performance, ***no*** amount of spoilage is viewed as "acceptable." Therefore, the accounting system should ***record separately*** even amounts of spoilage that are immaterial in dollar amount, and should associate these costs with specific production processes.

Accounting for such small amounts of spoilage in this manner is ***not necessary for financial statement purposes.*** Rather, the purpose is to focus attention throughout the organization on the zero-defects target, and to emphasize the importance of quality in a JIT system.

Measuring Quality Accounting systems in JIT companies measure ***quality,*** as well as costs and cycle times. One widely used measure of production quality is ***defects per million*** units produced. In some companies, defect rates have been reduced to less than one defective part per million units of production. Other measures of quality include merchandise returns, numbers of warranty claims, customer complaints, and the results of customer satisfaction polls.

A JIT system does not, in itself, ensure quality. Rather, it establishes ***striving for quality*** as a basic goal of the organization.

A Concluding Comment . . .

The principles of JIT manufacturing offer many benefits to manufacturing companies. Among the most significant are:

1 A reduction in unit cost through increased efficiency and the reduction or elimination of non-value-adding activities.

2 Constant improvement in product quality.

3 Greater challenge, variety, and responsibility for production workers.

4 Reduction in the risk that not all output can be sold.

The most commonly cited characteristic of JIT systems—maintenance of inventories at near-zero levels—is ***not appropriate for all companies.*** If a company does not have access to highly reliable sources of supply, it should maintain reasonable inventories of materials. If the company has a lengthy cycle time, or if it cannot achieve a nearly zero-defects level of production, it should consider maintaining an adequate inventory of finished goods to ensure prompt deliveries to customers. ***All*** companies, however, can benefit from the basic ***philosophy*** of the JIT approach, which is ***striving to eliminate inefficiency and to improve product quality.***

CASE IN POINT JIT and other applications of total quality management (TQM) are widely cited as contributing to the industrial rebirth of Japan. After World War II, Japan was a nation with a shattered economy and little manufacturing capacity. Throughout the 1950s, Japanese products were regarded as "cheap imitations" of American goods. Today, however, Japan is recognized worldwide as an efficient producer of high-quality products.

Interestingly, the concepts of JIT and TQM so successfully adopted by many Japanese companies are based in large part upon the management theories of W. Edwards Deming, an American statistician.

CHAPTER REVIEW

KEY TERMS INTRODUCED OR EMPHASIZED IN CHAPTER 22

*Activity-based costing (ABC) The technique of assigning the cost of each overhead activity to products in proportion to the extent that manufacture of the product drives that specific overhead activity. Also called ***transaction-based costing.***

* *Supplemental Topic, "The New Manufacturing Environment"*

Conversion costs   Manufacturing costs incurred in the process of converting direct materials into finished goods. Conversion costs include both direct labour and manufacturing overhead.

*****Cycle time**   The length of time for a product to pass completely through a specific manufacturing process, or the manufacturing process viewed as a whole. Used as a measure of efficiency in JIT systems.

Defects per million   The number of defective units per million units produced. Used as a measure of product quality.

Equivalent full units of production   A measure of the work done during an accounting period. Includes work done on beginning and ending inventories of work in process as well as work on units completely processed during the period.

Fixed cost   A cost that does not vary in direct response to changes in the level of activity.

Job cost sheet   A record used in a job order cost system to summarize the manufacturing costs (materials, labour, and overhead) applicable to each job, or batch of production. Job cost sheets may be viewed as a subsidiary ledger supporting the balance of the Work in Process Inventory control account.

Job order cost system   A cost accounting system under which the focal point of costing is a quantity of product known as a *job* or *lot.* Costs of direct materials, direct labour, and manufacturing overhead applicable to each job are compiled to arrive at average unit cost.

*****Just-in-time (JIT) manufacturing systems**   A modern approach to manufacturing aimed at reducing or eliminating non-value-adding activities, such as maintenance of inventories. Focuses upon both efficiency and product quality.

*****Manufacturing efficiency ratio**   Processing time stated as a percentage of cycle time. Used as a measure of efficiency in JIT systems.

*****Non-value-adding activity**   An activity within the manufacturing process that does not add value to the product. Storage of inventory is an example.

Overhead application rate   A device used to apply a "normal" amount of overhead costs to work in process. The rate is predetermined at the beginning of the year and expresses the percentage relationship between estimated total overhead for the year and the estimated total of some "cost driver," such as direct labour hours, direct labour costs, or machine hours. Use of the overhead application rate causes overhead to be charged to work in process in proportion to the amount of "cost driver" traceable to those units.

Over- or underapplied overhead   The difference between the actual manufacturing overhead incurred during the period and the amount applied to work in process by use of a predetermined overhead application rate.

Process cost summary   A schedule prepared for each production process or department in a process cost system. Shows the costs charged to the department during the period, the computation of unit manufacturing costs, and the allocation of departmental costs between units completed during the period and the ending inventory of work in process.

Process cost system   A cost accounting system used mostly in industries such as petroleum or chemicals characterized by continuous mass production. Costs are not assigned to specific units but to a manufacturing process or department.

*****Total quality management (TQM)**   An approach to eliminating wasteful activities and improving quality throughout the organization. The philosophy behind JIT manufacturing systems.

---

*   *Supplemental Topic, "The New Manufacturing Environment"*

Transaction-based costing See *activity-based costing.*

Value-adding activity An activity that, from the customers' viewpoint, adds value to the product. Actual manufacture and assembly functions are examples.

Variable cost A cost that changes in approximate proportion to some level of activity, such as the level of production. The cost of direct materials used is a variable cost.

Zero defects The goal of defect-free production. Although some defects actually do occur, they are so infrequent and are so quickly corrected as not to interfere with a JIT manufacturing system.

DEMONSTRATION PROBLEM FOR YOUR REVIEW

Sumasani Corp. manufactures EndAll, an electronic unit that plays a wide variety of video games on a television set. The units are entirely assembled in one production department. All manufacturing costs are incurred at a uniform rate throughout the production process. The following information is available for the month of March:

Beginning inventory of work in process		$154,000
Manufacturing costs incurred during March:		
Direct materials	$360,000	
Direct labour	90,000	
Manufacturing overhead	135,000	585,000
Total costs to be accounted for		$739,000

The beginning inventory of work in process consisted of 3,000 units, each 80% complete as of the beginning of March. In addition to completing these units, the department started and completed another 7,000 units during March, and also started work on an additional 2,000 units that were 70% complete at month-end.

INSTRUCTIONS
a Compute the equivalent full units of production during March.

b Prepare a process cost summary for the Production Department covering the month of March. (The company values its inventories using the FIFO method.)

c Prepare journal entries to record (1) the manufacturing costs charged to the Production Department during March (use one compound entry), and (2) the transfer of completed units to the finished goods warehouse.

SOLUTION TO DEMONSTRATION PROBLEM

a **Computation of Equivalent Full Units—Materials and Conversion Costs**

	Units	×	Portion Completed = in March	Equivalent Full Units Produced
Units in process at the beginning of March (80% complete at March 1)	3,000		20%	600
Units started and completed in March	7,000		100%	7,000
Units completed during March	10,000			
Units in process at the end of March (70% complete at March 31)	2,000		70%	1,400
Equivalent full units of production during March.............................				9,000

---

* *Supplemental Topic, "The New Manufacturing Environment"*

b

SUMASANI CORP.
Process Cost Summary—Production Department
For the Month Ended March 31, 19__

	Total Costs	Equivalent Full Units	Unit Cost
Costs charged to the department and unit costs:			
Work in process inventory, March 1	$154,000		
Manufacturing costs charged to the department during March:			
Direct materials used	360,000	9,000	$40
Direct labour	90,000	9,000	10
Manufacturing overhead	135,000	9,000	15
Unit cost per equivalent full unit processed during March..			$65
Total costs to be accounted for	$739,000		

	Total Costs	Equivalent Full Units	Unit Cost
Allocation of costs charged to department:			
Work in process inventory, end of March			
(2,000 units, 70% complete as to all costs;			
2,000 units × $65 × 70%)...........................	$ 91,000		
Cost of units completed (10,000 units):			
Total cost ($739,000 − $91,000).....................	648,000		
Unit cost ($648,000 ÷ 10,000 finished units).........			$64.80
Total costs to be accounted for	$739,000		

c   **General Journal**

(1) Work in Process Inventory: Production Dept......................	585,000	
Materials Inventory..		360,000
Direct labour..		90,000
Manufacturing Overhead		135,000
To summarize manufacturing costs charged to production in March.		
(2) Finished Goods Inventory	648,000	
Work in Process Inventory: Production Dept................		648,000
To record cost of 10,000 units of EndAll completed in March		
(unit cost = $648,000 ÷ 10,000 units = $64.80).		

ASSIGNMENT MATERIAL

DISCUSSION QUESTIONS

1 What is a cost accounting system?

2 What are the major objectives of a cost accounting system in a manufacturing company?

3 What factors should be taken into account in deciding whether to use a job order cost system or a process cost system in any given manufacturing situation?

4 Northwest Power produces electricity. Would you expect the company to use a job order or a process cost accounting system? Explain.

5 Rodeo Drive Jewellers makes custom jewellery for celebrities. Would you expect the company to use a job order or a process cost accounting system? Explain.

6 Describe the three kinds of charges on a job cost sheet. For what general ledger controlling account do job cost sheets constitute supporting detail?

7 What documents serve as the basis for charging the costs of direct materials used in production to the Work in Process Inventory account?

8 What documents serve as the basis for charging direct labour costs to specific jobs or production departments?

9 What is meant by underapplied overhead? By overapplied overhead?

10 Gerox Company applies manufacturing overhead on the basis of machine-hours, using a predetermined overhead rate. At the end of the current year the Manufacturing Overhead account has a credit balance. What are the possible explanations for this? What disposition should be made of this balance?

11 Taylor & Malone is a law firm. Would the concepts of a job order system or a process cost system be more appropriate for this type of service business? Explain.

12 Briefly explain the operation of a process cost system, including the manner in which the unit costs of finished goods are determined.

13 Silex Mfg. has two processing departments: Assembly and Packaging. Identify the four accounts most likely to be **credited** as costs are charged to the Work in Process Inventory account of the Packaging Department.

14 What is meant by the term **equivalent full units?** How is this concept used in computing average unit costs?

15 When must the equivalent full units of production figure for materials be computed separately from that for conversion costs? Explain.

16 If a department has no beginning inventory of work in process but has 10,000 units in process at month-end, will the equivalent full units of work performed be greater or smaller than the number of units completed during the month? Explain.

17 In a process cost system, is the average cost of producing an **equivalent full unit** during a given month always equal to the average cost of producing a **completed unit** during that month? Explain.

18 What is the difference between **fixed overhead costs** and **variable overhead costs?**

19 Explain why charging actual overhead costs to production, rather than using an overhead application rate, can cause distortions in unit costs if production volume fluctuates from month to month.

*20 Explain the distinction between **value-adding activities** and **non-value-adding activities** in a manufacturing business. Provide two examples of each type of activity.

*21 Explain why activity-based costing should provide a better indication of "actual" unit cost than does the use of a single overhead application rate.

*22 Briefly explain the nature and goals of a JIT manufacturing system.

---

* *Supplemental Topic, "The New Manufacturing Environment"*

*23 Why is the output of a JIT system likely to contain fewer defective units than the output of a traditional manufacturing system?

*24 Why is JIT often described as a "philosophy," rather than as an inventory-management technique?

MULTIPLE CHOICE QUESTIONS

1 If CustomCraft uses a **job order** cost system, each of the following is true, **except:**

a Individual job cost sheets accumulate all manufacturing costs applicable to each job, and together constitute a subsidiary ledger for the Work in Process Inventory account.

b Direct labour cost applicable to individual jobs is recorded when paid by a debit to Work in Process Inventory and a credit to Cash, as well as by entering the amount on the job cost sheets.

c The amount of direct materials used in individual jobs is recorded by debiting the Work in Process Inventory account and crediting the Materials Inventory account, as well as by entering the amount used on job cost sheets.

d The manufacturing overhead applied to each job is transferred from the Manufacturing Overhead account to the Work in Process Inventory account, as well as entered on the individual job cost sheets.

2 When a job cost system is in use, **underapplied** overhead:

a Represents the cost of manufacturing overhead that relates to unfinished jobs.

b Is indicated by a credit balance remaining at year-end in the Manufacturing Overhead account.

c Is closed out at year-end into the Cost of Goods Sold account if the amount is not material.

d Results when actual overhead costs incurred during a year are less than the amounts applied to individual jobs.

3 Indicate which of the following phrases correctly complete this sentence: "Equivalent full units of production . . . " (More than one answer may be correct.)

a Are a measure of the work done during a given accounting period.

b Represent only those units completed during the period and transferred out of the production department.

c Are the basis for determining per-unit manufacturing costs in a process cost accounting system.

d May be more or less than the number of units actually completed during the period.

4 Fogg Manufacturing has operations that involve three processing departments: Assembly, Painting, and Packaging. Debits to the Work in Process Inventory: Painting Department account could involve a credit to any of the following, **except:**

a Work in Process Inventory: Packaging Department.

b Direct Labour.

c Manufacturing Overhead.

d Work in Process Inventory: Assembly Department.

---

* *Supplemental Topic, "The New Manufacturing Environment"*

5 When **actual** overhead costs incurred are charged to processing departments each month:

 a The cost of infrequent items, such as a major plant refurbishing, is spread uniformly over all units produced throughout the year.

 b Under- or overapplied overhead may occur, but it is treated in the same manner as when an overhead application rate is used.

 c It is no longer necessary to compute the equivalent full units of production for individual departments.

 d The monthly per-unit cost of producing a product will vary from fluctuations in the level of production when a significant portion of overhead cost is fixed.

*6 Which of the following are more characteristic of JIT systems than of the "traditional" approach to manufacturing? (More than one answer may be correct.)

 a Use of activity-based costing procedures

 b Greater specialization by production workers

 c Shorter cycle times

 d Greater emphasis upon quality control inspections

EXERCISES

**EXERCISE 22-1
Accounting
Terminology**

Listed below are twelve technical accounting terms introduced or emphasized in this chapter.

Job order cost system	**Manufacturing efficiency ratio*	*Variable costs*
Process cost system	*Equivalent full units of production*	*Fixed costs*
Overapplied overhead	**Just-in-time manufacturing*	**Cycle time*
*Value-adding activity	**Activity-based costing*	**Defects per million*

Each of the following statements may (or may not) describe one of these technical terms. For each statement, indicate the term described, or answer "None" if the statement does not correctly describe any of the terms.

 a The type of cost accounting system likely to be used in a **Coca-Cola** bottling plant.

 b Manufacturing costs that change in direct proportion to the number of units manufactured.

 c A measure of the **quantity** of production work done during a time period, including work on partially completed units.

 d Time spent on value-adding activities as a percentage of cycle time.

 e Production activities such as the movement of work in process between workstations, inspection of finished goods, and reworking of defective units.

 f A debit balance remaining in the Manufacturing Overhead account at the end of the period.

 g Allocating different types of overhead activity to units produced based upon the percentage of cost driver activity relating to each product line.

 h The philosophy of minimizing non-value-adding activities throughout the manufacturing process and of producing a nearly defect-free product.

---

* *Supplemental Topic, "The New Manufacturing Environment"*

i The type of cost accounting system likely to be used by a construction company that builds several projects at one time.

j A period required for a unit of product to pass completely through a specific part of—or the entire—manufacturing process.

EXERCISE 22-2
Flow of Costs in a Cost Accounting System

For each of the four accounts listed below, prepare an example of a journal entry that would cause the account to be (1) debited and (2) credited. Assume perpetual inventory records are maintained. Include written explanations with your journal entries and use "XXX" in place of dollar amounts.

a Materials Inventory

b Direct Labour

c Manufacturing Overhead

d Finished Goods Inventory

EXERCISE 22-3
Flow of Costs in a Job Order Cost System

The information below is taken from the job cost sheets of Guangzhou Company:

Job Number	Manufacturing Costs as of June 30	Manufacturing Costs in July
101	$4,200	
102	3,240	
103	900	$1,950
104	2,250	3,900
105		5,700
106		3,630

During July, jobs no. 103 and 104 were completed, and jobs no. 101, 102, and 104 were delivered to customers. Jobs no. 105 and 106 are still in process at July 31. From this information, compute the following:

a The work in process inventory at June 30

b The finished goods inventory at June 30

c The cost of goods sold during July

d The work in process inventory at July 31

e The finished goods inventory at July 31

EXERCISE 22-4
Journal Entries in a Job Order Cost System

Riverside Engineering is a machine shop that uses a job order cost accounting system. Overhead is applied to individual jobs at a predetermined rate based on direct labour costs. The job cost sheet for job no. 321 appears as follows:

Job Cost Sheet

Job number: _321_ Date Started: _June 7_
Product: _2" Brass Check Valves_ Date Completed: _June 15_
Units Completed: _4,000_

Direct materials used	$ 7,720
Direct labour	1,400
Manufacturing overhead applied	3,080
Total cost of job no. 321..	$12,200
Unit cost ($12,200 ÷ 4,000 units)	$3.05

INSTRUCTIONS Prepare general journal entries to:

a Summarize the manufacturing costs charged to job no. 321. (Use one compound entry.)

b Record the completion of job no. 321.

c Record the credit sale of 2,100 units from job no. 321 at a unit sales price of $5. Record in a separate entry the related cost of goods sold.

EXERCISE 22-5
Computation of Equivalent Full Units

The following relates to the Assembly Department of Lawncraft Mowers during the month of May:

Units in process at May 1 (40% completed in April)	2,000
Units started and completed during May	15,000
Units in process at May 31 (90% completed).....................................	5,000

INSTRUCTIONS Determine the equivalent full units of production during the month of May, assuming that all costs are incurred uniformly as the units move through the production line.

EXERCISE 22-6
Preparing Journal Entries in a Process Cost System

Shamrock Industries uses a process cost system. Products are processed successively by the Cutting Department and the Assembly Department and are then transferred to the finished goods warehouse. Shown below is cost information for the Assembly Department during the month of June:

Cost of work in process at June 1		$ 19,000
Cost of units transferred in from Cutting Department during June		72,500
Manufacturing costs added in Assembly Department:		
Direct materials used	$44,000	
Direct labour	6,100	
Manufacturing overhead	17,400	67,500
Total costs to be accounted for		$159,000

The total cost of finished goods manufactured during June amounted to $136,300.

INSTRUCTIONS Prepare journal entries to summarize for the month of June (1) the transfer of production from the Cutting Department to the Assembly Department, (2) the manufacturing costs incurred by the Assembly Department, and (3) the transfer of completed units from the Assembly Department to the finished goods warehouse.

EXERCISE 22-7
Computing Unit Costs

Given below are the production data for Department No. 1 for the first month of operation:

Costs charged to Department No. 1:	
Direct materials used	$30,900
Direct labour	11,440
Manufacturing overhead	57,200
Total...	$99,540

During this first month, 3,000 units were placed into production; 2,800 units were completed and the remaining 200 units are *100% completed* as to direct material and *30% completed* as to direct labour and overhead.

INSTRUCTIONS You are to compute the following:

a Unit cost of direct material used.

b Equivalent full units of production for direct labour and manufacturing overhead.

c Unit cost of direct labour.

d Unit cost of manufacturing overhead.

e Total cost of the 200 units in process at month-end.

f Total cost of the 2,800 units completed during the month.

EXERCISE 22-8
Evaluating
Departmental
Performance

Shown below in the left-hand column are the unit costs relating to the manufacturing activities of the Packaging Department of Baker Labs in the month of July. (These unit costs are taken directly from the process cost summary on page 1052.) Assume that the right-hand column indicates the unit costs **budgeted** for the Packaging Department—that is, the unit costs that managers had **expected** the department to incur during the month.

	Unit Costs	
	Actual	*Budgeted*
Manufacturing cost charged to the Packaging Department:		
Units transferred in from the Mixing Department	*$2.00*	*$2.15*
Manufacturing costs added by the Packaging Department:		
Direct materials requisitioned	*.16*	*.16*
Direct labour	*.25*	*.20*
Manufacturing overhead (120% of direct labour cost)	*.30*	*.24*
Unit cost per equivalent unit processed during July	*$2.71*	*$2.75*

Based upon this information, did the Packaging Department perform as well during July as managers had expected? Explain.

*EXERCISE 22-9
Characteristics
of JIT Systems

Indicate whether the following characteristics are more closely associated with a JIT manufacturing system or with a traditional "supply push" system. Explain your reasons for each answer.

a High inventory turnover rate

b Low manufacturing efficiency ratio

c Thorough quality control inspection of each finished unit

d Short cycle time

e Continuous focus upon the production of a single type of product

f Low rate of defects in finished goods

g Increased emphasis upon product design

*EXERCISE 22-10
Evaluation of
JIT Systems

Just-in-time (JIT) manufacturing systems are receiving much attention in today's business world.

a Explain the nature of a JIT manufacturing system.

b Why is the quality of materials and finished products of greater importance in a JIT system than in a system that maintains sizable inventories?

---

* *Supplemental Topic, "The New Manufacturing Environment"*

c Why do JIT systems often utilize activity-based costing procedures?

d Identify four areas of potential cost savings often associated with JIT systems.

e Identify three separate conditions that might make it **unwise** for a company to attempt operating at the near-zero levels of materials and finished goods inventories often associated with JIT systems.

f Does the JIT philosophy offer any potential benefits to a company that decides **not** to minimize its inventory levels?

*EXERCISE 22-11
Measurement and Evaluation of Manufacturing Efficiency

The activities involved in the manufacture of a particular model piano at von Rohen Piano Co. are listed below, along with the average number of days required for each activity:

Activity	Days
Inspection of incoming shipments of materials	*2*
Direct materials kept in storage	*45*
Processing by Milling Department	*12.5*
Partially completed pianos and components kept in storage between processing activities	*20*
Processing by Staining and Finishing Department	*8*
Processing by Assembly Department	*3*
Inspection	*1*
Correcting defects	*4*
Tuning	*.5*
Storage of finished units awaiting sale	*33*
Packaging for shipment	*1*
Total cycle time	*130.0*

INSTRUCTIONS

a List the value-adding activities in the company's production cycle and the times required to complete these activities.

b Compute the manufacturing efficiency ratio for the entire production cycle, from the receipt of materials through the shipment of finished goods. (Round to the nearest percent.)

c Suggest several specific steps likely to increase the manufacturing efficiency ratio, and explain how each of these steps may reduce the company's overall costs.

PROBLEMS

Group A

PROBLEM 22A-1
Job Order Cost System: A Short Problem

Pelee Island Sailmakers uses a job order cost accounting system. Manufacturing overhead is charged to individual jobs through the use of a predetermined overhead rate based on direct labour costs. The following information appears in the company's Work in Process Inventory controlling account for the month of June:

* *Supplemental Topic, "The New Manufacturing Environment"*

Debits to account:

Balance, June 1	$ 7,200
Direct materials	12,000
Direct labour	9,000
Manufacturing overhead (applied to jobs as 150% of direct labour cost)	13,500
Total debits to account	$41,700

Credits to account:

Transferred to Finished Goods Inventory account............................	33,200
Balance, June 30	$ 8,500

INSTRUCTIONS

a Assuming that the direct labour charged to the jobs still in process at June 30 amounts to $2,100, compute the amount of manufacturing overhead and the amount of direct materials that have been charged to these jobs as of June 30.

b Prepare general journal entries to summarize:

1 The manufacturing costs (direct materials, direct labour, and overhead) charged to production during June.

2 The transfer of production completed during June to the Finished Goods Inventory account.

3 The cash sale of 90% of the merchandise completed during June at a total sales price of $46,500. Show the related cost of goods sold in a separate journal entry.

PROBLEM 22A-2
Job Order Cost System: A Comprehensive Problem

Georgia Woods, Inc., manufactures furniture to customers' specifications and uses a job order cost system. A predetermined overhead rate is used in applying manufacturing overhead to individual jobs. In Department One, overhead is applied on the basis of machine-hours, and in Department Two, on the basis of direct labour hours. At the beginning of the current year, management made the following budget estimates to assist in determining the overhead application rate:

	Department One	Department Two
Direct labour cost	$300,000	$225,000
Direct labour hours..	20,000	15,000
Manufacturing overhead	$420,000	$337,500
Machine-hours	12,000	7,500

Production of a batch of custom furniture ordered by City Furniture (job no. 58) was started early in the year and completed three weeks later on January 29. The records for this job show the following cost information:

	Department One	Department Two
Job order for City Furniture (job no. 58):		
Direct materials cost	$10,100	$ 7,600
Direct labour cost	$16,500	$11,100
Direct labour hours...	1,100	740
Machine-hours	750	500

Selected additional information for January is given below:

	Department One	Department Two
Direct labour hours—month of January	1,600	1,200
Machine-hours—month of January	1,100	600
Manufacturing overhead incurred in January	$39,010	$26,540

INSTRUCTIONS **a** Compute the predetermined overhead rate for each department.

    b What is the total cost of the furniture produced for City Furniture?

    c Prepare the entries required to record the sale (on account) of the furniture to City Furniture. The sales price of the order was $147,000.

    d Determine the over- or underapplied overhead for each department at the end of January.

PROBLEM 22A-3
Process Cost System: A Short but Comprehensive Problem

One of the primary products of Magic Touch is the Shutterbug, an instant camera, which is processed successively in the Assembly Department and the Lens Department, and then transferred to the company's sales warehouse. After having been shut down for three weeks as a result of a materials shortage, the company resumed production of Shutterbugs on May 1. The flow of *units of product* through the departments during May is shown below.

Assembly Department Work in Process		Lens Department Work in Process	
Started in process— 30,000 units	To Lens Dept.— 25,000 units	From Assembly Dept.—25,000 units	To warehouse— 21,000 units

Neither department had any units in process at May 1. Departmental manufacturing costs applicable to Shutterbug production for the month of May were as follows:

	Assembly Department	Lens Department
Units transferred from Assembly Department		$?
Direct materials	$164,700	67,800
Direct labour	67,500	45,200
Manufacturing overhead	118,800	135,600
Total manufacturing costs	$351,000	$?

Unfinished goods in each department at the end of May were on the average 40% complete, with respect to both direct materials and conversion costs.

INSTRUCTIONS **a** Determine the equivalent full units of production in each department during May.

    b Compute unit production costs in each department during May.

    c Prepare the necessary journal entries to record the transfer of product out of the Assembly Department and the Lens Department during May.

PROBLEM 22A-4
Process Costs: Cost Report and Journal Entries

Aladdin Electric manufactures several products, including an electric garage door opener called the Door Tender. Door Tenders are completely processed in one department and are then transferred to the finished goods warehouse. All manufacturing costs are applied to Door Tender units at a uniform rate throughout the production process. The following information is available for July:

Beginning inventory of work in process	$ 21,220
Manufacturing costs incurred in July:	
Direct materials used	56,100
Direct labour	29,920
Manufacturing overhead applied	82,280
Total costs to be accounted for	$189,520

The beginning inventory consisted of 400 units that had been 60% completed during June. In addition to completing these units, the department started and completed another 1,500 units during July and started work on 300 more units that were 70% completed at July 31.

INSTRUCTIONS
a Compute the equivalent full units of production in July.

b Prepare a process cost summary for the department for the month of July, as illustrated in this chapter. Use the July unit cost figures to determine the cost of the ending inventory of work in process. (This represents a *FIFO* flow assumption.)

c Prepare journal entries to record (1) the manufacturing costs charged to the department during July and (2) the transfer of 1,900 completed units to the finished goods warehouse.

PROBLEM 22A-5
Process Costs:
A Second
Comprehensive
Problem

Saf-T-File, Inc., manufactures metal filing cabinets and uses a process cost system. The cabinets pass through a series of production processes, one of which is the Lock Assembly Department. The costs charged to the Lock Assembly Department during April, along with a summary of the units worked on by the department, are shown below:

Costs charged to the Lock Assembly Department:

Work in process, April 1	$ 29,840
Cost of 2,000 units transferred in from the Drawer Assembly Department	
during April ($52 per unit)	104,000
Manufacturing costs added by the Lock Assembly Department during April:	
Direct materials	8,200
Direct labour	3,800
Manufacturing overhead (applied as 150% of direct labour costs)..........	5,700
Total costs to be accounted for	$151,540

Units worked on during April:

Work in process, April 1 (100% complete as to materials, 80% complete as	
to conversion costs)...	500
Units started and completed during April	1,600
Units completed and transferred to the Painting Department during April	2,100
Work in process, May 31 (100% complete as to materials, 50% complete	
as to conversion costs)...	400

INSTRUCTIONS
a Compute separately the equivalent full units of production during April for (1) materials and (2) conversion costs (direct labour and overhead).

b Prepare a process cost summary for April, following the format illustrated in this chapter. Use the April unit cost figures to value the ending inventory of work in process; the remainder of the $151,540 total cost to be accounted for may be assigned to units transferred from the Lock Assembly Department to the Painting Department (a *FIFO* flow assumption).

c Prepare journal entries to record:

1 Transfer of the 2,000 units from the Drawer Assembly Department into the Lock Assembly Department.

2 Manufacturing costs added by the Lock Assembly Department during April.

3 Transfer of the 2,100 completed units from the Lock Assembly Department to the Painting Department.

PROBLEM 22A-6
Manufacturing Overhead and Fluctuations in Production Volume

John Park is the founder and president of Park West Engineering. One of the company's principal products is sold exclusively to BigMart, a national chain of retail stores. BigMart buys a large quantity of the product in the first quarter of each year but buys successively smaller quantities in the second, third, and fourth quarters. Park West cannot produce in advance to meet the big first-quarter sales requirement, because BigMart frequently makes minor changes in the specifications for the product. Therefore, Park West must adjust its production schedules to fit BigMart's buying pattern.

In Park West's cost accounting system, unit costs are computed quarterly on the basis of actual materials, labour, and manufacturing overhead costs charged to work in process at the end of each quarter. At the close of the current year, Park received the following cost report, by quarters, for the year.

	First Quarter	Second Quarter	Third Quarter	Fourth Quarter
Direct materials used	$ 78,000	$ 60,000	$ 42,000	$22,000
Direct labour	80,000	60,000	40,000	20,000
Fixed overhead (actual)...................	30,000	30,000	30,000	30,000
Variable overhead (actual)	48,000	39,000	29,000	14,000
Total manufacturing cost	$236,000	$189,000	$141,000	$86,000
Equivalent full units produced	40,000	30,000	20,000	10,000
Unit production cost......................	$ 5.90	$ 6.30	$ 7.05	$ 8.60

Park is concerned about the steadily rising unit costs. He states, "We have a contract to produce 50,000 units for BigMart next quarter at a unit sales price of $8.50. If this sales price won't even cover our unit production costs, I'll have to cancel the contract. But before I take such drastic action, I'd like to study our method of computing unit costs to see if we might be doing something wrong."

INSTRUCTIONS

a As the first step in your study, determine the **unit cost** of each cost element (materials, labour, fixed overhead, and variable overhead) in the first quarter and in the fourth quarter of the current year.

b Based on your computation in part **a**, which cost element is primarily responsible for the increase in unit production costs? Explain why you think the unit cost for this cost element has been rising throughout the year.

c Compute an overhead application rate for Park West Engineering that expresses total overhead **for the year** (including both fixed and variable overhead) as a percentage of direct labour costs.

d Redetermine the unit production cost for each quarter using the overhead application rate to apply overhead costs.

e Determine the expected unit cost of producing 50,000 units next quarter. (Assume that unit costs for materials and direct labour remain the same as in the fourth quarter and use the overhead application rate to determine the unit cost of applied overhead.)

f Explain to Park how Park West might improve its procedures for determining unit production costs. Also explain whether Park West reasonably can expect to recover its production costs next quarter if it sells 50,000 units to BigMart at a unit sales price of $8.50.

Group B

PROBLEM 22B-1
Journal Entries
to Record
Basic Cost
Flows

The following information relates to the manufacturing operations of O'Shaughn-essy Mfg. Co. during the month of March. The company uses a job order cost accounting system.

a Purchases of direct materials during the month amount to $59,700. (All purchases were made on account.)

b Materials requisitions issued by the production department during the month total $56,200.

c Time cards of direct workers show 2,000 hours worked on various jobs during the month, for total direct labour cost of $30,000.

d Direct workers were paid $26,300 in March.

e Actual overhead costs for the month amount to $34,900 (for simplicity, you may credit Accounts Payable).

f Overhead is applied to jobs at a rate of $18 per direct labour hour.

g Jobs with total accumulated costs of $116,000 were completed during the month.

h During March, units costing $128,000 were sold for $210,000. (All sales were made on account.)

INSTRUCTIONS

Prepare general journal entries to summarize each of these transactions in the company's general ledger accounts.

PROBLEM 22B-2
Job Order Cost
System: A
Comprehensive
Problem

Precision Instruments, Inc., uses a job order cost system and applies manufacturing overhead to individual jobs by using predetermined overhead rates. In Department A overhead is applied on the basis of machine-hours, and in Department B on the basis of direct labour hours. At the beginning of the current year, management made the following budget estimates as a step toward determining the overhead application rates:

	Department A	Department B
Direct labour	$420,000	$300,000
Manufacturing overhead	$540,000	$412,500
Machine-hours	18,000	1,900
Direct labour hours	28,000	25,000

Production of 4,000 tachometers (job no. 399) was started in the middle of January and completed two weeks later. The cost records for this job show the following information:

	Department A	Department B
Job no. 399 (4,000 units of product):		
Cost of direct materials used on job	$6,800	$4,500
Direct labour cost	$8,100	7,200
Direct labour hours	540	600
Machine-hours	250	100

INSTRUCTIONS

a Determine the overhead rate that should be used for each department in applying overhead costs to job no. 399.

b What is the total cost of job no. 399, and the unit cost of the product manufactured on this production order?

c Prepare the journal entries required to record the sale (on account) of 1,000 of the tachometers to SkiCraft Boats. The total sales price was $19,500.

d Assume that actual overhead costs for the year were $517,000 in Department A and $424,400 in Department B. Actual machine-hours in Department A were 17,000, and actual direct labour hours in Department B were 26,000 during the year. On the basis of this information, determine the over- or underapplied overhead in each department for the year.

PROBLEM 22B-3
Process Costs: Journal Entries

After having been shut down for two months during a strike, Oshima Appliance Co. resumed operations on August 1. One of the company's products is a dishwasher that is successively processed by the Tub Department and the Motor Department before being transferred to the finished goods warehouse. Following are data concerning the units produced and costs incurred by the two manufacturing departments during August:

Production Summary—in Units

	Tub Department	Motor Department
Units placed in production	1,700	900
Less: Units in process, Aug. 31	800	400
Units completed during August	900	500

Costs Charged to the Departments

	Tub Department	Motor Department
Transferred in from Tub Department		$?
Direct materials used	$54,000	57,600
Direct labour	30,000	10,400
Manufacturing overhead	46,500	14,400

Due to the strike, there were no units in process at August 1 in either department. The units in process in both departments at August 31 are 75% complete with respect to both materials and conversion costs.

INSTRUCTIONS

a Compute the equivalent full units of production in August for each department.

b Compute the unit production costs for August in each department. (Include in the product costs of the Motor Department the cost of the 900 units transferred in from the Tub Department.)

c Use the August unit cost figures to determine the cost of the ending inventory of work in process in each department at August 31.

d Prepare the journal entries required to record the transfer of completed units out of each of the two departments during August.

PROBLEM 22B-4
Process Costs: A Comprehensive Problem

Universal Corp. has one production department and uses a process cost system. The following data is available as to the costs of production and the number of units worked on during the month of May:

Costs charged to the production department:

Work in process, May 1..	$ 25,400
Manufacturing costs added during May:	
Direct materials	137,400
Direct labour	56,000
Manufacturing overhead (applied as 180% of direct labour costs)..........	100,800
Total costs to be accounted for	$319,600

Units worked on during May:

Work in process, May 1 (40% complete as to materials, 60% complete as to conversion costs)	2,000
Units started and completed during May	8,000
Finished goods produced during May	10,000
Work in process, May 31 (75% complete as to materials, 80% complete as to conversion costs)..	3,000

INSTRUCTIONS **a** Compute separately the equivalent full units of production during May for (1) materials and (2) conversion costs (direct labour and overhead).

b Prepare a process cost summary for May, following the format illustrated in this chapter. Use the May unit cost figures to value the ending inventory of work in process.

c Prepare journal entries to record for the month:

1 The manufacturing costs charged to production.

2 The transfer of the completed units to the finished goods warehouse.

PROBLEM 22B-5
Process Costs:
A Second
Comprehensive
Problem

Dayton Chemical, Inc., manufactures a fertilizer concentrate, called PH Max. This product passes through four successive production processes, identified as Departments No. 1, 2, 3, and 4. After processing by Department No. 4, the product is transferred to a warehouse as finished goods inventory.

In Department No. 4, all direct materials needed to complete PH Max are added at the beginning of processing. The accounting department has accumulated the following information relating to processing in Department No. 4 during the month of April:

Costs charged to Department No. 4:

Work in process inventory, April 1 (40,000 units, 100% complete as to materials, 75% complete as to conversion costs)	$ 387,000
Cost of 140,000 units transferred in from Department No. 3 during April (unit cost = $5)	700,000
Manufacturing costs added in Department No. 4 during April:	
Direct materials added...	280,000
Direct labour	125,000
Manufacturing overhead	375,000
Total costs to be accounted for	$1,867,000

During April, the 40,000 units in process at April 1 and 90,000 of the units transferred in from Department No. 3 were completed and transferred to the warehouse. The remaining 50,000 units transferred in from Department No. 3 are still in process at April 30, and are 100% complete as to materials and 50% complete as to conversion costs (direct labour and overhead).

INSTRUCTIONS **a** Compute the equivalent full units of production during April.

b Prepare a process cost summary for Department No. 4 for the month of April. Use the April unit cost figures to determine the cost of work in process at April 30.

c Prepare journal entries to record:

1 The transfer of the 140,000 units from Department No. 3 into Department No. 4.

2 The manufacturing costs added by Department No. 4 during April.

3 The transfer of the completed units from Department No. 4 to the finished goods warehouse.

ANALYTICAL AND DECISION PROBLEMS AND CASES

*A&D 22-1
ABC

Rotron Mfg. Corp. manufactures two automotive products: airbags and passive-restraint seat belts. Shown below are the forecast amounts of three manufacturing overhead costs for the coming year:

Direct materials storage	$ 300,000
Supervision (indirect labour)	900,000
Quality control inspection of finished goods	1,200,000
Total	$2,400,000

The company also has developed the following forecasts of factors that might be useful in assigning overhead costs to units produced:

	Airbags	Seat Belts
Number of incoming materials shipments	12	24
Square metres of warehouse space used in direct materials storage	800	200
Units scheduled for manufacture	1,000,000	2,000,000
Direct labour hours	400,000	200,000
Machine-hours	300,000	50,000
Inspection (minutes per unit)	2.5	.25

INSTRUCTIONS **a** Assume that all overhead costs are assigned to production on the basis of direct labour hours. Determine the amount of the $2,400,000 in overhead costs listed above that will be assigned to *each unit* of (1) airbags and (2) seat belts scheduled for production in the coming year.

b Assume that Rotron uses activity-based costing. The following cost drivers are used in assigning the selected overhead costs to production:

Overhead Cost	Cost Driver
Direct materials storage costs	Square metres of storage space
Supervision	Direct labour hours
Quality control inspection	Total inspection time

---

* *Supplemental Topic, "The New Manufacturing Environment"*

Using these criteria, determine the per-unit amount of each of the three overhead costs that would be assigned to airbags and to seat belts. Also indicate for each product the total of these three per-unit costs.

c Which method of assigning overhead costs do you believe results in the more accurate measure of unit cost? Explain your reasoning.

d Identify two areas of potential cost savings relating to the manufacture of airbags. Indicate how cost savings might be achieved in each of these areas.

---

*A&D 22-2
Just-in-Time
Frozen Dinners

Healthy Times produces four types of frozen TV dinners that it sells to supermarkets and independent grocery stores. The company operates from two locations: a manufacturing plant and a refrigerated warehouse located a few blocks away. (Administrative offices are located in the manufacturing plant.)

The types of dinners to be produced each week is scheduled a week in advance, based upon customer orders. The **number** of dinners produced, however, is always the same. The company runs its production facilities at full capacity—20,000 units per day—to minimize fixed manufacturing costs per unit.

Every Friday, local suppliers deliver to Healthy Times' factory the fresh vegetables, chicken, fish, and other ingredients required for the following week's production. (Materials are abundant in the region.) These ingredients then are cut into meal-sized portions, "fresh frozen" using special equipment, and transported by truck to the refrigerated warehouse. The company maintains an inventory of frozen ingredients equal to approximately two weeks' production.

Every day, ingredients for 20,000 dinners are brought by truck from the warehouse to the factory. All dinners produced in a given production run must be of the same type. However, production workers can make the machinery "setup" changes necessary to produce a different type of frozen dinner in about 10 minutes.

Monday through Thursday, Healthy Times produces one type of dinner each day. On Friday, it manufactures whatever types of dinner are needed to "balance" its inventories. Completed frozen dinners are transported back to the refrigerated warehouse on a daily basis.

Frozen dinners are shipped daily from the warehouse to customers. All shipments are sent by independent carriers. Healthy Times usually maintains about a 10-day inventory of frozen dinners in the warehouse. Recently, however, daily sales have been averaging about 2,000 units less than the level of production, and the finished goods inventory has swelled to a 25-day supply.

Marsha Osaka, the controller of Healthy Times, recently read about the JIT inventory system used by Toyota in its Japanese production facilities. She is wondering whether a JIT system might benefit Healthy Times.

INSTRUCTIONS

a In **general terms,** describe a JIT manufacturing system and identify its basic goals.

b Identify any non-value-adding activities in Healthy Times' operations that might be reduced or eliminated in a JIT system. Also identify specific types of costs that might be reduced or eliminated.

c Assume that Healthy Times **does** adopt at JIT manufacturing system. Prepare a description of the company's operations under such a system. (Your description should be similar in depth to the description provided above.)

d Explain whether or not you think that a JIT system would work for Healthy Times. Provide specific reasons supporting your conclusion.

---

* *Supplemental Topic, "The New Manufacturing Environment"*

COMPREHENSIVE PROBLEM 6

APEX COMPUTER, INC.

JOB ORDER AND PROCESS COST ACCOUNTING SYSTEMS

Apex Computer, Inc., manufactures and sells 10 different models of small computers, each using different combinations of micro-processors, disc drives, number of expansion slots, and other features. Some models are lap-tops, some are desk-tops, and others are workstations designed for networking. Production departments that manufacture standardized computer components, such as keyboards or monitors, use process cost accounting systems. However, the Computer Assembly Department sequentially assembles batches of from 5,000 to 10,000 of whichever model computer is most in demand. Therefore, the Computer Assembly Department uses a job order cost accounting system.

In **Part 1** of this Comprehensive Problem, we look at the accounting practices of the Computer Assembly Department—a job order cost accounting system. In **Part 2,** we focus upon the Keyboard Assembly Department, which uses a process cost accounting system.

Computer Assembly Department

PART 1
Job Order Cost Accounting Systems

The Computer Assembly Department uses a *job order* cost accounting system, with each job representing assembly of between 5,000 and 10,000 units of a particular model of computer. Once assembly is completed, the computers are transferred to the Finished Goods Warehouse and are available for sale.

Late in May 1996, the Computer Assembly Department began job no. 2140, the assembly of 10,000 model AC10 lap-top computers. This job was partially complete on May 31, and was completed on June 9. The job cost sheet included the following costs for direct materials and for direct labour as of May 31 and June 9 (the June 9 costs include those charged through May 31):

	Costs Charged to Job as of:	
	May 31	*June 9*
Direct materials requisitioned	$ 657,200	$2,290,300
Manufactured component parts requisitioned	$1,058,000	$4,723,700
Number of manufactured component parts requisitioned	12,000	65,000
Direct labour	$ 12,000	$ 56,000

Accounting Policies and Other Data

1 Manufacturing overhead is applied to jobs at the predetermined rate of $2 per component part requisitioned.

2 Direct materials represent parts purchased from others in a ready-to-use condition. Therefore, requisition of these parts is recorded by crediting the Materials Inventory controlling account.

3 Manufactured component parts are manufactured by Apex's other production departments and stored in the Components Warehouse. The requisition of these parts is recorded by crediting the Work in Process Inventory, Components controlling account.

4 Units completed by the Computer Assembly Department are classified as finished goods.

5 The specific identification method is used in transferring costs from the Finished Goods Inventory account to the Cost of Goods Sold account.

INSTRUCTIONS

a Compute the total cost of completing job no. 2140, and the per-unit cost of the 10,000 lap-top computers manufactured.

b Prepare general journal entries to summarize:

1 The manufacturing costs charged to job no. 2140 through the end of May.

2 The manufacturing costs charged to job no. 2140 during June.

3 The completion of the job and the transfer of the computers to the Finished Goods Warehouse.

c On June 28, Apex sells 4,000 of the lap-top computers in job no. 2140 to MicroCity, a national computer retailer. The sales price was $1,200 per unit; terms, 2/10, n/30.

1 Prepare the journal entries to record this sale.

2 Briefly explain how the total costs charged to job no. 2140 (per part **a**) will be shown in Apex's financial statements for the month ended June 30, 1996.

d Assume that during 1996, actual manufacturing overhead for the Computer Assembly Department amounted to $2,372,740, and that during the year the department requisitioned for assembly a total of 1,180,340 component parts.

1 Compute the amount of over- or underapplied overhead for the year.

2 Prepare a journal entry to close the Manufacturing Overhead controlling account at year-end, assuming that the amount of over- or underapplied overhead was not material in dollar amount.

The Keyboard Assembly Department

PART 2
Process Cost Accounting Systems

One of the production departments of Apex Computer, Inc., that uses a process cost accounting system is the Keyboard Assembly Department. The plastic frames for keyboards are produced in Apex's Plastic Molding Department. Those frames are then transferred to the Keyboard Assembly Department, where the production process is completed. Completed keyboards are transferred to the Components Warehouse where they are stored until they are needed by the Computer Assembly Department.

The accounting department has accumulated the following information relating to processing in the Keyboard Assembly Department during the month of June, 1996:

Costs charged to Keyboard Assembly Department:	
Work in process inventory, June 1	*$ 47,696*
Cost of 16,600 plastic keyboard frames transferred in from Plastic Molding Department during June	*17,596*
Manufacturing costs added in Keyboard Assembly Department during June:	
Direct materials added	*157,700*
Direct labour	*40,040*
Manufacturing overhead	*48,048*
Total costs to be accounted for	*$311,080*
Keyboards worked on during June:	
Units in process, June 1 (100% complete as to direct materials, 30% complete as to conversion costs)	*4,000*
Units started and completed during June	*13,600*
Units completed and transferred to Components Warehouse during June	*17,600*
Units in process, June 30 (100% complete as to direct materials, 60% complete as to conversion costs)	*3,000*

Accounting Policies and Other Data

1 All direct materials needed to complete Keyboards are placed into production at the start of the manufacturing process.

2 The FIFO inventory method is used in valuing the ending inventories of work in process and in determining the cost of completed keyboards transferred to the Components Warehouse.

3 Transfers of completed keyboards to the Components Warehouse are recorded by debiting a controlling account entitled Work in Process Inventory, Components.

INSTRUCTIONS

a Compute separately the equivalent full units of production in June by the Keyboard Assembly Department with respect to (1) direct materials and (2) conversion costs.

b Prepare a process cost report for the Keyboard Assembly Department for the month of June.

c Prepare journal entries to record for June the:

1 Transfer of 16,600 plastic keyboard frames from the Plastic Department into the Keyboard Assembly Department.

2 Manufacturing costs incurred in the Keyboard Assembly Department.

3 Transfer of 17,600 completed keyboards from the Keyboard Assembly Department to the Components Warehouse. (Note: these keyboards are **not** viewed as finished goods.)

8 Managerial Accounting: Planning and Control

*M*anagers are responsible for planning and controlling the activities of the business. The functions of planning and control are closely related. Planning is the process of setting financial and operational goals for the business and deciding upon the strategies and actions for achieving these goals. Exercising control means monitoring actual operating results, comparing those results to the plan, and taking corrective action when actual results fall below expectation.

23 Cost-Volume-Profit Analysis

This chapter has two major objectives. Our first is to explain how various costs respond to changes in the level of business activity. An understanding of these relationships is essential to developing successful business strategies and to planning future operations. Our second objective is to show how managers may use cost-volume-profit analysis in a wide variety of business decisions. We illustrate and explain the use of a "break-even" graph—a basic tool of cost-volume-profit analysis. Also, we discuss the concept of "contribution margin." In tailoring this concept to specific managerial decisions, we show how contribution margin may be expressed on a per-unit basis, as a percentage of sales, and in relation to available units of a scarce resource.

Learning Objectives

After studying this chapter, you should be able to:

1 *Explain how fixed, variable, and semivariable costs respond to changes in the level of business activity.*

2 *Use the high-low method to separate the fixed and variable elements of a semivariable cost.*

3 *Prepare a cost-volume-profit (break-even) graph.*

4 *Explain contribution margin; compute contribution margin per unit and contribution margin ratio.*

5 *Determine the sales volume required to earn a desired level of operating income.*

6 *Use the contribution margin ratio to estimate the effect upon operating income of changes in sales volume.*

7 *Use cost-volume-profit relationships in evaluating various marketing strategies.*

8 *Determine the sales mix that will maximize the contribution margin per unit of a scarce resource.*

*O*ne of the most important analytical tools used by many managers is cost-volume-profit analysis (or *CVP analysis*). CVP analysis is a means of learning how costs and profits behave in response to changes in the level of business activity. An understanding of these relationships is essential in developing plans and budgets for future business operations. In addition, analysis assists managers in predicting the effects of various decisions and strategies upon the operating income of the business. In our discussion of cost-volume-profit relationships, the term *"cost" is used to describe both manufacturing costs and operating expenses.*

Cost-volume-profit analysis may be used by managers to answer questions such as the following:

■ What level of sales must be reached to cover all costs, that is, to break even?

■ How many units of a product must be sold to earn a given operating income?

■ What will happen to our profitability if we expand capacity?

■ What will be the effect of changing compensation of sales personnel from fixed monthly salaries to a straight commission of 10% on sales?

■ If we increase our spending on advertising to $100,000 per month, what increase in sales volume will be required to maintain our current level of income from operations?

Cost-volume-profit relationships are useful not only to management but also to creditors and investors. The ability of a business to pay its debts and to increase its dividend payments, for example, depends largely upon its ability to generate earnings. Assume that a company's sales volume is expected to increase by 10% during the next year. What will be the effect of this increase in sales volume upon the company's net income? The answer depends upon how the company's costs behave in response to this increase in the level of business activity.

The concepts of cost-volume-profit analysis may be applied to the business as a whole; to individual segments of the business such as a division, a branch, or a department; or to a particular product line.

Cost-Volume Relationships

To illustrate the relationships between costs and the level of activity, we shall first consider cost behaviour in a simple and familiar setting, the cost of operating a personal automobile. Suppose that someone tells you that the average annual cost of owning and operating an automobile is $2,700. Obviously, each individual driver does not incur an annual cost of exactly $2,700. In large part, the annual cost of owning an automobile depends upon how much you drive.

OBJECTIVE 1 Explain how fixed, variable, and semivariable costs respond to changes in the level of business activity.

The Activity Base   In studying cost behaviour, we first look for some measurable concept of volume or activity that serves as a *cost driver*—that is, has a strong influence on the amount of cost incurred. We then try to find out how costs change in response to changes in the level of this activity. The unit of measure used to define the selected cost driver is called the *activity base*.

An activity base may be units of key production input, such as tonnes of peaches processed or direct labour hours worked. (We have seen in prior chapters that manufacturing overhead costs often are expressed in terms of an activity base such as direct labour costs, direct labour hours, or machine-hours.) Alternatively, the activity base may be based upon output, such as equivalent full units of production, units sold, or dollars of sales revenue.

Most airlines consider passenger-kilometres flown to be their major cost driver and use this measurement as the activity base for studying the behaviour of their operating costs. Retail stores, on the other hand, usually find total dollar sales to be the most significant activity base in cost analysis. In our example involving the operation of an automobile, we will use ***kilometres driven*** during the year as our activity base.

Once an appropriate activity base has been selected, we can classify all operating costs into one of the following three broad categories.

Fixed Costs (or Fixed Expenses)   ***Fixed*** costs are those costs and expenses that ***do not change*** significantly in response to changes in the activity base. For example, the annual licensing fee is an example of a fixed cost in the operation of an automobile, as this cost remains constant regardless of the number of kilometres driven. In a business entity, fixed costs include monthly salaries to office workers and executives, property taxes, and many types of insurance protection.

Variable Costs (Variable Expenses)   A ***variable*** cost is one that rises or falls in direct proportion to changes in the activity base. For example, if the activity base increases by 10%, a variable cost increases by approximately 10%. In our example involving the operation of an automobile, gasoline is a variable cost that changes in response to the number of kilometres driven.

In manufacturing operations, the costs of direct materials and direct labour are variable costs with respect to the number of units manufactured. For an airline, fuel expense is a variable cost that responds to changes in the number of passenger-kilometres flown. In retailing, the cost of goods sold and sales commissions expense are examples of variable costs that respond closely to changes in total dollar sales.

Semivariable Costs (Semivariable Expenses)   ***Semivariable*** costs also are called ***mixed*** costs, because ***part of the cost is fixed*** and ***part is variable.*** A great many business costs are semivariable. Telephone expense, for example, includes both a fixed element (the "base rate" charged by the telephone company each month) and a variable element (the additional charges for long-distance calls).

The concept of a semivariable cost usually applies when we combine a variety of different costs into one broad category. For example, manufacturing overhead includes both fixed costs, such as property taxes, and variable costs, such as supplies used and utilities expense. Therefore, total manufacturing overhead behaves as a semivariable cost.

In our example involving the operation of an automobile, we will use depreciation to illustrate the concept of a semivariable cost. With respect to automobiles, some depreciation occurs simply with the passage of time, without regard to kilometres driven. This represents the "fixed portion" of depreciation expense. However, the more kilometres an automobile is driven each year, the faster it depreciates. Thus, part of the total depreciation expense is a variable cost. (A technique for determining the fixed and variable portions of a semivariable expense will be illustrated and explained later in this chapter.)

Automobile Costs—Graphic Analysis To illustrate cost-volume behaviour, we shall assume the following somewhat simplified data to describe the cost of owning and operating an automobile:

Type of Cost	*Amount*
Fixed costs:	
Insurance	*$450 per year*
Licence fee	*50 per year*
Variable costs:	
Gasoline, oil, servicing	*8 cents per kilometre*
Semivariable costs:	
Depreciation	*$1,000 per year plus 4 cents per kilometre*

We can express these cost-volume relationships graphically. The relation between volume (kilometres driven per year) and the three types of cost, both separately and combined, is shown in the following diagrams.

GRAPHIC ANALYSIS OF AUTOMOBILE COSTS

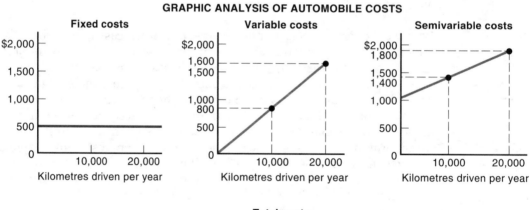

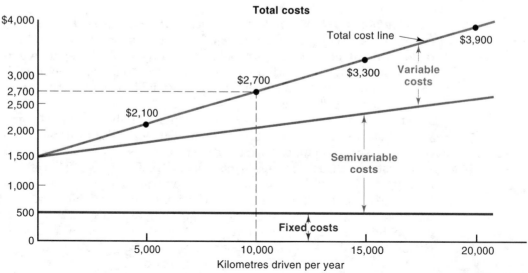

We can read from the total costs graph the estimated annual automobile cost for any assumed kilometres driven. For example, an owner who expects to drive 10,000 kilometres in a given year may estimate the total cost at $2,700 or 27.0 cents per kilometre. By combining all the fixed and variable elements of cost, we can generalize the cost-volume relationship and state simply that the cost of owning an automobile is ***$1,500 per year plus 12 cents per kilometre*** driven during the year.

The effect of volume on unit (per-kilometre) costs can be observed by converting total cost figures to average unit costs as follows:

Cost per Kilometre of Owning and Using an Automobile

Kilometres driven	5,000	10,000	15,000	20,000
Costs:				
Fully variable (8 cents per kilometre)	$ 400	$ 800	$1,200	$1,600
Semivariable:				
Variable portion (4 cents per kilometre)...........	200	400	600	800
Fixed portion.....................................	1,000	1,000	1,000	1,000
Completely fixed ($450 + $50).....................	500	500	500	500
Total costs...	$2,100	$2,700	$3,300	$3,900
Cost per kilometre...................................	$ 0.42	$ 0.27	$ 0.22	$0.195

Note decrease in cost per kilometre as use increases

The average unit-cost behaviour of operating an automobile may be presented graphically as shown below:

Average cost per kilometre of driving a car

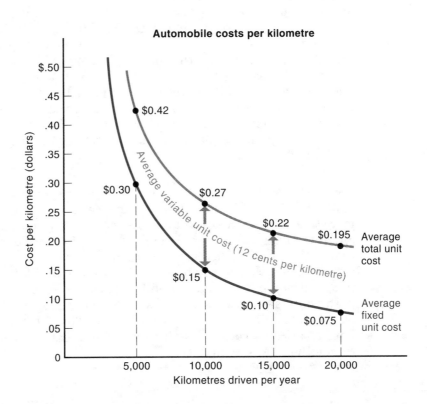

Automobile costs per kilometre

Behaviour of Unit Costs

Total variable costs rise and fall in approximate proportion to changes in the activity base. Therefore, variable costs *per unit remain relatively constant.* Notice in our preceding example that variable costs amount to 12 cents per kilometre, regardless of the number of kilometres driven.

Fixed costs, on the other hand, *do not* vary with changes in the activity base. Therefore, fixed costs *per unit decline as the level of activity increases.* Notice in our example that fixed costs amount to 30 cents per kilometre for an automobile driven 5,000 kilometres each year, but amount to only 15 cents per kilometre for an automobile driven 10,000 kilometres.

Cost Advantage for Intensive Use of Facilities

What does the behaviour of these unit costs mean to a business entity? In short, *a business can reduce its overall per-unit costs by using its facilities more intensively.* To illustrate, assume that an automobile plant incurs fixed costs of $8.4 million per month and has the capacity to produce 7,000 automobiles per month. The fixed cost per automobile manufactured is shown below at three different levels of production:

Fixed Costs per Month	Level of Production	Fixed Cost per Unit
$8,400,000	4,000 cars	$2,100
8,400,000	6,000 cars	1,400
8,400,000	7,000 cars	1,200

Notice that by producing 7,000 cars per month, the automaker's manufacturing costs are *$900 less* per automobile than if the automaker produces only 4,000 cars each month ($2,100 − $1,200 = $900). This "cost advantage" results from fully utilizing the company's production facilities and, therefore, spreading the company's fixed costs over as many units as possible. Unless overtime costs are incurred, *every business benefits from using its facilities more intensively.* This benefit is most apparent in business operations with relatively high fixed costs, such as automakers, utility companies, airlines, chemical manufacturers, and other companies with large investments in plant assets or large commitments to research and development.

CASE IN POINT General Motors is the world's largest automaker; it sells more than twice as many automobiles each year as does its archrival, Ford Motor Company. Yet for much of the late 1980s, Ford earned larger profits than GM. The variable costs of manufacturing an automobile were similar at Ford and GM. The key to Ford's impressive profitability was its ability to operate its plants at nearly full capacity. Weekend shifts were part of Ford's normal workweek. As a result, Ford incurred much lower fixed costs per car than did its domestic competitors. This "cost advantage" enabled Ford to price its cars competitively and still earn a higher profit margin than either GM or Chrysler.

Cost Behaviour in Business

Cost relationships in a business are seldom as simple as those in our example involving the operation of an automobile. However, the operating costs of all businesses exhibit variable, semivariable, and fixed characteristics.

Some business costs increase in lump-sum steps as shown in graph **(a)** below rather than in continuous increments. For example, when production reaches a point where another supervisor and crew must be added, a lump-sum addition to labour costs occurs at this point. Other costs may vary along a curve rather than a straight line, as in graph **(b).** For example, when overtime must be worked to increase production, the labour cost per unit may rise more rapidly than volume because of the necessity of paying an overtime premium to employees.

"Stair-step" and curvilinear costs

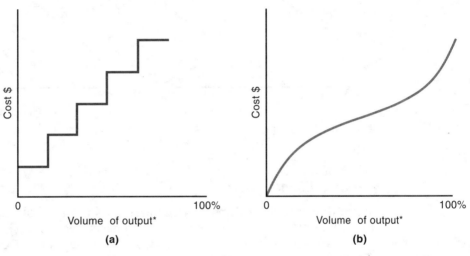

(a)

(b)

*Stated as a percentage of plant capacity

Taking all the possible variations of cost behaviour into account would add greatly to the complexity of cost-volume analysis. How far from reality are the assumed straight-line relationships? Fortunately, there are two factors that make straight-line approximations of cost behaviour useful for analytical purposes.

First, unusual patterns of cost behaviour tend to offset one another. If we were to plot actual total costs incurred by a business over a time period in which volume changes occurred, the result might appear as in the cost-volume graph **(a)** on the next page. Total cost often moves in close approximation to a straight-line pattern when the various "stair-step" and curvilinear cost patterns of individual costs are combined.

Second, unusual patterns of cost behaviour are most likely to occur at extremely high or extremely low levels of volume. For example, if output were increased to near 100% of plant capacity, variable costs would curve sharply upward because of payments for overtime. An extreme decline in volume, on the other hand, might require shutting down plants and extensive layoffs, thereby reducing some expenditures that are usually considered fixed costs. Most businesses, however, operate somewhere between perhaps 45% and 80% of capacity and try to avoid large fluctuations in volume. For a given business, the probability that volume will vary outside of a fairly narrow range is usually remote. The range over which output may be expected to vary is called the ***relevant range,*** as shown in graph (**b**) below. Within this relevant range, the assumption that total costs vary in straight-line relation to changes in volume is reasonably realistic for most companies.

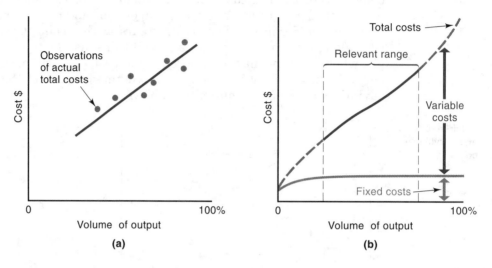

(a)   (b)

Analysis of Semivariable Costs: Determining the Fixed and Variable Elements

The study of relationships between costs and the level of activity is simplified when all costs may be classified either as fixed or variable. Therefore, we divide semivariable costs into two elements: (1) the fixed portion and (2) the variable portion.

OBJECTIVE 2 Use the high-low method to separate the fixed and variable elements of a semivariable cost.

Several mathematical techniques may be used to determine the fixed and variable elements of a semivariable cost or mixed cost. One approach, called the ***high-low method,*** is illustrated below.[1]

High-Low Method   To illustrate the high-low method, assume that some portion of the monthly maintenance cost of Ross Mfg. Co. is fixed and that some portion of this cost varies with the level of production. The levels of production and of maintenance cost for the first six months of the year are shown below:

Month	Equivalent Full Units of Production	Maintenance Cost
January	7,200	$4,790
February	7,000	4,700
March	7,700	5,100
April	8,400	5,430
May	9,000	5,700
June	8,600	5,600

---

[1]   Other approaches to determining the fixed and variable elements of a semivariable cost include the least squares method and regression analysis. These techniques are discussed in the cost accounting course.

To find the variable portion of this cost, we relate the change in the cost to the change in the activity base between the months of highest and lowest production activity:

	Equivalent Full Units of Production	Maintenance Cost
Highest level of activity base	9,000	$5,700
Lowest level of activity base	7,000	4,700
Changes	2,000	$1,000

Notice that a 2,000-unit increase in production caused a $1,000 increase in maintenance cost. Therefore, the variable element of this cost may be estimated at $1,000/2,000 units, or **$0.50 per equivalent full unit of production.**

To determine the fixed portion of the monthly maintenance cost, we take the total monthly cost at either the high point or low point and deduct the variable maintenance cost at that level of activity. This computation follows, starting with the total monthly maintenance cost at the high point of activity:

> Fixed Cost = Total Cost − Variable Cost
> = $5,700 − ($0.50 per unit × 9,000 units)
> = $5,700 − $4,500
> = $1,200 per month

We have now developed a **cost formula** for monthly maintenance cost: **$1,200 fixed cost + $0.50 per equivalent full unit of production.** This formula may be used in evaluating the reasonableness of maintenance costs incurred in past periods, and also in forecasting costs likely to be incurred in the future. For example, what amount of maintenance cost should Ross Mfg. Co. expect in a month in which the company has scheduled 8,000 equivalent full units of production? The answer is approximately **$5,200,** determined as follows:

Monthly fixed cost..	$1,200
Variable cost ($0.50 × 8,000 equivalent full units)	4,000
Total estimated maintenance cost	$5,200

Cost Classifications

Once semivariable costs and expenses have been subdivided into fixed and variable elements, we may summarize the relationships among revenue, costs (and expenses), and profit as follows:

Classifications used in CVP analysis

Revenue − Variable Costs − Fixed Costs = Operating Income

Remember, we are using the term **cost** to include both manufacturing costs **and** operating expenses.

Notice that this formula leads to the determination of **operating income,** rather than net income. This is because income taxes expense and nonoperating gains and losses do not meet the criteria of either variable costs or fixed costs. Therefore, the term **profit** in cost-volume-profit analysis always refers to **operating income, not net income.**

Cost-volume-profit analysis often is called **break-even analysis,** a reference to the point at which a business moves from a loss to a profit position. This **break-even point** may be defined as the level of activity at which operating income is equal to **zero;** thus, revenue is exactly equal to the sum of the variable costs and fixed costs.

Cost-Volume-Profit Analysis: An Illustration

A simple business situation will be used to illustrate the kinds of information that can be derived from cost-volume-profit analysis. Hannigan's Ice Cream Limited has a chain of stores located throughout a large city, selling an exclusive brand of ice cream products. Although the company sells many ice cream products of different size, we shall assume that volume of business is measured in litres of ice cream sold. The company buys its ice cream from the dairy that produces this exclusive brand for Hannigan's at a price of $4.20 per litre. Retail sales prices vary depending upon the item and quantity purchased by a customer, but revenue consistently **averages** $12 per litre of ice cream sold. Monthly operating statistics for a typical store are shown below:

HANNIGAN'S ICE CREAM LIMITED
Monthly Operating Data—
Typical Retail Store

	Fixed Expenses	Variable Expenses per Litre	Variable Expenses as Percentage of Sales Price
Average selling price		$12.00	100%
Cost of ice cream		$ 4.20	35.0%
Monthly operating expenses:			
Manager's salary	$2,400		
Wages	3,720+	.24	2.0
Store rent	1,600		
Utilities	180+	.06	.5
Insurance and depreciation	280		
Miscellaneous	820+	.30	2.5
Total expenses (except for income taxes)....	$9,000+	$4.80	40.0%
Unit contribution margin and contribution margin ratio (discussed on pages 1100–1101)................................		$7.20	60.0%

Note variable and fixed cost elements (margin note)

Notice that income taxes expense is not included among the monthly operating expenses. Income taxes are neither a fixed nor a variable cost because they depend upon the amount of taxable income, rather than sales volume.[2]

---

[2] Determination of the income taxes expense applicable to a corporation's pretax income is discussed in Chapter 18.

CVP analysis may be performed either by stating the cost-volume-profit relationships in the form of mathematical formulas or by illustrating them visually in a graph. Let us begin with graphic analysis.

Preparing and Using a Break-Even Graph

OBJECTIVE 3
Prepare a
cost-volume-
profit
(break-even)
graph.

A *cost-volume-profit* (or *break-even*) graph for a typical Hannigan's Ice Cream store, based on the preceding data, is shown below.

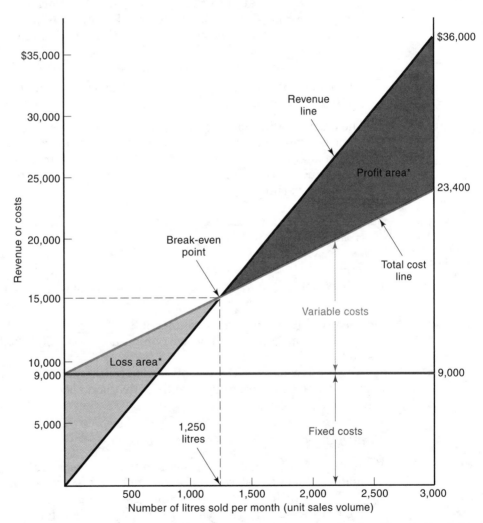

HANNIGAN'S ICE CREAM LIMITED
Monthly Cost-Volume-Profit Graph
Typical Retail Store

* Profit and loss areas represent operating income or loss before non-operating gains and losses and income taxes

The horizontal axis represents the activity base, which for a Hannigan's store is the number of litres of ice cream sold per month. Since none of the company's stores sells more than 3,000 litres per month, this is assumed to be the upper limit of the relevant range. The vertical axis of the graph is in dollars of revenue or costs (expenses).

The steps in drawing this graph are as follows:

1 Draw the total revenue line. This line runs from $0 revenue at zero sales volume to $36,000 in revenue at the maximum sales volume of 3,000 litres per month. (Notice that the revenue line increases at a rate of $12 per litre sold.)

2 Draw the fixed cost line. This is a horizontal line representing a constant $9,000 monthly amount at all volume levels.

3 Starting at the $9,000 fixed cost line, draw a line representing variable costs. This line will rise at the rate of $4.80 per litre of ice cream sold. Any two points may be used in drawing the variable cost line, such as $0 in variable costs at zero litres, and $14,400 in variable costs at 3,000 litres ($4.80 per litre × 3,000 litres = $14,400). **Remember,** however, to add the $9,000 in fixed costs to the variable costs in finding the points for drawing the variable cost line. When the variable cost line is drawn starting "on top" of the fixed costs, it *also serves as the total cost line.*

4 Label the point at which the revenue line crosses the total cost line as the **break-even point.**

The operating income or loss expected at any sales volume may be read from the cost-volume-profit graph. For example, the break-even point (zero profit) for a Hannigan's store is at **1,250** litres per month, or $15,000 in sales revenue. At this point, total revenue is exactly equal to total costs and expenses, as verified below:

Computation verifying the break-even point in our graph

Revenue (1,250 litres × $12 per litre)		$15,000
Costs and expenses:		
Fixed	$9,000	
Variable (1,250 litres × $4.80 per litre)	6,000	15,000
Operating income		$ -0-

On the other hand, if a sales volume of 3,000 litres per month is achieved, the monthly operating income will amount to $12,600 ($36,000 revenue, less $23,400 in total costs).

We will now explore the use of several mathematical formulas that will enable us to focus more quickly and easily upon specific cost-volume-profit relationships.

Contribution Margin: A Key Relationship

OBJECTIVE 4
Explain contribution margin; compute contribution margin per unit and contribution margin ratio.

Variable costs vary in direct proportion to revenue. Thus, the generation of an additional dollar of revenue also generates some amount of variable costs. The operating data for our Hannigan's ice cream stores indicate that variable costs (such as the cost of ice cream) account for 40% of the company's sales revenue. Thus, for every $100 in revenue, the company may expect to pay out $40 to cover the related variable costs. The remaining $60 is called the **contribution margin.**

The contribution margin is the **amount of revenue in excess of variable costs.** This portion of the revenue is available to cover the company's fixed costs and, after all fixed costs have been covered, provide an operating income. The allocation of the average revenue dollar between the variable costs relating to the sale and the contribution margin is illustrated below for a typical Hannigan's store:

40¢ of each revenue dollar is consumed by variable costs relating to the sale.

60¢ of each revenue dollar is available to cover fixed expenses and to contribute to operating income. This is called the **contribution margin**.

Contribution margin may be expressed either as a total dollar amount for the period (total revenue minus total variable costs) or as an amount per unit (unit sales price minus variable costs per unit). For example, the contribution margin **per litre** of ice cream sold at a typical Hannigan's store is **$7.20,** computed as follows:

$$\text{Unit Contribution Margin} = \text{Unit Sales Price} - \text{Variable Costs per Unit}$$
$$= \qquad \$12.00 \qquad - \qquad \$4.80$$
$$= \qquad \$7.20$$

Contribution Margin Ratio   In CVP analysis, it is often useful to express contribution margin as a **percentage of revenue.** This percentage, called the **contribution margin ratio,** may be computed using either the total contribution margin or the contribution margin per unit. The relationships are as follows:

$$\text{Contribution Margin Ratio} = \frac{\text{Total Contribution Margin}}{\text{Total Revenue}}$$

and/or

$$\text{Contribution Margin Ratio} = \frac{\text{Unit Contribution Margin}}{\text{Unit Sales Price}}$$

Using Hannigan's per-unit data, the contribution margin ratio of a typical Hannigan's store is **60%,** computed as follows:

$$\text{Contribution Margin Ratio} = \frac{\$7.20}{\$12.00} = 60\%$$

A contribution margin of 60% means that 60% of the revenue earned in a Hannigan's store contributes toward covering fixed costs and providing operating income. The other 40% of revenue earned is consumed by variable costs.

Let us now see how management makes use of such measurements as contribution margin and contribution margin ratio.

How Many Units Must We Sell?

The concept of contribution margin provides a quick means of determining the **unit sales volume** required for a business to break even or to earn any

OBJECTIVE 5
Determine
the sales
volume re-
quired to
earn a de-
sired level of
operating
income.

desired level of operating income. Break-even sales volume can be of vital importance, especially to companies deciding whether to introduce a new product line, build a new plant, or, in some cases, remain in business.

CASE IN POINT Chrysler Corporation in the United States, widely believed to be heading for bankruptcy during the early 1980s, undertook a severe cost-cutting program and altered marketing strategies in an effort to lower the company's break-even point. In 1981, Chrysler had a break-even point of 1,413,000 vehicles; sales amounted to 1,282,000 vehicles and the company incurred substantial losses. For 1982, the company was able to reduce its break-even point to 1,244,000 vehicles. Chrysler surprised many people in the financial community by returning to profitable operations in 1982 with sales of approximately 1,400,000 vehicles. This "turn-around year" may well have saved Chrysler Corp. Notice, however, that the 1982 sales volume would have resulted in a net loss had Chrysler not been able to lower its break-even point.

To illustrate the relationship between sales volume and contribution margin, assume that we want to know how many litres of ice cream a Hannigan's store must sell to break even. At the break-even point, the store must earn a contribution large enough to cover all fixed costs. The Hannigan's data show that the monthly fixed costs amount to *$9,000,* and that the contribution margin per litre of ice cream is *$7.20* ($12.00 sales price minus $4.80 variable costs). If the sale of each litre covers $7.20 of fixed costs, how many litres must be sold to cover monthly fixed costs of $9,000? The answer is 1,250 litres per month, as shown below:

$$\text{Sales Volume (in units)} = \frac{\$9,000}{\$7.20 \text{ per litre}} = \textbf{1,250 litres per month}$$

Notice that this answer corresponds to the sales volume shown in the cost-volume-profit graph.

The reasoning in our above analysis may be summarized by the following formula:

$$\text{Sales Volume (in units)} = \frac{\text{Fixed Costs} + \text{Target Operating Income}}{\text{Unit Contribution Margin}}$$

With this formula, we may find not only the break-even sales volume (at which operating income is zero), but also the unit sales volume needed to achieve **any desired level of operating income.** For example, how many litres of ice cream must be sold for a Hannigan's store to earn a monthly operating income of *$4,500?*

$$\text{Sales Volume (in units)} = \frac{\$9,000 + \$4,500}{\$7.20} = \textbf{1,875 litres per month}$$

Finding Required Dollar Sales Volume To find the **dollar sales volume** needed to earn a given level of operating income, we could first compute the required unit sales and then multiply our answer by the unit sales price. Using the data from our preceding example, a Hannigan's store expecting to earn a monthly operating income of $4,500 would need sales revenue of $22,500 (1,875 litres × $12 per litre).

As a more direct approach, we may compute the required dollar sales volume by substituting the *contribution margin ratio* for the contribution margin per unit in our sales volume formula. The formula then becomes:

$$\text{Sales Volume (in dollars)} = \frac{\text{Fixed Costs} + \text{Target Operating Income}}{\text{Contribution Margin Ratio}}$$

To illustrate, let us again compute the sales volume required for a Hannigan's store to earn a monthly operating income of $4,500:

$$\text{Sales Volume (in dollars)} = \frac{\$9,000 + \$4,500}{.60} = \$22,500 \text{ per month}$$

Margin of Safety The amount by which actual sales volume *exceeds* the break-even sales volume is called the margin of safety. This is the dollar amount by which sales could *decline* before the company will incur an operating loss. A typical Hannigan's store has a break-even sales volume of $15,000 per month.

$$\text{Sales Volume (in dollars)} = \frac{\$9,000}{.60} = \$15,000 \text{ per month}$$

Therefore, a store with actual sales of $22,500 has a *margin of safety* of $7,500; a store with sales of $25,000 has a margin of safety of ***$10,000*** ($25,000 − $15,000).

The margin of safety provides us with a quick means of estimating operating income at any sales volume above the break-even point, as shown below:

$$\text{Operating Income} = \text{Margin of Safety} \times \text{Contribution Margin Ratio}$$

The rationale for this formula stems from the fact that the margin of safety represents sales dollars *in excess of* the break-even point. Therefore, fixed costs have already been covered and the *entire contribution margin from these sales increases operating income.*

To illustrate this concept, let us estimate the operating income of a Hannigan's store with a sales volume of $22,500, which is $7,500 above the break-even point. The estimated operating income is ***$4,500*** ($7,500 × 60%). (Notice that this answer is consistent with our earlier computations.)

Changes in Operating Income The contribution margin ratio in our example is 60%, which means that 60 cents out of every revenue dollar goes toward covering fixed costs (which reduces an operating loss) or toward increasing operating income. Thus, every additional dollar of sales improves Hannigan's profit picture by 60 cents. Conversely, a $1 sales decline lowers profitability by 60 cents. This relationship may be summarized as follows:

OBJECTIVE 6 Use the contribution margin ratio to estimate the effect upon operating income of changes in sales volume.

$$\frac{\text{Change in}}{\text{Operating Income}} = \frac{\text{Change in}}{\text{Sales Volume}} \times \frac{\text{Contribution}}{\text{Margin Ratio}}$$

To illustrate, let us assume that the sales volume at a given ice cream store increases from $15,000 (the break-even point) to $22,500, an increase of $7,500. According to the above equation, the operating income of the store should increase by **$4,500** ($7,500 × 60%). This increase may be verified by reference to our earlier calculations. On page 1100, we showed that a sales volume of $15,000 is the break-even point for a Hannigan's store; operating income at this sales volume, therefore, is zero. Also, in an earlier section, we determined that the sales volume required to earn a target operating income of $4,500 is $22,500.

Using Cost-Volume-Profit Relationships

OBJECTIVE 7
Use cost-
volume-
profit rela-
tionships in
evaluating
various
marketing
strategies.

Cost-volume-profit relationships are widely used during the budgeting process to set sales targets, and to estimate costs and expenses. In addition, these relationships can provide information that is useful in a wide variety of planning decisions. To illustrate, let us consider several ways in which cost-volume-profit relationships might be used by the management of Hannigan's Ice Cream in planning marketing strategies:

1 **Question:** To increase volume, management is considering a policy of giving greater discounts on litre packages of ice cream. It is estimated that the effect of this pricing policy would be to reduce the selling price per litre by $1.20 (that is, from $12 per litre to $10.80). Management is interested in knowing the effect of such a price reduction on the **number of litres** of ice cream a store must sell to break even.

Analysis: The proposed change in sales price changes the contribution margin per litre of ice cream from $7.20 to $6.00, as shown below:

$$\text{Unit Contribution Margin} = \text{Unit Sales Price} - \text{Variable Costs per Unit}$$
$$= \$10.80 - \$4.80$$
$$= \$6.00$$

The fixed operating expenses remain unchanged by this pricing decision. Therefore, the unit sales volume **to break even** under the new pricing situation would be:

$$\text{Sales Volume (in units)} = \frac{\text{Fixed Costs} + \text{Target Operating Income}}{\text{Unit Contribution Margin}}$$
$$= \frac{\$9,000 + \$0}{\$6.00}$$
$$= \textbf{1,500 litres per month}$$

This new break-even point, 1,500 litres, is 20% higher than the present 1,250 litre break-even volume. Thus, management should be advised that the proposed pricing policy is desirable only if the unit sales volume per store can be expected to increase 20% per month as a result of the lower sales prices on litre packages.

2 **Question:** Management is considering a change in the method of compensating store managers. Instead of a fixed salary of $2,400 per month, it is proposed that managers be put on a salary of $1,740 per month plus a commission of 72 cents per litre of sales. The present average monthly operating income per store is $3,000 on sales of $20,000 (Proof: $20,000 × 60% − $9,000 = $3,000). What sales revenue per store will be necessary to

produce the same monthly income to Hannigan's under the proposed incentive compensation arrangement?

Analysis: This proposal involves a change in both the contribution margin ratio and the fixed monthly operating expenses. Adding 72 cents per litre to variable costs raises the total variable cost to $5.52 per litre and reduces the contribution margin ratio to 54%, as computed below:

$$\text{Contribution Margin Ratio} = \frac{\text{Unit Sales Price} - \text{Variable Costs per Unit}}{\text{Unit Sales Price}}$$

$$= \frac{\$12.00 - \$5.52}{\$12.00}$$

$$= 54\%$$

Cutting the manager's salary from $2,400 to $1,740 per month will reduce monthly fixed costs from $9,000 to $8,340. The sales volume required to produce a monthly operating income of $3,000 may be computed as follows:

$$\text{Sales Volume (in dollars)} = \frac{\text{Fixed Costs} + \text{Target Operating Income}}{\text{Contribution Margin Ratio}}$$

$$= \frac{\$8,340 + \$3,000}{.54}$$

$$= \$21,000 \text{ per month}$$

To produce the same $3,000 per month operating income under the new compensation plan, sales volume per store would have to be increased by $1,000 (or 83⅓ litres) over the current monthly sales volume of $20,000. The issue thus boils down to whether the incentive compensation arrangement will induce store managers to increase volume by more than 83⅓ litres per month. Cost-volume-profit analysis does not answer this question, but it provides the information that enables management to exercise its judgment intelligently.

3 *Question:* Hannigan's Ice Cream stores are now open 12 hours each day (from 9 A.M. to 9 P.M.). Management is considering a proposal to decrease store hours by opening two hours later each morning. It is estimated that this policy would reduce sales volume by an average of 125 litres per month and would cut fixed costs (utilities and wages) by $1,100 per month. Would it pay the company to change its store hours?

Analysis: The loss of 125 litres of sales per month would decrease revenue by $1,500 (125 × $12). This would result in the loss of contribution margin of $900 ($1,500 × 60%). Therefore, whether the reduction in store hours would increase operating income per store may be determined as follows:

Reduction in fixed costs	$1,100
Less: Loss of contribution margin ($1,500 × 60%)	900
Prospective increase in monthly operating income per store	$ 200

Importance of Sales Mix in Cost-Volume-Profit Analysis

In our example of Hannigan's Ice Cream Limited, we assumed that the contribution margin ratio ***averaged*** 60% of sales expressed in dollars and that the ***average*** selling price was $12 per litre of ice cream sold. Let us now change our example and assume that a detailed analysis indicated that ice cream is actually sold in the following varieties:

	Hand-packed Quarter-litre	Prepackaged Half-litre	Cones and Novelties
Unit sales price	$4.00	$5.00	$1.60
Less: Variable costs per unit..................	1.50	2.50	.40
Unit contribution margin.......................	$2.50	$2.50	$1.20
Contribution margin ratio (unit contribution margin ÷ sales price)	62.5%	50%	75%
Break-even sales volume, assuming that only the one type of product is sold (fixed costs, $9,000, divided by contribution margin ratio)	$14,400	$18,000	$12,000

Why would you prefer to sell only cones?

Earlier in this chapter we stated that Hannigan's Ice Cream is now selling a certain *mix* of the three sizes and that a sales volume of $15,000 is required to break even ($9,000 ÷ *average* contribution margin ratio of 60%). If ice cream were sold exclusively in quarter-litres, sales of $14,400 would be required to break even; if only half-litre packages were sold, the break-even sales volume would be $18,000; if only cones and novelties were sold, the break-even sales volume would be $12,000. The reason the break-even sales volume differs for each size is because each size yields a different contribution margin per dollar of sales (contribution margin ratio). *The higher the contribution margin ratio, the lower the sales volume that is required to cover a given amount of fixed costs.*

The amount of operating income earned by a business unit depends not only on the volume of sales and the ability to control costs, but also on the *quality* of sales. At any given sales volume, selling products with high contribution margin ratios is more profitable than selling products with low contribution margin ratios. Thus, sales with high contribution margin ratios are said to be *high-quality sales.* A shift from low-margin sales to high-margin sales can increase net income even though total sales volume may decline. On the other hand, a shift from high-margin to low-margin sales can cause operating income to fall even though total sales may increase.

Contribution Margin per Unit of Scarce Resource

OBJECTIVE 8 Determine the sales mix that will maximize the contribution margin per unit of a scarce resource.

The contribution margin approach is useful to management in deciding what products to manufacture (or purchase for resale) and what products to eliminate when certain factors of production are available only in limited quantity. One of the important functions of management is to develop the most profitable uses of such scarce resources as direct (raw) materials, skilled labour, high-cost equipment, and factory floor space.

Assume that you are offered two equally satisfactory jobs, one paying $6 per hour and one paying $9 per hour. Since your time is scarce and you wish to maximize the pay that you receive for an hour of your time, you would naturally choose the job paying $9 per hour. For the same reason, if a company has the capacity to utilize only 100,000 direct labour hours per year, management would want to use this capacity in such a way as *to produce the maximum contribution margin per hour of direct labour.*

To illustrate this concept, assume that Optic Corporation is considering the production of three products. The contribution margin per direct labour hour required to produce each of the three products is estimated as follows:

OPTIC CORPORATION
Contribution Margin per Hour of Direct Labour

Product	Unit Sales Price	−	Variable Expenses Per Unit	=	Unit Contribution Margin	÷	Direct Labour Hours Required per Unit Produced	=	Contribution Margin per Direct Labour Hour
A	$100		$60		$40		10		$ 4
B	80		50		30		5		6
C	60		40		20		2		10

Should output of product C be expanded?

Notice that the manufacture of a unit of product A requires 10 hours of direct labour and generates $40 in contribution margin; a unit of product B requires only 5 hours of direct labour and yields $30 of contribution margin; finally, product C requires only 2 hours of direct labour and yields $20 in contribution margin. Thus, product C produces the ***largest amount of contribution margin per hour of direct labour.*** Even though product A has the highest contribution margin per unit ($40) and the highest contribution margin ratio (40%), it is the least profitable of the three products in terms of contribution margin ***per hour of direct labour.***

When a company's total output is limited by the scarcity of one particular resource, the company should attempt to maximize the contribution margin per unit of this scarce resource. To illustrate this idea, the following table shows the amounts of contribution margin that Optic would earn if it devoted all 100,000 available direct labour hours exclusively to the manufacture of each of the three products under consideration:

Product	Total Capacity (Hours)	×	Contribution Margin per Hour of Direct Labour	=	Total Contribution Margin If Only One Product Is Manufactured
A	100,000		$ 4		$ 400,000
B	100,000		6		600,000
C	100,000		10		1,000,000

Which is the most profitable product?

This schedule clearly shows that the company can maximize its contribution margin and, therefore, its operating income by concentrating its manufacturing efforts on ***product C.***

In most cases, however, a company cannot simply devote all of its efforts to manufacturing the single product that is the most profitable. For example, the demand for product C may not be sufficient to allow the company to sell all the units of this product that it can produce. In this case, the company should produce units of product B after it has met the demand for product C. It should produce product A only after it has met the total demand for both products B and C.

Another consideration is that the production and sale of products A or B may be ***necessary to support the sales of product C.*** Often, the contribution margins are much lower on these "supporting" products. Gillette, for example, manufactures blade-razors that it sells at or below cost. Why? The answer is that the sale of razors promotes the sale of razor blades, which are products with a high contribution margin.

In conclusion, most companies are not able to devote all their manufacturing efforts to the single product that provides the highest contribution margin per unit of the resource that limits the company's production. However, if the sales of different products are independent of one another, the company will maximize its total contribution margin by first meeting the demand for those products with the highest contribution margins *per unit of this scarce resource.*

Assumptions Underlying Cost-Volume-Profit Analysis

In cost-volume-profit analysis, accountants assume the following:

1 Sales price per unit remains constant.
2 If more than one product is sold, the proportion of the various products sold (sales mix) is assumed to be constant.
3 Fixed costs (expenses) remain constant at all levels of sales within the assumed relevant range of activity.
4 Variable costs (expenses) remain constant as a percentage of sales revenue.
5 For a business engaged in manufacturing, the number of units produced is assumed to be equal to the number of units sold.

These assumptions simplify cost-volume-profit analysis. In actual practice, however, some of these assumptions may not hold true. However, cost-volume-profit analysis is still a useful planning tool for management. As changes take place in selling prices, sales mix, expenses, and production levels, management should update and revise its analysis.

Summary of Basic Cost-Volume-Profit Relationships

In this chapter, we have demonstrated a number of ratios and mathematical relationships that are useful in cost-volume-profit analysis. For your convenience, these relationships are summarized as follows:

Measurement	*Method of Computation*
Contribution margin	*Sales Revenue – Total Variable Costs*
Unit contribution margin	*Unit Sales Price – Variable Costs per Unit*
Contribution margin ratio	$\dfrac{\textit{Unit Sales Price – Variable Costs per Unit}}{\textit{Unit Sales Price}}$
	or
	$\dfrac{\textit{Sales – Total Variable Costs}}{\textit{Sales}}$
Sales volume (in units)	$\dfrac{\textit{Fixed costs + Target Operating Income}}{\textit{Unit Contribution Margin}}$
Sales volume (in dollars)	$\dfrac{\textit{Fixed costs + Target Operating Income}}{\textit{Contribution Margin Ratio}}$
Margin of safety	*Actual Sales Volume – Break-Even Sales Volume*
Operating income	*Margin of Safety* × *Contribution Margin Ratio*
Change in operating income	*Change in Sales Volume* × *Contribution Margin Ratio*

CHAPTER REVIEW

KEY TERMS INTRODUCED OR EMPHASIZED IN CHAPTER 23

Activity base   The scale used in measuring an activity that serves as a *cost driver* of variable and semivariable cost.

Break-even point   The level of sales at which a company neither earns an operating income nor incurs a loss. Revenue exactly covers costs and expenses.

Cost driver   A type of activity that has a causal effect in the occurrence of a particular cost.

Cost formula   A mathematical statement expressing the expected amount of a cost in terms of the fixed element of the cost and/or the portion of the cost that varies in response to changes in some activity base. For example, the cost formula for a semivariable cost might be: $2,500 per month, plus 5% of net sales.

Contribution margin   Sales minus variable costs. The portion of sales revenue that is not consumed by variable costs and, therefore, is available to cover fixed costs and contribute to operating income.

Contribution margin per unit   The excess of unit sales price over variable cost per unit; the dollar amount contributed by the sale *of each unit* toward covering fixed costs and generating operating income.

Contribution margin ratio   The contribution margin expressed as a percentage of sales price. Represents the percentage of each revenue dollar that is available to cover fixed costs or to provide an operating income.

Fixed costs   Costs and expenses that remain unchanged despite changes in the level of the activity base.

High-low method   A method of dividing a semivariable (or mixed) cost into its fixed and variable elements by relating the change in the cost to the change in the activity base between the highest and lowest levels of observed activity.

Margin of safety   Amount by which actual sales exceed the break-even point.

Relevant volume range   The span or range of output over which output is likely to vary and assumptions about cost behaviour are generally valid. Excludes extreme volume variations.

Semivariable costs   Costs and expenses that respond to change in the level of the activity base by less than a proportionate amount.

Variable costs   Costs and expenses that vary directly and proportionately with changes in the level of the activity base.

DEMONSTRATION PROBLEM FOR YOUR REVIEW

The management of Fresno Processing Limited has engaged you to assist in the development of information to be used for managerial decisions.

The company has the capacity to process 20,000 tonnes of cottonseed per year. The yield from a tonne of cottonseed is as shown below.

Product	Average Yield per Tonne* of Cottonseed	Average Selling Price	Total Revenue
Oil	200 kilograms	$ 0.50 per kg	$100
Meal	300 kilograms	160.00 per tonne	48
Hulls	400 kilograms	100.00 per tonne	40
Lint	100 kilograms	0.12 per kg	12
Total	1,000 kilograms		$200

*There are 1,000 kilograms in a tonne.

A special marketing study revealed that the company can expect to sell its entire output for the coming year at the average selling prices listed on the preceding page.

You have determined the company's cost structure to be as follows:

Cost of cottonseed:	*$80 per tonne*
Processing costs:	
Variable:	*$26 per tonne of cottonseed processed*
Fixed:	*$340,000 per year at all levels of production*
Marketing costs:	*All variable, $44 per tonne of all products sold*
Administrative costs:	*All fixed, $300,000 per year at all levels of production and sales activity*

INSTRUCTIONS

a Compute (1) the contribution margin per tonne and (2) the contribution margin ratio per tonne of cottonseed processed.

b Compute the break-even sales volume in (1) dollars and (2) tonnes of cottonseed.

c Assume that the company's budget calls for an operating income of $240,000. Compute the sales volume required to reach this profit objective, stated (1) in dollars and (2) in tonnes of cottonseed.

d Compute the maximum amount that the company can afford to pay per tonne of raw cottonseed and still break even by processing and selling 16,000 tonnes during the current year.

SOLUTION TO DEMONSTRATION PROBLEM

a (1) *Total revenue per tonne of cotton seed* *$200*

      Less: Variable Costs:

Cottonseed	*$80*	
Processing	*26*	
Marketing...	*44*	*150*
Unit contribution margin ($200 − $150)..................................		*$ 50*

(2) *Contribution margin ratio ($50 ÷ $200)* *25%*

b (1) *Break-even dollar sales volume:*

Fixed costs ($340,000 + $300,000)	*$ 640,000*
Contribution margin ratio (part a).....................................	*25%*
Break-even dollar sales volume ($640,000 ÷ .25)......................	*$2,560,000*

(2) *Break-even unit sales volume (in tonnes):*

Fixed costs (per above)	*$ 640,000*
Unit contribution margin (part a).....................................	*$ 50*
Break-even unit sales volume, stated in tonnes of	
cottonseed products ($640,000 ÷ $50).............................	*12,800*

     (Alternative computation: break-even dollar sales volume, $2,560,000, divided by unit sales price, $200, equals 12,800 tonnes.)

c (1) *Required dollar sales volume:*

Fixed expenses	$ 640,000
Add: Target operating income	240,000
Required contribution margin..	$ 880,000
Contribution margin ratio *(part a)*.................................	25%
Required dollar sales volume..	$3,520,000

(2) *Required unit sales volume:*

Required dollar sales volume [from (1)]	$3,520,000
Unit sales price	$ 200
Required unit sales volume, in tonnes ($3,520,000 ÷ $200)	17,600

(Alternative computation: required contribution margin to cover fixed expenses and target operating income, $880,000, [part c(1)], divided by unit contribution margin, $50 per tonne, equals 17,600 tonnes.)

d

Total revenue (16,000 tonnes × $200)		$3,200,000
Less: Costs other than cottonseed:		
Processing (16,000 tonnes × $26)........................	$416,000	
Marketing (16,000 tonnes × $44)	704,000	
Fixed costs	640,000	1,760,000
Maximum amount that can be paid for 16,000 tonnes of cottonseed, while allowing company to break even.....................		$1,440,000
Maximum amount that can be paid per tonne of cottonseed, while allowing company to break even ($1,440,000 ÷ 16,000 tonnes)		$90

ASSIGNMENT MATERIAL

DISCUSSION QUESTIONS

1 Why is it important for management to understand cost-volume-profit relationships?

2 What is an *activity base* and why is it important in analyzing cost behaviour?

3 What is the effect of an increase in activity upon:
   a Total variable costs.
   b Variable costs per unit of activity.

4 What is the effect of an increase in activity upon:
   a Total fixed costs.
   b Fixed costs per unit of activity.

5 The simplifying assumption that costs and volume vary in straight-line relationships makes the analysis of cost behaviour much easier. What factors make this a reasonable and useful assumption in many cases?

6 Define the *relevant range* of activity.

7 Explain how the high-low method determines:
   a The variable portion of a semivariable cost.
   b The fixed portion of a semivariable cost.

8 Define (a) *contribution margin* and (b) *contribution margin ratio*.

9 What important relationships are shown on a cost-volume-profit (break-even) graph?

10 Klein Company has an average contribution margin ratio of 35%. What dollar sales volume per month is necessary to produce a monthly operating income of $30,000, if fixed costs are $145,000 per month?

11 Explain how the unit contribution margin can be used to determine the unit sales required to break even.

12 Hurst Company has variable costs of $26 per unit and a contribution margin ratio of 35%. Compute the selling price per unit.

13 Define *margin of safety.*

14 Explain the probable effect upon operating income of a $19,000 increase in sales volume by a company with variable costs of $75 per unit and a contribution margin ratio of 40%.

15 An executive of a large steel company put the blame for lower net income for a recent fiscal period on the "shift in product mix to a higher proportion of export sales." Sales for the period increased slightly while net income declined by 28%. Explain how a change in product (sales) mix to a higher proportion in export sales would result in a lower level of net income.

16 Why is it helpful to know the approximate amount of contribution margin generated from the use of a scarce resource such as a machine-hour or an hour of direct labour?

17 The president of an airline blamed a profit squeeze on "unwise and unjustifiable promotional fares." He pointed out that 50% of the company's revenue came from "discount fares." Explain why discount fares tend to reduce net income and point out circumstances in which a discount from the regular price of a plane fare could *increase* net income.

MULTIPLE CHOICE QUESTIONS

1 During the current year, the net sales of Ridgeway, Inc., were 10% below last year's level. You should expect Ridgeway's semivariable costs to:

a Decrease in total, but increase as a percentage of net sales.

b Increase in total and increase as a percentage of net sales.

c Decrease in total and decrease as a percentage of net sales.

d Increase in total, but decrease as a percentage of net sales.

2 Shown below are the monthly high and low levels of direct labour hours and of total manufacturing overhead for Apex Mfg. Co.:

	Direct Labour Hours	Total Manufacturing Overhead
Highest observed level......................................	*6,000*	*$17,000*
Lowest observed level	*4,000*	*14,000*

In a month in which 5,000 direct labour hours are used, the *fixed element* of total manufacturing overhead costs should be approximately:

a $15,500.　　b $8,000.　　c $7,500.　　d $8,000 plus $1.50 per unit.

3 Marston Corporation sells a single product at a sales price of $50 per unit. Fixed costs total $15,000 per month, and variable costs amount to $20 per unit. If management reduces the sales price of this product by $5 per unit, the sales volume needed for the company to break-even will:

   a Increase by $5,000.　　c Increase by $2,000.

   b Increase by $4,500.　　d Remain unchanged.

4 Becker Auto Supply earns an average contribution margin ratio of 40% on its sales. The store manager estimates that by spending an additional $5,000 per month for radio advertising, the store will be able to increase its operating income by $3,000 per month. The manager is expecting the radio advertising to increase monthly dollar sales volume by:

   a $12,500.　　b $8,000.　　c $7,500.　　d Some other amount.

5 Elco Corporation manufactures two products. Data concerning these products is shown below:

	Product A	Product B
Total monthly demand for product.........................	1,000 units	500 units
Sales price per unit.......................................	$400	$500
Contribution margin ratio	30%	40%
Direct labour hours to manufacture each unit..............	5	10

   Elco's productive capacity is limited by the availability of only 6,500 direct labour hours each month. If the company is to maximize its operating income, how many units of product B should Elco produce each month?

   a None　　b 150　　c 500　　d Some other amount

EXERCISES

Listed below are nine technical accounting terms introduced in this chapter:

Variable costs	Relevant range	Contribution margin ratio
Break-even point	Fixed costs	Semivariable costs
Margin of safety	Sales mix	Unit contribution margin

Each of the following statements may (or may not) describe one of these technical terms. For each statement, indicate the accounting term described, or answer "None" if the statement does not correctly describe any of the terms.

a The level of sales at which revenue exactly equals costs and expenses.

b Costs that remain unchanged despite changes in sales volume.

c The span over which output is likely to vary and assumptions about cost behaviour generally remain valid.

d Contribution margin per unit expressed as a percentage of unit sales price.

e Unit sales price minus variable costs per unit.

f The amount by which sales volume exceeds the break-even point.

g Costs that respond to changes in sales volume by less than a proportionate amount.

h Operating income less variable costs.

EXERCISE 23-2
Patterns of
Cost Behaviour

Explain the effects of an increase in the volume of activity upon the following costs. (Assume volume remains within the relevant range.)

a Total variable costs

b Variable costs per unit

c Total fixed costs

d Fixed costs per unit

e Total semivariable costs

f Semivariable costs per unit

EXERCISE 23-3
Classification
of Various
Costs

Explain whether you regard each of the following costs or categories of costs as fixed, variable, or semivariable with respect to net sales. Briefly explain your reasoning. If you do not believe that a cost fits into any of these classifications, explain.

a The cost of goods sold.

b Salaries to salespeople. (These salaries include a monthly minimum amount, plus a commission on all sales.)

c Income taxes expense.

d Property taxes expense.

e Depreciation expense on a sales showroom, based upon the straight-line method of depreciation.

f Depreciation expense on a sales showroom, based upon the double-declining-balance method of depreciation.

EXERCISE 23-4
High-Low
Method of Cost
Analysis

The following information is available regarding the total manufacturing overhead of Drew Mfg. Co. for a recent four-month period:

	Machine-Hours	Manufacturing Overhead
March...	3,000	$122,250
April	2,500	114,000
May...	3,500	132,750
June	4,000	141,000

a Use the high-low method to determine:

1 The variable element of manufacturing overhead costs per machine-hour.

2 The fixed element of monthly overhead cost.

b Use the cost relationships determined in part **a** to estimate the total manufacturing overhead expected to be incurred at an activity level of 3,800 machine-hours.

EXERCISE 23-5
Using a Cost
Formula

City Ambulance Service estimates the monthly cost of responding to emergency calls to be $19,500 plus $110 per call.

a In a month in which the company responds to 125 emergency calls, determine the estimated:

1 Total cost of responding to emergency calls.

2 Average cost of responding to emergency calls.

b Assume that in a given month, the number of emergency calls was unusually low. Would you expect the average cost of responding to emergency calls during this month to be higher or lower than in other months? Explain.

EXERCISE 23-6
Using a Cost Formula

Through using the high-low method, Regency Hotels estimates the total costs of providing room service meals to amount to $5,950 per month, plus 30% of room service revenue.

a What is the contribution margin ratio of providing room service meals?

b What is the break-even point for room service operations in terms of total room service revenue?

c What would you expect to be the total cost of providing room service in a month in which room service revenue amounts to $15,000?

EXERCISE 23-7
Computing Required Sales Volume

Information concerning a product manufactured by Ames Brothers appears below:

Sales price per unit..	*$ 70*
Variable cost per unit...	*43*
Total fixed manufacturing and operating costs (per month)....................	*405,000*

Determine the following:

a The unit contribution margin

b The number of units that must be sold each month to break even

c The unit sales level that must be reached in order to earn an operating income of $270,000 per month

EXERCISE 23-8
Computing Sales Volume

Porter Corporation has fixed costs of $660,000, variable costs of $24 per unit, and a contribution margin ratio of 40%.

Compute the following:

a Unit sales price, and unit contribution margin for the above product

b The sales volume in units required for Porter Corporation to earn an operating income of $300,000

c The dollar sales volume required for Porter Corporation to earn an operating income of $300,000

EXERCISE 23-9
Computing Contribution Margin Ratio and Margin of Safety

The information shown below relates to the only product sold by Harper Company:

Sales price per unit..	*$ 24*
Variable cost per unit...	*18*
Fixed costs per year...	*240,000*

a Compute the contribution margin ratio and the dollar sales volume required to break even.

b Assuming that the company sells 75,000 units during the current year, compute the margin of safety sales volume (dollars).

EXERCISE 23-10
Relating Contribution Margin Ratio to Sales Price

Firebird Mfg. Co. has a contribution margin ratio of 45% and must sell 25,000 units at a price of $80 each in order to break even. Compute:

a Total fixed costs.

b Variable costs per unit.

EXERCISE 23-11
Computing the Break-Even Point

Malibu Corporation has fixed costs of $36,000 per month. It sells two products as follows:

	Sales Price	Variable Costs	Contribution Margin
Product no. 1	$10	$4	$6
Product no. 2	10	7	3

a What monthly dollar sales volume is required to break even if two units of product no. 1 are sold with one unit of product no. 2?

b What monthly dollar sales volume is required to break even if one unit of product no. 1 is sold with two units of product no. 2?

EXERCISE 23-12
Cost-Volume-Profit Relationships

For each of the six independent situations below, compute the missing amounts.

a Only one product is manufactured:

	Sales	Variable Costs	Contribution Margin per Unit	Fixed Costs	Operating Income	Units Sold
(1)	$_____	$120,000	$20	$_____	$25,000	4,000
(2)	180,000	_____	—	45,000	30,000	5,000
(3)	600,000	_____	30	150,000	90,000	_____

b Many products are manufactured:

	Sales	Variable Costs	Contribution Margin Ratio	Fixed Costs	Operating Income
(1)	$900,000	$720,000	___%	$_____	$95,000
(2)	600,000	_____	40%	_____	75,000
(3)	_____	_____	30%	90,000	60,000

EXERCISE 23-13
Evaluating a Marketing Strategy

Chaps & Saddles, a retailer of tack and western apparel, earns an average contribution margin of 45% on its sales volume. Recently, the advertising manager of a local "country" radio station offered to run numerous radio advertisements for Chaps & Saddles at a monthly cost of $1,800.

Compute the amount by which the proposed radio advertising campaign must increase Chaps & Saddles' monthly sales volume to:

a Pay for itself.

b Increase operating income by $1,000 per month. (Round computations to the nearest dollar.)

PROBLEMS

Group A

PROBLEM 23A-1
Using Cost-Volume-Profit Formulas

MURDER TO GO! writes and manufactures murder mystery parlour games that it sells to retail stores. Shown below is per-unit information relating to the manufacture and sale of this product.

Unit sales price	$	28
Variable cost per unit..		7
Fixed costs per year..		240,000

INSTRUCTIONS

Determine the following, showing as part of your answer the formula that you used in your computation. For example, the formula used to determine the contribution margin ratio (part a) is:

$$\text{Contribution Margin Ratio} = \frac{\text{Unit Sales Price} - \text{Variable Costs per Unit}}{\text{Unit Sales Price}}$$

a Contribution margin ratio

b Sales volume (in dollars) required to break even

c Sales volume (in dollars) required to earn an annual operating income of $450,000

d The margin of safety sales volume if annual sales total 40,000 units

e Operating income if annual sales total 40,000 units

PROBLEM 23A-2
Setting Sales Price and Computing the Break-Even Point

Thermal Tent, Inc., is a newly organized manufacturing business that plans to manufacture and sell 50,000 units per year of a new product. The following estimates have been made of the company's costs and expenses (other than income taxes):

	Fixed	*Variable per Unit*
Manufacturing costs:		
Direct materials		*$47*
Direct labour		*32*
Manufacturing overhead	*$340,000*	*4*
Period expenses:		
Selling expenses		*1*
Administrative expenses..	*200,000*	
Totals..	*$540,000*	*$84*

INSTRUCTIONS

a What should the company establish as the sales price per unit if it sets a budgeted operating income of $260,000 by producing and selling 50,000 units during the first year of operations?

b At the unit sales price computed in part **a**, how many units must the company produce and sell to break even? (Assume all units produced are sold.)

c What will be the margin of safety (in dollars) if the company produces and sells 50,000 units at the sales price computed in part **a**? Using the margin of safety, compute operating income at 50,000 units.

d Assume that the marketing manager feels that the price of this product must be no higher than $94 in order to ensure market penetration. Will setting the sales price at $94 enable Thermal Tent to break even, given the plans to manufacture and sell 50,000 units? Explain your answer.

PROBLEM 23A-3
Preparing a "Break-Even" Graph

Stop-n-Shop operates a parking lot containing 800 parking spaces. The lot is open 2,500 hours per year. The parking charge per car is 50 cents per hour; the average customer parks two hours. Stop-n-Shop rents the lot for $7,250 per month. The lot supervisor is paid $24,000 per year. Five employees who handle the parking of cars are paid $300 per week for 50 weeks, plus $600 each for the two-week vacation period. Employees rotate vacations during the slow months when four employees can handle the reduced load of traffic. Lot maintenance, payroll taxes, and other costs of operating the parking lot include fixed costs of $3,000 per month and variable costs of 5 cents per parking-space hour.

INSTRUCTIONS

a Draw a cost-volume-profit graph for Stop-n-Shop on an annual basis. Use thousands of parking-space hours as the measure of volume of activity. [Stop-n-Shop has an annual capacity of 2 million parking-space hours (800 spaces × 2,500 hours per year).]

b What is the contribution margin ratio? What is the annual break-even point in dollars of parking revenue?

c Suppose that the five employees were taken off the hourly wage basis and paid 30 cents per car parked, with the same vacation pay as before. (1) How would this change the contribution margin ratio and total fixed costs? (2) What annual sales revenue would be necessary to produce operating income of $300,000 under these circumstances?

PROBLEM 23A-4
Determining
Optimal Sales
Mix

Priestley Equipment Company manufactures three different products. The estimated demand for the products for the current year is such that production will not be able to keep pace with incoming orders. Some pertinent data for each product are listed below:

Product	Estimated Unit Sales	Sales Price	Direct Material Cost	Direct Labour Cost	Variable Manufacturing Overhead
A	15,000	$65	$9	$30	$2
B	8,000	37	3	15	1
C	2,500	55	6	20	1

Direct labour costs an average of $10 per hour.

INSTRUCTIONS

a Prepare a schedule showing the contribution margin per one unit of each product and also the contribution margin per one hour of direct labour applied to the production of each class of product.

b If you were able to reduce the production of one of the products in order to meet the demand for the others, what would that product be? Why? Assume that available direct labour hours represent the scarce resource that limits total output.

c Assume that the 45,000 hours of direct labour now used to produce product A are used to produce additional units of product C. What would be the effect on total contribution margin?

PROBLEM 23A-5
Cost-Volume-
Profit Analysis;
Preparing a
Graph

Simon Teguh is considering investing in a vending machine operation involving 20 vending machines located in various plants around the city. The machine manufacturer reports that similar vending machine routes have produced a sales volume ranging from 800 to 1,000 units per machine per month. The following information is made available to Teguh in evaluating the possible profitability of the operation.

1 An investment of $45,000 will be required, $9,000 for merchandise and $36,000 for the 20 machines.

2 The machines have a service life of five years and no salvage value at the end of that period. Depreciation will be computed on the straight-line basis.

3 The merchandise (candy and soft drinks) retails for an average of 75 cents per unit and will cost Teguh an average of 25 cents per unit.

4 Owners of the buildings in which the machines are located are paid a commission of 5 cents per unit of candy and soft drinks sold.

5 One person will be hired to service the machines. The salary will be $1,500 per month.

6 Other expenses are estimated at $600 per month. These expenses do not vary with the number of units sold.

INSTRUCTIONS

a Determine the unit contribution margin and the break-even volume in units and in dollars per month.

b Draw a monthly cost-volume-profit graph for sales volume up to 1,000 units per machine per month.

c What sales volume in units and in dollars per month will be necessary to produce an operating income equal to a 30% annual return on Teguh's $45,000 investment? (Round to the nearest unit.)

d Teguh is considering offering the building owners a flat rental of $30 per machine per month in lieu of the commission of 5 cents per unit sold. What effect would this change in commission arrangement have on his **monthly** break-even volume in terms of units?

Group B

PROBLEM 23B-1
Introduction to
Cost-Volume-
Profit Formulas

Shown below is information relating to the only product sold by EnviroPure, Inc.:

Unit sales price	$ 85
Variable cost per unit..	34
Fixed costs per year...	390,000

INSTRUCTIONS

Determine the following, showing as part of your answer the formula or relationships you used in your computations. For example, the formula used to determine the contribution margin ratio (part **a**) is:

$$\text{Contribution Margin Ratio} = \frac{\text{Unit Sales Price} - \text{Variable Costs per Unit}}{\text{Unit Sales Price}}$$

a Contribution margin ratio

b Dollar sales volume required to break even

c Dollar sales volume required to earn an annual operating income of $900,000

d The margin of safety if annual sales total 30,000 units

e Operating income if annual sales total 30,000 units

PROBLEM 23B-2
Estimating
Costs and
Profits

High Rollers, Inc., manufactures rollerskates. For the coming year, the company has budgeted the following costs for the production and sale of 30,000 pairs of skates.

	Budgeted Costs	Budgeted Costs per Pair	Percentage of Costs Considered Variable
Direct materials	$ 630,000	21	100%
Direct labour	300,000	10	100
Manufacturing overhead (fixed and variable).......	720,000	24	25
Selling and administrative expenses..............	600,000	20	20
Totals...	$2,250,000	$75	

INSTRUCTIONS

a Compute the sales price per unit that would result in a budgeted operating income of $900,000, assuming that the company produces and sells 30,000 pairs.

b Assuming that the company decides to sell the skates at a unit price of $121 per pair, compute the following:

1 Total fixed costs budgeted for the year

2 Variable costs per unit

3 The unit contribution margin

4 The number of pairs that must be produced and sold annually to break even at a sales price of $121 per pair

PROBLEM 23B-3
Drawing a Cost-Volume-Profit Graph

Rainbow Paints operates a chain of retail paint stores. Although the paint is sold under the Rainbow label, it is purchased from an independent paint manufacturer. Guy Walker, president of Rainbow Paints, is studying the advisability of opening another store. His estimates of monthly costs for the proposed location are:

Fixed costs:	
Occupancy costs	*$3,160*
Salaries	*3,640*
Other	*1,200*
Variable costs (including cost of paint)	*$6 per litre*

Although Rainbow stores sell several different types of paint, monthly sales revenue consistently averages $10 per litre sold.

INSTRUCTIONS

a Compute the contribution margin ratio and the break-even point in dollar sales and in litres sold for the proposed store.

b Draw a monthly cost-volume-profit graph for the proposed store, assuming 3,000 litres per month as the maximum sales potential.

c Walker thinks that the proposed store will sell between 2,200 and 2,600 litres of paint per month. Compute the amount of operating income that would be earned per month at each of these sales volumes.

PROBLEM 23B-4
Determining the Most Profitable Product Given Scarce Resources

Optical Instruments produces two models of binoculars. Information for each model is shown below:

	Model 100	Model 101
Sales price per unit	*$200*	*$135*
Costs and expenses per unit:		
Direct materials	*$51*	*$38*
Direct labour	*33*	*30*
Manufacturing overhead (applied at the rate of $18 per machine-hour, $\frac{1}{3}$ of which is fixed and $\frac{2}{3}$ variable)	*36*	*18*
Variable selling expenses	*30*	*15*
Total costs and expenses per unit	*150*	*101*
Profit per unit	*$ 50*	*$ 34*
Machine-hours required to produce one unit	*2*	*1*

Total manufacturing overhead amounts to $180,000 per month, one-third of which is fixed. The demand for either product is sufficient to keep the plant operating at full capacity of 10,000 machine-hours per month. Assume that *only one product is to be produced in the future.*

INSTRUCTIONS

a Prepare a schedule showing the contribution margin per machine-hour for each product.

b Explain your recommendation as to which of the two products should be discontinued.

PROBLEM 23B-5
Analyzing the Effects of Changes in Costs

Precision Systems manufactures tape decks and currently sells 18,500 units annually to producers of sound reproduction systems. Jay Wilson, president of the company, anticipates a 15% increase in the cost per unit of direct labour on January 1 of next year. He expects all other costs and expenses to remain unchanged. Wilson has asked you to assist him in developing the information he needs to formulate a reasonable product strategy for next year.

You are satisfied that volume is the primary factor affecting costs and expenses and have separated the semivariable costs into their fixed and variable segments. Beginning and ending inventories remain at a level of 1,000 units.

Below are the current-year data assembled for your analysis:

Sales price per unit..		$100
Variable costs per unit:		
Direct materials	$10	
Direct labour	20	
Manufacturing overhead and selling and administrative expenses	30	60
Contribution margin per unit (40%)..		$ 40
Fixed costs		$390,000

INSTRUCTIONS

a What increase in the selling price is necessary to cover the 15% increase in direct labour cost and still maintain the current contribution margin ratio of 40%?

b How many tape decks must be sold to maintain the current operating income of **$350,000** if the sales price remains at $100 and the 15% wage increase goes into effect?

c Wilson believes that an additional $700,000 of machinery (to be depreciated at 20% annually) will increase present capacity (20,000 units) by 25%. If all tape decks produced can be sold at the present price of $100 per unit and the wage increase goes into effect, how would the estimated operating income before capacity is increased compare with the estimated operating income after capacity is increased? Prepare schedules of estimated operating income at full capacity **before** and **after** the expansion.

ANALYTICAL AND DECISION PROBLEMS AND CASES

A&D 23-1
Iacocca's
Dilemma

Assume that you are part of the new management team that has taken over the management of a large diversified automobile manufacturer that is in serious financial condition. Despite several years of large losses, the company's previous management has made practically no changes in the company's operations. The automobiles manufactured by the company are satisfactory in terms of size, style, and fuel economy.

INSTRUCTIONS

a Suggest some actions you might consider in an effort to reduce:

1 Fixed costs.

2 Variable costs per automobile.

b Suggest some ways other than cost reductions by which the company may be able to lower its break-even point.

A&D 23-2
Evaluating
Marketing
Strategies

Purple Cow operates a chain of drive-ins selling primarily an exclusive brand of top quality ice cream products. The following information is taken from the records of a typical drive-in now operated by the company:

Average selling price of ice cream per litre		$ 14.80
Number of litres sold per month		*3,000*
Variable costs per litre:		
Ice cream	*$4.60*	
Supplies (cups, cones, toppings, etc.)	*2.20*	
Total variable expenses per litre		$ 6.80
Fixed costs per month:		
Rent on building		$ 2,200.00
Utilities and upkeep		*760.00*
Wages, including payroll taxes		*4,840.00*
Manager's salary, including payroll taxes but excluding any bonus		*2,500.00*
Other fixed expenses		*1,700.00*
Total fixed costs per month		*$12,000.00*

INSTRUCTIONS   **a**   Currently, all store managers have contracts calling for a bonus of 20 cents per litre for each litre sold **beyond** the break-even point. Compute the number of litres of ice cream that must be sold per month in order to earn a monthly operating income of $10,000 (round to the nearest litre).

b   In order to increase operating income, the company is considering the following two alternatives:

1   Reduce the selling price by an average of $2.00 per litre. This action is expected to increase the number of litres sold by 20%. (Under this plan, the manager would be paid a salary of $2,500 per month without a bonus.)

2   Spend $3,000 per month on advertising without any change in selling price. This action is expected to increase the number of litres sold by 10%. (Under this plan, the manager would be paid a salary of $2,500 per month without a bonus.)

Which of these two alternatives would result in the higher monthly operating income? How many litres must be sold per month under each alternative in order for a typical outlet to break even? Provide schedules in support of your answers.

c   Draft a memo to management indicating your recommendations with respect to these alternative marketing strategies.

CHAPTER

24 Measuring and Evaluating Segment Performance

In this chapter, we focus upon measuring the performance of a segment of a business organization, such as a division or a department. Emphasis is placed upon such topics as responsibility accounting, developing segmented income statements that show subtotals for contribution margin and segment margin, and the use of segment information in evaluating the performance of segments and segment managers.

As a Supplemental Topic we also explore variable costing—a technique for rearranging the information generated by a conventional cost accounting system into a format that is better suited to many types of managerial decisions.

Learning Objectives

After studying this chapter, you should be able to:

1 *Explain the need for segment information and describe a responsibility accounting system.*

2 *Prepare segment income statements showing contribution margin and segment margin.*

3 *Distinguish between traceable and common fixed costs.*

4 *Explain the usefulness of contribution margin and segment margin in making short-term and long-term decisions.*

*5 *Explain the differences between full costing and variable costing.*

*6 *Use a variable costing income statement in cost-volume-profit analysis.*

*7 *Explain why short-term fluctuation in the level of production may distort key measurements of segment performance under full costing.*

---

* *Supplemental Topic, "Variable Costing"*

SEGMENTS OF A BUSINESS

Most businesses are organized into a number of different subunits that perform different functions. For example, a manufacturing company typically has departments specializing in purchasing, production, sales, shipping, accounting, finance, and human resources. Production departments and sales departments often are further subdivided along different product lines or geographical areas. Organizing a business in this manner enables managers and employees to specialize in specific types of business activity. Also, this type of organization helps to establish clear lines of managerial responsibility.

Companies use many different names to describe their internal operating units, including divisions, departments, branches, product lines, and sales territories. In our discussion, we generally will use the term *segment* to describe a subunit within a business organization. A designated manager is responsible for directing the activities of each segment within a business organization. Therefore, we also describe segments of a business as *responsibility centres.*

In most business organizations, large responsibility centres are further subdivided into smaller ones. Consider, for example, a retail store within a chain such as Sears or Kmart. Each store is a responsibility centre under the control of a store manager. However, each store is further divided into many separate sales departments, such as appliances, automotive products, and sporting goods. Each sales department also is a responsibility centre, under the control of a department manager. These department managers report to, and are supervised by, the store manager.

The Need for Information about Segment Performance

An income statement measures the overall performance of a business entity. However, managers also need accounting information measuring the performance of *each segment* within the business organization. This segment information assists managers in:

OBJECTIVE 1
Explain the need for segment information and describe a responsibility accounting system.

1 **Planning and allocating resources.**   Management needs to know how well various segments of the business are performing in order to set future performance goals and to allocate resources to those segments offering the greatest profit potential. If one product line is more profitable than another, for example, the company's overall profitability may increase by allocating more production capacity to the more profitable product.

2 **Controlling operations.**   One use of segment data is to identify those portions of the business that are performing inefficiently or below expectations. When revenue lags, or costs become excessive, segment information helps to focus management's attention upon the segments responsible for the poor performance. If a segment of the business is unprofitable, perhaps it should be discontinued.

3 **Evaluating the performance of segment managers.**   As each segment is an area of managerial responsibility, the performance of the segment provides one basis for evaluating the skills of the segment manager.

Thus, measuring the performance of each segment in the business organization is an important function of any accounting system designed to meet the needs of management.

Profit Centres, Investment Centres, and Cost Centres

The segments of a business may be viewed as profit centres, as investment centres, or as cost centres.

Profit Centres A profit centre is a segment of the business that **generates revenue and incurs costs.**[1] Examples of profit centres include product lines, sales territories, retail outlets, and the specific sales departments within each retail outlet. Even an individual salesperson may be viewed as a profit centre within a business organization.

Profit centres are evaluated primarily upon their profitability. Thus, **segmented income statements** are prepared showing the revenue and costs applicable to each profit centre. The revenue and costs of each segment may then be compared with budgeted amounts, with the segment's performance in past periods, and, most importantly, with the profitability of other profit centres within the organization. For example, supermarkets view every product line as a separate profit centre. Because supermarkets have limited shelf space, they may discontinue even profitable product lines if the related shelf space can be used for still more profitable products.

Investment Centres Some profit centres also qualify as investment centres. An **investment centre** is a profit centre for which management is able to measure objectively the cost of the assets used in the centre's operations.

The performance of an investment centre may be evaluated using return on investment (ROI) measurements. The most common of these measures is **return on assets,** in which the operating income (or **segment margin**) of the segment is expressed as a percentage of the average total assets utilized by the segment during the period.

Not all profit centres can be evaluated as investment centres. For example, if a profit centre shares the use of common facilities with other segments of the business, it may be difficult to determine the "amount invested" in the profit centre. Thus, profit centres that share common facilities usually are evaluated upon their profitability, but this profitability is not expressed as a "return on investment."

To illustrate the distinction between investment centres and other profit centres, consider a hotel within a national hotel chain, and also the coffee shop within this hotel. Both the hotel and the coffee shop are profit centres. The hotel, however, is also an investment centre, because management can readily identify those assets used in the operations of the hotel. The assets utilized by the coffee shop, on the other hand, cannot be determined with anywhere near the same degree of objectivity. For example, the coffee shop uses a small portion of the land, building, and parking lot of the

---

[1] In this chapter, we will continue the convenient practice of using the term **costs** to describe both costs (such as the cost of goods sold) and expenses.

hotel. Any allocation of such assets among the subunits within the hotel (the coffee shop, dining room, lounge, and guest rooms) would be highly arbitrary. Thus, the coffee shop would be evaluated as a profit centre, but not as an investment centre.

Cost Centres   A *cost centre* is a segment of the business that incurs costs (or expenses) but does not directly generate revenue.[2] Production departments in a manufacturing company are examples of cost centres. Service departments, such as accounting, finance, maintenance, and the legal department also are cost centres. Service departments provide services to other segments within the business but do not sell goods or services directly to customers.

Cost centres are evaluated primarily upon (1) their ability to control costs and (2) the *quantity* and the *quality* of the services that they provide to the business organization. As cost centres do not directly generate revenue, segmented income statements are not prepared for these segments of the business. However, the accounting system must accumulate separately the costs incurred by each cost centre.

In some cases, costs provide an objective basis for evaluating the performance of a cost centre. For example, production departments are evaluated primarily upon the unit costs incurred in manufacturing inventory. For many cost centres, however, nonfinancial criteria are extremely important in assessing the segment's performance. In evaluating the performance of a maintenance department, for example, the question of whether plant assets are maintained in good operating order is an important consideration. Evaluating the performance of an accounting department is even more subjective. Management must compare the costs incurred by the department with the "value" of the department's services to the business. These services include not only meeting the company's financial and income tax reporting requirements, but also providing managers with the information necessary to run the business.

RESPONSIBILITY ACCOUNTING SYSTEMS

An accounting system designed to measure the performance of each responsibility centre within a business is termed a *responsibility accounting system.* Measuring performance along the lines of managerial responsibility is an important managerial tool. A responsibility accounting system holds individual managers accountable for the performance of the business segments under their control. In addition, such systems provide top management with information useful in identifying the strong and the weak segments throughout the business organization.

The operation of a responsibility accounting system involves three basic steps. First, *budgets* are prepared for each responsibility centre. These budgets serve as targets, with which the segment's actual performance will be compared. Second, the accounting system *measures the performance* of each responsibility centre. Third, timely *performance reports* are pre-

---

[2]   Cost centres sometimes generate insignificant amounts of revenue, but the direct generation of revenue is incidental to the basic purpose of the segment.

pared, comparing the actual performance of each segment with the budgeted amounts. Frequent performance reports help segment managers keep their segments' performance "on target," and they also assist top management in evaluating the performance of each segment and segment manager.

In this chapter, we emphasize the second step in the operation of a responsibility accounting system—measuring the performance of each responsibility centre. The use of budgets and of performance reports is discussed in the following chapter.

Responsibility Accounting: An Illustration

OBJECTIVE 2 Prepare segment income statements showing contribution margin and segment margin.

The diagram on the following page shows in condensed form how the monthly performance of profit centres is measured and reported in the responsibility accounting system. The company in our example, NuTech Electronics, is first segmented into two divisions: retail sales and special orders. The Retail Sales Division is further segmented into two stores; each store has two profit centres—a department that sells merchandise and a department that repairs electronic appliances for customers.[3]

As you read down the NuTech illustration, you are looking at smaller and smaller parts of the company. The recording of revenue and costs must begin at the **bottom** of the illustration—that is, for the **smallest** areas of managerial responsibility. If income statements are to be prepared for each profit centre in the 42nd St. Store, for example, NuTech's chart of accounts must be sufficiently detailed to measure separately the revenue and costs of these departments. The income statements for larger responsibility centres then may be prepared primarily by combining the amounts appearing in the income statements of the smaller subunits. Notice, for example, that the total sales of the 42nd St. Store ($200,000) are equal to the sum of the sales reported by the two profit centres within the store ($180,000 and $20,000).

Assigning Revenue and Costs to Segments of a Business

In segment income statements, revenue is assigned first to the profit centre responsible for earning that revenue. Assigning revenue to the proper department is relatively easy. Electronic cash registers, for example, automatically classify sales revenue by the department of origin.

In assigning costs to segments of a business, two concepts generally are applied:

1 **Costs are classified into the categories of variable costs and fixed costs.**[4] When costs are classified in this manner, a subtotal may be developed in the income statement showing the **contribution margin** of the business segment. Arranging an income statement in this

---

[3] NuTech also prepares segment income statements showing the profit centres in the Special Orders Division and in the Baker St. Store. To conserve space, these statements are not included in our illustration.

[4] In Chapter 23, we discussed techniques such as the "high-low method" for separating semivariable costs such as sales salaries and telephone expense into their variable and fixed elements.

ILLUSTRATION OF A RESPONSIBILITY ACCOUNTING SYSTEM

NUTECH ELECTRONICS

Segments defined as divisions

	Entire Company	Retail Division	Special Orders Division
Sales	$900,000	$500,000	$400,000
Variable costs	400,000	240,000	160,000
Contribution margins	$500,000	$260,000	$240,000
Fixed costs traceable to divisions	360,000	170,000	190,000
Division segment margins	$140,000	$ 90,000	$ 50,000
Common fixed costs	40,000		
Operating income	$100,000		
Income taxes expense	35,000		
Net income	$ 65,000		

Segments defined as stores in the Retail Division

	Retail Division	42nd St. Store	Baker St. Store
Sales	$500,000	$200,000	$300,000
Variable costs	240,000	98,000	142,000
Contribution margins	$260,000	$102,000	$158,000
Fixed costs traceable to stores	140,000	60,000	80,000
Store segment margins	$120,000	$ 42,000	$ 78,000
Common fixed costs	30,000		
Segment margin for division	$ 90,000		

Segments defined as profit centres (departments) in the 42nd St. Store

	42nd St. Store	Sales Department	Repairs Department
Sales	$200,000	$180,000	$ 20,000
Variable costs	98,000	90,000	8,000
Contribution margins	$102,000	$ 90,000	$ 12,000
Fixed costs traceable to departments	32,000	18,000	14,000
Departmental segment margins	$ 70,000	$ 72,000	$ (2,000)
Common fixed costs	28,000		
Segment margin for store	$ 42,000		

manner is termed the ***contribution margin approach*** and is widely used in preparing reports for use by managers.

2 Each segment is charged with only those costs that are directly traceable to that segment. A cost is "directly traceable" to a particular segment if that segment is ***solely responsible*** for the cost being incurred. Thus, traceable costs should ***disappear if the segment is discontinued.***

The question of whether a cost is traceable to a particular department is not always clear-cut. In assigning costs to segments of a business, accountants often must exercise professional judgment.

CASE IN POINT The sales department of a large manufacturing company used to request many "Rush" orders from the production department. To fill these rush orders, the production department had to work overtime, which caused the production department to incur labour costs well in excess of budgeted amounts. The company's controller modified the responsibility accounting system to charge the ***sales department*** with the extra labour cost of processing rush orders. After this change was made, the sales department made a greater effort to give the production department adequate notice of all sales orders. As a result, the number of costly rush orders was substantially reduced.

Variable Costs

In segmented income statements, variable costs are those costs that change in approximate proportion to changes in revenue such as sales volume. Examples of variable costs include the cost of goods sold and commissions paid to salespeople. Because variable costs are directly related to revenue, they usually are traceable to the profit centre generating the revenue. If a profit centre were eliminated, all of that centre's variable costs should disappear.

Contribution Margin

Contribution margin (revenue minus variable costs) is an important tool for cost-volume-profit analysis. For example, the effect of a change in sales volume upon operating income may be estimated by either (1) multiplying the change in unit sales by the contribution margin per unit or (2) multiplying the dollar change in sales volume by the contribution margin ratio. (To assist in this type of analysis, segmented income statements often include percentages, as well as dollar amounts. A segmented income statement with percentage columns is illustrated later.)

Contribution margin expresses the relationship between revenue and variable costs but ignores fixed costs. Thus, contribution margin is primarily a ***short-run*** planning tool. It is useful primarily in decisions relating to price changes, short-run promotional campaigns, or changes in the level of output that will not significantly affect fixed costs. For longer-term decisions, such as whether to build a new plant or close a particular profit centre, managers must consider fixed costs as well as contribution margin.

Fixed Costs

For a business to be profitable, total contribution margin must exceed total fixed costs. However, many fixed costs cannot be easily traced to specific

OBJECTIVE 3
Distinguish
between
traceable
and common
fixed costs.

segments of the business. Thus, a distinction is often drawn in segment income statements between **traceable fixed costs** and **common fixed costs.**

Traceable Fixed Costs

Traceable fixed costs are those that can be easily traced to a specific segment of the business, and that arise because of that segment's existence. In short, traceable fixed costs **could be eliminated** if the segment were closed. Examples of traceable fixed costs include the salaries of the segment's employees and depreciation and other costs relating to fixtures or equipment used exclusively by that segment.

In determining whether a specific profit centre adds to the profitability of the business, it is reasonable to deduct from the centre's contribution margin any traceable fixed costs. In a segmented income statement, contribution margin less traceable fixed costs is termed **segment margin,** as illustrated in the NuTech Electronics example earlier.

Common Fixed Costs

Common fixed costs (or indirect fixed costs) **jointly benefit several segments** of the business. The level of these fixed costs usually would not change significantly even if one of the segments deriving benefits from these costs were discontinued.

Consider, for example, a large department store, such as a Sears or a Zellers. Every department in the store derives some benefit from the store building. However, such costs as depreciation and property taxes on the store will continue at current levels even if one or more of the departments within the store is discontinued. Thus, from the viewpoint of the segments within the store, depreciation on the building is a common fixed cost.

Common fixed costs cannot be assigned to specific subunits except by arbitrary means, such as in proportion to relative sales volume or square metres of space occupied. In an attempt to measure the "overall profitability" of each profit centre, some businesses allocate common fixed costs to segments along with traceable costs. A more common approach, however, is to charge each profit centre only with those costs **directly traceable** to that segment of the business. In this text, we follow this latter approach.

Activity-based costing, discussed in the Supplemental Topic section following Chapter 22, greatly increases the portion of a company's total costs that are traceable to specific business segments.

Common Fixed Costs Include Costs Traceable to Service Departments In a segmented income statement, the category of traceable fixed costs usually includes only those fixed costs **traceable to profit centres.** Costs traceable to **service departments,** such as the accounting department, benefit many segments of the business. Thus, the costs of operating service departments are classified in a segmented income statement as common fixed costs. For example, the $28,000 in common fixed costs shown in the segmented income statement of NuTech's 42nd St. Store includes the costs of operating the store's accounting, security, and maintenance departments, as well as other "storewide" costs such as depreciation, utilities expense, and the store manager's salary.

Service departments are evaluated as cost centres. Therefore, the responsibility accounting system should accumulate separately the costs traceable to each service department.

Common Fixed Costs Are Traceable to Larger Responsibility Centres All costs are traceable to *some level* of the organization. To illustrate this concept, a portion of the responsibility accounting system of NuTech Electronics is repeated below, with emphasis upon the fixed costs in the 42nd St. Store:

Segments defined as stores in the Retail Division

	Retail Division	Segments 42nd St. Store	Baker St. Store
Sales	$500,000	$200,000	$300,000
Variable costs	240,000	98,000	142,000
Contribution margins	$260,000	$102,000	$158,000
Fixed costs traceable to stores	140,000	→ 60,000	80,000
Store segment margins	$120,000	$ 42,000	$ 78,000
Common fixed costs	30,000		
Segment margin for division	$ 90,000		

Segments defined as profit centres (departments) in the
42nd St. Store

	42nd St. Store	Segments Sales Department	Repairs Department
Sales	$200,000	$180,000	$ 20,000
Variable costs	98,000	90,000	8,000
Contribution margins	$102,000	$ 90,000	$ 12,000
Fixed costs traceable to departments	32,000	18,000	14,000
Departmental segment margins	$ 70,000	$ 72,000	$ (2,000)
Common fixed costs	28,000		
Segment margin for store.....................	$ 42,000		

We have made the point that certain "storewide" costs, such as the operation of the maintenance department and the store manager's salary, are not traceable to the specific profit centres within the store. These costs are, however, easily traceable to the 42nd St. Store. In the NuTech Electronics example, the $60,000 fixed costs are traceable to the 42nd Street store, $32,000 of which is traceable to the departments within the store. Therefore, whether these costs are classified as "traceable" or "common" depends upon whether we define the business segments as stores or as departments within the stores.

As we move up a responsibility reporting system to broader and broader areas of responsibility, common costs at the lower levels of managerial responsibility ***become traceable costs*** as they fall under the control of the managers of larger responsibility centres.

Segment Margin

OBJECTIVE 4 Explain the usefulness of contribution margin and segment margin in making short-term and long-term decisions.

We have mentioned that contribution margin is an excellent tool for evaluating the effects of short-run decisions upon profitability. ***Segment margin*** is a ***longer-run*** measure of profitability because it takes into consideration any fixed costs traceable to the segment. Thus, segment margin is more useful than contribution margin for making long-term decisions that involve changes in fixed costs. Examples of such "long-run" decisions include whether to expand plant capacity or eliminate a profit centre that is performing poorly.

To illustrate, assume that Pioneer Mfg. Ltd. manufactures and sells two products—car radios and cellular telephones. The company's monthly income statement, segmented by product line, is shown below. In this segmented income statement, we illustrate the common practice of including ***component percentages*** as well as dollar amounts.

			Product			
	Entire Company		Car Radios		Cellular Telephones	
	Dollars	%	Dollars	%	Dollars	%
Sales	$200,000	100	$100,000	100	$100,000	100
Variable costs	100,000	50	60,000	60	40,000	40
Contribution margins	$100,000	50	$ 40,000	40	$ 60,000	60
Fixed costs traceable to product lines	56,000	28	12,000	12	44,000	44
Product segment margins	$ 44,000	22	$ 28,000	28	$ 16,000	16
Common fixed costs	26,000	13				
Operating income	$ 18,000	9				
Income taxes expense	6,000	3				
Net income..........................	$ 12,000	6				

Which is the company's most profitable product? The answer depends upon whether you are making short-run decisions, which usually do not change fixed costs, or long-run decisions, in which changes in fixed costs become important factors.

First, let us consider short-run decisions. Assume that management believes a $2,000 per month radio advertising campaign would increase the monthly sales of whichever product is advertised by 10% ($10,000). Which product will it be most profitable to advertise? The answer is ***cellular telephones,*** because of the higher ***contribution margin ratio*** of this product (60% as compared to 40% for car radios). Selling an additional $10,000 of cellular telephones will generate $6,000 in contribution margin, whereas selling an additional $10,000 of radios will generate only $4,000.

Now let us take a longer-run view. Assume that the company must discontinue one of these products. Which product should the company ***continue to produce?*** The answer is ***car radios.*** After considering fixed costs traceable to each product, car radios contribute $28,000 to the company's operating income, whereas cellular telephones contribute only $16,000.

Stated another way, if the cellular telephone product line is discontinued, all the revenue, variable costs, and traceable fixed costs relating to this product should disappear. In short, the company would lose the $16,000 monthly **segment margin** now produced by this product line. This, of course, is preferable to losing the $28,000 monthly segment margin produced by the car radio product line.

In summary, in making short-run decisions that do not affect fixed costs, managers should attempt to generate the most **contribution margin** for the additional costs incurred. This usually means emphasizing those segments with the highest contribution margin ratios. In evaluating a segment as a long-term investment, however, managers must consider the ability of the segment to cover its fixed costs and the extent of the segment's contribution to the common fixed costs. Thus, in the long run managers should emphasize growth in those segments with the highest **segment margins** and **segment margin ratios.**

When a segment is evaluated as an investment centre, segment margin generally is used as the "income" figure in making any ROI computations. Thus, the return on assets for an investment centre would be computed as segment margin divided by the average assets utilized by the segment.

When Is a Segment "Unprofitable"?

In deciding whether a specific profit centre is "unprofitable," management should consider several factors. Segment margin, however, is a good starting point. Segment margin indicates whether the profit centre earns enough contribution margin to cover the fixed costs traceable to that segment of the business.

To illustrate, consider the segmented income statement for the 42nd St. Store of NuTech Electronics:

| | 42nd St. Store | Segments | |
		Sales Department	Repairs Department
Sales	$200,000	$180,000	$ 20,000
Variable costs.................................	98,000	90,000	8,000
Contribution margins	$102,000	$ 90,000	$ 12,000
Fixed costs traceable to departments	32,000	18,000	14,000
Departmental segment margins	$ 70,000	$ 72,000	$ (2,000)
Common fixed costs	28,000		
Segment margin for store.....................	$ 42,000		

According to this data, discontinuing the Repairs Department should eliminate the $20,000 in revenue, and also $22,000 in costs ($8,000 variable costs, plus $14,000 in traceable fixed costs). Thus, closing the Repairs Department might well increase the profitability of the store by **$2,000**— the negative segment margin reported by the Repairs Department.

In deciding whether or not to close the Repairs Department, managers should also consider other factors. For example, does the existence of the Repairs Department contribute to merchandise sales? What alternative use could be made of the space now used by the Repairs Department? These factors will be considered in greater depth in Chapter 26.

Evaluating Segment Managers

Some costs traceable to a segment are simply beyond the segment manager's immediate control. Examples include depreciation expense and property taxes on plant assets. If a segment is saddled with high costs that are beyond the segment manager's control, the segment may perform poorly even if the segment manager is doing an excellent job.

As a response to this problem, some companies subdivide the fixed costs traceable to each segment into the subcategories of **controllable fixed costs** and **committed fixed costs.** Controllable fixed costs are those under the segment manager's immediate control, such as salaries and advertising. Committed fixed costs are those which the segment manager cannot readily change, such as depreciation. In the segmented income statement, controllable fixed costs are deducted from contribution margin to arrive at a subtotal called **performance margin.** Committed fixed costs then are deducted to determine segment margin.

Subdividing traceable costs in this manner draws a distinction between the performance of the segment manager and the profitability of the segment as a long-term investment. The performance margin includes only the revenue and costs **under the segment manager's direct control** and is a useful tool in evaluating the manager's skill. Segment margin, however, remains the best measure of the segment's long-term profitability.

Arguments against Allocating Common Fixed Costs to Segments

We have mentioned that some companies follow a policy of allocating common fixed costs among the segments benefiting from these costs. The bases used for allocating common costs are necessarily arbitrary, such as relative sales volume, or square metres of floor space occupied by the segment. In a segmented income statement, segment margin less common fixed costs allocated to the segment usually is called "operating income."

We do **not** recommend this practice, for several reasons:

1 **Common fixed costs often would not change even if a segment were eliminated.**   Therefore, an allocation of these costs only distorts the amount contributed by each segment to the income of the company.

   To illustrate this point, assume that $10,000 in common costs are allocated to a segment that has a segment margin of only $4,000. Also assume that total common costs would not change even if the segment were eliminated. The allocation of common costs makes the segment **appear** to be unprofitable, showing an operating loss of $6,000 ($4,000 segment margin, less $10,000 in allocated common fixed costs). However, closing the segment would actually **reduce** the company's income by **$4,000,** as the segment's $4,000 segment margin would be lost, but common fixed costs would not change.

2 **Common fixed costs are not under the direct control of the segment managers.**   Therefore, allocating these costs to the segments does not assist in evaluating the performance of segment managers.

3 **Allocation of common fixed costs may imply changes in segment profitability that are unrelated to segment performance.**   To illustrate this point, assume that $50,000 in monthly common fixed costs

are allocated equally to each of five profit centres. Thus, each profit centre is charged with **$10,000** of these costs. Now assume that one of the profit centres is discontinued but that the monthly level of common fixed costs does not change. Each of the four remaining profit centres will now be charged with **$12,500** in common fixed costs ($50,000 ÷ 4). Thus, the continuing profit centres are made to appear less profitable because of an event (closure of the fifth profit centre) that is **unrelated** to their activities.

Nonfinancial Objectives and Information

So far, we have emphasized measuring the financial performance of segments within a business organization. In addition, many firms have **nonfinancial** objectives that they consider important to their basic goals. A responsibility accounting system may be designed to gather much nonfinancial information about each responsibility centre.

CASE IN POINT Among the factors used by McDonald's to evaluate a restaurant manager is the manager's performance on the company's QSC standards. "QSC" stands for "quality, service, and cleanliness." Each restaurant manager periodically is rated on these standards by a member of McDonald's supervisory staff. Among the many items listed on McDonald's QSC rating forms are:

Quality: Temperature, appearance, quantity, and taste of food servings.
Service: Appearance and general conduct of employees; use of proper procedures in greeting customers.
Cleanliness: Cleanliness in all areas in the kitchen, front counter, tables, and restrooms. Appearance of building exterior and parking lot.

■ ■ ■ ** Supplemental Topic*
Variable Costing

OBJECTIVE 5
Explain the differences between full costing and variable costing.

Our preceding examples of income statements showing contribution margin and segment margin are based upon the activities of merchandising companies. In a merchandising company, the entire cost of goods sold represents a variable cost. In the financial statements of a manufacturing company, however, the cost of goods sold is based upon manufacturing costs—some of which are variable, and some of which are fixed. The conventional practice of including both variable and fixed manufacturing costs in the valuation of inventories and in the cost of goods sold is called **full costing.** Full costing is the method **required** by generally accepted accounting principles.

For the purposes of making managerial decisions, it is often more useful to have an income statement in which variable and fixed costs are shown separately and a subtotal is shown indicating contribution margin. Arranging the income statement of a manufacturing company in this format involves a technique called **variable costing.**

Under variable costing, the cost of goods sold includes only *variable* manufacturing costs. Fixed manufacturing costs are viewed as *period costs* and are deducted separately in the income statement after the determination of contribution margin. Before discussing variable costing further, let us briefly review some of the basic concepts of accounting for manufacturing costs.

Full Costing: The Traditional View of Product Costs

In Chapter 21, we made the distinction between *product costs* and *period costs.* Product costs are the costs of manufacturing inventory and are debited to the Work-in-Process Inventory account. From this account, product costs flow into the Finished Goods Inventory account and then into the Cost of Goods Sold. Thus, product costs are offset against revenue in the period in which the related goods are *sold.* Period costs, on the other hand, are charged directly to expense accounts and are deducted from revenue in the period in which the *cost is incurred.*

Under full costing, *all manufacturing costs are treated as product costs,* regardless of whether these costs are "variable" or "fixed." As all manufacturing costs are "absorbed" into the cost of manufactured products, full costing often is termed *absorption* costing.

Variable Costing: A Different View of Product Costs

Some manufacturing costs are variable costs and some manufacturing costs are fixed costs. The costs of direct materials used and of direct labour, for example, are variable costs. Manufacturing overhead, on the other hand, consists primarily of fixed costs. Examples of "fixed" overhead costs include depreciation on plant assets and salaries to supervisors, security guards, and maintenance personnel.

Under variable costing, only the *variable* manufacturing costs are viewed as product costs; *fixed manufacturing costs are viewed as period costs.* Thus, fixed overhead costs are classified as expenses of the current period, rather than flowing into the inventory accounts and the Cost of Goods Sold account. The diagrams on the next page illustrate the flow of costs under full costing and variable costing.

In reports intended for use by managers, variable costing has two distinct advantages over full costing:

1 The format of the variable costing income statement easily lends itself to cost-volume-profit analysis.

2 Segment margin (or income from operations) is *not affected* by short-run fluctuations in the level of production.

Illustration of Variable Costing

The differences between variable costing and full costing may be further illustrated by preparing a partial income statement under each of these methods. Assume, for example, that on June 1, 1996, Hamilton Mfg. Ltd.

FLOW OF COSTS UNDER FULL AND VARIABLE COSTING

Full Costing

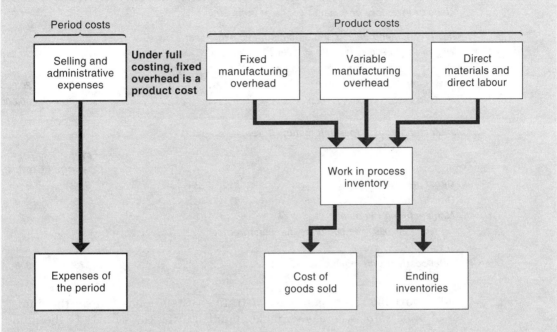

Variable Costing

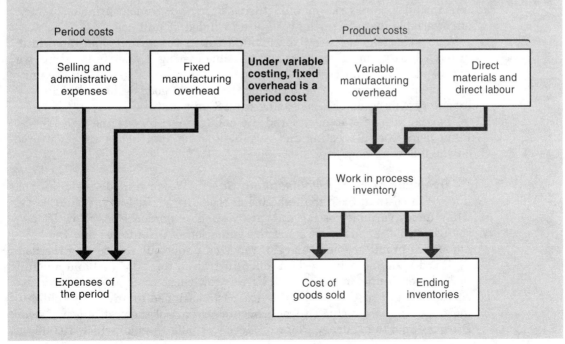

opened its Calgary Plant. Data for the first month of operations of this plant appear below:

Units manufactured and units sold:

Number of units manufactured (all completed by June 30)	11,000
Number of units sold	10,000
Units in inventory of finished goods at June 30.............................	1,000

Sales revenue and selling and administrative expenses:

Net sales (10,000 units sold @ $20)	$200,000
Selling and administrative expenses:	
Variable ($2 per unit sold)	20,000
Fixed	30,000

Manufacturing costs (per unit manufactured):

	Full Costing	Variable Costing
Direct materials	$ 4	$ 4
Direct labour	3	3
Manufacturing overhead:		
Fixed ($55,000 ÷ 11,000 units manufactured)...................	5	-0-
Variable	1	1
Total cost per unit manufactured	$13	$ 8

The variable selling and administrative costs are based upon the number of units **sold,** whereas variable manufacturing costs relate to the number of units **manufactured.**

Notice the difference in "total unit cost" under the two costing methods. Under full costing, the $55,000 in fixed manufacturing overhead is allocated to the 11,000 units produced. Thus, the cost assigned to each finished unit includes $5 of fixed manufacturing overhead. Under variable costing, only variable manufacturing costs are included in unit cost.

The treatment of these fixed manufacturing costs creates an important difference between full costing and variable costing. Under full costing, we will use the **$13** unit cost to determine the cost of goods sold and the ending inventory. Under variable costing, the cost of goods sold and ending inventory will be determined using the **$8** unit cost.

Partial income statements and the ending inventory at the Calgary Plant using the full costing and variable costing approaches are illustrated on the following page.

Treatment of Fixed Manufacturing Costs We have made the point that under full costing, fixed manufacturing costs are viewed as **product** costs, while under variable costing they are viewed as **period** costs. Now let us see what that means in terms of the valuation of inventories and the amount of profit (segment margin) reported under our two costing methods.

Fixed manufacturing costs in our illustration total $55,000 and amount to $5 for each unit manufactured. If we view these costs as **product costs**—the full costing approach—the costs assigned to any units sold during the period are deducted from revenue as part of the cost of goods sold. During June, the Calgary Plant produced 11,000 units, of which 10,000

FULL COSTING

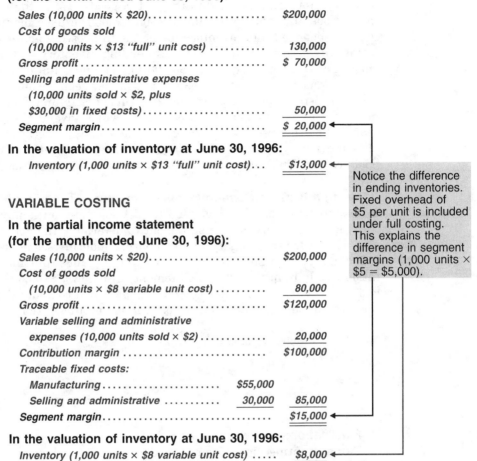

In the partial income statement
(for the month ended June 30, 1996):

Fixed overhead viewed as a product cost

Sales (10,000 units × $20)......................	$200,000
Cost of goods sold	
(10,000 units × $13 "full" unit cost)	130,000
Gross profit	$ 70,000
Selling and administrative expenses	
(10,000 units sold × $2, plus	
$30,000 in fixed costs)........................	50,000
Segment margin................................	$ 20,000

In the valuation of inventory at June 30, 1996:

Inventory (1,000 units × $13 "full" unit cost)...	$13,000

VARIABLE COSTING

In the partial income statement
(for the month ended June 30, 1996):

Sales (10,000 units × $20)......................		$200,000
Cost of goods sold		
(10,000 units × $8 variable unit cost)		80,000
Gross profit		$120,000
Variable selling and administrative		
expenses (10,000 units sold × $2)		20,000
Contribution margin		$100,000

Fixed overhead viewed as a period cost

Traceable fixed costs:		
Manufacturing......................	$55,000	
Selling and administrative	30,000	85,000
Segment margin................................		$15,000

In the valuation of inventory at June 30, 1996:

Inventory (1,000 units × $8 variable unit cost)	$8,000

> Notice the difference in ending inventories. Fixed overhead of $5 per unit is included under full costing. This explains the difference in segment margins (1,000 units × $5 = $5,000).

were sold. Under full costing, the per-unit cost is **$13,** including $5 per unit in fixed costs. Notice that the cost of goods sold in the full costing income statement is **$130,000** (10,000 units sold × $13), and ending inventory under full costing is **$13,000** (1,000 units × $13). Thus, **$50,000** of fixed manufacturing cost is **included in the cost of goods sold** (10,000 units sold × $5 per unit), and **$5,000** is **included in the ending inventory** of finished goods (1,000 units in inventory × $5 per unit).

Under variable costing, fixed manufacturing costs are treated as a **period cost.** The **entire $55,000 is deducted from revenue;** none is included in the cost assigned to inventory. (Notice that under variable costing, ending inventory is valued at only **$8** per unit, the **variable** costs of production.)

How do the different treatments accorded to fixed costs affect the amount of segment margin shown in the income statement? The answer is that fixed manufacturing costs may be **deferred to future periods** under the full costing method. Instead of being deducted from revenue immediately, fixed manufacturing costs relating to units in inventory are "carried forward" as part of the cost of this inventory. These costs will be "released" from inventory and included in the cost of goods sold in the period in which these goods are **sold.** In our illustration, $5,000 in fixed manufacturing cost was deferred into inventory under the full costing approach. This explains why both the value assigned to ending inventory and the reported amount of segment margin are $5,000 higher under full costing.

In summary, full costing results in a higher segment margin than does variable costing **when inventories are increasing** and fixed manufacturing costs are being deferred. In periods in which inventory **declines,** however, full costing results in a **lower** segment margin, because the fixed costs previously deferred into inventory are released into the Cost of Goods Sold account. This situation is illustrated later in this section.

Using a Variable Costing Income Statement The **variable costing** income statement readily lends itself to cost-volume-profit analysis. To illustrate, let us use this income statement to determine the dollar sales volume needed for the Calgary Plant to earn a monthly segment margin of $50,000. As a first step, we may compute the plant's contribution margin ratio directly from the income statement, as follows: $100,000 contribution margin ÷ $200,000 net sales = **50%.** We may then compute the required sales volume using the following cost-volume-profit relationships:

*OBJECTIVE 6
Use a variable costing income statement in CVP analysis.*

$$\text{Sales Volume} = \frac{\text{Fixed Costs} + \text{Target Segment Margin}}{\text{Contribution Margin Ratio}}$$

$$= \frac{\$85,000 + \$50,000}{.50} = \underline{\$270,000}$$

Fluctuations in the Level of Production

Two accounting measurements widely used in evaluating the performance of a manufacturing segment of a business are the unit cost of manufactured products and segment margin. A significant shortcoming in the full costing approach is that both of these performance measurements are affected by short-term fluctuation in the level of production. This complicates the process of evaluating the performance of a segment. The manager performing the evaluation must determine whether changes in unit cost and in segment margin represent important changes in performance or merely the effects of a temporary change in the number of units produced.

*OBJECTIVE 7
Explain why short-term fluctuation in the level of production may distort key measurements of segment performance under full costing.*

This problem arises because under full costing, fixed manufacturing costs are included in the cost of finished goods manufactured. If the level of production temporarily rises, fixed costs per unit will decline. If production temporarily declines, fixed costs per unit will increase. In either case, the changes in fixed costs per unit will also affect total **unit** manufacturing cost.

In addition to causing changes in unit cost, fluctuations in the level of production may cause some fixed costs to be deferred into inventory, or released from inventory. For example, if production rises **above** the level of current sales, some of the fixed costs of the period are **deferred** into inventory, rather than being offset against the revenue of the current period. If production temporarily falls **below** the level of sales, the fixed costs of prior periods are ***released*** from inventory and charged against the revenue of the current period.

Most accountants agree that short-term fluctuations in the level of production, by themselves, do ***not*** represent changes in the profitability of a segment. Profits result from sales, not merely from production. An advantage of variable costing is that unit cost, contribution margin, and segment margin—all important measurements of segment performance—are ***not affected*** by short-run fluctuations in the level of production.

To illustrate this point, we will use the operating data for the Jogman Division of Yato Mfg. Ltd. during 1996 and 1997, illustrated below and on the following page. In this illustration, sales, variable costs per unit, and total fixed costs remain ***unchanged*** in each of the two years. The only change is a temporary fluctuation in the level of production; during 1996, the division produces ***60,000*** units and in 1997 it produces only ***40,000*** units. (To simplify this illustration, we assume that the segment has no beginning inventory and that all selling and administrative expenses are fixed costs.)

Operating Data for the Jogman Division

	1996 & 1997
Annual unit sales......	50,000
Unit sales price	$ 18
Annual net sales (50,000 × $18)	900,000
Annual fixed costs:	
Manufacturing......	240,000
Selling and administrative	130,000

	1996	1997
Number of units manufactured	60,000	40,000
Cost per unit manufactured (full costing):		
Variable manufacturing costs	$ 7	$ 7
Fixed manufacturing costs ($240,000 divided by number of units manufactured during the year)	4	6
Total unit cost of finished goods manufactured (full costing)	$11	$13

Income Statements for the Jogman Division

Full Costing

	1996		1997	
Sales (50,000 units)......		$900,000		$900,000
Cost of goods sold:				
Beginning inventory	$ -0-		$110,000	
Cost of finished goods manufactured ...	660,000[a]		520,000[c]	
Cost of goods available for sale	$660,000		$630,000	
Less: Ending inventory	110,000[b]		-0-	
Cost of goods sold......		550,000		630,000
Gross profit......		$350,000		$270,000
Selling and administrative expenses......		130,000		130,000
Segment margin......		$220,000		$140,000

[a] 60,000 units @ $11 per unit.
[b] 10,000 units @ $11 per unit.
[c] 40,000 units @ $13 per unit.

Variable Costing

	1996		1997	
Sales (50,000 units).....................................		$900,000		$900,000
Variable cost of goods				
sold (50,000 units @ $7).............................		350,000		350,000
Contribution margin		**$550,000**		**$550,000**
Traceable fixed costs:				
Manufacturing...........................	$240,000		$240,000	
Selling and administrative	130,000	370,000	130,000	370,000
Segment margin.......................................		**$180,000**		**$180,000**

Analysis of the Illustration Remember the basic facts of our illustration: nothing has changed at the Jogman Division from 1996 to 1997 *except for the level of production.* Notice that in the variable costing income statements, the Jogman Division reports the *same amounts* of contribution margin and segment margin in 1996 and 1997. The unit cost of finished goods manufactured, $7, also remained unchanged. Thus, the key measurements of segment performance are *not affected* by the change in the level of production. Under variable costing, contribution margin and segment margin change only when there is a change in (1) sales revenue, (2) variable costs per unit, or (3) fixed costs incurred during the period.

Under full costing, however, changes in the level of production *can* cause significant changes in key measurements of performance. These changes result from both the change in fixed costs per unit and fixed costs being deferred into inventory or released from inventory. Let us now look at the reasons behind the fluctuation in the amounts of segment margin reported in our example under the full costing approach.

1996: *More units are produced than sold* Notice that under full costing in 1996, fixed manufacturing costs amounted to $4 per unit ($240,000 ÷ 60,000 units manufactured). During 1996, the Jogman Division manufactured 10,000 more units than it sold. Thus, under full costing, $40,000 in fixed manufacturing costs were deferred into ending inventory. This deferral of fixed costs explains why the segment margin reported in 1996 is $40,000 higher than the segment margin shown in the variable costing income statement.

1997: *Fewer units are produced than sold* Now consider the results reported under full costing in 1997. In this year, unit sales exceeded production by 10,000 units. As the inventory is drawn down, the $40,000 in fixed costs deferred in 1996 become part of the cost of goods sold in 1997. Thus, the segment margin is $40,000 lower than that shown under variable costing.

Summary Because the full costing method associates fixed manufacturing costs with units of production, the amount of fixed manufacturing cost offset against revenue varies with the relationship between the number of units produced and the number of units sold. If production temporarily exceeds unit sales, some fixed manufacturing costs are deferred to future periods, and segment margin will be higher than would be reported under variable costing. If fewer units are produced during the period than are sold, fixed costs deferred in prior periods are offset against current revenue as inventory is drawn down. Thus, segment margin reported for the current period will be lower than would result from variable costing.

Under variable costing, the level of production has **no effect** upon segment margin, because all fixed manufacturing costs are offset against revenue as they are incurred, **regardless** of the level of production.

In the long run, the total amounts of segment margin reported under full costing and variable costing should be very similar. Over the long run, the number of units produced tends to equal the number of units sold. In the short run, however, variable costing provides managers with the more reliable measurement of the performance of segments engaged in manufacturing activities.

Why Is Variable Costing Unacceptable for Use in Financial Statements?

We have shown that in several respects, variable costing may be more useful than full costing as a basis for many managerial decisions. Why then is variable costing not also used in external financial reporting? The answer to this question is that variable costing omits fixed manufacturing costs from the valuation of the ending inventory. Financial accountants argue that variable costing significantly understates the "full" cost of manufacturing this asset. As a result of understating ending inventories, variable costing may understate net income, especially for a growing business with steadily increasing inventories.

CHAPTER REVIEW

KEY TERMS INTRODUCED OR EMPHASIZED IN CHAPTER 24

***Absorption costing** See **full costing.**

Committed fixed costs Fixed costs that are traceable to a segment of a business but that, in the short run, cannot readily be changed by the segment manager.

Common fixed costs Fixed costs that are of joint benefit to several segments of a business. Thus, these common costs cannot be traced to the segments deriving benefit, except by arbitrary means.

Contribution margin Revenue less variable costs; also, the amount of revenue available to contribute toward fixed costs and operating income (or **segment margin**). The key statistic for most types of cost-volume-profit analysis.

Contribution margin approach Arranging a segmented income statement in a manner that develops **contribution margin** as a subtotal. Requires dividing costs and expenses into the categories of variable costs and fixed costs.

---

*   *Supplemental Topic, "Variable Costing"*

Controllable fixed costs Fixed costs that are under the direct control of the segment manager.

Cost centre A segment of the business that incurs costs but that does not directly generate revenue.

*****Direct costing** See **variable costing.**

*****Full costing** The traditional method of product costing in which both fixed and variable manufacturing costs are treated as product costs and charged to inventories. Also called **absorption costing.**

Investment centre A profit centre for which the amount of assets invested in the segment may be readily identified. When a profit centre meets this criterion, its performance may be evaluated using return on investment (ROI) techniques, such as return on assets.

Performance margin A subtotal in a segmented income statement designed to assist in evaluating the performance of a segment manager based solely upon revenue and expenses under the manager's control. Consists of contribution margin less the controllable fixed costs traceable to the segment.

Period costs Costs that are deducted as expense in the period in which they are incurred, rather than being debited to asset accounts.

Product costs Costs that become part of the inventory value of work-in-process and finished goods. These costs are deducted from revenue in the period that the related goods are sold.

Profit centre A segment of a business that directly generates revenue, as well as incurring costs.

Responsibility accounting system An accounting system that separately measures the performance of each responsibility centre in the organization.

Responsibility centre A segment of a business for which a particular manager is in charge and held responsible for the segment's performance.

Segment A subunit within a business organization. A segment of a business conducts specific types of business activity and is under the control of a designated manager.

Segment margin Revenue less variable costs and traceable fixed costs. A long-run measure of the profitability of a profit centre. Consists of the revenue and costs likely to disappear if the segment were eliminated.

Segmented income statement An income statement that subdivides the operating results of a business segment among the profit centres comprising that segment.

Traceable fixed costs Fixed costs that are directly traceable to a specific segment of a business. These costs usually would be eliminated if the segment were discontinued.

*****Variable costing** The technique of product costing in which only the variable manufacturing costs are regarded as product costs. Fixed manufacturing costs are treated as period costs. Useful for managerial purposes, but not acceptable for use in external financial reporting. Also called *direct costing.*

---

*   *Supplemental Topic, "Variable Costing"*

DEMONSTRATION PROBLEM FOR YOUR REVIEW

Burnham Mfg. Ltd. operates two plants that produce and sell a single product. Shown below are the operating results of both plants during 1996, the company's first year of operations:

	Riverville Plant	Truesdale Plant
Sales (40,000 units at $50)	$2,000,000	$2,000,000
Per unit costs:		
Variable manufacturing costs	$ 15	$ 18
Variable selling and administrative	3	4
Traceable fixed costs:		
Manufacturing overhead	$ 600,000	$ 400,000
Selling and administrative	150,000	150,000

During 1996, both plants produced 50,000 units, of which 40,000 were sold. Common fixed costs relating to both plants amount to $500,000.

INSTRUCTIONS

*a Determine the variable cost of goods sold at each plant, using variable costing.

b Prepare a partial income statement for Burnham Mfg. Ltd., segmented by plant and using the contribution margin approach (use the cost of goods sold amounts in a). Conclude this income statement with the company's income from operations.

*c Compute the cost of goods sold at each plant using full costing.

*d Prepare a partial income statement for the entire company determining income from operations using the full costing approach. (Show the cost of goods sold as a single figure.)

e Explain the difference in the amounts of income from operations reported in parts b and d.

SOLUTION TO DEMONSTRATION PROBLEM

a

	Riverville Plant	Truesdale Plant
Variable cost of goods sold (variable costing):		
Riverville Plant: $15 variable manufacturing		
costs × 40,000 units manufactured	$600,000	
Truesdale Plant: $18 variable manufacturing		
costs × 40,000 units manufactured		$720,000

---

*   *Supplemental Topic, "Variable Costing"*

b Segmented income statement:

	Burnham Mfg. Ltd.	Segments	
		Riverville Plant	Truesdale Plant
Sales..	$4,000,000	$2,000,000	$2,000,000
Variable costs:			
Cost of goods sold *(part a)*...................	$1,320,000	$ 600,000	$ 720,000
Selling and administrative....................	280,000	120,000	160,000
Total variable costs	$1,600,000	$ 720,000	$ 880,000
Contribution margin...........................	$2,400,000	$1,280,000	$1,120,000
Traceable fixed costs:			
Manufacturing	$1,000,000	$ 600,000	$ 400,000
Selling and administrative...................	300,000	150,000	150,000
Total traceable fixed costs	$1,300,000	$ 750,000	$ 550,000
Plant segment margins........................	$1,100,000	$ 530,000	$ 570,000
Common fixed costs	500,000		
Income from operations.......................	$ 600,000		

c

	Riverville Plant	Truesdale Plant
Cost of goods sold (full costing):		
Variable manufacturing costs:		
Riverville Plant ($15 × 40,000 units)......................	$ 600,000	
Truesdale Plant ($18 × 40,000 units)		$ 720,000
Fixed manufacturing costs:		
Riverville Plant ($600,000 ÷ 50,000 units =		
$12 per unit; $12 × 40,000 units sold)..................	480,000	
Truesdale Plant ($400,000 ÷ 50,000 units =		
$8 per unit; $8 × 40,000 units sold)		320,000
Cost of goods sold (full costing)	$1,080,000	$1,040,000

d

BURNHAM MFG. LTD.
Partial Income Statement—Full Costing
For the Year Ended December 31, 1996

Sales...		$4,000,000
Cost of goods sold [$1,080,000 + $1,040,000 *(part c)*]......................		2,120,000
Gross profit		$1,880,000
Selling and administrative expenses:		
Variable ($120,000 + $160,000).............................	$280,000	
Fixed ($150,000 + $150,000 + $500,000)	800,000	1,080,000
Income from operations...		$ 800,000

e The difference in the amount of income from operations is explained by the fixed manufacturing costs deferred into inventory under the full costing method, as follows. (The fixed manufacturing costs per unit were determined in part **c**).

Income from operations: variable costing *(part b)*		$600,000
Add: Fixed manufacturing costs deferred into inventory		
under full costing:		
Riverville Plant (10,000 units × $12 per unit)	$120,000	
Truesdale Plant (10,000 units × $8 per unit)	80,000	200,000
Income from operations: full costing *(part d)*.............................		$800,000

ASSIGNMENT MATERIAL

DISCUSSION QUESTIONS

1 What are some of the uses that management may make of accounting information about individual segments of the business?

2 Explain how a responsibility accounting system can assist managers in controlling the costs of a large business organization.

3 Distinguish among a *cost centre,* a *profit centre,* and an *investment centre,* and give an example of each.

4 Marshall's Grocery Store has a small bakery that sells coffee and baked goods at very low prices. (For example, coffee and one doughnut cost 50 cents.) The basic purpose of the bakery is to attract customers to the store and to make the store "smell like a bakery." In each period, costs traceable to the bakery exceed revenue. Would you evaluate the bakery as a cost centre or as a profit centre? Explain.

5 In general terms, describe the criteria that should be considered in evaluating the performances of a *cost centre.*

6 What is a *responsibility accounting system?*

7 The operation of a responsibility accounting system involves three basic steps. In this chapter, we emphasize the second step: measuring the performance of each responsibility centre. List all three steps in the logical sequence of occurrence.

8 In a responsibility accounting system, should the recording of revenue and costs begin at the largest areas of responsibility or the smallest? Explain.

9 In the segmented income statements illustrated in this chapter, two concepts are used in classifying costs. What are these concepts?

10 Distinguish between *traceable* and *common* fixed costs. Give an example of each type of fixed cost for an auto dealership that is segmented into a sales department and a service department.

11 How do the costs of operating *service departments* (organized as cost centres) appear in a segmented income statement?

12 DeskTop, Inc., operates a national sales organization. The income statements prepared for each sales territory are segmented by product line. In these income statements, the sales territory manager's salary is treated as a common fixed cost. Will this salary be viewed as a common fixed cost at all levels of the organization? Explain.

13 Assume that Department A has a higher contribution margin ratio, but a lower segment margin ratio, than Department B. If $10,000 in advertising is expected to increase the sales of either department by $50,000, in which department can the advertising dollars be spent to the best advantage?

14 Criticize the following statement: "In our business, we maximize profits by closing any department that does not show a segment margin ratio of at least 15%."

15 What is the relationship between contribution margin and segment margin? Explain how each of these measurements is useful in making managerial decisions.

16 What does a consistently negative segment margin imply will happen to the operating income of the business if the segment is closed? Why? Identify several other factors that should be considered in deciding whether or not to close the segment.

17 Briefly explain the distinction between **controllable** fixed costs and **committed** fixed costs. Also explain the nature and purpose of performance margin in a segmented income statement.

18 The controller of Fifties, a chain of drive-in restaurants, is considering modifying the monthly segmented income statements by charging all costs relating to operations of the corporate headquarters to the individual restaurants in proportion to each restaurant's gross revenue. Do you think that this would increase the usefulness of the segmented income statement in evaluating the performance of the restaurants or the restaurant managers? Explain.

*19 Distinguish between **variable costing** and **full costing.** Which method is used in external financial reporting?

*20 Explain why a variable costing income statement provides a better basis for cost-volume-profit analysis than does a full costing income statement.

*21 Rose Speakers, a division of Innovative Sound, temporarily increases production to exceed unit sales, thereby causing its inventory of finished goods to increase. Explain the effect of this action upon the segment margin reported by Rose under (a) full costing and (b) variable costing.

MULTIPLE CHOICE QUESTIONS

1 Which of the following is a common fixed cost to the sales departments in a department store?
  a Salaries of store security personnel.
  b Salaries of sales department managers.
  c Cost of goods sold.
  d Depreciation on fixtures used exclusively in a specific sales department.

2 In preparing an income statement that measures contribution margin and segment margin, two concepts are applied in classifying costs. One is whether the costs are variable or fixed. The other is whether the costs are:
  a Product costs or period costs.
  b Traceable to the segment.
  c Under the control of the segment manager.
  d Higher or lower than the budgeted amount.

* *Supplemental Topic, "Variable Costing"*

3 A subtotal used in evaluating the performance of a segment manager, as distinct from the performance of the segment, is:

   a Contribution margin, less traceable fixed costs.

   b Sales, less committed costs.

   c Contribution margin, plus fixed costs deferred into inventory.

   d Contribution margin, less controllable fixed costs.

4 An investment centre has annual sales of $500,000, a contribution margin ratio of 40%, and traceable fixed costs of $80,000. Average assets invested in the centre are $600,000. Which of the following statements are correct? (More than one answer may be correct.)

   a Variable costs amount to $300,000.

   b Segment margin amounts to $200,000.

   c Segment margin represents a 20% return on assets.

   d If $10,000 in additional advertising would result in $60,000 in additional sales, segment margin would increase by $14,000.

*5 During its first year of operations, Marco Mfg. Ltd. manufactured 5 million units, of which 4 million were sold. Manufacturing costs for the year were as follows:

Fixed manufacturing costs *$10,000,000*
Variable manufacturing costs . . . . *$3 per unit*

   Which of the following answers is correct? (In all cases, assume that unit sales for the year remain at 4 million; more than one answer may be correct.)

   a Under variable costing, income from operations will be $2,000,000 less than full costing.

   b Under full costing, the cost of goods sold would have been $2 million greater if Marco had manufactured only 4 million units during the year.

   c Under variable costing, the amount of manufacturing costs deducted from revenue during the year will be $12 million, regardless of the number of units manufactured.

   d Under full costing, Marco's net income would have been higher for the first year of operations if more units had been manufactured.

EXERCISES

EXERCISE 24-1
Accounting
Terminology

Listed below are nine technical accounting terms introduced or emphasized in this chapter:

Segment margin	**Variable costing*	*Common fixed costs*
Contribution margin	**Full costing*	*Traceable fixed costs*
Performance margin	*Product costs*	*Committed fixed costs*

Each of the following statements may (or may not) describe one of these technical terms. For each statement, indicate the accounting term described, or answer "None" if the statement does not correctly describe any of the terms.

   a The costs deducted from contribution margin to determine segment margin.

_____

*   *Supplemental Topic, "Variable Costing"*

b The method of assigning manufacturing costs to inventories and to the cost of goods sold that is required under generally accepted accounting principles.

c Fixed costs that are readily controllable by the segment manager.

d A subtotal in a segmented income statement, equal to segment margin plus committed fixed costs.

e The subtotal in a segmented income statement that is most useful in evaluating the short-run effect of various marketing strategies upon the income of the business.

f The subtotal in a segmented income statement that comes closest to indicating the change in income from operations that would result from closing a particular segment of the business.

g A technique that makes the income statement of a manufacturing segment readily suitable to cost-volume-profit analysis.

**EXERCISE 24-2
Types of Responsibility Centres**

Indicate whether each of the following should be evaluated as an investment centre, a profit centre (other than an investment centre), or a cost centre. Briefly explain the reasoning behind your answer.

a An individual restaurant within a chain of restaurants.

b A restaurant within a department store, owned by the department store.

c A kitchen within a hospital that prepares meals for patients. (Patients are billed for time spent in the hospital but are not charged separately for meals.)

**EXERCISE 24-3
Classification of Costs in a Segmented Income Statement**

The controller of Maxwell Department Store is preparing an income statement, segmented by sales departments and including subtotals for contribution margin, performance margin, and segment margin. Indicate the appropriate classification of the seven items (**a** through **g**) listed below. Select from the following cost classifications:

Variable costs
Traceable fixed costs—controllable
Traceable fixed costs—committed
Common fixed costs
None of the above

a Cost of operating the store's accounting department.

b Cost of advertising specific product lines (classify as a fixed cost).

c Sales taxes on merchandise sold.

d Depreciation on the hydraulic lifts used in the Automotive Service Department.

e Salaries of departmental sales personnel.

f Salary of the store manager.

g Cost of merchandise sold in the Sportswear Department.

**EXERCISE 24-4
Preparing a Segmented Income Statement**

MicroPress is segmented into two product lines—software and hardware. During the current year, the two product lines reported the following results (dollar amounts are stated in thousands):

	Software	Hardware
Sales	$450,000	$600,000
Variable costs (as a percentage of sales)	30%	58%
Traceable fixed costs	189,000	168,000

In addition, fixed costs common to both product lines (stated in thousands of dollars) amounted to $31,500.

Prepare a segmented income statement showing percentages as well as dollar amounts (stated in thousands). Conclude your statement with income from operations for the business, and with segment margin for each product line.

Exercises 5, 6, and 7 are based upon the following data:
Shown below is a segmented income statement for Drexel-Hall during the current month:

	Drexel-Hall		Store 1		Store 2		Store 3	
	Segments							
	Dollars	%	Dollars	%	Dollars	%	Dollars	%
Sales	$1,800,000	100	$600,000	100	$600,000	100	$600,000	100
Variable costs	1,080,000	60	372,000	62	378,000	63	330,000	55
Contribution margin	$ 720,000	40	$228,000	38	$222,000	37	$270,000	45
Traceable fixed								
costs: controllable	432,000	24	120,000	20	102,000	17	210,000	35
Performance margin	$ 288,000	16	$108,000	18	$120,000	20	$ 60,000	10
Traceable fixed								
costs: committed	180,000	10	48,000	8	66,000	11	66,000	11
Store segment								
margins..........	$ 108,000	6	$ 60,000	10	$ 54,000	9	$ (6,000)	(1)
Common fixed costs	36,000	2						
Income from opera-								
ations............	$ 72,000	4						

All stores are similar in size, carry similar products, and operate in similar neighbourhoods. **Store 1** was established first and was built at a lower cost than were Stores 2 and 3. This lower cost results in less depreciation expense for Store 1. **Store 2** follows a policy of minimizing both costs and sales prices. **Store 3** follows a policy of providing extensive customer service and charges slightly higher prices than the other two stores.

EXERCISE 24-5
Evaluation of Segments and Segment Managers

Use the data presented above for Drexel-Hall to answer the following questions:

a Assume that by spending an additional $15,000 per month in advertising a particular store, Drexel-Hall can increase the sales of that store by 10%. Which store should the company advertise to receive the maximum benefit from this additional advertising expenditure? Explain.

b From the viewpoint of top management, which is the most profitable of the three stores? Why?

c Which store manager seems to be pursuing the most effective strategy in managing his or her store? Why?

EXERCISE 24-6
Closing an Unprofitable Segment

Top management of Drexel-Hall is considering closing Store 3. The three stores are close enough together that management estimates closing Store 3 would cause sales at Store 1 to increase by $60,000, and sales at Store 2 to increase by $120,000. Closing Store 3 is not expected to cause any change in common fixed costs. (This exercise is based upon the data preceding Exercise 24-5.)

Compute the increase or decrease that closing Store 3 should cause in:

a Total monthly sales for Drexel-Hall Stores.

b The monthly segment margins of Stores 1 and 2.

c The company's monthly income from operations.

EXERCISE 24-7
Cost-Volume-Profit Analysis

The marketing manager of Drexel-Hall is considering two alternative advertising strategies, each of which would cost $15,000 per month. One strategy is to advertise the name Drexel-Hall, which is expected to increase the monthly sales at all stores by 5%. The other strategy is to emphasize the low prices available at Store 2, which is expected to increase monthly sales at Store 2 by $150,000, but to reduce sales by $30,000 per month at Stores 1 and 3.

Determine the expected effect of each strategy upon the company's overall income from operations. (This exercise is based upon the data preceding Exercise 24-5.)

*EXERCISE 24-8
Comparison of Full Costing and Variable Costing

The following are the manufacturing costs of Fisher Products during the first year of operations:

Variable manufacturing costs per unit:		
Direct materials used	$	12
Direct labour		7
Variable manufacturing overhead		2
Fixed manufacturing overhead		$2,700,000

INSTRUCTIONS

a Compute the cost of goods sold using the full costing approach, assuming that the company:

1 Manufactured and sold 180,000 units.

2 Manufactured 200,000 units and sold 180,000 units.

b Compute the cost of goods sold using the variable costing approach, under each of the two assumptions listed in part **a.**

c Explain why full costing resulted in different amounts for the cost of goods sold under the two different assumptions in part **a** regarding the number of units manufactured.

*EXERCISE 24-9
Full Costing vs. Variable Costing

Shown below are cost and sales data for Aluminum Products, Inc., at the end of its first year of operations:

Sales (100,000 units @ $50)	$5,000,000
Manufacturing costs (125,000 units):	
Variable	1,750,000
Fixed	2,125,000
Selling and administrative expenses (all fixed)	750,000

INSTRUCTIONS

a Compute the per-unit manufacturing cost that will be used in the valuation of inventory and in the determination of the cost of goods sold under (1) full costing and (2) variable costing.

b Compute the income from operations for the year, assuming the use of (1) full costing and (2) variable costing.

c Explain the cause of the different amounts of income from operations under the full costing and variable costing approaches.

---

* *Supplemental Topic, "Variable Costing"*

PROBLEMS

Group A

PROBLEM 24A-1
Types of Responsibility Centres and Basis for Evaluation

Listed below are segments of various well-known businesses:

1　Women's Sportswear department in a **Sears** store.

2　Holiday Inn-Crowne Plaza, the Montreal downtown hotel of **Holiday Inns, Inc.**

3　The housekeeping department in the Holiday Inn-Crowne Plaza.

4　The central accounting department of Holiday Inns, Inc.

5　A restaurant located within the Holiday Inn-Crowne Plaza.

6　Catering, Video, and Entertainment; the department of **Air Canada** responsible for in-flight food service.

7　The **Hertz** rental car centre at Pearson International Airport.

INSTRUCTIONS

a　Classify each of the above business segments as an investment centre, a profit centre (other than an investment centre), or a cost centre.

b　Briefly explain the criteria that are used in evaluating the performance of: (1) investment centres, (2) profit centres, and (3) cost centres.

PROBLEM 24A-2
Preparing and Using a Segmented Income Statement

Samantha First Designs has two product lines—jewellery and apparel (sweatshirts and T-shirts). Cost and revenue data for these two products during the current month are shown below.

	Product Lines	
	Jewellery	*Apparel*
Sales	$750,000	$375,000
Variable costs as a percentage of sales	60%	30%
Fixed costs traceable to product lines.........................	$120,000	$195,000

In addition to the costs shown above, the company incurs monthly fixed costs of $90,000 common to both product lines.

INSTRUCTIONS

a　Prepare a segmented income statement for the month. Carry your computations through segment margin for each product line, and through income from operations for the company viewed as a whole. Include columns to show percentages for all dollar amounts.

b　A marketing survey shows that a $60,000 monthly advertising campaign focused upon either product line should increase that product line's monthly sales by approximately $125,000. Do you recommend this additional advertising for either or both product lines? Show computations to support your conclusions.

c　Management is considering expanding its activities in one product line or the other. An investment of a given dollar amount is expected to increase the sales of the expanded product line by $375,000 per month. However, an expansion of this size will increase traceable fixed costs in proportion to the increase in sales. Which product line would you recommend expanding? Explain the basis for your conclusion.

PROBLEM 24A-3
Preparing Segmented Income Statements in a Responsibility Accounting System

Fit For Life, Inc., sells home exercise equipment. The company is segmented into two sales territories—Eastern and Western. Two products are sold in each territory—ThorTrak, a Nordic ski simulator, and ScanRow, a stationary rowing machine.

During January 1996, the following data are reported for the Eastern territory:

	ThorTrak	ScanRow
Sales	$300,000	$500,000
Contribution margin ratios	60%	52%
Traceable fixed costs	66,000	110,000

Common fixed costs in the Eastern territory amounted to $96,000 during the month.

During January, the Western territory reported sales of $400,000, variable costs of $180,000, and a segment margin of $120,000. Fit For Life incurred $84,000 in common fixed costs that were not traceable to the sales territories.

The two territories are evaluated as investment centres. Average assets invested in the territories are Western, $6,000,000; Eastern, $10,000,000.

INSTRUCTIONS

a Prepare the January income statement for the Eastern territory, segmented by product line. Include columns showing percentages, as well as dollar amounts.

b Prepare the January income statement for the company, showing as segments the two sales territories. Conclude your statement with income from operations for the company, and with segment margins for the two territories. Show percentages as well as dollar amounts.

c Compute the rate of return on average assets earned in each sales territory during the month of January.

d In part **a**, your income statement for the Eastern territory included $96,000 in common fixed costs. What happened to these common fixed costs in the segmented income statement shown in part **b**?

e The manager of the Eastern territory is authorized to spend an additional $30,000 per month in advertising one of the two products. Based upon marketing surveys, the manager estimates that this advertising would increase the sales of either product by $80,000. Upon which product should the manager focus this advertising campaign? Explain.

f Top management is considering investing several million dollars to expand operations in one of its two sales territories. Such an expansion would increase traceable fixed costs approximately in proportion to the increase in sales. Which territory appears to be the better candidate for this investment? Explain.

PROBLEM 24A-4
Allocating Costs among Segments

You are the chief accountant of Powell Department Store and are about to initiate a policy of preparing monthly income statements segmented by the store's 21 sales departments. Your objective is to provide the store manager with a basis for evaluating the performance of departmental managers and the contribution of each department to the profitability of the store.

Mark Ryan, manager of the automotive service department, suggests that each department should be charged only with its variable costs, and that department managers should be evaluated upon the department's contribution margin. He points out that departmental managers can influence a department's sales, but that fixed costs occur at the same levels regardless of the level of sales achieved.

Christine Ferrara, manager of the jewellery department, suggests that all costs of the store should be charged to the departments, as the departments are credited for all of the store's revenue. She believes that departments and departmental managers can most fairly be evaluated based upon departmental operating income—that is, revenue less all costs. She points out that many fixed costs are directly traceable to specific departments, and that common fixed costs could easily be allocated to departments based upon the relative square metres of floor space occupied by the department.

INSTRUCTIONS

a Separately evaluate each of these two suggestions.

b Explain and justify your own recommendations for the classifications of costs to be charged against departments in the segmented income statement. Explain which subtotals you consider most useful in evaluating (1) short-run marketing strategies, (2) the performance of departmental managers, and (3) the long-run profitability of a department.

*PROBLEM 24A-5
Full and Vari-
able Costing

Lathrop Corporation manufactures and sells a single product. The following costs were incurred during 1996, the company's first year of operations:

Variable costs per unit:

Direct materials used	$18
Direct labour	9
Variable manufacturing overhead	3
Variable selling and administrative expenses	7

Fixed costs for the year:

Manufacturing overhead	$900,000
Selling and administrative expenses	250,000

During the year, the company manufactured 90,000 units, of which 75,000 were sold at a price of $60 per unit. The 15,000 units in inventory at year-end were all finished goods.

INSTRUCTIONS

a Assuming that the company uses full costing:

1 Determine the per-unit cost of each finished good manufactured during 1996.

2 Prepare a partial income statement for the year, ending with income from operations.

b Assuming that the company uses variable costing:

1 Determine the per-unit cost of each finished good manufactured during 1996.

2 Prepare a partial income statement for the year, ending with income from operations.

c Explain why your income statements in parts **a** and **b** result in different amounts of income from operations. Indicate which costing approach is used for external financial reporting, and briefly explain the usefulness of the other approach.

d Using the data contained in the variable costing income statement, compute (1) the contribution margin per unit sold and (2) the unit sales volume that must be manufactured and sold annually for Lathrop Corporation to break even.

Group B

PROBLEM 24B-1
Types of Re-
sponsibility
Centres and
Basis for Eval-
uation

Listed below are segments of well-known businesses:

1 Disneyland, one of several amusement parks owned by **The Walt Disney Company.**

2 The Emporium on Main Street, a gift and souvenir shop in Disneyland.

3 Pirates of the Carribean (a ride in Disneyland; Disneyland charges visitors for admission to the park, but not for specific rides.)

4 Windsor Van plant of **Chrysler Canada Limited.**

---

* *Supplemental Topic, "Variable Costing"*

5 Subscriptions billing department of **Maclean's magazine.**

6 Shoe department in a **Sears** department store.

INSTRUCTIONS

a Indicate whether each segment represents an investment centre, a profit centre (other than an investment centre), or a cost centre.

b Briefly explain the criteria that are used in evaluating (1) investment centres, (2) profit centres (other than investment centres), and (3) cost centres.

PROBLEM 24B-2
Preparing and
Using a Seg-
mented Income
Statement

Kitchen Master Equipment Co. is organized into two divisions—Commercial Sales and Home Products. During June 1996, the company's net sales amount to $1,200,000, of which $750,000 are sales of the Commercial Sales Division. The Commercial Sales Division has a contribution margin ratio of 34%, and the Home Products Division, 50%. Fixed costs for the month totalled $240,000, of which $90,000 is traceable to each of the two divisions.

INSTRUCTIONS

a Prepare an income statement for the month, segmented by division. Conclude your income statement with the segment margin for each division, but show income from operations for the company viewed as a whole. Include columns showing percentages as well as columns showing dollar amounts.

b Compute the dollar sales volume required for the Home Products Division to earn a monthly segment margin of *$150,000.*

c A marketing study indicates that sales in the Home Products Division would increase by *5%* if advertising expenditures were increased by *$7,500* per month. Would you recommend this increase in advertising? Show computations to support your conclusion.

PROBLEM 24B-3
Analysis of
Segmented
Income State-
ments

The following are segmented income statements for Butterfield, Inc., for the month ended March 31, 1996:

| | Butterfield, Inc. | | Segments | | | |
| | | | Division 1 | | Division 2 | |
	Dollars	%	Dollars	%	Dollars	%
Sales	$450,000	100	$300,000	100	$150,000	100
Variable costs	225,000	50	180,000	60	45,000	30
Contribution margin	$225,000	50	$120,000	40	$105,000	70
Fixed costs traceable to						
divisions	135,000	30	63,000	21	72,000	48
Division segment margins	$ 90,000	20	$ 57,000	19	$ 33,000	22
Common fixed costs	45,000	10				
Income from operations	$ 45,000	10				

| | Division 1 | | Segments | | | |
| | | | Product A | | Product B | |
	Dollars	%	Dollars	%	Dollars	%
Sales	$300,000	100	$100,000	100	$200,000	100
Variable costs	180,000	60	52,000	52	128,000	64
Contribution margin	$120,000	40	$ 48,000	48	$ 72,000	36
Fixed costs traceable to						
products	42,000	14	26,000	26	16,000	8
Product segment margins	$ 78,000	26	$ 22,000	22	$ 56,000	28
Common fixed costs	21,000	7				
Segment margin for division	$ 57,000	19				

INSTRUCTIONS

a The company plans to initiate an advertising campaign for one of the two products in Division 1. The campaign would cost $10,000 per month and is expected to increase the sales of whichever product is advertised by $30,000 per month. Compute the expected increase in the segment margin of Division 1 assuming that (1) product A is advertised and (2) product B is advertised.

b Assume that the sales of both products by Division 1 are equal to total manufacturing capacity. To increase sales of either product, the company must increase manufacturing facilities, which means an increase in traceable fixed costs in approximate proportion to the expected increase in sales. In this case, which product line would you recommend expanding? Explain.

c The segmented income statement for Division 1 includes $21,000 in common fixed costs. What happens to these fixed costs in the income statements segmented by division?

d Assume that in April, the monthly sales in Division 2 increase to $200,000. Compute the expected effect of this change upon the operating income of the company (assume no other changes in revenue or cost behaviour).

e Prepare an income statement for Butterfield, Inc., segmented by divisions, under the assumption stated in part **d**. Organize this income statement in the format illustrated above, including columns for percentages.

PROBLEM 24B-4
Allocating Fixed Costs to Segments

You have just been hired as the controller of Land's End Hotel. The hotel prepares monthly segmented income statements in which all fixed costs are allocated among the various profit centres in the hotel, based upon the relative amounts of revenue generated by each profit centre.

Robert Chamberlain, manager of the hotel dining room, argues that this approach understates the profitability of his department. "Through developing a reputation as a fine restaurant, the dining room has significantly increased its revenue. Yet the more revenue we earn, the larger the percentage of the hotel's operating costs that are charged against our department. Also, whenever vacancies go up, rental revenue goes down, and the dining room is charged with a still greater percentage of overall operating costs. Our strong performance is concealed by poor performance in departments responsible for keeping occupancy rates up." Chamberlain suggests that fixed costs relating to the hotel should be allocated among the profit centres based upon the number of square metres occupied by each department.

Debra Mettenburg, manager of the Sunset Lounge, objects to Chamberlain's proposal. She points out that the lounge is very big, because it is designed for hotel guests to read, relax, and watch the sunset. Although the lounge does serve drinks, the revenue earned in the lounge is small in relation to its space. Many guests just come to the lounge for the free hors d'oeuvres and don't even order a drink. Chamberlain's proposal would cause the lounge to appear unprofitable; yet a hotel must have some "open space" for its guests to sit and relax.

INSTRUCTIONS

a Separately evaluate the points raised by each of the two managers.

b Suggest your own approach to allocating the hotel's fixed costs among the various profit centres.

*PROBLEM 24B-5
Full and Variable Costing

At the beginning of the current year, Tender Age, Inc., opened its Lewiston Plant to manufacture baby strollers. During the year, 200,000 strollers were manufactured, of which 175,000 were sold at a unit sales price of $150. Variable manufacturing costs for the year amounted to $9,000,000, and fixed manufacturing costs totalled

---

* *Supplemental Topic, "Variable Costing"*

$3,600,000. Variable selling and administrative expenses were $1,575,000, and traceable fixed selling and administrative expenses were $2,700,000.

INSTRUCTIONS

a Prepare a schedule showing variable, fixed, and total manufacturing costs per unit.

b Prepare partial income statements (ending with segment margin) for the Lewiston Plant for the current year using:

  1 Full costing

  2 Variable costing

c Briefly explain the difference in the amount of segment margin reported in the two income statements for the segment.

d Using the data contained in the variable costing income statement, compute (1) the contribution margin per unit sold and (2) the number of strollers that must be manufactured and sold annually for the Lewiston Plant to cover its fixed costs—that is, to break even.

ANALYTICAL AND DECISION PROBLEMS AND CASES

A&D 24-1
The Perfect Product: Low Fat, Low Cost

Fantasy Dairy prepares income statements that show the operating income of each of the company's major product segments—butter, ice cream, and milk. Depreciation on all plant assets is viewed as a common fixed cost. Common fixed costs are allocated to the various product segments based upon the amount of butterfat included in the product. Butter and ice cream are the highest in butterfat. This practice developed because the sales value of dairy products traditionally has varied with the amount of butterfat in the product.

Last year, however, the company added a new product segment—dehydrated milk. The manufacture of dehydrated milk requires large amounts of expensive equipment, but dehydrated milk contains almost no butterfat. After reviewing recent income statements, the company president stated, "The profitability of our butter and ice cream segments has really fallen off. It's a good thing that we started manufacturing dehydrated milk when we did, because that has become our most profitable product. It looks to me as if we should cut back our production of butter and ice cream, and expand our production of dehydrated milk."

INSTRUCTIONS

Discuss the validity of the president's statement and recommend a course of action that you feel the president should take.

*A&D 24-2
Congratulations!?

Advance Electronics opened its new Jefferson Plant at the beginning of the current year to manufacture a burglar alarm. During the year, the Jefferson Plant manufactured 120,000 burglar alarms, of which 100,000 were sold and 20,000 remain on hand as finished goods inventory. There was no work-in-process inventory at year-end. An income statement for the Jefferson Plant, prepared in conventional (full costing) form, is shown on the following page.

---

*   *Supplemental Topic, "Variable Costing"*

ADVANCE ELECTRONICS—JEFFERSON PLANT
Income Statement
For First Year of Operations

Sales (100,000 units @ $90)...		$9,000,000
Cost of goods sold:		
Manufacturing costs (120,000 units @ $63)	$7,560,000	
Less: Ending inventory (20,000 units @ $63)..................	1,260,000	6,300,000
Gross profit		$2,700,000
Selling and administrative expenses:		
Variable ($12 per unit sold)	$1,200,000	
Fixed	1,275,000	2,475,000
Segment margin..		$ 225,000

The $7,560,000 in total manufacturing costs consisted of the following cost elements:

Direct materials used		$2,700,000
Direct labour		2,160,000
Manufacturing overhead:		
Variable	$ 900,000	
Fixed	1,800,000	2,700,000
Total manufacturing costs		$7,560,000

The manager of the Jefferson Plant is proud of the $225,000 operating income reported for the first year of operations. However, the controller of Advance Electronics, an advocate of variable costing, makes the following statement: "The only reason that the Jefferson Plant shows a profit is that $300,000 of fixed costs are deferred in the ending inventory figure. Actually a sales volume of 100,000 units is below the break-even point."

INSTRUCTIONS

a Prepare a schedule showing each manufacturing cost on a per-unit basis. As a subtotal in your schedule, show the variable manufacturing cost per unit. The final cost in your schedule will be the total manufacturing cost per unit on a full-costing basis ($63).

b Prepare a revised income statement for the Jefferson Plant using the variable costing approach.

c Briefly explain the difference in the amount of segment margin reported in the two statements. Is the controller correct about the $1,260,000 ending inventory in the full costing statement including $300,000 of fixed manufacturing costs?

d Compute the contribution margin per unit sold.

e How many units must be produced and sold each year for the Jefferson Plant to break even—that is, to cover its fixed costs and expenses? (In computing the break-even point, assume all units produced are sold.) Is the controller correct that the Jefferson Plant failed to achieve the break-even point in unit sales volume during its first year of operations?

25 Budgeting and Standard Costs

Budgeting—preparing a written plan—provides the very foundation for the managerial functions of planning and control. In this chapter we discuss the uses of budgets and the importance of setting budgeted amounts at realistic levels. Next, we illustrate the mechanics of preparing a master budget for a manufacturing business. The concept of "flexible budgets" also is explained and illustrated. Another major topic in the chapter is the use of standard costs—an important tool in achieving control over business operations. We show how standard costs may be incorporated into a cost accounting system to inform management on a continuing basis how well actual business performance is "measuring up" to the budget. This chapter builds upon your understanding of responsibility accounting, cost accounting systems, and cost-volume-profit relationships.

Learning Objectives

After studying this chapter, you should be able to:

1. Discuss the benefits that a company may derive from a formal budgeting process.
2. Explain two "philosophies" that may be used in setting budgeted amounts.
3. Describe the elements of a master budget.
4. Prepare any of the budgets or supporting schedules included in a master budget.
5. Prepare a flexible budget and explain its usefulness.
6. Explain how standard costs assist managers in controlling the costs of a business.
7. Compute the materials, labour, and overhead variances and explain the meaning of each cost variance.

BUDGETING: THE BASIS FOR PLANNING AND CONTROL

A budget is a comprehensive *financial plan* setting forth the expected route for achieving the financial and operational goals of an organization. Budgeting is an essential step in effective financial planning. Even the smallest business will benefit from preparing a formal written plan for its future operations, including the expected levels of sales, expenses, net income, cash receipts, and cash outlays.

The use of a budget is a key element of financial planning and also of the managerial function of controlling costs. To control costs, the managers of all units of the company compare actual costs incurred with the budgeted amounts and take action to correct excessive costs. Thus, controlling costs means keeping actual costs in line with a financial plan.

Virtually all economic entities—businesses, governmental agencies, universities, churches, and individuals—engage in some form of budgeting. For example, a university or college student with limited financial resources may prepare a list of expected monthly cash payments to see that they do not exceed expected monthly cash receipts. This list is a simple form of cash budget. Business managers must plan (budget) to achieve profit objectives as well as to meet the financial obligations of the business as they become due. Administrators of nonprofit organizations and governmental agencies must plan to accomplish the objectives of the organization with the available resources.

While all businesses engage in some degree of planning, the extent to which plans are formalized in written budgets varies from one business to another. Large well-managed companies generally have carefully developed budgets for every aspect of their operations. Inadequate or sloppy budgeting is a characteristic of companies with weak or inexperienced management.

Benefits Derived from Budgeting

A budget is a forecast of future events. In fact, the process of budgeting is often called *financial forecasting.* Careful planning and preparation of a formal budget benefit a company in many ways, including:

OBJECTIVE 1 Discuss the benefits that a company may derive from a formal budgeting process.

1 **Enhanced managerial perspective.** On a day-to-day basis, most managers focus their attention upon the routine problems of running the business. In preparing a budget, however, managers are forced to consider all aspects of a company's internal activities and also to make estimates of future economic conditions, including costs, interest rates, demand for the company's products, and the level of competition. Thus, budgeting increases management's awareness of the company's internal and external economic environment.

2 **Advance warning of problems.** Since the budget shows the expected results of future operations, management is forewarned of financial problems. If, for example, the budget shows that the company will run short of cash during the summer months, management has advance warning of the need to hold down expenditures or to obtain additional financing.

3 Coordination of activities. Preparation of a budget provides management with an opportunity to coordinate the activities of the various departments (segments) within the business. For example, the production department should be budgeted to produce approximately the same quantity of goods as the sales department is budgeted to sell. A written budget shows departmental managers in quantitative terms exactly what is expected of their departments during the upcoming period.

4 Performance evaluation. Budgets show the expected costs and expenses for each department as well as the expected output, such as revenue to be earned or units to be produced. Thus, the budgets provide a yardstick with which each department's actual performance may be measured.

advantage + disadvantage

Establishing Budgeted Amounts

OBJECTIVE 2 Explain two "philosophies" that may be used in setting budgeted amounts.

Comparisons of actual performance with budgeted amounts are widely used in evaluating the performance of segments (departments) and of segment managers. There are today two basic philosophies as to the levels at which budgeted amounts should be set. We will identify these philosophies as (1) the **behavioural** approach and (2) the **total quality management** approach. We will first discuss the behavioural approach, which currently is the more widely used budgeting philosophy.

The "Behavioural" Approach The assumption underlying the behavioural approach is that segment managers will be most highly motivated if they view the budget as a *"fair"* basis for evaluating their performance. Therefore, budgeted amounts are set at **reasonable and achievable levels;** that is, at levels that **can be achieved** through **reasonably efficient** operations. A segment that operates in a highly efficient manner should be able to **exceed** the budgeted level of performance. Failure to stay "within the budget," in contrast, is viewed as an unacceptable level of performance.

The "Total Quality Management" Approach A basic premise of total quality management is that every individual and segment of the organization constantly should strive for improvement. The entire organization is committed to the goal of **completely eliminating** inefficiency and non-value-adding activities. In short, the organization strives to achieve **perfection** in all aspects of its operations.

As a step toward achieving this goal, budgeted amounts may be set at levels representing **absolute efficiency.** Segments generally will fall somewhat short of achieving this level of performance. However, even small failures to achieve the budgeted performance serve to direct management's attention toward those areas in which there is "room for improvement."

Selecting and Using a Budgeting Approach The approach used in setting budget amounts reflects the philosophy and goals of top management. Under either approach, however, segment managers should **participate**

actively in the budgeting process. Segment managers generally are the best source of information as to the levels of performance that can be achieved within their segments. Also, these managers should understand both the intended purpose of the budget and the philosophy underlying the development of budgeted amounts.

In comparing actual performance with budgeted amounts, top management should consider the philosophy used in developing the budgeted amounts. If a behavioural approach was employed, a highly efficient segment often may *exceed* the budgeted level of performance. If a total quality management approach was used, a highly efficient segment should fall *slightly short* of the budget standards.

In the remainder of this chapter and in our assignment material, we will assume that budgeted amounts are set at *reasonable and achievable levels* (that is, the behavioural approach). Using this approach will enable us to illustrate and discuss actual levels of performance both above and below budgeted levels.

The Budget Period

As a general rule, the period covered by a budget should be long enough to show the effect of managerial policies but short enough so that estimates can be made with reasonable accuracy. This suggests that different types of budgets should be made for different time spans.

Capital expenditures budgets, which summarize plans for major investments in plant and equipment, might be prepared to cover plans for as long as 5 to 10 years. Projects such as building a new factory or an oil refinery require many years of planning and expenditures before the new facilities are ready for use.

Most *operating budgets* and *financial budgets* cover a period of one fiscal year. Companies often divide these annual budgets into four quarters, with budgeted figures for each quarter. The first quarter is then subdivided into budgeted figures for each month, while only quarterly figures are shown for the last three quarters. As the end of the quarter nears, the budget for the next quarter is reviewed, revised for any changes in economic conditions, and divided into monthly budget figures. This process assures that the budget is reviewed at least several times each year and that the budgeted figures for the months just ahead are based upon current conditions and estimates. In addition, budgeted figures for relatively short periods of time enable managers to compare actual performance to the budget without waiting until year-end.

Continuous Budgeting   An increasing number of companies follow a policy of continuous budgeting, whereby a new month is added to the end of the budget as the current month draws to a close. Thus, the budget always covers the upcoming 12 months. The principal advantage of continuous budgeting is that it "stabilizes" the planning horizon at one year ahead. Also, continuous budgeting forces managers into a continuous review and reassessment of the budget estimates and the company's current progress.

The Master Budget: A "Package" of Related Budgets

OBJECTIVE 3
Describe the elements of a master budget.

The "budget" is not a single document. Rather, the ***master budget*** consists of a number of interrelated budgets that together summarize all the planned activities of the business. The elements of a master budget vary, depending upon the size and nature of the business. However, a typical master budget for a manufacturing business includes:

1 Operating budgets
  a Sales forecast
  b Production schedule (stated in number of units to be produced)
  c Manufacturing expense budget
  d Operating expense budget
  e Budgeted income statement
2 Capital expenditures budget
3 Financial budgets
  a Cash budget
  b Budgeted balance sheet

Some elements of the master budget are ***segmented by responsibility centres.*** The budgeted income statement, for example, is segmented to indicate the budgeted revenue and expenses of each profit centre. The cash budget is segmented to show the budgeted cash flows for each cost centre as well as each revenue centre. The production schedule and manufacturing cost budget may be segmented to indicate the unit production and manufacturing costs budgeted for each production process. The portion of the budget relating to an individual responsibility centre is called a ***responsibility budget.*** As explained in Chapter 24, responsibility budgets are an important element of a responsibility accounting system.

The many budgets and schedules comprising the master budget are closely interrelated. Some of these relationships are illustrated in the diagram on the following page.

Steps in Preparing a Master Budget

OBJECTIVE 4
Prepare any of the budgets or supporting schedules included in a master budget.

Some parts of the master budget should not be prepared until other parts have been completed. For example, the budgeted financial statements are not prepared until the sales, manufacturing, and operating expense budgets are available. A logical sequence of steps for preparing the annual elements of the master budget is described below. (Through the use of colour, these steps also are illustrated in our diagram of the elements of the budget.)

1 **Prepare a sales forecast.**   The sales forecast is the starting point in the preparation of a master budget. This forecast is based upon past experience, estimates of general business and economic conditions, and expected levels of competition. A forecast of the expected level of sales is a prerequisite to scheduling production and to budgeting revenue and variable costs.

To emphasize the central role of the sales forecast in the budgeting

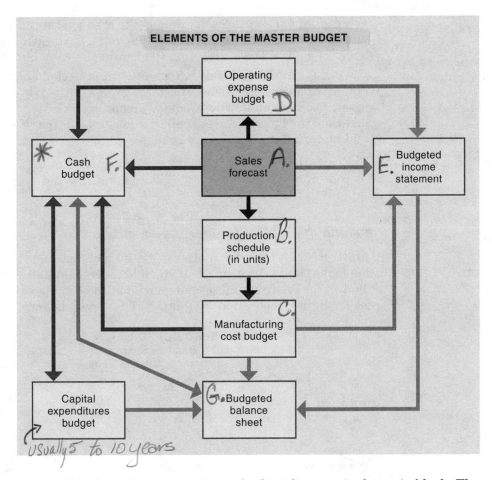

ELEMENTS OF THE MASTER BUDGET

process, the sales forecast in our budget diagram is shown in black. The arrows indicate that information "flows" from this forecast into several other budgets.

2 **Prepare budgets for production, manufacturing costs, and operating expenses.** Once the level of sales has been forecast, production may be scheduled and estimates made of the expected manufacturing costs and operating expenses for the year (black arrows). These elements of the master budget depend upon both the level of sales and cost-volume relationships.

3 **Prepare a budgeted income statement.** The budgeted income statement is based upon the sales forecast, the manufacturing costs comprising the cost of goods sold, and the budgeted operating expenses (light blue arrows).

4 **Prepare a cash budget.** The cash budget is a forecast of the cash receipts and cash payments for the budget period. As shown by the dark blue arrows in the budget diagram, the cash budget is affected by many of the other budget estimates.

The budgeted level of cash receipts depends upon the sales forecast, credit terms offered by the company, and the company's experience in collecting accounts receivable from customers. Budgeted cash payments depend upon the forecasts of manufacturing costs, operating expenses, and capital expenditures, as well as the credit terms offered by suppliers. Anticipated borrowing, debt repayment, cash dividends, and issuances of capital stock also are reflected in the cash budget.

5 **Prepare a budgeted balance sheet.** A projected balance sheet cannot be prepared until the effects of cash transactions upon various asset, liability, and owners' equity accounts have been determined. In addition, the balance sheet is affected by budgeted capital expenditures and budgeted net income (gray arrows).

The capital expenditures budget covers a span of many years. This budget is continuously reviewed and updated, but it is not prepared anew on an annual basis.

Preparing the Master Budget: An Illustration

To illustrate the preparation of a master budget, assume that Berg Corporation makes and sells a single product. Management has asked for a master budget for the first and second quarter of the coming year. The balance sheet for Berg Corporation at January 1 is shown below:

BERG CORPORATION
Balance Sheet
January 1, Current Year

Assets

Current assets:		
Cash..		$ 75,000
Receivables		82,000
Inventories:		
Direct materials	$ 25,000	
Finished goods (FIFO method)	52,000	77,000
Prepayments		21,000
Total current assets		$255,000
Plant and equipment:		
Buildings and equipment	$970,000	
Less: Accumulated depreciation	420,000	
Total plant and equipment		550,000
Total assets		$805,000

Liabilities & Shareholders' Equity

Current liabilities:		
Notes payable, 12% ($40,000 payable quarterly).............................		$160,000
Other current payables		78,000
Income taxes payable		25,000
Total current liabilities		$263,000
Shareholders' equity:		
Capital stock, no par, 100,000 shares issued and outstanding	$350,000	
Retained earnings	192,000	542,000
Total liabilities & shareholders' equity		$805,000

Sales of the company's product are seasonal; sales during the second quarter are expected to exceed first-quarter sales by 50%. However, the economies of a stable level of production have led management to schedule production of *120,000* units in both the first and second quarters.

Operating Budget Estimates The various operating budgets (except for the budgeted income statement) for each of the first two quarters are shown below:

BERG CORPORATION
Operating Budget Estimates
First and Second Quarters of the Current Year

Schedule		1st Quarter	2nd Quarter
A1	*Sales forecast:*		
	Selling price per unit:..............................	$ 3.00	$ 3.00
	Budgeted sales (in units)	100,000	150,000
	Budgeted sales (in dollars)	$300,000	$450,000
A2	*Production schedule (in units):*		
	Budgeted sales (A1)	100,000	150,000
	Add: Ending inventory of finished goods	50,000	20,000
	Units budgeted to be available for sale	150,000	170,000
	Less: Beginning inventory of finished goods	30,000	50,000
	Planned production of finished goods	120,000	120,000

		Per Quarter
A3	*Manufacturing cost estimates:*	
	Variable costs:	
	Per unit manufactured:	
	Direct materials	$ 0.50
	Direct labour	0.60
	Variable manufacturing overhead............................	0.30
	Fixed costs (per quarter):	
	Manufacturing overhead	$ 42,000
A4	*Manufacturing cost budget (for 120,000 units):*	
	Direct materials used ($0.50 per unit).........................	$ 60,000
	Direct labour ($0.60 per unit)..................................	72,000
	Variable manufacturing overhead ($0.30 per unit)	36,000
	Fixed manufacturing overhead	42,000
	Total cost of finished goods manufactured	$210,000
	Cost per unit ($210,000 ÷ 120,000 units)	$1.75

Schedule		1st Quarter	2nd Quarter
A5	*Ending finished goods inventory:*		
	50,000 units at $1.75 (A4)	$ 87,500	
	20,000 units at $1.75 (A4)		$ 35,000
A6	*Operating expense budget:*		
	Variable expenses ($0.30 × units sold)..............	$ 30,000	$ 45,000
	Fixed expenses	70,000	70,000
	Total selling and administrative expense	$100,000	$115,000

Estimates of unit sales and sales prices per unit (Schedule *A1*) are based upon future marketing plans and forecasts of future economic conditions. The production schedule (Schedule *A2*) reflects both the decision to stabilize production and a decision to reduce the inventory of finished goods from its January 1 level of 30,000 to 20,000 units at the end of the second quarter. (Notice that the inventory of finished goods must rise to 50,000 units at the end of the first quarter in order to meet the budgeted sales and ending inventory of the second quarter.)

The cost estimates in Schedule *A3* provide the basis for budgeting manufacturing costs. Schedule *A4,* the manufacturing budget, indicates the budgeted cost of producing 120,000 finished units in each quarter.

Schedule *A5* shows the dollar value of the ending inventories of finished goods that will be on hand if the targets in the sales budget and the manufacturing budget are met. Schedule *A6,* the operating expense budget, summarizes numerous estimates made by departmental managers in light of the budgeted sales volume.

Budgeted Income Statement The budgeted income statements for each quarter shown below are based upon the estimates in Schedules *A1* through *A6*. In addition, these income statements include budgeted amounts for interest expense and income taxes expense. The $160,000 note payable in the January 1 balance sheet is a bank loan payable in quarterly instalments of $40,000, plus accrued interest, due at the end of each quarter. Interest at 12% per year, or 3% per quarter, is computed on the outstanding balance of $160,000 during the first quarter, and on $120,000 during the second quarter. Income tax expense is budgeted at 40% of income before income taxes.

BERG CORPORATION
Budgeted Income Statements
First Two Quarters of Current Year

	1st Quarter	2nd Quarter
Sales (A1)...	$300,000	$450,000
Cost of goods sold:		
Finished goods, beginning inventory	$ 52,000	$ 87,500
Cost of finished goods manufactured (A4)...............	210,000	210,000
Cost of goods available for sale	$262,000	$297,500
Less: Finished goods, ending inventory (A5)	87,500	35,000
Cost of goods sold.....................................	$174,500	$262,500
Gross profit...	$125,500	$187,500
Operating expenses:		
Selling and administrative expenses (A6)...............	$100,000	$115,000
Interest expense.......................................	4,800	3,600
Total operating expenses	$104,800	$118,600
Income before income taxes	$ 20,700	$ 68,900
Income taxes (40% of income before income taxes).......	8,280	27,560
Net income...	$ 12,420	$ 41,340

Here is what quarterly income should be

The budgeted income statement shows the effects that our budgeted activities are expected to have upon revenue, expense, and net income. We are now ready to estimate the cash flows required by implementing our operating budgets and also to determine the effects of the budgeted activities upon balance sheet accounts.

Financial Budget Estimates The estimates and data necessary to prepare a cash budget and budgeted balance sheet for each quarter follow. (The amounts used in the preparation of the cash budget are shown in black.)

BERG CORPORATION
Financial Budget Estimates
First and Second Quarters of Current Year

Schedule		1st Quarter	2nd Quarter
B1	Budgeted direct materials purchases and inventory:		
	Direct materials used (A4)	$ 60,000	$ 60,000
	Desired ending inventory	40,000	40,000
	Direct materials available for use	$100,000	$100,000
	Less: Inventory at beginning of quarter	25,000	40,000
	Budgeted direct materials purchases.................	$ 75,000	$ 60,000

B2   *Means of financing costs and expenses:*

	Total	Current Payables	Expiration of Prepayments	Depreciation
First quarter:				
Direct materials purchases (B1)	$ 75,000	$ 75,000		
Direct labour (A4)..............	72,000	72,000		
Manufacturing overhead— variable and fixed (A4)........	78,000	64,000	$4,400	$ 9,600
Selling and administrative expense (A6)	100,000	94,600	3,000	2,400
Total	$325,000	$305,600	$7,400	$12,000
Second quarter:				
Direct materials purchases (B1)	$ 60,000	$ 60,000		
Direct labour (A4)..............	72,000	72,000		
Manufacturing overhead— variable and fixed (A4)........	78,000	64,400	$4,000	$ 9,600
Selling and administrative expense (A6)	115,000	109,500	3,100	2,400
Total	$325,000	$305,900	$7,100	$12,000

		1st Quarter	2nd Quarter
B3	Payments on current payables:		
	Balance at beginning of quarter......................	$ 78,000	$101,500
	Increase in payables during quarter (B2)	305,600	305,900
	Total payables during quarter.....................	$383,600	$407,400
	Estimated balance at end of quarter (given)	101,500	85,000
	Payments on current payables during quarter	$282,100	$322,400

Schedule		1st Quarter	2nd Quarter
B4	**Prepayments budget:**		
	Balance at beginning of quarter.....................	$ 21,000	$ 15,600
	Estimated cash expenditure during quarter..........	2,000	12,000
	Total prepayments	$ 23,000	$ 27,600
	Expiration of prepayments (B2).....................	7,400	7,100
	Prepayments at end of quarter.....................	$ 15,600	$ 20,500
B5	**Debt service budget:**		
	Liability to bank at beginning of quarter..............	$160,000	$120,000
	Interest expense for the quarter.....................	4,800	3,600
	Total principal plus accrued interest	$164,800	$123,600
	Cash payments (principal and interest)..............	44,800	43,600
	Liability to bank at end of quarter...................	$120,000	$ 80,000
B6	**Budgeted income taxes:**		
	Income tax liability at beginning of quarter...........	$ 25,000	$ 8,280
	Estimated income taxes for the quarter (per budgeted income statement)...........	8,280	27,560
	Total accrued income tax liability	$ 33,280	$ 35,840
	Cash payments (tax liability at beginning of quarter)	25,000	8,280
	Income tax liability at end of quarter	$ 8,280	$ 27,560
B7	**Estimated cash receipts from customers:**		
	Balance of receivables at beginning of year	$ 82,000	
	Collections on first-quarter sales of $300,000 ($\frac{2}{3}$ in first quarter and $\frac{1}{3}$ in second)........	200,000	$100,000
	Collections on second-quarter sales of $450,000 ($\frac{2}{3}$ in second quarter)		300,000
	Cash receipts from customers	$282,000	$400,000
B8	**Budgeted accounts receivable:**		
	Balance at the beginning of the quarter	$ 82,000	$100,000
	Sales on open account during quarter (A1)...........	300,000	450,000
	Total accounts receivable.........................	$382,000	$550,000
	Less: Estimated collections on accounts receivable (B7).....................................	282,000	400,000
	Estimated accounts receivable balance at end of quarter	$100,000	$150,000

Let us now briefly discuss each of these schedules:

Schedule B1 In our manufacturing budget *(A4),* we estimated the cost of direct materials expected to be **used** in our manufacturing process at $60,000. In preparing a cash budget, however, we need to know the cost of direct materials to be **purchased** each quarter, rather than used. In budgeting purchases of direct materials, we must consider both the expected use of direct materials and the desired direct materials inventory at the end of each quarter.

Let us assume that the production supervisor feels that the January 1 inventory of direct materials of $25,000 is too low. The supervisor recommends that the direct materials inventory be increased to $40,000 and maintained at that level. Schedule *B1* calculates the purchases of direct materials required to achieve this desired inventory level while allowing for the use of $60,000 of direct materials each quarter.

Schedule B2 The next step in preparing a cash budget is to estimate the portion of our budgeted costs and expenses that must be *paid in cash* in the near future. Costs and expenses may be financed in any of three ways: through (1) current payables (including accounts payable, accrued expenses payable, and immediate cash payments), (2) expiration of prepaid expenses, and (3) depreciation of plant assets.

Schedule *B2* shows how the budgeted costs and expenses of Berg are expected to be financed. The column headed "Current Payables" indicates the portion of the costs and expenses to be paid in cash or financed by current liabilities. Examples of these items include purchases of direct materials (whether for cash or on account), factory payrolls, and utilities bills. The column headed "Expiration of Prepayments" includes costs and expenses stemming from the expiration of short-term prepayments, such as unexpired insurance and prepaid rent.

The budgeted manner of financing the costs and expenses listed in Schedule *B2* is based upon an analysis of the prepaid expenses at the beginning of the first quarter and upon computations of depreciation on plant assets. All costs and expenses other than those resulting from depreciation or the expiration of prepayments require future cash payments and, therefore, are listed as current payables.

Schedule B3 The purpose of this schedule is to estimate the cash payments required each quarter for the costs and expenses classified as current payables in Schedule *B2*. The starting point in Schedule *B3* is the balance of the current payables at the beginning of the first quarter ($78,000), which is taken from the January 1 balance sheet presented earlier. To this amount, we add the $305,600 shown in Schedule *B2* as the total current payables budgeted to arise during the first quarter. From this subtotal ($383,600), we subtract the estimated balance of current payables at the end of the quarter to determine the cash payments to be made during the first quarter. The $101,500 balance of current payables at the end of the first quarter was estimated by Berg's treasurer after an analysis of suppliers' credit terms.

Similar computations are made for the second quarter. The beginning balance of current payables for the second quarter is the ending balance from the first quarter. Again, the amount payable at the end of the second quarter ($85,000) was estimated by the treasurer.

Schedule B4 This schedule budgets the expected cash payments for prepaid expenses during the period. These payments were estimated by the treasurer after considering the amount of prepaid expenses at January 1 and the expiration of these items indicated in Schedule *B2*.

Schedule B5 This schedule summarizes the cash payments required on Berg's bank loan during the budget period. The loan agreement calls for quarterly payments of $40,000 plus the interest accrued during the quarter. Interest is computed at an annual rate of 12%, or 3% per quarter. Thus, the interest amounts to $4,800 for the first quarter ($160,000 loan × 3%) and $3,600 in the second ($120,000 outstanding balance × 3%).

Schedule B6 The budgeted cash payments for income tax expense are summarized in Schedule *B6*. Each quarter, Berg makes income tax payments equal to its income tax liability at the beginning of that quarter.

Schedule B7 All of Berg's sales are made on account. Therefore, the sole source of the company's cash receipts is the collection of accounts receivable. The credit manager estimates that two-thirds of the sales in any quarter will be collected in that quarter and that the remaining one-third will be collected in the following quarter. Schedule *B7* indicates the budgeted cash collections under these assumptions. (Losses from uncollectible accounts are ignored in our example.)

Schedule B8 This schedule indicates the effect that credit sales (from the sales budget) and collections from customers (Schedule *B7*) are expected to have upon the balance of accounts receivable. The balances shown for accounts receivable at the end of each quarter are carried forward to the budgeted balance sheets on the next page.

Cash Budget The information derived from the financial budget schedules is the basis for the following quarterly cash budget.

BERG CORPORATION
Cash Budget
First Two Quarters of Current Year

	1st Quarter	*2nd Quarter*
Projected cash flow and ending cash balance — Cash balance at beginning of quarter	$ 75,000	$ 3,100
Cash receipts:		
Cash received from customers (*B7*)	282,000	400,000
Total cash available	$357,000	$403,100
Cash payments:		
Payment of current payables (*B3*)	$282,100	$322,400
Prepayments (*B4*)	2,000	12,000
Payments on notes, including interest (*B5*)	44,800	43,600
Income tax payments (*B6*)	25,000	8,280
Total payments.......................................	$353,900	$386,280
Cash balance at end of the quarter.......................	$ 3,100	$ 16,820

The cash budget is an important tool for forecasting whether the company will be able to meet its obligations as they mature. Often the cash budget may indicate a need for short-term borrowing or other measures to generate or conserve cash in order to keep the company solvent. Remember that one of the principal reasons for preparing budgets is to give advance warning of potential problems such as cash shortages.

Budgeted Balance Sheet We now have the necessary information to forecast the financial position of Berg Corporation at the end of each of the next two quarters. The budgeted balance sheets are illustrated on the following page. Budget schedules from which various figures on the balance sheets have been derived are indicated parenthetically.

BERG CORPORATION
Budgeted Balance Sheets
As of the End of First Two Quarters of Current Year

Projected quarterly balance sheet

Assets	*1st Quarter*	*2nd Quarter*
Current assets:		
Cash (per cash budget)	$ 3,100	$ 16,820
Receivables (B8)	100,000	150,000
Inventories:		
Direct materials (B1)	40,000	40,000
Finished goods (A5)	87,500	35,000
Prepayments (B4)	15,600	20,500
Total current assets	$246,200	$262,320
Plant and equipment:		
Buildings and equipment	$970,000	$970,000
Less: Accumulated depreciation (B2)	(432,000)	(444,000)
Total plant and equipment	$538,000	$526,000
Total assets	$784,200	$788,320

Liabilities & Shareholders' Equity		
Current liabilities:		
Notes payable, 12% (B5)	$120,000	$ 80,000
Other current payables (B3)	101,500	85,000
Income taxes payable (B6)	8,280	27,560
Total current liabilities	$229,780	$192,560
Shareholders' equity:		
Capital stock, no par, 100,000 shares issued		
and outstanding	$350,000	$350,000
Retained earnings, beginning of quarter	192,000	204,420
Net income for the quarter (per budgeted		
income statements)	12,420	41,340
Total shareholders' equity	$554,420	$595,760
Total liabilities & shareholders' equity	$784,200	$788,320

Using Budgets Effectively

Earlier in this chapter, we noted several ways in which budgeting benefits an organization. One benefit, an increased awareness by managers of the company's operations and its business environment, may be received even if the completed budget is promptly filed and forgotten. In preparing a budget, managers are forced to consider carefully all aspects of the company's activities. This study and analysis should, in itself, enable managers to do a better job of managing.

The primary benefits of budgeting, however, stem from the uses made of the budgeted information. Among these benefits are (1) advance warning of conditions that require advance corrective action, (2) coordination of the activities of all the departments within the organization, and (3) the creation of standards for evaluating the performance of company personnel. Let us consider how the master budget for Berg Corporation might serve these functions.

An Advance Warning of Potential Trouble   One of the major concerns of the management of Berg was the ability of the company to meet the quarterly payments on its loan obligations. The cash budget for the first two quarters of the year indicates that the cash position of the company at the end of each quarter will be precariously low. A cash balance of $3,100 is forecast at the end of the first quarter, and a balance of $16,820 at the end of the second quarter. If all goes well the payments *can* be met, but there is little margin for error in the estimates.

When confronted with such a forecast, management should take steps in advance to prevent the cash balance from dropping as low as the budgeted amounts. It may be possible to obtain longer credit terms from suppliers and thus reduce payments on accounts payable during the first two quarters. The company may decide to let inventories fall below scheduled levels in order to reduce cash payments relating to manufacturing costs. An extension of the terms of the note payable might be sought, or the possibility of long-term financing might be considered. If any or all of these steps were taken, it would be necessary to revise the budget estimates accordingly. The fact that management is *forewarned* of this condition several months before it happens illustrates one of the prime values of budgeting.

Coordination of the Activities of Departments The budget provides a comprehensive plan for all the departments to work together in a coordinated manner. For example, the production department knows the quantity of goods that must be produced to meet the expected needs of the sales department. The purchasing department knows the quantities of direct materials that must be ordered to meet the requirements of the production department. Responsibility budgets inform every segment manager of the level of performance expected of his or her responsibility centre during the budget period.

A Yardstick for Evaluating Managerial Performance Comparison of actual results with budgeted amounts is a common means of evaluating the performance of segment managers. As discussed in Chapter 24, the evaluation of performance should be based only upon those revenues and costs that are *under the control* of the person being evaluated. Therefore, in a responsibility budget, budgeted fixed costs should be subdivided into the categories of *controllable costs* and *committed costs.*

Performance may become difficult to evaluate if the actual level of activity (either sales or production) differs substantially from the level originally budgeted. Assume, for example, that sales for the first quarter are considerably higher than forecast. Not only will revenue differ substantially from the originally budgeted amount, but so will variable costs, production levels, cash flows, and the March 31 balance sheet amounts. Thus, the usefulness of the original budget as a yardstick for evaluating performance is greatly reduced. The solution to this problem lies in *flexible budgeting.*

Flexible Budgeting

A *flexible budget* is one that can be easily adjusted to show budgeted revenue, costs, and cash flows at different levels of activity. Thus, if a change in volume lessens the usefulness of the original budget, a new bud-

*OBJECTIVE 5
Prepare a
flexible bud-
get and ex-
plain its
usefulness.*

get may be prepared quickly that reflects the actual level of activity for the period.

To illustrate the usefulness of a flexible budget, assume that Harold Stone, Berg's production manager, is presented with the following performance report at the end of the first quarter of the current year. This performance report compares the manufacturing costs originally budgeted for the quarter (Schedule *A4*) with the actual results.

BERG CORPORATION
Performance Report for Production Department
For the Quarter Ended March 31, 19___

	Budgeted	Actual	Over or (Under) Budget
Manufacturing costs:			
Direct materials used	$ 60,000	$ 63,800	$ 3,800
Direct labour	72,000	76,500	4,500
Variable overhead	36,000	38,000	2,000
Fixed overhead............................	42,000	42,400	400
Total manufacturing costs	$210,000	$220,700	$10,700

Is this good or poor performance?

At first glance, it appears that the production manager's cost control performance is quite poor, since all production costs exceeded the budgeted amounts. However, we have deliberately omitted one piece of information from this performance report. To meet unexpectedly high customer demand for the company's product, the production department produced **130,000** units, instead of the **120,000** units originally budgeted for the first quarter.

Under these circumstances, we should reevaluate our conclusions concerning the manager's ability to control manufacturing costs. At this higher level of production, variable manufacturing costs should naturally exceed the originally budgeted amounts. In order to evaluate the performance of the production manager, the budget must be adjusted to indicate the levels of cost that should be incurred in manufacturing 130,000 units.

Flexible budgeting may be viewed as combining the concepts of budgeting and cost-volume-profit analysis. Using the cost-volume-profit estimates in Schedule *A3*, the manufacturing cost budget for Berg may be revised to reflect any level of production. For example, in the following schedule these relationships are used to forecast quarterly manufacturing costs at three different levels of production:

	Level of Production (In Units)		
	110,000	120,000	130,000
Manufacturing cost estimates from Schedule A3:			
Variable costs:			
Direct materials ($0.50 per unit)	$ 55,000	$ 60,000	$ 65,000
Direct labour ($0.60 per unit)......................	66,000	72,000	78,000
Manufacturing overhead ($0.30 per unit).............	33,000	36,000	39,000
Fixed costs:			
Manufacturing overhead	42,000	42,000	42,000
Total manufacturing costs	$196,000	$210,000	$224,000

Notice that budgeted *variable* manufacturing costs change with the level of production, but that budgeted *fixed* costs remain the same.

Let us modify the performance report for the production department to reflect the actual *130,000* unit level of production achieved during the first quarter:

BERG CORPORATION
Performance Report for Production Department
For the Quarter Ended March 31, 19__

	Level of Production (In Units)			Actual Costs Over or (Under) Flexible Budget
	Originally Budgeted 120,000	Flexible Budget 130,000	Actual 130,000	
Manufacturing costs:				
Direct materials used	$ 60,000	$ 65,000	$ 63,800	$(1,200)
Direct labour	72,000	78,000	76,500	(1,500)
Variable overhead	36,000	39,000	38,000	(1,000)
Fixed overhead................	42,000	42,000	42,400	400
Total manufacturing costs	$210,000	$224,000	$220,700	$(3,300)

Flexible budget shows a different picture

This comparison paints quite a different picture from the performance report on the preceding page. Considering the actual level of production, the production manager has kept all manufacturing costs below budgeted amounts, with the exception of fixed overhead (most of which may be committed costs).

The techniques of flexible budgeting also may be applied to profit centres by applying cost-volume-profit relationships to the actual level of *sales* achieved.

Computers and Flexible Budgeting   Adjusting the entire budget to reflect a different level of sales or production would be a sizable task in a manual system. In a computer-based system, however, it can be done quickly and easily. Once the cost-volume-profit relationships have been entered into the budgeting program, the computer almost instantly can perform the computations to generate a complete master budget for any level of business activity.

Many businesses use their budgeting software to generate complete budgets under many different assumptions. These companies use this software as a planning tool to assess the expected impact of changes in sales, production, or other key variables upon all aspects of their business operations.

STANDARD COSTS: FOCUSING ATTENTION ON COST VARIANCES

In Chapter 22 we saw how cost accounting systems are used to determine the actual cost to manufacture products or to perform specific manufacturing processes. A cost accounting system becomes even more useful when it includes the budgeted amounts for direct materials, direct labour, and manufacturing overhead to serve as standards for comparison with the actual costs. The budgeted amounts used in a cost accounting system are called *standard costs.* Standard costs may be used in both job order and process cost accounting systems.

OBJECTIVE 6
Explain how
standard
costs assist
managers in
controlling
the costs of
a business.

The standard cost is the cost that *should be* incurred to produce a product *under normal conditions.* Thus, comparison of actual costs with the predetermined standard alerts managers to those areas in which the actual costs appear excessive. Assume, for example, that the standard (budgeted) cost of making a product is $10 per unit. If job no. 430, which requires 1,000 units of the product, has an average unit cost of $12.50, management should investigate immediately to determine why actual costs exceeded the standard by such a large margin (25%).

Cost accountants often speak of the "standard" materials cost and the "standard" labour cost: Remember that these "standard" costs are actually *budgeted* costs.

Establishing and Revising Standards

Standard costs are established during the budgeting process. Along with the budget, standard costs should be reviewed periodically and revised if significant changes occur in production methods or the prices paid for materials, labour, or overhead. When actual costs exceed standard costs because of waste or inefficiency, however, the standard costs should *not* be revised upward. The standard cost for direct materials, for example, would not be changed if some of the materials placed in production were spoiled because of carelessness by employees. The standard cost for direct material would be changed, however, if the price of the materials were increased by the supplier. Similarly, the standard cost for labour would not be changed merely because excessive hours of labour were wasted; but it would be changed if laboursaving equipment were installed or if new contracts with labour ·unions called for increased wage rates.

Cost Variances

Even though standard costs are carefully set and are revised as conditions change, actual costs will still vary somewhat from standard costs. The differences between standard costs and actual costs are called *cost vari-ances.* Cost variances for materials, labour, and overhead result from a variety of different causes. Thus, in evaluating the efficiency of manufacturing operations, these cost variances should be measured and analyzed. As might be expected, different managers within the organization are responsible for different types of cost variances.

When standard costs are used in a cost accounting system, the costs charged to the Work in Process Inventory, Finished Goods Inventory, and Cost of Goods Sold accounts are *standard costs, not actual costs.* Any differences between the actual and standard costs are recorded in *cost variance accounts.* A separate cost variance account is used for each type of cost variance. Thus, the cost accounting system provides managers with information as to the *nature and amount* of all differences between the actual and budgeted manufacturing costs.

A cost variance is said to be ***favourable*** when actual costs are less than standard costs. When actual costs exceed standard costs, the cost variance is said to be ***unfavourable.***

Illustration of Standard Costs

To illustrate the use of standard costs and the computation of cost variances, assume that product C is one of the products produced by Briar Mfg. Ltd. The company produces an average of **6,000 units** of product C per month. The standard manufacturing cost per unit, assuming production at the average level of 6,000 units per month, is shown below:

Direct materials (3 kilograms @ $5.00)		$15
Direct labour (2.0 hours @ $12.00 per hour)		24
Manufacturing overhead (based upon 12,000 standard direct labour hours):		
Fixed ($120,000 ÷ 6,000 units)	$20	
Variable	1	21
Standard cost per unit of finished goods		$60

During March, Briar Mfg. Ltd. deliberately reduced the level of its finished goods inventory by scheduling and producing only 5,000 units of product C. Actual manufacturing costs incurred during March were as follows:

Direct materials (14,500 kilograms @ $5.20)		$ 75,400
Direct labour (9,800 hours × $13)		127,400
Manufacturing overhead:		
Fixed	$122,020	
Variable	6,180	128,200
Total manufacturing costs incurred in March		$331,000

There was no work in process at either the beginning or the end of March.

By comparing the actual costs incurred in March to the standard costs, we can determine the net cost variance for the month:

Actual costs (above)	$331,000
Standard cost for producing 5,000 units (5,000 units × $60)	300,000
Net unfavourable cost variance (excess of actual costs over standard costs)	$ 31,000

Actual costs incurred during the month ***exceeded*** the standard cost of producing 5,000 units by ***$31,000.*** In planning corrective action, management needs to know the specific causes of this $31,000 unfavourable cost variance. By comparing each element of manufacturing cost (direct materials, direct labour, and overhead) to the related standard costs, we can explain the net cost variance for March in greater detail. Let us begin by determining the portion of this variance that is attributable to the price and the quantity of direct materials used in March.

Materials Price and Materials Quantity Variances

OBJECTIVE 7
Compute the
materials,
labour, and
overhead
variances
and explain
the meaning
of each cost
variance.

In establishing the standard material cost for each unit of product, two factors were considered: (1) the **quantity** of direct materials that should have been used in making a unit of finished product and (2) the **prices** that should have been paid in acquiring this quantity of direct materials. Therefore, the total materials cost variance may result from differences between standard and actual **quantities** of direct materials used or between standard and actual **prices paid** for direct materials, or from a combination of these two factors. This can be illustrated by the following diagram:

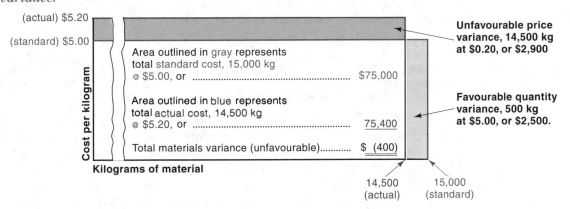

(actual) $5.20
(standard) $5.00

Cost per kilogram

Area outlined in gray represents total standard cost, 15,000 kg @ $5.00, or $75,000

Area outlined in blue represents total actual cost, 14,500 kg @ $5.20, or 75,400

Total materials variance (unfavourable)............ $ (400)

Kilograms of material

14,500 (actual)   15,000 (standard)

Unfavourable price variance, 14,500 kg at $0.20, or $2,900

Favourable quantity variance, 500 kg at $5.00, or $2,500.

The $400 excess of actual materials cost over the standard materials cost was caused by two factors: (1) a $2,900 unfavourable **materials price variance** and (2) a $2,500 favourable **materials quantity variance.**

The unfavourable **materials price variance** results from the fact that each of the 14,500 kilograms of direct material used during the period cost **20 cents more** than the standard $5 price. The materials price variance is the responsibility of the manager responsible for purchasing materials—namely, the purchasing agent.

A formula for computing the materials price variance is illustrated below:

Materials Price Variance = Actual Quantity Used × (Standard Price − Actual Price)
= 14,500 kilograms × ($5.00 − $5.20)
= −$2,900 (or $2,900 Unfavourable)

(All of our variance formulas result in a negative number when the variance is unfavourable, and a positive number when the variance is favourable.)

The favourable **materials quantity variance** of $2,500 resulted from the production department using **500 fewer kilograms of material** than allowed by the 3-kilogram per-unit standard in producing 5,000 units of finished product. This variance indicates that the production supervisors are doing a good job in seeing that materials are used efficiently in the production process. The materials quantity variance may be computed as shown below:

Materials Quantity Variance = Standard Price × (Standard Quantity − Actual Quantity)
= $5 × (15,000 kilograms − 14,500 kilograms)
= $2,500 Favourable

The two materials cost variances may be summarized as follows:

Actual Quantity at Actual Price 14,500 kg × $5.20 $75,400	Actual Quantity at Standard Price 14,500 kg × $5.00 $72,500	Standard Quantity at Standard Price 15,000 kg × $5.00 $75,000

Materials Price Variance
$2,900 Unfavourable

Materials Quantity Variance
$2,500 Favourable

Total Materials Variance, $400 Unfavourable

The journal entry to record the cost of materials used during March, and the related cost variances, is shown below:

Work in Process Inventory (standard cost).....................	75,000	
Materials Price Variance (unfavourable).......................	2,900	
Materials Quantity Variance (favourable).................		2,500
Materials Inventory (actual cost)		75,400

To record cost of direct materials used in March.

Notice that the Work in Process account is debited for the **standard cost** of materials used, but that the Materials Inventory account is credited for the actual cost of materials used. The differences between the standard and actual costs of materials used are recorded in the two **cost variance accounts.**[1] Unfavourable variances are recorded by debit entries, because they represent costs in excess of the standard cost; favourable variances are recorded by credit entries, because they represent cost savings relative to the standard amounts.

Labour Rate and Labour Efficiency Variances

Briar incurred actual direct labour costs of $127,400 in March, although the standard labour cost of producing 5,000 finished units is only $120,000 (5,000 units × 2 labour hours per unit × $12 per hour). Thus, the company incurred an unfavourable total labour cost variance of **$7,400.** We can gain additional insight into the reasons for this excessive labour cost by dividing the total labour variance into a labour rate variance and a labour efficiency variance.

Actual labour costs are a function of (1) the wage rate paid to direct labour workers and (2) the number of direct labour hours worked. A **labour rate variance** shows the extent to which differences between actual and standard hourly wage **rates** contribute to the total labour variance. The **labour efficiency variance** indicates the extent to which the total labour variance results from differences between the budgeted and actual number of **labour hours** required in the production process.

The labour rate variance is equal to the actual number of hours worked, multiplied by the difference between the standard and actual hourly wage rates. The computation of the labour rate variance for Briar in March is as follows:

Labour Rate Variance = Actual Labour Hours × (Standard Hourly Rate − Actual Hourly Rate)
= 9,800 hours × ($12.00 − $13.00)
= −$9,800 (or $9,800 Unfavourable)

---

[1] An alternative is to record the materials price variance at the time that the materials are purchased. Such alternatives are discussed in the cost accounting course.

An ***unfavourable*** labour rate variance may result from using highly paid employees to perform lower payscale jobs or from poor scheduling of production that results in unnecessary overtime.[2] The production manager is responsible for assigning employees to production tasks and also for scheduling production. Therefore, the production manager is responsible for labour rate variances.

The labour efficiency variance (also called labour usage variance) is a measure of workers' productivity. This variance is favourable if workers are able to complete the scheduled production in fewer hours than are allowed by the standard. An unfavourable labour efficiency variance represents excessive labour costs resulting from wasted time or low levels of hourly productivity. The labour efficiency variance is computed by multiplying the standard hourly wage rate by the difference between the standard and actual number of direct labour hours used, as shown below:

Labour Efficiency Variance = Standard Hourly Rate × (Standard Hours − Actual Hours)
= $12.00 per hour × (10,000 hours − 9,800 hours)
= $2,400 Favourable

The ***favourable*** labour efficiency variance indicates that direct workers were able to complete the scheduled level of production in ***less time*** than was allowed in the standard cost estimates. Production managers are responsible for the productivity of direct workers and, therefore, for the labour efficiency variance.

The two labour cost variances may be summarized as follows:

Actual Hours at Actual Rate 9,800 hr × $13.00 $127,400	Actual Hours at Standard Rate 9,800 hr × $12.00 $117,600	Standard Hours at Standard Rate 10,000 hr × $12.00 $120,000
	Labour Rate Variance $9,800 Unfavourable	Labour Efficiency Variance $2,400 Favourable	

Total Labour Variance, $7,400 Unfavourable

The journal entry to record direct labour costs relating to work performed in March is:

Work in Process Inventory (standard cost)	120,000	
Labour Rate Variance	9,800	
Labour Efficiency Variance		2,400
Direct Labour (actual cost)		127,400

To record cost of direct labour used in March.

Both the labour rate and the labour efficiency variances are controllable by the production manager. Often, these variances are closely related. For example, assume that during March the production manager decided to use more highly skilled workers to manufacture product C. This strategy could explain both the unfavourable labour rate variance and the favourable labour efficiency variance, as the more highly skilled workers receive a higher hourly wage and also should work faster than less skilled workers.

---

[2]   If the scheduled level of production requires overtime even with efficient scheduling, the overtime wage rate should be reflected in the standard cost.

In this case, however, the production manager's strategy did not pay off. The cost savings resulting from increased productivity ($2,400) were not sufficient to offset the additional costs from the higher hourly wage rates ($9,800). After reviewing these cost variances, the production manager probably will return to the approach of using lower paid workers in the production of product C.

Manufacturing Overhead Variances

The difference between actual manufacturing overhead costs and the standard overhead cost charged to production is called the **overhead variance.** Whereas direct materials and direct labour are **variable** costs, manufacturing overhead consists primarily of **fixed** costs. Therefore, the analysis of the overhead variance differs somewhat from the analysis of the materials and labour variances. The total overhead variance may be subdivided into three or four subvariances. In our discussion, however, we will follow the more common accounting practice of dividing the total overhead variance into two elements: the spending variance and the volume variance.[3]

The Overhead Spending Variance The most important element of the overhead variance is the **spending variance**—that is, the difference between overhead shown in a **flexible budget** and actual overhead expenditures during the period. The overhead spending variance of Briar Mfg. Ltd. in March may be computed as follows:

Overhead per flexible budget at 5,000 units of production:		
Fixed	*$120,000*	
Variable ($1 per unit × 5,000 units)	*5,000*	*$125,000*
Actual overhead in March:		
Fixed	*$122,020*	
Variable	*6,180*	*128,200*
Overhead spending variance (unfavourable)		*$ (3,200)*

The overhead spending variance is the responsibility of the production manager. Presumably, most of the overhead spending variance represents differences between budgeted and actual amounts of **controllable** overhead costs. For this reason, the spending variance is sometimes called the **controllable** overhead variance. If a significant portion of the spending variance results from differences between the budgeted and actual amounts of **committed** costs, the overhead cost standards should be revised.

The Volume Variance The overhead spending variance has shown us the difference between the amount of overhead included in a flexible budget and the actual overhead costs incurred. The **volume variance** represents the difference between overhead **applied to work in process** (at standard cost) and the overhead per the flexible budget.

---

[3] "Three-way" and "four-way" analysis of the overhead variance will be illustrated and explained in the cost accounting course.

In a standard cost system, overhead is applied (debited) to the Work in Process Inventory account using a standard per-unit cost. On page 1178, we computed the standard per-unit cost of manufacturing overhead at $21. Thus, the Work in Process Inventory account will be debited with $21 in overhead costs for each unit produced.

A temporary problem may arise when overhead is applied at a standard per-unit amount. Using a standard unit cost to apply overhead means that the total amount of applied overhead will *vary directly with the number of units produced.* In essence, a standard cost system treats overhead as a *variable cost.* In reality, however, overhead consists primarily of *fixed costs.*

To illustrate the temporary distortions that may result from using a standard unit cost to apply overhead to Work in Process Inventory, let us compare applied overhead to flexible budget overhead for Briar at three different levels of monthly production.

	Actual Production (In Units)		
	5,000	6,000	7,000
Overhead applied to Work in Process			
Inventory using $21 per unit standard cost	$105,000	$126,000	$147,000
Overhead per flexible budget:			
Fixed	$120,000	$120,000	$120,000
Variable ($1 per unit)	5,000	6,000	7,000
Total overhead per flexible budget	$125,000	$126,000	$127,000
Volume variances—favourable (unfavourable)	$ (20,000)	$ –0–	$ 20,000

Notice that when actual production is 6,000 units per month, the "normal" level of production, there is no volume variance. This is because our $21 standard cost figure *assumes* the 6,000 unit per month level of production. As shown on page 1178, the $21 per-unit standard cost *includes $20 per-unit in fixed costs* ($120,000 budgeted fixed overhead ÷ 6,000 units). Whenever actual production is less than 6,000 units, less than $120,000 in fixed overhead costs will be applied to production. In March, for example, only *5,000* units were produced. Thus, use of a standard cost that includes *$20* per unit in fixed overhead applies only *$100,000* in fixed overhead costs to work in process. The remaining $20,000 in fixed overhead budgeted for the month is recorded as an *unfavourable* volume variance. This unfavourable volume variance actually represents *underapplied overhead.*

The situation reverses whenever actual production exceeds the normal level. When actual monthly production is *greater* than 6,000 units, use of a standard unit cost applies *more than* $120,000 in fixed overhead costs to work in process. Comparison of the applied overhead to the budget then indicates a *favourable* volume variance. This favourable variance should be viewed as *overapplied* overhead.

The key point is that *volume variances represent over- or underapplied overhead;* they occur automatically whenever actual production differs from the average level of production assumed in computing the standard overhead cost per unit. Over time, actual production should average approximately the level used in developing the standard cost. Thus, the favourable and unfavourable volume variances should "balance out" over the year.

As long as the production department is producing the desired number of units, volume variances do **not** indicate either strong or poor performance. Volume variances are the natural result of variations in the scheduled level of production from month to month. Scheduled production may vary from month to month because of such factors as seasonal sales demand, an effort to increase or decrease inventories, or holidays and vacations. Thus, unless the production department fails to produce the scheduled number of units, no manager should be considered "responsible" for a volume variance.

Summary of the Overhead Cost Variances The two overhead variances incurred in March by Briar Mfg. Ltd. may be summarized as follows:

Actual Overhead		Overhead per Flexible Budget		Overhead Applied at Standard Cost
Fixed .	$122,020	Fixed	$120,000	5,000 units × $21
Variable	6,180	Variable (5,000 × $1)	5,000	
Total . .	$128,200	Total.	$125,000	$105,000

Spending Variance
$3,200 Unfavourable

Volume Variance
$20,000 Unfavourable

Total Overhead Variance, $23,200 Unfavourable

The journal entry to apply overhead costs to production in March, and to record the overhead cost variances, is:

Work in Process Inventory (standard cost).	105,000	
Overhead Spending Variance.	3,200	
Overhead Volume Variance.	20,000	
Manufacturing Overhead (actual).		128,200

To assign overhead costs to 5,000 units of production at standard rate of $21 per unit, and to record overhead cost variances.

Valuation of Finished Goods

In a standard cost system, only standard costs are debited to the Work in Process Inventory account. Thus, finished goods manufactured are valued at standard cost as they are transferred into the Finished Goods Inventory account and the Cost of Goods Sold account. The entry made at the end of March to record the completion of 5,000 units of product C is shown below:

Finished Goods Inventory: Product C	300,000	
Work in Process Inventory: Product C.		300,000

To record completion during March of 5,000 units of product C at standard cost (5,000 units × $60 per unit = $300,000).

Notice that the inventory of finished goods is valued at **standard cost.** As units of product C are sold, this standard cost will be transferred into the Cost of Goods Sold account.

Disposition of Cost Variance Accounts The balances in the variance accounts represent differences between actual manufacturing costs and the standard costs used in the valuation of finished goods inventory and the cost of goods sold. These balances are allowed to accumulate in the variance accounts from month to month. Hopefully, the favourable and unfavourable variances will "balance out" over the year, and only a small balance will remain in each variance account at year-end. In this case, the variance accounts are simply closed into the cost of goods sold, since most of the difference between actual and standard cost is applicable to goods sold during the year.

However, if the net cost variance for the year is ***material in dollar amount,*** it should be apportioned among the Work in Process Inventory, Finished Goods Inventory, and Cost of Goods Sold accounts in order to restate these accounts at actual cost.

Evaluation of Cost Variances

We have now computed six separate cost variances to explain in greater detail the $31,000 net unfavourable cost variance incurred by Briar Mfg. Ltd. in March. These variances are summarized below:

Cost variances:		
Materials price variance—unfavourable	$ (2,900)	
Materials quantity variance—favourable	2,500	
Total materials variance—unfavourable		$ (400)
Labour rate variance—unfavourable	$ (9,800)	
Labour efficiency variance—favourable	2,400	
Total labour variance—unfavourable		(7,400)
Overhead spending variance—unfavourable	$ (3,200)	
Overhead volume variance—unfavourable	(20,000)	
Total labour variance—unfavourable		(23,200)
Net unfavourable cost variance in March		$(31,000)

This summary should assist managers in identifying problem areas and in controlling costs in future months. For example, the unfavourable materials price variance highlights the fact that the purchasing department should be able to purchase the direct materials used in product C at a lower cost. The favourable materials quantity variance, in contrast, indicates that the production department is using materials in a very efficient manner.

However, the production manager has a serious problem with respect to labour rates. The large unfavourable labour variance indicates that the strategy of using more highly paid workers in manufacturing product C is not cost effective. Therefore, the manager should change this strategy and return to using lower payscale workers in the manufacture of this product.

The overhead spending variance also indicates excessive levels of expenditures. Now that managers are alerted to this problem, they should look more carefully for opportunities to reduce overhead costs. The large negative volume variance should not be a matter of concern—this variance resulted automatically from the deliberate action of scheduling only 5,000 units of production in March. As soon as production returns to the normal level of 6,000 units per month, this variance will disappear.

Summary of Cost Variances

For your convenience, the six cost variances discussed in this chapter are summarized as follows:

Variance	Computation	Responsible Manager
Materials:		
Price variance	Actual Quantity × (Standard Price − Actual Price)	Purchasing agent
Quantity variance	Standard Price × (Standard Quantity − Actual Quantity)	Production manager
Labour:		
Rate variance	Actual Hours × (Standard Hourly Rate − Actual Hourly Rate)	Production manager
Efficiency (usage) variance	Standard Hourly Rate × (Standard Hours − Actual Hours)	Production manager
Overhead:		
Spending variance	Overhead per Flexible Budget − Actual Overhead	Production manager (to extent variance relates to controllable costs)
Volume variance	Applied Overhead (at Standard Rate) − Overhead per Flexible Budget	None—this variance results from scheduling production at any level other than "normal"

CHAPTER REVIEW

KEY TERMS INTRODUCED OR EMPHASIZED IN CHAPTER 25

Budget A plan or forecast for a future period expressed in quantitative terms. Establishes objectives and aids in evaluating subsequent performance.

Continuous budgeting A technique of extending the budget period by one month as each month passes. Therefore, the budget always covers the upcoming 12 months.

Cost variance A difference between the actual level of cost incurred and the standard (budgeted) level for the cost. The total cost variance may be subdivided into separate cost variances indicating the amount of variance attributable to specific causal factors.

Flexible budget A budget that can readily be revised to reflect budgeted amounts given the actual levels of activity (sales and production) achieved during the period. Makes use of cost-volume-profit relationships to restate the master budget for the achieved level of activity.

Labour efficiency variance The portion of the total labour variance caused by a difference between the standard and actual number of labour hours to complete the task. Computed as *Standard hourly rate × (Standard hours − Actual hours)*. Also called labour usage variance.

Labour rate variance The portion of the total labour variance caused by a difference between the standard hourly wage rate and the rate actually paid to workers. Usually stems from overtime or using workers at a different payscale than assumed in developing the standard cost. Computed as *Actual hours × (Standard hourly rate – Actual hourly rate).*

Master budget   An overall financial and operating plan, including budgets for all aspects of business operations and for all responsibility centres.

Materials price variance   The portion of the total materials variance caused by paying a different price to purchase materials than was assumed in the standard cost. Computed as *Actual quantity × (Standard unit price – Actual unit price).*

Materials quantity variance   The portion of the total materials variance caused by using more or less material in the production process than is called for in the standards. Computed as *Standard unit price × (Standard quantity – Actual quantity).*

Overhead spending variance   The portion of the total overhead variance caused by incurring more overhead costs than are indicated in a flexible budget prepared for the actual level of activity achieved.

Performance report   A schedule comparing the actual and budgeted performance of a particular responsibility centre.

Responsibility budget   A portion of the master budget showing the budgeted performance of a particular responsibility centre within the organization.

Standard cost   The budgeted cost that should be incurred under normal, efficient conditions.

Standard cost system   An accounting system in which inventories and the cost of goods sold are valued at standard costs, and cost variances are separately accumulated in cost variance accounts. A tool for promptly alerting management to significant cost variances.

Volume variance   The portion of the total overhead variance that results from a difference between the actual level of production and the "normal" level assumed in computing the standard unit cost. In effect, the volume variance is a misallocation of fixed overhead costs and often is not relevant in evaluating segment performance.

ASSIGNMENT MATERIAL

DISCUSSION QUESTIONS

1 Explain the relationship between the managerial functions of *planning* and *controlling costs.*

2 Briefly explain at least three ways in which a business may expect to benefit from preparing a formal budget.

3 Criticize the following quotation:
   "At our company, budgeted revenue is set so high and budgeted expenses so low that no department can ever meet the budget. This way, department managers can never relax; they are motivated to keep working harder no matter how well they are already doing."

4 Identify at least five budgets or schedules that are often included in the master budget of a manufacturing business.

5 List in a logical sequence the major steps in the preparation of a master budget.

6 Why is the preparation of a sales forecast one of the earliest steps in preparing a master budget?

7 What are **responsibility budgets?** What responsibility segments would serve as the basis for preparing responsibility sales budgets in a large retail store, such as **The Bay** or **Zellers?**

8 What is a **flexible budget?** Explain how a flexible budget increases the usefulness of budgeting as a means of evaluating performance.

9 It has been suggested that approximately one-third of the total federal budget is considered "controllable." What is meant by a budgeted expenditure being controllable? Give two examples of government expenditures that may be considered "noncontrollable."

10 Define **standard costs** and briefly indicate how they may be used by management in planning and control.

11 What is wrong with the following statement: "There are three basic kinds of cost accounting systems: job order, process, and standard"?

12 Once standard costs are established, what conditions would require that standards be revised?

13 List the variances from standard cost that are generally computed for direct materials, direct labour, and manufacturing overhead.

14 Would a production manager be equally responsible for an unfavourable materials price variance and an unfavourable materials quantity variance? Explain.

15 What is meant by a favourable labour efficiency variance? How is the labour efficiency variance computed?

16 Explain the cause of an unfavourable and of a favourable overhead **volume variance.**

17 Why is an unfavourable overhead volume variance not usually considered in evaluating the performance of the production department manager?

MULTIPLE CHOICE QUESTIONS

1 Which of the following statements correctly describe relationships within the master budget? (More than one answer may be correct.)

   a The manufacturing budget is based in large part upon the sales forecast.

   b In many elements of the master budget, the amounts budgeted for the upcoming quarter are reviewed and subdivided into monthly budget figures.

   c The manufacturing cost budget affects the budgeted income statement, the cash budget, and the budgeted balance sheet.

   d The capital expenditures budget has a greater effect upon the budgeted income statement than it does upon the budgeted balance sheet.

2 During the first quarter of its operations, Morris Mfg. Ltd. expects to sell 50,000 units and create an ending inventory of 20,000 units. Variable manufacturing costs are budgeted at $10 per unit, and fixed manufacturing costs at $100,000 per quarter. The company's treasurer expects that 80% of the variable manufacturing costs will require cash payment during the quarter and that 20% will be financed through accounts payable and accrued liabilities. Only 50% of the fixed manufacturing costs are expected to require cash payments during the quarter.

   In the cash budget, payments for manufacturing costs during the quarter will total:

   a $800,000   b $610,000   c $600,000   d $450,000

3 Rodgers Mfg. Ltd. prepares a flexible budget. The original budget forecast sales of 100,000 units @ $20, and operating expenses of $300,000 fixed, plus $2 per unit. Production was budgeted at 100,000 units. Actual sales and production for the period totalled 110,000 units. When the budget is adjusted to reflect these new activity levels, which of the following budgeted amounts will increase, but by *less than* 10%?

a Sales revenue.

b Variable manufacturing costs.

c Fixed manufacturing costs.

d Total operating expenses.

4 For the number of equivalent full units actually produced, the flexible budget called for the use of 9,500 kilograms of materials at a standard cost of $10 per kilogram. The production department actually used 10,000 kilograms of materials costing $9.90 per kilogram. The production manager should be considered responsible for:

a An unfavourable cost variance of $4,000.

b A favourable price variance of $1,000.

c An unfavourable quantity variance of $5,000.

d None of the above; the flexible budget should be adjusted to reflect the use of 10,000 kilograms of material.

5 An unfavourable volume variance indicates that:

a Total fixed overhead exceeded budgeted amounts.

b Variable overhead per unit exceeded budgeted amounts.

c The production department failed to produce the quantity of units called for in the production schedule.

d The actual production for the period was less than the normal volume used in establishing the standard unit cost.

EXERCISES

EXERCISE 25-1
Accounting
Terminology
Listed below are nine technical accounting terms introduced in this chapter:

Overhead spending variance	*Materials price variance*	*Materials quantity variance*
Labour rate variance	*Master budget*	*Standard costs*
Labour efficiency variance	*Flexible budget*	*Volume variance*

Each of the following statements may (or may not) describe one of these technical terms. For each statement, indicate the accounting term described, or answer "None" if the statement does not correctly describe any of the terms.

a The additional cost or cost savings resulting from the actual number of required hours of direct labour differing from standard.

b A budget showing cost levels that departmental managers may not exceed without written permission from top management.

c The budgeted costs of producing a product under normal conditions.

d An overall financial plan for the operation of a business, which includes separate budgets or supporting schedules for each aspect of business operations.

e A variance that is always favourable when more units are sold than are produced during the period.

f The difference between actual manufacturing overhead and the level of overhead budgeted for the level of output actually achieved.

g A budget that may be readily adjusted to show budgeted amounts at different possible levels of output.

h The difference between the standard and actual unit cost of materials used, multiplied by the actual quantity of materials used.

EXERCISE 25-2
Budgeting Purchases and Cash Payments

The following information is taken from the manufacturing budget and budgeted financial statements of Wexler Fabrication:

Direct materials inventory, Jan. 1	$ 62,000
Direct materials inventory, Dec. 31	75,000
Direct materials budgeted for use during the year	220,000
Accounts payable to suppliers of direct materials, Jan. 1	48,000
Accounts payable to suppliers of direct materials, Dec. 31	60,000

INSTRUCTIONS

Compute the budgeted amounts for:

a Purchases of direct materials during the year.

b Cash payments during the year to suppliers of direct materials.

EXERCISE 25-3
Budgeting Cash Receipts

Sales on account for the first two months of the current year are budgeted as follows:

January	$600,000
February	800,000

All sales are made on terms of 2/10, n/30; collections on accounts receivable are typically made as follows:

Collections within the month of sale:	
Within discount period	60%
After discount period	15%
Collections within the month following sale:	
Within discount period	15%
After discount period	7%
Returns, allowances, and uncollectibles	3%
Total	100%

INSTRUCTIONS

Compute the estimated cash collections on accounts receivable for the month of **February.**

EXERCISE 25-4
Preparing a Flexible Budget

The flexible budget at the 70,000-unit and the 80,000-unit level of activity is shown below:

	70,000 Units	80,000 Units	90,000 Units
Sales	$1,400,000	$1,600,000	$
Cost of goods sold	840,000	960,000	
Gross profit	$ 560,000	$ 640,000	$
Operating expenses ($90,000 fixed)	370,000	410,000	
Operating income	$ 190,000	$ 230,000	$
Income taxes (30% of operating income)	57,000	69,000	
Net income	$ 133,000	$ 161,000	$

INSTRUCTIONS Complete the flexible budget at the 90,000-unit level of activity. Assume that the cost of goods sold and variable operating expenses vary directly with sales and that income taxes remain at 30% of operating income.

EXERCISE 25-5
More on
Flexible Bud-
geting

The cost accountant for Amalfi Leather Goods prepared the following monthly performance report relating to the Finishing Department:

	Budgeted Production (10,000 Units)	Actual Production (11,000 Units)	Variances Favourable	Variances Unfavourable
Direct materials used	$300,000	$320,000		$20,000
Direct labour	100,000	115,000		15,000
Variable manufacturing overhead.................	20,000	21,500		1,500
Fixed manufacturing overhead................	150,000	149,200	$800	

INSTRUCTIONS Prepare a revised performance report in which the variances are computed by comparing the actual costs incurred with estimated costs *using a flexible budget* for 11,000 units of production.

EXERCISE 25-6
Relationships
among Stan-
dard Costs,
Actual Costs,
and Cost Vari-
ances

The standard costs and variances for direct materials, direct labour, and manufacturing overhead for the month of May are given below:

	Standard Cost	Variances Unfavourable	Variances Favourable
Direct materials	$ 90,000		
Price variance...........................		$4,500	
Quantity variance........................			$2,700
Direct labour	180,000		
Rate variance			1,800
Efficiency variance		5,400	
Manufacturing overhead	270,000		
Spending variance.......................			3,600
Volume variance.........................			2,400

INSTRUCTIONS Determine the *actual costs* incurred during the month of May for direct materials, direct labour, and manufacturing overhead.

EXERCISE 25-7
Computing
Materials Cost
Variances

One of the products of Hearts & Flowers is a one-kilogram box of chocolate flavoured candy, packaged in a box bearing the customer's logo. (Minimum order, 100 boxes.) The standard cost of the chocolate candy used is $2 per kilogram. During November, 20,000 of these one-kilogram boxes were produced, requiring 20,800 kilograms of chocolate flavoured candy at a total direct materials cost of $42,640.

Determine the materials price variance and quantity variance with respect to the candy used producing this product.

EXERCISE 25-8
Computing
Labour Cost
Variances

One of the most popular products of Loring Glassworks is a hand-decorated vase. The company's standard cost system calls for .75 hours of direct labour per vase, at a standard wage rate of $8.25. During September, Loring produced 4,000 vases at an actual direct labour cost of $24,464 for 2,780 direct labour hours.

INSTRUCTIONS a What was the average hourly pay rate of the direct workers producing the vases in September?

b Compute the labour rate and efficiency variances for the month.

c Was using workers on the payscale indicated in part **a** an effective strategy? Explain.

EXERCISE 25-9 **Computing** **Overhead Cost** **Variances**	From the following information for Alfred Industries, compute the overhead spending variance and the volume variance.

Standard manufacturing overhead based on normal
  monthly volume:

Fixed ($300,000 ÷ 20,000 units)................................	$15.00	
Variable ($100,000 ÷ 20,000 units)	5.00	$20.00
Units actually produced in current month		18,000 units
Actual overhead costs incurred (including $300,000 fixed)...................		$383,800

EXERCISE 25-10 **Elements of** **the Materials** **Cost Variances**	The following computation of the materials variances of Weitzen Foods is incomplete. The missing data is labelled *(a)* through *(d)*.

Materials price variance = 3,640 kilograms × [(a) standard price –
  $9.00 actual price].. $910 Unfavourable

Materials quantity variance = (b) × [3,800 kilograms – (c) actual
  quantity] .... $ (d)

INSTRUCTIONS	Supply the missing data for items *(a)* through *(d)*. Prepare a caption describing the item, as well as indicating the dollar amount or physical quantity. Briefly explain each answer, including how you determined the amount.

EXERCISE 25-11 **Computing** **Materials and** **Labour Vari-** **ances**	Nolan Mills uses a standard cost system. During May, Nolan manufactured 15,000 pillowcases, using 27,000 metres of fabric costing $3.05 per metre and incurring direct labour costs of $22,440 for 3,300 hours of direct labour. The standard cost per pillowcase assumes 1.75 metres of fabric at $3.10 per metre, and 0.2 hours of direct labour at $6.95 per hour.

INSTRUCTIONS	**a** Compute both the price variance and quantity variance relating to direct materials used in the manufacture of pillowcases in May. **b** Compute both the rate variance and efficiency variance for direct labour costs incurred in manufacturing pillowcases in May.

EXERCISE 25-12 **Causes of Cost** **Variances**	For each of the following variances, briefly explain at least one probable cause and indicate the departmental manager (if any) responsible for the variance. **a** A favourable materials price variance. **b** An unfavourable labour rate variance. **c** A favourable volume variance. **d** An unfavourable materials quantity variance.

PROBLEMS

Group A

PROBLEM 25A-1 **Budgeting** **Manufacturing** **Overhead**	Yung Hsin, Inc., manufactures a component that is processed successively by Department A and Department B. Manufacturing overhead is applied to units of production at the following standard costs:

	Manufacturing Overhead Per Unit		
	Fixed	Variable	Total
Department A	$14.40	$6.80	$21.20
Department B	10.40	4.90	15.30

These standard manufacturing overhead costs per unit are based on a normal volume of production of 5,000 units per month. In January, variable manufacturing overhead is expected to be *15%* above standard in Department B because of scheduled repairs to equipment. The company plans to produce 4,500 units during January.

INSTRUCTIONS Prepare a budget for manufacturing overhead costs in January. Use column headings as follows: Total, Department A, and Department B.

PROBLEM 25A-2
Short Budgeting Problem

Harmony Corporation at present manufactures and sells a single product. In preparing the budget for the first quarter, the company's cost accountant has assembled the following information:

	Units	Dollars
Sales (budgeted)	150,000	$12,150,000
Finished goods inventory, Jan. 1 (actual)	30,000	1,080,000
Finished goods inventory, Mar. 31 (budgeted)	20,000	?
Cost of finished goods manufactured (budgeted manufacturing cost is $39 per unit)	?	?

The company uses the first-in, first-out method of pricing its inventory of finished goods.

INSTRUCTIONS Compute the following budgeted quantities or dollar amounts:
a Planned production of finished goods (in units).
b Cost of finished goods manufactured.
c Finished goods inventory, Mar. 31.
d Cost of goods sold.

PROBLEM 25A-3
Preparing a Cash Budget

Barnum Distributors wants a projection of cash receipts and cash payments for the month of November. On November 28, a note will be payable in the amount of $98,500, including interest. The cash balance on November 1 is $29,600. Accounts payable to merchandise creditors at the end of October were $217,000.

The company's experience indicates that 70% of sales will be collected during the month of sale, 20% in the month following the sale, and 7% in the second month following the sale; 3% will be uncollectible. The company sells various products at an average price of $11 per unit. Selected sales figures are shown below:

	Units
September—actual	40,000
October—actual	60,000
November—estimated	80,000
December—estimated	50,000
Total estimated for the current year	800,000

Because purchases are payable within 15 days, approximately 50% of the purchases in a given month are paid in the following month. The average cost of units purchased is $7 per unit. Inventories at the end of each month are maintained at a level of 2,000 units plus 10% of the number of units that will be sold in the following month. The inventory on October 1 amounted to 8,000 units.

Budgeted operating expenses for November are $220,000. Of this amount, $90,000 is considered fixed (including depreciation of $35,000). All operating expenses, other than depreciation, are paid in the month in which they are incurred.

The company expects to sell fully depreciated equipment in November for $8,400 cash.

INSTRUCTIONS Prepare a cash budget for the month of November, supported by schedules of cash collections on accounts receivable and cash payments for purchases of merchandise.

**PROBLEM 25A-4
Preparing and
Using a Flexi-
ble Budget**

Four Flags is a retail department store. The following cost-volume relationships were used in developing a flexible budget for the company for the current year:

	Yearly Fixed Expenses	Variable Expenses per Sales Dollar
Cost of goods sold...		$0.600
Selling and promotion expense	$ 210,000	0.082
Building occupancy expense..................................	186,000	0.022
Buying expense	150,000	0.040
Delivery expense	111,000	0.010
Credit and collection expense...............................	72,000	0.002
Administrative expense.......................................	531,000	0.003
Totals..	$1,260,000	$0.759

Management expected to attain a sales level of $12 million during the current year. At the end of the year the actual results achieved by the company were as follows:

Net sales..	$10,500,000
Cost of goods sold...	6,180,000
Selling and promotion expense	1,020,000
Building occupancy expense.......................................	420,000
Buying expense	594,000
Delivery expense	183,000
Credit and collection expense....................................	90,000
Administrative expense...	564,000

INSTRUCTIONS **a** Prepare a schedule comparing the actual results with flexible budget amounts developed for the actual sales volume of $10,500,000. Organize your schedule as a partial multiple-step income statement, ending with operating income. Include separate columns for (1) flexible budget amounts, (2) actual amounts, and (3) any amount over or (under) budget. Use the cost-volume relationships given in the problem to compute the flexible budget amounts.

b Write a statement evaluating the company's performance in relation to the plan reflected in the flexible budget.

PROBLEM 25A-5
Basic Standard
Cost Problem

AgriChem Industries manufactures fertilizer concentrate and uses a cost system. The fertilizer is produced in 500-kilogram batches; the normal level of production is 250 batches of fertilizer per month. The standard costs per batch are shown below:

		Standard Costs per Batch
Direct materials:		
Various chemicals (500 kg per batch @ $0.60/kg)		*$300*
Direct labour:		
Preparation and blending (25 hrs. per batch @ $7.00/hr.)		*175*
Manufacturing overhead:		
Fixed ($50,000 per month ÷ 250 batches)	*$200*	
Variable (per batch).	*25*	*225*
Total standard cost per batch of fertilizer.		*$700*

During January, the company temporarily reduced the level of production to 200 batches of fertilizer. Actual costs incurred in January were as follows:

Direct materials (102,500 kg @ $0.57/kg).	*$ 58,425*
Direct labour (4,750 hrs. @ $6.80/hr.)	*32,300*
Manufacturing overhead	*54,525*
Total actual costs (200 batches).	*$145,250*
Standard cost of 200 batches (200 batches × $700 per batch)	*140,000*
Net unfavourable cost variance	*$ 5,250*

INSTRUCTIONS

You have been engaged to explain in detail the elements of the $5,250 net unfavourable cost variance, and to record the manufacturing costs for January in the company's standard cost accounting system.

a As a first step, compute the materials price and quantity variances, the labour rate and efficiency variances, and the overhead spending and volume variances for the month.

b Prepare journal entries to record the flow of manufacturing costs through the standard cost system and the related cost variances. Make separate entries to record the costs of direct materials used, direct labour, and manufacturing overhead. Work in Process Inventory is to be debited only with standard costs.

PROBLEM 25A-6
Computation,
Recording, and
Analysis of
Cost Variances

Heritage Furniture Co. uses a standard cost system. One of the company's most popular products is an oak entertainment centre that looks like an old ice box but houses a television, stereo, or other electronic components. The per-unit standard costs of the entertainment centre, assuming a "normal" volume of 1,000 units per month, are as follows:

Direct materials, 100 board feet of wood at $1.30 per foot		*$130.00*
Direct labour, 5 hours at $8.00 per hour		*40.00*
Manufacturing overhead (applied at $22 per unit)		
Fixed ($15,000 ÷ 1,000 units of normal production).	*$15.00*	
Variable	*7.00*	*22.00*
Total standard unit cost		*$192.00*

During July, 800 entertainment centres were scheduled and produced at the following actual unit costs:

Direct materials, 110 board feet at $1.20 per foot	*$132.00*
Direct labour, $5\frac{1}{2}$ hours at $7.80 per hour	*42.90*
Manufacturing overhead, $18,480 ÷ 800 units	*23.10*
Total actual unit cost	*$198.00*

INSTRUCTIONS

a Compute the following cost variances for the month of July:

  1 Materials price variance.

  2 Materials quantity variance.

  3 Labour rate variance.

  4 Labour efficiency variance.

  5 Overhead spending variance.

  6 Volume variance.

b Prepare journal entries to assign manufacturing costs to the Work in Process Inventory account and to record cost variances for July. Use separate entries for (1) direct materials, (2) direct labour, and (3) overhead costs.

c Comment upon any significant problems or areas of cost savings revealed by your computation of cost variances. Also comment on any possible causal relationships between significant favourable and unfavourable cost variances.

Group B

PROBLEM 25B-1
Budgeting Labour Costs

Sun Valley Naturals manufactures a product that is first dry roasted and then packed for shipment to customers. The standard direct labour cost per kilogram of product in each process follows:

Process	Direct Labour Hours per Kilogram	Standard Direct Labour Cost per Hour
Dry roasting...	*.024*	*$7.50*
Packing...	*.015*	*6.00*

The budget for November calls for the production of 150,000 kilograms of product. The expected labour cost in the dry roasting department is expected to be 7% above standard for the month of November as a result of higher wage rates and inefficiencies in the scheduling of work. The expected cost of labour in the packing room is expected to be 5% below standard because of a new arrangement of equipment.

INSTRUCTIONS

Prepare a budget for direct labour costs for November. Use column headings as follows: Total, Dry Roasting, and Packing.

PROBLEM 25B-2
Budgeting Production Inventories, and the Cost of Sales

Welsh Scientific manufactures and sells a single product. In preparing the budget for the current quarter, the company's controller has assembled the following information:

	Units	Dollars
Sales (budgeted)	*126,000*	*$4,410,000*
Finished goods inventory, beginning of the quarter	*31,200*	*594,000*
Finished goods inventory, end of the quarter	*24,000*	*?*
Cost of finished goods manufactured (budgeted man-		
ufacturing cost is $20 per unit)	*?*	*?*

The company uses the weighted-average method of pricing its inventory of finished goods.

INSTRUCTIONS Compute the following budgeted quantities or dollar amounts:

a Planned production of finished goods (in units).

b Cost of finished goods manufactured.

c Finished goods inventory, end of the quarter.

d Cost of goods sold.

PROBLEM 25B-3
Flexible
Budgeting

Braemar Saddlery uses departmental budgets and performance reports in planning and controlling its manufacturing operations. The following annual performance report for the custom saddle production department was presented to the president of the company.

	Budgeted Costs for 5,000 Units		Actual Costs Incurred	Over or (Under) Budget
	Per Unit	Total		
Variable manufacturing costs:				
Direct materials	$ 30.00	$150,000	$171,000	$21,000
Direct labour	48.00	240,000	261,500	21,500
Indirect labour	15.00	75,000	95,500	20,500
Indirect materials, supplies, etc...........	9.00	45,000	48,400	3,400
Total variable manufacturing costs	$102.00	$510,000	$576,400	$66,400
Fixed manufacturing costs:				
Lease rental.............................	$ 9.00	$ 45,000	$ 45,000	None
Salaries of supervisors	24.00	120,000	125,000	$ 5,000
Depreciation and other	15.00	75,000	78,600	3,600
Total fixed manufacturing costs	$ 48.00	$240,000	$248,600	$ 8,600
Total manufacturing costs	$150.00	$750,000	$825,000	$75,000

Although a production volume of 5,000 saddles was originally budgeted for the year, the actual volume of production achieved for the year was **6,000** saddles. The company does not use standard costs; direct materials and direct labour are charged to production at actual cost. Manufacturing overhead is applied to production at the predetermined rate of 150% of the actual direct labour cost.

After a quick glance at the performance report showing an unfavourable manufacturing cost variance of $75,000, the president said to the accountant: "Fix this thing so it makes sense. It looks as though our production people really blew the budget. Remember that we exceeded our budgeted production schedule by a significant margin. I want this performance report to show a better picture of our ability to control costs."

INSTRUCTIONS a Prepare a revised performance report for the year on a flexible budget basis. Use the same format as the production report above, but revise the budgeted cost figures to reflect the actual production level of **6,000** saddles.

b In a few sentences compare the original performance report with the revised report.

c What is the amount of over- or underapplied manufacturing overhead for the year? (Note that a standard cost system is not used.)

PROBLEM 25B-4
Preparing a
Cash Budget

Jake Marley, owner of Marley Wholesale, is negotiating with the bank for a $200,000, 90-day, 12% loan effective July 2 of the current year. If the bank grants the loan, the proceeds will be $194,000, which Marley intends to use on July 2 as follows: pay accounts payable, $150,000; purchase equipment, $16,000; add to bank balance, $28,000.

The current working capital position of Marley Wholesale, according to financial statements as of June 30, is as follows:

Cash in bank...	$ 20,000
Receivables (net of allowance for doubtful accounts)	160,000
Merchandise inventory..	90,000
Total current assets	$270,000
Accounts payable (including accrued operating expenses)	150,000
Working capital..	$120,000

The bank loan officer asks Marley to prepare a forecast of his cash receipts and cash payments for the next three months to demonstrate that the loan can be repaid at the end of September.

Marley has made the following estimates, which are to be used in preparing a three-month cash budget: Sales (all on open account) for July, $300,000; August, $360,000; September, $270,000; and October, $200,000. Past experience indicates that 80% of the receivables generated in any month will be collected in the month following the sale, 19% in the second month following the sale, and 1% will prove uncollectible. Marley expects to collect $120,000 of the June 30 receivables in July, and the remaining $40,000 in August.

Cost of goods sold has averaged consistently about 65% of sales. Operating expenses are budgeted at $36,000 per month plus 8% of sales. With the exception of $4,400 per month depreciation expense, all operating expenses and purchases are on open account and are paid in the month following their incurrence.

Merchandise inventory at the end of each month should be sufficient to cover the following month's sales.

INSTRUCTIONS

a Prepare a monthly cash budget showing estimated cash receipts and cash payments for July, August, and September, and the cash balance at the end of each month. Supporting schedules should be prepared for estimated collections on receivables, estimated merchandise purchases, and estimated payments for operating expenses and of accounts payable for merchandise purchases.

b On the basis of this cash forecast, write a brief report to Marley explaining whether he will be able to repay the $200,000 bank loan at the end of September.

PROBLEM 25B-5
Using Standard Costs

Canadian Hardwood Products uses standard costs in a process cost system. At the end of the current month, the following information is prepared by the company's cost accountant:

	Direct Materials	Direct Labour	Manufacturing Overhead
Actual costs incurred.............................	$96,000	$82,500	$123,240
Standard costs	90,000	84,000	115,500
Materials price variance (favourable)	2,400		
Materials quantity variance (unfavourable)..........	8,400		
Labour rate variance (favourable)		3,000	
Labour efficiency variance (unfavourable)		1,500	
Overhead spending variance (unfavourable)			3,240
Overhead volume variance (unfavourable)			4,500

The total standard cost per unit of finished product is $30. During the current month, 9,000 units were completed and transferred to the finished goods inventory and 8,800 units were sold. The inventory of work in process at the end of the month consists of 1,000 units that are 65% completed. There was no inventory in process at the beginning of the month.

INSTRUCTIONS

a Prepare journal entries to record all variances and the costs incurred (at standard) in the Work in Process account. Prepare separate compound entries for (1) direct materials, (2) direct labour, and (3) manufacturing overhead.

b Prepare journal entries to record (1) the transfer of units finished to the Finished Goods Inventory account and (2) the cost of goods sold (at standard) for the month.

c Assuming that the company operated at 90% of its normal capacity during the current month, what is the amount of the fixed manufacturing overhead per month?

PROBLEM 25B-6
Computing and Recording Cost Variances

The accountants for Polyglaze, Inc., have developed the following information regarding the standard cost and the actual cost of a product manufactured in June:

	Standard Cost	Actual Cost
Direct materials:		
Standard: 10 grams at $0.15 per gram	$1.50	
Actual: 11 grams at $0.16 per gram		$1.76
Direct labour:		
Standard: .50 hours at $10.00 per hour	5.00	
Actual: .45 hours at $10.40 per hour		4.68
Manufacturing overhead:		
Standard: $5,000 fixed cost and $5,000 variable cost for 10,000 units normal monthly volume	1.00	
Actual: $5,000 fixed cost and $4,600 variable cost for 8,000 units actually produced in June		1.20
Total unit cost	$7.50	$7.64

INSTRUCTIONS

a Compute the materials price variance and the materials quantity variance, indicating whether each is favourable or unfavourable. Prepare the journal entry to record the cost of direct materials used during June in the Work in Process account (at standard).

b Compute the labour rate variance and the labour efficiency variance, indicating whether each is favourable or unfavourable. Prepare the journal entry to record the cost of direct labour used during June in the Work in Process account (at standard).

c Compute the overhead spending variance and the overhead volume variance, indicating whether each is favourable or unfavourable. Prepare the journal entry to assign overhead cost to production in June.

ANALYTICAL AND DECISION PROBLEMS AND CASES

A&D 25-1
It's Not My Fault

Cabinets, Cabinets, Inc., is a large manufacturer of modular kitchen cabinets, sold primarily to builders and developers. The company uses standard costs in a responsibility accounting system. Standard production costs have been developed for each type of cabinet; these costs, and any cost variances, are charged to the production department. A budget also has been developed for the sales department. The sales department is credited with the gross profit (measured at standard costs) and is charged with selling expenses and any variations between budgeted and actual selling expenses.

In early April, the manager of the sales department asked the production department to fill a "rush" order of kitchen cabinets for a tract of 120 homes. The sales manager stated that the entire order must be completed by May 31. The manager of the production department argued that an order of this size would take 12 weeks to produce. The sales manager answered, "The customer needs it on May 31, or we don't get the business. Do you want to be responsible for our losing a customer who makes orders of this size?"

Of course, the production manager did not want to take that responsibility. Therefore, he gave in and processed the rush order by having production personnel work overtime through April and May. As a result of the overtime, the performance reports for the production department in those months showed large, unfavourable labour rate variances. The production manager, who in the past had prided himself on "coming in under budget," now has very ill feelings toward the sales manager. He also has stated that the production department will never again accept a "rush" order.

INSTRUCTIONS

a Identify any problem that you see in the company's standard cost system or in the manner in which cost variances are assigned to the responsible managers.

b Make recommendations for changing the cost accounting system to reduce or eliminate any problems that you have identified.

**A&D 25-2
Determination
and Use of
Standard Costs**

Armstrong Chemical began operations in January. The company manufactures an acrylic floor wax called Tough-Coat. The following standard cost estimates were developed several months before the company began operations, based upon an estimated production of 1,000,000 units:

Direct material X-1 (one gram)	$1.00
Direct material X-2 (one kilogram)	.50
Direct labour	.80
Manufacturing overhead ($1,400,000 ÷ 1,000,000 units)	1.40
Total estimated standard cost per unit	$3.70

During the year, 1,000,000 units of Tough-Coat were actually produced and 900,000 units were sold. Actual costs incurred during the year were:

Direct material X-1 purchased, 1,200,000 grams @ $0.70	$ 840,000
Direct material X-2 purchased, 1,150,000 kilograms @ $0.50	575,000
Direct labour	880,000
Manufacturing overhead	1,400,000
Total production cost incurred during the year	$3,695,000

The company's inventories at the end of the year consisted of the following, with the Finished Goods inventory stated at standard cost:

Direct materials:		
Material X-1, 200,000 grams @ $0.70	$140,000	
Material X-2, 100,000 kilograms @ $0.50	50,000	$190,000
Finished Goods:		
Tough-Coat, 100,000 units @ $3.70 standard cost		370,000
Total inventory at December 31		$560,000

The independent public accountant who has been engaged to audit the company's financial statements wants to adjust the valuation of Finished Goods inventory to "a revised standard cost" that would take into account the favourable price variance on direct material X-1 and the 10% wage increase early in the year. (An unfavourable quantity variance on material X-2 was caused by spoilage in production; the public accountant feels no adjustment to the standard should be made for this type of item.)

The president of the company objects on the following grounds: "Such a revision is not necessary because the cost of direct material X-1 already shows signs of going up and the wage increase was not warranted because the productivity of workers did not increase one bit. Furthermore, if we revise our inventory figure of $560,000, our operating income will be reduced from the current level of $50,000." You are called in by the president to help resolve the controversy.

INSTRUCTIONS

a Do you agree with the president that revision of the $3.70 standard cost figure is not necessary?

b Assume that you conclude that the standards for this first year of operations should be revised. Compute a "revised standard cost per unit" and determine the value to be assigned to the ending inventory of finished units using this revised standard cost.

c What effect would this revaluation of Finished Goods inventory have upon the company's operating income?

d Using the *original* standards, compute the following:

1 Materials price variance and quantity variance for material X-1

2 Materials price variance and quantity variance for material X-2

3 Total direct labour variance (do not separate into rate variance and usage variance.)

4 Total manufacturing overhead variance

26 Relevant Information, Incremental Analysis, and Capital Budgeting

In this chapter, we discuss several analytical techniques that aid managers in making a variety of business decisions. First, we explain the nature of "relevant" information and show how incremental analysis is used to identify and evaluate this information. Emphasis is given to the relevance of opportunity costs and to the irrelevance of sunk costs.

Our second major topic is capital budgeting—the process of planning and evaluating proposals for investments in plant assets. We illustrate and explain the widely used capital budgeting techniques of payback period, return on average investment, and discounting future cash flows.

We also emphasize the need for managers to be aware of (1) nonfinancial considerations, (2) the long-run implications of their actions, and (3) the possible existence of additional, more advantageous courses of action.

Learning Objectives

After studying this chapter you should be able to:

1 *Identify the financial information relevant to a particular business decision.*

2 *Use incremental analysis to evaluate alternative courses of action.*

3 *Discuss the relevance of opportunity costs, sunk costs, and out-of-pocket costs in making business decisions.*

4 *Determine the effect upon operating income of discontinuing a product line.*

5 *Explore a decision: be aware of the nonfinancial considerations, and creatively search for a better course of action.*

6 *Evaluate capital budgeting proposals using (a) the payback period, (b) return on average investment, and (c) discounted future cash flows.*

THE CONCEPT OF RELEVANT INFORMATION

OBJECTIVE 1
Identify the
financial
information
relevant to a
particular
business
decision.

Many types of information may be relevant to a given business decision. For example, information as to the number of jobs to be created or the expected effect of a decision upon the environment or upon public opinion may be quite relevant. Our discussion, however, will be limited to relevant *financial* information—namely, costs and revenue.

All business decisions involve a choice among alternative courses of action. The only information relevant to a decision is that information *which varies among the alternative courses of action being considered.* Costs, revenue, or other factors that *do not vary* among alternative courses of action *are not relevant* to the decision.

To illustrate the concept of relevant information, assume that the sawmill of Sierra Lumber is closed because of a labour strike expected to last for several months. During the strike, Sierra Lumber is incurring costs at the mill of $15,000 per week. (These costs include depreciation, interest expense, and salaries to nonstriking employees.) Assume also that a film company has offered to rent the mill for one week at a price of $10,000 in order to shoot scenes for a new version of the movie, *Gone with the Wind*. If the mill is rented to the film company, Sierra's management estimates that clean-up costs will amount to approximately $2,000 after shooting is completed. Based solely upon this information, would it be profitable to rent the closed sawmill to the film company?

If the mill is rented to the film company, the profitability of the mill during that week may be measured as follows:

Revenue		$10,000
Costs and expenses:		
Weekly sawmill expenses	$15,000	
Clean-up cost	2,000	17,000
Operating income (loss)		$ (7,000)

However, not all the information in this analysis is *relevant* to the decision at hand. The $15,000 in weekly sawmill expenses will continue *whether or not* the mill is rented to the film company.

OBJECTIVE 2
Use incre-
mental
analysis to
evaluate al-
ternative
courses of
action.

The relevant factors in this decision are the *differences* between the costs incurred and revenue earned under the alternative courses of action (renting or not renting.) These differences are often called the *incremental* costs and revenue. An incremental analysis of the Sierra Lumber decision is shown as follows:

	Reject Offer	Accept Offer	Incremental Analysis
Revenue	$ 0	$10,000	$10,000
Costs and expenses:			
Weekly sawmill expenses	(15,000)	(15,000)	
Estimated clean-up costs	0	(2,000)	(2,000)
Operating income (loss)	$(15,000)	$ (7,000)	$ 8,000

The incremental analysis shows that accepting the film company's offer results in $10,000 of incremental revenue, but only $2,000 in incremental costs. Thus, renting the sawmill to the company will benefit Sierra by reducing its operating loss for the week by $8,000.

Accepting Special Orders

A more commonplace example of the need to identify relevant information is the decision of whether to accept an order for an additional volume of business at special terms.

To illustrate, assume that one product of Zing Golf Products is golf balls. The company has the capacity to produce 2 million golf balls per month, but actually manufactures only 800,000 balls per month, as this is all that it is able to sell. The balls normally sell for **$1.25** apiece; the cost of manufacturing 800,000 balls in a month amounts to $480,000, or **$0.60** per ball, as shown below:

Manufacturing costs:	
Variable ($0.20 per ball × 800,000 balls).....................................	$160,000
Fixed	320,000
Total cost of manufacturing 800,000 balls per month......................	$480,000
Average manufacturing cost per ball ($480,000 ÷ 800,000 balls)................	$0.60

Now assume that Zing Golf Products receives an offer from a foreign company to purchase 500,000 "private label" golf balls per month. These balls will be imprinted with the name of the foreign company, not with Zing's name. In fact, golfers who purchase the balls will never know that they were manufactured by Zing. These balls will be sold only in the foreign country, and will not affect Zing's regular sales to its own customers. However, the foreign country offers to pay Zing only **$250,000** (or 50 cents per ball) for this special order. Would it be profitable for Zing to accept this order?

At first glance, it appears unprofitable for Zing to accept this special order. Not only is the sales price of $0.50 per ball much less than the regular sales price, it is even less than Zing's $0.60 average per-unit cost of manufacturing golf balls. Let us look, however, at the incremental monthly revenue and manufacturing costs that should result from accepting this special order:

		Production Level	
	Normal (800,000 Balls)	**With Special Order (1,300,000 Balls)**	**Incremental Analysis**
Sales:			
Regular sales @ $1.25	$1,000,000	$1,000,000	$ –0–
Special order......................		250,000	250,000
Manufacturing costs:			
Variable ($0.20 per ball)............	(160,000)	(260,000)	(100,000)
Fixed manufacturing costs per month	(320,000)	(320,000)	–0–
Gross profit on golf ball sales	$ 520,000	$ 670,000	$150,000

A special order is profitable if incremental revenue exceeds incremental costs

This analysis shows that accepting the special order will generate incremental revenue of $250,000 and incremental costs of only $100,000. Therefore, accepting the special order will *increase* Zing's monthly gross profit on golf ball sales *by $150,000.*

The relevant factors in this type of decision are the incremental revenue that will be earned and the additional (incremental) costs that will be incurred by accepting the special order. The only incremental costs of filling the special order are the related *variable* manufacturing costs; accepting the order will *not* increase fixed manufacturing costs. Thus, the $0.60 "average manufacturing cost," which includes fixed costs per unit, is *not relevant* to the decision.[1]

In evaluating the merits of a special order such as the one received by Zing, managers should consider the effect that filling the order might have upon the company's regular sales volume and sales prices. Obviously, it would not be wise for Zing to sell golf balls at 50 cents apiece to a domestic company that might then try to sell the balls to Zing's regular customers for less than Zing's regular sales price ($1.25 per ball). Management should also consider how Zing's large regular customers might react if "word gets out" about Zing accepting this special order. Might these customers also demand the $0.50 per-ball price?

In summary, incremental analysis is a useful tool for evaluating the effects of expected short-term changes in revenue and in costs. Managers should always be alert, however, to the long-run implications of their actions.

Make or Buy Decisions

In many manufacturing operations, a company must decide whether (1) to produce a certain component part required in the assembly of its finished products or (2) to buy the component part from outside suppliers. If the company is currently producing a component part that could be purchased at a lower cost from outsiders, profits *may* be increased by a decision to buy the part and utilize the company's own manufacturing resources for other purposes.

For example, if a company can buy for $5 per unit a part that costs the company $6 per unit to produce, the choice seems to be clearly in favour of buying. But the astute reader will quickly raise the question, "What is included in the cost of $6 per unit?" Assume that the $6 unit cost of producing a normal required volume of 10,000 units per month was determined as follows:

Manufacturing costs:	
Direct materials	$ 8,000
Direct labour	12,500
Variable overhead	10,000
Fixed overhead per month	29,500
Total cost of manufacturing 10,000 units per month........................	$60,000
Average manufacturing cost per unit ($60,000 ÷ 10,000 units)	$6

[1] In our discussion, we evaluate only the *profitability* of accepting this order. Some countries have "antidumping" laws that legally prohibit a foreign company from selling its products in that country at a price below the average "full" manufacturing cost per unit. Zing should, of course, consider the legal as well as economic implications of accepting this order.

A review of operations indicates that if the production of this part were discontinued, all the cost of direct materials and direct labour plus $9,000 of variable overhead would be eliminated. In addition, $2,500 of the fixed overhead would be eliminated. These, then, are the **relevant costs** in producing the 10,000 units of the component part, and we can summarize them as follows:

Is it cheaper to make or to buy?

Manufacturing costs for 10,000 units:	Make the Part	Buy the Part	Incremental Analysis
Direct materials	$ 8,000		$ 8,000
Direct labour	12,500		12,500
Variable overhead	10,000	$ 1,000	9,000
Fixed overhead..................................	29,500	27,000	2,500
Purchase price of part, $5 per unit		50,000	(50,000)
Total cost to make or buy part..................	$60,000	$78,000	$(18,000)

Our analysis shows that making the part will cost $60,000 per month, while buying the part will cost $78,000. Thus, the company will save $18,000 per month by continuing to make the part.

In our example, we assumed that only part ($9,000) of the variable overhead incurred in producing the part would be eliminated if the part were purchased. We also assumed that $2,500 of the fixed overhead could be eliminated if the part were purchased. The purpose of these assumptions was to show that not all variable costs are incremental and that some fixed costs may be incremental in a given situation.

Opportunity Costs

OBJECTIVE 3 Discuss the relevance of opportunity costs, sunk costs, and out-of-pocket costs in making business decisions.

At this stage of our discussion, it is appropriate to introduce the topic of opportunity costs. An **opportunity cost** is the benefit that could have been obtained **by following another course of action.** For example, assume that you pass up a summer job that pays $2,400 in order to attend summer school. The $2,400 may be viewed as an opportunity cost of attending summer school.

Opportunity costs are **not recorded** in the accounting records, but they are an important factor in many business decisions. Ignoring opportunity costs is a common source of error in cost analyses. In our preceding example, we determined that the company could save $18,000 per month by continuing to manufacture a particular part, rather than buying it from an outside supplier. Assume, however, that the production facilities used to make the part could instead be used to manufacture a product that would increase the company's profitability by $25,000 per month. Obviously, the company should not forgo a $25,000 profit in order to save $18,000. When this $25,000 **opportunity cost** is considered, it becomes evident that the company should buy the part and use its productive facilities to produce the more profitable product.

Sunk Costs versus Out-of-Pocket Costs

The only costs relevant to a decision are those costs that vary if one course of action is taken rather than another. A **sunk cost** is one that has **al-**

ready been incurred by past actions. Sunk costs are *not relevant* to decisions because they *cannot be changed* regardless of what decision is made. The term *out-of-pocket cost* is often used to describe costs that have *not yet* been incurred and *may vary* among the alternative courses of action. Out-of-pocket costs, therefore, are relevant in making decisions.

Scrap or Rebuild Defective Units

To illustrate the irrelevance of sunk costs, assume that 500 television sets that cost $80,000 to manufacture are found to be defective and management must decide what to do with them. These sets may be sold "as is" for $30,000 or they can be rebuilt and placed in good condition at an additional out-of-pocket cost of $60,000. If the sets are rebuilt, they can be sold for the regular price of $100,000. Should the sets be sold "as is" or rebuilt?

Regardless of whether the sets are sold or rebuilt, the $80,000 sunk cost has already been incurred. The relevant considerations in the decision to sell the sets in their present condition or to rebuild are the *incremental revenue* and the *incremental cost.* By rebuilding the sets, the company will realize $70,000 more revenue than if the sets are sold "as is." The incremental cost necessary to obtain this incremental revenue is the $60,000 cost of rebuilding the sets. Thus, the company will be $10,000 better off ($70,000 − $60,000) if it rebuilds the sets.

Whether to Discontinue an Unprofitable Product Line

OBJECTIVE 4 Determine the effect upon operating income of discontinuing a product line.

Management often must decide whether a company's overall profitability can be improved by discontinuing one or more product lines. The concepts of incremental analysis and of opportunity costs play important roles in such decisions.

To illustrate, assume that Auto Sound Co. manufactures three products: an economy model car radio, a deluxe car radio that includes a tape deck, and speakers for automobile sound systems. In recent years, increased competition has forced the company to reduce the sales price of its deluxe radios to the point that this product line now has a negative segment margin. A partial income statement for the current month, segmented by product lines, appears below:

AUTO SOUND CO.
Partial Income Statement, Segmented by Product Line
For the Current Month

		Products		
	Auto Sound Co.	Economy Radios	Deluxe Radios	Speakers
Sales	$600,000	$300,000	$100,000	$200,000
Variable costs	320,000	170,000	70,000	80,000
Contribution margins	$280,000	$130,000	$ 30,000	$120,000
Fixed costs traceable to product lines	100,000	30,000	40,000	30,000
Product segment margins	$180,000	$100,000	$ (10,000)	$ 90,000
Common fixed costs	80,000			
Income from operations	$100,000			

Should the deluxe radio be discontinued?

Management is considering whether or not to discontinue deluxe radios. As discussed in Chapter 24, the revenue, variable costs, and fixed costs traceable to a business segment are likely to disappear if that segment is discontinued. Thus, discontinuing the deluxe radio should *eliminate* the $10,000 negative monthly segment margin of that product line. At first glance, we might assume that Auto Sound's monthly operating income should then increase by this amount. However, several other factors must be considered. Two such factors are:

1 How will discontinuing the sale of deluxe radios affect sales of the company's *other products?*

2 What *alternative use* might be made of the production facilities now used in manufacturing deluxe radios?

Competing Products and Complementary Products Many companies offer customers several products that compete directly with one another. For example, Auto Sound's economy model and deluxe model radios are competing products—most customers will buy one or the other, but not both. If the deluxe radio is discontinued, it is logical to expect some increase in the sales of economy radios. Some customers, no longer able to buy the deluxe model, will instead purchase the economy model. Assume that management estimates that sales of the economy radio will *increase by 5%* if the deluxe radio is discontinued.

Companies often also sell complementary products. Complementary products are those for which sales of one may contribute to sales of the other. Assume, for example, that many buyers of Auto Sound Co.'s deluxe radios also buy a set of the company's speakers. Therefore, discontinuing the sale of deluxe radios can be expected to reduce sales of speakers. Management estimates that speaker sales will *decline by 20%* if the deluxe radio is discontinued.

Incremental Analysis To illustrate the effects of expected changes in the sales of other products, we will temporarily assume that no alternative use will be made of the facilities now used in manufacturing deluxe radios. In this case, an incremental analysis of the expected effects of discontinuing the deluxe radio product line is shown below:

Increases in monthly operating income expected from discontinuing the deluxe radio product line:

Elimination of negative monthly segment margin of deluxe radio product line	$10,000
Additional contribution margin from expected 5% increase in sales of economy radios ($130,000 × 5%)	6,500
Total expected increases in operating income	$16,500

Decreases in monthly operating income expected from discontinuing deluxe radio product line:

Decrease in contribution margin from expected 20% decrease in speaker sales ($120,000 × 20%)	(24,000)
Estimated increase (decrease) in monthly operating income if deluxe radio product line is discontinued	$(7,500)

This analysis indicates that although the deluxe radio line has a negative segment margin, discontinuing this product would cause the company's monthly operating income to *decrease* by $7,500. The reason that operating income would decline is not the disappearance of the revenue and costs relating to the deluxe radio segment of the business, but rather the expected loss in contribution margin from sales of speakers—a highly profitable complementary product.

The loss in contribution margin from speaker sales is an *opportunity cost* of discontinuing the deluxe radio line. However, continuing to produce the deluxe radios also may involve an opportunity cost—namely the segment margin of a more profitable product line that might be produced in place of deluxe radios.

Alternative Use of the Facilities   Let us now assume that if the deluxe radio line is discontinued Auto Sound Co. will use the related production facilities to manufacture car phones. Management estimates that the manufacture and sale of car phones will produce a positive segment margin of $50,000 per month. Sales of car phones are not expected to have any effect upon sales of economy radios or speakers. Therefore, the effects of discontinuing the deluxe radios upon these two product lines remains the same as in our preceding analysis. An incremental analysis of manufacturing car phones instead of deluxe car radios follows:

Increases in monthly operating income expected from manufacturing
car phones instead of deluxe radios:

Elimination of negative monthly segment margin of deluxe radio product line	*$10,000*
Expected monthly segment margin from new car phone product line	*50,000*
Additional contribution margin from expected 5% increase in sales of economy radios ($130,000 × 5%)	*6,500*
Total expected increases in operating income	*$66,500*

Decreases in monthly operating income expected from manufacturing
car phones instead of deluxe radios:

Decrease in contribution margin from expected 20% decline in speaker sales ($120,000 × 20%)	*(24,000)*
Estimated increase in operating income if deluxe radio product line is discontinued..	*$42,500*

This analysis indicates that operating income will *increase* by $42,500 per month if the company uses its production facilities to manufacture car phones instead of deluxe radios.

Other Factors to Be Considered   There are, of course, other factors to consider in a decision of whether to discontinue a product line. Perhaps a company wants to avoid laying-off employees, especially if these workers may be needed in the near future to produce new products. Perhaps a company wants to maintain a reputation for offering its customers a "full line" of products, or "state-of-the-art" products, even if it cannot earn a profit from every product line. Perhaps an "unprofitable" product line is an effective "loss leader," which attracts customers who also buy the compa-

OBJECTIVE 5
*Explore a
decision: be
aware of the
nonfinancial
considera-
tions, and
creatively
search for a
better course
of action.*

ny's profitable products. (Auto Sound's deluxe radio is an effective "loss leader," because sales of this product generate enough contribution margin from additional sales of speakers to more than cover the losses of the deluxe radio segment.)

Looking for Better Alternatives Incremental analysis is an excellent tool for evaluating alternative courses of action. However, managers should not automatically follow the first course of action that holds a promise of increased profitability. Rather, managers and accountants should always be alert to the possibility of even more satisfactory alternatives. Often, a careful review of the incremental analysis of one possible decision will offer clues to additional, more profitable alternatives.

Consider, for example, our incremental analysis on the preceding page. The principal benefit to be derived from discontinuing the deluxe radio product line is that the company's production facilities can be used more profitably in manufacturing car phones. The one drawback in discontinuing the deluxe radios is the expected loss in contribution margin from a decline in speaker sales. These facts suggest an alternative course of action: perhaps Auto Sound should continue to sell deluxe radios, but should ***buy*** these radios from an outside supplier ***instead of manufacturing them.*** The company could then use its production facilities to manufacture car phones, while continuing to sell deluxe radios and speakers at the current sales level. The effects of this alternative also may be evaluated through the technique of incremental analysis.

CAPITAL BUDGETING

OBJECTIVE 6
*Evaluate
capital bud-
geting pro-
posals using
(a) the pay-
back period,
(b) return
on average
investment,
and (c) dis-
counted fu-
ture cash
flows.*

In terms of dollar amounts, some of the most significant decisions made by management involve expenditures to acquire plant assets. The process of planning and evaluating proposals for investment in plant assets is called ***capital budgeting.*** Capital budgeting decisions are complicated by the fact that the decision must be made from estimates of future operating results, which by their nature involve a considerable degree of uncertainty. Yet these decisions are crucial to the long-run financial health of a business enterprise. Not only are large amounts of money committed for long periods of time, but many capital budgeting decisions are difficult or impossible to reverse once the funds have been committed and the project has begun. Thus, companies may benefit from good capital budgeting decisions and suffer from poor ones for many years.

Many nonfinancial factors are considered in making capital budgeting decisions. For example, many companies give high priority to creating new jobs and avoiding layoffs. However, it is also essential that investments in plant assets earn a satisfactory return on the funds invested. Without this return, investors will not be willing to make funds available to finance the project and the company will not be able to generate sufficient funds for future investment projects.

Capital budgeting is a broad field, involving many sophisticated techniques for evaluating the financial and nonfinancial considerations. We shall limit our discussion in this area to three of the most common techniques of evaluating investment opportunities: payback period, return on average investment, and discounted cash flow analysis.

To illustrate these techniques, let us assume that Tanner Corporation is considering several alternative investments, including the purchase of equipment to produce a new product. The equipment costs $450,000, has a 10-year service life, and has an estimated salvage value of $50,000. Tanner Corporation estimates that production and sale of the new product will increase the company's net income by $50,000 per year, computed as follows:

Estimated sales of new product...		$400,000
Deduct estimated expenses:		
Depreciation on new equipment [($450,000 – $50,000) ÷ 10 years] .	$ 40,000	
Manufacturing costs other than depreciation	220,000	
Additional selling and general expenses.........................	60,000	320,000
Estimated increase in before-tax income		$ 80,000
Less: Additional income taxes ($37\frac{1}{2}$%)...		30,000
Estimated increase in net income		$ 50,000

Most capital budgeting techniques involve analysis of the estimated annual net cash flows pertaining to the investment. Annual net cash flow is the excess of cash receipts over cash payments in a given year. In our example, assume that all revenue is received in cash and all expenses other than depreciation are paid in cash. Tanner Corporation should expect an annual **net cash flow of $90,000** from sales of the new product ($400,000 − $220,000 − $60,000 − $30,000). Note that annual net cash flow exceeds estimated net income ($50,000) by the amount of the depreciation expense ($40,000). This is because none of the cash received from revenue is paid out for depreciation expense. (Other differences which may exist between net income and net cash flow were discussed in Chapter 19.)

Payback Period

The **payback period** is the length of time necessary to recover the entire cost of an investment from the resulting annual net cash flow. In our example, the payback period is computed as follows:

$$\frac{\textbf{Amount to Be Invested}}{\textbf{Estimated Annual Net Cash Flow}} = \frac{\$450,000}{\$90,000} = \textbf{5 years}$$

In selecting among alternative investment opportunities, a short payback period is considered desirable because the sooner the amount of the investment is recovered, the sooner the funds may be put to other use. A short payback period also reduces the risk that changes in economic conditions will prevent full recovery of the investment. Before an investment can be considered profitable, the life of the investment must exceed the payback period. However, the payback period ignores the total life and, therefore, the total profitability of the investment. For this reason, the payback period should never be the only factor considered in a major capital budgeting decision.

Return on Average Investment

The **return on investment (ROI)** is the average annual net income from an investment expressed as a percentage of the **average** amount invested. Tanner Corporation will have to invest $450,000 in the new equipment, but each year depreciation will reduce the carrying value of this asset by $40,000. Since the annual cash flow will exceed net income by this amount, we may view depreciation expense as providing for the recovery of the amount originally invested. Thus, the amount invested in the equipment at any given time is represented by the carrying value (cost less accumulated depreciation) of the asset.

When straight-line depreciation is used, the carrying value of an asset decreases uniformly over the asset's life. Thus, the average carrying value is equal to an amount halfway between the asset's original cost and its salvage value. (When the expected salvage value is zero, the average investment is simply one-half of the original investment.) Mathematically, the average amount invested over the life of an asset may be determined as follows:

$$\text{Average Investment} = \frac{\text{Original Cost} + \text{Salvage Value}}{2}$$

Thus, Tanner Corporation will have an average investment in the new equipment of ($450,000 + $50,000) ÷ 2, or $250,000. We may compute the expected rate of return on this average investment as follows:

$$\frac{\text{Average Estimated Net Income}}{\text{Average Investment}} = \frac{\$50,000}{\$250,000} = 20\%$$

In deciding whether 20% is a satisfactory rate of return, Tanner Corporation should consider such factors as the rate of return available from alternative investment opportunities, the risk involved in actually realizing the expected rate of return, the corporation's cost of capital, and the nonfinancial factors relating to the investment. In comparing alternative investment opportunities, management usually prefers the investment with the **lowest risk, highest rate of return,** and **shortest payback period.** Of course, the same investment is seldom superior to all others in every respect. Thus, managers must consider many subjective factors in making their decisions.

A weakness in the concept of return on average investment is the failure to consider the **timing** of the future cash flows. Computing the average annual net income, for example, ignores the question of whether the cash receipts will occur early or late in the life of the investment. Also, computing the average investment in the equipment fails to consider whether the purchase price of the equipment must be paid in advance or in instalments stretching over a period of years. A technique that does take into account the timing of cash flows is called **discounting** future cash flows.

Discounting Future Cash Flows

As explained in Chapter 16, the present value of a future cash flow is the amount that a knowledgeable investor would pay today for the right to receive that future amount. The exact amount of the present value depends upon (1) the amount of the future payment, (2) the length of time until the future amount will be received, and (3) the rate of return required by the investor. ***Discounting*** is the process of determining the present value of cash flows.

The use of present value tables to discount future cash flows is demonstrated in Appendix A, entitled Applications of Present Value, located at the end of Chapter 16. (Readers who are not familiar with the concept of present value and with the use of present value tables should read this appendix before continuing with this chapter.) For your convenience, the two present value tables presented in the appendix are repeated below and on the following page.

Table 1 shows the present value of a single lump-sum payment of $1 to be received *n* periods (years) in the future. ***Table 2*** shows the present value of a $1 annuity—that is, $1 to be received each year for *n* consecutive years. For illustrative purposes, both tables have been kept short. They include only selected discount rates and extend for a limited number of periods. However, the tables contain the appropriate rates and periods for all problem material in this chapter.

The discount rate may be viewed as the investor's required rate of return. The present value of the future cash flows is the maximum amount that the investor may pay for the investment and still expect to earn the required rate of return. Therefore, an investment is considered desirable when its cost is less than the present value of the expected future cash flows. Conversely, an investment is undesirable when its cost is greater than the present value of expected future cash flows.

TABLE 1
Present Values of $1 Due in *n* Periods*

Number of Periods (n)	Discount Rate								
	1%	1½%	5%	6%	8%	10%	12%	15%	20%
1	.990	.985	.952	.943	.926	.909	.893	.870	.833
2	.980	.971	.907	.890	.857	.826	.797	.756	.694
3	.971	.956	.864	.840	.794	.751	.712	.658	.579
4	.961	.942	.823	.792	.735	.683	.636	.572	.482
5	.951	.928	.784	.747	.681	.621	.567	.497	.402
6	.942	.915	.746	.705	.630	.564	.507	.432	.335
7	.933	.901	.711	.665	.583	.513	.452	.376	.279
8	.923	.888	.677	.627	.540	.467	.404	.327	.233
9	.914	.875	.645	.592	.510	.424	.361	.284	.194
10	.905	.862	.614	.558	.463	.386	.322	.247	.162
20	.820	.742	.377	.312	.215	.149	.104	.061	.026
24	.788	.700	.310	.247	.158	.102	.066	.035	.013
36	.699	.585	.173	.123	.063	.032	.017	.007	.001

* The present value of $1 is computed by the formula $p = 1/(1 + i)^n$, where p is the present value of $1, i is the discount rate, and n is the number of periods until the future cash flow will occur. Amounts in this table have been rounded to three decimal places and are shown for a limited number of periods and discount rates. Many calculators are programmed to use this formula and can compute present values when the future amount is entered along with values for i and n.

TABLE 2
Present Values of $1 to Be Received Periodically for *n* Periods

Number of Periods (n)	Discount Rate								
	1%	1½%	5%	6%	8%	10%	12%	15%	20%
1	0.990	0.985	0.952	0.943	0.926	0.909	0.893	0.870	0.833
2	1.970	1.956	1.859	1.833	1.783	1.736	1.690	1.626	1.528
3	2.941	2.912	2.723	2.673	2.577	2.487	2.402	2.283	2.106
4	3.902	3.854	3.546	3.465	3.312	3.170	3.037	2.855	2.589
5	4.853	4.783	4.329	4.212	3.993	3.791	3.605	3.352	2.991
6	5.795	5.697	5.076	4.917	4.623	4.355	4.111	3.784	3.326
7	6.728	6.598	5.786	5.582	5.206	4.868	4.564	4.160	3.605
8	7.652	7.486	6.463	6.210	5.747	5.335	4.968	4.487	3.837
9	8.566	8.361	7.108	6.802	6.247	5.759	5.328	4.772	4.031
10	9.471	9.222	7.722	7.360	6.710	6.145	5.650	5.019	4.192
20	18.046	17.169	12.462	11.470	9.818	8.514	7.469	6.259	4.870
24	21.243	20.030	13.799	12.550	10.529	8.985	7.784	6.434	4.937
36	30.108	27.661	16.547	14.621	11.717	9.677	8.192	6.623	4.993

The higher the discount rate being used, the lower will be the resulting present value. Therefore the investor will be interested in the investment only at a lower price. The "appropriate" discount rate for determining the present value of a specific investment depends upon the nature of that investment, the alternative investment opportunities available, and the investor's cost of capital.

Let us now apply the concept of discounting cash flows to our continuing example of the Tanner Corporation. We shall assume that Tanner Corporation requires a 15% annual rate of return on investments in new plant assets. The $450,000 investment in equipment is expected to produce annual net cash flows of $90,000 for 10 years. *Table 2* indicates that the present value of $1 to be received annually for 10 years, discounted at an annual rate of 15%, is *5.019.* Therefore, the present value of $90,000 received annually for 10 years is $90,000 × 5.019 or *$451,710.*

In addition to the annual cash flows, Tanner Corporation expects to receive $50,000 in salvage value for the equipment at the end of the tenth year. Referring to *Table 1,* we see that the present value of $1 due in 10 years, discounted at 15% per year, is *.247.* Thus, the present value of $50,000 to be received 10 years hence is $50,000 × .247, or *$12,350.* We may now analyze the proposal to invest in the equipment as follows:

Present value of expected annual cash flows ($90,000 × 5.019)	*$451,710*
Present value of proceeds from disposal of equipment ($50,000 × .247)	*12,350*
Total present value of future cash flows	*$464,060*
Amount to be invested (payable in advance)	*450,000*
Net present value of proposed investment	*$ 14,060*

This analysis indicates that the present value of the expected net cash flows from the investment, discounted at an annual rate of 15%, amounts to $464,060. This is the maximum amount which Tanner Corporation could afford to invest in the project and still expect to earn the required 15% annual rate of return. Since the actual cost of the investment is only $450,000, Tanner Corporation can expect to earn more than 15%.

The *net present value* of the proposal is the difference between the total present value of the net cash flows and the cost of the investment. When the net present value is equal to zero, the investment provides a rate of return *exactly equal* to the rate used in discounting the cash flows. A *positive* net present value means that the investment provides a rate of return *greater than the discount rate;* a *negative* net present value means that the investment yields a return of *less* than the discount rate. Since the discount rate is usually the minimum rate of return required by the investor, proposals with a positive net present value are considered acceptable and those with a negative net present value are viewed as unacceptable.

Replacement of Old Equipment

A problem often facing management is whether it should buy new and more efficient equipment or whether it should continue to use existing equipment. Assume, for example, that Ardmore Limited is meeting increasing competition in the sale of product Q. The sales manager believes the source of the trouble is that competitors have installed more efficient equipment, which has enabled them to reduce prices. The issue raised therefore is whether Ardmore should: (1) buy new equipment at a cost of $120,000, or (2) continue using its present equipment. We will make the simplifying assumption that both the new equipment and present equipment have a remaining useful life of five years and neither will have any residual value. The new equipment will produce substantial savings in direct labour, direct materials, and manufacturing overhead costs. The company does not believe the use of new equipment will have any effect on sales volume, so the decision rests entirely on whether cost savings are possible.

The old equipment has a book value of $100,000 but can be sold for only $20,000 if it is replaced. At first glance, the resulting $80,000 loss on disposal appears to be a good reason for not replacing the old equipment. However, the cost of the old equipment is a *sunk cost* and is not relevant to the decision. If the old machinery is sold, its book value contributes to the amount of the loss; if the old machinery is retained, its book value will be recognized as expense through future charges to depreciation. Thus, this cost cannot be avoided by Ardmore regardless of which decision is made. From a present value standpoint, there is some benefit to recognizing this sunk cost as a loss in the current period inasmuch as the related tax reduction will occur this year rather than over the remaining life of the equipment.

In deciding whether to replace the old equipment, Ardmore should determine the *present value of the incremental net cash flows* resulting from replacement of the old machinery. This present value may then be compared with the cost of the new equipment to determine whether the investment will provide the required rate of return. To compute the incremental annual net cash flow from replacing the old equipment, management must consider both the annual cash savings in manufacturing costs and the difference in annual income taxes. Income taxes will differ under the alternative courses of action because of differences in (1) variable manufacturing costs and (2) annual depreciation expense.

Let us assume that the new machinery will result in a $34,000 annual cash savings in variable manufacturing costs. However, annual depreciation on the new equipment will be $24,000 ($120,000 ÷ 5 years), whereas annual depreciation on the old equipment is $20,000 ($100,000 ÷ 5 years).[2] This $4,000 increase in depreciation expense means that purchase of the new equipment will *increase* taxable income by $30,000 per year ($34,000 cost savings less $4,000 additional depreciation). Assuming a tax rate of 40%, purchase of the new equipment will increase annual income tax expense by $12,000 ($30,000 × 40%). The incremental annual *net cash flow* from owning the new machinery, therefore, amounts to *$22,000* ($34,000 cost savings less $12,000 additional income tax expense).

We shall assume that Ardmore requires a 12% return on investments in plant assets. Referring to the annuity table *(Table 2),* we see that the present value of $1 received annually for five years discounted at an annual rate of 12%, is *3.605.* Therefore, $22,000 received annually for five years, discounted at an annual rate of 12%, has a present value of *$79,310* ($22,000 × 3.605). In addition to the present value of the annual net cash flows, however, we must consider two other factors: (1) the proceeds from sale of the old equipment and (2) the tax savings resulting from the loss on disposal.

The $20,000 proceeds from sale of the old equipment will be received immediately and, therefore, have a present value of *$20,000.* The $80,000 loss on disposal results in a $32,000 reduction in income taxes payable at the end of the first year ($80,000 × 40%). The present value of $32,000 one year hence discounted at 12% is *$28,576* ($32,000 × .893), as determined from a present value table *(Table 1).*

We may now determine the net present value of the proposal to replace the old equipment with new equipment as follows:

Present value of incremental annual cash flows ($22,000 × 3.605)	$ 79,310
Present value of proceeds from sale of old equipment	20,000
Present value of tax savings from loss on disposal ($32,000 × .893)	28,576
Total present value	$127,886
Amount to be invested	120,000
Net present value	$ 7,886

Since the total present value of all future cash flows from acquiring the new equipment exceeds the cost of the investment, Ardmore should replace the old equipment with new.

---

[2]   In order to focus on the essential issues and to simplify the calculations, it is assumed that the depreciation expenses are the same for income tax purposes.

Concluding Comments

We have merely scratched the surface in discussing the possible kinds of analyses that might be prepared in making decisions. The brief treatment in this chapter, however, has been sufficient to establish the basic principles that lie behind such analyses. The most profitable course of action is determined by studying the costs and revenue that are *incremental* to the particular alternatives under consideration. The relevant information generally involves making *estimates* about the future. As a result, such information is subject to some degree of error. Of course it is important to remember that many nonfinancial factors may be brought into the decision picture after the quantitative analysis has been made.

CHAPTER REVIEW

KEY TERMS INTRODUCED OR EMPHASIZED IN CHAPTER 26

Capital budgeting   The process of planning and evaluating proposals for investments in plant assets.

Discount rate   The required rate of return used by an investor to discount future cash flows to their present value.

Discounted cash flows   The present value of expected future cash flows.

Incremental (or differential) cost   The difference between the total costs of alternative courses of action.

Incremental (or differential) revenue   The difference between the revenue amounts provided by alternative courses of action.

Net present value   The excess of the present value of the net cash flows expected from an investment over the amount to be invested. Net present value is one method of ranking alternative investment opportunities.

Opportunity cost   The benefit foregone by not pursuing an alternative course of action. Opportunity costs are not recorded in the accounting records, but are important in making many types of business decisions.

Payback period   The length of time necessary to recover the cost of an investment through the cash flows generated by that investment. Payback period is one criterion used in making capital budgeting decisions.

Present value   The amount of money today that is considered equivalent to a cash inflow or outflow expected to take place in the future. The present value of money is always less than the future amount, since money on hand today can be invested to become the equivalent of a larger amount in the future.

Relevant information   Information that should be given consideration in making a specific decision and that varies among the alternative courses of action being considered.

Return on average investment   The average annual net income from an investment expressed as a percentage of the average amount invested. Return on average investment is one method of ranking alternative investment opportunities according to their relative profitability.

Sunk cost   A cost that has irrevocably been incurred by past actions. Sunk costs are irrelevant to decisions regarding future actions.

ASSIGNMENT MATERIAL

DISCUSSION QUESTIONS

1 What is the basic characteristic of "relevant" information?

2 A company regularly sells 100,000 washing machines at an average price of $250. The average cost of producing these machines is $180. Under what circumstances might the company accept an order for 20,000 washing machines at $175 per machine?

3 The Shandl Corporation produces a large number of products. The costs per unit for one product, a fishing reel, are shown below:

Direct materials and direct labour $7.00
Variable factory overhead 4.00
Fixed factory overhead 2.00

The company recently decided to buy 10,000 fishing reels from another manufacturer for $12.50 per unit because "it was cheaper than our cost of $13.00 per unit." Evaluate the decision only on the basis of the cost data given.

4 Define *opportunity costs* and explain why they represent a common source of error in making cost analyses.

5 What is the difference between a *sunk cost* and an *out-of-pocket cost?*

6 Briefly explain the factors you would want to know before deciding to discontinue the production of a major line of products.

7 Indicate several reasons why management might decide *not* to discontinue a product line that consistently incurs a negative segment margin.

8 What is *capital budgeting?* Why are capital budgeting decisions crucial to the long-run financial health of a business enterprise?

9 A company invests $100,000 in plant assets with an estimated 20-year service life and no salvage value. These assets contribute $10,000 to annual net income when depreciation is computed on a straight-line basis. Assume that all revenue and expenses (other than depreciation) are on a cash basis. Compute the payback period and explain your computation.

10 What is the major shortcoming of using the payback period as the only criterion in making capital budgeting decisions?

11 What factors should an investor consider in appraising the adequacy of the rate of return from a specific investment proposal?

12 Discounting a future cash flow at 15% results in a lower present value than does discounting the same cash flow at 10%. Explain why.

13 What factors determine the present value of a future cash flow?

14 Discounting cash flows takes into consideration one characteristic of the earnings stream that is ignored in the computation of return on average investment. What is this characteristic and why is it important?

15 Explain why the book value of existing equipment is not relevant in deciding whether the equipment should be scrapped (without realizing any proceeds) or continued in use.

MULTIPLE CHOICE QUESTIONS

The following data relate to questions 1 and 2

One of Phoenix Computer's products is WizardCard. The company currently produces and sells 30,000 WizardCards per month, although it has the plant capacity to produce 50,000 units per month. At the 30,000 unit-per-month level of production, the per-unit cost of manufacturing WizardCards is $45, consisting of $15 in variable costs and $30 in fixed costs. Phoenix sells WizardCards to retail stores for $90 each. Computer Marketing Corp. has offered to purchase 10,000 WizardCards per month at a reduced price. Phoenix can manufacture these additional units with no change in fixed manufacturing costs.

1 In deciding whether to accept this special order from Computer Marketing Corp., Phoenix should be **least** concerned with:

   a What Computer Marketing Corp. intends to do with the WizardCards.

   b The $45 average cost of manufacturing WizardCards.

   c The opportunity cost of not accepting the order.

   d The incremental cost of manufacturing an additional 10,000 WizardCards per month.

2 Assume that Phoenix decides to accept the special order at a unit sales price that will add $400,000 per month to its operating income. The unit price of the special order will be:

   a $85   b $70   c $55   d Some other amount

3 The contribution margin ratios and monthly segment margins of three products sold by Bockus Video Game Corp. are as follows:

	Product 1	Product 2	Product 3
Contribution margin ratio	20%	40%	60%
Monthly segment margin........................	$(4,000)	$15,000	$10,000

Management is considering discontinuing product 1. This action is expected to eliminate all costs traceable to product 1, increase monthly sales of product 2 by $10,000, decrease monthly sales of product 3 by $5,000, and have no effect on common fixed costs. Based upon these facts, discontinuing product 1 should cause the company's monthly operating income to:

   a Increase by $4,000   c Decrease by $3,000

   b Increase by $9,000   d None of the above

4 Western Mfg. Ltd. is considering two capital budgeting proposals, each with a 10-year life, and each requiring an initial cash outlay of $50,000. Proposal A shows a higher return on average investment than Proposal B, but Proposal B shows the higher net present value. The most probable explanation is that:

   a Expected cash inflows tend to occur earlier in Proposal B.

   b Total expected cash inflows are greater in Proposal B.

   c The payback period is shorter in Proposal A.

   d The discounted future cash flows approach makes no provision for recovery of the original $50,000 investment.

5 Copy Centre is considering replacing its old copying machine, which has a $3,200 book value, with a new one. Discounted cash flow analysis of the proposal to acquire the new machine shows an estimated net present value of $2,800. If the new machine is acquired, the old machine will have no resale value and will be given away. The loss on disposal of the old machine:

a Is an opportunity cost of purchasing the new machine.

b Exceeds the net present value of the new machine, indicating that the new machine should not be acquired.

c Has already been deducted from future revenue in arriving at the $2,800 net present value of the new machine.

d Is a sunk cost and is not relevant to the decision at hand, except as it affects the timing of income tax payments.

EXERCISES

EXERCISE 26-1
Accounting
Terminology

Listed below are nine technical accounting terms introduced or emphasized in this chapter:

Opportunity cost	*Sunk cost*	*Out-of-pocket cost*
Net present value	*Payback period*	*Incremental analysis*
Capital budgeting	*Estimated useful life*	*Relevant information*

Each of the following statements may (or may not) describe one of these technical terms. For each statement, indicate the accounting term described, or answer "None" if the statement does not correctly describe any of the terms.

a Examination of differences between costs to be incurred and revenues to be earned under alternative courses of action.

b A cost incurred in the past that cannot be changed as a result of future actions.

c Costs and revenues that are expected to vary, depending upon the course of action decided upon.

d The benefit foregone by not pursuing an alternative course of action.

e The process of planning and evaluating proposals for investments in plant assets.

f The average annual net income from an investment expressed as a percentage of the average amount invested.

g Length of time necessary to recover the entire cost of an investment from resulting annual net cash flow.

h A cost that has not yet been incurred that will require payment and may vary among alternative courses of action.

EXERCISE 26-2
Incremental
Analysis: Accepting a Special Order

Marrion Corp. manufactures and sells 110,000 laser printers each month. The principal component part in a laser printer is the engine, and Marrion's plant has the capacity to produce 150,000 engines per month. The costs of manufacturing these printer engines (up to 150,000 engines per month) are as follows:

Variable costs per unit:	
Direct materials	*$42*
Direct labour	*19*
Variable manufacturing overhead...	*4*
Fixed costs per month:	
Fixed manufacturing overhead	*$1,430,000*

Desk-Mate Printers has offered to buy 20,000 printer engines per month from Marrion, to be used in the Desk-Mate laser printer.

INSTRUCTIONS   Compute the following:

a   The average unit cost of manufacturing each printer engine, assuming that Marrion manufactures only enough printer engines for its own laser printers.

b   The incremental unit cost of producing additional printer engines.

c   The per-unit sales price that Marrion should charge Desk-Mate in order to earn $500,000 in monthly pretax income on the sale of printer engines to Desk-Mate.

EXERCISE 26-3
Incremental Analysis: Make or Buy Decision

The cost to Smyth Company of manufacturing 10,000 units of a particular product is $230,000, including $80,000 of fixed costs and $150,000 of variable costs. The company can buy the part from an outside supplier for $18.00 per unit, but the fixed manufacturing overhead now allocated to the part will remain unchanged. Should the company buy the part or continue to manufacture it? Prepare a comparative schedule in the format illustrated in this chapter.

EXERCISE 26-4
Sunk Costs: Scrap or Rework Decision

Road Master Shocks has 20,000 units of a defective product on hand that cost $123,500 to manufacture. The company can either sell this product as scrap for $4.18 per unit or it can sell the product for $10 per unit by reworking the units and correcting the defects at a cost of $119,200. What should the company do? Prepare a schedule in support of your recommendation.

EXERCISE 26-5
Whether to Close a Department

The Wine Cellar sells wine and operates a small sandwich deli. Typical monthly operating data is shown below:

	Total	Wine Sales	Deli
Sales	$39,000	$35,000	$4,000
Variable costs (including cost of goods sold)	15,500	14,000	1,500
Contribution margin	$23,500	$21,000	$2,500
Fixed costs traceable to departments	9,000	6,000	3,000
Departmental segment margins	$14,500	$15,000	$ (500)
Common fixed costs	7,500		
Income from operations	$ 7,000		

Tim Johnson, owner of The Wine Cellar, is considering closing the deli and renting the related floor space to a film developing company for $1,200 per month. However, Johnson has read in a trade journal that without a deli, wine sales should be expected to decline by 10%. Also, the fixed costs traceable to the deli include $1,100 in monthly salary to an employee that Johnson will retain even if he closes the deli.

Prepare a schedule showing the expected effect upon monthly operating income of closing the deli and renting the related floor space. Based upon this analysis, make a recommendation as to whether or not to close the deli.

EXERCISE 26-6
Discounting Cash Flows

Using the tables in this chapter, determine the present value of the following cash flows, discounted at an annual rate of 15%:

a $10,000 to be received 20 years from today

b $15,000 to be received annually for 10 years

c $10,000 to be received annually for 5 years, with an additional $12,000 salvage value expected at the end of the fifth year.

d $30,000 to be received annually for the first 3 years, followed by $20,000 received annually for the next 2 years (total of 5 years in which cash is received)

EXERCISE 26-7
Capital
Budgeting

Bowman Corporation is considering an investment in special-purpose equipment to enable the company to obtain a four-year government contract for the manufacture of a special item. The equipment costs $300,000 and would have no salvage value when its use is discontinued at the end of the four years. Estimated annual operating results of the project are:

Revenue from contract sales...		$325,000
Expenses other than depreciation..................................	$225,000	
Depreciation (straight-line basis)....................................	75,000	300,000
Increase in net income from contract work		$ 25,000

All revenue and all expenses other than depreciation will be received or paid in cash in the same period as recognized for accounting purposes. Compute for the proposal to undertake the contract work the following:

a Payback period.

b Return on average investment.

c Net present value of the proposal to undertake contract work, discounted at an annual rate of 12%.

EXERCISE 26-8
Another Capi-
tal Budgeting
Exercise

Pack & Carry is debating whether or not to invest in new equipment to manufacture a line of high-quality luggage. The new equipment would cost $900,000, with an estimated four-year life and no salvage value. The estimated annual operating results with the new equipment are as follows:

Revenue from sales of new luggage line		$975,000
Expenses other than depreciation..................................	$675,000	
Depreciation (straight-line basis)....................................	225,000	900,000
Increase in net income from the new line.......................................		$ 75,000

All revenue from the new luggage line and all expenses (except depreciation) will be received or paid in cash in the same period as recognized for accounting purposes. You are to compute the following for the investment in the new equipment to produce the new luggage line:

a Annual cash flow.

b Payback period.

c Return on average investment.

d *Total* present value of the expected future annual cash inflows, discounted at an annual rate of 12%.

e *Net* present value of the proposed investment.

PROBLEMS

Group A

PROBLEM 26A-1
Evaluating a
Special Order

D. Lawrance designs and manufactures fashionable men's clothing. For the coming year, the company has scheduled production of 30,000 suede jackets. The budgeted costs for this product are as folllows:

	Unit Costs (30,000 Units)	Total
Variable manufacturing costs	$51	$1,530,000
Variable selling expenses	15	450,000
Fixed manufacturing costs	8	240,000
Fixed operating expenses	6	180,000
Total costs and expenses	$80	$2,400,000

The management of D. Lawrance is considering a special order from Discount House for an additional 10,000 jackets. These jackets would carry the Discount House label, rather than that of D. Lawrance. In all other respects, they would be identical to the regular D. Lawrance jackets.

Although D. Lawrance sells its regular jackets to retail stores at a price of $120 each, Discount House has offered to pay only $69 per jacket. However, no sales commissions are involved on this special order, so D. Lawrance would incur variable selling expenses of only $3 per unit on these jackets, rather than the regular $15. Accepting the order would cause no change in D. Lawrance's fixed costs or fixed operating expenses. D. Lawrance has enough plant capacity to produce 45,000 jackets per year.

INSTRUCTIONS

a Using incremental revenue and incremental costs, compute the expected effect of accepting this special order upon D. Lawrance's operating income.

b Briefly discuss any other factors that you believe D. Lawrance's management should consider in deciding whether to accept this special order. You may include nonfinancial as well as financial considerations.

PROBLEM 26A-2
Make or Buy Decision

Guaranteed Tools manufactures an electric motor that it uses in several of its products. Management is considering whether to continue manufacturing the motors, or whether to buy them from an outside source. The following information is available:

1 The company needs 10,000 motors per year. The motors can be purchased from an outside supplier at a cost of $20 per unit.

2 The cost of manufacturing the motors is $25 per unit, computed as follows:

Direct materials	$ 65,000
Direct labour	55,000
Manufacturing overhead:	
Variable	70,000
Fixed	60,000
Total manufacturing costs	$250,000
Cost per unit ($250,000 ÷ 10,000 units)	$25

3 Discontinuing the manufacture of motors will eliminate all of the direct materials and direct labour costs, but will eliminate only 60% of the variable manufacturing overhead costs.

4 If the motors are purchased from an outside source, certain machinery used in the production of motors will be sold at its book value. The sale of this machinery will reduce fixed manufacturing overhead costs by $3,600 for depreciation and $400 for property taxes. No other reductions in fixed overhead will result from discontinuing production of the motors.

INSTRUCTIONS

a Prepare a schedule to determine the incremental cost or benefit of buying the motors from the outside supplier. Based on this schedule, would you recommend that the company manufacture the motors or buy them from the outside source?

b Assume that if the motors are purchased from the outside source, the factory space previously used to produce motors can be used to manufacture an additional 7,000 power trimmers per year. Power trimmers have an estimated contribution margin of $8 per unit. The manufacture of the additional power trimmers would have no effect upon fixed manufacturing overhead. Would this new assumption change your recommendation as to whether to make or buy the motors? In support of your conclusion, prepare a schedule showing the incremental cost or benefit of buying the motors from the outside source and using the factory space to produce additional power trimmers.

PROBLEM 26A-3
Discontinuing
a Product Line

Ski West is a small airline flying out of Victoria. The company has only enough planes to service three routes, connecting Victoria with Edmonton, and with Whistler and Vancouver. Typical monthly operating data for these three routes are summarized below:

	Edmonton		Whistler		Vancouver	
Passengers per month.............	1,000		1,200		900	
	Dollars	%	Dollars	%	Dollars	%
Sales	$400,000	100	$240,000	100	$270,000	100
Variable costs.....................	40,000	10	12,000	5	13,500	5
Contribution margins	$360,000	90	$228,000	95	$256,500	95
Traceable fixed costs	408,000	102	96,000	40	113,400	42
Segment margins.................	$ (48,000)	(12)	$132,000	55	$143,100	53

Management is concerned about the losses incurred each month on the Edmonton route, and also has an opportunity to use the plane now serving Edmonton to establish a new Victoria to Calgary route. Management estimates that the new route would generate a positive monthly segment margin of $50,000. However, many of the passengers flying the Edmonton route with Ski West also "book through" on either the Whistler or Vancouver flights. Ski West's management knows that cancelling service to Edmonton will cause a loss of passengers on the Whistler and Vancouver routes.

By studying ticket sales, Ski West's managerial accountants have learned that 45% of the passengers flying Ski West from Edmonton continue on Ski West to Whistler, and that 36% fly Ski West into Vancouver. A marketing survey indicates that if the Edmonton route is cancelled, Ski West will still receive 60% of the business of those Edmonton passengers who travel from Victoria to Whistler or Vancouver.

INSTRUCTIONS

a Using the data about numbers of passengers, prepare a schedule showing the percentage by which monthly passenger volume is expected to decline on (1) the Whistler route, and (2) the Vancouver route, assuming that the Edmonton route is cancelled.

b Prepare a schedule showing the estimated effect of replacing the Edmonton route with service to Calgary upon the monthly operating income of Ski West. Changes in the contribution margin generated from the Whistler and Vancouver routes are expected to coincide with the changes in passenger volume.

c Make a recommendation as to whether the Edmonton route should be discontinued. Also raise any points that you believe should be considered by management.

PROBLEM 26A-4
Capital Budgeting

Micro Technology is considering two alternative proposals for modernizing its production facilities. To provide a basis for selection, the cost accounting department has developed the following data regarding the expected annual operating results for the two proposals.

	Proposal 1	Proposal 2
Required investment in equipment	$360,000	$350,000
Estimated service life of equipment	8 years	7 years
Estimated salvage value	–0–	$ 14,000
Estimated annual cost savings (net cash flow).................	$ 75,000	$ 76,000
Depreciation on equipment (straight-line basis)	$ 45,000	$ 48,000
Estimated increase in annual net income	$ 30,000	$ 28,000

INSTRUCTIONS

a For each proposal, compute the (1) payback period, (2) return on average investment, and (3) net present value, discounted at an annual rate of 12%. (Round the payback period to the nearest tenth of a year and the return on investment to the nearest tenth of a percent.)

b Based on your analysis in part **a**, state which proposal you would recommend and explain the reasons for your choice.

PROBLEM 26A-5
Capital Budgeting Using Three Models

Marengo is a popular restaurant located in the Chilton Resort. Management feels that enlarging the facility to incorporate a large outdoor seating area will enable Marengo to continue to attract existing customers as well as handle large banquet parties that now must be turned away. Two proposals are currently under consideration. Proposal A involves a temporary walled structure and umbrellas used for sun protection; Proposal B entails a more permanent structure with a full awning cover for use even in inclement weather. Although the useful life of each alternative is estimated to be 10 years, Proposal B results in higher salvage value due to the awning protection. The accounting department of Chilton Resort and the manager of Marengo have assembled the following data regarding the two proposals:

	Proposal A	Proposal B
Required investment..	$400,000	$500,000
Estimated life of fixtures......................................	10 years	10 years
Estimated salvage value	$ 20,000	$ 50,000
Estimated annual net cash flow	$ 80,000	$ 95,000
Depreciation (straight-line basis)	$ 38,000	$ 45,000
Estimated annual net income	?	?

INSTRUCTIONS

a For each proposal, compute the (1) payback period, (2) return on average investment, and (3) net present value discounted at management's required rate of return of 15%. Round the payback period to the nearest tenth of a year and the return on investment to the nearest tenth of a percent.

b Based upon your analysis in part **a**, state which proposal you would recommend and explain the reasons for your choice.

PROBLEM 26A-6
Capital Budgeting— Computing Annual Net Cash Flow

Toying With Nature wants to take advantage of children's current fascination with dinosaurs by adding several scale-model dinosaurs to its existing product line. Annual sales of the dinosaurs are estimated at 80,000 units at a price of $6 per unit. Variable manufacturing costs are estimated at $2.50 per unit, incremental fixed manufacturing costs (excluding depreciation) at $45,000 annually, and additional selling and general expenses related to the dinosaurs at $55,000 annually.

To manufacture the dinosaurs, the company must invest $350,000 in design molds and special equipment. Since toy fads wane in popularity rather quickly,

Toying With Nature anticipates the special equipment will have a three-year service life with only a $20,000 salvage value. Depreciation will be computed on a straight-line basis. All revenue and expenses other than depreciation will be received or paid in cash. The company's income tax rate is 40%.

INSTRUCTIONS

a Prepare a schedule showing the estimated increase in annual net income from the planned manufacture and sale of dinosaur toys.

b Compute the annual net cash flow expected from this project.

c Compute for this project (1) payback period, (2) return on average investment, and (3) net present value, discounted at an annual rate of 15%. Round the payback period to the nearest tenth of a year and the return on average investment to the nearest tenth of a percent.

Group B

PROBLEM 26B-1
Evaluating a Special Order

Never Bored Game Limited sells 600,000 units per year of a particular board game at $12.00 each. The current unit cost of the game sets is broken down as follows:

Direct materials	*$2.50*
Direct labour	*2.70*
Variable manufacturing overhead	*1.60*
Fixed manufacturing overhead	*2.20*
Total	*$9.00*

At the beginning of the current year, Never Bored receives a special order for 10,000 of these games per month, *for one year only* at a sales price of $8.00 per unit. A new machine with an estimated life of five years would have to be purchased for $30,000 to produce the additional units. Management thinks that it will not be able to use the new machine beyond one year and that it will have to be sold for a salvage value of approximately $20,000.

INSTRUCTIONS

Compute the estimated increase or decrease in annual operating income that will result from accepting this special order.

PROBLEM 26B-2
Make or Buy Decision

Precision Heating & Cooling manufactures thermostats that it uses in several of its products. Management is considering whether to continue manufacturing thermostats, or to buy them from an outside source. The following information is available:

1 The company needs 80,000 thermostats per year. Thermostats can be purchased from an outside supplier at a cost of $6 per unit.

2 The cost of manufacturing thermostats is $7.50 per unit, computed as follows:

Direct materials	*$156,000*
Direct labour	*132,000*
Manufacturing overhead:	
Variable	*168,000*
Fixed	*144,000*
Total manufacturing costs	*$600,000*
Cost per unit ($600,000 ÷ 80,000 units)	*$7.50*

3 Discontinuing the manufacture of the thermostats will eliminate all of the direct materials and direct labour costs, but will eliminate only 60% of the variable overhead costs.

4 If the thermostats are purchased from an outside source, certain machinery used in the production of thermostats will be sold at its book value. The sale of this machinery will reduce fixed overhead costs by $8,400 for depreciation and $800 for property taxes. No other reductions in fixed overhead will result from discontinuing production of the thermostats.

INSTRUCTIONS

a Prepare a schedule to determine the incremental cost or benefit of buying thermostats from the outside supplier. Based on this schedule, would you recommend that the company manufacture thermostats or buy them from the outside source?

b Assume that if thermostats are purchased from the outside source, the factory space previously used to produce thermostats can be used to manufacture an additional 6,000 heat-flow regulators per year. These regulators have an estimated contribution margin of $18 per unit. The manufacture of the additional heat-flow regulators would have no effect upon fixed overhead.

Would this new assumption change your recommendation as to whether to make or buy thermostats? In support of your conclusion, prepare a schedule showing the incremental cost or benefit of buying thermostats from the outside source and using the factory space to produce additional heat-flow regulators.

PROBLEM 26B-3
Discontinuing a Product Line—Any Ideas?

Quest Corporation began business about 10 years ago manufacturing and selling ski equipment. Later it introduced a line of golf clubs, which has since become its biggest selling and most profitable product. Over the years, competition from Europe has forced the company to reduce its sales price on skis, and this product line now consistently has a negative segment margin. The company also makes a unique ski binding, which has remained profitable. Typical monthly operating data for these three product lines are shown below:

	Golf Clubs Dollars	%	Skis Dollars	%	Ski Bindings Dollars	%
Sales	$500,000	100	$300,000	100	$160,000	100
Variable costs	215,000	43	225,000	75	80,000	50
Contribution margins	$285,000	57	$ 75,000	25	$ 80,000	50
Traceable fixed costs	110,000	22	90,000	30	68,800	43
Segment margins	$175,000	35	$ (15,000)	(5)	$ 11,200	7

Management is considering discontinuing the manufacture and sale of skis. All costs traceable to the product line would be eliminated if the product line is discontinued. Skis and bindings are sold to the same stores; therefore, management estimates that discontinuing the sale of skis would cause a 20% decline in sales of ski bindings. Golf clubs are sold to different customers, so management does not believe that golf club sales would be affected by discontinuing skis. All three product lines are manufactured in the same plant, which is operating at between 90% and 95% of capacity, due to the increasing demand for golf clubs.

INSTRUCTIONS

a Prepare a schedule showing the estimated effect of discontinuing the manufacture and sale of skis upon Quest's monthly operating income.

b Prepare a schedule determining the expected monthly segment margin of the ski bindings product line, assuming that the ski product line is discontinued and that sales of ski bindings decline by 20%.

c Draft a memo summarizing your recommendations as to Quest's best course of action. Bring out any points that you think management should consider. Perhaps you have noticed factors that management may be overlooking.

PROBLEM 26B-4
Capital
Budgeting

Banner Equipment Co. is evaluating two alternative investment opportunities. The controller of the company has prepared the following analysis of the two investment proposals:

	Proposal A	Proposal B
Required investment in equipment	$220,000	$240,000
Estimated service life of equipment	5 years	6 years
Estimated salvage value	$ 10,000	–0–
Estimated annual net cash flow	$ 60,000	$ 60,000
Depreciation on equipment (straight-line basis)	$ 42,000	$ 40,000
Estimated annual net income	$ 18,000	$ 20,000

INSTRUCTIONS

a For each proposed investment, compute the (1) payback period, (2) return on average investment, and (3) net present value, discounted at an annual rate of 12%. (Round the payback period to the nearest tenth of a year and the return on investment to the nearest tenth of a percent.)

b Based upon your computations in part **a,** which proposal do you consider to be the better investment? Explain.

PROBLEM 26B-5
Capital Budgeting Using
Three Models

V. S. Yogurt is considering two possible expansion plans. Proposal A involves opening 10 stores in northern Ontario at a total cost of $3,150,000. Under another strategy, Proposal B, V. S. Yogurt would focus on southern Ontario and open six stores for a total cost of $2,500,000. Selected data regarding the two proposals has been assembled by the controller of V. S. Yogurt as follows:

	Proposal A	Proposal B
Required investment...	$3,150,000	$2,500,000
Estimated life of store locations..............................	7 years	7 years
Estimated salvage value	–0–	$ 400,000
Estimated annual net cash flow	$ 750,000	$ 570,000
Depreciation on equipment (straight-line basis)	$ 450,000	$ 300,000
Estimated annual net income	?	?

INSTRUCTIONS

a For each proposal, compute the (1) payback period, (2) return on average investment, and (3) net present value, discounted at management's required rate of return of 15%. Round the payback period to the nearest tenth of a year and the return on investment to the nearest tenth of a percent.

b Based upon your analysis in part **a,** state which proposal you would recommend and explain the reasoning behind your choice.

PROBLEM 26B-6
Another Capital Budgeting
Problem

Rothmore Appliance Limited is planning to introduce a built-in blender to its line of small home appliances. Annual sales of the blender are estimated at 10,000 units at a price of $35 per unit. Variable manufacturing costs are estimated at $15 per unit, incremental fixed manufacturing costs (other than depreciation) at $40,000 annually, and incremental selling and general expenses relating to the blenders at $50,000 annually.

To build the blenders, the company must invest $240,000 in molds, patterns, and special equipment. Since the company expects to change the design of the blender every four years, this equipment will have a four-year service life with no salvage value. Depreciation will be computed on a straight-line basis. All revenue and expenses other than depreciation will be received or paid in cash. The company's income tax rate is 40%.

INSTRUCTIONS　**a**　Prepare a schedule showing the estimated annual net income from the proposal to manufacture and sell the blenders.

b　Compute the annual net cash flow expected from the proposal.

c　Compute for this proposal the (1) payback period (round to the nearest tenth of a year), (2) return on average investment (round to the nearest tenth of a percent), and (3) net present value, discounted at an annual rate of 15%.

ANALYTICAL AND DECISION PROBLEMS AND CASES

A&D 26-1
Relevant Information and Opportunity Costs

McFriendly Software recently developed new spreadsheet software, Easy-Calc, which it intends to market by mail through ads in computer magazines. Just prior to introducing Easy-Calc, McFriendly receives an unexpected offer from Jupiter Computer to buy all rights to the software for $10 million cash.

a　Is the $10 million offer "relevant" financial information?

b　Describe McFriendly's opportunity cost if it (1) accepts Jupiter's offer, and (2) turns down the offer and markets Easy-Calc itself. Would these opportunity costs be recorded in McFriendly's accounting records? If so, explain the journal entry to record these costs.

c　Briefly describe the extent to which the dollar amounts of the two opportunity costs described in part **b** are known to management at the time of the decision of whether to accept Jupiter's offer.

d　Might there be any other opportunity costs to consider at the time of making this decision? If so, explain briefly.

A&D 26-2
How Much Is That Laser in the Window?

The management of Metro Printers is considering a proposal to replace some existing equipment with a new highly efficient laser printer. The existing equipment has a current book value of $2,200,000 and a remaining life (if not replaced) of 10 years. The laser printer has a cost of $1,300,000 and an expected useful life of 10 years. The purchase price of the laser printer will be paid in cash at the time of its acquisition. The laser printer would increase the company's annual cash flow by reducing operating costs and by increasing the company's ability to generate revenue. Susan Mills, controller of Metro Printers, has prepared the following estimates of the laser printer's effect upon annual earnings and cash flow:

Estimated increase in annual cash flow (before income taxes):		
Incremental revenue	$140,000	
Cost savings (other than depreciation)	110,000	$250,000
Reduction in annual depreciation expense:		
Depreciation on existing equipment	$220,000	
Depreciation on laser printer	130,000	90,000
Estimated increase in income before income taxes		$340,000
Increase in annual income taxes (40%)		136,000
Estimated increase in annual net income		$204,000
Estimated increase in annual net cash flow ($250,000 − $136,000)		$114,000

Don Adams, a director of Metro Printers, makes the following observation: "These estimates look fine, but won't we take a huge loss in the current year on the sale of our existing equipment? After the invention of the laser printer, I doubt that our old equipment can be sold for much at all." In response, Mills provides the following information about the expected loss on the sale of the existing equipment:

Book value of existing printing equipment....................................	$2,200,000
Estimated current sales price, net of removal costs...........................	200,000
Estimated loss on sale, before income taxes	$2,000,000
Reduction in current year's income taxes as a result of loss (40%)...........	800,000
Loss on sale of existing equipment, net of tax savings.......................	$1,200,000

Adams replies, "Good grief, our loss would be almost as great as the cost of the laser itself. Add this $1,200,000 loss to the $1,300,000 cost of the laser, we're into this new equipment for $2,500,000. I'd go along with a cost of $1,300,000, but $2,500,000 is out of the question. Besides, I am not sure this proposed investment meets the minimum rate of return required by the company."

INSTRUCTIONS a Assuming the following, should the management of Metro Printers go ahead with this proposal?

1 The $200,000 sales price of the existing equipment will be received in cash immediately.

2 The income tax benefit from selling the equipment will be realized one year from today.

3 The annual net cash flows may be regarded as received at year-end for each of the next ten years.

b Is the cost to Metro Printers of acquiring the laser printer $2,500,000, as Adams suggests? Explain fully.

Index

Internal control *(Cont.)*
    computer-based systems, in, 307
    defined, 9, 299
    fraud, 9
    guidelines to achieving, 300–306
    limitations and costs, 307–308
    payrolls, over, 551–553
    prevention of fraud, 308
    relationship to accounting system, 299
Internal control procedure
    subsidiary ledgers, 226
International Accounting Standards Committee, 13, 593
Inventoriable costs, 1003
Inventory, 1004
    chapter coverage of, 441–464
    current asset, as a, 442
    current replacement cost, 454
    defined, 220, 442
    effects of errors in inventory valuation, 458–459
    finished goods, 442, 1005, 1013
    flow assumptions, 444–451
    (see also Inventory flow assumptions)
    flow of costs in, 442–452, 1005–1008
    goods in transit, 455
    income taxes, 450–451
    just-in-time inventory systems, 451–452, 1058–1063
    lower-of-cost-and-market rule, 453–454
    management of, 462
    manufacturing concern, in a, 442, 1005–1008, 1013
    market value, 454
    materiality, 234, 453
    materials, 442, 1005–1013
    net realizable value, 454
    operating cycle, 442
    periodic inventory systems
    (see Periodic inventory systems)
    perpetual inventory systems
    (see Perpetual inventory systems)
    physical counts of, 230–231, 452
    shrinkage losses, 230–231, 452–453
    statement of changes in financial position, 882
    subsidiary ledgers, 223, 227, 229–230, 443, 446–448
    turnover rate, 463, 950–951
    work in process, 442, 1005, 1013
Inventory flow assumptions
    average-cost (moving average) method, 445–446, 449–450, 457
    estimating techniques
      gross profit method, 460–461
      retail method, 461–462

Inventory flow assumptions *(Cont.)*
    evaluation of methods, 448–450
    first-in, first-out (FIFO), 446–447, 450, 457–458
    last-in, first-out (LIFO), 447–448, 450, 457–458
    specific identification, 449, 456–457
Investee, 811
Investing activities (in statement of changes in financial position), 880, 886
Investment of owner's equity, 18
Investment centres, 1125–1126
    return on assets, 1125
    return on investment (ROI), 1125
Investments in corporate securities (stocks and bonds)
    chapter coverage of, 803–824
    marketable securities, 804–811
    purposes of control, for
      consolidated financial statements *(see* Consolidated financial statements)
    significant influence for, equity method, 811–813
    summary of accounting methods, 824
Investor(s), 5
    defined, 26
    users of information, as, 26–28
Invoice, 245, 305–306
Invoice approval form (voucher), 306, 360–365
Irregularities, 308
Ivaco, 678

Job cost sheet, 1035–1036
Job order cost accounting systems
    characteristics of, 1034–1035
    direct labour, 1040
    direct materials, 1037
    flow of costs in, 1035–1042
    indirect labour, 1040
    job cost sheets in, 1035–1036
    overhead application in, 1040–1042
    overhead costs, 1040
    service industries, in, 1040–1042
Johnson & Johnson, 453
Journal entries
    compound, 65
    educational devices, as, 77
    illustrated, 66
    posting, 67–70
    usefulness to management of, 77
Journalizing, 65
Journals
    cross-reference, 67
    general, 65–70, 291
    special, 77, 291–293
Judgment
    (see Professional judgment)
Junk bonds, 743, 767

Just-in-time inventory systems, 451–452, 1058–1063
    accounting implications, 1061
    equipment reliability, 1061
    product quality, 1060
    scrap, 1062
    spoilage, 1062

K mart, 103

Labour cost variances, 1180–1182
Labour costs, 1003
Labour efficiency variance, 1180–1181
Labour rate variance, 1180–1181
Land, 487
Land improvements, 488
Last-in, first-out (LIFO) inventory valuation method
    (see Inventory flow assumptions)
Leases, 760
    capital, 760
    CICA Handbook, 761
    operating, 760
Ledger
    general, 55–63, 223
    subsidiary, 223–226, 229–230
Ledger account(s), 55
    balance column, 62
    chart of, 63, 294
    comparisons with data base, 297
    credit, 55
    cross-reference, 67
    date column, 62
    debit, 55
    defined, 55
    expenses, 106
    explanation column, 62
    financial statement order, 63, 113
    illustrated, 56–58, 110–113
    manufacturing costs, 1005
    recording transactions in, 58–62
    reference column, 62
    responsibility accounting systems, in, 294, 1127
    revenue, 106
    running balance form of, 62
    sequence and numbering, 63
    T format, 62
    usefulness to management of, 77
Legal capital, 666
Lessee, 760
Lessor, 760
Leverage, use of, 945–946
Liabilities, 4
    accrued, 540–542
    bonds payable
      (see Bonds payable)
    chapter coverage of, 533–560, 740–769
    collateral, 534

STUDENT REPLY CARD

In order to improve future editions, we are seeking your comments on
ACCOUNTING: The Basis for Business Decisions, Seventh Canadian Edition,
Volume 3, by Meigs, Meigs, and Lam.
Please answer the following questions and return this form via Business Reply
Mail. Your opinions matter. Thank you in advance for sharing them with us!

Name of your college or university: _____

Major program of study: _____

Course title: _____

Were you required to buy this book? _____ yes _____ no

Did you buy this book new or used? _____ new _____ used ($_____)

Do you plan to keep or sell this book? _____ keep _____ sell

Is the order of topic coverage consistent with what was taught in your course?

Are there chapters or sections of this text that were not assigned for your course?
Please specify:

Were there topics covered in your course that are not included in the text?
Please specify:

What did you like most about this text?

What did you like least?

If you would like to say more, we would appreciate hearing from you. Please write
to us at the address shown on the reverse of this page.

- - - - - - - - - - - - - - - - - *cut here* - - - - - - - - - - - - - - - - - -

Postage will be paid by

- - - - - - - - - - - - - - *fold here* - - - - - - - - - - - - - - -

0183560299-L1N9B6-BR01

Attn.: Sponsoring Editor
College Division

MCGRAW-HILL RYERSON LIMITED
300 WATER ST
WHITBY ON   L1N 9Z9

tape shut

cut here

15 A-3 (b) Retained earnings, $7,230,000
15 A-4 (a) Net income, $420,000
15 A-5 (1) Total shareholders' equity, $743,600
15 A-6 (b) Total shareholders' equity, $8,792,800
15 A-7 (a) Total contributed capital, $4,990,000;
      (b) retained earnings, $874,000

15 B-1 (a) Income before extraordinary items,
      $11,820,000
15 B-2 (a) Retained earnings, $606,800
15 B-3 (b) Retained earnings, $8,220,000
15 B-4 (a) Net income, $190,000
15 B-5 (1) Total shareholders' equity, $4,578,000
15 B-6 (b) Total shareholders' equity, $9,318,000
15 B-7 (b) Retained earnings, $469,800

16-1 (c) Bond interest expense, $1,500,000
16-2 (b) Long-term liabilities, $58,880,000
16-3 (b) Carrying value of bond liability, bonds
      issued at 101, $60,560,000
16-4 (c) (1) Long-term liabilities, $29,570,000
16-5 (c) (1) Long-term liabilities, $80,800,000
16-6 (b) Gain on retirement of bonds, $8,800
16-7 (b) Loss on early retirement of bonds, $76,480
16-8 (a) (2) Amortization of discount, $5,400
16-9 (c) Long-term liabilities, $9,473,818
16-10 (c) Long-term liabilities, $10,189,225
16-11 (c) Liability, bonds issued at discount,
      $8,706,000
16-12 No key figure
16-13 (d) Lease payment obligation, $23,870
16-14 (a) Total liabilities, $1,088,620

CP-4 (c) (1) Net income, $383,710; (c) (3) total
      assets, $32,067,410

Appendix A

1 (d) Present value, $96,120
2 (a) Issuance price, $9,428,500
3 (c) Liability, Dec. 31, $23,197
4 (a) Present value of payments, 10-year lease,
      $8,032,300
5 (d) Lease payment obligation, Dec. 31, $40,184
6 (b) (2) Discount on Notes Receivable, $259,920

17 A-1 (b) (2) Gain on sale, $3,700
17 A-2 No key figure
17 A-3 (b) Market value, $305,000
17 A-4 (b) (3) Carrying value, Dec. 31, 1996,
      $4,995,000
17 A-5 (c) Consolidated total assets, $7,525,000
17 A-6 Consolidated total assets, $3,928,000
17 A-7 Consolidated total assets, $1,204,000

17 B-1 (b) (2) Loss on sale, $5,600
17 B-2 No key figure

17 B-3 (b) Market value, $224,000
17 B-4 (b) (3) Carrying value, Dec. 31, 1997,
      $1,710,000
17 B-5 (c) Consolidated total assets, $10,670,000
17 B-6 Consolidated total assets, $7,760,000
17 B-7 Consolidated total assets, $1,326,000

18 A-1 No key figure
18 A-2 No key figure
18 A-3 Taxable income, $79,920
18 A-4 (a) Capital cost allowance, $225,000
18 A-5 (a) Accounting income, $969,000

18 B-1 No key figure
18 B-2 No key figure
18 B-3 Taxable income, $75,470
18 B-4 (a) Capital cost allowance, $160,000
18 B-5 (a) Accounting income, $150,000

19 A-1 No key figure
19 A-2 Cash provided by operating activities, $514,000
19 A-3 (b) Cash provided by operating activities,
      $155,000
19 A-4 Cash provided by operating activities, $155,000
19 A-5 (b) Cash provided by operating activities,
      $204,000
19 A-6 (c) Cash provided by operating activities,
      $166,000
19 A-7 (c) Cash used in investing activities, $80,000

19 B-1 No key figure
19 B-2 No key figure
19 B-3 (b) Cash provided by operating activities,
      $144,000
19 B-4 Cash provided by operating activities, $144,000
19 B-5 (b) Cash provided by operating activities,
      $1,020,000
19 B-6 (c) Cash provided by operating activities,
      $1,000
19 B-7 (c) Cash provided by operating activities,
      $580,000

20-1 (a) Net sales, 1995, $2,520,000
20-2 (a) Net income, Sub Zero, 7%
20-3 (c) Operating cycle, 119.8 days
20-4 (a) (6) Return on average assets, 16%
20-5 (a) (3) Operating expenses, $270,000
20-6 (a) (6) Operating cycle, Mondo, 192 days
20-7 (a) (6) Operating cycle, Imports, 168 days
20-8 (b) (3) Working capital, $1,296,000
20-9 No key figure
20-10 Total assets, $1,000; net sales, $1,280
20-11 (c) Price-earnings ratio, Continental, 9.1 times
20-12 (a) (9) Interest coverage ratio, PepsiCo, 2.9
      times

CP-5 Part 1: No key figure
      Part 2: (a) (6) Accounts receivable turnover
      rate, 1992, 42 days

INTRODUCTION
À L'ALGÈBRE LINÉAIRE
ET À SES APPLICATIONS

Introduction à l'algèbre linéaire et ses applications

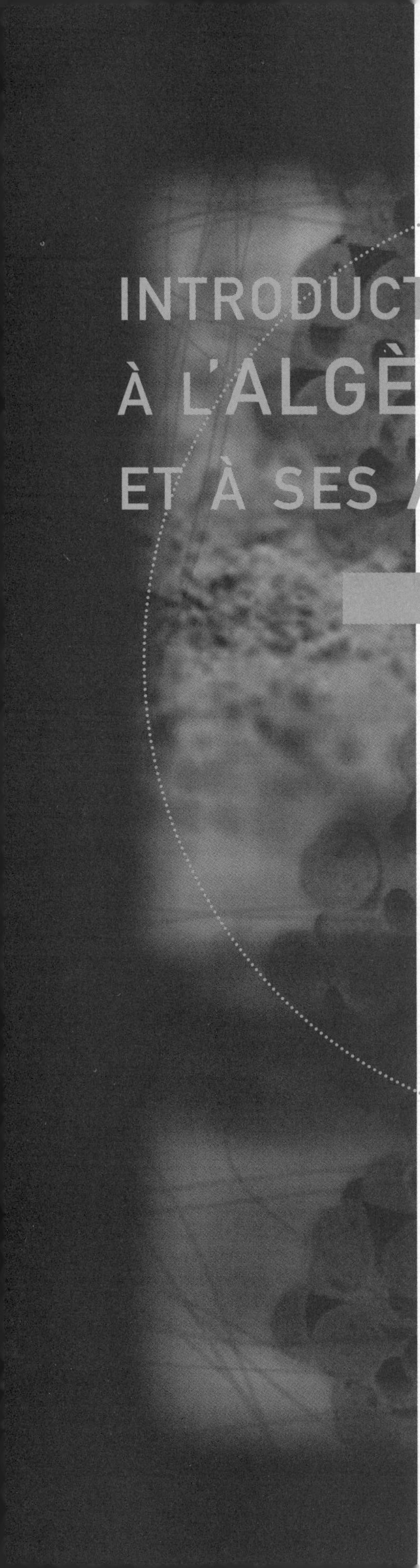

INTRODUCTION
À L'ALGÈBRE LINÉAIRE
ET À SES APPLICATIONS

LUC AMYOTTE

professeur de mathématiques
au cégep de Drummondville

ERPI

ÉDITIONS DU RENOUVEAU
PÉDAGOGIQUE INC.

5757, RUE CYPIHOT
SAINT-LAURENT (QUÉBEC) H4S 1R3
TÉL.: (514) 334-2690
TÉLÉC.: (514) 334-4720
COURRIEL: erpidlm@erpi.com

Luc Amyotte est professeur de mathématiques au cégep de Drummond-ville depuis 1977. En plus d'un brevet d'enseignement, il possède un baccalauréat en mathématiques, un baccalauréat en administration des affaires, un baccalauréat en sciences économiques, une maîtrise en mathématiques et une maîtrise en didactique des mathématiques. Il est l'auteur de *Méthodes quantitatives – Applications à la recherche en sciences humaines* et de *Méthodes quantitatives – Formation complémentaire*, deux livres publiés également aux Éditions du Renouveau Pédagogique.

Supervision éditoriale : Jacqueline Leroux
Révision linguistique : Pierrette Mayer
Correction d'épreuves : Sylvie Chapleau et Jacqueline Leroux
Conception graphique : Sylvie Mailhot
Édition électronique : Caractéra
Couverture : alibi/acapella
Photographies : Alfred Pasieka, SPL/Publiphoto (ADN – couverture) ; NASA (navette spatiale – couverture) ; Science Photo Library/Publiphoto (p. 2, 67, 220, 276, 308, 356) ; Archives Snark/Publiphoto (p. 164, en haut) ; J. L. Charmet/Explorer/Publiphoto (p. 164, en bas) ; Stock Montage, Inc. (p. 26)

Dépôt légal : 2e trimestre 1999
Bibliothèque nationale du Québec
Bibliothèque nationale du Canada
Imprimé au Canada

ISBN 2-7613-1089-6

123456789 II 5432109
20126 ABCD   VO-7

Avant-propos

De nos jours, le hasard ne favorise l'invention que pour des esprits préparés aux découvertes par de patientes études et de persévérants efforts.

Louis Pasteur

PARTICULARITÉS DE L'ALGÈBRE LINÉAIRE

Comme son titre l'indique, Introduction à l'algèbre linéaire et à ses applications *est un texte d'initiation à la théorie et aux applications de l'algèbre linéaire. L'étude de l'algèbre linéaire fait partie de plusieurs programmes parce que peu de sujets sont aussi utiles à autant de disciplines (biologie, physique, chimie, sciences économiques et administratives, nutrition, démographie, etc.). En plus d'avoir de nombreuses applications, l'algèbre linéaire sert à illustrer l'axiomatique parce qu'elle a notamment pour objet l'étude de structures mathématiques. Ces deux particularités de l'algèbre linéaire ont été une véritable source d'inspiration lors de la rédaction du présent manuel.*

CARACTÉRISTIQUES PÉDAGOGIQUES DU MANUEL

À l'instar de Stendhal, beaucoup d'étudiants considèrent que les mathématiques sont «la patrie du bâillement et du raisonnement triste». À l'encontre de cette opinion très répandue, Introduction à l'algèbre linéaire et à ses applications *comporte des caractéristiques qui facilitent l'étude de l'algèbre et la rendent plus agréable.*

- *Chaque chapitre débute par une citation visant à éveiller l'intérêt de l'élève, suivie d'une série de questions importantes auxquelles il devra tenter de répondre après avoir terminé la lecture du chapitre.*

- *Dans chaque chapitre, l'auteur trace le portrait d'un mathématicien ou d'une mathématicienne. Il indique sa contribution au thème développé de même que la place qu'il occupe dans son époque. Cette section apporte une dimension humaine à ce que plusieurs considèrent comme un sujet aride. Ainsi, l'élève apprendra que la discrimination religieuse ou sexuelle a joué un rôle considérable dans la carrière de plusieurs mathématiciens et mathématiciennes, que le génie mathématique de certains s'est révélé précocement, que d'autres ont travaillé dans des universités sans recevoir aucune rémunération, pour le simple plaisir de faire des mathématiques, etc.*

- *La plupart des chapitres comportent aussi une section portant sur un aspect particulier de l'évolution du thème principal. Par exemple, au chapitre 2, il est question de la façon dont Arthur Cayley en est venu à la définition de la multiplication de matrices ; au chapitre 3, l'élève apprendra pourquoi, contrairement à la logique, les déterminants sont apparus avant les matrices et quels mathématiciens ont contribué à leur essor ; au chapitre 4, l'élève pourra prendre connaissance d'un extrait du texte original de Gabriel Cramer où ce dernier présente – de façon très limpide pour l'époque – la règle qui porte son nom ; au chapitre 7, il est question du rôle crucial d'un article de Carl Friedrich Gauss dans l'acceptation des nombres complexes et une anecdote à propos de ces nombres relatée par Isaac Asimov est citée en entier ; au chapitre 10, il est fait état de la longue évolution que le concept d'espace vectoriel a dû suivre avant d'occuper une place de choix en mathématiques, etc.*

- *Bien qu'on y respecte le formalisme mathématique, l'ouvrage est écrit dans un langage accessible. Les explications sont détaillées et complètes. Chaque mot clé est bien identifié dans le texte et défini en marge, et une liste des mots clés est présentée à la fin de chaque chapitre. On trouve également un glossaire des mots clés à la fin du manuel.*

- *Chaque chapitre comporte un résumé des principales notions. La lecture de cette synthèse aidera l'élève à déterminer quels concepts il a bien assimilés et lesquels il ne comprend pas parfaitement. Plusieurs résumés comportent un ou des tableaux synoptiques qui permettent de trouver rapidement les informations requises pour faire les exercices.*

- *De nombreux exemples illustrent la théorie. Ils sont généralement suivis d'exercices, de sorte que l'élève pourra vérifier rapidement s'il a bien saisi les notions traitées.*

- *Chaque chapitre se termine par des exercices récapitulatifs. Ceux-ci comprennent non seulement des exercices simples, mais également des applications à différentes disciplines et des exercices de nature plus théorique (démonstration d'un théorème, explication d'un concept ou d'une marche à suivre, etc.). Les exercices récapitulatifs sont gradués de I (facile) à III (difficile). Les divers domaines d'application sont indiqués par une icône :*

 pour les sciences de la vie (biologie, nutrition, etc.) ;

 pour la physique et l'ingénierie ;

 pour la chimie ;

 pour les sciences administratives et économiques.

Les solutions des exercices récapitulatifs sont données en fin de volume.

- *Un aide-mémoire accompagne le manuel. Il constitue un précieux outil de référence pour l'exécution des exercices et la préparation des examens. On y trouve non seulement un résumé des notions présentées dans le manuel, mais également une liste des principaux symboles, l'alphabet grec, la définition des fonctions trigonométriques, etc.*

MATÉRIEL COMPLÉMENTAIRE

Les professeurs qui adoptent le manuel peuvent se procurer un guide d'enseignement chez l'éditeur. On y trouve les solutions détaillées de tous les exercices proposés dans le manuel.

Remerciements

Un ouvrage de cette envergure est le fruit de la collaboration de plusieurs personnes. Je tiens à souligner tout particulièrement l'aide précieuse de mes collègues du département de mathématiques du cégep de Drummondville, notamment Chantal Baril, Louise Gaudet et Ginette Villiard, qui ont lu le manuscrit et l'ont utilisé pour leur enseignement, Josée Hamel, qui a lu le manuscrit et a vérifié tous les exemples et exercices, de même que Yvon Boulanger, Carole Côté et Josée Mercier, qui ont lu le manuscrit. Toutes ces personnes m'ont fait de nombreuses suggestions et elles ont ainsi grandement contribué à la qualité de l'ouvrage.

Je tiens également à remercier les personnes qui ont travaillé à l'évaluation du manuscrit : Yvonne Bolduc, Daniel Chaput, Louise Dagenais, Jean-Pierre Leclercq, Jacques Marion, Pierre Ripeau et Claude St-Hilaire. Leurs suggestions et commentaires ont été très appréciés.

Un grand merci à Jean-Pierre Albert qui m'a fait confiance encore une fois et m'a constamment épaulé tout au long de la rédaction. Merci également à Sylvain Giroux pour les consultations qu'il a réalisées auprès de professeurs de cégeps et d'universités, et pour ses recherches en bibliothèque.

Je veux aussi signaler la qualité du travail de Pierrette Mayer à la révision linguistique. La minutie avec laquelle elle a accompli sa tâche mérite d'être soulignée.

Le mot de la fin est pour ma conjointe Carole. Je veux lui dire encore une fois combien sa patience et ses nombreux encouragements me sont précieux.

Luc Amyotte

Table des matières

CHAPITRE 5

Vecteurs du plan

CHAPITRE 8

Vecteurs de l'espace

CHAPITRE 9

Droite et plan de l'espace

CHAPITRE 10

Espaces vectoriels

Langage matriciel

Algebra is the intellectual instrument for rendering clear the quantitative aspects of the world.

Alfred North Whitehead

À LA FIN DU PRÉSENT CHAPITRE, VOUS DEVRIEZ ÊTRE
EN MESURE DE RÉPONDRE AUX QUESTIONS SUIVANTES:

- Qu'est-ce qu'une matrice?
- Comment note-t-on les éléments d'une matrice?
- À quelles conditions deux matrices sont-elles égales?
- Quels sont les différents types de matrices?
- Qu'est-ce qu'un théorème?

UN PORTRAIT de James Joseph Sylvester

James Joseph naquit à Londres, le 3 septembre 1814, dans une famille juive. À l'instar de son frère aîné, il ajouta à son nom le patronyme de Sylvester, sous lequel il est mieux connu. Le génie mathématique du jeune homme se manifesta très tôt. À quatorze ans, il fut l'élève du mathématicien De Morgan, à l'Université de Londres. À quinze ans, il entra au Royal Institution de Liverpool, où il étudia pendant deux ans. Dès la première année, il gagna un prix de mathématiques, de même qu'une bourse de 500 $ – somme rondelette pour l'époque – pour avoir trouvé la solution d'un difficile problème d'analyse combinatoire, soumis par une société américaine d'actuaires. Il était tellement en avance sur ses confrères qu'on créa pour lui seul une classe spéciale de mathématiques. En 1831, il entra à l'Université de Cambridge mais, malgré ses succès, il n'obtint pas de diplôme parce qu'il était juif et qu'il ne remplissait donc pas les prescriptions de l'Église d'Angleterre sur le «minimum de croyance religieuse nécessaire aux personnes rationnelles». Ce n'est qu'en 1872 que l'Université lui décerna des diplômes de baccalauréat et de maîtrise honoris causa.

À l'âge de 24 ans, Sylvester devint professeur de philosophie naturelle (science et physique) au University College de Londres, qu'il quitta deux ans plus tard pour aller enseigner à l'Université de Virginie, où il ne resta que trois mois : un conflit avec des élèves et ses positions antiesclavagistes l'obligèrent à démissionner. De retour en Angleterre, même s'il était Fellow de la Royal Society depuis 1839, Sylvester ne put trouver un poste d'enseignant digne de son talent. Il choisit donc de pratiquer le droit et l'actuariat pendant une dizaine d'années. Il continua toutefois de donner des cours particuliers à quelques étudiants, notamment à Florence Nightingale, celle qui allait donner ses lettres de noblesse à la profession d'infirmière. En 1855, Sylvester accepta un poste de professeur dans une école militaire. Il occupa cette fonction pendant quelques années avant de s'installer à l'Université Johns Hopkins, où il fonda l'American Journal of Mathematics et travailla activement au développement des programmes d'études supérieures en mathématiques aux États-Unis. En 1884, âgé de 70 ans, il retourna en Angleterre pour enseigner les mathématiques à l'Université d'Oxford.

On a dit de Sylvester qu'il possédait une très vaste culture, qu'il avait lu dans le texte les œuvres marquantes de la littérature latine, grecque, anglaise, française, allemande et italienne et qu'il prenait toujours plaisir à agrémenter ses articles scientifiques d'une citation tirée des classiques. Dans toute l'histoire, Sylvester et Leibniz sont reconnus pour avoir introduit le plus grand nombre de termes nouveaux en mathématiques. Sylvester travailla pendant de nombreuses années avec un autre Britannique, son ami Arthur Cayley. On considère, à juste titre, ces deux mathématiciens comme les fondateurs de la théorie des invariants algébriques.

1.1 LES MATRICES : UNE APPROCHE INTUITIVE

Si vous avez déjà lu les pages consacrées aux sports dans un journal, vous avez sans doute vu des tableaux semblables au tableau 1.1.

TABLEAU 1.1 **Classement des équipes de la section Est (16 août 1997)**

	Parties jouées	Parties gagnées	Parties perdues	Moyenne
ATLANTA	122	75	47	0,615
FLORIDE	119	69	50	0,580
NEW YORK	120	67	53	0,558
MONTRÉAL	119	60	59	0,504
PHILADELPHIE	117	42	75	0,359

Ce tableau, qui présente le classement des équipes de la section Est de la Ligue nationale de baseball, le 16 août 1997, constitue un exemple de matrice. Une matrice est un tableau de nombres, c'est-à-dire un ensemble ordonné de nombres disposés en lignes et en colonnes. Les informations contenues dans une matrice s'interprètent selon la position de chaque nombre. Ainsi, dans le tableau 1.1, la deuxième colonne donne le nombre de parties gagnées par chaque équipe tandis que la quatrième ligne donne les résultats de l'équipe de Montréal. Le 16 août 1997, l'équipe d'Atlanta avait gagné 75 parties sur 122, d'où une moyenne de 0,615. Quant à l'équipe montréalaise, elle avait accumulé 59 défaites en 119 parties.

Les matrices sont employées couramment pour classer de l'information numérique sous une forme concise. Ainsi, une entreprise pourrait présenter au moyen du tableau 1.2 l'inventaire de trois produits qu'elle distribue et stocke dans deux entrepôts. Dans ce cas également, l'interprétation des

TABLEAU 1.2

Inventaire par entrepôt

	Entrepôt 1	Entrepôt 2
PRODUIT *A*	85	87
PRODUIT *B*	72	40
PRODUIT *C*	36	22

nombres dépend de leur position dans la matrice. Comme le nombre 22 est situé à l'intersection de la troisième ligne et de la deuxième colonne, on sait que l'entreprise dispose de 22 unités du produit *C* dans son deuxième entrepôt.

Le tableau 1.3 présente un autre exemple de matrice, qui fait état de la migration interprovinciale entre les recensements de 1986 et de 1991, dans les provinces de l'Atlantique. La matrice indique notamment que 530 personnes ont quitté Terre-Neuve entre 1986 et 1991 pour s'établir à l'Île-du-Prince-Édouard, alors que 195 personnes ont migré en sens inverse.

TABLEAU 1.3   **Migration interprovinciale entre les recensements de 1986 et de 1991, provinces de l'Atlantique**

	Résidence (1991)			
Résidence (1986)	Terre-Neuve	Île-du-Prince-Édouard	Nouvelle-Écosse	Nouveau-Brunswick
TERRE-NEUVE	0	530	6 250	1 685
ÎLE-DU-PRINCE-ÉDOUARD	195	0	2 320	1 535
NOUVELLE-ÉCOSSE	3 110	2 110	0	7 900
NOUVEAU-BRUNSWICK	1 170	1 190	8 945	0

SOURCE: Statistique Canada, *Les Canadiens en mouvement*, n° 96-309 F au catalogue, 1994, p. 65.

À l'aide du tableau 1.3, on peut construire la matrice de migration nette (tableau 1.4).

TABLEAU 1.4   **Migration interprovinciale nette entre les recensements de 1986 et de 1991, provinces de l'Atlantique**

	Résidence (1991)			
Résidence (1986)	Terre-Neuve	Île-du-Prince-Édouard	Nouvelle-Écosse	Nouveau-Brunswick
TERRE-NEUVE	0	335	3 140	515
ÎLE-DU-PRINCE-ÉDOUARD	−335	0	210	345
NOUVELLE-ÉCOSSE	−3 140	−210	0	−1 045
NOUVEAU-BRUNSWICK	−515	−345	1 045	0

SOURCE: Statistique Canada, *Les Canadiens en mouvement*, n° 96-309 F au catalogue, 1994, p. 65.

On peut tirer diverses informations de cette dernière matrice. Par exemple, le nombre de personnes qui ont quitté Terre-Neuve pour l'Île-du-Prince-Édouard excède par 335 le nombre de personnes qui ont migré en sens inverse. Le solde migratoire net de l'Île-du-Prince-Édouard est de −220 (soit 335 − 210 − 345) personnes. Cela signifie que les mouvements de population dans les provinces de l'Atlantique, entre les deux recensements, ont provoqué une perte nette de 220 habitants pour l'Île-du-Prince-Édouard, au profit des autres provinces de l'Atlantique.

Les matrices constituent donc un puissant outil de description. Mais il y a plus ! Elles sont aussi un objet d'étude théorique ; elles permettent notamment de représenter un système d'équations linéaires et de le résoudre.

En mathématiques, on a parfois besoin de résoudre des équations linéaires (c'est-à-dire des équations du premier degré) à plusieurs inconnues. Par exemple, si on veut résoudre le système

$$2x - 3y = 5$$
$$-2x + 4y = 6$$

on peut se servir d'une matrice pour représenter les coefficients des inconnues (tableau 1.5).

Nous aurons l'occasion au chapitre 2 de résoudre de tels systèmes d'équations.

TABLEAU 1.5

Matrice des coefficients

	x	y
Première équation	2	−3
Deuxième équation	−2	4

EXERCICE 1.1

1. Examinez, à la page suivante, la matrice qui présente les notes de quatre élèves à un cours d'algèbre.

    a) Que représente la deuxième colonne de la matrice ?

    b) Que représente la troisième ligne de la matrice ?

    c) Interprétez les nombres suivants de la matrice des notes :

        i) 75

        ii) 80

NOTES AU COURS D'ALGÈBRE			
	Examen 1	Examen 2	Examen 3
Carole	90	95	80
Alexis	85	90	88
Jérémie	92	82	89
Olga	75	83	86

2. Donnez la matrice des coefficients du système d'équations linéaires suivant. N'oubliez pas que l'interprétation des éléments d'une matrice dépend de leur position.

$$2x + 3y - z = 8$$
$$z + 4y = 2$$
$$y + 2x - 3z = -7$$

Un peu d'histoire

C'est en 1850, dans un article du mathématicien britannique James Joseph Sylvester (1814-1897) que le mot matrice fut pour la première fois employé pour désigner un tableau de nombres. Sylvester voulait distinguer le concept de matrice de celui de déterminant (que nous aborderons au chapitre 3). Il choisit le terme matrice (du mot latin *mater* qui signifie « mère ») pour indiquer qu'une matrice représente la « mère d'un déterminant ». C'est toutefois un collègue et ami de Sylvester, le mathématicien Arthur Cayley (1821-1895), qui établit une véritable théorie des matrices. Dans une publication célèbre de 1858, intitulée *A Memoir on the Theory of Matrices*, Cayley définit les principaux termes et les opérations fondamentales de l'algèbre matricielle. Cet ouvrage contient également les démonstrations des principales propriétés des matrices.

Avant d'aborder les principales opérations sur les matrices et les applications du calcul matriciel, il faut connaître le vocabulaire matriciel de base. Vous devrez donc patienter encore un peu avant de passer à l'aspect pratique des matrices et du calcul matriciel.

MATRICE

Une matrice $A = \left[a_{ij} \right]_{m \times n}$ est un tableau de mn nombres disposés sur m lignes et n colonnes.

FORMAT

Le format d'une matrice indique le nombre de ses lignes et de ses colonnes. Une matrice de format $m \times n$ compte m lignes et n colonnes.

Une **matrice** de **format** $m \times n$ est un tableau de mn nombres disposés sur m lignes et n colonnes. On note généralement une matrice par une lettre majuscule, telle A, et on indique si nécessaire son format en indice : par exemple, $A_{m \times n}$. Une matrice de format $m \times n$, ou plus simplement une matrice $m \times n$, s'écrit en abrégé[1] $A = \left[a_{ij} \right]_{m \times n}$ et a la forme générale suivante :

$$A = \begin{bmatrix} a_{11} & a_{12} & \cdots & a_{1j} & \cdots & a_{1n} \\ a_{21} & a_{22} & \cdots & a_{2j} & \cdots & a_{2n} \\ \vdots & \vdots & & \vdots & & \vdots \\ a_{i1} & a_{i2} & \cdots & a_{ij} & \cdots & a_{in} \\ \vdots & \vdots & & \vdots & & \vdots \\ a_{m1} & a_{m2} & \cdots & a_{mj} & \cdots & a_{mn} \end{bmatrix} = \left[a_{ij} \right]_{m \times n}$$

ÉLÉMENT D'UNE MATRICE

Un élément d'une matrice est un nombre de cette matrice. L'élément situé à l'intersection de la i-ième ligne et de la j-ième colonne d'une matrice A est notée a_{ij}.

Les nombres d'une matrice sont appelés **éléments**. L'élément situé à l'intersection de la i-ième ligne et de la j-ième colonne est noté a_{ij} : c'est le terme général de la matrice. À titre d'exemple, a_{24} (qui se prononce « a deux quatre » et non « a vingt-quatre ») est l'élément situé à l'intersection de la deuxième ligne et de la quatrième colonne de la matrice A. On emploie donc le nom de la matrice en minuscule pour en désigner les éléments. Ainsi, les éléments d'une matrice B sont notés b_{ij}, ceux d'une matrice C sont notés c_{ij}, etc.

MATRICE LIGNE

Une matrice ligne est une matrice de format $1 \times n$.

MATRICE COLONNE

Une matrice colonne est une matrice de format $m \times 1$.

Pour des raisons évidentes, une matrice $1 \times n$ est appelée **matrice ligne**, et une matrice $m \times 1$ est appelée **matrice colonne**. Dans une matrice ligne ou une matrice colonne, un seul indice suffit pour noter les éléments. Ainsi, une matrice ligne $1 \times n$ s'écrit $A = \left[a_j \right]_{1 \times n} = \begin{bmatrix} a_1 & a_2 & \dots & a_n \end{bmatrix}$.

Exemple

1. Étudions les caractéristiques de la matrice

$$A = \begin{bmatrix} 2 & -3 & 0 & 10 & 12{,}1 \\ 10 & 2 & 4 & 8 & 1{,}5 \\ \frac{1}{4} & 6 & 5 & 1 & 4{,}7 \end{bmatrix}$$

---

1. Dans certains manuels, on utilise des parenthèses plutôt que des crochets pour représenter les matrices. Ainsi, on trouve la notation $A = \left(a_{ij} \right)_{m \times n}$ plutôt que $A = \left[a_{ij} \right]_{m \times n}$. Nous avons choisi d'employer des crochets.

La matrice A est de format 3×5 puisqu'elle comporte trois lignes et cinq colonnes, et elle compte donc 15 éléments. L'élément situé à l'intersection de la troisième ligne et de la quatrième colonne, soit 1, est noté a_{34}.

2. La matrice $B = \begin{bmatrix} b_{ij} \end{bmatrix}_{2 \times 2}$, définie par $b_{ij} = i + 3^j$, s'écrit

$$B = \begin{bmatrix} b_{11} & b_{12} \\ b_{21} & b_{22} \end{bmatrix} = \begin{bmatrix} 1 + 3^1 & 1 + 3^2 \\ 2 + 3^1 & 2 + 3^2 \end{bmatrix} = \begin{bmatrix} 4 & 10 \\ 5 & 11 \end{bmatrix}$$

EXERCICE 1.2

1. Soit la matrice

$$B = \begin{bmatrix} 2 & -1 & 0 \\ 0 & 3 & 4 \\ 0{,}2 & 1 & 8 \\ 9 & 10 & \tfrac{1}{2} \end{bmatrix}$$

a) Quel est le format de la matrice B?

b) Que vaut b_{21}? b_{43}? b_{34}?

c) Dans cette matrice, comment note-t-on le nombre 10? le nombre 8?

2. Écrivez la matrice $C = \begin{bmatrix} c_{ij} \end{bmatrix}_{3 \times 3}$ où $c_{ij} = (-1)^{i+j}(2^i)(j)$.

MATRICE CARRÉE

Une matrice carrée est une matrice qui comporte un même nombre de lignes et de colonnes. On dit d'une matrice carrée qu'elle est d'ordre n lorsqu'elle comporte n lignes et n colonnes; elle est alors notée $A = \begin{bmatrix} a_{ij} \end{bmatrix}_{n \times n}$.

ORDRE D'UNE MATRICE CARRÉE

L'ordre d'une matrice carrée est le nombre de ses lignes (ou de ses colonnes).

DIAGONALE PRINCIPALE

La diagonale principale d'une matrice carrée $A = \begin{bmatrix} a_{ij} \end{bmatrix}_{n \times n}$ est formée des éléments a_{ii} de A.

TRACE

La trace d'une matrice carrée d'ordre n, soit $A = \begin{bmatrix} a_{ij} \end{bmatrix}_{n \times n}$, est la somme des éléments de la diagonale principale de A: $\operatorname{Tr}(A) = \displaystyle\sum_{i=1}^{n} a_{ii}$.

Une matrice $n \times n$ comporte un même nombre de lignes et de colonnes. Elle présente donc une forme carrée plutôt que rectangulaire. C'est pourquoi on appelle **matrice carrée** d'**ordre** n toute matrice $n \times n$. Une telle matrice a la forme générale suivante:

$$A = \begin{bmatrix} a_{ij} \end{bmatrix}_{n \times n} = \begin{bmatrix} \mathbf{a_{11}} & a_{12} & \cdots & a_{1i} & \cdots & a_{1n} \\ a_{21} & \mathbf{a_{22}} & \cdots & a_{2i} & \cdots & a_{2n} \\ \vdots & \vdots & & \vdots & & \vdots \\ a_{i1} & a_{i2} & \cdots & \mathbf{a_{ii}} & \cdots & a_{in} \\ \vdots & \vdots & & \vdots & & \vdots \\ a_{n1} & a_{n2} & \cdots & a_{ni} & \cdots & \mathbf{a_{nn}} \end{bmatrix}$$

Étant donné la forme carrée de cette matrice, tous les éléments a_{ii} (inscrits en gras) sont situés sur une diagonale. C'est pourquoi on appelle **diagonale principale** de la matrice l'ensemble des éléments a_{ii}. La **trace** d'une matrice carrée A, notée $\operatorname{Tr}(A)$, est la somme des éléments de sa diagonale principale.

Exemple

Les matrices A, B et C suivantes sont des matrices carrées d'ordre 1, 2 et 3 respectivement.

$$A = \begin{bmatrix} 4 \end{bmatrix} \quad B = \begin{bmatrix} 2 & 3 \\ 0 & 5 \end{bmatrix} \quad C = \begin{bmatrix} 1 & 3 & 7 \\ 8 & -6 & -1 \\ 0{,}5 & 5 & 3 \end{bmatrix}$$

De plus,

$\text{Tr}(A) = 4$, $\text{Tr}(B) = 2 + 5 = 7$ et $\text{Tr}(C) = 1 + (-6) + 3 = -2$

EXERCICE 1.3

Évaluez si possible la trace de chacune des matrices

$$A = \begin{bmatrix} 2 & -1 & 0 \\ 0 & 3 & 4 \\ 0{,}2 & 1 & 8 \\ 9 & 10 & \frac{1}{2} \end{bmatrix} \quad B = \begin{bmatrix} 1 & 4 & -3 \\ 2 & 3 & 2 \\ -1 & 2 & -1{,}4 \end{bmatrix} \quad C = \begin{bmatrix} 1{,}3 & 1{,}4 \\ 2 & -8{,}1 \end{bmatrix}$$

$$D = \begin{bmatrix} 0 & 0 & 0 \end{bmatrix} \quad E = \begin{bmatrix} 1 \\ 1 \\ 1 \\ 1 \end{bmatrix}$$

En général, la trace d'une matrice carrée $A = \begin{bmatrix} a_{ij} \end{bmatrix}_{n \times n}$ est donnée par

$$\text{Tr}(A) = a_{11} + a_{22} + \cdots + a_{nn} = \sum_{i=1}^{n} a_{ii}$$

Le nouveau symbole que nous venons d'introduire, Σ, est la lettre majuscule sigma de l'alphabet grec, qui correspond à S, la première lettre du mot « somme ». L'expression $\sum_{i=1}^{n} a_{ii}$ signifie « effectuer la somme des a_{ii} en laissant i prendre les valeurs entières de 1 jusqu'à n ». La notation Σ est couramment utilisée en mathématiques pour abréger l'écriture d'une somme de termes.

Exemple

1. On abrège l'écriture de $3^1 + 3^2 + 3^3 + 3^4 + 3^5 + 3^6 + 3^7 + 3^8$

   au moyen de l'expression $\displaystyle\sum_{i=1}^{8} 3^i$, alors que

   $$2 + 4 + 6 + 8 + 10 + \cdots + 98 + 100 = \sum_{i=1}^{50} 2i$$

   Inversement, pour développer l'expression $\displaystyle\sum_{i=4}^{9} (2i + 1)a_i$, on écrit

   la somme de tous les termes de la forme $(2i + 1)a_i$ en donnant à
   i les valeurs entières allant de 4 à 9 :

   $$\sum_{i=4}^{9} (2i + 1)a_i = 9a_4 + 11a_5 + 13a_6 + 15a_7 + 17a_8 + 19a_9$$

2. La somme des éléments de la deuxième colonne d'une matrice

   $A = \left[a_{ij}\right]_{m \times n}$ s'écrit $\displaystyle\sum_{i=1}^{m} a_{i2}$, alors que la somme des éléments de

   la troisième ligne s'écrit $\displaystyle\sum_{j=1}^{n} a_{3j}$.

EXERCICE 1.4

1. Développez l'expression $\displaystyle\sum_{i=4}^{7} (i^2 + 1)$.

2. Écrivez la somme $3 + 5 + 7 + \cdots + 35$ au moyen de la notation Σ.

3. Exprimez la somme des éléments de la i-ième ligne d'une matrice
   $A = \left[a_{ij}\right]_{m \times n}$ au moyen de la notation Σ.

ÉGALITÉ DE DEUX MATRICES

Deux matrices $A = \left[a_{ij}\right]_{m \times n}$ et
$B = \left[b_{ij}\right]_{p \times q}$ sont égales si et
seulement si elles ont le même
format ($m = p$ et $n = q$) et que leurs
éléments correspondants sont égaux
($a_{ij} = b_{ij}$).

Lorsque nous étudierons le calcul matriciel (chapitre 2), nous aurons besoin
du concept d'**égalité de deux matrices**. Deux matrices $A = \left[a_{ij}\right]_{m \times n}$ et
$B = \left[b_{ij}\right]_{p \times q}$ sont égales si et seulement si :
- elles ont le même format, c'est-à-dire que $m = p$ et $n = q$;
- tous les éléments correspondants sont égaux, c'est-à-dire que $a_{ij} = b_{ij}$
  pour toutes les valeurs de i et de j.

1. Soit les deux matrices

$$A = \begin{bmatrix} 0 & 0 \\ 0 & 0 \\ 0 & 0 \end{bmatrix} \quad \text{et} \quad B = \begin{bmatrix} 0 & 0 & 0 \\ 0 & 0 & 0 \end{bmatrix}$$

Ces matrices ne sont pas égales parce qu'elles n'ont pas le même format : A est une matrice 3×2, alors que B est une matrice 2×3.

2. Soit les matrices

$$C = \begin{bmatrix} x & 0 & 1 \\ 2 & y & -2 \end{bmatrix} \quad \text{et} \quad D = \begin{bmatrix} 8 & 0 & z \\ 2 & \frac{1}{4} & -2 \end{bmatrix}$$

Ces deux matrices sont de format 2×3. De plus, leurs éléments correspondants sont égaux si et seulement si $x = 8$, $y = \frac{1}{4}$ et $z = 1$. Ainsi, les matrices C et D sont égales si et seulement si $x = 8$, $y = \frac{1}{4}$ et $z = 1$.

EXERCICE 1.5

Examinez les matrices

$$A = \begin{bmatrix} x^2 & 0 \\ 1 & x \end{bmatrix} \quad \text{et} \quad B = \begin{bmatrix} 1 & 0 \\ 2 & -1 \end{bmatrix}$$

Existe-t-il une valeur de x pour laquelle les matrices A et B sont égales ? Si oui, donnez cette valeur. Sinon, comment modifier la matrice B de manière qu'elle soit égale à A pour une valeur de x ?

1.3 QUELQUES MATRICES PARTICULIÈRES

Tout au long de ce manuel, nous ferons appel à différents types de matrices particulières, que nous définissons dans la présente section.

MATRICE NULLE

Une matrice nulle est une matrice dont tous les éléments valent zéro. La matrice nulle de format $m \times n$ est notée $O_{m \times n}$.

Une **matrice nulle** est une matrice dont tous les éléments valent zéro. Comme nous le verrons plus loin, cette matrice joue le rôle d'élément neutre pour l'addition de matrices. Une matrice nulle est donc de la forme $A = \begin{bmatrix} a_{ij} \end{bmatrix}_{m \times n}$ où $a_{ij} = 0$ pour toutes les valeurs de i et de j. La matrice nulle de format $m \times n$ est notée $O_{m \times n} = \begin{bmatrix} 0 \end{bmatrix}_{m \times n}$.

Exemple

Les matrices $O_{1 \times 1}$, $O_{1 \times 2}$ et $O_{3 \times 2}$ sont des matrices nulles de format 1×1, 1×2 et 3×2, respectivement.

$$O_{1 \times 1} = \begin{bmatrix} 0 \end{bmatrix} \quad O_{1 \times 2} = \begin{bmatrix} 0 & 0 \end{bmatrix} \quad O_{3 \times 2} = \begin{bmatrix} 0 & 0 \\ 0 & 0 \\ 0 & 0 \end{bmatrix}$$

MATRICE TRIANGULAIRE SUPÉRIEURE

Une matrice triangulaire supérieure est une matrice carrée dont tous les éléments situés sous la diagonale principale sont nuls.

MATRICE TRIANGULAIRE INFÉRIEURE

Une matrice triangulaire inférieure est une matrice carrée dont tous les éléments situés au-dessus de la diagonale principale sont nuls.

Une matrice carrée dont tous les éléments situés sous la diagonale principale sont nuls est appelée **matrice triangulaire supérieure**. De façon analogue, une matrice carrée dont tous les éléments situés au-dessus de la diagonale principale sont nuls est une **matrice triangulaire inférieure**. En langage symbolique, une matrice $A = \begin{bmatrix} a_{ij} \end{bmatrix}_{n \times n}$ est une matrice triangulaire supérieure si et seulement si $a_{ij} = 0$ pour tout $i > j$, et A est une matrice triangulaire inférieure si et seulement si $a_{ij} = 0$ pour tout $i < j$.

Exemple

Les matrices A, B et C suivantes sont des matrices triangulaires supérieures, d'ordre 1, 3 et 4 respectivement. Les matrices A et D sont des matrices triangulaires inférieures, d'ordre 1 et 5 respectivement.

$$A = \begin{bmatrix} 4 \end{bmatrix} \quad B = \begin{bmatrix} 1 & 2 & 0 \\ 0 & 5 & 0 \\ 0 & 0 & 4 \end{bmatrix} \quad C = \begin{bmatrix} -1 & 8 & 0 & 9 \\ 0 & 0 & 1 & 8 \\ 0 & 0 & 3 & 4 \\ 0 & 0 & 0 & 5 \end{bmatrix}$$

$$D = \begin{bmatrix} 1 & 0 & 0 & 0 & 0 \\ 2 & 3 & 0 & 0 & 0 \\ 4 & 5 & 6 & 0 & 0 \\ 6 & 8 & 3 & 4 & 0 \\ 9 & 2 & -1 & 4 & -3 \end{bmatrix}$$

MATRICE DIAGONALE

Une matrice diagonale est une matrice carrée dont tous les éléments non situés sur la diagonale principale sont nuls.

MATRICE SCALAIRE

Une matrice scalaire est une matrice diagonale dans laquelle tous les éléments de la diagonale principale sont identiques.

Une matrice carrée dont tous les éléments non situés sur la diagonale principale sont nuls est appelée **matrice diagonale**. Ainsi, la matrice $A = \begin{bmatrix} a_{ij} \end{bmatrix}_{n \times n}$ est diagonale si et seulement si $a_{ij} = 0$ pour tout $i \neq j$.

Une matrice diagonale dont tous les éléments de la diagonale principale sont identiques est appelée **matrice scalaire**.

MATRICE IDENTITÉ

Une matrice identité est une matrice scalaire dans laquelle tous les éléments de la diagonale principale valent 1. La matrice identité d'ordre n est notée I_n.

Une matrice scalaire d'ordre n dont tous les éléments de la diagonale principale valent 1 s'appelle **matrice identité** d'ordre n. Nous verrons bientôt que la matrice identité joue le rôle d'élément neutre pour la multiplication de matrices. On note la matrice identité d'ordre n par I_n.

Exemple

Soit les matrices

$$A = \begin{bmatrix} 4 \end{bmatrix} \quad B = \begin{bmatrix} 1 & 0 & 0 \\ 0 & 5 & 0 \\ 0 & 0 & 4 \end{bmatrix} \quad C = \begin{bmatrix} 8 & 0 \\ 0 & 8 \end{bmatrix} \quad I_2 = \begin{bmatrix} 1 & 0 \\ 0 & 1 \end{bmatrix}$$

$$O_{3 \times 3} = \begin{bmatrix} 0 & 0 & 0 \\ 0 & 0 & 0 \\ 0 & 0 & 0 \end{bmatrix} \quad I_5 = \begin{bmatrix} 1 & 0 & 0 & 0 & 0 \\ 0 & 1 & 0 & 0 & 0 \\ 0 & 0 & 1 & 0 & 0 \\ 0 & 0 & 0 & 1 & 0 \\ 0 & 0 & 0 & 0 & 1 \end{bmatrix}$$

La matrice B est une matrice diagonale d'ordre 3. Les matrices A, C et $O_{3 \times 3}$ sont des matrices scalaires d'ordre 1, 2 et 3 respectivement. Les matrices I_2 et I_5 sont les matrices identité d'ordre 2 et 5 respectivement.

EXERCICE 1.6

1. Quelle est la matrice scalaire d'ordre 5 dont la trace vaut 15 ?

2. Complétez : Si $I_n = \begin{bmatrix} \delta_{ij} \end{bmatrix}_{n \times n}$, alors[2]

$$\delta_{ij} = \begin{cases} \underline{} & \text{si } i = j \\ \underline{} & \text{si } i \neq j \end{cases}$$

3. Complétez : Si $A = \begin{bmatrix} a_{ij} \end{bmatrix}_{n \times n}$ est une matrice scalaire, alors

$$a_{ij} = \begin{cases} \underline{} & \text{si } i = j \\ \underline{} & \text{si } i \neq j \end{cases}$$

---

2. La notation δ_{ij} est appelée *symbole de Kronecker* en l'honneur du mathématicien allemand Leopold Kronecker (1823-1891). Celui-ci considérait que les mathématiques ne doivent reposer que sur les entiers et les processus finis. On lui doit une phrase célèbre : « Les entiers sont l'œuvre de Dieu, tout le reste est invention humaine. »

Une matrice symétrique est une matrice carrée $A = \begin{bmatrix} a_{ij} \end{bmatrix}_{n \times n}$, telle que $a_{ij} = a_{ji}$ pour toutes les valeurs de i et de j.

MATRICE ANTISYMÉTRIQUE

Une matrice antisymétrique est une matrice carrée $A = \begin{bmatrix} a_{ij} \end{bmatrix}_{n \times n}$ telle que $a_{ij} = -a_{ji}$ pour toutes les valeurs de i et de j.

Une matrice carrée $A = \begin{bmatrix} a_{ij} \end{bmatrix}_{n \times n}$ est appelée **matrice symétrique** si et seulement si $a_{ij} = a_{ji}$ pour toutes les valeurs de i et de j. Elle est nommée **matrice antisymétrique** si et seulement si $a_{ij} = -a_{ji}$ pour toutes les valeurs de i et de j.

Ainsi, la forme générale d'une matrice symétrique d'ordre 2 est

$$\begin{bmatrix} a & c \\ c & b \end{bmatrix}$$

alors que celle d'une matrice antisymétrique d'ordre 2 est

$$\begin{bmatrix} 0 & -a \\ a & 0 \end{bmatrix}$$

Exemple

La plupart des cartes routières contiennent une matrice des distances entre les villes principales, comme celle du tableau ci-dessous. Cette matrice est bien sûr symétrique. En effet, la distance entre Québec et Montréal est évidemment la même qu'entre Montréal et Québec.

DISTANCE EN KILOMÈTRES

	Chicoutimi	Montréal	Québec	Rouyn	Sherbrooke
Chicoutimi	0	476	206	1 120	420
Montréal	476	0	270	644	156
Québec	206	270	0	914	214
Rouyn	1 120	644	914	0	800
Sherbrooke	420	156	214	800	0

SOURCE: Ministère de l'Énergie, des Mines et des Ressources, *Canada : Carte de planification des vacances*, Ottawa, 1977.

Par contre, la matrice de migration interprovinciale nette entre les provinces de l'Atlantique (tableau 1.4, p. 4) est une matrice antisymétrique.

MATRICE ÉCHELONNÉE

Une matrice échelonnée est une matrice dont toutes les lignes nulles sont situées sous les lignes non nulles, où le premier élément non nul de chaque ligne, le pivot, vaut 1 et où le pivot de chaque ligne se trouve à droite du pivot de la ligne précédente.

PIVOT

Le pivot d'une ligne d'une matrice est le premier élément non nul de cette ligne.

Une **matrice échelonnée** possède les trois propriétés suivantes :

1) Toutes les lignes nulles de la matrice (c'est-à-dire constituées entièrement de zéros) sont situées sous les lignes qui comptent des éléments non nuls.

2) Le **pivot** d'une ligne, soit le premier élément non nul de cette ligne, vaut 1.

3) Le pivot d'une ligne est toujours situé à droite du pivot de la ligne précédente.

Une **matrice échelonnée réduite** est une matrice échelonnée qui possède une quatrième propriété :

4) Dans toute colonne qui contient un pivot, tous les éléments autres que le pivot sont nuls.

MATRICE ÉCHELONNÉE RÉDUITE
Une matrice échelonnée réduite est une matrice échelonnée telle que, dans une colonne contenant un pivot, tous les éléments valent zéro à l'exception du pivot lui-même.

Au chapitre 4, nous ferons appel aux matrices échelonnées pour résoudre des systèmes d'équations par la méthode de Gauss, et aux matrices échelonnées réduites pour appliquer la méthode de Gauss-Jordan.

Exemple

Les matrices A, B, C, D et E suivantes sont des matrices échelonnées.

$$A = \begin{bmatrix} 1 & 3 & 0 \\ 0 & 1 & 0 \\ 0 & 0 & 0 \end{bmatrix} \quad B = \begin{bmatrix} 1 & 3 & 6 & 5 \\ 0 & 1 & 6 & 0 \\ 0 & 0 & 0 & 1 \end{bmatrix} \quad C = \begin{bmatrix} 0 & 0 & 0 \\ 0 & 0 & 0 \\ 0 & 0 & 0 \end{bmatrix}$$

$$D = \begin{bmatrix} 1 & 0 & 0 & 4 & 3 \\ 0 & 0 & 1 & 3 & 8 \end{bmatrix} \quad E = \begin{bmatrix} 1 & 0 \\ 0 & 1 \\ 0 & 0 \\ 0 & 0 \end{bmatrix}$$

Mais seules les matrices C, D et E sont échelonnées réduites. En effet, dans les matrices A et B, la deuxième colonne contient un autre élément non nul que le pivot, soit 3. Les matrices A et B ne possèdent donc pas la quatrième propriété.

Les matrices F, G, H et K suivantes ne sont pas des matrices échelonnées.

$$F = \begin{bmatrix} 2 & 3 & 0 \\ 0 & 1 & 0 \\ 0 & 0 & 0 \end{bmatrix} \quad G = \begin{bmatrix} 1 & 3 & 6 & 5 \\ 1 & 1 & 6 & 0 \\ 0 & 0 & 0 & 1 \end{bmatrix}$$

$$H = \begin{bmatrix} 0 & 0 & 0 & 0 & 1 \\ 0 & 0 & 1 & 3 & 8 \end{bmatrix} \quad K = \begin{bmatrix} 1 & 0 \\ 0 & 0 \\ 0 & 1 \\ 0 & 0 \end{bmatrix}$$

EXERCICE 1.7

Expliquez pourquoi les matrices F, G, H et K de l'exemple précédent ne sont pas des matrices échelonnées.

1.4 LES PREUVES EN MATHÉMATIQUES

THÉORÈME

Un théorème est une proposition générale qui découle de propositions déjà démontrées, de définitions ou d'axiomes.

CONTRE-EXEMPLE

Un contre-exemple est un cas particulier (un exemple) qui infirme (contredit) un énoncé général. Il sert à montrer qu'un énoncé est faux.

Tout au long de ce manuel, vous allez devoir démontrer (ou prouver, montrer) des théorèmes. Un **théorème** est une proposition générale qui découle d'autres propositions déjà démontrées, de définitions ou d'axiomes. L'énoncé d'un théorème comporte une ou plusieurs hypothèses (A) et une conclusion (B). Il est essentiel de bien distinguer les hypothèses de la conclusion. Généralement, on peut énoncer un théorème sous la forme « Si A, alors B » où A représente les hypothèses et B, la conclusion.

Lorsqu'on fait une démonstration, on veut prouver par une suite d'arguments logiques que la conclusion découle des hypothèses, c'est-à-dire que « A implique B », ce qu'on écrit sous la forme symbolique $A \Rightarrow B$. Chaque étape de la démonstration exige une justification. En outre, il ne suffit pas de montrer que la proposition s'applique dans un ou plusieurs cas particuliers : il faut montrer qu'elle est toujours vraie. Un exemple, aussi convaincant soit-il, ne constitue jamais une preuve d'un énoncé. Par contre, on peut prouver la fausseté d'un énoncé par un exemple qui l'infirme : c'est ce que les mathématiciens appellent un **contre-exemple**.

En mathématiques, la démonstration de théorèmes est une activité importante. Elle demande beaucoup de savoir-faire et d'ingéniosité mais, avec le temps, vous verrez que prouver un théorème est très stimulant puisque cela représente chaque fois un défi à relever.

À propos des démonstrations mathématiques, André Joyal, mathématicien québécois de renommée internationale, a tenu les propos suivants au journaliste Normand Baillargeon du quotidien *Le Devoir*[3] :

> L'objectif serait que chacun comprenne ce qu'est une théorie, comment, à partir d'axiomes et de règles de déduction, on peut arriver par le raisonnement déductif à démontrer des choses qui ne sont pas évidentes. Il ne s'agit pas de faire des élèves des géomètres, ni même des mathématiciens, mais bien des citoyens qui puissent juger par eux-mêmes, qui auront fait l'expérience d'une démonstration et appris que le savoir humain ne repose pas entièrement sur l'observation empirique, qu'on peut comprendre la nature par le raisonnement, sans en faire l'expérience directe. Faire une démonstration plutôt que d'imposer une vérité est une exigence au cœur de la démocratie. Celui qui avance une proposition a la responsabilité d'en faire la démonstration s'il veut convaincre les autres. Les mathématiques sont démocratiques en ce sens : elles convainquent sans avoir recours ni à la force ni à l'argument d'autorité.
>
> [...]
>
> ... une démonstration, une preuve est une stratégie qui permet à celui qui défend une proposition de la défendre jusqu'au bout avec succès et qui peut faire face à un opposant pouvant défendre le contraire.

---

3. N. Baillargeon. « Le langage des maths », *Le Devoir*, 17 novembre 1997, p. B1.

PREUVE

Une preuve est un raisonnement servant à établir la vérité d'une proposition à l'aide d'énoncés considérés comme vrais.

En mathématiques, une **preuve** (ou une *démonstration*) comporte les éléments suivants, présentés dans l'ordre indiqué :

- L'énoncé qu'on veut prouver.
- Le mot *Preuve* pour indiquer le début de l'argumentation.
- L'argumentation ou le raisonnement (le cœur de la preuve).
- Un symbole pour indiquer la fin de la démonstration[4]. Dans ce manuel nous employons l'icône ∎.

En guise d'initiation, voici la démonstration de deux théorèmes. Il ne faut pas croire que toutes les preuves mathématiques soient aussi simples.

Théorème 1.1

La trace de la matrice identité d'ordre n est n.

Avant d'aborder la preuve, distinguons les hypothèses et la conclusion en reformulant le théorème : « Si A est une matrice identité d'ordre n, alors la trace de A est n. » L'hypothèse est : la matrice A est une matrice identité d'ordre n ; et la conclusion est : la trace de A est n.

Pour prouver le théorème 1.1, il ne suffit pas de vérifier que la proposition est vraie pour la matrice identité d'ordre 1, 2 ou 5. Il faut montrer que cet énoncé est vrai quel que soit l'ordre n.

Preuve

Si A est une matrice identité d'ordre n, alors $A = I_n$ et les n éléments de sa diagonale principale valent tous 1. Par conséquent,

$$\text{Tr}(A) = \text{Tr}(I_n) = \underbrace{1 + 1 + \cdots + 1}_{n \text{ termes}} = n$$

De manière plus formelle, on écrit

$$\text{Tr}(A) = \sum_{i=1}^{n} a_{ii} = \sum_{i=1}^{n} 1 = n \qquad \blacksquare$$

Le théorème 1.2 qui suit comporte l'expression « si et seulement si », qu'on retrouve dans l'énoncé de plusieurs théorèmes. On peut réécrire ce théorème sous la forme symbolique $A \Leftrightarrow B$, soit une double implication (ou biconditionnelle) qu'on lit « A est équivalent à B ». Dans un tel cas, le théorème comprend deux parties : $A \Rightarrow B$ (une affirmation qu'on lit « A implique B » ou « B est une conséquence de A » ou encore « Si A, alors B »)

---

4. Autrefois, on utilisait le sigle QED (*Quod erat demonstrandum*) qui signifie « Ce qu'il fallait démontrer ». Ce sigle fut ensuite remplacé en français par le sigle CQFD (Ce qu'il fallait démontrer), ce que certaines mauvaises langues ont associé à « Ce qui fait dormir » ou mieux encore « Ce que le frère disait ». Aujourd'hui, on emploie plutôt une icône.

et $A \Leftarrow B$ (une affirmation qu'on lit «B implique A» ou «A est une conséquence de B» ou encore «Si B, alors A»). La démonstration comportera donc elle aussi deux parties.

Théorème 1.2

Une matrice est diagonale si et seulement si elle est à la fois triangulaire inférieure et triangulaire supérieure.

Preuve

($\Rightarrow$) Distinguons l'hypothèse et la conclusion : si A est une matrice diagonale (hypothèse), alors A est une matrice triangulaire inférieure et triangulaire supérieure (conclusion).

Si A est une matrice diagonale, alors A est une matrice carrée dont tous les éléments n'appartenant pas à la diagonale principale sont nuls. Par conséquent, tous les éléments situés au-dessus de la diagonale principale sont nuls : la matrice A est triangulaire inférieure. De plus, tous les éléments situés au-dessous de la diagonale principale sont nuls : la matrice A est triangulaire supérieure. La matrice A est donc à la fois triangulaire supérieure et triangulaire inférieure.

Nous venons de prouver la conclusion : A est une matrice triangulaire inférieure et triangulaire supérieure, étant donné l'hypothèse : A est une matrice diagonale. Dans la deuxième partie de la preuve, hypothèse et conclusion sont inversées.

($\Leftarrow$) Distinguons l'hypothèse et la conclusion : si A est une matrice triangulaire inférieure et triangulaire supérieure (hypothèse), alors A est une matrice diagonale (conclusion).

Soit A, une matrice à la fois triangulaire inférieure et triangulaire supérieure. Les éléments de A situés au-dessus de la diagonale principale sont nuls parce que A est triangulaire inférieure. De plus, les éléments situés au-dessous de la diagonale principale sont nuls parce que la matrice est triangulaire supérieure. Par conséquent, tous les éléments qui ne sont pas sur la diagonale principale de A sont nuls et, en vertu de la définition de matrice diagonale, A est une matrice diagonale. ∎

EXERCICE 1.8

Montrez que toute matrice diagonale est symétrique.

RÉSUMÉ

La théorie des matrices fut élaborée au milieu du XIXe siècle par deux mathématiciens anglais, Cayley et Sylvester. Les matrices permettent de présenter de l'information numérique sous forme de tableau, de manière concise. L'interprétation des différents éléments d'une matrice dépend essentiellement de leur position.

On dit d'une matrice A qu'elle est de format $m \times n$ si elle compte mn éléments disposés sur m lignes et n colonnes. On note généralement une telle matrice $A = \left[a_{ij} \right]_{m \times n}$. Deux matrices sont égales si et seulement si elles sont parfaitement identiques : il faut qu'elles aient le même format et que leurs éléments correspondants soient égaux.

Il existe plusieurs types de matrices. Le nom de ces matrices est souvent descriptif. Une matrice carrée a la forme d'un carré. Une matrice diagonale ne comporte des éléments non nuls que sur sa diagonale principale. Une matrice nulle n'est formée que de zéros. Une matrice ligne ne compte qu'une seule ligne. Une matrice colonne est formée d'une seule colonne. On trouve un triangle de nombres dans une matrice triangulaire. Tous les éléments d'une matrice symétrique sont disposés de manière symétrique par rapport à la diagonale principale. Etc.

La rigueur en mathématiques repose essentiellement sur des fondements méthodologiques. Toute affirmation doit être étayée par une démonstration construite à l'aide d'arguments logiques faisant appel à des théorèmes déjà prouvés, à des axiomes ou à des définitions. Faire une preuve consiste donc à établir une suite d'arguments logiques qui permettent de déduire une conclusion des hypothèses. Une preuve mathématique commence par l'énoncé à prouver, suivi du mot « Preuve » – qui sert à indiquer le début de la preuve elle-même – puis de l'argumentation. On marque la fin de la démonstration par un symbole comme ■.

EXERCICES RÉCAPITULATIFS

1. (I) Un fabricant de composants électroniques vend deux produits différents à trois clients. Les deux produits sont fabriqués dans des usines différentes. Les coûts de transport de chaque produit, pour chaque client, sont indiqués dans le schéma suivant.

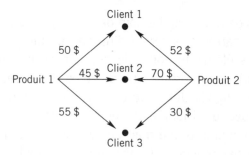

a) Présentez les informations contenues dans le schéma sous la forme d'une matrice A de format 2 × 3.

b) Quelle information la deuxième ligne de la matrice contient-elle?

c) Quelle information la troisième colonne de la matrice contient-elle?

d) Quelle information a_{12} donne-t-il?

2. (I) Une entreprise compte 524 employés: 1 président, 3 vice-présidents, 20 cadres intermédiaires et 500 syndiqués. Leurs salaires annuels de base sont les suivants: le président reçoit 500 000 $, chaque vice-président, 200 000 $, chaque cadre intermédiaire, 100 000 $ et chaque syndiqué, 40 000 $. En plus de leur salaire de base, les employés reçoivent une prime annuelle et des actions de la compagnie. La prime annuelle correspond à 10 % du salaire de base, et chaque employé reçoit une action par tranche de 1 000 $ de salaire. La valeur d'une action est de 5 $. Construisez la matrice de la rémunération des employés de l'entreprise de manière que les lignes représentent les catégories d'emploi et les colonnes, les différentes modalités de rémunération (dans l'ordre où ces données ont été présentées).

3. (I) Si $A = \left[a_{ij} \right]_{n \times n}$, quelle est la relation (<, > ou =) entre les indices i et j des éléments de A situés:

a) sur la diagonale principale?

b) au-dessous de la diagonale principale?

c) au-dessus de la diagonale principale?

4. (I) Soit les matrices

$$A = \begin{bmatrix} 2 & 6 & 0 & 1 & 4 \\ -6 & -1 & 2 & 3 & 9 \\ 2 & 1 & 5 & 2 & 10 \\ 0 & 1 & 2 & 5 & 7 \end{bmatrix}$$

$$B = \begin{bmatrix} 1 & 2 & 4 \\ 2 & -1 & 7 \\ 4 & 7 & 0 \end{bmatrix} \quad C = \begin{bmatrix} 2 & 0 \\ 0 & 2 \end{bmatrix}$$

$$D = \begin{bmatrix} 0 & 2 & -4 \\ -2 & 0 & -6 \\ 4 & 6 & 0 \end{bmatrix} \quad E = \begin{bmatrix} 1 \\ 2 \\ 5 \\ -9 \end{bmatrix}$$

$$F = \begin{bmatrix} 2 & 4 & 6 \end{bmatrix} \quad G = \begin{bmatrix} 1 \end{bmatrix}$$

$$H = \begin{bmatrix} 1 & 5 & \frac{1}{2} & 0 & 2 & 7 \\ 0 & 1 & 6 & 3 & \frac{3}{4} & 3 \end{bmatrix}$$

$$K = \begin{bmatrix} 1 & 3 & 4 \\ 0 & 0 & 1 \\ 0 & 0 & 0 \end{bmatrix} \quad L = \begin{bmatrix} 1 & 0 & 0 & 0 \\ 2 & 8 & 0 & 0 \\ 2 & 4 & 7 & 0 \\ 2 & 1 & 3 & 5 \end{bmatrix}$$

$$M = \begin{bmatrix} 1 & 4 \\ 0 & -2 \end{bmatrix} \quad N = \begin{bmatrix} 0 & 0 & 0 \\ 0 & 0 & 0 \end{bmatrix}$$

$$P = \begin{bmatrix} 1 & 0 & 0 \\ 0 & 2 & 0 \\ 0 & 0 & 3 \end{bmatrix} \quad Q = \begin{bmatrix} 0 & 1 \\ \pi & 0 \end{bmatrix}$$

a) Donnez le format de chaque matrice et, s'il y a lieu, calculez-en la trace.

b) Si possible, donnez la valeur de chacun des éléments suivants: a_{53}; a_{35}; b_{23}; b_{11}; c_{22}; d_{12}; e_{31}; e_{13}; h_{16}.

Lesquelles des matrices données sont:

c) des matrices carrées?

d) des matrices lignes?

e) des matrices colonnes?

f) des matrices nulles?

g) des matrices triangulaires inférieures?

h) des matrices triangulaires supérieures?

i) des matrices diagonales?

j) des matrices scalaires?

k) des matrices identités?

l) des matrices symétriques?

m) des matrices antisymétriques?

n) des matrices échelonnées?

o) des matrices échelonnées réduites?

5. (I) Construisez la matrice des coefficients de chacun des systèmes d'équations suivants.

a) $2x + 3y - z + w = 6$
$5x + w + 3z = 2$
$-3x - 2z + 3y + 5w = 9$
$4w = 12$

b) $x + y - 5 = 0$
$2x + 3y + 4 = 0$

6. (I) Quelle est la forme générale d'une matrice diagonale: a) d'ordre 3? b) d'ordre n?

7. (I) Quelle est la forme générale d'une matrice antisymétrique d'ordre 3?

8. (I) Une matrice 2×2 échelonnée réduite peut avoir la forme

$$\begin{bmatrix} 1 & k \\ 0 & 0 \end{bmatrix}$$

où k est une constante. Quelles sont les autres formes possibles d'une matrice 2×2 échelonnée réduite?

9. (I) Construisez les matrices $O_{3 \times 1}$, $O_{2 \times 3}$ et I_3.

10. (I) Dites si chaque énoncé est vrai ou faux. Justifiez votre réponse.

a) Toutes les colonnes d'une matrice comportent le même nombre d'éléments.

b) Une matrice 50×60 compte plus de lignes que de colonnes.

c) Il n'y a que deux matrices lignes 1×6 qui soient échelonnées.

d) Il n'y a que deux matrices colonnes 6×1 qui soient échelonnées.

e) La seule matrice diagonale d'ordre 3 qui soit échelonnée réduite est I_3.

f) Une matrice $\left[a_{ij} \right]_{3 \times 2}$ peut être antisymétrique.

g) $\begin{bmatrix} 1 & 1 & 1 \end{bmatrix} = \begin{bmatrix} 1 & 1 \end{bmatrix}$

h) La trace d'une matrice antisymétrique vaut 0.

i) Une matrice diagonale est nécessairement échelonnée.

j) Les éléments de la diagonale principale d'une matrice carrée A sont notés a_{ii}.

k) La matrice $A = \left[a_{ij} \right]_{n \times n}$ où $a_{ij} = i \times j$ est symétrique.

l) La matrice $A = \left[a_{ij} \right]_{n \times n}$ où $a_{ij} = i - j$ est antisymétrique.

m) Une matrice de format 8×4 compte 12 éléments.

n) La somme de tous les éléments d'une matrice antisymétrique est égale à la trace de cette matrice.

o) Les matrices d'ordre 1 sont des matrices scalaires.

11. (I) Énoncez les critères d'égalité de deux matrices A et B.

12. (I) Pour quelles valeurs des paramètres x et y les matrices A et B sont-elles égales?

$$A = \begin{bmatrix} 2x + 3 & 8 \\ y & 4 \end{bmatrix} \quad B = \begin{bmatrix} x^2 & 8 \\ -5 & 4 \end{bmatrix}$$

13. (I) Donnez la forme générale d'une matrice à la fois symétrique et antisymétrique.

14. (I) Construisez les matrices A et B suivantes:

$$A = \left[a_{ij} \right]_{2 \times 3} \quad \text{où } a_{ij} = (-1)^{i+j} j^2$$
$$B = \left[b_{ij} \right]_{3 \times 3} \quad \text{où } b_{ij} = i + 2j$$

15. (I) Donnez l'expression du terme général (a_{ij}; b_{ij}; c_{ij}; d_{ij}) de chacune des matrices suivantes:

$$A = \begin{bmatrix} 2 & 2 & 2 \\ 2 & 2 & 2 \\ 2 & 2 & 2 \end{bmatrix} \quad B = \begin{bmatrix} 1 & 1 & 1 & 1 \\ 2 & 2 & 2 & 2 \\ 3 & 3 & 3 & 3 \\ 4 & 4 & 4 & 4 \end{bmatrix}$$

$$C = \begin{bmatrix} 1 & 0 & 0 & 0 \\ 0 & 4 & 0 & 0 \\ 0 & 0 & 9 & 0 \\ 0 & 0 & 0 & 16 \end{bmatrix} \quad D = \begin{bmatrix} 1 & -1 & 1 \\ -1 & 1 & -1 \\ 1 & -1 & 1 \end{bmatrix}$$

16. (I) Le schéma suivant donne des informations sur la migration interprovinciale entre les recensements de 1986 et de 1991, dans les provinces de l'Ouest canadien.

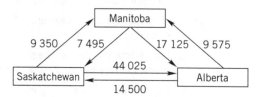

a) Présentez la migration interprovinciale nette sous forme matricielle.

b) Faites la somme de tous les nombres de la matrice. Expliquez le résultat.

c) Quelle province affiche le solde migratoire interprovincial net le plus élevé?

d) Quelle province affiche le solde migratoire interprovincial net le plus faible?

17. (II) Lorsque plusieurs espèces animales vivent dans un même écosystème, elles entrent généralement en compétition pour leur alimentation. Lorsque deux animaux se disputent la même nourriture, le gagnant est celui qui réussit à s'approprier l'objet de convoitise. Supposons qu'un animal de l'espèce i l'emporte sur un animal de l'espèce j dans une proportion de $c_{ij} = i/(i + j)$.

a) Construisez la matrice de compétition, $C = \left[c_{ij} \right]_{3 \times 3}$, entre trois espèces animales d'un même écosystème.

b) Quelle espèce gagne le plus souvent lorsqu'elle est en compétition avec les autres espèces?

c) Que vaut $c_{ij} + c_{ji}$? Expliquez le résultat.

18. (II) Au cours du dernier mois, trois revendeurs de service interurbain se sont livré une concurrence féroce. Ces trois entreprises détiennent la totalité du marché. L'entreprise 1 a conservé 80 % de sa clientèle mais en a perdu 10 % au profit de l'entreprise 2. L'entreprise 2 a retenu 75 % de sa clientèle mais en a perdu 5 % au profit de l'entreprise 3. Enfin, l'entreprise 3 détient toujours 90 % de sa clientèle mais elle en a perdu 5 % au profit de l'entreprise 2. La matrice de transition $T = \left[t_{ij} \right]_{3 \times 3}$, qui représente les mouvements de la clientèle, est définie par

t_{ij} = part de la clientèle de j qui passe à i

Construisez la matrice de transition du marché de l'interurbain.

19. (I) Au jeu d'échecs, on joue à deux sur un échiquier formé de 64 cases alternativement noires et blanches, qui forment 8 lignes et 8 colonnes. Chaque joueur dispose de 16 pièces (un roi, une reine, deux fous, deux cavaliers, deux tours et huit pions). Un joueur possède des pièces blanches (les Blancs) et l'autre des pièces noires (les Noirs). La position initiale des pièces sur l'échiquier est indiquée dans la figure suivante.

Étant donné la forme de l'échiquier, on peut représenter le jeu d'échecs par une matrice. On détermine d'abord la valeur des pièces comme suit.

VALEUR DES PIÈCES

Pièce	Couleur	
	Blanc	Noir
Roi	9	−9
Reine	8	−8
Fou	4	−4
Cavalier	2	−2
Tour	5	−5
Pion	1	−1

On note la position de chacune des cases de l'échiquier comme si celui-ci constituait une matrice; puis on associe à chaque case occupée le nombre correspondant à la valeur de la pièce qui s'y trouve, et à chaque case libre la valeur 0. Si on note la matrice par $A = \left[a_{ij} \right]_{8 \times 8}$, alors, par exemple, $a_{85} = 9$ parce qu'au début du jeu le roi blanc se trouve à l'intersection de la huitième ligne et de la cinquième colonne.

a) Complétez la matrice suivante qui représente la position initiale des pièces sur un jeu d'échecs.

$$\begin{bmatrix} \_ & -2 & -4 & -8 & \_ & \_ & \_ & -5 \\ -1 & -1 & -1 & \_ & \_ & \_ & \_ & \_ \\ 0 & 0 & 0 & 0 & 0 & 0 & 0 & 0 \\ 0 & 0 & 0 & 0 & 0 & 0 & 0 & 0 \\ 0 & 0 & 0 & 0 & 0 & 0 & 0 & 0 \\ 0 & 0 & 0 & 0 & 0 & 0 & 0 & 0 \\ \_ & \_ & \_ & \_ & \_ & \_ & \_ & \_ \\ \_ & \_ & \_ & \_ & 9 & \_ & \_ & \_ \end{bmatrix}$$

b) Voici la matrice représentant la position des pièces sur l'échiquier après plusieurs coups. Quelle notation matricielle emploie-t-on pour désigner le roi noir dans cet échiquier?

$$A = \begin{bmatrix} 0 & 0 & 0 & 0 & 0 & 0 & 0 & 0 \\ 0 & -8 & 0 & 0 & 0 & 0 & 0 & 0 \\ 0 & -1 & 0 & 0 & 0 & 0 & 0 & -1 \\ -1 & 0 & 0 & -9 & 0 & 0 & -1 & 0 \\ 0 & 0 & -1 & 1 & -4 & 0 & 0 & 0 \\ 0 & 0 & 1 & 0 & 8 & 0 & 1 & 0 \\ 0 & 1 & 0 & 0 & 0 & 1 & 0 & 0 \\ 0 & 0 & 0 & 0 & 0 & 4 & 9 & 0 \end{bmatrix}$$

c) Quelles sont les pièces restantes des Blancs?

d) Quelle matrice obtiendra-t-on si les Blancs déplacent leur fou dans la case située au-dessus de leur roi?

20. (I) La théorie des graphes est la branche des mathématiques qui étudie les réseaux (sociaux, électriques, de communication, de transport, etc.). Un graphe simple est un ensemble fini de points (appelés sommets) et de liens entre ces points (des segments de droite appelés arêtes). La matrice d'adjacence d'un graphe simple est $A = \begin{bmatrix} a_{ij} \end{bmatrix}_{n \times n}$ où $a_{ij} = 1$ si les points i et j sont reliés par une arête, et $a_{ij} = 0$ dans le cas contraire. Voici un graphe simple et sa matrice d'adjacence.

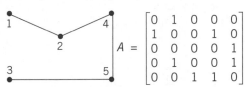

$$A = \begin{bmatrix} 0 & 1 & 0 & 0 & 0 \\ 1 & 0 & 0 & 1 & 0 \\ 0 & 0 & 0 & 0 & 1 \\ 0 & 1 & 0 & 0 & 1 \\ 0 & 0 & 1 & 1 & 0 \end{bmatrix}$$

a) Combien de points le graphe compte-t-il?

b) Quel est le format de la matrice d'adjacence du graphe?

c) Quel est le format de la matrice d'adjacence d'un graphe simple qui compte: i) huit points? ii) n points?

d) La matrice d'adjacence du graphe simple illustré précédemment est symétrique. Peut-on dire que la matrice d'adjacence de n'importe quel graphe simple est symétrique? Si vous répondez oui, justifiez votre réponse. Si vous répondez non, donnez un contre-exemple.

e) Quelle est la matrice d'adjacence du graphe simple suivant?

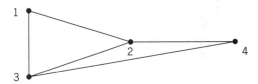

f) Construisez un graphe simple dont la matrice d'adjacence est

$$A = \begin{bmatrix} 0 & 1 & 0 \\ 1 & 0 & 1 \\ 0 & 1 & 0 \end{bmatrix}$$

g) Pourquoi la matrice suivante ne peut-elle pas être la matrice d'adjacence d'un graphe simple?

$$A = \begin{bmatrix} 0 & 1 & 1 \\ 1 & 0 & 1 \\ 0 & 1 & 0 \end{bmatrix}$$

21. (I) Prouvez chacun des énoncés suivants. Au préalable, distinguez les hypothèses et la conclusion.

a) Une matrice nulle carrée est une matrice scalaire.

b) Une matrice scalaire dont la trace vaut zéro est une matrice nulle.

c) La diagonale principale d'une matrice anti-symétrique ne comporte que des zéros.

22. (I) Montrez que deux matrices scalaires de même format sont égales si et seulement si leurs traces sont égales.

CHAPITRE 2

Opérations sur les matrices

Tel est l'avantage d'une langue bien construite que sa notation
simplifiée est souvent à l'origine de théories profondes.

Pierre Simon, marquis de Laplace

À LA FIN DU PRÉSENT CHAPITRE, VOUS DEVRIEZ ÊTRE
EN MESURE DE RÉPONDRE AUX QUESTIONS SUIVANTES:

• Comment additionne-t-on deux matrices?

• Comment multiplie-t-on deux matrices?

• Qu'est-ce que la transposée d'une matrice?

• Quelles sont les principales propriétés des opérations
  sur les matrices?

• Comment représente-t-on un système d'équations linéaires
  au moyen de matrices?

• Qu'est-ce que l'inverse d'une matrice?

• Comment résout-on un système d'équations linéaires
  au moyen de matrices?

UN PORTRAIT de Arthur Cayley

Arthur Cayley naquit en 1821 à Richmond, en Angleterre. Entré au Trinity College de l'Université de Cambridge à l'âge de 17 ans, le jeune Cayley démontra rapidement son immense talent pour les mathématiques. Il obtint son diplôme avec les plus hautes distinctions et devint Fellow du Trinity College. Un des examinateurs, impressionné par les prouesses de Cayley, écrivit à côté de son nom qu'il se trouvait dans une classe à part, au-dessus du premier.

Cayley devait toutefois penser à gagner sa vie, et aucun poste de professeur n'était disponible pour un laïc. Il s'inscrivit alors en droit et devint avocat. Il exerça cette profession pendant quatorze ans, ce qui ne l'empêcha pas de publier près de 300 articles portant sur différents sujets en mathématiques durant cette période.

En 1863, grâce à un legs de Lady Sadler, l'Université de Cambridge ouvrit une chaire de mathématiques pures, dont Cayley devint le premier titulaire. Il occupa ce poste de professeur jusqu'à sa mort en 1895.

Cayley toucha à presque toutes les branches des mathématiques pures, mais il manifesta un intérêt particulier pour l'algèbre et la géométrie (euclidienne et non euclidienne). Ainsi, il fut le premier à étudier la géométrie à n dimensions, il inventa le calcul matriciel, il élabora la théorie des invariants algébriques et il apporta une contribution importante à la théorie des déterminants.

Son collègue et ami J. J. Sylvester dit de lui qu'il embellissait tout ce qu'il touchait («nihil tetigit quod non ornavit»). D'ailleurs, la collaboration de Cayley et de Sylvester dans l'élaboration de la théorie des invariants fut si étroite qu'on les désigne souvent comme les invariant twins (les «jumeaux invariants»).

Cayley compte parmi les trois auteurs les plus prolifiques en mathématiques, les autres étant L. Euler et A.-L. Cauchy. Son œuvre mathématique se compose de 13 volumes d'environ 600 pages chacun ; on y dénombre 966 articles spécialisés.

2.1 ADDITION DE DEUX MATRICES

Au chapitre précédent, nous avons établi le vocabulaire qui va nous servir dans l'étude de l'algèbre[1] matricielle. De même qu'il est possible d'effectuer des opérations mathématiques sur les nombres réels, il est possible d'effectuer des opérations sur les matrices. Dans le présent chapitre, nous allons aborder l'addition de matrices, la multiplication d'une matrice par un scalaire, la transposition d'une matrice et la multiplication de deux matrices. Nous présenterons également les principales propriétés de ces opérations.

Vous savez additionner deux nombres réels, voyons maintenant comment additionner deux matrices.

Exemple

Après les récentes coupes effectuées dans les budgets affectés à l'éducation, James, Jasmine et Julien ont vu leurs prêts et bourses diminuer de façon importante. Ils doivent s'astreindre à un régime minceur et réduire leurs dépenses reliées à des services ou produits considérés comme moins essentiels, tels que les loisirs (cinéma, sports, etc.), le tabac, l'alcool et les friandises. Comme ils suivent un cours d'algèbre linéaire, ils ont décidé de représenter leurs dépenses du mois de septembre sous forme matricielle.

DÉPENSES EN SEPTEMBRE

	Loisirs	Tabac	Alcool	Friandises
James	20 $	50 $	50 $	12 $
Jasmine	15 $	0 $	0 $	25 $
Julien	25 $	0 $	25 $	18 $

---

1. Le mot algèbre a pour origine le terme arabe *al-jabr*, qui signifie « reconstruction ». Ce mot a été employé pour la première fois par le mathématicien Al-Khwarizmi pour décrire le transfert d'un terme d'un membre à l'autre membre d'une équation. Initialement, l'algèbre avait donc pour objet la résolution d'équations ou de systèmes d'équations. On a longtemps considéré cette branche des mathématiques comme « l'arithmétique des lettres ».

Toutefois, au XIXᵉ siècle, des mathématiciens, plus enclins à la théorie qu'au simple calcul, ont enrichi l'algèbre. Ils en ont fait la partie des mathématiques qui étudie les ensembles munis d'opérations et de propriétés (associativité, commutativité, distributivité, fermeture, etc.) et ont ainsi créé le concept de structure algébrique. Les espaces vectoriels, que nous aborderons au chapitre 10, constituent un exemple de structure algébrique.

Ils ont ensuite fait la même chose pour le mois d'octobre.

Dépenses en octobre

	Loisirs	Tabac	Alcool	Friandises
James	16 $	24 $	30 $	20 $
Jasmine	15 $	0 $	0 $	23 $
Julien	21 $	0 $	19 $	16 $

Jasmine a alors eu l'idée de combiner ces deux matrices afin de mesurer leurs dépenses individuelles totales par poste budgétaire, au cours des deux mois. Voici les calculs qu'elle a effectués et les résultats qu'elle a obtenus.

Dépenses en septembre et en octobre

	Loisirs	Tabac	Alcool	Friandises
James	20 $ + 16 $	50 $ + 24 $	50 $ + 30 $	12 $ + 20 $
Jasmine	15 $ + 15 $	0 $ + 0 $	0 $ + 0 $	25 $ + 23 $
Julien	25 $ + 21 $	0 $ + 0 $	25 $ + 19 $	18 $ + 16 $

Dépenses en septembre et en octobre

	Loisirs	Tabac	Alcool	Friandises
James	36 $	74 $	80 $	32 $
Jasmine	30 $	0 $	0 $	48 $
Julien	46 $	0 $	44 $	34 $

En combinant les deux matrices comme elle l'a fait, Jasmine les a en fait additionnées. Elle a calculé la somme des éléments qui occupent une même position dans la matrice des dépenses de septembre et dans celle d'octobre. Cet exemple nous amène à la définition de l'addition de deux matrices.

ADDITION DE DEUX MATRICES

L'addition de deux matrices de même format, $A = \begin{bmatrix} a_{ij} \end{bmatrix}_{m \times n}$ et $B = \begin{bmatrix} b_{ij} \end{bmatrix}_{m \times n}$, est une opération matricielle dont le résultat est la matrice $A + B = \begin{bmatrix} a_{ij} + b_{ij} \end{bmatrix}_{m \times n}$.

L'**addition**[2] **de deux matrices** de même format, $A = \begin{bmatrix} a_{ij} \end{bmatrix}_{m \times n}$ et $B = \begin{bmatrix} b_{ij} \end{bmatrix}_{m \times n}$, est une opération matricielle dont le résultat (la somme) est la matrice $A + B = \begin{bmatrix} a_{ij} + b_{ij} \end{bmatrix}_{m \times n}$.

---

2. En théorie, il faut distinguer les mots addition et somme, de même que les mots multiplication et produit. Les termes addition et multiplication désignent des opérations, alors que les termes somme et produit désignent les résultats de ces opérations. Dans ce manuel, nous ne nous attarderons pas à cette distinction.

$$A + B = \begin{bmatrix} a_{11} & a_{12} & \cdots & a_{1j} & \cdots & a_{1n} \\ a_{21} & a_{22} & \cdots & a_{2j} & \cdots & a_{2n} \\ \vdots & \vdots & & \vdots & & \vdots \\ a_{i1} & a_{i2} & \cdots & a_{ij} & \cdots & a_{in} \\ \vdots & \vdots & & \vdots & & \vdots \\ a_{m1} & a_{m2} & \cdots & a_{mj} & \cdots & a_{mn} \end{bmatrix} + \begin{bmatrix} b_{11} & b_{12} & \cdots & b_{1j} & \cdots & b_{1n} \\ b_{21} & b_{22} & \cdots & b_{2j} & \cdots & b_{2n} \\ \vdots & \vdots & & \vdots & & \vdots \\ b_{i1} & b_{i2} & \cdots & b_{ij} & \cdots & b_{in} \\ \vdots & \vdots & & \vdots & & \vdots \\ b_{m1} & b_{m2} & \cdots & b_{mj} & \cdots & b_{mn} \end{bmatrix}$$

$$= \begin{bmatrix} a_{11} + b_{11} & a_{12} + b_{12} & \cdots & a_{1j} + b_{1j} & \cdots & a_{1n} + b_{1n} \\ a_{21} + b_{21} & a_{22} + b_{22} & \cdots & a_{2j} + b_{2j} & \cdots & a_{2n} + b_{2n} \\ \vdots & \vdots & & \vdots & & \vdots \\ a_{i1} + b_{i1} & a_{i2} + b_{i2} & \cdots & a_{ij} + b_{ij} & \cdots & a_{in} + b_{in} \\ \vdots & \vdots & & \vdots & & \vdots \\ a_{m1} + b_{m1} & a_{m2} + b_{m2} & \cdots & a_{mj} + b_{mj} & \cdots & a_{mn} + b_{mn} \end{bmatrix}$$

L'élément situé à l'intersection de la i-ième ligne et de la j-ième colonne de la matrice somme est donc égal à la somme des éléments qui se trouvent à l'intersection de la i-ième ligne et de la j-ième colonne dans les deux matrices à additionner. Il est à noter que le résultat de l'addition de deux matrices de format $m \times n$ est également une matrice de format $m \times n$. C'est pourquoi on dit que l'opération d'addition dans l'univers des matrices de format $m \times n$ possède la propriété de fermeture.

En vertu de la définition de l'addition de deux matrices, on ne peut additionner que des matrices de même format. Si deux matrices sont de formats différents, on dit qu'il y a **incompatibilité pour l'addition** ou encore que l'addition n'est pas définie pour ces deux matrices.

INCOMPATIBILITÉ POUR L'ADDITION

Si deux matrices n'ont pas le même format, on dit qu'elles sont incompatibles pour l'addition.

L'expression $\underbrace{A + B}_{\substack{\text{Addition} \\ \text{de matrices}}} = \begin{bmatrix} a_{ij} \underbrace{+}_{\substack{\text{Addition} \\ \text{de réels}}} b_{ij} \end{bmatrix}_{m \times n}$ contient deux signes d'addition. Le

premier représente l'addition de deux matrices et le second, l'addition de deux nombres réels[3]. L'addition des matrices A et B est une opération sur deux éléments d'un ensemble (les matrices de format $m \times n$) dont le résultat appartient au même ensemble. L'addition des éléments a_{ij} et b_{ij} est une opération sur deux éléments d'un autre ensemble (les nombres réels) dont le résultat appartient à cet autre ensemble. On emploie le même symbole (le signe « + ») pour désigner ces deux opérations différentes (qui portent sur des ensembles différents) seulement parce qu'elles sont intimement liées. Il importe que vous sachiez reconnaître ces deux sens du signe « + » pour bien comprendre les démonstrations des propriétés des matrices, que nous présenterons bientôt.

---

3. Les éléments d'une matrice peuvent être des nombres complexes. Cependant, à l'exception du chapitre 7, nous nous limiterons aux matrices réelles dans ce manuel.

Exemple

Soit les matrices

$$A = \begin{bmatrix} 1 & 4 \\ 3 & 2 \end{bmatrix} \quad O_{2 \times 2} = \begin{bmatrix} 0 & 0 \\ 0 & 0 \end{bmatrix} \quad B = \begin{bmatrix} -1 & 2 \\ 6 & -4 \end{bmatrix}$$

$$C = \begin{bmatrix} 1 & 6 \\ 2 & 3 \\ 4 & 9 \end{bmatrix} \quad O_{3 \times 2} = \begin{bmatrix} 0 & 0 \\ 0 & 0 \\ 0 & 0 \end{bmatrix}$$

$$D = \begin{bmatrix} d_{ij} \end{bmatrix}_{m \times n} \text{ où } d_{ij} = i^2 + j^2 \quad E = \begin{bmatrix} e_{ij} \end{bmatrix}_{m \times n} \text{ où } e_{ij} = 2ij$$

L'addition des matrices A et C n'est pas définie parce que ces matrices ne sont pas de même format : A est une matrice 2×2 alors que C est une matrice 3×2. De même, l'addition des matrices C et $O_{2 \times 2}$ n'est pas définie.

Par contre,

$$A + B = \begin{bmatrix} 1 + (-1) & 4 + 2 \\ 3 + 6 & 2 + (-4) \end{bmatrix} = \begin{bmatrix} 0 & 6 \\ 9 & -2 \end{bmatrix}$$

$$A + O_{2 \times 2} = \begin{bmatrix} 1 + 0 & 4 + 0 \\ 3 + 0 & 2 + 0 \end{bmatrix} = \begin{bmatrix} 1 & 4 \\ 3 & 2 \end{bmatrix} = A$$

$$C + O_{3 \times 2} = \begin{bmatrix} 1 + 0 & 6 + 0 \\ 2 + 0 & 3 + 0 \\ 4 + 0 & 9 + 0 \end{bmatrix} = \begin{bmatrix} 1 & 6 \\ 2 & 3 \\ 4 & 9 \end{bmatrix} = C$$

Les deux dernières opérations portent à croire que les matrices nulles jouent le rôle d'élément neutre pour l'addition. Cette intuition est juste, mais la propriété reste à démontrer !

Enfin, si on pose $F = D + E$, alors $F = \begin{bmatrix} f_{ij} \end{bmatrix}_{m \times n}$ où

$$f_{ij} = d_{ij} + e_{ij} = (i^2 + j^2) + 2ij = (i + j)^2$$

Ainsi, $f_{31} = (3 + 1)^2 = 16$ et $f_{45} = (4 + 5)^2 = 81$. De plus, comme $f_{ij} = (i + j)^2 = (j + i)^2 = f_{ji}$, la matrice F est symétrique.

EXERCICE 2.1

Soit les matrices

$$A = \begin{bmatrix} 3 & 5 & -8 \\ 1 & 0 & 4 \\ 6 & 7 & 7 \end{bmatrix} \quad B = \begin{bmatrix} -1 & 5 & -7 \\ 9 & 3 & 2 \\ -5 & 5 & 4 \end{bmatrix} \quad C = \begin{bmatrix} 1 & 4 \\ 2 & 0 \\ -1 & 4 \end{bmatrix}$$

$$D = \begin{bmatrix} d_{ij} \end{bmatrix}_{3 \times 3} \text{ où } d_{ij} = (-1)^i \, j^2$$

Effectuez si possible les opérations suivantes.

a) $A + C$

b) $A + B$

c) $B + A$. Comparez le résultat avec celui que vous avez obtenu en b. Que constatez-vous? D'après vous, s'agit-il d'une coïncidence ou est-ce une propriété générale de l'addition de matrices?

d) $B + D$

2.2 MULTIPLICATION D'UNE MATRICE PAR UN SCALAIRE

La deuxième opération sur les matrices que nous définissons est la multiplication d'une matrice par un scalaire.

Exemple

James, Jasmine et Julien ont continué de comptabiliser leurs dépenses pendant quatre mois, et ils ont obtenu la matrice suivante:

DÉPENSES DE SEPTEMBRE À DÉCEMBRE

	Loisirs	Tabac	Alcool	Friandises
James	84 $	100 $	120 $	60 $
Jasmine	48 $	0 $	0 $	80 $
Julien	72 $	0 $	88 $	64 $

James a alors eu l'idée de calculer la dépense mensuelle moyenne de chacun d'eux par poste budgétaire. Voici le résultat.

DÉPENSES MENSUELLES MOYENNES

	Loisirs	Tabac	Alcool	Friandises
James	21 $	25 $	30 $	15 $
Jasmine	12 $	0 $	0 $	20 $
Julien	18 $	0 $	22 $	16 $

Comme la période compte quatre mois, James a multiplié chaque élément de la matrice par $\frac{1}{4}$. Il a donc multiplié chaque élément de la matrice par un scalaire (le nombre $\frac{1}{4}$). Cet exemple nous amène à la définition de la multiplication d'une matrice par un scalaire.

MULTIPLICATION D'UNE MATRICE
PAR UN SCALAIRE

La multiplication d'une matrice
$A = \left[a_{ij} \right]_{m \times n}$ par un scalaire
(un nombre) k est une opération
dont le résultat est la matrice
$kA = \left[ka_{ij} \right]_{m \times n}$.

La **multiplication d'une matrice** $A = \left[a_{ij} \right]_{m \times n}$ **par un scalaire** (un nombre) k donne une nouvelle matrice de même format que A, notée $kA = \left[ka_{ij} \right]_{m \times n}$. On multiplie donc chaque élément de la matrice A par le nombre k pour obtenir le produit kA.

$$A = \begin{bmatrix} a_{11} & a_{12} & \dots & a_{1j} & \dots & a_{1n} \\ a_{21} & a_{22} & \dots & a_{2j} & \dots & a_{2n} \\ \vdots & \vdots & & \vdots & & \vdots \\ a_{i1} & a_{i2} & \dots & a_{ij} & \dots & a_{in} \\ \vdots & \vdots & & \vdots & & \vdots \\ a_{m1} & a_{m2} & \dots & a_{mj} & \dots & a_{mn} \end{bmatrix} \Rightarrow kA = \begin{bmatrix} ka_{11} & ka_{12} & \dots & ka_{1j} & \dots & ka_{1n} \\ ka_{21} & ka_{22} & \dots & ka_{2j} & \dots & ka_{2n} \\ \vdots & \vdots & & \vdots & & \vdots \\ ka_{i1} & ka_{i2} & \dots & ka_{ij} & \dots & ka_{in} \\ \vdots & \vdots & & \vdots & & \vdots \\ ka_{m1} & ka_{m2} & \dots & ka_{mj} & \dots & ka_{mn} \end{bmatrix}$$

Exemple

Soit les matrices

$$A = \begin{bmatrix} 1 & 4 \\ 3 & 2 \end{bmatrix} \quad \text{et} \quad B = \begin{bmatrix} -1 & 2 \\ 6 & -4 \end{bmatrix}$$

Alors,

$$5A = \begin{bmatrix} 5 \times 1 & 5 \times 4 \\ 5 \times 3 & 5 \times 2 \end{bmatrix} = \begin{bmatrix} 5 & 20 \\ 15 & 10 \end{bmatrix}$$

$$(-1)B = \begin{bmatrix} (-1)(-1) & (-1)(2) \\ (-1)(6) & (-1)(-4) \end{bmatrix} = \begin{bmatrix} 1 & -2 \\ -6 & 4 \end{bmatrix}$$

Par ailleurs,

$$B + (-1)B = \begin{bmatrix} -1 & 2 \\ 6 & -4 \end{bmatrix} + \begin{bmatrix} 1 & -2 \\ -6 & 4 \end{bmatrix} = \begin{bmatrix} 0 & 0 \\ 0 & 0 \end{bmatrix} = O_{2 \times 2}$$

MATRICE OPPOSÉE

La matrice opposée d'une matrice
$A = \left[a_{ij} \right]_{m \times n}$ est la matrice
$-A = \left[-a_{ij} \right]_{m \times n}$. La somme de
deux matrices opposées est la
matrice nulle de format $m \times n$,
c'est-à-dire que $A + (-A) = O_{m \times n}$.

On note la matrice $(-1)A$ par $-A$ et on appelle $-A$ **matrice opposée** de A. Les matrices opposées possèdent une propriété intéressante : si $A = \left[a_{ij} \right]_{m \times n}$, alors $-A = \left[-a_{ij} \right]_{m \times n}$ et $A + (-A) = A - A = O_{m \times n}$. La matrice $-A$ joue donc le rôle d'inverse additif de la matrice A.

Soit les matrices

$$A = \begin{bmatrix} 3 & 5 & -8 \\ 1 & 0 & 4 \\ 6 & 7 & 7 \end{bmatrix} \quad B = \begin{bmatrix} -1 & 5 & -7 \\ 9 & 3 & 2 \\ -5 & 5 & 4 \end{bmatrix} \quad C = \begin{bmatrix} 1 & 4 \\ 2 & 0 \\ -1 & 4 \end{bmatrix}$$

$$D = \begin{bmatrix} d_{ij} \end{bmatrix}_{3 \times 3} \text{ où } d_{ij} = i + j$$

Effectuez si possible les opérations suivantes.

a) $-2C$

b) $3A + 2B$

c) $3D + 4C$

d) $-2A + D$

2.3 TRANSPOSITION D'UNE MATRICE

TRANSPOSÉE D'UNE MATRICE

La transposée d'une matrice $A = \begin{bmatrix} a_{ij} \end{bmatrix}_{m \times n}$ est la matrice $A^t = \begin{bmatrix} a_{ji} \end{bmatrix}_{n \times m}$, obtenue en interchangeant les lignes et les colonnes de la matrice A.

La transposition d'une matrice est l'une des opérations dont nous nous servirons dans les chapitres subséquents. La **transposée** d'une matrice A, notée A^t (ou A^T), est la matrice obtenue en interchangeant les lignes et les colonnes de la matrice A. Ainsi, la première ligne de A devient la première colonne de A^t, etc. Si $A = \begin{bmatrix} a_{ij} \end{bmatrix}_{m \times n}$, alors $A^t = \begin{bmatrix} a_{ji} \end{bmatrix}_{n \times m}$: la transposition d'une matrice de format $m \times n$ donne une matrice de format $n \times m$.

Exemple

Soit les matrices

$$A = \begin{bmatrix} 3 & 2 \\ 2 & 1 \end{bmatrix} \quad B = \begin{bmatrix} 0 & 4 \\ -4 & 0 \end{bmatrix} \quad C = \begin{bmatrix} 1 & 4 & 5 \\ 1 & -3 & 7 \end{bmatrix}$$

$$D = \begin{bmatrix} d_{ij} \end{bmatrix}_{3 \times 4} \text{ où } d_{ij} = 2i - j$$

Alors,

$$A^t = \begin{bmatrix} 3 & 2 \\ 2 & 1 \end{bmatrix} \quad B^t = \begin{bmatrix} 0 & -4 \\ 4 & 0 \end{bmatrix} \quad C^t = \begin{bmatrix} 1 & 1 \\ 4 & -3 \\ 5 & 7 \end{bmatrix}$$

$$D^t = \begin{bmatrix} d_{ji} \end{bmatrix}_{4 \times 3} \text{ où } d_{ji} = 2i - j$$

À la section 1.3, nous avons dit qu'une matrice symétrique est une matrice carrée $A = \left[a_{ij} \right]_{n \times n}$ telle que $a_{ij} = a_{ji}$ pour toutes les valeurs de i et de j. Nous pouvons maintenant reformuler cette définition en faisant appel au concept de transposée : une **matrice symétrique** est une matrice A telle que $A = A^t$.

Par ailleurs, nous avons dit qu'une matrice antisymétrique est une matrice carrée $A = \left[a_{ij} \right]_{n \times n}$ telle que $a_{ij} = -a_{ji}$ pour toutes les valeurs de i et de j. Nous pouvons également reformuler cette définition à l'aide du concept de transposée : une **matrice antisymétrique** est une matrice A telle que $A = -A^t$ ou, ce qui est équivalent, $A^t = -A$. Ces deux définitions – qu'on retrouve dans l'article d'Arthur Cayley intitulé *A Memoir on the Theory of Matrices* – sont très utiles pour prouver quelques-unes des propriétés des matrices symétriques et des matrices antisymétriques.

MATRICE SYMÉTRIQUE

Une matrice A est une matrice symétrique si et seulement si $A = A^t$.

MATRICE ANTISYMÉTRIQUE

Une matrice A est une matrice antisymétrique si et seulement si $A = -A^t$ ou, ce qui est équivalent, si et seulement si $A^t = -A$.

EXERCICE 2.3

Soit les matrices

$$A = \begin{bmatrix} 3 & 5 & -8 \\ 1 & 0 & 4 \\ 6 & 7 & 7 \end{bmatrix} \quad B = \begin{bmatrix} 3 & -4 & 2 \\ 2 & 5 & 8 \end{bmatrix} \quad C = \begin{bmatrix} 1 & 4 \\ 2 & 0 \\ -1 & 4 \end{bmatrix}$$

$$D = \left[d_{ij} \right]_{3 \times 3} \text{ où } d_{ij} = i + j$$

Effectuez si possible les opérations suivantes.

a) $3B^t - 2C$

b) $3A^t + 2B$

c) $(B^t)^t$. Que constatez-vous ? D'après vous, s'agit-il d'une coïncidence ou est-ce une propriété générale des matrices ?

d) $(A + D)^t$

e) $A^t + D^t$. Comparez le résultat avec celui que vous avez obtenu en *d*. Que constatez-vous ? D'après vous, s'agit-il d'une coïncidence ou est-ce une propriété générale des matrices ?

2.4 PROPRIÉTÉS DE L'ADDITION, DE LA MULTIPLICATION PAR UN SCALAIRE ET DE LA TRANSPOSITION

Les opérations que nous venons de définir possèdent des propriétés intéressantes, qui découlent pour la plupart des propriétés correspondantes des opérations sur les nombres réels. Il va sans dire que les propriétés d'une opération sur des matrices ne sont vérifiées que si l'opération est définie. Ainsi, l'affirmation $A + B = B + A$ a un sens seulement si les matrices A et B sont de même format.

Le théorème 2.1 énonce les principales propriétés des opérations définies précédemment. On suppose que A, B et C sont des matrices de format $m \times n$, et que r et s sont des scalaires (ou nombres réels).

Théorème 2.1

1) $A + B = B + A$ (commutativité de l'addition)

2) $(A + B) + C = A + (B + C)$ (associativité de l'addition)

3) $A + O_{m \times n} = A$ (existence d'un élément neutre pour l'addition)

4) $A + (-A) = O_{m \times n}$ (A et $-A$ sont des matrices opposées)

5) $r(A + B) = rA + rB$ (distributivité de la multiplication par un scalaire par rapport à l'addition)

6) $(r + s)A = rA + sA$

7) $(rs)A = r(sA)$

8) $0A = O_{m \times n}$

9) $1A = A$

10) $(A^t)^t = A$

11) $(kA)^t = kA^t$

12) $(A + B)^t = A^t + B^t$

Nous allons maintenant prouver les propriétés 1, 3, 8 et 10 du théorème 2.1. Nous vous laissons démontrer les autres propriétés en guise d'exercice.

Propriété 1 Si A et B sont deux matrices de format $m \times n$, alors
$$A + B = B + A$$

Preuve

Si $A = \left[a_{ij} \right]_{m \times n}$ et $B = \left[b_{ij} \right]_{m \times n}$, alors

$$
\begin{aligned}
A + B &= \left[a_{ij} + b_{ij} \right]_{m \times n} \quad \text{(définition de l'addition de deux matrices)} \\
&= \left[b_{ij} + a_{ij} \right]_{m \times n} \quad \text{(commutativité de l'addition dans les réels)} \\
&= B + A \quad \text{(définition de l'addition de deux matrices)} \quad \blacksquare
\end{aligned}
$$

Propriété 3 Si A est une matrice de format $m \times n$, alors $A + O_{m \times n} = A$.

Preuve

Si $A = \left[a_{ij} \right]_{m \times n}$, alors

$$A + O_{m \times n} = \left[a_{ij} + 0 \right]_{m \times n} \quad \text{(définition de l'addition de deux matrices)}$$

$$= \begin{bmatrix} a_{ij} \end{bmatrix}_{m \times n} \qquad \text{(0 est l'élément neutre pour l'addition dans}$$

(0 est l'élément neutre pour l'addition dans les réels)

$$= A \qquad \text{(définition de } A\text{)} \qquad \blacksquare$$

Propriété 8 Si A est une matrice de format $m \times n$, alors $0A = O_{m \times n}$.

Preuve

Si $A = \begin{bmatrix} a_{ij} \end{bmatrix}_{m \times n}$, alors

$$0A = \begin{bmatrix} 0 \times a_{ij} \end{bmatrix}_{m \times n} \qquad \text{(définition de la multiplication d'une matrice par un scalaire)}$$

$$= \begin{bmatrix} 0 \end{bmatrix}_{m \times n} \qquad \text{(0 est l'élément absorbant pour la multiplication dans les réels)}$$

$$= O_{m \times n} \qquad \text{(définition de } O_{m \times n}\text{)} \qquad \blacksquare$$

Propriété 10 Si A est une matrice de format $m \times n$, alors $(A^t)^t = A$.

Preuve

$$A = \begin{bmatrix} a_{ij} \end{bmatrix}_{m \times n} \Rightarrow \underbrace{A^t = \begin{bmatrix} a_{ji} \end{bmatrix}_{n \times m}}_{\substack{\text{Définition de la} \\ \text{transposée}}} \Rightarrow \underbrace{(A^t)^t = \begin{bmatrix} a_{ij} \end{bmatrix}_{m \times n}}_{\substack{\text{Définition de la} \\ \text{transposée}}} \Rightarrow (A^t)^t = A \qquad \blacksquare$$

EXERCICE 2.4

Prouvez la propriété 7 du théorème 2.1 : $(rs)A = r(sA)$.

2.5 MULTIPLICATION DE DEUX MATRICES

Nous avons introduit les opérations d'addition de deux matrices et de multiplication d'une matrice par un scalaire de manière intuitive, à l'aide d'un exemple simple. La multiplication de deux matrices n'est pas aussi facile à définir.

Exemple

Le coût total, noté c, de q unités d'un bien dont le prix unitaire est de p \$ est égal au produit $c = qp$ \$. Ainsi, le coût total de 3 sacs de croustilles à 1,79 \$ l'unité est $c = qp$ \$ $= 3 \times 1,79$ \$ $= 5,37$ \$.

Voyons comment généraliser, à l'aide de la multiplication de matrices, le calcul du coût de divers biens ayant des prix différents.

Chaque semaine, James, Jasmine et Julien achètent quatre denrées alimentaires, dont les quantités sont indiquées dans la matrice suivante.

MATRICE DES QUANTITÉS (NOMBRE D'UNITÉS)

	Denrée 1	Denrée 2	Denrée 3	Denrée 4
James	4	3	1	0
Jasmine	2	4	2	3
Julien	3	3	3	1

Les prix unitaires des denrées varient d'une semaine à l'autre. La matrice des prix pour les deux dernières semaines est la suivante.

MATRICE DES PRIX UNITAIRES

	Semaine 1	Semaine 2
Denrée 1	1,50 $	1,40 $
Denrée 2	2,00 $	2,25 $
Denrée 3	0,75 $	0,80 $
Denrée 4	1,25 $	1,15 $

Nous voulons représenter les dépenses hebdomadaires de chacune des trois personnes sous forme matricielle. Comme nous l'avons fait lorsque nous n'avions qu'une quantité et qu'un prix, nous voulons déterminer la matrice des coûts, notée C, en calculant le produit de la matrice des quantités, notée Q, par la matrice des prix, notée P.

Déterminons d'abord le format de la matrice des coûts. Comme il y a trois consommateurs et deux périodes d'une semaine, cette matrice est de format 3×2 ; par conséquent, $C = \left[c_{ij} \right]_{3 \times 2}$. La première ligne de C représente les dépenses de James, la deuxième celles de Jasmine et la troisième celles de Julien. La première colonne représente les dépenses des trois personnes au cours de la première semaine et la deuxième colonne, les dépenses pendant la deuxième semaine.

Les dépenses totales de Julien la première semaine sont donc notées par c_{31} et celles de Jasmine, la deuxième semaine, par c_{22}.

Évaluons chacun de ces éléments:

$$c_{31} = 3 \times 1,50\ \$ + 3 \times 2,00\ \$ + 3 \times 0,75\ \$ + 1 \times 1,25\ \$$$
$$= 14,00\ \$$$

$$c_{22} = 2 \times 1,40\ \$ + 4 \times 2,25\ \$ + 2 \times 0,80\ \$ + 3 \times 1,15\ \$$$
$$= 16,85\ \$$$

Pour évaluer c_{31}, nous avons dû effectuer une opération qui consiste en quelque sorte à « multiplier » la *troisième* ligne de la matrice des quantités par la *première* colonne de la matrice des prix.

$$C = QP = \begin{bmatrix} 4 & 3 & 1 & 0 \\ 2 & 4 & 2 & 3 \\ \mathbf{3} & \mathbf{3} & \mathbf{3} & \mathbf{1} \end{bmatrix} \begin{bmatrix} \mathbf{1,50} & 1,40 \\ \mathbf{2,00} & 2,25 \\ \mathbf{0,75} & 0,80 \\ \mathbf{1,25} & 1,15 \end{bmatrix}$$

Ainsi, $c_{31} = q_{31} \times p_{11} + q_{32} \times p_{21} + q_{33} \times p_{31} + q_{34} \times p_{41}$.

L'élément de la matrice des coûts situé à l'intersection de la *i*-ième ligne et de la *j*-ième colonne, soit c_{ij}, s'obtient donc en « multipliant » de la même façon la *i*-ième ligne de la matrice des quantités par la *j*-ième colonne de la matrice des prix:

$$c_{ij} = q_{i1} \times p_{1j} + q_{i2} \times p_{2j} + q_{i3} \times p_{3j} + q_{i4} \times p_{4j}$$

La matrice des coûts est donc

$$C = \begin{bmatrix} 12,75 & 13,15 \\ 16,25 & 16,85 \\ 14,00 & 14,50 \end{bmatrix}$$

Par conséquent, la deuxième semaine, James a dépensé 13,15 \$ pour l'achat des quatre denrées.

MULTIPLICATION DE DEUX MATRICES

La multiplication de deux matrices $A = \begin{bmatrix} a_{ij} \end{bmatrix}_{m \times n}$ et $B = \begin{bmatrix} b_{ij} \end{bmatrix}_{n \times p}$ est une opération matricielle dont le résultat est la matrice

$$AB = \begin{bmatrix} \sum_{k=1}^{n} a_{ik} b_{kj} \end{bmatrix}_{m \times p}.$$

Nous sommes maintenant en mesure de définir de manière formelle le produit matriciel. Soit deux matrices $A = \begin{bmatrix} a_{ij} \end{bmatrix}_{m \times n}$ et $B = \begin{bmatrix} b_{ij} \end{bmatrix}_{n \times p}$, alors le **produit des matrices** A et B, dans cet ordre, est la matrice $C = AB = \begin{bmatrix} c_{ij} \end{bmatrix}_{m \times p}$, définie comme suit:

$$AB = \begin{bmatrix} a_{11} & a_{12} & \cdots & a_{1j} & \cdots & a_{1n} \\ a_{21} & a_{22} & \cdots & a_{2j} & \cdots & a_{2n} \\ \vdots & \vdots & & \vdots & & \vdots \\ \mathbf{a_{i1}} & \mathbf{a_{i2}} & \cdots & \mathbf{a_{ij}} & \cdots & \mathbf{a_{in}} \\ \vdots & \vdots & & \vdots & & \vdots \\ a_{m1} & a_{m2} & \cdots & a_{mj} & \cdots & a_{mn} \end{bmatrix} \begin{bmatrix} b_{11} & b_{12} & \cdots & \mathbf{b_{1j}} & \cdots & b_{1p} \\ b_{21} & b_{22} & \cdots & \mathbf{b_{2j}} & \cdots & b_{2p} \\ \vdots & \vdots & & \vdots & & \vdots \\ b_{i1} & b_{i2} & \cdots & \mathbf{b_{ij}} & \cdots & b_{ip} \\ \vdots & \vdots & & \vdots & & \vdots \\ b_{n1} & b_{n2} & \cdots & \mathbf{b_{nj}} & \cdots & b_{np} \end{bmatrix}$$

$$
= \begin{bmatrix}
c_{11} & c_{12} & \cdots & c_{1j} & \cdots & c_{1p} \\
c_{21} & c_{22} & \cdots & c_{2j} & \cdots & c_{2p} \\
\vdots & \vdots & & \vdots & & \vdots \\
c_{i1} & c_{i2} & \cdots & \boldsymbol{c_{ij}} & \cdots & c_{ip} \\
\vdots & \vdots & & \vdots & & \vdots \\
c_{m1} & c_{m2} & \cdots & c_{mj} & \cdots & c_{mp}
\end{bmatrix}
$$

où $c_{ij} = a_{i1}b_{1j} + a_{i2}b_{2j} + a_{i3}b_{3j} + \cdots + a_{in}b_{nj} = \displaystyle\sum_{k=1}^{n} a_{ik}b_{kj}$.

Autrement dit, $C = AB = \left[\displaystyle\sum_{k=1}^{n} a_{ik}b_{kj} \right]_{m \times p}$.

Il n'est pas nécessaire d'employer cette formule pour calculer le produit de deux matrices. Il suffit de se rappeler que pour trouver l'élément du produit matriciel AB situé à l'intersection de la i-ième ligne et de la j-ième colonne, soit c_{ij}, on « multiplie » en quelque sorte la i-ième ligne de la matrice A par la j-ième colonne de la matrice B, dans cet ordre. Par contre, il faut employer la formule contenant le symbole de sommation pour prouver les principales propriétés de la multiplication de deux matrices.

On sait qu'on ne peut additionner deux matrices que si elles ont le même format. Il existe également une condition que les formats des deux matrices doivent satisfaire pour qu'on puisse multiplier celles-ci : le produit matriciel AB, où A est une matrice $m \times n$ et B une matrice $r \times p$, est défini seulement si $n = r$, c'est-à-dire si le nombre de colonnes de la matrice A est égal au nombre de lignes de la matrice B. Dans ce cas, la matrice AB est de dimension $m \times p$:

$$
A_{m \times n} B_{n \times p} = C_{m \times p}
$$

Si A est une matrice de format 2×3 et B une matrice de format 3×5, alors AB est une matrice de format 2×5. Par contre, le produit BA n'est pas défini puisque le nombre de colonnes de B n'est pas égal au nombre de lignes de A.

Cette dernière constatation nous amène à faire une remarque importante au sujet du produit matriciel. On sait que $ab = ba$ pour n'importe quels nombres réels a et b; par contre, il existe des matrices A et B telles que $AB \neq BA$: contrairement à la multiplication de réels, la multiplication de matrices n'est pas commutative. Il faut donc être très prudent; n'étant pas des nombres réels, les matrices n'en possèdent pas toutes les propriétés.

Soit les matrices

$$A = \begin{bmatrix} 3 & 5 & -8 \\ 1 & 0 & 4 \\ 6 & 7 & 7 \end{bmatrix} \quad B = \begin{bmatrix} 3 & -4 & 2 \\ 2 & 5 & 8 \end{bmatrix} \quad C = \begin{bmatrix} 1 & 4 \\ 2 & 0 \\ -1 & 4 \end{bmatrix}$$

$$D = \begin{bmatrix} d_{ij} \end{bmatrix}_{3 \times 3} \text{ où } d_{ij} = (-1)^i \, j^2$$

Donnez le format des produits matriciels qui sont définis.

a) AC

b) CA

c) BC

d) CB

e) AD

f) BA

g) $(BA)(DC)$

Illustrons maintenant le produit matriciel à l'aide d'un exemple numérique.

Exemple

Soit les matrices

$$A = \begin{bmatrix} 1 & 2 \\ -1 & 3 \end{bmatrix} \quad B = \begin{bmatrix} 4 & -4 & 2 \\ 2 & 5 & 5 \end{bmatrix}$$

Le produit AB est une matrice de format 2×3, tandis que le produit BA n'est pas défini en raison du format des matrices.

Si on pose $C = AB$, alors l'élément c_{11} est tiré de la première ligne de la matrice A et de la première colonne de la matrice B de la façon suivante : $c_{11} = 1 \times 4 + 2 \times 2 = 8$. En procédant de la même façon pour tous les éléments du produit matriciel, on obtient :

$c_{11} = 1 \times 4 + 2 \times 2 = 8$ $\qquad c_{12} = 1 \times (-4) + 2 \times 5 = 6$

$c_{13} = 1 \times 2 + 2 \times 5 = 12$ $\qquad c_{21} = -1 \times 4 + 3 \times 2 = 2$

$c_{22} = -1 \times (-4) + 3 \times 5 = 19$ $\qquad c_{23} = -1 \times 2 + 3 \times 5 = 13$

Par conséquent,

$$C = \begin{bmatrix} 8 & 6 & 12 \\ 2 & 19 & 13 \end{bmatrix}$$

Soit les matrices

$$A = \begin{bmatrix} 3 & 5 & -8 \\ 1 & 0 & 4 \\ 6 & 7 & 7 \end{bmatrix} \quad B = \begin{bmatrix} 3 & -4 & 2 \\ 2 & 5 & 8 \end{bmatrix} \quad C = \begin{bmatrix} 1 & 4 \\ 2 & 0 \\ -1 & 4 \end{bmatrix}$$

$$D = \begin{bmatrix} d_{ij} \end{bmatrix}_{3 \times 3} \text{ où } d_{ij} = (-1)^i \, j^2$$

Effectuez, si possible, les opérations suivantes.

a) AC

b) CA

c) BC

d) CB

e) AD

f) DA. Comparez le résultat avec celui que vous avez obtenu en *e*. Que constatez-vous? Cela vous étonne-t-il?

La multiplication de matrices a de nombreuses applications. Elle sert notamment à décrire la propagation d'une maladie contagieuse transmissible par contact direct entre deux individus.

Exemple

Un premier groupe de trois personnes, atteintes d'une maladie contagieuse, a été en contact direct avec un deuxième groupe de cinq personnes. On désigne la matrice des contacts directs entre les individus des premier et deuxième groupes par $A = \begin{bmatrix} a_{ij} \end{bmatrix}_{3 \times 5}$ où

$$a_{ij} = \begin{cases} 0 & \text{si l'individu } i \text{ n'a pas été directement en contact avec } j \\ 1 & \text{si l'individu } i \text{ a été directement en contact avec } j \end{cases}$$

Les individus du deuxième groupe qui ont eu des contacts directs avec ceux du premier groupe peuvent à leur tour infecter les individus d'un troisième groupe avec lesquels ils entrent en contact. On dit alors que les individus du troisième groupe ont été indirectement en contact avec ceux du premier groupe. Si les individus du deuxième groupe ont eu des contacts directs avec les quatre individus d'un troisième groupe, on désigne la matrice des contacts directs entre les individus des deuxième et troisième groupes par $B = \begin{bmatrix} b_{ij} \end{bmatrix}_{5 \times 4}$ où

$$b_{ij} = \begin{cases} 0 & \text{si l'individu } i \text{ n'a pas été directement en contact avec } j \\ 1 & \text{si l'individu } i \text{ a été directement en contact avec } j \end{cases}$$

Soit les matrices de contacts directs

$$A = \begin{bmatrix} 0 & 0 & 1 & 0 & 1 \\ 0 & 0 & 1 & 1 & 0 \\ 1 & 0 & 0 & 1 & 1 \end{bmatrix} \quad \text{et} \quad B = \begin{bmatrix} 0 & 0 & 1 & 0 \\ 1 & 0 & 0 & 0 \\ 0 & 1 & 0 & 0 \\ 1 & 0 & 0 & 1 \\ 0 & 1 & 0 & 0 \end{bmatrix}$$

Par exemple, $a_{23} = 1$ indique que l'individu 2 du premier groupe a été directement en contact avec l'individu 3 du deuxième groupe. Par contre, l'individu 1 du premier groupe n'a pas eu de contact direct avec l'individu 4 du deuxième groupe puisque $a_{14} = 0$. De façon similaire, la cinquième ligne de la matrice B indique que seul l'individu 2 du troisième groupe a été directement en contact avec l'individu 5 du deuxième groupe.

On construit la matrice qui donne le nombre de contacts indirects entre les individus des premier et troisième groupes en calculant le produit matriciel $C = AB$. On a

$$c_{ij} = \sum_{k=1}^{5} a_{ik} b_{kj} = a_{i1} b_{1j} + a_{i2} b_{2j} + a_{i3} b_{3j} + a_{i4} b_{4j} + a_{i5} b_{5j}$$

Or,

$$a_{ik} b_{kj} = \begin{cases} 0 & \text{si l'individu } k \text{ (2}^{\text{e}}\text{ gr.) n'a pas été directement} \\ & \text{en contact avec } i \text{ (1}^{\text{er}}\text{ gr.) ou } j \text{ (3}^{\text{e}}\text{ gr.)} \\ 1 & \text{si l'individu } k \text{ (2}^{\text{e}}\text{ gr.) a été directement en contact} \\ & \text{avec } i \text{ (1}^{\text{er}}\text{ gr.) et } j \text{ (3}^{\text{e}}\text{ gr.)} \end{cases}$$

de sorte que $a_{ik} b_{kj}$ vaut 1 si l'individu j (3e gr.) a été indirectement en contact avec l'individu i (1er gr.) par l'intermédiaire de l'individu k (2e gr.).

Par conséquent, c_{ij} représente le nombre de contacts indirects de la personne j (3e gr.) avec la personne i (1er gr.) par l'intermédiaire des personnes du deuxième groupe.

$$C = AB = \begin{bmatrix} 0 & 0 & 1 & 0 & 1 \\ 0 & 0 & 1 & 1 & 0 \\ 1 & 0 & 0 & 1 & 1 \end{bmatrix} \begin{bmatrix} 0 & 0 & 1 & 0 \\ 1 & 0 & 0 & 0 \\ 0 & 1 & 0 & 0 \\ 1 & 0 & 0 & 1 \\ 0 & 1 & 0 & 0 \end{bmatrix} = \begin{bmatrix} 0 & 2 & 0 & 0 \\ 1 & 1 & 0 & 1 \\ 1 & 1 & 1 & 1 \end{bmatrix}$$

Ainsi, la personne 2 du troisième groupe a eu 2 contacts indirects avec la personne 1 du premier groupe puisque $c_{12} = 2$.

EXERCICE 2.7

Combien de contacts indirects avec la maladie la personne 2 du troisième groupe a-t-elle eus en tout?

Vous savez que la multiplication de matrices ne possède pas les mêmes propriétés que la multiplication dans les réels. Par exemple, $ab = ba$ pour n'importe quels nombres réels a et b. Par contre, nous avons vu que la multiplication de matrices n'est pas commutative : il existe des matrices A et B telles que $AB \neq BA$.

De façon analogue, l'expression a^n est définie pour tout nombre réel a et tout nombre naturel n. Mais l'expression $A^n = \underbrace{AA \cdots A}_{n \text{ facteurs}}$ n'est définie que si

A est une matrice carrée[4].

EXERCICE 2.8

Soit les matrices

$$A = \begin{bmatrix} 3 & 5 & -8 \\ 1 & 0 & 4 \\ 6 & 7 & 7 \end{bmatrix} \quad \text{et} \quad B = \begin{bmatrix} 3 & -4 & 2 \\ 2 & 5 & 8 \end{bmatrix}$$

Effectuez si possible les opérations suivantes.

a) B^4

b) A^2

Lorsque nous avons défini les matrices particulières à la section 1.3, nous avons dû omettre deux types de matrices parce que nous n'avions pas encore vu la multiplication de matrices. Une **matrice** carrée A d'ordre n est

---

4. Cette affirmation repose sur l'associativité de la multiplication de matrices, une propriété que nous énoncerons dans la prochaine section.

dite **idempotente**[5] si $A^2 = A$. Une **matrice** carrée d'ordre n est dite **nilpotente**[6] s'il existe un entier positif k tel que $A^k = O_{n \times n}$; le plus petit entier k qui satisfait cette égalité est appelé **indice de nilpotence** de A.

Exemple

Les matrices $A = \begin{bmatrix} 3 & -1 \\ 6 & -2 \end{bmatrix}$, $B = \begin{bmatrix} 1 & 0 & 0 \\ 0 & 0 & 1 \\ 0 & 0 & 1 \end{bmatrix}$ et $O_{n \times n}$ sont des matrices idempotentes. En effet, il est facile de vérifier que $A^2 = A$, $B^2 = B$ et $O_{n \times n}^2 = O_{n \times n}$.

Quant à la matrice $C = \begin{bmatrix} 1 & -1 \\ 1 & -1 \end{bmatrix}$, elle est nilpotente d'indice 2 puisque $C^2 = O_{2 \times 2}$.

La matrice C n'est pas nulle, et pourtant $CC = C^2 = O_{2 \times 2}$. Voilà un autre résultat surprenant de la multiplication de deux matrices. Le produit de deux nombres réels est 0 si et seulement si l'un des deux nombres est nul. Par contre, le produit de deux matrices peut être la matrice nulle sans qu'aucune des deux matrices ne soit nulle :

$$A_{m \times n} B_{n \times p} = O_{m \times p} \not\Rightarrow A_{m \times n} = O_{m \times n} \quad \text{ou} \quad B_{n \times p} = O_{n \times p}$$

EXERCICE 2.9

Déterminez si les matrices suivantes sont idempotentes ou nilpotentes.

$$A = \begin{bmatrix} \frac{1}{2} & \frac{3}{4} \\ \frac{1}{3} & \frac{1}{2} \end{bmatrix} \qquad B = \begin{bmatrix} 0 & 1 & 1 \\ 0 & 0 & 2 \\ 0 & 0 & 0 \end{bmatrix} \qquad O_{3 \times 2} \qquad O_{4 \times 4}$$

---

5. Le sens de ce mot est facile à retenir : idempotente veut dire identique dans ses puissances.
6. Le sens de ce mot est facile à retenir : nilpotente veut dire nulle pour une certaine puissance.

Nous avons déjà souligné que le mathématicien Arthur Cayley (1821-1895) élabora une véritable théorie des matrices. Dans une publication de 1858, intitulée *A Memoir on the Theory of Matrices*, il définit les principaux termes et les opérations fondamentales de l'algèbre matricielle. De plus, il y démontre plusieurs propriétés de l'algèbre matricielle. Ainsi, il écrit que deux matrices de même format sont égales lorsque leurs éléments correspondants sont égaux, que la somme de deux matrices est la matrice dont les éléments sont égaux à la somme des éléments correspondants des deux matrices à additionner, que le produit d'une matrice par un scalaire s'obtient en multipliant chaque élément de la matrice par ce scalaire. Cayley affirme également que l'addition de matrices est associative et convertible (commutative).

Cet article contient en outre la définition de la transposée d'une matrice et la proposition, non prouvée, $(AB)^t = B^t A^t$. Cayley y définit également les concepts de matrice symétrique et de matrice antisymétrique de la façon suivante : Si $A^t = A$, alors la matrice A est dite symétrique ; si $A^t = -A$, alors la matrice A est dite antisymétrique. Il poursuit en démontrant que toute matrice carrée s'écrit comme la somme d'une matrice symétrique et d'une matrice antisymétrique.

Cayley élabora le langage matriciel parce qu'il cherchait un moyen de représenter succinctement l'effet de deux transformations successives, soit

$$x' = a_{11}x + a_{12}y$$
$$y' = a_{21}x + a_{22}y$$

suivie de

$$x'' = b_{11}x' + b_{12}y'$$
$$y'' = b_{21}x' + b_{22}y'$$

Cayley construisit les matrices des coefficients de ces deux transformations :

$$A = \begin{bmatrix} a_{11} & a_{12} \\ a_{21} & a_{22} \end{bmatrix} \quad \text{et} \quad B = \begin{bmatrix} b_{11} & b_{12} \\ b_{21} & b_{22} \end{bmatrix}$$

Il voulut par la suite exprimer la matrice des coefficients de la transformation liant les variables x'' et y'' aux variables x et y.

Si, dans la seconde transformation, on substitue à x' et à y' leurs valeurs dans la première transformation, on obtient :

$$x'' = b_{11}(a_{11}x + a_{12}y) + b_{12}(a_{21}x + a_{22}y)$$
$$= (b_{11}a_{11} + b_{12}a_{21})x + (b_{11}a_{12} + b_{12}a_{22})y$$

$$y'' = b_{21}(a_{11}x + a_{12}y) + b_{22}(a_{21}x + a_{22}y)$$
$$= (b_{21}a_{11} + b_{22}a_{21})x + (b_{21}a_{12} + b_{22}a_{22})y$$

La matrice des coefficients de la transformation des variables x et y en x'' et y'' est donc

$$\begin{bmatrix} b_{11}a_{11} + b_{12}a_{21} & b_{11}a_{12} + b_{12}a_{22} \\ b_{21}a_{11} + b_{22}a_{21} & b_{21}a_{12} + b_{22}a_{22} \end{bmatrix}$$

Cayley choisit donc de définir la multiplication de deux matrices de façon que le produit BA soit égal à cette dernière matrice. C'est cette définition que nous avons présentée dans la section 2.5.

Cayley poursuit son article en affirmant que la multiplication de deux matrices est associative, mais qu'elle n'est pas commutative.

Par cette publication remarquable, Arthur Cayley jeta les fondements de l'algèbre matricielle et il éveilla l'intérêt de la communauté mathématique de son époque pour l'étude de structures algébriques abstraites.

2.6 PROPRIÉTÉS DE LA MULTIPLICATION DE MATRICES

La multiplication de matrices possède, comme les autres opérations, plusieurs propriétés intéressantes. Celles-ci sont toutefois un peu plus – sinon beaucoup plus – difficiles à prouver à cause de la complexité de la définition du produit matriciel. C'est pourquoi nous nous contenterons d'en démontrer seulement quelques-unes. Nous vous demanderons de prouver les autres propriétés en guise d'exercice ou simplement de les illustrer.

Le théorème 2.2 énonce d'autres propriétés des opérations sur les matrices. On suppose que A, B, C, D, E et F sont des matrices telles que les opérations en question sont définies. De plus, r est un scalaire.

Théorème 2.2

1) Il existe des matrices A et B telles que $AB \neq BA$ (la multiplication de matrices n'est pas commutative).

2) $(AB)C = A(BC)$ (associativité de la multiplication de matrices)

3) $r(AB) = (rA)B = A(rB)$

4) $A_{m \times n}I_n = A_{m \times n}$ et $I_n B_{n \times p} = B_{n \times p}$ (existence d'un élément neutre pour la multiplication)

5) $A(B + C) = AB + AC$ et $(D + E)F = DF + EF$ (distributivité de la multiplication de matrices par rapport à l'addition)

6) $(AB)^t = B^t A^t$

7) $O_{m \times n}A_{n \times p} = O_{m \times p}$ et $A_{n \times p}O_{p \times q} = O_{n \times q}$

8) $A_{m \times n}B_{n \times p} = O_{m \times p} \not\Rightarrow A_{m \times n} = O_{m \times n}$ ou $B_{n \times p} = O_{n \times p}$

La formulation de certaines propriétés, comme la propriété 4, comporte deux égalités : l'une pour la multiplication à droite et l'autre pour la multiplication à gauche. C'est la non-commutativité de la multiplication de matrices qui nous oblige à faire cette distinction.

Exemple

La propriété 1 du théorème 2.2 énonce essentiellement que la multiplication de deux matrices n'est pas nécessairement commutative même lorsque le produit matriciel est défini. Pour prouver cette proposition, il suffit de trouver un contre-exemple infirmant l'égalité $AB = BA$; autrement dit, il faut trouver deux matrices A et B telles que $AB \neq BA$.

Soit les matrices

$$A = \begin{bmatrix} 3 & -4 & 2 \\ 2 & 5 & 8 \end{bmatrix} \quad \text{et} \quad B = \begin{bmatrix} 1 & 4 \\ 2 & 0 \\ -1 & 4 \end{bmatrix}$$

Le produit AB est une matrice de format 2×2, alors que BA est une matrice de format 3×3. Comme deux matrices de formats différents ne peuvent être égales, $AB \neq BA$.

Pour montrer la fausseté d'un énoncé, il suffit de trouver un contre-exemple. Cependant, on ne peut jamais prouver qu'un énoncé général est vrai en donnant un ou même plusieurs exemples.

La preuve de la deuxième propriété du théorème 2.2 n'est pas très compliquée, mais elle est ennuyeuse comme la pluie. C'est pourquoi nous nous contenterons d'illustrer cette propriété par un exemple.

Exemple

Soit les matrices

$$A = \begin{bmatrix} 3 & -4 & 2 \\ 2 & 5 & 8 \end{bmatrix} \quad B = \begin{bmatrix} 1 & 4 \\ 2 & 0 \\ -1 & 4 \end{bmatrix} \quad C = \begin{bmatrix} 3 & -2 \\ 1 & 2 \end{bmatrix}$$

On veut vérifier que $(AB)C = A(BC)$. Or,

$$(AB)C = \left(\begin{bmatrix} 3 & -4 & 2 \\ 2 & 5 & 8 \end{bmatrix} \begin{bmatrix} 1 & 4 \\ 2 & 0 \\ -1 & 4 \end{bmatrix} \right) \begin{bmatrix} 3 & -2 \\ 1 & 2 \end{bmatrix}$$

$$= \begin{bmatrix} -7 & 20 \\ 4 & 40 \end{bmatrix} \begin{bmatrix} 3 & -2 \\ 1 & 2 \end{bmatrix}$$

$$= \begin{bmatrix} -1 & 54 \\ 52 & 72 \end{bmatrix}$$

et

$$A(BC) = \begin{bmatrix} 3 & -4 & 2 \\ 2 & 5 & 8 \end{bmatrix} \left(\begin{bmatrix} 1 & 4 \\ 2 & 0 \\ -1 & 4 \end{bmatrix} \begin{bmatrix} 3 & -2 \\ 1 & 2 \end{bmatrix} \right)$$

$$= \begin{bmatrix} 3 & -4 & 2 \\ 2 & 5 & 8 \end{bmatrix} \begin{bmatrix} 7 & 6 \\ 6 & -4 \\ 1 & 10 \end{bmatrix}$$

$$= \begin{bmatrix} -1 & 54 \\ 52 & 72 \end{bmatrix}$$

Ainsi, nous avons vérifié que la deuxième propriété du théorème 2.2 est vraie pour les trois matrices données. Toutefois, il ne s'agit pas d'une preuve valable de cette propriété pour toutes les matrices dont le produit est défini.

Nous allons prouver les propriétés 4, 6 et 8 du théorème 2.2. À vous de démontrer les propriétés 3, 5 et 7, en guise d'exercice.

La propriété 4 est particulièrement importante. Elle affirme essentiellement que la matrice identité joue le rôle d'élément neutre pour la multiplication.

Nous ferons bientôt appel à cette propriété pour résoudre un système d'équations linéaires.

Propriété 4 $A_{m \times n} I_n = A_{m \times n}$ et $I_n B_{n \times p} = B_{n \times p}$

Preuve

La matrice identité est définie par $I_n = \left[\delta_{ij} \right]_{n \times n}$ où $\delta_{ij} = \begin{cases} 1 & \text{pour } i = j \\ 0 & \text{pour } i \neq j \end{cases}$.

Si $A = \left[a_{ij} \right]_{m \times n}$ et $A I_n = C = \left[c_{ij} \right]_{m \times n}$, alors, selon la définition du produit matriciel,

$$\begin{aligned}
c_{ij} &= \sum_{k=1}^{n} a_{ik} \delta_{kj} \\
&= a_{i1} \delta_{1j} + a_{i2} \delta_{2j} + \cdots + a_{ij} \delta_{jj} + \cdots + a_{in} \delta_{nj} \\
&= a_{i1}(0) + a_{i2}(0) + \cdots + a_{ij}(1) + \cdots + a_{in}(0) \\
&= a_{ij}
\end{aligned}$$

Par conséquent, $A I_n = C = \left[c_{ij} \right]_{m \times n} = \left[a_{ij} \right]_{m \times n} = A$.

La seconde partie de la preuve est analogue.   ◼

La propriété 6 surprend à première vue. Pourquoi faut-il inverser l'ordre des matrices lorsqu'on prend la transposée du produit de deux matrices? En d'autres mots, pourquoi n'a-t-on pas $(AB)^t = A^t B^t$? La raison en est fort simple: il arrive que le produit $A^t B^t$ ne soit pas défini même si le produit AB l'est. En effet, si A est une matrice de format $m \times n$ et B une matrice de format $n \times p$, alors le format de A^t est $n \times m$ et le format de B^t est $p \times n$. Les matrices $(AB)^t$ et $B^t A^t$ sont définies, mais $A^t B^t$ ne l'est pas nécessairement. De plus, le format de $B^t A^t$ est le même que celui de $(AB)^t$, soit $p \times m$. Toutefois, il ne suffit pas que deux matrices aient le même format pour qu'elles soient égales, il faut de plus que les éléments correspondants des deux matrices soient égaux.

Avant de démontrer la propriété 6, illustrons-la à l'aide d'un exemple.

Exemple

Soit les matrices

$$A = \begin{bmatrix} 3 & -4 & 2 \\ 2 & 5 & 8 \end{bmatrix} \quad \text{et} \quad B = \begin{bmatrix} 1 & 4 \\ 2 & 0 \\ -1 & 4 \end{bmatrix}$$

On veut vérifier que $(AB)^t = B^t A^t$. D'une part,

$$AB = \begin{bmatrix} -7 & 20 \\ 4 & 40 \end{bmatrix} \Rightarrow (AB)^t = \begin{bmatrix} -7 & 4 \\ 20 & 40 \end{bmatrix}$$

et, d'autre part,

$$B^t A^t = \begin{bmatrix} 1 & 2 & -1 \\ 4 & 0 & 4 \end{bmatrix} \begin{bmatrix} 3 & 2 \\ -4 & 5 \\ 2 & 8 \end{bmatrix} = \begin{bmatrix} -7 & 4 \\ 20 & 40 \end{bmatrix}$$

Par conséquent, pour les matrices A et B données, $(AB)^t = B^t A^t$.

Propriété 6 $(AB)^t = B^t A^t$

Preuve

Si $A = \begin{bmatrix} a_{ij} \end{bmatrix}_{m \times n}$ et $B = \begin{bmatrix} b_{ij} \end{bmatrix}_{n \times p}$, alors les matrices $(AB)^t$ et $B^t A^t$ ont le même format, soit $p \times m$. La première condition pour que deux matrices soient égales est donc satisfaite.

Il reste à vérifier que les éléments correspondants de $(AB)^t$ et de $B^t A^t$ sont égaux. Or, l'élément situé à l'intersection de la i-ième ligne et de la j-ième colonne du produit AB est

$$a_{i1} b_{1j} + a_{i2} b_{2j} + \cdots + a_{in} b_{nj}$$

D'après la définition de la transposée d'une matrice, cette valeur se situe à l'intersection de la j-ième ligne et de la i-ième colonne de la matrice $(AB)^t$.

L'élément de la matrice $B^t A^t$ situé à l'intersection de la j-ième ligne et de la i-ième colonne s'obtient en « multipliant » en quelque sorte la j-ième ligne de B^t, c'est-à-dire la j-ième colonne de B, par la i-ième colonne de A^t, soit la i-ième ligne de A. Selon la définition du produit matriciel, cet élément est donc

$$b_{1j} a_{i1} + b_{2j} a_{i2} + \cdots + b_{nj} a_{in}$$

Or,

$$b_{1j} a_{i1} + b_{2j} a_{i2} + \cdots + b_{nj} a_{in} = (a_{i1} b_{1j} + a_{i2} b_{2j} + \cdots + a_{in} b_{nj})$$

Ainsi, les éléments situés respectivement à l'intersection de la j-ième ligne et de la i-ième colonne de $(AB)^t$ et de $B^t A^t$ sont égaux. Par conséquent, les éléments correspondants de $(AB)^t$ et de $B^t A^t$ sont égaux et $(AB)^t = B^t A^t$.   ∎

Propriété 8 $\quad A_{m \times n}B_{n \times p} = O_{m \times p} \nRightarrow A_{m \times n} = O_{m \times n}$ ou $B_{n \times p} = O_{n \times p}$

Preuve

Il suffit de trouver deux matrices non nulles dont le produit est une matrice nulle. Or, le produit des matrices $A = \begin{bmatrix} 1 & 0 \\ 0 & 0 \end{bmatrix}$ et $B = \begin{bmatrix} 0 & 0 \\ 1 & 0 \end{bmatrix}$ est la matrice $O_{2 \times 2} = \begin{bmatrix} 0 & 0 \\ 0 & 0 \end{bmatrix}$. Donc, $AB = O_{2 \times 2}$, mais ni A ni B n'est une matrice nulle. $\quad\blacksquare$

La démonstration de certaines propriétés de la multiplication de matrices exige qu'on fasse appel à la notation Σ.

PROPRIÉTÉS DE LA NOTATION Σ

1) Si r est une constante, alors $\displaystyle\sum_{i=1}^{n} r = nr$.

(addition de n termes égaux à r)

2) Si r est une constante, alors $\displaystyle\sum_{i=1}^{n} ra_i = r\sum_{i=1}^{n} a_i$

(mise en évidence de la constante r)

3) $\displaystyle\sum_{i=1}^{n} (a_i + b_i) = \sum_{i=1}^{n} a_i + \sum_{i=1}^{n} b_i$

(commutativité et associativité de l'addition)

4) $\displaystyle\sum_{i=1}^{n} a_i = \sum_{k=1}^{n} a_k = \sum_{l=1}^{n} a_l = \cdots$

(possibilité de renommer un indice de sommation)

5) $\displaystyle\sum_{i=1}^{n} \sum_{j=1}^{m} a_{ij} = \sum_{j=1}^{m} \sum_{i=1}^{n} a_{ij}$

(possibilité de changer l'ordre des sommations lorsque les indices de sommation sont indépendants)

6) $\displaystyle\sum_{i=1}^{n} \sum_{j=1}^{m} a_{ij} b_i = \sum_{i=1}^{n} \left(b_i \sum_{j=1}^{m} a_{ij} \right)$

(mise en évidence du terme dont l'indice est indépendant de celui de la sommation)

Familiarisez-vous avec les trois premières propriétés de la notation Σ en faisant l'exercice qui suit.

EXERCICE 2.10

Soit A et B, deux matrices carrées de même ordre, et k, un scalaire. Montrez que :

a) $\text{Tr}(A + B) = \text{Tr}(A) + \text{Tr}(B)$

b) $\text{Tr}(kA) = k\text{Tr}(A)$

Examinons les trois dernières propriétés de la notation Σ à l'aide d'un exemple et d'un exercice.

Exemple

Si A et B sont des matrices carrées de même ordre, alors
$$\text{Tr}(AB) = \text{Tr}(BA)$$

Preuve

Si $A = \begin{bmatrix} a_{ij} \end{bmatrix}_{n \times n}$, $B = \begin{bmatrix} b_{ij} \end{bmatrix}_{n \times n}$, $C = AB = \begin{bmatrix} c_{ij} \end{bmatrix}_{n \times n}$ et $D = BA = \begin{bmatrix} d_{ij} \end{bmatrix}_{n \times n}$, alors

$$c_{ii} = \sum_{k=1}^{n} a_{ik}b_{ki} \quad \text{et} \quad \text{Tr}(AB) = \sum_{i=1}^{n} c_{ii} = \sum_{i=1}^{n} \sum_{k=1}^{n} a_{ik}b_{ki}$$

$$d_{ii} = \sum_{k=1}^{n} b_{ik}a_{ki} \quad \text{et} \quad \text{Tr}(BA) = \sum_{i=1}^{n} d_{ii} = \sum_{i=1}^{n} \sum_{k=1}^{n} b_{ik}a_{ki}$$

Or, k et i n'étant que les noms des indices, on peut les changer à volonté. Ainsi, dans l'expression de la trace du produit BA, on peut remplacer i par k et k par i, c'est-à-dire nommer les deux indices différemment. De plus, les valeurs de i et de k sont indépendantes de sorte que

$$\text{Tr}(BA) = \sum_{i=1}^{n} \sum_{k=1}^{n} b_{ik}a_{ki} = \sum_{k=1}^{n} \sum_{i=1}^{n} b_{ki}a_{ik} = \sum_{i=1}^{n} \sum_{k=1}^{n} a_{ik}b_{ki} = \text{Tr}(AB)$$

∎

EXERCICE 2.11

Une matrice de probabilité est une matrice $P = \left[p_{ij} \right]_{n \times n}$ qui possède les deux propriétés suivantes :

- tous les éléments de P sont non négatifs, c'est-à-dire que $p_{ij} \geq 0$ pour toutes les valeurs de i et de j;
- la somme des éléments de n'importe quelle colonne de P vaut 1 :

$$\sum_{i=1}^{n} p_{ij} = 1.$$

Complétez la démonstration de la proposition suivante :

Si P est une matrice de probabilité, alors P^2 est également une matrice de probabilité.

Preuve

Si $P = \left[p_{ij} \right]_{n \times n}$ est une matrice de probabilité, alors $P^2 = C = \left[c_{ij} \right]_{n \times n}$ où $c_{ij} = \sum_{k=1}^{n} p_{ik} p_{kj}$. Il est clair que $c_{ij} \geq 0$ parce que _____.

Il ne reste donc qu'à vérifier que la somme des éléments d'une colonne quelconque de P^2 vaut 1, c'est-à-dire que $\sum_{i=1}^{n} c_{ij} = 1$ quelle que soit la valeur de j. Or,

$$\sum_{i=1}^{n} c_{ij} = \sum_{i=1}^{n} \sum_{k=1}^{n} p_{ik} p_{kj} = \sum_{k=1}^{n} \sum_{i=1}^{n} p_{ik} p_{kj} \quad \text{(parce que _____)}$$

$$= \sum_{k=1}^{n} \left(p_{kj} \sum_{i=1}^{n} p_{ik} \right) \quad \text{(parce que _____).}$$

De plus, $\sum_{i=1}^{n} p_{ik} = 1$ parce que _____. Par conséquent,

$$\sum_{k=1}^{n} \left(p_{kj} \sum_{i=1}^{n} p_{ik} \right) = \sum_{k=1}^{n} p_{kj} = 1 \quad \text{(parce que _____).}$$

On en conclut que $\sum_{i=1}^{n} c_{ij} = 1$ et que la matrice P^2 est une matrice de probabilité. ∎

À la section 1.1 du chapitre 1, nous avons souligné qu'il est possible de représenter un système d'équations linéaires à l'aide du langage matriciel. La forme générale d'un système d'équations linéaires comportant n équations et n inconnues est la suivante:

$$a_{11}x_1 + a_{12}x_2 + \cdots + a_{1n}x_n = b_1$$
$$a_{21}x_1 + a_{22}x_2 + \cdots + a_{2n}x_n = b_2$$
$$\vdots \qquad \vdots \qquad \cdots \qquad \vdots \qquad \vdots$$
$$a_{n1}x_1 + a_{n2}x_2 + \cdots + a_{nn}x_n = b_n$$

Dans ce système, les inconnues sont x_1, x_2, ... et x_n, alors que b_1, b_2, ... et b_n sont des constantes et que a_{ij} est le coefficient de l'inconnue x_j dans la i-ième équation.

On peut écrire ce système sous la forme matricielle $AX = B$ où $A = \begin{bmatrix} a_{ij} \end{bmatrix}_{n \times n}$ est la matrice des coefficients, $X = \begin{bmatrix} x_i \end{bmatrix}_{n \times 1}$ la matrice des inconnues, et $B = \begin{bmatrix} b_i \end{bmatrix}_{n \times 1}$ la matrice des constantes:

$$\begin{matrix} A & X & = & B \end{matrix}$$
$$\begin{bmatrix} a_{11} & a_{12} & \dots & a_{1n} \\ a_{21} & a_{22} & \dots & a_{2n} \\ \vdots & \vdots & \dots & \vdots \\ a_{n1} & a_{n2} & \dots & a_{nn} \end{bmatrix} \begin{bmatrix} x_1 \\ x_2 \\ \vdots \\ x_n \end{bmatrix} = \begin{bmatrix} b_1 \\ b_2 \\ \vdots \\ b_n \end{bmatrix}$$

Exemple

Le système d'équations

$$2x + 3y = 13$$
$$3x + 4y = -6$$

s'écrit sous la forme matricielle $AX = B$:

$$\begin{matrix} A & X & = & B \end{matrix}$$
$$\begin{bmatrix} 2 & 3 \\ 3 & 4 \end{bmatrix} \begin{bmatrix} x \\ y \end{bmatrix} = \begin{bmatrix} 13 \\ -6 \end{bmatrix}$$

En effet,

$$AX = B \Leftrightarrow \begin{bmatrix} 2x + 3y \\ 3x + 4y \end{bmatrix} = \begin{bmatrix} 13 \\ -6 \end{bmatrix} \Leftrightarrow \begin{matrix} 2x + 3y = 13 \\ 3x + 4y = -6 \end{matrix}$$

On résout l'équation à une seule inconnue $ax = b$ où $a \neq 0$ en multipliant chaque membre par l'inverse de a, soit a^{-1}. Puisque $a \neq 0$, alors

$$ax = b \Rightarrow a^{-1}ax = a^{-1}b \Rightarrow 1x = a^{-1}b \Rightarrow x = a^{-1}b$$

Les équations $ax = b$ et $AX = B$ se ressemblent par leur forme. Il est donc naturel de penser qu'on peut résoudre l'équation matricielle en employant à peu près la même méthode que pour résoudre l'équation à une seule inconnue.

Pour ce faire, il faut d'abord définir le concept de matrice inverse. Si A et D sont des matrices carrées d'ordre n telles que $AD = DA = I_n$, alors on dit que D est la **matrice inverse**[7] de A. En général, la matrice inverse, ou l'inverse, d'une matrice A est notée A^{-1}.

MATRICE INVERSE

La matrice inverse d'une matrice carrée A d'ordre n est, si elle existe, la matrice, notée A^{-1}, telle que $AA^{-1} = A^{-1}A = I_n$.

Exemple

Soit $A = \begin{bmatrix} 2 & 3 \\ 3 & 4 \end{bmatrix}$. On a $\begin{bmatrix} 2 & 3 \\ 3 & 4 \end{bmatrix}\begin{bmatrix} -4 & 3 \\ 3 & -2 \end{bmatrix} = \begin{bmatrix} 1 & 0 \\ 0 & 1 \end{bmatrix}$ et

$\begin{bmatrix} -4 & 3 \\ 3 & -2 \end{bmatrix}\begin{bmatrix} 2 & 3 \\ 3 & 4 \end{bmatrix} = \begin{bmatrix} 1 & 0 \\ 0 & 1 \end{bmatrix}$. Par conséquent, la matrice

$\begin{bmatrix} -4 & 3 \\ 3 & -2 \end{bmatrix}$ est la matrice inverse de $\begin{bmatrix} 2 & 3 \\ 3 & 4 \end{bmatrix}$. On écrit donc

$A^{-1} = \begin{bmatrix} -4 & 3 \\ 3 & -2 \end{bmatrix}$.

Nous avons vu que le système d'équations

$$2x + 3y = 13$$
$$3x + 4y = -6$$

s'écrit sous la forme matricielle $AX = B$ où

$$A = \begin{bmatrix} 2 & 3 \\ 3 & 4 \end{bmatrix} \quad X = \begin{bmatrix} x \\ y \end{bmatrix} \quad B = \begin{bmatrix} 13 \\ -6 \end{bmatrix}$$

On peut donc résoudre ce système de la façon suivante:

$$AX = B \Rightarrow \underbrace{A^{-1}AX = A^{-1}B}_{\substack{\text{Multiplication par } A^{-1} \\ \text{par la gauche}}} \Rightarrow \underbrace{I_2X = A^{-1}B}_{\text{Définition de } A^{-1}} \Rightarrow \underbrace{X = A^{-1}B}_{\substack{\text{Théorème 2.2,} \\ \text{prop. 4}}}$$

---

7. Au prochain chapitre, nous prouverons que toute matrice inversible ne possède qu'une seule matrice inverse. C'est pourquoi nous utilisons l'expression « la matrice inverse » plutôt que « une matrice inverse ».

Par conséquent,

$$\begin{bmatrix} x \\ y \end{bmatrix} = \begin{bmatrix} -4 & 3 \\ 3 & -2 \end{bmatrix} \begin{bmatrix} 13 \\ -6 \end{bmatrix} = \begin{bmatrix} -70 \\ 51 \end{bmatrix}$$

On en déduit que $x = -70$ et $y = 51$ est la solution du système d'équations donné.

Au chapitre 3, nous verrons comment trouver la matrice inverse d'une matrice carrée inversible d'ordre n. Pour le moment, nous nous contentons de souligner que la matrice inverse de $A = \begin{bmatrix} a & b \\ c & d \end{bmatrix}$ est

$$A^{-1} = \frac{1}{ad - bc} \begin{bmatrix} d & -b \\ -c & a \end{bmatrix}$$

si $ad - bc \neq 0$.

EXERCICE 2.12

1. Résolvez le système d'équations linéaires suivant à l'aide de la multiplication de matrices et de l'inverse de la matrice des coefficients.

$$x + y = 5$$
$$2x - y = 1$$

2. Vérifiez que C est la matrice inverse de A si

$$A = \begin{bmatrix} 1 & 1 & 1 \\ 1 & -1 & -1 \\ 1 & -1 & 1 \end{bmatrix} \quad \text{et} \quad C = \begin{bmatrix} 0,5 & 0,5 & 0 \\ 0,5 & 0 & -0,5 \\ 0 & -0,5 & 0,5 \end{bmatrix}$$

3. Résolvez le système d'équations linéaires suivant à l'aide de la multiplication de matrices et de l'inverse de la matrice des coefficients. Servez-vous du résultat obtenu en 2.

$$x + y + z = 3$$
$$x - y - z = -1$$
$$x - y + z = 1$$

RÉSUMÉ

On définit sur les matrices les opérations d'addition, de multiplication par un scalaire, de transposition et de multiplication de la façon suivante.

- Addition : si $A = \left[a_{ij}\right]_{m \times n}$ et $B = \left[b_{ij}\right]_{m \times n}$, alors
$$A + B = \left[a_{ij} + b_{ij}\right]_{m \times n}$$

- Multiplication par un scalaire : si $A = \left[a_{ij}\right]_{m \times n}$ et si k est un scalaire, alors $kA = \left[ka_{ij}\right]_{m \times n}$.

- Transposition : si $A = \left[a_{ij}\right]_{m \times n}$, alors $A^t = \left[a_{ji}\right]_{n \times m}$.

- Multiplication de matrices : si $A = \left[a_{ij}\right]_{m \times n}$ et $B = \left[b_{ij}\right]_{n \times p}$, alors
$$AB = \left[\sum_{k=1}^{n} a_{ik}b_{kj}\right]_{m \times p}$$

Il ressort de ces définitions que les opérations sont définies seulement si certaines conditions sont satisfaites : on peut additionner deux matrices uniquement si elles ont le même format ; on peut calculer le produit AB uniquement si le nombre de colonnes de A est égal au nombre de lignes de B, etc. À cause de cette dernière restriction, l'opération qui consiste à élever une matrice A à une puissance entière positive n n'est pas toujours définie. En fait, l'expression A^n n'est définie que pour une matrice carrée.

Le concept de transposée d'une matrice sert à définir les notions de matrice symétrique et de matrice antisymétrique. En effet, une matrice carrée A est symétrique si $A^t = A$ et elle est antisymétrique si $A^t = -A$ ou, ce qui est équivalent, si $A = -A^t$. On emploie ces deux nouvelles définitions pour démontrer plusieurs des propriétés de la transposée. Nous avons de plus défini deux autres types de matrices. Comme leur nom l'indique, une matrice idempotente est une matrice dont le carré (puissance 2) est égal à la matrice elle-même, et une matrice nilpotente donne la matrice nulle lorsqu'on l'élève à une certaine puissance.

Les théorèmes 2.1 (p. 35) et 2.2 (p. 47) énoncent les principales propriétés des opérations matricielles. Ils stipulent notamment que la matrice nulle et la matrice identité jouent le rôle d'élément neutre pour l'addition et la multiplication respectivement. On note que les opérations sur les matrices ne possèdent pas exactement les mêmes propriétés que les opérations sur les réels. Ainsi, l'addition et la multiplication de deux nombres réels donnent toujours un nombre réel, mais la somme et le produit de deux matrices ne sont pas nécessairement définis.

Les opérations matricielles se distinguent des opérations sur les réels de nombreuses autres façons. Par exemple, le produit matriciel n'est pas commutatif et il existe des matrices non nulles dont le produit est la matrice nulle.

On peut représenter le système d'équations linéaires

$$
\begin{aligned}
a_{11}x_1 + a_{12}x_2 + \cdots + a_{1n}x_n &= b_1 \\
a_{21}x_1 + a_{22}x_2 + \cdots + a_{2n}x_n &= b_2 \\
\vdots \qquad \vdots \qquad \cdots \qquad \vdots \quad &\quad \vdots \\
a_{n1}x_1 + a_{n2}x_2 + \cdots + a_{nn}x_n &= b_n
\end{aligned}
$$

sous la forme matricielle $AX = B$. Dans cette dernière équation, $A = \left[a_{ij}\right]_{n \times n}$ est la matrice des coefficients, $X = \left[x_i\right]_{n \times 1}$ la matrice des inconnues, et $B = \left[b_i\right]_{n \times 1}$ la matrice des constantes. Étant donné la forme de l'équation matricielle $AX = B$, il est naturel de penser qu'on peut la résoudre en employant à peu près la même méthode que pour résoudre l'équation $ax = b$, soit en multipliant chaque membre par l'inverse de A. La matrice inverse de A, notée A^{-1}, est la matrice qui satisfait l'équation $AA^{-1} = A^{-1}A = I_n$. En particulier, si $ad - bc \neq 0$

$$
A = \begin{bmatrix} a & b \\ c & d \end{bmatrix} \implies A^{-1} = \frac{1}{ad - bc}\begin{bmatrix} d & -b \\ -c & a \end{bmatrix}
$$

MOTS CLÉS

EXERCICES RÉCAPITULATIFS

1. (I) Soit les matrices

$$
A = \begin{bmatrix} -1 & 2 & 3 \\ 0 & -5 & 4 \\ 4 & -2 & 1 \end{bmatrix} \quad B = \begin{bmatrix} 5 & -2 \\ 3 & 0 \\ -4 & 2 \end{bmatrix}
$$

$$
C = \begin{bmatrix} 5 & -3 & 1 \\ 0 & 6 & -4 \\ 1 & 2 & 7 \end{bmatrix} \quad D = \begin{bmatrix} 10 & -4 \\ 6 & 3 \\ 8 & 5 \end{bmatrix}
$$

$$
E = \begin{bmatrix} 1 & 2 & 7 \\ -1 & -2 & 3 \end{bmatrix}
$$

$$
F = \begin{bmatrix} 2 & -1 & 5 & 4 \end{bmatrix} \quad G = \begin{bmatrix} 4 \\ 6 \\ 8 \\ 12 \end{bmatrix}
$$

Effectuez si possible les opérations suivantes. Si une opération n'est pas définie, donnez-en la raison.

a) $A + C$

b) $2A - 3C$

c) $2 + E$

d) $3F + 0,25G^t$

e) $2F - G$

f) $B^t - D^t + E$

g) $D + E^t$

h) $D^t + E$

i) $A + O_{3 \times 3}$

j) $E + O_{3 \times 2}$

2. (I) Soit les matrices

$$A = \left[a_{ij}\right]_{3 \times 3} \quad \text{où} \quad a_{ij} = i^2$$

$$B = \left[b_{ij}\right]_{3 \times 3} \quad \text{où} \quad b_{ij} = i + 2j$$

Déterminez la matrice C telle que $C = A + B$.

3. (I) En supposant que les opérations soient définies, simplifiez l'expression

$$5(2B + 2A^t + 6B)^t + 5A - 8B^t$$

4. (II) Soit $P = \left[p_{ij}\right]_{m \times n}$ et $R = \left[r_{ij}\right]_{m \times n}$, les matrices de prix de m produits disponibles dans n points de vente, pour les années 1996 et 1997 respectivement. Soit $Q = \left[q_{ij}\right]_{m \times n}$ et $S = \left[s_{ij}\right]_{m \times n}$, les matrices des quantités de ces m produits vendues dans les n points de vente, pour les années 1996 et 1997 respectivement.

a) Que représente p_{23}? r_{43}? q_{32}?

b) Que représente la troisième colonne de la matrice S? la quatrième ligne de S?

c) Peut-on additionner les matrices P et Q? Cette opération a-t-elle un sens? Justifiez votre réponse.

d) Peut-on additionner les matrices P et R? Cette opération a-t-elle un sens? Justifiez votre réponse.

e) Peut-on calculer $\frac{1}{2}(P + R)$? Cette opération a-t-elle un sens? Justifiez votre réponse.

f) Peut-on additionner les matrices Q et S? Cette opération a-t-elle un sens? Justifiez votre réponse.

g) Peut-on calculer $\frac{1}{2}(Q + S)$? Cette opération a-t-elle un sens? Justifiez votre réponse.

5. (I) Démontrez les propriétés 2, 4, 5, 11 et 12 du théorème 2.1.

6. (I) Démontrez que les éléments de la diagonale principale d'une matrice antisymétrique sont tous nuls.

7. (I) Démontrez que pour toute matrice carrée A:

a) $S = \frac{1}{2}(A + A^t)$ est une matrice symétrique.

b) $N = \frac{1}{2}(A - A^t)$ est une matrice antisymétrique.

c) $A = S + N$, c'est-à-dire que toute matrice carrée s'écrit comme la somme d'une matrice symétrique et d'une matrice antisymétrique.

8. (I) Trouvez la matrice X qui vérifie l'équation $2X + 3(A + B) = CD$ où

$$A = \begin{bmatrix} -1 & 3 \\ 6 & 8 \end{bmatrix} \qquad B = \begin{bmatrix} 2 & 3 \\ -1 & 5 \end{bmatrix}$$

$$C = \begin{bmatrix} 4 & 2 & 1 \\ 3 & -2 & 3 \end{bmatrix} \qquad D = \begin{bmatrix} 1 & 2 \\ -2 & 4 \\ -1 & 6 \end{bmatrix}$$

9. (I) Soit les matrices

$$A = \begin{bmatrix} 2 & 0 \\ 0 & 3 \end{bmatrix} \qquad B = \begin{bmatrix} -1 & 0 & 0 \\ 0 & 4 & 0 \\ 0 & 0 & 2 \end{bmatrix}$$

$$C = \left[c_{ij}\right]_{n \times n} \quad \text{où} \quad c_{ij} = 0 \text{ pour tout } i \neq j$$

a) Qu'ont en commun ces trois matrices?

b) Calculez A^2. Que constatez-vous?

c) Calculez A^3. Que constatez-vous?

d) Calculez B^3. Que constatez-vous?

e) Calculez C^2.

f) Soit k un entier positif. Calculez C^k.

10. (I) Soit les matrices

$$A = \begin{bmatrix} -1 & 2 & 3 \\ 0 & -5 & 4 \\ 4 & -2 & 1 \end{bmatrix} \qquad B = \begin{bmatrix} 1 & 0 \\ 1 & 1 \end{bmatrix}$$

$$C = \begin{bmatrix} 5 & -3 & 1 \\ 0 & 6 & -4 \\ 1 & 2 & 7 \end{bmatrix} \qquad D = \begin{bmatrix} 1 & 0 \\ -1 & 1 \end{bmatrix}$$

$$E = \begin{bmatrix} 10 & -4 \\ 6 & 3 \\ 8 & 5 \end{bmatrix} \quad F = \begin{bmatrix} 1 & 2 & 7 \\ -1 & -2 & 3 \end{bmatrix}$$

$$G = \begin{bmatrix} 2 & -1 & 5 & 4 \end{bmatrix} \quad H = \begin{bmatrix} 3 \\ 6 \\ 8 \\ 1 \end{bmatrix}$$

Effectuez si possible les opérations suivantes. Si une opération n'est pas définie, donnez-en la raison.

a) BD

b) $O_{3 \times 2}D$

c) $FE - 2A$

d) A^2

e) E^2

f) $3 + GH$

g) EF

h) F^tE^t. Comparez le résultat avec celui que vous avez obtenu en g.

i) I_3E

j) CI_3

k) AEF

11. (I) Si A est une matrice de format $m \times n$, et B une matrice telle que les produits AB et BA sont définis, quel est le format de B?

12. (I) Soit $M = \begin{bmatrix} a & 1 \\ 0 & a \end{bmatrix}$ où a est un nombre réel.

Calculez:

a) M^2

b) M^3

c) M^k où k est un entier positif.

13. (I) En supposant que chaque opération soit définie, simplifiez chacune des expressions suivantes.

a) $(5AB^t)^t$

b) $(A^t + B)^t + 4B^t$

c) $\left[(A^t + A)(A^t - A)\right]^t$

14. (I) Démontrez que si $AB = A$ et $BA = B$, alors AB est une matrice idempotente.

15. (I) Vérifiez que la matrice $D = \begin{bmatrix} -22 & -3 & -25 \\ 40 & 6 & 44 \\ 16 & 3 & 16 \end{bmatrix}$

est une matrice nilpotente d'indice de nilpotence de 3.

16. (I) Dites si les énoncés suivants sont vrais ou faux et justifiez votre réponse.

a) On peut toujours additionner deux matrices qui comportent le même nombre de lignes.

b) Si A ou B est une matrice nulle, alors le produit AB est une matrice nulle, s'il est défini.

c) Si le produit matriciel AB est une matrice nulle, alors A ou B est nécessairement une matrice nulle.

d) Si le produit matriciel AB est défini, alors $AB = BA$.

e) Si le produit matriciel AB est défini, alors $(AB)^t = A^tB^t$.

f) Si A est une matrice nilpotente d'ordre n, alors $A^2 = O_{n \times n}$.

g) Le produit de deux matrices carrées est toujours défini.

h) Si A est la transposée de B, et B la transposée de C, alors $A = C$.

i) La matrice $A = \begin{bmatrix} 1 & 0 & 0 \\ 0 & 1 & 0 \\ 1 & 0 & 0 \end{bmatrix}$ est une matrice idempotente.

j) Si A est une matrice triangulaire inférieure, alors A^t est une matrice triangulaire supérieure.

k) L'expression A^2 est toujours définie.

l) Si le produit matriciel AB est défini, alors le produit matriciel BA l'est aussi.

m) Si les opérations AB et $A + B$ sont définies, alors les matrices A et B sont des matrices carrées de même ordre.

n) Si A et B sont des matrices carrées de même ordre, alors

$$(A + B)^2 = A^2 + 2AB + B^2$$

o) Si A est une matrice idempotente, alors A^n l'est également.

17. (I) Démontrez que si $ABA = A$, alors BA est une matrice idempotente.

18. (II) Démontrez que si A et B sont deux matrices diagonales de même ordre, alors le produit AB est aussi une matrice diagonale et, de plus, $AB = BA$.

19. (II) Démontrez que le produit de deux matrices triangulaires supérieures de même ordre est une matrice triangulaire supérieure.

20. (II) Démontrez que si A est une matrice carrée d'ordre n telle que $A^t A = I_n$, alors $(I_n - A)^t (I_n + A)$ est une matrice antisymétrique.

21. (I) À la fin de leur premier cours d'algèbre linéaire, James, Jasmine et Julien ont construit la matrice A de leurs notes à chacun des examens.

NOTES À CHACUN DES EXAMENS

	1er examen	2e examen	3e examen	4e examen
James	90,0	85,0	80,5	90,0
Jasmine	88,5	86,5	84,0	89,5
Julien	78,5	87,0	83,5	98,0

a) Donnez le sens des éléments a_{24}, a_{32} et a_{13} de la matrice A.

b) Donnez le sens de la ligne formée des éléments a_{2j} de la matrice A.

c) Donnez le sens de la colonne formée des éléments a_{i4} de la matrice A.

d) Si le professeur a accordé la même pondération (25 %) à chaque examen, donnez le sens du produit matriciel AB où $B = \begin{bmatrix} 0,25 & 0,25 & 0,25 & 0,25 \end{bmatrix}^t$.

e) Quelle opération faut-il effectuer sur la matrice A pour obtenir la note finale des trois élèves si chacun des deux premiers examens compte pour 20 % de la note finale et si chacun des deux derniers compte pour 30 % de la note finale.

22. (I) La valeur (en dollars) des ventes effectuées par deux vendeurs pour trois modèles de voitures, durant les mois de septembre et octobre, est donnée par les matrices A et B suivantes.

Septembre

	Compact	Inter-médiaire	De luxe
G. Tremblay	100 000	50 000	40 000
O. Dupuis	80 000	60 000	80 000

$= A$

Octobre

	Compact	Inter-médiaire	De luxe
G. Tremblay	80 000	20 000	90 000
O. Dupuis	90 000	40 000	120 000

$= B$

a) Quels sont la valeur et le sens de a_{21}?

b) Quels sont la valeur et le sens de b_{13}?

c) Donnez le sens de $A + B$.

d) Quelle opération matricielle faut-il effectuer pour trouver la moyenne mensuelle des ventes par modèle et par vendeur pour les mois de septembre et octobre?

e) Quelle opération matricielle faut-il effectuer pour trouver la commission de 1 % de chaque vendeur sur chaque modèle de voiture, pour le mois d'octobre?

f) Interprétez le produit $A \begin{bmatrix} 1 & 1 & 1 \end{bmatrix}^t$.

g) Si la commission des vendeurs est de 1 % pour le modèle compact, de 1,5 % pour le modèle intermédiaire et de 2 % pour le modèle de luxe, quelle opération matricielle faut-il effectuer pour obtenir la commission totale de chaque vendeur pour le mois d'octobre?

23. (I) Une de vos amies revient d'un voyage en Europe. Ayant visité la France, l'Angleterre et l'Allemagne, elle rapporte 20 francs, 5 livres sterling et 10 marks.

a) Représentez ces informations par une matrice ligne M.

Votre amie se rend à la banque pour échanger ses devises étrangères contre des dollars canadiens. On lui offre 0,25 $ par franc, 2 $ par livre et 0,90 $ par mark.

b) Représentez ces informations par une matrice colonne C.

c) Calculez MC. Quelle information cette matrice donne-t-elle?

24. (I) Le portefeuille d'actions d'un individu comporte trois titres. La matrice A représente le nombre d'actions de chaque titre et la matrice B, le cours de chaque action en dollars pour une semaine donnée (du lundi au vendredi).

$$A = \begin{bmatrix} 100 & 150 & 125 \end{bmatrix}$$

$$B = \begin{bmatrix} 1,90 & 1,95 & 2,00 & 2,05 & 2,05 \\ 3,10 & 3,08 & 3,14 & 3,12 & 3,09 \\ 0,85 & 0,90 & 0,92 & 0,94 & 1,00 \end{bmatrix}$$

a) Calculez *AB*. Que représente cette matrice?

b) Quand le portefeuille de l'individu a-t-il atteint sa plus grande valeur?

25. (I) Un bijoutier fabrique des bagues et des boucles d'oreille. Chaque bague exige 1,5 heure de travail, 5 grammes d'or et 4 pierres précieuses. Chaque paire de boucles d'oreille exige 1 heure de travail, 2 grammes d'or et 2 pierres précieuses.

a) Représentez ces informations par une matrice *Q* de format 2 × 3.

Le coût de chacun des intrants (main-d'œuvre, or et pierres précieuses) est respectivement de 18 $/heure, 12 $/g d'or et 25 $ par pierre précieuse.

b) Représentez ces informations par une matrice colonne *U*.

c) Quelle opération matricielle faut-il effectuer sur les matrices *Q* et *U* pour obtenir le coût de fabrication de chaque type de bijoux? Si on désigne par *C* la matrice des coûts, que vaut *C*?

Le bijoutier vend ses bagues 300 $ l'unité et ses boucles d'oreille 125 $ la paire.

d) Représentez ces informations par une matrice colonne *R*.

e) Quelle opération matricielle faut-il effectuer sur les matrices *R* et *C* pour obtenir le profit unitaire réalisé sur la vente de chaque type de bijoux? Quel est le profit unitaire réalisé sur la vente de chaque type de bijoux?

26. (I) Le propriétaire de deux pâtisseries fabrique des baguettes de pain, des brioches et des gâteaux. Pour chaque douzaine de baguettes, de brioches et de gâteaux, il faut combiner les quantités suivantes de farine, de sucre et de beurre:

QUANTITÉS (EN KILOGRAMMES)
D'INGRÉDIENTS REQUIS
POUR UNE DOUZAINE

INGRÉDIENT	Baguettes	Brioches	Gâteaux
Farine	2,5	0,5	1,1
Sucre	0,1	0,5	0,8
Beurre	0,2	0,4	0,8

Les quantités produites par chacune des pâtisseries sont données par la matrice suivante.

PRODUCTION (EN DOUZAINES)
DE CHAQUE PÂTISSERIE

PRODUIT	Pâtisserie 1	Pâtisserie 2
Baguettes	10	30
Brioches	20	10
Gâteaux	10	10

a) Quelle opération matricielle faut-il effectuer pour connaître la quantité de chaque ingrédient qui doit être livrée à chacune des pâtisseries pour que celles-ci puissent produire les quantités habituelles de baguettes, de brioches et de gâteaux?

b) Quelle quantité de sucre faut-il livrer à la pâtisserie 1?

c) Quelle quantité de farine faut-il livrer à la pâtisserie 2?

27. (I) Un auteur de manuels scolaires a écrit un livre d'algèbre, un livre de calcul et un livre de statistiques, codés respectivement 1, 2 et 3. Au début de l'année, les deux entrepôts de l'éditeur renferment 10 000 exemplaires des livres de cet auteur, dont 3 000 copies du manuel de calcul et 1 000 copies du manuel de statistiques. Le premier des deux entrepôts contient 4 000 exemplaires des ouvrages de l'auteur, dont 1 000 copies du manuel d'algèbre et 2 000 copies du manuel de calcul.

a) Écrivez la matrice *A* de l'inventaire des ouvrages de l'auteur dans les deux entrepôts de l'éditeur. Les éléments de la matrice doivent respecter l'ordre utilisé dans le tableau suivant.

INVENTAIRE DES LIVRES
DE L'AUTEUR

	Algèbre (1)	Calcul (2)	Statistiques (3)
Entrepôt 1			
Entrepôt 2			

b) L'éditeur prévoit vendre au cours de l'année 30 % des exemplaires de chaque ouvrage stockés dans chacun des deux entrepôts. Si les prévisions de l'éditeur se réalisent, quelle opération matricielle sur *A* permet de dresser l'inventaire à la fin de l'année?

c) Si les prévisions de l'éditeur se réalisent, quelle sera la matrice d'inventaire à la fin de l'année?

d) Quelle matrice *V* donne la prévision du nombre d'exemplaires de chaque ouvrage vendus pour chaque entrepôt?

e) L'éditeur vend les manuels d'algèbre 20 $ l'unité, les manuels de calcul 25 $ l'unité et les manuels de statistiques 30 $ l'unité. Écrivez la matrice des prix $P = \left[p_{ij} \right]_{3 \times 1}$.

f) Comment doit-on interpréter la matrice $R = VP$?

g) Que vaut la matrice *R*?

 28. (II) Une diététicienne, qui travaille dans un hôpital, fait préparer trois types de déjeuners pour répondre aux différents besoins alimentaires des patients. Chaque déjeuner contient deux aliments composés de protéines, de fibres et de matières grasses. Les quantités (en grammes) de chacune de ces composantes, par portion de 30 g d'un aliment, sont données par la matrice *A*.

$$A = \begin{array}{cc} \text{Aliment 1} & \text{Aliment 2} \\ \left[\begin{array}{cc} 3 & 5 \\ 13 & 1 \\ 1 & 2 \end{array} \right] & \begin{array}{l} \text{Protéines} \\ \text{Fibres} \\ \text{Gras} \end{array} \end{array}$$

Chaque déjeuner contient au total 30 g des deux aliments, dans les proportions indiquées par la matrice *B*.

$$B = \begin{array}{c} \begin{array}{ccc} \text{Déjeuner} & \text{Déjeuner} & \text{Déjeuner} \\ 1 & 2 & 3 \end{array} \\ \left[\begin{array}{ccc} 0,8 & 0,6 & 0,4 \\ 0,2 & 0,4 & 0,6 \end{array} \right] \begin{array}{l} \text{Aliment 1} \\ \text{Aliment 2} \end{array} \end{array}$$

a) Interprétez la valeur de a_{21} dans le contexte donné. N'oubliez pas d'indiquer les unités de mesure dans votre réponse.

b) Interprétez la valeur de b_{13} dans le contexte donné. N'oubliez pas d'indiquer les unités de mesure dans votre réponse.

c) Que représente la deuxième colonne de la matrice *A*?

d) Pouvez-vous interpréter le produit matriciel *BA*? Si oui, calculez ce produit et donnez-en le sens.

e) Pouvez-vous interpréter le produit matriciel *AB*? Si oui, calculez ce produit et donnez-en le sens.

 29. (II) Trois revendeurs de service interurbain se partagent un marché. L'entreprise 1 détient 50 % du marché et l'entreprise 2 en détient 30 %, ce qui ne laisse que 20 % du marché à la troisième entreprise.

a) Représentez ces informations par la matrice $P^{(0)} = \left[p_i^{(0)} \right]_{3 \times 1}$ où $p_i^{(0)}$ = part du marché détenue initialement par l'entreprise *i*.

Au cours du dernier mois, les trois revendeurs de service interurbain se sont livré une concurrence féroce. L'entreprise 1 a conservé 80 % de sa clientèle et elle en a perdu 10 % au profit de l'entreprise 2; celle-ci a retenu 75 % de sa clientèle et elle en a perdu 5 % au profit de l'entreprise 3. Enfin, l'entreprise 3 a gardé 90 % de sa clientèle, mais elle en a perdu 5 % au profit de l'entreprise 2.

La matrice de transition $T = \left[t_{ij} \right]_{3 \times 3}$, qui représente ces mouvements de la clientèle, est définie par

t_{ij} = part de la clientèle de *j* qui passe à *i*

b) Construisez la matrice de transition *T*.

c) Que vaut la somme des éléments de chaque colonne de *T*? Pourquoi obtient-on ce résultat?

d) La matrice *T* est-elle une matrice de probabilité (voir l'exercice 2.11, p. 53)? Justifiez votre réponse.

e) Que vaut $TP^{(0)}$? Qu'indique cette matrice? Proposez une notation.

f) Si la matrice de transition est la même de mois en mois, quelle part du marché chaque entreprise détiendra-t-elle à la fin du deuxième mois? Proposez une notation.

g) Quelle expression matricielle représente la part du marché de chacune des trois entreprises à la fin du *n*-ième mois? Proposez une notation.

 30. (III) P. H. Leslie[8] a proposé un modèle démographique pour décrire l'évolution de la taille d'une population de femelles de diverses espèces animales. Voici les principaux éléments de ce modèle.

On divise la population étudiée en *n* classes d'âges, notées C_1, C_2, C_3, ..., C_n, et on choisit une même amplitude pour toutes les classes. Par exemple, pour les êtres humains, on pourrait définir 20 classes d'amplitude 5, soit $C_1 = [0, 5[$, $C_2 = [5, 10[$, $C_3 = [10, 15[$, ..., $C_{20} = [95, 100[$.

8. P. H. Leslie. «On the Use of Matrices in Certain Population Mathematics», *Biometrika*, 1945, vol. 33, p. 183 à 212.

La structure par âge d'une population, après t observations, correspond au nombre de femelles dans chacune des classes d'âge. On suppose que les observations de la population se font à des intervalles de temps correspondant à l'amplitude des classes d'âge. Dans le cas des êtres humains, on ferait donc des observations tous les 5 ans.

On représente la structure par âge après t observations par une matrice $X^{(t)}$ de format $n \times 1$:

$$X^{(t)} = \begin{bmatrix} x_1^{(t)} \\ x_2^{(t)} \\ x_3^{(t)} \\ \vdots \\ x_n^{(t)} \end{bmatrix}$$

où $x_i^{(t)}$ désigne le nombre de femelles dans la classe d'âge C_i après t observations. L'objectif du modèle est de prédire la structure d'âge d'une population à l'aide d'une cohorte initiale $X^{(0)}$.

Si aucun décès ne survient entre deux observations, les femelles enregistrées dans la classe d'âge C_i à la première de ces observations se retrouveraient toutes dans la classe d'âge C_{i+1} à la seconde observation. Pour que le modèle soit réaliste, on définit un taux de survie s_i entre deux classes d'âge : seule une fraction s_i des femelles de la classe C_i se retrouveront dans la classe C_{i+1}. Il va sans dire que $0 \leq s_i \leq 1$. En particulier, comme la dernière classe d'âge est C_n, on a $s_n = 0$.

De plus, entre deux observations, les femelles d'une classe d'âge C_i donnent naissance à des descendantes. On note d_i le nombre moyen de descendantes nées d'une femelle de la classe d'âge C_i entre deux observations et ayant survécu jusqu'à la seconde de ces observations. Ainsi, $d_i x_i^{(0)}$ représente le nombre total de telles descendantes nées des femelles de la cohorte initiale qui appartiennent à la classe d'âge C_i. Il s'agit des descendantes nées avant la première observation ($t = 1$) et ayant survécu jusqu'au moment de cette observation.

Nous sommes maintenant en mesure de construire le modèle. Le nombre d'individus dans la première classe d'âge à $t = 1$, soit à la première observation, est égal au nombre total de descendantes survivantes des femelles de toutes les classes d'âge, c'est-à-dire

$$x_1^{(1)} = d_1 x_1^{(0)} + d_2 x_2^{(0)} + d_3 x_3^{(0)} + \cdots + d_n x_n^{(0)}$$

C'est la première équation du modèle.

Quant au nombre de femelles de chacune des autres classes d'âge C_i (pour $i > 1$) au temps $t = 1$, il est égal au nombre de femelles survivantes issues de la classe d'âge C_{i-1} au temps $t = 0$. Donc $x_i^{(1)} = s_{i-1} x_{i-1}^{(0)}$ pour $i > 1$, ce qui donne $n - 1$ autres équations.

Le modèle compte donc n équations, qu'on peut écrire sous la forme matricielle $X^{(1)} = A X^{(0)}$ où la matrice A porte le nom de matrice de Leslie.

a) Donnez l'expression générale d'une matrice de Leslie.

b) En supposant que la matrice de Leslie demeure la même entre deux observations, exprimez $X^{(2)}$ en fonction de A et de $X^{(0)}$.

c) Exprimez $X^{(k)}$ en fonction de A et de $X^{(0)}$.

La matrice de Leslie[9] pour la population de truites femelles du *Hunt Creek*, au Michigan, est

$$\begin{bmatrix} 0 & 0 & 37 & 64 & 82 \\ 0{,}06 & 0 & 0 & 0 & 0 \\ 0 & 0{,}34 & 0 & 0 & 0 \\ 0 & 0 & 0{,}16 & 0 & 0 \\ 0 & 0 & 0 & 0{,}08 & 0 \end{bmatrix}$$

L'amplitude des classes d'âge est de un an et on observe cette population une fois par année. Au temps $t = 0$, la structure d'âge est donnée par

$$X^{(0)} = \begin{bmatrix} 10\,000 \\ 600 \\ 200 \\ 50 \\ 5 \end{bmatrix}$$

d) Donnez le sens du nombre 0,06 dans la matrice de Leslie.

e) Donnez le sens du nombre 82 dans la matrice de Leslie.

f) À partir de quel âge les truites de la population étudiée se reproduisent-elles ?

g) Donnez le sens du nombre 600 dans la matrice $X^{(0)}$ de la structure d'âge de la cohorte initiale.

h) Donnez la structure d'âge de la population de truites au temps $t = 1$.

9. M. R. Cullen. *Mathematics for the Biosciences*, Boston, PWS-Kent, 1983, p. 633.

31. (III) Un carré magique est une matrice carrée A formée d'entiers non négatifs et telle que la somme des éléments de chaque ligne ou de chaque colonne est une même constante, notée $S(A)$. Par exemple, la matrice

$$A = \begin{bmatrix} 1 & 0 & 4 \\ 4 & 1 & 0 \\ 0 & 4 & 1 \end{bmatrix}$$

est un carré magique pour lequel $S(A) = 5$.

Démontrez que si A et B sont des carrés magiques d'ordre n, alors:

a) $A + B$ est un carré magique et

$$S(A + B) = S(A) + S(B)$$

b) AB est un carré magique et

$$S(AB) = S(A) \times S(B)$$

32. (I) Démontrez les propriétés 3, 5 et 7 du théorème 2.2.

33. (II) Soit A une matrice carrée d'ordre n.

a) Simplifiez l'expression

$$(I_n - A)(I_n + A + A^2 + \cdots + A^{k-1})$$

b) En supposant que la matrice $(I_n - A)$ admet une matrice inverse et que $S_k = (I_n + A + A^2 + \cdots + A^{k-1})$, montrez que $S_k = (I_n - A)^{-1}(I_n - A^k)$.

Les questions qui suivent s'adressent à ceux et celles qui connaissent le concept de limite.

c) Si $\lim\limits_{k \to \infty} A^k = O_{n \times n}$, que vaut $\lim\limits_{k \to \infty} S_k$?

d) Si $A = \begin{bmatrix} a & 0 \\ 0 & b \end{bmatrix}$ où $0 < a < 1$ et $0 < b < 1$, que valent A^2, A^3, ..., A^k, $\lim\limits_{k \to \infty} A^k$ et $\lim\limits_{k \to \infty} S_k$?

34. (I) Si $A = \begin{bmatrix} 1 & -1 \\ 1 & 1 \end{bmatrix}$, que vaut A^{-1}?

35. (I) Vérifiez que la matrice inverse de $A = \begin{bmatrix} a & b \\ c & d \end{bmatrix}$ où $ad - bc \neq 0$ est $A^{-1} = \dfrac{1}{ad - bc} \begin{bmatrix} d & -b \\ -c & a \end{bmatrix}$.

36. (I) Soit les matrices

$$A = \begin{bmatrix} 1 & 1 \\ 0 & 0 \end{bmatrix} \quad B = \begin{bmatrix} 0 & 1 \\ 0 & -1 \end{bmatrix}$$

$$C = \begin{bmatrix} 5 & 8 \\ 2 & 3 \end{bmatrix} \quad D = \begin{bmatrix} 2 & 3 \\ 5 & 8 \end{bmatrix}$$

a) Que vaut AB?

b) La matrice A admet-elle une matrice inverse?

c) Vérifiez que $AC = AD$.

d) Servez-vous de l'égalité obtenue en c pour montrer qu'il existe des matrices M, N et P telles que $MN = MP \nRightarrow N = P$.

37. (I) Résolvez chacun des systèmes d'équations linéaires suivants en faisant appel au produit matriciel et à la matrice inverse de la matrice des coefficients.

a) $3x + 2y = 8$
   $5x - 4y = 6$

b) $-2x + 3y = 11$
   $6x - 2y = 2$

c) $x + 5y = 6$
   $8x - 7y = 1$

38. (I) Vérifiez que la matrice C donnée est la matrice inverse de A et servez-vous de ce résultat pour résoudre le système d'équations linéaires donné.

$$A = \begin{bmatrix} 1 & 2 & 3 \\ 1 & 3 & 5 \\ 2 & 5 & 9 \end{bmatrix} \quad C = \begin{bmatrix} 2 & -3 & 1 \\ 1 & 3 & -2 \\ -1 & -1 & 1 \end{bmatrix}$$

$$x + 2y + 3z = 10$$
$$x + 3y + 5z = 5$$
$$2x + 5y + 9z = 20$$

39. (I) Donnez les principales différences entre les matrices et les nombres réels en ce qui a trait aux opérations d'addition et de multiplication.

Déterminants et inversion de matrices

... logically the idea of a matrix precedes that of a determinant but historically the order was the reverse and this is why the basic properties of matrices were already clear by the time that matrices were introduced.

M. Kline

À LA FIN DU PRÉSENT CHAPITRE, VOUS DEVRIEZ ÊTRE
EN MESURE DE RÉPONDRE AUX QUESTIONS SUIVANTES:

- Qu'est-ce qu'un déterminant?
- Comment calcule-t-on un déterminant?
- Quelles sont les principales propriétés des déterminants?
- Quand une matrice admet-elle une matrice inverse?
- Quelle est la formule pour trouver l'inverse d'une matrice?
- Quelles sont les principales propriétés de l'inverse d'une matrice?
- Comment peut-on résoudre un système d'équations linéaires à l'aide de l'inverse de la matrice des coefficients?

UN PORTRAIT de Augustin-Louis Cauchy

Augustin-Louis Cauchy naquit à Paris le 21 août 1789 et il mourut à Sceaux le 25 mai 1857. Son père fut un ami des illustres mathématiciens Laplace et Lagrange. Ce dernier s'intéressa au talent du jeune Augustin-Louis, qui allait devenir le plus célèbre mathématicien français du XIXe siècle. Ainsi, en 1801, Lagrange déclara : « Vous voyez ce petit jeune homme, eh bien ! il nous remplacera tous tant que nous sommes pauvres géomètres. » Puis il ajouta à l'intention du père : « Ne lui laissez pas ouvrir un livre de mathématiques, ni écrire un chiffre avant qu'il ait achevé ses études littéraires. »[1]

En 1805, à l'âge de 16 ans, Cauchy entra à l'École polytechnique de Paris, et il poursuivit ensuite ses études à l'École nationale des ponts et chaussées. Il exerça quelque temps le métier d'ingénieur, mais sa santé fragile et sa préférence marquée pour les questions abstraites, et non les problèmes concrets, l'amenèrent à réorienter sa carrière vers les mathématiques. À partir de 1815, il donna des cours d'analyse à l'École polytechnique et, en 1816, il devint membre de l'Académie des sciences. Au cours de sa longue carrière, Cauchy enseigna également au Collège de France et à la Sorbonne. Sur le plan politique, il fut conservateur et royaliste. C'est pourquoi, après la Révolution de 1830, il dut s'expatrier pendant quelques années à Turin, à Fribourg et à Prague, où le roi Charles X, en exil, lui conféra le titre de baron. Cauchy revint en France en 1838.

Cauchy a laissé de nombreuses publications d'une grande importance ; près d'une vingtaine de concepts et de théorèmes portent d'ailleurs son nom. On lui doit 7 livres, plus de 700 articles scientifiques et plus de 150 rapports traitant de diverses branches des mathématiques : géométrie, analyse réelle et complexe, équations différentielles, physique mathématique, théorie des nombres, probabilités, théorie des déterminants, etc. À cet égard, le volume de ses publications incluses dans les Comptes Rendus de l'Académie des sciences était si considérable que l'Académie fixa une limite de quatre pages par article afin de réduire les frais d'impression, limite toujours en vigueur aujourd'hui.

1. B. Belhoste. *Cauchy. Un mathématicien légitimiste au XIXe siècle*, Paris, Belin, 1984, p. 18.

On attribue souvent à Cauchy l'introduction de la rigueur du raisonnement en mathématiques. Si on s'était depuis toujours permis de publier des articles fondés sur des intuitions, avec son arrivée cela devient pratiquement impossible : tout devait désormais être prouvé à l'aide d'une argumentation rigoureuse.

En calcul différentiel et intégral, les définitions de limite et de dérivée qu'on trouve dans les manuels modernes, ainsi que certains critères de convergence des séries, correspondent essentiellement à des notions définies dans les notes de cours de Cauchy.

3.1 ALGORITHME DE CALCUL D'UN DÉTERMINANT

À la fin du chapitre 2, nous avons abordé un sujet très important, à savoir la résolution d'un système d'équations linéaires. Nous avons montré comment résoudre un système de deux équations à deux inconnues à l'aide d'un produit matriciel : on multiplie, par la gauche, chaque membre de l'équation matricielle $AX = B$ par la matrice inverse de A, soit A^{-1}. La solution du système s'écrit alors sous la forme $X = A^{-1}B$. On peut généraliser cette méthode à tout système d'équations qui comporte autant d'équations que d'inconnues, à la condition que la matrice des coefficients admette une matrice inverse.

Toutefois, nous n'avons pas encore répondu à deux questions importantes :

- Quelles conditions garantissent l'existence de la matrice inverse d'une matrice carrée d'ordre n ?
- Quelle est l'expression de l'inverse d'une matrice d'ordre n quelconque si cet inverse existe ?

Pour répondre à ces deux questions, nous étudierons un nouveau concept, soit le déterminant d'une matrice. Nous allons d'abord présenter un algorithme de calcul d'un déterminant, puis la définition formelle du déterminant d'une matrice et les principales propriétés des déterminants, notamment celles qui en simplifient le calcul. Pour terminer, nous allons voir comment évaluer une matrice inverse à l'aide des déterminants et comment résoudre un système d'équations linéaires par la méthode de la matrice inverse.

DÉTERMINANT

Le déterminant est une fonction qui associe un nombre réel à toute matrice carrée A. On le note det A ou $|A|$. Une matrice est inversible si et seulement si son déterminant est différent de zéro.

ORDRE D'UN DÉTERMINANT

L'ordre du déterminant d'une matrice carrée est identique à l'ordre de la matrice.

Le **déterminant** d'une matrice carrée A d'ordre n est un nombre réel, associé à cette matrice. Par analogie, on dit du déterminant d'une matrice carrée d'ordre n qu'il est d'**ordre** n. Le déterminant d'une matrice A est noté det A ou encore $|A|$. La dernière notation (deux barres verticales) est identique au symbole de la valeur absolue, mais le contexte permet généralement de distinguer les deux concepts.

La valeur du déterminant d'une matrice A sert entre autres à « déterminer » si A admet une matrice inverse. En effet, nous allons démontrer qu'une matrice carrée A dont le déterminant est différent de zéro admet une matrice inverse. Cette propriété a son analogue dans les nombres réels : seuls les nombres différents de zéro possèdent un inverse. Une **matrice** carrée dont le déterminant est différent de zéro est dite **régulière**, ou *non singulière*, alors qu'une matrice carrée dont le déterminant vaut zéro est dite **singulière**.

Avant d'aborder la définition formelle d'un déterminant, voyons d'abord un algorithme de calcul. Il consiste à écrire un déterminant d'ordre n sous la forme d'une somme de déterminants d'ordre $n - 1$, puis à écrire chacun de ceux-ci sous la forme d'une somme de déterminants d'ordre $n - 2$, et ainsi de suite jusqu'à ce qu'on obtienne une somme de déterminants d'ordre 2. C'est pourquoi on qualifie cet algorithme de récursif. Donc, si on connaît la formule de calcul d'un déterminant d'ordre 2, on peut calculer à l'aide de celle-ci n'importe quel déterminant, quel que soit son ordre.

MATRICE RÉGULIÈRE

Une matrice régulière (ou non singulière) est une matrice carrée dont le déterminant est différent de zéro.

MATRICE SINGULIÈRE

Une matrice singulière est une matrice carrée dont le déterminant vaut zéro.

Déterminant d'ordre 1

Le déterminant d'une matrice carrée d'ordre 1 est la valeur de l'unique élément de cette matrice : si $A = \left[a_{ij} \right]_{1 \times 1} = \left[a_{11} \right]$, alors $|A| = a_{11}$. De plus, si $a_{11} \neq 0$, alors $A^{-1} = \left[1/a_{11} \right]$. En effet, $\left[a_{11} \right] \left[1/a_{11} \right] = \left[1 \right] = I_1$ et $\left[1/a_{11} \right] \left[a_{11} \right] = \left[1 \right] = I_1$.

Déterminant d'ordre 2

Si $A = \left[a_{ij} \right]_{2 \times 2} = \begin{bmatrix} a_{11} & a_{12} \\ a_{21} & a_{22} \end{bmatrix}$, alors le déterminant de A est

$|A| = \begin{vmatrix} a_{11} & a_{12} \\ a_{21} & a_{22} \end{vmatrix} = a_{11} a_{22} - a_{21} a_{12}$, soit le produit des éléments de la diagonale principale moins le produit des éléments de la diagonale secondaire. Cette formule est représentée par le schéma suivant.

$$\begin{vmatrix} a_{11} & a_{12} \\ a_{21} & a_{22} \end{vmatrix} = a_{11} a_{22} - a_{21} a_{12}$$

Au chapitre 2, nous avons établi que la matrice inverse de la matrice $A = \begin{bmatrix} a & b \\ c & d \end{bmatrix}$ est

$$A^{-1} = \frac{1}{ad - bc} \begin{bmatrix} d & -b \\ -c & a \end{bmatrix}$$

à la condition que $ad - bc \neq 0$. Or, $|A| = ad - bc$. Par conséquent, la matrice inverse d'une matrice carrée d'ordre 2 existe seulement si le déterminant de celle-ci est différent de 0. Si *A* est une matrice carrée d'ordre 2 telle que $|A| \neq 0$, alors la matrice inverse de *A* est

$$A^{-1} = \frac{1}{|A|} \begin{bmatrix} d & -b \\ -c & a \end{bmatrix}$$

Exemple

Soit les matrices

$$A = \begin{bmatrix} -3 \end{bmatrix} \quad B = \begin{bmatrix} 2 & 3 \\ 1 & 4 \end{bmatrix} \quad C = \begin{bmatrix} -1 & -5 \\ 1 & -4 \end{bmatrix}$$

$$D = \begin{bmatrix} 2 & 4 \\ 6 & 12 \end{bmatrix} \quad E = \begin{bmatrix} 5 & -3 \\ -2 & \frac{1}{2} \end{bmatrix}$$

Alors,

$|A| = -3$ et $A^{-1} = \begin{bmatrix} -\frac{1}{3} \end{bmatrix}$

$|B| = \begin{vmatrix} 2 & 3 \\ 1 & 4 \end{vmatrix} = 2 \times 4 - 1 \times 3 = 5$ et $B^{-1} = \frac{1}{5} \begin{bmatrix} 4 & -3 \\ -1 & 2 \end{bmatrix}$

$|C| = \begin{vmatrix} -1 & -5 \\ 1 & -4 \end{vmatrix} = -1 \times (-4) - 1 \times (-5) = 9$ et $C^{-1} = \frac{1}{9} \begin{bmatrix} -4 & 5 \\ -1 & -1 \end{bmatrix}$

$|D| = \begin{vmatrix} 2 & 4 \\ 6 & 12 \end{vmatrix} = 2 \times 12 - 6 \times 4 = 0$ et D^{-1} n'existe pas.

$|E| = \begin{vmatrix} 5 & -3 \\ -2 & \frac{1}{2} \end{vmatrix} = 5(\frac{1}{2}) - (-2)(-3) = -3,5$ et

$E^{-1} = \frac{1}{-3,5} \begin{bmatrix} \frac{1}{2} & 3 \\ 2 & 5 \end{bmatrix}$

Par conséquent, seule la matrice *D* est une matrice singulière, toutes les autres matrices sont régulières (ou non singulières). De plus, on note que le déterminant de chaque matrice est un nombre réel positif, négatif ou nul.

EXERCICE 3.1

Calculez le déterminant des matrices suivantes et donnez, si possible, leur matrice inverse.

$$A = \begin{bmatrix} -2 & -3 \\ -1 & -4 \end{bmatrix} \quad B = \begin{bmatrix} -1 & -1 \\ 1 & 1 \end{bmatrix}$$

Déterminant d'ordre 3

Un déterminant d'ordre 3 s'écrit sous la forme d'une somme de déterminants d'ordre 2. Si

$$A = \begin{bmatrix} a_{11} & a_{12} & a_{13} \\ a_{21} & a_{22} & a_{23} \\ a_{31} & a_{32} & a_{33} \end{bmatrix}$$

alors le déterminant de A est donné par

$$|A| = \begin{vmatrix} a_{11} & a_{12} & a_{13} \\ a_{21} & a_{22} & a_{23} \\ a_{31} & a_{32} & a_{33} \end{vmatrix} = a_{11} \begin{vmatrix} a_{22} & a_{23} \\ a_{32} & a_{33} \end{vmatrix} - a_{12} \begin{vmatrix} a_{21} & a_{23} \\ a_{31} & a_{33} \end{vmatrix} + a_{13} \begin{vmatrix} a_{21} & a_{22} \\ a_{31} & a_{32} \end{vmatrix}$$

Vous vous demandez sans doute comment retenir une formule aussi compliquée. Regardons de plus près comment chacun des termes de cette somme est formé.

On note d'abord que les signes des différents termes de la somme alternent $(+, -, +)$. De plus, le premier terme est le produit du premier élément de la première ligne de la matrice A (soit a_{11}) par un déterminant d'ordre 2. Ce déterminant est celui de la matrice résiduelle obtenue en supprimant la ligne et la colonne de A où se trouve l'élément a_{11}.

$$\begin{array}{ccc} a_{11} & a_{12} & a_{13} \\ a_{21} & a_{22} & a_{23} \\ a_{31} & a_{32} & a_{33} \end{array} \rightarrow \begin{array}{cc} a_{22} & a_{23} \\ a_{32} & a_{33} \end{array}$$

Quant au deuxième terme, c'est le produit du deuxième élément de la première ligne de la matrice A (soit a_{12}) par un déterminant d'ordre 2. Ce déterminant est celui de la matrice résiduelle obtenue en supprimant la ligne et la colonne de A où se trouve l'élément a_{12}.

$$\begin{array}{ccc} a_{11} & a_{12} & a_{13} \\ a_{21} & a_{22} & a_{23} \\ a_{31} & a_{32} & a_{33} \end{array} \rightarrow \begin{array}{cc} a_{21} & a_{23} \\ a_{31} & a_{33} \end{array}$$

Enfin, le troisième terme est le produit du troisième élément de la première ligne de la matrice A (soit a_{13}) par un déterminant d'ordre 2. Ce déterminant est celui de la matrice résiduelle obtenue en supprimant la ligne et la colonne de A où se trouve l'élément a_{13}.

$$\begin{array}{ccc} a_{11} & a_{12} & a_{13} \\ a_{21} & a_{22} & a_{23} \\ a_{31} & a_{32} & a_{33} \end{array} \rightarrow \begin{array}{cc} a_{21} & a_{22} \\ a_{31} & a_{32} \end{array}$$

$$\begin{vmatrix} 5 & -2 & -3 \\ 4 & 3 & -1 \\ -1 & 1 & 2 \end{vmatrix} = 5 \begin{vmatrix} 3 & -1 \\ 1 & 2 \end{vmatrix} - (-2) \begin{vmatrix} 4 & -1 \\ -1 & 2 \end{vmatrix} + (-3) \begin{vmatrix} 4 & 3 \\ -1 & 1 \end{vmatrix}$$

$$= 5 \times (6 + 1) + 2 \times (8 - 1) - 3 \times (4 + 3)$$

$$= 28$$

EXERCICE 3.2

Évaluez le déterminant de chacune des matrices

$$A = \begin{bmatrix} 1 & 2 & 3 \\ 4 & -1 & -2 \\ 1 & 5 & 2 \end{bmatrix} \quad \text{et} \quad B = \begin{bmatrix} -4 & 4 & -4 \\ 1 & -1 & 1 \\ 2 & 3 & -5 \end{bmatrix}$$

RÈGLE DE SARRUS

La règle de Sarrus constitue une méthode pratique pour calculer le déterminant d'une matrice $A = \begin{bmatrix} a_{ij} \end{bmatrix}_{3 \times 3}$. Elle consiste à ajouter d'abord les deux premières colonnes du déterminant à évaluer à la droite de celui-ci, puis à calculer la somme des produits des éléments situés sur une même flèche, chaque produit étant affecté du signe indiqué dans le schéma suivant.

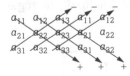

La méthode que nous venons d'expliquer s'applique au calcul de tout déterminant, quel qu'en soit l'ordre. Toutefois, dans le cas d'un déterminant d'ordre 3, on peut également employer la **règle de Sarrus**[2], qui permet de représenter la formule du déterminant par un schéma simple. On répète, à droite du déterminant à calculer, les deux premières colonnes, puis on effectue les opérations indiquées dans le schéma, à savoir la somme ou la différence des produits des éléments reliés par une même flèche.

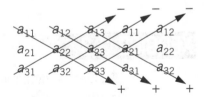

Si $A = \begin{bmatrix} a_{ij} \end{bmatrix}_{3 \times 3}$, alors

$$|A| = a_{11} a_{22} a_{33} + a_{12} a_{23} a_{31} + a_{13} a_{21} a_{32}$$
$$- a_{31} a_{22} a_{13} - a_{32} a_{23} a_{11} - a_{33} a_{21} a_{12}$$

2. Le mathématicien français Pierre Frédéric Sarrus (1798-1861) enseigna l'analyse à l'Université de Strasbourg. Il est particulièrement connu pour la technique de calcul d'un déterminant d'ordre trois qui porte son nom, mais il apporta sa contribution aux mathématiques sur de nombreux autres plans. On lui doit entre autres la notation $F(x) \big|_a^b$, qui sert à désigner l'expression $F(b) - F(a)$ dans l'évaluation d'une intégrale. En 1842, Sarrus obtint le grand prix de l'Académie des sciences pour un mémoire dans lequel il donna la première démonstration exacte d'un résultat important, appelé aujourd'hui *lemme fondamental du calcul des variations*.

Évaluons le déterminant de la matrice A en appliquant la règle de Sarrus.

$$A = \begin{bmatrix} 5 & -2 & -3 \\ 4 & 3 & -1 \\ -1 & 1 & 2 \end{bmatrix}$$

Il faut d'abord ajouter deux colonnes à cette matrice, puis inscrire les flèches et les signes.

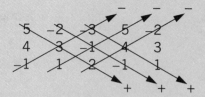

Par conséquent,

$$\det A = 5 \times 3 \times 2 + (-2) \times (-1) \times (-1) + (-3) \times 4 \times 1$$
$$-(-1) \times 3 \times (-3) - 1 \times (-1) \times 5 - 2 \times 4 \times (-2)$$
$$= 28$$

EXERCICE 3.3

Évaluez le déterminant des matrices A et B à l'aide de la règle de Sarrus.

$$A = \begin{bmatrix} 1 & 1 & -2 \\ 4 & -1 & -2 \\ 1 & 5 & 2 \end{bmatrix} \quad B = \begin{bmatrix} -2 & 3 & -4 \\ 1 & -1 & 1 \\ -1 & 2 & -3 \end{bmatrix}$$

Déterminant d'ordre 4 ou supérieur à 4

Le calcul d'un déterminant d'ordre 4 ou supérieur à 4 est analogue au calcul d'un déterminant d'ordre 3. Si $A = \begin{bmatrix} a_{ij} \end{bmatrix}_{4 \times 4}$, alors

$$|A| = \begin{vmatrix} a_{11} & a_{12} & a_{13} & a_{14} \\ a_{21} & a_{22} & a_{23} & a_{24} \\ a_{31} & a_{32} & a_{33} & a_{34} \\ a_{41} & a_{42} & a_{43} & a_{44} \end{vmatrix} = a_{11}\begin{vmatrix} a_{22} & a_{23} & a_{24} \\ a_{32} & a_{33} & a_{34} \\ a_{42} & a_{43} & a_{44} \end{vmatrix} - a_{12}\begin{vmatrix} a_{21} & a_{23} & a_{24} \\ a_{31} & a_{33} & a_{34} \\ a_{41} & a_{43} & a_{44} \end{vmatrix}$$

$$+ a_{13}\begin{vmatrix} a_{21} & a_{22} & a_{24} \\ a_{31} & a_{32} & a_{34} \\ a_{41} & a_{42} & a_{44} \end{vmatrix} - a_{14}\begin{vmatrix} a_{21} & a_{22} & a_{23} \\ a_{31} & a_{32} & a_{33} \\ a_{41} & a_{42} & a_{43} \end{vmatrix}$$

On note d'abord que les signes des différents termes de la somme alternent $(+, -, +, -)$. De plus, le premier terme est le produit du premier élément de la première ligne de la matrice A (soit a_{11}) par un déterminant d'ordre 3. Ce déterminant est celui de la matrice résiduelle obtenue en supprimant la ligne et la colonne de A où se trouve l'élément a_{11}.

$$\begin{array}{cccc} \cancel{a_{11}} & \cancel{a_{12}} & \cancel{a_{13}} & \cancel{a_{14}} \\ a_{21} & a_{22} & a_{23} & a_{24} \\ a_{31} & a_{32} & a_{33} & a_{34} \\ a_{41} & a_{42} & a_{43} & a_{44} \end{array} \rightarrow \begin{array}{ccc} a_{22} & a_{23} & a_{24} \\ a_{32} & a_{33} & a_{34} \\ a_{42} & a_{43} & a_{44} \end{array}$$

De façon analogue, le deuxième terme de la somme est le produit du deuxième élément de la première ligne de A (soit a_{12}) par le déterminant de la matrice résiduelle obtenue en supprimant la première ligne et la deuxième colonne de A.

$$\begin{array}{cccc} \cancel{a_{11}} & a_{12} & \cancel{a_{13}} & \cancel{a_{14}} \\ a_{21} & a_{22} & a_{23} & a_{24} \\ a_{31} & a_{32} & a_{33} & a_{34} \\ a_{41} & a_{42} & a_{43} & a_{44} \end{array} \rightarrow \begin{array}{ccc} a_{21} & a_{23} & a_{24} \\ a_{31} & a_{33} & a_{34} \\ a_{41} & a_{43} & a_{44} \end{array}$$

Quant aux troisième et quatrième termes, on constate qu'ils sont formés comme les deux premiers. En général, pour évaluer un déterminant d'ordre 4, il faut calculer quatre déterminants d'ordre 3 et, pour trouver la valeur de chacun de ceux-ci, on doit calculer trois déterminants d'ordre 2.

Exemple

$$\begin{vmatrix} 1 & -1 & 0 & 2 \\ -1 & 1 & 0 & 1 \\ 2 & 0 & 1 & 2 \\ 2 & 1 & -2 & -1 \end{vmatrix} = 1\begin{vmatrix} 1 & 0 & 1 \\ 0 & 1 & 2 \\ 1 & -2 & -1 \end{vmatrix} - (-1)\begin{vmatrix} -1 & 0 & 1 \\ 2 & 1 & 2 \\ 2 & -2 & -1 \end{vmatrix}$$

$$+ 0\begin{vmatrix} -1 & 1 & 1 \\ 2 & 0 & 2 \\ 2 & 1 & -1 \end{vmatrix} - 2\begin{vmatrix} -1 & 1 & 0 \\ 2 & 0 & 1 \\ 2 & 1 & -2 \end{vmatrix}$$

$$= 1\left(1\begin{vmatrix} 1 & 2 \\ -2 & -1 \end{vmatrix} - 0\begin{vmatrix} 0 & 2 \\ 1 & -1 \end{vmatrix} + 1\begin{vmatrix} 0 & 1 \\ 1 & -2 \end{vmatrix}\right)$$

$$+ 1\left(-1\begin{vmatrix} 1 & 2 \\ -2 & -1 \end{vmatrix} - 0\begin{vmatrix} 2 & 2 \\ 2 & -1 \end{vmatrix} + 1\begin{vmatrix} 2 & 1 \\ 2 & -2 \end{vmatrix}\right)$$

$$+ 0 - 2\left(-1\begin{vmatrix} 0 & 1 \\ 1 & -2 \end{vmatrix} - 1\begin{vmatrix} 2 & 1 \\ 2 & -2 \end{vmatrix} + 0\begin{vmatrix} 2 & 0 \\ 2 & 1 \end{vmatrix}\right)$$

$$= 1(1 \times 3 - 0 + 1 \times (-1))$$
$$+ 1(-1 \times 3 - 0 + 1 \times (-6))$$
$$+ 0 - 2(-1 \times (-1) - 1 \times (-6) + 0)$$
$$= -21$$

On remarque que la présence de zéros dans un déterminant réduit considérablement les calculs à effectuer.

Il n'est sûrement pas nécessaire de donner un autre exemple pour vous convaincre que le calcul d'un déterminant d'ordre 4 ou, en général, d'ordre n demande du temps. Pour évaluer un déterminant d'ordre n, on généralise la méthode que nous avons exposée : alternance des signes, somme de produits d'un élément de la première ligne par le déterminant de la matrice résiduelle (d'ordre $n - 1$) obtenue en supprimant la ligne et la colonne où se trouve l'élément en question.

L'application de cette méthode au calcul d'un déterminant d'ordre n exige d'effectuer un nombre considérable d'opérations[3]. Le tableau 3.1 donne le nombre d'opérations à réaliser pour quelques valeurs de n et le temps que mettrait un ordinateur qui effectue un million d'opérations à la seconde pour calculer un déterminant en employant la méthode indiquée.

TABLEAU 3.1 — **Nombre d'opérations et temps requis pour calculer un déterminant, selon l'ordre de ce dernier**

Ordre du déterminant	Nombre d'opérations	Temps requis
5	326	$3,26 \times 10^{-4}$ secondes
10	9 864 101	9,86 secondes
15	$3,55 \times 10^{12}$	41 jours
20	$6,61 \times 10^{18}$	210 000 années
50	$8,27 \times 10^{64}$	$2,62 \times 10^{51}$ années

SOURCE : S. Friedberg et A. Insel. *Introduction to Linear Algebra with Applications*, Englewood Cliffs, Prentice-Hall Inc., 1986, p. 231.

3. Le nombre d'opérations est d'environ $e \times n! = e \times n \times (n - 1) \times (n - 2) \times \cdots \times 1$ où $e \approx 2,718\ 28$ est un nombre irrationnel, appelé *nombre de Néper*.

Les déterminants possèdent des propriétés qui en facilitent grandement l'évaluation. En vertu de l'une de ces propriétés, on peut développer tout déterminant selon n'importe quelle ligne ou colonne. Cette opération consiste à écrire le déterminant sous la forme d'une somme de termes dont chacun est le produit d'un élément de la matrice (situé sur une ligne ou une colonne donnée) par le déterminant de la matrice résiduelle obtenue en supprimant la ligne et la colonne où se trouve cet élément. On attribue un signe (+ ou −) à chaque produit (ou terme de la somme) de la façon indiquée par la matrice des signes.

Matrice des signes

$$\begin{bmatrix} + & - & + & - & \cdots \\ - & + & - & + & \cdots \\ + & - & + & - & \cdots \\ - & + & - & + & \cdots \\ \cdots & \cdots & \cdots & \cdots & \cdots \end{bmatrix}$$

On constate que, dans cette matrice, il y a alternance des signes d'une ligne ou d'une colonne à l'autre.

Voici un exemple qui illustre la propriété selon laquelle on peut développer un déterminant suivant n'importe quelle ligne ou colonne.

Exemple

Soit la matrice

$$A = \begin{bmatrix} 1 & 2 & 3 \\ 4 & -1 & -2 \\ 1 & 5 & 2 \end{bmatrix}$$

Il s'agit de vérifier qu'on obtient bien la même valeur pour le déterminant de A qu'on développe celui-ci selon la première ligne, la deuxième ligne ou la troisième colonne.

Le développement du déterminant de A selon la première ligne donne

$$\begin{vmatrix} \mathbf{1} & \mathbf{2} & \mathbf{3} \\ 4 & -1 & -2 \\ 1 & 5 & 2 \end{vmatrix} = 1\begin{vmatrix} -1 & -2 \\ 5 & 2 \end{vmatrix} - 2\begin{vmatrix} 4 & -2 \\ 1 & 2 \end{vmatrix} + 3\begin{vmatrix} 4 & -1 \\ 1 & 5 \end{vmatrix}$$

$$= 1 \times 8 - 2 \times 10 + 3 \times 21$$
$$= 51$$

Le développement du déterminant de A selon la deuxième ligne donne

$$\begin{vmatrix} 1 & 2 & 3 \\ \mathbf{4} & \mathbf{-1} & \mathbf{-2} \\ 1 & 5 & 2 \end{vmatrix} = -4 \begin{vmatrix} 2 & 3 \\ 5 & 2 \end{vmatrix} + (-1) \begin{vmatrix} 1 & 3 \\ 1 & 2 \end{vmatrix} - (-2) \begin{vmatrix} 1 & 2 \\ 1 & 5 \end{vmatrix}$$

$$= -4 \times (-11) - 1 \times (-1) + 2 \times 3$$
$$= 51$$

Le développement du déterminant de A selon la troisième colonne donne

$$\begin{vmatrix} 1 & 2 & \mathbf{3} \\ 4 & -1 & \mathbf{-2} \\ 1 & 5 & \mathbf{2} \end{vmatrix} = 3 \begin{vmatrix} 4 & -1 \\ 1 & 5 \end{vmatrix} - (-2) \begin{vmatrix} 1 & 2 \\ 1 & 5 \end{vmatrix} + 2 \begin{vmatrix} 1 & 2 \\ 4 & -1 \end{vmatrix}$$

$$= 3 \times 21 + 2 \times 3 + 2 \times (-9)$$
$$= 51$$

Dans les trois cas, on obtient det $A = 51$.

EXERCICE 3.4

Développez le déterminant de la matrice A de l'exemple précédent selon la troisième ligne et la deuxième colonne, et vérifiez que det $A = 51$ dans chaque cas.

La propriété que nous venons d'énoncer permet de réduire le temps nécessaire pour calculer le déterminant de certaines matrices, particulièrement si on développe celui-ci selon la ligne ou la colonne qui comporte le plus de zéros.

Exemple

Le calcul de

$$\begin{vmatrix} 1 & -1 & 0 & 2 \\ -1 & 0 & 0 & 1 \\ 0 & 0 & 1 & 0 \\ 2 & 0 & -2 & -1 \end{vmatrix}$$

est plus rapide si on développe le déterminant selon la deuxième colonne ou la troisième ligne, qui comportent chacune trois zéros.

Le développement du déterminant selon la deuxième colonne est

$$\begin{vmatrix} 1 & \mathbf{-1} & 0 & 2 \\ -1 & \mathbf{0} & 0 & 1 \\ 0 & \mathbf{0} & 1 & 0 \\ 2 & \mathbf{0} & -2 & -1 \end{vmatrix} = -(-1)\begin{vmatrix} -1 & 0 & 1 \\ 0 & 1 & 0 \\ 2 & -2 & -1 \end{vmatrix} + 0\begin{vmatrix} 1 & 0 & 2 \\ 0 & 1 & 0 \\ 2 & -2 & -1 \end{vmatrix}$$

$$- 0\begin{vmatrix} 1 & 0 & 2 \\ -1 & 0 & 1 \\ 2 & -2 & -1 \end{vmatrix} + 0\begin{vmatrix} 1 & 0 & 2 \\ -1 & 0 & 1 \\ 0 & 1 & 0 \end{vmatrix}$$

$$= -(-1)\begin{vmatrix} -1 & 0 & 1 \\ 0 & 1 & 0 \\ 2 & -2 & -1 \end{vmatrix}$$

Il est à noter que, dans ce développement, les signes attribués aux différents termes sont conformes à ceux de la matrice des signes (p. 77). En développant le déterminant selon la deuxième colonne, qui comporte trois zéros, on a un seul déterminant d'ordre 3 à évaluer. Comme la deuxième ligne de celui-ci compte plus de zéros que les autres lignes ou les colonnes, on développe ce déterminant d'ordre 3 selon la deuxième ligne, ce qui réduit encore une fois le nombre de calculs à effectuer.

$$-(-1)\begin{vmatrix} -1 & 0 & 1 \\ \mathbf{0} & \mathbf{1} & \mathbf{0} \\ 2 & -2 & -1 \end{vmatrix}$$

$$= -(-1)\left(-0\begin{vmatrix} 0 & 1 \\ -2 & -1 \end{vmatrix} + 1\begin{vmatrix} -1 & 1 \\ 2 & -1 \end{vmatrix} - 0\begin{vmatrix} -1 & 0 \\ 2 & -2 \end{vmatrix}\right)$$

$$= -1$$

Par conséquent, $\begin{vmatrix} 1 & -1 & 0 & 2 \\ -1 & 0 & 0 & 1 \\ 0 & 0 & 1 & 0 \\ 2 & 0 & -2 & -1 \end{vmatrix} = -1.$

EXERCICE 3.5

Soit les matrices

$$A = \begin{bmatrix} 5 & 0 \\ 3 & 3 \end{bmatrix} \quad B = \begin{bmatrix} -7 & 9 & 5 \\ 0 & -1 & 7 \\ 0 & 0 & 2 \end{bmatrix} \quad C = \begin{bmatrix} 3 & 0 & 0 & 0 \\ -1 & 2 & 0 & 0 \\ 2 & 6 & -4 & 0 \\ 2 & 1 & -2 & -5 \end{bmatrix}$$

$$D = \begin{bmatrix} 5 & 0 \\ 3 & 0 \end{bmatrix} \quad E = \begin{bmatrix} -2 & 0 & 3 \\ 6 & 0 & -4 \\ 5 & 0 & 2 \end{bmatrix} \quad F = \begin{bmatrix} 3 & 3 & 0 & -1 \\ -1 & 2 & 0 & 6 \\ 2 & -6 & 0 & -7 \\ 2 & -5 & 0 & -5 \end{bmatrix}$$

a) De quel type les matrices A, B et C sont-elles?

b) Calculez le déterminant des matrices A, B et C.

c) Calculez le produit des éléments de la diagonale principale de chacune des matrices A, B et C.

d) Comparez les résultats obtenus en b et en c. Émettez une hypothèse sur la façon de calculer la valeur du déterminant d'une matrice triangulaire.

e) Montrez que l'hypothèse formulée en d ne se vérifie pas nécessairement pour une matrice non triangulaire. (Vous pouvez employer la matrice de l'exemple précédent.)

f) Qu'ont en commun les matrices D, E et F?

g) Calculez le déterminant des matrices D, E et F.

h) À la lumière des résultats obtenus en g, émettez une hypothèse sur la valeur du déterminant d'une matrice qui possède la caractéristique identifiée en f.

3.3 DÉFINITION FORMELLE DU DÉTERMINANT D'UNE MATRICE CARRÉE

Nous avons besoin de deux nouveaux concepts pour définir formellement le déterminant[4] d'une matrice carrée, à savoir le mineur et le cofacteur d'un élément de la matrice.

MINEUR

Le mineur, noté M_{ij}, de l'élément a_{ij} d'une matrice carrée A est égal au déterminant de la matrice résiduelle obtenue en supprimant la i-ième ligne et la j-ième colonne de A.

COFACTEUR

Le cofacteur A_{ij} d'un élément a_{ij} d'une matrice carrée A est égal au mineur associé à a_{ij}, multiplié par 1 ou -1 selon la position de cet élément: $A_{ij} = (-1)^{i+j} M_{ij}$.

Si $A = \begin{bmatrix} a_{ij} \end{bmatrix}_{n \times n}$, alors le **mineur** associé à l'élément a_{ij} (situé à l'intersection de la i-ième ligne et de la j-ième colonne), noté M_{ij}, est le déterminant de la matrice résiduelle obtenue en supprimant la i-ième ligne et la j-ième colonne de A.

Le **cofacteur** de l'élément a_{ij} est $A_{ij} = (-1)^{i+j} M_{ij}$. En d'autres termes, le cofacteur de a_{ij} est égal au mineur M_{ij} multiplié par 1 ou -1 selon la position de l'élément a_{ij} dans la matrice. Dans ce cas, multiplier par 1 ou -1 revient à attribuer au mineur le signe donné par la matrice des signes

---

4. Il s'agit d'une définition récursive. On peut aussi définir un déterminant en faisant appel aux permutations et aux produits élémentaires. Les personnes intéressées peuvent consulter H. Anton et C. Rorres. *Elementary Linear Algebra: Applications Version*, New York, John Wiley & Sons, 6e éd., 1994, p. 79-85.

(p. 77). On désigne les cofacteurs d'une matrice B par B_{ij}, ceux d'une matrice C par C_{ij}, etc. Par conséquent, dans la mesure du possible, on s'abstient d'employer la lettre M pour désigner une matrice afin d'éviter la confusion qui pourrait en résulter entre les mineurs et les cofacteurs.

Ainsi, on définit le déterminant d'une matrice A d'ordre n par

$$\det A = a_{11}A_{11} + a_{12}A_{12} + \cdots + a_{1n}A_{1n}$$

On abrège l'écriture de cette expression de det A en employant la notation Σ :

$$\det A = \sum_{k=1}^{n} a_{1k}A_{1k} \quad \text{(développement selon la 1}^{\text{re}}\text{ ligne)}^{5}$$

Nous avons déjà souligné qu'on peut développer un déterminant selon n'importe quelle ligne ou colonne de sorte que

$$\det A = \sum_{k=1}^{n} a_{ik}A_{ik} \quad \text{(développement selon la }i\text{-ième ligne)}$$

et

$$\det A = \sum_{k=1}^{n} a_{kj}A_{kj} \quad \text{(développement selon la }j\text{-ième colonne)}$$

Exemple

Si $A = \begin{bmatrix} 5 & -2 & -3 \\ 4 & 3 & -1 \\ -1 & 1 & 2 \end{bmatrix}$, alors $M_{23} = \begin{vmatrix} 5 & -2 \\ -1 & 1 \end{vmatrix}$. En effet, si on supprime la deuxième ligne et la troisième colonne de la matrice A, on obtient

$$\begin{matrix} 5 & -2 & -3 \\ 4 & 3 & -1 \\ -1 & 1 & 2 \end{matrix} \quad \rightarrow \quad \begin{matrix} 5 & -2 \\ -1 & 1 \end{matrix}$$

Par conséquent, $M_{23} = \begin{vmatrix} 5 & -2 \\ -1 & 1 \end{vmatrix} = 5(1) - (-1)(-2) = 3$. Quant au cofacteur de l'élément a_{23}, il est donné par $A_{23} = (-1)^{2+3}M_{23} = -3$.

---

5. On comprend ici le sens du mot cofacteur A_{ij} : il s'agit du « facteur avec » l'élément a_{ij} dans le développement d'un déterminant.

1. Soit $A = \begin{bmatrix} 1 & 2 \\ 3 & 4 \end{bmatrix}$. Calculez le cofacteur de chaque élément de A.

2. Soit $A = \begin{bmatrix} 1 & 2 & 3 \\ 4 & -1 & -2 \\ 1 & 5 & 2 \end{bmatrix}$. Calculez M_{31}, A_{22} et $a_{32}A_{32}$.

3. Soit $A = \begin{bmatrix} -1 & 4 & 3 & -2 \\ 0 & 2 & -4 & 4 \\ 2 & 1 & 6 & -3 \\ 3 & -2 & -1 & 7 \end{bmatrix}$. Calculez M_{43} et A_{43}.

4. Soit $A = \begin{bmatrix} 0 & 1 & -2 \\ 4 & -2 & 3 \end{bmatrix}$. Calculez M_{11} et A_{11}.

3.4 PROPRIÉTÉS DES DÉTERMINANTS

Nous avons déjà donné la propriété des déterminants qui permet d'évaluer ceux-ci en les développant selon n'importe quelle ligne ou colonne. Le théorème 3.1 énonce une dizaine d'autres propriétés des déterminants. Nous allons en prouver certaines et nous vous laissons en démontrer d'autres en guise d'exercice. Nous avons omis les preuves qui sortent du cadre du présent manuel. Toutefois, nous illustrerons par un exemple chaque propriété non démontrée.

Théorème 3.1

Dans les énoncés qui suivent, A et B désignent des matrices carrées d'ordre n, et c est un scalaire.

1) $\det A = \sum_{k=1}^{n} a_{1k}A_{1k} = \sum_{k=1}^{n} a_{ik}A_{ik} = \sum_{k=1}^{n} a_{kj}A_{kj}$. On peut développer un déterminant selon la première ligne, la i-ième ligne ou la j-ième colonne.

2) Si la matrice B résulte de l'interversion de deux lignes ou de deux colonnes de la matrice A, alors $\det B = -\det A$.

3) Le déterminant d'une matrice triangulaire est égal au produit des éléments de la diagonale principale de celle-ci, c'est-à-dire que si A est triangulaire, alors

$$\det A = a_{11} \times a_{22} \times a_{33} \times \cdots \times a_{nn} = \prod_{i=1}^{n} a_{ii}$$

La notation Π d'un produit est analogue à la notation Σ d'une somme.

4) $\det A^t = \det A$.

5) Le déterminant d'une matrice qui comporte une ligne (ou une colonne) contenant seulement des zéros vaut 0.

6) Si B est une matrice obtenue en multipliant une ligne (ou une colonne) d'une matrice A par une constante c, alors le déterminant de B est donné par $\det B = c \det A$.

7) $\det (cA) = c^n \det A$.

8) Le déterminant d'une matrice qui comporte deux lignes (ou deux colonnes) identiques vaut 0.

9) Le déterminant d'une matrice qui comporte deux lignes (ou deux colonnes) dont l'une est un multiple de l'autre vaut 0.

10) Si B est une matrice obtenue en ajoutant un multiple d'une ligne (ou d'une colonne) d'une matrice A à une autre ligne (ou à une autre colonne) de A, alors $\det B = \det A$.

11) Le déterminant du produit de deux matrices est égal au produit des déterminants des deux matrices, c'est-à-dire que

$$\det AB = \det A \times \det B$$

Propriété 1 $\det A = \displaystyle\sum_{k=1}^{n} a_{1k}A_{1k} = \sum_{k=1}^{n} a_{ik}A_{ik} = \sum_{k=1}^{n} a_{kj}A_{kj}$

La propriété 1 du théorème 3.1 affirme essentiellement qu'on peut développer un déterminant selon n'importe quelle ligne ou colonne. Nous avons déjà montré qu'on tire parti au maximum de cette propriété en développant le déterminant selon la ligne ou la colonne qui comporte le plus grand nombre de zéros. On réduit ainsi considérablement le temps nécessaire pour le calcul du déterminant. La preuve de la propriété 1 fait appel à un raisonnement par récurrence et elle sort du cadre du présent manuel[6].

Propriété 2   Si B est la matrice obtenue en intervertissant deux lignes (ou deux colonnes) d'une matrice A, alors $\det B = -\det A$.

La preuve de la propriété 2 sort également du cadre du présent manuel[7]. Cette propriété n'est pas d'une très grande utilité dans le calcul des déterminants, mais elle est indispensable pour démontrer quelques autres propriétés énoncées dans le théorème 3.1. Nous nous contentons d'en illustrer l'emploi par un exemple.

---

6. Les personnes désireuses de connaître la démonstration peuvent consulter les ouvrages de Noble (p. 201) et de Grossman (p. 134) mentionnés dans la bibliographie.
7. Les personnes désireuses de connaître la démonstration peuvent consulter les ouvrages de Noble (p. 203) et de Grossman (p. 122) mentionnés dans la bibliographie.

Soit les matrices

$$A = \begin{bmatrix} 1 & 2 & 3 \\ 4 & -1 & -2 \\ 1 & 5 & 2 \end{bmatrix} \quad B = \begin{bmatrix} 4 & -1 & -2 \\ 1 & 2 & 3 \\ 1 & 5 & 2 \end{bmatrix}$$

$$C = \begin{bmatrix} 2 & 3 & 4 & -1 & 3 \\ 0 & -2 & 3 & 7 & 3 \\ 0 & 0 & 5 & 6 & 3 \\ 0 & 0 & 0 & -1 & 4 \\ 0 & 0 & 0 & 0 & 3 \end{bmatrix} \quad D = \begin{bmatrix} 4 & 3 & 2 & -1 & 3 \\ 3 & 3 & 0 & 7 & -2 \\ 5 & 3 & 0 & 6 & 0 \\ 0 & 4 & 0 & -1 & 0 \\ 0 & 3 & 0 & 0 & 0 \end{bmatrix}$$

La matrice B résulte de l'interversion des première et deuxième lignes de la matrice A. À la page 77, on a calculé que det $A = 51$. Par conséquent, det $B = -51$.

De façon similaire, la matrice D résulte de l'interversion des première et troisième colonnes et des deuxième et cinquième colonnes de la matrice C. Comme il y a deux interversions, det $D = -(-\det C) = 60$. Il est à noter que l'application de la propriété 3 permet d'évaluer rapidement le déterminant de la matrice C, cette dernière étant triangulaire.

Propriété 3 Le déterminant d'une matrice triangulaire est égal au produit des éléments de la diagonale principale de celle-ci, c'est-à-dire que si A est triangulaire alors

$$\det A = a_{11} \times a_{22} \times a_{33} \times \cdots \times a_{nn} = \prod_{i=1}^{n} a_{ii}$$

Preuve

Nous allons démontrer la propriété 3 pour une matrice A triangulaire supérieure. La preuve dans le cas d'une matrice triangulaire inférieure est similaire[8].

Si A est une matrice triangulaire supérieure d'ordre n, alors

$$A = \begin{bmatrix} a_{11} & a_{12} & \cdots & a_{1i} & \cdots & a_{1n} \\ 0 & a_{22} & \cdots & a_{2i} & \cdots & a_{2n} \\ \vdots & \vdots & & \vdots & & \vdots \\ 0 & 0 & \cdots & a_{ii} & \cdots & a_{in} \\ \vdots & \vdots & & \vdots & & \vdots \\ 0 & 0 & \cdots & 0 & \cdots & a_{nn} \end{bmatrix}$$

---

8. Nous donnons une preuve intuitive. Quant à la preuve formelle, elle fait appel à un raisonnement par récurrence portant sur l'ordre de la matrice.

En développant les déterminants successifs selon la première colonne, on obtient

$$\det A = \begin{vmatrix} a_{11} & a_{12} & \cdots & a_{1i} & \cdots & a_{1n} \\ 0 & a_{22} & \cdots & a_{2i} & \cdots & a_{2n} \\ \vdots & \vdots & & \vdots & & \vdots \\ 0 & 0 & \cdots & a_{ii} & \cdots & a_{in} \\ \vdots & \vdots & & \vdots & & \vdots \\ 0 & 0 & \cdots & 0 & \cdots & a_{nn} \end{vmatrix}$$

$$= a_{11} \begin{vmatrix} a_{22} & \cdots & a_{2i} & \cdots & a_{2n} \\ \vdots & & \vdots & & \vdots \\ 0 & \cdots & a_{ii} & \cdots & a_{in} \\ \vdots & & \vdots & & \vdots \\ 0 & \cdots & 0 & \cdots & a_{nn} \end{vmatrix}$$

$$= a_{11} \times a_{22} \begin{vmatrix} a_{33} & \cdots & a_{3i} & \cdots & a_{3n} \\ \vdots & & \vdots & & \vdots \\ 0 & \cdots & a_{ii} & \cdots & a_{in} \\ \vdots & & \vdots & & \vdots \\ 0 & \cdots & 0 & \cdots & a_{nn} \end{vmatrix}$$

$$= \cdots$$

$$= a_{11} \times a_{22} \times a_{33} \times \cdots \times a_{(n-2)(n-2)} \begin{vmatrix} a_{(n-1)(n-1)} & a_{(n-1)n} \\ 0 & a_{nn} \end{vmatrix}$$

$$= a_{11} \times a_{22} \times a_{33} \times \ldots \times a_{nn}$$

$$= \prod_{i=1}^{n} a_{ii}$$

∎

EXERCICE 3.7

Calculez le déterminant de chaque matrice.

a) $A = \begin{bmatrix} a & b & c \\ 0 & d & e \\ 0 & 0 & f \end{bmatrix}$

b) $B = \begin{bmatrix} -2 & 0 & 0 & 0 \\ 4 & -6 & 0 & 0 \\ 12 & 4 & 5 & 0 \\ 9 & 1 & 2 & -3 \end{bmatrix}$

Propriété 4 $\det A^t = \det A$

Preuve

L'énoncé 1 du théorème 3.1 affirme qu'on peut évaluer un déterminant en le développant selon n'importe quelle ligne ou colonne. Développer le déterminant d'une matrice A selon la première ligne, cela équivaut à développer le déterminant de la transposée de A selon la première colonne[9]. Par conséquent, det A^t = det A. ∎

L'énoncé 4 est particulièrement intéressant du fait qu'il implique que toute propriété des déterminants relative aux lignes demeure vraie si on remplace le mot ligne par le mot colonne. Ainsi, en prouvant un énoncé – portant sur les déterminants – qui contient le mot ligne, on démontre du même coup l'énoncé obtenu en remplaçant le mot ligne par le mot colonne.

Propriété 5 Le déterminant d'une matrice qui comporte une ligne (ou une colonne) formée seulement de zéros vaut 0.

Preuve

Nous allons d'abord montrer que la propriété 5 est vraie dans le cas d'une ligne nulle. Si A est une matrice carrée d'ordre n dont la i-ième ligne est formée seulement de zéros, alors $a_{ik} = 0$ pour $k = 1, 2, 3, ..., n$. Si on développe le déterminant de A selon la i-ième ligne, on obtient

$$\det A = \sum_{k=1}^{n} a_{ik} A_{ik} = \sum_{k=1}^{n} 0 \times A_{ik} = 0$$

En vertu de la propriété 4, le même raisonnement s'applique au cas où la matrice A comporte une colonne dont tous les éléments valent zéro. ∎

Propriété 6 Si on multiplie une ligne (ou une colonne) d'une matrice A par une constante c, alors le déterminant de la matrice B résultante est donné par det $B = c$ det A.

Preuve

Si A est une matrice carrée d'ordre n, alors

$$A = \begin{bmatrix} a_{11} & a_{12} & \cdots & a_{1j} & \cdots & a_{1n} \\ a_{21} & a_{22} & \cdots & a_{2j} & \cdots & a_{2n} \\ \vdots & \vdots & & \vdots & & \vdots \\ a_{i1} & a_{i2} & \cdots & a_{ij} & \cdots & a_{in} \\ \vdots & \vdots & & \vdots & & \vdots \\ a_{n1} & a_{n2} & \cdots & a_{nj} & \cdots & a_{nn} \end{bmatrix}$$

Si on multiplie la i-ième ligne de A par une constante c, il en résulte la matrice

$$B = \begin{bmatrix} a_{11} & a_{12} & \cdots & a_{1j} & \cdots & a_{1n} \\ a_{21} & a_{22} & \cdots & a_{2j} & \cdots & a_{2n} \\ \vdots & \vdots & & \vdots & & \vdots \\ ca_{i1} & ca_{i2} & \cdots & ca_{ij} & \cdots & ca_{in} \\ \vdots & \vdots & & \vdots & & \vdots \\ a_{n1} & a_{n2} & \cdots & a_{nj} & \cdots & a_{nn} \end{bmatrix}$$

---

9. En fait, ce n'est pas tout à fait aussi simple que cela. On devrait prouver la propriété 4 à l'aide d'un raisonnement par récurrence. Toutefois, l'essence de la preuve réside dans l'argument indiqué.

En développant le déterminant de B selon la i-ième ligne, on obtient

$$\det B = \sum_{k=1}^{n} ca_{ik}B_{ik} = c \sum_{k=1}^{n} a_{ik}B_{ik}$$

Or, on constate que $B_{ik} = A_{ik}$ quelle que soit la valeur de k. Par conséquent,

$$\det B = c \sum_{k=1}^{n} a_{ik}B_{ik} = c \sum_{k=1}^{n} a_{ik}A_{ik} = c \det A \qquad \blacksquare$$

Exemple

Soit les matrices

$$A = \begin{bmatrix} 1 & 2 & 3 \\ 4 & -1 & -2 \\ 1 & 5 & 2 \end{bmatrix} \quad \text{et} \quad B = \begin{bmatrix} 2 & 4 & 6 \\ -12 & 3 & 6 \\ 1 & 5 & 2 \end{bmatrix}$$

On obtient la matrice B en multipliant la première ligne de A par 2 et la deuxième ligne de A par -3. On a déjà calculé (p. 77) que $\det A = 51$. Donc, on a $\det B = 2(-3) \det A = -306$.

Propriété 7 $\det(cA) = c^n \det A$

Preuve

Si A est une matrice carrée d'ordre n, la matrice cA est le résultat de la multiplication de chaque ligne de A par la constante c. En vertu de la propriété 6, chaque fois qu'on multiplie une ligne d'une matrice A par une constante, on obtient le déterminant de la matrice résultante en multipliant $\det A$ par cette constante. Donc, si on multiplie chacune des n lignes de A par une constante c, pour obtenir le déterminant de la matrice cA résultante, on doit multiplier $\det A$ par la constante c à n reprises, ce qui équivaut à multiplier $\det A$ par c^n. Ainsi, $\det(cA) = c^n \det A$. $\blacksquare$

EXERCICE 3.8

Si A est une matrice carrée d'ordre 5 dont le déterminant vaut 4, que valent $\det(-2A)$ et $\det(3A)$?

On peut employer la propriété 7 (th. 3.1) pour montrer que le déterminant de la transposée d'une matrice antisymétrique A d'ordre k est donné par det $A^t = (-1)^k$ det A.

Preuve

Si A est une matrice antisymétrique d'ordre k, alors $A^t = -A$. Par conséquent, on a det $(A^t) = $ det $(-A) = (-1)^k$ det A. ∎

EXERCICE 3.9

Montrez qu'une matrice antisymétrique d'ordre k où k est impair est une matrice singulière. (Utilisez la propriété 4 (th. 3.1) et le résultat de l'exemple précédent.)

Propriété 8 Le déterminant d'une matrice qui comporte deux lignes (ou deux colonnes) identiques vaut 0.

Preuve

La propriété 8 est une conséquence directe de la propriété 2.

Soit A, une matrice comportant deux lignes identiques, et soit B la matrice obtenue en intervertissant les deux lignes identiques de A. Il est clair que les matrices A et B sont égales puisque les deux lignes interverties sont identiques; d'où det $B = $ det A.

Par ailleurs, d'après la propriété 2, on a det $B = -$det A parce que B résulte de l'interversion de deux lignes de A. Par conséquent, det $A = -$det A. Donc, det $A = 0$. ∎

Exemple

Soit les matrices

$$A = \begin{bmatrix} 1 & 2 & 3 \\ 4 & -1 & -2 \\ 1 & 2 & 3 \end{bmatrix} \quad \text{et} \quad B = \begin{bmatrix} 2 & 3 & 4 & -1 & 3 \\ 0 & 3 & 3 & 7 & 3 \\ 9 & 3 & 5 & 6 & 3 \\ 6 & 4 & 6 & -1 & 4 \\ -7 & 3 & 4 & 1 & 3 \end{bmatrix}$$

Comme les première et troisième lignes de la matrice A sont identiques, alors det $A = 0$. De même, puisque les deuxième et cinquième colonnes de la matrice B sont identiques, on a det $B = 0$.

Propriété 9   Le déterminant d'une matrice qui comporte deux lignes (ou deux colonnes) dont l'une est un multiple de l'autre vaut 0.

Voici d'abord un exemple qui illustre cette propriété des déterminants.

Exemple

La quatrième colonne de la matrice A suivante est égale à trois fois la première colonne.

$$A = \begin{bmatrix} 2 & 2 & 4 & 6 & 3 \\ 0 & 5 & 3 & 0 & 3 \\ 9 & 7 & 5 & 27 & 3 \\ 6 & -1 & 6 & 18 & 4 \\ -7 & 3 & 4 & -21 & 3 \end{bmatrix}$$

Par conséquent, en vertu de la propriété 9, on a det $A = 0$.

EXERCICE 3.10

Démontrez, à l'aide des propriétés 6 et 8 (th. 3.1), la propriété 9: le déterminant d'une matrice qui comporte deux lignes (ou deux colonnes) dont l'une est un multiple de l'autre vaut 0.

Propriété 10   Si B est une matrice obtenue en ajoutant un multiple d'une ligne (ou d'une colonne) d'une matrice A à une autre ligne (ou à une autre colonne) de A, alors det $B =$ det A.

Nous allons d'abord montrer comment employer la propriété 10 pour simplifier le calcul d'un déterminant.

Exemple

Nous avons déjà souligné qu'il est avantageux de développer un déterminant selon la ligne ou la colonne qui comporte le plus grand nombre de zéros. Nous allons maintenant, à l'aide de la propriété 10, introduire des zéros dans une ligne ou dans une colonne du déterminant à calculer. Pour indiquer qu'on a additionné a fois la p-ième ligne à la i-ième ligne, on inscrit, à côté de la i-ième ligne, l'expression $L_i \rightarrow L_i + aL_p$. Ainsi,

$$
\begin{vmatrix} 1 & 2 & 3 \\ 4 & -1 & -2 \\ 1 & 5 & 2 \end{vmatrix} = \begin{vmatrix} 1 & 2 & 3 \\ 0 & -9 & -14 \\ 0 & 3 & -1 \end{vmatrix} \begin{matrix} \\ L_2 \rightarrow L_2 - 4L_1 \\ L_3 \rightarrow L_3 - L_1 \end{matrix}
$$

$$
= \begin{vmatrix} 1 & 2 & 3 \\ 0 & -9 & -14 \\ 0 & 0 & -\frac{17}{3} \end{vmatrix} \begin{matrix} \\ \\ L_3 \rightarrow L_3 + (\frac{1}{3})L_2 \end{matrix}
$$

$$
= 1 \times (-9) \times (-\frac{17}{3}) \quad \text{(propriété 3)}
$$

$$
= 51
$$

Ce résultat est exactement le même que celui qu'on a obtenu à la page 77.

EXERCICE 3.11

Calculez, à l'aide des propriétés 3 et 10 (th. 3.1), le déterminant de la matrice

$$
A = \begin{bmatrix} 1 & 3 & 2 & -1 \\ -1 & -2 & 2 & 6 \\ 2 & 4 & -3 & 2 \\ -2 & -7 & 4 & 1 \end{bmatrix}
$$

L'application de la propriété 10 (th. 3.1) réduit considérablement le nombre d'opérations à réaliser pour calculer le déterminant d'une matrice carrée d'ordre n. En effet, si on fait appel à la propriété 10 pour transformer une matrice A en matrice triangulaire, et si on calcule ensuite le déterminant de A à l'aide de la propriété 3, le nombre d'opérations à effectuer est d'environ $n^3/3$ opérations[10] au lieu de $e \times n!$ opérations. D'après le tableau 3.1 (p. 76), le temps de calcul, par un ordinateur, d'un déterminant d'ordre 15 passerait ainsi de 41 jours à moins d'une seconde.

---

10. C. G. Cullen. *Linear Algebra with Applications*, Reading, Addison Wesley Longman Inc., 2e éd., 1997, p. 113.

Complétez la preuve de la propriété 10.

Propriété 10

Si B est une matrice obtenue en ajoutant un multiple d'une ligne (ou d'une colonne) d'une matrice A à une autre ligne (ou à une autre colonne) de A, alors det B = det A.

Preuve

D'après la propriété _____, il suffit de montrer que la propriété 10 est vraie dans le cas où B est obtenue en modifiant une ligne de A. Soit les matrices

$$A = \begin{bmatrix} a_{11} & a_{12} & \cdots & a_{1j} & \cdots & a_{1n} \\ a_{21} & a_{22} & \cdots & a_{2j} & \cdots & a_{2n} \\ \vdots & \vdots & & \vdots & & \vdots \\ a_{i1} & a_{i2} & \cdots & a_{ij} & \cdots & a_{in} \\ \vdots & \vdots & & \vdots & & \vdots \\ a_{p1} & a_{p2} & \cdots & a_{pj} & \cdots & a_{pn} \\ \vdots & \vdots & & \vdots & & \vdots \\ a_{n1} & a_{n2} & \cdots & a_{nj} & \cdots & a_{nn} \end{bmatrix}$$

$$B = \begin{bmatrix} a_{11} & a_{12} & \cdots & a_{1j} & \cdots & a_{1n} \\ a_{21} & a_{22} & \cdots & a_{2j} & \cdots & a_{2n} \\ \vdots & \vdots & & \vdots & & \\ a_{i1}+ca_{p1} & a_{i2}+ca_{p2} & \cdots & a_{ij}+ca_{pj} & \cdots & a_{in}+ca_{pn} \\ \vdots & \vdots & & \vdots & & \vdots \\ a_{p1} & a_{p2} & \cdots & a_{pj} & \cdots & a_{pn} \\ \vdots & \vdots & & \vdots & & \vdots \\ a_{n1} & a_{n2} & \cdots & a_{nj} & \cdots & a_{nn} \end{bmatrix}$$

La matrice B résulte de l'addition de $c \times$ la _____-ième ligne de A à la _____-ième ligne de A. Il faut montrer que det B = det A.

Or, det B = _____ (développement selon la i-ième ligne) parce que les cofacteurs des éléments de la i-ième ligne de B sont égaux aux cofacteurs des éléments de la i-ième ligne de A.

Donc det $B = \left(\sum_{k=1}^{n} a_{ik}A_{ik} \right) + c \left(\sum_{k=1}^{n} a_{pk}A_{ik} \right)$. Cette expression correspond à la somme de deux déterminants, dont le premier est _____. Soit D la matrice associée au deuxième déterminant. On obtient alors det B = det A + c det D. Il suffit donc de montrer que det D = 0. Or, la seule chose qui distingue les matrices A et D, c'est la i-ième ligne. En effet, la i-ième ligne de D est identique à la p-ième ligne de A. Par conséquent, la matrice D comporte deux lignes identiques, à savoir les _____ et _____ lignes. En vertu de la propriété _____, det $D = 0$.

Comme det $B =$ det $A + c$ det D et que det $D = 0$, alors det $B =$ det A.
∎

Étant donné l'importance de la propriété 10, nous en illustrons l'application par deux autres exemples.

Exemple

1. On peut montrer, à l'aide des propriétés des déterminants (th. 3.1), que

$$\begin{vmatrix} x^2 & xy & xz \\ x+2 & y+2 & z+2 \\ 3 & 3 & 3 \end{vmatrix} = 0$$

En effet,

$$\begin{vmatrix} x^2 & xy & xz \\ x+2 & y+2 & z+2 \\ 3 & 3 & 3 \end{vmatrix} = x \begin{vmatrix} x & y & z \\ x+2 & y+2 & z+2 \\ 3 & 3 & 3 \end{vmatrix} \text{(propriété 6)}$$

$$= x \begin{vmatrix} x & y & z \\ 2 & 2 & 2 \\ 3 & 3 & 3 \end{vmatrix} \begin{matrix} L_2 \to L_2 - L_1 \\ \text{(propriété 10)} \end{matrix}$$

$$= 0 \qquad \text{(propriété 9 : la 2}^e \text{ ligne est un multiple de la 3}^e \text{ et vice versa)}$$

2. On peut montrer, à l'aide des propriétés des déterminants (th. 3.1) que

$$\begin{vmatrix} 1+a_1 & a_2 & \cdots & a_n \\ a_1 & 1+a_2 & \cdots & a_n \\ \vdots & \vdots & & \vdots \\ a_1 & a_2 & \cdots & 1+a_n \end{vmatrix} = 1 + a_1 + a_2 + \cdots + a_n$$

Preuve

Si on ajoute à la première colonne du déterminant chacune des autres colonnes, en vertu de la propriété 10 (th. 3.1), on obtient

$$\begin{vmatrix} 1 + a_1 & a_2 & \cdots & a_n \\ a_1 & 1 + a_2 & \cdots & a_n \\ \vdots & \vdots & & \vdots \\ a_1 & a_2 & \cdots & 1 + a_n \end{vmatrix}$$

$$= \begin{vmatrix} 1 + a_1 + a_2 + \cdots + a_n & a_2 & \cdots & a_n \\ 1 + a_1 + a_2 + \cdots + a_n & 1 + a_2 & \cdots & a_n \\ \vdots & \vdots & & \vdots \\ 1 + a_1 + a_2 + \cdots + a_n & a_2 & \cdots & 1 + a_n \end{vmatrix}$$

Toujours d'après la propriété 10, on ne modifie pas la valeur du déterminant en soustrayant la première ligne de chacune des autres lignes,

$$\begin{vmatrix} 1 + a_1 + a_2 + \cdots + a_n & a_2 & \cdots & a_n \\ 1 + a_1 + a_2 + \cdots + a_n & 1 + a_2 & \cdots & a_n \\ \vdots & & \vdots & \vdots \\ 1 + a_1 + a_2 + \cdots + a_n & a_2 & \cdots & 1 + a_n \end{vmatrix}$$

$$= \begin{vmatrix} 1 + a_1 + a_2 + \cdots + a_n & a_2 & \cdots & a_n \\ 0 & 1 & \cdots & 0 \\ \vdots & \vdots & & \vdots \\ 0 & 0 & \cdots & 1 \end{vmatrix}$$

Comme le dernier déterminant est celui d'une matrice triangulaire, il est égal au produit des éléments de sa diagonale principale, soit

$$(1 + a_1 + a_2 + \cdots + a_n) \times 1 \times \cdots \times 1$$

Par conséquent,

$$\begin{vmatrix} 1 + a_1 & a_2 & \cdots & a_n \\ a_1 & 1 + a_2 & \cdots & a_n \\ \vdots & \vdots & & \vdots \\ a_1 & a_2 & \cdots & 1 + a_n \end{vmatrix} = 1 + a_1 + a_2 + \cdots + a_n \quad \blacksquare$$

EXERCICE 3.13

Montrer, en appliquant les propriétés des déterminants, que

$$\begin{vmatrix} a & a+1 & a+2 & e \\ b & b+1 & b+2 & f \\ c & c+1 & c+2 & g \\ d & d+1 & d+2 & h \end{vmatrix} = 0$$

Propriété 11   Le déterminant du produit de deux matrices est égal au produit des déterminants des deux matrices, c'est-à-dire que

$$\det AB = \det A \times \det B$$

La démonstration de la propriété 11 sort du cadre du présent manuel[11]. Nous nous contentons de souligner que nous nous servirons de cette propriété pour montrer qu'une matrice est singulière, et nous l'illustrons par un exemple.

Exemple

Si A et B sont des matrices carrées d'ordre 4 telles que $\det A = 5$ et $\det B = 2$, alors, en vertu de la propriété 11 (th. 3.1),

$$\det AB = \det A \times \det B = 5 \times 2 = 10$$

EXERCICE 3.14

1. Montrez, en faisant appel à la définition de matrice inverse et à la propriété 11 (th. 3.1), que les matrices singulières n'admettent pas de matrice inverse. Faites une preuve par l'absurde : supposez qu'une matrice singulière admet une matrice inverse et montrez que cette hypothèse mène à une contradiction.

2. Déduisez de la proposition prouvée en 1 que seules les matrices régulières peuvent admettre une matrice inverse.

---

11. Les personnes désireuses de connaître la démonstration peuvent consulter les manuels de Noble (p. 206-207) et de Grossman (p. 138) mentionnés dans la bibliographie.

Un peu d'histoire

Nous avons défini un déterminant comme une fonction qui associe un nombre réel à chaque matrice carrée. On pourrait en déduire que le concept de matrice est antérieur au concept de déterminant. Toutefois, l'histoire ne se déroule pas toujours selon un ordre logique. Nous avons souligné que l'étude des matrices en tant que tableaux de nombres débute en 1850 avec J. J. Sylvester (1814-1897). Pourtant, on mentionne les déterminants dans des écrits beaucoup plus anciens. Ainsi, un mathématicien japonais, Seki Kowa, aussi appelé Seki Takakazu (1642-1708), employa ce concept dès 1683. C'est dans une lettre que G. W. Leibniz (1646-1716) adressa, en 1693, au marquis de L'Hospital (1661-1704) qu'on trouve toutefois la première référence, par un Occidental, à la méthode des déterminants pour la résolution d'un système d'équations.

Dans une publication posthume, *Treatise of Algebra* (1748), C. Maclaurin (1698-1746) donne une règle pour résoudre un système d'équations linéaires (jusqu'à quatre équations à quatre inconnues) à l'aide de déterminants. En 1750, le mathématicien suisse G. Cramer (1704-1752) publie *Introduction à l'analyse des courbes algébriques*. On y retrouve la règle énoncée par Maclaurin, exprimée dans une notation tellement supérieure à celle de Maclaurin que l'appellation «règle de Cramer» a survécu jusqu'à aujourd'hui. La règle de Cramer est l'un des résultats les plus importants de l'histoire des mathématiques. Pendant de nombreuses années, elle fut enseignée dans les cours d'algèbre et de théorie des équations mais, à cause du grand nombre d'opérations requises, elle est tombée en désuétude.

A. T. Vandermonde (1735-1796) fut le premier à étudier les déterminants dans un autre contexte que la recherche des solutions d'un système d'équations linéaires. Il fut suivi en cela par d'autres mathématiciens éminents, dont P. S. Laplace (1749-1827) – à qui l'on doit le développement d'un déterminant à l'aide des cofacteurs – et J. L. Lagrange (1736-1813). Il fallut toutefois attendre la publication en 1815 d'un mémoire (de 84 pages) du mathématicien français A. L. Cauchy (1789-1857) pour une présentation systématique et moderne des déterminants et de leurs propriétés. C'est en fait dans ce mémoire qu'on trouve la première preuve de la règle générale du déterminant d'un produit de matrices, c'est-à-dire que : le déterminant du produit de deux matrices est égal au produit des déterminants des deux matrices : det AB = det A × det B. Cauchy y montre également que les formules du volume de certains polyèdres s'écrivent à l'aide des déterminants et, ce faisant, il ouvre la porte à l'utilisation des déterminants en dehors du champ de l'algèbre. Cauchy fut l'un des auteurs les plus prolifiques en mathématiques ; il a notamment beaucoup contribué à la théorie des déterminants. On lui doit entre autres le terme déterminant (dans son sens actuel), la présentation des éléments sous la forme d'un tableau carré et l'emploi d'indices doubles pour désigner la position des éléments dans le tableau.

En 1825, H. F. Scherk (1798-1885) démontra plusieurs autres propriétés des déterminants, notamment : le déterminant d'une matrice dont une ligne peut être exprimée comme une combinaison linéaire des autres lignes vaut 0 et le déterminant d'une matrice triangulaire est égal au produit des éléments de la diagonale principale de la matrice.

Les déterminants ont également leur place en dehors du champ de l'algèbre. Les mathématiciens C. G. Jacobi (1804-1851) et H. Wronski (1778-1853), qui les employèrent en calcul différentiel et intégral, ont donné leur nom à des déterminants particuliers, soit le jacobien et le wronskien.

Ainsi, la théorie des déterminants était déjà bien établie lorsque Cayley (1821-1895) exposa la théorie des matrices, au milieu du XIXe siècle. En fait, Cayley reconnut simplement la possibilité d'étudier les tableaux de nombres indépendamment des déterminants. En plus de nombreuses contributions à la théorie des matrices et des déterminants, on doit à Cayley la notation d'un déterminant à l'aide de deux barres verticales.

Enfin, on ne saurait passer sous silence la contribution de C. Dodgson (1832-1898), qui publia en 1867 *An Elementary Theory of Determinants*. On y trouve les conditions pour qu'un système d'équations admette une solution unique ou une infinité de solutions ou qu'il n'en admette aucune. Bien qu'il fut un très grand logicien et mathématicien, Dodgson est surtout connu comme l'auteur d'un classique de la littérature anglaise, *Alice aux pays des merveilles*, qu'il publia sous le nom de plume de Lewis Carroll.

Nous allons maintenant répondre aux deux questions que nous avions formulées en début de chapitre:

- Quelles conditions garantissent l'existence de la matrice inverse d'une matrice carrée d'ordre n?

- Quelle est l'expression de l'inverse d'une matrice d'ordre n quelconque si cet inverse existe?

Vous avez prouvé dans l'exercice 3.14 que les matrices singulières n'admettent pas de matrice inverse. Par conséquent, seules les matrices régulières (ou non singulières) peuvent admettre une matrice inverse. Il s'agit maintenant de montrer que toute matrice régulière admet une matrice inverse. Mais faites d'abord l'exercice 3.15, où nous vous demandons de compléter la preuve d'un théorème dont nous aurons besoin.

EXERCICE 3.15

Complétez la preuve du théorème 3.2.

Théorème 3.2

Si A est une matrice carrée d'ordre n, alors

$$a_{i1}A_{k1} + a_{i2}A_{k2} + \cdots + a_{in}A_{kn} = \begin{cases} \det A & \text{pour } i = k \\ 0 & \text{pour } i \neq k \end{cases}$$

Preuve

Soit la matrice

$$A = \begin{bmatrix} a_{11} & a_{12} & \cdots & a_{1j} & \cdots & a_{1n} \\ a_{21} & a_{22} & \cdots & a_{2j} & \cdots & a_{2n} \\ \vdots & \vdots & & \vdots & & \vdots \\ a_{i1} & a_{i2} & \cdots & a_{ij} & \cdots & a_{in} \\ \vdots & \vdots & & \vdots & & \vdots \\ a_{n1} & a_{n2} & \cdots & a_{nj} & \cdots & a_{nn} \end{bmatrix}$$

Si $i = k$,

$$a_{i1}A_{k1} + a_{i2}A_{k2} + \cdots + a_{in}A_{kn} = a_{i1}A_{i1} + a_{i2}A_{i2} + \cdots + a_{in}A_{in}$$

D'après la propriété _____ (th. _____),

$$a_{i1}A_{i1} + a_{i2}A_{i2} + \cdots + a_{in}A_{in} = \det A \quad (\text{développement } \underline{\hspace{2cm}})$$

Par conséquent, si $i = k$,

$$a_{i1}A_{k1} + a_{i2}A_{k2} + \cdots + a_{in}A_{kn} = \underline{\hspace{2cm}}$$

Par contre, si $i \neq k$, l'expression $a_{i1}A_{k1} + a_{i2}A_{k2} + \cdots + a_{in}A_{kn}$ représente le déterminant d'une matrice B identique à la matrice A à l'exception de la k-ième ligne :

$$A = \begin{bmatrix} a_{11} & a_{12} & \cdots & a_{1j} & \cdots & a_{1n} \\ a_{21} & a_{22} & \cdots & a_{2j} & \cdots & a_{2n} \\ \vdots & \vdots & & \vdots & & \vdots \\ a_{i1} & a_{i2} & \cdots & a_{ij} & \cdots & a_{in} \\ \vdots & \vdots & & \vdots & & \vdots \\ a_{k1} & a_{k2} & \cdots & a_{kj} & \cdots & a_{kn} \\ \vdots & \vdots & & \vdots & & \vdots \\ a_{n1} & a_{n2} & \cdots & a_{nj} & \cdots & a_{nn} \end{bmatrix} \begin{matrix} \\ \\ \\ \leftarrow i\text{-ième ligne} \\ \\ \leftarrow k\text{-ième ligne} \\ \\ \end{matrix}$$

$$B = \begin{bmatrix} a_{11} & a_{12} & \cdots & a_{1j} & \cdots & a_{1n} \\ a_{21} & a_{22} & \cdots & a_{2j} & \cdots & a_{2n} \\ \vdots & \vdots & & \vdots & & \vdots \\ a_{i1} & a_{i2} & \cdots & a_{ij} & \cdots & a_{in} \\ \vdots & \vdots & & \vdots & & \vdots \\ a_{i1} & a_{i2} & \cdots & a_{ij} & \cdots & a_{in} \\ \vdots & \vdots & & \vdots & & \vdots \\ a_{n1} & a_{n2} & \cdots & a_{nj} & \cdots & a_{nn} \end{bmatrix} \begin{matrix} \\ \\ \\ \leftarrow i\text{-ième ligne} \\ \\ \leftarrow k\text{-ième ligne} \\ \\ \end{matrix}$$

La k-ième ligne de la matrice B est identique à la _____ ligne de la matrice A. Les _____ et _____ lignes de la matrice B sont donc _____. En vertu de la propriété _____ (th. 3.1), det $B = $ _____.

Par conséquent, si $i \neq k$, $a_{i1}A_{k1} + a_{i2}A_{k2} + \cdots + a_{in}A_{kn} = 0$. ∎

La **matrice adjointe**, ou *adjointe*, d'une matrice A est la transposée de la matrice des cofacteurs des éléments de A. Elle est notée adj A. Ainsi,

$$\text{adj } A = \begin{bmatrix} A_{11} & A_{12} & \cdots & A_{1j} & \cdots & A_{1n} \\ A_{21} & A_{22} & \cdots & A_{2j} & \cdots & A_{2n} \\ \vdots & \vdots & & \vdots & & \vdots \\ A_{i1} & A_{i2} & \cdots & A_{ij} & \cdots & A_{in} \\ \vdots & \vdots & & \vdots & & \vdots \\ A_{n1} & A_{n2} & \cdots & A_{nj} & \cdots & A_{nn} \end{bmatrix}^t = \begin{bmatrix} A_{11} & A_{21} & \cdots & A_{i1} & \cdots & A_{n1} \\ A_{12} & A_{22} & \cdots & A_{i2} & \cdots & A_{n2} \\ \vdots & \vdots & & \vdots & & \vdots \\ A_{1j} & A_{2j} & \cdots & A_{ij} & \cdots & A_{nj} \\ \vdots & \vdots & & \vdots & & \vdots \\ A_{1n} & A_{2n} & \cdots & A_{in} & \cdots & A_{nn} \end{bmatrix}$$

L'adjointe de la matrice $A = \begin{bmatrix} -5 & 1 \\ -3 & 2 \end{bmatrix}$ est donnée par

$$\text{adj } A = \begin{bmatrix} A_{11} & A_{12} \\ A_{21} & A_{22} \end{bmatrix}^t = \begin{bmatrix} A_{11} & A_{21} \\ A_{12} & A_{22} \end{bmatrix} = \begin{bmatrix} 2 & -1 \\ 3 & -5 \end{bmatrix}$$

L'adjointe de la matrice $B = \begin{bmatrix} -1 & 1 & -3 \\ 2 & 1 & -1 \\ 3 & -2 & 4 \end{bmatrix}$ est donnée par

$$\text{adj } B = \begin{bmatrix} B_{11} & B_{21} & B_{31} \\ B_{12} & B_{22} & B_{32} \\ B_{13} & B_{23} & B_{33} \end{bmatrix}$$

$$= \begin{bmatrix} \begin{vmatrix} 1 & -1 \\ -2 & 4 \end{vmatrix} & -\begin{vmatrix} 1 & -3 \\ -2 & 4 \end{vmatrix} & \begin{vmatrix} 1 & -3 \\ 1 & -1 \end{vmatrix} \\ -\begin{vmatrix} 2 & -1 \\ 3 & 4 \end{vmatrix} & \begin{vmatrix} -1 & -3 \\ 3 & 4 \end{vmatrix} & -\begin{vmatrix} -1 & -3 \\ 2 & -1 \end{vmatrix} \\ \begin{vmatrix} 2 & 1 \\ 3 & -2 \end{vmatrix} & -\begin{vmatrix} -1 & 1 \\ 3 & -2 \end{vmatrix} & \begin{vmatrix} -1 & 1 \\ 2 & 1 \end{vmatrix} \end{bmatrix}$$

$$= \begin{bmatrix} 2 & 2 & 2 \\ -11 & 5 & -7 \\ -7 & 1 & -3 \end{bmatrix}$$

EXERCICE 3.16

Trouvez la matrice adjointe de chacune des matrices

$$A = \begin{bmatrix} 2 & -1 \\ -4 & -5 \end{bmatrix} \quad B = \begin{bmatrix} 1 & 2 \\ -4 & -8 \end{bmatrix} \quad C = \begin{bmatrix} 1 & 1 & 1 \\ 2 & 1 & -1 \\ 1 & -2 & 2 \end{bmatrix}$$

Nous sommes maintenant en mesure de démontrer le théorème 3.3.

Théorème 3.3

Si A est une matrice régulière, alors la matrice inverse de A est donnée par $A^{-1} = \dfrac{1}{\det A} \text{adj } A$.

Preuve

Le théorème 3.3 découle directement du théorème 3.2 et de la définition de la matrice inverse et du produit matriciel.

Il faut montrer que $A\left(\dfrac{1}{\det A}\text{adj }A\right) = I_n$ et que $\left(\dfrac{1}{\det A}\text{adj }A\right)A = I_n$. Nous nous contenterons de prouver la première égalité, la preuve de la deuxième égalité étant similaire.

Si A est une matrice régulière d'ordre n, alors

$$A\left(\frac{1}{|A|}\text{adj }A\right) = \frac{1}{|A|}A(\text{adj }A)$$

$$= \frac{1}{|A|}\begin{bmatrix} a_{11} & a_{12} & \cdots & a_{1j} & \cdots & a_{1n} \\ a_{21} & a_{22} & \cdots & a_{2j} & \cdots & a_{2n} \\ \vdots & \vdots & & \vdots & & \vdots \\ a_{i1} & a_{i2} & \cdots & a_{ij} & \cdots & a_{in} \\ \vdots & \vdots & & \vdots & & \vdots \\ a_{n1} & a_{n2} & \cdots & a_{nj} & \cdots & a_{nn} \end{bmatrix}\begin{bmatrix} A_{11} & A_{21} & \cdots & A_{j1} & \cdots & A_{n1} \\ A_{12} & A_{22} & \cdots & A_{j2} & \cdots & A_{n2} \\ \vdots & \vdots & & \vdots & & \vdots \\ A_{1i} & A_{2i} & \cdots & A_{ji} & \cdots & A_{ni} \\ \vdots & \vdots & & \vdots & & \vdots \\ A_{1n} & A_{2n} & \cdots & A_{jn} & \cdots & A_{nn} \end{bmatrix}$$

On obtient l'élément c_{ij}, situé à l'intersection de la i-ième ligne et de la j-ième colonne de ce produit, en multipliant en quelque sorte la i-ième ligne de la matrice A par la j-ième colonne de adj A. Donc,

$$c_{ij} = \frac{1}{|A|}(a_{i1}A_{j1} + a_{i2}A_{j2} + \cdots + a_{in}A_{jn})$$

Or, en vertu du théorème 3.2,

$$a_{i1}A_{j1} + a_{i2}A_{j2} + \cdots + a_{in}A_{jn} = \begin{cases} \det A & \text{pour } i = j \\ 0 & \text{pour } i \neq j \end{cases}$$

de sorte que

$$c_{ij} = \begin{cases} 1 & \text{pour } i = j \\ 0 & \text{pour } i \neq j \end{cases}$$

ce qui correspond à la définition des éléments de la matrice identité.

Par conséquent, $A\left(\dfrac{1}{\det A}\text{adj }A\right) = I_n$. On peut montrer de façon analogue que $\left(\dfrac{1}{\det A}\text{adj }A\right)A = I_n$. Donc, $A^{-1} = \dfrac{1}{\det A}\text{adj }A$. ∎

Le déterminant de la matrice $A = \begin{bmatrix} -5 & 1 \\ -3 & 2 \end{bmatrix}$ vaut -7. Comme det A est différent de zéro, la matrice A est régulière et sa matrice inverse est donnée par

$$A^{-1} = \frac{1}{|A|}\,\text{adj } A = \frac{1}{-7}\begin{bmatrix} 2 & -1 \\ 3 & -5 \end{bmatrix} = \begin{bmatrix} -\frac{2}{7} & \frac{1}{7} \\ -\frac{3}{7} & \frac{5}{7} \end{bmatrix}$$

Le déterminant de la matrice $B = \begin{bmatrix} -1 & 1 & -3 \\ 2 & 1 & -1 \\ 3 & -2 & 4 \end{bmatrix}$ vaut 8. Comme det B est différent de zéro, la matrice B est inversible et sa matrice inverse est donnée par

$$B^{-1} = \frac{1}{|B|}\,\text{adj } B = \frac{1}{8}\begin{bmatrix} 2 & 2 & 2 \\ -11 & 5 & -7 \\ -7 & 1 & -3 \end{bmatrix} = \begin{bmatrix} \frac{1}{4} & \frac{1}{4} & \frac{1}{4} \\ -\frac{11}{8} & \frac{5}{8} & -\frac{7}{8} \\ -\frac{7}{8} & \frac{1}{8} & -\frac{3}{8} \end{bmatrix}$$

EXERCICE 3.17

Trouvez, si elle existe, la matrice inverse de chacune des matrices suivantes. (Les matrices adjointes ont été calculées à l'exercice 3.16.)

$$A = \begin{bmatrix} 2 & -1 \\ -4 & -5 \end{bmatrix} \quad B = \begin{bmatrix} 1 & 2 \\ -4 & -8 \end{bmatrix} \quad C = \begin{bmatrix} 1 & 1 & 1 \\ 2 & 1 & -1 \\ 1 & -2 & 2 \end{bmatrix}$$

MATRICE INVERSIBLE

Une matrice est dite inversible si elle admet une matrice inverse.

On déduit du théorème 3.3 et des propositions prouvées dans l'exercice 3.14 que les matrices régulières (dont le déterminant est non nul), et elles seules, admettent une matrice inverse. C'est pourquoi on dit qu'une matrice régulière est une **matrice inversible** : elle admet une matrice inverse.

Les matrices inversibles possèdent des propriétés intéressantes, que nous avons regroupées dans le théorème 3.4.

Théorème 3.4

Dans les énoncés qui suivent, A et B sont des matrices carrées inversibles d'ordre n; C, D, E et F sont des matrices pour lesquelles les opérations matricielles sont définies; k est une constante différente de 0.

1) Si $AC = D$ et $EB = F$, alors $C = A^{-1}D$ et $E = FB^{-1}$.

2) La matrice inverse d'une matrice régulière A est unique.

3) $(A^{-1})^{-1} = A$.

4) $(AB)^{-1} = B^{-1}A^{-1}$

5) $(A^t)^{-1} = (A^{-1})^t$

6) $(kA)^{-1} = \dfrac{1}{k}A^{-1}$

7) $\det(A^{-1}) = \dfrac{1}{\det A}$

Nous allons esquisser les preuves des quatre premières propriétés en vous laissant le soin de justifier chaque étape. Les démonstrations des propriétés 5, 6 et 7 font l'objet d'exercices.

Propriété 1 Si $AC = D$ et $EB = F$, alors $C = A^{-1}D$ et $E = FB^{-1}$.

Preuve

$$AC = D \Rightarrow A^{-1}AC = A^{-1}D \Rightarrow I_nC = A^{-1}D \Rightarrow C = A^{-1}D$$

De façon analogue,

$$EB = F \Rightarrow EBB^{-1} = FB^{-1} \Rightarrow EI_n = FB^{-1} \Rightarrow E = FB^{-1} \qquad \blacksquare$$

Propriété 2 La matrice inverse d'une matrice régulière A est unique.

Preuve

Employons un raisonnement par l'absurde. Soit une matrice régulière A qui possède deux matrices inverses, à savoir P et Q telles que $P \neq Q$. Alors,

$$P = PI_n = P(AQ) = (PA)Q = I_nQ = Q$$

Ce résultat contredit l'hypothèse $P \neq Q$. Par conséquent, la matrice inverse d'une matrice régulière est unique. $\qquad \blacksquare$

Propriété 3 $(A^{-1})^{-1} = A$

Nous allons donner deux démonstrations légèrement différentes de cette propriété.

Preuve 1

$$A = AI_n = A(A^{-1}(A^{-1})^{-1}) = (AA^{-1})(A^{-1})^{-1} = I_n(A^{-1})^{-1} = (A^{-1})^{-1} \quad \blacksquare$$

Preuve 2

Soit B, la matrice inverse de A^{-1}, c'est-à-dire $B = (A^{-1})^{-1}$. Il faut montrer que $B = A$. Or, en vertu de la définition de matrice inverse et de matrice identité,

$$BA^{-1} = I_n \Rightarrow (BA^{-1})A = I_nA \Rightarrow B(A^{-1}A) = A \Rightarrow BI_n = A \Rightarrow B = A$$

Par conséquent, $(A^{-1})^{-1} = A$. $\qquad\qquad\qquad\qquad\qquad\qquad\qquad\qquad\blacksquare$

Propriété 4 $(AB)^{-1} = B^{-1}A^{-1}$

Preuve

Il faut vérifier que $(AB)(B^{-1}A^{-1}) = I_n = (B^{-1}A^{-1})(AB)$. Or,

$$(AB)(B^{-1}A^{-1}) = A(BB^{-1})A^{-1} = AI_nA^{-1} = AA^{-1} = I_n$$

On montre de façon analogue que $(B^{-1}A^{-1})(AB) = I_n$.

Par conséquent, $B^{-1}A^{-1}$ est la matrice inverse de AB, c'est-à-dire que $(AB)^{-1} = B^{-1}A^{-1}$. $\qquad\qquad\qquad\qquad\qquad\qquad\qquad\qquad\qquad\blacksquare$

EXERCICE 3.18

Prouvez les propriétés 5 et 6 (th. 3.4).

3.7 RÉSOLUTION D'UN SYSTÈME D'ÉQUATIONS LINÉAIRES PAR LA MÉTHODE DE LA MATRICE INVERSE

Un système d'équations linéaires (n équations à n inconnues) s'écrit sous la forme $AX = B$, qui s'apparente à celle d'une équation à une inconnue $ax = b$. L'analogie porte à croire qu'on peut résoudre un système d'équations $AX = B$ de la même manière qu'on résout une équation $ax = b$, soit en multipliant par un inverse de façon à obtenir $X = A^{-1}B$. On ne peut évidemment appliquer cette méthode que si la matrice A des coefficients admet une matrice inverse, c'est-à-dire si le déterminant de A est différent de zéro ou encore si la matrice A est régulière.

Soit le système d'équations linéaires

$$
\begin{aligned}
-x + y - 3z &= 4 \\
2x + y - z &= 8 \\
3x - 2y + 4z &= 12
\end{aligned}
$$

La matrice des coefficients est $A = \begin{bmatrix} -1 & 1 & -3 \\ 2 & 1 & -1 \\ 3 & -2 & 4 \end{bmatrix}$. Comme le déterminant de la matrice des coefficients est différent de zéro (det $A = 8$), la matrice A est inversible et son inverse est donné par

$$
A^{-1} = \frac{1}{|A|} \text{adj } A = \frac{1}{8} \begin{bmatrix} 2 & 2 & 2 \\ -11 & 5 & -7 \\ -7 & 1 & -3 \end{bmatrix} = \begin{bmatrix} \frac{1}{4} & \frac{1}{4} & \frac{1}{4} \\ -\frac{11}{8} & \frac{5}{8} & -\frac{7}{8} \\ -\frac{7}{8} & \frac{1}{8} & -\frac{3}{8} \end{bmatrix}
$$

La solution du système d'équations est $X = A^{-1}B$, c'est-à-dire

$$
\begin{bmatrix} x \\ y \\ z \end{bmatrix} = \begin{bmatrix} \frac{1}{4} & \frac{1}{4} & \frac{1}{4} \\ -\frac{11}{8} & \frac{5}{8} & -\frac{7}{8} \\ -\frac{7}{8} & \frac{1}{8} & -\frac{3}{8} \end{bmatrix} \begin{bmatrix} 4 \\ 8 \\ 12 \end{bmatrix} = \begin{bmatrix} 6 \\ -11 \\ -7 \end{bmatrix}
$$

Par conséquent, la solution du système est $x = 6$, $y = -11$ et $z = -7$.

Il est conseillé de vérifier l'exactitude de la solution d'un système d'équations en substituant les valeurs de x, y et z dans chacune des équations. Si on obtient une égalité dans chaque cas, alors la solution est exacte.

EXERCICE 3.19

Résoudre le système d'équations linéaires suivant à l'aide de la méthode de la matrice inverse.

$$
\begin{aligned}
x + y + z &= 3 \\
2x + y - z &= -1 \\
3x + y - 2z &= -2
\end{aligned}
$$

Un système d'équations linéaires (n équations à n inconnues) s'écrit sous la forme $AX = B$, qui s'apparente à celle d'une équation à une inconnue $ax = b$. L'analogie porte à croire qu'on peut résoudre un système d'équations $AX = B$ de la même manière qu'on résout une équation $ax = b$, soit en multipliant par un inverse de façon à obtenir $X = A^{-1}B$. Deux questions se posent alors :

- Quelles conditions doivent être satisfaites pour que la matrice A^{-1} existe ?
- Quelle formule faut-il employer pour trouver la matrice A^{-1} ?

C'est en tentant de répondre à ces deux questions que les mathématiciens en sont venus à introduire le concept de déterminant. Celui-ci est une fonction qui associe une valeur numérique à toute matrice carrée. Un déterminant est dit d'ordre n si la matrice qui lui est associée est d'ordre n. Il est défini de manière récursive : le déterminant d'ordre n s'exprime comme une somme de déterminants d'ordre $n - 1$, qui s'expriment chacun comme une somme de déterminants d'ordre $n - 2$ et ainsi de suite.

La valeur du déterminant d'une matrice A est donnée par

$$\det A = \sum_{k=1}^{n} a_{ik}A_{ik} \quad \text{(développement selon la i-ième ligne)}$$

ou encore

$$\det A = \sum_{k=1}^{n} a_{kj}A_{kj} \quad \text{(développement selon la j-ième colonne)}$$

Dans cette définition, A_{ik} est le cofacteur de l'élément a_{ik} de la matrice A. Ce cofacteur est égal au produit de $(-1)^{i+k}$ et du déterminant de la matrice d'ordre $n - 1$ obtenue en supprimant la i-ième ligne et la k-ième colonne de la matrice A.

Le calcul d'un déterminant à l'aide de la formule ci-dessus peut prendre un temps considérable comme l'indique le tableau 3.1 (p. 76). C'est pourquoi il faut tirer parti des propriétés des déterminants (th. 3.1, p. 82) pour réduire autant que possible le nombre des opérations à effectuer.

Lorsque le déterminant d'une matrice A est différent de zéro, A admet une matrice inverse, donnée par

$$A^{-1} = \frac{1}{|A|} \text{adj } A = \frac{1}{|A|} \begin{bmatrix} A_{11} & A_{12} & \cdots & A_{1j} & \cdots & A_{1n} \\ A_{21} & A_{22} & \cdots & A_{2j} & \cdots & A_{2n} \\ \vdots & \vdots & & \vdots & & \vdots \\ A_{i1} & A_{i2} & \cdots & A_{ij} & \cdots & A_{in} \\ \vdots & \vdots & & \vdots & & \vdots \\ A_{n1} & A_{n2} & \cdots & A_{nj} & \cdots & A_{nn} \end{bmatrix}^t$$

Les matrices inverses présentent des propriétés intéressantes, regroupées dans le théorème 3.4 (p. 102).

Le calcul de l'inverse d'une matrice A à l'aide de la matrice adjointe de A demande beaucoup de temps, d'où la nécessité de trouver des « raccourcis ». Il serait également utile de connaître une méthode plus efficace de résolution d'un système d'équations linéaires. Le chapitre 4 traite de ces deux sujets.

MOTS CLÉS

EXERCICES RÉCAPITULATIFS

1. (I) Évaluez si possible chacune des expressions suivantes.

   a) $\det \begin{bmatrix} -5 \end{bmatrix}$

   b) $\begin{vmatrix} 4 & 6 \\ 5 & 2 \end{vmatrix}$

   c) $\det \begin{bmatrix} -1 & 3 \\ -2 & -4 \end{bmatrix}$

   d) $\begin{vmatrix} 1 & -4 & 0 \\ 0 & 0,5 & -1 \\ 2 & 3 & 2 \end{vmatrix}$

   e) $\det \begin{bmatrix} 0 & 0 & 0 \\ 0 & 0 & 0 \end{bmatrix}$

   f) $\begin{vmatrix} 0 & 1 & 0 & 1 \\ 1 & 0 & 0 & 1 \\ 1 & 0 & 1 & 0 \\ 0 & 0 & 1 & 0 \end{vmatrix}$

   g) $\det(5I_4)$

   h) $\det(O_{n \times n})$

   i) $\begin{vmatrix} 1 & -4 & 2 \\ -1 & 2 & 5 \\ 2 & -2 & 1 \end{vmatrix}$ (Appliquez la règle de Sarrus.)

2. (I) Calculez les mineurs M_{12}, M_{22} et M_{23} et les cofacteurs correspondants pour les matrices

$$A = \begin{bmatrix} -1 & 2 & 3 \\ 4 & -5 & 7 \\ 1 & 3 & -1 \end{bmatrix} \text{ et } B = \begin{bmatrix} 0 & 1 & 2 & 3 \\ 2 & 0 & 1 & 4 \\ 5 & 0 & 2 & 2 \\ 0 & 5 & 0 & 1 \end{bmatrix}$$

3. (I) Soit la matrice

$$A = \begin{bmatrix} 0 & 5 & -2 & 1 & -3 & 6 \\ 1 & -1 & -3 & 0 & 2 & 4 \\ 3 & 9 & 6 & 0 & 1 & 1 \\ -6 & 7 & 7 & 0 & 1 & 6 \\ 2 & 5 & 4 & 0 & 8 & 0 \\ 1 & 2 & 6 & 0 & 3 & 1 \end{bmatrix}$$

a) Exprimez les cofacteurs A_{32} et A_{53} sous la forme de déterminants. (N'effectuez pas les calculs.)

b) Si on vous demandait de calculer le déterminant de la matrice A, suivant quelle ligne ou quelle colonne développeriez-vous le déterminant?

4. (I) Soit les matrices

$$A = \begin{bmatrix} 1 & 2 \\ 0 & 0 \end{bmatrix} \quad \text{et} \quad B = \begin{bmatrix} 0 & 0 \\ 3 & 4 \end{bmatrix}$$

a) Que vaut det A?

b) Que vaut det B?

c) Que vaut det $(A + B)$?

d) Dites si l'énoncé suivant est vrai ou faux: « Le déterminant de la somme de deux matrices est égal à la somme des déterminants des deux matrices. »

e) Dites si l'énoncé suivant est vrai ou faux: « La somme de deux matrices singulières de même ordre est une matrice singulière. »

5. (I) Dites si les énoncés suivants sont vrais ou faux et justifiez votre réponse.

a) Le déterminant d'une matrice idempotente vaut 0 ou 1.

b) Le déterminant d'une matrice nilpotente vaut 0.

c) det $(A + B) = $ det $A + $ det B

d) det $(-A) = -$det A

e) Si A est une matrice régulière, alors det $(AA^t) > 0$.

f) La somme de deux matrices régulières est une matrice régulière. (Indice: Que vaut $A + (-A)$?)

g) Si le produit de deux matrices carrées A et B est une matrice régulière, alors A et B sont aussi des matrices régulières.

h) Une matrice A est régulière si et seulement si sa transposée, A^t, est régulière.

i) Le déterminant d'une matrice carrée échelonnée vaut 1.

j) Une matrice triangulaire dont la diagonale principale ne compte aucun zéro est régulière.

6. (I) Exprimez le déterminant de la matrice B en fonction du déterminant de la matrice A.

a) $A = \begin{bmatrix} a & b & c \\ 3 & 2 & 4 \\ 1 & 1 & 1 \end{bmatrix} \quad B = \begin{bmatrix} 3 & 2 & 4 \\ a & b & c \\ 1 & 1 & 1 \end{bmatrix} \; L_1 \leftrightarrow L_2$

b) $A = \begin{bmatrix} 2 & 2 & 2 \\ 1 & 2 & 3 \\ -1 & -4 & -8 \end{bmatrix} \quad B = \begin{bmatrix} -4 & -4 & -4 \\ 3 & 6 & 9 \\ -1 & -4 & -8 \end{bmatrix}$

$|B| = -6|A|$

c) $A = \begin{bmatrix} a & b & c \\ 2 & 4 & 6 \\ 1 & 1 & 1 \end{bmatrix}$

$B = \begin{bmatrix} a + 2k & b + 4k & c + 6k \\ 2 & 4 & 6 \\ 1 & 1 & 1 \end{bmatrix}$

d) $A = \begin{bmatrix} a_{ij} \end{bmatrix}_{5 \times 5} \quad B = 3A$

e) $A = \begin{bmatrix} 1 & 2 & 5 \\ 1 & 3 & 6 \\ 1 & 4 & 7 \end{bmatrix} \quad B = \begin{bmatrix} 1 & 0 & 5 \\ 1 & 1 & 6 \\ 1 & 2 & 7 \end{bmatrix}$

7. (III) Montrez qu'une matrice carrée d'ordre n qui compte plus de $n^2 - n$ zéros est singulière. (Indice: montrez qu'une telle matrice compte au moins une ligne formée entièrement de zéros.)

8. (II) Soit $A = \begin{bmatrix} a_{ij} \end{bmatrix}_{n \times n}$ une matrice nilpotente d'indice k.

a) Montrez que la matrice A est singulière.

b) Montrez que, pour toute valeur x,

$$(I_n + xA + x^2 A^2 + \cdots + x^{k-1} A^{k-1})(I_n - xA) = I_n$$

9. (I) Évaluez chaque déterminant en faisant appel aux propriétés des déterminants.

a) $\begin{vmatrix} 0 & 5 & -2 & 0 & -3 & 6 \\ 1 & -1 & -3 & 0 & 2 & 4 \\ 3 & 9 & 6 & 0 & 1 & 1 \\ -6 & 7 & 7 & 0 & 1 & 6 \\ 2 & 5 & 4 & 0 & 8 & 0 \\ 1 & 2 & 6 & 0 & 3 & 1 \end{vmatrix}$

b)
$$\begin{vmatrix} 2 & 5 & -2 & 0 & -3 & 6 \\ 0 & -1 & -3 & 0 & 2 & 4 \\ 0 & 0 & 6 & -2 & 1 & 1 \\ 0 & 0 & 0 & 4 & 1 & 6 \\ 0 & 0 & 0 & 0 & 7 & 0 \\ 0 & 0 & 0 & 0 & 0 & 1 \end{vmatrix}$$

c)
$$\begin{vmatrix} 2 & 1 & -2 & 1 \\ 1 & 2 & -4 & 1 \\ 1 & 4 & -8 & 0 \\ 0 & -3 & 6 & 0 \end{vmatrix}$$

d)
$$\begin{vmatrix} 2 & -2 & 8 & 6 & 3 \\ 3 & 0 & -1 & -6 & -1 \\ 3 & 0 & 0 & 4 & 0 \\ 1 & 0 & 0 & 2 & 0 \\ -1 & 0 & 1 & 1 & 0 \end{vmatrix}$$

e)
$$\begin{vmatrix} x_1 y_1 & x_1 y_2 & x_1 y_3 & \cdots & x_1 y_n \\ x_2 y_1 & x_2 y_2 & x_2 y_3 & \cdots & x_2 y_n \\ x_3 y_1 & x_3 y_2 & x_3 y_3 & \cdots & x_3 y_n \\ \vdots & \vdots & \vdots & & \vdots \\ x_n y_1 & x_n y_2 & x_n y_3 & \cdots & x_n y_n \end{vmatrix}$$

(Indice : Étudiez deux cas, soit $n = 1$ et $n > 1$.)

f) det C où $C = \begin{bmatrix} 0 & 1 & 0 & \cdots & 0 \\ 0 & 0 & 1 & \cdots & 0 \\ \vdots & \vdots & \vdots & & \vdots \\ 0 & 0 & 0 & & 1 \\ 1 & 0 & 0 & \cdots & 0 \end{bmatrix}_{n \times n}$

(Indice : Calculez C_{n1}.)

10. (I) Calculez chaque déterminant en faisant appel au théorème 3.1.

a)
$$\begin{vmatrix} 1 & 3 & 2 & -1 \\ 1 & 1 & 2 & 6 \\ 2 & 2 & -3 & 2 \\ 2 & 3 & 4 & 1 \end{vmatrix}$$

b)
$$\begin{vmatrix} 3 & 3 & 2 & -1 \\ 1 & 1 & 3 & -2 \\ 2 & 2 & -2 & 2 \\ -2 & 3 & -1 & 1 \end{vmatrix}$$

11. (I) Évaluez le déterminant de la matrice $A = \left[a_{ij} \right]_{n \times n}$ où :

a) $a_{ij} = \begin{cases} 2 & \text{pour } i \le j \\ 0 & \text{pour } i > j \end{cases}$

b) $a_{ij} = \begin{cases} i & \text{pour } i = j \\ 0 & \text{pour } i \ne j \end{cases}$

12. (I) Soit $H = \begin{bmatrix} a & d & g \\ b & e & h \\ c & f & i \end{bmatrix}$ et det $H = -4$. Évaluez le déterminant de chacune des matrices suivantes.

a) $A = \begin{bmatrix} a & b & c \\ d & e & f \\ g & h & i \end{bmatrix}$

b) $B = \begin{bmatrix} g & a & d \\ h & b & e \\ i & c & f \end{bmatrix}$

c) $C = \begin{bmatrix} 3a & d & -g \\ 3b & e & -h \\ 3c & f & -i \end{bmatrix}$

d) $D = \begin{bmatrix} a & d & g \\ (4b + 3a) & (4e + 3d) & (4h + 3g) \\ c & f & i \end{bmatrix}$

13. (I) Soit A et B, deux matrices carrées d'ordre n, dont l'une est singulière. Montrez que le produit AB est aussi une matrice singulière.

14. (II) Utilisez le fait que les nombres 12 388, 69 426, 82 935, 42 218 et 21 394 sont des multiples de 19 pour montrer que le déterminant de la matrice A suivante est aussi un multiple de 19.

$$A = \begin{bmatrix} 1 & 2 & 3 & 8 & 8 \\ 6 & 9 & 4 & 2 & 6 \\ 8 & 2 & 9 & 3 & 5 \\ 4 & 2 & 2 & 1 & 8 \\ 2 & 1 & 3 & 9 & 4 \end{bmatrix}$$

15. (II) Soit la matrice $T = \left[a_{ij} \right]_{5 \times 5}$ où $a_{ij} = \begin{cases} b & \text{pour } i = j \\ c & \text{pour } i \ne j \end{cases}$.

a) Construisez la matrice T.

b) Montrez que det $T = (b - c)^4 (b + 4c)$.

16. (I) Soit les matrices

$$A = \begin{bmatrix} a_{11} & a_{12} & \cdots & b_{1j} + c_{1j} & \cdots & a_{1n} \\ a_{21} & a_{22} & \cdots & b_{2j} + c_{2j} & \cdots & a_{2n} \\ \vdots & \vdots & & \vdots & & \vdots \\ a_{i1} & a_{i2} & \cdots & b_{ij} + c_{ij} & \cdots & a_{in} \\ \vdots & \vdots & & \vdots & & \vdots \\ a_{n1} & a_{n2} & \cdots & b_{nj} + c_{nj} & \cdots & a_{nn} \end{bmatrix}$$

$$B = \begin{bmatrix} a_{11} & a_{12} & \cdots & b_{1j} & \cdots & a_{1n} \\ a_{21} & a_{22} & \cdots & b_{2j} & \cdots & a_{2n} \\ \vdots & \vdots & & \vdots & & \vdots \\ a_{i1} & a_{i2} & \cdots & b_{ij} & \cdots & a_{in} \\ \vdots & \vdots & & \vdots & & \vdots \\ a_{n1} & a_{n2} & \cdots & b_{nj} & \cdots & a_{nn} \end{bmatrix}$$

$$C = \begin{bmatrix} a_{11} & a_{12} & \cdots & c_{1j} & \cdots & a_{1n} \\ a_{21} & a_{22} & \cdots & c_{2j} & \cdots & a_{2n} \\ \vdots & \vdots & & \vdots & & \vdots \\ a_{i1} & a_{i2} & \cdots & c_{ij} & \cdots & a_{in} \\ \vdots & \vdots & & \vdots & & \vdots \\ a_{n1} & a_{n2} & \cdots & c_{nj} & \cdots & a_{nn} \end{bmatrix}$$

Montrez que det A = det B + det C.

17. (I) (Cet exercice s'adresse à ceux qui connaissent le calcul différentiel.) Le wronskien de deux fonctions dérivables $f(x)$ et $g(x)$ est défini par

$$W(x) = \begin{vmatrix} f(x) & g(x) \\ f'(x) & g'(x) \end{vmatrix}$$

Quel est le wronskien de chacune des paires de fonctions suivantes ?

a) $f(x) = 1$ et $g(x) = x$.

b) $f(x) = x^2$ et $g(x) = x^3$.

c) $f(x) = \sin x$ et $g(x) = \cos x$.

18. (I) Trouvez, si elle existe, la matrice inverse de chaque matrice.

a) $A = \begin{bmatrix} 1 & 2 \\ 2 & -3 \end{bmatrix}$

b) $B = \begin{bmatrix} 2 & -1 \\ 3 & 1 \end{bmatrix}$

c) $C = \begin{bmatrix} a & 2 \\ 2 & a \end{bmatrix}$

d) $D = \begin{bmatrix} 1 & -1 & 1 \\ 1 & 1 & 1 \\ 2 & 0 & 2 \end{bmatrix}$

e) $E = \begin{bmatrix} -3 & 5 & -6 \\ 2 & -3 & 5 \\ 5 & 2 & -3 \end{bmatrix}$

f) $F = \begin{bmatrix} 1 & 2 \\ 3 & 4 \\ -1 & 2 \end{bmatrix}$

g) $G = \begin{bmatrix} 3 & 2 & 5 \\ 1 & 2 & 0 \\ 2 & -1 & 1 \end{bmatrix}$

19. (II) Si A est une matrice régulière d'ordre n, montrez que det $(A^{-1}) = \dfrac{1}{\det A}$.

20. (I) Soit A et B deux matrices carrées d'ordre 4 telles que det $A = -3$ et det $B = 2{,}5$. À l'aide des propriétés des déterminants, évaluez si possible chacune des expressions suivantes.

a) det AB

b) det $(A - B)$

c) det (A^3)

d) det $((AB)^{-1})$

e) det $3B^2$

f) det (AB^t)

21. (I) Soit la matrice

$$A = \begin{bmatrix} 1 & 0 & 1 \\ 2 & x & 0 \\ x & 3 & 1 \end{bmatrix}$$

a) Pour quelle(s) valeur(s) de x la matrice A n'est-elle pas inversible ?

b) Exprimez A^{-1} en fonction de x.

c) Pour quelle(s) valeur(s) de x le déterminant de la matrice A vaut-il 14 ?

22. (I) Soit les matrices

$$A = \begin{bmatrix} 1 & 2 & x \\ 0 & -1 & y \\ 0 & 0 & 1 \end{bmatrix} \quad B = \begin{bmatrix} 1 & 1 & x \\ 1 & x & 1 \\ x & 1 & 1 \end{bmatrix}$$

$$C = \begin{bmatrix} 1 & a & a^2 \\ 1 & b & b^2 \\ 1 & c & c^2 \end{bmatrix} \quad D = \begin{bmatrix} 1 & 1 & 1 \\ a & b & c \\ bc & ac & ab \end{bmatrix}$$

$$E = \begin{bmatrix} 1 & 1 & 1 \\ a & b & c \\ b+c & a+c & a+b \end{bmatrix}$$

$$F = \begin{bmatrix} a & ab \\ b & a^2 + b^2 \end{bmatrix}$$

a) Montrez que la matrice A est inversible quelles que soient les valeurs de x et y.

b) Exprimez A^{-1} en fonction de x et y.

c) Montrez que la matrice B est inversible pour toutes les valeurs de x à l'exception de $x = 1$ et $x = -2$.

d) Montrez que det $C = (b - a)(c - b)(c - a)$ en appliquant les propriétés des déterminants.

e) À quelles conditions la matrice C est-elle inversible ?

f) Montrez, sans développer le déterminant, que $(a - b)$ est un facteur de det D.

g) Montrez que la matrice E n'est pas inversible. (Indice : ajoutez la deuxième ligne à la troisième ligne et comparez le résultat avec la première ligne).

h) Montrez que la matrice F est inversible seulement si $a \neq 0$.

23. (II) Montrez que la matrice identité est la seule matrice idempotente dont le déterminant est différent de 0.

24. (I) Dites si les énoncés suivants sont vrais ou faux et justifiez votre réponse.

a) Si elle existe, la matrice inverse d'une matrice antisymétrique est aussi une matrice antisymétrique.

b) Si elle existe, la matrice inverse d'une matrice symétrique est aussi une matrice symétrique.

c) Toutes les matrices idempotentes sont régulières.

25. (I) Soit $A = \begin{bmatrix} a_{ij} \end{bmatrix}_{n \times n}$ une matrice diagonale d'ordre n.

a) À quelles conditions la matrice A est-elle inversible ?

b) Donnez l'expression de l'inverse d'une matrice diagonale inversible ?

26. (II) Dans *A Memoir on the Theory of Matrices*, Arthur Cayley affirme que : «... le produit de deux matrices [carrées de même ordre] peut être zéro [la matrice nulle] sans que chacun des deux facteurs soient nuls [des matrices

nulles], si et seulement si l'une ou les deux matrices sont indéterminées [singulières][12] ». Même si Cayley fut un très grand mathématicien, la deuxième partie de son énoncé (*si et seulement* ...) est fausse. En effet, il faut que les deux matrices soient singulières. Prouvez ce dernier énoncé.

27. (I) Soit A et B, deux matrices carrées de même ordre. Montrez que, si B est inversible, det $(B^{-1}AB) = $ det A.

28. (I) Calculez $(AB)^{-1}$ où

$$A^{-1} = \begin{bmatrix} 2 & 4 & 1 \\ 1 & 2 & 1 \\ 3 & 4 & 2 \end{bmatrix} \text{ et } B^{-1} = \begin{bmatrix} 1 & 2 & -1 \\ 3 & 6 & 0 \\ 0 & 4 & 2 \end{bmatrix}$$

29. (I) Une matrice carrée d'ordre n est dite orthogonale si sa transposée est égale à son inverse.

a) Montrez que la matrice I_n est orthogonale.

b) Vérifiez que $A = \begin{bmatrix} \sin \theta & \cos \theta \\ -\cos \theta & \sin \theta \end{bmatrix}$ est une matrice orthogonale.

c) Montrez que le déterminant d'une matrice orthogonale vaut 1 ou −1.

30. (I) Soit A et B, deux matrices non singulières telles que $AB = BA$. Montrez que

a) $AB^{-1} = B^{-1}A$

b) $A^{-1}B^{-1} = B^{-1}A^{-1}$

c) $A^t B^t = B^t A^t$

31. (I) Une façon sécuritaire de transmettre de l'information confidentielle consiste à coder cette information. Ainsi, pour coder le message *BONJOUR LUC*, on convertit d'abord les lettres en chiffres en adoptant une convention comme : $A = 1$, $B = -1$, $C = 2$, $D = -2$ et ainsi de suite, le symbole 0 désignant un espace ou une apostrophe.

$$\begin{array}{ccccccccccc} B & O & N & J & O & U & R & & L & U & C \\ -1 & 8 & -7 & -5 & 8 & 11 & -9 & 0 & -6 & 11 & 2 \end{array}$$

On peut également coder cette information de manière sécuritaire à l'aide du produit matriciel. Soit la matrice de codage

---

12. J.-P. Colette. *Histoire des mathématiques*, tome 2, Montréal, Éditions du Renouveau Pédagogique, 1979, p. 250.

$$A = \begin{bmatrix} 1 & 1 & 1 \\ 2 & 1 & 2 \\ -1 & -1 & 0 \end{bmatrix}$$

Comme la matrice A est d'ordre 3, on divise le message en segments de trois caractères et on forme la matrice B du message, dont chaque colonne correspond à un segment.

$$B = \begin{bmatrix} B & J & R & U \\ O & O & \_ & C \\ N & U & L & \_ \end{bmatrix} = \begin{bmatrix} -1 & -5 & -9 & 11 \\ 8 & 8 & 0 & 2 \\ -7 & 11 & -6 & 0 \end{bmatrix}$$

En calculant le produit AB, on obtient la matrice du message codé

$$AB = \begin{bmatrix} 0 & 14 & -15 & 13 \\ -8 & 20 & -30 & 24 \\ -7 & -3 & 9 & -13 \end{bmatrix}$$

Le message codé est donc le suivant:

0 –8 –7 14 20 –3 –15 –30 9 13 24 –13

a) Quelle lettre a-t-on employée pour noter la matrice du message?

b) Comment a-t-on noté la matrice du message codé?

c) Comment décode-t-on un message? (Autrement dit, quelle opération matricielle doit-on effectuer sur le message codé pour retrouver le message original?)

d) Codez le message « ADIEU » à l'aide de la matrice A.

e) Carole a reçu de son amoureux le message suivant, codé à l'aide de la matrice A.

–2 –7 2 –9 –18 10 15 23 –12

Décodez ce message.

f) Quelle caractéristique fondamentale une matrice doit-elle posséder pour qu'on puisse l'employer comme matrice de codage?

g) Pourquoi la matrice $C = \begin{bmatrix} 1 & 1 & 1 \\ 2 & 1 & 2 \\ -1 & -1 & -1 \end{bmatrix}$ ne peut-elle pas être employée pour coder un message?

32. (I) Résoudre si possible chaque système d'équations linéaires à l'aide de la méthode de la matrice inverse.

a) $\begin{aligned} a - 2b - 3c &= -1 \\ 2a - b - 2c &= 2 \\ 3a - b - 3c &= 3 \end{aligned}$

b) $\begin{aligned} x_1 - x_2 + 2x_3 &= 6 \\ 2x_1 + x_2 - 3x_3 &= 5 \\ 3x_1 \phantom{{}+ x_2} - x_3 &= 8 \end{aligned}$

c) $\begin{aligned} 2x + 4y - 4z &= -4 \\ 3x - 3y - 8z &= 20 \\ x + 2y + 2z &= 0 \end{aligned}$

d) $\begin{aligned} x + y + z + w &= 2 \\ 2x - 3y + 4z - w &= -10 \\ x + 2y + 2z + 3w &= 20 \end{aligned}$

Résolution de systèmes d'équations linéaires

Comme le soleil éclipse les étoiles par sa brillance, l'homme savant éclipse la gloire des autres hommes s'il propose des problèmes d'algèbre, et plus encore s'il les résout.

Brahmagupta

À LA FIN DU PRÉSENT CHAPITRE, VOUS DEVRIEZ ÊTRE EN MESURE DE RÉPONDRE AUX QUESTIONS SUIVANTES:

- Comment représente-t-on un système d'équations linéaires à l'aide d'une matrice augmentée?

- Quelles sont les trois opérations élémentaires de ligne qui préservent l'ensemble solution d'un système d'équations linéaires?

- À quelle condition deux matrices sont-elles équivalentes?

- En quoi la méthode d'élimination gaussienne et la méthode de Gauss-Jordan sont-elles supérieures à la règle de Cramer pour résoudre un système d'équations linéaires?

- Comment distingue-t-on un système d'équations linéaires compatible d'un système incompatible?

- À quoi reconnaît-on un système d'équations linéaires qui compte une infinité de solutions?

- Comment procède-t-on pour trouver l'inverse d'une matrice à l'aide de la méthode de Gauss-Jordan?

UN PORTRAIT de Carl Friedrich Gauss

Carl Friedrich Gauss naquit à Brunswick, en Allemagne, le 23 avril 1777 dans une famille très modeste, et il mourut à Göttingen le 23 février 1855. On sait bien peu de choses de l'enfance de celui qu'on a appelé le Prince des mathématiciens et qui est, selon plusieurs, l'un des trois plus grands mathématiciens de tous les temps, avec Archimède et Newton. Il existe quelques anecdotes sur la précocité du jeune Gauss; on dit par exemple que, dès l'âge de trois ans, il découvrit une erreur de calcul dans la comptabilité de son père et qu'il apprit seul à lire et à compter. De plus, il aurait, à l'âge de dix ans, étonné fortement son professeur d'arithmétique. Ce dernier aurait demandé à ses élèves d'additionner une suite de termes formant une progression arithmétique (comme la somme des 1 000 premiers entiers). À peine avait-il fini d'énoncer le problème que le jeune Gauss aurait inscrit sa réponse sur son ardoise et aurait déposé celle-ci sur le bureau du professeur. Il suffit de quelques minutes pour résoudre un tel problème à l'aide de la formule de la somme d'une progression arithmétique[1]. Toutefois, le jeune Gauss ne connaissait probablement pas cette formule : il l'aurait découverte par lui-même de manière quasi instantanée. Ces anecdotes font partie de la légende de Gauss, mais selon Bühler, un biographe de Gauss, il est impossible de les confirmer.

Deux professeurs de l'école élémentaire que fréquenta Gauss, à savoir Büttner et Bartels, remarquèrent le talent du jeune prodige et le firent entrer à l'école secondaire. En 1791, Bartels présenta Gauss au duc de Brunswick qui remit à celui-ci une bourse pour lui permettre de s'inscrire au Collegium Carolinum puis à l'Université de Göttingen. C'est au cours de ses études à Göttingen que Gauss conçut la méthode des moindres carrés et découvrit comment inscrire un polygone de 17 côtés dans un cercle avec

---

1. $$\begin{aligned} S &= 1 + 2 + \cdots + 999 + 1000 \\ S &= 1000 + 999 + \cdots + 2 + 1 \\ \hline 2S &= 1001 + 1001 + \cdots + 1001 + 1001 \end{aligned}$$

   $$2S = 1000 \times 1001 \Rightarrow S = (1000 \times 1001)/2$$

   En général, $\displaystyle\sum_{k=1}^{n} \left[a + (k-1)d \right] = na + \frac{n(n-1)}{2}d$

seulement une règle et un compas. Cette dernière découverte est la première inscription du journal mathématique de Gauss, qu'il commença en 1796 et qui contient 146 énoncés extrêmement brefs (le dernier daté de 1814) mais d'une grande profondeur. Plusieurs de ces énoncés servirent de base au développement de champs de recherche importants. Leopold Kronecker, un illustre mathématicien allemand, affirma d'ailleurs que, au XIXᵉ siècle, la majorité des idées novatrices en mathématiques pouvaient être associées à Gauss.

En 1799, Gauss soutint sa thèse de doctorat à l'Université de Helmstedt. Intitulée Demonstratio nova theorematis omnem functionem algebraicam rationalem integram unius variabilis in factores reales primi vel secundi gradus resolvi posse[2], elle représente, malgré son titre, la première preuve véritable du théorème fondamental de l'algèbre. Au cours de sa vie, Gauss proposa trois autres preuves de ce théorème, la dernière alors qu'il avait plus de 70 ans. En 1801, Gauss publia son œuvre maîtresse en théorie des nombres, Disquisitiones arithmeticæ. Ses écrits sont cependant peu nombreux, conformément à sa devise : Pauca sed matura (Peu de fruits, mais des fruits mûrs), qu'il respecta tout au long de sa vie.

Lors de l'étude des orbites des astéroïdes Cérès et Pallas, Gauss mit au point une méthode de résolution d'un système d'équations linéaires. Les calculs qu'il dut effectuer pour déterminer l'orbite de Pallas l'amenèrent à résoudre un système de six équations linéaires à six inconnues. Dans Disquisitio de elementis ellipticis Palladis (1810), Gauss décrit une méthode de résolution de ce système d'équations (eliminatio vulgaris). Il montre comment remplacer le système d'équations à résoudre par un système équivalent dont seule la première équation comporte six inconnues, la seconde n'en comportant que cinq, la troisième quatre et ainsi de suite, de sorte que la dernière équation ne comporte qu'une seule inconnue. La solution de cette dernière équation est évidente et on résout facilement les autres en effectuant une suite de substitutions, à rebours.

Signalons pour terminer que Gauss fit également de nombreuses et importantes contributions en géodésie, en électricité et magnétisme, et en astronomie. D'ailleurs, le gouvernement allemand a reconu l'apport considérable de Gauss

---

2. Nouvelle démonstration du théorème selon lequel toute fonction algébrique à coefficients rationnels s'exprime sous la forme d'un produit de facteurs réels du premier ou du second degré.

en faisant imprimer sur le billet de dix marks l'effigie de Gauss et une courbe normale (appelée aussi courbe de Laplace-Gauss), à l'allure caractéristique et dont l'importance en probabilités et statistique est bien connue.

4.1 IMPORTANCE DE LA RÉSOLUTION DE SYSTÈMES D'ÉQUATIONS LINÉAIRES

Il est courant d'avoir à résoudre un système d'équations linéaires à plusieurs inconnues, notamment en biologie, en chimie, en physique et en sciences économiques.

Exemple

1. Un technicien doit administrer 2 g de protéines et 0,5 g de gras à un animal de laboratoire. Il dispose de deux produits dont la composition est donnée dans le tableau suivant.

Produit	Protéines (%)	Gras (%)
A	5	3
B	10	1

Si on note x la quantité (en grammes) du produit A et y la quantité (en grammes) du produit B qui doivent entrer dans le mélange, alors on obtient le système d'équations

$$0,05x + 0,10y = 2 \quad \text{(quantité requise de protéines)}$$
$$0,03x + 0,01y = 0,5 \quad \text{(quantité requise de gras)}$$

2. La température d'une tige métallique isolée est maintenue à 25 °C à l'une de ses extrémités et à 50 °C à l'autre extrémité. On veut déterminer la température de la tige aux trois points x, y, z, qui divisent la tige en quatre parties égales.

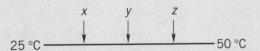

On suppose que la température en x, y ou z est égale à la moyenne des températures aux deux points les plus proches. Par conséquent, on obtient les équations

$$x = \frac{25 + y}{2}, \ y = \frac{x + z}{2} \ \text{et} \ z = \frac{y + 50}{2}$$

qui s'écrivent également sous la forme

$$
\begin{aligned}
2x - \ y \qquad\ &= 25 \\
x - 2y + \ z &= \ \ 0 \\
-y + 2z &= 50
\end{aligned}
$$

3. En économie, les courbes de l'offre et de la demande d'un produit en donnent le prix et la quantité d'équilibre. L'offre décrit la quantité (Q) d'un bien en fonction du prix (P): plus le prix est élevé plus la quantité offerte est grande et, inversement, plus le prix est bas, plus la quantité offerte est faible. L'offre est souvent représentée par une droite de pente positive. Par exemple, l'offre d'un produit est donnée par une équation telle que $Q = 40 + 32P$. Quant à la demande, elle est souvent représentée par une droite de pente négative. Par exemple, la demande d'un produit est donnée par une équation telle que $Q = 300 - 20P$. Il est à noter que la quantité demandée diminue lorsque le prix augmente, ce qui explique que le coefficient de P (le prix) est négatif dans la dernière équation. L'équilibre de l'offre et de la demande est atteint lorsque le système suivant, formé des équations linéaires qui les représentent, admet une solution.

$$
\begin{aligned}
Q &= \ \ 40 + 32P \\
Q &= 300 - 20P
\end{aligned}
$$

4. On fait appel aux lois de Kirchhoff[3] pour trouver la valeur du courant dans un circuit électrique comme celui-ci:

---

3. L'Allemand Gustav Kirchhoff (1824-1887) fut un grand physicien. Vous trouverez l'énoncé des lois qui portent son nom dans tout bon manuel de physique traitant d'électricité, comme celui de H. Benson. *Physique II, Électricité et magnétisme*, Saint-Laurent, Éditions du Renouveau Pédagogique, 1993, p. 116-117.

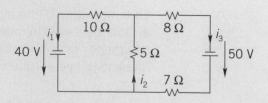

Le système formé des équations obtenues en appliquant ces lois est

$$i_1 - i_2 + i_3 = 0$$
$$5 i_2 + 15 i_3 = 50$$
$$10 i_1 + 5 i_2 \quad = 40$$

5. Toute réaction chimique est représentée par une équation. Par exemple, si on combine une certaine quantité d'azote et une certaine quantité d'hydrogène, on obtient le composé NH_3. Pour établir l'équation de cette réaction, il faut déterminer les quantités requises de chaque composante et la quantité obtenue du produit final. Autrement dit, on doit trouver les plus petites valeurs entières de x, y et z qui vérifient l'équation $xN_2 + yH_2 \rightarrow zNH_3$. Pour que le nombre d'atomes de chacun des éléments du membre de droite soit égal au nombre d'atomes contenus dans le composé du membre de gauche, il faut que $2x = z$ (même nombre d'atomes d'azote) et que $2y = 3z$ (même nombre d'atomes d'hydrogène).

$$xN_2 + yH_2 \rightarrow zNH_3 \qquad xN_2 + yH_2 \rightarrow zNH_3$$
$$2 \; x \qquad = \; z \qquad\qquad 2 \; y = 3 \; z$$

Le système formé des équations associées à cette réaction est donc

$$2x \quad - \; z = 0$$
$$2y - 3z = 0$$

Nous avons déjà vu comment résoudre les systèmes d'équations des quatre premiers exemples par la méthode de la matrice inverse. Nous avons toutefois souligné que cette méthode n'est pas très efficace et qu'elle ne s'applique pas dans tous les cas. Ainsi, on ne peut l'employer pour résoudre le système d'équations de l'exemple 5, qui compte deux équations et trois inconnues, puisque la matrice des coefficients n'est pas une matrice carrée.

C'est pourquoi nous présentons d'autres façons de résoudre un système d'équations linéaires. Nous allons étudier d'abord la règle de Cramer, pour des raisons historiques et parce que les ingénieurs l'affectionnent particulièrement.

La règle de Cramer n'est pas plus efficace que la méthode de la matrice inverse, mais on peut l'utiliser pour résoudre un système d'équations avec paramètres, elle donne une formule générale pour la valeur de chacune des inconnues et elle permet de distinguer les cas où un système d'équations admet une solution unique ou une infinité de solutions ou encore lorsqu'il n'admet aucune solution.

Nous étudierons ensuite les méthodes d'élimination gaussienne et de Gauss-Jordan, qui s'avèrent beaucoup plus efficaces et permettent de résoudre des systèmes comme celui de l'exemple 5.

4.2 RÈGLE DE CRAMER

La **règle de Cramer**, qui est une méthode de résolution d'un système d'équations linéaires, exige l'évaluation du déterminant de la matrice des coefficients. Par conséquent, on peut l'appliquer seulement si cette matrice est une matrice carrée, c'est-à-dire si le système d'équations linéaires comporte autant d'équations que d'inconnues.

4.2.1 ÉNONCÉ DE LA RÈGLE DE CRAMER

RÈGLE DE CRAMER

La règle de Cramer est une méthode de résolution d'un système d'équations linéaires comportant autant d'équations que d'inconnues. Elle fait appel au calcul de déterminants et elle fournit une expression symbolique pour les inconnues lorsque le système d'équations linéaires admet une solution unique.

Un système d'équations linéaires qui compte autant d'équations que d'inconnues s'écrit sous la forme

$$
\begin{aligned}
a_{11}x_1 + a_{12}x_2 + a_{13}x_3 + \cdots + a_{1n}x_n &= b_1 \\
a_{21}x_1 + a_{22}x_2 + a_{23}x_3 + \cdots + a_{2n}x_n &= b_2 \\
a_{31}x_1 + a_{32}x_2 + a_{33}x_3 + \cdots + a_{3n}x_n &= b_3 \\
\vdots \qquad\quad \vdots \qquad\quad \vdots \qquad\qquad\quad \vdots \qquad\quad \vdots \\
a_{n1}x_1 + a_{n2}x_2 + a_{n3}x_3 + \cdots + a_{nn}x_n &= b_n
\end{aligned}
$$

et la matrice des coefficients est

$$
A = \begin{bmatrix}
a_{11} & a_{12} & a_{13} & \cdots & a_{1n} \\
a_{21} & a_{22} & a_{23} & \cdots & a_{2n} \\
a_{31} & a_{32} & a_{33} & \cdots & a_{3n} \\
\vdots & \vdots & \vdots & & \vdots \\
a_{n1} & a_{n2} & a_{n3} & \cdots & a_{nn}
\end{bmatrix}
$$

Les matrices des inconnues et des constantes sont respectivement

$$
X = \begin{bmatrix} x_1 \\ x_2 \\ x_3 \\ \vdots \\ x_n \end{bmatrix} \quad \text{et} \quad B = \begin{bmatrix} b_1 \\ b_2 \\ b_3 \\ \vdots \\ b_n \end{bmatrix}
$$

Il est souvent commode de représenter une matrice colonne par la transposée d'une matrice ligne. Ainsi, on écrit souvent les matrices des inconnues et des constantes de la façon suivante :

$$
X = \begin{bmatrix} x_1 & x_2 & x_3 & \cdots & x_n \end{bmatrix}^t \quad \text{et} \quad B = \begin{bmatrix} b_1 & b_2 & b_3 & \cdots & b_n \end{bmatrix}^t
$$

L'**ensemble solution** (noté S) d'un système d'équations linéaires $AX = B$ est l'ensemble des matrices qui vérifient cette équation matricielle : si $X_1 \in S$, alors $AX_1 = B$. Un tel ensemble solution peut compter un seul élément, une infinité d'éléments ou encore être vide. Selon le cas, on dit que le système d'équations admet une solution unique, une infinité de solutions ou encore qu'il n'admet aucune solution.

Théorème 4.1   Règle de Cramer

Soit $AX = B$, un système d'équations linéaires comportant n équations à n inconnues $(x_1, x_2, \cdots, x_n)$. On note Δ le déterminant de la matrice A, et Δ_{x_i} le déterminant de la matrice obtenue en remplaçant la i-ième colonne de A par la matrice B des constantes.

- Si $\Delta \neq 0$, alors le système d'équations admet une solution unique, donnée par $x_i = \dfrac{\Delta_{x_i}}{\Delta}$ (pour $i = 1, 2, \cdots, n$).

- Si $\Delta = 0$ et $\Delta_{x_i} = 0$ pour **toutes les valeurs** de i, alors le système d'équations admet une infinité de solutions.

- Si $\Delta = 0$ et $\Delta_{x_i} \neq 0$ pour **au moins une valeur** de i, alors le système d'équations n'admet aucune solution.

Un **système d'équations** est dit **compatible** ou **incompatible** selon qu'il admet au moins une solution ou qu'il n'en admet aucune.

4.2.2 ILLUSTRATION DE LA RÈGLE DE CRAMER

Avant d'aborder la preuve du théorème 4.1, nous illustrons par des exemples simples les trois cas à considérer.

Exemple

1. Soit le système d'équations linéaires

$$2x + 3y = 8$$
$$7x - 5y = -3$$

Alors,

$$A = \begin{bmatrix} 2 & 3 \\ 7 & -5 \end{bmatrix} \quad X = \begin{bmatrix} x \\ y \end{bmatrix} \quad B = \begin{bmatrix} \mathbf{8} \\ \mathbf{-3} \end{bmatrix}$$

de sorte que

$$\Delta = \begin{vmatrix} 2 & 3 \\ 7 & -5 \end{vmatrix} = -31 \quad \Delta_x = \begin{vmatrix} \mathbf{8} & 3 \\ \mathbf{-3} & -5 \end{vmatrix} = -31 \quad \Delta_y = \begin{vmatrix} 2 & \mathbf{8} \\ 7 & \mathbf{-3} \end{vmatrix} = -62$$

Comme $\Delta = -31 \neq 0$, le système admet une solution unique, à savoir

$$x = \frac{\Delta_x}{\Delta} = \frac{-31}{-31} = 1 \quad \text{et} \quad y = \frac{\Delta_y}{\Delta} = \frac{-62}{-31} = 2$$

Voici une interprétation géométrique de ce système d'équations compatible. L'équation $2x + 3y = 8$ s'écrit également sous la forme $y = -\frac{2}{3}x + \frac{8}{3}$. Cette équation est celle de la droite de pente $-\frac{2}{3}$ et d'ordonnée à l'origine $\frac{8}{3}$. L'équation $7x - 5y = -3$ définit elle aussi une droite et, si on trace ces deux droites dans un même plan cartésien, on obtient le graphique suivant.

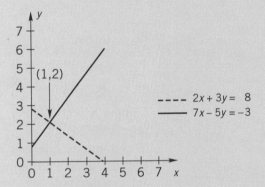

Il est clair que la solution du système d'équations est représentée par le point d'intersection des deux droites. Comme il n'y a qu'un seul point d'intersection, le système d'équations admet une solution unique, correspondant à une valeur unique de chacune des inconnues. Ainsi, l'ensemble solution du système est $S = \left\{ \begin{bmatrix} 1 & 2 \end{bmatrix}^t \right\}$, dont l'unique élément est la matrice qui vérifie le système d'équations $AX = B$. Par conséquent, $X = \begin{bmatrix} x & y \end{bmatrix}^t = \begin{bmatrix} 1 & 2 \end{bmatrix}^t$, et la solution du système s'écrit également sous la forme $x = 1$ et $y = 2$. Le système d'équations est donc compatible.

2. Soit le système d'équations linéaires

$$\begin{aligned} 2x + 3y &= 8 \\ 4x + 6y &= 12 \end{aligned}$$

Si on représente ces équations dans un même plan cartésien, on obtient le graphique suivant.

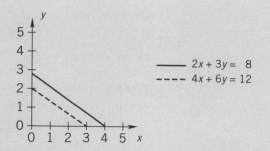

On constate que les deux droites sont parallèles, ce qui signifie qu'aucun couple de valeurs de x et de y ne vérifie simultanément les deux équations. Par conséquent, le système d'équations n'admet pas de solution. L'application de la règle de Cramer permet de vérifier ce résultat géométrique. On a

$$A = \begin{bmatrix} 2 & 3 \\ 4 & 6 \end{bmatrix} \quad X = \begin{bmatrix} x \\ y \end{bmatrix} \quad B = \begin{bmatrix} 8 \\ 12 \end{bmatrix}$$

de sorte que

$$\Delta = \begin{vmatrix} 2 & 3 \\ 4 & 6 \end{vmatrix} = 0 \quad \Delta_x = \begin{vmatrix} 8 & 3 \\ 12 & 6 \end{vmatrix} = 12 \quad \Delta_y = \begin{vmatrix} 2 & 8 \\ 4 & 12 \end{vmatrix} = -8$$

Comme $\Delta = 0$ et qu'au moins un des Δ_{x_i} est différent de zéro (en fait, $\Delta_x = 12 \neq 0$ et $\Delta_y = -8 \neq 0$), en vertu de la règle de Cramer, le système d'équations n'admet aucune solution. L'ensemble solution est donc l'ensemble vide : $S = \varnothing$, et le système d'équations est incompatible.

3. Soit le système d'équations linéaires

$$2x + 3y = 8$$
$$4x + 6y = 16$$

Si on représente ces équations dans un même plan cartésien, on obtient le graphique suivant.

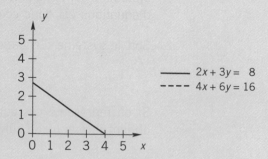

On constate que les deux droites se confondent, c'est-à-dire que les deux équations définissent une seule et même droite. Il existe une infinité de couples de valeurs de x et de y qui vérifient simultanément ces deux équations puisque la droite qui les représente comporte une infinité de points. Par conséquent, le système d'équations admet une infinité de solutions, ce qu'on peut vérifier à l'aide de la règle de Cramer. On a

$$A = \begin{bmatrix} 2 & 3 \\ 4 & 6 \end{bmatrix} \quad X = \begin{bmatrix} x \\ y \end{bmatrix} \quad B = \begin{bmatrix} 8 \\ 16 \end{bmatrix}$$

de sorte que

$$\Delta = \begin{vmatrix} 2 & 3 \\ 4 & 6 \end{vmatrix} = 0 \quad \Delta_x = \begin{vmatrix} 8 & 3 \\ 16 & 6 \end{vmatrix} = 0 \quad \Delta_y = \begin{vmatrix} 2 & 8 \\ 4 & 16 \end{vmatrix} = 0$$

Comme $\Delta = 0$ et que tous les Δ_{x_i} valent zéro, en vertu de la règle de Cramer, le système d'équations admet une infinité de solutions, soit l'ensemble des points de la droite $2x + 3y = 8$. En isolant y dans cette équation, on obtient $y = \dfrac{8 - 2x}{3}$.

L'ensemble solution est $S = \left\{ \begin{bmatrix} k & \dfrac{8 - 2k}{3} \end{bmatrix}^t \middle| k \in \mathbb{R} \right\}$. Ainsi, la matrice $\begin{bmatrix} 1 & 2 \end{bmatrix}^t$ appartient à l'ensemble solution, puisque si $k = 1$ alors $\dfrac{8 - 2k}{3} = \dfrac{8 - 2(1)}{3} = 2$, et il en est de même pour la matrice $\begin{bmatrix} 2 & 4/3 \end{bmatrix}^t$. Ces deux matrices sont des solutions particulières du système d'équations linéaires, qui en compte une infinité. Par contre, la matrice $\begin{bmatrix} 3 & 2 \end{bmatrix}^t$ n'appartient pas à l'ensemble solution parce que si $k = 3$ alors $\dfrac{8 - 2k}{3} = \dfrac{8 - 2(3)}{3} = \dfrac{2}{3} \neq 2$.

Puisqu'il compte au moins une solution, le système d'équations est compatible.

EXERCICE 4.1

Résolvez chaque système d'équations en faisant appel à la règle de Cramer et dites s'il s'agit d'un système compatible ou incompatible.

a) $x - 2y = 1$
   $x + \ y = 0$

b) $4x + 3y = 15$
   $8x + 6y = 12$

c) $4x_1 + 3x_2 = 15$
     $8x_1 + 6x_2 = 30$

d) $x - 2y + 3z = 6$
     $-2x + y - z = -1$
     $-3x + 2y - 2z = -3$

4.2.3 DÉMONSTRATION DE LA RÈGLE DE CRAMER

Nous nous contentons de démontrer le premier cas de la règle de Cramer.

Théorème 4.1 : premier cas

Soit $AX = B$, un système d'équations linéaires comportant n équations à n inconnues. Si $\Delta = \det A \neq 0$, alors $x_i = \dfrac{\Delta_{x_i}}{\Delta}$ pour $i = 1, 2, ..., n$.

Preuve

Si $\Delta \neq 0$, alors, en vertu du théorème 3.3, $A^{-1} = \dfrac{1}{\det A} \operatorname{adj} A$. Ainsi, l'ensemble solution est donné par $X = A^{-1}B = \left(\dfrac{1}{\det A} \operatorname{adj} A \right) B$ où X est une matrice de format $n \times 1$. L'élément situé sur la i-ième ligne de la matrice X, noté x_i, est donc identique à l'élément situé sur la i-ième ligne du produit $A^{-1}B = \left(\dfrac{1}{\det A} \operatorname{adj} A \right) B = \dfrac{1}{\det A} \left[(\operatorname{adj} A) B \right]$. On obtient cet élément en multipliant en quelque sorte la i-ième ligne de la matrice adjointe de A par la matrice colonne B, puis en divisant le résultat par le déterminant de la matrice des coefficients. Par conséquent,

$$x_i = \frac{A_{1i}b_1 + A_{2i}b_2 + A_{3i}b_3 + \cdots + A_{ni}b_n}{\det A} = \frac{\displaystyle\sum_{k=1}^{n} A_{ki}b_k}{\Delta}$$

Le numérateur ressemble fort au développement selon la i-ième colonne du déterminant d'une matrice. Il s'agit en fait du développement (selon la i-ième colonne) du déterminant, noté Δ_{x_i}, de la matrice obtenue en remplaçant la i-ième colonne de A par la colonne des constantes. Ainsi,

$$x_i = \frac{\Delta_{x_i}}{\Delta}$$

∎

On donne souvent à un théorème important le nom d'un mathématicien qui a contribué à l'établir. Il ne faut pas en déduire pour autant que ce mathématicien ait présenté le résultat qu'il a obtenu sous la forme employée de nos jours. Il arrive même que ce mathématicien n'ait obtenu qu'un résultat partiel. Pour vous convaincre de la différence qui peut exister entre les formulations originale et moderne, lisez l'énoncé de la règle de Cramer contenu dans *Introduction à l'analyse des lignes courbes algébriques*[4], paru en 1750 :

Soient plusieurs inconnues *z*, *y*, *x*, *v*, &c., et autant d'équations

$$A^1 = Z^1z + Y^1y + X^1x + V^1v + \&c.$$
$$A^2 = Z^2z + Y^2y + X^2x + V^2v + \&c.$$
$$A^3 = Z^3z + Y^3y + X^3x + V^3v + \&c.$$
$$A^4 = Z^4z + Y^4y + X^4x + V^4v + \&c.$$
$$\&c.$$

où les lettres A^1, A^2, A^3, A^4, &c., ne marquent pas, comme à l'ordinaire, les puissances d'*A*, mais le premier membre, supposé connu, de la première, seconde, troisième, quatrième, &c. équation.

[...]

L'examen de ces Formules fournit cette Règle générale. Le nombre des équations et des inconnues étant *n*, on trouvera la valeur de chaque inconnue en formant *n* fractions dont le dénominateur commun a autant de termes qu'il y a de divers arrangements de *n* choses différentes. Chaque terme est composé des lettres *ZYXV*, &c., toujours écrites dans le même ordre, mais auxquelles on distribue, comme exposants, les *n* premiers chiffres rangés en toutes les manières possibles. Ainsi, lorsqu'on a trois inconnues, le dénominateur a 6 termes [soit $3 \times 2 \times 1$], composés des trois lettres *ZYX*, qui reçoivent successivement les exposants 123, 132, 213, 231, 312, 321. On donne à ces termes les signes + ou −, selon la Règle

---

4. G. Cramer, *in* T. Muir. *The Theory of Determinants in the Historical Order of Development*, New York, Dover Publications Inc., 1960, 2 vol., p. 12-13.

suivante. Quand un exposant est suivi dans le même terme, médiatement ou immédiatement, d'un exposant plus petit que lui, j'appellerai cela un *dérangement*. Qu'on compte, pour chaque terme, le nombre de dérangements : s'il est pair ou nul, le terme aura le signe + ; s'il est impair, le terme aura le signe −. Par ex. dans le terme $Z^1Y^2X^3$ il n'y a aucun dérangement ; ce terme aura donc le signe +. Le terme $Z^3Y^1X^2$ a aussi le signe +, parce qu'il a deux dérangements, 3 avant 1 et 3 avant 2. Mais le terme $Z^3Y^2X^1$, qui a trois dérangements, 3 avant 2, 3 avant 1, et 2 avant 1, aura le signe −.

Le dénominateur commun étant ainsi formé, on aura la valeur de *z* en donnant à ce dénominateur le numérateur qui se forme en changeant, dans tous ces termes, *Z* en *A*. Et la valeur d'*y* est la fraction qui a le même dénominateur et pour numérateur la quantité qui résulte quand on change *Y* en *A*, dans tous les termes du dénominateur. Et on trouve d'une manière semblable la valeur des autres inconnues.

4.2.4 Résolution d'un système d'équations linéaires avec paramètres

La règle de Cramer s'emploie pour résoudre un système d'équations avec paramètres, soit une famille de systèmes d'équations.

Exemple

PARAMÈTRE

Un paramètre désigne, par opposition au terme « inconnue », un coefficient en fonction duquel on cherche à exprimer les solutions d'un système d'équations. Il s'agit donc d'une constante symbolique qu'on pourra fixer librement.

On veut résoudre le système d'équations suivant où *k* est un **paramètre**, c'est-à-dire une quantité en fonction de laquelle on cherche à exprimer la solution du système d'équations.

$$kx + 2y = k$$
$$\tfrac{1}{2}x + ky = k - \tfrac{1}{2}$$

Il est clair que la solution de ce système d'équations dépend du paramètre *k*. Pour appliquer la règle de Cramer, il faut d'abord évaluer Δ, Δ_x et Δ_y :

$$\Delta = \begin{vmatrix} k & 2 \\ \tfrac{1}{2} & k \end{vmatrix} = k^2 - 1 = (k-1)(k+1)$$

$$\Delta_x = \begin{vmatrix} k & 2 \\ k - \tfrac{1}{2} & k \end{vmatrix} = k^2 - 2k + 1 = (k-1)^2$$

$$\Delta_y = \begin{vmatrix} k & k \\ \tfrac{1}{2} & k - \tfrac{1}{2} \end{vmatrix} = k^2 - k = k(k-1)$$

Pour résoudre le système, il faut analyser deux possibilités : ou bien le déterminant de la matrice des coefficients est non nul ou bien il est nul. Or, $\Delta = 0$ si $k = 1$ ou $k = -1$, et $\Delta \neq 0$ pour les autres valeurs de k. On divise donc la solution en trois parties.

Premier cas : $k \neq 1$ et $k \neq -1$

Si $k \neq 1$ et $k \neq -1$, alors $\Delta \neq 0$ et, en vertu de la règle de Cramer, le système admet une solution unique pour chaque valeur de k différente de 1 et de -1 :

$$x = \frac{\Delta_x}{\Delta} = \frac{(k-1)^2}{(k-1)(k+1)} = \frac{k-1}{k+1}$$

$$y = \frac{\Delta_y}{\Delta} = \frac{k(k-1)}{(k-1)(k+1)} = \frac{k}{k+1}$$

Ainsi, la solution du système d'équations est $x = \frac{1}{3}$ et $y = \frac{2}{3}$ pour $k = 2$, et $x = \frac{1}{2}$ et $y = \frac{3}{4}$ pour $k = 3$.

Deuxième cas : $k = 1$

Si $k = 1$, alors $\Delta = 0$, $\Delta_x = 0$ et $\Delta_y = 0$, et, en vertu de la règle de Cramer, le système d'équations admet une infinité de solutions.

Troisième cas : $k = -1$

Si $k = -1$, alors $\Delta = 0$, $\Delta_x = 4 \neq 0$ et $\Delta_y = 2 \neq 0$. Comme au moins un des $\Delta_{x_i} \neq 0$ (en fait les deux sont différents de zéro), en vertu de la règle de Cramer, le système d'équations n'admet aucune solution pour $k = -1$, c'est-à-dire qu'il est incompatible pour cette valeur de k.

EXERCICE 4.2

Résolvez le système d'équations suivant où k est un paramètre.

$$kx - ky = 1$$
$$x + ky = k$$

La méthode d'élimination gaussienne – nommée ainsi en l'honneur de C. F. Gauss – est une méthode de résolution d'un système d'équations linéaires plus efficace que celle de la matrice inverse et que la règle de Cramer.

n peu d'histoire

Gauss n'est pas le véritable inventeur de la méthode d'élimination gaussienne. Toutefois, c'est lui qui l'a fait connaître en Occident. Des mathématiciens chinois du IIIᵉ siècle avant notre ère appliquaient déjà une méthode d'élimination similaire à celle de Gauss. On retrouve la méthode chinoise dans un vieux traité de mathématiques intitulé *Neuf chapitres dans l'art des mathématiques*. Il faut cependant souligner que Gauss ne connaissait pas ce résultat des mathématiciens chinois et qu'il l'a en quelque sorte redécouvert.

4.3.1 OPÉRATIONS ÉLÉMENTAIRES DE LIGNE

Avant de présenter la méthode d'élimination gaussienne de manière formelle, nous en illustrons les principes à l'aide d'un exemple simple.

Exemple

Soit les deux systèmes d'équations

$$\begin{array}{rl} 2x + y - z = 1 \\ x + y + z = 6 \\ -x - y + z = 0 \end{array} \quad \text{et} \quad \begin{array}{rl} x + y + z = 6 \\ y + 3z = 11 \\ z = 3 \end{array}$$

On peut vérifier que l'ensemble solution de ces deux systèmes est identique : $S = \left\{ \begin{bmatrix} 1 & 2 & 3 \end{bmatrix}^{t} \right\}$. Or, il est évidemment beaucoup plus facile de résoudre le deuxième système que le premier. En effet, la valeur de z étant donnée par la troisième équation du deuxième système, on trouve la valeur de y en remplaçant z par sa valeur dans la deuxième équation :

$$y + 3z = 11 \Rightarrow y = 11 - 3z \Rightarrow y = 11 - 3(3) \Rightarrow y = 2$$

Les valeurs de y et de z étant connues, on trouve la valeur de x par substitution dans la première équation :

$$x + y + z = 6 \Rightarrow x = 6 - y - z \Rightarrow x = 6 - 2 - 3 \Rightarrow x = 1$$

La question qui se pose maintenant est de savoir comment passer du premier système d'équations au deuxième ou, de façon générale, comment passer d'un système d'équations complexe à un système d'équations facile à résoudre. Si on arrive à répondre à cette question – quel que soit le système d'équations linéaires – on aura établi une stratégie efficace pour résoudre un système d'équations linéaires.

Il est clair qu'on peut intervertir les première et deuxième lignes du premier système d'équations sans changer l'ensemble solution puisque celui-ci ne dépend nullement de l'ordre des équations. Ainsi,

$$\begin{array}{ll} 2x + y - z = 1 & x + y + z = 6 \\ x + y + z = 6 \quad \text{et} \quad 2x + y - z = 1 \\ -x - y + z = 0 & -x - y + z = 0 \end{array}$$

SYSTÈMES D'ÉQUATIONS ÉQUIVALENTS

Deux systèmes d'équations linéaires sont équivalents s'ils ont exactement le même ensemble solution.

sont des **systèmes d'équations équivalents**, car ils admettent le même ensemble solution. On note l'équivalence de deux systèmes d'équations à l'aide du symbole ~, placé entre les deux systèmes.

Si on additionne la première ligne du nouveau système à la troisième ligne, on ne change pas non plus l'ensemble solution, puisqu'on ajoute ainsi des quantités égales à chaque membre d'une équation : on ajoute $x + y + z$ au membre de gauche et la valeur de cette expression, soit 6, au membre de droite.

On a donc

$$\begin{array}{ll} x + y + z = 6 & x + y + z = 6 \\ 2x + y - z = 1 \quad \sim \quad 2x + y - z = 1 \\ -x - y + z = 0 & 2z = 6 \end{array}$$

En vertu du même argument, en additionnant −2 fois la première ligne à la deuxième ligne, on obtient l'équivalence

$$\begin{array}{ll} x + y + z = 6 & x + y + z = 6 \\ 2x + y - z = 1 \quad \sim \quad -y - 3z = -11 \\ 2z = 6 & 2z = 6 \end{array}$$

De même, la multiplication de la troisième ligne par $\frac{1}{2}$ et de la deuxième ligne par −1 ne change pas la solution du système d'équations parce que cette opération est effectuée simultanément sur chaque membre d'une équation. On a donc l'équivalence

$$\begin{array}{rl} x + y + z = 6 \\ -y - 3z = -11 \\ 2z = 6 \end{array} \quad \sim \quad \begin{array}{rl} x + y + z = 6 \\ y + 3z = 11 \\ z = 3 \end{array}$$

Ainsi, on a montré l'équivalence entre les deux systèmes donnés :

$$\begin{array}{rl} 2x + y - z = 1 \\ x + y + z = 6 \\ -x - y + z = 0 \end{array} \quad \sim \quad \begin{array}{rl} x + y + z = 6 \\ y + 3z = 11 \\ z = 3 \end{array}$$

L'exemple précédent illustre les opérations qu'il est possible de faire sur les lignes d'un système d'équations sans changer l'ensemble solution de celui-ci. Ces trois opérations, appelées **opérations élémentaires de ligne**, sont :

1) l'interversion de deux lignes,

2) la multiplication d'une ligne par une constante différente de zéro,

3) l'addition d'un multiple d'une ligne à une autre ligne.

Nous emploierons les notations suivantes pour désigner chacune de ces opérations :

1) $L_i \leftrightarrow L_j$ représente l'interversion des i-ième et j-ième lignes ;

2) $L_i \rightarrow kL_i$ représente la multiplication de la i-ième ligne par une constante k différente de zéro ;

3) $L_i \rightarrow L_i + kL_j$ représente l'addition de k fois la j-ième ligne à la i-ième ligne.

4.3.2 MATRICE AUGMENTÉE D'UN SYSTÈME D'ÉQUATIONS LINÉAIRES

Un système d'équations linéaires comportant m équations à n inconnues s'écrit sous la forme

$$\begin{array}{l} a_{11}x_1 + a_{12}x_2 + a_{13}x_3 + \cdots + a_{1n}x_n = b_1 \\ a_{21}x_1 + a_{22}x_2 + a_{23}x_3 + \cdots + a_{2n}x_n = b_2 \\ a_{31}x_1 + a_{32}x_2 + a_{33}x_3 + \cdots + a_{3n}x_n = b_3 \\ \quad\vdots \qquad\quad \vdots \qquad\quad \vdots \qquad\qquad \vdots \qquad \vdots \\ a_{m1}x_1 + a_{m2}x_2 + a_{m3}x_3 + \cdots + a_{mn}x_n = b_m \end{array}$$

L'analogie suivante fait ressortir le caractère redondant de cette représentation d'un système d'équations. On sait que dans l'écriture du nombre 111 les trois chiffres 1 n'ont pas la même signification : le premier 1, à droite, représente une unité, le second une dizaine, et le troisième une centaine. En général, la position d'un chiffre dans un nombre indique clairement par elle-même la valeur qu'il faut attribuer à ce chiffre. Il en est ainsi pour un système d'équations : on peut abréger l'écriture d'un système d'équations à l'aide du langage matriciel parce que les informations fournies par la position des éléments dans la matrice n'ont pas à être explicitées. Ainsi, on écrit en abrégé le système d'équations de m équations à n inconnues à l'aide de sa **matrice augmentée**, notée $\begin{bmatrix} A \mid B \end{bmatrix}$, c'est-à-dire la matrice des coefficients des inconnues à laquelle on ajoute la colonne des constantes :

MATRICE AUGMENTÉE

La matrice augmentée $\begin{bmatrix} A \mid B \end{bmatrix}$ d'un système d'équations linéaires ($AX = B$) est la matrice des coefficients (A) à laquelle on ajoute la matrice des constantes (B).

$$\begin{bmatrix} A \mid B \end{bmatrix} = \left[\begin{array}{ccccc|c} a_{11} & a_{12} & a_{13} & \cdots & a_{1n} & b_1 \\ a_{21} & a_{22} & a_{23} & \cdots & a_{2n} & b_2 \\ a_{31} & a_{32} & a_{33} & \cdots & a_{3n} & b_3 \\ \vdots & \vdots & \vdots & & \vdots & \vdots \\ a_{m1} & a_{m2} & a_{m3} & \cdots & a_{mn} & b_m \end{array} \right]$$

Il est clair que l'écriture du système d'équations linéaires sous cette forme abrégée n'entraîne aucune perte d'information.

Exemple

La matrice augmentée du système d'équations linéaires

$$\begin{array}{rcl} 2x + 3y + z + 4w &=& 5 \\ -x + 2y - 3z - 2w &=& 8 \\ 5x - 4y \phantom{{}- 3z} - 4w &=& 6 \end{array}$$

est

$$\left[\begin{array}{cccc|c} 2 & 3 & 1 & 4 & 5 \\ -1 & 2 & -3 & -2 & 8 \\ 5 & -4 & 0 & -4 & 6 \end{array} \right]$$

Il est à noter que l'absence d'une inconnue dans une équation s'exprime par un 0, à la position appropriée, dans la matrice augmentée, tout comme l'absence de dizaine dans le nombre 205 s'exprime par un 0 à la deuxième position du nombre.

EXERCICE 4.3

Soit la matrice augmentée

$$\left[\begin{array}{cc|c} 2 & -1 & 8 \\ 0 & -2 & -4 \\ 1 & 0 & 2 \end{array} \right]$$

Dites combien d'inconnues et d'équations comporte le système d'équations linéaires représenté par cette matrice augmentée, et écrivez ce système sous sa forme non abrégée.

4.3.3 MATRICES ÉQUIVALENTES

La matrice augmentée d'un système d'équations linéaires contient exactement la même information que celui-ci. De plus, on peut effectuer des opérations élémentaires sur les lignes de la matrice augmentée tout comme on le fait sur les équations d'un système d'équations. C'est pourquoi on dit de deux **matrices** qu'elles sont **équivalentes** si on peut obtenir l'une des matrices en effectuant des opérations élémentaires de ligne sur l'autre matrice.

La méthode d'**élimination gaussienne** consiste à résoudre un système d'équations linéaires en effectuant des opérations élémentaires de ligne sur la matrice augmentée du système de manière à la transformer en une matrice échelonnée équivalente. Le système d'équations représenté par cette dernière matrice est facile à résoudre en remplaçant, à rebours, les inconnues par leur valeur.

Avant d'aborder l'exemple qui suit, vous devriez relire les définitions de matrice échelonnée et de pivot énoncées au chapitre 1.

MATRICES ÉQUIVALENTES

Deux matrices sont équivalentes si on peut obtenir l'une des matrices en effectuant une série d'opérations élémentaires de ligne sur l'autre.

ÉLIMINATION GAUSSIENNE

La méthode d'élimination gaussienne, qui sert à résoudre un système d'équations linéaires, consiste à trouver une matrice échelonnée équivalente à la matrice augmentée du système, puis à effectuer, à rebours, une série de substitutions de manière à déterminer l'ensemble solution.

Exemple

Soit le système d'équations

$$3x + 2y + 4z = -1$$
$$2x - y + 2z = -2$$
$$-x + y + 2z = 2$$

La matrice augmentée de ce système est

$$\left[A \,|\, B \right] = \begin{bmatrix} 3 & 2 & 4 & -1 \\ 2 & -1 & 2 & -2 \\ -1 & 1 & 2 & 2 \end{bmatrix}$$

On se propose de trouver une matrice échelonnée équivalente à $\left[A \,|\, B \right]$:

$$\left[A \,|\, B \right] = \begin{bmatrix} 3 & 2 & 4 & -1 \\ 2 & -1 & 2 & -2 \\ -1 & 1 & 2 & 2 \end{bmatrix} \sim \begin{bmatrix} * & * & * & * \\ 0 & * & * & * \\ 0 & 0 & * & * \end{bmatrix}$$

Il existe plusieurs façons d'atteindre cet objectif. En voici une.

$$\begin{bmatrix} 3 & 2 & 4 & | & -1 \\ 2 & -1 & 2 & | & -2 \\ -1 & 1 & 2 & | & 2 \end{bmatrix} \sim \begin{bmatrix} -1 & 1 & 2 & | & 2 \\ 2 & -1 & 2 & | & -2 \\ 3 & 2 & 4 & | & -1 \end{bmatrix} \begin{matrix} L_3 \leftrightarrow L_1 \\ \\ \end{matrix}$$

$$\sim \begin{bmatrix} -1 & 1 & 2 & | & 2 \\ 0 & 1 & 6 & | & 2 \\ 0 & 5 & 10 & | & 5 \end{bmatrix} \begin{matrix} \\ L_2 \to L_2 + 2L_1 \\ L_3 \to L_3 + 3L_1 \end{matrix}$$

$$\sim \begin{bmatrix} 1 & -1 & -2 & | & -2 \\ 0 & 1 & 6 & | & 2 \\ 0 & 1 & 2 & | & 1 \end{bmatrix} \begin{matrix} L_1 \to -L_1 \\ \\ L_3 \to \frac{1}{5}L_3 \end{matrix}$$

$$\sim \begin{bmatrix} 1 & -1 & -2 & | & -2 \\ 0 & 1 & 6 & | & 2 \\ 0 & 0 & -4 & | & -1 \end{bmatrix} \begin{matrix} \\ \\ L_3 \to L_3 - L_2 \end{matrix}$$

$$\sim \begin{bmatrix} 1 & -1 & -2 & | & -2 \\ 0 & 1 & 6 & | & 2 \\ 0 & 0 & 1 & | & \frac{1}{4} \end{bmatrix} \begin{matrix} \\ \\ L_3 \to -\frac{1}{4}L_3 \end{matrix}$$

Une fois qu'on a obtenu une matrice échelonnée, il reste à réécrire chacune des lignes de la matrice augmentée sous la forme d'une équation, puis à résoudre le système d'équations résultant par substitution à rebours.

Ainsi, la dernière ligne de la matrice échelonnée indique que $z = \frac{1}{4}$, et la deuxième ligne indique que $y + 6z = 2$. Si on remplace z par sa valeur dans cette équation, on obtient

$$y + 6z = 2 \implies y = 2 - 6z \implies y = 2 - 6(\tfrac{1}{4}) \implies y = \tfrac{1}{2}$$

De façon analogue, la première ligne de la matrice augmentée échelonnée donne

$$x - y - 2z = -2 \implies x = y + 2z - 2 \implies x = \tfrac{1}{2} + 2(\tfrac{1}{4}) - 2 = -1$$

Les valeurs de x, y et z qui vérifient le système d'équations sont donc $x = -1$, $y = \frac{1}{2}$ et $z = \frac{1}{4}$.

L'algorithme servant à résoudre un système d'équations par élimination gaussienne est simple. Il comprend généralement les étapes suivantes[5]. On

---

5. Diverses situations peuvent se présenter ; par exemple on peut obtenir à l'une ou l'autre étape une colonne formée partiellement de zéros. Cependant, l'assimilation de l'algorithme général permet de résoudre de tels cas particuliers.

construit d'abord la matrice augmentée (où les * représentent des nombres quelconques) du système d'équations à résoudre.

$$\left[\begin{array}{ccccc|c} * & * & * & \cdots & * & * \\ * & * & * & \cdots & * & * \\ * & * & * & \cdots & * & * \\ \vdots & \vdots & \vdots & & \vdots & \vdots \\ * & * & * & \cdots & * & * \end{array}\right]$$

On remplace tous les éléments de la première colonne situés sous la première ligne par des zéros. Pour ce faire, on multiplie la première ligne par une constante telle que le pivot (le premier élément non nul d'une ligne) de cette ligne prenne la valeur 1 (ou on intervertit la première ligne avec une ligne dont le pivot est 1)[6]. On ajoute ensuite un multiple approprié de la première ligne à chacune des autres lignes de façon que tous les éléments de la première colonne situés sous la première ligne soient 0.

$$\left[\begin{array}{ccccc|c} * & * & * & \cdots & * & * \\ * & * & * & \cdots & * & * \\ * & * & * & \cdots & * & * \\ \vdots & \vdots & \vdots & & \vdots & \vdots \\ * & * & * & \cdots & * & * \end{array}\right] \sim \left[\begin{array}{ccccc|c} 1 & * & * & \cdots & * & * \\ 0 & * & * & \cdots & * & * \\ 0 & * & * & \cdots & * & * \\ \vdots & \vdots & \vdots & & \vdots & \vdots \\ 0 & * & * & \cdots & * & * \end{array}\right]$$

À partir de ce moment, on n'opère plus sur la première ligne ni à l'aide de la première ligne. On reprend la première étape avec la deuxième ligne. Ainsi, on multiplie la deuxième ligne par une constante telle que le pivot de cette ligne prenne la valeur 1 (ou on intervertit la deuxième ligne avec une ligne dont le pivot est 1)[7]. On ajoute ensuite un multiple approprié de la deuxième ligne à chacune des autres lignes de façon que tous les éléments de la deuxième colonne situés sous la deuxième ligne soient 0.

$$\left[\begin{array}{ccccc|c} * & * & * & \cdots & * & * \\ * & * & * & \cdots & * & * \\ * & * & * & \cdots & * & * \\ \vdots & \vdots & \vdots & & \vdots & \vdots \\ * & * & * & \cdots & * & * \end{array}\right] \sim \left[\begin{array}{ccccc|c} 1 & * & * & \cdots & * & * \\ 0 & * & * & \cdots & * & * \\ 0 & * & * & \cdots & * & * \\ \vdots & \vdots & \vdots & & \vdots & \vdots \\ 0 & * & * & \cdots & * & * \end{array}\right] \sim \left[\begin{array}{ccccc|c} 1 & * & * & \cdots & * & * \\ 0 & 1 & * & \cdots & * & * \\ 0 & 0 & * & \cdots & * & * \\ \vdots & \vdots & \vdots & & \vdots & \vdots \\ 0 & 0 & * & \cdots & * & * \end{array}\right]$$

À partir de ce moment, on n'opère plus sur la deuxième ligne ni à l'aide de la deuxième ligne. On reprend la première étape avec la troisième ligne, puis la quatrième et ainsi de suite jusqu'à ce qu'on obtienne une matrice augmentée échelonnée. On écrit ensuite, une à une, en commençant par

---

6. Lorsqu'on effectue des opérations élémentaires de ligne, on évite autant que possible d'introduire des fractions dans la matrice parce que cela augmente le risque d'erreur dans les étapes subséquentes. Malheureusement, il n'existe pas de règle qui s'applique à tous les cas. Seule l'expérience permet d'acquérir quelques trucs.
7. Songez à ce qu'il faut faire si tous les éléments de la deuxième colonne situés sous la première ligne valent 0.

la dernière, les équations représentées par les lignes de cette matrice. Le système formé de ces équations est facile à résoudre par substitution.

Bien qu'en théorie la méthode d'élimination gaussienne ait comme objectif l'obtention d'une matrice échelonnée, il n'est pas vraiment nécessaire que le pivot de chaque ligne soit égal à 1. On réduit le nombre d'opérations à effectuer si on laisse tomber cette exigence, comme le montre l'exemple suivant.

Exemple

On veut résoudre par élimination gaussienne le système d'équations.

$$
\begin{aligned}
2x - \ \ y + \ \ z + 2w &= -1 \\
x + \ \ y + 2z - \ \ w &= \ \ 2 \\
3y - 3z + \ \ w &= -2 \\
-x - \ \ y - 2z - 4w &= \tfrac{1}{2}
\end{aligned}
$$

En construisant la matrice augmentée de ce système d'équations et en effectuant des opérations élémentaires de ligne, on obtient

$$
\begin{bmatrix}
2 & -1 & 1 & 2 & -1 \\
1 & 1 & 2 & -1 & 2 \\
0 & 3 & -3 & 1 & -2 \\
-1 & -1 & -2 & -4 & \tfrac{1}{2}
\end{bmatrix}
\sim
\begin{bmatrix}
1 & 1 & 2 & -1 & 2 \\
2 & -1 & 1 & 2 & -1 \\
0 & 3 & -3 & 1 & -2 \\
-1 & -1 & -2 & -4 & \tfrac{1}{2}
\end{bmatrix}
\begin{matrix} \\ L_2 \leftrightarrow L_1 \\ \\ \\ \end{matrix}
$$

$$
\sim
\begin{bmatrix}
1 & 1 & 2 & -1 & 2 \\
0 & -3 & -3 & 4 & -5 \\
0 & 3 & -3 & 1 & -2 \\
0 & 0 & 0 & -5 & \tfrac{5}{2}
\end{bmatrix}
\begin{matrix} \\ L_2 \to L_2 - 2L_1 \\ \\ L_4 \to L_4 + L_1 \end{matrix}
$$

$$
\sim
\begin{bmatrix}
1 & 1 & 2 & -1 & 2 \\
0 & -3 & -3 & 4 & -5 \\
0 & 0 & -6 & 5 & -7 \\
0 & 0 & 0 & -5 & \tfrac{5}{2}
\end{bmatrix}
\begin{matrix} \\ \\ L_3 \to L_3 + L_2 \\ \\ \end{matrix}
$$

Il n'est pas vraiment nécessaire d'effectuer d'autres opérations élémentaires de ligne, de manière à aboutir à une matrice échelonnée. On peut procéder immédiatement à une substitution à rebours.

De la dernière ligne de la matrice, on tire

$$
-5w = \tfrac{5}{2} \quad \Rightarrow \quad w = -\tfrac{1}{2}
$$

De la troisième ligne, on tire

$$
-6z + 5w = -7 \quad \Rightarrow \quad z = \frac{-7 - 5w}{-6} = \frac{3}{4}
$$

De la deuxième ligne, on tire

$$-3y - 3z + 4w = -5 \quad \Rightarrow \quad y = \frac{-5 + 3z - 4w}{-3} = \frac{1}{4}$$

De la première ligne, on tire

$$x + y + 2z - w = 2 \quad \Rightarrow \quad x = 2 - y - 2z + w = -\tfrac{1}{4}$$

L'ensemble solution du système d'équations est donc

$$S = \left\{ \begin{bmatrix} -\tfrac{1}{4} & \tfrac{1}{4} & \tfrac{3}{4} & -\tfrac{1}{2} \end{bmatrix}^t \right\}$$

ou, si on préfère, $x = -\tfrac{1}{4}$, $y = \tfrac{1}{4}$, $z = \tfrac{3}{4}$ et $w = -\tfrac{1}{2}$.

Si on vous demande de résoudre un système d'équations par élimination gaussienne, il n'est donc pas nécessaire que vous calculiez une matrice échelonnée équivalente à la matrice augmentée. Il suffit que vous trouviez une matrice équivalente qui permette la substitution à rebours.

EXERCICE 4.4

Résolvez chaque système d'équations par la méthode d'élimination gaussienne.

a) $2x - y = 6$
$\quad x + 3y = 2$

b) $3x + y - z = -1$
$\quad x + 2y + 2z = 5$
$\quad -x + 3y + z = 3$

c) $3x_1 + 4x_2 + x_3 = 5$
$\quad 2x_1 + x_2 - 3x_3 = -6$
$\quad 5x_1 - 3x_2 - 4x_3 = 1$

4.3.4 SYSTÈME D'ÉQUATIONS INCOMPATIBLE OU ADMETTANT UNE INFINITÉ DE SOLUTIONS

Contrairement à la règle de Cramer, la méthode d'élimination gaussienne s'applique même aux systèmes dont le nombre d'équations est différent du nombre d'inconnues. De plus, cette méthode permet de déterminer l'ensemble solution d'un système d'équations qui admet une infinité de solutions.

1. La règle de Cramer ne permet pas de résoudre le système d'équations

$$\begin{aligned} -x + 2y &= 5 \\ 2x + 3y &= 4 \\ 3x + y &= -1 \end{aligned}$$

Cependant, à l'aide de la méthode d'élimination gaussienne, on obtient

$$\begin{bmatrix} -1 & 2 & \Big| & 5 \\ 2 & 3 & \Big| & 4 \\ 3 & 1 & \Big| & -1 \end{bmatrix} \sim \begin{bmatrix} -1 & 2 & \Big| & 5 \\ 0 & 7 & \Big| & 14 \\ 0 & 7 & \Big| & 14 \end{bmatrix} \begin{matrix} \\ L_2 \to L_2 + 2L_1 \\ L_3 \to L_3 + 3L_1 \end{matrix}$$

$$\sim \begin{bmatrix} -1 & 2 & \Big| & 5 \\ 0 & 7 & \Big| & 14 \\ 0 & 0 & \Big| & 0 \end{bmatrix} \begin{matrix} \\ \\ L_3 \to L_3 - L_2 \end{matrix}$$

On tire de la deuxième ligne de la dernière matrice $7y = 14$, soit $y = 2$, et, de la première ligne, on tire $-x + 2y = 5$, d'où $x = -1$. Par conséquent, la solution du système est $x = -1$ et $y = 2$.

2. Soit le système d'équations

$$\begin{aligned} x + y + z + w &= 4 \\ x + 2y + 2z - w &= 4 \\ 3x + 5y + 5z - w &= 12 \\ 2x + 3y + 3z &= 8 \end{aligned}$$

En construisant la matrice augmentée de ce système et en effectuant des opérations élémentaires de ligne, on obtient

$$\begin{bmatrix} 1 & 1 & 1 & 1 & \Big| & 4 \\ 1 & 2 & 2 & -1 & \Big| & 4 \\ 3 & 5 & 5 & -1 & \Big| & 12 \\ 2 & 3 & 3 & 0 & \Big| & 8 \end{bmatrix} \sim \begin{bmatrix} 1 & 1 & 1 & 1 & \Big| & 4 \\ 0 & 1 & 1 & -2 & \Big| & 0 \\ 0 & 2 & 2 & -4 & \Big| & 0 \\ 0 & 1 & 1 & -2 & \Big| & 0 \end{bmatrix} \begin{matrix} \\ L_2 \to L_2 - L_1 \\ L_3 \to L_3 - 3L_1 \\ L_4 \to L_4 - 2L_1 \end{matrix}$$

$$\sim \begin{bmatrix} 1 & 1 & 1 & 1 & \Big| & 4 \\ 0 & 1 & 1 & -2 & \Big| & 0 \\ 0 & 0 & 0 & 0 & \Big| & 0 \\ 0 & 0 & 0 & 0 & \Big| & 0 \end{bmatrix} \begin{matrix} \\ \\ L_3 \to L_3 - 2L_2 \\ L_4 \to L_4 - L_2 \end{matrix}$$

Le système d'équations représenté par la matrice augmentée échelonnée compte deux équations et quatre inconnues. On fixe arbitrairement la valeur de deux des inconnues, en fonction desquelles on calcule ensuite la valeur des deux autres inconnues. On choisit généralement comme inconnues libres les inconnues associées aux colonnes sans pivot. Dans le cas présent, il s'agit des troisième et quatrième colonnes. On pose donc $z = r$ et $w = k$, où r et k sont des constantes arbitraires. On tire alors de la deuxième ligne

$$y + z - 2w = 0 \quad \Rightarrow \quad y = -z + 2w = -r + 2k$$

puis, de la première ligne,

$$x + y + z + w = 4$$

Par conséquent,

$$x = 4 - y - z - w = 4 - (-r + 2k) - r - k = 4 - 3k$$

L'ensemble solution du système est

$$S = \left\{ \begin{bmatrix} 4 - 3k & -r + 2k & r & k \end{bmatrix}^t \mid r \text{ et } k \in \mathbb{R} \right\}$$

Le système admet donc une infinité de solutions et, en attribuant des valeurs à r et à k, on obtient une solution particulière. Ainsi, en posant $r = 1$ et $k = 2$, on obtient la solution $\begin{bmatrix} -2 & 3 & 1 & 2 \end{bmatrix}^t$ ou encore $x = -2$, $y = 3$, $z = 1$ et $w = 2$.

On a choisi de paramétrer les inconnues z et w, mais on aurait pu également paramétrer les inconnues y et z. On aurait alors obtenu un ensemble solution équivalent, soit

$$S' = \left\{ \begin{bmatrix} 4 - \dfrac{3s + 3t}{2} & s & t & \dfrac{s + t}{2} \end{bmatrix}^t \;\middle|\; s \text{ et } t \in \mathbb{R} \right\}.$$

On vérifie facilement l'équivalence des ensembles solutions S et S' en posant $r = t$ et $k = \dfrac{s + t}{2}$. On a alors

$$s = -r + 2k \quad \text{et} \quad 4 - \frac{3s + 3t}{2} = 4 - 3k$$

3. Soit le système d'équations

$$\begin{array}{rcr}
x + z &=& 2 \\
2x + y + z &=& 1 \\
x + y &=& 0
\end{array}$$

En construisant la matrice augmentée de ce système et en effectuant des opérations élémentaires de ligne, on obtient

$$\begin{bmatrix} 1 & 0 & 1 & 2 \\ 2 & 1 & 1 & 1 \\ 1 & 1 & 0 & 0 \end{bmatrix} \sim \begin{bmatrix} 1 & 0 & 1 & 2 \\ 0 & 1 & -1 & -3 \\ 0 & 1 & -1 & -2 \end{bmatrix} \begin{array}{l} \\ L_2 \to L_2 - 2L_1 \\ L_3 \to L_3 - L_1 \end{array}$$

$$\sim \begin{bmatrix} 1 & 0 & 1 & 2 \\ 0 & 1 & -1 & -3 \\ 0 & 0 & 0 & 1 \end{bmatrix} \begin{array}{l} \\ \\ L_3 \to L_3 - L_2 \end{array}$$

Si on exprime la dernière ligne de la matrice échelonnée sous forme d'équation, on obtient $0x + 0y + 0z = 1$, ce qui est évidemment impossible. Par conséquent, le système d'équations n'admet aucune solution.

EXERCICE 4.5

Résolvez chaque système d'équations par la méthode d'élimination gaussienne.

a)
$$\begin{aligned}
x_1 + x_2 + x_3 &= 3 \\
x_1 - x_2 + x_3 &= 1 \\
x_1 - 3x_2 + x_3 &= -1
\end{aligned}$$

b)
$$\begin{aligned}
3x + 2y - 2z &= 5 \\
2x - y - 3z &= -2 \\
-x + 4y + 4z &= 1
\end{aligned}$$

c)
$$\begin{aligned}
a + 2b - c &= 5 \\
-2a - 4b + 2c &= -10
\end{aligned}$$

Nous avons établi que le système d'équations de l'exemple 2 (p. 137) admet une infinité de solutions. Nous avons paramétré la solution générale en posant $z = r$ et $w = k$. Ce faisant, nous avons considéré les **inconnues** z et w comme **libres**. Les autres **inconnues** du système, soit x et y, sont alors **liées** aux inconnues libres: on les exprime en fonction des inconnues libres.

Le nombre d'inconnues libres dans un système d'équations qui admet une infinité de solutions correspond au nombre d'inconnues de ce système, moins le nombre de lignes non nulles de la matrice augmentée échelonnée ou, ce qui est équivalent, au nombre de colonnes sans pivot de la matrice des coefficients échelonnée. Le choix des inconnues libres n'est pas totalement arbitraire. Ainsi, dans l'exemple 2 (p. 137), on aurait pu faire un autre choix que w et z pour les inconnues libres, mais, afin de ne pas commettre d'erreur, il est préférable de choisir comme inconnues liées les inconnues associées au pivot de chaque ligne non nulle de la matrice échelonnée équivalente à la matrice augmentée du système.

INCONNUES LIBRES

Lorsqu'un système d'équations linéaires admet plus d'une solution, les inconnues paramétrées sont appelées inconnues libres.

INCONNUES LIÉES

Lorsqu'un système d'équations linéaires admet plus d'une solution, les inconnues exprimées en fonction des inconnues libres sont appelées inconnues liées.

Exemple

On veut résoudre le système d'équations

$$\begin{aligned}
x + y + z + w &= 4 \\
2x + 2y + 3z + 4w &= 11 \\
2x + 2y + 2z + 2w &= 8 \\
z + 2w &= 3
\end{aligned}$$

En construisant la matrice augmentée de ce système d'équations et en effectuant des opérations élémentaires de ligne, on obtient

$$\begin{bmatrix} 1 & 1 & 1 & 1 & | & 4 \\ 2 & 2 & 3 & 4 & | & 11 \\ 2 & 2 & 2 & 2 & | & 8 \\ 0 & 0 & 1 & 2 & | & 3 \end{bmatrix} \sim \begin{bmatrix} 1 & 1 & 1 & 1 & | & 4 \\ 0 & 0 & 1 & 2 & | & 3 \\ 0 & 0 & 0 & 0 & | & 0 \\ 0 & 0 & 1 & 2 & | & 3 \end{bmatrix} \begin{matrix} \\ L_2 \rightarrow L_2 - 2L_1 \\ L_3 \rightarrow L_3 - 2L_1 \\ \end{matrix}$$

$$\sim \begin{bmatrix} 1 & 1 & 1 & 1 & | & 4 \\ 0 & 0 & 1 & 2 & | & 3 \\ 0 & 0 & 0 & 0 & | & 0 \\ 0 & 0 & 0 & 0 & | & 0 \end{bmatrix} \begin{matrix} \\ \\ \\ L_4 \rightarrow L_4 - L_2 \end{matrix}$$

Le système d'équations représenté par la matrice augmentée éche-lonnée compte deux équations mais quatre inconnues. La solution de ce système comporte donc deux inconnues libres et deux incon-nues liées. Comme les pivots sont situés dans les première et troisième colonnes, on choisit les inconnues x et z comme incon-nues liées et on exprime celles-ci en fonction des inconnues libres y et w. Ainsi, on pose $w = k$ et $y = r$, et on tire de la deuxième ligne

$$z + 2w = 3 \quad \Rightarrow \quad z = 3 - 2w = 3 - 2k$$

puis on tire de la première ligne

$$x + y + z + w = 4$$

Par conséquent,

$$x = 4 - y - z - w = 4 - r - (3 - 2k) - k = 1 - r + k$$

L'ensemble solution du système est donc

$$S = \left\{ \begin{bmatrix} 1 - r + k & r & 3 - 2k & k \end{bmatrix}^t \mid r \text{ et } k \in \mathbb{R} \right\}$$

ou, si on préfère, $x = 1 - r + k$, $y = r$, $z = 3 - 2k$ et $w = k$.

4.3.5 Caractérisation des systèmes d'équations linéaires

La règle de Cramer énonce des critères qui permettent de distinguer entre un système d'équations qui admet une solution unique ($\Delta \neq 0$), un système d'équations qui admet une infinité de solutions ($\Delta = 0$ et $\Delta_{x_i} = 0$ pour tous les i) et un système d'équations qui n'admet aucune solution ($\Delta = 0$ et $\Delta_{x_i} \neq 0$ pour au moins un i). Il existe aussi des critères pour faire ces mêmes distinctions lorsqu'on résout un système d'équations à l'aide de la méthode d'élimination gaussienne. Mais pour les énoncer, il faut d'abord définir un nouveau concept, à savoir le rang d'une matrice.

Le **rang**[8] d'une matrice A est le nombre de lignes non nulles (ou le nombre de pivots) d'une matrice échelonnée équivalente à A.

RANG

Le rang d'une matrice A est égal au nombre de lignes non nulles (ou au nombre de pivots) d'une matrice échelonnée équivalente à A.

8. On peut également définir le rang d'une matrice comme l'ordre de la plus grande sous-matrice de A (une matrice formée en supprimant des lignes ou des colonnes de A) dont le déterminant est non nul.

Exemple

Pour évaluer le rang de la matrice A donnée, on effectue des opérations élémentaires de ligne de manière à réduire A à une matrice échelonnée.

$$A = \begin{bmatrix} 1 & 2 & 3 \\ 2 & 1 & 1 \\ 1 & -1 & -2 \end{bmatrix} \sim \begin{bmatrix} 1 & 2 & 3 \\ 0 & -3 & -5 \\ 0 & -3 & -5 \end{bmatrix} \begin{matrix} \\ L_2 \to L_2 - 2L_1 \\ L_3 \to L_3 - L_1 \end{matrix}$$

$$\sim \begin{bmatrix} 1 & 2 & 3 \\ 0 & -3 & -5 \\ 0 & 0 & 0 \end{bmatrix} \begin{matrix} \\ \\ L_3 \to L_3 - L_2 \end{matrix}$$

$$\sim \begin{bmatrix} 1 & 2 & 3 \\ 0 & 1 & {}^5\!/_3 \\ 0 & 0 & 0 \end{bmatrix} \begin{matrix} \\ L_2 \to (-{}^1\!/_3)L_2 \\ \\ \end{matrix}$$

Comme la matrice échelonnée équivalente à la matrice A compte deux lignes non nulles (ou deux pivots), le rang de A est 2.

EXERCICE 4.6

Déterminez le rang de chacune des matrices

$$A = \begin{bmatrix} 1 & 2 & 3 \\ 2 & 4 & 6 \\ 3 & 6 & 9 \end{bmatrix} \qquad B = \begin{bmatrix} -1 & 8 & 2 & 9 \\ 0 & 2 & 1 & 8 \\ 0 & 4 & 2 & 16 \\ 0 & 0 & 0 & 5 \end{bmatrix}$$

$$C = \begin{bmatrix} 1 & 2 & 5 & 0 & 3 \\ 0 & 2 & 2 & 4 & 6 \\ 0 & 0 & -1 & 2 & 1 \\ 0 & 0 & 3 & -5 & 0 \\ 0 & 0 & 0 & 0 & 1 \end{bmatrix} \qquad D = \begin{bmatrix} 1 & 2 & 3 & 1 \\ 1 & 1 & 2 & 4 \end{bmatrix}$$

Le concept de rang permet d'énoncer le théorème suivant, dont nous ne donnerons pas la preuve.

Théorème 4.2

Si $AX = B$ est un système d'équations linéaires (m équations à n inconnues) dont la matrice des coefficients A est une matrice de format

$m \times n$, de rang p, et si $\begin{bmatrix} A \mid B \end{bmatrix}$, la matrice augmentée du système, est de rang q, alors ce système :

- n'admet aucune solution lorsque $p < q$;
- admet une infinité de solutions lorsque $p = q$ et $p < n$;
- admet une solution unique lorsque $p = q = n$.

De plus, lorsque le système admet une infinité de solutions, la solution générale comporte $n - q$ inconnues libres.

Exemple

1. Soit le système d'équations linéaires

$$
\begin{aligned}
x + y + z &= 4 \\
2x + 3y + 2z &= 10 \\
3x + 4y + 3z &= 14
\end{aligned}
$$

En construisant la matrice augmentée de ce système et en effectuant des opérations élémentaires de ligne, on obtient

$$
\begin{bmatrix} 1 & 1 & 1 & 4 \\ 2 & 3 & 2 & 10 \\ 3 & 4 & 3 & 14 \end{bmatrix} \sim \begin{bmatrix} 1 & 1 & 1 & 4 \\ 0 & 1 & 0 & 2 \\ 0 & 1 & 0 & 2 \end{bmatrix} \begin{matrix} \\ L_2 \to L_2 - 2L_1 \\ L_3 \to L_3 - 3L_1 \end{matrix}
$$

$$
\sim \begin{bmatrix} 1 & 1 & 1 & 4 \\ 0 & 1 & 0 & 2 \\ 0 & 0 & 0 & 0 \end{bmatrix} \begin{matrix} \\ \\ L_3 \to L_3 - L_2 \end{matrix}
$$

Le rang de la matrice augmentée échelonnée est égal au rang de la matrice des coefficients : $p = q = 2$. De plus, puisque le système d'équations compte trois inconnues ($n = 3$), alors $p = 2 < 3 = n$. En vertu du théorème 4.2, le système d'équations admet une infinité de solutions et il possède une seule inconnue libre ($n - q = 1$). L'ensemble solution du système est

$$
S = \left\{ \begin{bmatrix} 2 - k & 2 & k \end{bmatrix}^t \mid k \in \mathbb{R} \right\}
$$

2. Soit le système d'équations linéaires

$$
\begin{aligned}
x + y + z &= 4 \\
2x + 3y + 2z &= 10 \\
3x + 4y + 3z &= 12
\end{aligned}
$$

En construisant la matrice augmentée de ce système et en effectuant des opérations élémentaires de ligne, on obtient

$$
\begin{bmatrix} 1 & 1 & 1 & | & 4 \\ 2 & 3 & 2 & | & 10 \\ 3 & 4 & 3 & | & 12 \end{bmatrix} \sim \begin{bmatrix} 1 & 1 & 1 & | & 4 \\ 0 & 1 & 0 & | & 2 \\ 0 & 1 & 0 & | & 0 \end{bmatrix} \begin{matrix} \\ L_2 \to L_2 - 2L_1 \\ L_3 \to L_3 - 3L_1 \end{matrix}
$$

$$
\sim \begin{bmatrix} 1 & 1 & 1 & | & 4 \\ 0 & 1 & 0 & | & 2 \\ 0 & 0 & 0 & | & -2 \end{bmatrix} \begin{matrix} \\ \\ L_3 \to L_3 - L_2 \end{matrix}
$$

$$
\sim \begin{bmatrix} 1 & 1 & 1 & | & 4 \\ 0 & 1 & 0 & | & 2 \\ 0 & 0 & 0 & | & 1 \end{bmatrix} \begin{matrix} \\ \\ L_3 \to -\tfrac{1}{2}L_3 \end{matrix}
$$

Le rang de la matrice augmentée échelonnée est $q = 3$, alors que le rang de la matrice des coefficients est $p = 2$. En vertu du théorème 4.2, le système d'équations n'admet aucune solution puisque $p = 2 < 3 = q$.

EXERCICE 4.7

Pour chacune des matrices augmentées échelonnées suivantes, indiquez si le système d'équations qu'elle représente admet une seule solution ou une infinité de solutions, ou encore s'il n'admet aucune solution. Si le système admet une infinité de solutions, précisez le nombre d'inconnues libres.

a) $\begin{bmatrix} 1 & 2 & | & 3 \\ 0 & 1 & | & 0 \end{bmatrix}$

b) $\begin{bmatrix} 1 & -2 & 3 & | & 4 \\ 0 & 0 & 0 & | & 1 \\ 0 & 0 & 0 & | & 0 \end{bmatrix}$

c) $\begin{bmatrix} 1 & -2 & -3 & 2 & 4 & | & -3 \\ 0 & 0 & 1 & 2 & 3 & | & 6 \\ 0 & 0 & 0 & 0 & 0 & | & 0 \\ 0 & 0 & 0 & 0 & 0 & | & 0 \\ 0 & 0 & 0 & 0 & 0 & | & 0 \end{bmatrix}$

MÉTHODE DE GAUSS-JORDAN

La méthode de Gauss-Jordan, qui sert à résoudre un système d'équations linéaires, est une extension de la méthode d'élimination gaussienne et elle consiste à calculer une matrice échelonnée réduite équivalente à la matrice augmentée du système. La méthode de Gauss-Jordan sert également à trouver l'inverse d'une matrice régulière.

La **méthode de Gauss-Jordan** est une extension de la méthode d'élimination gaussienne. Elle consiste à effectuer des opérations élémentaires de ligne de manière à transformer la matrice augmentée du système d'équations à résoudre en une matrice échelonnée réduite[9]. Toutefois, vous constaterez vous-même que la méthode de Gauss-Jordan est moins efficace que la méthode d'élimination gaussienne :

> [...] un ordinateur met environ 50 % plus de temps à résoudre un grand système d'équations par la méthode de Gauss-Jordan qu'il n'en met pour résoudre le même système par la méthode d'élimination de Gauss (substitution à rebours). En effet, le nombre d'opérations arithmétiques à effectuer est d'environ 50 % plus élevé dans le premier cas[10].

Wilhelm Jordan (1842-1899) était un professeur allemand de géodésie et un auteur prolifique. Dans *Handbuch der Vermessungskunde* (Manuel de géodésie), il décrit une méthode de résolution d'un système d'équations linéaires qui s'apparente à l'élimination gaussienne et qui portera par la suite le nom de méthode de Gauss-Jordan. Ce manuel a été très populaire ; il a connu cinq éditions et il a été traduit en italien, en russe et en français. On a dit de Jordan qu'il était un professeur très apprécié de ses élèves parce qu'il savait faire les liens entre la théorie et la pratique.

4.4.1 RÉSOLUTION D'UN SYSTÈME D'ÉQUATIONS LINÉAIRES PAR LA MÉTHODE DE GAUSS-JORDAN

L'exemple suivant illustre l'application de la méthode de Gauss-Jordan à la résolution d'un système d'équations linéaires.

---

9. Vous auriez avantage à revoir la définition de matrice échelonnée réduite (chap. 1).
10. Traduction d'un extrait de J. B. Fraleigh et R. A. Beauregard. *Linear Algebra*, Reading, Addison-Wesley Publishing Company, 3e éd., 1995, p. 62.

Soit le système d'équations

$$3x + 2y + 4z = -1$$
$$2x - y + 2z = -2$$
$$-x + y + 2z = 2$$

En construisant la matrice augmentée de ce système et en effectuant des opérations élémentaires de ligne, on obtient

$$\begin{bmatrix} A & | & B \end{bmatrix} = \begin{bmatrix} 3 & 2 & 4 & -1 \\ 2 & -1 & 2 & -2 \\ -1 & 1 & 2 & 2 \end{bmatrix}$$

On veut trouver une matrice échelonnée réduite équivalente à cette matrice augmentée.

$$\begin{bmatrix} 3 & 2 & 4 & -1 \\ 2 & -1 & 2 & -2 \\ -1 & 1 & 2 & 2 \end{bmatrix} \sim \begin{bmatrix} -1 & 1 & 2 & 2 \\ 2 & -1 & 2 & -2 \\ 3 & 2 & 4 & -1 \end{bmatrix} \begin{matrix} L_3 \leftrightarrow L_1 \\ \\ \end{matrix}$$

$$\sim \begin{bmatrix} -1 & 1 & 2 & 2 \\ 0 & 1 & 6 & 2 \\ 0 & 5 & 10 & 5 \end{bmatrix} \begin{matrix} \\ L_2 \rightarrow L_2 + 2L_1 \\ L_3 \rightarrow L_3 + 3L_1 \end{matrix}$$

$$\sim \begin{bmatrix} 1 & -1 & -2 & -2 \\ 0 & 1 & 6 & 2 \\ 0 & 1 & 2 & 1 \end{bmatrix} \begin{matrix} L_1 \rightarrow -L_1 \\ \\ L_3 \rightarrow \frac{1}{5}L_3 \end{matrix}$$

$$\sim \begin{bmatrix} 1 & -1 & -2 & -2 \\ 0 & 1 & 6 & 2 \\ 0 & 0 & -4 & -1 \end{bmatrix} \begin{matrix} \\ \\ L_3 \rightarrow L_3 - L_2 \end{matrix}$$

$$\sim \begin{bmatrix} 1 & -1 & -2 & -2 \\ 0 & 1 & 6 & 2 \\ 0 & 0 & 1 & \frac{1}{4} \end{bmatrix} \begin{matrix} \\ \\ L_3 \rightarrow -\frac{1}{4}L_3 \end{matrix}$$

$$\sim \begin{bmatrix} 1 & -1 & 0 & -\frac{3}{2} \\ 0 & 1 & 0 & \frac{1}{2} \\ 0 & 0 & 1 & \frac{1}{4} \end{bmatrix} \begin{matrix} L_1 \rightarrow L_1 + 2L_3 \\ L_2 \rightarrow L_2 - 6L_3 \\ \\ \end{matrix}$$

$$\sim \begin{bmatrix} 1 & 0 & 0 & -1 \\ 0 & 1 & 0 & \frac{1}{2} \\ 0 & 0 & 1 & \frac{1}{4} \end{bmatrix} \begin{matrix} L_1 \rightarrow L_1 + L_2 \\ \\ \end{matrix}$$

On tire directement de la dernière matrice, qui est échelonnée réduite, la solution du système d'équations, à savoir $x = -1$, $y = \frac{1}{2}$ et $z = \frac{1}{4}$.

Résolvez chaque système d'équations à l'aide de la méthode de Gauss-Jordan.

a) $2x - 3y = 5$
$4x + 3y = 1$

b) $a - 3b \quad\quad = -5$
$3a - b + 2c = 7$
$5a - 2b + 4c = 10$

4.4.2 DÉTERMINATION DE L'INVERSE D'UNE MATRICE PAR LA MÉTHODE DE GAUSS-JORDAN

La méthode de Gauss-Jordan sert également à trouver l'inverse d'une matrice carrée A d'ordre n. Dans ce cas, on augmente la matrice A de la matrice identité d'ordre n et on effectue des opérations élémentaires de ligne pour passer de $\left[A \mid I_n\right]$ à $\left[I_n \mid C\right]$. Si cette transformation est possible, on obtient une matrice C qui est l'inverse de la matrice A. Cet algorithme de calcul de l'inverse d'une matrice est beaucoup plus efficace que l'application de la formule $A^{-1} = \dfrac{1}{\det A} \text{adj } A$.

Voici la justification de la méthode de Gauss-Jordan. On note les colonnes de la matrice inverse X_1, X_2, $\cdots$, X_n, et on note B_i la matrice colonne formée de zéros à l'exception de l'élément de la i-ième ligne, qui est 1. Si on juxtapose les matrices B_i en allant de $i = 1$ à $i = n$, on obtient la matrice identité. Par conséquent, $AA^{-1} = I_n \Rightarrow AX_i = B_i$. Il s'agit donc de résoudre simultanément n systèmes d'équations ayant tous la même matrice des coefficients. On peut appliquer la méthode de Gauss-Jordan à la matrice A augmentée de toutes les matrices B_i, c'est-à-dire à la matrice A augmentée de la matrice identité. Dans le résultat final, la partie de droite de la matrice augmentée est la solution de tous ces systèmes d'équations ; elle représente donc la matrice C telle que $AC = I_n$, soit la matrice inverse de A.

Exemple

On veut trouver l'inverse de la matrice

$$A = \begin{bmatrix} 3 & 2 & 4 \\ 2 & -1 & 2 \\ -1 & 1 & 2 \end{bmatrix}$$

On applique la méthode de Gauss-Jordan à la matrice A augmentée de la matrice identité.

$$\left[\begin{array}{ccc|ccc} 3 & 2 & 4 & 1 & 0 & 0 \\ 2 & -1 & 2 & 0 & 1 & 0 \\ -1 & 1 & 2 & 0 & 0 & 1 \end{array}\right] \sim \left[\begin{array}{ccc|ccc} -1 & 1 & 2 & 0 & 0 & 1 \\ 2 & -1 & 2 & 0 & 1 & 0 \\ 3 & 2 & 4 & 1 & 0 & 0 \end{array}\right] \begin{array}{l} L_1 \leftrightarrow L_3 \end{array}$$

$$\sim \left[\begin{array}{ccc|ccc} -1 & 1 & 2 & 0 & 0 & 1 \\ 0 & 1 & 6 & 0 & 1 & 2 \\ 0 & 5 & 10 & 1 & 0 & 3 \end{array}\right] \begin{array}{l} L_2 \to L_2 + 2L_1 \\ L_3 \to L_3 + 3L_1 \end{array}$$

$$\sim \left[\begin{array}{ccc|ccc} -1 & 1 & 2 & 0 & 0 & 1 \\ 0 & 1 & 6 & 0 & 1 & 2 \\ 0 & 0 & -20 & 1 & -5 & -7 \end{array}\right] \begin{array}{l} L_3 \to L_3 - 5L_2 \end{array}$$

$$\sim \left[\begin{array}{ccc|ccc} -1 & 1 & 2 & 0 & 0 & 1 \\ 0 & 1 & 6 & 0 & 1 & 2 \\ 0 & 0 & 1 & -0,05 & 0,25 & 0,35 \end{array}\right] \begin{array}{l} L_3 \to (-0,05)L_3 \end{array}$$

$$\sim \left[\begin{array}{ccc|ccc} -1 & 1 & 0 & 0,1 & -0,5 & 0,3 \\ 0 & 1 & 0 & 0,3 & -0,5 & -0,1 \\ 0 & 0 & 1 & -0,05 & 0,25 & 0,35 \end{array}\right] \begin{array}{l} L_1 \to L_1 - 2L_3 \\ L_2 \to L_2 - 6L_3 \end{array}$$

$$\sim \left[\begin{array}{ccc|ccc} -1 & 0 & 0 & -0,2 & 0 & 0,4 \\ 0 & 1 & 0 & 0,3 & -0,5 & -0,1 \\ 0 & 0 & 1 & -0,05 & 0,25 & 0,35 \end{array}\right] \begin{array}{l} L_1 \to L_1 - L_2 \end{array}$$

$$\sim \left[\begin{array}{ccc|ccc} 1 & 0 & 0 & 0,2 & 0 & -0,4 \\ 0 & 1 & 0 & 0,3 & -0,5 & -0,1 \\ 0 & 0 & 1 & -0,05 & 0,25 & 0,35 \end{array}\right] \begin{array}{l} L_1 \to -L_1 \end{array}$$

$$\sim \left[\begin{array}{c|c} I_3 & A^{-1} \end{array}\right]$$

Par conséquent,

$$A^{-1} = \begin{bmatrix} 0,2 & 0 & -0,4 \\ 0,3 & -0,5 & -0,1 \\ -0,05 & 0,25 & 0,35 \end{bmatrix}$$

EXERCICE 4.9

Trouvez l'inverse de la matrice $\begin{bmatrix} -1 & 2 \\ -3 & 1 \end{bmatrix}$ à l'aide de la méthode de Gauss-Jordan.

Nous avons vu dans les sections précédentes comment résoudre un système d'équations, mais ce n'est là qu'une des étapes de la résolution d'un problème concret comme celui-ci.

> Vous travaillez chez un marchand de café. Un client vous demande 5 kg de café sans préciser la composition du mélange. Vous disposez de trois sortes de grains dont les prix sont respectivement de 6 $, 8 $ et 10 $ le kilogramme. Le client vous a également dit qu'il veut payer exactement 40 $. Comment pouvez-vous le satisfaire ?

Pour résoudre les problèmes de ce genre, nous vous suggérons d'adopter la marche à suivre que voici :

1) Faire une première lecture du problème pour en avoir une idée d'ensemble.

2) Relire le problème pour en dégager les éléments clés : la question posée, les inconnues, les relations entre les différentes inconnues, les contraintes, etc.

3) Attribuer un symbole à chaque quantité inconnue :
$x = $ ....
$y = $ ....
$z = $ ....
etc.

4) Écrire sous forme d'équations les liens entre les inconnues.

5) Résoudre le système d'équations.

6) Répondre à la question posée et s'assurer que les contraintes sont respectées. Ainsi, certains problèmes exigent que les inconnues prennent des valeurs entières, d'autres des valeurs non négatives, etc.

L'exemple suivant illustre cette technique de résolution d'un problème concret.

Exemple

> Vous travaillez chez un marchand de café. Un client vous demande 5 kg de café sans préciser la composition du mélange. Vous disposez de trois sortes de grains dont les prix sont respectivement de 6 $, 8 $ et 10 $ le kilogramme. Le client vous a également dit qu'il veut payer exactement 40 $. Comment pouvez-vous le satisfaire ?

Après avoir lu le problème, vous constatez qu'on vous demande de faire un mélange de trois sortes de café dont les proportions ne sont pas données. Les quantités des trois types de grains sont donc des inconnues, qu'il faut nommer:

x = quantité de café à 6 $ le kilogramme
y = quantité de café à 8 $ le kilogramme
z = quantité de café à 10 $ le kilogramme

La donnée du problème contient deux informations: une information sur le coût total de l'achat et une information sur la masse du mélange. Les liens entre les variables doivent donc être établis en fonction de ces deux informations. Comme le mélange pèse 5 kg, on en déduit que la somme des quantités des trois sortes de café est égale à cette masse, ce qui se traduit par l'équation $x + y + z = 5$. On dit également que le coût total doit être de 40 $ et celui-ci s'obtient en faisant la somme des coûts du café de la première sorte, de la deuxième sorte et de la troisième sorte. Or, le coût est égal au prix multiplié par la quantité, soit respectivement $6x$, $8y$ et $10z$.

Par conséquent, on pose l'équation $6x + 8y + 10z = 40$. Comme on ne dispose d'aucune autre information, il faut résoudre le système d'équations

$$\begin{array}{rrrr} x + & y + & z = & 5 \\ 6x + & 8y + & 10z = & 40 \end{array}$$

La matrice augmentée de ce système est

$$\left[\begin{array}{ccc|c} 1 & 1 & 1 & 5 \\ 6 & 8 & 10 & 40 \end{array}\right]$$

et on applique la méthode d'élimination gaussienne pour résoudre le système.

$$\left[\begin{array}{ccc|c} 1 & 1 & 1 & 5 \\ 6 & 8 & 10 & 40 \end{array}\right] \sim \left[\begin{array}{ccc|c} 1 & 1 & 1 & 5 \\ 0 & 2 & 4 & 10 \end{array}\right] L_2 \to L_2 - 6L_1$$

$$\sim \left[\begin{array}{ccc|c} 1 & 1 & 1 & 5 \\ 0 & 1 & 2 & 5 \end{array}\right] L_2 \to \tfrac{1}{2}L_2$$

Le système d'équations admet une infinité de solutions. Si on pose $z = k$, on obtient par substitution à rebours $y + 2z = 5 \Rightarrow y = 5 - 2k$.

De plus,

$x + y + z = 5 \Rightarrow x = 5 - y - z = 5 - (5 - 2k) - k \Rightarrow x = k$

L'ensemble solution du système est donc

$$S = \left\{ \begin{bmatrix} k & 5 - 2k & k \end{bmatrix}^t \mid k \in \mathbb{R} \right\}$$

Toutefois, l'ensemble solution du système ne donne pas nécessairement la réponse à la question posée. À cause du contexte, les inconnues ne prennent que des valeurs non négatives parce qu'elles représentent des quantités de café. Il faut donc réduire l'ensemble solution aux valeurs telles que $k \geq 0$ et $5 - 2k \geq 0$. Par conséquent, la réponse à la question est donnée par l'ensemble

$$S' = \left\{ \begin{bmatrix} k & 5 - 2k & k \end{bmatrix}^t \mid 0 \leq k \leq 2,5 \right\}$$

Ainsi, vous pourriez satisfaire le client en lui donnant 2 kg de café à 6 \$/kg, 1 kg de café à 8 \$/kg et 2 kg de café à 10 \$/kg, ou encore 1 kg de café à 6 \$/kg, 3 kg de café à 8 \$/kg et 1 kg de café à 10 \$/kg. Toute autre combinaison faisant partie de l'ensemble S' devrait également satisfaire le client.

EXERCICE 4.10

Puisqu'il existe une infinité de façons de satisfaire le client de l'exemple précédent, vous demandez à ce dernier de vous donner plus d'informations.

a) S'il vous dit qu'il aime particulièrement le café à 10 \$/kg, et qu'il souhaite en avoir le plus possible, quel mélange allez-vous lui offrir ?

b) S'il vous dit qu'il veut avoir deux fois plus de café à 8 \$/kg que de café à 10 \$/kg, quel mélange allez-vous lui offrir ?

c) S'il vous dit qu'il souhaite avoir plus de café à 10 \$/kg que de café à 6 \$/kg, pouvez-vous le satisfaire ?

d) S'il vous dit qu'il souhaite avoir 3 kg de plus de café à 6 \$/kg que de café à 8 \$/kg, pouvez-vous le satisfaire ?

Voici un dernier exemple tiré du domaine de la chimie.

Exemple

Pour équilibrer l'équation chimique $N_2 + H_2 \rightarrow NH_3$, il faut déterminer les quantités minimales de chaque composante requises pour obtenir le produit final. On note x la quantité de N_2, y la quantité de H_2 et z la quantité de NH_3. Il faut donc trouver les plus petites valeurs entières de x, y et z qui vérifient $xN_2 + yH_2 \rightarrow zNH_3$. Pour que le nombre d'atomes de chaque élément dans le membre de droite soit égal au nombre d'atomes du même élément dans le membre de gauche, il faut que $2x = z$ (même nombre d'atomes d'azote) et que $2y = 3z$ (même nombre d'atomes d'hydrogène). On a donc le système d'équations

$$
\begin{aligned}
2x \quad - \quad z &= 0 \\
2y - 3z &= 0
\end{aligned}
$$

En construisant la matrice augmentée de ce système et en effectuant des opérations élémentaires de ligne sur cette dernière, on obtient

$$
\left[\begin{array}{ccc|c} 2 & 0 & -1 & 0 \\ 0 & 2 & -3 & 0 \end{array}\right] \sim \left[\begin{array}{ccc|c} 1 & 0 & -0{,}5 & 0 \\ 0 & 1 & -1{,}5 & 0 \end{array}\right] \begin{array}{l} L_1 \to L_1/2 \\ L_2 \to L_2/2 \end{array}
$$

Comme le rang de la matrice augmentée est égal au rang de la matrice des coefficients et qu'il est inférieur au nombre d'inconnues, il y a théoriquement une infinité de solutions. L'ensemble solution est $S = \left\{ \begin{bmatrix} 0{,}5k & 1{,}5k & k \end{bmatrix}^t \mid k \in \mathbb{R} \right\}$. Toutefois, on cherche la plus petite valeur de k pour laquelle les trois inconnues sont des entiers positifs. Cette valeur étant $k = 2$, la formule chimique recherchée est $N_2 + 3H_2 \to 2NH_3$.

RÉSUMÉ

Que ce soit en physique, en chimie, en biologie ou en sciences économiques, la résolution de problèmes nécessite souvent la recherche des solutions d'un système d'équations linéaires. Au chapitre 2, nous avons vu comment résoudre un système d'équations linéaires par la méthode de la matrice inverse. Mais cette méthode n'est pas tout à fait satisfaisante parce que :

- elle ne donne pas une formule générale pour déterminer la valeur de chacune des inconnues ;

- elle ne permet pas de résoudre les systèmes d'équations linéaires dont le nombre d'équations est différent du nombre d'inconnues ;

- elle demande beaucoup de temps dès que le système à résoudre comporte un grand nombre d'équations.

Bien qu'elle comporte des calculs également longs à exécuter, la règle de Cramer est utile parce qu'elle fournit une expression symbolique pour les inconnues lorsque le système d'équations linéaires admet une solution unique $\left(x_i = \dfrac{\Delta_{x_i}}{\Delta} \text{ où } \Delta \neq 0 \right)$. Si le déterminant de la matrice des coefficients est égal à zéro, la règle de Cramer permet de distinguer un système d'équations qui admet une infinité de solutions d'un système qui n'en admet aucune. Enfin, la règle de Cramer peut être employée pour résoudre un système d'équations avec paramètres. La règle de Cramer est énoncée dans le théorème 4.1 à la page 120.

La règle de Cramer, tout comme la méthode de la matrice inverse, n'est pas applicable à un système d'équations n'ayant pas le même nombre d'équations et d'inconnues. Heureusement, les méthodes d'élimination gaussienne et de Gauss-Jordan comblent cette lacune. Dans les deux cas, on effectue des opérations élémentaires de ligne pour transformer la matrice augmentée du système en une matrice échelonnée (élimination gaussienne) ou en une matrice échelonnée réduite (méthode de Gauss-Jordan). Les opérations élémentaires de ligne sont au nombre de trois :

1) l'interversion de deux lignes : $L_i \leftrightarrow L_j$,

2) la multiplication d'une ligne par une constante différente de zéro : $L_i \rightarrow kL_i$,

3) l'addition d'un multiple d'une ligne à une autre ligne : $L_i \rightarrow L_i + kL_j$.

Dans le cas de l'élimination gaussienne, la substitution à rebours, en commençant par la dernière ligne de la matrice échelonnée, permet de résoudre facilement un système d'équations. Cette méthode permet, comme la règle de Cramer, de distinguer entre les systèmes qui admettent une solution unique et une infinité de solutions, ou qui n'admettent aucune solution. Ces caractéristiques sont énoncées dans le théorème 4.2 à la page 141.

Parce qu'elle exige un plus grand nombre de calculs que l'élimination gaussienne, la méthode de Gauss-Jordan est surtout utile pour déterminer l'inverse d'une matrice carrée A d'ordre n. On effectue des opérations élémentaires de ligne sur la matrice A augmentée de la matrice identité d'ordre n de manière à transformer $\left[A \mid I_n \right]$ en $\left[I_n \mid C \right]$. Si cette transformation est possible, on obtient ainsi $C = A^{-1}$.

En pratique, le système à résoudre est formé d'équations qu'il faut d'abord établir à l'aide des données d'un problème tiré d'un contexte particulier. Il est alors fortement recommandé de respecter la marche à suivre que voici :

1) Faire une première lecture du problème pour en avoir une idée d'ensemble.

2) Relire le problème pour en dégager les éléments clés : la question posée, les inconnues, les relations entre les différentes inconnues, les contraintes, etc.

3) Attribuer un symbole à chaque quantité inconnue :

$x = $ ....

$y = $ ....

$z = $ ....

etc.

4) Écrire sous forme d'équations les liens entre les inconnues.

5) Résoudre le système d'équations.

6) Répondre à la question posée et s'assurer que les contraintes sont respectées. Ainsi, certains problèmes exigent que les inconnues prennent des valeurs entières, d'autres des valeurs non négatives, etc.

EXERCICES RÉCAPITULATIFS

1. (I) Résolvez chaque système d'équations en faisant appel à la règle de Cramer.

a) $\begin{aligned} x - 5y &= 2 \\ 3x + y &= 3 \end{aligned}$

b) $\begin{aligned} 2x + 3y &= 4 \\ 6x + 4y &= -8 \end{aligned}$

c) $\begin{aligned} 2x - 4y &= 0 \\ 3x - 6y &= 3 \end{aligned}$

d) $\begin{aligned} 3x + 2y - 5z &= 2 \\ x + 2y &= 3 \\ 2x - y + z &= -3 \end{aligned}$

e) $\begin{aligned} 3x + 6y + 2z &= 0 \\ 6x - 3y + 5z &= 0 \\ 4x + 3y + 3z &= 0 \end{aligned}$

f) $\begin{aligned} x_1 + x_2 - x_3 &= 4 \\ 2x_1 - 3x_2 + 2x_3 &= 3 \\ -x_1 + 9x_2 - 7x_3 &= 2 \end{aligned}$

g) $2x^2 + 3y^2 = 13$
$4x^2 - 3y^2 = -1$

(Indice : Remplacez x^2 et y^2 respective-ment par x_1 et x_2 pour obtenir un système d'équations linéaires.)

h) $\dfrac{1}{x} - \dfrac{1}{y} + \dfrac{1}{z} = 4$

$\dfrac{2}{x} - \dfrac{1}{y} - \dfrac{3}{z} = 2$

$\dfrac{1}{x} + \dfrac{2}{y} + \dfrac{2}{z} = 2$

2. (I) Résolvez chaque système d'équations avec paramètre (k) et interprétez les résultats.

a) $(2 - k)x + 3y = 0$
$(6 + k)y = 0$

b) $(k + 1)x - \quad y = 1$
$x + (k - 1)y = 2$

c) $4x - ky = k$
$kx - 9y = k + 3$

d) $x + y = 3k$
$kx + y = k$

e) $x + ky = 2k$
$kx + \quad y = 1 + k^2$

3. (I) Soit le circuit électrique

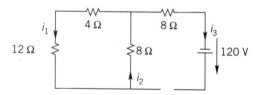

En appliquant les lois de Kirchhoff à ce circuit, on obtient le système d'équations

$$i_1 - i_2 + i_3 = 0$$
$$8i_2 + 8i_3 = 120$$
$$16i_1 + 8i_2 = 0$$

Quelles sont les valeurs des courants i_1, i_2 et i_3 ?

4. (I) Représentez, par des droites dans un plan cartésien, un système de trois équations li-néaires à deux inconnues illustrant le cas donné.

a) Un système dont l'unique solution est $\begin{bmatrix} 2 & 2 \end{bmatrix}^t$. Les trois droites sont-elles néces-sairement distinctes ?

b) Un système qui n'admet aucune solution. Les droites représentant les équations sont-elles nécessairement parallèles ?

c) Un système qui admet une infinité de solu-tions.

5. (I) Soit le triangle

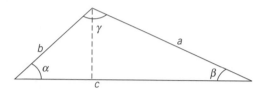

On note que $a\cos\beta + b\cos\alpha = c$. De façon analogue, on constate que $c\cos\beta + b\cos\gamma = a$ et $a\cos\gamma + c\cos\alpha = b$. En considérant les cosi-nus des angles comme des inconnues, à l'aide de la règle de Cramer, démontrez la loi des cosi-nus, à savoir $\cos\gamma = \dfrac{a^2 + b^2 - c^2}{2ab}$ ou, selon la formule habituelle, $c^2 = a^2 + b^2 - 2ab\cos\gamma$.

6. (III) Après avoir lu l'extrait du texte de Cramer (p. 125) sur la formulation de sa règle, essayez d'en déduire une définition d'un déterminant d'ordre n autre que la définition récursive pré-sentée au chapitre 3.

7. (I) Soit le système d'équations linéaires

$$x + y = a$$
$$-2x + ay = b$$

Quelles valeurs prennent les paramètres a et b :

a) si le système d'équations admet une solu-tion unique ?

b) si le système d'équations n'admet aucune solution ?

c) si le système d'équations admet une infinité de solutions ?

8. (I) Déterminez l'ensemble solution de chaque système d'équations à l'aide de la méthode d'élimination gaussienne.

a) $3x - 4y = 4$
$6x - 4y = 8$

b) $3x + 2y - 5z = 2$
$x + 2y = 3$

c) $3x + 6y + 2z = 4$
$-6x - 12y - 4z = -8$
$9x + 18y + 4z = 12$

d) $x_1 - x_2 + 2x_3 = 6$
$2x_1 + x_2 - 3x_3 = 5$
$3x_1 \quad - x_3 = 8$

e) $a - 2b - 3c = -1$
$2a - b - 2c = 2$
$3a - b - 3c = 3$

f) $2x + y - 3z = 1$
$x - y + 2z = -2$
$4x - y - z = -3$
$x \quad + 2z = 3$

g) $x_1 - x_2 + x_3 - x_4 = 1$
$x_1 + x_2 - x_3 + x_4 = 2$
$x_1 - x_2 - x_3 - x_4 = -1$
$x_1 + x_2 + x_3 - x_4 = -3$

h) $x_1 - x_2 + 4x_3 + 3x_4 = -3$
$-x_1 \quad + 2x_3 \quad = -1$
$2x_1 \quad - 6x_3 + 5x_4 = 9$
$-x_1 + x_2 + x_3 + x_4 = 2$

9. (I) Soit le système d'équations $2x - y + 3z = 4$ et $x + 2y - z = 7$. Lesquels des ensembles suivants correspondent à l'ensemble solution de ce système.

a) $S = \left\{ \begin{bmatrix} 5 - k & k & k - 2 \end{bmatrix}^t \mid k \in \mathbb{R} \right\}$

b) $S = \left\{ \begin{bmatrix} k & k + 3 & 2k - 1 \end{bmatrix}^t \mid k \in \mathbb{R} \right\}$

c) $S = \left\{ \begin{bmatrix} 3 - k & k + 2 & k \end{bmatrix}^t \mid k \in \mathbb{R} \right\}$

d) $S = \left\{ \begin{bmatrix} k & 5 - k & 3 - k \end{bmatrix}^t \mid k \in \mathbb{R} \right\}$

10. (I) Soit le système d'équations

$$x + y + z + w = 4$$
$$2x + y - z + 2w = 4$$
$$-x + 2y - 2z + w = 0$$
$$x + 2y - z + 2w = 4$$

a) Quel est l'ensemble solution de ce système d'équations?

b) Est-ce que $x = 1$, $y = 1$, $z = 1$ et $w = 1$ est une solution du système d'équations?

c) Est-ce que $x = 2$, $y = -2$, $z = 3$ et $w = 4$ est une solution du système d'équations?

d) Si $w = 6$, quelles valeurs de x, y et z vérifient le système d'équations?

11. (I) Trouvez les valeurs de A, B et C qui vérifient les équations suivantes[11] quelle que soit la valeur de x. (Indice: Réduisez les fractions du membre de droite au même dénominateur, posez l'égalité entre les numérateurs et comparez les coefficients de chaque puissance de x dans l'un et l'autre membre de cette égalité.)

a) $\dfrac{2}{x^2 - 4} = \dfrac{A}{x - 2} + \dfrac{B}{x + 2}$

b) $\dfrac{x - 1}{x^3 - x^2 - 6x} = \dfrac{A}{x} + \dfrac{B}{x + 2} + \dfrac{C}{x - 3}$

c) $\dfrac{2x - 1}{x^3 - x^2 - x + 1} = \dfrac{A}{x + 1} + \dfrac{B}{x - 1} + \dfrac{C}{(x - 1)^2}$

d) $\dfrac{x^2 + 2x + 7}{x^3 + x^2 - 2} = \dfrac{A}{x - 1} + \dfrac{Bx + C}{x^2 + 2x + 2}$

12. (II) Soit le système d'équations $AX = O_{n \times 1}$

$$a_{11}x_1 + a_{12}x_2 + a_{13}x_3 + \cdots + a_{1n}x_n = 0$$
$$a_{21}x_1 + a_{22}x_2 + a_{23}x_3 + \cdots + a_{2n}x_n = 0$$
$$a_{31}x_1 + a_{32}x_2 + a_{33}x_3 + \cdots + a_{3n}x_n = 0$$
$$\vdots \qquad \vdots \qquad \vdots \qquad \qquad \vdots \qquad \vdots$$
$$a_{n1}x_1 + a_{n2}x_2 + a_{n3}x_3 + \cdots + a_{nn}x_n = 0$$

Ce système est dit homogène parce que sa matrice des constantes est une matrice colonne nulle.

a) Le système d'équations admet une solution évidente. Quelle est-elle?

b) Le système peut-il admettre plus d'une solution? Justifiez votre réponse.

c) Montrez que si $K = \begin{bmatrix} k_1 & k_2 & k_3 & \cdots & k_n \end{bmatrix}^t$ et $J = \begin{bmatrix} j_1 & j_2 & j_3 & \cdots & j_n \end{bmatrix}^t$ sont des solutions distinctes du système d'équations, alors $K + J$ est aussi une solution du système.

d) Montrez que si $K = \begin{bmatrix} k_1 & k_2 & k_3 & \cdots & k_n \end{bmatrix}^t$ est une solution du système d'équations et si c est une constante, alors cK est aussi une solution du système.

e) Montrez que tout système d'équations homogène qui possède plus d'une solution en admet une infinité.

13. (II) Soit X_1 et X_2 deux solutions distinctes du système d'équations linéaires $AX = B$, à m équations et n inconnues. Montrez que:

a) $X_1 - X_2$ est une solution de $AX = O_{m \times 1}$.

---

11. Vous utiliserez cette stratégie, appelée décomposition en fractions partielles, en calcul intégral. Nous vous invitons à consulter le théorème sur les fractions partielles dans n'importe quel bon livre de calcul intégral.

b) $X_1 + k(X_1 - X_2)$ où k est une constante différente de 0 est une solution de $AX = B$.

c) Un système d'équations linéaires qui possède plus d'une solution en admet une infinité.

14. (I) Quel est le nombre d'inconnues libres de chaque système d'équations?

a) $2x + 5y = 12$
$-x + 2y = 5$

b) $x + y + z + w = 8$
$2x + 2y + 3z + 4w = 11$
$2x + 2y + 2z + 2w = 16$
$z + 2w = -5$

c) $3x + 2y - z = -5$
$2x + y + 2z = -2$
$-x - y + 3z = 3$

15. (I) Soit $S = \{[r \quad 2r \quad 2r + 5]^t \mid r \in \mathbb{R}\}$ l'ensemble solution d'un système d'équations.

a) Combien d'inconnues le système d'équations compte-t-il?

b) Combien d'inconnues libres le système d'équations compte-t-il?

c) Est-ce que $[1 \quad 2 \quad 7]^t$ est une solution particulière du système d'équations?

d) Est-ce que $[3 \quad 6 \quad 11]^t$ est une solution particulière du système d'équations?

e) Est-ce que $[-1 \quad -2 \quad 4]^t$ est une solution particulière du système d'équations?

f) Montrez que

$S' = \{[k/2 \quad k \quad k + 5]^t \mid k \in \mathbb{R}\}$

représente également l'ensemble solution de ce système d'équations.

g) Montrez que

$S'' = \{[(m - 5)/2 \quad m + 5 \quad m]^t \mid m \in \mathbb{R}\}$

ne représente pas l'ensemble solution de ce système d'équations.

16. (I) Soit la représentation matricielle $AX = B$ d'un système d'équations linéaires dont la matrice A des coefficients est une matrice carrée d'ordre n, dont la matrice des inconnues est X et dont la matrice des constantes est B. Complétez le tableau qui suit en y inscrivant les chiffres appropriés, selon la liste donnée à la fin du tableau. Un chiffre peut être utilisé plus d'une fois ou ne pas être utilisé du tout.

NATURE DES SOLUTIONS D'UN SYSTÈME D'ÉQUATIONS LINÉAIRES $AX = B$

Matrice A	Type de système	Nature des solutions selon la matrice B	
		$B \neq O_{n \times 1}$	$B = O_{n \times 1}$
$\|A\| \neq 0$ La matrice A est _____. Le rang de A est _____. Le rang de $[A \mid B]$ est _____.	Le système d'équations est _____.	_____	_____
$\|A\| = 0$ La matrice A n'est pas _____. Le rang de $[A \mid B]$ est_____.	Le système d'équations est compatible.	_____	_____
$\|A\| = 0$ La matrice A est _____. Le rang de $[A \mid B]$ est plus grand que celui de A.	Le système d'équations est _____.	_____	Ne s'applique pas.

1) L'unique solution du système d'équations est $X \neq O_{n \times 1}$.

2) L'unique solution du système d'équations est $X = O_{n \times 1}$.

3) Le système d'équations admet une infinité de solutions, dont $X = O_{n \times 1}$.

4) Le système d'équations admet une infinité de solutions toutes différentes de $O_{n \times 1}$.

5) Le système d'équations n'admet aucune solution.

6) compatible

7) incompatible

8) égal à n

9) plus grand que n

10) plus petit que n

11) singulière

12) régulière

17. (I) Trouvez, si elle existe, la matrice inverse de chaque matrice en faisant appel à la méthode de Gauss-Jordan.

a) $\begin{bmatrix} 2 & 2 \\ -1 & 4 \end{bmatrix}$

b) $\begin{bmatrix} -1 & -1 \\ 3 & 2 \end{bmatrix}$

c) $\begin{bmatrix} 1 & 2 & 3 \\ -1 & 2 & 0 \\ 0 & 4 & 3 \end{bmatrix}$

d) $\begin{bmatrix} 1 & 1 & -1 \\ -1 & 0 & 0 \\ 1 & 0 & 1 \end{bmatrix}$

18. (I) En économie, on obtient les prix et les quantités d'équilibre (équilibre simultané sur les marchés) de produits en résolvant le système formé des équations de l'offre et de la demande des biens. On dit d'un produit qu'il est un substitut d'un autre produit si la demande du premier augmente lorsque le prix du second augmente, les consommateurs substituant alors un bien à l'autre. Deux biens sont dits complémentaires si l'augmentation du prix de l'un entraîne une réduction de la demande de l'autre, les consommateurs achetant simultanément ces deux biens.

Les équations de l'offre et de la demande pour les marchés du bœuf et du porc sont les suivantes.

	Marché du porc	Marché du bœuf
Demande	$Q_p = 109 - 3P_p + P_b$	$Q_b = 204 + 5P_p - 8P_b$
Offre	$Q_p = -60 + 40P_p$	$Q_b = -10 + 70P_b$

a) De quelle façon la quantité offerte de porc (Q_p) varie-t-elle lorsque le prix du porc (P_p) augmente?

b) La quantité de porc demandée augmente-t-elle lorsque le prix du porc augmente?

c) La quantité de porc demandée augmente-t-elle lorsque le prix du bœuf (P_b) augmente? Qu'en concluez-vous à propos de la nature économique des deux biens (porc et bœuf)? Le porc et le bœuf sont-ils des substituts l'un de l'autre ou des biens complémentaires?

d) Quels sont les prix d'équilibre du bœuf (P_b) et du porc (P_p) ainsi que les quantités d'équilibre du bœuf (Q_b) et du porc (Q_p) sur les deux marchés?

Les équations de l'offre et de la demande pour les marchés des chemises d'hommes et des cravates sont les suivantes.

	Marché des chemises	Marché des cravates
Demande	$Q_c = 540 - 4P_c - 6P_r$	$Q_r = 240 - 2P_c - 2P_r$
Offre	$Q_c = -60 + 3P_c$	$Q_r = -90 + 5P_r$

e) De quelle façon la quantité offerte de chemises (Q_c) varie-t-elle lorsque le prix des chemises (P_c) augmente?

f) La quantité de chemises demandée augmente-t-elle lorsque le prix des chemises augmente?

g) La quantité de chemises demandée augmente-t-elle lorsque le prix des cravates (P_r) augmente? Qu'en concluez-vous à propos de la nature économique des deux biens (chemises et cravates)? Les chemises et les cravates sont-elles des biens dont l'un est un substitut de l'autre ou des biens complémentaires?

h) Quels sont les prix d'équilibre des chemises (P_c) et des cravates (P_r) ainsi que les quantités d'équilibre des chemises (Q_c) et des cravates (Q_r) sur les deux marchés?

19. (I) Quelle quantité de lait contenant 1 % de matières grasses doit-on mélanger avec de la crème contenant 15 % de matières grasses pour obtenir 5 litres de lait contenant 3 % de matières grasses?

20. (I) Une solution A contient 6 g de sel et 9 g de sucre par litre. Une solution B contient 15 g de sel et 21 g de sucre par litre. Quelle quantité de chaque solution faut-il mélanger pour obtenir une solution contenant 9 g de sel et 13 g de sucre par litre?

21. (I) Un manufacturier produit trois modèles différents (A, B et C) d'un même bien. L'usine comprend trois départements (1, 2 et 3) qui jouent tous un rôle dans la fabrication de chaque modèle et où le nombre d'heures de travail maximal est respectivement de 780, 600 et 320 heures par jour. Le tableau qui suit présente le temps requis (en heures) par chaque département pour réaliser sa part de la fabrication d'une unité du produit, selon le modèle. Combien d'unités de chaque modèle l'usine doit-elle produire pour que le nombre d'heures de travail effectuées soit égal au nombre d'heures maximal?

TEMPS (h) REQUIS POUR FABRIQUER UNE UNITÉ, SELON LE DÉPARTEMENT ET LE MODÈLE

Département	Modèle		
	A	B	C
1	0,1	0,4	0,6
2	0,2	0,2	0,4
3	0,1	0,2	0,1

22. (I) Le propriétaire d'un chenil fait l'élevage de trois races de chiens: dalmatiens, labradors et bergers anglais. Il possède 30 bêtes, et il y a trois fois plus de bergers anglais que de dalmatiens et deux fois plus de labradors que de dalmatiens. Combien de chiens de chaque race l'éleveur possède-t-il?

23. (I) Un entrepreneur a construit 100 maisons comptant, selon le modèle, une, deux ou trois salles de bain. Chaque salle de bain comprend une seule toilette, et l'entrepreneur a installé 200 toilettes en tout. De plus, il a construit autant de maisons comptant deux salles de bain que de maisons en comptant une ou trois. Combien de maisons de chaque modèle a-t-il fabriquées?

24. (I) Dans un treillis métallique, la température à un point d'intersection est égale à la température moyenne des extrémités et des points d'intersection immédiatement voisins. Déterminez la température à chaque point d'intersection des treillis suivants pour les températures indiquées.

a)

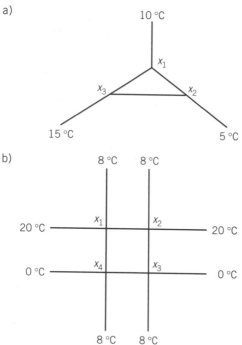

b)

25. (I) Un individu a investi 5 000 $ dans deux fonds dont les rendements ont été respectivement de 4 % et de 9 %. Si le deuxième fonds lui a rapporté 60 $ de plus que le premier, combien a-t-il investi dans chaque fonds?

26. (I) Un club de golf compte 500 membres répartis en trois catégories selon leur cotisation annuelle. Les membres de la catégorie A, qui

peuvent jouer en tout temps, paient une cotisation annuelle de 1 000 $; ceux de la catégorie B, qui ne sont autorisés à jouer que du lundi au vendredi, paient 600 $; ceux de la catégorie C, qui ne sont autorisés à jouer que du lundi au jeudi, paient 400 $. Le club de golf compte autant de membres de la catégorie B que des deux autres catégories réunies, et 100 membres de plus de la catégorie B que de la catégorie C. Quel revenu le club de golf tire-t-il des cotisations?

27. (I) Le même club de golf (voir n° 26) vend également des cartes d'un jour dont les prix sont les suivants: 25 $ pour les personnes qui commencent à jouer avant midi, 20 $ pour celles qui commencent à jouer entre midi et 15 heures, et 15 $ pour celles qui commencent à jouer après 15 heures. Si 95 golfeurs ont dépensé au total 2 050 $ pour des cartes d'un jour et s'ils ont acheté cinq cartes à 25 $ de plus qu'ils n'ont acheté de cartes des deux autres types, combien le club de golf a-t-il vendu de cartes de chaque type?

28. (I) Un individu a acheté un portefeuille qui comprend des actions de trois compagnies. Après un an, la valeur de ce portefeuille avait chuté de 100 $, toutes les actions ayant subi une variation: celles de la première et de la deuxième compagnie ont diminué respectivement de 1 $ et de 2 $, et celles de la troisième compagnie ont augmenté de 0,50 $. Après deux ans, la valeur du même portefeuille a augmenté de 200 $ par rapport à sa valeur initiale: les actions de la première compagnie ayant augmenté de 1 $, celles de la deuxième compagnie de 0,50 $ et celles de la troisième compagnie de 1,50 $.

a) Les informations données permettent-elles de trouver le nombre d'actions de chaque compagnie dans le portefeuille?

b) Si on précise que le portefeuille compte 60 actions de la première compagnie, cette information supplémentaire permet-elle de trouver le nombre d'actions de chaque compagnie dans le portefeuille?

c) Si on donne plutôt comme information supplémentaire que le portefeuille compte 200 actions de la deuxième compagnie, est-il alors possible de déterminer le nombre d'actions de chaque compagnie dans le portefeuille?

29. (I) Un commerçant souhaite offrir à ses clients un mélange composé d'amandes, de noix d'acajou et de pistaches. Il vend les amandes 5 $/kg, les noix d'acajou 8 $/kg et les pistaches 6 $/kg. Si le mélange doit coûter 6 $/kg et comporter trois fois moins de noix d'acajou que de pistaches, quelle quantité d'amandes doit contenir chaque kilogramme du mélange?

30. (I) Une portion de 100 g de pommes de terre contient 100 cal (calories) et 5 g de protéines; une portion de 100 g de maïs contient 150 cal et 10 g de protéines; une portion de 100 g de bœuf haché contient 300 cal et 25 g de protéines. Vous voulez combiner ces trois aliments pour préparer un « pâté chinois » contenant 800 cal et 50 g de protéines.

a) Existe-t-il plusieurs façons de confectionner le « pâté chinois » (c'est-à-dire de déterminer le nombre de portions de 100 g de chaque aliment)? Donnez la solution générale de ce problème.

b) Est-il possible de confectionner un « pâté chinois » végétarien en éliminant simplement le bœuf haché? Justifiez votre réponse en déterminant le nombre de portions de 100 g de pommes de terre et de maïs ou en expliquant pourquoi cela est impossible.

c) Est-il possible de confectionner un « pâté chinois » qui ne contiennent pas de pommes de terre? Justifiez votre réponse en déterminant le nombre de portions de 100 g de bœuf haché et de maïs ou en expliquant pourquoi cela est impossible.

d) Est-il possible de confectioner un « pâté chinois » ne contenant pas de maïs? Justifiez votre réponse en déterminant le nombre de portions de 100 g de bœuf haché et de pommes de terre ou en expliquant pourquoi cela est impossible.

Le prix d'une portion de 100 g de pommes de terre est de 0,40 $; le prix d'une portion de 100 g de maïs est de 0,20 $; le prix d'une portion de 100 g de bœuf haché est de 0,80 $.

e) Si le plat que vous avez préparé coûte 2,20 $, combien de portions de 100 g de chaque aliment contient-il?

f) Est-il possible de préparer un « pâté chinois » qui coûte 1,50 $ en respectant les contraintes relatives au nombre de calories et à la quantité de protéines?

g) Quel est le coût minimal d'un « pâté chinois » si on respecte les contraintes relatives au nombre de calories et à la quantité de protéines?

31. (I) Vous avez décidé de vous remettre en forme en pratiquant trois types d'activité physique: la marche rapide, la natation et le vélo d'appartement. Vous pouvez consacrer au total 2 heures par semaine à ces différentes activités qui, cependant, ne vous procurent pas toutes la même satisfaction. Vous avez défini une mesure de la satisfaction associée à chaque activité: une heure de marche vous procure trois unités de satisfaction; une heure de natation, deux unités de satisfaction; une heure de vélo, une unité de satisfaction. Enfin, vous voulez brûler 2 000 cal durant chaque période de deux heures. Une heure de marche entraîne une dépense de 500 cal; une heure de natation, une dépense de 1 000 cal; une heure de vélo, une dépense de 1 500 cal.

a) Pouvez-vous planifier un programme d'activité physique qui vous permette de respecter les contraintes relatives au temps et à la dépense énergétique et vous procure quatre unités de satisfaction?

b) Existe-t-il un programme d'activité qui respecte les contraintes énoncées et vous permette de faire une demi-heure de vélo? Si oui, décrivez ce programme; sinon, justifiez votre réponse.

c) Existe-t-il un programme d'activité qui vous permet d'atteindre vos objectifs en faisant plus d'une heure de vélo? Si oui, décrivez ce programme; sinon, justifiez votre réponse.

32. (I) Les mobiles illustrés en *a* et *b* sont constitués d'objets reliés entre eux par des tiges rigides et des fils dont la masse est négligeable. Le moment de force d'un objet par rapport à un point est égal au produit du poids [en newtons (N)] de l'objet et de sa distance horizontale à ce point. Un mobile est en équilibre statique lorsque la somme des moments de force des objets situés à gauche d'un point est égale à la somme des moments de force des objets situés à droite de ce point. Pour quelles valeurs de *x* et de *y* les mobiles illustrés en *a* et *b* sont-ils en équilibre statique?

a)

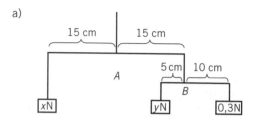

b)

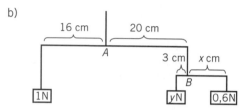

 33. (I) Équilibrez les équations chimiques suivantes.

a) $NO_2 + H_2O \rightarrow HNO_3 + NO$

b) $Cu_2S + O_2 \rightarrow Cu + SO_2$

c) $Fe_2O_3 + HCl \rightarrow FeCl_3 + H_2O$

 34. (I) Dans le n° 29 des exercices récapitulatifs du chapitre 2, nous avons présenté un modèle qui décrit l'évolution de la part du marché de l'interurbain détenue par trois revendeurs, à l'aide de la matrice de répartition

$$P^{(0)} = \left[p_i^{(0)} \right]_{3 \times 1}$$

où $p_i^{(0)}$ est la part du marché initialement détenue par la compagnie i. La matrice de répartition après n mois est

$$P^{(n)} = \left[p_i^{(n)} \right]_{3 \times 1}$$

où $p_i^{(n)}$ est la part du marché détenue par la compagnie i après n mois.

La matrice de transition qui décrit les mouvements de la clientèle d'une compagnie à l'autre entre deux mois consécutifs est

$$T = \begin{bmatrix} 0,80 & 0,20 & 0,05 \\ 0,10 & 0,75 & 0,05 \\ 0,10 & 0,05 & 0,90 \end{bmatrix}$$

où t_{ij} est la part de la clientèle de j qui passe à i.

Si la matrice de transition est la même de mois en mois, alors $P^{(n)} = TP^{(n-1)}$. À long terme, le marché s'équilibre, c'est-à-dire que

$$P^{(n)} = P^{(n-1)} = P = \begin{bmatrix} p_1 & p_2 & p_3 \end{bmatrix}^t$$

À l'état d'équilibre, les parts du marché détenues par les divers revendeurs vérifient donc l'équation matricielle $P = TP$ et l'équation

linéaire $p_1 + p_2 + p_3 = 1$. On peut donc trouver ces parts du marché en résolvant un système d'équations linéaires à quatre équations et trois inconnues.

a) Pourquoi l'équation $p_1 + p_2 + p_3 = 1$ doit-elle être satisfaite ?

b) Écrivez le système d'équations qui permet de trouver les parts du marché détenues par les divers revendeurs à l'état d'équilibre.

c) Résolvez le système d'équations.

d) Les parts du marché détenues par les trois revendeurs à l'état d'équilibre sont-elles fonction des parts du marché qu'ils détenaient initialement ?

La fusion des compagnies 2 et 3 a donné naissance à une nouvelle compagnie 2, et la nouvelle matrice de transition est

$$T' = \begin{bmatrix} 0,8 & 0,1 \\ 0,2 & 0,9 \end{bmatrix}$$

e) Interprétez les nombres 0,1 et 0,8 de la matrice de transition T'.

f) Quelle part du marché chaque compagnie détient-elle à l'état d'équilibre dans le nouveau contexte ?

 35. (II) Les économistes ont conçu des modèles simples pour décrire les différents types d'économies. Ces modèles se présentent habituellement sous la forme d'un système d'équations reliant les variables et les paramètres étudiés. La première équation d'un de ces modèles exprime le produit intérieur brut (Y) d'une économie comme la somme des dépenses des consommateurs (C), des dépenses d'investissement (I_0) et des dépenses gouvernementales (G_0). La deuxième équation exprime les dépenses des consommateurs comme la somme de deux éléments, soit une dépense autonome (a), indépendante du produit intérieur brut, et une dépense qui représente une fraction (b) du produit intérieur brut. Le paramètre b représente la propension marginale à consommer. Les variables I_0 et G_0 sont dites exogènes parce qu'elles sont déterminées à l'extérieur du modèle ; on peut donc considérer ces variables comme des paramètres, au même titre que a et b. Les variables Y et C sont dites endogènes parce qu'elles sont déterminées à l'intérieur du modèle. On souhaite trouver la valeur des variables endogènes en fonction des variables exogènes et des paramètres.

a) Écrivez les deux équations du modèle.

b) Résolvez le modèle, c'est-à-dire trouvez l'expression de chaque variable endogène en fonction des variables exogènes I_0 et G_0 et des paramètres a et b.

c) Que valent Y et C lorsque $I_0 = 100$, $G_0 = 200$, $a = 50$ et $b = 0,8$?

d) Quel est l'effet sur le produit intérieur brut d'une augmentation de 0,8 à 0,9 de la propension marginale à consommer?

36. (II) Une variante du modèle présenté au n° 35 intègre un système de taxation. Elle comporte trois équations: la première porte sur le produit intérieur brut, la deuxième sur les dépenses des consommateurs et la troisième sur les taxes. Dans ce modèle, le produit intérieur brut (Y) d'une économie est encore une fois égal à la somme des dépenses des consommateurs (C), des dépenses d'investissement (I_0) et des dépenses gouvernementales (G_0). Les dépenses des consommateurs sont égales à la somme de deux éléments: une dépense autonome (a), indépendante du produit intérieur brut, et une dépense qui représente une fraction (b) du revenu disponible, c'est-à-dire du produit intérieur brut moins les taxes (T). Les taxes sont égales à la somme de deux éléments: un montant fixe (d) et une fraction (t) du produit intérieur brut. Les variables endogènes du modèle sont Y, C et T, alors que les variables exogènes et les paramètres sont I_0, G_0, a, b, d et t.

a) Écrivez les trois équations du modèle.

b) Résolvez le modèle, c'est-à-dire trouvez l'expression de chacune des variables endogènes Y, C et T en fonction des variables exogènes I_0 et G_0 et des paramètres a, b, d et t.

37. (I) Dites si chaque énoncé est vrai ou faux, et justifiez votre réponse.

a) La méthode d'élimination gaussienne est plus rapide que la méthode de Gauss-Jordan pour résoudre un système d'équations linéaires.

b) On peut faire appel à la règle de Cramer pour résoudre un système d'équations linéaires qui comporte moins d'équations que d'inconnues.

c) Le rang de la matrice augmentée d'un système d'équations linéaires est parfois plus petit que le rang de la matrice des coefficients de ce système.

d) Un système d'équations qui compte moins d'équations que d'inconnues admet nécessairement une infinité de solutions.

e) Un système d'équations qui compte plus d'équations que d'inconnues est nécessairement incompatible.

f) Un système d'équations linéaires qui compte le même nombre d'équations que d'inconnues est nécessairement compatible.

g) La valeur totale de 19 pièces choisies dans une pile de pièces de 5 ¢, de 10 ¢ et de 25 ¢ peut être de 2,15 $ lorsque le nombre de pièces de 25 ¢ est trois fois plus élevé que le nombre de pièces de 10 ¢.

h) Un système d'équations qui compte moins d'équations que d'inconnues n'admet jamais une solution unique.

i) (III) Le rang d'une matrice carrée non singulière d'ordre n est égal à n.

j) Tout système d'équations linéaires compatible admet une solution unique.

k) Si un système de n équations linéaires à n inconnues admet une solution unique, alors, en supprimant l'une des équations, on obtient un système qui admet lui aussi une solution unique.

l) Si un système de n équations linéaires à n inconnues admet une solution unique, alors, en lui ajoutant une équation, on obtient un système qui admet lui aussi une solution unique.

38. (I) Nommez un cas où on préfère employer la règle de Cramer plutôt que la méthode d'élimination gaussienne pour résoudre un système d'équations.

39. (I) Nommez trois cas où on préfère employer la méthode d'élimination gaussienne plutôt que la règle de Cramer pour résoudre un système d'équations linéaires.

Vecteurs du plan

Mais ce qui a surtout immortalisé le nom de [Descartes,] ce grand homme, c'est l'application qu'il a su faire de l'algèbre à la géométrie, idée des plus vastes et des plus heureuses que l'esprit humain ait jamais eues, et qui sera toujours la clef des plus profondes recherches, non seulement dans la géométrie, mais dans toutes les sciences physico-mathématiques.

Jean Le Rond d'Alembert

À LA FIN DU PRÉSENT CHAPITRE, VOUS DEVRIEZ ÊTRE EN MESURE DE RÉPONDRE AUX QUESTIONS SUIVANTES:

- Qu'est-ce qu'un vecteur?
- Quelles sont les principales caractéristiques d'un vecteur?
- À quelles conditions deux vecteurs sont-ils égaux?
- Comment est-ce qu'on effectue les différentes opérations sur des vecteurs?
- Qu'est-ce qu'une combinaison linéaire?
- À quelles conditions des vecteurs sont-ils linéairement indépendants?
- Y a-t-il un lien entre les matrices et les vecteurs du plan?
- Que représentent les composantes d'un vecteur algébrique?
- Comment trouve-t-on l'angle entre deux vecteurs?
- Quelles caractéristiques un ensemble de vecteurs doit-il posséder pour former une base d'un espace vectoriel?

UN PORTRAIT de René Descartes

Cogito, ergo sum *(« Je pense, donc je suis »)*. *Cette phrase célèbre est tirée du fameux* Discours de la méthode pour bien conduire sa raison et chercher la vérité dans les sciences *(1637) de René Descartes. Né en France en 1596, dans une famille noble, et mort à Stockholm en 1650, Descartes est considéré à juste titre comme l'un des fondateurs de la philosophie moderne et l'inventeur de la géométrie analytique.*

La santé du jeune Descartes était fragile. C'est pourquoi il n'entra à l'école (le collège La Flèche) qu'à l'âge de huit ans. Conscient du fait que le garçon a besoin de beaucoup de sommeil, le recteur lui permit de rester au lit aussi longtemps qu'il le souhaitait. Descartes conserva cette pratique toute sa vie et il affirmait que les longs moments passés au lit le matin lui permettaient de rester en santé et constituaient des moments privilégiés de réflexion.

Après des études universitaires en droit à l'Université de Poitiers, Descartes s'engagea quelque temps comme mercenaire dans les armées de différentes nations. Cela lui permit de voyager partout en Europe et de rencontrer de nombreux mathématiciens et scientifiques. Sa carrière militaire fut apparemment brillante puisqu'on lui offrit un poste de lieutenant général, qu'il refusa pour se consacrer à la philosophie.

Page de titre du *Discours de la méthode*

Descartes vécut plus de vingt ans en Hollande (1628-1649), où il écrivit son œuvre maîtresse : le Discours de la méthode. *Il raconta souvent que l'inspiration lui en était venue dans la nuit du 10 novembre 1619, le dernier de trois rêves qu'il avait fait alors lui ayant indiqué le chemin à suivre pour comprendre la nature.*

Le Discours de la méthode *tient lieu de préface à trois essais scientifiques : la Dioptrique, où est énoncée la loi de la réfraction de Snell, les Météores, un traité de météorologie où Descartes présente notamment une explication des couleurs de l'arc-en-ciel, et la Géométrie. C'est dans ce dernier essai que Descartes expose l'idée, révolutionnaire pour l'époque, d'établir un lien entre l'algèbre et la géométrie et de résoudre algébriquement des problèmes géométriques.*

Descartes affirme essentiellement que tout point du plan – qu'on nomme aujourd'hui plan cartésien en son honneur – est complètement déterminé par les distances (x et y) de ce point à deux axes. En s'appuyant sur cette observation, il décrit des courbes – ou ensembles de points – du plan au moyen d'équations algébriques. Il emploie ensuite celles-ci pour étudier les propriétés des courbes qu'elles représentent. Descartes affirme également, sans expliciter, qu'il aurait pu déterminer de façon similaire des points et des fonctions de l'espace par un système de trois coordonnées.

La Géométrie est divisée en trois livres. Le premier traite des opérations arithmétiques d'un point de vue géométrique ; le second présente une classification des courbes du plan ; et le troisième porte sur les racines des équations. Dans ce dernier livre, Descartes énonce que le nombre de racines d'un polynôme est égal au degré de ce polynôme (théorème fondamental de l'algèbre), et il démontre un théorème important (règle des signes de Descartes) qui permet de déterminer le nombre de racines positives d'un polynôme en fonction du nombre de changements de signe des coefficients de ce polynôme.

Descartes contribua également à fixer certains éléments de la notation mathématique moderne : l'utilisation des exposants et l'emploi du symbole $\sqrt{\ }$ pour désigner une racine et du signe + pour désigner l'addition. C'est également Descartes qui introduisit l'usage des premières lettres de l'alphabet (a, b, c, ...) pour désigner des constantes et des dernières lettres (..., x, y, z) pour désigner des variables ou des inconnues.

Invité à la cour de Catherine de Suède à l'automne 1649, Descartes mourut d'une infection pulmonaire quelque temps après. L'hiver suédois et les leçons de philosophie qu'il devait donner à la reine à cinq heures du matin ont probablement eu raison de celui qui aimait tant faire la grasse matinée pour s'adonner à ses méditations.

5.1 IMPORTANCE DU CONCEPT DE VECTEUR

Quoi qu'en ait pensé Lord Kelvin, qui affirmait que les vecteurs ne sont en rien essentiels, ces derniers ont de nombreuses applications. Conçus en premier lieu pour résoudre des problèmes de physique, et plus particulièrement de mécanique, les vecteurs ont bientôt été appliqués à d'autres domaines du savoir, notamment la biologie et l'économie.

En mécanique – la branche de la physique qui s'intéresse au mouvement – on a rapidement adopté un segment de droite orienté comme représentation géométrique d'un **vecteur**. Grâce à ce modèle, les physiciens ont pu distinguer les quantités physiques qui ne comportent qu'une grandeur (masse, longueur, volume, etc.), et qu'on appelle **scalaires**[1], des quantités physiques qui comportent une grandeur et une direction (vitesse, force, accélération, etc.), et qu'on appelle vecteurs.

VECTEUR

Pour les physiciens, un vecteur est une quantité qui possède une grandeur et une direction.

SCALAIRE

Pour les physiciens, un scalaire est une quantité physique qui ne comporte qu'une grandeur. Pour les mathématiciens, un scalaire est un nombre.

Ainsi, on représente un vent de 5 km/h venant du sud par le vecteur $\vec{u}$, et un vent du nord-ouest de 10 km/h par le vecteur $\vec{v}$.

On a noté chacun des vecteurs $\vec{u}$ et $\vec{v}$ par une lettre minuscule surmontée d'une flèche. De plus, le segment de droite qui représente le vecteur $\vec{v}$ est deux fois plus long que celui qui représente le vecteur $\vec{u}$ parce que l'intensité du vent du nord-ouest est deux fois plus grande : la longueur du vecteur $\vec{u}$ est de 5 unités, alors que celle du vecteur $\vec{v}$ est de 10 unités.

---

1. Le terme *scalaire* vient du mot anglais *scale*, qui veut dire « échelle ». Le prix Nobel de physique (1929) Louis de Broglie a écrit : « On les nomme grandeurs scalaires parce qu'elles suggèrent l'image d'une échelle de valeurs indépendamment de toute idée d'orientation. »

Par ailleurs, les physiciens décrivent les forces qui s'exercent sur un objet en mouvement sur un plan incliné par un schéma du type suivant, où les vecteurs représentent des forces.

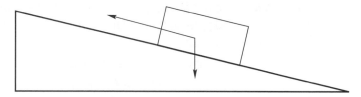

Les biologistes n'ont pas tardé à appliquer les principes élaborés par les physiciens à l'étude des corps vivants (dont le corps humain) en mouvement : ils ont créé la biomécanique. Le schéma qui suit illustre l'utilisation des vecteurs dans cette discipline.

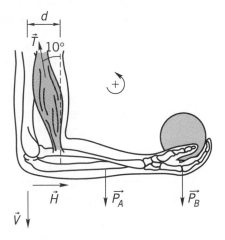

La représentation géométrique d'un vecteur adoptée par les physiciens se transpose naturellement dans un système de coordonnées à deux dimensions (le plan) ou à trois dimensions (l'espace). On peut alors étudier les vecteurs d'un point de vue algébrique et en généraliser l'application en les étendant à des espaces à *n* dimensions. Détachés de leur support géométrique, les vecteurs servent à décrire des réalités qui ne sont pas purement physiques ni géométriques. (Les notions de grandeur et de direction associées aux vecteurs géométriques n'ont plus alors nécessairement de sens.) Ainsi, en économie, on parle de vecteur prix et de vecteur quantité ; en démographie, on présente la structure par âge d'une population à l'aide d'un vecteur ; en biologie marine, on divise un écosystème en cinq groupes (phytoplancton, zooplancton, prédateurs de zooplancton, petits carnivores, grands carnivores), et on représente la biomasse de chacun par une composante d'un vecteur qui en comporte cinq. Et ce ne sont là que quelques exemples.

Bien qu'à l'origine il ait été associé à sa représentation géométrique, le concept de vecteur est maintenant doté d'un support algébrique. Pour tenir compte de ces deux facettes, nous étudierons les vecteurs géométriques et les vecteurs algébriques.

VECTEUR GÉOMÉTRIQUE

Un vecteur géométrique est un être mathématique qui possède une grandeur et une direction et qu'on peut représenter géométriquement par un segment de droite orienté (une flèche).

SUPPORT D'UN VECTEUR

Le support d'un vecteur est la droite qui porte ce vecteur.

On représente un **vecteur géométrique** par un segment de droite orienté, c'est-à-dire une flèche. La droite qui porte un vecteur est appelée **support** de ce vecteur. Un vecteur géométrique est caractérisé par les éléments suivants :

- une origine (le point d'application du vecteur) ;
- une extrémité (le point d'arrivée du vecteur ou la tête de la flèche) ;
- une longueur (la distance entre l'origine et l'extrémité du vecteur) ;
- une direction (l'angle ou les angles formés par le vecteur et un ou des axes de coordonnées). Dans le plan, la direction est donnée par l'angle, mesuré dans le sens contraire des aiguilles d'une montre, que fait le vecteur avec une demi-droite horizontale issue de l'origine du vecteur et ayant la même orientation que l'axe des abscisses.

Traditionnellement, on distinguait les mots sens et direction : cette dernière constituait la caractéristique commune à toutes les droites parallèles au vecteur, chaque direction comprenant alors deux sens opposés (par exemple de gauche à droite ou de droite à gauche sur un axe horizontal, et de haut en bas ou de bas en haut sur un axe vertical). Pourtant, on emploie couramment des expressions comme « en direction de Montréal », où le terme direction inclut la notion de sens. C'est pourquoi nous ne distinguerons pas ces deux mots. Dans le présent manuel, l'expression « direction[2] d'un vecteur » signifie « direction orientée » : elle traduit également l'idée de sens.

On note généralement un vecteur[3] par une seule lettre surmontée d'une flèche ($\vec{u}$, $\vec{v}$, $\vec{w}$, $\vec{F}$, $\vec{T}$, ...) ou encore par deux lettres majuscules surmontées d'une flèche ($\overrightarrow{AB}$, $\overrightarrow{CD}$, $\overrightarrow{EF}$, ...). Dans ce dernier cas, la première lettre représente l'origine du vecteur et la seconde, son extrémité. Par exemple, le vecteur $\overrightarrow{AB}$ a pour origine le point A et pour extrémité le point B. On peut interpréter un vecteur comme le déplacement de l'origine de ce vecteur vers son extrémité. Ainsi, le vecteur $\overrightarrow{AB}$ s'interprète

---

2. Les physiciens et la plupart des mathématiciens nord-américains ont laissé tomber la distinction entre direction et sens, pour ne garder que le mot direction. Il est difficile d'évaluer numériquement un sens, alors qu'il est facile d'évaluer une direction orientée définie par la mesure d'un ou de plusieurs angles. Certains auteurs emploient l'expression « orientation » pour désigner ce que nous appelons la direction.
3. On pourrait, comme le font plusieurs auteurs, distinguer les termes *vecteur libre*, *vecteur glissant* et *vecteur lié*. Nous avons délibérément choisi de ne pas faire cette distinction. Dans ce qui suit, chaque vecteur est considéré comme un représentant d'une classe d'équivalence, soit la classe des vecteurs qui ont la même longueur et la même direction que le vecteur en question. Nous ne traiterons donc que de vecteurs libres.

comme le déplacement de *A* vers *B*, dont la grandeur est égale à la longueur du vecteur.

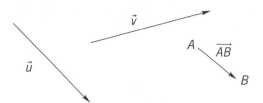

MODULE D'UN VECTEUR

Le module d'un vecteur est égal à la longueur de ce vecteur. Les termes *norme*, *intensité* et *grandeur* sont synonymes de module. On note le module d'un vecteur $\vec{u}$ par $\|\vec{u}\|$.

La longueur d'un vecteur est appelée indifféremment **module**, *norme*, *intensité* ou *grandeur* du vecteur. Le module d'un vecteur $\vec{v}$ est noté $\|\vec{v}\|$ (ou $|\vec{v}|$), celui de $\overrightarrow{AB}$ est noté $\|\overrightarrow{AB}\|$ (ou $|\overrightarrow{AB}|$). La longueur de la flèche représentant un vecteur est censée être proportionnelle au module du vecteur. Ainsi, un vecteur de module 5 est représenté par un segment de droite orienté d'une longueur de 5 unités. Le module d'un vecteur $\vec{v}$ est donc un scalaire (un nombre réel) non négatif : $\|\vec{v}\| \geq 0$.

VECTEUR NUL

Le vecteur nul, noté $\vec{0}$, est un vecteur dont le module vaut zéro. C'est le seul vecteur dont la direction est indéterminée.

Le vecteur de module 0 est appelé **vecteur nul** et il est noté $\vec{0}$. On peut évidemment se demander quelle est la direction du vecteur nul ? Pour des raisons pratiques, on s'entend pour dire que la direction du vecteur nul est indéterminée.

ÉGALITÉ DE DEUX VECTEURS GÉOMÉTRIQUES

Deux vecteurs géométriques sont égaux si et seulement s'ils ont le même module et la même direction.

Le concept d'**égalité de deux vecteurs géométriques** se fonde sur les caractéristiques des vecteurs : module et direction. Deux vecteurs $\vec{u}$ et $\vec{v}$ sont égaux[4] ($\vec{u} = \vec{v}$) si et seulement s'ils satisfont aux conditions suivantes :

• Ils ont le même module (la même longueur) : $\|\vec{u}\| = \|\vec{v}\|$.

• Ils ont la même direction : s'il s'agit de vecteurs du plan, ils sont parallèles et forment un même angle avec une demi-droite horizontale (la partie positive de l'axe des abscisses).

En vertu de cette définition, il n'est pas nécessaire que deux vecteurs aient la même origine ni la même extrémité pour être égaux. Par contre, il faut être capable de faire coïncider les origines et les extrémités respectives des deux vecteurs en appliquant une **translation** (déplacement rigide parallèle) à l'un d'entre eux.

TRANSLATION

Une translation d'un objet géométrique est un déplacement rigide et parallèle de cet objet : chaque point de l'objet est déplacé sur une même distance et dans une même direction.

---

4. L'expression « équipollents » serait plus juste : les deux vecteurs représentent une même classe d'équivalence. Toutefois, le terme « vecteurs égaux » est tellement répandu dans la littérature que nous lui avons accordé la préférence.

Exemple

Soit les vecteurs

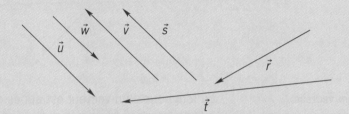

Les vecteurs $\vec{u}$ et $\vec{v}$ ne sont pas égaux bien qu'ils soient parallèles et de même longueur, car ils n'ont pas la même direction. Le vecteur $\vec{u}$ pointe dans la direction sud-est, et le vecteur $\vec{v}$ dans la direction nord-ouest. Il est impossible d'effectuer une translation du vecteur $\vec{u}$ sur le vecteur $\vec{v}$ de manière à faire coïncider à la fois leurs extrémités et leurs origines respectives.

Les vecteurs $\vec{u}$ et $\vec{w}$ ne sont pas égaux parce que, bien qu'ils aient la même direction, ils n'ont pas la même longueur. Les vecteurs $\vec{u}$ et $\vec{r}$ ont la même longueur, mais ils ne sont pas parallèles. Par conséquent, ils n'ont pas la même direction et ils ne sont donc pas égaux. Les vecteurs $\vec{u}$ et $\vec{t}$ n'ont ni la même longueur ni la même direction. Ils ne sont donc pas égaux.

Par contre, les vecteurs $\vec{v}$ et $\vec{s}$ sont égaux parce qu'ils ont la même longueur et la même direction. En effet, il est possible d'effectuer une translation du vecteur $\vec{v}$ sur le vecteur $\vec{s}$ de manière que les origines et les extrémités respectives des deux vecteurs coïncident.

EXERCICE 5.1

Soit le parallélogramme *ABCD* suivant.

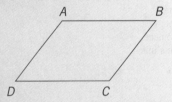

a) Les vecteurs $\overrightarrow{AD}$ et $\overrightarrow{AB}$ sont-ils égaux ? Justifiez votre réponse.

b) Les vecteurs $\overrightarrow{AD}$ et $\overrightarrow{CB}$ sont-ils égaux ? Justifiez votre réponse.

c) Trouvez un vecteur égal au vecteur $\overrightarrow{CD}$.

En vertu de la définition de l'égalité de deux vecteurs, on peut toujours déplacer un vecteur de façon que son origine coïncide avec l'origine du plan cartésien. La **direction d'un vecteur du plan** est alors donnée par l'angle, mesuré[5] dans le sens contraire des aiguilles d'une montre, que fait ce vecteur avec la partie positive de l'axe des abscisses.

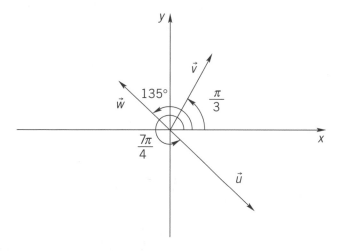

Ainsi, dans le schéma, la direction du vecteur $\vec{u}$ est de 315° (ou de $7\pi/4$) par rapport à la demi-droite $x \geq 0$, alors que la direction du vecteur $\vec{v}$ est de 60° (ou de $\pi/3$) et que celle du vecteur $\vec{w}$ est de 135° (ou de $3\pi/4$).

L'**angle entre deux vecteurs** $\vec{u}$ et $\vec{v}$ est le plus petit angle θ déterminé par ces vecteurs lorsque (après translation ou non) leurs origines coïncident. Par conséquent, $0 \leq \theta \leq \pi$ ou $0° \leq \theta \leq 180°$, selon que l'angle est mesuré en radians ou en degrés. Dans le schéma précédent, l'angle déterminé par les vecteurs $\vec{u}$ et $\vec{v}$ est de $7\pi/12$ (ou de 105°)[6].

Deux vecteurs ont la même direction lorsqu'ils déterminent un angle de 0°. Deux vecteurs ont des **directions contraires** ou *opposées* lorsqu'ils déterminent un angle de π ou de 180°. Ainsi, les vecteurs $\vec{u}$ et $\vec{w}$ du schéma précédent ont des directions contraires.

EXERCICE 5.2

Tracez deux vecteurs, dont l'un a une direction de 120° et l'autre une direction de $11\pi/6$.

---

5. On mesure un angle en degrés (°) ou en radians (rad). Dans le présent manuel, lorsqu'un angle est mesuré en radians, nous omettons d'écrire l'unité de mesure comme c'est souvent l'usage. Ainsi, on écrit un angle de π et non de π rad.
6. L'autre angle est de $360° - \theta = 255°$ (ou de $2\pi - \theta = 17\pi/12$).

Il est particulièrement facile de tracer des vecteurs du plan sur du papier graphique à coordonnées polaires (c'est-à-dire comportant une série de cercles concentriques sur lesquels on a indiqué des angles remarquables). Ainsi, la figure qui suit représente le vecteur $\vec{r}$ de longueur 8 et de direction $5\pi/4$, le vecteur $\vec{s}$ de longueur 5 et de direction $\pi/6$, et le vecteur $\vec{t}$ de longueur 7 et de direction $5\pi/3$.

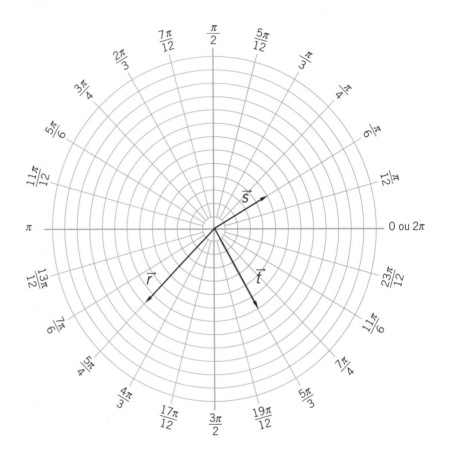

5.3 OPÉRATIONS SUR LES VECTEURS GÉOMÉTRIQUES DU PLAN

Nous sommes maintenant en mesure de définir différentes opérations sur les vecteurs géométriques du plan, soit l'addition de deux vecteurs, la multiplication d'un vecteur par un scalaire et le produit scalaire.

5.3.1 ADDITION DE DEUX VECTEURS

VECTEUR RÉSULTANT

Le vecteur résultant, ou la *résultante*, de deux vecteurs $\vec{u}$ et $\vec{v}$ est la somme de ces deux vecteurs, soit $\vec{u} + \vec{v}$.

Le résultat de l'addition, ou la somme, de deux vecteurs géométriques $\vec{u}$ et $\vec{v}$ est appelé **vecteur résultant** ou *résultante* des deux vecteurs, et on le note $\vec{u} + \vec{v}$. Il existe deux méthodes pour additionner deux vecteurs : la méthode du parallélogramme et la méthode du triangle.

MÉTHODE DU PARALLÉLOGRAMME

Méthode employée pour additionner deux vecteurs géométriques non parallèles. Elle consiste à faire coïncider les origines des deux vecteurs, puis à compléter le parallélogramme dont deux côtés correspondent à ces vecteurs. La somme recherchée est le vecteur correspondant à la diagonale du parallélogramme issue de l'origine des vecteurs à additionner.

Pour additionner deux vecteurs $\vec{u}$ et $\vec{v}$ par la **méthode du parallélogramme**, il faut d'abord faire coïncider les origines respectives des deux vecteurs, puis compléter le parallélogramme dont deux des côtés correspondent aux vecteurs $\vec{u}$ et $\vec{v}$. Le vecteur résultant correspond à la diagonale issue de l'origine commune des deux vecteurs, comme l'indique le schéma suivant.

Si les vecteurs $\vec{u}$ et $\vec{v}$ représentent des forces, alors le vecteur $\vec{u} + \vec{v}$ représente la force résultante, c'est-à-dire la force unique qui a le même effet que les deux forces combinées.

Toutefois, la méthode du parallélogramme ne peut servir à additionner deux vecteurs parallèles. C'est pourquoi on lui préfère la méthode du triangle. Pour additionner deux vecteurs $\vec{u}$ et $\vec{v}$ par la **méthode du triangle**, il faut d'abord faire coïncider l'origine du deuxième vecteur avec l'extrémité du premier. La résultante est le vecteur dont l'origine coïncide avec celle du premier vecteur et dont l'extrémité coïncide avec celle du deuxième vecteur, comme l'indique le schéma suivant.

MÉTHODE DU TRIANGLE

Méthode employée pour additionner deux vecteurs géométriques. Elle consiste, en premier lieu, à faire coïncider l'origine du deuxième vecteur avec l'extrémité du premier. Le vecteur résultant est le vecteur allant de l'origine du premier vecteur à l'extrémité du second.

On constate que le résultat est identique qu'on emploie l'une ou l'autre méthode.

EXERCICE 5.3

Soit les vecteurs

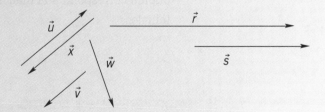

Tracez chacun des vecteurs résultants suivants.

a) $\vec{u} + \vec{w}$. Employez la méthode du parallélogramme.

b) $\vec{v} + \vec{r}$. Employez la méthode du triangle.

c) $\vec{u} + \vec{v}$. Peut-on employer la méthode du parallélogramme ?

d) $\vec{r} + \vec{s}$.

e) $\vec{u} + \vec{x}$. Quel nom donne-t-on au vecteur résultant ? Proposez un nom et une notation pour le vecteur $\vec{x}$ qui dénote sa relation au vecteur $\vec{u}$.

f) $\vec{u} + \vec{O}$. Que suggère ce résultat à propos du vecteur nul ?

n peu d'histoire

L'histoire du concept de vecteur est intimement liée à celle de la physique. Ainsi, des physiciens de la Grèce antique considéraient que la vitesse d'un objet dans une direction peut être représentée par un vecteur. L'auteur anonyme de *Mechanica*, un traité de physique datant du IVe siècle avant notre ère, affirme que le déplacement d'un corps s'effectue selon la diagonale du parallélogramme dont deux côtés adjacents représentent les vitesses de déplacement du corps dans ces directions. Toutefois, c'est un mathématicien flamand, Simon Stevin (1548-1620), qui formula le premier le principe d'addition des forces dans son traité de statique (*De beghinselen der weeghcoust*) publié en 1586 et traduit en latin (*Hypomnemata mathematica*), vingt ans plus tard, par W. Snell (1591-1626). Il montre que la force résultante de deux autres forces issues d'une même origine correspond à la diagonale du parallélogramme formé par les forces initiales.

5.3.2 PROPRIÉTÉS DE L'ADDITION DE VECTEURS

L'addition de vecteurs possède des propriétés intéressantes, énoncées dans le théorème 5.1.

Si $\vec{u}$, $\vec{v}$ et $\vec{w}$ sont des vecteurs du plan, alors

1) $\vec{u} + \vec{v}$ est un vecteur (fermeture).

2) $\vec{u} + \vec{v} = \vec{v} + \vec{u}$ (commutativité).

3) $(\vec{u} + \vec{v}) + \vec{w} = \vec{u} + (\vec{v} + \vec{w})$ (associativité).

4) $\vec{u} + \vec{0} = \vec{0} + \vec{u} = \vec{u}$. (Le vecteur nul est l'élément neutre pour l'addition de vecteurs.)

Voici des arguments informels qui devraient vous convaincre de la vérité de ces quatre énoncés.

La première propriété découle directement de la définition de l'addition de deux vecteurs : la somme de deux vecteurs est un vecteur.

La preuve de la deuxième propriété repose essentiellement sur le graphique suivant, où les deux méthodes d'addition sont appliquées.

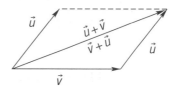

Quant à la preuve de la troisième propriété, elle s'appuie sur la comparaison des deux graphiques suivants, qui met en évidence le fait que

$$(\vec{u} + \vec{v}) + \vec{w} = \vec{u} + (\vec{v} + \vec{w})$$

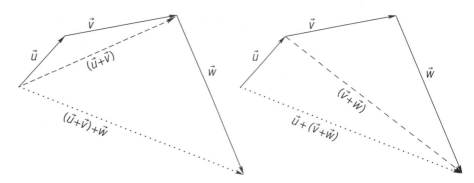

La quatrième propriété découle du fait que le vecteur nul représente un déplacement nul.

Règle de Chasles

La méthode du triangle convient particulièrement lorsqu'on souhaite additionner plus de deux vecteurs. Dans ce cas, on juxtapose l'extrémité de chaque vecteur avec l'origine du suivant. La résultante est le vecteur joignant l'origine du premier vecteur à l'extrémité du dernier vecteur.

Exemple

Soit les vecteurs

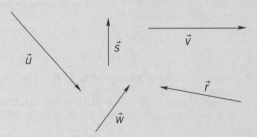

On obtient la somme $\vec{u} + \vec{v} + \vec{w} + \vec{r} + \vec{s}$ en joignant l'origine du vecteur $\vec{u}$ et l'extrémité du vecteur $\vec{s}$ après avoir appliqué des translations à tous les vecteurs, sauf $\vec{u}$, de manière que l'extrémité de chaque vecteur coïncide avec l'origine du vecteur suivant.

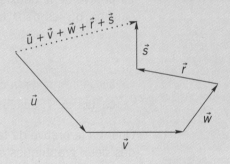

RÈGLE DE CHASLES

La règle de Chasles s'énonce comme suit : si A, B et C sont des points du plan ou de l'espace, alors
$$\overrightarrow{AB} + \overrightarrow{BC} = \overrightarrow{AC}$$
La généralisation de cette règle, appliquée à un nombre quelconque de points, est
$$\overrightarrow{AB} + \overrightarrow{BC} + \overrightarrow{CD} + \cdots + \overrightarrow{PQ} + \overrightarrow{QR} = \overrightarrow{AR}$$

Le procédé décrit ci-dessus donne la **règle de Chasles**, qui s'énonce comme suit : si A, B et C désignent trois points, alors
$$\overrightarrow{AB} + \overrightarrow{BC} = \overrightarrow{AC}$$

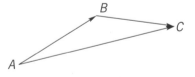

On peut évidemment étendre cette règle à plus de deux vecteurs. Si A, B, C, D, $\cdots$, P, Q, R désignent des points du plan (ou, comme nous le verrons plus tard, de l'espace), alors
$$\overrightarrow{AB} + \overrightarrow{BC} + \overrightarrow{CD} + \cdots + \overrightarrow{PQ} + \overrightarrow{QR} = \overrightarrow{AR}$$

Cette règle est simple à mémoriser. En effet, on peut considérer que le vecteur $\overrightarrow{AB}$ représente un déplacement de A à B, le vecteur $\overrightarrow{BC}$ un déplacement de B à C, le vecteur $\overrightarrow{CD}$ un déplacement de C à D, $\cdots$, le vecteur $\overrightarrow{QR}$ un déplacement de Q à R. La somme de ces vecteurs représente donc une suite de déplacements équivalente à un déplacement unique de A à R. On en conclut que la somme de ces vecteurs est le vecteur $\overrightarrow{AR}$.

Ainsi, il est clair que $\overrightarrow{AA}$ représente un déplacement de A à A, c'est-à-dire un déplacement nul ; d'où $\overrightarrow{AA} = \vec{O}$, le vecteur nul.

Le mathématicien français Michel Chasles (1793-1880) enseigna à l'École polytechnique et à la Sorbonne. En 1837, il publia un ouvrage qui contribua grandement à sa renommée : l'*Aperçu historique sur l'origine et le développement des méthodes en géométrie*, qui constitue une des premières et des plus remarquables histoires de la géométrie.

Chasles était toutefois extrêmement chauvin. Lorsqu'un certain Vrain-Denis Lucas lui présenta des lettres soi-disant écrites par Pascal, dans lesquelles ce dernier formule la loi de la gravitation, Chasles s'empressa de les acheter. Il était convaincu de pouvoir ainsi montrer que la découverte de la loi de la gravitation est attribuable à un Français (Pascal) plutôt qu'à un Anglais (Newton). Entre 1861 et 1869, il acheta de Lucas, à prix fort (140 000 francs), plus de 27 000 lettres, dont 175 lettres de Pascal adressées à Newton, 139 de Pascal à Galilée, six d'Alexandre le Grand à Aristote, une de Cléopâtre à César, une de Marie-Madeleine à Lazare et une de Lazare à Saint-Pierre. Bien que toutes ces lettres aient été écrites en français et sur du papier, Chasles ne se rendit pas compte de la supercherie. Lorsqu'il présenta les prétendues lettres de Pascal à l'Académie des sciences, on lui fit remarquer que l'écriture ne ressemblait pas du tout à celle de Pascal. Ce n'est qu'après plusieurs années de controverse, que Chasles reconnut s'être fait duper. Quant à l'auteur des contrefaçons, Vrain-Denis Lucas, il fut condamné à deux ans de pénitencier.

5.3.3 MODULE ET DIRECTION D'UN VECTEUR RÉSULTANT

Voyons maintenant comment déterminer le module et la direction du vecteur résultant de $\vec{u}$ et de $\vec{v}$, c'est-à-dire de la somme de ces deux vecteurs du plan.

On note θ l'angle entre les vecteurs $\vec{u}$ et $\vec{v}$, α l'angle entre les vecteurs $\vec{u}$ et $\vec{u} + \vec{v}$, et β la direction du vecteur $\vec{u}$.

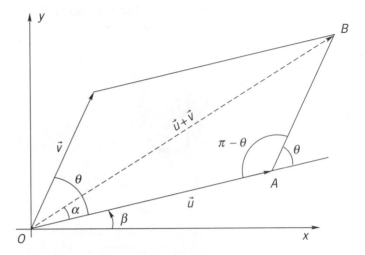

En appliquant la loi des cosinus au triangle OAB, on obtient

$$OB^2 = OA^2 + AB^2 - 2(OA)(AB)\cos(\pi - \theta)$$

On en déduit que

$$OB = \sqrt{OA^2 + AB^2 - 2(OA)(AB)\cos(\pi - \theta)}$$

Si on exprime la longueur des segments de droite en fonction des modules des vecteurs correspondants, alors la longueur du vecteur résultant est

$$\|\vec{u} + \vec{v}\| = \sqrt{\|\vec{u}\|^2 + \|\vec{v}\|^2 - 2\|\vec{u}\|\,\|\vec{v}\|\cos(\pi - \theta)}$$

Comme $\cos(\pi - \theta) = -\cos\theta$, la longueur du vecteur résultant est donnée par

$$\|\vec{u} + \vec{v}\| = \sqrt{\|\vec{u}\|^2 + \|\vec{v}\|^2 + 2\|\vec{u}\|\,\|\vec{v}\|\cos\theta}$$

Si on applique à nouveau la loi des cosinus pour l'angle α du même triangle, on obtient

$$\|\vec{v}\|^2 = \|\vec{u} + \vec{v}\|^2 + \|\vec{u}\|^2 - 2\|\vec{u}\|\,\|\vec{u} + \vec{v}\|\cos\alpha$$

Donc, l'angle α entre les vecteurs $\vec{u}$ et $\vec{u} + \vec{v}$ est donné par

$$\alpha = \text{arc } \cos\left(\frac{\|\vec{u} + \vec{v}\|^2 + \|\vec{u}\|^2 - \|\vec{v}\|^2}{2\|\vec{u}\|\,\|\vec{u} + \vec{v}\|}\right)$$

On tire également du graphique précédent que la direction du vecteur résultant $\vec{u} + \vec{v}$ est $\alpha + \beta$.

Il n'est pas utile de retenir ces formules, mais il est important de comprendre la marche à suivre pour trouver la norme et la direction de la somme de deux vecteurs. Ces informations seront d'ailleurs beaucoup plus faciles à obtenir dans le cas de vecteurs algébriques.

Soit les vecteurs $\vec{u}$ et $\vec{v}$ suivants, tracés dans un plan cartésien.

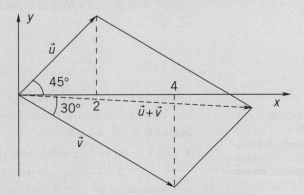

Pour trouver la longueur et la direction du vecteur $\vec{u} + \vec{v}$, il faut d'abord calculer la longueur des vecteurs $\vec{u}$ et $\vec{v}$. Or,

$$\|\vec{u}\| \cos 45° = 2 \quad \Rightarrow \quad \|\vec{u}\| = \frac{2}{\cos 45°} = 2\sqrt{2}$$

et de manière analogue,

$$\|\vec{v}\| \cos 30° = 4 \quad \Rightarrow \quad \|\vec{v}\| = \frac{4}{\cos 30°} = \frac{8}{3}\sqrt{3}$$

On en déduit que

$$\|\vec{u} + \vec{v}\| = \sqrt{\|\vec{u}\|^2 + \|\vec{v}\|^2 + 2\|\vec{u}\|\,\|\vec{v}\|\cos\theta}$$

$$= \sqrt{8 + \frac{64}{3} + 2(2\sqrt{2})\left(\frac{8}{3}\sqrt{3}\right)\cos 75°}$$

$$\approx 6,0$$

L'angle entre les vecteurs $\vec{u}$ et $\vec{u} + \vec{v}$ est

$$\alpha = \text{arc } \cos\left(\frac{\|\vec{u} + \vec{v}\|^2 + \|\vec{u}\|^2 - \|\vec{v}\|^2}{2\|\vec{u}\|\,\|\vec{u} + \vec{v}\|}\right) \approx 47,9°$$

Par conséquent, la direction du vecteur résultant $\vec{u} + \vec{v}$ est d'environ 357° (soit 45° − 47,9° = −2,9°, ou 357,1°).

EXERCICE 5.4

Soit le vecteur $\vec{u}$ de longueur 4 et de direction 60°, et le vecteur $\vec{v}$ de longueur 8 et de direction 120°.

a) Calculez la longueur et la direction du vecteur $-\vec{u}$.

b) Calculez la longueur et la direction du vecteur $\vec{u} + \vec{v}$.

c) Calculez la longueur et la direction du vecteur $\vec{u} - \vec{v}$.

5.3.4 MULTIPLICATION D'UN VECTEUR PAR UN SCALAIRE

La multiplication d'un vecteur par un scalaire est la deuxième opération sur les vecteurs que nous définissons. Le **produit d'un vecteur $\vec{u}$ par un scalaire** k est un vecteur, noté $k\vec{u}$, qui possède les propriétés suivantes :

• $\|k\vec{u}\| = |k|\,\|\vec{u}\|$, c'est-à-dire que la longueur du vecteur $k\vec{u}$ est égale à $|k|$ fois la longueur du vecteur $\vec{u}$.

• Le vecteur $k\vec{u}$ est parallèle au vecteur $\vec{u}$.

• Les vecteurs $\vec{u}$ et $k\vec{u}$ ont la même direction si $k > 0$ et des directions contraires si $k < 0$. Si $k = 0$, le vecteur $k\vec{u}$ est le vecteur nul, c'est-à-dire que $0\vec{u} = \vec{0}$.

Il est à noter que la multiplication par un scalaire est une opération sur deux entités qui n'appartiennent pas au même ensemble : k est un scalaire et $\vec{u}$ est un vecteur. Le résultat de cette opération est toutefois un vecteur.

Vous devriez être en mesure de déduire de la définition donnée ci-dessus que deux vecteurs non nuls $\vec{u}$ et $\vec{v}$ sont parallèles si et seulement s'il existe un scalaire k tel que $k\vec{u} = \vec{v}$ ou $k\vec{v} = \vec{u}$, c'est-à-dire si le vecteur $\vec{v}$ (ou $\vec{u}$) s'exprime comme le produit du vecteur $\vec{u}$ (ou $\vec{v}$) par un scalaire k.

Exemple

Soit les vecteurs $\vec{u}$, $-\vec{u}$, $2\vec{u}$ et $-\frac{1}{2}\vec{u}$ suivants.

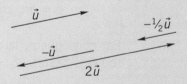

On remarque que ces quatre vecteurs sont parallèles. La norme du vecteur $2\vec{u}$ est deux fois plus grande que celle du vecteur $\vec{u}$, alors que la norme du vecteur $-\frac{1}{2}\vec{u}$ n'est que la moitié de celle du vecteur $\vec{u}$. On note également que le vecteur $2\vec{u}$ a la même direction que le vecteur $\vec{u}$, alors que le vecteur $-\frac{1}{2}\vec{u}$ est de direction contraire. Enfin, on constate que le vecteur $\vec{u} + (-\vec{u}) = \vec{u} - \vec{u} = \vec{0}$. Le vecteur $-\vec{u}$ est donc le **vecteur opposé** de $\vec{u}$.

Il ressort de la définition du produit d'un vecteur par un scalaire que l'opposé d'un vecteur $\overrightarrow{AB}$ est le vecteur $\overrightarrow{BA}$. On en tire une relation très importante, à laquelle nous ferons fréquemment appel :

$$-\overrightarrow{AB} = \overrightarrow{BA}$$

En effet, le vecteur $\overrightarrow{BA}$ est parallèle au vecteur $\overrightarrow{AB}$ et il a la même longueur que $\overrightarrow{AB}$ mais il est de direction contraire.

Cette propriété et la règle de Chasles permettent de simplifier diverses expressions vectorielles.

Exemple

On simplifie l'expression $\overrightarrow{AB} - \overrightarrow{CB} + \overrightarrow{CD}$ comme suit :

$$\overrightarrow{AB} - \overrightarrow{CB} + \overrightarrow{CD} = \overrightarrow{AB} - (-\overrightarrow{BC}) + \overrightarrow{CD} = \overrightarrow{AB} + \overrightarrow{BC} + \overrightarrow{CD} = \overrightarrow{AD}$$

5.3.5 PROPRIÉTÉS DE LA MULTIPLICATION D'UN VECTEUR PAR UN SCALAIRE

Tout comme pour l'addition, la multiplication d'un vecteur par un scalaire présente des propriétés intéressantes, que nous avons regroupées dans le théorème 5.2.

Théorème 5.2

Si $\vec{u}$ et $\vec{v}$ sont des vecteurs du plan et a et b des scalaires, alors

1) $1\vec{u} = \vec{u}$

2) $a\vec{0} = \vec{0}$

3) $(ab)\vec{u} = a(b\vec{u})$

4) $(a + b)\vec{u} = a\vec{u} + b\vec{u}$

5) $a(\vec{u} + \vec{v}) = a\vec{u} + a\vec{v}$

VECTEUR UNITAIRE

Un vecteur unitaire est un vecteur dont le module (la longueur) vaut 1.

6) Si $\vec{u} \neq 0$, alors le vecteur $\dfrac{1}{\|\vec{u}\|}\vec{u}$ est un **vecteur unitaire**, c'est-à-dire un vecteur de longueur 1.

Nous nous contentons de démontrer la propriété 6.

Propriété 6 Le vecteur $\dfrac{1}{\|\vec{u}\|}\vec{u}$ est un vecteur unitaire si $\vec{u} \neq \vec{0}$.

Preuve

Comme $\vec{u} \neq \vec{0}$, alors $\|\vec{u}\| \neq 0$ et l'expression $\dfrac{1}{\|\vec{u}\|}\vec{u}$ est définie. On veut

montrer que le module du vecteur $\dfrac{1}{\|\vec{u}\|}\vec{u}$ vaut 1. Or,

$$\left\|\dfrac{1}{\|\vec{u}\|}\vec{u}\right\| = \left|\dfrac{1}{\|\vec{u}\|}\right| \|\vec{u}\| = \dfrac{1}{\|\vec{u}\|} \|\vec{u}\| = 1$$

Par conséquent, $\dfrac{1}{\|\vec{u}\|}\vec{u}$ est un vecteur unitaire. ∎

5.3.6 COMBINAISON LINÉAIRE DE VECTEURS

On peut combiner l'addition de vecteurs et la multiplication d'un vecteur par un scalaire. Ainsi, l'expression $3\vec{u} + 4\vec{v} - 2\vec{w}$ est définie.

EXERCICE 5.5

Soit les vecteurs

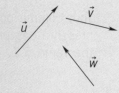

Tracez les vecteurs :

a) $3\vec{u}$ b) $-2\vec{w}$ c) $3\vec{u} + 4\vec{v} - 2\vec{w}$

COMBINAISON LINÉAIRE

Une combinaison linéaire des n vecteurs $\vec{u_1}$, $\vec{u_2}$, ..., $\vec{u_n}$ est une expression de la forme

$$a_1\vec{u_1} + a_2\vec{u_2} + \cdots + a_n\vec{u_n}$$

où a_1, a_2, ..., a_n sont des scalaires.

Toute expression de la forme $a_1\vec{u_1} + a_2\vec{u_2} + \cdots + a_n\vec{u_n}$, où a_1, a_2, ..., a_n sont des scalaires, est une **combinaison linéaire** des n vecteurs $\vec{u_1}$, $\vec{u_2}$, ..., $\vec{u_n}$. La notion de combinaison linéaire est un concept clé auquel nous ferons souvent appel. Souvenez-vous qu'il s'agit de la « combinaison » de l'addition de vecteurs et de la multiplication d'un vecteur par un scalaire.

Le théorème 5.3 énonce une propriété fondamentale des vecteurs du plan.

Théorème 5.3

Si $\vec{u}$ et $\vec{v}$ sont deux vecteurs non nuls et non parallèles du plan, alors tout vecteur $\vec{w}$ du plan s'écrit comme une combinaison linéaire des vecteurs $\vec{u}$ et $\vec{v}$.

Preuve

On distingue trois cas.

Premier cas : $\vec{w} = \vec{0}$.

$\vec{w} = \vec{0} \Rightarrow \vec{w} = \vec{0} + \vec{0} = 0\vec{u} + 0\vec{v}$, cette dernière somme étant une combinaison linéaire des vecteurs $\vec{u}$ et $\vec{v}$.

Deuxième cas : Le vecteur $\vec{w}$ est parallèle à l'un des vecteurs $\vec{u}$ et $\vec{v}$.

Si $\vec{w}$ est parallèle à $\vec{u}$, alors $\vec{w} = a\vec{u} = a\vec{u} + \vec{0} = a\vec{u} + 0\vec{v}$. De façon similaire, si $\vec{w}$ est parallèle à $\vec{v}$, alors $\vec{w} = a\vec{v} = a\vec{v} + \vec{0} = a\vec{v} + 0\vec{u}$. Par conséquent, si le vecteur $\vec{w}$ est parallèle à l'un des vecteurs $\vec{u}$ et $\vec{v}$, il s'écrit comme une combinaison linéaire des vecteurs $\vec{u}$ et $\vec{v}$.

Troisième cas : Le vecteur $\vec{w}$ n'est parallèle ni à $\vec{u}$ ni à $\vec{v}$.

Comme aucun des trois vecteurs n'est parallèle à l'un des deux autres vecteurs, il est possible de les tracer dans le plan de façon que leurs origines coïncident, comme l'indique le schéma suivant.

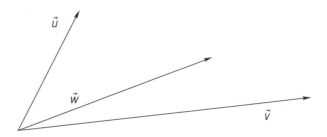

La longueur des vecteurs et leur position relative pourraient être différentes mais cela ne changerait essentiellement rien à l'argument qui suit.

On construit le parallélogramme ayant comme diagonale le vecteur $\vec{w}$ et dont les côtés correspondent à des vecteurs respectivement parallèles aux vecteurs $\vec{u}$ et $\vec{v}$. Alors $\vec{w} = a\vec{u} + b\vec{v}$ où a et b sont des scalaires.

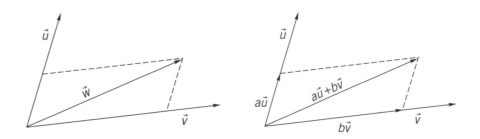

Il est possible que l'un ou l'autre des coefficients a et b soit négatif, comme l'indique le schéma suivant.

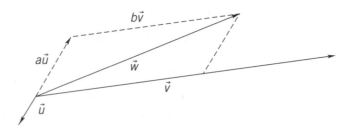

Tout vecteur du plan s'écrit donc comme une combinaison linéaire de deux vecteurs non nuls non parallèles du plan. ∎

5.3.7 INDÉPENDANCE LINÉAIRE DE PLUSIEURS VECTEURS

VECTEURS LINÉAIREMENT INDÉPENDANTS

Des vecteurs $\vec{u_1}$, $\vec{u_2}$, ..., $\vec{u_n}$ sont dits linéairement indépendants si et seulement si *la seule* combinaison linéaire de ces vecteurs qui soit égale au vecteur nul est celle où tous les coefficients (ou scalaires) sont nuls. De manière plus formelle, n vecteurs $\vec{u_1}$, $\vec{u_2}$, ..., $\vec{u_n}$ sont dits linéairement indépendants si et seulement si

$a_1\vec{u_1} + a_2\vec{u_2} + \cdots + a_n\vec{u_n} = \vec{0}$
$\Rightarrow\ a_1 = 0,\ a_2 = 0,\ ...,\ a_n = 0$

VECTEURS LINÉAIREMENT DÉPENDANTS

Des vecteurs $\vec{u_1}$, $\vec{u_2}$, ..., $\vec{u_n}$ sont linéairement dépendants si et seulement s'il existe une combinaison linéaire de ces vecteurs égale au vecteur nul et telle qu'au moins un des coefficients est différent de zéro, c'est-à-dire s'il existe une combinaison linéaire égale au vecteur nul et différente de celle où tous les coefficients sont nuls.

Le concept d'indépendance linéaire est étroitement lié à celui de combinaison linéaire. On dit que n **vecteurs** $\vec{u_1}$, $\vec{u_2}$, ..., $\vec{u_n}$ sont **linéairement indépendants** si et seulement si *la seule* combinaison linéaire de ces vecteurs égale au vecteur nul est celle où tous les coefficients (ou scalaires) sont nuls.

De manière plus formelle, n vecteurs $\vec{u_1}$, $\vec{u_2}$, ..., $\vec{u_n}$ sont dits linéairement indépendants si et seulement si

$$a_1\vec{u_1} + a_2\vec{u_2} + \cdots + a_n\vec{u_n} = \vec{0} \quad \Rightarrow \quad a_1 = 0,\ a_2 = 0,\ ...,\ a_n = 0$$

Il est clair que toute combinaison linéaire de vecteurs où tous les coefficients sont nuls est égale au vecteur nul. Pour montrer que des vecteurs sont linéairement indépendants, il faut montrer que cette combinaison linéaire particulière est *la seule* qui soit égale au vecteur nul.

Si des **vecteurs** ne sont pas linéairement indépendants, on dit qu'ils sont **linéairement dépendants**. Par conséquent, les vecteurs $\vec{u_1}$, $\vec{u_2}$, ..., $\vec{u_n}$ sont linéairement dépendants si et seulement s'il existe une combinaison linéaire de ces vecteurs qui soit égale au vecteur nul et dans laquelle au moins un des coefficients est différent de zéro, c'est-à-dire si et seulement s'il existe une combinaison linéaire égale au vecteur nul et différente de celle où tous les coefficients sont nuls.

Exemple

Dans le schéma suivant, les vecteurs $\vec{u}$ et $\vec{v}$ sont linéairement indépendants, alors que les vecteurs $\vec{u}$ et $\vec{w}$ sont linéairement dépendants.

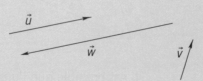

En effet, on note que les vecteurs $\vec{u}$ et $\vec{v}$ ne sont pas parallèles, alors que les vecteurs $\vec{u}$ et $\vec{w}$ le sont.

Si $\vec{u}$ et $\vec{v}$ étaient des vecteurs linéairement dépendants, alors il existerait une combinaison linéaire $a\vec{u} + b\vec{v} = \vec{0}$ telle que $a \neq 0$ ou $b \neq 0$. Sans perte de généralité, on peut supposer que $a \neq 0$. Il s'ensuit que

$$a\vec{u} + b\vec{v} = \vec{0} \quad \Rightarrow \quad a\vec{u} = \vec{0} - b\vec{v} = -b\vec{v} \quad \Rightarrow \quad \vec{u} = -\frac{b}{a}\vec{v}$$

Cela revient à dire que les vecteurs $\vec{u}$ et $\vec{v}$ sont parallèles, ce qui contredit l'hypothèse. Par conséquent, les vecteurs $\vec{u}$ et $\vec{v}$ sont linéairement indépendants.

En fait, deux vecteurs non nuls du plan qui ne sont pas parallèles sont toujours linéairement indépendants.

Par ailleurs, comme les vecteurs $\vec{u}$ et $\vec{w}$ sont parallèles, il existe un scalaire k tel que $k\vec{u} = \vec{w}$, d'où $k\vec{u} - \vec{w} = \vec{0}$. Il existe donc une combinaison linéaire des vecteurs $\vec{u}$ et $\vec{w}$ qui est égale au vecteur nul et telle qu'au moins un des coefficients est différent de zéro. En effet, le coefficient de $\vec{w}$ vaut -1. Par conséquent, en vertu de la définition de l'indépendance linéaire, les vecteurs $\vec{u}$ et $\vec{w}$ sont linéairement dépendants.

En fait, deux vecteurs parallèles du plan sont toujours linéairement dépendants.

EXERCICE 5.6

À l'aide du théorème 5.3 et des résultats présentés dans l'exemple précédent, montrez que tout vecteur du plan s'écrit comme une combinaison linéaire de deux vecteurs linéairement indépendants.

5.3.8 PRODUIT SCALAIRE ET ANGLE ENTRE DEUX VECTEURS

PRODUIT SCALAIRE

Le produit scalaire est une opération sur deux vecteurs, dont le résultat est un scalaire. Le produit scalaire de deux vecteurs $\vec{u}$ et $\vec{v}$ est donné par l'expression

$$\vec{u} \cdot \vec{v} = \|\vec{u}\| \, \|\vec{v}\| \cos \theta$$

où θ représente l'angle déterminé par les vecteurs $\vec{u}$ et $\vec{v}$.

La troisième opération, soit le produit scalaire, est une opération sur deux vecteurs et son résultat est un scalaire. Le **produit scalaire** de deux vecteurs $\vec{u}$ et $\vec{v}$, noté $\vec{u} \cdot \vec{v}$ (lire « u point v » ou « u scalaire v »), est donné par l'expression

$$\vec{u} \cdot \vec{v} = \|\vec{u}\| \, \|\vec{v}\| \cos \theta$$

où θ représente l'angle déterminé par les vecteurs $\vec{u}$ et $\vec{v}$.

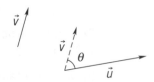

Par conséquent, $0 \le \theta \le \pi$ ou $0° \le \theta \le 180°$ selon que l'angle est mesuré en radians ou en degrés.

Exemple

Si l'angle entre deux vecteurs $\vec{u}$ et $\vec{v}$ est de 60° et si les modules de ces vecteurs sont respectivement de 3 et de 5, alors

$$\vec{u} \cdot \vec{v} = \|\vec{u}\| \|\vec{v}\| \cos \theta = 3 \times 5 \times \cos 60° = 3 \times 5 \times 0{,}5 = 7{,}5$$

La formule du produit scalaire sert également à calculer l'angle entre deux vecteurs non nuls dont on connaît les modules et le produit scalaire :

$$\vec{u} \cdot \vec{v} = \|\vec{u}\| \|\vec{v}\| \cos \theta \;\; \Rightarrow \;\; \cos \theta = \frac{\vec{u} \cdot \vec{v}}{\|\vec{u}\| \|\vec{v}\|} \;\; \Rightarrow \;\; \theta = \text{arc} \cos \frac{\vec{u} \cdot \vec{v}}{\|\vec{u}\| \|\vec{v}\|}$$

EXERCICE 5.7

Complétez le tableau suivant dans lequel $\vec{u}$ et $\vec{v}$ sont des vecteurs et θ est l'angle entre ces deux vecteurs.

	$\|\vec{u}\|$	$\|\vec{v}\|$	θ	$\vec{u} \cdot \vec{v}$	
a)	4	8	30°	____	
b)	3	4	____	0	Que peut-on dire de $\vec{u}$ et de $\vec{v}$?
c)	2	2	____	−4	Que peut-on dire de $\vec{u}$ et de $\vec{v}$?

5.3.9 PROPRIÉTÉS DU PRODUIT SCALAIRE

Le produit scalaire possède des propriétés intéressantes, que nous avons regroupées dans le théorème 5.4.

Théorème 5.4

Soit trois vecteurs $\vec{u}$, $\vec{v}$ et $\vec{w}$, et un scalaire a.

1) $\vec{u} \cdot \vec{v} = \vec{v} \cdot \vec{u}$ (commutativité)
2) $\vec{u} \cdot (\vec{v} + \vec{w}) = \vec{u} \cdot \vec{v} + \vec{u} \cdot \vec{w}$ (distributivité du produit scalaire par rapport à l'addition de vecteurs)

3) $a(\vec{u} \cdot \vec{v}) = (a\vec{u}) \cdot \vec{v} = \vec{u} \cdot (a\vec{v})$

4) $\vec{u} \cdot \vec{0} = 0$

5) $\vec{u} \cdot \vec{u} = \|\vec{u}\|^2$

6) Deux vecteurs non nuls $\vec{u}$ et $\vec{v}$ sont perpendiculaires si et seulement si $\vec{u} \cdot \vec{v} = 0$.

Nous allons démontrer immédiatement les propriétés 1, 5 et 6, et nous prouverons plus loin la propriété 2. Nous vous laissons le soin de faire les autres démonstrations, en guise d'exercice.

Propriété 1 $\vec{u} \cdot \vec{v} = \vec{v} \cdot \vec{u}$

Preuve

$\vec{u} \cdot \vec{v} = \|\vec{u}\| \|\vec{v}\| \cos \theta$ (définition du produit scalaire)

$= \|\vec{v}\| \|\vec{u}\| \cos \theta$ (commutativité de la multiplication dans les réels)

$= \vec{v} \cdot \vec{u}$ (définition du produit scalaire)   ∎

Propriété 5 $\vec{u} \cdot \vec{u} = \|\vec{u}\|^2$

Preuve

$\vec{u} \cdot \vec{u} = \|\vec{u}\| \|\vec{u}\| \cos \theta$ (définition du produit scalaire)

$= \|\vec{u}\|^2 \cos 0°$ (l'angle entre $\vec{u}$ et $\vec{u}$ vaut 0°)

$= \|\vec{u}\|^2$ (cos 0° = 1)   ∎

Propriété 6   Deux vecteurs non nuls $\vec{u}$ et $\vec{v}$ sont perpendiculaires si et seulement si $\vec{u} \cdot \vec{v} = 0$.

Preuve

($\Rightarrow$) Si $\vec{u}$ et $\vec{v}$ sont perpendiculaires, alors

$\vec{u} \cdot \vec{v} = \|\vec{u}\| \|\vec{v}\| \cos \theta$ (définition du produit scalaire)

$= \|\vec{u}\| \|\vec{v}\| \cos 90°$ (l'angle entre deux vecteurs perpendiculaires vaut 90°)

$= \|\vec{u}\| \|\vec{v}\| (0)$

$= 0$

($\Leftarrow$) $\vec{u} \cdot \vec{v} = 0 \Rightarrow \|\vec{u}\| \|\vec{v}\| \cos \theta = 0$

Or, un produit de nombres réels ne vaut zéro que si au moins l'un des facteurs vaut zéro. Comme les vecteurs $\vec{u}$ et $\vec{v}$ sont non nuls, leurs modules sont différents de zéro. Il faut donc que cos $\theta = 0$, d'où $\theta = 90°$. Les vecteurs $\vec{u}$ et $\vec{v}$ sont donc perpendiculaires.   ∎

Deux vecteurs sont orthogonaux si
et seulement si leur produit scalaire
est zéro. Dans le plan ou l'espace,
des vecteurs orthogonaux non nuls
sont perpendiculaires.

On appelle **vecteurs orthogonaux**[7] deux vecteurs dont le produit scalaire vaut zéro. Il découle de la propriété 6 que deux vecteurs non nuls du plan (ou de l'espace) sont orthogonaux si et seulement s'ils sont perpendiculaires.

EXERCICE 5.8

Prouvez la propriété 4 du théorème 5.4.

Dans l'exercice 5.6, vous avez montré que tout vecteur du plan s'écrit comme une combinaison linéaire de deux vecteurs linéairement indépendants. Par conséquent, deux vecteurs du plan linéairement indépendants forment en quelque sorte le matériau avec lequel on construit l'ensemble des vecteurs du plan (ou l'espace de tous les vecteurs du plan). Ces deux vecteurs constituent ce qu'on appelle un **système générateur** parce que l'ensemble de leurs combinaisons linéaires engendre l'ensemble de tous les vecteurs du plan. C'est pourquoi on dit que deux vecteurs linéairement indépendants forment une base de l'espace des vecteurs (ou l'espace vectoriel) du plan. Nous généraliserons les concepts de base et d'espace vectoriel dans un chapitre subséquent. Notons toutefois que, pour former une **base d'un espace vectoriel**, un ensemble de vecteurs doit posséder les deux caractéristiques suivantes :

SYSTÈME GÉNÉRATEUR

Un ensemble de vecteurs est un
système générateur d'un espace
vectoriel si tout vecteur de cet
espace s'écrit comme une
combinaison linéaire des vecteurs
de l'ensemble.

BASE D'UN ESPACE VECTORIEL

Une base d'un espace vectoriel
est un ensemble de vecteurs
linéairement indépendants de
cet espace, qui forment un système
générateur de l'espace.

- les vecteurs de l'ensemble doivent être linéairement indépendants ;

- les vecteurs doivent former un système générateur.

Si la base d'un espace vectoriel est telle que le produit scalaire de chaque paire de vecteurs distincts vaut 0, on dit qu'il s'agit d'une **base orthogonale**. Dans le cas des vecteurs du plan, deux vecteurs perpendiculaires non nuls forment une base orthogonale.

BASE ORTHOGONALE

Une base orthogonale d'un espace
vectoriel est une base formée de
vecteurs orthogonaux deux à deux.

BASE ORTHONORMÉE

Une base orthonormée d'un espace
vectoriel est une base formée de
vecteurs orthogonaux unitaires.

Si les vecteurs d'une base orthogonale sont unitaires, on dit qu'ils forment une **base orthonormée**.

5.4 PREUVES VECTORIELLES EN GÉOMÉTRIE

On peut faire appel aux vecteurs pour démontrer, de façon élégante, certains théorèmes de la géométrie euclidienne.

---

7. Orthogonal a pour étymologie deux mots grecs, soit *orthos* qui veut dire « droit » et *gônos* qui veut dire « angle » ; des vecteurs orthogonaux forment un angle droit.

Exemple

Les diagonales d'un parallélogramme se coupent en leur milieu.

Preuve

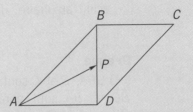

Soit un parallélogramme *ABCD* quelconque. On note *P* le milieu du segment de droite *BD* (l'une des deux diagonales du parallélogramme). On veut montrer que *P* est le milieu du segment *AC*, c'est-à-dire que $\overrightarrow{AP} = \frac{1}{2}\overrightarrow{AC}$ ou, ce qui est équivalent, $2\overrightarrow{AP} = \overrightarrow{AC}$.

Or, d'une part, $\overrightarrow{AP} = \overrightarrow{AB} + \overrightarrow{BP}$ et, d'autre part, $\overrightarrow{AP} = \overrightarrow{AD} + \overrightarrow{DP}$, de sorte que

$$2\overrightarrow{AP} = \overrightarrow{AB} + \overrightarrow{BP} + \overrightarrow{AD} + \overrightarrow{DP} = \overrightarrow{AB} + \overrightarrow{AD} + \overrightarrow{BP} + \overrightarrow{DP}$$

En vertu de la définition de l'addition de deux vecteurs (méthode du parallélogramme), $\overrightarrow{AB} + \overrightarrow{AD} = \overrightarrow{AC}$. De plus, comme *P* est le milieu du segment *BD*, on a $\overrightarrow{BP} + \overrightarrow{DP} = \vec{0}$.

Par conséquent, $2\overrightarrow{AP} = \overrightarrow{AC}$, d'où $\overrightarrow{AP} = \frac{1}{2}\overrightarrow{AC}$. Ainsi, en vertu de la définition de la multiplication par un scalaire, le point *P* divise la deuxième diagonale *AC* en deux parties égales. Le point *P* est donc situé à l'intersection des deux diagonales, qu'il divise en deux parties égales. Les diagonales du parallélogramme se coupent donc en leur milieu. ∎

EXERCICE 5.9

Montrez que le segment de droite qui joint les milieux de deux côtés d'un triangle est parallèle au troisième côté et deux fois plus court que ce dernier.

Le théorème suivant s'avère utile dans certaines démonstrations vectorielles.

Théorème 5.5

Trois points distincts A, B et C sont colinéaires (c'est-à-dire situés sur une même droite) si et seulement si, pour tout autre point O, appelé point auxiliaire, il existe un scalaire k pour lequel

$$\overrightarrow{OC} = k\overrightarrow{OA} + (1 - k)\overrightarrow{OB}$$

Preuve

($\Rightarrow$) Si A, B et C sont trois points distincts et colinéaires, alors les vecteurs $\overrightarrow{BC}$ et $\overrightarrow{BA}$ sont parallèles, de sorte qu'il existe un scalaire k tel que $\overrightarrow{BC} = k\overrightarrow{BA}$. Par conséquent,

$$
\begin{aligned}
\overrightarrow{OC} &= \overrightarrow{OB} + \overrightarrow{BC} \\
&= \overrightarrow{OB} + k\overrightarrow{BA} \\
&= \overrightarrow{OB} + k(\overrightarrow{BO} + \overrightarrow{OA}) \\
&= \overrightarrow{OB} + k(-\overrightarrow{OB} + \overrightarrow{OA}) \\
&= k\overrightarrow{OA} + (1 - k)\overrightarrow{OB}
\end{aligned}
$$

($\Leftarrow$) Si A, B et C sont trois points distincts tels que, pour tout autre point O, il existe un scalaire k pour lequel $\overrightarrow{OC} = k\overrightarrow{OA} + (1 - k)\overrightarrow{OB}$, alors

$$
\begin{aligned}
\overrightarrow{BC} &= \overrightarrow{BO} + \overrightarrow{OC} \\
&= -\overrightarrow{OB} + k\overrightarrow{OA} + (1 - k)\overrightarrow{OB} \\
&= k\overrightarrow{OA} - k\overrightarrow{OB} \\
&= k(\overrightarrow{OA} - \overrightarrow{OB}) \\
&= k(\overrightarrow{OA} + \overrightarrow{BO}) \\
&= k\overrightarrow{BA}
\end{aligned}
$$

Par conséquent, $\overrightarrow{BC}$ et $\overrightarrow{BA}$ sont parallèles et les points A, B et C sont colinéaires. ∎

BARYCENTRE

Le barycentre d'un ensemble de n points P_1, P_2, ..., P_n du plan est tout point P tel que

$$\overrightarrow{PP_1} + \overrightarrow{PP_2} + \cdots + \overrightarrow{PP_n} = \vec{0}$$

On appelle **barycentre** d'un ensemble de n points P_1, P_2, ..., P_n du plan n'importe quel point P tel que $\overrightarrow{PP_1} + \overrightarrow{PP_2} + \cdots + \overrightarrow{PP_n} = \vec{0}$. On peut montrer (n° 16 des exercices récapitulatifs) que le barycentre P d'un ensemble de n points du plan, P_1, P_2, ..., P_n, vérifie l'équation vectorielle

$$\overrightarrow{OP} = \tfrac{1}{n}\,(\overrightarrow{OP_1} + \overrightarrow{OP_2} + \cdots + \overrightarrow{OP_n})$$

où O est un point auxiliaire. En mécanique, le barycentre correspond au centre de masse.

Exemple

Les médianes d'un triangle se coupent au barycentre du triangle, qui est situé aux deux tiers de chaque médiane, à partir du sommet.

Preuve

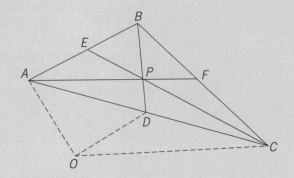

Soit un triangle *ABC* et un point auxiliaire *O*. Si *P* est le barycentre du triangle, alors $\overrightarrow{OP} = \frac{1}{3}(\overrightarrow{OA} + \overrightarrow{OB} + \overrightarrow{OC})$.

Si on note *D*, *E* et *F* les milieux des côtés du triangle, alors

$$\overrightarrow{OD} = \overrightarrow{OA} + \overrightarrow{AD} = \overrightarrow{OA} + \frac{1}{2}\overrightarrow{AC} = \overrightarrow{OA} + \frac{1}{2}(\overrightarrow{AO} + \overrightarrow{OC}) = \frac{1}{2}(\overrightarrow{OA} + \overrightarrow{OC})$$

Par conséquent, $\overrightarrow{OA} + \overrightarrow{OC} = 2\overrightarrow{OD}$. De façon similaire, on montre que $\overrightarrow{OA} + \overrightarrow{OB} = 2\overrightarrow{OE}$ et $\overrightarrow{OB} + \overrightarrow{OC} = 2\overrightarrow{OF}$.

On en déduit les trois égalités

$$\overrightarrow{OP} = \frac{1}{3}\overrightarrow{OB} + \frac{2}{3}\overrightarrow{OD}$$
$$\overrightarrow{OP} = \frac{1}{3}\overrightarrow{OC} + \frac{2}{3}\overrightarrow{OE}$$
$$\overrightarrow{OP} = \frac{1}{3}\overrightarrow{OA} + \frac{2}{3}\overrightarrow{OF}$$

En vertu du théorème 5.5, le point *P* est situé sur chacun des segments *BD*, *CE* et *AF*. Le barycentre *P* est donc un point de chacune des médianes du triangle et, par conséquent, il est situé à l'intersection des médianes. De plus,

$$\overrightarrow{BP} = \overrightarrow{BO} + \overrightarrow{OP}$$
$$= \overrightarrow{BO} + \frac{1}{3}\overrightarrow{OB} + \frac{2}{3}\overrightarrow{OD}$$
$$= \frac{2}{3}\overrightarrow{BO} + \frac{2}{3}\overrightarrow{OD}$$
$$= \frac{2}{3}\overrightarrow{BD}$$

De façon similaire, $\overrightarrow{AP} = \frac{2}{3}\overrightarrow{AF}$ et $\overrightarrow{CP} = \frac{2}{3}\overrightarrow{CE}$.

Par conséquent, les médianes d'un triangle se coupent au barycentre du triangle, qui est situé aux deux tiers de chaque médiane, à partir du sommet. ∎

Lorsque nous avons abordé la notion de direction d'un vecteur, nous avons tracé des vecteurs dans un plan cartésien en faisant coïncider leur origine avec le point $O(0, 0)$. Nous allons reprendre ce procédé pour exprimer les vecteurs géométriques sous forme algébrique. Définissons d'abord deux vecteurs à l'aide desquels il est possible d'exprimer tout vecteur du plan.

5.5.1 COMPOSANTES D'UN VECTEUR

On note $\vec{i}$ le vecteur dont l'origine est le point $(0, 0)$ et dont l'extrémité est le point $(1, 0)$. Ce vecteur est un vecteur unitaire ayant comme support l'axe des abscisses. De plus, on note $\vec{j}$ le vecteur dont l'origine est le point $(0, 0)$ et dont l'extrémité est le point $(0, 1)$. Ce vecteur est un vecteur unitaire ayant comme support l'axe des ordonnées.

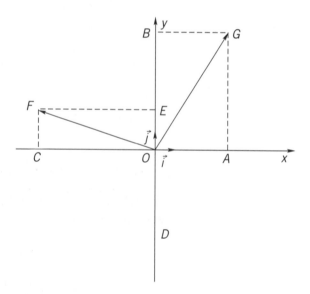

Soit les points du plan $A(a, 0)$, $B(0, b)$, $C(c, 0)$, $D(0, d)$, $E(0, e)$, $F(c, e)$ et $G(a, b)$. Il est clair que $\overrightarrow{OA} = a\vec{i} = a\vec{i} + 0\vec{j}$. En effet, le vecteur $\overrightarrow{OA}$ a la même direction que le vecteur $\vec{i}$ et son module est égal à a fois celui du vecteur $\vec{i}$. De façon analogue,

$$\overrightarrow{OB} = b\vec{j} = 0\vec{i} + b\vec{j}$$
$$\overrightarrow{OC} = c\vec{i} = c\vec{i} + 0\vec{j}$$
$$\overrightarrow{OD} = d\vec{j} = 0\vec{i} + d\vec{j}$$
$$\overrightarrow{OE} = e\vec{j} = 0\vec{i} + e\vec{j}$$

Il est à noter que $c < 0$; donc, les vecteurs $\overrightarrow{OC}$ et $\vec{i}$ sont de directions contraires.

Par exemple, le vecteur $\overrightarrow{OA}$ qui joint le point $(0, 0)$ au point $(3, 0)$ s'écrit $\overrightarrow{OA} = 3\vec{i} = 3\vec{i} + 0\vec{j}$. De même, le vecteur $\overrightarrow{OD}$ qui joint le point $(0, 0)$ au point $(0, -5)$ s'écrit $\overrightarrow{OD} = -5\vec{j} = 0\vec{i} - 5\vec{j}$.

Mais il y a plus! Par exemple, le vecteur $\overrightarrow{OG}$ qui joint le point $(0, 0)$ au point (a, b) s'écrit $\overrightarrow{OG} = \overrightarrow{OA} + \overrightarrow{OB} = a\vec{i} + b\vec{j}$. De même, le vecteur $\overrightarrow{OF}$ qui joint le point $(0, 0)$ au point (c, e) s'écrit $\overrightarrow{OF} = \overrightarrow{OC} + \overrightarrow{OE} = c\vec{i} + e\vec{j}$.

Ces deux derniers exemples portent à croire qu'en général le vecteur $\overrightarrow{OX}$ qui joint le point $(0, 0)$ au point $X(x, y)$ s'écrit $\overrightarrow{OX} = x\vec{i} + y\vec{j}$, cette somme étant une combinaison linéaire des vecteurs $\vec{i}$ et $\vec{j}$. On appelle le vecteur $\overrightarrow{OX}$ **vecteur position** ou *rayon vecteur* du point (x, y).

Tout vecteur du plan issu de l'origine [soit le point $O(0, 0)$] comporte donc deux composantes (une en $\vec{i}$ et l'autre en $\vec{j}$) dont les coefficients sont les coordonnées de l'extrémité du vecteur.

Mais qu'en est-il d'un vecteur qui n'est pas issu de l'origine? Comment peut-on trouver ses composantes?

VECTEUR POSITION

Le vecteur position, ou *rayon vecteur*, d'un point X est le vecteur $\overrightarrow{OX}$ issu de l'origine et dont l'extrémité est le point X.

Exemple

On veut trouver les composantes du vecteur issu du point A $(2, 1)$ et dont l'extrémité est le point B $(4, -2)$.

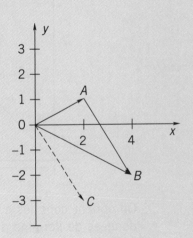

$$\overrightarrow{AB} = \overrightarrow{AO} + \overrightarrow{OB}$$
$$= -\overrightarrow{OA} + \overrightarrow{OB}$$
$$= -(2\vec{i} + \vec{j}) + 4\vec{i} - 2\vec{j}$$
$$= -2\vec{i} + 4\vec{i} - \vec{j} - 2\vec{j}$$
$$= 2\vec{i} - 3\vec{j}$$
$$= \overrightarrow{OC}$$

En s'inspirant de l'exemple précédent, on écrit le vecteur $\overrightarrow{AB}$ allant du point $A(a_1, a_2)$ au point $B(b_1, b_2)$ comme suit :

$$\overrightarrow{AB} = \overrightarrow{AO} + \overrightarrow{OB}$$
$$= -\overrightarrow{OA} + \overrightarrow{OB}$$
$$= -(a_1\vec{i} + a_2\vec{j}) + b_1\vec{i} + b_2\vec{j}$$
$$= (b_1 - a_1)\vec{i} + (b_2 - a_2)\vec{j}$$

On obtient donc chaque composante du vecteur $\overrightarrow{AB}$ en soustrayant la composante correspondante du vecteur $\overrightarrow{OA}$ de celle du vecteur $\overrightarrow{OB}$.

Selon une autre interprétation du résultat donné ci-dessus, on obtient le vecteur $\overrightarrow{AB}$ en effectuant un déplacement horizontal d'une longueur $b_1 - a_1$, suivi d'un déplacement vertical d'une longueur $b_2 - a_2$. Sous forme vectorielle, ces déplacements s'écrivent respectivement $(b_1 - a_1)\vec{i}$ et $(b_2 - a_2)\vec{j}$. Le vecteur $\overrightarrow{AB}$ est égal à la somme de ces deux déplacements : $\overrightarrow{AB} = (b_1 - a_1)\vec{i} + (b_2 - a_2)\vec{j}$.

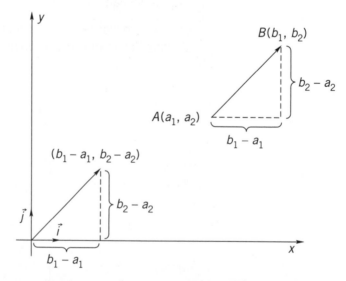

On obtient donc les composantes du vecteur $\overrightarrow{AB}$ en soustrayant les coordonnées de l'origine du vecteur des coordonnées correspondantes de son extrémité.

Ainsi, on peut déplacer n'importe quel vecteur du plan de façon que son origine coïncide avec le point (0, 0) et son extrémité avec le point $X(x, y)$. Le vecteur s'écrit alors comme une combinaison linéaire des vecteurs $\vec{i}$ et $\vec{j}$:

$$\overrightarrow{OX} = x\vec{i} + y\vec{j}$$

Il est à noter que les vecteurs $\vec{i}$ et $\vec{j}$ sont linéairement indépendants et unitaires, et qu'ils forment un système générateur. Autrement dit, ils constituent une base orthonormée de l'ensemble des vecteurs du plan.

EXERCICE 5.10

Pour chaque paire de points A et B donnée, exprimez le vecteur $\overrightarrow{AB}$ comme une combinaison linéaire des vecteurs $\vec{i}$ et $\vec{j}$.

a) $A(0, 0)$ et $B(3, 5)$

b) $A(0, 0)$ et $B(-2, 0)$

c) $A(0, 0)$ et $B(0, -4)$

d) $A(4, 8)$ et $B(0, 0)$

e) $A(8, -4)$ et $B(-1, 3)$

f) $A(-1, -2)$ et $B(1, 4)$

5.5.2 RELATION ENTRE LES VECTEURS ALGÉBRIQUES ET LES MATRICES

Soyons maintenant audacieux ! Ne retenons que les coefficients du vecteur $\overrightarrow{OX} = x\vec{i} + y\vec{j}$ et écrivons ce dernier sous la forme matricielle[8] $\overrightarrow{OX} = \begin{bmatrix} x & y \end{bmatrix}$. Mais attention à la notation ! L'expression (x, y) représente un point du plan cartésien alors que $\begin{bmatrix} x & y \end{bmatrix}$ représente le vecteur qui joint l'origine (0, 0) du plan cartésien au point (x, y). Les scalaires x et y sont appelés **composantes du vecteur**. Les vecteurs du plan ainsi exprimés sous forme algébrique sont appelés **vecteurs algébriques**. On donne à l'ensemble des vecteurs algébriques du plan, noté $\mathbb{R}^2$, le nom d'**espace euclidien de dimension deux**.

Mais ce n'est pas tout ! Il existe une équivalence entre les opérations définies sur les matrices et les opérations ou relations définies sur les

COMPOSANTES D'UN VECTEUR

Les composantes d'un vecteur sont les coordonnées du point associé à l'extrémité de ce vecteur lorsque ce dernier est issu de l'origine. Les composantes du vecteur $\overrightarrow{OX} = \begin{bmatrix} x & y \end{bmatrix}$ sont donc les scalaires x et y.

VECTEUR ALGÉBRIQUE DU PLAN

Un vecteur algébrique du plan est un vecteur exprimé sous forme algébrique (une matrice de format 1×2) à l'aide de ses composantes.

ESPACE EUCLIDIEN DE DIMENSION DEUX

L'espace euclidien de dimension deux, noté $\mathbb{R}^2$, est l'ensemble de tous les vecteurs algébriques du plan cartésien.

---

8. Il existe plusieurs notations pour écrire un vecteur algébrique. Dans la littérature, on trouve (x, y), $\langle x, y \rangle$, $[x, y]$ et $\begin{bmatrix} x & y \end{bmatrix}$. Bien que la première de ces notations ait été couramment employée il y a quelques années, elle présente l'inconvénient d'être identique à la représentation d'un point dans le plan cartésien. Récemment, beaucoup d'auteurs ont opté pour l'une ou l'autre des trois dernières notations, qui éliminent le risque de confusion. Nous avons adopté la notation matricielle parce qu'elle établit un lien entre les vecteurs et les matrices tout en permettant de faire la distinction entre vecteurs et points.

TABLEAU 5.1 **Relations et opérations sur les vecteurs**

	Forme vectorielle	Forme algébrique (matricielle)
Vecteurs	$\vec{u} = u_1\vec{i} + u_2\vec{j}$ et $\vec{v} = v_1\vec{i} + v_2\vec{j}$	$\vec{u} = \begin{bmatrix} u_1 & u_2 \end{bmatrix}$ et $\vec{v} = \begin{bmatrix} v_1 & v_2 \end{bmatrix}$
Vecteur nul	$\vec{0} = 0\vec{i} + 0\vec{j}$	$\vec{0} = \begin{bmatrix} 0 & 0 \end{bmatrix}$
Égalité	$\vec{u} = \vec{v} \Rightarrow u_1\vec{i} + u_2\vec{j} = v_1\vec{i} + v_2\vec{j}$ $\Rightarrow (u_1 - v_1)\vec{i} + (u_2 - v_2)\vec{j} = \vec{0}$ $\Rightarrow u_1 - v_1 = 0$ et $u_2 - v_2 = 0$ $\Rightarrow u_1 = v_1$ et $u_2 = v_2$	$\vec{u} = \vec{v} \Rightarrow \begin{bmatrix} u_1 & u_2 \end{bmatrix} = \begin{bmatrix} v_1 & v_2 \end{bmatrix}$ $\Rightarrow u_1 = v_1$ et $u_2 = v_2$
Addition	$\vec{u} + \vec{v} = (u_1\vec{i} + u_2\vec{j}) + (v_1\vec{i} + v_2\vec{j})$ $= (u_1 + v_1)\vec{i} + (u_2 + v_2)\vec{j}$	$\vec{u} + \vec{v} = \begin{bmatrix} u_1 & u_2 \end{bmatrix} + \begin{bmatrix} v_1 & v_2 \end{bmatrix}$ $= \begin{bmatrix} u_1 + v_1 & u_2 + v_2 \end{bmatrix}$
Multiplication par un scalaire	$k\vec{u} = k(u_1\vec{i} + u_2\vec{j}) = ku_1\vec{i} + ku_2\vec{j}$	$k\vec{u} = k\begin{bmatrix} u_1 & u_2 \end{bmatrix} = \begin{bmatrix} ku_1 & ku_2 \end{bmatrix}$

vecteurs, comme l'indique le tableau 5.1 ci-dessus. N'oubliez pas que les vecteurs $\vec{i}$ et $\vec{j}$ sont linéairement indépendants et que, par conséquent, la seule combinaison linéaire de ces vecteurs qui soit égale au vecteur nul est la combinaison où tous les coefficients sont nuls.

Voici, en clair, les propriétés énoncées dans le tableau 5.1 :

- Tout vecteur du plan (ou tout vecteur appartement à $\mathbb{R}^2$) comporte deux composantes, la première selon le vecteur $\vec{i}$ (la composante horizontale) et la seconde selon le vecteur $\vec{j}$ (la composante verticale).

- Les composantes du vecteur nul valent zéro.

- Deux vecteurs sont égaux si et seulement si leurs composantes correspondantes sont égales.

- Chaque composante du vecteur résultant est égale à la somme des composantes correspondantes des vecteurs additionnés.

- Chaque composante du produit d'un vecteur par un scalaire est égale au produit de la composante correspondante du vecteur par le scalaire.

- On peut interpréter tout vecteur[9] du plan comme une matrice ligne de format 1×2 et, inversement, toute matrice ligne de format 1×2 comme un vecteur du plan.

Il est important de rappeler encore une fois que le vecteur $\vec{u} = \begin{bmatrix} u_1 & u_2 \end{bmatrix}$ peut représenter un vecteur géométrique issu du point $(0, 0)$, dont l'extré-

---

9. Il s'agit d'un vecteur ligne, mais on aurait également pu utiliser un vecteur colonne, soit une matrice colonne de dimension 2×1. Ainsi, dans un système d'équations linéaires, on aurait pu utiliser les expressions vecteur des inconnues et vecteur des constantes, plutôt que matrice des inconnues et matrice des constantes.

mité est le point (u_1, u_2); en d'autres termes, les composantes d'un vecteur correspondent aux coordonnées de l'extrémité de ce vecteur lorsque l'origine de celui-ci coïncide avec l'origine du plan cartésien. Par ailleurs, les matrices lignes ne servent pas uniquement à exprimer sous forme algébrique les vecteurs géométriques représentés par des flèches. Les matrices lignes de format 1×2 sont employées bien sûr pour écrire les composantes d'un vecteur géométrique mais on peut également les utiliser pour coder d'autres types d'informations – par exemple la liste des prix (ou des quantités) de deux biens – comme nous l'avons fait dans les premiers chapitres de ce manuel. Dans ce cas, la représentation géométrique (grandeur et direction) d'un vecteur algébrique n'a pas de sens.

Nous étendrons le concept de vecteur aux matrices lignes de format 1×3, puis à celles de format $1 \times n$. Puisqu'on emploie indifféremment vecteur ou matrice ligne, on peut considérer que les propriétés de l'addition de vecteurs (th. 5.1) et de la multiplication d'un vecteur par un scalaire (th. 5.2) sont prouvées. En effet, au chapitre 2, nous avons démontré toutes ces propriétés pour les matrices en général, et donc pour les matrices de format 1×2 (ou $1 \times n$) en particulier, qu'on identifie à des vecteurs. Voilà une belle illustration de l'efficacité des mathématiques.

Exemple

Soit les points $A(2, 1)$, $B(4, -2)$ et $C(-1, 4)$. Pour trouver les composantes du vecteur $\overrightarrow{AB} + \overrightarrow{AC}$, il faut d'abord trouver les composantes de chacun des vecteurs $\overrightarrow{AB}$ et $\overrightarrow{AC}$. Le vecteur $\overrightarrow{AB}$ est donné par l'expression

$$\overrightarrow{AB} = \overrightarrow{AO} + \overrightarrow{OB} = -\overrightarrow{OA} + \overrightarrow{OB} = -\begin{bmatrix} 2 & 1 \end{bmatrix} + \begin{bmatrix} 4 & -2 \end{bmatrix} = \begin{bmatrix} 2 & -3 \end{bmatrix}$$

On montre de façon similaire que $\overrightarrow{AC} = \begin{bmatrix} -3 & 3 \end{bmatrix}$. Par conséquent,

$$\overrightarrow{AB} + \overrightarrow{AC} = \begin{bmatrix} 2 & -3 \end{bmatrix} + \begin{bmatrix} -3 & 3 \end{bmatrix} = \begin{bmatrix} -1 & 0 \end{bmatrix}$$

5.5.3 RELATION ENTRE LES COMPOSANTES, LE MODULE ET LA DIRECTION D'UN VECTEUR

La trigonométrie et le théorème de Pythagore permettent de faire le lien entre les composantes d'un vecteur, son module et sa direction.

Le vecteur $\vec{u} = \begin{bmatrix} u_1 & u_2 \end{bmatrix}$ correspond, dans le plan, au vecteur issu du point $(0, 0)$ et ayant comme extrémité le point (u_1, u_2). On note θ la direction de ce vecteur.

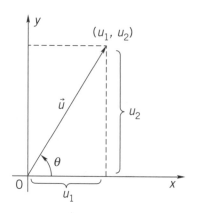

NORME EUCLIDIENNE D'UN VECTEUR DE $\mathbb{R}^2$

La norme euclidienne d'un vecteur $\vec{u} = \begin{bmatrix} u_1 & u_2 \end{bmatrix} \in \mathbb{R}^2$ est $\|\vec{u}\| = \sqrt{u_1^2 + u_2^2}$.

Le graphique indique clairement que :

- $\|\vec{u}\| = \sqrt{u_1^2 + u_2^2}$ (c'est ce qu'on appelle la **norme euclidienne d'un vecteur de $\mathbb{R}^2$**) ;

- $u_1 = \|\vec{u}\| \cos \theta$ et $u_2 = \|\vec{u}\| \sin \theta$;

- $\text{tg } \theta = \dfrac{u_2}{u_1}$, d'où $\theta = \text{arc tg}\dfrac{u_2}{u_1}$.

On dit que $\|\vec{u}\| \cos \theta$ est la composante horizontale du vecteur $\vec{u}$ et que $\|\vec{u}\| \sin \theta$ est la composante verticale du vecteur $\vec{u}$. Les physiciens notent respectivement ces composantes u_x et u_y.

La fonction tangente étant une fonction périodique de période 180° (ou π), il faut déterminer la valeur de l'angle qui correspond au quadrant où se trouve le vecteur.

Grâce aux formules données ci-dessus, on peut trouver le module et la direction d'un vecteur dont on connaît les composantes. De même, si on connaît le module et la direction d'un vecteur, on peut trouver ses composantes.

Comme nous allons faire appel régulièrement aux fonctions trigonométriques, il est utile de consulter le tableau 5.2 (p. 200), qui donne les valeurs exactes de ces fonctions pour des angles remarquables.

Exemple

Les composantes du vecteur $\vec{u} = \begin{bmatrix} u_1 & u_2 \end{bmatrix}$ dont le module est 3 et dont la direction est de $5\pi/4$ sont données par

$$u_1 = \|\vec{u}\| \cos \theta = 3\cos\frac{5\pi}{4} = -\frac{3\sqrt{2}}{2}$$

et

$$u_2 = \|\vec{u}\| \sin \theta = 3\sin\frac{5\pi}{4} = -\frac{3\sqrt{2}}{2}$$

Par conséquent,

$$\vec{u} = \left[-\frac{3\sqrt{2}}{2} \quad -\frac{3\sqrt{2}}{2} \right] \approx \left[-2,12 \quad -2,12 \right]$$

Pour trouver la direction du vecteur $\vec{w} = \begin{bmatrix} 1 & 2 \end{bmatrix}$, il faut déterminer la valeur de l'angle θ_1 tel que

$$\theta_1 = \text{arc tg}\frac{w_2}{w_1} = \text{arc tg}\frac{2}{1} = \text{arc tg } 2 \approx 63,4° \quad \text{ou} \quad 243,4°$$

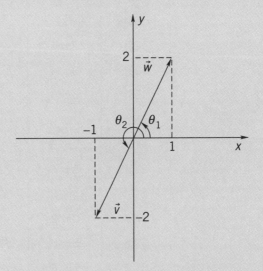

On choisit $\theta_1 \approx 63,4°$ parce que le vecteur $\vec{w}$ est dans le premier quadrant.

De même, la direction du vecteur $\vec{v} = \begin{bmatrix} -1 & -2 \end{bmatrix}$ est donnée par

$\theta_2 = \text{arc tg}\frac{v_2}{v_1} = \text{arc tg}\frac{-2}{-1} = \text{arc tg } 2 \approx 63,4°$ ou $243,4°$. On choisit

$\theta_2 \approx 243,4°$ parce que le vecteur $\vec{v}$ est situé dans le troisième quadrant.

Lorsqu'on cherche la direction d'un vecteur, il est plus facile de choisir le bon angle si on représente le vecteur dans un plan cartésien.

EXERCICE 5.11

a) Quelles sont les composantes du vecteur $\vec{u}$ dont le module vaut 4, et la direction 60° ?

TABLEAU 5.2 **Valeurs exactes* des fonctions trigonométriques pour des angles remarquables**

θ (en degrés)	θ (en radians)	$\sin\theta$	$\cos\theta$	$\text{tg}\,\theta$	$\text{cotg}\,\theta$	$\sec\theta$	$\text{cosec}\,\theta$
0°	0	0	1	0	$\mp\infty$	1	$\mp\infty$
30°	$\pi/6$	$1/2$	$\sqrt{3}/2$	$\sqrt{3}/3$	$\sqrt{3}$	$2\sqrt{3}/3$	2
45°	$\pi/4$	$\sqrt{2}/2$	$\sqrt{2}/2$	1	1	$\sqrt{2}$	$\sqrt{2}$
60°	$\pi/3$	$\sqrt{3}/2$	$1/2$	$\sqrt{3}$	$\sqrt{3}/3$	2	$2\sqrt{3}/3$
90°	$\pi/2$	1	0	$\pm\infty$	0	$\pm\infty$	1
120°	$2\pi/3$	$\sqrt{3}/2$	$-1/2$	$-\sqrt{3}$	$-\sqrt{3}/3$	-2	$2\sqrt{3}/3$
135°	$3\pi/4$	$\sqrt{2}/2$	$-\sqrt{2}/2$	-1	-1	$-\sqrt{2}$	$\sqrt{2}$
150°	$5\pi/6$	$1/2$	$-\sqrt{3}/2$	$-\sqrt{3}/3$	$-\sqrt{3}$	$-2\sqrt{3}/3$	2
180°	π	0	-1	0	$\mp\infty$	-1	$\pm\infty$
210°	$7\pi/6$	$-1/2$	$-\sqrt{3}/2$	$\sqrt{3}/3$	$\sqrt{3}$	$-2\sqrt{3}/3$	-2
225°	$5\pi/4$	$-\sqrt{2}/2$	$-\sqrt{2}/2$	1	1	$-\sqrt{2}$	$-\sqrt{2}$
240°	$4\pi/3$	$-\sqrt{3}/2$	$-1/2$	$\sqrt{3}$	$\sqrt{3}/3$	-2	$-2\sqrt{3}/3$
270°	$3\pi/2$	-1	0	$\pm\infty$	0	$\mp\infty$	-1
300°	$5\pi/3$	$-\sqrt{3}/2$	$1/2$	$-\sqrt{3}$	$-\sqrt{3}/3$	2	$-2\sqrt{3}/3$
315°	$7\pi/4$	$-\sqrt{2}/2$	$\sqrt{2}/2$	-1	-1	$\sqrt{2}$	$-\sqrt{2}$
330°	$11\pi/6$	$-1/2$	$\sqrt{3}/2$	$-\sqrt{3}/3$	$-\sqrt{3}$	$2\sqrt{3}/3$	-2
360°	2π	0	1	0	$\mp\infty$	1	$\mp\infty$

* Les symboles $\pm\infty$ et $\mp\infty$ indiquent le comportement de la fonction pour des valeurs voisines de l'angle où la fonction n'est pas définie.

b) Quelles sont les composantes du vecteur $\vec{v}$ dont le module vaut 8, et la direction 120°?

c) Quels sont le module et la direction de chacun des vecteurs $\vec{u} + \vec{v}$ et $\vec{u} - \vec{v}$? Comparez votre réponse avec la solution de l'exercice 5.4. Laquelle des deux méthodes vous paraît la plus simple?

5.5.4 COMBINAISON LINÉAIRE DE VECTEURS ALGÉBRIQUES

Nous avons déjà montré que tout vecteur du plan s'écrit comme une combinaison linéaire de deux vecteurs linéairement indépendants. Pour trouver cette combinaison linéaire, il faut résoudre un système d'équations linéaires.

Exemple

Pour exprimer le vecteur $\vec{w} = \begin{bmatrix} -3 & -6 \end{bmatrix}$ comme une combinaison linéaire des vecteurs $\vec{u} = \begin{bmatrix} 3 & 2 \end{bmatrix}$ et $\vec{v} = \begin{bmatrix} -3 & -4 \end{bmatrix}$, il faut résoudre le système d'équations linéaires correspondant à l'équation vectorielle $a\vec{u} + b\vec{v} = \vec{w}$, soit $a\begin{bmatrix} 3 & 2 \end{bmatrix} + b\begin{bmatrix} -3 & -4 \end{bmatrix} = \begin{bmatrix} -3 & -6 \end{bmatrix}$.

Il faut donc résoudre le système d'équations

$$3a - 3b = -3$$
$$2a - 4b = -6$$

En appliquant la règle de Cramer, on obtient

$$\Delta = \begin{vmatrix} 3 & -3 \\ 2 & -4 \end{vmatrix} = -6 \quad \Delta_a = \begin{vmatrix} -3 & -3 \\ -6 & -4 \end{vmatrix} = -6 \quad \Delta_b = \begin{vmatrix} 3 & -3 \\ 2 & -6 \end{vmatrix} = -12$$

d'où $a = \dfrac{\Delta_a}{\Delta} = 1$ et $b = \dfrac{\Delta_b}{\Delta} = 2$

Par conséquent, $\vec{w} = a\vec{u} + b\vec{v} = \vec{u} + 2\vec{v}$ c'est-à-dire que $\begin{bmatrix} -3 & -6 \end{bmatrix} = \begin{bmatrix} 3 & 2 \end{bmatrix} + 2\begin{bmatrix} -3 & -4 \end{bmatrix}$.

EXERCICE 5.12

1. Exprimez le vecteur $\vec{w} = \begin{bmatrix} 1 & -1 \end{bmatrix}$ comme une combinaison linéaire des vecteurs $\vec{u} = \begin{bmatrix} 3 & 1 \end{bmatrix}$ et $\vec{v} = \begin{bmatrix} 2 & 1 \end{bmatrix}$.

2. Exprimez le vecteur $\vec{w} = \begin{bmatrix} 1 & -1 \end{bmatrix}$ comme une combinaison linéaire des vecteurs $\vec{u} = \begin{bmatrix} 3 & 1 \end{bmatrix}$ et $\vec{v} = \begin{bmatrix} -6 & -2 \end{bmatrix}$. Que constatez-vous ? Pourquoi en est-il ainsi ?

5.5.5 INDÉPENDANCE LINÉAIRE

Un ensemble de n vecteurs algébriques $\vec{u_1}$, $\vec{u_2}$, ..., $\vec{u_n}$ sont dits linéairement indépendants si et seulement si

$$a_1 \vec{u_1} + a_2 \vec{u_2} + \cdots + a_n \vec{u_n} = \vec{0} \quad \Rightarrow \quad a_1 = 0, \ a_2 = 0, \ ..., \ a_n = 0$$

Exemple

Les vecteurs $\vec{u} = \begin{bmatrix} 3 & 2 \end{bmatrix}$ et $\vec{v} = \begin{bmatrix} -3 & -4 \end{bmatrix}$ sont linéairement indépendants. En effet, si $a\vec{u} + b\vec{v} = \vec{0}$, alors

$$a\begin{bmatrix} 3 & 2 \end{bmatrix} + b\begin{bmatrix} -3 & -4 \end{bmatrix} = \begin{bmatrix} 0 & 0 \end{bmatrix}$$

$$\begin{bmatrix} 3a & 2a \end{bmatrix} + \begin{bmatrix} -3b & -4b \end{bmatrix} = \begin{bmatrix} 0 & 0 \end{bmatrix}$$

$$\begin{bmatrix} 3a - 3b & 2a - 4b \end{bmatrix} = \begin{bmatrix} 0 & 0 \end{bmatrix}$$

On a donc le système d'équations

$$3a - 3b = 0$$
$$2a - 4b = 0$$

Ce système admet évidemment au moins une solution, soit $a = 0$ et $b = 0$. Il faut cependant s'assurer qu'il s'agit là de la seule solution possible. Or, le déterminant de la matrice des coefficients vaut -6. En vertu de la règle de Cramer, le système admet une seule solution, qui doit donc être $a = 0$ et $b = 0$. Par conséquent, les vecteurs $\vec{u} = \begin{bmatrix} 3 & 2 \end{bmatrix}$ et $\vec{v} = \begin{bmatrix} -3 & -4 \end{bmatrix}$ sont linéairement indépendants.

Par contre, les vecteurs $\vec{u} = \begin{bmatrix} 3 & 2 \end{bmatrix}$ et $\vec{w} = \begin{bmatrix} -6 & -4 \end{bmatrix}$ sont linéairement dépendants. En effet, si $a\vec{u} + b\vec{w} = \vec{0}$, alors

$$a\begin{bmatrix} 3 & 2 \end{bmatrix} + b\begin{bmatrix} -6 & -4 \end{bmatrix} = \begin{bmatrix} 0 & 0 \end{bmatrix}$$

$$\begin{bmatrix} 3a & 2a \end{bmatrix} + \begin{bmatrix} -6b & -4b \end{bmatrix} = \begin{bmatrix} 0 & 0 \end{bmatrix}$$

$$\begin{bmatrix} 3a - 6b & 2a - 4b \end{bmatrix} = \begin{bmatrix} 0 & 0 \end{bmatrix}$$

On a donc le système d'équations

$$3a - 6b = 0$$
$$2a - 4b = 0$$

Le déterminant de la matrice des coefficients de ce système vaut 0. De plus, le système admet évidemment la solution $a = 0$ et $b = 0$. En vertu de la règle de Cramer, il admet donc une infinité de solutions. Ainsi, $a = 2$ et $b = 1$ est également une solution particulière du système d'équations. Par conséquent, les vecteurs $\vec{u} = \begin{bmatrix} 3 & 2 \end{bmatrix}$ et $\vec{w} = \begin{bmatrix} -6 & -4 \end{bmatrix}$ ne sont pas linéairement indépendants. Il existe en effet une combinaison linéaire de ces deux vecteurs qui est égale au vecteur nul et telle qu'au moins l'un des coefficients est différent de zéro, par exemple $2\vec{u} + \vec{w} = \vec{0}$.

5.5.6 PRODUIT SCALAIRE DE VECTEURS ALGÉBRIQUES

Les vecteurs algébriques du plan étant équivalents aux matrices, ils possèdent exactement les mêmes propriétés que ces dernières. Toutefois, les vecteurs du plan sont des matrices particulières (des matrices lignes de format 1 × 2) et, de ce fait, ils présentent des caractéristiques qui leur sont propres. Ainsi, certains concepts vectoriels n'ont pas d'équivalent dans le langage matriciel. C'est le cas du produit scalaire, que nous devrons donc traiter à part.

PRODUIT SCALAIRE

Le produit scalaire de deux vecteurs $\vec{u} = \begin{bmatrix} u_1 & u_2 \end{bmatrix}$ et $\vec{v} = \begin{bmatrix} v_1 & v_2 \end{bmatrix}$ est donné par $\vec{u} \cdot \vec{v} = u_1 v_1 + u_2 v_2$.

Théorème 5.6

Le **produit scalaire** des vecteurs $\vec{u} = \begin{bmatrix} u_1 & u_2 \end{bmatrix}$ et $\vec{v} = \begin{bmatrix} v_1 & v_2 \end{bmatrix}$ est donné par

$$\vec{u} \cdot \vec{v} = u_1 v_1 + u_2 v_2$$

Preuve

On trace les vecteurs $\vec{u}$ et $\vec{v}$ dans un plan cartésien en faisant coïncider leur origine avec l'origine du système d'axes. Le vecteur allant de l'extrémité de $\vec{u}$ à l'extrémité de $\vec{v}$ est le vecteur $\vec{v} - \vec{u}$.

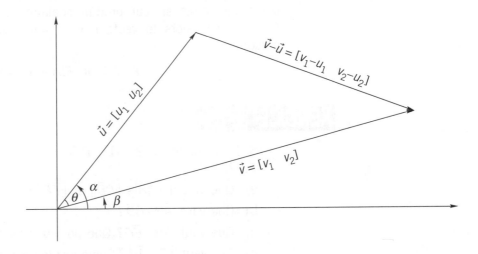

En vertu de la loi des cosinus, $\|\vec{v} - \vec{u}\|^2 = \|\vec{u}\|^2 + \|\vec{v}\|^2 - 2\|\vec{u}\|\,\|\vec{v}\|\cos\theta$, d'où

$$\|\vec{u}\|\,\|\vec{v}\|\cos\theta = \tfrac{1}{2}(\|\vec{u}\|^2 + \|\vec{v}\|^2 - \|\vec{v} - \vec{u}\|^2)$$

Le membre de gauche de cette équation est précisément l'expression du produit scalaire des vecteurs $\vec{u}$ et $\vec{v}$, de sorte que

$$
\begin{aligned}
\vec{u} \cdot \vec{v} &= \|\vec{u}\|\,\|\vec{v}\|\cos\theta \\
&= \tfrac{1}{2}(\|\vec{u}\|^2 + \|\vec{v}\|^2 - \|\vec{v} - \vec{u}\|^2) \\
&= \tfrac{1}{2}\left[u_1^2 + u_2^2 + v_1^2 + v_2^2 - ((v_1 - u_1)^2 + (v_2 - u_2)^2) \right] \\
&= \tfrac{1}{2}(u_1^2 + u_2^2 + v_1^2 + v_2^2 - v_1^2 + 2u_1 v_1 - u_1^2 - v_2^2 + 2u_2 v_2 - u_2^2) \\
&= u_1 v_1 + u_2 v_2
\end{aligned}
$$

On aurait pu également démontrer ce résultat en faisant appel à une identité trigonométrique fondamentale :

$$\vec{u} \cdot \vec{v} = \|\vec{u}\| \, \|\vec{v}\| \cos \theta$$
$$= \|\vec{u}\| \, \|\vec{v}\| \cos(\alpha - \beta)$$
$$= \|\vec{u}\| \, \|\vec{v}\| \, (\cos \alpha \cos \beta + \sin \alpha \sin \beta)$$
$$= (\|\vec{u}\| \cos \alpha)(\|\vec{v}\| \cos \beta) + (\|\vec{u}\| \sin \alpha)(\|\vec{v}\| \sin \beta)$$
$$= u_1 v_1 + u_2 v_2 \qquad \blacksquare$$

Exemple

Si $\vec{u} = \begin{bmatrix} 3 & -2 \end{bmatrix}$ et $\vec{v} = \begin{bmatrix} -3 & -4 \end{bmatrix}$, alors

$$\vec{u} \cdot \vec{v} = \begin{bmatrix} 3 & -2 \end{bmatrix} \cdot \begin{bmatrix} -3 & -4 \end{bmatrix} = 3(-3) + (-2)(-4) = -1$$

Selon la propriété 6 (th. 5.4, p. 186), deux vecteurs $\vec{u}$ et $\vec{v}$ non nuls sont perpendiculaires si leur produit scalaire vaut zéro. Par conséquent, si $\vec{u} = \begin{bmatrix} a & b \end{bmatrix}$, alors le vecteur $\vec{v} = \begin{bmatrix} -kb & ka \end{bmatrix}$ est perpendiculaire à $\vec{u}$ puisque

$$\vec{u} \cdot \vec{v} = a(-kb) + b(ka) = 0$$

EXERCICE 5.13

Soit les points $A(2, -1)$, $B(3, 5)$, $C(4, -2)$, $D(3, 5)$, $E(4, -3)$, et $F(-2, -2)$.

a) Que valent $\|\overrightarrow{AB}\|$, $\|\overrightarrow{CD}\|$ et $\|\overrightarrow{EF}\|$?

b) Que vaut $\overrightarrow{AB} \cdot \overrightarrow{CD}$?

c) Que vaut $\overrightarrow{AB} \cdot \overrightarrow{EF}$? Que pouvez-vous dire des deux vecteurs ?

d) Que vaut $\overrightarrow{AB} \cdot \overrightarrow{AB}$? Comparez le résultat avec $\|\overrightarrow{AB}\|^2$. S'agit-il d'une coïncidence ?

e) Trouvez un vecteur unitaire perpendiculaire au vecteur $\overrightarrow{CD}$. Est-ce que ce vecteur est unique ? Justifiez votre réponse.

5.5.7 ANGLE ENTRE DEUX VECTEURS

On peut exprimer le produit scalaire de deux vecteurs $\vec{u} = \begin{bmatrix} u_1 & u_2 \end{bmatrix}$ et $\vec{v} = \begin{bmatrix} v_1 & v_2 \end{bmatrix}$ de deux façons, soit $\vec{u} \cdot \vec{v} = \|\vec{u}\| \, \|\vec{v}\| \cos \theta$ (où θ représente l'angle déterminé par les deux vecteurs) et $\vec{u} \cdot \vec{v} = u_1 v_1 + u_2 v_2$. Si $\vec{u}$ et $\vec{v}$ sont non nuls, on obtient une formule de l'angle qu'ils déterminent en comparant les deux expressions de leur produit scalaire :

$$u_1 v_1 + u_2 v_2 = \|\vec{u}\| \, \|\vec{v}\| \cos\theta \quad \Rightarrow \quad \theta = \text{arc } \cos\frac{u_1 v_1 + u_2 v_2}{\|\vec{u}\| \, \|\vec{v}\|}$$

Exemple

Pour trouver l'angle entre les vecteurs $\vec{u} = \begin{bmatrix} 3 & -2 \end{bmatrix}$ et $\vec{v} = \begin{bmatrix} -3 & -4 \end{bmatrix}$, on calcule d'abord leur produit scalaire :

$$\vec{u} \cdot \vec{v} = \begin{bmatrix} 3 & -2 \end{bmatrix} \cdot \begin{bmatrix} -3 & -4 \end{bmatrix} = 3(-3) + (-2)(-4) = -1$$

De plus,

$$\vec{u} \cdot \vec{v} = \|\vec{u}\| \, \|\vec{v}\| \cos\theta$$

Par conséquent,

$$\cos\theta = \frac{\vec{u} \cdot \vec{v}}{\|\vec{u}\| \, \|\vec{v}\|} = \frac{-1}{(\sqrt{13}) \times 5} \quad \Rightarrow \quad \theta \approx 93{,}2°$$

On peut aussi employer le produit scalaire pour trouver la direction d'un vecteur $\vec{u}$. Selon la position de l'extrémité du rayon vecteur, la direction de $\vec{u}$ correspond à l'angle θ déterminé par $\vec{u}$ et le vecteur $\vec{i}$ ou encore à l'angle $360° - \theta$ (ou $2\pi - \theta$).

Exemple

Pour trouver la direction du vecteur $\vec{u} = \begin{bmatrix} 1 & \sqrt{3} \end{bmatrix}$, on calcule l'angle θ_1 déterminé par $\vec{u}$ et le vecteur $\vec{i} = \begin{bmatrix} 1 & 0 \end{bmatrix}$:

$$\vec{u} \cdot \vec{i} = \|\vec{u}\| \, \|\vec{i}\| \cos\theta_1 \quad \Rightarrow \quad \cos\theta_1 = \frac{\vec{u} \cdot \vec{i}}{\|\vec{u}\| \, \|\vec{i}\|}$$

Par conséquent,

$$\theta_1 = \text{arc } \cos\frac{\vec{u} \cdot \vec{i}}{\|\vec{u}\| \, \|\vec{i}\|} = \text{arc } \cos\tfrac{1}{2} = 60° \quad \left(\text{ou } \frac{\pi}{3}\right)$$

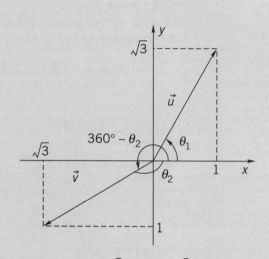

Par ailleurs, le vecteur $\vec{v} = \begin{bmatrix} -\sqrt{3} & -1 \end{bmatrix}$ étant situé dans le troisième quadrant, sa direction est égale à $360° - \theta_2$ où

$$\theta_2 = \text{arc cos}\frac{\vec{v} \cdot \vec{i}}{\|\vec{v}\|\|\vec{i}\|} = \text{arc cos}\left(\frac{-\sqrt{3}}{2}\right) \quad \Rightarrow \quad \theta_2 = 150°$$

Par conséquent, la direction de $\vec{v}$ est de 210° (ou de $7\pi/6$).

EXERCICE 5.14

Soit $\vec{u} = \begin{bmatrix} -1 & \sqrt{3} \end{bmatrix}$ et $\vec{v} = \begin{bmatrix} 2 & -2 \end{bmatrix}$.

a) Quel est l'angle entre ces deux vecteurs?

b) Quelle est la direction de chacun de ces vecteurs?

5.5.8 PROJECTION D'UN VECTEUR SUR UN AUTRE VECTEUR

PROJECTION ORTHOGONALE

La projection orthogonale de $\vec{u}$ sur $\vec{v}$, notée $\vec{u}_{\vec{v}}$, est le vecteur

$\vec{u}_{\vec{v}} = \frac{\vec{u} \cdot \vec{v}}{\vec{v} \cdot \vec{v}}\vec{v}$. On utilise également l'expression *vecteur projection*.

Soit $\vec{u}$ et $\vec{v}$ deux vecteurs non nuls. Le *vecteur projection* ou la **projection orthogonale** de $\vec{u}$ sur $\vec{v}$, notée $\vec{u}_{\vec{v}}$, est représentée dans la figure suivante.

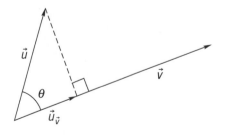

Le module du vecteur $\vec{u}_{\vec{v}}$ est égal à $|\|\vec{u}\| \cos\theta|$. De plus, ce vecteur a la même direction que le vecteur $\vec{v}$ si $0 \le \theta \le \pi/2$, et il est de direction contraire à $\vec{v}$ si $\pi/2 < \theta \le \pi$. Par conséquent,

$$\vec{u}_{\vec{v}} = \|\vec{u}\| \cos\theta \frac{1}{\|\vec{v}\|} \vec{v}$$

$$= \|\vec{u}\| \|\vec{v}\| \cos\theta \frac{1}{\|\vec{v}\|^2} \vec{v}$$

$$= \frac{\vec{u} \cdot \vec{v}}{\vec{v} \cdot \vec{v}} \vec{v}$$

Exemple

La projection orthogonale du vecteur $\vec{u} = \begin{bmatrix} -2 & 2 \end{bmatrix}$ sur le vecteur $\vec{v} = \begin{bmatrix} 3 & 4 \end{bmatrix}$ est donnée par

$$\vec{u}_{\vec{v}} = \frac{\vec{u} \cdot \vec{v}}{\vec{v} \cdot \vec{v}} \vec{v} = \frac{2}{25} \begin{bmatrix} 3 & 4 \end{bmatrix} = \begin{bmatrix} 0{,}24 & 0{,}32 \end{bmatrix}$$

EXERCICE 5.15

Quelle est la projection orthogonale du vecteur $\vec{v} = \begin{bmatrix} 3 & 4 \end{bmatrix}$ sur le vecteur $\vec{u} = \begin{bmatrix} -2 & 2 \end{bmatrix}$?

À l'aide du concept de projection, on peut démontrer géométriquement la distributivité du produit scalaire sur l'addition de vecteurs (propriété 2 du théorème 5.4), c'est-à-dire $\vec{u} \cdot (\vec{v} + \vec{w}) = \vec{u} \cdot \vec{v} + \vec{u} \cdot \vec{w}$.

Preuve

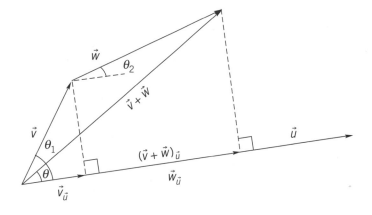

Soit les vecteurs $\vec{u}$, $\vec{v}$, $\vec{w}$ et les angles θ, θ_1 et θ_2 représentés dans la figure.

$$\begin{aligned}
\vec{u} \cdot (\vec{v} + \vec{w}) &= \|\vec{u}\|\,\|\vec{v} + \vec{w}\|\cos\theta \\
&= \|\vec{u}\|\,(\|\vec{v}_{\vec{u}}\| + \|\vec{w}_{\vec{u}}\|) \\
&= \|\vec{u}\|\,(\|\vec{v}\|\cos\theta_1 + \|\vec{w}\|\cos\theta_2) \\
&= \|\vec{u}\|\,\|\vec{v}\|\cos\theta_1 + \|\vec{u}\|\,\|\vec{w}\|\cos\theta_2 \\
&= \vec{u} \cdot \vec{v} + \vec{u} \cdot \vec{w} \qquad\blacksquare
\end{aligned}$$

La distributivité du produit scalaire sur l'addition de vecteurs étant établie, on peut donner une autre preuve de la formule suivante du produit scalaire des vecteurs $\vec{u} = \begin{bmatrix} u_1 & u_2 \end{bmatrix}$ et $\vec{v} = \begin{bmatrix} v_1 & v_2 \end{bmatrix}$:

$$\vec{u} \cdot \vec{v} = u_1 v_1 + u_2 v_2$$

Preuve

Si on écrit les vecteurs $\vec{u}$ et $\vec{v}$ comme des combinaisons linéaires des vecteurs $\vec{i}$ et $\vec{j}$, qui sont des vecteurs perpendiculaires de longueur 1, on a

$$\begin{aligned}
\vec{u} \cdot \vec{v} &= \begin{bmatrix} u_1 & u_2 \end{bmatrix} \cdot \begin{bmatrix} v_1 & v_2 \end{bmatrix} \\
&= (u_1\vec{i} + u_2\vec{j}) \cdot (v_1\vec{i} + v_2\vec{j}) \\
&= u_1 v_1 \vec{i} \cdot \vec{i} + u_1 v_2 \vec{i} \cdot \vec{j} + u_2 v_1 \vec{j} \cdot \vec{i} + u_2 v_2 \vec{j} \cdot \vec{j} \\
&= u_1 v_1(1) + u_1 v_2(0) + u_2 v_1(0) + u_2 v_2(1) \\
&= u_1 v_1 + u_2 v_2 \qquad\blacksquare
\end{aligned}$$

EXERCICE 5.16

Donnez une preuve « algébrique » (en vous servant de vecteurs algébriques) de la propriété 2 (th. 5.4), soit $\vec{u} \cdot (\vec{v} + \vec{w}) = \vec{u} \cdot \vec{v} + \vec{u} \cdot \vec{w}$.

RÉSUMÉ

En physique, on distingue les quantités scalaires, qui ne possèdent qu'une grandeur, des quantités vectorielles, qui possèdent une grandeur et une direction (mesurée par un angle). On représente les vecteurs par une ou deux lettres surmontées d'une flèche : $\vec{u}$, $\vec{F}$, $\overrightarrow{AB}$, et ainsi de suite. La longueur d'un vecteur $\vec{u}$ est notée $\|\vec{u}\|$. Les vecteurs géométriques, représentés par un segment de droite orienté, et les vecteurs algébriques, définis par leurs composantes dans un plan cartésien, sont soumis à une algèbre particulière.

	Représentation géométrique	**Représentation algébrique**
VECTEURS		$\|\vec{u}\| = \sqrt{u_1^2 + u_2^2}$ et $\|\vec{v}\| = \sqrt{v_1^2 + v_2^2}$ $\theta = \text{arc tg} \dfrac{u_2}{u_1}$ et $\varphi = \text{arc tg} \dfrac{v_2}{v_1}$ Attention! Choisissez l'angle dans le bon quadrant. Ne vous fiez pas qu'à votre calculatrice. $\vec{u} = \begin{bmatrix} u_1 & u_2 \end{bmatrix} = \begin{bmatrix} \|\vec{u}\|\cos\theta & \|\vec{u}\|\sin\theta \end{bmatrix}$ $\vec{v} = \begin{bmatrix} v_1 & v_2 \end{bmatrix} = \begin{bmatrix} \|\vec{v}\|\cos\varphi & \|\vec{v}\|\sin\varphi \end{bmatrix}$ $\vec{w} = \begin{bmatrix} c - a & d - b \end{bmatrix}$
ÉGALITÉ DE DEUX VECTEURS	 $\vec{u} = \vec{v} = \vec{w} \neq \vec{t}$ Deux vecteurs sont égaux si et seulement s'ils ont le même module et la même direction.	Si $\vec{u} = \begin{bmatrix} u_1 & u_2 \end{bmatrix}$ et $\vec{v} = \begin{bmatrix} v_1 & v_2 \end{bmatrix}$, alors $\vec{u} = \vec{v}$ si et seulement si $u_1 = v_1$ et $u_2 = v_2$
ADDITION DE VECTEURS		Si $\vec{u} = \begin{bmatrix} u_1 & u_2 \end{bmatrix}$ et $\vec{v} = \begin{bmatrix} v_1 & v_2 \end{bmatrix}$, alors $\vec{u} + \vec{v} = \begin{bmatrix} u_1 + v_1 & u_2 + v_2 \end{bmatrix}$.
MULTIPLICATION PAR UN SCALAIRE	 $a > 0$ et $b < 0$	Si $\vec{u} = \begin{bmatrix} u_1 & u_2 \end{bmatrix}$ et si $k \in \mathbb{R}$, alors $k\vec{u} = \begin{bmatrix} ku_1 & ku_2 \end{bmatrix}$.
PRODUIT SCALAIRE	 $\vec{u} \cdot \vec{v} = \|\vec{u}\|\,\|\vec{v}\|\cos\theta$ où $0 \leq \theta \leq \pi$	Si $\vec{u} = \begin{bmatrix} u_1 & u_2 \end{bmatrix}$ et $\vec{v} = \begin{bmatrix} v_1 & v_2 \end{bmatrix}$, alors $\vec{u} \cdot \vec{v} = u_1 v_1 + u_2 v_2$.
ANGLE ENTRE DEUX VECTEURS NON NULS		$\theta = \text{arc cos} \dfrac{\vec{u} \cdot \vec{v}}{\|\vec{u}\|\,\|\vec{v}\|}$ où $0 \leq \theta \leq \pi$

	Représentation géométrique	Représentation algébrique
PROJECTION ORTHOGONALE	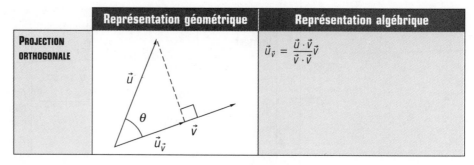	$\vec{u}_{\vec{v}} = \dfrac{\vec{u} \cdot \vec{v}}{\vec{v} \cdot \vec{v}}\vec{v}$

Les principales propriétés des opérations sur les vecteurs sont énoncées dans les théorèmes 5.1 à 5.4.

Toute expression de la forme $a_1\vec{u_1} + a_2\vec{u_2} + \cdots + a_n\vec{u_n}$, où a_1, a_2, ..., a_n sont des scalaires, est une combinaison linéaire des n vecteurs $\vec{u_1}$, $\vec{u_2}$, ..., $\vec{u_n}$. La figure suivante représente une combinaison de deux vecteurs non parallèles.

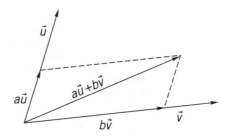

On dit que n vecteurs, $\vec{u_1}$, $\vec{u_2}$, ..., $\vec{u_n}$, sont linéairement indépendants si et seulement si **la seule** combinaison linéaire de ces vecteurs qui est égale au vecteur nul est celle où tous les coefficients (les scalaires) sont nuls.

De manière plus formelle, n vecteurs $\vec{u_1}$, $\vec{u_2}$, ..., $\vec{u_n}$ sont dits linéairement indépendants si et seulement si

$$a_1\vec{u_1} + a_2\vec{u_2} + \cdots + a_n\vec{u_n} = \vec{0} \quad \Rightarrow \quad a_1 = 0, \ a_2 = 0, \ ..., \ a_n = 0$$

Des vecteurs non linéairement indépendants sont dits linéairement dépendants. Ainsi, des vecteurs $\vec{u_1}$, $\vec{u_2}$, ..., $\vec{u_n}$ sont linéairement dépendants si et seulement s'il existe une combinaison linéaire de ces vecteurs qui est égale au vecteur nul et dont au moins l'un des coefficients est différent de zéro, c'est-à-dire si et seulement s'il existe une combinaison linéaire égale au vecteur nul et différente de celle où tous les coefficients sont nuls.

Deux vecteurs du plan, non nuls et non parallèles, sont linéairement indépendants, alors que deux vecteurs parallèles sont linéairement dépendants.

Une base d'un espace vectoriel est un ensemble de vecteurs linéairement indépendants dont les combinaisons linéaires engendrent tous les éléments de cet espace. Deux vecteurs linéairement indépendants du plan forment une base de l'espace des vecteurs du plan.

EXERCICES RÉCAPITULATIFS

1. (I) À l'aide d'une règle et d'un rapporteur, estimez la norme et la direction des vecteurs représentés dans le graphique ci-contre (échelle : une unité = 1 cm).

2. (I) Tracez les vecteurs présentant les caractéristiques suivantes : $\vec{u}$ a une longueur de 3 unités et une direction de $7\pi/6$; $\vec{v}$ a une longueur de 5 unités et une direction de 315° ; $\vec{w}$ a une longueur de 2 unités et une direction de $\pi/4$.

3. (I) Une rivière coule d'ouest en est et la vitesse du courant est de 6 kn (nœuds). Un bateau, capable d'atteindre une vitesse de 8 kn en eau calme, part de la rivière sud et se dirige franc nord.

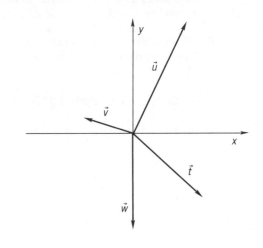

a) Représentez, dans un même graphique, la vitesse du bateau, $\vec{v_b}$, la vitesse du courant, $\vec{v_c}$, et la vitesse réelle ($\vec{v_r}$) du bateau. (Indice : Quelle opération faut-il effectuer sur les vecteurs $\vec{v_b}$ et $\vec{v_c}$ pour obtenir le vecteur $\vec{v_r}$?)

b) Le vecteur $\vec{v_r}$ est-il plus long que le vecteur $\vec{v_b}$? Justifiez votre réponse.

4. (I) Soit les vecteurs

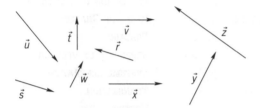

a) Nommez deux vecteurs égaux.

b) Nommez deux vecteurs opposés.

c) Tracez le vecteur $\vec{s} + \vec{t}$ en employant la méthode du parallélogramme.

d) Tracez les vecteurs $\vec{w} + \vec{v}$ et $\vec{u} + \vec{v} + \vec{w} + \vec{t}$.

e) Nommez un vecteur égal à $2\vec{w}$.

f) Nommez un vecteur égal à $\vec{w} + 2\vec{r}$.

g) Tracez les vecteurs $3\vec{w} - 2\vec{v}$ et $\vec{u} + 2\vec{v} - \vec{w}$.

h) Vérifiez graphiquement que $\vec{w} + \vec{v} = \vec{v} + \vec{w}$ et que $2(\vec{w} + \vec{v}) = 2\vec{w} + 2\vec{v}$.

5. (I) La direction et la longueur d'un vecteur $\vec{u}$ sont respectivement $\pi/6$ et 3, alors que la direction et la longueur d'un vecteur $\vec{v}$ sont respectivement $\pi/3$ et 5.

a) Tracez les vecteurs $\vec{u}$ et $\vec{v}$.

b) Tracez le vecteur $\vec{u} + \vec{v}$.

c) Quelles sont la direction et la longueur du vecteur $\vec{u} + \vec{v}$?

6. (I) Exprimez les caractéristiques (longueur et direction) du vecteur $-\vec{u}$ en fonction de celles de $\vec{u}$.

7. (I) Si $\|\vec{u}\| = 5$, que valent $\|4\vec{u}\|$ et $\|-6\vec{u}\|$?

8. (I) Soit un parallélogramme $ABCD$.

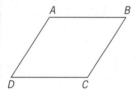

Que vaut $\overrightarrow{AD} - \overrightarrow{BC}$? $\overrightarrow{AB} + \overrightarrow{AD} + \overrightarrow{CB}$? $\overrightarrow{AD} + \overrightarrow{DC} - \overrightarrow{AB}$?

9. (I) Remplacez chaque expression par un vecteur unique.

a) $\overrightarrow{AB} - \overrightarrow{CB} + \overrightarrow{DE} - \overrightarrow{DC} - \overrightarrow{AE}$

b) $\overrightarrow{AB} - \overrightarrow{CD} + \overrightarrow{AD} + 4\overrightarrow{BA} - \overrightarrow{BC}$

10. (I) Remplacez chaque expression par un vecteur unique.

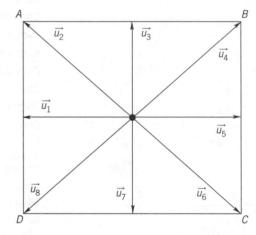

a) $\vec{u_1} - \vec{u_3}$

b) $\vec{u_1} + \vec{u_3} + \vec{u_5}$

c) $\vec{u_4} - \vec{u_8}$

d) $2\vec{u_3} - \vec{u_4}$

e) $\vec{u_6} + \vec{u_8}$

f) $\vec{u_2} - \vec{u_1} + \vec{u_5}$

11. (I) Quelle est la longueur du vecteur $\dfrac{k}{\|\vec{u}\|}\vec{u}$ où k est un scalaire différent de zéro et $\vec{u} \neq \vec{0}$. À l'aide du résultat, décrivez l'opération que vous devriez faire sur le vecteur $\vec{u}$ pour obtenir un vecteur de longueur 5 et de direction contraire à $\vec{u}$.

12. (II) Soit un rectangle $ABCD$.

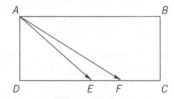

a) Soit E, le milieu du segment CD. Exprimez le vecteur $\overrightarrow{AE}$ comme une combinaison linéaire des vecteurs $\overrightarrow{AB}$ et $\overrightarrow{BC}$.

b) Si F divise le segment CD de telle façon que la longueur du segment DF représente une fraction x (où $0 < x < 1$) de la longueur du segment *DC*, exprimez le vecteur $\overrightarrow{AF}$ comme une combinaison linéaire des vecteurs $\overrightarrow{AB}$ et $\overrightarrow{BC}$.

13. (I) Illustrez à l'aide d'un graphique le fait que le vecteur $\vec{u} - \vec{v}$ correspond à l'une des diagonales du parallélogramme déterminé par deux vecteurs $\vec{u}$ et $\vec{v}$ issus d'une même origine.

14. (II) Soit trois points *A*, *B* et *C* non colinéaires. Montrez que le vecteur $\dfrac{1}{\|\overrightarrow{AB}\|}\overrightarrow{AB} + \dfrac{1}{\|\overrightarrow{AC}\|}\overrightarrow{AC}$ divise l'angle de sommet *A* en deux angles égaux. (Indice : Les diagonales d'un losange correspondent aux bissectrices des angles.)

15. (I) Soit trois points colinéaires *A*, *B* et *C*. Quel est l'ordre relatif de ces points si $\overrightarrow{AB}$ et $\overrightarrow{BC}$ ont la même direction ? (Énumérez toutes les possibilités.)

16. (II) Montrez que le barycentre *P* d'un ensemble de *n* points du plan, P_1, P_2, ..., P_n, vérifie l'équation vectorielle

$$\overrightarrow{OP} = \tfrac{1}{n}(\overrightarrow{OP_1} + \overrightarrow{OP_2} + \cdots + \overrightarrow{OP_n})$$

où *O* est un point auxiliaire.

17. (III) Soit un quadrilatère *ABCD*. En joignant les milieux des côtés adjacents de ce quadrilatère, on obtient un autre quadrilatère, soit *EFGH*.

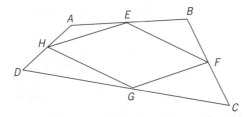

a) Montrez que *EFGH* est un parallélogramme en prenant un point auxiliaire *O*.

b) Montrez que le barycentre des points *EFGH* est identique au barycentre des points *ABCD*. (Indice : faites appel au résultat démontré au n° 16).

18. (I) Donnez une démonstration vectorielle de chaque énoncé. (Indice : Faites appel au produit scalaire.)

a) Tout angle inscrit dans un demi-cercle est un angle droit.

b) Les diagonales d'un losange (un parallélogramme dont les quatre côtés ont la même longueur) se coupent à angle droit.

19. (II) Montrez que trois vecteurs quelconques du plan sont linéairement dépendants.

20. (I) Exprimez les vecteurs $\vec{u}$, $\vec{v}$, $\vec{w}$, comme une combinaison linéaire des vecteurs $\vec{i}$ et $\vec{j}$.

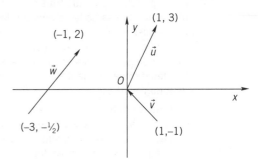

21. (I) Si $\overrightarrow{AB} = \overrightarrow{CD}$ pour les points *A*(1, 3), *B*(−1,5) et *C*(3, −2), quelles sont les coordonnées du point *D*?

22. (I) Soit les points *A*(2, −1), *B*(3, −3), *C*(−1, −1), *D*(2, 2) et *E*(4, −2).

a) Donnez les composantes de chacun des vecteurs suivants : $\overrightarrow{AB}$, $\overrightarrow{CB}$, $\overrightarrow{CD}$, $\overrightarrow{ED}$, $\overrightarrow{AE}$ et $\overrightarrow{AB} - \overrightarrow{CB} + \overrightarrow{CD} - \overrightarrow{ED}$. Expliquez pourquoi les deux derniers vecteurs sont égaux.

b) Calculez le module des vecteurs $\overrightarrow{AB}$, $\overrightarrow{CB}$ et $\overrightarrow{ED}$.

23. (I) Soit les vecteurs $\vec{u} = \begin{bmatrix} 4 & 1 \end{bmatrix}$, $\vec{v} = \begin{bmatrix} -3 & 2 \end{bmatrix}$ et $\vec{w} = \begin{bmatrix} 6 & -4 \end{bmatrix}$.

a) Représentez les trois vecteurs dans un même plan cartésien.

b) Donnez les composantes de $\vec{u} + \vec{v}$.

c) Donnez les composantes de $3\vec{u} + 2\vec{v} - 4\vec{w}$.

d) Donnez les composantes de $5\vec{u} - 2\vec{v} - \vec{w}$.

e) Évaluez $\|\vec{u} - \vec{v}\|$.

f) Quelle est la direction de chacun des vecteurs $\vec{u}$, $\vec{v}$ et $\vec{w}$?

g) À l'aide du résultat obtenu en *f*, évaluez l'angle entre $\vec{u}$ et $\vec{v}$.

h) À l'aide du résultat obtenu en *f*, évaluez l'angle entre $\vec{v}$ et $\vec{w}$. Que pouvez-vous dire de ces deux vecteurs?

24. (I) Calculez la longueur de chacune des diagonales du parallélogramme dont les deux côtés non parallèles correspondent respectivement aux vecteurs $\vec{u} = \begin{bmatrix} 4 & 1 \end{bmatrix}$ et $\vec{v} = \begin{bmatrix} 1 & 3 \end{bmatrix}$.

25. (I) Quelles sont les composantes du vecteur dont le module est 5 et la direction de 75°?

26. Donnez les composantes du vecteur unitaire de direction $7\pi/12$.

27. (I) Un golfeur a effectué trois roulés sur un vert plat avant que sa balle ne pénètre dans le trou. Le premier roulé a fait avancer la balle de huit mètres en direction franc nord; le deuxième roulé, de deux mètres en direction sud-est; le troisième roulé, d'une distance de un mètre en direction nord-est.

    a) Illustrez cette situation dans un plan cartésien (l'axe des x est l'axe est-ouest, l'axe des y est l'axe nord-sud) en représentant chaque roulé par un vecteur.

    b) Donnez les composantes des vecteurs représentant les trois roulés.

    c) Que représente la somme des trois vecteurs?

    d) À quelle distance du trou la balle était-elle lorsque le golfeur a effectué son premier roulé?

28. (I) Le graphique suivant représente les deux forces $\vec{F_1}$ et $\vec{F_2}$ qui s'exercent sur un objet et dont la résultante a pour support l'axe des abscisses. Déterminez l'intensité de la force $\vec{F_2}$.

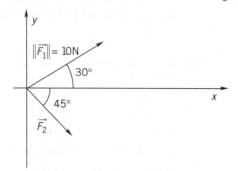

29. (I) Un système de forces est en équilibre si la somme des forces est nulle.

    a) Le système de forces $\vec{F_1} = \begin{bmatrix} 1 & 1 \end{bmatrix}$, $\vec{F_2} = \begin{bmatrix} 4 & -2 \end{bmatrix}$ et $\vec{F_3} = \begin{bmatrix} -1 & 3 \end{bmatrix}$ est-il en équilibre?

    b) Quelle force $\vec{F_4}$ faut-il ajouter au système décrit en *a* pour obtenir un système en équilibre?

    c) Trois enfants se disputent un jouet. Le schéma suivant indique l'intensité et la direction des forces exercées par deux des enfants dans le cas où l'objet est placé à l'origine du plan cartésien. Quelle force (direc-

tion et intensité) doit exercer le troisième enfant pour que le jouet reste à l'origine?

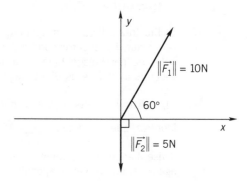

    d) Quelle force exerce le troisième enfant, si la résultante des forces a une intensité de 3 N et une direction de $2\pi/3$?

30. (II) À l'aide de la définition d'un système de forces en équilibre (voir l'exercice précédent), déterminez la tension dans chaque corde, c'est-à-dire $\|\vec{T_1}\|$ et $\|\vec{T_2}\|$.

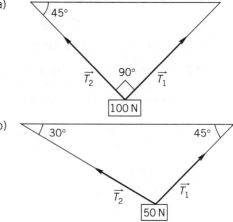

31. (I) À l'aide de trois électrocardiogrammes (ECG), il est possible de déterminer l'axe électrique du cœur en calculant une somme vectorielle. On obtient un ECG en plaçant des électrodes en différents endroits du corps. On nomme *dérivation* la disposition des électrodes sur le corps. Les dérivations standards permettent de mesurer le signal cardiaque entre deux électrodes placées sur deux membres. La première de ces dérivations consiste à placer une électrode à chaque poignet du sujet; la seconde consiste à placer une électrode au poignet droit et une autre à la cheville gauche du sujet; la troisième consiste à placer des électrodes au poignet gauche et à la cheville gauche du sujet.

Voici la représentation d'une révolution cardiaque typique, donnée par un ECG.

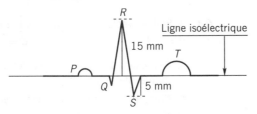

Ligne isoélectrique

Dans ce tracé, $R = 15$ mm et $S = -5$ mm. On mesure la longueur de R et de S (affectée d'un signe) sur les trois tracés obtenus pour les trois dérivations standards.

L'axe électrique du cœur est donné par la somme vectorielle $\vec{D} = \vec{D_1} + \vec{D_2} + \vec{D_3}$. Pour chaque ECG, la longueur du vecteur $\vec{D_i}$ est $|D_i|$ où $D_i = R_i + S_i$ [pour le graphique donné, $D_i = R_i + S_i = 15 + (-5) = 10$ mm]. La direction du vecteur $\vec{D_1}$ est de 0° ou 180° selon que D_1 est positif ou négatif ; la direction de $\vec{D_2}$ est de 300° ou 120° selon que D_2 est positif ou négatif ; la direction de $\vec{D_3}$ est de 240° ou 60° selon que D_3 est positif ou négatif.

On dit que l'axe électrique du cœur est normal lorsque la direction de $\vec{D}$ est comprise entre 270° et 360° ; il est droit lorsque la direction de $\vec{D}$ est comprise entre 90° et 270° ; il est dévié à gauche lorsque la direction de $\vec{D}$ est comprise entre 0° et 90°.

Déterminez la nature de chacun des axes électriques correspondant aux données suivantes :

a) $D_1 = 12$, $D_2 = -10$, $D_3 = 18$

b) $R_1 = 25$, $S_1 = -7$, $R_2 = 28$, $S_2 = -6$, $R_3 = 24$, $S_3 = -4$

32. (I) Montrez que $\vec{u} \cdot \vec{u} \geq 0$, où l'égalité est vérifiée seulement pour le vecteur nul.

33. (I) Soit $\vec{u}$ et $\vec{v}$ deux vecteurs non nuls. Démontrez que ces deux vecteurs déterminent un angle aigu lorsque leur produit scalaire est positif.

34. (I) Complétez la preuve de l'inégalité du triangle[10].

$$\|\vec{u} + \vec{v}\| \leq \|\vec{u}\| + \|\vec{v}\|$$

---

10. Le nom de cette inégalité tire son origine du fait bien connu que, dans un triangle, la somme des longueurs de deux côtés est plus grande que la longueur du troisième côté. Or, si $\vec{u}$ et $\vec{v}$ sont des vecteurs, alors $\vec{u} + \vec{v}$ représente le troisième côté du triangle déterminé par $\vec{u}$ et $\vec{v}$. Les longueurs respectives des côtés sont donc $\|\vec{u}\|$, $\|\vec{v}\|$ et $\|\vec{u} + \vec{v}\|$, d'où l'inégalité $\|\vec{u} + \vec{v}\| \leq \|\vec{u}\| + \|\vec{v}\|$.

Preuve

Comme $\|\vec{u} + \vec{v}\| \geq 0$, $\|\vec{u}\| \geq 0$ et $\|\vec{v}\| \geq 0$, il faut montrer que $\|\vec{u} + \vec{v}\|^2 \leq (\|\vec{u}\| + \|\vec{v}\|)^2$. Or,

$$\|\vec{u} + \vec{v}\|^2 = (\vec{u} + \vec{v}) \cdot (\vec{u} + \vec{v})$$
$$= \vec{u} \cdot \vec{u} + \vec{u} \cdot \vec{v} + \vec{v} \cdot \vec{u} + \vec{v} \cdot \vec{v}$$
$$= \vec{u} \cdot \vec{u} + \vec{u} \cdot \vec{v} + \vec{u} \cdot \vec{v} + \vec{v} \cdot \vec{v}$$
$$= \|\vec{u}\|^2 + \underline{\quad} \|\vec{u}\| \|\vec{v}\| \underline{\quad} + \underline{\quad}$$

De plus, $\cos\theta \leq \underline{\quad}$. Par conséquent,

$$\|\vec{u} + \vec{v}\|^2 \leq \|\vec{u}\|^2 + \underline{\quad} \|\vec{u}\| \|\vec{v}\| + \underline{\quad}$$
$$\|\vec{u} + \vec{v}\|^2 \leq (\|\vec{u}\| + \underline{\quad})^2$$

Donc, $\|\vec{u} + \vec{v}\| \leq \|\vec{u}\| + \|\vec{v}\|$ ∎

35. (I) Le travail effectué par une force $\vec{F}$ appliquée sur un objet qu'on déplace, dans la direction d'un vecteur $\vec{D}$, sur une distance $\|\vec{D}\|$ est donné par l'expression $\vec{F} \cdot \vec{D}$. Une personne pousse une tondeuse à gazon sur une distance de 30 mètres en appliquant une force de 100 N. Si la poignée de la tondeuse forme un angle de 30° avec le sol, quel travail la personne effectue-t-elle ?

36. (I) Soit $\vec{u}$ et $\vec{v}$ des vecteurs non nuls, démontrez que $|\vec{u} \cdot \vec{v}| = \|\vec{u}\| \|\vec{v}\|$ si et seulement si $\vec{u}$ et $\vec{v}$ sont parallèles.

37. (I) La direction et la longueur d'un vecteur $\vec{u}$ sont respectivement $\pi/6$ et 3, alors que la direction et la longueur d'un vecteur $\vec{v}$ sont respectivement $\pi/3$ et 5.

a) Donnez les composantes de chacun des vecteurs $\vec{u}$ et $\vec{v}$.

b) Donnez les composantes de la somme de $\vec{u}$ et $\vec{v}$.

c) Quelles sont la direction et la longueur du vecteur $\vec{u} + \vec{v}$? Comparez les résultats avec ceux que vous avez obtenus au n° 5.

38. (I) Soit les vecteurs $\vec{u} = \begin{bmatrix} 2 & 3 \end{bmatrix}$, $\vec{v} = \begin{bmatrix} -6 & 4 \end{bmatrix}$ et $\vec{w} = \begin{bmatrix} \frac{\sqrt{3}}{2} & -\frac{1}{2} \end{bmatrix}$.

a) Montrez que $\vec{u}$ et $\vec{v}$ sont des vecteurs perpendiculaires.

b) Exprimez le vecteur $\vec{r} = \begin{bmatrix} 4 & 3 \end{bmatrix}$ comme une combinaison linéaire des vecteurs $\vec{u}$ et $\vec{v}$.

c) Exprimez le vecteur $\vec{s} = \begin{bmatrix} a & b \end{bmatrix}$ comme une combinaison linéaire des vecteurs $\vec{u}$ et $\vec{v}$.

d) Les vecteurs $\vec{u}$ et $\vec{v}$ forment-ils une base de $\mathbb{R}^2$? Si oui, cette base est-elle orthogonale ? Est-elle orthonormée ?

e) Trouvez un vecteur $\vec{t}$ qui forme, avec le vecteur $\vec{w}$, une base orthonormée de $\mathbb{R}^2$. (Il existe deux possibilités.)

39. (I) Montrez que les points $A(1, 2)$, $B(3, 4)$ et $C(5, 2)$ sont les sommets d'un triangle rectangle. Quel point est le sommet de l'angle droit ? Quelles sont les mesures des deux autres angles ?

40. (I) Déterminez, si possible, le nombre a tel que les vecteurs $\begin{bmatrix} a & 4 \end{bmatrix}$ et $\begin{bmatrix} a & -9 \end{bmatrix}$ sont :
a) perpendiculaires ;
b) parallèles.

41. (I) Lesquelles des expressions suivantes n'ont aucun sens ? Justifiez votre réponse.
a) $2\vec{u} - 3\vec{v} = \vec{w}$
b) $2\vec{u} + \vec{v} = 0$
c) $2\vec{u} + 3\vec{u} = 5\vec{u}$
d) $3\vec{u} - 2\|\vec{v}\| = 4\vec{w}$
e) $2\|\vec{u}\| - 3\|\vec{v}\| = 10$
f) $\vec{u} < 5$
g) $\vec{u} < \vec{v}$
h) $\|\vec{u}\| < \|\vec{v}\|$
i) $\vec{u} \cdot (\vec{v} \cdot \vec{w}) = (\vec{u} \cdot \vec{v}) \cdot \vec{w}$

42. (I) Dites si chaque énoncé est vrai ou faux. Justifiez votre réponse.
a) $\vec{u} \cdot \vec{v} = \vec{u} \cdot \vec{w} \Rightarrow \vec{v} = \vec{w}$.
b) $\|\vec{u} + \vec{v}\| = \|\vec{u}\| + \|\vec{v}\|$ si $\vec{u}$ et $\vec{v}$ sont des vecteurs parallèles.
c) $|\vec{u} \cdot \vec{v}| \leq \|\vec{u}\| \|\vec{v}\|$.
d) Deux vecteurs égaux ont la même origine.
e) Deux vecteurs opposés ont des directions contraires.
f) $\overrightarrow{AB} = \overrightarrow{BA}$
g) $\|\overrightarrow{AB}\| = \|\overrightarrow{BA}\|$
h) Toute paire de vecteurs du plan constitue une base de $\mathbb{R}^2$.
i) Si $\|\vec{u} + \vec{v}\| = 0$, alors $\|\vec{u}\| = \|\vec{v}\|$.
j) Le vecteur nul peut faire partie d'une base de $\mathbb{R}^2$.
k) $k\vec{u} = \vec{0}$ si et seulement si $k = 0$.
l) La projection orthogonale d'un vecteur $\vec{u}$ sur un vecteur $\vec{v}$, notée $\vec{u}_{\vec{v}}$, ne vaut jamais $\vec{0}$.

m) Deux vecteurs parallèles de même longueur sont nécessairement égaux.

43. (I) Soit les vecteurs $\vec{s} = \begin{bmatrix} 4 & -3 \end{bmatrix}$, $\vec{t} = \begin{bmatrix} 2 & 2 \end{bmatrix}$, $\vec{u} = \begin{bmatrix} -1 & 1 \end{bmatrix}$, $\vec{v} = \begin{bmatrix} 1 & -3 \end{bmatrix}$ et $\vec{w} = \begin{bmatrix} -3 & -4 \end{bmatrix}$.

a) Représentez tous ces vecteurs dans un même plan cartésien.

b) Calculez le module de chaque vecteur.

c) Calculez la direction de chaque vecteur.

d) Trouvez un vecteur $\vec{a}$ tel que les vecteurs $\vec{a}$, $\vec{s}$ et $\vec{t}$ déterminent un triangle.

e) Donnez les composantes des vecteurs $\vec{u} + 3\vec{s}$, $-3\vec{u} + 2\vec{w} + \vec{t}$ et $5\vec{s} + 3\vec{t} - 2\vec{u}$.

f) Évaluez $\vec{u} \cdot \vec{v}$, $\vec{s} \cdot \vec{t}$, $\vec{u} \cdot 3\vec{s}$ et $2\vec{u} \cdot (3\vec{s} + 4\vec{t})$.

g) Quel est l'angle entre les vecteurs $\vec{u}$ et $\vec{v}$? Entre les vecteurs $\vec{s}$ et $\vec{t}$?

h) Montrez que les vecteurs $\vec{s}$ et $\vec{w}$ sont orthogonaux.

i) Montrez que le vecteur $\vec{w}$ est perpendiculaire (on dit aussi *normal*) à la droite d'équation $3x + 4y = 12$. (Indice : trouvez deux points de cette droite et montrez qu'un vecteur joignant ces deux points est perpendiculaire au vecteur $\vec{w}$.)

j) Exprimez le vecteur $\vec{v}$ comme une combinaison linéaire des vecteurs $\vec{u}$ et $\vec{s}$.

k) Exprimez le vecteur $\vec{v}$ comme une combinaison linéaire des vecteurs $\vec{w}$ et $\vec{t}$.

l) Exprimez le vecteur $\vec{s}$ comme une combinaison linéaire des vecteurs $\vec{u}$, $\vec{w}$ et $\vec{t}$. Existe-t-il plus d'une possibilité ?

m) Les vecteurs $\vec{u}$, $\vec{w}$ et $\vec{s}$ sont-ils linéairement indépendants ?

n) Pourquoi les vecteurs $\vec{u}$, $\vec{w}$ et $\vec{s}$ ne forment-ils pas une base de $\mathbb{R}^2$?

o) Peut-on exprimer le vecteur $\vec{v}$ comme une combinaison linéaire des vecteurs $\vec{u}$ et $\vec{p}$ où $\vec{p} = \begin{bmatrix} 2 & -2 \end{bmatrix}$? Justifiez votre réponse.

p) Pourquoi les vecteurs $\vec{u}$ et $\vec{p}$ ne forment-ils pas une base de $\mathbb{R}^2$?

q) Montrez que tout vecteur du plan $\vec{r} = \begin{bmatrix} a & b \end{bmatrix}$ s'écrit comme une combinaison linéaire des vecteurs $\vec{u}$ et $\vec{s}$. Que peut-on dire des vecteurs $\vec{u}$ et $\vec{s}$?

r) Montrez que les vecteurs $\vec{u}$ et $\vec{s}$ sont linéairement indépendants.

s) Sachant que les vecteurs $\vec{u}$ et $\vec{s}$ sont linéairement indépendants et qu'ils constituent un système générateur de $\mathbb{R}^2$, que peut-on en conclure?

t) Les vecteurs $\vec{t}$ et $\vec{s}$ forment-ils une base de $\mathbb{R}^2$?

u) Donnez les composantes du vecteur dont le module est quatre fois plus grand que le module de $\vec{v}$ et dont la direction est contraire à celle du vecteur $\vec{v}$.

v) Donnez les composantes des deux vecteurs unitaires perpendiculaires au vecteur $\vec{v}$.

w) Donnez les composantes des deux vecteurs unitaires qui forment chacun un angle de 45° avec le vecteur $\vec{v}$.

x) Quelle est la projection orthogonale du vecteur $\vec{s}$ sur le vecteur $\vec{t}$?

y) Quelle est la projection orthogonale du vecteur $\vec{s}$ sur le vecteur $\vec{w}$? Qu'en concluez-vous?

44. (II) Soit les vecteurs $\vec{u} = \begin{bmatrix} \cos\alpha & \sin\alpha \end{bmatrix}$ et $\vec{v} = \begin{bmatrix} \cos\beta & \sin\beta \end{bmatrix}$ où $0 \le \alpha \le \beta \le 2\pi$.

a) Quelle est la longueur des vecteurs $\vec{u}$ et $\vec{v}$?

b) Tracez les vecteurs $\vec{u}$ et $\vec{v}$ dans un même plan cartésien.

c) Que représente $\beta - \alpha$?

d) Déterminez le produit scalaire de $\vec{u}$ et $\vec{v}$.

e) Établissez une identité trigonométrique pour $\cos(\beta - \alpha)$.

45. (II) Les logiciels graphiques permettent le traitement d'images dans le plan: projection, élongation, réflexion par rapport à un axe, rotation. On fait appel aux matrices et aux vecteurs pour modéliser ces transformations. Dans ce cas-ci, nous employons des vecteurs colonnes (ou matrices colonnes).

Soit le vecteur $\vec{u} = \begin{bmatrix} a \\ b \end{bmatrix}$ représenté dans un plan cartésien.

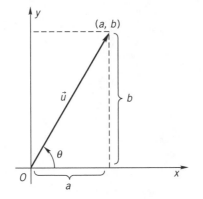

a) Tracez, dans un même plan cartésien, le vecteur correspondant au produit matriciel $\begin{bmatrix} 1 & 0 \\ 0 & 0 \end{bmatrix} \begin{bmatrix} a \\ b \end{bmatrix}$ et le vecteur $\vec{u} = \begin{bmatrix} a \\ b \end{bmatrix}$. Donnez une interprétation géométrique du produit de la matrice $\begin{bmatrix} 1 & 0 \\ 0 & 0 \end{bmatrix}$ par le vecteur $\vec{u} = \begin{bmatrix} a \\ b \end{bmatrix}$.

b) Tracez, dans un même plan cartésien, le vecteur correspondant au produit matriciel $\begin{bmatrix} 0 & 0 \\ 0 & 1 \end{bmatrix} \begin{bmatrix} a \\ b \end{bmatrix}$ et le vecteur $\vec{u} = \begin{bmatrix} a \\ b \end{bmatrix}$. Donnez une interprétation géométrique du produit de la matrice $\begin{bmatrix} 0 & 0 \\ 0 & 1 \end{bmatrix}$ par le vecteur $\vec{u} = \begin{bmatrix} a \\ b \end{bmatrix}$.

c) Tracez, dans un même plan cartésien, le vecteur correspondant au produit matriciel $\begin{bmatrix} -1 & 0 \\ 0 & 1 \end{bmatrix} \begin{bmatrix} a \\ b \end{bmatrix}$ et le vecteur $\vec{u} = \begin{bmatrix} a \\ b \end{bmatrix}$. Vérifiez que cette opération constitue une réflexion du vecteur $\vec{u} = \begin{bmatrix} a \\ b \end{bmatrix}$ par rapport à l'axe des ordonnées.

d) Quelle matrice carrée d'ordre 2 permet d'exprimer la réflexion du vecteur $\vec{u} = \begin{bmatrix} a \\ b \end{bmatrix}$ par rapport à l'axe des abscisses?

e) Quelle matrice carrée d'ordre 2 permet d'exprimer la réflexion du vecteur $\vec{u} = \begin{bmatrix} a \\ b \end{bmatrix}$ par rapport à la droite d'équation $y = x$, c'est-à-dire de transformer $\begin{bmatrix} a \\ b \end{bmatrix}$ en $\begin{bmatrix} b \\ a \end{bmatrix}$?

f) Quel est l'effet de l'opération $\begin{bmatrix} 2 & 0 \\ 0 & 2 \end{bmatrix} \begin{bmatrix} a \\ b \end{bmatrix}$?

g) Quel est l'effet de l'opération $\begin{bmatrix} k & 0 \\ 0 & k \end{bmatrix} \begin{bmatrix} a \\ b \end{bmatrix}$ si k est un scalaire positif? si k est un scalaire négatif?

h) Montrez que $\begin{bmatrix} \cos\varphi & -\sin\varphi \\ \sin\varphi & \cos\varphi \end{bmatrix} \begin{bmatrix} a \\ b \end{bmatrix}$ applique une rotation d'un angle φ au vecteur $\vec{u} = \begin{bmatrix} a \\ b \end{bmatrix}$. (Indice : Vérifiez que le vecteur $\vec{w} = \begin{bmatrix} \cos\varphi & -\sin\varphi \\ \sin\varphi & \cos\varphi \end{bmatrix} \begin{bmatrix} a \\ b \end{bmatrix}$ a la même longueur que $\vec{u}$, et que la direction de $\vec{w}$ est $\theta + \varphi$ où θ désigne la direction de $\vec{u}$.)

Droite du plan

The early study of Euclid made me a hater of geometry, and yet, in spite of this repugnance, which had become a second nature in me, whenever I went far enough into any mathematical question, I found I touched, at last, a geometrical bottom.

James Joseph Sylvester

À LA FIN DU PRÉSENT CHAPITRE, VOUS DEVRIEZ ÊTRE EN MESURE DE RÉPONDRE AUX QUESTIONS SUIVANTES:

- De quelles façons peut-on caractériser une droite du plan?
- Comment trouve-t-on le point d'intersection de deux droites concourantes et l'angle qu'elles déterminent?
- Comment évalue-t-on la distance d'un point à une droite du plan?
- Comment calcule-t-on la distance entre deux droites parallèles du plan?
- Comment peut-on interpréter les coefficients de l'équation normale d'une droite du plan?

On sait peu de choses à propos d'Euclide. Ses contemporains n'ont laissé de lui aucun dessin, peinture ou buste, de sorte que nous n'avons pas de portrait réaliste de cet illustre mathématicien ; nous devons donc nous contenter de représentations – comme celle de gauche – issues de l'imagination d'artistes ayant vécu bien après lui. Euclide était vraisemblablement d'origine grecque. Il serait né aux environs de l'an 330 avant notre ère et serait mort aux environs de l'an 275. Il aurait reçu sa formation à Athènes, mais c'est à Alexandrie qu'il fonda l'école de mathématiques où il enseigna.

Euclide aurait été une personne affable et scrupuleusement honnête. On raconte que, en guise de réponse à un élève qui le questionnait sur l'utilité de la géométrie, il aurait ordonné à un esclave de donner de l'argent à ce dernier puisqu'il tenait tant à ce que ses études lui rapportent.

Les travaux mathématiques d'Euclide ont d'abord été traduits en latin et en arabe, puis ces versions ont été traduites dans diverses langues d'Europe. L'ouvrage le plus connu d'Euclide, les Éléments, est divisé en treize livres. Les six premiers livres traitent de géométrie plane ; les trois suivants, d'algèbre et de théorie des nombres ; le dixième, des nombres irrationnels ; et les trois derniers, des solides géométriques. Cet ouvrage didactique, qui couvre l'ensemble des connaissances mathématiques accumulées par les anciens Grecs, a connu un énorme succès. À l'exception de la Bible et du Coran, les Éléments est sans doute le livre le plus édité[1] et le plus étudié des deux derniers millénaires. Dans certains pays, ce traité servait encore à l'enseignement de la géométrie au début du XXᵉ siècle.

La popularité des Éléments tient non seulement à son contenu, mais également à sa forme. L'exposé d'Euclide est extrêmement clair et rigoureux. La démarche axiomatique proposée dans les Éléments sert encore aujourd'hui de modèle. En effet, l'ouvrage commence par une série de 23 définitions, suivies de 5 postulats (des énoncés acceptés comme vrais parce qu'ils constituent des évidences) et de 5 notions communes (parfois

---

1. R. E. Moritz cite Riccardi, qui affirme avoir répertorié près de 2 000 éditions de l'ouvrage d'Euclide.

appelées axiomes), viennent ensuite des théorèmes, tous démontrés. La structure logique du traité, fondée sur un nombre restreint d'hypothèses et de définitions, a largement contribué à sa renommée, et elle a valu à son auteur une place de choix dans l'histoire des mathématiques.

Il fallut d'ailleurs attendre les travaux de Gerolamo Saccheri (1667-1733) pour la formulation d'une géométrie non euclidienne remettant en question le cinquième postulat d'Euclide. Cette géométrie fut développée notamment par Bernhard Riemann (1826-1866) et elle trouva finalement son utilité dans les travaux d'Albert Einstein (1879-1955) sur la relativité.

Plusieurs termes mathématiques encore en usage comportent le qualificatif euclidien, en l'honneur du grand mathématicien de la Grèce antique : algorithme euclidien, anneau euclidien, distance euclidienne, division euclidienne, espace vectoriel euclidien, géométrie euclidienne, norme euclidienne.

6.1 TERMINOLOGIE DE BASE

Les vecteurs du plan ont de nombreuses applications. Dans le présent chapitre, nous adoptons une approche vectorielle pour étudier les différentes caractéristiques d'une droite du plan. Au chapitre 7, nous aborderons une deuxième application des vecteurs du plan : les nombres complexes.

La droite est le lieu géométrique le plus simple qui s'exprime sous la forme d'une équation. Il existe toutefois plusieurs façons de caractériser une droite.

Ainsi, dès les premières pages des *Éléments*, immédiatement après les définitions, Euclide énonce cinq postulats[2], dont les deux premiers portent sur la droite. Le premier affirme qu'on ne peut conduire qu'une seule droite d'un point à un autre point. Toute droite est donc complètement déterminée par deux de ses points.

Nous désignons une droite, ou son équation, par le symbole Δ auquel on ajoute au besoin un indice[3]. Le schéma suivant représente la droite Δ passant par deux points (x_1, y_1) et (x_2, y_2).

---

2. Pour Euclide, un postulat est un énoncé primitif, qui n'a pas besoin d'être démontré parce qu'il paraît incontestable.
3. Le symbole Δ se prononce « delta ». Il s'agit de la lettre majuscule de l'alphabet grec qui correspond à *d* et qui est l'initiale du mot « droite ».

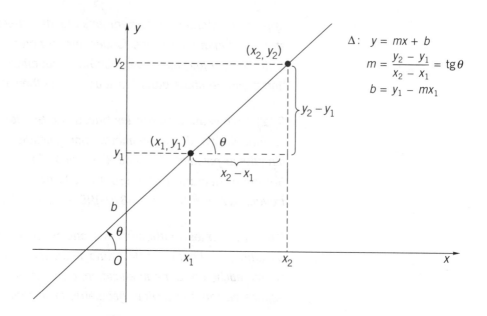

On sait qu'on peut calculer la distance d entre les points $(x_1,\ y_1)$ et $(x_2,\ y_2)$ en appliquant le théorème de Pythagore :

$$d = \sqrt{(x_2 - x_1)^2 + (y_2 - y_1)^2}$$

L'expression $\Delta : y = mx + b$ désigne une droite Δ de pente m et d'ordonnée à l'origine b. Si on se déplace entre deux points distincts, $(x_1,\ y_1)$ et $(x_2,\ y_2)$, d'une même droite, le quotient de la variation des ordonnées sur la variation des abscisses est la **pente** de la droite. Ce quotient est constant quels que soient les points distincts de la droite. La pente est donc donnée par l'expression

$$m = \frac{y_2 - y_1}{x_2 - x_1}$$

Donc, si on se déplace sur une droite, la pente indique de quelle quantité augmente l'ordonnée lorsque l'abscisse augmente d'une unité.

La pente d'une droite est également donnée par l'expression $m = \operatorname{tg} \theta$ où θ représente l'angle ($0° \leq \theta < 180°$ ou $0 \leq \theta < \pi$) déterminé par la droite et l'axe des abscisses. L'angle θ se mesure dans le sens contraire des aiguilles d'une montre, depuis l'axe jusqu'à la droite. Cet angle est appelé **angle d'inclinaison** de la droite. L'angle d'inclinaison d'une droite verticale est de 90°, alors que celui d'une droite horizontale est de 0°.

Exemple

L'angle d'inclinaison des droites Δ_1, Δ_2, Δ_3 et Δ_4 est respective-ment de 40°, 160°, 90° et 0°.

PENTE D'UNE DROITE

La pente d'une droite du plan est le quotient de la variation des ordonnées sur la variation des abscisses. La pente m de la droite qui passe par deux points $(x_1,\ y_1)$ et $(x_2,\ y_2)$ est donnée par

$$m = \frac{y_2 - y_1}{x_2 - x_1}$$

ANGLE D'INCLINAISON D'UNE DROITE

L'angle d'inclinaison d'une droite Δ est l'angle θ entre la droite Δ et l'axe des abscisses, cet angle étant mesuré dans le sens contraire des aiguilles d'une montre. De plus, $0° \leq \theta < 180°$ ou $0 \leq \theta < \pi$.

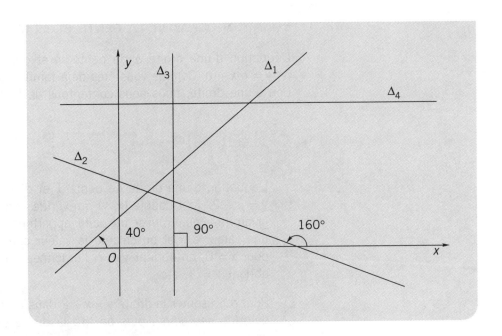

ORDONNÉE À L'ORIGINE D'UNE DROITE

L'ordonnée à l'origine d'une droite est l'ordonnée du point d'intersection de la droite avec l'axe des y. Une droite de pente m qui passe par un point (x_1, y_1) a comme ordonnée à l'origine $b = y_1 - mx_1$.

L'**ordonnée à l'origine**, notée b, d'une droite Δ est égale à l'ordonnée du point d'intersection de la droite avec l'axe des y. Une droite de pente m qui passe par un point (x_1, y_1) a pour ordonnée à l'origine $b = y_1 - mx_1$.

Une droite est donc complètement déterminée par sa pente et son ordonnée à l'origine. Autrement dit, il n'existe qu'une seule droite de pente m et d'ordonnée à l'origine b.

Il y a lieu de distinguer deux cas particuliers, soit les droites horizontales et les droites verticales. L'équation d'une droite horizontale est $y = b$, c'est-à-dire que sa pente est nulle ($m = 0$). L'équation d'une droite verticale est $x = a$: sa pente n'est pas définie. Il faut garder à l'esprit que les règles générales énoncées dans le présent chapitre ne s'appliquent pas nécessairement à ces deux cas particuliers.

Une droite est également complètement déterminée par son angle d'inclinaison et l'un de ses points. De plus, nous verrons qu'il est possible de caractériser une droite en adoptant une approche vectorielle.

6.2 DIFFÉRENTES FORMES DE L'ÉQUATION D'UNE DROITE DU PLAN

Dans les prochaines sections, nous verrons différentes façons d'écrire l'équation d'une droite, qui dépendent chacune de la perspective adoptée pour caractériser la droite. Nous verrons ensuite certaines particularités des droites: point d'intersection de deux droites concourantes, distance d'une droite à l'origine, distance d'un point à une droite, distance entre deux droites parallèles, et angle entre deux droites concourantes.

6.2.1 ÉQUATION DONNANT LA PENTE ET L'ORDONNÉE À L'ORIGINE

L'équation d'une droite Δ de pente m et d'ordonnée à l'origine b s'écrit $\Delta : y = mx + b$. Comme vous êtes déjà familier avec cette forme de l'équation d'une droite, nous nous contentons de l'illustrer par un exemple.

Exemple

L'équation d'une droite de pente 1 et d'ordonnée à l'origine 2 est $y = x + 2$. Tout couple (x, y) qui vérifie cette équation appartient à la droite. Pour trouver un point appartenant à la droite, on donne une valeur à x et on calcule la valeur correspondante de y. Ainsi, pour $x = 0$, on obtient $y = 2$, l'ordonnée à l'origine. Pour $x = 1$, on obtient $y = 3$, etc.

Pour représenter la droite $y = x + 2$ dans un plan cartésien, on trace deux de ses points puis on tire la droite qui passe par ces deux points.

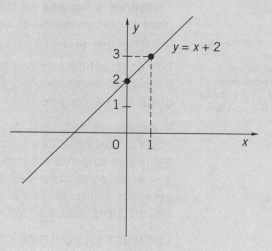

EXERCICE 6.1

Soit la droite de pente -2 et d'ordonnée à l'origine 2.

a) Écrivez l'équation de cette droite qui donne la pente et l'ordonnée à l'origine.

b) Le point $(2, 2)$ appartient-il à la droite ?

c) Tracez la droite dans un plan cartésien.

Si deux droites d'un plan cartésien se coupent en un seul point, on dit que ce sont des **droites concourantes**. Pour trouver le point d'intersection de deux droites concourantes, il faut résoudre le système d'équations formé des équations des droites.

Exemple

Pour déterminer le point d'intersection des droites $\Delta_1 : y = 2x + 3$ et $\Delta_2 : y = x - 4$, on pose l'égalité entre les ordonnées :

$$2x + 3 = x - 4$$

On obtient ainsi $x = -7$ et, en remplaçant x par sa valeur dans l'équation de l'une des droites, on a $y = -11$. Le point d'intersection des deux droites est donc $(-7, -11)$.

6.2.2 ÉQUATION DONNANT L'ANGLE D'INCLINAISON ET L'ORDONNÉE À L'ORIGINE

Une droite est complètement déterminée par son angle d'inclinaison θ et son ordonnée à l'origine. L'équation d'une telle droite peut donc s'écrire sous la forme $y = (\text{tg}\theta)x + b$, qui n'est en fait qu'une variante de la forme $y = mx + b$. En effet, la pente d'une droite est égale à la tangente de l'angle d'inclinaison. On peut donc exprimer l'angle d'inclinaison en fonction de la pente :

$$\text{tg}\theta = m \ \Rightarrow \ \theta = \text{arc tg}\,m \ \text{ où } \ 0° \le \theta < 180° \ (\text{ou } 0 \le \theta < \pi)$$

Exemple

L'équation de la droite dont l'angle d'inclinaison est de 30° et l'ordonnée à l'origine −1 est donnée par

$$y = (\text{tg}30°)x + (-1) = \frac{\sqrt{3}}{3}x - 1$$

EXERCICE 6.2

1. Quel est l'angle d'inclinaison de la droite $y = 2x - 4$?

2. Quel est l'angle d'inclinaison de la droite $y = -x + 1$?

6.2.3 ÉQUATION DONNANT LA PENTE ET UN POINT

Une droite est entièrement déterminée par sa pente et l'un de ses points. Si (x, y) est un point quelconque de la droite et si (x_1, y_1) est un point dont on connaît les coordonnées, alors $m = \dfrac{y - y_1}{x - x_1}$. De cette expression de la pente, on déduit l'équation d'une droite $(y - y_1) = m(x - x_1)$, qui donne la pente et un point.

Exemple

L'équation de la droite de pente 2 qui passe par le point $(3, 1)$ est $(y - 1) = 2(x - 3)$.

EXERCICE 6.3

1. Écrivez l'équation de la droite $y = 2x - 8$ qui donne la pente et un point.

2. Écrivez l'équation de la droite $(y - 3) = 3(x - 2)$ qui donne la pente et l'ordonnée à l'origine.

6.2.4 ÉQUATION DONNANT DEUX POINTS DISTINCTS

Une droite est entièrement déterminée par deux de ses points. Si (x, y) est un point quelconque d'une droite et si (x_1, y_1) et (x_2, y_2) sont deux points distincts de cette droite, alors, comme la pente est constante, on a l'équation

$$\frac{y - y_1}{x - x_1} = \frac{y_2 - y_1}{x_2 - x_1}$$

Exemple

L'équation de la droite passant par les points $(1, 2)$ et $(-2, 3)$ est donnée par

$$\frac{y - y_1}{x - x_1} = \frac{y_2 - y_1}{x_2 - x_1} \quad \Rightarrow \quad \frac{y - 2}{x - 1} = \frac{3 - 2}{-2 - 1} \quad \Rightarrow \quad \frac{y - 2}{x - 1} = -\frac{1}{3}$$

EXERCICE 6.4

Soit la droite qui passe par les points $(-1, 3)$ et $(-4, -2)$.

a) Écrivez l'équation de cette droite qui donne deux points distincts.

b) Quelle est la pente de la droite?

c) Quel est l'angle d'inclinaison de la droite?

d) Le point $(2, 8)$ appartient-il à la droite?

e) Le point $(1, 6)$ appartient-il à la droite?

f) Quel est le point d'intersection de la droite donnée avec la droite qui passe par les points $(1, 2)$ et $(2, 2)$?

6.2.5 ÉQUATION VECTORIELLE

Nous allons maintenant faire appel au concept de vecteur pour définir une droite. Comme dans les sections précédentes, il faut identifier ce qui détermine de façon unique et non équivoque une droite particulière.

Un vecteur $\vec{d} = \begin{bmatrix} d_1 & d_2 \end{bmatrix}$ définit une famille de droites parallèles, formée de toutes les droites qui pourraient servir de support à ce vecteur. Le vecteur $\vec{d}$ est parallèle à la droite particulière Δ dont on veut trouver l'équation. Tout vecteur parallèle à une droite est un **vecteur directeur** de cette droite. Le qualificatif « directeur » évoque le fait que ce vecteur donne la direction de la droite, c'est-à-dire l'angle d'inclinaison θ de la droite. En effet,

VECTEUR DIRECTEUR D'UNE DROITE

Un vecteur directeur d'une droite est un vecteur $\vec{d}$ parallèle à cette droite.

$$m = \operatorname{tg}\theta = \frac{d_2}{d_1} \quad \Rightarrow \quad \theta = \operatorname{arc\,tg}\frac{d_2}{d_1} \quad \text{où} \quad 0° \leq \theta < 180° \text{ ou } 0 \leq \theta < \pi$$

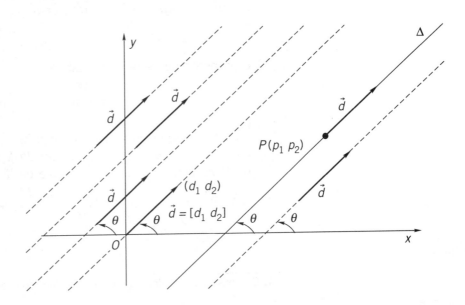

La figure indique clairement que la droite Δ est entièrement déterminée par un point $P(p_1, p_2)$ et un vecteur directeur $\vec{d} = \begin{bmatrix} d_1 & d_2 \end{bmatrix}$, c'est-à-dire que Δ est la seule droite qui passe par le point P et dont $\vec{d}$ est un vecteur directeur.

Si $X(x, y)$ est un point quelconque de la droite Δ, alors le vecteur $\overrightarrow{PX}$ est parallèle à la droite et au vecteur $\vec{d}$. Par conséquent, $\overrightarrow{PX} = k\vec{d}$. Or,

$$\overrightarrow{PX} = \overrightarrow{PO} + \overrightarrow{OX} = -\overrightarrow{OP} + \overrightarrow{OX} = -\begin{bmatrix} p_1 & p_2 \end{bmatrix} + \begin{bmatrix} x & y \end{bmatrix}$$

et

$$k\vec{d} = k\begin{bmatrix} d_1 & d_2 \end{bmatrix}$$

Par conséquent,

$$-\begin{bmatrix} p_1 & p_2 \end{bmatrix} + \begin{bmatrix} x & y \end{bmatrix} = k\begin{bmatrix} d_1 & d_2 \end{bmatrix}$$

ÉQUATION VECTORIELLE D'UNE DROITE DU PLAN

L'équation vectorielle de la droite dont $\vec{d} = \begin{bmatrix} d_1 & d_2 \end{bmatrix}$ est un vecteur directeur et qui passe par le point $P(p_1, p_2)$ est

$\begin{bmatrix} x & y \end{bmatrix} = \begin{bmatrix} p_1 & p_2 \end{bmatrix} + k\begin{bmatrix} d_1 & d_2 \end{bmatrix}$

où $k \in \mathbb{R}$.

On tire de cette équation l'**équation vectorielle** de la droite qui a comme vecteur directeur $\vec{d} = \begin{bmatrix} d_1 & d_2 \end{bmatrix}$ et qui passe par le point $P(p_1, p_2)$:

$$\begin{bmatrix} x & y \end{bmatrix} = \begin{bmatrix} p_1 & p_2 \end{bmatrix} + k\begin{bmatrix} d_1 & d_2 \end{bmatrix} \quad \text{où} \quad k \in \mathbb{R}$$

Il est à noter que l'équation vectorielle d'une droite n'est pas unique : une droite a plus d'un vecteur directeur et une infinité de points. De plus, deux droites sont parallèles si et seulement si leurs vecteurs directeurs sont parallèles[4].

Exemple

L'équation vectorielle de la droite qui passe par le point $A(-1, 3)$ et qui a comme vecteur directeur $\vec{d} = \begin{bmatrix} -2 & 1 \end{bmatrix}$ est

$$\begin{bmatrix} x & y \end{bmatrix} = \begin{bmatrix} -1 & 3 \end{bmatrix} + k\begin{bmatrix} -2 & 1 \end{bmatrix} \quad \text{où} \quad k \in \mathbb{R}$$

et la pente de cette droite est

$$m = \operatorname{tg} \theta = \frac{d_2}{d_1} = -\frac{1}{2}$$

Pour savoir si le point $B(4, 1)$ appartient à la droite, il faut déterminer s'il existe une unique valeur de k telle que les coordonnées de B vérifient l'équation vectorielle de la droite. Or,

$$\begin{bmatrix} 4 & 1 \end{bmatrix} = \begin{bmatrix} -1 & 3 \end{bmatrix} + k\begin{bmatrix} -2 & 1 \end{bmatrix} \Rightarrow 4 = -1 - 2k \text{ et } 1 = 3 + k$$

---

4. On considère que deux droites confondues sont parallèles.

d'où $k = -5/2$ et $k = -2$. Comme k ne peut prendre qu'une seule valeur à la fois, on en conclut que le point B n'appartient pas à la droite.

Par contre, le point $C(-5, 5)$ appartient à la droite. En effet, si on remplace k par 2 dans l'équation vectorielle de la droite, on obtient $x = -5$ et $y = 5$.

Les points A et C appartenant à la droite, $\overrightarrow{AC} = \begin{bmatrix} -4 & 2 \end{bmatrix}$ est un autre vecteur directeur de la droite. L'équation vectorielle de la droite s'écrit donc également

$$\begin{bmatrix} x & y \end{bmatrix} = \begin{bmatrix} -1 & 3 \end{bmatrix} + t\begin{bmatrix} -4 & 2 \end{bmatrix} \quad \text{où} \quad t \in \mathbb{R}$$

ou encore

$$\begin{bmatrix} x & y \end{bmatrix} = \begin{bmatrix} -5 & 5 \end{bmatrix} + r\begin{bmatrix} -4 & 2 \end{bmatrix} \quad \text{où} \quad r \in \mathbb{R}$$

L'équation vectorielle d'une droite n'est pas unique!

EXERCICE 6.5

Soit les points $A(1, -1)$ et $B(-2, 0)$.

a) Quelles sont les composantes du vecteur $\overrightarrow{AB}$?

b) Quel nom donne-t-on au vecteur $\overrightarrow{AB}$ relativement à la droite qui passe par les points A et B?

c) Donnez l'équation vectorielle de la droite qui passe par les points A et B.

d) Quelle est la pente de la droite?

e) Vérifiez que le point $C(-14, 4)$ appartient à la droite.

f) Quelles sont les composantes du vecteur $\overrightarrow{AC}$?

g) Que constatez-vous à propos des vecteurs $\overrightarrow{AB}$ et $\overrightarrow{AC}$? Tirez-en une règle générale qui permette de vérifier si trois points sont colinéaires, c'est-à-dire situés sur une même droite.

6.2.6 ÉQUATIONS PARAMÉTRIQUES

ÉQUATIONS PARAMÉTRIQUES D'UNE DROITE DU PLAN

Les équations paramétriques de la droite Δ dont $\vec{d} = \begin{bmatrix} d_1 & d_2 \end{bmatrix}$ est un vecteur directeur et qui passe par le point $P(p_1, p_2)$ sont

$$\Delta : \begin{cases} x = p_1 + kd_1 \\ y = p_2 + kd_2 \end{cases} \quad \text{où } k \in \mathbb{R}$$

Comme l'équation vectorielle d'une droite contient un paramètre, on peut exprimer chacune des variables x et y en fonction de ce paramètre. Les deux équations ainsi obtenues sont appelées **équations paramétriques** de la droite:

$$\begin{bmatrix} x & y \end{bmatrix} = \begin{bmatrix} p_1 & p_2 \end{bmatrix} + k\begin{bmatrix} d_1 & d_2 \end{bmatrix} \quad \Rightarrow \quad \begin{cases} x = p_1 + kd_1 \\ y = p_2 + kd_2 \end{cases} \quad \text{où} \quad k \in \mathbb{R}$$

Il est à noter qu'encore une fois p_1 et p_2 représentent les coordonnées d'un point de la droite (ou, ce qui est équivalent, les composantes du rayon vecteur de ce point), et que d_1 et d_2 représentent les composantes d'un vecteur directeur de la droite.

Exemple

Pour trouver les équations paramétriques de la droite $y = 2x - 1$, il faut déterminer un vecteur directeur et un point de la droite. On obtient le vecteur directeur à l'aide de deux points de la droite. Si $x = 0$ alors $y = -1$, et si $x = 1$ alors $y = 1$. Par conséquent, les points $A(0, -1)$ et $B(1, 1)$ appartiennent à la droite, et le vecteur $\vec{AB} = \begin{bmatrix} 1 & 2 \end{bmatrix}$ est un vecteur directeur de la droite. Si on utilise le point A, les équations paramétriques de la droite sont : $x = k$ et $y = -1 + 2k$ où $k \in \mathbb{R}$. Si on utilise le point B, on a plutôt $x = 1 + t$ et $y = 1 + 2t$ où $t \in \mathbb{R}$. Même si ces paires d'équations sont apparemment différentes, elles représentent toutes les deux la même droite. En effet, il suffit de remplacer k par $1 + t$ pour se convaincre de leur équivalence.

EXERCICE 6.6

1. Montrez que les paires d'équations paramétriques $x = 1 + t$ et $y = 3 - 2t$ où $t \in \mathbb{R}$ et $x = 3 - 2k$ et $y = -1 + 4k$ où $k \in \mathbb{R}$ décrivent une même droite.

2. Quelle est la pente de la droite dont les équations paramétriques sont $x = -2 - 3k$ et $y = 2 + 5k$ où $k \in \mathbb{R}$?

3. Quelle particularité la droite dont les équations paramétriques sont $x = 2$ et $y = k$ où $k \in \mathbb{R}$ présente-t-elle ?

4. Quelles sont les équations paramétriques de la droite horizontale qui passe par le point $(1, 3)$?

6.2.7 ÉQUATION SYMÉTRIQUE

Si on isole le paramètre dans les équations paramétriques d'une droite, on obtient l'équation symétrique de cette droite :

$$x = p_1 + kd_1 \quad \Rightarrow \quad \begin{cases} k = \dfrac{x - p_1}{d_1} \\ k = \dfrac{y - p_2}{d_2} \end{cases} \quad \Rightarrow \quad \dfrac{x - p_1}{d_1} = \dfrac{y - p_2}{d_2}$$

ÉQUATION SYMÉTRIQUE D'UNE DROITE DU PLAN

L'équation symétrique de la droite Δ qui passe par le point $P(p_1,\ p_2)$ et dont $\vec{d} = \begin{bmatrix} d_1 & d_2 \end{bmatrix}$ est un vecteur directeur tel que $d_1 \neq 0$ et $d_2 \neq 0$ est

$$\Delta : \dfrac{x - p_1}{d_1} = \dfrac{y - p_2}{d_2}$$

L'**équation symétrique** de la droite qui a comme vecteur directeur $\vec{d} = \begin{bmatrix} d_1 & d_2 \end{bmatrix}$ et qui passe par le point $P(p_1,\ p_2)$ est donc

$$\dfrac{x - p_1}{d_1} = \dfrac{y - p_2}{d_2}$$

Il est à noter que, dans cette équation également, p_1 et p_2 représentent les coordonnées d'un point de la droite, et d_1 et d_2, les composantes d'un vecteur directeur de la droite. Évidemment, cette équation d'une droite n'a de sens que si $d_1 \neq 0$ et $d_2 \neq 0$.

Exemple

Pour trouver l'équation symétrique d'une droite, il faut déterminer un vecteur directeur et un point de celle-ci. Par exemple, si on souhaite écrire l'équation symétrique de la droite passant par le point (1, 3) et dont l'angle d'inclinaison est de 30°, on peut choisir comme vecteur directeur n'importe quel vecteur dont la direction est de 30°. On sait qu'un vecteur de direction θ s'écrit sous la forme $\vec{d} = \|\vec{d}\| \begin{bmatrix} \cos\theta & \sin\theta \end{bmatrix}$. Par conséquent, on peut choisir le vecteur $\begin{bmatrix} \cos 30° & \sin 30° \end{bmatrix} = \begin{bmatrix} \sqrt{3}/2 & 1/2 \end{bmatrix}$ comme vecteur directeur de la droite. L'équation symétrique de la droite qui passe par le point (1, 3) et qui a un angle d'inclinaison de 30° est donc

$$\dfrac{x - 1}{\sqrt{3}/2} = \dfrac{y - 3}{1/2}$$

EXERCICE 6.7

Soit la droite d'équation $y = \frac{2}{3}x - 1$.

a) Quelle est l'équation symétrique de cette droite ? (Indice : Réécrivez l'équation donnée sous la forme $\dfrac{x - p_1}{d_1} = \dfrac{y - p_2}{d_2}$.)

b) À l'aide de l'équation symétrique de la droite, montrez que le vecteur $\vec{d} = \begin{bmatrix} 3 & 2 \end{bmatrix}$ est un vecteur directeur de celle-ci.

6.2.8 ÉQUATION CARTÉSIENNE

On peut déterminer l'équation d'une droite en employant un vecteur perpendiculaire à celle-ci plutôt qu'un vecteur directeur. La figure qui suit indique clairement que tout vecteur $\vec{n} = \begin{bmatrix} a & b \end{bmatrix}$ définit une famille de droites parallèles qui sont toutes perpendiculaires à $\vec{n}$. Pour distinguer la droite Δ, par exemple, de toutes les autres droites perpendiculaires au vecteur $\vec{n} = \begin{bmatrix} a & b \end{bmatrix}$, il suffit d'en déterminer un point $P(p_1, p_2)$.

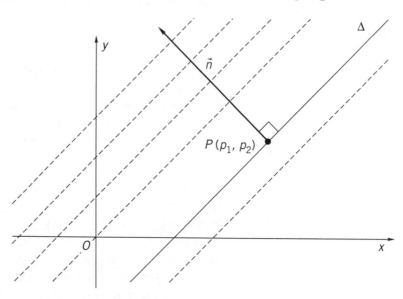

VECTEUR NORMAL À UNE DROITE

Un vecteur normal à une droite est un vecteur $\vec{n}$ perpendiculaire à cette droite.

On dit de tout vecteur perpendiculaire à une droite que c'est un **vecteur normal**[5] à cette droite, d'où le choix de la notation $\vec{n}$. En particulier, on désigne un vecteur normal unitaire par $\vec{n_u}$.

Si $X(x, y)$ est un point quelconque d'une droite Δ, alors le vecteur $\overrightarrow{PX}$ est porté par cette droite et il est perpendiculaire au vecteur $\vec{n} = \begin{bmatrix} a & b \end{bmatrix}$. Or, le produit scalaire de deux vecteurs perpendiculaires vaut zéro. Par conséquent,

$$\vec{n} \cdot \overrightarrow{PX} = 0$$
$$\vec{n} \cdot (\overrightarrow{PO} + \overrightarrow{OX}) = 0$$
$$\vec{n} \cdot (-\overrightarrow{OP} + \overrightarrow{OX}) = 0$$
$$\vec{n} \cdot \overrightarrow{OX} = \vec{n} \cdot \overrightarrow{OP}$$
$$\begin{bmatrix} a & b \end{bmatrix} \cdot \begin{bmatrix} x & y \end{bmatrix} = \begin{bmatrix} a & b \end{bmatrix} \cdot \begin{bmatrix} p_1 & p_2 \end{bmatrix}$$
$$ax + by = ap_1 + bp_2$$

Comme a, b, p_1 et p_2 sont connus, on peut remplacer l'expression $ap_1 + bp_2$ par une constante c.

---

5. Le mot « normal » vient du latin *norma*, qui signifie « équerre ». Son étymologie évoque l'idée de perpendicularité, clairement représentée dans le graphique.

ÉQUATION CARTÉSIENNE D'UNE DROITE DU PLAN

L'équation cartésienne d'une droite perpendiculaire au vecteur $\vec{n} = \begin{bmatrix} a & b \end{bmatrix}$ et passant par le point $P(p_1, p_2)$ est $ax + by = c$ où $c = ap_1 + bp_2$.

Par conséquent, l'**équation cartésienne** d'une droite perpendiculaire au vecteur $\vec{n} = \begin{bmatrix} a & b \end{bmatrix}$ et passant par le point $P(p_1,\ p_2)$ est

$$ax + by = c \quad \text{où} \quad c = ap_1 + bp_2$$

Il est à noter que le vecteur $\vec{n} = \begin{bmatrix} a & b \end{bmatrix}$ est normal à la droite d'équation $ax + by = c$, c'est-à-dire que les coefficients des deux variables de l'équation cartésienne sont les composantes d'un vecteur normal à la droite.

Il existe donc un moyen simple pour vérifier si deux droites sont parallèles : il suffit de déterminer si leurs vecteurs normaux sont parallèles.

Exemple

L'équation cartésienne de la droite $y = \frac{2}{3}x - 2$ est $2x - 3y = 6$. On déduit de cette dernière équation que le vecteur $\vec{n} = \begin{bmatrix} 2 & -3 \end{bmatrix}$ est normal à la droite. Il est à noter que l'équation cartésienne d'une droite n'est pas unique. Par exemple, les équations $-4x + 6y = -12$, $\frac{2}{3}x - y = 2$ décrivent elles aussi la même droite.

La droite $6x - 9y = 7$ est parallèle à la droite $2x - 3y = 6$. En effet, le vecteur $\vec{n_1} = \begin{bmatrix} 6 & -9 \end{bmatrix}$ est normal à la première droite, et $\vec{n_2} = \begin{bmatrix} 2 & -3 \end{bmatrix}$ est normal à la deuxième droite. Ces deux vecteurs étant parallèles, puisque $\vec{n_1} = 3\,\vec{n_2}$, les deux droites sont parallèles.

EXERCICE 6.8

Montrez que $\vec{d} = \begin{bmatrix} b & -a \end{bmatrix}$ est un vecteur directeur de la droite d'équation $ax + by = c$. (Indice : Montrez que le vecteur $\vec{d} = \begin{bmatrix} b & -a \end{bmatrix}$ est perpendiculaire à un vecteur normal à la droite.)

6.2.9 ÉQUATION NORMALE

Pour déterminer l'équation cartésienne d'une droite, on emploie un vecteur normal à cette droite, de module quelconque. Si on choisit un vecteur unitaire, on obtient alors l'équation normale de la droite. Si $\vec{n} = \begin{bmatrix} a & b \end{bmatrix}$ est un vecteur perpendiculaire à la droite dont on veut établir l'équation, alors le vecteur unitaire de même direction (même angle φ par rapport à la partie positive de l'axe des abscisses) que $\vec{n}$ est

$$\vec{n_u} = \frac{1}{\|\vec{n}\|}\vec{n} = \frac{1}{\sqrt{a^2 + b^2}}\begin{bmatrix} a & b \end{bmatrix} = \begin{bmatrix} \dfrac{a}{\sqrt{a^2 + b^2}} & \dfrac{b}{\sqrt{a^2 + b^2}} \end{bmatrix}$$

ou encore

$$\vec{n_u} = \begin{bmatrix} \cos\varphi & \sin\varphi \end{bmatrix}$$

L'équation normale d'une droite
perpendiculaire au vecteur unitaire

$\vec{n_u} = \left[\dfrac{a}{\sqrt{a^2 + b^2}} \quad \dfrac{b}{\sqrt{a^2 + b^2}} \right]$ et

passant par le point $P(p_1, p_2)$ est

$\dfrac{a}{\sqrt{a^2 + b^2}} x + \dfrac{b}{\sqrt{a^2 + b^2}} y = h$

ou encore

$(\cos\varphi)x + (\sin\varphi)y = h$

où φ représente la direction du
vecteur $\vec{n_u}$ et

$h = \dfrac{a}{\sqrt{a^2 + b^2}} p_1 + \dfrac{b}{\sqrt{a^2 + b^2}} p_2$

On obtient l'équation normale de la droite en écrivant son équation carté-sienne à l'aide de ce vecteur unitaire. Par conséquent, l'**équation normale** d'une

droite perpendiculaire au vecteur unitaire $\vec{n_u} = \left[\dfrac{a}{\sqrt{a^2 + b^2}} \quad \dfrac{b}{\sqrt{a^2 + b^2}} \right]$ (de

direction φ) et passant par le point $P(p_1, p_2)$ est

$$\frac{a}{\sqrt{a^2 + b^2}} x + \frac{b}{\sqrt{a^2 + b^2}} y = h$$

ou encore

$$(\cos\varphi)x + (\sin\varphi)y = h$$

La valeur du paramètre h est donnée par

$$h = \frac{a}{\sqrt{a^2 + b^2}} p_1 + \frac{b}{\sqrt{a^2 + b^2}} p_2 = (\cos\varphi)p_1 + (\sin\varphi)p_2$$

Comme il n'existe que deux vecteurs unitaires (de directions contraires) perpendiculaires à une droite donnée, il n'y a que deux expressions possibles pour l'équation normale d'une droite. De plus, nous verrons sous peu comment interpréter la constante h. Souvenez-vous donc de l'expression de cette constante.

Exemple

On veut établir l'équation normale d'une droite dont l'angle d'incli-naison est de 120° et qui passe par le point $P(-1, 1)$. Tout vecteur normal à cette droite a une direction de 30° (soit 120° − 90°) ou de 210° (soit 120° + 90°). Par conséquent, le vecteur

$$\vec{n_u} = \left[\cos 30° \quad \sin 30°\right] = \left[\sqrt{3}/2 \quad 1/2\right]$$

est un vecteur unitaire perpendiculaire à la droite. L'équation normale de la droite perpendiculaire au vecteur $\vec{n_u} = \left[\sqrt{3}/2 \quad 1/2\right]$ et pas-sant par le point $P(-1, 1)$ est

$$\frac{\sqrt{3}}{2} x + \frac{1}{2} y = \frac{\sqrt{3}}{2}(-1) + \frac{1}{2}(1)$$

c'est-à-dire

$$\frac{\sqrt{3}}{2} x + \frac{1}{2} y = \frac{1 - \sqrt{3}}{2}$$

On sait qu'il existe deux expressions de l'équation normale d'une droite. La seconde est

$$-\frac{\sqrt{3}}{2} x - \frac{1}{2} y = \frac{\sqrt{3} - 1}{2}$$

EXERCICE 6.9

Soit les points $A(-1, -1)$ et $B(1, 3)$.

a) Quelles sont les composantes du vecteur $\overrightarrow{AB}$?

b) Trouvez un vecteur unitaire perpendiculaire au vecteur $\overrightarrow{AB}$. (Indice : Utilisez le résultat de l'exercice 6.8 pour trouver un vecteur perpendiculaire à $\overrightarrow{AB}$.)

c) Déterminez l'équation normale de la droite qui passe par les points A et B.

6.3 DISTANCES

Il arrive souvent qu'on veuille calculer la distance entre des lieux géométriques du plan : distance d'une droite à l'origine, distance d'un point à une droite, distance entre deux droites parallèles, etc.

6.3.1 DISTANCE D'UNE DROITE À L'ORIGINE

On calcule facilement la distance d'une droite à l'origine, soit la distance au point (0, 0), à l'aide de l'équation normale de la droite.

Soit la droite Δ dont l'équation normale est $\dfrac{a}{\sqrt{a^2 + b^2}}x + \dfrac{b}{\sqrt{a^2 + b^2}}y = h$.

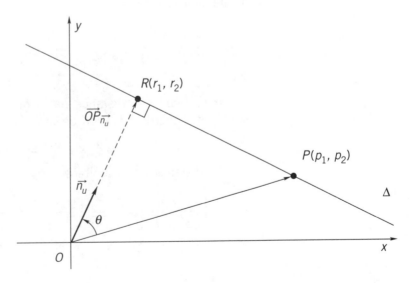

Le point R de la droite Δ le plus proche de l'origine est le point tel que le vecteur $\overrightarrow{OR}$ est perpendiculaire à la droite, donc parallèle au vecteur unitaire

$\vec{n_u} = \left[a/\sqrt{a^2 + b^2} \quad b/\sqrt{a^2 + b^2} \right]$. Si $P(p_1, p_2)$ est un point connu de la droite, alors la distance de la droite à l'origine est égale à la longueur du vecteur projection de $\overrightarrow{OP}$ sur $\vec{n_u}$, c'est-à-dire à $\left\| \overrightarrow{OP}_{\vec{n_u}} \right\|$. En vertu de la définition du vecteur projection, on a

$$\left\| \overrightarrow{OP}_{\vec{n_u}} \right\| = \left\| \frac{\overrightarrow{OP} \cdot \vec{n_u}}{\vec{n_u} \cdot \vec{n_u}} \vec{n_u} \right\| = \frac{\left| \overrightarrow{OP} \cdot \vec{n_u} \right|}{\|\vec{n_u}\|^2} \|\vec{n_u}\| = \frac{\left| \overrightarrow{OP} \cdot \vec{n_u} \right|}{1^2} \times 1 = \left| \overrightarrow{OP} \cdot \vec{n_u} \right|$$

Par ailleurs,

$$\overrightarrow{OP} \cdot \vec{n_u} = \begin{bmatrix} p_1 & p_2 \end{bmatrix} \cdot \left[\frac{a}{\sqrt{a^2 + b^2}} \quad \frac{b}{\sqrt{a^2 + b^2}} \right]$$

$$= \frac{a}{\sqrt{a^2 + b^2}} p_1 + \frac{b}{\sqrt{a^2 + b^2}} p_2$$

On note que cette dernière expression est précisément celle de la constante h de l'équation normale d'une droite. Par conséquent,

$$\left\| \overrightarrow{OP}_{\vec{n_u}} \right\| = \left| \overrightarrow{OP} \cdot \vec{n_u} \right| = |h|$$

La distance d'une droite à l'origine est donc égale à la valeur absolue de la constante h de l'équation normale de cette droite, soit

$$\frac{a}{\sqrt{a^2 + b^2}} x + \frac{b}{\sqrt{a^2 + b^2}} y = h$$

Si on utilise plutôt l'équation cartésienne de la droite, $ax + by = c$, alors la distance de la droite à l'origine est égale à $\left| \dfrac{c}{\sqrt{a^2 + b^2}} \right|$, comme on peut facilement le vérifier.

Exemple

Pour trouver la distance de la droite $y = \frac{3}{2}x + 5$ à l'origine, on écrit d'abord l'équation de la droite sous sa forme cartésienne :

$$y = \tfrac{3}{2}x + 5 \quad \Rightarrow \quad 3x - 2y = -10$$

La distance de la droite à l'origine est

$$\left| \frac{c}{\sqrt{a^2 + b^2}} \right| = \left| \frac{-10}{\sqrt{3^2 + (-2)^2}} \right| = \frac{10}{\sqrt{13}} = \frac{10\sqrt{13}}{13} \approx 2{,}8 \text{ unités}$$

L'équation normale d'une droite et l'expression de la distance de la droite à l'origine permettent de trouver le point R (voir le graphique précédent) d'une droite le plus proche de l'origine. D'une part, le point $R(r_1, r_2)$ appartenant à la droite et ses coordonnées doivent vérifier l'équation

$$\frac{a}{\sqrt{a^2 + b^2}}r_1 + \frac{b}{\sqrt{a^2 + b^2}}r_2 = h$$

D'autre part, la distance de R à l'origine est donnée par $\sqrt{r_1^2 + r_2^2} = |h|$, d'où

$$r_1^2 + r_2^2 = h^2$$

En résolvant les deux équations pour r_1 et r_2, on obtient les coordonnées du point R.

Il existe bien d'autres façons de déterminer le point R. Nous vous demandons d'en donner une autre dans l'exercice récapitulatif n° 15.

EXERCICE 6.10

Quelles sont les coordonnées du point de la droite $x + y = 1$ le plus proche de l'origine ?

6.3.2 DISTANCE D'UN POINT À UNE DROITE

La distance d'un point $Q(q_1, q_2)$ à une droite $\Delta: ax + by = c$ est égale à

$$\frac{|\overrightarrow{PQ} \cdot \vec{n}|}{\|\vec{n}\|} = \left|\frac{aq_1 + bq_2 - c}{\sqrt{a^2 + b^2}}\right|$$

où $P(p_1, p_2)$ est un point de la droite Δ et $\vec{n} = \begin{bmatrix} a & b \end{bmatrix}$ est un vecteur normal à la droite.

On démontre cette formule en appliquant un raisonnement similaire à celui qui a servi à trouver la distance d'une droite à l'origine (voir l'exercice 6.11).

Exemple

La distance entre le point $Q(5, 3)$ et la droite $4x + 2y = -3$ est égale à

$$\left|\frac{aq_1 + bq_2 - c}{\sqrt{a^2 + b^2}}\right| = \left|\frac{4(5) + 2(3) - (-3)}{\sqrt{4^2 + 2^2}}\right| = \frac{29}{\sqrt{20}} \approx 6,5 \text{ unités}$$

1. Montrez que la distance du point $Q(q_1, q_2)$ à la droite $\Delta : ax + by = c$ est égale à

$$\frac{\left|\overrightarrow{PQ} \cdot \vec{n}\right|}{\|\vec{n}\|} = \left|\frac{aq_1 + bq_2 - c}{\sqrt{a^2 + b^2}}\right|$$

où $P(p_1, p_2)$ est un point de la droite. Reportez-vous au graphique suivant et rappelez-vous que $ap_1 + bp_2 = c$ puisque P appartient à la droite Δ.

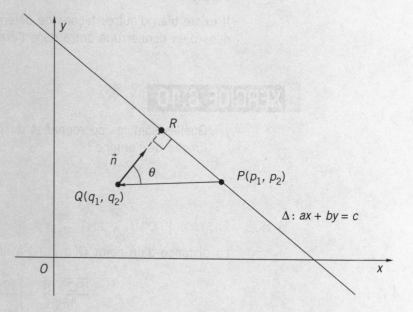

2. Quelle est la distance du point $Q(5, 3)$ à la droite dont l'angle d'inclinaison est de 120° et dont l'ordonnée à l'origine est 8 ?

6.3.3 DISTANCE ENTRE DEUX DROITES PARALLÈLES

Deux droites sont parallèles si et seulement si leurs vecteurs normaux sont parallèles. Ainsi, les droites $\Delta_1 : a_1x + b_1y = f_1$ et $\Delta_2 : a_2x + b_2y = f_2$ sont parallèles s'il existe un réel $k \neq 0$ tel que

$$\overrightarrow{n_1} = k\overrightarrow{n_2} \quad \Rightarrow \quad \begin{bmatrix} a_1 & b_1 \end{bmatrix} = k\begin{bmatrix} a_2 & b_2 \end{bmatrix} = \begin{bmatrix} ka_2 & kb_2 \end{bmatrix}$$

De plus, les droites Δ_1 et Δ_2 sont confondues si $f_1 = kf_2$. Il est possible de réécrire les équations de deux droites parallèles de façon que les coefficients des variables soient les mêmes pour les deux droites. Ainsi,

$$\Delta_1 : ax + by = c_1 \quad \text{et} \quad \Delta_2 : ax + by = c_2$$

La distance entre ces deux droites est égale à la distance d'un point $Q(q_1, q_2)$ de la droite Δ_2 à la droite Δ_1, soit $\left| \dfrac{aq_1 + bq_2 - c_1}{\sqrt{a^2 + b^2}} \right|$. Cette expression est bien sûr indépendante du choix du point Q de la droite Δ_2.

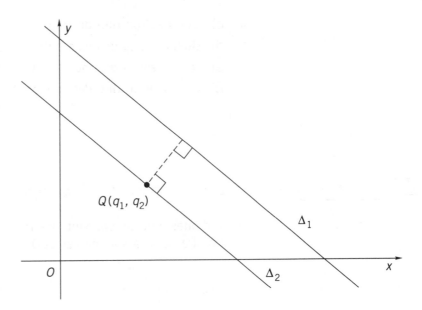

Exemple

Soit les droites $\Delta_1 : 2x - 3y = -1$ et $\Delta_2 : -4x + 6y = -8$. Ces droites sont parallèles puisque leurs vecteurs normaux le sont. En effet,

$$\vec{n_2} = \begin{bmatrix} -4 & 6 \end{bmatrix} = -2 \begin{bmatrix} 2 & -3 \end{bmatrix} = -2\vec{n_1}$$

La distance entre les deux droites est égale à la distance d'un point $Q(q_1, q_2)$ de la droite Δ_2 à la droite Δ_1. Le point $Q(2, 0)$, par exemple, appartient à la droite Δ_2. La distance entre les deux droites vaut donc

$$\left| \frac{aq_1 + bq_2 - c_1}{\sqrt{a^2 + b^2}} \right| = \left| \frac{2(2) + (-3)(0) - (-1)}{\sqrt{2^2 + (-3)^2}} \right| = \frac{5}{\sqrt{13}} \approx 1,4 \text{ unité}$$

Soit les points $A(2, 4)$, $B(4, 7)$, $C(1, 3)$ et $D(-1, 0)$.

a) Quelle est l'équation cartésienne de la droite Δ_1 qui passe par les points A et B?

b) Quelle est l'équation normale de la droite Δ_2 qui passe par les points C et D?

c) Que peut-on dire de la position relative des droites Δ_1 et Δ_2?

d) Quelle est la distance entre les droites Δ_1 et Δ_2?

e) Quelle est la distance entre les droites Δ_2 et Δ_3: $6x - 4y = -6$?

f) Que peut-on dire des droites Δ_2 et Δ_3?

6.4 ANGLE ENTRE DEUX DROITES CONCOURANTES

Deux droites qui se coupent déterminent deux angles supplémentaires, c'est-à-dire dont la somme est 180° ou π.

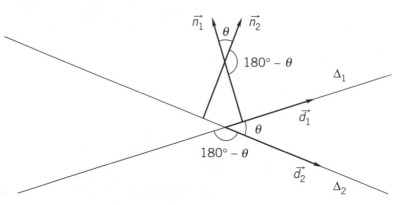

Le graphique indique clairement que les angles déterminés par Δ_1 et Δ_2 sont égaux aux angles déterminés par les vecteurs normaux ou les vecteurs directeurs des deux droites. Or, on sait que l'angle α entre deux vecteurs $\vec{v_1}$ et $\vec{v_2}$ est donné par

$$\alpha = \text{arc cos}\left(\frac{\vec{v_1} \cdot \vec{v_2}}{\|\vec{v_1}\| \, \|\vec{v_2}\|}\right)$$

Par conséquent, selon qu'on prend des vecteurs normaux ou des vecteurs directeurs, les angles déterminés par Δ_1 et Δ_2 sont donnés par

$$\theta = \text{arc cos}\left(\frac{\vec{d_1} \cdot \vec{d_2}}{\|\vec{d_1}\| \, \|\vec{d_2}\|}\right) \quad \text{et} \quad 180° - \theta$$

$$\text{ou} \quad \theta = \text{arc cos}\left(\frac{\vec{n_1} \cdot \vec{n_2}}{\|\vec{n_1}\| \, \|\vec{n_2}\|}\right) \quad \text{et} \quad 180° - \theta$$

Toutefois, on définit l'angle entre deux droites comme le plus petit angle qu'elles déterminent ; il s'agit d'un angle aigu ou droit. Comme

$$\cos(180° - \theta) = -\cos\theta$$

l'angle entre deux droites est donc défini par

$$\theta = \text{arc cos}\left|\frac{\vec{d_1} \cdot \vec{d_2}}{\|\vec{d_1}\| \, \|\vec{d_2}\|}\right| \quad \text{ou} \quad \theta = \text{arc cos}\left|\frac{\vec{n_1} \cdot \vec{n_2}}{\|\vec{n_1}\| \, \|\vec{n_2}\|}\right|$$

Exemple

Pour trouver l'angle entre les droites

$$\Delta_1 : 4x - 3y = 5 \quad \text{et} \quad \Delta_2 : 3x - 2y = -3$$

on détermine d'abord des vecteurs normaux chacun à l'une des droites. Or, $\vec{n_1} = \begin{bmatrix} 4 & -3 \end{bmatrix}$ est un vecteur normal à la droite Δ_1 et $\vec{n_2} = \begin{bmatrix} 3 & -2 \end{bmatrix}$ est un vecteur normal à la droite Δ_2. Par conséquent, l'angle entre ces deux droites est

$$\theta = \text{arc cos}\left|\frac{\vec{n_1} \cdot \vec{n_2}}{\|\vec{n_1}\| \, \|\vec{n_2}\|}\right| = \text{arc cos}\left|\frac{18}{5\sqrt{13}}\right| \approx 3,2°$$

EXERCICE 6.13

Soit les points $A(1, 5)$, $B(4, -1)$, $C(2, 3)$ et $D(-1, 4)$. Quel est l'angle entre la droite Δ_1 qui passe par les points A et B et la droite Δ_2 qui passe par les points C et D?

RÉSUMÉ

Une droite du plan est complètement déterminée par deux caractéristiques, qui peuvent être :

- deux points ;
- la pente et l'ordonnée à l'origine ;
- la pente et un point ;
- l'angle d'inclinaison et un point ;
- un vecteur directeur et un point ;
- un vecteur normal et un point.

Ces différentes façons de caractériser une droite permettent d'écrire l'équation d'une droite sous différentes formes, présentées dans le tableau 6.1.

TABLEAU 6.1 **Les différentes formes de l'équation d'une droite Δ du plan**

	Informations requises	Équation
PENTE ET ORDONNÉE À L'ORIGINE	Pente : m Ordonnée à l'origine : b	$y = mx + b$
PENTE ET POINT	Pente : m $A(x_1, y_1) \in \Delta$	$(y - y_1) = m(x - x_1)$
DEUX POINTS DISTINCTS	$A(x_1, y_1)$ et $B(x_2, y_2) \in \Delta$	$\dfrac{y - y_1}{x - x_1} = \dfrac{y_2 - y_1}{x_2 - x_1}$
ANGLE D'INCLINAISON ET ORDONNÉE À L'ORIGINE	Angle d'inclinaison : θ Ordonnée à l'origine : b	$y = (\operatorname{tg}\theta)x + b$
ÉQUATION VECTORIELLE	Vecteur directeur $\vec{d} = \begin{bmatrix} d_1 & d_2 \end{bmatrix}$ et un point $P(p_1, p_2) \in \Delta$	$\begin{bmatrix} x & y \end{bmatrix} = \begin{bmatrix} p_1 & p_2 \end{bmatrix} + k\begin{bmatrix} d_1 & d_2 \end{bmatrix}$ où $k \in \mathbb{R}$
ÉQUATIONS PARAMÉTRIQUES	Vecteur directeur $\vec{d} = \begin{bmatrix} d_1 & d_2 \end{bmatrix}$ et un point $P(p_1, p_2) \in \Delta$	$x = p_1 + kd_1$ $y = p_2 + kd_2$ où $k \in \mathbb{R}$
ÉQUATION SYMÉTRIQUE	Vecteur directeur $\vec{d} = \begin{bmatrix} d_1 & d_2 \end{bmatrix}$ et un point $P(p_1, p_2) \in \Delta$	$\dfrac{x - p_1}{d_1} = \dfrac{y - p_2}{d_2}$ si $d_1 \neq 0$ et $d_2 \neq 0$
ÉQUATION CARTÉSIENNE	Vecteur normal $\vec{n} = \begin{bmatrix} a & b \end{bmatrix}$ et un point $P(p_1, p_2) \in \Delta$	$ax + by = c$ où $c = ap_1 + bp_2$
ÉQUATION NORMALE	Vecteur normal unitaire $\vec{n_u} = \begin{bmatrix} \dfrac{a}{\sqrt{a^2 + b^2}} & \dfrac{b}{\sqrt{a^2 + b^2}} \end{bmatrix}$ et un point $P(p_1, p_2) \in \Delta$	$\dfrac{a}{\sqrt{a^2 + b^2}}x + \dfrac{b}{\sqrt{a^2 + b^2}}y = \dfrac{c}{\sqrt{a^2 + b^2}}$ où $c = ap_1 + bp_2$

L'équation cartésienne d'une droite fournit plusieurs informations utiles. Ainsi de l'équation $\Delta : ax + by = c$, on tire les renseignements suivants :

- $\vec{n} = \begin{bmatrix} a & b \end{bmatrix}$ est un vecteur normal à Δ.
- $\vec{d} = \begin{bmatrix} -b & a \end{bmatrix}$ est un vecteur directeur de Δ.
- La distance de la droite Δ à l'origine est égale à $\left| \dfrac{c}{\sqrt{a^2 + b^2}} \right|$ ou $\dfrac{c}{\|\vec{n}\|}$.
- La pente de la droite Δ est $m = -\dfrac{a}{b}$.

- L'angle d'inclinaison de la droite Δ est donné par $\theta = \text{arc tg}\left(-\dfrac{a}{b}\right)$.

- La droite Δ est parallèle à n'importe quelle droite dont l'équation est $\Delta_0 : kax + kby = c_0$ où k est un nombre réel non nul.

- La distance entre les droites Δ et Δ_0 est égale à $\left|\dfrac{aq_1 + bq_2 - c}{\sqrt{a^2 + b^2}}\right|$ où $Q(q_1, q_2)$ est un point de Δ_0. Cette distance est identique à la distance entre la droite Δ et le point $Q(q_1, q_2)$.

L'angle entre deux droites concourantes Δ_1 et Δ_2 est, par définition, le plus petit angle θ déterminé par les deux droites, et il est donné par l'expression

$$\theta = \text{arc cos}\left|\frac{\vec{d_1} \cdot \vec{d_2}}{\|\vec{d_1}\| \, \|\vec{d_2}\|}\right| \quad \text{ou} \quad \theta = \text{arc cos}\left|\frac{\vec{n_1} \cdot \vec{n_2}}{\|\vec{n_1}\| \, \|\vec{n_2}\|}\right|$$

où $\vec{d_1}$ et $\vec{n_1}$ sont respectivement un vecteur directeur et un vecteur normal de Δ_1, alors que $\vec{d_2}$ et $\vec{n_2}$ sont respectivement un vecteur directeur et un vecteur normal de Δ_2.

Il est à noter que la pente de la droite qui passe par deux points $A(x_1, y_1)$ et $B(x_2, y_2)$, et dont l'angle d'inclinaison est θ (où $0 \leq \theta < 180°$), est $m = \dfrac{y_2 - y_1}{x_2 - x_1} = \text{tg}\theta$. L'angle θ est la plus petite valeur positive donnée par l'expression $\theta = \text{arc tg}(d_2/d_1)$ où $\vec{d} = \begin{bmatrix} d_1 & d_2 \end{bmatrix}$ est un vecteur directeur de la droite. L'ordonnée à l'origine de cette droite est $b = y_1 - mx_1$.

Si la direction d'un vecteur unitaire normal à une droite Δ passant par le point $P(p_1, p_2)$ est φ, l'équation normale de Δ s'écrit
$$(\cos\varphi)x + (\sin\varphi)y = h$$
où $h = (\cos\varphi)p_1 + (\sin\varphi)p_2$.

MOTS CLÉS

1. (I) Quelle est l'équation (qui donne la pente et l'ordonnée à l'origine) de la droite passant par les points donnés ?

   a) $A(2, 5)$ et $B(-1, -1)$.

   b) $A(3, 0)$ et $B(5, -2)$.

   c) $A(4, -3)$ et $B(-4, 1)$.

   d) $A(5, 3)$ et $B(5, 1)$.

   e) $A(2, 1)$ et $B(2, 4)$.

   f) $A(2, 1)$ et $B(5, 1)$.

2. (I) Un vendeur d'automobiles reçoit un salaire de base de 300 $ par semaine plus une commission de 100 $ par voiture vendue. Quelle est l'équation de la rémunération hebdomadaire totale, R (salaire de base et commission), de ce vendeur en fonction du nombre x de voitures vendues par semaine ?

3. (I) Une troupe de théâtre a obtenu une subvention de 50 000 $ pour monter une pièce. Chaque représentation rapporte 10 000 $, mais les frais fixes (décors, costumes, répétitions, etc.) s'élèvent à 150 000 $ et les frais variables (salaires des comédiens, des placiers, des éclairagistes, etc.), à 8 000 $ par représentation.

   a) Quel revenu total (R) rapportent x représentations de la pièce ?

   b) Quelles dépenses (D) la troupe de théâtre doit-elle payer pour x représentations de la pièce ?

   c) Représentez les fonctions $D(x)$ et $R(x)$ dans un même plan cartésien.

   d) Quel profit total (P) la troupe de théâtre tire-t-elle de x représentations de la pièce ?

   e) Interprétez le point d'intersection des droites représentant les fonctions $C(x)$ et $R(x)$.

   f) La troupe de théâtre rentre-t-elle dans ses frais si elle donne 25 représentations ? Justifiez votre réponse.

   g) Quel est le seuil de rentabilité de la pièce, c'est-à-dire le nombre de représentations pour lequel le profit est nul ?

4. (I) Quel est l'angle d'inclinaison de chacune des droites définies au n° 1 ?

5. (I) Les ingénieurs expriment la déclivité d'une route au moyen d'un pourcentage. Une déclivité de 1 % signifie que la route monte de 1 m pour chaque 100 m de distance horizontale. On note y la distance verticale parcourue sur une route en fonction de la distance horizontale x parcourue.

   a) Quelle est la déclivité d'une route si l'équation de la distance verticale est $y = 0,15x$?

   b) Quelle est l'équation de la distance verticale si la route présente une déclivité de 10 % ?

   c) Quel est l'angle d'inclinaison d'une route qui présente une déclivité de 10 % ?

6. (I) Évaluez la pente d'une droite qui présente les caractéristiques suivantes.

   a) La droite a un angle d'inclinaison de 30°.

   b) Le vecteur $\vec{d} = \begin{bmatrix} -1 & -2 \end{bmatrix}$ est parallèle à la droite.

   c) L'ordonnée à l'origine de la droite est 4 et la droite passe par le point $(1, 1)$.

   d) Si on se déplace d'un point à un autre de la droite, la valeur de l'ordonnée augmente de 5 unités, alors que la valeur de l'abscisse augmente de 3 unités.

   e)

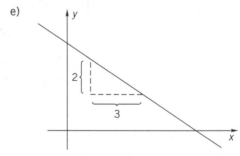

7. (II) Démontrez que l'angle φ entre deux droites concourantes de pente m_1 et m_2, respectivement, vérifie l'équation $\operatorname{tg}\varphi = \dfrac{m_2 - m_1}{1 + m_1 m_2}$. Utilisez ensuite ce résultat pour montrer que deux droites de pentes respectives m_1 et m_2 sont perpendiculaires si $m_1 = -\dfrac{1}{m_2}$. Appliquez l'identité $\operatorname{tg}(A + B) = \dfrac{\operatorname{tg}A + \operatorname{tg}B}{1 - \operatorname{tg}A \operatorname{tg}B}$ et reportez-vous au graphique suivant.

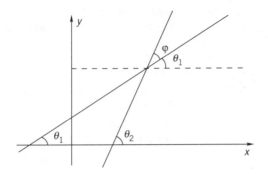

8. (I) Déterminez l'équation de la droite (qui donne la pente et un point) qui satisfait aux conditions suivantes.

a) Droite de pente 3 qui passe par le point $A(-1, 3)$.

b) Droite qui passe par le point $(2, 4)$ et dont l'angle d'inclinaison est de $90°$.

c) Droite qui passe par le point $(-1, -2)$ et dont l'angle d'inclinaison est de $2\pi/3$.

d) Droite parallèle au vecteur $\vec{d} = \begin{bmatrix} 1 & 4 \end{bmatrix}$, qui passe par le point $(1, 1)$.

9. (I) a) À l'aide des propriétés des déterminants, montrez que

$$\begin{vmatrix} 1 & x_1 & y_1 \\ 1 & x_2 & y_2 \\ 1 & x & y \end{vmatrix} = (x_2 - x_1)(y - y_1) \\ - (x - x_1)(y_2 - y_1)$$

b) Montrez que l'équation de la droite (qui donne deux points) qui passe par deux points (x_1, y_1) et (x_2, y_2) est donnée par

$$\begin{vmatrix} 1 & x_1 & y_1 \\ 1 & x_2 & y_2 \\ 1 & x & y \end{vmatrix} = 0$$

10. (I) Déterminez un vecteur directeur, l'équation vectorielle, les équations paramétriques et l'équation symétrique de chacune des droites définies au n° 1.

11. (I) Quelle est l'équation vectorielle de chacune des droites suivantes?

a) La droite dont l'ordonnée à l'origine est 4 et dont $\vec{d} = \begin{bmatrix} 3 & -5 \end{bmatrix}$ est un vecteur directeur.

b) La droite dont l'angle d'inclinaison est de $135°$ et qui passe par le point $(6, 1)$.

c) La droite qui passe par le point $(4, 0)$ et qui détermine avec les axes de coordonnées un triangle dont l'aire est de 20 unités².

d) La droite dont l'abscisse à l'origine est le double de l'ordonnée à l'origine et qui détermine avec les axes de coordonnées un triangle dont l'aire est de 25 unités².

12. (I) Déterminez l'équation vectorielle, les équations paramétriques, l'équation symétrique et l'équation cartésienne de la droite qui présente les caractéristiques données.

a) La droite qui passe par le point $(1, 2)$ et dont $\vec{d} = \begin{bmatrix} 4 & 2 \end{bmatrix}$ est un vecteur directeur.

b) La droite qui passe par le point $(-1, 1)$ et dont $\vec{d} = \begin{bmatrix} 3 & 0 \end{bmatrix}$ est un vecteur directeur.

c) La droite perpendiculaire à $\vec{n} = \begin{bmatrix} -2 & 3 \end{bmatrix}$ et passant par le point $(2, 4)$.

d) La droite perpendiculaire à $\vec{n} = \begin{bmatrix} -1 & 1 \end{bmatrix}$ et passant par le point $(2, 3)$.

e) La droite de pente 3 et d'ordonnée à l'origine 4.

13. (I) Quelles sont les équations vectorielle, paramétriques, symétrique et cartésienne de la droite qui passe par un point $P(p_1, p_2)$ et dont $\vec{d} = \begin{bmatrix} d_1 & d_2 \end{bmatrix}$ est un vecteur directeur?

14. (I) Soit la droite d'équation

$$\begin{bmatrix} x & y \end{bmatrix} = \begin{bmatrix} 2 & 3 \end{bmatrix} + k\begin{bmatrix} 1 & 4 \end{bmatrix}$$

où $k \in \mathbb{R}$.

a) Quel point de la droite obtient-on en posant $k = 2$? $k = 6$?

b) Que représente le lieu géométrique formé par les points obtenus en posant $k \in \begin{bmatrix} 2, 6 \end{bmatrix}$?

15. (II) Soit la droite d'équation $\Delta_1 : 3x + 2y = 5$ et le point $P(3, 6)$, extérieur à cette droite.

a) Quelle est la distance du point P à la droite Δ_1?

b) Quelle est l'équation cartésienne de la droite Δ_2 qui passe par le point P et qui est perpendiculaire à Δ_1?

c) Quelles sont les coordonnées du point d'intersection A des droites Δ_1 et Δ_2?

d) Que peut-on dire du point A par rapport au point P?

e) En prenant comme modèle la marche à suivre suggérée par les questions a à d, établissez une méthode pour trouver le point d'une droite le plus proche d'un point donné, extérieur à la droite.

16. (I) Pour quelle valeur du scalaire p les droites Δ_1 et Δ_2 sont-elles parallèles?

    a) $\Delta_1 : 2x + 3y = 8$ et $\Delta_2 : x + py = 5$.

    b) $\Delta_1 : y = 3x + 12$ et $\Delta_2 : px + 3y = 5$.

    c) La droite Δ_1 a pour vecteur normal $\vec{n_1} = \begin{bmatrix} 1 & p \end{bmatrix}$, et la droite Δ_2 passe par les points $A(1, -3)$ et $B(-1, 4)$.

    d) La droite Δ_1 a pour équation symétrique $\dfrac{x-1}{3} = \dfrac{y+4}{2}$, et la droite Δ_2 a comme vecteur directeur $\vec{d_2} = \begin{bmatrix} -1 & p \end{bmatrix}$.

17. (I) Pour quelle valeur du scalaire p les droites Δ_1 et Δ_2 définies au n° 16 sont-elles perpendiculaires?

18. (I) Quelle est la distance du point $Q(2, 4)$ à chacune des droites définies au n° 12?

19. (I) Quelle est la distance du point d'intersection de $\Delta_1 : -x + 2y = 2$ et de $\Delta_2 : 2x - 3y = 4$ à la droite $\Delta_3 : 3x - 2y = -4$?

20. (II) Un point $P(x_0, y_0)$ décrit une trajectoire telle que sa distance à la droite $\Delta_1 : x + y = 4$ est constante et égale à 2 unités.

    a) Tracez le lieu géométrique que décrit le point en se déplaçant dans le plan. (Il existe deux solutions.)

    b) Quelle est l'équation de la trajectoire du point P?

21. (II) Soit les droites $\Delta_1 : 4x - 3y = 1$ et $\Delta_2 : 3x - 4y = -1$, dont le point d'intersection est noté A. On désigne par $\vec{d_1}$ et $\vec{d_2}$ un vecteur directeur de Δ_1 et de Δ_2 respectivement.

    a) Trouvez l'équation cartésienne de la droite Δ_3 qui passe par le point A et dont un vecteur directeur est $\dfrac{1}{\|\vec{d_1}\|} \vec{d_1} + \dfrac{1}{\|\vec{d_2}\|} \vec{d_2}$.

    b) Montrez que tout point de la droite Δ_3 est situé à égale distance des droites Δ_1 et Δ_2.

    c) Quelle est la valeur de l'angle entre les droites Δ_1 et Δ_2?

    d) Quelle est la valeur de l'angle entre les droites Δ_1 et Δ_3?

    e) Que représente la droite Δ_3 par rapport à l'angle entre les droites Δ_1 et Δ_2?

22. (I) Montrez que les droites $\Delta_1 : ax - by = c_1$ et $\Delta_2 : bx + ay = c_2$ sont perpendiculaires.

23. (I) Quelle est l'équation normale de chacune des droites données.

    a) La droite qui passe par les points $A(1, 4)$ et $B(2, 3)$.

    b) La droite qui passe par le point $(-1, 2)$ et dont l'angle d'inclinaison est de 60°.

    c) La droite de pente 4 qui passe par le point $(-2, 1)$.

    d) La droite dont l'équation symétrique est $\dfrac{x-1}{3} = \dfrac{y+4}{2}$.

    e) La droite qui passe par le milieu du segment de droite joignant les points $A(2, 4)$ et $B(4, -3)$, et qui est perpendiculaire à ce segment.

    f) La droite dont l'ordonnée à l'origine est -3 et qui est parallèle à la droite d'équations paramétriques

$$\Delta_1 : \begin{cases} x = 4 + 2k \\ y = -2 + 3k \end{cases} \text{ où } k \in \mathbb{R}$$

24. (I) Donnez deux vecteurs unitaires normaux à chacune des droites suivantes.

    a) $y = \tfrac{1}{2}x + 3$

    b) $x = 3 + 2k$ et $y = 5 - 4k$ où $k \in \mathbb{R}$

    c) $3x - 2y = 6$

25. (I) Soit les droites

$$\Delta_1 : \frac{a}{\sqrt{a^2 + b^2}} x + \frac{b}{\sqrt{a^2 + b^2}} y = h_1$$

et

$$\Delta_2 : \frac{a}{\sqrt{a^2 + b^2}} x + \frac{b}{\sqrt{a^2 + b^2}} y = h_2$$

    a) Quelle est la forme des équations des droites Δ_1 et Δ_2?

    b) Pourquoi les droites Δ_1 et Δ_2 sont-elles parallèles?

    c) Montrez que la distance entre les droites Δ_1 et Δ_2 est égale à $|h_1 - h_2|$.

26. (I) a) Tracez deux droites parallèles distinctes dans un même plan cartésien.

    b) Tracez deux droites confondues dans un même plan cartésien.

c) Tracez deux droites concourantes dans un même plan cartésien.

d) Comparez les trois cas représentés en *a*, *b* et *c* avec les trois possibilités quant au nombre de solutions d'un système d'équations linéaires de deux équations à deux inconnues.

27. (I) Si les droites Δ_1 et Δ_2 données sont parallèles (distinctes ou confondues), trouvez la distance entre ces droites; si Δ_1 et Δ_2 sont concourantes, trouvez leur point d'intersection.

a) $\Delta_1 : 3x + 2y = 8$ et $\Delta_2 : -x + 2y = 4$.

b) $\Delta_1 : 2x - 3y = 4$ et $\Delta_2 : -4x + 6y = 7$.

c) $\Delta_1 : \dfrac{x - 1}{3} = \dfrac{y + 4}{2}$ et $\Delta_2 : 2x - 3y = 3$.

d) $\Delta_1 : \begin{cases} x = 4 + 2k \\ y = -2 + 3k \end{cases}$ où $k \in \mathbb{R}$ et

$\Delta_2 : \begin{cases} x = -1 + 4t \\ y = 1 - 2t \end{cases}$ où $t \in \mathbb{R}$.

e) $\Delta_1 : \begin{cases} x = -3 + 2k \\ y = -6 + 3k \end{cases}$ où $k \in \mathbb{R}$ et

$\Delta_2 : \begin{cases} x = -1 + 4t \\ y = -3 + 6t \end{cases}$ où $t \in \mathbb{R}$.

f) $\Delta_1 : x - 2y = 4$ et $\Delta_2 :$ la droite dont l'angle d'inclinaison est de 135° et qui passe par le point (1, 3).

g) $\Delta_1 : \begin{cases} x = 4 - k \\ y = -3 + 2k \end{cases}$ où $k \in \mathbb{R}$ et

$\Delta_2 : y = -2x + 5$.

h) Δ_1 passe par les points $A(1, 4)$ et $B(2, 3)$, et Δ_2 passe par les points $C(2, -4)$ et $D(-1, -1)$.

i) $\Delta_1 : \begin{cases} x = 4 - k \\ y = -3 + 2k \end{cases}$ où $k \in \mathbb{R}$ et

$\Delta_2 : 2x + y = 6$.

28. (I) Trouvez l'angle entre les droites Δ_1 et Δ_2 données.

a) Une droite Δ_1 dont l'angle d'inclinaison est de 40° et une droite Δ_2 dont l'angle d'inclinaison est de $5\pi/6$.

b) $\Delta_1 : 2x - 4y = 3$ et $\Delta_2 : x + 2y = 4$.

c) $\Delta_1 : \begin{cases} x = 4 - k \\ y = -3 + 2k \end{cases}$ où $k \in \mathbb{R}$ et

$\Delta_2 : y = 3x + 5$.

d) Une droite Δ_1 dont $\vec{d_1} = \begin{bmatrix} 1 & 4 \end{bmatrix}$ est un vecteur directeur et une droite Δ_2 dont $\vec{n_2} = \begin{bmatrix} -2 & 3 \end{bmatrix}$ est un vecteur normal.

29. (I) Soit $\Delta_1 : x + 2y = 3$, $\Delta_2 : x - y = 2$ et $\Delta_3 : 3x + y = 4$. Soit A le point d'intersection des droites Δ_1 et Δ_3, B le point d'intersection des droites Δ_2 et Δ_3, et C le point d'intersection des droites Δ_1 et Δ_2.

a) Quelles sont les coordonnées des points A, B et C?

b) Tracez les droites Δ_1, Δ_2 et Δ_3 dans un même plan cartésien.

c) Quelle est la valeur des angles du triangle déterminé par les droites Δ_1, Δ_2 et Δ_3?

d) Quel est le périmètre du triangle déterminé par Δ_1, Δ_2 et Δ_3?

30. (II) Soit une droite $\Delta_1 : a_1x + b_1y = c_1$ qui passe par un point P_1 et une droite $\Delta_2 : a_2x + b_2y = c_2$ qui passe par un point P_2. À l'aide des informations données, dites si les droites Δ_1 et Δ_2 sont concourantes, parallèles confondues ou parallèles distinctes.

a) Il existe un réel k tel que $\begin{bmatrix} a_1 & b_1 \end{bmatrix} = k\begin{bmatrix} a_2 & b_2 \end{bmatrix}$ et $c_1 \neq kc_2$.

b) $\begin{bmatrix} a_1 & b_1 \end{bmatrix} \cdot \begin{bmatrix} b_2 & -a_2 \end{bmatrix} = 0$ et $P_2 \in \Delta_1$.

c) $\begin{bmatrix} a_1 & b_1 \end{bmatrix} \cdot \begin{bmatrix} a_2 & b_2 \end{bmatrix} = 0$.

31. (I) Soit les droites Δ_1, Δ_2, Δ_3 et Δ_4 dont les équations sont

$$\Delta_1 : \begin{cases} x = 4 - 2k \\ y = 2 - 3k \end{cases} \text{ où } k \in \mathbb{R}$$

$$\Delta_2 : y = -\tfrac{2}{3}x + 5$$

$$\Delta_3 : \dfrac{x - 1}{2} = \dfrac{y + 4}{3}$$

$$\Delta_4 : x + 3y = 5$$

a) Tracez les quatre droites dans un même plan cartésien.

b) Trouvez les coordonnées manquantes des points $P(x, 4)$ et $Q(-1, y)$ de la droite Δ_1.

c) Trouvez les coordonnées manquantes des points $R(x, 2)$ et $S(3, y)$ de la droite Δ_3.

d) Quelles sont les coordonnées des points d'intersection de la droite Δ_3 avec les axes de coordonnées?

e) À laquelle des quatre droites le point $T(2, 1)$ appartient-il?

f) Quel est l'angle d'inclinaison de Δ_4?

g) Quelle est l'équation cartésienne de la droite Δ_1?

h) Quels sont la pente et l'angle d'inclinaison de la droite Δ_1?

i) Les droites Δ_1 et Δ_2 sont-elles parallèles ou concourantes? Si elles sont concourantes, quel est leur point d'intersection et quelle est la valeur de l'angle entre elles? Si les droites Δ_1 et Δ_2 sont parallèles, calculez la distance qui les sépare.

j) Les droites Δ_1 et Δ_3 sont-elles parallèles ou concourantes? Si elles sont concourantes, quel est leur point d'intersection et quelle est la valeur de l'angle entre elles? Si les droites Δ_1 et Δ_3 sont parallèles, calculez la distance qui les sépare.

k) Les droites Δ_1 et Δ_4 sont-elles parallèles ou concourantes? Si elles sont concourantes, quel est leur point d'intersection et quelle est la valeur de l'angle entre elles? Si les droites Δ_1 et Δ_4 sont parallèles, calculez la distance qui les sépare.

l) Quelle est l'équation symétrique de Δ_4?

m) Quelles sont les équations paramétriques de la droite Δ_3?

n) Quelle est l'équation vectorielle de la droite Δ_5 qui passe par le point $(1, 1)$ et qui est perpendiculaire à Δ_3?

o) Quelle est la distance du point $(2, -4)$ à la droite Δ_4?

p) Quel point de la droite Δ_4 est le plus proche du point $(2, -4)$?

q) Quel point de la droite Δ_2 est le plus proche de l'origine?

r) Pour quelles valeurs de k les points de Δ_1 appartiennent-ils au segment de droite joignant les points $A(2, -1)$ et $B(14, 17)$?

s) Tracez le lieu géométrique des points de la droite Δ_1 tels que $k \leq 1$.

t) Montrez que les droites Δ_2 et Δ_3 sont perpendiculaires.

32. (I) Dites si chaque énoncé est vrai ou faux, et justifiez votre réponse.

a) La droite $\Delta_1 : \begin{cases} x = 1 + 2k \\ y = 2 - 5k \end{cases}$ où $k \in \mathbb{R}$ est perpendiculaire à la droite $\Delta_2 : y = \frac{2}{5}x + 3$.

b) La distance de la droite $\Delta : -3x + 4y = 5$ à l'origine vaut 1.

c) Une droite est complètement déterminée par son angle d'inclinaison.

d) Si le vecteur $\vec{n} = \begin{bmatrix} n_1 & n_2 \end{bmatrix}$ est normal à une droite Δ, alors l'angle d'inclinaison de cette droite est $\theta = \operatorname{arc\,tg}\left(-\dfrac{n_2}{n_1}\right)$.

e) Si les angles d'inclinaison de deux droites concourantes Δ_1 et Δ_2 sont respectivement θ et φ, alors l'angle entre ces deux droites vaut $|\theta - \varphi|$ ou $\pi - |\theta - \varphi|$. (Justifiez votre réponse à l'aide d'un graphique.)

f) Tout vecteur normal à une droite est perpendiculaire à un vecteur directeur de cette droite.

g) L'équation normale d'une droite est un cas particulier de l'équation cartésienne de cette droite.

h) Les droites $\Delta_1 : \begin{cases} x = 1 + 2k \\ y = 2 - 5k \end{cases}$ où $k \in \mathbb{R}$ et $\Delta_2 : 10x - 4y = 16$ sont confondues.

i) Deux droites sont parallèles si leurs vecteurs normaux respectifs sont perpendiculaires.

j) Si a et b sont des constantes différentes de zéro, l'équation cartésienne de la droite Δ dont l'ordonnée à l'origine est b et dont l'abscisse à l'origine est a s'écrit sous la forme $\dfrac{1}{a}x + \dfrac{1}{b}y = 1$.

Nombres complexes

À l'inverse des autres sciences, l'algèbre a une manière toute
spéciale et bien caractéristique de traiter les impossibilités ;
si tel problème d'algèbre est impossible, si telle équation
est insoluble, l'algèbre, au lieu de s'arrêter là pour passer
à une autre question, accorde droit de cité à ces solutions
impossibles et en enrichit son domaine au lieu de les exclure.
Le moyen qu'elle emploie est le symbole.

De Campou

À LA FIN DU PRÉSENT CHAPITRE, VOUS DEVRIEZ ÊTRE
EN MESURE DE RÉPONDRE AUX QUESTIONS SUIVANTES :

- Qu'est-ce qu'un nombre complexe ?

- Comment représente-t-on graphiquement un nombre
complexe ?

- Quelles sont les différentes formes d'un nombre complexe ?

- Comment est-ce qu'on effectue les opérations sur les
nombres complexes ?

- Quelles opérations s'effectuent plus facilement sous
la forme trigonométrique ?

- Quel rôle jouent le théorème de Moivre et son corollaire ?

UN PORTRAIT de Abraham de Moivre

Abraham de Moivre vit le jour le 26 mai 1667 à Vitry, en France. Il eut le malheur de naître dans une famille protestante au moment où la lutte contre le protestantisme était en recrudescence. De Moivre fut d'ailleurs emprisonné pour des motifs religieux après avoir fait des études en mathématiques et en physique à Paris. Dès sa libération, à l'âge de 21 ans, il quitta la France pour l'Angleterre et ne retourna jamais dans son pays natal, ce qui ne l'empêcha pas de rester profondément attaché à ses origines françaises. En effet, il connaissait par cœur les œuvres de Rabelais et de Molière et il aurait même déclaré que, si on lui avait donné le choix, il aurait préféré être Molière plutôt que Newton. Sa nomination à l'Académie des sciences de Paris, au crépuscule de sa vie, le rendit tellement heureux qu'il dit de cette élection qu'elle était sa «lettre de noblesse».

De Moivre mit la main, à Londres, sur une copie du célèbre Philosophiæ Naturalis Principia Mathematica d'Isaac Newton. Il en détacha toutes les pages pour pouvoir les lire une à une entre deux cours privés. De Moivre et Newton devinrent d'ailleurs d'excellents amis. Ce dernier reconnut la compétence de Moivre et n'hésita pas à lui envoyer des élèves en leur disant: «Go to M. De Moivre; he knows these things better than I do[1].»

De Moivre fut un mathématicien extrêmement talentueux. Il publia de nombreux mémoires et ouvrages, dont le plus célèbre est sans doute Doctrine of Chances, dédicacé à son grand ami Newton. Cette œuvre fit l'objet de trois éditions, la première étant datée de 1718. La deuxième édition contient une démonstration du fait que $\int_0^\infty e^{-x^2}\,dx = \sqrt{\pi}/2$, ce qui mène à la première utilisation d'une loi normale de probabilité. De Moivre publia également un traité d'actuariat, Annuity Upon Lives, dont la première édition en 1725 fut suivie de six autres, notamment en italien et en allemand.

---

1. «Allez voir M. de Moivre. Il connaît ces choses bien mieux que moi.» C. B. Boyer. *A History of Mathematics*, New York, John Wiley & Sons, 1968, p. 466.

De Moivre s'intéressa aussi à la trigonométrie et on lui doit la formule qui porte aujourd'hui son nom, soit

$$[\rho(cos\theta + i\ sin\theta)]^n = \rho^n(cosn\theta + i\ sinn\theta)$$

De Moivre fit partie, en 1712, d'une commission, plutôt partiale, formée par la Société Royale pour déterminer à qui, de Newton ou de Leibniz, revenait le titre d'inventeur du calcul différentiel et intégral.

De Moivre reçut de nombreux honneurs au cours de sa vie. Il fut nommé membre de la Société Royale en 1697, Fellow de l'Académie des sciences de Berlin en 1735, puis associé «étranger» de l'Académie des sciences de Paris en 1754.

En dépit de cette reconnaissance apparente, de la quantité et de la qualité de ses publications, et de l'influence de ses puissants amis au sein de la communauté scientifique, de Moivre ne réussit jamais à obtenir un poste de professeur dans une université. Il dut se contenter des maigres revenus que lui rapportaient ses cours privés et ses travaux de consultant auprès de compagnies d'assurances.

Vers la fin de sa vie, de Moivre affirma avoir besoin de dormir chaque jour 15 minutes de plus que la veille. Quelque temps après, le 27 novembre 1754, il mourut durant son sommeil, à l'âge vénérable de 87 ans.

7.1 FORME CARTÉSIENNE D'UN NOMBRE COMPLEXE

On sait qu'il n'existe aucun nombre réel qui vérifie l'équation $x^2 + 1 = 0$. Pour contourner cette difficulté, les mathématiciens, comme ils l'ont souvent fait au cours de l'histoire, ont simplement inventé une solution en créant un nouveau système de nombres, soit les nombres complexes. Ces nombres servent non seulement à résoudre des équations algébriques, mais également à résoudre certaines équations différentielles. Ils ont en outre des applications en physique, notamment en électricité.

Le symbole i représente le nombre complexe qui vérifie l'équation $i^2 = -1$. Ce nombre i est appelé unité imaginaire. Mais ce qualificatif ne doit pas faire croire que i est plus mystérieux que n'importe quel autre nombre. Tous les nombres ne sont-ils pas des symboles, des fruits de l'imagination humaine?

Une petite anecdote

Isaac Asimov fut un grand vulgarisateur scientifique et l'auteur de nombreux ouvrages de science-fiction. Dans l'extrait qui suit, il raconte la discussion qu'il a eue avec un professeur de sociologie alors qu'il étudiait à l'université. Asimov avait l'habitude d'assister au cours de ce professeur pour accompagner un ami.

« Les mathématiciens, dit le professeur, sont des mystiques, car ils croient en l'existence de nombres qui n'ont aucune réalité. »

D'habitude, n'étant pas inscrit à ce cours, je m'asseyais dans un coin et je baillais d'ennui. Mais cette fois je me levai d'un bond et dis : « Quels nombres ? »

Le professeur regarda dans ma direction et répondit : « La racine carrée de moins un. Ce nombre n'existe pas. Les mathématiciens le qualifient d'imaginaire tout en lui attribuant une existence qui relève de la mystique. »

« Il n'y a rien de mystique là-dedans », dis-je avec emportement. « La racine carrée de moins un est aussi réelle que n'importe quel autre nombre. »

Le professeur sourit à l'idée qu'il avait devant lui quelqu'un qui pourrait lui servir à faire étalage de sa supériorité intellectuelle. (Comme j'ai moi-même donné des cours depuis, je sais exactement ce qu'il ressentait.) Il dit, sur un ton doucereux : « Nous avons parmi nous un jeune mathématicien qui veut prouver le caractère réel de la racine carrée de moins un. Alors, jeune homme, donnez-moi la racine carrée de moins un d'un bâton de craie ! »

Je rougis et bafouillai : « Eh bien ! Alors… »

« Cela règle la question », dit le professeur, qui s'imaginait s'être acquitté de sa mission avec adresse et en douceur.

Mais j'élevai la voix : « Je vais le faire. Je vais vous donner la racine carrée de moins un d'un bâton de craie si vous me donnez un demi-bâton de craie. »

Le professeur sourit de nouveau et répondit : « Très bien. » Il brisa en deux un bâton de craie neuf et me tendit l'une des deux moitiés, en ajoutant : « À vous maintenant de remplir votre partie du contrat. »

«Ah! Un instant! dis-je. Vous n'avez pas rempli la vôtre. Ce que vous m'avez donné, c'est un bâton de craie et non un demi-bâton de craie.» Je levai la main pour montrer le morceau de craie à la classe. «N'êtes-vous pas tous d'accord que ceci est un bâton de craie? Il ne s'agit certainement pas de deux ou trois bâtons.»

Le professeur ne souriait plus. «Un instant! Un bâton de craie est un bâton de longueur standard. Le morceau que vous tenez a une longueur égale à la moitié de la longueur standard.»

Je répondis: «Vous me balancez de but en blanc une définition arbitraire. Même si je l'accepte, pouvez-vous soutenir que ce morceau de craie est bien une moitié d'un bâton, et non les 48 centièmes ou les 52 centièmes d'un bâton? Et puis, croyez-vous être réellement qualifié pour discuter de la racine carrée de moins un alors que vous n'avez pas une idée très claire de ce qu'est une moitié?»

À ce moment, le professeur avait déjà perdu sa belle sérénité. Il me fut impossible de répliquer à son dernier argument: «Foutez-moi le camp d'ici!» Je sortis en riant et, par la suite, j'attendis mon ami dans le corridor[2].

L'ensemble des **nombres complexes**, noté $\mathbb{C}$, est défini comme suit:

$$\mathbb{C} = \{a + bi \mid a \text{ et } b \in \mathbb{R} \text{ et } i^2 = -1\}$$

On emploie généralement la lettre z pour désigner un nombre complexe. Dans l'expression $z = a + bi$, le membre de droite est appelé **forme cartésienne** (ou encore *rectangulaire* ou *algébrique*) **du nombre complexe** z. Comme cette forme ressemble à un binôme en i, on la qualifie également de *binomiale*. Tout nombre complexe exprimé sous forme cartésienne comporte deux parties. Si $z = a + bi$, le nombre a est appelé **partie réelle** de z, ce qu'on écrit $a = \text{Re}(z)$, alors que le nombre b est appelé **partie imaginaire** de z, ce qu'on écrit $b = \text{Im}(z)$.

---

2. I. Asimov. *Asimov on Numbers*, New York, Pocket books, 1977, p. 115-116.

Voici cinq nombres complexes ainsi que leur partie réelle et leur partie imaginaire.

z	Re(z)	Im(z)
$2 + 3i$	2	3
$5 - 2i$	5	-2
$-3 + i$	-3	1
$4i$	0	4
8	8	0

La dernière ligne du tableau indique clairement que les nombres réels sont des nombres complexes dont la partie imaginaire est nulle. Ainsi, les nombres réels constituent un sous-ensemble des nombres complexes.

Encore une fois, ne vous laissez pas impressionner par la terminologie. Les nombres complexes appartiennent tout autant à la réalité que les nombres réels. Vous est-il déjà venu à l'idée que les nombres irrationnels sont moins conformes à la raison que les nombres rationnels? Les nombres complexes ne sont pas plus «complexes» ou difficiles à manipuler que les nombres réels. Le choix des termes (positif, négatif, réel, imaginaire, complexe) servant à désigner des ensembles de nombres n'a pas été des plus heureux. À l'origine, chaque ensemble de nombres a revêtu un caractère plus ou moins mystérieux ou douteux. Avec le temps, les nouveaux nombres sont devenus d'usage courant, on leur a trouvé diverses applications et leur aspect un peu magique a disparu. Ils n'ont pas perdu pour autant leur nom initial, qui maintient le mystère chez les non-initiés. C'est ce que le grand mathématicien Gauss soutenait quand il écrivait:

> Si les unités 1, −1 et $\sqrt{-1}$ avaient été appelées directe, inverse, et latérale, plutôt que positive, négative et imaginaire, toute la mystique entourant ces nombres n'aurait probablement pas eu lieu[3].

Les nombres complexes n'ont donc rien de «complexe»!

7.2 SOLUTION D'UNE ÉQUATION QUADRATIQUE

La solution générale d'une équation quadratique $ax^2 + bx + c = 0$ est donnée par la formule quadratique:

$$x = \frac{-b \pm \sqrt{b^2 - 4ac}}{2a}$$

---

3. J. P. Colette. *Histoire des mathématiques*, tome 2, Montréal, Éditions du Renouveau Pédagogique, 1979, p. 182.

Cette solution est un nombre réel seulement si le discriminant, $b^2 - 4ac$, est positif ou nul. Toutefois, les équations quadratiques dont le discriminant est négatif admettent comme solutions des nombres complexes.

Exemple

L'équation $x^2 - 4x + 8 = 0$ n'a pas de solution dans les réels parce que $b^2 - 4ac = 16 - 32 = -16 < 0$. Toutefois, elle admet deux solutions complexes, données par la formule quadratique :

$$x = \frac{4 \pm \sqrt{16 - 32}}{2} = \frac{4 \pm \sqrt{-16}}{2} = \frac{4 \pm \sqrt{16\,i^2}}{2} = \frac{4 \pm 4i}{2} = 2 \pm 2i$$

EXERCICE 7.1

Résolvez chaque équation quadratique.

a) $x^2 - 2x + 5 = 0$

b) $x^2 - 6x + 10 = 0$

7.3 OPÉRATIONS SUR LES NOMBRES COMPLEXES

Comme les nombres complexes sont représentés par des binômes en i, les relations et les opérations d'addition et de multiplication sur les nombres complexes sont définies de la même façon que dans le cas des binômes, à la différence qu'on remplace i^2 par -1.

Soit $z_1 = a_1 + b_1 i$ et $z_2 = a_2 + b_2 i$ deux nombres complexes, et k un nombre réel.

1) $z_1 = z_2$ si et seulement si $a_1 = a_2$ et $b_1 = b_2$
   (égalité de deux nombres complexes)

2) $z_1 + z_2 = (a_1 + a_2) + (b_1 + b_2)i \in \mathbb{C}$
   (addition de deux nombres complexes)

3) $z_1 - z_2 = (a_1 - a_2) + (b_1 - b_2)i \in \mathbb{C}$
   (soustraction de deux nombres complexes)

4) $kz_1 = ka_1 + kb_1 i \in \mathbb{C}$
   (multiplication d'un nombre complexe par un scalaire réel)

5) $z_1 z_2 = (a_1 + b_1 i)(a_2 + b_2 i)$

$\qquad = a_1 a_2 + a_1 b_2 i + a_2 b_1 i + b_1 b_2 i^2$

$\qquad = (a_1 a_2 - b_1 b_2) + (a_1 b_2 + a_2 b_1)i \in \mathbb{C}$

(multiplication de deux nombres complexes)

Exemple

1. $(2 + 3i) + (5 - 2i) = (2 + 5) + (3 - 2)i = 7 + i$

2. $(8 - 6i) - (3 + 4i) = (8 - 3) + (-6 - 4)i = 5 - 10i$

3. $(2 + 3i) + (0 + 0i) = (2 + 0) + (3 + 0)i = 2 + 3i$

   En général, $(a + bi) + (0 + 0i) = a + bi$, de sorte que le nombre $0 + 0i = 0$ est l'élément neutre pour l'addition dans $\mathbb{C}$.

4. $(2 + 3i)(5 - 2i) = 2(5) + 2(-2i) + (3i)(5) + (3i)(-2i)$

   $\qquad\qquad\qquad = 10 - 4i + 15i - 6i^2$

   $\qquad\qquad\qquad = 10 + 11i - 6(-1)$

   $\qquad\qquad\qquad = 16 + 11i$

5. $(2 + 3i)(1 + 0i) = 2(1) + 2(0i) + (3i)(1) + (3i)(0i) = 2 + 3i$

   En général, $(a + bi)(1 + 0i) = a + bi$, de sorte que le nombre $1 + 0i = 1$ est l'élément neutre pour la multiplication dans $\mathbb{C}$.

6. $(-3i)^7 = (-3)^7 i^7 = -2\,187(i)(i^6) = -2\,187(i)(i^2)^3 = 2\,187i$

CONJUGUÉ D'UN NOMBRE COMPLEXE

Le conjugué d'un nombre complexe $z = a + bi$ est noté $\bar{z}$ et il est donné par $\bar{z} = a - bi$.

Le **conjugué d'un nombre complexe** $z = a + bi$ est le nombre complexe $\bar{z} = a - bi$. La multiplication d'un nombre complexe par son conjugué donne un nombre réel. En effet,

$$z\bar{z} = (a + bi)(a - bi) = a^2 - abi + abi - b^2 i^2 = a^2 + b^2 \in \mathbb{R}$$

Cette propriété sert dans la division de deux nombres complexes. Pour effectuer l'opération z_1/z_2 (où $z_2 \neq 0$), on multiplie le numérateur et le dénominateur par le conjugué de z_2. L'exemple qui suit indique que le quotient de deux nombres complexes est un nombre complexe.

Exemple

1. $\dfrac{5 - 2i}{4 + 3i} = \left(\dfrac{5 - 2i}{4 + 3i}\right)\left(\dfrac{4 - 3i}{4 - 3i}\right) = \dfrac{14 - 23i}{25} = \dfrac{14}{25} + \dfrac{-23}{25}i$

2. $\dfrac{1}{3 - 2i} = \left(\dfrac{1}{3 - 2i}\right)\left(\dfrac{3 + 2i}{3 + 2i}\right) = \dfrac{3 + 2i}{13} = \dfrac{3}{13} + \dfrac{2}{13}i$

MODULE D'UN NOMBRE COMPLEXE

Le module du nombre complexe $z = a + bi$ est noté $|z|$ et il est donné par $|z| = \sqrt{a^2 + b^2}$.

Le **module du nombre complexe** $z = a + bi$ est le nombre réel noté $|z|$ et défini par $|z| = \sqrt{a^2 + b^2}$. On peut également exprimer le module d'un nombre complexe z en fonction du nombre z et de son conjugué. En effet, si $z = a + bi$, alors

$$z\bar{z} = (a + bi)(a - bi) = a^2 - abi + abi - b^2i^2 = a^2 + b^2 = |z|^2$$

de sorte que $|z| = \sqrt{z\bar{z}}$.

L'inverse, $1/z$, d'un nombre complexe z non nul est noté z^{-1} et il est égal à $\bar{z}/|z|^2$. En effet, si z est un nombre complexe non nul, alors

$$\frac{1}{z} = \left(\frac{1}{z}\right)\left(\frac{\bar{z}}{\bar{z}}\right) = \frac{\bar{z}}{|z|^2}$$

Vous devriez vérifier que cette dernière expression est un nombre complexe, c'est-à-dire qu'elle s'écrit sous la forme $a + bi$. On déduit de la dernière égalité que, si $z_2 \neq 0$, alors

$$\frac{z_1}{z_2} = \frac{z_1\bar{z_2}}{|z_2|^2}$$

EXERCICE 7.2

Soit $z_1 = 4 - 2i$, $z_2 = 2 - 5i$ et $z_3 = 3 + 3i$. Évaluez chaque expression.

a) $3z_1 - 4z_2$

b) $z_1 z_2$

c) $i^{13}z_3$

d) $\bar{z_1}$

NOMBRES COMPLEXES

257

e) $\dfrac{z_1 z_3}{z_2}$

f) $\left|\dfrac{1}{z_3}\right|$

g) $\text{Re}\left(\dfrac{z_2 + z_3}{i}\right)$

h) $\text{Im}\left(\dfrac{2z_1 - 3z_2}{i}\right)$

Tout comme l'ensemble des nombres réels ($\mathbb{R}$), l'ensemble des nombres complexes ($\mathbb{C}$), muni des opérations d'addition et de multiplication, forme une structure algébrique particulière appelée corps.

Un corps $\langle E, +, \cdot \rangle$ est un ensemble non vide muni de deux opérations (généralement appelées addition et multiplication) qui possèdent les propriétés suivantes.

1) Si $x \in E$ et $y \in E$, alors $x + y \in E$ (fermeture par rapport à l'addition).

2) Si $x \in E$ et $y \in E$, alors $x + y = y + x$ (commutativité de l'addition).

3) Si x, y et $z \in E$, alors $(x + y) + z = x + (y + z)$ (associativité de l'addition).

4) Il existe un élément $e_0 \in E$ tel que $x + e_0 = x$ pour tout $x \in E$ (existence d'un élément neutre pour l'addition).

5) Pour tout $x \in E$, il existe un $y \in E$ tel que $x + y = e_0$. (Chaque élément x d'un corps E a un opposé y.)

6) Si $x \in E$ et $y \in E$, alors $x \cdot y \in E$ (fermeture par rapport à la multiplication).

7) Si x, y et $z \in E$, alors $(x \cdot y) \cdot z = x \cdot (y \cdot z)$ (associativité de la multiplication).

8) Il existe un élément $e_1 \in E \backslash \{e_0\}$ tel que $x \; e_1 = x$ pour tout $x \in E$ (existence d'un élément neutre, e_1, pour la multiplication, différent de e_0).

9) Pour tout $x \in E \backslash \{e_0\}$, il existe un $y \in E$ tel que $x \cdot y = e_1$. (Chaque élément $x \neq e_0$ d'un corps E a un inverse.)

10) Si x, y et $z \in E$, alors $x \cdot (y + z) = x \cdot y + x \cdot z$ (distributivité de la multiplication par rapport à l'addition).

Si le cœur vous en dit, essayez de prouver que les nombres complexes forment un corps. Nous reviendrons sur la notion de structure algébrique au dernier chapitre.

Soyons maintenant audacieux! Traitons les parties réelle et imaginaire d'un nombre complexe comme si elles étaient les composantes d'un vecteur algébrique. Cela permet de constater la similitude entre les concepts d'égalité de deux nombres complexes et de deux vecteurs du plan, de même qu'entre les concepts d'addition, de module et de multiplication par un scalaire réel dans l'un et l'autre ensemble.

Ces similarités incitent à représenter les nombres complexes comme des vecteurs géométriques dans un plan cartésien, alors appelé **plan d'Argand** ou *plan des complexes*. Dans un plan d'Argand, l'axe des abscisses est l'axe des réels et l'axe des ordonnées est l'axe des imaginaires.

Ainsi, tout nombre complexe $z = a + bi$ s'écrit sous la forme vectorielle $z = \begin{bmatrix} a & b \end{bmatrix}$. Il est à noter qu'on désigne par z, et non par $\vec{z}$, le vecteur représentant un nombre complexe z.

PLAN D'ARGAND

Un plan d'Argand est un plan cartésien où l'axe horizontal est appelé axe des réels et l'axe vertical est appelé axe des imaginaires. Un tel plan sert à la représentation graphique des nombres complexes interprétés comme des vecteurs.

Exemple

On représente les nombres complexes $z_1 = 2 + 3i$, $z_2 = -2 + i$, $z_3 = 4 - 2i$ et $z_4 = \begin{bmatrix} -3 & -3 \end{bmatrix}$ dans un plan d'Argand, comme suit.

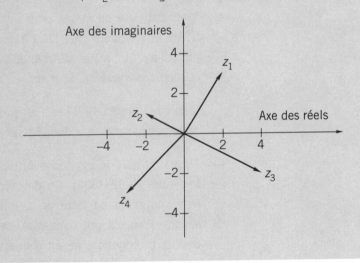

EXERCICE 7.3

Représentez les nombres complexes $z_1 = 3i$, $z_2 = 1 - 4i$ et $z_3 = \begin{bmatrix} -4 & 0 \end{bmatrix}$ dans un plan d'Argand.

Un peu d'histoire

L'histoire des nombres complexes débute en 1545 avec la publication de *Ars Magna* de J. Cardan. Cet ouvrage contient la première mention de la racine d'un nombre négatif et l'utilisation de celle-ci dans des calculs. D'autres mathématiciens, dont Leibniz, Euler et Descartes, employèrent par la suite les nombres complexes sans toutefois leur accorder une véritable légitimité.

En 1806, J. R. Argand (1768-1822) publia, sous le couvert de l'anonymat, *Essai sur une manière de représenter les quantités imaginaires dans les constructions géométriques*. Dans cet ouvrage, il donne une description géométrique des nombres complexes et des opérations sur ces nombres. De plus, il utilise les nombres complexes pour prouver des théorèmes de trigonométrie, de géométrie et d'algèbre. Mais, au moment de sa parution, le livre d'Argand ne retint pas l'attention des mathématiciens.

Il en avait été de même pour un article de l'arpenteur danois C. Wessel (1745-1818), publié dès 1799 dans les mémoires de l'Académie royale du Danemark. À l'instar d'Argand, Wessel y décrit les nombres complexes comme des vecteurs du plan.

Bien que l'article de Wessel ait précédé le livre d'Argand, par un concours de circonstances on a donné le nom de ce dernier au plan des complexes.

Argand fit part de ses découvertes au célèbre mathématicien Adrien-Marie Legendre (1752-1833). Ce dernier exposa les idées d'Argand dans une lettre adressée au frère de J.-F. Français, sans toutefois en nommer la source. Français prit connaissance de la correspondance entre son frère décédé et Legendre et, en s'appuyant sur les informations qu'elle contenait, il publia, en 1813, un mémoire dans les *Annales de mathématiques pures et appliquées*, la toute première revue savante entièrement consacrée aux mathématiques. À la fin de son mémoire, Français affirme que les principales idées qu'il y présente ne sont pas de lui, mais d'un mathématicien inconnu cité dans une lettre de Legendre. Il termine en demandant à cet inconnu de se manifester.

Ayant pris connaissance de l'article de Français, Argand écrivit à J. D. Gergonne (1771-1859), le fondateur des *Annales*, pour lui dire qu'il était le mathématicien inconnu cité par Français. Il donne également un résumé du livre qu'il a publié. Cette lettre fut suivie d'un article d'Argand dans les *Annales*. C'est donc grâce à l'honnêteté intellectuelle remarquable de J.-F. Français qu'Argand occupe une petite place dans l'histoire des mathématiques.

L'acceptation générale des nombres complexes a certainement été facilitée par l'existence de modèles géométriques, dont ceux de J. R. Argand et de C. Wessel, mais elle a été retardée à cause du manque de notoriété de ces deux individus. Ce fut grâce à l'autorité morale de l'illustre C. F. Gauss que les nombres complexes furent admis comme de véritables entités mathématiques. Dans un article célèbre, publié en 1831, celui-ci écrit que les représentations géométriques des nombres complexes leur donnent un sens qui satisfait l'intuition et qu'il n'est pas besoin d'autre justification pour accepter ces nombres.

Comme le fait remarquer Crowe, c'est cette publication de Gauss qui donna leur pleine légitimité aux nombres complexes.

> Cependant, l'acceptation du concept [de la représentation des nombres complexes] ne se fit que très lentement et ces idées attirèrent peu l'attention avant la publication de l'article de Gauss, en 1831. Il n'est pas étonnant que cette notion soit passée inaperçue jusqu'à ce que Gauss n'intervienne. Les historiens des sciences ont montré à maintes reprises que les idées radicalement nouvelles ne retiennent généralement pas l'attention en vertu de leur seul mérite. Les mathématiciens qui ont traité des nombres complexes avant Gauss étaient tous peu connus ; en fait ils sont entrés dans l'histoire en raison d'une unique découverte d'importance. Mais lorsque Gauss a écrit sur le sujet, il l'a fait avec toute l'autorité que lui conférait la célébrité qu'il avait acquise grâce à ses travaux impressionnants dans des domaines traditionnels et à sa prédiction, largement diffusée, de la position où l'astéroïde Cérès allait réapparaître après qu'on l'ait perdu dans l'ombre du Soleil[4].

On doit à de grands mathématiciens une partie de la terminologie et du symbolisme relatifs aux nombres complexes. Descartes a été le premier à

---

4. M. J. Crowe. *A History of Vector Analysis ; the Evolution of the Idea of a Vectorial System*, New York, Dover Publications, Inc., 1994, p. 11.

employer le mot « imaginaire » ; Gauss a introduit le terme « complexe » pour désigner les nombres de la forme $a + bi$, qu'il traite comme des points du plan et non comme des vecteurs ; Euler a créé le symbole i ; Cauchy a donné aux mots « conjugué » et « module » leur sens mathématique.

7.5 FORME TRIGONOMÉTRIQUE DES NOMBRES COMPLEXES

Nous avons défini le module d'un nombre complexe $z = a + bi$ par $|z| = \sqrt{a^2 + b^2}$. On désigne aussi le module d'un nombre complexe z par le symbole ρ (la lettre grecque rho, qui correspond à r), qui évoque la longueur du *rayon* vecteur représentant ce nombre. Dans le cas des nombres complexes, la direction de ce vecteur est appelée **argument**. L'argument d'un nombre complexe z, noté Arg(z), est donc l'angle, mesuré dans le sens contraire des aiguilles d'une montre, que détermine le vecteur géométrique avec l'axe des réels.

ARGUMENT D'UN NOMBRE COMPLEXE

L'argument d'un nombre complexe z est égal à l'angle θ, mesuré dans le sens contraire des aiguilles d'une montre, que détermine le vecteur représentant ce nombre complexe avec l'axe des réels dans un plan d'Argand. On écrit $\theta = \text{Arg}(z)$ où $0 \leq \theta < 2\pi$ ou encore $0° \leq \theta < 360°$ selon que l'angle est mesuré en radians ou en degrés.

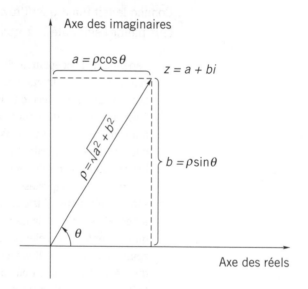

FORME TRIGONOMÉTRIQUE D'UN NOMBRE COMPLEXE

La forme trigonométrique (ou polaire) d'un nombre complexe $z = a + bi$ est donnée par l'une des expressions suivantes :

$$z = \rho\cos\theta + i\rho\sin\theta$$
$$= \rho(\cos\theta + i\sin\theta)$$
$$= \rho\operatorname{cis}\theta$$

où $\rho = |z| = \sqrt{a^2 + b^2}$ et $\theta = \operatorname{arc\,tg}\dfrac{b}{a}$.

On appelle **forme trigonométrique** ou *polaire* **d'un nombre complexe** l'expression de ce nombre en fonction de son module et de son argument :

$$z = \rho\cos\theta + i\rho\sin\theta = \rho(\cos\theta + i\sin\theta)$$

qui s'écrit également sous la forme abrégée

$$z = \rho\operatorname{cis}\theta \quad \text{où} \quad \operatorname{cis}\theta = \cos\theta + i\sin\theta$$

On passe de la forme cartésienne à la forme trigonométrique, et vice versa, à l'aide des équations suivantes :

$$\rho = |z| = \sqrt{a^2 + b^2} \qquad \theta = \text{arc tg}\frac{b}{a}$$
$$a = \rho\cos\theta \qquad\qquad b = \rho\sin\theta$$

Ces équations sont essentiellement identiques aux équations présentées à la section 5.5.3. Les fonctions sinus et cosinus étant périodiques de période 2π, ou 360°, on choisit la valeur de l'argument dans l'intervalle $0 \leq \theta < 2\pi$ ou $0° \leq \theta < 360°$ selon que l'angle θ est mesuré en radians ou en degrés.

Exemple

Pour exprimer le nombre complexe $z_1 = 2 - 2i$ sous forme trigonométrique, il faut d'abord calculer son module et son argument :

$$\rho = \sqrt{2^2 + (-2)^2} = 2\sqrt{2}$$
$$\theta = \text{arc tg}\left(\frac{-2}{2}\right) = \text{arc tg}(-1) = \frac{3\pi}{4} \quad \text{ou} \quad \frac{7\pi}{4}$$

Comme l'extrémité du rayon vecteur du nombre z_1 est située dans le quatrième quadrant, l'argument est $\theta = 7\pi/4$ ou 315°. Par conséquent,

$$z_1 = 2 - 2i = 2\sqrt{2}\,\text{cis}\left(\frac{7\pi}{4}\right)$$

Par ailleurs, pour écrire le nombre complexe $z_2 = 3\,\text{cis}(30°)$ sous forme cartésienne, il faut d'abord calculer la partie réelle et la partie imaginaire de ce nombre :

$$\text{Re}(z) = 3\cos(30°) = \frac{3\sqrt{3}}{2}$$
$$\text{Im}(z) = 3\sin(30°) = \frac{3}{2}$$

Par conséquent, $z_2 = \frac{3\sqrt{3}}{2} + \frac{3}{2}i$.

EXERCICE 7.4

Exprimez chaque nombre complexe sous la forme indiquée.

a) $z_1 = -\sqrt{3} - i$, sous la forme trigonométrique.

b) $z_2 = 4\,\text{cis}(330°)$, sous la forme cartésienne.

Il est facile d'effectuer les opérations d'addition et de soustraction sur des nombres complexes exprimés sous forme cartésienne ou vectorielle, mais il est impossible d'effectuer directement ces opérations sur des nombres complexes exprimés sous forme trigonométrique.

Par contre, la forme trigonométrique convient parfaitement pour les opérations de multiplication, de division, d'élévation à une puissance et d'extraction d'une racine.

Théorème 7.1

Si $z_1 = \rho_1 \operatorname{cis} \theta_1$ et $z_2 = \rho_2 \operatorname{cis} \theta_2$, alors $z_1 z_2 = \rho_1 \rho_2 \operatorname{cis}(\theta_1 + \theta_2)$.

Preuve

Si $z_1 = \rho_1 \operatorname{cis} \theta_1$ et $z_2 = \rho_2 \operatorname{cis} \theta_2$, alors

$$
\begin{aligned}
z_1 z_2 &= (\rho_1 \cos\theta_1 + i\rho_1 \sin\theta_1)(\rho_2 \cos\theta_2 + i\rho_2 \sin\theta_2) \\
&= \rho_1 \rho_2 \cos\theta_1 \cos\theta_2 - \rho_1 \rho_2 \sin\theta_1 \sin\theta_2 \\
&\quad + i(\rho_1 \rho_2 \cos\theta_1 \sin\theta_2 + \rho_1 \rho_2 \cos\theta_2 \sin\theta_1) \\
&= \rho_1 \rho_2 \left[(\cos\theta_1 \cos\theta_2 - \sin\theta_1 \sin\theta_2) + i(\cos\theta_1 \sin\theta_2 + \cos\theta_2 \sin\theta_1) \right] \\
&= \rho_1 \rho_2 \left[\cos(\theta_1 + \theta_2) + i\sin(\theta_1 + \theta_2) \right] \\
&= \rho_1 \rho_2 \operatorname{cis}(\theta_1 + \theta_2)
\end{aligned}
$$

Cette dernière expression est un nombre complexe exprimé sous forme trigonométrique. Ainsi, le module du produit de deux nombres complexes est égal au produit des modules de ces nombres, alors que l'argument du produit est égal à la somme des arguments des deux nombres. ∎

Exemple

Soit $z_1 = 5\operatorname{cis}(200°)$ et $z_2 = 8\operatorname{cis}(220°)$. Les fonctions sinus et cosinus étant périodiques de période 360°, on a

$$z_1 z_2 = (5)(8)\operatorname{cis}(200° + 220°) = 40\operatorname{cis}(420°) = 40\operatorname{cis}(60°)$$

EXERCICE 7.5

Que vaut z^3 si $z = 5\operatorname{cis}(200°)$?

On peut également montrer que si $z_1 = \rho_1 \mathrm{cis}\,\theta_1$, si $z_2 = \rho_2 \mathrm{cis}\,\theta_2$ et si $z_2 \neq 0$, alors

$$\frac{1}{z_2} = \frac{1}{\rho_2}\mathrm{cis}(-\theta_2) \quad \text{et} \quad \frac{z_1}{z_2} = \frac{\rho_1}{\rho_2}\mathrm{cis}(\theta_1 - \theta_2)$$

Exemple

Soit $z_1 = 5\,\mathrm{cis}(200°)$ et $z_2 = 8\,\mathrm{cis}(220°)$. Les fonctions sinus et cosinus étant périodiques de période 360°, on a

$$\frac{z_1}{z_2} = \frac{5}{8}\mathrm{cis}(200° - 220°) = \frac{5}{8}\mathrm{cis}(-20°) = \frac{5}{8}\mathrm{cis}(340°)$$

EXERCICE 7.6

Prouvez que si $z_1 = \rho_1 \mathrm{cis}\,\theta_1$, si $z_2 = \rho_2 \mathrm{cis}\,\theta_2$ et si $z_2 \neq 0$ alors

$$\frac{1}{z_2} = \frac{1}{\rho_2}\mathrm{cis}(-\theta_2) \quad \text{et} \quad \frac{z_1}{z_2} = \frac{\rho_1}{\rho_2}\mathrm{cis}(\theta_1 - \theta_2)$$

(Indice : Tracez un plan d'Argand et représentez-y un nombre complexe et son conjugué. Quel est le lien entre les modules et les arguments des deux nombres ?)

7.7 LE THÉORÈME DE MOIVRE ET SON COROLLAIRE

Le théorème de Moivre est l'une des conséquences directes du théorème 7.1. Il indique comment élever un nombre complexe à une puissance entière.

Théorème 7.2 (Théorème de Moivre)

Si $z = \rho\,\mathrm{cis}\,\theta$ et si n est un entier positif, alors

$$z^n = (\rho\,\mathrm{cis}\,\theta)^n = \rho^n \mathrm{cis}(n\theta)$$

ou, ce qui est équivalent,

$$\left[\rho(\cos\theta + i\sin\theta)\right]^n = \rho^n(\cos n\theta + i\sin n\theta)$$

Preuve[5]

Si $z = \rho \operatorname{cis} \theta$, alors, en vertu du théorème 7.1,

$$z^n = \underbrace{zz \ldots z}_{n \text{ facteurs}}$$

$$= \underbrace{(\rho \operatorname{cis} \theta)(\rho \operatorname{cis} \theta) \ldots (\rho \operatorname{cis} \theta)}_{n \text{ facteurs}}$$

$$= \underbrace{\rho \rho \ldots \rho}_{n \text{ facteurs}} \operatorname{cis}(\underbrace{\theta + \theta + \cdots + \theta}_{n \text{ termes}})$$

$$= \rho^n \operatorname{cis}(n\theta)$$

Le théorème 7.2 se généralise aux entiers négatifs. En effet, si $z \neq 0$ et si $n < 0$, alors $-n > 0$ et

$$z^n = (z^{-1})^{-n} = \left(\frac{1}{\rho} \operatorname{cis}(-\theta) \right)^{-n} = \left(\frac{1}{\rho} \right)^{-n} \operatorname{cis}(-n)(-\theta) = \rho^n \operatorname{cis}(n\theta) \qquad \blacksquare$$

Exemple

Pour évaluer $(1 + i)^{10}$, il est préférable d'écrire ce nombre complexe sous forme trigonométrique avant d'appliquer le théorème de Moivre. Étant donné que $1 + i = \sqrt{2} \operatorname{cis}(45°)$,

$$(1 + i)^{10} = (\sqrt{2} \operatorname{cis}(45°))^{10} = 32 \operatorname{cis}(450°) = 32 \operatorname{cis}(90°) = 32i$$

EXERCICE 7.7

Évaluez chaque expression.

a) $\left[3 \operatorname{cis}(20°) \right]^{12}$

b) $(2 - 2i)^6$

c) $(-\sqrt{3} + i)^{-7}$

On peut déduire du théorème de Moivre un corollaire[6] important, qui permet de déterminer les n racines n-ièmes de tout nombre complexe différent de zéro.

---

5. Il ne s'agit pas ici d'une preuve formelle, il s'agit plutôt d'un argument heuristique, néanmoins satisfaisant. Une preuve formelle aurait exigé le recours à l'induction mathématique, une technique de démonstration usuelle en mathématiques.

6. Un corollaire est une proposition qui découle directement d'un théorème déjà démontré.

RACINE *N*-IÈME D'UN NOMBRE
COMPLEXE

On appelle racine *n*-ième d'un
nombre complexe *z* différent de zéro
tout nombre complexe *w* tel que
$w^n = z$, et on écrit $w = z^{1/n}$.

On appelle **racine *n*-ième d'un nombre complexe** *z* différent de zéro tout nombre complexe *w* tel que $w^n = z$, et on écrit $w = z^{1/n}$.

Nous allons donner deux preuves différentes du corollaire du théorème de Moivre.

Théorème 7.3 (corollaire du théorème de Moivre)

Si $z = \rho\operatorname{cis}\theta$, alors $z^{1/n} = \rho^{1/n}\operatorname{cis}\left(\dfrac{\theta + 2k\pi}{n}\right)$ où $k = 0, 1, ..., n - 1$.

Preuve 1

Si on pose $w = \rho^{1/n}\operatorname{cis}\left(\dfrac{\theta + 2k\pi}{n}\right)$ où $k = 0, 1, ..., n - 1$, il faut vérifier

que $w^n = z$. Or, en vertu du théorème de Moivre et de la périodicité des fonctions sinus et cosinus, on a

$$
\begin{aligned}
w^n &= \left[\rho^{1/n}\operatorname{cis}\left(\frac{\theta + 2k\pi}{n}\right)\right]^n \\
&= (\rho^{1/n})^n\operatorname{cis}\left[n\left(\frac{\theta + 2k\pi}{n}\right)\right] \\
&= \rho\operatorname{cis}(\theta + 2k\pi) \\
&= \rho\operatorname{cis}(\theta) \\
&= z
\end{aligned}
$$

Par conséquent, $z^{1/n} = \rho^{1/n}\operatorname{cis}\left(\dfrac{\theta + 2k\pi}{n}\right)$ où $k = 0, 1, ..., n - 1$. ∎

Preuve 2

Si $w = r\operatorname{cis}\alpha$ est une racine *n*-ième de $z = \rho\operatorname{cis}\theta$, alors $w^n = z$. En vertu du théorème de Moivre, il faut donc que

$$
w^n = r^n\operatorname{cis}(n\alpha) = \rho\operatorname{cis}\theta = z
$$

Cette égalité est vraie seulement si les modules des deux nombres complexes sont égaux, c'est-à-dire si $r^n = \rho$ ou, ce qui est équivalent, si $r = \rho^{1/n}$.

Il faut également que les arguments des deux nombres soient égaux, ou qu'ils diffèrent par un multiple entier de 2π étant donné la périodicité des fonctions sinus et cosinus, c'est-à-dire qu'on doit avoir $n\alpha = \theta + 2k\pi$ où *k* est un entier ou encore $\alpha = (\theta + 2k\pi)/n$ où *k* est un entier.

Donc,

$$
w = \rho^{1/n}\operatorname{cis}\left(\frac{\theta + 2k\pi}{n}\right)
$$

où k est un entier. Si on limite les valeurs de k à $k = 0, 1, ..., n - 1$, on obtient quand même toutes les valeurs de w, les autres valeurs de k donnant des résultats identiques aux premiers. Ainsi, w est le même pour $k = 0$ ou $k = n$.

Par conséquent,

$$w = z^{1/n} = \rho^{1/n} \operatorname{cis}\left(\frac{\theta + 2k\pi}{n}\right) \quad \text{où} \quad k = 0, 1, ..., n - 1 \qquad \blacksquare$$

Exemple

Pour trouver les racines quatrièmes de $z = (1 + i)$, il faut d'abord écrire ce nombre complexe sous sa forme trigonométrique, soit $z = \sqrt{2}\operatorname{cis}(\pi/4)$, puis appliquer le corollaire du théorème de Moivre. On désigne les quatre racines quatrièmes de z par w_k où $k = 0, 1, 2, 3$ et on a

$$w_k = (\sqrt{2})^{1/4} \operatorname{cis}\left[\frac{(\pi/4) + 2k\pi}{4}\right] \quad \text{où} \quad k = 0, 1, 2, 3$$

Ainsi,

$$w_0 = 2^{1/8} \operatorname{cis}\left(\frac{\pi}{16}\right)$$

$$w_1 = 2^{1/8} \operatorname{cis}\left(\frac{9\pi}{16}\right)$$

$$w_2 = 2^{1/8} \operatorname{cis}\left(\frac{17\pi}{16}\right)$$

$$w_3 = 2^{1/8} \operatorname{cis}\left(\frac{25\pi}{16}\right)$$

sont les quatre racines quatrièmes de $z = (1 + i)$. Il est d'ailleurs facile de vérifier que $(w_k)^4 = (1 + i)$.

EXERCICE 7.8

Trouvez les racines n-ièmes de chacun des nombres complexes suivants.

a) $z = 64\operatorname{cis}120°$, $n = 6$

b) $z = (-\sqrt{3} - 3i)$, $n = 4$

Les nombres complexes constituent une extension des nombres réels. Ils permettent notamment de résoudre toutes les équations quadratiques, de la forme $ax^2 + bx + c = 0$, et notamment celles dont le discriminant, $b^2 - 4ac$, est négatif.

Il s'est écoulé presque 300 ans entre le *Arc Magna* de Cardan et l'article de 1831 de Gauss, et il a fallu tout ce temps pour venir à bout du scepticisme qu'entretenaient les mathématiciens à l'endroit des nombres complexes. L'invention d'une représentation graphique a certes été déterminante dans l'acceptation de ces nombres en tant qu'entités mathématiques à part entière.

L'ensemble des nombres complexes est défini par

$$\mathbb{C} = \{a + bi \mid a \text{ et } b \in \mathbb{R} \text{ et } i^2 = -1\}$$

Un nombre complexe $z = a + bi$ est essentiellement un binôme en i formé d'une partie réelle $\left[\text{Re}(z) = a\right]$ et d'une partie imaginaire $\left[\text{Im}(z) = b\right]$. Les relations et les opérations sur les nombres complexes sont donc définies de la même façon que les relations et les opérations sur les binômes, à la différence que $i^2 = -1$.

Les nombres complexes peuvent être interprétés comme des vecteurs du plan. Le plan complexe, aussi nommé plan d'Argand, comporte un axe horizontal, appelé axe des réels, et un axe vertical, appelé axe des imaginaires.

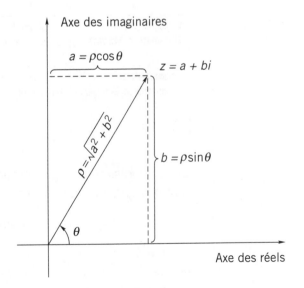

TABLEAU 7.1

Opérations et relations sur les nombres complexes

	Forme cartésienne (binomiale)	Forme trigonométrique (polaire)
NOMBRES	$z = a + bi$ $z_1 = a_1 + b_1 i$ $z_2 = a_2 + b_2 i$	$z = \rho \operatorname{cis} \theta$ $z_1 = \rho_1 \operatorname{cis} \theta_1$ $z_2 = \rho_2 \operatorname{cis} \theta_2$
ÉGALITÉ	$z_1 = z_2 \Leftrightarrow \begin{cases} a_1 = a_2 \\ b_1 = b_2 \end{cases}$	$z_1 = z_2 \Leftrightarrow \begin{cases} \rho_1 = \rho_2 \\ \theta_1 = \theta_2 + 2k\pi \end{cases}$
ADDITION	$z_1 + z_2 = (a_1 + a_2)$ $+ (b_1 + b_2)i$	Employer la forme cartésienne
MULTIPLICATION	$z_1 z_2 = (a_1 a_2 - b_1 b_2)$ $+ (a_1 b_2 + a_2 b_1)i$	$z_1 z_2 = \rho_1 \rho_2 \operatorname{cis}(\theta_1 + \theta_2)$
CONJUGUÉ	$\bar{z} = a - bi$	$\bar{z} = \rho \operatorname{cis}(-\theta)$
MODULE	$|z| = \sqrt{a^2 + b^2}$	ρ
ARGUMENT	$\operatorname{Arg}(z) = \operatorname{arc\ tg} \dfrac{b}{a}$	θ
INVERSE	Si $z \neq 0$, alors $\dfrac{1}{z} = z^{-1} = \dfrac{\bar{z}}{|z|^2}$	Si $z \neq 0$, alors $\dfrac{1}{z} = z^{-1} = \dfrac{1}{\rho} \operatorname{cis}(-\theta)$
DIVISION	Si $z_2 \neq 0$, alors $\dfrac{z_1}{z_2} = \dfrac{z_1 \bar{z_2}}{|z_2|^2}$	Si $z_2 \neq 0$, alors $\dfrac{z_1}{z_2} = \dfrac{\rho_1}{\rho_2} \operatorname{cis}(\theta_1 - \theta_2)$
PUISSANCE N-IÈME (THÉORÈME DE MOIVRE)	Employer la forme trigonométrique lorsque $n > 3$	$(\rho \operatorname{cis} \theta)^n = \rho^n \operatorname{cis}(n\theta)$
RACINE N-IÈME (COROLLAIRE DE MOIVRE)	Employer la forme trigonométrique	Si $z = \rho \operatorname{cis} \theta$, alors $z^{1/n} = \rho^{1/n} \operatorname{cis}\left(\dfrac{\theta + 2k\pi}{n}\right)$ où $k = 0, 1, \dots, n - 1$

De la représentation graphique des nombres complexes, on déduit leur forme trigonométrique, soit

$$z = \rho \cos \theta + i\rho \sin \theta = \rho(\cos \theta + i \sin \theta) = \rho \operatorname{cis} \theta$$

L'angle θ est appelé argument de z et on écrit $\theta = \operatorname{Arg}(z)$. Cet angle est mesuré dans le sens contraire des aiguilles d'une montre et sa valeur appartient à l'intervalle $0 \leq \theta < 2\pi$.

Les formes cartésienne et trigonométrique d'un nombre complexe sont liées par les équations :

$$\rho = |z| = \sqrt{a^2 + b^2} \qquad \theta = \text{arc tg}\frac{b}{a}$$

$$a = \rho\cos\theta \qquad\qquad b = \rho\sin\theta$$

MOTS CLÉS

EXERCICES RÉCAPITULATIFS

1. (I) Résoudre chaque équation quadratique.

a) $x^2 + 4 = 0$

b) $x^2 + 4x + 6 = 0$

c) $3x^2 - 5x + 4 = 0$

2. (I) Trouvez deux nombres complexes dont la somme est 8, et le produit 20.

3. (I) Soit $z_1 = 5 + 5i$, $z_2 = -2 + 3i$ et $z_3 = 3 - i$. Évaluez chaque expression.

a) $z_1 + 3z_2 - 2z_3$

b) $z_1 z_2$

c) $(z_2 + z_3)i$

d) $(z_1)^3$

e) i^{43}

f) i^{33}

g) i^{26}

h) $|z_1 + 3z_2 - 2z_3|$

i) $\text{Re}(4z_1 - 2z_2 + z_3)$

j) $\text{Im}(z_1 z_3)$

k) $\overline{z_1} + \overline{z_2}$

l) $\overline{z_1 + z_2}$. Comparez le résultat avec celui que vous avez obtenu en *k*. Croyez-vous qu'il s'agit d'une coïncidence ?

m) $\overline{z_1}\,\overline{z_2}$

n) $\overline{z_1 z_2}$. Comparez le résultat avec celui que vous avez obtenu en *m*. Croyez-vous qu'il s'agit d'une coïncidence ?

o) $\dfrac{z_1}{z_2}$

p) $\dfrac{z_1 + 3z_2}{z_2 - z_3}$

q) $(z_1)^{-1}$

4. (II) Pour quelle valeur entière de *n* l'expression $(n + i)^4$ représente-t-elle un entier ?

5. (I) Trouvez la valeur de *z* qui vérifie l'équation donnée.

a) $(4 - 5i)z + 3 - i = 2 + 3z$

b) $i\bar{z} = 2 + 2i$

6. (I) Soit les matrices suivantes, dont les éléments sont des nombres complexes.

$$A = \begin{bmatrix} 2 + i & 2 - 3i \\ 3 - 2i & i \end{bmatrix}$$

$$B = \begin{bmatrix} 2 - i & 4 + 2i \\ 1 + i & 2 - i \end{bmatrix}$$

$$C = \begin{bmatrix} 1 - i & 2i & 2 - i \\ 4 & 3 + i & 3 \end{bmatrix}$$

$$D = \begin{bmatrix} 0 & i \\ i & 0 \end{bmatrix}$$

Évaluez si possible chacune des expressions suivantes.

a) $A + B$

b) $2A + iB$

c) $2A + C$

d) AB

e) CB

f) AC

g) D^2

h) D^3

i) D^5

7. (II) Soit z_1 et z_2 deux nombres complexes. Montrez que :

a) $\overline{z_1} + \overline{z_2} = \overline{z_1 + z_2}$

b) $\overline{z_1}\,\overline{z_2} = \overline{z_1 z_2}$

c) $z_1 \in \mathbb{R} \Leftrightarrow z_1 = \overline{z_1}$

8. (III) Si $p(z) = a_0 + a_1 z + a_2 z^2 + \cdots + a_n z^n$ est un polynôme à coefficients réels ($a_k \in \mathbb{R}$), alors les racines de ce polynôme sont les valeurs de z telles que $p(z) = 0$. Servez-vous des égalités prouvées au n° 7 pour démontrer que si z est une racine du polynôme alors $\overline{z}$ en est aussi une racine, c'est-à-dire que l'ensemble des racines d'un polynôme à coefficients réels est formé de paires de nombres conjugués.

9. (I) Représentez les nombres complexes $z_1 = 5 + 5i$, $z_2 = -2 + 3i$ et $z_3 = 3 - i$ dans un plan d'Argand.

10. (I) Écrivez chacun des nombres complexes suivants sous forme trigonométrique.

a) $z_1 = -5 + 5i$

b) $z_2 = -2i$

c) $z_3 = 4$

d) $z_4 = -3\sqrt{3} - 3i$

e) $z_5 = 1 - \sqrt{3}i$

11. (I) Écrivez chacun des nombres complexes suivants sous forme cartésienne.

a) $z_1 = 4\operatorname{cis}(\pi/2)$

b) $z_2 = \operatorname{cis}(150°)$

c) $z_3 = 3\operatorname{cis}(11\pi/6)$

d) $z_4 = 2\operatorname{cis}(\pi)$

12. (II) On considère les nombres complexes $z_1 = \operatorname{cis}(30°)$, $z_2 = 2\operatorname{cis}(45°)$, $z_3 = \operatorname{cis}(\theta)$ et $z_4 = 2 - 3i$ comme des vecteurs dans un plan d'Argand.

a) Quel est le module de chaque vecteur ?

b) Quel est l'argument de chaque vecteur ?

c) Que vaut $z_1 z_2$?

d) Comparez les modules de z_2 et de $z_1 z_2$.

e) Comparez les arguments de z_2 et de $z_1 z_2$.

f) Représentez z_1, z_2 et $z_1 z_2$ dans un plan d'Argand.

g) Quel est l'effet géométrique de la multiplication de z_1 par i ?

h) Quel est l'effet géométrique de la division de z_1 par i ?

i) Quel est l'effet géométrique de la multiplication de z_2 par z_1 ?

j) Quel est l'effet géométrique de la multiplication de z_2 par z_3 ?

k) Par quel nombre complexe faut-il multiplier z_2 pour que le rayon vecteur qui représente ce nombre subisse une rotation de 60° ?

l) Quel nombre complexe obtient-on en faisant tourner le rayon vecteur qui représente z_4 autour de l'origine, d'un angle de 150° ?

13. (I) Évaluez chaque expression.

a) $\left[2\operatorname{cis}\left(\dfrac{5\pi}{6}\right)\right]\left[5\operatorname{cis}\left(\dfrac{5\pi}{3}\right)\right]$

b) $\dfrac{\left[3\operatorname{cis}(60°)\right]\left[5\operatorname{cis}(25°)\right]}{\left[2\operatorname{cis}(130°)\right]\left[6\operatorname{cis}(40°)\right]}$

c) $\left[3\operatorname{cis}\left(\dfrac{11\pi}{6}\right)\right]^5$

d) $\left[2\operatorname{cis}\left(\dfrac{\pi}{3}\right)\right]^{-6}$

e) $\dfrac{\left[6\operatorname{cis}(15°)\right]^7}{\left[4\operatorname{cis}(45°)\right]^3}$. Exprimez votre réponse sous forme cartésienne.

f) $(-1 + i)^{20}$. Exprimez votre réponse sous forme cartésienne.

g) $\left(\frac{\sqrt{3}}{2} - \frac{1}{2}i \right)^{-10}$. Exprimez votre réponse sous forme cartésienne.

h) $(1 + i + i^2 + i^3 + i^4)^{100}$

14. (I) Pour quelle valeur entière et positive de n l'expression $(\sqrt{3} + i)^n$ est-elle un nombre réel ?

15. (I) Établissez une identité trigonométrique pour chacune des fonctions $\cos 2\theta$ et $\sin 2\theta$ en comparant l'expression de $(\cos\theta + i\sin\theta)^2$ obtenue à l'aide du théorème de Moivre et le résultat de $(\cos\theta + i\sin\theta)(\cos\theta + i\sin\theta)$.

16. (I) Trouvez toutes les racines n-ièmes demandées pour chacun des nombres complexes suivants.

a) $z_1 = 1$, $n = 4$

b) $z_2 = 1 + i$, $n = 3$

c) $z_3 = 3\sqrt{3} - 3i$, $n = 6$

17. (I) Trouvez toutes les solutions de chacune des équations suivantes.

a) $z^4 - 81 = 0$

b) $z^6 - 19z^3 - 216 = 0$

18. (I) Dites si chaque énoncé est vrai ou faux, et justifiez votre réponse. Les symboles z, z_1 et z_2 représentent des nombres complexes.

a) $z_1^3 = z_2^3 \Rightarrow z_1 = z_2$

b) $\text{Re}(iz) = \text{Im}(z)$

c) $\text{Im}\left(\frac{z}{i} \right) = -\text{Re}(z)$

d) $\bar{\bar{z}} = z$

e) $z - \bar{z} \in \mathbb{R}$

f) $z + \bar{z} \in \mathbb{R}$

Vecteurs de l'espace

Le mathématicien prépare d'avance des moules que le physicien
viendra plus tard remplir.

H. Tayne

À LA FIN DU PRÉSENT CHAPITRE, VOUS DEVRIEZ ÊTRE
EN MESURE DE RÉPONDRE AUX QUESTIONS SUIVANTES:

- Quelles sont les principales différences entre les vecteurs
  de l'espace et les vecteurs du plan?

- Comment définit-on la direction d'un vecteur de l'espace?

- Comment calcule-t-on le module d'un vecteur de l'espace
  dont on connaît les composantes?

- Qu'est-ce que le produit vectoriel?

- Quelle relation existe-t-il entre le produit vectoriel et l'aire
  d'un parallélogramme?

- À quoi sert le produit mixte?

UN PORTRAIT de Josiah Willard Gibbs

Josiah Willard Gibbs naquit en 1839 à New Haven, dans le Connecticut. Il fit de brillantes études à l'Université Yale, où son père enseignait la théologie. Il obtint des prix de latin et de mathématiques, et décrocha un diplôme de premier cycle à 19 ans et un doctorat (Ph. D.) en ingénierie à 24 ans. Gibbs reçut en fait le premier diplôme de doctorat en génie décerné par l'Université Yale, et le deuxième diplôme de doctorat décerné par une université américaine. Sa thèse portait sur la conception d'engrenages. Après avoir étudié la physique en Europe (Paris, Berlin et Heidelberg) pendant trois ans, Gibbs occupa, à compter de 1871, la chaire de physique-mathématique de l'Université Yale, poste qu'il conserva jusqu'à sa mort, le 28 avril 1903. Toutefois, au cours des neuf premières années, on ne lui versa aucun salaire sous prétexte qu'il n'avait pas besoin d'argent.

En 1881, Gibbs publia, à compte d'auteur, une brochure intitulée Elements of Vector Analysis, dans laquelle il introduit un système de vecteurs à trois dimensions. Cet ouvrage de vulgarisation destiné à ses élèves connut un vif succès. Gibbs y présente une adaptation brillante des travaux de W. R. Hamilton sur les quaternions et de J. C. Maxwell en physique. Les notes de cours de Gibbs constituent un traité d'analyse vectorielle simple à comprendre et orienté vers les applications à la physique, notamment à l'électricité et au magnétisme. E. B. Wilson, l'un des élèves de Gibbs, vit à ce que ces notes de cours connaissent une plus large diffusion en les faisant publier sous la forme d'un livre. Vector Analysis parut en 1901 et devint la référence de l'époque en analyse vectorielle.

C'est dans Vector Analysis que Gibbs introduisit les symboles $\vec{i}$, $\vec{j}$ et $\vec{k}$ pour désigner les vecteurs unitaires de l'espace portés par les axes de coordonnées. Il y donna également les définitions et les notations modernes du produit scalaire ($\vec{u} \cdot \vec{v}$) et du produit vectoriel ($\vec{u} \times \vec{v}$), et montra que le produit vectoriel n'est pas commutatif, en fait $\vec{u} \times \vec{v} = -\vec{v} \times \vec{u}$.

Gibbs fit de nombreuses contributions scientifiques en dehors de l'analyse vectorielle. Ainsi, on a donné son nom à un phénomène d'oscillation au voisinage d'un point de discontinuité dans l'approximation d'une fonction *par une série de Fourier. De plus, Gibbs jeta les bases de la thermodynamique chimique moderne, et il détint un brevet sur un système de freinage des trains. Josiah Willard Gibbs est considéré à juste titre comme l'un des premiers scientifiques américains de réputation internationale.*

8.1 VECTEURS GÉOMÉTRIQUES DE L'ESPACE

Les vecteurs géométriques de l'espace possèdent essentiellement les mêmes propriétés que les vecteurs géométriques du plan, dont ils sont une généralisation. Ils résultent du passage d'un univers bidimensionnel à un univers tridimensionnel.

- Deux vecteurs de l'espace $\vec{u}$ et $\vec{v}$ sont égaux s'ils ont la même longueur et la même direction. Les vecteurs de l'espace sont libres. Ainsi, les translations sont permises : on peut déplacer des vecteurs de façon que leurs origines respectives coïncident avec l'origine d'un système de coordonnées cartésiennes de l'espace. Dans l'espace, il faut cependant trois angles (appelés angles directeurs), plutôt qu'un seul (comme dans le plan), pour caractériser la direction d'un vecteur.

- La somme de deux vecteurs $\vec{u}$ et $\vec{v}$ s'obtient en joignant l'origine de $\vec{u}$ à l'extrémité de $\vec{v}$ après avoir déplacé $\vec{v}$ de façon que son origine coïncide avec l'extrémité de $\vec{u}$. La règle de Chasles est donc valable pour les vecteurs de l'espace, c'est-à-dire que

$$\overrightarrow{AB} + \overrightarrow{BC} + \cdots + \overrightarrow{PQ} + \overrightarrow{QR} = \overrightarrow{AR}$$

- Le produit du vecteur $\vec{u}$ par le scalaire k, noté $k\vec{u}$, est un vecteur de longueur $\|k\vec{u}\| = |k|\,\|\vec{u}\|$, qui a la même direction que $\vec{u}$ si k est positif et une direction contraire (ou opposée) à celle de $\vec{u}$ si k est négatif. Si $k = 0$, alors $k\vec{u} = \vec{0}$.

- L'angle entre deux vecteurs $\vec{u}$ et $\vec{v}$ est défini comme le plus petit angle θ déterminé par ces deux vecteurs lorsqu'ils sont issus d'une même origine.

- Le produit scalaire des vecteurs $\vec{u}$ et $\vec{v}$ est défini par $\vec{u} \cdot \vec{v} = \|\vec{u}\|\,\|\vec{v}\|\cos\theta$ où θ est l'angle entre ces deux vecteurs.

- Deux vecteurs sont orthogonaux si et seulement si leur produit scalaire est nul.

- Toute expression $a_1\overrightarrow{u_1} + a_2\overrightarrow{u_2} + \cdots + a_n\overrightarrow{u_n}$, où a_1, a_2, ..., a_n sont des scalaires, est une combinaison linéaire des n vecteurs $\overrightarrow{u_1}$, $\overrightarrow{u_2}$, ..., $\overrightarrow{u_n}$.

- On dit que n vecteurs $\overrightarrow{u_1}$, $\overrightarrow{u_2}$, ..., $\overrightarrow{u_n}$ sont linéairement indépendants si et seulement si

$$a_1\overrightarrow{u_1} + a_2\overrightarrow{u_2} + \cdots + a_n\overrightarrow{u_n} = \vec{0} \quad \Rightarrow \quad a_1 = 0,\ a_2 = 0,\ ...,\ a_n = 0$$

Il existe néanmoins quelques différences entre les vecteurs de l'espace et les vecteurs du plan. Ainsi, bien que deux vecteurs non parallèles de l'espace soient linéairement indépendants, ils ne forment pas une base de l'espace. En effet, deux **vecteurs** de l'espace sont nécessairement **coplanaires** et ils ne peuvent pas engendrer un vecteur n'appartenant pas au plan qu'ils déterminent. Ainsi, on ne peut pas écrire le vecteur $\vec{w}$ représenté dans la figure suivante comme une combinaison linéaire des vecteurs $\vec{u}$ et $\vec{v}$, qui sont coplanaires. En effet, toute combinaison linéaire de deux vecteurs $\vec{u}$ et $\vec{v}$ non parallèles donne un vecteur qui appartient à un plan parallèle au plan déterminé par $\vec{u}$ et $\vec{v}$.

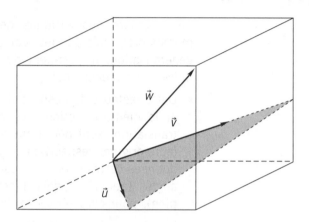

Il faut donc trois vecteurs non coplanaires pour engendrer les vecteurs de l'espace, noté $\mathbb{R}^3$ et appelé **espace euclidien de dimension trois**. Les vecteurs $\vec{u}$, $\vec{v}$ et $\vec{w}$ représentés dans la figure ne sont pas coplanaires; ils engendrent l'ensemble des vecteurs de l'espace.

Nous allons voir sous peu qu'on peut également définir des opérations spécifiques aux vecteurs de l'espace, soit le produit vectoriel et le produit mixte.

Exemple

La figure suivante représente un parallélépipède rectangle[1] dont les arêtes mesurent respectivement 3, 4 et 5 unités.

VECTEURS COPLANAIRES

Des vecteurs sont dits coplanaires s'ils appartiennent à un même plan lorsqu'ils sont issus d'une même origine.

ESPACE EUCLIDIEN DE DIMENSION TROIS

L'espace euclidien de dimension trois est l'ensemble des vecteurs de l'espace.

---

1. Un parallélépipède rectangle est un polyèdre à six faces rectangulaires, parallèles deux à deux.

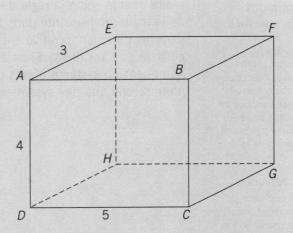

Il est clair que $\overrightarrow{AD} = \overrightarrow{EH}$, $\overrightarrow{AC} = \overrightarrow{EG}$, $\overrightarrow{AB} = -\overrightarrow{CD}$, $\overrightarrow{AE} + \overrightarrow{EC} = \overrightarrow{AC}$, $\overrightarrow{EF} + \overrightarrow{EH} = \overrightarrow{EG}$, etc. De plus, en vertu du théorème de Pythagore,

$$\|\overrightarrow{AH}\| = \sqrt{4^2 + 3^2} = \sqrt{25} = 5 \text{ unités}$$
$$\|\overrightarrow{DG}\| = \sqrt{5^2 + 3^2} = \sqrt{34} \approx 5{,}8 \text{ unités}$$

Enfin, toujours d'après le théorème de Pythagore, on a

$$\begin{aligned}
\|\overrightarrow{AG}\|^2 &= \|\overrightarrow{AH}\|^2 + \|\overrightarrow{HG}\|^2 \\
&= \|\overrightarrow{AE}\|^2 + \|\overrightarrow{EH}\|^2 + \|\overrightarrow{HG}\|^2 \\
&= 3^2 + 4^2 + 5^2 \\
&= 50
\end{aligned}$$

d'où $\|\overrightarrow{AG}\| = \sqrt{50}$ unités.

EXERCICE 8.1

Soit le parallélépipède de l'exemple précédent.

a) Trouvez un vecteur égal à chacune des sommes suivantes :
$$\overrightarrow{AB} + \overrightarrow{DH} \text{ et } \overrightarrow{AD} + \overrightarrow{HG} + \overrightarrow{CB}$$

b) Que valent $\|\overrightarrow{AD} + \overrightarrow{HG}\|$ et $\|\overrightarrow{EC}\|$?

8.2 SYSTÈME DE COORDONNÉES DE L'ESPACE

SYSTÈME D'AXES DIRECT

Un système d'axes direct est un système d'axes orienté selon la règle de la main droite.

Tout comme on le fait dans le plan, il est possible d'établir un système de coordonnées dans l'espace. On choisit d'abord un point de l'espace, noté O, comme origine du système de coordonnées cartésiennes. On trace ensuite trois axes perpendiculaires, nommés axe des x, axe des y et axe des z. L'axe des z est habituellement vertical et les deux autres axes sont horizontaux. Par convention, on choisit un **système d'axes** dit **direct**, c'est-à-dire orienté selon la **règle de la main droite**. Dans un tel système, l'index de la main droite pointe dans la direction positive de l'axe des x, le majeur dans la direction positive de l'axe des y et le pouce dans la direction positive de l'axe des z. Si on applique la même règle avec la main gauche, on obtient un **système d'axes** dit **rétrograde**. Dans le présent manuel, nous n'utiliserons que des systèmes d'axes directs.

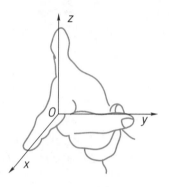

EXERCICE 8.2

Identifiez correctement la direction positive des axes de manière à obtenir un système direct.

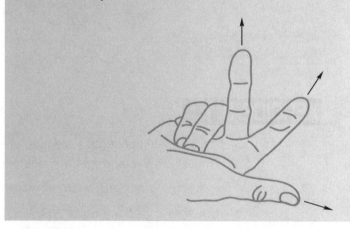

On définit, à l'aide des trois axes, trois plans de coordonnées perpendiculaires : le plan xy qui contient l'axe des x et l'axe des y ; le plan xz qui contient l'axe des x et l'axe des z ; et le plan yz qui contient l'axe des y et l'axe des z. Un point de l'espace est défini de façon unique par les distances orientées à chacun des plans de coordonnées. La première coordonnée d'un point (appelée abscisse) donne la distance orientée du point au plan yz ; la seconde coordonnée, appelée ordonnée, donne la distance orientée du point au plan xz ; et la troisième coordonnée, appelée **cote**, donne la distance orientée du point au plan xy.

Exemple

Le graphique suivant représente les points $P(2, 3, 5)$ et $Q(4, -5, -2)$ et le vecteur $\overrightarrow{PQ}$ dans un système de coordonnées direct de l'espace.

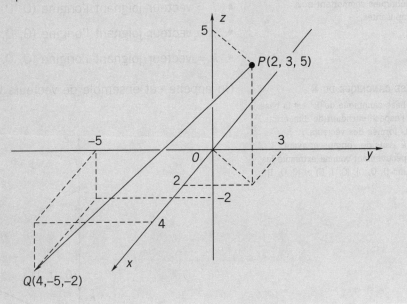

EXERCICE 8.3

Placez les points $P(2, 2, 2)$ et $Q(-2, -4, 1)$ et tracez le vecteur $\overrightarrow{PQ}$ dans un système de coordonnées cartésiennes.

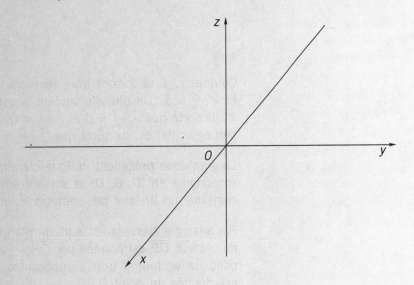

ESPACE EUCLIDIEN DE DIMENSION TROIS

L'espace euclidien de dimension trois est l'ensemble des vecteurs algébriques comportant trois composantes.

Tout comme les vecteurs du plan, les vecteurs de l'**espace euclidien de dimension trois** s'écrivent sous forme algébrique. On définit d'abord trois vecteurs de l'espace qui serviront de base:

- $\vec{i}$ = vecteur joignant l'origine (0, 0, 0) au point (1, 0, 0);
- $\vec{j}$ = vecteur joignant l'origine (0, 0, 0) au point (0, 1, 0);
- $\vec{k}$ = vecteur joignant l'origine (0, 0, 0) au point (0, 0, 1).

On appelle cet ensemble de vecteurs **base canonique de** $\mathbb{R}^3$.

BASE CANONIQUE DE $\mathbb{R}^3$

La base canonique de $\mathbb{R}^3$ est la base de l'espace euclidien de dimension trois formée des vecteurs $\vec{i}$, $\vec{j}$ et $\vec{k}$ issus de l'origine et ayant respectivement comme extrémité les points (1, 0, 0), (0, 1, 0) et (0, 0, 1).

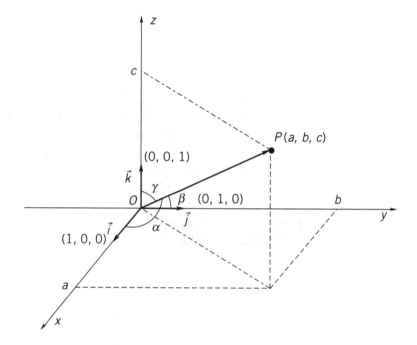

Comme $\vec{i}$, $\vec{j}$ et $\vec{k}$ sont trois vecteurs unitaires, on a $\vec{i} \cdot \vec{i} = 1$, $\vec{j} \cdot \vec{j} = 1$ et $\vec{k} \cdot \vec{k} = 1$. De plus, le vecteur $\vec{i}$ est perpendiculaire aux vecteurs $\vec{j}$ et $\vec{k}$, de sorte que $\vec{i} \cdot \vec{j} = 0$ et $\vec{i} \cdot \vec{k} = 0$. Les vecteurs $\vec{j}$ et $\vec{k}$ sont également perpendiculaires, de sorte que $\vec{j} \cdot \vec{k} = 0$.

Le graphique précédent indique clairement qu'un rayon vecteur $\overrightarrow{OP}$, ayant son origine en (0, 0, 0) et son extrémité en (a, b, c), s'écrit comme une combinaison linéaire des vecteurs $\vec{i}$, $\vec{j}$ et $\vec{k}$: $\overrightarrow{OP} = a\vec{i} + b\vec{j} + c\vec{k}$.

Par analogie avec les vecteurs du plan, la forme algébrique (ou matricielle) du vecteur $\overrightarrow{OP}$ est donnée par $\overrightarrow{OP} = \begin{bmatrix} a & b & c \end{bmatrix}$. Le rayon vecteur $\overrightarrow{OP}$ est donc un vecteur à trois composantes, qui correspondent chacune à une coordonnée du point P.

On calcule la longueur du vecteur $\overrightarrow{OP} = \begin{bmatrix} a & b & c \end{bmatrix}$ en appliquant le théorème de Pythagore : $\|\overrightarrow{OP}\| = \sqrt{a^2 + b^2 + c^2}$. Des constatations qui précèdent et de la distributivité du produit scalaire par rapport à l'addition de vecteurs, on déduit que $\overrightarrow{OP} \cdot \vec{i} = a$, $\overrightarrow{OP} \cdot \vec{j} = b$ et $\overrightarrow{OP} \cdot \vec{k} = c$.

Quant à la direction du vecteur $\overrightarrow{OP} = \begin{bmatrix} a & b & c \end{bmatrix}$, elle est donnée par les **angles directeurs**, α, β et γ, entre $\overrightarrow{OP}$ et les vecteurs $\vec{i}$, $\vec{j}$ et $\vec{k}$ respectivement. La valeur de chacun de ces angles se calcule à l'aide du produit scalaire. Ainsi, la valeur de l'angle entre les vecteurs $\overrightarrow{OP}$ et $\vec{i}$ est tirée de $\overrightarrow{OP} \cdot \vec{i} = \|\overrightarrow{OP}\| \|\vec{i}\| \cos \alpha$. Par conséquent,

$$\alpha = \text{arc cos}\left(\frac{\overrightarrow{OP} \cdot \vec{i}}{\|\overrightarrow{OP}\| \|\vec{i}\|}\right) = \text{arc cos}\left(\frac{\overrightarrow{OP} \cdot \vec{i}}{\|\overrightarrow{OP}\|}\right) = \text{arc cos}\left(\frac{a}{\sqrt{a^2 + b^2 + c^2}}\right)$$

De façon analogue,

$$\beta = \text{arc cos}\left(\frac{b}{\sqrt{a^2 + b^2 + c^2}}\right) \quad \text{et} \quad \gamma = \text{arc cos}\left(\frac{c}{\sqrt{a^2 + b^2 + c^2}}\right)$$

Comme les angles directeurs représentent des angles entre deux vecteurs, on choisit les valeurs comprises entre 0° et 180° (ou entre 0 radian et π radians).

Les **cosinus directeurs** du vecteur $\overrightarrow{OP} = \begin{bmatrix} a & b & c \end{bmatrix}$ sont égaux aux cosinus des angles directeurs :

$$\cos \alpha = \frac{a}{\sqrt{a^2 + b^2 + c^2}}, \quad \cos \beta = \frac{b}{\sqrt{a^2 + b^2 + c^2}} \quad \text{et} \quad \cos \gamma = \frac{c}{\sqrt{a^2 + b^2 + c^2}}$$

ANGLES DIRECTEURS D'UN VECTEUR

Les angles directeurs d'un vecteur $\vec{u} = \begin{bmatrix} u_1 & u_2 & u_3 \end{bmatrix}$ de l'espace donnent la direction de ce vecteur. Ils sont notés α, β et γ, et représentent respectivement les angles que $\vec{u}$ détermine avec les vecteurs $\vec{i}$, $\vec{j}$ et $\vec{k}$ de la base canonique de $\mathbb{R}^3$. Les angles directeurs de $\vec{u}$ sont donnés par

$$\alpha = \text{arc cos}\left(\frac{u_1}{\sqrt{u_1^2 + u_2^2 + u_3^2}}\right)$$

$$\beta = \text{arc cos}\left(\frac{u_2}{\sqrt{u_1^2 + u_2^2 + u_3^2}}\right)$$

$$\gamma = \text{arc cos}\left(\frac{u_3}{\sqrt{u_1^2 + u_2^2 + u_3^2}}\right)$$

COSINUS DIRECTEURS D'UN VECTEUR

Les cosinus directeurs d'un vecteur sont les cosinus des angles directeurs de ce vecteur.

Exemple

La longueur du vecteur $\vec{u} = \begin{bmatrix} 2 & -3 & -5 \end{bmatrix}$ est donnée par $\|\vec{u}\| = \sqrt{2^2 + (-3)^2 + (-5)^2} = \sqrt{38} \approx 6{,}2$ unités, et les cosinus directeurs de $\vec{u}$ sont :

$$\cos \alpha = \frac{2}{\sqrt{38}} \qquad \cos \beta = \frac{-3}{\sqrt{38}} \qquad \cos \gamma = \frac{-5}{\sqrt{38}}$$

De plus, les angles directeurs du vecteur $\vec{u}$ sont :

$$\alpha = \text{arc cos}\left(\frac{2}{\sqrt{38}}\right) \approx 71{,}1°$$

$$\beta = \text{arc cos}\left(\frac{-3}{\sqrt{38}}\right) \approx 119{,}1°$$

$$\gamma = \text{arc cos}\left(\frac{-5}{\sqrt{38}}\right) \approx 144{,}2°$$

1. En employant les valeurs des cosinus directeurs de $\vec{u}$ déterminées dans l'exemple précédent, calculez $\cos^2\alpha + \cos^2\beta + \cos^2\gamma$.

2. Soit α, β et γ, les angles directeurs d'un vecteur $\vec{v} = \begin{bmatrix} a & b & c \end{bmatrix}$. Exprimez le vecteur $\vec{w} = \begin{bmatrix} \cos\alpha & \cos\beta & \cos\gamma \end{bmatrix}$ en fonction de $\vec{v}$. Quel est le module du vecteur $\vec{w}$?

3. Soit α, β et γ, les angles directeurs d'un vecteur de l'espace. Montrez que $\cos^2\alpha + \cos^2\beta + \cos^2\gamma = 1$.

Par analogie avec les vecteurs du plan, le vecteur joignant les points $A(a_1, a_2, a_3)$ et $B(b_1, b_2, b_3)$ s'écrit comme une combinaison linéaire des vecteurs $\vec{i}$, $\vec{j}$ et $\vec{k}$:

$$\begin{aligned}
\vec{AB} &= \vec{AO} + \vec{OB} \\
&= -\vec{OA} + \vec{OB} \\
&= -(a_1\vec{i} + a_2\vec{j} + a_3\vec{k}) + (b_1\vec{i} + b_2\vec{j} + b_3\vec{k}) \\
&= (b_1 - a_1)\vec{i} + (b_2 - a_2)\vec{j} + (b_3 - a_3)\vec{k}
\end{aligned}$$

On écrit le vecteur $\vec{AB}$ sous forme algébrique (ou matricielle) en ne conservant que les coefficients des vecteurs $\vec{i}$, $\vec{j}$ et $\vec{k}$, c'est-à-dire que

$$\vec{AB} = \begin{bmatrix} b_1 - a_1 & b_2 - a_2 & b_3 - a_3 \end{bmatrix}$$

On peut interpréter la forme algébrique de $\vec{AB}$ en fonction d'un déplacement de A vers B. Ainsi, le vecteur $\vec{AB}$ s'obtient en effectuant un déplacement selon l'axe des x d'une distance de $b_1 - a_1$, suivi d'un déplacement selon l'axe des y d'une distance de $b_2 - a_2$ et d'un déplacement selon l'axe des z d'une distance de $b_3 - a_3$. Sous forme vectorielle, ces déplacements s'écrivent respectivement $(b_1 - a_1)\vec{i}$, $(b_2 - a_2)\vec{j}$ et $(b_3 - a_3)\vec{k}$. Le vecteur $\vec{AB}$ est la somme de ces trois déplacements:

$$\begin{aligned}
\vec{AB} &= (b_1 - a_1)\vec{i} + (b_2 - a_2)\vec{j} + (b_3 - a_3)\vec{k} \\
&= \begin{bmatrix} b_1 - a_1 & b_2 - a_2 & b_3 - a_3 \end{bmatrix}
\end{aligned}$$

La longueur du vecteur $\vec{AB}$ est donnée par

$$\|\vec{AB}\| = \sqrt{(b_1 - a_1)^2 + (b_2 - a_2)^2 + (b_3 - a_3)^2}$$

ce qui correspond à la distance entre les points A et B.

Quels sont les composantes, le module, les cosinus directeurs et les angles directeurs du vecteur qui a pour origine $A(1, 4, -6)$ et pour extrémité $B(-1, 3, 2)$?

Les vecteurs de $\mathbb{R}^3$ étant des matrices de format 1×3, l'égalité de deux vecteurs algébriques et les opérations d'addition et de multiplication par un scalaire sont définies de la même façon que pour les matrices; de plus, les propriétés de ces opérations sont de ce fait déjà démontrées. Que les mathématiques sont efficaces! La définition du produit scalaire de deux vecteurs de $\mathbb{R}^3$ est simplement une extension de la définition du produit scalaire de deux vecteurs de $\mathbb{R}^2$. Le tableau 8.1 indique clairement que les seules différences notables entre les vecteurs de $\mathbb{R}^2$ et de $\mathbb{R}^3$ sont les suivantes:

- un vecteur de $\mathbb{R}^2$ compte deux composantes alors qu'un vecteur de $\mathbb{R}^3$ en compte trois;
- la direction d'un vecteur de $\mathbb{R}^2$ est donnée par un angle alors que celle d'un vecteur de $\mathbb{R}^3$ est donnée par trois angles.

TABLEAU 8.1   **Parallèle entre les relations et les opérations sur les vecteurs de $\mathbb{R}^2$ et de $\mathbb{R}^3$**

	Vecteurs de $\mathbb{R}^2$	**Vecteurs de $\mathbb{R}^3$**
VECTEURS	$\vec{u} = \begin{bmatrix} u_1 & u_2 \end{bmatrix}$ et $\vec{v} = \begin{bmatrix} v_1 & v_2 \end{bmatrix}$	$\vec{u} = \begin{bmatrix} u_1 & u_2 & u_3 \end{bmatrix}$ et $\vec{v} = \begin{bmatrix} v_1 & v_2 & v_3 \end{bmatrix}$
VECTEUR NUL	$\vec{0} = \begin{bmatrix} 0 & 0 \end{bmatrix}$	$\vec{0} = \begin{bmatrix} 0 & 0 & 0 \end{bmatrix}$
ÉGALITÉ	$\vec{u} = \vec{v} \Leftrightarrow u_1 = v_1$ et $u_2 = v_2$	$\vec{u} = \vec{v} \Leftrightarrow u_1 = v_1,\ u_2 = v_2$ et $u_3 = v_3$
MODULE	$\|\vec{u}\| = \sqrt{u_1^2 + u_2^2}$	$\|\vec{u}\| = \sqrt{u_1^2 + u_2^2 + u_3^2}$
DIRECTION DU VECTEUR $\vec{u}$	$\theta = \text{arc tg}\, \dfrac{u_2}{u_1}$	$\alpha = \text{arc cos}\left(\dfrac{u_1}{\sqrt{u_1^2 + u_2^2 + u_3^2}} \right)$ $\beta = \text{arc cos}\left(\dfrac{u_2}{\sqrt{u_1^2 + u_2^2 + u_3^2}} \right)$ $\gamma = \text{arc cos}\left(\dfrac{u_3}{\sqrt{u_1^2 + u_2^2 + u_3^2}} \right)$
ADDITION	$\vec{u} + \vec{v} = \begin{bmatrix} u_1 + v_1 & u_2 + v_2 \end{bmatrix}$	$\vec{u} + \vec{v} = \begin{bmatrix} u_1 + v_1 & u_2 + v_2 & u_3 + v_3 \end{bmatrix}$
MULTIPLICATION PAR UN SCALAIRE k	$k\vec{u} = \begin{bmatrix} ku_1 & ku_2 \end{bmatrix}$	$k\vec{u} = \begin{bmatrix} ku_1 & ku_2 & ku_3 \end{bmatrix}$
PRODUIT SCALAIRE	$\vec{u} \cdot \vec{v} = u_1 v_1 + u_2 v_2$	$\vec{u} \cdot \vec{v} = u_1 v_1 + u_2 v_2 + u_3 v_3$
ANGLE ENTRE DEUX VECTEURS $\vec{u}$ ET $\vec{v}$	$\varphi = \text{arc cos}\, \dfrac{\vec{u} \cdot \vec{v}}{\|\vec{u}\|\,\|\vec{v}\|}$	$\varphi = \text{arc cos}\, \dfrac{\vec{u} \cdot \vec{v}}{\|\vec{u}\|\,\|\vec{v}\|}$
PROJECTION ($\vec{u}_{\vec{v}}$)	$\vec{u}_{\vec{v}} = \dfrac{\vec{u} \cdot \vec{v}}{\vec{v} \cdot \vec{v}}\vec{v}$	$\vec{u}_{\vec{v}} = \dfrac{\vec{u} \cdot \vec{v}}{\vec{v} \cdot \vec{v}}\vec{v}$

Les propriétés des vecteurs du plan énoncées dans les théorèmes 5.1 (p. 175), 5.2 (p. 181) et 5.4 (p. 186) restent valables pour les vecteurs de l'espace. En particulier, il est utile de se rappeler que le produit scalaire de deux vecteurs non nuls est zéro si et seulement si les deux vecteurs sont perpendiculaires.

Exemple

Si $\vec{u} = \begin{bmatrix} 1 & 2 & 3 \end{bmatrix}$, $\vec{v} = \begin{bmatrix} -1 & -1 & 1 \end{bmatrix}$ et $\vec{w} = \begin{bmatrix} 1 & 3 & 7 \end{bmatrix}$, alors

$$3\vec{u} + 2\vec{v} + \vec{w} = 3\begin{bmatrix} 1 & 2 & 3 \end{bmatrix} + 2\begin{bmatrix} -1 & -1 & 1 \end{bmatrix} + \begin{bmatrix} 1 & 3 & 7 \end{bmatrix}$$
$$= \begin{bmatrix} 2 & 7 & 18 \end{bmatrix}$$

Les vecteurs $\vec{u}$ et $\vec{v}$ sont perpendiculaires parce que leur produit scalaire vaut 0. En effet,

$$\vec{u} \cdot \vec{v} = 1(-1) + 2(-1) + 3(1) = 0$$

L'angle entre les vecteurs $\vec{u}$ et $\vec{w}$ est donné par

$$\varphi = \arccos \frac{\vec{u} \cdot \vec{w}}{\|\vec{u}\| \, \|\vec{w}\|}$$
$$= \arccos \frac{1(1) + 2(3) + 3(7)}{(\sqrt{1^2 + 2^2 + 3^2})(\sqrt{1^2 + 3^2 + 7^2})}$$
$$= \arccos \frac{28}{\sqrt{826}}$$
$$\approx 13{,}0°$$

On peut exprimer le vecteur $\vec{w}$ comme une combinaison linéaire des vecteurs $\vec{u}$ et $\vec{v}$. En effet,

$$\vec{w} = a\vec{u} + b\vec{v} \quad \Rightarrow \quad \begin{bmatrix} 1 & 3 & 7 \end{bmatrix} = \begin{bmatrix} a - b & 2a - b & 3a + b \end{bmatrix}$$

On tire de la dernière égalité le système d'équations

$$a - b = 1$$
$$2a - b = 3$$
$$3a + b = 7$$

dont la solution est $a = 2$ et $b = 1$. Ainsi, $\vec{w} = 2\vec{u} + \vec{v}$.

Les vecteurs $\vec{u}$, $\vec{v}$ et $\vec{w}$ ne sont donc pas linéairement indépendants. En effet, nous venons de montrer que $\vec{w} = 2\vec{u} + \vec{v}$, d'où on tire $\vec{w} - 2\vec{u} - \vec{v} = \vec{0}$. Il existe donc une combinaison linéaire des vecteurs $\vec{u}$, $\vec{v}$ et $\vec{w}$ qui est égale au vecteur nul et dont au moins l'un des coefficients est non nul. Par conséquent, ces trois vecteurs n'étant pas linéairement indépendants, ils ne forment pas une base de $\mathbb{R}^3$.

EXERCICE 8.6

Soit les vecteurs $\vec{u} = \begin{bmatrix} 1 & 2 & 3 \end{bmatrix}$, $\vec{v} = \begin{bmatrix} -1 & -1 & 1 \end{bmatrix}$ et $\vec{w} = \begin{bmatrix} 2 & 1 & -2 \end{bmatrix}$.

a) Que vaut $\vec{u} - 2\vec{v} + 3\vec{w}$?

b) Exprimez le vecteur $\vec{s} = \begin{bmatrix} 4 & 1 & 2 \end{bmatrix}$ comme une combinaison linéaire des vecteurs $\vec{u}$, $\vec{v}$ et $\vec{w}$.

c) Quel est l'angle entre les vecteurs $\vec{u}$ et $\vec{w}$?

d) Les vecteurs $\vec{u}$, $\vec{v}$ et $\vec{w}$ sont-ils linéairement indépendants ? Justifiez votre réponse.

e) Les vecteurs $\vec{u}$, $\vec{v}$ et $\vec{w}$ forment-ils un système générateur de $\mathbb{R}^3$?

f) Que peut-on dire des vecteurs $\vec{u}$, $\vec{v}$ et $\vec{w}$?

8.4 PRODUIT VECTORIEL

Nous abordons maintenant une opération propre aux vecteurs de l'espace, soit le produit vectoriel. Tout comme le produit mixte, que nous présenterons plus loin, le produit vectoriel est défini seulement pour des vecteurs de $\mathbb{R}^3$. Par contre, on peut transformer tout vecteur de $\mathbb{R}^2$ en un vecteur de l'espace en y ajoutant une cote égale à zéro. Il ne faut cependant pas en conclure que $\mathbb{R}^2$ est un sous-ensemble de $\mathbb{R}^3$. En effet, les vecteurs de $\mathbb{R}^2$ n'ont que deux composantes alors que ceux de $\mathbb{R}^3$ en ont trois. Toutefois, on peut considérer que $\mathbb{R}^2$ est équivalent à un sous-ensemble W de $\mathbb{R}^3$, soit le sous-ensemble formé des vecteurs dont la cote est nulle.

8.4.1 DÉFINITION DU PRODUIT VECTORIEL

PRODUIT VECTORIEL

Le produit vectoriel des vecteurs
$\vec{u} = \begin{bmatrix} u_1 & u_2 & u_3 \end{bmatrix}$ et
$\vec{v} = \begin{bmatrix} v_1 & v_2 & v_3 \end{bmatrix}$ est un vecteur
noté $\vec{u} \times \vec{v}$ et défini par

$$\vec{u} \times \vec{v} = \begin{vmatrix} \vec{i} & \vec{j} & \vec{k} \\ u_1 & u_2 & u_3 \\ v_1 & v_2 & v_3 \end{vmatrix}$$

Le **produit vectoriel** de $\vec{u} = \begin{bmatrix} u_1 & u_2 & u_3 \end{bmatrix}$ et $\vec{v} = \begin{bmatrix} v_1 & v_2 & v_3 \end{bmatrix}$ est un vecteur noté $\vec{u} \times \vec{v}$. On définit ce vecteur à l'aide d'un déterminant[2] dont la première ligne est formée des symboles $\vec{i}$, $\vec{j}$ et $\vec{k}$, dans cet ordre, dont la deuxième ligne est formée des composantes du vecteur $\vec{u}$ et dont la troisième ligne est formée des composantes du vecteur $\vec{v}$. On obtient l'expression du produit vectoriel en développant ce déterminant selon la première ligne :

---

2. Il ne s'agit pas d'un véritable déterminant : un déterminant est un nombre et non un vecteur. Toutefois, cet emploi abusif du concept de déterminant pour définir le produit vectoriel est toléré, et même largement répandu, parce que c'est un moyen vraiment commode de se souvenir de l'expression du produit vectoriel. De plus, on pourra faire appel aux propriétés des déterminants pour prouver certaines propriétés du produit vectoriel.

$$\vec{u} \times \vec{v} = \begin{vmatrix} \vec{i} & \vec{j} & \vec{k} \\ u_1 & u_2 & u_3 \\ v_1 & v_2 & v_3 \end{vmatrix}$$

$$= (u_2 v_3 - u_3 v_2)\vec{i} - (u_1 v_3 - u_3 v_1)\vec{j} + (u_1 v_2 - u_2 v_1)\vec{k}$$

$$= \begin{bmatrix} u_2 v_3 - u_3 v_2 & u_3 v_1 - u_1 v_3 & u_1 v_2 - u_2 v_1 \end{bmatrix}$$

Il est à noter que l'ordre des vecteurs dans un produit vectoriel a de l'importance. Ainsi, pour calculer le produit vectoriel $\vec{u} \times \vec{v}$, on place les composantes de $\vec{u}$ dans la deuxième ligne du déterminant, et celles de $\vec{v}$ dans la troisième ligne. Par contre, pour calculer le produit vectoriel $\vec{v} \times \vec{u}$, on place les composantes de $\vec{v}$ dans la deuxième ligne, et celles de $\vec{u}$ dans la troisième ligne.

Exemple

Si $\vec{u} = \begin{bmatrix} 1 & 2 & 3 \end{bmatrix}$ et $\vec{v} = \begin{bmatrix} -1 & -1 & 2 \end{bmatrix}$, alors

$$\vec{u} \times \vec{v} = \begin{vmatrix} \vec{i} & \vec{j} & \vec{k} \\ u_1 & u_2 & u_3 \\ v_1 & v_2 & v_3 \end{vmatrix}$$

$$= \begin{vmatrix} \vec{i} & \vec{j} & \vec{k} \\ 1 & 2 & 3 \\ -1 & -1 & 2 \end{vmatrix}$$

$$= 7\vec{i} - 5\vec{j} + \vec{k}$$

$$= \begin{bmatrix} 7 & -5 & 1 \end{bmatrix}$$

et

$$\vec{v} \times \vec{u} = \begin{vmatrix} \vec{i} & \vec{j} & \vec{k} \\ v_1 & v_2 & v_3 \\ u_1 & u_2 & u_3 \end{vmatrix}$$

$$= \begin{vmatrix} \vec{i} & \vec{j} & \vec{k} \\ -1 & -1 & 2 \\ 1 & 2 & 3 \end{vmatrix}$$

$$= -7\vec{i} + 5\vec{j} - \vec{k}$$

$$= \begin{bmatrix} -7 & 5 & -1 \end{bmatrix}$$

Cet exemple montre bien que le produit vectoriel n'est pas commutatif : $\vec{u} \times \vec{v} \neq \vec{v} \times \vec{u}$.

Toutefois, on note que $\vec{u} \times \vec{v} = -\vec{v} \times \vec{u}$. En fait, il s'agit là d'une propriété générale du produit vectoriel, dont la démonstration découle directement des propriétés des déterminants, même si, comme nous l'avons déjà souligné, le produit vectoriel n'est pas un véritable déterminant. En effet, si on intervertit deux lignes d'un déterminant, on en change le signe.

Soit les vecteurs $\vec{u} = \begin{bmatrix} 1 & 2 & 3 \end{bmatrix}$ et $\vec{w} = \begin{bmatrix} -2 & -4 & -6 \end{bmatrix}$.

a) Vérifiez que les vecteurs $\vec{u}$ et $\vec{w}$ sont parallèles.

b) Que vaut $\vec{u} \times \vec{w}$?

c) Le résultat obtenu en b) est-il fortuit ou est-ce une caractéristique des vecteurs parallèles ? Justifiez votre réponse.

Le théorème 8.1 énonce une propriété particulièrement importante du produit vectoriel.

Théorème 8.1

Le produit vectoriel, $\vec{u} \times \vec{v}$, de deux vecteurs $\vec{u}$ et $\vec{v}$ non nuls et non parallèles est un vecteur perpendiculaire aux vecteurs $\vec{u}$ et $\vec{v}$.

Preuve

Soit $\vec{u} = \begin{bmatrix} u_1 & u_2 & u_3 \end{bmatrix}$ et $\vec{v} = \begin{bmatrix} v_1 & v_2 & v_3 \end{bmatrix}$. Pour démontrer que le vecteur $\vec{u} \times \vec{v}$ est perpendiculaire au vecteur $\vec{u}$, il faut montrer que le produit scalaire de ces deux vecteurs est 0, c'est-à-dire que $\vec{u} \cdot (\vec{u} \times \vec{v}) = 0$. Or,

$$\begin{aligned} \vec{u} \cdot (\vec{u} \times \vec{v}) &= \begin{bmatrix} u_1 & u_2 & u_3 \end{bmatrix} \cdot \begin{bmatrix} u_2 v_3 - u_3 v_2 & u_3 v_1 - u_1 v_3 & u_1 v_2 - u_2 v_1 \end{bmatrix} \\ &= u_1(u_2 v_3 - u_3 v_2) + u_2(u_3 v_1 - u_1 v_3) + u_3(u_1 v_2 - u_2 v_1) \\ &= u_1 u_2 v_3 - u_1 u_3 v_2 + u_2 u_3 v_1 - u_2 u_1 v_3 + u_3 u_1 v_2 - u_3 u_2 v_1 \\ &= 0 \end{aligned}$$

Par conséquent, $\vec{u} \times \vec{v}$ est perpendiculaire à $\vec{u}$.

On applique le même raisonnement pour montrer que $\vec{u} \times \vec{v}$ est perpendiculaire à $\vec{v}$. ∎

Grâce à ce théorème, il est très facile de trouver un vecteur perpendiculaire à deux vecteurs donnés : il suffit de calculer un produit vectoriel.

Exemple

Pour trouver un vecteur perpendiculaire aux vecteurs $\vec{u} = \begin{bmatrix} -2 & 1 & 2 \end{bmatrix}$ et $\vec{v} = \begin{bmatrix} 1 & 1 & 4 \end{bmatrix}$, il suffit de calculer le produit vectoriel de ces deux vecteurs :

$$\vec{u} \times \vec{v} = \begin{vmatrix} \vec{i} & \vec{j} & \vec{k} \\ u_1 & u_2 & u_3 \\ v_1 & v_2 & v_3 \end{vmatrix}$$

$$= \begin{vmatrix} \vec{i} & \vec{j} & \vec{k} \\ -2 & 1 & 2 \\ 1 & 1 & 4 \end{vmatrix}$$

$$= 2\vec{i} + 10\vec{j} - 3\vec{k}$$

$$= \begin{bmatrix} 2 & 10 & -3 \end{bmatrix}$$

Le vecteur $\begin{bmatrix} 2 & 10 & -3 \end{bmatrix}$ est donc perpendiculaire aux vecteurs $\begin{bmatrix} -2 & 1 & 2 \end{bmatrix}$ et $\begin{bmatrix} 1 & 1 & 4 \end{bmatrix}$.

EXERCICE 8.8

Quels sont les deux vecteurs unitaires perpendiculaires aux vecteurs $\vec{u} = \begin{bmatrix} 3 & 2 & 3 \end{bmatrix}$ et $\vec{v} = \begin{bmatrix} -2 & -4 & 1 \end{bmatrix}$?

8.4.2 DIRECTION DU PRODUIT VECTORIEL

Le théorème 8.1 indique que le produit vectoriel de deux vecteurs est un vecteur perpendiculaire à ces deux vecteurs, et donc perpendiculaire au plan qu'ils déterminent. Or, en théorie, un vecteur perpendiculaire à un plan peut avoir l'une ou l'autre de deux directions opposées. Laquelle de ces directions est celle du produit vectoriel? L'analyse des produits vectoriels de toutes les paires de vecteurs formées avec $\vec{i}$, $\vec{j}$ et $\vec{k}$ permet de déduire une règle simple pour déterminer la direction d'un produit vectoriel.

D'après la définition du produit vectoriel,

$$\vec{i} \times \vec{j} = \vec{k} \qquad \vec{j} \times \vec{k} = \vec{i} \qquad \vec{k} \times \vec{i} = \vec{j}$$
$$\vec{j} \times \vec{i} = -\vec{k} \qquad \vec{k} \times \vec{j} = -\vec{i} \qquad \vec{i} \times \vec{k} = -\vec{j}$$

En effet, par exemple,

$$\vec{i} \times \vec{j} = \begin{vmatrix} \vec{i} & \vec{j} & \vec{k} \\ 1 & 0 & 0 \\ 0 & 1 & 0 \end{vmatrix} = 0\vec{i} + 0\vec{j} + \vec{k} = \vec{k}$$

La direction du vecteur $\vec{i} \times \vec{j}$ est indiquée par le pouce lorsqu'on referme la main droite en parcourant l'angle θ entre les vecteurs $\vec{i}$ et $\vec{j}$, depuis $\vec{i}$ jusqu'à $\vec{j}$, le poignet de la main droite étant situé à l'origine commune des deux vecteurs. Il en est de même pour la direction de tout produit vectoriel de deux vecteurs distincts de la base canonique. C'est donc cette règle,

La règle de la main droite sert à déterminer la direction du produit vectoriel. Ainsi, la direction de $\vec{u} \times \vec{v}$ est indiquée par le pouce lorsqu'on referme la main droite en parcourant l'angle θ entre les deux vecteurs, depuis $\vec{u}$ jusqu'à $\vec{v}$, le poignet de la main droite étant situé à l'origine commune des deux vecteurs.

appelée **règle de la main droite**, qui sert à déterminer la direction du produit vectoriel. Exercez-vous avec les graphiques suivants.

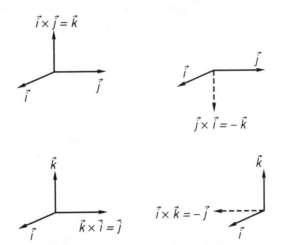

En général, la direction de $\vec{u} \times \vec{v}$ est indiquée par le pouce lorsqu'on referme la main droite en parcourant l'angle θ entre ces deux vecteurs, depuis $\vec{u}$ jusqu'à $\vec{v}$, le poignet de la main droite étant situé à l'origine commune des deux vecteurs. La figure suivante illustre cette technique.

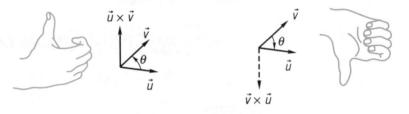

La direction du vecteur $\vec{u} \times \vec{v}$ est également donnée par la direction du pouce de la main droite lorsque l'index pointe dans la direction du premier vecteur, $\vec{u}$, et le majeur dans la direction du deuxième vecteur, $\vec{v}$. La figure suivante illustre cette technique.

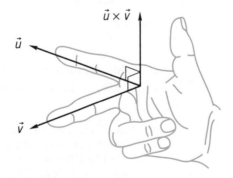

La règle de la vis est équivalente à la règle de la main droite. Elle sert à déterminer la direction du produit vectoriel. Ainsi, la direction du produit vectoriel $\vec{u} \times \vec{v}$ correspond à la direction dans laquelle se déplace une vis placée à l'origine commune des deux vecteurs lorsqu'on la fait tourner de $\vec{u}$ vers $\vec{v}$ en parcourant l'angle entre ces deux vecteurs.

Il existe une troisième façon de déterminer la direction du vecteur $\vec{u} \times \vec{v}$, soit la **règle de la vis**. Il suffit d'imaginer une vis placée à l'origine commune des deux vecteurs. On tourne la vis en parcourant l'angle entre les vecteurs $\vec{u}$ et $\vec{v}$, depuis $\vec{u}$ jusqu'à $\vec{v}$. La direction dans laquelle la vis se déplace (elle rentre dans le plan ou elle en sort) est la direction du vecteur $\vec{u} \times \vec{v}$.

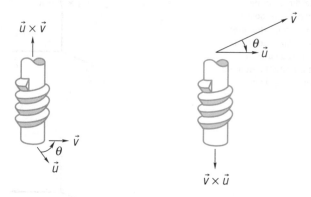

8.4.3 Interprétation géométrique du produit vectoriel

Tout comme pour le produit scalaire, il est possible d'exprimer le produit vectoriel de deux vecteurs non seulement en fonction de ses composantes, mais également en fonction des modules des deux vecteurs et de l'angle entre ces derniers. Pour cela, on a besoin du théorème suivant, appelé « identité de Lagrange[3] ».

Théorème 8.2 (Identité de Lagrange)

$$\|\vec{u} \times \vec{v}\|^2 = \|\vec{u}\|^2 \|\vec{v}\|^2 - (\vec{u} \cdot \vec{v})^2$$

Preuve

Si on pose $\vec{u} = \begin{bmatrix} u_1 & u_2 & u_3 \end{bmatrix}$ et $\vec{v} = \begin{bmatrix} v_1 & v_2 & v_3 \end{bmatrix}$, on a, d'une part,

$$\|\vec{u} \times \vec{v}\|^2 = \left\| \begin{bmatrix} u_2 v_3 - u_3 v_2 & u_3 v_1 - u_1 v_3 & u_1 v_2 - u_2 v_1 \end{bmatrix} \right\|^2$$
$$= (u_2 v_3 - u_3 v_2)^2 + (u_3 v_1 - u_1 v_3)^2 + (u_1 v_2 - u_2 v_1)^2$$

et, d'autre part,

$$\|\vec{u}\|^2 \|\vec{v}\|^2 - (\vec{u} \cdot \vec{v})^2$$
$$= (u_1^2 + u_2^2 + u_3^2)(v_1^2 + v_2^2 + v_3^2) - (u_1 v_1 + u_2 v_2 + u_3 v_3)^2$$

On déduit l'identité à prouver en développant le membre de droite de chacune des deux égalités. ∎

---

3. Le mathématicien Joseph Louis Lagrange (1736-1813) naquit à Turin, en Italie. Il occupa des postes de professeur de mathématiques à Turin et à Berlin avant d'accepter un poste similaire à l'École polytechnique. Inventeur du calcul des variations, auteur de nombreux traités, dont le plus célèbre est la *Mécanique analytique*, président influent de la commission qui a mis au point le système métrique, Lagrange est considéré comme le plus grand mathématicien de son époque et l'un des plus grands de toute l'histoire.

PRODUIT VECTORIEL

Le produit vectoriel de vecteurs $\vec{u}$ et $\vec{v}$ déterminant un angle θ est

$$\vec{u} \times \vec{v} = (\|\vec{u}\| \, \|\vec{v}\| \sin\theta)\vec{n}$$

où $\vec{n}$ est un vecteur unitaire perpendiculaire à chacun des vecteurs $\vec{u}$ et $\vec{v}$ et dont la direction est donnée par la règle de la main droite.

Si $\vec{u}$ et $\vec{v}$ sont des vecteurs non nuls et non parallèles, alors le **produit vectoriel** est donné par $\vec{u} \times \vec{v} = (\|\vec{u}\| \, \|\vec{v}\| \sin\theta)\vec{n}$ où θ représente l'angle entre les vecteurs $\vec{u}$ et $\vec{v}$, et $\vec{n}$ est un vecteur unitaire perpendiculaire à ces deux vecteurs et dont la direction est donnée par la règle de la main droite.

Preuve

Il faut montrer que $(\|\vec{u}\| \, \|\vec{v}\| \sin\theta)\vec{n}$ est un vecteur dont la direction et le module sont identiques à ceux du vecteur $\vec{u} \times \vec{v}$.

Or, $\|\vec{u}\| > 0$, $\|\vec{v}\| > 0$ et $\sin\theta > 0$ puisque $0° < \theta < 180°$. Donc, $(\|\vec{u}\| \, \|\vec{v}\| \sin\theta)\vec{n}$ a la même direction que $\vec{n}$ qui, par définition, a la même direction que $\vec{u} \times \vec{v}$. De plus, en vertu de l'identité de Lagrange,

$$\begin{aligned}
\|\vec{u} \times \vec{v}\|^2 &= \|\vec{u}\|^2 \|\vec{v}\|^2 - (\vec{u} \cdot \vec{v})^2 \\
&= \|\vec{u}\|^2 \|\vec{v}\|^2 - (\|\vec{u}\| \, \|\vec{v}\| \cos\theta)^2 \\
&= \|\vec{u}\|^2 \|\vec{v}\|^2 - \|\vec{u}\|^2 \|\vec{v}\|^2 \cos^2\theta \\
&= \|\vec{u}\|^2 \|\vec{v}\|^2 (1 - \cos^2\theta) \\
&= \|\vec{u}\|^2 \|\vec{v}\|^2 \sin^2\theta
\end{aligned}$$

Comme $0° < \theta < 180°$, alors $\sin\theta > 0$ et, par conséquent,

$$\|\vec{u} \times \vec{v}\| = \|\vec{u}\| \, \|\vec{v}\| \sin\theta$$

De plus, comme $\vec{n}$ est un vecteur unitaire,

$$\|\vec{u} \times \vec{v}\| = \|\vec{u}\| \, \|\vec{v}\| \sin\theta \|\vec{n}\|$$

Par conséquent, les vecteurs $\vec{u} \times \vec{v}$ et $(\|\vec{u}\| \, \|\vec{v}\| \sin\theta)\vec{n}$ ont le même module.

Nous avons établi que les vecteurs $\vec{u} \times \vec{v}$ et $(\|\vec{u}\| \, \|\vec{v}\| \sin\theta)\vec{n}$ ont le même module et la même direction. Ces deux vecteurs sont donc égaux, c'est-à-dire que

$$\vec{u} \times \vec{v} = (\|\vec{u}\| \, \|\vec{v}\| \sin\theta)\vec{n} \qquad \blacksquare$$

EXERCICE 8.9

Montrez que deux vecteurs non nuls sont parallèles si et seulement si leur produit vectoriel est le vecteur nul.

Le théorème 8.3 donne lieu à une interprétation géométrique intéressante. Soit un parallélogramme dont les côtés non parallèles sont déterminés par deux vecteurs $\vec{u}$ et $\vec{v}$ issus d'une même origine. L'aire de ce parallélogramme est égale au module du produit vectoriel de $\vec{u}$ et $\vec{v}$, soit $\|\vec{u} \times \vec{v}\|$.

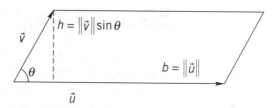

$h = \|\vec{v}\| \sin \theta$

$\vec{v}$

θ

$b = \|\vec{u}\|$

$\vec{u}$

En effet, l'aire d'un parallélogramme est égale au produit de la base par la hauteur : $A = bh$. Or, la figure indique clairement que

$$A = bh = \|\vec{u}\| \, \|\vec{v}\| \sin \theta = \|\vec{u} \times \vec{v}\|$$

Exemple

L'aire du parallélogramme dont deux côtés non parallèles sont déterminés par $\vec{u} = \begin{bmatrix} -2 & 1 & 2 \end{bmatrix}$ et $\vec{v} = \begin{bmatrix} 1 & 1 & 4 \end{bmatrix}$ est égale à $\|\vec{u} \times \vec{v}\|$. Or,

$$\vec{u} \times \vec{v} = \begin{vmatrix} \vec{i} & \vec{j} & \vec{k} \\ u_1 & u_2 & u_3 \\ v_1 & v_2 & v_3 \end{vmatrix}$$

$$= \begin{vmatrix} \vec{i} & \vec{j} & \vec{k} \\ -2 & 1 & 2 \\ 1 & 1 & 4 \end{vmatrix}$$

$$= 2\vec{i} + 10\vec{j} - 3\vec{k}$$

$$= \begin{bmatrix} 2 & 10 & -3 \end{bmatrix}$$

Par conséquent, l'aire du parallélogramme vaut $\|\vec{u} \times \vec{v}\|$, soit

$$\sqrt{2^2 + 10^2 + (-3)^2} = \sqrt{113} \approx 10{,}6 \text{ unités carrées}$$

EXERCICE 8.10

Trouvez l'aire du triangle dont deux côtés sont déterminés par $\vec{u} = \begin{bmatrix} 1 & 2 & 3 \end{bmatrix}$ et $\vec{v} = \begin{bmatrix} 2 & -1 & 2 \end{bmatrix}$. (Indice : Quel est le lien entre l'aire d'un triangle et l'aire du parallélogramme qui a deux côtés en commun avec le triangle ?)

8.4.4 INTERPRÉTATION PHYSIQUE DU PRODUIT VECTORIEL

Lorsqu'on veut changer un pneu, on desserre d'abord les boulons de la roue au moyen d'une clé. Plus le manche de la clé est long, plus le travail est facile parce que le moment de force dépend de la force exercée et de la distance entre le boulon et le point d'application de cette force.

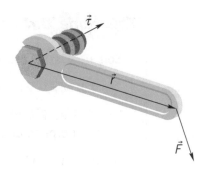

Soit $\vec{\tau}$, le moment de force d'une force $\vec{F}$ qui agit à une distance $\|\vec{r}\|$ de son point d'application, où $\vec{r}$ représente le rayon vecteur issu de l'axe de rotation. Le moment de force $\vec{\tau}$ est donné par l'expression $\vec{\tau} = \vec{r} \times \vec{F}$, et son intensité, $\tau = \|\vec{\tau}\|$, s'exprime en newtons-mètres (N·m). L'intensité du moment de force est égale au module du produit vectoriel :

$$\tau = \|\vec{\tau}\| = \|\vec{r}\|\,\|\vec{F}\|\sin\theta$$

où θ représente l'angle entre $\vec{F}$ et $\vec{r}$.

Exemple

L'intensité du moment de force qu'exerce sur un boulon une force de 50 N appliquée à l'extrémité d'une clé de 1 m de longueur lorsque la force fait un angle de 60° avec la clé est donnée par $\tau = \|\vec{\tau}\| = \|\vec{r}\|\,\|\vec{F}\|\sin\theta = (1)(50)\sin 60° = (50)(\sqrt{3}/2) \approx 43,3$ N·m.

EXERCICE 8.11

1. Montrez que si on double la longueur d'une clé, on double l'intensité du moment de force associé à une force appliquée à l'extrémité de la clé.

2. Quel angle une force agissant à l'extrémité d'une clé doit-elle déterminer avec le manche de la clé pour que le moment de force soit maximal ?

8.4.5 PROPRIÉTÉS DU PRODUIT VECTORIEL

Le produit vectoriel possède, comme les autres opérations vectorielles, des propriétés intéressantes, que nous avons regroupées dans le théorème 8.4. Nous avons déjà prouvé certaines de ces propriétés, et les autres sont faciles à démontrer. Il suffit généralement d'appliquer la définition du produit vectoriel et d'appliquer les propriétés des déterminants.

Théorème 8.4

Soit $\vec{u}$, $\vec{v}$ et $\vec{w}$ des vecteurs de $\mathbb{R}^3$ et k un scalaire.

1) $\vec{u} \times \vec{v} = -\vec{v} \times \vec{u}$.

2) Si $\vec{u}$ et $\vec{v}$ sont non nuls et non parallèles, alors le vecteur $\vec{u} \times \vec{v}$ est perpendiculaire à $\vec{u}$ et à $\vec{v}$.

3) $\vec{u} \times (\vec{v} + \vec{w}) = \vec{u} \times \vec{v} + \vec{u} \times \vec{w}$ et $(\vec{u} + \vec{v}) \times \vec{w} = \vec{u} \times \vec{w} + \vec{v} \times \vec{w}$.

4) $k(\vec{u} \times \vec{v}) = (k\vec{u}) \times \vec{v} = \vec{u} \times (k\vec{v})$.

5) $\vec{u} \times \vec{0} = \vec{0} \times \vec{u} = \vec{0}$.

6) $\vec{u} \times \vec{u} = \vec{0}$.

7) Deux vecteurs non nuls $\vec{u}$ et $\vec{v}$ sont parallèles si et seulement si $\vec{u} \times \vec{v} = \vec{0}$.

8.5 PRODUIT MIXTE

Le **produit mixte** est une opération portant sur trois vecteurs de $\mathbb{R}^3$. Le qualificatif «mixte» évoque la relation entre ce produit et les produits vectoriel et scalaire. Le produit mixte est un scalaire.

8.5.1 DÉFINITION DU PRODUIT MIXTE

PRODUIT MIXTE

Le produit mixte des vecteurs
$\vec{u} = \begin{bmatrix} u_1 & u_2 & u_3 \end{bmatrix}$,
$\vec{v} = \begin{bmatrix} v_1 & v_2 & v_3 \end{bmatrix}$ et
$\vec{w} = \begin{bmatrix} w_1 & w_2 & w_3 \end{bmatrix}$ est
un scalaire noté $\vec{u} \cdot (\vec{v} \times \vec{w})$
et défini par

$$\vec{u} \cdot (\vec{v} \times \vec{w}) = \begin{vmatrix} u_1 & u_2 & u_3 \\ v_1 & v_2 & v_3 \\ w_1 & w_2 & w_3 \end{vmatrix}$$

Le produit mixte de trois vecteurs $\vec{u}$, $\vec{v}$ et $\vec{w}$ de $\mathbb{R}^3$ est égal à $\vec{u} \cdot (\vec{v} \times \vec{w})$. Il est à noter que l'ordre des vecteurs est important puisque le produit vectoriel n'est pas commutatif.

Exemple

Si $\vec{u} = \begin{bmatrix} 1 & 2 & 3 \end{bmatrix}$, $\vec{v} = \begin{bmatrix} 2 & -1 & 2 \end{bmatrix}$ et $\vec{w} = \begin{bmatrix} 1 & 1 & 2 \end{bmatrix}$, alors

$$\vec{v} \times \vec{w} = \begin{vmatrix} \vec{i} & \vec{j} & \vec{k} \\ 2 & -1 & 2 \\ 1 & 1 & 2 \end{vmatrix} = -4\vec{i} - 2\vec{j} + 3\vec{k} = \begin{bmatrix} -4 & -2 & 3 \end{bmatrix}$$

d'où $\vec{u} \cdot (\vec{v} \times \vec{w}) = \begin{bmatrix} 1 & 2 & 3 \end{bmatrix} \cdot \begin{bmatrix} -4 & -2 & 3 \end{bmatrix} = 1$.

Le théorème 8.5 permet de simplifier le calcul du produit mixte.

Théorème 8.5

Si $\vec{u} = \begin{bmatrix} u_1 & u_2 & u_3 \end{bmatrix}$, $\vec{v} = \begin{bmatrix} v_1 & v_2 & v_3 \end{bmatrix}$ et $\vec{w} = \begin{bmatrix} w_1 & w_2 & w_3 \end{bmatrix}$, alors

$$\vec{u} \cdot (\vec{v} \times \vec{w}) = \begin{vmatrix} u_1 & u_2 & u_3 \\ v_1 & v_2 & v_3 \\ w_1 & w_2 & w_3 \end{vmatrix}$$

Preuve

$$\vec{v} \times \vec{w} = \begin{vmatrix} \vec{i} & \vec{j} & \vec{k} \\ v_1 & v_2 & v_3 \\ w_1 & w_2 & w_3 \end{vmatrix}$$

$$= (v_2 w_3 - v_3 w_2)\vec{i} - (v_1 w_3 - v_3 w_1)\vec{j} + (v_1 w_2 - v_2 w_1)\vec{k}$$

$$= \begin{bmatrix} v_2 w_3 - v_3 w_2 & v_3 w_1 - v_1 w_3 & v_1 w_2 - v_2 w_1 \end{bmatrix}$$

Par conséquent,

$$\vec{u} \cdot (\vec{v} \times \vec{w}) = u_1(v_2 w_3 - v_3 w_2) + u_2(v_3 w_1 - v_1 w_3) + u_3(v_1 w_2 - v_2 w_1)$$

Le membre de gauche de cette équation est égal au développement selon la première ligne du déterminant

$$\begin{vmatrix} u_1 & u_2 & u_3 \\ v_1 & v_2 & v_3 \\ w_1 & w_2 & w_3 \end{vmatrix}$$

Par conséquent,

$$\vec{u} \cdot (\vec{v} \times \vec{w}) = \begin{vmatrix} u_1 & u_2 & u_3 \\ v_1 & v_2 & v_3 \\ w_1 & w_2 & w_3 \end{vmatrix} \qquad \blacksquare$$

EXERCICE 8.12

Soit $\vec{u} = \begin{bmatrix} 2 & -2 & 3 \end{bmatrix}$, $\vec{v} = \begin{bmatrix} 1 & -1 & 2 \end{bmatrix}$ et $\vec{w} = \begin{bmatrix} 1 & 3 & -2 \end{bmatrix}$. Évaluez $\vec{u} \cdot (\vec{v} \times \vec{w})$.

8.5.2 Propriétés du produit mixte

Le produit mixte possède, comme les autres opérations vectorielles, des propriétés intéressantes, que nous avons regroupées dans le théorème 8.6.

Soit $\vec{u}$, $\vec{v}$ et $\vec{w}$, des vecteurs de $\mathbb{R}^3$.

1) $\vec{u} \cdot (\vec{v} \times \vec{w}) = (\vec{u} \times \vec{v}) \cdot \vec{w}$.

2) $\vec{u} \cdot (\vec{u} \times \vec{v}) = 0$ et $\vec{v} \cdot (\vec{u} \times \vec{v}) = 0$.

3) $\vec{u} \cdot (\vec{v} \times \vec{w}) = 0$ si et seulement si les trois vecteurs sont coplanaires (ou linéairement dépendants).

Nous allons démontrer chaque propriété.

Propriété 1 $\vec{u} \cdot (\vec{v} \times \vec{w}) = (\vec{u} \times \vec{v}) \cdot \vec{w}$

Preuve

D'une part,

$$\vec{u} \cdot (\vec{v} \times \vec{w}) = \begin{vmatrix} u_1 & u_2 & u_3 \\ v_1 & v_2 & v_3 \\ w_1 & w_2 & w_3 \end{vmatrix}$$

$$= u_1(v_2 w_3 - v_3 w_2) + u_2(v_3 w_1 - v_1 w_3) + u_3(v_1 w_2 - v_2 w_1)$$

et, d'autre part,

$$(\vec{u} \times \vec{v}) \cdot \vec{w} = \begin{bmatrix} u_2 v_3 - u_3 v_2 & u_3 v_1 - u_1 v_3 & u_1 v_2 - u_2 v_1 \end{bmatrix} \cdot \begin{bmatrix} w_1 & w_2 & w_3 \end{bmatrix}$$

$$= (u_2 v_3 - u_3 v_2) w_1 + (u_3 v_1 - u_1 v_3) w_2 + (u_1 v_2 - u_2 v_1) w_3$$

Les membres de droite des deux égalités sont égaux. Par conséquent, $\vec{u} \cdot (\vec{v} \times \vec{w}) = (\vec{u} \times \vec{v}) \cdot \vec{w}$. ∎

Propriété 2 $\vec{u} \cdot (\vec{u} \times \vec{v}) = 0$ et $\vec{v} \cdot (\vec{u} \times \vec{v}) = 0$

Preuve

Comme le déterminant compte deux lignes identiques,

$$\vec{u} \cdot (\vec{u} \times \vec{v}) = \begin{vmatrix} u_1 & u_2 & u_3 \\ u_1 & u_2 & u_3 \\ v_1 & v_2 & v_3 \end{vmatrix} = 0$$

De façon analogue, $\vec{v} \cdot (\vec{u} \times \vec{v}) = 0$. ∎

Propriété 3 $\vec{u} \cdot (\vec{v} \times \vec{w}) = 0$ si et seulement si les trois vecteurs sont coplanaires (ou linéairement dépendants).

Preuve

($\Rightarrow$) Si $\vec{u} \cdot (\vec{v} \times \vec{w}) = 0$, alors $\vec{u}$ est perpendiculaire à $\vec{v} \times \vec{w}$. Le vecteur $\vec{u}$ appartient donc au plan qui contient les vecteurs $\vec{v}$ et $\vec{w}$. Par conséquent, les trois vecteurs sont coplanaires.

($\Leftarrow$) Si les vecteurs $\vec{u}$, $\vec{v}$ et $\vec{w}$ sont coplanaires, alors on peut supposer que l'un de ces vecteurs s'écrit comme une combinaison linéaire des deux autres. On peut donc poser, sans perte de généralité, que $\vec{w} = a\vec{u} + b\vec{v}$. Par conséquent,

$$\vec{u} \cdot (\vec{v} \times \vec{w}) = \begin{vmatrix} u_1 & u_2 & u_3 \\ v_1 & v_2 & v_3 \\ w_1 & w_2 & w_3 \end{vmatrix}$$

$$= \begin{vmatrix} u_1 & u_2 & u_3 \\ v_1 & v_2 & v_3 \\ au_1 + bv_1 & au_2 + bv_2 & au_3 + bv_3 \end{vmatrix}$$

$$= \begin{vmatrix} u_1 & u_2 & u_3 \\ v_1 & v_2 & v_3 \\ 0 & 0 & 0 \end{vmatrix} L_3 \to L_3 - aL_1 - bL_2$$

$$= 0 \qquad \blacksquare$$

EXERCICE 8.13

Vérifiez, à l'aide du produit mixte, que les vecteurs $\vec{u} = \begin{bmatrix} 2 & -2 & 3 \end{bmatrix}$, $\vec{v} = \begin{bmatrix} 1 & -1 & 2 \end{bmatrix}$ et $\vec{w} = \begin{bmatrix} 1 & -1 & 0 \end{bmatrix}$ sont coplanaires.

8.5.3 INTERPRÉTATION GÉOMÉTRIQUE DU PRODUIT MIXTE

On sait que le module du produit vectoriel est égal à l'aire d'un parallélogramme ; la valeur absolue du produit mixte est quant à elle égale au volume d'un parallélépipède.

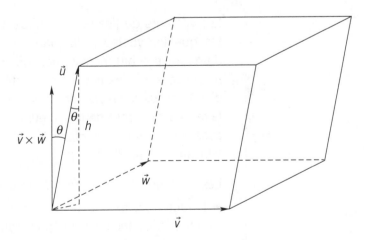

En effet, le volume d'un parallélépipède est égal au produit de l'aire de la base et de la hauteur. Or, la base est un parallélogramme d'aire

$A = \|\vec{v} \times \vec{w}\|$, et la hauteur est donnée par $h = \|\vec{u}\| |\cos\theta|$. Le volume du parallélépipède est donc

$$V = Ah = \|\vec{v} \times \vec{w}\| \, \|\vec{u}\| \, |\cos\theta| = \|\vec{u}\| \, \|\vec{v} \times \vec{w}\| \, |\cos\theta| = |\vec{u} \cdot (\vec{v} \times \vec{w})|$$

Exemple

Si $\vec{u} = \begin{bmatrix} -1 & 2 & 3 \end{bmatrix}$, $\vec{v} = \begin{bmatrix} 2 & 2 & 2 \end{bmatrix}$ et $\vec{w} = \begin{bmatrix} 1 & 1 & 2 \end{bmatrix}$, alors le volume du parallélépipède déterminé par ces trois vecteurs est égal à la valeur absolue du produit mixte de ces trois vecteurs. Or,

$$\vec{u} \cdot (\vec{v} \times \vec{w}) = \begin{vmatrix} u_1 & u_2 & u_3 \\ v_1 & v_2 & v_3 \\ w_1 & w_2 & w_3 \end{vmatrix} = \begin{vmatrix} -1 & 2 & 3 \\ 2 & 2 & 2 \\ 1 & 1 & 2 \end{vmatrix} = -6$$

Le volume du parallélépipède est égal à $|-6| = 6$ unités cubes.

EXERCICE 8.14

Le volume d'un tétraèdre (un polyèdre formé de quatre faces triangulaires) vaut $\frac{1}{6}$ du volume du parallélépipède avec lequel il partage trois arêtes. Quel est le volume du tétraèdre qui a pour sommets les points $A(1, 1, 1)$, $B(2, 2, 3)$, $C(3, -1, 1)$ et $D(4, 3, 2)$?

RÉSUMÉ

Les vecteurs de l'espace possèdent essentiellement les mêmes propriétés que les vecteurs du plan. On transpose simplement les concepts d'un univers bidimensionnel ($\mathbb{R}^2$) à un univers tridimensionnel ($\mathbb{R}^3$). Ainsi, dans $\mathbb{R}^3$, les notions d'égalité de vecteurs, de module d'un vecteur, d'addition de vecteurs, de multiplication par un scalaire, de produit scalaire, d'angle entre deux vecteurs et de projection orthogonale sont analogues aux notions correspondantes définies dans $\mathbb{R}^2$, comme l'indique le tableau 8.1 (p. 285).

Les vecteurs de l'espace présentent toutefois certaines particularités :

• Il faut trois axes (axe des abscisses, axe des ordonnées et axe des cotes) pour localiser un point ou un vecteur dans l'espace.

• Il faut trois composantes pour décrire un vecteur.

- Il faut trois angles (les angles directeurs) pour donner la direction d'un vecteur.
- Il faut trois vecteurs linéairement indépendants (non coplanaires) pour former une base de $\mathbb{R}^3$.
- Le produit vectoriel et le produit mixte sont des opérations spécifiques aux vecteurs de $\mathbb{R}^3$.

On utilise généralement un système d'axes direct, c'est-à-dire orienté selon la règle de la main droite. La règle de la main droite sert également à déterminer la direction du produit vectoriel de deux vecteurs de $\mathbb{R}^3$.

Le produit vectoriel de $\vec{u} = \begin{bmatrix} u_1 & u_2 & u_3 \end{bmatrix}$ et $\vec{v} = \begin{bmatrix} v_1 & v_2 & v_3 \end{bmatrix}$, formant un angle θ, est le vecteur, noté $\vec{u} \times \vec{v}$, défini par

$$\vec{u} \times \vec{v} = \begin{vmatrix} \vec{i} & \vec{j} & \vec{k} \\ u_1 & u_2 & u_3 \\ v_1 & v_2 & v_3 \end{vmatrix} = (\|\vec{u}\| \, \|\vec{v}\| \sin\theta)\vec{n}$$

où $\vec{n}$ est un vecteur unitaire perpendiculaire à chacun des vecteurs $\vec{u}$ et $\vec{v}$, et dont la direction est donnée par la règle de la main droite. Par conséquent, lorsqu'on cherche les composantes d'un vecteur perpendiculaire à deux vecteurs $\vec{u}$ et $\vec{v}$, il suffit de calculer le produit vectoriel de ces deux vecteurs. Ainsi, $\vec{u} \times \vec{v}$ est un vecteur perpendiculaire à $\vec{u}$ et à $\vec{v}$.

Le module du produit vectoriel de deux vecteurs correspond en physique à l'intensité d'un moment de force et, en géométrie, à l'aire du parallélogramme dont deux côtés non parallèles correspondent aux deux vecteurs.

Les principales propriétés du produit vectoriel sont regroupées dans le théorème 8.4 (p. 296). Il faut notamment retenir que le produit vectoriel n'est pas commutatif, que le produit vectoriel de deux vecteurs parallèles est le vecteur nul et, surtout, que le produit vectoriel de deux vecteurs non nuls et non parallèles est un vecteur perpendiculaire à chacun de ces deux vecteurs.

Le produit mixte des vecteurs $\vec{u} = \begin{bmatrix} u_1 & u_2 & u_3 \end{bmatrix}$, $\vec{v} = \begin{bmatrix} v_1 & v_2 & v_3 \end{bmatrix}$ et $\vec{w} = \begin{bmatrix} w_1 & w_2 & w_3 \end{bmatrix}$ est un scalaire noté $\vec{u} \cdot (\vec{v} \times \vec{w})$ et défini par

$$\vec{u} \cdot (\vec{v} \times \vec{w}) = \begin{vmatrix} u_1 & u_2 & u_3 \\ v_1 & v_2 & v_3 \\ w_1 & w_2 & w_3 \end{vmatrix}$$

Les principales propriétés du produit mixte sont regroupées dans le théorème 8.6 (p. 298). Il faut notamment retenir que le produit mixte de trois vecteurs coplanaires vaut 0. Pour vérifier si trois vecteurs de $\mathbb{R}^3$ sont coplanaires (et donc linéairement dépendants), il suffit de montrer que leur produit mixte est nul. Enfin, la valeur absolue du produit mixte de trois vecteurs est égale au volume du parallélépipède engendré par ces trois vecteurs.

EXERCICES RÉCAPITULATIFS

1. (I) Le parallélépipède suivant a six faces rectangulaires et ses arêtes mesurent respectivement 4, 5 et 6 cm.

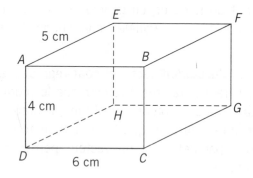

a) Complétez : $\overrightarrow{AF} = \overrightarrow{A\_} + \overrightarrow{B\_} + \overrightarrow{GF}$.

b) Que vaut $\overrightarrow{AB} + \overrightarrow{AE}$?

c) Est-ce que $\overrightarrow{HD} + \overrightarrow{HG} = -(\overrightarrow{BA} + \overrightarrow{BF})$? Justifiez votre réponse.

d) Remplacez l'expression $\overrightarrow{GD} - \overrightarrow{AD} - \overrightarrow{GB} + \overrightarrow{AH}$ par un seul vecteur.

e) Que vaut $\|\overrightarrow{DG}\|$?

f) Que vaut $\|\overrightarrow{HB}\|$?

g) Que vaut $\|\overrightarrow{CD} - \overrightarrow{AD} - \overrightarrow{CH} + \overrightarrow{FH} + \overrightarrow{GF}\|$?

h) Montrez que $\overrightarrow{AC} + \overrightarrow{AH} + \overrightarrow{AF} = 2\overrightarrow{AG}$.

2. (I) Les points $A(0, 0, 0)$, $B(3, 2, 1)$ et $C(4, -6, 4)$ sont les sommets d'un triangle de l'espace.

a) Quelle est la distance entre le point B et le plan xy ?

b) Quelle est la distance entre le point B et l'origine ?

c) Localisez les points A, B et C dans l'espace et tracez le triangle qu'ils déterminent.

d) Quelle est la distance entre le point B et l'axe des abscisses ?

e) Quelle est la distance entre les points B et C ?

3. (I) Les points $A(-2, 0, 0)$, $B(2, 2, 0)$, $C(-1, -5, 0)$ et $D(\frac{1}{2}, -\frac{1}{2}, 3)$ sont les sommets d'un tétraèdre (du grec *tetra*: quatre et *hedra*: base ; il s'agit d'un solide à quatre faces).

a) Localisez les quatre points dans l'espace et tracez le tétraèdre.

b) Quelle est la hauteur du tétraèdre, soit la distance entre le sommet D et la base du tétraèdre ?

4. (I) Tracez les vecteurs géométriques représentés par $\vec{u} = \begin{bmatrix} 3 & -1 & 4 \end{bmatrix}$ et $\vec{v} = \begin{bmatrix} -2 & 1 & -3 \end{bmatrix}$ dans un système de coordonnées cartésiennes de l'espace.

5. (I) Exprimez les vecteurs suivants sous la forme $\begin{bmatrix} a_1 & a_2 & a_3 \end{bmatrix}$.

a) $\vec{u} = 2\vec{i} + 3\vec{j} + 4\vec{k}$

b) $\vec{v} = \vec{i} - \vec{k}$

c) $\vec{w} = 3\vec{j} - 2\vec{k}$

d) Le vecteur $\vec{t}$ a pour origine le point $A(2, 1, 4)$ et pour extrémité le point B dont l'abscisse est deux fois plus grande que l'ordonnée, dont la cote est supérieure de deux unités à la somme de l'abscisse et de l'ordonnée, et dont la somme des coordonnées vaut huit.

6. (I) Exprimez chacun des vecteurs suivants comme une combinaison linéaire des vecteurs $\vec{i}$, $\vec{j}$ et $\vec{k}$.

a) $\vec{u} = \begin{bmatrix} 1 & 2 & 4 \end{bmatrix}$

b) $\vec{v} = \begin{bmatrix} -2 & 0 & 1 \end{bmatrix}$

c) $\vec{w} = \begin{bmatrix} 0 & -2 & 0 \end{bmatrix}$

7. (I) Soit les points $A(1, 2, -3)$, $B(4, -2, 5)$, $C(-5, -2, 3)$, $D(-6, -2, -5)$, $E(4, -4, -3)$ et $F(2, -1, 3)$.

a) Quelles sont les composantes et le module de chacun des vecteurs $\overrightarrow{AB}$, $\overrightarrow{CD}$ et $\overrightarrow{EF}$?

b) Pour chacun des vecteurs $\overrightarrow{AB}$, $\overrightarrow{CD}$ et $\overrightarrow{EF}$, trouvez un vecteur unitaire qui ait la même direction.

c) Que représentent les composantes de chacun des vecteurs unitaires déterminés en *b* ?

d) Quels sont les angles directeurs de chacun des vecteurs $\overrightarrow{AB}$, $\overrightarrow{CD}$ et $\overrightarrow{EF}$?

e) Quelles sont les composantes de
$$2\,\overrightarrow{AB} + 3\,\overrightarrow{CD}$$

f) Quelles sont les composantes de
$$-4\,\overrightarrow{EF} + \overrightarrow{AB} - 2\,\overrightarrow{DC}$$

8. (I) Soit les points $A(2, 1, -3)$, $B(2, -3, 4)$ et $C(1, 3, 5)$.

a) Quelles sont les coordonnées du point D tel que $\overrightarrow{AB} = \overrightarrow{CD}$?

b) Quelles sont les coordonnées du point D tel que $\overrightarrow{AD} + \overrightarrow{AB} = \overrightarrow{AC}$?

c) Quelles sont les coordonnées du point D tel que $\overrightarrow{CD}$ est un vecteur dont la direction est opposée à celle de $\overrightarrow{AB}$ et dont le module est quatre fois plus grand que celui de $\overrightarrow{AB}$?

9. (I) Soit les vecteurs
$$\vec{s} = \begin{bmatrix} 4 & 1 & 2 \end{bmatrix}$$
$$\vec{t} = \begin{bmatrix} 3 & -1 & 2 \end{bmatrix}$$
$$\vec{u} = \begin{bmatrix} 1 & -2 & 4 \end{bmatrix}$$
$$\vec{v} = \begin{bmatrix} -2 & 1 & 1 \end{bmatrix}$$
$$\vec{w} = \begin{bmatrix} -3 & 6 & -12 \end{bmatrix}$$

a) Que vaut $3\vec{u} + 2\vec{s} - 4\vec{t}$?

b) Que vaut $-\vec{w} + 4\vec{v} - 3\vec{t}$?

c) Que vaut $\|3\vec{t} + 2\vec{v} - \vec{w}\|$?

d) Que vaut $\|-\vec{u} + 3\vec{v} - 2\vec{w}\|$?

e) Que vaut $\vec{s} \cdot \vec{t}$?

f) Que vaut $\vec{u} \cdot \vec{t}$?

g) Que vaut $2\vec{s} \cdot (2\vec{v} - 3\vec{u})$?

h) Que vaut $(3\vec{t} + \vec{v}) \cdot (\vec{s} + 2\vec{w})$?

i) Quel est l'angle entre les vecteurs $\vec{u}$ et $\vec{v}$? Que peut-on dire de ces vecteurs ?

j) Quel est l'angle entre les vecteurs $\vec{u}$ et $\vec{w}$? Que peut-on dire de ces vecteurs ?

k) Quel est l'angle entre les vecteurs $\vec{s} - \vec{t}$ et $\vec{u} + 3\vec{v}$?

l) Quels sont les cosinus directeurs de $\vec{u}$?

m) Quels sont les angles directeurs de $\vec{v}$?

n) Peut-on exprimer le vecteur $\vec{t}$ comme une combinaison linéaire des vecteurs $\vec{u}$ et $\vec{v}$? Justifiez votre réponse.

o) Les vecteurs $\vec{t}$, $\vec{u}$ et $\vec{v}$ sont-ils linéairement indépendants ? Justifiez votre réponse.

p) Les vecteurs $\vec{t}$, $\vec{u}$ et $\vec{v}$ forment-ils un système générateur de $\mathbb{R}^3$? Justifiez votre réponse.

q) Les vecteurs $\vec{t}$, $\vec{u}$ et $\vec{v}$ forment-ils une base de $\mathbb{R}^3$? Justifiez votre réponse.

r) Peut-on exprimer le vecteur $\vec{w}$ comme une combinaison linéaire des vecteurs $\vec{u}$ et $\vec{v}$? Justifiez votre réponse.

s) Les vecteurs $\vec{u}$, $\vec{v}$ et $\vec{w}$ forment-ils une base de $\mathbb{R}^3$? Justifiez votre réponse.

t) Quel est le vecteur unitaire de direction contraire au vecteur $\vec{v}$?

u) Servez-vous du produit scalaire pour trouver un vecteur non nul $\vec{p} = \begin{bmatrix} p_1 & p_2 & p_3 \end{bmatrix}$ qui soit perpendiculaire à chacun des vecteurs $\vec{s}$ et $\vec{t}$.

10. (I) Si les angles directeurs d'un vecteur $\vec{u}$ sont α, β, et γ, quels sont les angles directeurs du vecteur $-\vec{u}$?

11. (I) Quel est l'angle entre $\vec{u} = \begin{bmatrix} k & -k & k \end{bmatrix}$ et $\vec{v} = \begin{bmatrix} -k & k & k \end{bmatrix}$ où k est un nombre réel différent de zéro?

12. (I) Dites si un vecteur peut avoir les angles suivants comme angles directeurs. (Indice: Servez-vous du résultat de l'exercice 8.4.)

a) $\alpha = \pi/4$, $\beta = \pi/4$ et $\gamma = \pi/3$

b) $\alpha = \pi/4$, $\beta = \pi/6$ et $\gamma = \pi/3$

c) $\alpha = \pi/3$, $\beta = \pi/3$ et $\gamma = \pi/4$

13. (I) Déterminez les angles directeurs manquants.

a) $\alpha = 30°$, $\beta = \gamma$

b) $\alpha = \pi/3$, $\beta = 5\pi/6$

c) $\alpha = \pi/3$, $\gamma = 2\pi/3$

14. (I) Quels sont les deux vecteurs unitaires dont tous les angles directeurs sont égaux?

15. (I) Soit le triangle dont les sommets sont les points $A(2, 1, -1)$, $B(3, 0, 4)$ et $C(4, 5, 6)$.

a) Quel est le périmètre de ce triangle?

b) Quelle est la mesure de l'angle θ issu du point A?

16. (I) Montrez que le triangle dont les sommets sont les points $A(2, 1, 4)$, $B(4, 4, 10)$ et $C(5, -5, 6)$ est un triangle rectangle isocèle dont l'angle droit est issu du point A.

17. (I) Pour quelles valeurs de k les points $A(1, 2, 1)$, $B(-2, -2, 1)$ et $C(k, 0, -1)$ déterminent-ils un triangle rectangle dont l'hypoténuse est le segment de droite AB?

18. (I) Pour quelle(s) valeur(s) réelle(s) de k (si elles existent), les vecteurs $\vec{u}$ et $\vec{v}$ sont-ils perpendiculaires?

a) $\vec{u} = \begin{bmatrix} 2 & 3 & -1 \end{bmatrix}$ et $\vec{v} = \begin{bmatrix} k & 3 & 4 \end{bmatrix}$

b) $\vec{u} = \begin{bmatrix} k & 2 & 1 \end{bmatrix}$ et $\vec{v} = \begin{bmatrix} k & -k & -3 \end{bmatrix}$

c) $\vec{u} = \begin{bmatrix} k & 2 & 1 \end{bmatrix}$ et $\vec{v} = \begin{bmatrix} k & 4 & k \end{bmatrix}$

19. (I) Un marchand de fruits et légumes, qui a vendu q_1 kg de pommes de terre, q_2 kg de carottes et q_3 kg de navets, a réalisé un profit de π_1 \$/kg de pommes de terre, π_2 \$/kg de carottes et π_3 \$/kg de navets.

a) Écrivez les informations données sous forme vectorielle:

$$\vec{q} = \begin{bmatrix} & & \end{bmatrix} \quad \text{et} \quad \vec{\pi} = \begin{bmatrix} & & \end{bmatrix}$$

b) Comment doit-on interpréter le produit scalaire $\vec{q} \cdot \vec{\pi}$ d'un point de vue économique?

20. (II) Montrez que si le vecteur $\vec{u}$ est orthogonal à chacun des vecteurs $\vec{v}$ et $\vec{w}$ alors il est également orthogonal à toute combinaison linéaire des vecteurs $\vec{v}$ et $\vec{w}$.

21. (II) Montrez que

$$\|\vec{u} + \vec{v}\|^2 = \|\vec{u}\|^2 + 2\vec{u} \cdot \vec{v} + \|\vec{v}\|^2$$

22. (I) Utilisez le résultat prouvé au n° 21 pour montrer que $\|\vec{u} + \vec{v}\|^2 = \|\vec{u}\|^2 + \|\vec{v}\|^2$ si et seulement si $\vec{u}$ est orthogonal à $\vec{v}$.

23. (II) Soit $\vec{u}$ et $\vec{v}$ deux vecteurs perpendiculaires. Exprimez $\|a\vec{u} + b\vec{v}\|$ en fonction de $\|\vec{u}\|$ et de $\|\vec{v}\|$.

24. (I) Selon une loi de la réflexion, l'angle de réflexion d'un rayon lumineux qui frappe un miroir est égal à l'angle d'incidence du rayon. Montrez que, dans le cas d'un miroir placé dans le plan xy et d'un rayon incident $\vec{a} = \begin{bmatrix} a_1 & a_2 & a_3 \end{bmatrix}$, le rayon réfléchi est donné par $\vec{b} = \begin{bmatrix} a_1 & a_2 & -a_3 \end{bmatrix}$.

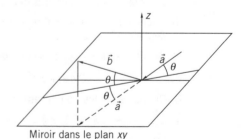

Miroir dans le plan xy

25. (II) La représentation géométrique d'une molécule de tétrafluorocarbone (CF_4) est un tétraèdre régulier (soit un polyèdre formé de quatre triangles équilatéraux). Les atomes de fluor sont situés aux sommets du tétraèdre et l'atome de carbone occupe le centre.

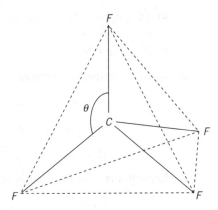

On suppose que les atomes de fluor de la molécule sont situés aux points $A(0, 0, 0)$, $B(1, 1, 0)$, $D(1, 0, 1)$ et $E(0, 1, 1)$, et que l'atome de carbone est situé au point $C(\frac{1}{2}, \frac{1}{2}, \frac{1}{2})$.

a) Vérifiez que le triangle ABD est équilatéral.

b) Vérifiez que l'atome de carbone est situé à égale distance de chacun des atomes de fluor.

c) Trouvez la valeur de l'angle de liaison θ entre l'atome de carbone et deux atomes de fluor (voir la figure).

d) Dans la molécule de tétrafluorocarbone, chaque atome de fluor exerce une force d'attraction sur les électrons de la liaison avec le carbone à cause de l'électronégativité plus forte de celui-ci. Montrez que la somme des forces qui s'exercent sur les électrons de l'atome de carbone est nulle, de sorte que la molécule est non polaire. Comme tous les atomes de fluor sont identiques, on peut supposer que chaque force est représentée par un vecteur issu de l'atome de carbone et ayant comme extrémité un sommet du tétraèdre.

26. (I) Déterminez si les points A, B et C donnés sont situés sur une même droite. (Indice : Quelle caractéristique doivent posséder les vecteurs $\overrightarrow{AB}$ et $\overrightarrow{AC}$ pour que les points A, B et C soient colinéaires ?)

a) $A(2, 4, 6)$, $B(-1, 3, 4)$, $C(1, 0, 1)$

b) $A(2, 4, 6)$, $B(-1, 3, 4)$, $C(11, 7, 12)$

c) $A(-5, 2, 1)$, $B(1, -3, 2)$, $C(13, -13, 4)$

d) $A(-2, 3, -4)$, $B(2, 3, 5)$, $C(4, 1, -3)$

27. (I) Soit $\vec{s} = \begin{bmatrix} 4 & 1 & 2 \end{bmatrix}$, $\vec{t} = \begin{bmatrix} 3 & -1 & 2 \end{bmatrix}$ et $\vec{u} = \begin{bmatrix} 1 & -2 & 4 \end{bmatrix}$. Évaluez si possible chacune des expressions suivantes.

a) $\vec{s} \times \vec{t}$

b) $\vec{u} \times \vec{t}$

c) $\vec{s} \times \vec{u}$

d) $(\vec{s} \times \vec{t}) \times \vec{u}$

e) $\vec{s} \times (\vec{t} \times \vec{u})$. Le produit vectoriel est-il associatif ?

f) $(\vec{s} \cdot \vec{t}) \times \vec{u}$

g) $\vec{s} \cdot (\vec{t} \times \vec{u})$

28. (I) Trouvez un vecteur unitaire qui soit perpendiculaire à chacun des vecteurs $\vec{u} = \begin{bmatrix} 1 & 3 & 4 \end{bmatrix}$ et $\vec{v} = \begin{bmatrix} -1 & -2 & 3 \end{bmatrix}$.

29. (I) Trouvez un vecteur de longueur cinq qui soit perpendiculaire à chacun des vecteurs $\vec{u} = \begin{bmatrix} 2 & -3 & 1 \end{bmatrix}$ et $\vec{v} = \begin{bmatrix} 1 & 4 & 1 \end{bmatrix}$.

30. (I) Quelle est l'aire du parallélogramme dont deux côtés non parallèles correspondent aux vecteurs $\vec{u} = \begin{bmatrix} 2 & 3 & -1 \end{bmatrix}$ et $\vec{v} = \begin{bmatrix} 3 & 6 & -1 \end{bmatrix}$?

31. (II) Un arpenteur géomètre a tracé le plan suivant d'un terrain de forme triangulaire.

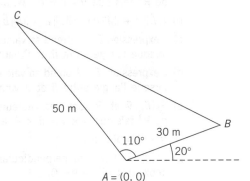

a) Quelles sont les coordonnées des sommets B et C du triangle ?

b) Quel est le périmètre du triangle ?

c) Transformez les coordonnées des sommets du triangle en coordonnées de l'espace.

d) Évaluez l'aire du triangle à l'aide du produit vectoriel.

32. (I) Soit $P(x_0, y_0)$, $Q(x_1, y_1)$ et $R(x_2, y_2)$, trois points non colinéaires du plan. À l'aide du produit vectoriel, montrez que l'aire A du triangle PQR est donnée par

$$A = \frac{1}{2} |(x_1 - x_0)(y_2 - y_0) - (x_2 - x_0)(y_1 - y_0)|$$

33. (I) Un poisson pesant 20 N est suspendu à l'extrémité d'une canne à pêche de 1,5 m qui forme un angle de 60° avec l'horizontale. Quelle est l'intensité du moment de force exercé par le poisson sur le manche de la canne à pêche?

34. (I) Quel est le volume du parallélépipède dont les arêtes correspondent aux vecteurs $\vec{u} = \begin{bmatrix} 2 & 3 & -1 \end{bmatrix}$, $\vec{v} = \begin{bmatrix} 3 & 6 & -1 \end{bmatrix}$ et $\vec{w} = \begin{bmatrix} 1 & 2 & 1 \end{bmatrix}$?

35. (I) Les points $A(1, 2, -1)$, $B(3, 3, -4)$, $C(2, 2, 1)$ et $D(5, 3, 0)$ sont-ils situés dans un même plan? (Indice: Quel est le volume du parallélépipède dont les arêtes correspondent aux vecteurs $\overrightarrow{AB}$, $\overrightarrow{AC}$ et $\overrightarrow{AD}$?)

36. (I) Quel est le volume du tétraèdre décrit au n° 3? au n° 25?

37. (I) Dites si chaque énoncé est vrai ou faux et justifiez votre réponse.
a) Si $\vec{u}$, $\vec{v}$ et $\vec{w}$ sont des vecteurs non nuls de $\mathbb{R}^3$ tels que $\vec{u} \cdot \vec{v} = \vec{u} \cdot \vec{w}$, alors $\vec{v} = \vec{w}$.
b) $(\|\vec{b}\|\vec{a} + \|\vec{a}\|\vec{b}) \cdot (\|\vec{b}\|\vec{a} - \|\vec{a}\|\vec{b}) = 0$.
c) L'expression $\vec{u} \cdot \vec{v}$ prend sa valeur maximale lorsque l'angle entre $\vec{u}$ et $\vec{v}$ vaut 0°.
d) L'expression $\vec{u} \cdot \vec{v}$ prend sa valeur minimale lorsque l'angle entre $\vec{u}$ et $\vec{v}$ vaut 90°.
e) Si $\vec{u}$, $\vec{v}$ et $\vec{w}$ sont des vecteurs non nuls de $\mathbb{R}^3$ tels que $\vec{u} \times \vec{v} = \vec{u} \times \vec{w}$, alors $\vec{v} = \vec{w}$.
f) $\vec{u} \times \vec{v} = \vec{v} \times \vec{u}$.
g) Si $\vec{u}$, $\vec{v}$ et $\vec{w}$ sont perpendiculaires deux à deux, $\vec{u} \times (\vec{v} \times \vec{w}) = \vec{0}$.
h) L'expression $\vec{u} \times (\vec{v} \cdot \vec{w})$ est définie.
i) Si $\vec{u} \cdot (\vec{v} \times \vec{w}) = 5$, alors $(\vec{u} \times \vec{w}) \cdot \vec{v} = -5$.
j) Le produit mixte de trois vecteurs quelconques est un scalaire positif.

k) $\|\vec{u} \times \vec{v}\| = \|\vec{u}\| \|\vec{v}\| \sin\theta$ où θ est l'angle entre $\vec{u}$ et $\vec{v}$.
l) $(\vec{u} \times \vec{v})_{\vec{v}} = \vec{0}$.

38. (II) Montrez que les vecteurs
$$\vec{u} = \begin{bmatrix} u_1 & u_2 & u_3 \end{bmatrix}$$
$$\vec{v} = \begin{bmatrix} v_1 & v_2 & v_3 \end{bmatrix}$$
$$\vec{w} = \begin{bmatrix} w_1 & w_2 & w_3 \end{bmatrix}$$
forment une base de $\mathbb{R}^3$ si et seulement si
$$\begin{vmatrix} u_1 & v_1 & w_1 \\ u_2 & v_2 & w_2 \\ u_3 & v_3 & w_3 \end{vmatrix} \neq 0$$

39. (II) Soit les vecteurs $\vec{u} = \begin{bmatrix} 2 & 1 & 3 \end{bmatrix}$ et $\vec{v} = \begin{bmatrix} -2 & 1 & 1 \end{bmatrix}$.
a) Vérifiez que les vecteurs $\vec{u}$ et $\vec{v}$ sont orthogonaux.
b) Trouvez un vecteur $\vec{w}$ qui forme avec $\vec{u}$ et $\vec{v}$ une base orthogonale de $\mathbb{R}^3$.
c) Formez une base orthonormée en partant des vecteurs $\vec{u}$, $\vec{v}$ et $\vec{w}$.

40. (I) Pourquoi le produit vectoriel n'est-il pas défini dans $\mathbb{R}^2$?

41. (I) Quelle est la nature (scalaire, vecteur, non défini) de chacune des expressions suivantes?
a) $\vec{u} \cdot \vec{v}$
b) $k\vec{u}$
c) $\vec{u} \times \|\vec{v}\|$
d) $\vec{u} \times (\vec{v} \cdot \vec{w})$
e) $\vec{u} \cdot (\vec{v} \times \vec{w})$
f) $k(\vec{v} \cdot \vec{w})$
g) $k(\vec{u} \times \vec{v})$
h) $\|\vec{u} \times \vec{v}\|$

Droite et plan de l'espace

L'algèbre n'est qu'une géométrie écrite,
la géométrie n'est qu'une algèbre figurée.

Sophie Germain

À LA FIN DU PRÉSENT CHAPITRE, VOUS DEVRIEZ ÊTRE
EN MESURE DE RÉPONDRE AUX QUESTIONS SUIVANTES:

- Comment caractérise-t-on une droite et un plan de l'espace?

- Quelles sont les différentes formes de l'équation d'une droite ou d'un plan de l'espace?

- Quelles sont les différentes positions relatives de droites et de plans de l'espace?

- Quelles sont les formules de la distance entre points, droites et plans de l'espace?

- Comment trouve-t-on l'intersection de deux droites, de deux plans ou d'une droite et d'un plan de l'espace?

- Comment trouve-t-on l'angle entre deux droites concourantes ou entre deux plans sécants de l'espace?

UN PORTRAIT de William Rowan Hamilton

William Rowan Hamilton naquit sur le coup de minuit le 4 août 1805 dans la ville irlandaise de Dublin. Ses parents moururent alors qu'il était très jeune et il fut élevé par un oncle excentrique, féru de linguistique. Le jeune Hamilton avait une facilité impressionnante pour l'apprentissage des langues. Ainsi, à quatorze ans, il en maîtrisait déjà quatorze, dont l'anglais, le latin, le grec, l'hébreu, le français, l'italien, le sanscrit et l'arabe. Dès l'âge de dix ans, il découvrit les œuvres majeures de grands mathématiciens tels qu'Euclide, Newton et Laplace. Hamilton était un véritable prodige et, lors de son séjour au Trinity College de Dublin, il reçut des prix d'excellence en mathématiques, en physique, en grec et en prose anglaise.

Hamilton réalisa ses premières expériences de physique et d'astronomie à l'âge de douze ans. En 1823, il présenta un premier mémoire d'optique, dans lequel il exposa les fondements du principe de moindre action, connu aujourd'hui sous le nom de principe de moindre action d'Hamilton. Ce mémoire, revu et augmenté, fut publié en 1828 sous le titre de A Theory of Systems of Rays. C'est sans doute pour ses découvertes remarquables en optique que, dès l'âge de 22 ans, avant même d'avoir obtenu son diplôme, il fut nommé professeur d'astronomie au Trinity College et astronome royal d'Irlande.

À la suite d'importants travaux sur les nombres complexes, Hamilton inventa les quaternions, qui forment un ensemble de nombres où, chose remarquable, la multiplication n'est pas commutative. Cette découverte força les mathématiciens à abandonner leur croyance au principe général de la commutativité. Inutile de dire que la communauté mathématique s'enflamma pour les quaternions, mais cet enthousiasme fut de courte durée. On se rendit vite compte que les quaternions sont difficiles à manipuler et qu'ils n'ont qu'une utilité limitée en physique. Le concept de quaternion fut précurseur de la notion de vecteur. Toutefois, bien que le mot vecteur fut introduit par Hamilton, c'est à J. W. Gibbs qu'on attribue généralement la paternité de l'algèbre vectorielle sous sa forme actuelle.

Hamilton reçut de nombreux honneurs au cours de sa vie. Il fut anobli en 1835 et nommé fellow de la National Academy of Sciences of the United States, devenant ainsi le premier étranger à porter ce titre. Toutefois, Hamilton connut de graves difficultés au cours des dernières années de sa vie. Il vécut en reclus et sombra dans l'alcool. La théorie des quaternions tomba en désuétude malgré tous les efforts qu'il fit pour la soutenir. Hamilton mourut le 2 septembre 1865.

Le nom d'Hamilton demeure associé à plusieurs concepts mathématiques : principe de moindre action d'Hamilton, fonction hamiltonienne, théorème de Cayley-Hamilton, graphe hamiltonien et équations différentielles d'Hamilton-Jacobi.

9.1 DROITE DE L'ESPACE

Il est possible, comme on le fait pour la droite du plan, d'adopter une approche vectorielle pour caractériser la droite et le plan de l'espace. Nous allons présenter les différentes formes d'équations employées pour décrire une droite et un plan de l'espace et, comme au chapitre 6, nous allons traiter des concepts de distance (entre un point et une droite ou un plan, entre deux droites, entre deux plans, entre un plan et une droite), d'angle (entre deux droites concourantes, entre une droite et un plan, et entre deux plans) et d'intersection (entre deux droites, entre deux ou plusieurs plans, entre une droite et un plan).

9.1.1 ÉQUATION VECTORIELLE D'UNE DROITE DE L'ESPACE

Comme on peut le constater dans la figure qui suit, une droite de l'espace est entièrement déterminée par un vecteur directeur et un point. Si $\vec{d} = \begin{bmatrix} d_1 & d_2 & d_3 \end{bmatrix}$ est un vecteur directeur d'une droite Δ, si $P(p_1, p_2, p_3)$ est un point connu de cette droite et si $X(x, y, z)$ en est un point quelconque, alors le vecteur $\overrightarrow{PX}$ est parallèle au vecteur $\vec{d}$. On en déduit que

$$\overrightarrow{PX} = k\vec{d} \quad \Rightarrow \quad \overrightarrow{PO} + \overrightarrow{OX} = k\vec{d} \quad \Rightarrow \quad \overrightarrow{OX} = \overrightarrow{OP} + k\vec{d}$$

Si on écrit la dernière égalité à l'aide des composantes des différents vecteurs, on obtient l'**équation vectorielle d'une droite de l'espace**, soit

$$\begin{bmatrix} x & y & z \end{bmatrix} = \begin{bmatrix} p_1 & p_2 & p_3 \end{bmatrix} + k\begin{bmatrix} d_1 & d_2 & d_3 \end{bmatrix} \quad \text{où} \quad k \in \mathbb{R}$$

ÉQUATION VECTORIELLE D'UNE DROITE DE L'ESPACE

L'équation vectorielle d'une droite Δ qui passe par le point $P(p_1, p_2, p_3)$ et dont $\vec{d} = \begin{bmatrix} d_1 & d_2 & d_3 \end{bmatrix}$ est un vecteur directeur est

$$\begin{bmatrix} x & y & z \end{bmatrix} = \begin{bmatrix} p_1 & p_2 & p_3 \end{bmatrix}$$
$$+ k\begin{bmatrix} d_1 & d_2 & d_3 \end{bmatrix}$$

où $k \in \mathbb{R}$.

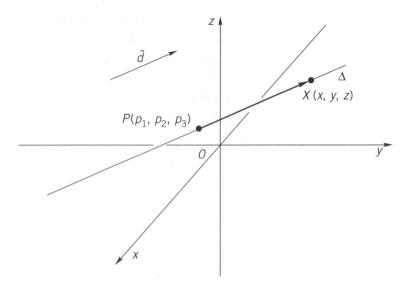

Cette équation n'est pas unique parce qu'elle dépend du point P et du vecteur directeur $\vec{d}$ employés. Le choix d'un autre point ou d'un autre vecteur directeur de la droite conduit à une formulation différente de l'équation vectorielle de la droite Δ.

Exemple

Le vecteur $\overrightarrow{AB} = \begin{bmatrix} 3 & 4 & -3 \end{bmatrix}$ est un vecteur directeur de la droite Δ qui passe par les points $A(2, -3, 1)$ et $B(5, 1, -2)$. Si on choisit le point A pour formuler l'équation vectorielle de la droite Δ, on obtient

$$\begin{bmatrix} x & y & z \end{bmatrix} = \begin{bmatrix} 2 & -3 & 1 \end{bmatrix} + k\begin{bmatrix} 3 & 4 & -3 \end{bmatrix} \quad \text{où} \quad k \in \mathbb{R}$$

Par contre, si on choisit le point B, l'équation vectorielle de Δ s'écrit

$$\begin{bmatrix} x & y & z \end{bmatrix} = \begin{bmatrix} 5 & 1 & -2 \end{bmatrix} + t\begin{bmatrix} 3 & 4 & -3 \end{bmatrix} \quad \text{où} \quad t \in \mathbb{R}$$

Même si les deux équations présentent des différences, elles n'en décrivent pas moins la même droite, soit la droite qui passe par les points A et B.

Pour trouver un autre point de la droite Δ, on remplace k par une valeur réelle quelconque. Pour $k = 2$, on obtient $x = 8$, $y = 5$ et $z = -5$. Par conséquent, le point $(8, 5, -5)$ appartient à la droite Δ.

Le point $C(-1, -7, 4)$ appartient aussi à la droite Δ. En effet, si on remplace x, y et z respectivement par -1, -7 et 4 dans l'équation de cette droite, on obtient $k = -1$. Par contre, le point

$E(-4, 0, 8)$ n'appartient pas à la droite Δ parce qu'il n'existe aucune valeur de k qui vérifie l'équation de la droite. En effet, si $x = -4$, alors $k = -2$; mais cette valeur de k donne $y = -11$ et non $y = 0$. Par conséquent, le point E n'appartient pas à la droite Δ.

EXERCICE 9.1

Soit les points $A(1, -1, 1)$ et $B(-2, -3, -4)$.

a) Quelle est l'équation vectorielle de la droite Δ qui passe par les points A et B?

b) Trouvez un point de la droite Δ, distinct de A et de B.

c) Vérifiez que le point $C(-5, -5, -9)$ appartient à la droite Δ.

d) Vérifiez que le point $D(1, 2, 3)$ n'appartient pas à la droite Δ.

e) Montrez que $\begin{bmatrix} x & y & z \end{bmatrix} = \begin{bmatrix} 4 & 1 & 6 \end{bmatrix} + t\begin{bmatrix} 3 & 2 & 5 \end{bmatrix}$ où $t \in \mathbb{R}$ représente également la droite Δ.

9.1.2 ÉQUATIONS PARAMÉTRIQUES D'UNE DROITE DE L'ESPACE

Si on exprime chacune des coordonnées d'un point $X(x, y, z)$ d'une droite en fonction du paramètre k de l'équation vectorielle de celle-ci, on obtient les **équations paramétriques d'une droite de l'espace**, soit

$$x = p_1 + kd_1$$
$$y = p_2 + kd_2$$
$$z = p_3 + kd_3$$

où $k \in \mathbb{R}$.

Il faut se rappeler que p_1, p_2 et p_3 représentent les coordonnées d'un point P de la droite (et, par le fait même, les composantes du rayon vecteur $\overrightarrow{OP}$) et que d_1, d_2 et d_3 représentent les composantes d'un vecteur directeur de la droite.

ÉQUATIONS PARAMÉTRIQUES D'UNE DROITE DE L'ESPACE

Les équations paramétriques d'une droite Δ qui passe par le point $P(p_1, p_2, p_3)$ et dont $\vec{d} = \begin{bmatrix} d_1 & d_2 & d_3 \end{bmatrix}$ est un vecteur directeur sont

$$x = p_1 + kd_1$$
$$y = p_2 + kd_2$$
$$z = p_3 + kd_3$$

où $k \in \mathbb{R}$.

Exemple

Les équations paramétriques de la droite passant par le point $A(1, 2, 3)$ et ayant comme vecteur directeur $\vec{d} = \begin{bmatrix} 5 & -6 & -4 \end{bmatrix}$ sont

$$x = 1 + 5k \quad y = 2 - 6k \quad z = 3 - 4k \quad \text{où } k \in \mathbb{R}$$

Quelles sont les équations paramétriques de la droite Δ qui passe par les points $A(0, 1, 2)$ et $B(5, 3, 2)$?

9.1.3 Équations symétriques d'une droite de l'espace

Si on isole le paramètre k dans chacune des équations paramétriques d'une droite, on a

$$\left.\begin{array}{l} x = p_1 + kd_1 \\ y = p_2 + kd_2 \\ z = p_3 + kd_3 \end{array}\right\} \quad \Rightarrow \quad \left\{\begin{array}{l} k = \dfrac{x - p_1}{d_1} \\[2mm] k = \dfrac{y - p_2}{d_2} \\[2mm] k = \dfrac{z - p_3}{d_3} \end{array}\right.$$

à la condition que d_1, d_2 et d_3 soient tous différents de zéro.

ÉQUATIONS SYMÉTRIQUES D'UNE DROITE DE L'ESPACE

Les équations symétriques d'une droite Δ qui passe par le point $P(p_1, p_2, p_3)$ et dont $\vec{d} = \begin{bmatrix} d_1 & d_2 & d_3 \end{bmatrix}$ est un vecteur directeur sont

$$\frac{x - p_1}{d_1} = \frac{y - p_2}{d_2} = \frac{z - p_3}{d_3}$$

à la condition que les composantes du vecteur directeur soient toutes différentes de zéro.

De ces trois équations, on déduit les **équations symétriques d'une droite de l'espace** passant par le point $P(p_1, p_2, p_3)$ et ayant comme vecteur directeur $\vec{d} = \begin{bmatrix} d_1 & d_2 & d_3 \end{bmatrix}$:

$$\frac{x - p_1}{d_1} = \frac{y - p_2}{d_2} = \frac{z - p_3}{d_3} \quad \text{où} \quad d_1 \neq 0, \ d_2 \neq 0 \text{ et } d_3 \neq 0$$

Exemple

La droite Δ_1 dont les équations symétriques sont

$$\Delta_1 : \frac{x - 2}{-1} = \frac{y - 3}{4} = \frac{z + 5}{6}$$

passe par le point $(2, 3, -5)$ et $\vec{d_1} = \begin{bmatrix} -1 & 4 & 6 \end{bmatrix}$ en est un vecteur directeur.

La droite Δ_2 parallèle à Δ_1 et passant par le point $P(1, -2, 4)$ a également $\vec{d_1}$ comme vecteur directeur. Les équations symétriques de Δ_2 sont donc

$$\Delta_2 : \frac{x - 1}{-1} = \frac{y + 2}{4} = \frac{z - 4}{6}$$

Par ailleurs, la droite $\Delta_3 : x - 9 = y = z + 12$ a comme vecteur directeur $\vec{d_3} = \begin{bmatrix} 1 & 1 & 1 \end{bmatrix}$ et elle passe par le point $(9, 0, -12)$.

Mais qu'en est-il des équations symétriques d'une droite dont un vecteur directeur a au moins une composante nulle ? Les divisions par zéro étant interdites, il faut reformuler les équations symétriques d'une telle droite, comme l'indique l'exemple suivant.

Exemple

Les équations paramétriques de la droite Δ qui passe par le point $(1, 2, 3)$ et dont $\vec{d} = \begin{bmatrix} -5 & 0 & 4 \end{bmatrix}$ est un vecteur directeur sont

$$x = 1 - 5k \quad y = 2 \quad z = 3 + 4k \quad \text{où} \quad k \in \mathbb{R}$$

Si on isole k dans ces équations, on obtient les équations symétriques de Δ :

$$\frac{x - 1}{-5} = \frac{z - 3}{4} \quad \text{et} \quad y = 2$$

EXERCICE 9.3

1. Quelles sont les équations symétriques de la droite Δ_1 qui passe par le point $(4, 2, 0)$ et dont $\vec{d_1} = \begin{bmatrix} 1 & 3 & 5 \end{bmatrix}$ est un vecteur directeur ?

2. Quelles sont les équations symétriques de la droite Δ_2 qui passe par les points $A(3, 2, 1)$ et $B(2, 5, 3)$?

3. Quelles sont les équations symétriques de la droite Δ_3 qui passe par le point $(4, 9, -14)$ et dont $\vec{d_3} = \begin{bmatrix} 0 & -2 & 4 \end{bmatrix}$ est un vecteur directeur ?

4. Quelles sont les équations symétriques de la droite Δ_4 qui passe par le point $(2, 1, 3)$ et dont $\vec{d_4} = \begin{bmatrix} 0 & 0 & -4 \end{bmatrix}$ est un vecteur directeur ?

9.1.4 POSITION RELATIVE DE DEUX DROITES DE L'ESPACE

Il est intéressant d'étudier la position relative de deux droites : dans l'espace, deux droites peuvent être parallèles (distinctes ou confondues), concourantes ou gauches.

Deux droites ayant des vecteurs directeurs parallèles sont elles aussi parallèles. Elles sont distinctes si elles n'ont aucun point commun ; dans le cas contraire, elles sont dites confondues (elles sont composées exactement des mêmes points). Dans la figure qui suit, les droites Δ_1, Δ_2 et Δ_3 ont un même vecteur directeur, soit $\vec{d}$: elles sont donc parallèles. Les droites Δ_1 et Δ_2 sont distinctes parce qu'elles n'ont aucun point commun, alors que les droites Δ_1 et Δ_3 sont confondues parce qu'elles ont un point commun (en fait, tous leurs points sont communs).

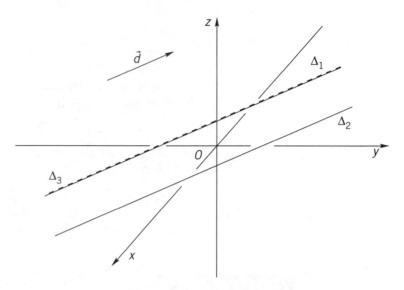

DROITES GAUCHES

Deux droites de l'espace sont dites gauches si elles ne sont pas parallèles et qu'elles ne se coupent pas.

Les vecteurs directeurs de deux droites non parallèles ne sont pas parallèles. Deux droites sont dites concourantes si elles ne sont pas parallèles et qu'elles se coupent en un point de l'espace, alors que deux **droites** sont dites **gauches** si elles ne sont pas parallèles et qu'elles ne se coupent pas. Dans la figure qui suit, les droites Δ_1 et Δ_2 ne sont pas parallèles parce que leurs vecteurs directeurs ne le sont pas, et elles sont gauches parce qu'elles n'ont aucun point commun : Δ_1 passe au-dessus de Δ_2. Les droites Δ_1 et Δ_3 ne sont pas parallèles parce que leurs vecteurs directeurs ne le sont pas, et elles sont concourantes parce qu'elles se rencontrent au point P.

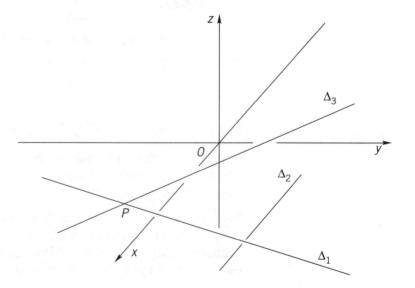

Pour déterminer si deux droites se coupent et, le cas échéant, trouver leur point d'intersection, il faut résoudre un système d'équations. Si le système admet une solution unique, les droites sont concourantes; s'il admet une infinité de solutions, les droites sont parallèles confondues; s'il n'admet aucune solution, les droites sont parallèles distinctes lorsque leurs vecteurs directeurs sont parallèles, et elles sont gauches lorsque leurs vecteurs directeurs ne sont pas parallèles. Les exemples qui suivent illustrent chacun de ces cas.

Exemple

1. Les droites Δ_1 et Δ_2 ont comme équations paramétriques

$$\Delta_1 : x = 1 + 5k_1 \quad y = 2 - 6k_1 \quad z = 3 - 4k_1 \quad \text{où} \quad k_1 \in \mathbb{R}$$
$$\Delta_2 : x = 8 + k_2 \quad y = -2 + k_2 \quad z = 1 + k_2 \quad \text{où} \quad k_2 \in \mathbb{R}$$

Les vecteurs $\vec{d_1} = \begin{bmatrix} 5 & -6 & -4 \end{bmatrix}$ et $\vec{d_2} = \begin{bmatrix} 1 & 1 & 1 \end{bmatrix}$ sont respectivement des vecteurs directeurs de Δ_1 et de Δ_2. Comme ces vecteurs ne sont pas parallèles ($\vec{d_1} \neq k\vec{d_2}$), les deux droites ne sont pas parallèles. Il reste à déterminer si elles sont concourantes ou gauches, c'est-à-dire qu'il faut vérifier si elles ont un point commun.

On suppose que (x, y, z) est le point d'intersection de Δ_1 et de Δ_2. Les coordonnées de ce point doivent donc vérifier les équations paramétriques de chacune des deux droites. Par conséquent,

$$1 + 5k_1 = 8 + k_2 \quad 2 - 6k_1 = -2 + k_2 \quad 3 - 4k_1 = 1 + k_2$$

On résout ce système de trois équations à deux inconnues par la méthode d'élimination gaussienne :

$$\begin{bmatrix} 5 & -1 & 7 \\ -6 & -1 & -4 \\ -4 & -1 & -2 \end{bmatrix} \sim \begin{bmatrix} 5 & -1 & 7 \\ 0 & -\tfrac{11}{5} & \tfrac{22}{5} \\ 0 & -\tfrac{9}{5} & \tfrac{18}{5} \end{bmatrix} \begin{array}{l} L_2 \to L_2 + \tfrac{6}{5}L_1 \\ L_3 \to L_3 + \tfrac{4}{5}L_1 \end{array}$$

$$\sim \begin{bmatrix} 5 & -1 & 7 \\ 0 & -\tfrac{11}{5} & \tfrac{22}{5} \\ 0 & 0 & 0 \end{bmatrix} \begin{array}{l} \\ \\ L_3 \to L_3 - \tfrac{9}{11}L_2 \end{array}$$

La solution du système d'équations est donc $k_1 = 1$ et $k_2 = -2$. En remplaçant k_1 et k_2 par leur valeur dans les équations de Δ_1 ou de Δ_2, on obtient le point d'intersection des deux droites : $(6, -4, -1)$. Par conséquent, les droites Δ_1 et Δ_2 sont concourantes.

On calcule l'angle θ entre deux droites concourantes de l'espace de vecteur directeur $\vec{d_1}$ et $\vec{d_2}$ respectivement, de la même façon que pour deux droites du plan (chap. 6). Ainsi, l'angle entre deux droites concourantes de l'espace est donné par

$$\theta = \arccos\frac{\left|\vec{d_1} \cdot \vec{d_2}\right|}{\left\|\vec{d_1}\right\| \left\|\vec{d_2}\right\|}$$

Par conséquent, l'angle entre les droites Δ_1 et Δ_2 est donné par

$$\theta = \arccos\frac{\left|\vec{d_1} \cdot \vec{d_2}\right|}{\left\|\vec{d_1}\right\| \left\|\vec{d_2}\right\|} = \arccos\frac{5}{\sqrt{77}\,\sqrt{3}} \approx 70,8°$$

2. Les droites Δ_2 et Δ_3 ont comme équations paramétriques

$$\Delta_2 : x = 8 + k_2 \qquad y = -2 + k_2 \qquad z = 1 + k_2 \qquad \text{où} \quad k_2 \in \mathbb{R}$$
$$\Delta_3 : x = 3 + 2k_3 \qquad y = 2k_3 \qquad\quad z = 7 + 2k_3 \qquad \text{où} \quad k_3 \in \mathbb{R}$$

Les vecteurs $\vec{d_2} = \begin{bmatrix} 1 & 1 & 1 \end{bmatrix}$ et $\vec{d_3} = \begin{bmatrix} 2 & 2 & 2 \end{bmatrix}$ sont respectivement des vecteurs directeurs des droites Δ_2 et Δ_3. Comme ces vecteurs sont parallèles ($\vec{d_3} = 2\vec{d_2}$), les droites Δ_2 et Δ_3 le sont également. Il reste à déterminer si ces droites sont distinctes ou confondues. En posant $k_2 = 0$, on obtient le point $(8, -2, 1)$ de la droite Δ_2. Ce point n'appartient pas à Δ_3 parce que, si (x, y, z) est un point de la droite Δ_3 et si $x = 8$, alors $k_3 = \frac{5}{2}$; mais, pour cette valeur de k_3, $y = 5$ et $z = 12$. Or, $(8, -2, 1) \neq (8, 5, 12)$. Le point $(8, -2, 1)$ n'appartient donc pas à Δ_3. Les droites Δ_2 et Δ_3 sont parallèles, et il existe au moins un point de Δ_2 qui est extérieur à Δ_3. Les droites Δ_2 et Δ_3 sont donc des droites parallèles distinctes.

3. Les droites Δ_1 et Δ_3 ont comme équations paramétriques

$$\Delta_1 : x = 1 + 5k_1 \qquad y = 2 - 6k_1 \qquad z = 3 - 4k_1 \qquad \text{où} \quad k_1 \in \mathbb{R}$$
$$\Delta_3 : x = 3 + 2k_3 \qquad y = 2k_3 \qquad\quad z = 7 + 2k_3 \qquad \text{où} \quad k_3 \in \mathbb{R}$$

Les vecteurs $\vec{d_1} = \begin{bmatrix} 5 & -6 & -4 \end{bmatrix}$ et $\vec{d_3} = \begin{bmatrix} 2 & 2 & 2 \end{bmatrix}$ sont respectivement des vecteurs directeurs de Δ_1 et de Δ_3. Comme ces vecteurs ne sont pas parallèles ($\vec{d_1} \neq k\vec{d_3}$), les droites Δ_1 et Δ_3 ne sont pas parallèles. Il reste à déterminer si ces droites sont concourantes ou gauches, c'est-à-dire qu'il faut vérifier si elles ont un point commun.

On suppose que (x, y, z) est le point d'intersection de Δ_1 et Δ_3. Ce point doit donc vérifier les équations paramétriques de chacune des deux droites. Par conséquent,

$$1 + 5k_1 = 3 + 2k_3 \qquad 2 - 6k_1 = 2k_3 \qquad 3 - 4k_1 = 7 + 2k_3$$

On résout ce système de trois équations à deux inconnues par la méthode d'élimination gaussienne :

$$\begin{bmatrix} 5 & -2 & | & 2 \\ -6 & -2 & | & -2 \\ -4 & -2 & | & 4 \end{bmatrix} \sim \begin{bmatrix} 5 & -2 & | & 2 \\ 3 & 1 & | & 1 \\ 1 & \frac{1}{2} & | & -1 \end{bmatrix} \begin{matrix} \\ L_2 \to -\frac{1}{2}L_2 \\ L_3 \to -\frac{1}{4}L_3 \end{matrix}$$

$$\sim \begin{bmatrix} 1 & \frac{1}{2} & | & -1 \\ 3 & 1 & | & 1 \\ 5 & -2 & | & 2 \end{bmatrix} \begin{matrix} L_1 \leftrightarrow L_3 \\ \\ \end{matrix}$$

$$\sim \begin{bmatrix} 1 & \frac{1}{2} & | & -1 \\ 0 & -\frac{1}{2} & | & 4 \\ 0 & -\frac{9}{2} & | & 7 \end{bmatrix} \begin{matrix} \\ L_2 \to L_2 - 3L_1 \\ L_3 \to L_3 - 5L_1 \end{matrix}$$

$$\sim \begin{bmatrix} 1 & \frac{1}{2} & | & -1 \\ 0 & -\frac{1}{2} & | & 4 \\ 0 & 0 & | & -29 \end{bmatrix} \begin{matrix} \\ \\ L_3 \to L_3 - 9L_2 \end{matrix}$$

Le système d'équations n'admet aucune solution. Par conséquent, les droites Δ_1 et Δ_3 n'ont aucun point commun (x, y, z) : elles ne sont ni parallèles ni concourantes. Les droites Δ_1 et Δ_3 sont donc des droites gauches.

4. Les droites Δ_2 et Δ_4 ont comme équations paramétriques

$$\Delta_2 : x = 8 + k_2 \quad y = -2 + k_2 \quad z = 1 + k_2 \quad \text{où} \quad k_2 \in \mathbb{R}$$
$$\Delta_4 : x = 10 - k_4 \quad y = -k_4 \quad z = 3 - k_4 \quad \text{où} \quad k_4 \in \mathbb{R}$$

Les vecteurs $\vec{d_2} = \begin{bmatrix} 1 & 1 & 1 \end{bmatrix}$ et $\vec{d_4} = \begin{bmatrix} -1 & -1 & -1 \end{bmatrix}$ sont respectivement des vecteurs directeurs des droites Δ_2 et Δ_4. Comme ces vecteurs sont parallèles ($\vec{d_2} = -\vec{d_4}$), les droites Δ_2 et Δ_4 le sont également. Il reste à déterminer si ces droites sont distinctes ou confondues. En posant $k_2 = 0$, on obtient le point $(8, -2, 1)$ de la droite Δ_2. Or, ce point appartient aussi à la droite Δ_4 (pour $k_4 = 2$). Par conséquent, les droites Δ_2 et Δ_4 sont parallèles et elles ont au moins un point commun. Ce sont donc des droites parallèles confondues.

EXERCICE 9.4

Soit les droites définies dans l'exercice 9.3.

a) Que peut-on dire de la position relative des droites Δ_1 et Δ_2 ? Si ces droites sont concourantes, trouvez l'angle qu'elles déterminent.

b) Que peut-on dire de la position relative des droites Δ_1 et Δ_3? Si ces droites sont concourantes, trouvez l'angle qu'elles déterminent.

9.1.5 DISTANCE D'UN POINT À UNE DROITE

On peut faire appel au produit vectoriel pour trouver la distance d'un point à une droite. Le graphique suivant représente une droite Δ passant par un point P et de vecteur directeur $\vec{d}$, et un point Q extérieur à cette droite.

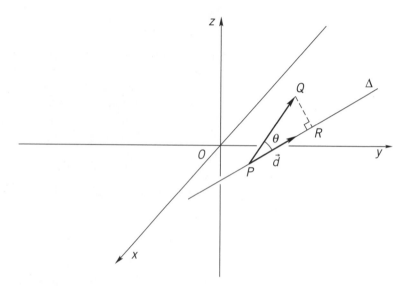

La distance du point Q à la droite Δ est donnée par $\|\overrightarrow{QR}\| = \|\overrightarrow{PQ}\| \sin\theta$. Or,

$$\|\overrightarrow{PQ} \times \vec{d}\| = \|\overrightarrow{PQ}\| \|\vec{d}\| \sin\theta \quad \Rightarrow \quad \frac{\|\overrightarrow{PQ} \times \vec{d}\|}{\|\vec{d}\|} = \|\overrightarrow{PQ}\| \sin\theta$$

La distance d'un point Q à une droite Δ passant par un point P et de vecteur directeur $\vec{d}$ est donc donnée par

$$\frac{\|\overrightarrow{PQ} \times \vec{d}\|}{\|\vec{d}\|}$$

On peut également vouloir déterminer les coordonnées du point R de la droite Δ qui est le plus proche d'un point Q extérieur à cette droite. La figure indique clairement que $\overrightarrow{PR} = \overrightarrow{PQ}_{\vec{d}}$, d'où on tire

$$\overrightarrow{OR} = \overrightarrow{OP} + \overrightarrow{PR} = \overrightarrow{OP} + \overrightarrow{PQ}_{\vec{d}}$$

Cette relation permet de trouver les composantes du rayon vecteur $\overrightarrow{OR}$ et, par le fait même, les coordonnées du point R.

Exemple

On cherche la distance du point $Q(1, 2, 4)$ à la droite Δ dont les équations paramétriques sont

$$x = 1 + k \quad y = 3k \quad z = 3 - 2k \quad \text{où} \quad k \in \mathbb{R}$$

Il faut d'abord déterminer un vecteur directeur et un point de Δ. Or, en posant $k = 0$, on obtient le point $P(1, 0, 3)$ de la droite. De plus, $\vec{d} = \begin{bmatrix} 1 & 3 & -2 \end{bmatrix}$ est un vecteur directeur de Δ. Ainsi, $\overrightarrow{PQ} = \begin{bmatrix} 0 & 2 & 1 \end{bmatrix}$, $\|\vec{d}\| = \sqrt{14}$ et

$$\overrightarrow{PQ} \times \vec{d} = \begin{vmatrix} \vec{i} & \vec{j} & \vec{k} \\ 0 & 2 & 1 \\ 1 & 3 & -2 \end{vmatrix} = -7\vec{i} + \vec{j} - 2\vec{k} \quad \Rightarrow \quad \|\overrightarrow{PQ} \times \vec{d}\| = \sqrt{54}$$

Par conséquent, la distance du point $Q(1, 2, 4)$ à la droite Δ est

$$\frac{\|\overrightarrow{PQ} \times \vec{d}\|}{\|\vec{d}\|} = \frac{\sqrt{54}}{\sqrt{14}} = \sqrt{\frac{27}{7}} \approx 1{,}96 \text{ unité}$$

De plus, si R est le point de la droite Δ le plus proche de Q, alors

$$\begin{aligned}
\overrightarrow{OR} &= \overrightarrow{OP} + \overrightarrow{PR} \\
&= \overrightarrow{OP} + \overrightarrow{PQ}_{\vec{d}} \\
&= \overrightarrow{OP} + \frac{\overrightarrow{PQ} \cdot \vec{d}}{\vec{d} \cdot \vec{d}} \vec{d} \\
&= \begin{bmatrix} 1 & 0 & 3 \end{bmatrix} + \tfrac{4}{14} \begin{bmatrix} 1 & 3 & -2 \end{bmatrix} \\
&= \begin{bmatrix} \tfrac{9}{7} & \tfrac{6}{7} & \tfrac{17}{7} \end{bmatrix}
\end{aligned}$$

Par conséquent, $R\left(\tfrac{9}{7}, \tfrac{6}{7}, \tfrac{17}{7}\right)$ est le point de la droite Δ qui est le plus proche du point $Q(1, 2, 4)$. La distance entre Q et R est égale à

$$\sqrt{(1 - \tfrac{9}{7})^2 + (2 - \tfrac{6}{7})^2 + (4 - \tfrac{17}{7})^2} = \sqrt{\tfrac{27}{7}} \text{ unité}$$

et cette valeur est exactement la distance du point Q à la droite Δ.

EXERCICE 9.5

Soit la droite Δ dont les équations symétriques sont

$$\frac{x - 3}{2} = \frac{y + 1}{3} = z$$

a) À l'aide des constantes de ces équations, trouvez un vecteur directeur et un point de la droite Δ.

b) Quelle est la distance du point $Q_1(-1, 2, -3)$ à la droite Δ?

c) Quel est le point de Δ le plus proche du point Q_1?

d) Quelle est la distance du point $Q_2(5, 2, 1)$ à la droite Δ? Que peut-on dire du point Q_2?

9.1.6 Distance entre deux droites parallèles

La distance entre deux droites parallèles Δ_1 et Δ_2 est égale à la distance entre un point P_2 de la droite Δ_2 et la droite Δ_1. On applique donc le procédé décrit dans la section précédente pour calculer une telle distance.

Exemple

Soit les droites :

$$\Delta_1 : x - 8 = y + 2 = z - 1$$
$$\Delta_2 : x = 3 + 2k_2 \quad y = 2k_2 \quad z = 7 + 2k_2 \quad \text{où} \quad k_2 \in \mathbb{R}$$

La droite Δ_1 est définie par ses équations symétriques, alors que la droite Δ_2 est définie par ses équations paramétriques. Le vecteur $\vec{d_1} = \begin{bmatrix} 1 & 1 & 1 \end{bmatrix}$ est un vecteur directeur de la droite Δ_1 et $\vec{d_2} = \begin{bmatrix} 2 & 2 & 2 \end{bmatrix}$ est un vecteur directeur de Δ_2. Comme ces deux vecteurs sont parallèles ($\vec{d_2} = 2\vec{d_1}$), les droites Δ_1 et Δ_2 le sont également. Pour trouver la distance entre ces deux droites, on calcule la distance entre un point P_2 de la droite Δ_2 et la droite Δ_1.

Or, $P_1(8, -2, 1)$ appartient à Δ_1 et $P_2(3, 0, 7)$ appartient à Δ_2. Par conséquent, la distance entre les deux droites est égale à

$$\frac{\left\|\overrightarrow{P_1P_2} \times \vec{d_1}\right\|}{\left\|\vec{d_1}\right\|}$$

De plus, $\overrightarrow{P_1P_2} = \begin{bmatrix} -5 & 2 & 6 \end{bmatrix}$, d'où

$$\overrightarrow{P_1P_2} \times \vec{d_1} = \begin{vmatrix} \vec{i} & \vec{j} & \vec{k} \\ -5 & 2 & 6 \\ 1 & 1 & 1 \end{vmatrix} = -4\vec{i} + 11\vec{j} - 7\vec{k}$$

La distance entre les deux droites vaut donc

$$\frac{\left\|\overrightarrow{P_1P_2} \times \vec{d_1}\right\|}{\left\|\vec{d_1}\right\|} = \frac{\sqrt{186}}{\sqrt{3}} \approx 7,9 \text{ unités}$$

EXERCICE 9.6

Soit les droites Δ_1 et Δ_2 dont les équations sont respectivement

$$\Delta_1 : x - 8 = y + 2 = z - 1$$

$$\Delta_2 : \frac{x + 2}{3} = \frac{y - 1}{3} = \frac{z}{3}$$

a) Vérifiez que les deux droites sont parallèles.

b) Quelle est la distance entre les deux droites?

Nous aborderons le concept de distance entre deux droites gauches lorsque nous traiterons de la distance entre deux plans parallèles puisque ces deux notions sont reliées.

9.2 PLAN DE L'ESPACE

Nous avons vu, à la section 9.1, qu'une droite est entièrement déterminée par deux points distincts ou par un point et un vecteur directeur. Mais on peut également concevoir une droite comme l'intersection de deux plans non parallèles, comme l'indique le graphique qui suit. C'est pourquoi nous allons examiner différentes façons de décrire un plan de l'espace. Tout comme nous avons utilisé le symbole Δ (la majuscule grecque delta correspondant à D, pour *droite*) pour représenter une droite, nous allons désigner un plan par le symbole π (la lettre grecque correspondant à p, pour *plan*).

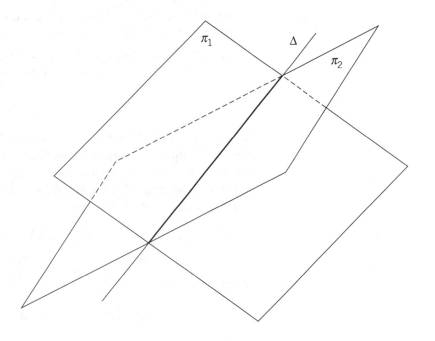

L'étude du plan de l'espace présente plusieurs similarités avec l'étude de la droite du plan puisque le plan est un objet à deux dimensions dans un univers à trois dimensions, alors que la droite du plan est un objet à une dimension dans un univers à deux dimensions. Il n'est donc pas étonnant que les résultats obtenus pour le plan de l'espace ne diffèrent des résultats obtenus pour la droite du plan que par l'ajout d'une troisième coordonnée ou d'une troisième composante. De plus, les stratégies employées sont très similaires.

9.2.1 ÉQUATION CARTÉSIENNE D'UN PLAN

VECTEUR NORMAL À UN PLAN

Un vecteur normal à un plan est un vecteur perpendiculaire à ce plan.

Un vecteur de l'espace définit une famille de plans parallèles, tous perpendiculaires à ce vecteur. On dit d'un vecteur perpendiculaire à un plan que c'est un **vecteur normal** à ce plan et on le note $\vec{n} = \begin{bmatrix} a & b & c \end{bmatrix}$. Des plans parallèles se distinguent par le fait qu'ils ont des vecteurs normaux parallèles. De façon similaire, deux plans perpendiculaires se distinguent par le fait que leurs vecteurs normaux respectifs sont mutuellement perpendiculaires.

Pour déterminer un plan particulier, il faut donc en donner un point $P(p_1,\ p_2,\ p_3)$ et un vecteur normal.

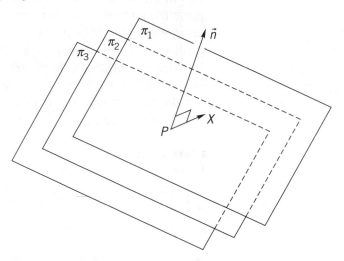

La figure indique clairement que tout vecteur d'un plan (ou parallèle à un plan) est perpendiculaire à un vecteur normal à ce plan. En particulier, si $X(x,\ y,\ z)$ est un point quelconque du plan, alors le vecteur $\vec{n}$ est perpendiculaire au vecteur $\overrightarrow{PX}$. On en déduit que le produit scalaire des vecteurs $\vec{n}$ et $\overrightarrow{PX}$ est nul, c'est-à-dire que

$$\vec{n} \cdot \overrightarrow{PX} = 0 \quad \Rightarrow \quad \vec{n} \cdot (\overrightarrow{PO} + \overrightarrow{OX}) = 0 \quad \Rightarrow \quad \vec{n} \cdot \overrightarrow{PO} + \vec{n} \cdot \overrightarrow{OX} = 0$$

$$\Rightarrow \quad \vec{n} \cdot \overrightarrow{OX} = -\vec{n} \cdot \overrightarrow{PO} \quad \Rightarrow \quad \vec{n} \cdot \overrightarrow{OX} = \vec{n} \cdot \overrightarrow{OP}$$

Par conséquent,

$$\begin{bmatrix} a & b & c \end{bmatrix} \cdot \begin{bmatrix} x & y & z \end{bmatrix} = \begin{bmatrix} a & b & c \end{bmatrix} \cdot \begin{bmatrix} p_1 & p_2 & p_3 \end{bmatrix}$$

d'où

$$ax + by + cz = ap_1 + bp_2 + cp_3$$

Cette équation s'écrit, plus simplement, sous la forme

$$ax + by + cz = d \quad \text{où} \quad d = ap_1 + bp_2 + cp_3$$

L'**équation cartésienne d'un plan** π passant par un point $P(p_1, p_2, p_3)$ et de vecteur normal $\vec{n} = \begin{bmatrix} a & b & c \end{bmatrix}$ est donc donnée par

$$\pi : ax + by + cz = d \quad \text{où} \quad d = ap_1 + bp_2 + cp_3$$

Si on compare cette équation avec l'équation cartésienne d'une droite du plan, on remarque des similarités autant dans la manière de construire ces équations que dans les équations elles-mêmes.

Il est également à noter que la forme de l'équation cartésienne d'un plan varie en fonction du choix du vecteur normal. Enfin, les coefficients de x, y et z dans cette équation représentent les composantes d'un vecteur normal au plan.

Il est souvent plus simple de reconstruire l'équation cartésienne d'un plan à l'aide du principe de base (un vecteur $\vec{n}$ normal à un plan est perpendiculaire à tout vecteur $\overrightarrow{PX}$ de ce plan, d'où $\vec{n} \cdot \overrightarrow{PX} = 0$) que de se rappeler la formule générale.

Exemple

Un plan π est complètement déterminé par trois points non colinéaires de ce plan. Pour trouver l'équation cartésienne du plan qui passe par les points $A(2, 4, 1)$, $B(-1, 3, 2)$ et $C(3, 1, -2)$, il faut d'abord trouver un vecteur normal à ce plan. Or, les vecteurs $\overrightarrow{AB}$ et $\overrightarrow{AC}$ étant des vecteurs de ce plan, leur produit vectoriel est perpendiculaire à chacun d'eux et, par conséquent, au plan qui les contient :

$$\vec{n} = \overrightarrow{AB} \times \overrightarrow{AC} = \begin{vmatrix} \vec{i} & \vec{j} & \vec{k} \\ -3 & -1 & 1 \\ 1 & -3 & -3 \end{vmatrix} = \begin{bmatrix} 6 & -8 & 10 \end{bmatrix}$$

Si on choisit $A(2, 4, 1)$ comme point connu du plan, on obtient l'équation

$$6x - 8y + 10z = (6)(2) + (-8)(4) + (10)(1) = -10$$

Par conséquent, l'équation cartésienne du plan π est donnée par

$$\pi : 6x - 8y + 10z = -10$$

Trouver un point particulier du plan π est un jeu d'enfant. En effet, il suffit de fixer la valeur de la ou des variables libres, puis de calculer la valeur de la variable liée. Ainsi, en remplaçant x et y par 0 dans l'équation du plan π, on obtient $z = -1$. Par conséquent, le point $(0, 0, -1)$ appartient à π. On aurait également pu effectuer la substitution $y = 1$ et $z = -5$ dans la même équation, ce qui donne $x = 8$. Le point $(8, 1, -5)$ appartient donc lui aussi au plan π.

L'équation cartésienne d'un plan n'a pas une forme unique. On aurait obtenu une formulation différente de l'équation du même plan si on avait utilisé l'un des vecteurs $\overrightarrow{BA} \times \overrightarrow{BC}$ et $\overrightarrow{CA} \times \overrightarrow{CB}$ comme vecteur normal.

Si on choisit $\overrightarrow{BA} \times \overrightarrow{BC}$ comme vecteur normal, on obtient l'équation cartésienne

$$\pi: -6x + 8y - 10z = 10$$

EXERCICE 9.7

Soit le plan π_1 dont l'équation cartésienne est donnée par

$$\pi_1: 2x + 3y + z = 6$$

a) Lesquels des points suivants appartiennent au plan π_1 : $A(1, 1, 1)$, $B(2, 1, -2)$, $C(3, -2, 6)$ ou $D(2, -1, 5)$?

b) Quel point d'abscisse 3 et de cote 9 appartient au plan π_1?

c) Donnez un vecteur normal au plan π_1.

d) Trouvez un vecteur unitaire normal au plan π_1.

e) Déterminez l'équation cartésienne du plan π_2 qui passe par le point $E = (1, 2, -4)$ et qui est parallèle au plan π_1.

9.2.2 ÉQUATION NORMALE D'UN PLAN

L'équation normale d'un plan se calcule à l'aide d'un vecteur unitaire normal à ce plan, tout comme l'équation normale d'une droite du plan s'obtient à l'aide d'un vecteur unitaire normal à cette droite (chap. 6).

ÉQUATION NORMALE D'UN PLAN

L'équation normale d'un plan est l'équation cartésienne de ce plan obtenue avec un vecteur unitaire normal à ce plan.

L'**équation normale d'un plan** π passant par le point $P = (p_1, p_2, p_3)$ et de vecteur normal unitaire

$$\vec{n_u} = \left[\frac{a}{\sqrt{a^2 + b^2 + c^2}} \quad \frac{b}{\sqrt{a^2 + b^2 + c^2}} \quad \frac{c}{\sqrt{a^2 + b^2 + c^2}} \right]$$

est donnée par

$$\pi: \frac{a}{\sqrt{a^2 + b^2 + c^2}}x + \frac{b}{\sqrt{a^2 + b^2 + c^2}}y + \frac{c}{\sqrt{a^2 + b^2 + c^2}}z = h$$

où $h = \dfrac{ap_1 + bp_2 + cp_3}{\sqrt{a^2 + b^2 + c^2}}$.

En partant de l'équation cartésienne $\pi\colon ax + by + cz = d$, on obtient

$$h = \frac{d}{\sqrt{a^2 + b^2 + c^2}}$$

On note encore une fois la similarité entre les équations normales d'un plan de l'espace et d'une droite du plan.

Exemple

L'équation normale du plan π d'équation cartésienne

$$\pi\colon 6x - 8y + 10z = -12$$

est donnée par

$$\pi\colon \frac{6}{\sqrt{200}}x - \frac{8}{\sqrt{200}}y + \frac{10}{\sqrt{200}}z = -\frac{12}{\sqrt{200}}$$

ou, après rationalisation des dénominateurs,

$$\pi\colon \frac{3\sqrt{2}}{10}x - \frac{2\sqrt{2}}{5}y + \frac{\sqrt{2}}{2}z = -\frac{3\sqrt{2}}{5}$$

EXERCICE 9.8

Trouvez l'équation normale du plan π qui passe par les points $A(2, 1, 1)$, $B(0, 1, -2)$ et $C(1, -1, 1)$.

9.2.3 DISTANCE D'UN PLAN À L'ORIGINE

Par analogie avec l'équation normale d'une droite du plan, il y a lieu de penser que la valeur absolue de la constante de l'équation normale d'un plan de l'espace représente la distance de ce plan à l'origine. Prouvons ce résultat.

Théorème 9.1

La distance entre l'origine et le plan π d'équation normale

$$\pi\colon \frac{a}{\sqrt{a^2 + b^2 + c^2}}x + \frac{b}{\sqrt{a^2 + b^2 + c^2}}y + \frac{c}{\sqrt{a^2 + b^2 + c^2}}z = h$$

est égale à $|h|$.

Preuve

Soit un plan π situé dans un système de coordonnées cartésiennes.

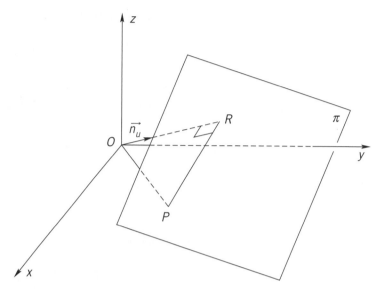

Dans le graphique, on note R le point de π le plus proche de l'origine, $P = (p_1,\ p_2,\ p_3)$ un point connu de π, et

$$\vec{n_u} = \left[\frac{a}{\sqrt{a^2 + b^2 + c^2}} \quad \frac{b}{\sqrt{a^2 + b^2 + c^2}} \quad \frac{c}{\sqrt{a^2 + b^2 + c^2}} \right]$$

un vecteur unitaire normal à π.

La distance du plan π à l'origine est égale à la longueur du vecteur $\overrightarrow{OR}$. Or ce vecteur est le vecteur projection de $\overrightarrow{OP}$ sur $\vec{n_u}$. Par conséquent, la distance du plan π à l'origine est donnée par

$$\left\| \overrightarrow{OR} \right\| = \left\| \overrightarrow{OP}_{\vec{n_u}} \right\| = \left\| \frac{\overrightarrow{OP} \cdot \vec{n_u}}{\vec{n_u} \cdot \vec{n_u}} \vec{n_u} \right\| = \left| \frac{\overrightarrow{OP} \cdot \vec{n_u}}{\vec{n_u} \cdot \vec{n_u}} \right| \left\| \vec{n_u} \right\| = \left| \frac{\overrightarrow{OP} \cdot \vec{n_u}}{1} \right| 1$$

$$= \left| \frac{ap_1}{\sqrt{a^2 + b^2 + c^2}} + \frac{bp_2}{\sqrt{a^2 + b^2 + c^2}} + \frac{cp_3}{\sqrt{a^2 + b^2 + c^2}} \right|$$

$$= \left| \frac{ap_1 + bp_2 + cp_3}{\sqrt{a^2 + b^2 + c^2}} \right|$$

$$= |h| \qquad \blacksquare$$

Exemple

La distance à l'origine du plan π d'équation cartésienne

$$\pi:\ 2x - y + 3z = 6$$

est égale à

$$|h| = \left| \frac{d}{\sqrt{a^2 + b^2 + c^2}} \right| = \left| \frac{6}{\sqrt{2^2 + (-1)^2 + 3^2}} \right| \approx 1{,}6 \text{ unité}$$

EXERCICE 9.9

Quelle est la distance à l'origine du plan π qui passe par les points $A(3, 1, 2)$, $B(0, 1, -2)$ et $C(1, -1, 1)$?

9.2.4 DISTANCE ENTRE UN POINT ET UN PLAN OU ENTRE DEUX PLANS PARALLÈLES

Si on compare la démonstration du théorème 9.1 et l'argument présenté à la section 6.3.1, la similarité du raisonnement saute aux yeux. La seule différence réside dans le fait que, dans le théorème 9.1, le vecteur normal compte trois composantes.

On établit aisément, en s'appuyant sur cette similitude, la formule de la distance d'un point quelconque de l'espace $Q(q_1, q_2, q_3)$ à un plan passant par le point P et d'équation cartésienne π: $ax + by + cz = d$:

$$\frac{\left| \overrightarrow{PQ} \cdot \vec{n} \right|}{\|\vec{n}\|} = \left| \frac{aq_1 + bq_2 + cq_3 - d}{\sqrt{a^2 + b^2 + c^2}} \right|$$

où $\vec{n} = \begin{bmatrix} a & b & c \end{bmatrix}$ est un vecteur normal au plan π.

Un argument analogue à celui qui est employé pour résoudre l'exercice 6.11 permet de prouver ce résultat. Encore une fois, il s'agit d'une simple généralisation du concept correspondant présenté dans le cadre de l'étude de la droite du plan.

Il est à noter que, dans le cas où le point Q appartient au plan π, la distance vaut 0 et que, dans le cas où le point Q coïncide avec l'origine, on obtient le résultat prouvé dans le théorème 9.1.

De plus, il n'est pas étonnant que la distance entre deux plans parallèles π_1 et π_2 (c'est-à-dire entre deux plans dont les vecteurs normaux sont parallèles) soit égale à la distance entre un point Q_1 du plan π_1 et le plan π_2.

Exemple

Les plans $\pi_1 : 2x - y + 3z = 1$ et $\pi_2 : -4x + 2y - 6z = -15$ ont respectivement comme vecteur normal $\vec{n_1} = \begin{bmatrix} 2 & -1 & 3 \end{bmatrix}$ et $\vec{n_2} = \begin{bmatrix} -4 & 2 & -6 \end{bmatrix}$. Comme $\vec{n_2} = -2\,\vec{n_1}$, ces vecteurs sont parallèles. Par conséquent, les plans π_1 et π_2 sont parallèles. Le point $Q_1(0, -1, 0)$ appartenant au plan π_1, la distance entre π_1 et π_2 est égale à la distance entre le point Q_1 et le plan π_2 :

$$\left| \frac{aq_1 + bq_2 + cq_3 - d}{\sqrt{a^2 + b^2 + c^2}} \right| = \left| \frac{(-4)(0) + (2)(-1) + (-6)(0) - (-15)}{\sqrt{(-4)^2 + 2^2 + (-6)^2}} \right|$$

$$= \left| \frac{13}{\sqrt{56}} \right|$$

$$\approx 1{,}7 \text{ unité}$$

La distance entre les plans parallèles $\pi_1 : ax + by + cz = d_1$ et $\pi_2 : ax + by + cz = d_2$ est aussi donnée par l'expression

$$\left| \frac{d_1 - d_2}{\sqrt{a^2 + b^2 + c^2}} \right|$$

Cette formule ne s'applique que si les coefficients de x, y et z sont égaux dans les deux équations des plans parallèles. La preuve de cette formule est demandée à l'exercice 9.10.

EXERCICE 9.10

1. Quelle est la distance entre le point $D(2, 1, 1)$ et le plan π qui passe par les points $A(3, 1, 2)$, $B(0, 1, -2)$ et $C(1, -1, 1)$?

2. Montrez que la distance entre les plans parallèles $\pi_1 : ax + by + cz = d_1$ et $\pi_2 : ax + by + cz = d_2$ est égale à

$$\left| \frac{d_1 - d_2}{\sqrt{a^2 + b^2 + c^2}} \right|$$

Il est intéressant, tout comme dans le cas d'une droite, de déterminer le point R d'un plan π qui est le plus proche d'un point Q extérieur à ce plan.

Nous avons établi, dans un contexte similaire, que le vecteur $\overrightarrow{QR}$ est le vecteur projection de $\overrightarrow{QP}$ sur $\vec{n_u}$, soit $\overrightarrow{QP}_{\vec{n_u}}$, où $\vec{n_u}$ est un vecteur unitaire normal au plan π et P est un point connu de π. Par conséquent,

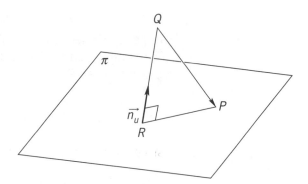

$\overrightarrow{OR} = \overrightarrow{OQ} + \overrightarrow{QR} = \overrightarrow{OQ} + \overrightarrow{QP}_{\vec{n_u}}$. Comme Q, P et $\vec{n_u}$ sont connus, il est facile de déterminer le vecteur position $\overrightarrow{OR}$ et, par le fait même, les coordonnées du point R du plan qui est le plus proche de Q.

Exemple

Soit R le point du plan $\pi\colon 2x - y + 3z = 8$ le plus proche du point $Q(0, -1, 0)$. Le point $P(4, 0, 0)$ appartient à π et $\vec{n} = \begin{bmatrix} 2 & -1 & 3 \end{bmatrix}$ est un vecteur normal au plan, de sorte que

$$\vec{n_u} = \frac{1}{\|\vec{n}\|}\vec{n} = \begin{bmatrix} \dfrac{2}{\sqrt{14}} & \dfrac{-1}{\sqrt{14}} & \dfrac{3}{\sqrt{14}} \end{bmatrix}$$

est un vecteur unitaire normal à π. Pour appliquer la formule

$$\overrightarrow{OR} = \overrightarrow{OQ} + \overrightarrow{QR} = \overrightarrow{OQ} + \overrightarrow{QP}_{\vec{n_u}}$$

il faut trouver les composantes du vecteur $\overrightarrow{QP}_{\vec{n_u}}$. Or,

$$\overrightarrow{QP}_{\vec{n_u}} = \frac{\overrightarrow{QP} \cdot \vec{n_u}}{\vec{n_u} \cdot \vec{n_u}}\vec{n_u}$$

$$= \frac{\begin{bmatrix} 4 & 1 & 0 \end{bmatrix} \cdot \begin{bmatrix} \dfrac{2}{\sqrt{14}} & \dfrac{-1}{\sqrt{14}} & \dfrac{3}{\sqrt{14}} \end{bmatrix}}{1} \begin{bmatrix} \dfrac{2}{\sqrt{14}} & \dfrac{-1}{\sqrt{14}} & \dfrac{3}{\sqrt{14}} \end{bmatrix}$$

$$= \begin{bmatrix} 1 & -0,5 & 1,5 \end{bmatrix}$$

Par conséquent,

$$\overrightarrow{OR} = \overrightarrow{OQ} + \overrightarrow{QR} = \overrightarrow{OQ} + \overrightarrow{QP}_{\vec{n_u}} = \begin{bmatrix} 0 & -1 & 0 \end{bmatrix} + \begin{bmatrix} 1 & -0,5 & 1,5 \end{bmatrix}$$

$$= \begin{bmatrix} 1 & -1,5 & 1,5 \end{bmatrix}$$

On en conclut que le point $R(1, -1,5, 1,5)$ est le point du plan $\pi\colon 2x - y + 3z = 8$ qui est le plus proche du point $Q(0, -1, 0)$.

On peut vérifier que la distance du point Q au plan π vaut $\sqrt{3,5}$ unité. Cette valeur est exactement celle de la distance entre les points Q et R.

9.2.5 Position relative d'une droite et d'un plan

Il existe deux possibilités quant à la position relative d'une droite et d'un plan de l'espace: la droite est parallèle au plan (elle appartient alors au plan ou elle n'a aucun point commun avec le plan) ou elle coupe le plan en un seul point. Dans le premier cas, il est possible d'évaluer la distance entre la droite et le plan, alors que dans le second cas on détermine plutôt les coordonnées du point d'intersection et l'angle que forme la droite avec le plan.

Comment détermine-t-on si une droite est parallèle à un plan? Une droite est parallèle à un plan si tout vecteur directeur de la droite est perpendiculaire à un vecteur normal au plan.

Exemple

1. Soit la droite Δ et le plan π_1 dont les équations sont

$$\Delta : \begin{bmatrix} x & y & z \end{bmatrix} = \begin{bmatrix} 2 & -3 & 1 \end{bmatrix} + k \begin{bmatrix} 3 & 4 & -3 \end{bmatrix} \quad \text{où} \quad k \in \mathbb{R}$$
$$\pi_1 : 2x - y + 3z = 8$$

Le vecteur $\vec{d} = \begin{bmatrix} 3 & 4 & -3 \end{bmatrix}$ est un vecteur directeur de la droite Δ, alors que le vecteur $\vec{n_1} = \begin{bmatrix} 2 & -1 & 3 \end{bmatrix}$ est un vecteur normal au plan π_1. Comme $\vec{d} \cdot \vec{n_1} = -7 \neq 0$, les vecteurs $\vec{d}$ et $\vec{n_1}$ ne sont pas perpendiculaires. Par conséquent, la droite Δ coupe le plan π_1, c'est-à-dire qu'il existe un point commun à la droite et au plan. Les coordonnées de ce point vérifient à la fois l'équation de la droite et l'équation du plan. En remplaçant x, y et z dans l'équation du plan π_1 par leurs valeurs, tirées de l'équation de la droite ($x = 2 + 3k$, $y = -3 + 4k$ et $z = 1 - 3k$), on obtient

$$2(2 + 3k) - (-3 + 4k) + 3(1 - 3k) = 8 \quad \Rightarrow \quad k = \tfrac{2}{7}$$

En substituant cette valeur à k dans l'équation de la droite, on obtient le point d'intersection de la droite Δ avec le plan π_1, soit $(\tfrac{20}{7}, -\tfrac{13}{7}, \tfrac{1}{7})$.

2. Soit la droite Δ et le plan π_2 dont les équations sont

$$\Delta : \begin{bmatrix} x & y & z \end{bmatrix} = \begin{bmatrix} 2 & -3 & 1 \end{bmatrix} + k\begin{bmatrix} 3 & 4 & -3 \end{bmatrix} \quad \text{où} \quad k \in \mathbb{R}$$
$$\pi_2 : 3y + 4z = 10$$

Le vecteur $\vec{d} = \begin{bmatrix} 3 & 4 & -3 \end{bmatrix}$ est un vecteur directeur de la droite Δ, alors que le vecteur $\vec{n_2} = \begin{bmatrix} 0 & 3 & 4 \end{bmatrix}$ est un vecteur normal au plan π_2. Comme $\vec{d} \cdot \vec{n_2} = 0$, les vecteurs $\vec{d}$ et $\vec{n_2}$ sont perpendiculaires. Par conséquent, la droite Δ est parallèle au plan π_2. Dans ce cas, la distance entre la droite Δ et le plan π_2 est égale à la distance entre un point de la droite et le plan. Le point $Q = (2, -3, 1)$ appartient à Δ et la distance entre ce point et le plan est égale à

$$\left| \frac{aq_1 + bq_2 + cq_3 - d}{\sqrt{a^2 + b^2 + c^2}} \right| = \left| \frac{(0)(2) + (3)(-3) + (4)(1) - 10}{\sqrt{0^2 + 3^2 + 4^2}} \right|$$

$$= 3 \text{ unités}$$

La droite Δ est donc située à trois unités du plan π_2.

EXERCICE 9.11

Soit les droites Δ_1 et Δ_2 et le plan π définis par

$$\Delta_1 : \frac{x-2}{-1} = \frac{y-3}{4} = \frac{z+5}{6}$$
$$\Delta_2 : \begin{bmatrix} x & y & z \end{bmatrix} = \begin{bmatrix} 2 & -3 & 1 \end{bmatrix} + k\begin{bmatrix} 3 & 4 & -3 \end{bmatrix} \quad \text{où} \quad k \in \mathbb{R}$$
$$\pi : 2x - y + z = 4$$

Pour chacune des deux droites, trouvez, selon le cas, le point d'intersection de la droite avec le plan ou la distance entre la droite et le plan.

ANGLE ENTRE UNE DROITE ET UN PLAN

L'angle entre une droite et un plan est l'angle θ ($0° < \theta \leq 90°$) complémentaire au plus petit angle α déterminé par la droite et un vecteur normal au plan.

Dans le cas d'une droite qui coupe un plan, l'**angle entre la droite et le plan** est l'angle θ ($0° < \theta \leq 90°$) complémentaire au plus petit angle α entre la droite et un vecteur normal au plan.

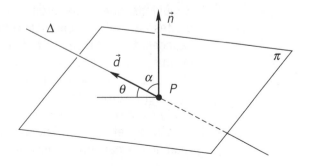

En vertu de l'identité trigonométrique $\sin\theta = \cos(90° - \theta)$,

$$\sin\theta = \cos(90° - \theta) = \cos\alpha = \frac{|\vec{n} \cdot \vec{d}|}{\|\vec{n}\|\,\|\vec{d}\|}$$

On en déduit que l'angle θ entre Δ et π est donné par

$$\theta = \text{arc sin} \frac{|\vec{n} \cdot \vec{d}|}{\|\vec{n}\|\,\|\vec{d}\|}$$

Exemple

Soit la droite Δ et le plan π dont les équations sont

$$\Delta: \begin{bmatrix} x & y & z \end{bmatrix} = \begin{bmatrix} 2 & -3 & 1 \end{bmatrix} + k\begin{bmatrix} 3 & 4 & -3 \end{bmatrix} \quad \text{où} \quad k \in \mathbb{R}$$
$$\pi: 2x - y + 3z = 8$$

Le vecteur $\vec{d} = \begin{bmatrix} 3 & 4 & -3 \end{bmatrix}$ est un vecteur directeur de la droite Δ, alors que $\vec{n} = \begin{bmatrix} 2 & -1 & 3 \end{bmatrix}$ est un vecteur normal au plan π. Comme $\vec{n} \cdot \vec{d} = -7 \neq 0$, les vecteurs $\vec{d}$ et $\vec{n}$ ne sont pas perpendiculaires. Par conséquent, la droite Δ coupe le plan π.

L'angle entre la droite Δ et le plan π est donné par

$$\theta = \text{arc sin} \frac{|\vec{n} \cdot \vec{d}|}{\|\vec{n}\|\,\|\vec{d}\|} = \text{arc sin} \frac{|-7|}{\sqrt{14}\,\sqrt{34}} \approx 18{,}7°$$

EXERCICE 9.12

Quel est l'angle entre la droite $\Delta: \dfrac{x - 2}{-1} = \dfrac{y - 3}{4} = \dfrac{z + 5}{3}$ et le plan $\pi: 2x - y + z = 4$?

9.2.6 DISTANCE ENTRE DEUX DROITES GAUCHES

Rappelons que deux droites non parallèles (les vecteurs directeurs des droites ne sont pas parallèles) qui ne se coupent pas sont appelées droites gauches. La distance entre deux droites gauches Δ_1 et Δ_2 est par définition la plus courte distance possible entre deux points appartenant, l'un à Δ_1 et l'autre à Δ_2. Le segment de droite joignant ces deux points est nécessairement perpendiculaire à la fois à Δ_1 et à Δ_2 ; il est donc parallèle au produit vectoriel des vecteurs directeurs $\vec{d_1}$ et $\vec{d_2}$ de ces deux droites. Les droites Δ_1 et Δ_2 sont donc parallèles à tout plan dont $\vec{d_1} \times \vec{d_2}$ est un vecteur normal. Par conséquent, Δ_1 et Δ_2 sont incluses dans deux plans parallèles π_1 et π_2, et la distance entre ces droites est égale à la distance entre les deux plans. Pour trouver la distance entre deux droites gauches, il faut donc calculer la distance entre les deux plans parallèles qui contiennent ces droites.

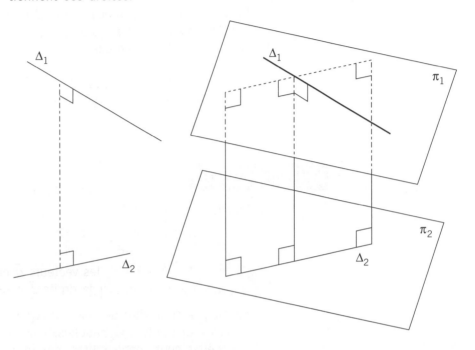

Exemple

Soit les droites Δ_1 et Δ_2 dont les équations sont

$$\Delta_1 : \begin{bmatrix} x & y & z \end{bmatrix} = \begin{bmatrix} 2 & -3 & 1 \end{bmatrix} + k_1 \begin{bmatrix} 3 & 4 & -3 \end{bmatrix} \quad \text{où} \quad k_1 \in \mathbb{R}$$

$$\Delta_2 : \begin{bmatrix} x & y & z \end{bmatrix} = \begin{bmatrix} 1 & 1 & 2 \end{bmatrix} + k_2 \begin{bmatrix} 1 & 2 & -2 \end{bmatrix} \quad \text{où} \quad k_2 \in \mathbb{R}$$

Les vecteurs $\vec{d_1} = \begin{bmatrix} 3 & 4 & -3 \end{bmatrix}$ et $\vec{d_2} = \begin{bmatrix} 1 & 2 & -2 \end{bmatrix}$ sont des vecteurs directeurs des droites Δ_1 et Δ_2 respectivement. Comme ces vecteurs ne sont pas parallèles ($\vec{d_1} \neq k\vec{d_2}$), les droites ne le sont pas non plus. En fait, Δ_1 et Δ_2 sont des droites gauches parce qu'elles n'ont aucun point commun (vérifiez ce fait). Ces droites sont toutes deux perpendiculaires au vecteur $\vec{n} = \vec{d_1} \times \vec{d_2} = \begin{bmatrix} -2 & 3 & 2 \end{bmatrix}$. Le plan π_1 qui passe par le point (2, −3, 1) de Δ_1 et dont $\vec{n} = \begin{bmatrix} -2 & 3 & 2 \end{bmatrix}$ est un vecteur normal contient donc la droite Δ_1. De façon similaire, le plan π_2 qui passe par le point (1, 1, 2) de Δ_2 et dont $\vec{n} = \begin{bmatrix} -2 & 3 & 2 \end{bmatrix}$ est un vecteur normal contient la droite Δ_2. Les plans π_1 et π_2 sont parallèles, et la distance entre Δ_1 et Δ_2 est égale à la distance entre ces deux plans, dont les équations cartésiennes respectives sont

$$\pi_1 : -2x + 3y + 2z = -11$$
$$\pi_2 : -2x + 3y + 2z = 5$$

En vertu du résultat prouvé au n° 2 de l'exercice 9.10, la distance entre les plans π_1 et π_2, qui est égale à la distance entre les droites Δ_1 et Δ_2, est donnée par

$$\left| \frac{d_1 - d_2}{\sqrt{a^2 + b^2 + c^2}} \right| = \left| \frac{-11 - 5}{\sqrt{(-2)^2 + 3^2 + 2^2}} \right| = \frac{16}{\sqrt{17}} \approx 3{,}9 \text{ unités}$$

EXERCICE 9.13

Soit les droites

$$\Delta_1 : \frac{x - 1}{5} = \frac{y - 2}{-6} = \frac{z - 3}{-4}$$
$$\Delta_2 : x - 8 = y + 2 = z - 1$$
$$\Delta_3 : \begin{bmatrix} x & y & z \end{bmatrix} = \begin{bmatrix} 3 & 0 & 7 \end{bmatrix} + k \begin{bmatrix} 2 & 2 & 2 \end{bmatrix} \quad \text{où} \quad k \in \mathbb{R}$$

a) Que peut-on dire des droites Δ_1 et Δ_2? Si ces droites sont parallèles distinctes ou gauches, calculez la distance qui les sépare; si elles sont concourantes, déterminez leur point d'intersection.

b) Que peut-on dire des droites Δ_1 et Δ_3? Si ces droites sont parallèles distinctes ou gauches, calculez la distance qui les sépare; si elles sont concourantes, déterminez leur point d'intersection.

c) Que peut-on dire des droites Δ_2 et Δ_3? Si ces droites sont parallèles distinctes ou gauches, calculez la distance qui les sépare; si elles sont concourantes, déterminez leur point d'intersection.

9.2.7 INTERSECTION DE DEUX OU PLUSIEURS PLANS

Deux plans parallèles se distinguent par le fait que leurs vecteurs normaux sont parallèles. Deux plans parallèles sont distincts s'ils n'ont aucun point commun, et ils sont confondus s'ils ont un point commun (deux plans confondus sont formés exactement des mêmes points).

Par contre, deux plans dont les vecteurs normaux ne sont pas parallèles sont des **plans sécants** : leur intersection est une droite.

PLANS SÉCANTS

Deux plans sont dits sécants si leur intersection est une droite.

On peut faire appel aux équations cartésiennes de plans sécants pour déterminer l'équation de la droite suivant laquelle ils se coupent. L'équation cartésienne d'un plan est une équation linéaire. Par conséquent, on peut employer les méthodes présentées au chapitre 4 pour résoudre le système

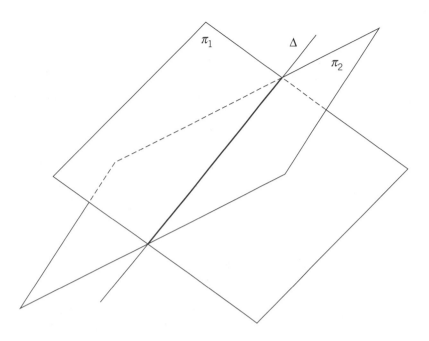

formé des équations des plans et trouver ainsi, s'il y a lieu, l'intersection de deux ou plusieurs plans.

Exemple

Soit les plans

$$\pi_1 : 2x - y + z = 4$$
$$\pi_2 : -4x + 2y - 2z = 6$$
$$\pi_3 : 6x - 3y + 3z = 12$$
$$\pi_4 : x + 2y - 3z = 6$$

Les plans π_1, π_2 et π_3 sont parallèles parce que leurs vecteurs normaux respectifs $\overrightarrow{n_1} = \begin{bmatrix} 2 & -1 & 1 \end{bmatrix}$, $\overrightarrow{n_2} = \begin{bmatrix} -4 & 2 & -2 \end{bmatrix}$ et $\overrightarrow{n_3} = \begin{bmatrix} 6 & -3 & 3 \end{bmatrix}$ sont parallèles. De plus, le point $(0, 0, 4)$ appartient à chacun des plans π_1 et π_3, mais il n'appartient pas au plan π_2. Par conséquent, π_1 et π_3 sont des plans parallèles confondus, alors que π_1 et π_2 sont des plans parallèles distincts.

Les plans π_1 et π_4 sont sécants parce que leurs vecteurs normaux respectifs $\overrightarrow{n_1} = \begin{bmatrix} 2 & -1 & 1 \end{bmatrix}$ et $\overrightarrow{n_4} = \begin{bmatrix} 1 & 2 & -3 \end{bmatrix}$ ne sont pas parallèles. L'intersection de ces deux plans est une droite, dont on détermine les équations paramétriques en résolvant le système formé des équations cartésiennes des deux plans :

$$\begin{bmatrix} 2 & -1 & 1 & | & 4 \\ 1 & 2 & -3 & | & 6 \end{bmatrix} \sim \begin{bmatrix} 1 & 2 & -3 & | & 6 \\ 2 & -1 & 1 & | & 4 \end{bmatrix} L_1 \leftrightarrow L_2$$

$$\sim \begin{bmatrix} 1 & 2 & -3 & | & 6 \\ 0 & -5 & 7 & | & -8 \end{bmatrix} L_2 \to L_2 - 2L_1$$

Ce système admet une infinité de solutions, car il comporte une inconnue libre. De la deuxième ligne de la matrice augmentée, on tire $-5y + 7z = -8$. Si on pose $z = k$, alors

$$y = \frac{8 + 7z}{5} = \frac{8 + 7k}{5} = {}^{8}\!/_{5} + {}^{7}\!/_{5}\,k$$

En remplaçant y et z par leur valeur dans l'équation associée à la première ligne de la matrice augmentée, on obtient

$$x = {}^{14}\!/_{5} + {}^{1}\!/_{5}\,k$$

Les équations paramétriques de la droite d'intersection sont donc

$$x = {}^{14}\!/_{5} + {}^{1}\!/_{5}\,k \quad y = {}^{8}\!/_{5} + {}^{7}\!/_{5}\,k \quad z = k \quad \text{où} \quad k \in \mathbb{R}$$

Il s'agit de la droite passant par le point $P({}^{14}\!/_{5},\ {}^{8}\!/_{5},\ 0)$ et de vecteur directeur $\vec{d} = \begin{bmatrix} {}^{1}\!/_{5} & {}^{7}\!/_{5} & 1 \end{bmatrix}$.

EXERCICE 9.14

Soit les plans

$$\pi_1 : x - y + z = 3$$
$$\pi_2 : 2x - 2y + 2z = 7$$
$$\pi_3 : 2x + y + z = 2$$
$$\pi_4 : -4x + 4y - 4z = -12$$

Répondez aux questions suivantes pour les plans:

a) π_1 et π_2

b) π_1 et π_3

c) π_1 et π_4

Les deux plans sont-ils parallèles ou sécants? S'ils sont parallèles, calculez la distance qui les sépare et dites s'ils sont distincts ou confondus; si les deux plans sont sécants, déterminez l'équation vectorielle de la droite suivant laquelle ils se coupent.

Pour déterminer l'intersection de trois plans ou plus, il faut résoudre le système formé des équations cartésiennes de ces plans. Si le système d'équations n'admet aucune solution, il n'existe pas de point commun à tous les plans : leur intersection est vide. Si le système d'équations admet une infinité de solutions, l'intersection des plans est une droite (la solution du système comporte une seule inconnue libre) ou un plan (tous les plans sont confondus et la solution du système comporte deux inconnues libres). Si le système d'équations admet une solution unique, l'intersection des plans est formée d'un seul point dont les coordonnées vérifient l'équation cartésienne de chacun des plans.

Exemple

1. Soit les plans

$$\pi_1 : -x + y + 2z = 2$$
$$\pi_2 : 2x - y + 2z = -2$$
$$\pi_3 : 3x + 2y + 4z = -1$$

On détermine l'intersection des plans π_1, π_2 et π_3 en résolvant le système formé des équations cartésiennes de chacun de ces plans.

$$\left[\begin{array}{ccc|c} -1 & 1 & 2 & 2 \\ 2 & -1 & 2 & -2 \\ 3 & 2 & 4 & -1 \end{array}\right] \sim \left[\begin{array}{ccc|c} -1 & 1 & 2 & 2 \\ 0 & 1 & 6 & 2 \\ 0 & 5 & 10 & 5 \end{array}\right] \begin{array}{l} \\ L_2 \to L_2 + 2L_1 \\ L_3 \to L_3 + 3L_1 \end{array}$$

$$\sim \left[\begin{array}{ccc|c} 1 & -1 & -2 & -2 \\ 0 & 1 & 6 & 2 \\ 0 & 1 & 2 & 1 \end{array}\right] \begin{array}{l} L_1 \to -L_1 \\ \\ L_3 \to \frac{1}{5}L_3 \end{array}$$

$$\sim \left[\begin{array}{ccc|c} 1 & -1 & -2 & -2 \\ 0 & 1 & 6 & 2 \\ 0 & 0 & -4 & -1 \end{array}\right] \begin{array}{l} \\ \\ L_3 \to L_3 - L_2 \end{array}$$

$$\sim \left[\begin{array}{ccc|c} 1 & -1 & -2 & -2 \\ 0 & 1 & 6 & 2 \\ 0 & 0 & 1 & \frac{1}{4} \end{array}\right] \begin{array}{l} \\ \\ L_3 \to -\frac{1}{4}L_3 \end{array}$$

De la dernière ligne de la matrice augmentée, on tire $z = \frac{1}{4}$ et, de la deuxième ligne, on tire $y + 6z = 2$. En remplaçant z par sa valeur dans cette équation, on obtient

$$y + 6z = 2 \implies y = 2 - 6z \implies y = 2 - 6(\tfrac{1}{4}) \implies y = \tfrac{1}{2}$$

Un raisonnement analogue donne

$$x - y - 2z = -2 \implies x = y + 2z - 2 \implies x = -1$$

Ainsi, les valeurs de x, y et z qui vérifient le système d'équations sont $x = -1$, $y = \frac{1}{2}$ et $z = \frac{1}{4}$.

Le point d'intersection des plans π_1, π_2 et π_3 est donc $(-1, \frac{1}{2}, \frac{1}{4})$.

2. Soit les plans

$$\pi_1 : -x + y + 2z = 2$$
$$\pi_2 : 2x - y + 2z = -2$$
$$\pi_4 : x + 4z = 3$$

Pour trouver l'intersection des plans π_1, π_2 et π_4, on résout le système d'équations formé des équations de ces plans par la méthode d'élimination gaussienne.

$$\begin{bmatrix} -1 & 1 & 2 & | & 2 \\ 2 & -1 & 2 & | & -2 \\ 1 & 0 & 4 & | & 3 \end{bmatrix} \sim \begin{bmatrix} -1 & 1 & 2 & | & 2 \\ 0 & 1 & 6 & | & 2 \\ 0 & 1 & 6 & | & 5 \end{bmatrix} \begin{matrix} \\ L_2 \to L_2 + 2L_1 \\ L_3 \to L_3 + L_1 \end{matrix}$$

$$\sim \begin{bmatrix} -1 & 1 & 2 & | & 2 \\ 0 & 1 & 6 & | & 2 \\ 0 & 0 & 0 & | & 3 \end{bmatrix} \begin{matrix} \\ \\ L_3 \to L_3 - L_2 \end{matrix}$$

Comme ce système d'équations n'admet aucune solution, il n'existe pas de point commun aux trois plans : leur intersection est vide. De plus, comme les vecteurs normaux de ces plans ne sont pas parallèles deux à deux, aucun des trois plans n'est parallèle à l'un des deux autres. Ainsi, les plans π_1 et π_2 sont sécants, de même que les plans π_1 et π_4, et les plans π_2 et π_4.

EXERCICE 9.15

Associez chaque système d'équations à la représentation graphique qui décrit le mieux la relation entre les plans π_1, π_2 et π_3.

a) $\pi_1 : -x + y + 2z = 2$
$\pi_2 : 2x - 2y - 4z = -6$
$\pi_3 : x - y + 6z = 5$

A)

b) $\pi_1 : -x + y + 2z = 2$
$\pi_2 : x + y + z = 3$
$\pi_3 : 2x - 2y - 4z = -4$

B)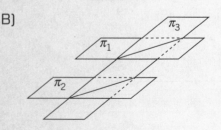

c) $\pi_1 : -x + y + 2z = 2$
$\pi_2 : x + y + z = 3$
$\pi_3 : x + 3y + 4z = 8$

C)

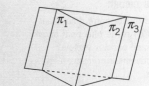

d) $\pi_1 : -x + y + 2z = 2$
$\pi_2 : x + y + z = 3$
$\pi_3 : x + 3y + 4z = 12$

D)

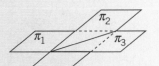

e) $\pi_1 : -x + y + 2z = 2$
$\pi_2 : 2x - y + 2z = -2$
$\pi_3 : 3x + 2y + 4z = -1$

E)

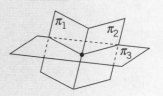

f) $\pi_1 : -x + y + 2z = 2$
$\pi_2 : x - y - 2z = 2$
$\pi_3 : 3x - 3y - 6z = 18$

F)

9.2.8 ANGLE ENTRE DEUX PLANS

On définit l'angle θ entre deux plans sécants π_1 et π_2 comme le plus petit angle ($0° < \theta \leq 90°$) formé par la trace sur les plans π_1 et π_2 d'un plan

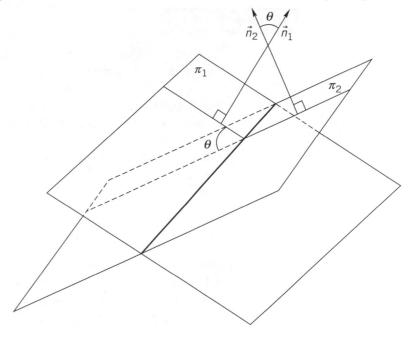

ANGLE DIÈDRE

L'angle dièdre entre deux plans π_1 et π_2 est le plus petit angle déterminé par des vecteurs respectivement normaux à π_1 et à π_2.

perpendiculaire à π_1 et à π_2, c'est-à-dire d'un plan parallèle à tout vecteur normal à π_1 et à π_2. Cet angle, appelé **angle dièdre**, est égal au plus petit angle entre deux vecteurs normaux aux plans π_1 et π_2 respectivement, car deux angles dont les côtés sont mutuellement perpendiculaires sont égaux.

Par conséquent,

$$\theta = \text{arc } \cos \frac{|\vec{n_1} \cdot \vec{n_2}|}{\|\vec{n_1}\| \, \|\vec{n_2}\|}$$

Si les plans sont parallèles, l'angle entre les plans vaut évidemment 0°.

Exemple

L'angle dièdre entre les plans

$$\pi_1 : 2x - y + z = 4 \text{ et } \pi_2 : x + 2y - 2z = 6$$

est donné par

$$\theta = \text{arc } \cos \frac{|\vec{n_1} \cdot \vec{n_2}|}{\|\vec{n_1}\| \, \|\vec{n_2}\|}$$

$$= \text{arc } \cos \frac{\left| \begin{bmatrix} 2 & -1 & 1 \end{bmatrix} \cdot \begin{bmatrix} 1 & 2 & -2 \end{bmatrix} \right|}{\left\| \begin{bmatrix} 2 & -1 & 1 \end{bmatrix} \right\| \left\| \begin{bmatrix} 1 & 2 & -2 \end{bmatrix} \right\|}$$

$$= \text{arc } \cos \frac{|-2|}{\sqrt{6} \, \sqrt{9}}$$

$$\approx 74,2°$$

EXERCICE 9.16

1. Soit les plans $\pi_1 : x - y + z = 3$ et $\pi_2 : 2x - y - 3z = 7$. Quel est l'angle dièdre? Que peut-on dire des deux plans?

2. Soit les plans $\pi_1 : x - y + z = 3$ et $\pi_3 : -2x + 2y - 2z = 5$. Quel est l'angle dièdre? Que peut-on dire des deux plans?

3. Soit les plans $\pi_1 : x - y + z = 3$ et $\pi_4 : x + y + z = 8$. Quel est l'angle dièdre?

9.2.9 ÉQUATION VECTORIELLE D'UN PLAN

Il existe d'autres façons de déterminer un plan que d'en donner un vecteur normal et un point. En effet, tout vecteur d'un plan s'écrit comme une combinaison linéaire de deux vecteurs linéairement indépendants et parallèles à ce plan. Si $\vec{u} = \begin{bmatrix} u_1 & u_2 & u_3 \end{bmatrix}$ et $\vec{v} = \begin{bmatrix} v_1 & v_2 & v_3 \end{bmatrix}$ sont deux vecteurs linéairement indépendants et parallèles à un plan π, si $P(p_1, p_2, p_3)$ est un point connu de π et si $X(x, y, z)$ en est un point quelconque, alors le vecteur $\overrightarrow{PX}$ s'écrit comme une combinaison linéaire des vecteurs $\vec{u}$ et $\vec{v}$:

$$\overrightarrow{PX} = r\vec{u} + s\vec{v} \quad \Rightarrow \quad \overrightarrow{PO} + \overrightarrow{OX} = r\vec{u} + s\vec{v} \quad \Rightarrow \quad \overrightarrow{OX} = \overrightarrow{OP} + r\vec{u} + s\vec{v}$$

où r et $s \in \mathbb{R}$.

Si on écrit cette dernière équation à l'aide des composantes des vecteurs, on obtient l'**équation vectorielle d'un plan** :

$$\begin{bmatrix} x & y & z \end{bmatrix} = \begin{bmatrix} p_1 & p_2 & p_3 \end{bmatrix} + r\begin{bmatrix} u_1 & u_2 & u_3 \end{bmatrix} + s\begin{bmatrix} v_1 & v_2 & v_3 \end{bmatrix}$$

où r et $s \in \mathbb{R}$.

Exemple

Soit le plan π d'équation cartésienne $\pi: 2x + 3y + z = 6$. En posant $x = y = 0$, on obtient $z = 6$. Le point $A(0, 0, 6)$ appartient donc au plan π. On montre de façon analogue que les points $B(3, 0, 0)$ et $C(0, 2, 0)$ appartiennent aussi à ce plan. Comme les vecteurs $\overrightarrow{AB} = \begin{bmatrix} 3 & 0 & -6 \end{bmatrix}$ et $\overrightarrow{AC} = \begin{bmatrix} 0 & 2 & -6 \end{bmatrix}$ ne sont pas parallèles, ils sont linéairement indépendants. On connaît donc deux vecteurs linéairement indépendants et un point de π; on peut donc écrire l'équation vectorielle de ce plan :

$$\begin{bmatrix} x & y & z \end{bmatrix} = \begin{bmatrix} 0 & 0 & 6 \end{bmatrix} + r\begin{bmatrix} 3 & 0 & -6 \end{bmatrix} + s\begin{bmatrix} 0 & 2 & -6 \end{bmatrix}$$

où r et $s \in \mathbb{R}$.

La forme de cette équation varie, comme celle de l'équation vectorielle d'une droite. Ainsi, en choisissant le point B, plutôt que le point A, et les vecteurs $\overrightarrow{AB}$ et $\overrightarrow{BC}$, on obtient l'équation vectorielle :

$$\begin{bmatrix} x & y & z \end{bmatrix} = \begin{bmatrix} 3 & 0 & 0 \end{bmatrix} + g\begin{bmatrix} 3 & 0 & -6 \end{bmatrix} + k\begin{bmatrix} -3 & 2 & 0 \end{bmatrix}$$

où g et $k \in \mathbb{R}$.

Bien qu'elles n'aient pas la même forme, les deux équations décrivent le même plan.

EXERCICE 9.17

Quelle est l'équation vectorielle du plan qui passe par les points $A(2, 1, 6)$, $B(3, -2, 1)$ et $C(1, 2, 4)$?

9.2.10 Équations paramétriques d'un plan

Si, dans l'équation vectorielle d'un plan, on exprime les valeurs de x, y et z en fonction des paramètres r et s, on obtient les **équations paramétriques d'un plan** :

$$x = p_1 + ru_1 + sv_1$$
$$y = p_2 + ru_2 + sv_2$$
$$z = p_3 + ru_3 + sv_3$$

où $\vec{u} = \begin{bmatrix} u_1 & u_2 & u_3 \end{bmatrix}$ et $\vec{v} = \begin{bmatrix} v_1 & v_2 & v_3 \end{bmatrix}$ sont deux vecteurs linéairement indépendants et parallèles au plan, $P = (p_1, p_2, p_3)$ est un point du plan, et r et s sont des scalaires réels. Tout comme dans le cas de l'équation vectorielle, la formulation des équations paramétriques n'est pas unique, car elle dépend du choix du point et des vecteurs.

Exemple

Les équations paramétriques du plan de l'exemple précédent sont

$$x = 3r \quad y = 2s \quad z = 6 - 6r - 6s \quad \text{où} \quad r \text{ et } s \in \mathbb{R}$$

EXERCICE 9.18

Soit le plan π dont les équations paramétriques sont

$$x = 2 + 3r + s \quad y = -1 + r - 2s \quad z = 3 + 2r - 3s \quad \text{où} \quad r \text{ et } s \in \mathbb{R}$$

a) Trouvez un point du plan π.

b) Quel point du plan π obtient-on en posant $r = 2$ et $s = -1$?

c) Le point $A(1, 2, 3)$ appartient-il au plan π ?

d) Trouvez deux vecteurs $\vec{u}$ et $\vec{v}$ linéairement indépendants et parallèles au plan π.

e) Que peut-on dire du vecteur $\vec{u} \times \vec{v}$ par rapport au plan π ?

f) Quelle est l'équation cartésienne du plan π ?

La droite et le plan de l'espace constituent deux applications des vecteurs de $\mathbb{R}^3$.

Pour définir complètement une droite Δ de l'espace, il faut donner:

- soit un point et un vecteur directeur de la droite;

- soit deux points de la droite (si A et B sont deux points distincts d'une droite, alors $\overrightarrow{AB}$ est un vecteur directeur de cette droite);

- soit deux plans sécants. (Si π_1 et π_2 sont deux plans sécants dont $\overrightarrow{n_1}$ et $\overrightarrow{n_2}$ sont respectivement des vecteurs normaux, alors $\overrightarrow{n_1} \times \overrightarrow{n_2}$ est un vecteur directeur de la droite Δ suivant laquelle les plans se coupent. On obtient un point de Δ en résolvant le système formé des équations des plans.)

Si $\vec{d} = \begin{bmatrix} d_1 & d_2 & d_3 \end{bmatrix}$ est un vecteur directeur d'une droite Δ, si $P(p_1, p_2, p_3)$ est un point connu de cette droite et si $X(x, y, z)$ en est un point quelconque, alors $\overrightarrow{PX}$ est parallèle à $\vec{d}$. On déduit de ce résultat (tableau 9.1) les différentes équations d'une droite de l'espace.

TABLEAU 9.1   **Équations d'une droite de l'espace**

ÉQUATION DE BASE	$\overrightarrow{PX} = k\vec{d}$ où $k \in \mathbb{R}$
ÉQUATION VECTORIELLE	$\begin{bmatrix} x & y & z \end{bmatrix} = \begin{bmatrix} p_1 & p_2 & p_3 \end{bmatrix} + k\begin{bmatrix} d_1 & d_2 & d_3 \end{bmatrix}$ où $k \in \mathbb{R}$
ÉQUATIONS PARAMÉTRIQUES	$x = p_1 + kd_1 \quad y = p_2 + kd_2 \quad z = p_3 + kd_3$ où $k \in \mathbb{R}$
ÉQUATIONS SYMÉTRIQUES	$\dfrac{x - p_1}{d_1} = \dfrac{y - p_2}{d_2} = \dfrac{z - p_3}{d_3}$ dans le cas où les composantes de $\vec{d}$ sont non nulles.

Deux droites parallèles se distinguent par le fait que leurs vecteurs directeurs sont parallèles, et deux droites concourantes ou gauches, par le fait que leurs vecteurs directeurs ne sont pas parallèles. Deux droites parallèles sont confondues si elles sont formées exactement des mêmes points et elles sont distinctes si elles n'ont aucun point commun. Deux droites non parallèles sont concourantes si elles ont un point commun; dans le cas contraire, les deux droites sont gauches.

Pour définir complètement un plan π, il faut donner:

- soit un point du plan et un vecteur normal au plan;

- soit trois points non colinéaires du plan (si *A*, *B* et *C* sont trois points non colinéaires de π, alors $\overrightarrow{AB} \times \overrightarrow{AC}$ est un vecteur normal à π);
- soit deux vecteurs linéairement indépendants et parallèles au plan, et un point du plan. (Si $\vec{u}$ et $\vec{v}$ sont deux vecteurs linéairement indépendants et parallèles à π, alors $\vec{u} \times \vec{v}$ est un vecteur normal à π.)

Soit $\vec{u} = \begin{bmatrix} u_1 & u_2 & u_3 \end{bmatrix}$ et $\vec{v} = \begin{bmatrix} v_1 & v_2 & v_3 \end{bmatrix}$ deux vecteurs linéairement indépendants et parallèles au plan π, soit $\vec{n} = \begin{bmatrix} a & b & c \end{bmatrix}$ un vecteur normal au plan π, soit $P(p_1, p_2, p_3)$ un point connu du plan π et $X(x, y, z)$ un point quelconque de π. Alors,

- $\overrightarrow{PX}$ est perpendiculaire à $\vec{n}$;
- $\overrightarrow{PX}$ s'écrit comme une combinaison linéaire de $\vec{u}$ et de $\vec{v}$.

On déduit de ces résultats (tableau 9.2) les différentes équations d'un plan de l'espace.

TABLEAU 9.2 **Équations d'un plan de l'espace**

ÉQUATIONS DE BASE	$\overrightarrow{PX} \cdot \vec{n} = 0$ ou $\overrightarrow{PX} = r\vec{u} + s\vec{v}$ où r et $s \in \mathbb{R}$
ÉQUATION CARTÉSIENNE	$ax + by + cz = d$ où $d = ap_1 + bp_2 + cp_3$
ÉQUATION NORMALE	$\dfrac{a}{\sqrt{a^2 + b^2 + c^2}}x + \dfrac{b}{\sqrt{a^2 + b^2 + c^2}}y + \dfrac{c}{\sqrt{a^2 + b^2 + c^2}}z = h$ où $h = \dfrac{ap_1 + bp_2 + cp_3}{\sqrt{a^2 + b^2 + c^2}}$
ÉQUATION VECTORIELLE	$\begin{bmatrix} x & y & z \end{bmatrix} = \begin{bmatrix} p_1 & p_2 & p_3 \end{bmatrix} + r\begin{bmatrix} u_1 & u_2 & u_3 \end{bmatrix} + s\begin{bmatrix} v_1 & v_2 & v_3 \end{bmatrix}$ où r et $s \in \mathbb{R}$
ÉQUATIONS PARAMÉTRIQUES	$x = p_1 + ru_1 + sv_1$ $y = p_2 + ru_2 + sv_2$ où r et $s \in \mathbb{R}$ $z = p_3 + ru_3 + sv_3$

Deux plans parallèles se distinguent par le fait que leurs vecteurs normaux sont parallèles, tandis que deux plans perpendiculaires se distinguent par le fait que leurs vecteurs normaux sont perpendiculaires. Une droite parallèle à un plan a un vecteur directeur qui est perpendiculaire à un vecteur normal au plan. Une droite parallèle à un plan avec lequel elle a un point commun est entièrement incluse dans ce plan.

Les concepts de distance, d'angle (tableaux 9.3 et 9.4) et d'intersection sont tout aussi intéressants, qu'il s'agisse de droites ou de plans.

TABLEAU 9.3

**Distance
dans l'espace**

D'UN POINT Q À UNE DROITE Δ	$\dfrac{\left\lVert \overrightarrow{PQ} \times \vec{d} \right\rVert}{\lVert \vec{d} \rVert}$ où $P \in \Delta$ et $\vec{d}$ est un vecteur directeur de Δ
ENTRE DEUX DROITES PARALLÈLES Δ_1 ET Δ_2	$\dfrac{\left\lVert \overrightarrow{P_1 P_2} \times \overrightarrow{d_1} \right\rVert}{\lVert \overrightarrow{d_1} \rVert}$ où $P_1 \in \Delta_1$, $P_2 \in \Delta_2$ et $\overrightarrow{d_1}$ est un vecteur directeur de Δ_1
D'UN PLAN π: $ax + by + cz = d$ À L'ORIGINE	$\dfrac{\lvert d \rvert}{\sqrt{a^2 + b^2 + c^2}}$
D'UN POINT $Q(q_1, q_2, q_3)$ À UN PLAN π: $ax + by + cz = d$	$\dfrac{\lvert \overrightarrow{PQ} \cdot \vec{n} \rvert}{\lVert \vec{n} \rVert}$ ou $\left\lvert \dfrac{aq_1 + bq_2 + cq_3 - d}{\sqrt{a^2 + b^2 + c^2}} \right\rvert$ où $\vec{n} = \begin{bmatrix} a & b & c \end{bmatrix}$ est un vecteur normal à π et $P \in \pi$.
ENTRE DEUX PLANS PARALLÈLES π_1: $ax + by + cz = d_1$ et π_2: $ax + by + cz = d_2$	$\left\lvert \dfrac{d_1 - d_2}{\sqrt{a^2 + b^2 + c^2}} \right\rvert$
D'UNE DROITE Δ À UN PLAN PARALLÈLE π: $ax + by + cz = d$	$\left\lvert \dfrac{aq_1 + bq_2 + cq_3 - d}{\sqrt{a^2 + b^2 + c^2}} \right\rvert$ où $Q(q_1, q_2, q_3) \in \Delta$
ENTRE DEUX DROITES GAUCHES Δ_1 ET Δ_2	Distance entre les deux plans parallèles qui contiennent chacun l'une des deux droites.

TABLEAU 9.4

**Angle θ
dans l'espace**

ENTRE DEUX DROITES CONCOURANTES Δ_1 ET Δ_2	$\theta = \arccos \dfrac{\lvert \overrightarrow{d_1} \cdot \overrightarrow{d_2} \rvert}{\lVert \overrightarrow{d_1} \rVert \, \lVert \overrightarrow{d_2} \rVert}$ où $\overrightarrow{d_1}$ et $\overrightarrow{d_2}$ sont respectivement des vecteurs directeurs des droites Δ_1 et Δ_2.
ENTRE UNE DROITE Δ ET UN PLAN π	$\theta = \arcsin \dfrac{\lvert \vec{n} \cdot \vec{d} \rvert}{\lVert \vec{n} \rVert \, \lVert \vec{d} \rVert}$ où $\vec{n}$ est un vecteur normal à π et $\vec{d}$, un vecteur directeur de Δ.
ENTRE DEUX PLANS π_1 ET π_2 (ANGLE DIÈDRE)	$\theta = \arccos \dfrac{\lvert \overrightarrow{n_1} \cdot \overrightarrow{n_2} \rvert}{\lVert \overrightarrow{n_1} \rVert \, \lVert \overrightarrow{n_2} \rVert}$ où $\overrightarrow{n_1}$ et $\overrightarrow{n_2}$ sont respectivement des vecteurs normaux aux plans π_1 et π_2.

Pour trouver le point R d'une droite Δ le plus proche d'un point Q extérieur à Δ, il faut résoudre l'équation vectorielle $\overrightarrow{OR} = \overrightarrow{OP} + \overrightarrow{PQ}_{\vec{d}}$ où P est un point de Δ et $\vec{d}$, un vecteur directeur de Δ.

Pour trouver le point R d'un plan π le plus proche d'un point Q extérieur à π, il faut résoudre l'équation vectorielle $\overrightarrow{OR} = \overrightarrow{OQ} + \overrightarrow{QP}_{\vec{n}_u}$ où P est un point de π et $\vec{n}_u$ est un vecteur unitaire normal à π.

On détermine l'intersection de plans ou de droites en résolvant simultanément les équations des différents plans et droites. Si le système formé de ces équations admet une solution unique, alors l'intersection est un point de l'espace. Si le système admet une infinité de solutions, alors l'intersection est une droite (une inconnue libre) ou un plan (deux inconnues libres). Si le système n'admet aucune solution, l'intersection est vide : les plans et droites n'ont pas de point commun.

MOTS CLÉS

EXERCICES RÉCAPITULATIFS

1. (I) Déterminez l'équation vectorielle de la droite donnée.

   a) La droite Δ_1 passant par les points $A(-1, -3, 2)$ et $B(4, 2, 2)$.

   b) La droite Δ_2 passant par le point $C(2, 4, 6)$ et parallèle au vecteur $\vec{d_2} = \begin{bmatrix} 1 & 3 & -1 \end{bmatrix}$.

   c) La droite Δ_3 passant par le point $D(-1, -2, 3)$ et perpendiculaire au plan xz.

   d) La droite Δ_4 passant par le point $E(3, -2, 1)$ et perpendiculaire à chacun des vecteurs $\vec{u} = \begin{bmatrix} -1 & 4 & 0 \end{bmatrix}$ et $\vec{v} = \begin{bmatrix} 2 & 4 & -2 \end{bmatrix}$.

   e) La droite Δ_5 passant par l'origine et parallèle à la droite Δ_6 dont l'équation vectorielle est

   $$\begin{bmatrix} x & y & z \end{bmatrix} = \begin{bmatrix} 4 & 1 & 1 \end{bmatrix} + k_6 \begin{bmatrix} 2 & -1 & 2 \end{bmatrix}$$

   où $k_6 \in \mathbb{R}$.

2. (I) Lesquels des points $A(-1, -7, 8)$, $B(4, -2, 5)$, $C(5, 5, 3)$ et $D(1, -3, 5)$ appartiennent à la droite

   $$\Delta : \begin{bmatrix} x & y & z \end{bmatrix} = \begin{bmatrix} 3 & 1 & 2 \end{bmatrix} + k \begin{bmatrix} 2 & 4 & -3 \end{bmatrix}$$

   où $k \in \mathbb{R}$?

3. (I) Donnez un point et un vecteur directeur de chacune des droites suivantes.

   a) $\Delta_1 : \begin{bmatrix} x & y & z \end{bmatrix} = \begin{bmatrix} 3 & 1 & 2 \end{bmatrix} + k_1 \begin{bmatrix} 2 & 4 & -3 \end{bmatrix}$ où $k_1 \in \mathbb{R}$.

   b) $\Delta_2 : \begin{bmatrix} x & y & z \end{bmatrix} = k_2 \begin{bmatrix} -1 & 2 & -2 \end{bmatrix}$ où $k_2 \in \mathbb{R}$.

   c) $\Delta_3 : x = 4 - 2k_3 \quad y = 2 - k_3 \quad z = k_3$ où $k_3 \in \mathbb{R}$.

   d) $\Delta_4 : x = 3 - 4k_4 \quad y = k_4 \quad z = 2$ où $k_4 \in \mathbb{R}$.

e) $\Delta_5 : \dfrac{x-1}{3} = \dfrac{y+1}{2} = \dfrac{z+4}{-5}$.

f) $\Delta_6 : \dfrac{x}{3} = \dfrac{y-4}{2}$ et $z = 6$.

4. (I) Trouvez les coordonnées manquantes en supposant que le point donné appartient à la droite.

a) $P_1(4,\ b_1,\ c_1)$ et $\Delta_1 : \dfrac{x-1}{3} = \dfrac{y+1}{2} = \dfrac{z+4}{-5}$.

b) $P_2(a_2,\ 5,\ c_2)$ et $\Delta_2 : x = 4 + 3k_2 \quad y = 2 + 3k_2$
$z = 5 + 5k_2$ où $k_2 \in \mathbb{R}$.

c) $P_3(a_3,\ b_3,\ 4)$ et
$\Delta_3 : \begin{bmatrix} x & y & z \end{bmatrix} = \begin{bmatrix} 1 & 1 & 1 \end{bmatrix} + k_3 \begin{bmatrix} 1 & -1 & 1 \end{bmatrix}$
où $k_3 \in \mathbb{R}$.

5. (I) Donnez les équations paramétriques et symétriques de chacune des droites définies au n° 1.

6. (II) Soit $\vec{d}$ un vecteur directeur d'une droite Δ, et $\overrightarrow{OP}$ et $\overrightarrow{OQ}$ les vecteurs position respectifs de deux points de la droite Δ. Montrez que $\overrightarrow{OP} \times \vec{d} = \overrightarrow{OQ} \times \vec{d}$.

7. (I) Donnez l'équation vectorielle de chacune des droites suivantes.

a) $\Delta_1 : \dfrac{x-1}{3} = \dfrac{y+1}{2} = \dfrac{z+4}{-5}$.

b) $\Delta_2 : x = 4 - 2k_2 \quad y = 2 - k_2 \quad z = k_2$ où $k_2 \in \mathbb{R}$.

c) $\Delta_3 : x = 2 + 3k_3 \quad y = 5 - 8k_3 \quad z = 2$ où $k_3 \in \mathbb{R}$.

d) $\Delta_4 : \dfrac{y+2}{3} = \dfrac{z-5}{-1} \quad x = 4$.

e) La droite Δ_5 passant par le point $A(2,\ 1,\ -1)$ et parallèle à la droite Δ d'équations paramétriques $\Delta : x = 4 - k \quad y = 3 + k \quad z = 2 - 4k$ où $k \in \mathbb{R}$.

f) La droite Δ_6, qui passe par le point d'intersection des droites

$\Delta_7 : x - 2 = \dfrac{y+1}{2} = \dfrac{z-3}{3}$

$\Delta_8 : \begin{bmatrix} x & y & z \end{bmatrix} = \begin{bmatrix} 5 & 1 & 4 \end{bmatrix} + k_8 \begin{bmatrix} 3 & 2 & 1 \end{bmatrix}$

où $k_8 \in \mathbb{R}$ et qui est parallèle au vecteur dont les angles directeurs sont $\alpha = \pi/3$, $\beta = 2\pi/3$ et $\gamma = \pi/4$.

8. (I) Déterminez la distance entre le point et la droite donnés.

a) $Q_1(2,\ 1,\ -3)$ et $\Delta_1 : \dfrac{x-1}{3} = \dfrac{y+1}{2} = \dfrac{z+4}{-5}$.

b) $Q_2(3,\ 2,\ -1)$ et $\Delta_2 : x = 4 + 3k_2 \quad y = 2 + 3k_2$
$z = 5 + 5k_2$ où $k_2 \in \mathbb{R}$.

c) $Q_3(-1,\ 3,\ -1)$ et
$\Delta_3 : \begin{bmatrix} x & y & z \end{bmatrix} = \begin{bmatrix} 1 & 1 & 1 \end{bmatrix} + k_3 \begin{bmatrix} 1 & -1 & 1 \end{bmatrix}$
où $k_3 \in \mathbb{R}$.

d) $Q_4(2,\ 3,\ -2)$ et la droite Δ_4 qui passe par les points $A(1,\ -1,\ 1)$ et $B(2,\ 2,\ 3)$.

9. (II) Soit P et Q deux points distincts d'une droite Δ de l'espace, et soit R un point extérieur à cette droite.

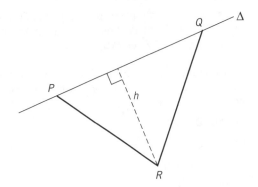

Donnez deux expressions de l'aire du triangle PQR et montrez que la distance du point R à la droite Δ est égale à

$$h = \dfrac{\left\| \overrightarrow{RP} \times \overrightarrow{RQ} \right\|}{\left\| \overrightarrow{PQ} \right\|}$$

10. (I) Déterminez la position relative (parallèles distinctes, parallèles confondues, concourantes ou gauches) des deux droites données. Si ce sont des droites parallèles, déterminez la distance qui les sépare ; si ce sont des droites concourantes, déterminez leur point d'intersection et l'angle qu'elles forment.

a) $\Delta_1 : x = 8 + 2k_1 \quad y = 7 + 2k_1 \quad z = 10 + 3k_1$ où $k_1 \in \mathbb{R}$.

$\Delta_2 : x = 4 + 3k_2 \quad y = 2 + 3k_2 \quad z = 5 + 5k_2$ où $k_2 \in \mathbb{R}$.

b) $\Delta_3 : x = 1 + 2k_3 \quad y = 3 - 3k_3 \quad z = 2 + k_3$ où $k_3 \in \mathbb{R}$.

$\Delta_4 : \dfrac{x-3}{-4} = \dfrac{y+2}{6} = \dfrac{z}{-2}$.

c) $\Delta_5 : \begin{bmatrix} x & y & z \end{bmatrix} = \begin{bmatrix} 1 & 1 & 1 \end{bmatrix} + k_5 \begin{bmatrix} 1 & -1 & 1 \end{bmatrix}$ où $k_5 \in \mathbb{R}$.

$\Delta_6 : x = 5 + 2k_6 \quad y = -3 - 2k_6 \quad z = 5 + 2k_6$ où $k_6 \in \mathbb{R}$.

d) $\Delta_7 : \dfrac{x-2}{2} = y + 1 = 1 - z$

$\Delta_8 : \dfrac{x+1}{3} = \dfrac{y-2}{-3} = \dfrac{z+1}{2}$

e) $\Delta_9 : \dfrac{x-3}{-6} = \dfrac{y-2}{4} = \dfrac{z+1}{3}$

$\Delta_{10} : x = 5 + 14k_{10} \quad y = 4 - 6k_{10} \quad z = 7 + 2k_{10}$ où $k_{10} \in \mathbb{R}$.

f) $\Delta_{11} : x = k_{11} \quad y = k_{11} \quad z = k_{11}$ où $k_{11} \in \mathbb{R}$.

$\Delta_{12} : x = 4 + 3k_{12} \quad y = 4 + 3k_{12} \quad z = 4 + 5k_{12}$
où $k_{12} \in \mathbb{R}$.

g) La droite Δ_{13} qui passe par les points $A(1, 1, 1)$ et $B(2, 0, 0)$, et la droite Δ_{14} qui passe par les points $C(0, 2, 3)$ et $D(4, -3, -1)$.

h) La droite Δ_{15} qui passe par les points $E(1, -1, 1)$ et $F(2, 2, 3)$ et la droite Δ_{16} qui passe par les points $G(5, 3, 7)$ et $H(6, 6, 9)$.

11. (I) Soit la droite $\Delta : x = 2 + k \quad y = 1 - 2k \quad z = -2 - k$ où $k \in \mathbb{R}$. Quel est le point de Δ le plus proche du point Q?

a) $Q(0, 0, 0)$

b) $Q(2, 3, -1)$

c) $Q(3, -1, -3)$

d) $Q(1, 1, -5)$

12. (II) Soit la droite Δ dont les équations paramétriques sont

$$x = p_1 + d_1 k$$
$$y = p_2 + d_2 k$$
$$z = p_3 + d_3 k$$

où $k \in \mathbb{R}$.

Donnez une interprétation géométrique (passe par l'origine, est parallèle à l'un des plans de coordonnées, est parallèle à l'un des axes de coordonnées, etc.) de la droite Δ pour les valeurs données de divers coefficients.

a) $d_2 = 0$

b) $p_1 = p_2 = p_3 = 0$

c) $d_1 = d_3 = 0$

d) $d_2 = d_3 = 0$

e) $d_1 = 0$

13. (III) Soit la droite Δ dont les équations paramétriques sont

$$x = p_1 + d_1 k \quad y = p_2 + d_2 k \quad z = p_3 + d_3 k$$

où $k \in \mathbb{R}$.

Montrez que cette droite coupe l'axe des abscisses lorsque $p_2 d_3 = p_3 d_2 \neq 0$.

14. (I) Soit a, b et c trois nombres réels non nuls. Montrez que la droite Δ passant par le point $A(a, b, c)$ et de vecteur directeur $\vec{d} = \begin{bmatrix} a & b & c \end{bmatrix}$ passe par l'origine.

15. (I) Montrez que les équations symétriques de la droite qui passe par les points $A(a_1, b_1, c_1)$ et $B(a_2, b_2, c_2)$

(dont les coordonnées correspondantes sont distinctes) s'écrivent sous la forme

$$\frac{x - a_1}{a_2 - a_1} = \frac{y - b_1}{b_2 - b_1} = \frac{z - c_1}{c_2 - c_1}$$

16. (I) Quelle est l'expression du paramètre k tel que le vecteur $\vec{d}$ est perpendiculaire au vecteur $\overrightarrow{OX}$ lorsque $\overrightarrow{OX} = \overrightarrow{OP} + k\vec{d}$ où $\vec{d} \neq \vec{0}$.

17. (II) Montrez que tous les points $X(x, y, z)$ de la droite qui passe par les points $P(p_1, p_2, p_3)$ et $Q(q_1, q_2, q_3)$ vérifient les équations paramétriques

$$x = (1 - k)p_1 + kq_1$$
$$y = (1 - k)p_2 + kq_2$$
$$z = (1 - k)p_3 + kq_3$$

où $k \in \mathbb{R}$.

18. (I) Lesquels des plans suivants sont parallèles?
$\pi_1 : 3x + 2y - 5z = 3$;
$\pi_2 : x - 2y - z = 3$;
$\pi_3 : 3x - 6y - 3z = 8$;
$\pi_4 : -3x - 2y + 5z = 2$;
$\pi_5 : x - 2y - z = 6$;
$\pi_6 : -3x - 2y - 5z = 7$;
$\pi_7 : -x + 2y + z = 1$;
$\pi_8 : 6x + 4y - 10z = 5$

19. (I) Lesquels des plans suivants sont perpendiculaires?
$\pi_1 : 3x + 2y - 5z = 3$;
$\pi_2 : x + y + z = 2$;
$\pi_3 : -x + y = 8$;
$\pi_4 : -2x - 7y - 4z = 2$

20. (I) Lesquelles des droites suivantes sont parallèles au plan $\pi : -x + 2y + z = 1$?

$\Delta_1 : \dfrac{x - 3}{2} = \dfrac{y - 3}{3} = \dfrac{z - 3}{-4}$;

$\Delta_2 : \dfrac{x - 5}{3} = \dfrac{y + 3}{2} = \dfrac{z + 3}{-1}$;

$\Delta_3 : \dfrac{x - 3}{2} = \dfrac{y - 3}{-1} \quad z = 3$;

$\Delta_4 : \begin{bmatrix} x & y & z \end{bmatrix} = \begin{bmatrix} 4 & 1 & 1 \end{bmatrix} + k_4 \begin{bmatrix} 3 & 1 & 1 \end{bmatrix}$
où $k_4 \in \mathbb{R}$;

$\Delta_5 : x = 4 - 2k_5 \quad y = 2 - k_5 \quad z = 4 + 3k_5$
où $k_5 \in \mathbb{R}$.

21. (I) Lesquelles des droites suivantes sont perpendiculaires au plan $\pi : -x + 2y + z = 1$?

$\Delta_1 : \dfrac{x + 1}{2} = \dfrac{y - 2}{2} = \dfrac{z}{-4}$;

$\Delta_2 : 5 - x = \dfrac{y + 3}{2} = z + 3$;

$\Delta_3 : \dfrac{x - 3}{2} = \dfrac{y - 3}{-1}$ $z = 3$;

$\Delta_4 : \begin{bmatrix} x & y & z \end{bmatrix} = \begin{bmatrix} 4 & 1 & 1 \end{bmatrix} + k_4 \begin{bmatrix} 2 & -4 & -2 \end{bmatrix}$
où $k_4 \in \mathbb{R}$;

$\Delta_5 : x = 4 - 2k_5$ $\quad y = 2 + 4k_5$ $\quad z = 4 + 2k_5$
où $k_5 \in \mathbb{R}$.

22. (I) Déterminez l'équation cartésienne du plan donné.

a) Le plan π_1 passant par les points $A(-1, -3, 2)$, $B(4, 2, 2)$ et $C(-3, 1, 1)$.

b) Le plan π_2 passant par le point $D(1, 2, -3)$ et perpendiculaire au vecteur $\vec{n} = \begin{bmatrix} -1 & 4 & 2 \end{bmatrix}$.

c) Le plan π_3 passant par le point $E(1, 1, -3)$ et parallèle au plan $\pi_4 : 3x + 2y - 5z = 3$.

d) Le plan π_5 passant par le point $F(2, 4, 6)$ et perpendiculaire à la droite

$$\Delta_1 : \dfrac{x + 1}{3} = \dfrac{y - 2}{-4} = \dfrac{z + 3}{5}$$

e) Le plan π_6 passant par le point d'intersection des droites

$$\Delta_2 : \dfrac{x + 1}{3} = \dfrac{y - 2}{4} = \dfrac{z + 3}{5}$$

$$\Delta_3 : \dfrac{x - 3}{-1} = \dfrac{y - 3}{3} = \dfrac{z}{2}$$

et perpendiculaire à Δ_2.

f) Le plan π_7 passant par le point $G(2, -1, 1)$ et perpendiculaire aux plans $\pi_8 : x + 2y - z = 3$ et $\pi_9 : 2x + y + z = 2$.

g) Le plan π_{10} passant par le point $H(1, 1, 2)$ et contenant la droite

$$\Delta_4 : \begin{bmatrix} x & y & z \end{bmatrix} = \begin{bmatrix} 4 & 1 & 1 \end{bmatrix} + k_4 \begin{bmatrix} 3 & 1 & 1 \end{bmatrix}$$

où $k_4 \in \mathbb{R}$.

h) Le plan π_{11} passant par les points $I(4, 2, -1)$ et $J(2, 2, 3)$, et parallèle à l'axe des abscisses.

23. (I) Soit les plans

$$\pi_1 : 2x + 3y + z = 2$$

$$\pi_2 : x + y + z = 3$$

a) Pour quelle valeur de b le plan

$$\pi_3 : 6x + by + 3z = -7$$

est-il parallèle au plan π_1 ?

b) Pour quelle valeur de a et de b, le plan

$$\pi_4 : ax + by + 5z = -7$$

est-il perpendiculaire à chacun des plans π_1 et π_2 ?

c) Lesquels des points suivants appartiennent au plan $\pi_2 : A(0, 2, 1)$, $B(2, 2, 1)$, $C(-2, -3, 8)$ et $D(-4, 4, 3)$?

d) Quel point d'abscisse 2 et d'ordonnée 4 appartient au plan π_1 ?

24. (I) Quelle est l'équation normale de chacun des plans suivants ?

a) $\pi_1 : 6x + 2y + 3z = -7$.

b) Le plan π_2 passant par le point $A(2, -3, 4)$ et parallèle au plan π_1.

c) Le plan π_3 passant par les points $P(a, 0, 0)$, $Q(0, b, 0)$ et $R(0, 0, c)$ où a, b et c sont des constantes différentes de zéro.

25. (II) Soit les droites

$$\Delta_1 : \dfrac{x + 1}{3} = \dfrac{y - 2}{4} = \dfrac{z + 3}{5}$$

$$\Delta_2 : x + r = y - 3 = z - 2$$

et les plans

$$\pi_1 : 2x + y - 2z = s \text{ et } \pi_2 : -6x + ty - 10z = 12$$

a) Pour quelle(s) valeur(s) de s la droite Δ_1 est-elle parallèle au plan π_1 ?

b) Pour quelle(s) valeur(s) de s la droite Δ_1 appartient-elle au plan π_1 ?

c) Pour quelle(s) valeur(s) de s la droite Δ_1 est-elle située à cinq unités du plan π_1 ?

d) Pour quelle(s) valeur(s) de t la droite Δ_1 est-elle parallèle au plan π_2 ? Quelle est alors la distance entre la droite et le plan ?

e) Pour quelle(s) valeur(s) de t la droite Δ_1 est-elle perpendiculaire au plan π_2 ?

f) Pour quelle(s) valeur(s) de r les droites Δ_1 et Δ_2 sont-elles concourantes ? Quel est alors le point d'intersection de ces deux droites ?

26. (I) Quelle est la distance à l'origine de chacun des plans donnés au n° 22 ?

27. (I) Quelle est la distance entre les lieux géométriques suivants ?

a) $\pi_1 : -4x - 6y + 2z = -7$ et $\pi_2 : 2x + 3y - z = -7$.

b) $A(2, -3, 4)$ et $\pi_3 : x + 3y - z = -7$.

c) $B(-1, -1, 3)$ et $\pi_4 : x + y - 2z = 4$.

d) $C(2, 1, -1)$ et $\pi_5 : 2x - 3y - 4z = 5$.

e) $\pi_6 : -x + 2y + z = 3$ et $\pi_7 : 2x - 4y - 2z = -6$.

f) $\pi_8 : x + 2y + z = 3$ et $\pi_9 : 2x + 4y + 2z = -5$.

g) $\pi_{10}: x + y + 4z = 6$ et $\pi_{11}: 2x + y - 2z = 4$.

h) Le point $D(-2, 1, 1)$ et le plan π_{12} qui passe par les points $A(2, -3, 4)$, $B(-1, -1, 3)$ et $C(2, 1, -1)$.

28. (II) Trouvez l'erreur que contient chaque raisonnement.

a) Le point $Q(2, 1, 3)$ appartient au plan

$$\pi_1: 3x + 2y - z = 5$$

Par conséquent, la distance entre le plan π_1 et le plan $\pi_2: 4x - 2y + z = 7$ est égale à

$$\left| \frac{aq_1 + bq_2 + cq_3 - d}{\sqrt{a^2 + b^2 + c^2}} \right|$$

$$= \left| \frac{(4)(2) + (-2)(1) + (1)(3) - 7}{\sqrt{4^2 + (-2)^2 + 1^2}} \right|$$

$$= \frac{2}{\sqrt{21}}$$

$$\approx 0,4 \text{ unité}$$

b) La distance entre les plans $\pi_1: 3x + 2y - z = 5$ et $\pi_2: 6x + 4y - 2z = 8$ est égale à

$$\left| \frac{d_1 - d_2}{\sqrt{a^2 + b^2 + c^2}} \right| = \left| \frac{5 - 8}{\sqrt{3^2 + 2^2 + (-1)^2}} \right|$$

$$= \frac{3}{\sqrt{14}}$$

$$\approx 0,8 \text{ unité}$$

c) Soit un point $Q(-1, 2, -3)$ de la droite

$$\Delta: \frac{x + 1}{3} = \frac{y - 2}{4} = \frac{z + 3}{5}$$

La distance entre cette droite et le plan

$$\pi: 4x - 2y + z = -5$$

est égale à

$$\left| \frac{aq_1 + bq_2 + cq_3 - d}{\sqrt{a^2 + b^2 + c^2}} \right|$$

$$= \left| \frac{(4)(-1) + (-2)(2) + (1)(-3) - (-5)}{\sqrt{4^2 + (-2)^2 + 1^2}} \right|$$

$$= \frac{6}{\sqrt{21}}$$

$$\approx 1,3 \text{ unité}$$

29. (I) Quel point du plan $\pi: x + y + z = 5$ est le plus proche de l'origine?

30. (I) Dans chaque cas, trouvez le point du plan le plus proche du point $Q(2, -1, 3)$.

a) $\pi_1: -4x - 6y + 2z = -7$.

b) $\pi_2: x + y - 2z = 6$.

c) $\pi_3: 2x + 3y + z = 4$.

d) Le plan π_4 passant par l'origine et parallèle à chacun des vecteurs

$$\vec{u} = \begin{bmatrix} -1 & 3 & 1 \end{bmatrix} \text{ et } \vec{v} = \begin{bmatrix} 3 & 1 & 1 \end{bmatrix}$$

31. (I) Trouvez la distance entre deux droites données.

a) $\Delta_1: \dfrac{x - 1}{2} = \dfrac{y + 1}{2} = 3 - z$ et

$$\Delta_2: \begin{bmatrix} x & y & z \end{bmatrix} = \begin{bmatrix} 1 & 2 & -1 \end{bmatrix} + k_2 \begin{bmatrix} 1 & -1 & 3 \end{bmatrix}$$
où $k_2 \in \mathbb{R}$.

b) $\Delta_3: \dfrac{x + 1}{-2} = \dfrac{y - 2}{2} = \dfrac{z - 1}{2}$ et

$$\Delta_4: x = 3 - 4k_4 \quad y = k_4 \quad z = 2$$
où $k_4 \in \mathbb{R}$.

c) $\Delta_5: \dfrac{x + 2}{-1} = \dfrac{y + 2}{3} = \dfrac{z + 1}{2}$ et

$$\Delta_6: \dfrac{x - 1}{2} = \dfrac{y - 4}{-6} = \dfrac{z + 2}{-4}.$$

32. (I) Trouvez l'intersection des lieux géométriques donnés.

a) Le plan $\pi_1: 3x + 2y - z = 5$ et les axes de coordonnées.

b) $\pi_2: x + 2y - z = 5$, $\pi_3: x - y + 2z = 8$ et $\pi_4: 3x + 3y = 6$.

c) $\pi_5: x + y - z = 5$ et
$$\Delta_1: \begin{bmatrix} x & y & z \end{bmatrix} = \begin{bmatrix} 1 & 2 & -1 \end{bmatrix} + k_1 \begin{bmatrix} 1 & -1 & 3 \end{bmatrix}$$
où $k_1 \in \mathbb{R}$.

d) $\pi_6: x + y + z = 5$ et
$$\Delta_2: \begin{bmatrix} x & y & z \end{bmatrix} = \begin{bmatrix} 6 & 3 & -4 \end{bmatrix} + k_2 \begin{bmatrix} 2 & 1 & -3 \end{bmatrix}$$
où $k_2 \in \mathbb{R}$.

e) $\pi_7: 2x + y - z = 5$ et $\Delta_3: \dfrac{x + 2}{-1} = \dfrac{y + 2}{3} = \dfrac{z + 1}{2}$.

f) $\pi_8: 2x - y + 3z = 6$ et
$$\Delta_4: \dfrac{x - 1}{-2} = \dfrac{y - 2}{2} = \dfrac{z - 5}{2}.$$

33. (III) L'équation $\pi: \vec{n} \cdot \overrightarrow{QX} = 0$ est celle du plan passant par le point Q et de vecteur normal $\vec{n}$ où $\vec{n} \neq \vec{0}$. L'équation $\Delta: \overrightarrow{PX} = k\vec{d}$ où $k \in \mathbb{R}$ est celle de la droite passant par le point P et de vecteur directeur $\vec{d}$ où $\vec{d} \neq \vec{0}$.

a) Montrez que la droite Δ est parallèle au plan π si $\vec{n} \cdot \vec{d} = 0$.

b) Montrez que, si $\vec{n} \cdot \vec{d} \neq 0$, le vecteur position du point d'intersection R de la droite Δ avec le plan π est égal à

$$\overrightarrow{OP} + \left(\frac{\vec{n} \cdot \overrightarrow{PQ}}{\vec{n} \cdot \vec{d}}\right)\vec{d}$$

c) Montrez que la distance entre le point P de Δ et le point d'intersection R de la droite Δ avec le plan π est égale à

$$\left|\frac{\vec{n} \cdot \overrightarrow{PQ}}{\vec{n} \cdot \vec{d}}\right| \|\vec{d}\|$$

34. (I) Trouvez l'angle entre les deux lieux géométriques donnés.

a) $\pi_1 : 3x + 2y - z = 5$ et $\pi_2 : x - y + 2z = 8$.

b) $\pi_3 : 3x + 2y + z = 5$ et $\Delta_1 : \dfrac{x-1}{2} = \dfrac{y+1}{2} = 3 - z$.

c) $\pi_4 : \begin{bmatrix} x & y & z \end{bmatrix} = \begin{bmatrix} 2 & -3 & 4 \end{bmatrix} + r\begin{bmatrix} -1 & 3 & 2 \end{bmatrix} + s\begin{bmatrix} 2 & 1 & 2 \end{bmatrix}$

où r et s sont des nombres réels et
$\pi_5 : x - y - z = 5$

d) $\pi_6 : x - y + 2z = 8$ et
$\Delta_2 : x = 3 - 4k_2 \quad y = k_2 \quad z = 2 \quad$ où $k_2 \in \mathbb{R}$.

35. (I) Déterminez l'équation vectorielle et les équations paramétriques de chaque plan.

a) $\pi_1 : -4x - 6y + 2z = -7$.

b) $\pi_2 : x + y - 2z = 6$.

c) Le plan π_3 qui contient les droites

$$\Delta_1 : \frac{x+1}{2} = \frac{y-2}{-6} = \frac{z+3}{-4} \quad \text{et}$$

$$\Delta_2 : \frac{x-3}{-1} = \frac{y-3}{3} = \frac{z}{2}$$

d) Le plan π_4 passant par le point $(-1, 3, 2)$ et parallèle au plan yz.

e) Le plan π_5 passant par le point $(2, 4, -2)$ et perpendiculaire à l'axe des ordonnées.

36. (I) Déterminez les équations demandées.

a) Les équations symétriques de la droite Δ_1 passant par le point $A(-1, -3, 2)$ et perpendiculaire au plan $\pi_1 : 3x + 2y - 5z = 3$.

b) Les équations paramétriques de la droite d'intersection, Δ_2, des plans $\pi_2 : x - y + z = 3$ et $\pi_3 : x + y + z = 6$.

c) L'équation vectorielle de la droite d'intersection, Δ_3, des plans

$$\pi_4 : 2x + y - z = 3 \quad \text{et} \quad \pi_5 : x + 2y + z = 6$$

d) L'équation vectorielle de la droite d'intersection, Δ_4, des plans

$\pi_6 : \begin{bmatrix} x & y & z \end{bmatrix} = \begin{bmatrix} 2 & -3 & 4 \end{bmatrix} + r\begin{bmatrix} -1 & 3 & 2 \end{bmatrix} + s\begin{bmatrix} 2 & 1 & 2 \end{bmatrix}$

où r et $s \in \mathbb{R}$ et
$\pi_7 : x - y - z = 5$.

e) Les équations symétriques de la droite Δ_5 passant par le point $(1, 1, 1)$ et parallèle aux plans

$\pi_8 : \begin{bmatrix} x & y & z \end{bmatrix} = \begin{bmatrix} 1 & -3 & 4 \end{bmatrix} + r\begin{bmatrix} -1 & 3 & 2 \end{bmatrix} + s\begin{bmatrix} 2 & 1 & 2 \end{bmatrix}$

$\pi_9 : \begin{bmatrix} x & y & z \end{bmatrix} = \begin{bmatrix} 1 & 2 & 1 \end{bmatrix} + k\begin{bmatrix} 1 & -3 & 2 \end{bmatrix} + t\begin{bmatrix} 1 & 1 & 2 \end{bmatrix}$

où k, r, s et t sont des nombres réels.

37. (II) Présentez trois approches différentes pour vérifier si quatre points sont coplanaires.

38. (I) Montrez que les points $A(1, 2, -4)$, $B(3, -1, 1)$, $C(-1, -1, 9)$ et $D(2, -2, 6)$ sont coplanaires.

39. (II) Quelle est l'équation du plan dont tous les points sont équidistants des points $A(2, 4, 1)$ et $B(6, 2, 3)$. (Indice : le plan recherché est nécessairement perpendiculaire au vecteur $\overrightarrow{AB}$ et il passe par le milieu du segment de droite AB.)

40. (II) Un plan π, situé à une distance p de l'origine, coupe les axes de coordonnées aux points $A(a, 0, 0)$, $B(0, b, 0)$ et $C(0, 0, c)$ où a, b et c sont des constantes différentes de zéro. Montrez que

$$\frac{1}{p^2} = \frac{1}{a^2} + \frac{1}{b^2} + \frac{1}{c^2}$$

41. (II) Soit A, B et C trois points non colinéaires de l'espace. Expliquez pourquoi l'équation vectorielle $\overrightarrow{AX} \cdot (\overrightarrow{AB} \times \overrightarrow{AC}) = 0$ décrit l'ensemble des points $X(x, y, z)$ du plan qui passe par A, B et C. (Indice : vous pouvez fonder votre argumentation sur l'interprétation d'un produit scalaire nul ou encore vous servir de l'interprétation géométrique du produit mixte.)

42. (I) Complétez.

Pour définir l'ensemble des points $X(x, y, z)$ d'un plan de l'espace, il faut déterminer :

• soit _____ points _____ du plan ;

• soit un point du plan et un vecteur _____ au plan ;

• soit _____ vecteurs linéairement _____ et parallèles au plan et un _____ du plan.

43. (II) Chacune des trois méthodes décrites au n° 42 s'écrit sous forme vectorielle. Associez une méthode à chacune des expressions vectorielles suivantes. Justifiez votre choix.

- $\vec{n} \cdot \overrightarrow{PX} = 0$
- $\overrightarrow{PX} = k_1 \vec{u} + k_2 \vec{v}$ où k_1 et $k_2 \in \mathbb{R}$
- $\overrightarrow{AX} \cdot (\overrightarrow{AB} \times \overrightarrow{AC}) = 0$

44. (I) Dites si chaque énoncé est vrai ou faux, et justifiez votre réponse.

a) Si $\vec{d}$ est un vecteur directeur d'une droite Δ et si A est un point de cette droite, alors tout point $X(x, y, z)$ de la droite Δ vérifie l'équation vectorielle $\vec{d} \times \overrightarrow{AX} = \vec{0}$.

b) Deux droites parallèles à une troisième sont parallèles entre elles.

c) Deux droites qui en coupent une troisième sont concourantes.

d) Deux plans parallèles à une même droite sont parallèles entre eux.

e) Deux plans parallèles à un troisième sont parallèles entre eux.

f) Deux plans perpendiculaires à un troisième sont parallèles entre eux.

g) Deux droites perpendiculaires à un même plan sont parallèles entre elles.

h) La distance du plan $\pi \colon 2x - 3y + 4z = 5$ à l'origine est de 5 unités.

i) Les deux droites
$\Delta_1 \colon \begin{bmatrix} x & y & z \end{bmatrix} = \begin{bmatrix} 2 & 1 & 2 \end{bmatrix} + k_1 \begin{bmatrix} 1 & 1 & 2 \end{bmatrix}$
où $k_1 \in \mathbb{R}$
$\Delta_2 \colon \begin{bmatrix} x & y & z \end{bmatrix} = \begin{bmatrix} 1 & 4 & 4 \end{bmatrix} + k_2 \begin{bmatrix} -1 & 1 & 0 \end{bmatrix}$
où $k_2 \in \mathbb{R}$ sont concourantes et perpendiculaires.

j) Un plan est entièrement déterminé par trois points non colinéaires.

k) L'intersection de trois plans non parallèles est un point de l'espace.

l) Le plan $\pi \colon 2x + 4z = 0$ passe par l'origine et il est perpendiculaire à l'axe des y.

m) Trois points quelconques de l'espace sont coplanaires.

n) L'équation $a(x - p_1) + b(y - p_2) + c(z - p_3) = 0$ décrit le plan passant par le point $P(p_1, p_2, p_3)$ et de vecteur normal $\vec{n} = \begin{bmatrix} a & b & c \end{bmatrix}$.

o) Le plan $\pi \colon by + cz = d$ où b, c et d sont des constantes différentes de zéro est parallèle à l'axe des abscisses.

p) Soit a, b et c, trois constantes différentes de zéro. L'équation

$$\frac{x}{a} + \frac{y}{b} + \frac{z}{c} = 1$$

décrit le plan π qui coupe les axes de coordonnées aux points $A(a, 0, 0)$, $B(0, b, 0)$ et $C(0, 0, c)$.

q) L'équation d'un plan parallèle au plan xz est de la forme $y = k$ où k est une constante réelle.

45. (I) Soit les droites
$\Delta_1 \colon \dfrac{x - 2}{2} = y - 4 = \dfrac{z + 3}{-3}$;

Δ_2 : la droite qui passe par les points $(7, 7, -7)$ et $(10, 9, -8)$;

$\Delta_3 \colon \begin{bmatrix} x & y & z \end{bmatrix} = \begin{bmatrix} 3 & 2 & -3 \end{bmatrix} + k_3 \begin{bmatrix} 3 & 2 & -1 \end{bmatrix}$
où $k_3 \in \mathbb{R}$.

a) Quelle est l'équation vectorielle de la droite Δ_1 ?

b) Lesquels des points suivants appartiennent à la droite Δ_1 : $A(2, 4, -3)$, $B(6, 6, -9)$ et $C(0, 3, 0)$?

c) Donnez un vecteur directeur de la droite Δ_2.

d) Quelles sont les équations paramétriques de la droite Δ_2 ?

e) Quelles sont les équations symétriques de la droite Δ_3 ?

f) Montrez que les droites Δ_2 et Δ_3 sont parallèles. Quelle est la distance entre ces deux droites ?

g) Montrez que les droites Δ_1 et Δ_2 sont concourantes. Quels sont le point d'intersection de ces deux droites et l'angle qu'elles déterminent ?

h) Quelle est la distance entre la droite Δ_1 et le point $Q(2, 1, 4)$?

i) Quel point de la droite Δ_1 est le plus proche du point Q ?

j) Quelle est la distance entre les droites Δ_1 et Δ_3 ?

k) Quelle est l'équation vectorielle du plan π_1 qui contient les droites Δ_1 et Δ_2 ?

l) Quelles sont les équations paramétriques du plan π_1 défini en k ?

m) Quelle est l'équation cartésienne du plan π_1 défini en k ?

n) Quelle est la distance entre le plan π_1 et l'origine ?

o) Quel point du plan π_1 est le plus proche de l'origine ?

p) Quel est l'angle entre l'axe des cotes et le plan π_1 ?

q) Quelle est l'équation vectorielle de la droite d'intersection (Δ_4) du plan π_1 et du plan π_2 qui passe par les points $D(2, 3, -1)$, $E(1, 4, 2)$ et $F(3, 2, -1)$?

r) Quel est l'angle dièdre entre les plans π_1 et π_2?

s) Quelle est l'équation cartésienne du plan π_3 passant par le point $G(1, 2, 1)$ et perpendiculaire à la droite d'intersection des plans π_1 et π_2?

t) Quel est le point d'intersection de la droite Δ_3 et du plan π_3, et quel est l'angle entre Δ_3 et π_3?

u) Montrez que la droite $\Delta_5 : \dfrac{x-4}{6} = \dfrac{y+7}{-6} = z - 2$ appartient au plan π_3.

Espaces vectoriels

But, as for everything else, so for a mathematical theory –
beauty can be perceived but not explained.

Arthur Cayley

À LA FIN DU PRÉSENT CHAPITRE, VOUS DEVRIEZ ÊTRE
EN MESURE DE RÉPONDRE AUX QUESTIONS SUIVANTES:

- Qu'est-ce qu'un espace euclidien de dimension n?
- Qu'est-ce qu'un espace vectoriel?
- Comment montre-t-on qu'un ensemble est un sous-espace vectoriel?
- Qu'est-ce qu'une base d'un espace vectoriel?
- Qu'ont en commun deux bases d'un même espace vectoriel de dimension finie?
- Comment trouve-t-on une base de l'espace vectoriel engendré par un ensemble de vecteurs de R^n?

UN PORTRAIT de Emmy Noether

Emmy Noether naquit le 23 mars 1882 dans la ville universitaire allemande d'Erlangen. Bien qu'elle fût très douée pour les mathématiques et que son père, Max Noether, fût un mathématicien réputé, elle ne fut pas admise comme étudiante à l'université après ses études secondaires parce qu'en Allemagne, à cette époque, seuls les hommes avaient accès aux études supérieures. On permit tout au plus à Emmy Noether de suivre des cours comme auditrice libre pendant deux ans (1900-1902). Heureusement, grâce à l'évolution des normes, elle put soutenir sa thèse de doctorat en 1907. Cette thèse, intitulée Sur les systèmes d'invariants complets pour les formes biquadratiques ternaires, constitua le prélude à ses travaux subséquents sur l'axiomatisation de l'algèbre.

Noether fut victime de discrimination toute sa vie, en raison de son sexe et de son origine ethnique. Ainsi, elle n'arriva pas à décrocher un poste de professeur après ses études. On venait d'admettre les femmes comme étudiantes, mais de là à leur permettre d'enseigner !

Noether poursuivit quand même ses travaux en algèbre de manière indépendante. En 1915, elle fut invitée à l'Université de Göttingen par le célèbre mathématicien David Hilbert (1862-1943) pour faire de la recherche en mathématiques et en physique, notamment en relativité. En 1919, grâce aux efforts de Hilbert, elle fut nommée «professeur associé non officiel», un poste auquel n'était attachée aucune rémunération.

Pourtant, Albert Einstein écrivit dès 1918 :

> À la lecture des derniers travaux de Fraülein Noether, je me suis encore dit qu'on se montre grandement injuste en ne lui accordant pas officiellement le titre de professeur.
>
> Cela n'aurait pas fait de mal à la vieille garde de Göttingen d'adopter quelques-unes des idées de Noether. De toute évidence, elle est très compétente[1].

---

1. Traduction d'un extrait de A. Calaprice. *The Quotable Einstein*, Princeton, Princeton University Press, 1996, p. 75.

En 1922, le poste de professeur associé de Noether devint enfin « officiel », et elle fut dès lors rémunérée. Malheureusement, en 1933, à la suite des purges effectuées par les nazis dans les universités, elle dut quitter Göttingen à cause de ses origines juives. Elle se réfugia aux États-Unis et enseigna au Bryn Mawr College, de même qu'à l'Institute for Advanced Study de l'Université Princeton.

Emmy Noether mourut, le 14 avril 1935, d'une infection postopératoire. Dans son édition du 4 mai 1935, le New York Times *rapporte les propos suivants d'Albert Einstein à propos de la contribution d'Emmy Noether à l'algèbre :*

> *Selon les mathématiciens les plus reconnus, Fraülein Noether est le plus grand génie créateur en mathématiques que l'ouverture des études supérieures aux femmes ait produit. En algèbre, un domaine auquel se sont intéressés les mathématiciens les plus doués des derniers siècles, elle a inventé des méthodes qui se sont avérées extrêmement importantes pour le développement de la dernière génération de mathématiciens[2].*

---

2. Traduction d'un extrait de L. M. Osen. *Women in Mathematics*, Cambridge, MIT Press, 1974, p. 151.

10.1 ESPACE EUCLIDIEN DE DIMENSION *n* OU $\mathbb{R}^n$

Maintenant que vous connaissez bien les espaces euclidiens de dimension deux et trois, nous allons aborder l'espace euclidien de dimension *n*, dont $\mathbb{R}^2$ et $\mathbb{R}^3$ sont des représentants. Par la suite, nous présenterons le concept plus général encore d'espace vectoriel.

Nous entrons ici dans le royaume des mathématiques pures, théoriques et abstraites. Nous allons essentiellement dégager des caractéristiques importantes, communes à plusieurs ensembles munis d'opérations. Nous déduirons des théorèmes valables pour tous les ensembles qui présentent une même structure mathématique (les mêmes caractéristiques communes). Cette structure, d'une importance capitale, porte le nom d'espace vectoriel.

ESPACE EUCLIDIEN DE DIMENSION *n*

L'espace euclidien de dimension *n*, noté $\mathbb{R}^n$, est l'ensemble de tous les vecteurs algébriques à *n* composantes réelles (ou *n*-uplets), soit l'ensemble des matrices de format $1 \times n$ dont les éléments sont des nombres réels. En langage symbolique,

$$\mathbb{R}^n = \left\{ \begin{bmatrix} x_1 & x_2 & x_3 & \cdots & x_n \end{bmatrix} \mid x_i \in \mathbb{R} \right\}$$

L'**espace euclidien de dimension *n***, noté $\mathbb{R}^n$, est l'ensemble des vecteurs algébriques comportant *n* composantes réelles (appelés *n*-uplets), soit l'ensemble des matrices de format $1 \times n$ dont les éléments sont des nombres réels. En langage symbolique,

$$\mathbb{R}^n = \left\{ \begin{bmatrix} x_1 & x_2 & x_3 & \cdots & x_n \end{bmatrix} \mid x_i \in \mathbb{R} \right\}$$

En particulier, $\mathbb{R}^n$ compte un vecteur nul, noté $\vec{0}$, formé de *n* composantes valant toutes zéro.

Les concepts d'égalité, d'addition et de multiplication par un scalaire dans $\mathbb{R}^n$ sont donc définis de la même façon que pour les matrices. Notamment, si $\vec{u} = \begin{bmatrix} u_1 & u_2 & \cdots & u_n \end{bmatrix}$ et $\vec{v} = \begin{bmatrix} v_1 & v_2 & \cdots & v_n \end{bmatrix}$ appartiennent à $\mathbb{R}^n$ et si k est un nombre réel, alors :

- $\vec{u} = \vec{v}$ si et seulement si $u_i = v_i$ pour $i = 1, 2, \ldots, n$ (égalité de deux vecteurs) ;

- $\vec{u} + \vec{v} = \begin{bmatrix} u_1 + v_1 & u_2 + v_2 & \cdots & u_n + v_n \end{bmatrix} \in \mathbb{R}^n$ (addition de deux vecteurs) ;

- $k\vec{u} = \begin{bmatrix} ku_1 & ku_2 & \cdots & ku_n \end{bmatrix} \in \mathbb{R}^n$ (multiplication d'un vecteur par un scalaire).

Exemple

1. Les vecteurs $\vec{u} = \begin{bmatrix} 3 & -1 & 2 & 5 \end{bmatrix}$ et $\vec{v} = \begin{bmatrix} x & y & z & w \end{bmatrix}$ appartiennent à $\mathbb{R}^4$. Ils sont égaux si et seulement si $x = 3$, $y = -1$, $z = 2$ et $w = 5$.

2. Les vecteurs $\vec{w} = \begin{bmatrix} 3 & 2 & 5 & -4 & 1 \end{bmatrix}$ et $\vec{t} = \begin{bmatrix} -4 & 1 & 5 & 4 & -2 \end{bmatrix}$ appartiennent à $\mathbb{R}^5$. Leur somme est

$$\vec{w} + \vec{t} = \begin{bmatrix} 3-4 & 2+1 & 5+5 & -4+4 & 1-2 \end{bmatrix}$$
$$= \begin{bmatrix} -1 & 3 & 10 & 0 & -1 \end{bmatrix}$$

Le produit du vecteur $\vec{w}$ par le scalaire 2 est

$$2\vec{w} = \begin{bmatrix} 2(3) & 2(2) & 2(5) & 2(-4) & 2(1) \end{bmatrix}$$
$$= \begin{bmatrix} 6 & 4 & 10 & -8 & 2 \end{bmatrix}$$

PRODUIT SCALAIRE DE DEUX VECTEURS DE $\mathbb{R}^n$

Le produit scalaire, $\vec{u} \cdot \vec{v}$, de deux vecteurs de $\mathbb{R}^n$,
$\vec{u} = \begin{bmatrix} u_1 & u_2 & \cdots & u_n \end{bmatrix}$ et
$\vec{v} = \begin{bmatrix} v_1 & v_2 & \cdots & v_n \end{bmatrix}$,
est un scalaire :

$$\vec{u} \cdot \vec{v} = u_1 v_1 + u_2 v_2 + \cdots + u_n v_n$$

NORME EUCLIDIENNE D'UN VECTEUR DE $\mathbb{R}^n$

La norme euclidienne d'un vecteur
$\vec{u} = \begin{bmatrix} u_1 & u_2 & \cdots & u_n \end{bmatrix} \in \mathbb{R}^n$
est donnée par

$$\|\vec{u}\| = \sqrt{u_1^2 + u_2^2 + \cdots + u_n^2}$$
$$= \sqrt{\sum_{i=1}^{n} u_i^2}$$

VECTEURS ORTHOGONAUX

Deux vecteurs sont orthogonaux si et seulement si leur produit scalaire est zéro.

Comme les vecteurs de $\mathbb{R}^n$ sont des matrices particulières, on peut également définir des concepts qui leur sont propres, tels le **produit scalaire** ($\vec{u} \cdot \vec{v}$) et la **norme euclidienne** ($\|\vec{u}\|$). Il s'agit de l'application à des vecteurs comportant n composantes des définitions données pour $\mathbb{R}^2$ et $\mathbb{R}^3$. Si $\vec{u} = \begin{bmatrix} u_1 & u_2 & \cdots & u_n \end{bmatrix}$ et $\vec{v} = \begin{bmatrix} v_1 & v_2 & \cdots & v_n \end{bmatrix}$ sont des vecteurs de $\mathbb{R}^n$, alors :

- $\vec{u} \cdot \vec{v} = u_1 v_1 + u_2 v_2 + \cdots + u_n v_n$ (produit scalaire) ;

- $\|\vec{u}\| = \sqrt{u_1^2 + u_2^2 + \cdots + u_n^2} = \sqrt{\sum_{i=1}^{n} u_i^2}$ (norme euclidienne).

Comme pour les vecteurs de $\mathbb{R}^2$ et de $\mathbb{R}^3$, on dit que deux **vecteurs** de $\mathbb{R}^n$ sont **orthogonaux** si et seulement si leur produit scalaire vaut zéro. Dans $\mathbb{R}^2$ et dans $\mathbb{R}^3$, nous avons montré que des vecteurs non nuls sont orthogonaux si et seulement s'ils sont perpendiculaires ; toutefois, dans $\mathbb{R}^n$ (où $n > 3$), il n'est pas possible de donner une interprétation géométrique du concept d'orthogonalité.

Exemple

Soit les vecteurs

$$\vec{u} = \begin{bmatrix} 3 & -1 & 2 & 5 \end{bmatrix}$$
$$\vec{v} = \begin{bmatrix} 2 & 3 & 4 & -1 \end{bmatrix}$$
$$\vec{w} = \begin{bmatrix} 3 & 1 & 1 & -2 \end{bmatrix}$$

alors

$$\vec{u} \cdot \vec{v} = 3(2) + (-1)(3) + 2(4) + 5(-1) = 6$$

Les vecteurs $\vec{u}$ et $\vec{w}$ sont orthogonaux parce que

$$\vec{u} \cdot \vec{w} = 3(3) + (-1)(1) + 2(1) + 5(-2) = 0$$

La norme euclidienne de $\vec{u}$ est

$$\|\vec{u}\| = \sqrt{3^2 + (-1)^2 + 2^2 + 5^2} = \sqrt{39}$$

EXERCICE 10.1

Soit les vecteurs

$$\vec{r} = \begin{bmatrix} 1 & 3 & 5 & 7 & 9 \end{bmatrix} \qquad \vec{s} = \begin{bmatrix} 1 & -1 & 1 & -1 & 1 & -1 \end{bmatrix}$$
$$\vec{t} = \begin{bmatrix} 2 & -1 \end{bmatrix} \qquad \vec{u} = \begin{bmatrix} 1 & -4 & 3 & -8 \end{bmatrix}$$
$$\vec{v} = \begin{bmatrix} -1 & 1 & -1 & -1 \end{bmatrix} \qquad \vec{w} = \begin{bmatrix} 5 & 12 & -8 & -2 \end{bmatrix}$$

a) Identifiez la dimension de l'espace euclidien $\mathbb{R}^n$ auquel appartient chaque vecteur.

b) Évaluez, si possible, les expressions suivantes.
   i) $\|\vec{s}\|$
   ii) $\vec{r} + \vec{s}$
   iii) $2\vec{u} + 3\vec{v} - 4\vec{w}$
   iv) $\vec{v} \cdot \vec{w}$
   v) $\vec{s} \cdot \vec{r}$

c) Vérifiez que les vecteurs $\vec{u}$ et $\vec{v}$ sont orthogonaux.

COMBINAISON LINÉAIRE

Une combinaison linéaire des n vecteurs $\overrightarrow{u_1}$, $\overrightarrow{u_2}$, ..., $\overrightarrow{u_n}$ est une expression de la forme

$$a_1\overrightarrow{u_1} + a_2\overrightarrow{u_2} + \cdots + a_n\overrightarrow{u_n}$$

où a_1, a_2, ..., a_n sont des scalaires.

VECTEURS LINÉAIREMENT INDÉPENDANTS

Des vecteurs $\overrightarrow{u_1}$, $\overrightarrow{u_2}$, ..., $\overrightarrow{u_n}$ sont dits linéairement indépendants si et seulement si *la seule* combinaison linéaire de ces vecteurs égale au vecteur nul est celle où tous les coefficients (les scalaires) sont nuls. De manière plus formelle, n vecteurs $\overrightarrow{u_1}$, $\overrightarrow{u_2}$, ..., $\overrightarrow{u_n}$ sont dits linéairement indépendants si et seulement si

$$a_1\overrightarrow{u_1} + a_2\overrightarrow{u_2} + \cdots + a_n\overrightarrow{u_n} = \vec{0}$$

$$\Rightarrow \quad a_1 = 0,\ a_2 = 0,\ ...,\ a_n = 0$$

Les notions de combinaison linéaire et d'indépendance linéaire sont également pertinentes dans $\mathbb{R}^n$.

On appelle **combinaison linéaire** des m vecteurs, $\overrightarrow{u_1}$, $\overrightarrow{u_2}$, ..., $\overrightarrow{u_m}$, de $\mathbb{R}^n$ toute expression de la forme $a_1\overrightarrow{u_1} + a_2\overrightarrow{u_2} + \cdots + a_m\overrightarrow{u_m}$, où a_1, a_2, ..., a_m sont des scalaires.

De plus, m **vecteurs**, $\overrightarrow{u_1}$, $\overrightarrow{u_2}$, ..., $\overrightarrow{u_m}$, sont dits **linéairement indépendants** si et seulement si *la seule* combinaison linéaire de ces vecteurs égale au vecteur nul est celle où tous les coefficients (les scalaires) sont nuls.

De manière plus formelle, m vecteurs $\vec{u_1}$, $\vec{u_2}$, ..., $\vec{u_m}$ sont linéairement indépendants si et seulement si

$$a_1 \vec{u_1} + a_2 \vec{u_2} + \cdots + a_m \vec{u_m} = \vec{0} \quad \Rightarrow \quad a_1 = 0,\ a_2 = 0,\ ...,\ a_m = 0$$

Des **vecteurs** qui ne sont pas linéairement indépendants sont dits **linéairement dépendants**.

Exemple

Soit les vecteurs

$$\vec{r} = \begin{bmatrix} 0 & 1 & 1 & -1 & 1 & 0 \end{bmatrix}$$
$$\vec{s} = \begin{bmatrix} 1 & -1 & 1 & -1 & 1 & -1 \end{bmatrix}$$
$$\vec{u} = \begin{bmatrix} 1 & 0 & 1 & 0 & 1 & 0 \end{bmatrix}$$

On veut montrer que ces vecteurs sont linéairement indépendants. De l'équation vectorielle $a\vec{r} + b\vec{s} + c\vec{u} = \vec{0}$, on tire le système de six équations à trois inconnues

$$\begin{aligned} b + c &= 0 \\ a - b &= 0 \\ a + b + c &= 0 \\ -a - b &= 0 \\ a + b + c &= 0 \\ -b &= 0 \end{aligned}$$

Ce système d'équations admet au moins une solution, soit $a = 0$, $b = 0$ et $c = 0$. Pour montrer que les vecteurs $\vec{r}$, $\vec{s}$ et $\vec{u}$ sont linéairement indépendants, il faut vérifier que cette solution est la seule possible.

On résout le système d'équations par la méthode d'élimination gaussienne.

$$\left[\begin{array}{ccc|c} 0 & 1 & 1 & 0 \\ 1 & -1 & 0 & 0 \\ 1 & 1 & 1 & 0 \\ -1 & -1 & 0 & 0 \\ 1 & 1 & 1 & 0 \\ 0 & -1 & 0 & 0 \end{array}\right] \sim \left[\begin{array}{ccc|c} 1 & 1 & 1 & 0 \\ 1 & -1 & 0 & 0 \\ 0 & 1 & 1 & 0 \\ -1 & -1 & 0 & 0 \\ 1 & 1 & 1 & 0 \\ 0 & -1 & 0 & 0 \end{array}\right] \begin{array}{l} L_1 \leftrightarrow L_3 \end{array}$$

$$\sim \left[\begin{array}{ccc|c} 1 & 1 & 1 & 0 \\ 0 & -2 & -1 & 0 \\ 0 & 1 & 1 & 0 \\ 0 & 0 & 1 & 0 \\ 0 & 0 & 0 & 0 \\ 0 & -1 & 0 & 0 \end{array}\right] \begin{array}{l} \\ L_2 \rightarrow L_2 - L_1 \\ \\ L_4 \rightarrow L_4 + L_1 \\ L_5 \rightarrow L_5 - L_1 \\ \\ \end{array}$$

$$\sim \begin{bmatrix} 1 & 1 & 1 & | & 0 \\ 0 & -1 & 0 & | & 0 \\ 0 & 1 & 1 & | & 0 \\ 0 & 0 & 1 & | & 0 \\ 0 & 0 & 0 & | & 0 \\ 0 & -2 & -1 & | & 0 \end{bmatrix} \begin{matrix} \\ L_2 \leftrightarrow L_6 \\ \\ \\ \\ \\ \end{matrix}$$

$$\sim \begin{bmatrix} 1 & 1 & 1 & | & 0 \\ 0 & -1 & 0 & | & 0 \\ 0 & 0 & 1 & | & 0 \\ 0 & 0 & 1 & | & 0 \\ 0 & 0 & 0 & | & 0 \\ 0 & 0 & -1 & | & 0 \end{bmatrix} \begin{matrix} \\ \\ L_3 \rightarrow L_3 + L_2 \\ \\ \\ L_6 \rightarrow L_6 - 2L_2 \end{matrix}$$

$$\sim \begin{bmatrix} 1 & 1 & 1 & | & 0 \\ 0 & -1 & 0 & | & 0 \\ 0 & 0 & 1 & | & 0 \\ 0 & 0 & 0 & | & 0 \\ 0 & 0 & 0 & | & 0 \\ 0 & 0 & 0 & | & 0 \end{bmatrix} \begin{matrix} \\ \\ \\ L_4 \rightarrow L_4 - L_3 \\ \\ L_6 \rightarrow L_6 + L_3 \end{matrix}$$

On obtient facilement, par substitution à rebours, $a = 0$, $b = 0$ et $c = 0$. Il n'existe donc qu'une seule combinaison linéaire des vecteurs $\vec{r}$, $\vec{s}$ et $\vec{u}$ qui est égale au vecteur nul, soit celle où tous les coefficients valent zéro. Par conséquent, ces trois vecteurs sont linéairement indépendants.

EXERCICE 10.2

Soit les vecteurs

$$\vec{r} = \begin{bmatrix} 0 & 1 & 1 & -1 & 1 & 0 \end{bmatrix} \quad \vec{s} = \begin{bmatrix} 1 & -1 & 1 & -1 & 1 & -1 \end{bmatrix}$$

$$\vec{u} = \begin{bmatrix} 1 & 0 & 1 & 0 & 1 & 0 \end{bmatrix} \quad \vec{v} = \begin{bmatrix} 1 & 0 & 0 & 2 & 0 & 1 \end{bmatrix}$$

a) Montrez que ces quatre vecteurs sont linéairement dépendants.

b) Exprimez le vecteur $\vec{v}$ comme une combinaison linéaire des vecteurs $\vec{r}$, $\vec{s}$ et $\vec{u}$.

L'espace euclidien $\mathbb{R}^n$ sert de modèle pour l'élaboration du concept d'espace vectoriel. Essentiellement, on retient les propriétés importantes des deux opérations (addition et multiplication par un scalaire) sur $\mathbb{R}^n$ pour définir un espace vectoriel.

Un **espace vectoriel** sur le corps[3] des réels $\mathbb{R}$ est un ensemble V – dont les éléments sont appelés vecteurs – muni de deux opérations, soit l'addition de deux vecteurs (notée $\vec{u} + \vec{v}$ ou $\vec{u} \oplus \vec{v}$) et la multiplication d'un vecteur par un scalaire (notée $a\vec{u}$ ou $a \odot \vec{u}$)[4], qui vérifient les dix propriétés suivantes.

Soit $\vec{u}$, $\vec{v}$ et $\vec{w} \in V$, et soit a et $b \in \mathbb{R}$.

1) $\vec{u} + \vec{v} \in V$ (fermeture de l'espace V par rapport à l'addition de vecteurs).

2) $\vec{u} + \vec{v} = \vec{v} + \vec{u}$ (commutativité de l'addition de vecteurs).

3) $(\vec{u} + \vec{v}) + \vec{w} = \vec{u} + (\vec{v} + \vec{w})$ (associativité de l'addition de vecteurs).

4) Il existe un vecteur $\vec{0} \in V$ tel que $\vec{u} + \vec{0} = \vec{u}$ (existence d'un élément neutre pour l'addition, soit un vecteur nul appartenant à V).

5) Il existe un vecteur $-\vec{u} \in V$, tel que $\vec{u} + (-\vec{u}) = \vec{0}$ (existence d'un opposé, noté $-\vec{u}$, appartenant à V pour tout vecteur $\vec{u}$ de V).

6) $a\vec{u} \in V$ (fermeture de l'espace V par rapport à la multiplication d'un vecteur par un scalaire).

7) $(ab)\vec{u} = a(b\vec{u})$ (associativité mixte).

8) $a(\vec{u} + \vec{v}) = a\vec{u} + a\vec{v}$ (distributivité de la multiplication d'un vecteur par un scalaire par rapport à l'addition de vecteurs).

9) $(a + b)\vec{u} = a\vec{u} + b\vec{u}$ (distributivité de la multiplication d'un vecteur par un scalaire par rapport à l'addition de scalaires).

10) $1\vec{u} = \vec{u}$.

---

3. Voir la définition de *corps* à la page 258. Nous pourrions utiliser n'importe quel corps de scalaires, par exemple $\mathbb{C}$, à la place du corps des réels. Toutefois, dans le présent manuel, nous nous limitons à l'étude des espaces vectoriels sur $\mathbb{R}$.

4. L'opération $\oplus$ est appelée *loi de composition interne* parce qu'il s'agit d'une opération sur deux éléments de l'espace, et l'opération $\odot$ est appelée *loi de composition externe* parce qu'il s'agit d'une opération sur un élément du corps et un élément de l'espace vectoriel. Dans ce manuel, on réserve les symboles $\oplus$ et $\odot$ pour des opérations autres que les opérations habituelles de l'espace vectoriel étudié.

C'est à Hermann Grassmann (1809-1877) qu'on doit le concept d'espace vectoriel. Grassmann fut le premier à étudier les espaces de dimension supérieure à trois, dans *Die lineale Ausdehnungslehre* («Théorie de l'étendue linéaire»), paru en 1844. Il y élabora les notions d'indépendance linéaire et de base; il montra que tout vecteur s'écrit comme une combinaison linéaire unique des vecteurs de la base et que des vecteurs orthogonaux non nuls sont linéairement indépendants. Cet ouvrage, révolutionnaire pour son époque, passa d'abord inaperçu parce que Grassmann, autodidacte, n'enseigna jamais à l'université et qu'il vécut en marge des milieux de la recherche mathématique. L'*Ausdehnungslehre* ne fut reconnu à sa juste valeur qu'environ 30 ans après sa parution, soit vers 1870, quelques années seulement avant la mort de son auteur. La première définition axiomatique d'espace vectoriel date cependant de 1888; elle fut donnée par le mathématicien italien Giuseppe Peano (1858-1932) dans *Calcolo geometrico*. Peano y définit notamment le concept de dimension d'un espace vectoriel. Mais ce n'est qu'avec la thèse de doctorat de Stefan Banach (1892-1945), déposée en 1920 et publiée en 1922, que le concept d'espace vectoriel prit véritablement sa place dans la boîte à outils des mathématiciens. Banach démontra clairement l'avantage de faire appel aux structures algébriques pour prouver du même coup diverses propriétés de plusieurs ensembles vérifiant tous un nombre restreint d'axiomes, plutôt que de prouver ces propriétés pour chaque ensemble particulier.

Ainsi, quel que soit les autres noms qu'on puisse lui attribuer, tout ensemble muni de deux opérations possédant les dix propriétés énoncées est aussi un espace vectoriel, et ses éléments sont appelés vecteurs.

Il faut se rappeler qu'un espace vectoriel n'est pas simplement un ensemble: c'est un ensemble muni de deux opérations. Mais il arrive qu'on parle d'un espace vectoriel sans nommer explicitement ces opérations. Il est alors sous-entendu qu'il s'agit des opérations habituelles d'addition et de multiplication par un scalaire définies sur l'ensemble en question.

Pour montrer qu'un ensemble muni de deux opérations est un espace vectoriel, il faut montrer qu'il vérifie les dix propriétés énoncées plus haut, ce qui demande généralement beaucoup de temps. Par contre, pour montrer qu'un ensemble n'est pas un espace vectoriel, il suffit de prouver que l'une des dix propriétés n'est pas satisfaite pour cet ensemble. Il suffit donc de donner un seul contre-exemple pour montrer qu'un ensemble n'est pas un espace vectoriel.

Exemple

1. L'ensemble des matrices de format $m \times n$ muni des opérations d'addition matricielle et de multiplication d'une matrice par un scalaire, définies au chapitre 2, forme un espace vectoriel. Nous en avons déjà fait la preuve, sans le dire, lorsque nous avons démontré le théorème 2.1 (p. 35).

2. Les matrices de format $1 \times n$ constituent un cas particulier des matrices de format $m \times n$; elles forment donc un espace vectoriel. Par ailleurs, $\mathbb{R}^n$ étant défini comme l'ensemble des matrices de format $1 \times n$, il constitue aussi un espace vectoriel.

3. L'ensemble $P_n = \left\{ a_0 + a_1 x + a_2 x^2 + \cdots + a_n x^n \middle| a_i \in \mathbb{R} \right\}$ est l'ensemble des polynômes en x à coefficients réels de degré inférieur ou égal à n, plus la constante 0. On peut abréger l'écriture d'un élément de P_n à l'aide de la notation Σ:

$$p(x) = a_0 + a_1 x + a_2 x^2 + \cdots + a_n x^n = \sum_{i=0}^{n} a_i x^i$$

Il faut se rappeler que deux polynômes

$$p(x) = \sum_{i=0}^{n} a_i x^i \in P_n \quad \text{et} \quad q(x) = \sum_{i=0}^{n} b_i x^i \in P_n$$

sont égaux si et seulement si $a_i = b_i$ pour $i = 1, 2, \ldots, n$.

On définit comme suit l'addition et la multiplication par un scalaire dans P_n.

Si $p(x) = \sum_{i=0}^{n} a_i x^i \in P_n$, si $q(x) = \sum_{i=0}^{n} b_i x^i \in P_n$ et si $k \in \mathbb{R}$, alors

- $p(x) + q(x) = \sum_{i=0}^{n} (a_i + b_i) x^i$;

- $kp(x) = \sum_{i=0}^{n} (ka_i) x^i$.

On veut démontrer que P_n est un espace vectoriel pour les opérations d'addition et de multiplication par un scalaire.

Preuve

Il faut vérifier que les dix propriétés des espaces vectoriels sont satisfaites. Il est utile de se rappeler que les coefficients de tout polynôme sont des nombres réels et que, par conséquent, les propriétés de l'addition et de la multiplication dans les réels s'appliquent.

1) Si $p(x) = \displaystyle\sum_{i=0}^{n} a_i x^i \in P_n$ et $q(x) = \displaystyle\sum_{i=0}^{n} b_i x^i \in P_n$, alors

$$p(x) + q(x) = \sum_{i=0}^{n} (a_i + b_i) x^i$$

Comme $(a_i + b_i) \in \mathbb{R}$, alors $p(x) + q(x) \in P_n$.

2) Si $p(x) = \displaystyle\sum_{i=0}^{n} a_i x^i \in P_n$ et $q(x) = \displaystyle\sum_{i=0}^{n} b_i x^i \in P_n$, alors

$$p(x) + q(x) = \sum_{i=0}^{n} (a_i + b_i) x^i = \sum_{i=0}^{n} (b_i + a_i) x^i = q(x) + p(x)$$

3) Si $p(x) = \displaystyle\sum_{i=0}^{n} a_i x^i \in P_n$, si $q(x) = \displaystyle\sum_{i=0}^{n} b_i x^i \in P_n$ et si

$r(x) = \displaystyle\sum_{i=0}^{n} c_i x^i \in P_n$, alors

$$\begin{aligned}
\left[p(x) + q(x) \right] + r(x) &= \left[\sum_{i=0}^{n} (a_i + b_i) x^i \right] + \sum_{i=0}^{n} c_i x^i \\
&= \sum_{i=0}^{n} \left[(a_i + b_i) + c_i \right] x^i \\
&= \sum_{i=0}^{n} \left[a_i + (b_i + c_i) \right] x^i \\
&= \sum_{i=0}^{n} a_i x^i + \left[\sum_{i=0}^{n} (b_i + c_i) x^i \right] \\
&= p(x) + \left[q(x) + r(x) \right]
\end{aligned}$$

4) Si $p(x) = \displaystyle\sum_{i=0}^{n} a_i x^i \in P_n$, alors $o(x) = \displaystyle\sum_{i=0}^{n} 0 x^i = 0 \in P_n$ et

$$p(x) + o(x) = \sum_{i=0}^{n} (a_i + 0) x^i = \sum_{i=0}^{n} a_i x^i = p(x)$$

Le polynôme $o(x) = \displaystyle\sum_{i=0}^{n} 0 x^i$ est le vecteur nul de P_n.

5) Si $p(x) = \sum_{i=0}^{n} a_i x^i \in P_n$, alors $q(x) = \sum_{i=0}^{n} (-a_i) x^i \in P_n$ et $p(x) + q(x) = o(x)$. Chaque polynôme de P_n possède donc un opposé qui appartient lui aussi à P_n.

6) Si $p(x) = \sum_{i=0}^{n} a_i x^i \in P_n$ et si $k \in \mathbb{R}$, alors

$$kp(x) = \sum_{i=0}^{n} (ka_i) x^i \in P_n$$

parce que $(ka_i) \in \mathbb{R}$.

7) Si $p(x) = \sum_{i=0}^{n} a_i x^i \in P_n$ et si k et $g \in \mathbb{R}$, alors

$$
\begin{aligned}
(kg) p(x) &= \sum_{i=0}^{n} \left[(kg) a_i \right] x^i \\
&= \sum_{i=0}^{n} \left[k(ga_i) \right] x^i \\
&= k \sum_{i=0}^{n} (ga_i) x^i \\
&= k \left[gp(x) \right]
\end{aligned}
$$

8) Si $p(x) = \sum_{i=0}^{n} a_i x^i \in P_n$, si $q(x) = \sum_{i=0}^{n} b_i x^i \in P_n$ et si $k \in \mathbb{R}$, alors

$$
\begin{aligned}
k \left[p(x) + q(x) \right] &= k \sum_{i=0}^{n} (a_i + b_i) x^i \\
&= \sum_{i=0}^{n} \left[k(a_i + b_i) \right] x^i \\
&= \sum_{i=0}^{n} (ka_i + kb_i) x^i \\
&= \sum_{i=0}^{n} (ka_i) x^i + \sum_{i=0}^{n} (kb_i) x^i \\
&= kp(x) + kq(x)
\end{aligned}
$$

9) Si $p(x) = \sum_{i=0}^{n} a_i x^i \in P_n$ et si k et $g \in \mathbb{R}$, alors

$$
\begin{aligned}
(k + g) p(x) &= \sum_{i=0}^{n} \left[(k + g) a_i \right] x^i \\
&= \sum_{i=0}^{n} (ka_i + ga_i) x^i
\end{aligned}
$$

$$= \sum_{i=0}^{n} (ka_i)x^i + \sum_{i=0}^{n} (ga_i)x^i$$
$$= kp(x) + gp(x)$$

10) Si $p(x) = \sum_{i=0}^{n} a_i x^i \in P_n$, alors

$$1\,p(x) = \sum_{i=0}^{n} (1\,a_i)x^i = \sum_{i=0}^{n} a_i x^i = p(x)$$

On en conclut que P_n muni des opérations d'addition et de multiplication par un scalaire, telles qu'elles ont été définies, forme un espace vectoriel. ■

4. Au chapitre 7, nous avons donné deux interprétations de l'ensemble $\mathbb{C}$ des nombres complexes muni des opérations habituelles d'addition et de multiplication par un scalaire, en le considérant comme un ensemble de vecteurs et comme un ensemble de polynômes. Ces deux ensembles formant des espaces vectoriels, les nombres complexes constituent aussi un espace vectoriel sur les réels.

5. L'ensemble $\mathbb{Z}_{2 \times 2} = \left\{ \left[a_{ij} \right]_{2 \times 2} \big| a_{ij} \in \mathbb{Z} \right\}$ est l'ensemble des matrices carrées d'ordre 2 dont les éléments sont des entiers. Cet ensemble muni des opérations d'addition matricielle et de multiplication d'une matrice par un scalaire n'est pas un espace vectoriel sur $\mathbb{R}$. Pour le prouver, il suffit de montrer que l'une des dix propriétés des espaces vectoriels n'est pas satisfaite. Or,

$$A = \begin{bmatrix} 1 & 0 \\ 0 & 1 \end{bmatrix} \in \mathbb{Z}_{2 \times 2} \text{ et } \tfrac{1}{2} \in \mathbb{R}, \text{ mais } \tfrac{1}{2}A = \begin{bmatrix} \tfrac{1}{2} & 0 \\ 0 & \tfrac{1}{2} \end{bmatrix} \notin \mathbb{Z}_{2 \times 2}$$

La propriété 6 n'est donc pas satisfaite. Par conséquent, $\mathbb{Z}_{2 \times 2}$ n'est pas un espace vectoriel sur les réels.

6. Soit $W = \left\{ \begin{bmatrix} a & b \end{bmatrix} \big| a \text{ et } b \in \mathbb{R} \right\}$ muni des opérations $\oplus$ et $\odot$ définies comme suit :

$$\begin{bmatrix} a & b \end{bmatrix} \oplus \begin{bmatrix} c & d \end{bmatrix} = \begin{bmatrix} a + c & d \end{bmatrix} \text{ (addition)}$$
$$k \odot \begin{bmatrix} a & b \end{bmatrix} = \begin{bmatrix} ka & kb \end{bmatrix} \text{ (multiplication par un scalaire)}$$

L'ensemble W n'est pas un espace vectoriel parce que l'addition n'est pas commutative. En effet,

$$\begin{bmatrix} 1 & 2 \end{bmatrix} \oplus \begin{bmatrix} 3 & 5 \end{bmatrix} = \begin{bmatrix} 4 & 5 \end{bmatrix} \text{ et } \begin{bmatrix} 3 & 5 \end{bmatrix} \oplus \begin{bmatrix} 1 & 2 \end{bmatrix} = \begin{bmatrix} 4 & 2 \end{bmatrix}$$

Puisque $\begin{bmatrix} 4 & 2 \end{bmatrix} \neq \begin{bmatrix} 4 & 5 \end{bmatrix}$, on a

$$\begin{bmatrix} 1 & 2 \end{bmatrix} \oplus \begin{bmatrix} 3 & 5 \end{bmatrix} \neq \begin{bmatrix} 3 & 5 \end{bmatrix} \oplus \begin{bmatrix} 1 & 2 \end{bmatrix}$$

La propriété 2 n'étant pas satisfaite, l'ensemble W n'est donc pas un espace vectoriel lorsqu'il est muni des opérations $\oplus$ et $\odot$ définies ci-dessus.

EXERCICE 10.3

1. Montrez que l'ensemble des vecteurs de $\mathbb{R}^4$ dont la quatrième composante est nulle est un espace vectoriel pour les opérations habituelles d'addition vectorielle et de multiplication par un scalaire.

2. Montrez que l'ensemble des vecteurs de $\mathbb{R}^4$ dont la quatrième composante vaut 2 n'est pas un espace vectoriel pour les opérations habituelles d'addition vectorielle et de multiplication par un scalaire.

Étant donné que la définition d'un espace vectoriel comporte la définition de deux opérations, soit l'addition de vecteurs et la multiplication d'un vecteur par un scalaire, on peut étendre les concepts de combinaison linéaire et d'indépendance linéaire aux espaces vectoriels.

Exemple

Les matrices

$$A = \begin{bmatrix} 1 & -2 \\ 2 & 2 \end{bmatrix} \quad B = \begin{bmatrix} 1 & -1 \\ 1 & -1 \end{bmatrix} \quad C = \begin{bmatrix} -1 & 0 \\ 0 & 4 \end{bmatrix}$$

sont des éléments de l'espace vectoriel des matrices carrées d'ordre 2. Ces trois matrices sont linéairement dépendantes parce qu'il existe une combinaison linéaire de A, B et C qui est égale à la matrice nulle et dont les coefficients ne sont pas tous nuls. En effet, $-A + 2B + C = O_{2 \times 2}$.

EXERCICE 10.4

Montrez que les polynômes $p(x) = 1 + x$, $q(x) = 1 + x^2$ et $r(x) = x$ sont des vecteurs linéairement indépendants de l'espace P_n.

10.2.1 Propriétés des espaces vectoriels

Les espaces vectoriels possèdent des propriétés intéressantes, regroupées dans le théorème 10.1. Nous allons prouver les deux premières; vous pourrez démontrer les autres en guise d'exercice.

> ### Théorème 10.1
>
> Si V est un espace vectoriel dont le vecteur nul est noté $\vec{0}$, alors :
>
> 1) $k\vec{0} = \vec{0}$ pour tout scalaire k;
> 2) $0\vec{v} = \vec{0}$ pour tout vecteur $\vec{v} \in V$;
> 3) $k\vec{v} = \vec{0} \Rightarrow k = 0$ ou $\vec{v} = \vec{0}$;
> 4) $(-1)\vec{v} = -\vec{v}$ pour tout vecteur $\vec{v} \in V$.

Propriété 1 Si V est un espace vectoriel dont le vecteur nul est noté $\vec{0}$, alors $k\vec{0} = \vec{0}$ pour tout scalaire k.

Preuve

Si k est un scalaire et V un espace vectoriel, alors, en raison de l'existence d'un vecteur nul dans V, de l'existence de l'opposé de tout vecteur de V ainsi que des propriétés d'associativité et de distributivité dans un espace vectoriel, on a

$$
\begin{aligned}
k\vec{0} &= k\vec{0} + \vec{0} \\
&= k\vec{0} + \left[k\vec{0} + (-k\vec{0}) \right] \\
&= (k\vec{0} + k\vec{0}) + (-k\vec{0}) \\
&= k(\vec{0} + \vec{0}) + (-k\vec{0}) \\
&= k\vec{0} + (-k\vec{0}) \\
&= \vec{0} \qquad\qquad\blacksquare
\end{aligned}
$$

Propriété 2 Si V est un espace vectoriel dont le vecteur nul est noté $\vec{0}$, alors $0\vec{v} = \vec{0}$ pour tout vecteur $\vec{v} \in V$.

Preuve

Si $\vec{v} \in V$, alors

$$
\begin{aligned}
0\vec{v} &= 0\vec{v} + \vec{0} \\
&= 0\vec{v} + \left[0\vec{v} + (-0\vec{v}) \right] \\
&= (0\vec{v} + 0\vec{v}) + (-0\vec{v}) \\
&= \left[(0 + 0)\vec{v} \right] + (-0\vec{v}) \\
&= 0\vec{v} + (-0\vec{v}) \\
&= \vec{0} \qquad\qquad\blacksquare
\end{aligned}
$$

Il ne faut pas oublier que, lorsqu'on prouve une propriété générale des espaces vectoriels, on prouve par la même occasion cette propriété pour chaque espace vectoriel particulier. Ainsi, les propriétés énoncées dans le théorème 10.1 sont valables pour l'espace des matrices de format $m \times n$, l'espace euclidien $\mathbb{R}^n$, l'espace des polynômes P_n, etc.

EXERCICE 10.5

Démontrez la propriété 3 du théorème 10.1.

10.2.2 SOUS-ESPACE VECTORIEL

SOUS-ESPACE VECTORIEL

Un sous-espace vectoriel S d'un espace vectoriel V est un sous-ensemble non vide de V qui est aussi un espace vectoriel pour les opérations définies sur V.

Si un sous-ensemble non vide S d'un espace vectoriel V est lui-même un espace vectoriel pour les opérations définies sur V, on dit que S est un **sous-espace vectoriel** de V ou, plus simplement, un *sous-espace* de V. Le cinquième exemple de la page 367 montre bien qu'un sous-ensemble (en l'occurrence $\mathbb{Z}_{2 \times 2}$) d'un espace vectoriel (en l'occurrence l'espace des matrices carrées d'ordre 2) ne forme pas nécessairement un espace vectoriel. Il est donc pertinent de se demander à quelles conditions un sous-ensemble d'un espace vectoriel constitue lui aussi un espace vectoriel, c'est-à-dire à quelles conditions un sous-ensemble d'un espace vectoriel est un sous-espace vectoriel. Le théorème 10.2 apporte une réponse à cette question.

Théorème 10.2

Un sous-ensemble non vide S d'un espace vectoriel V est un sous-espace de V s'il est fermé pour l'addition de vecteurs et la multiplication d'un vecteur par un scalaire, c'est-à-dire que S est un sous-espace de V lorsque :

- $S \neq \varnothing$;
- $S \subseteq V$;
- $\vec{u} + \vec{v} \in S$ pour tout $\vec{u} \in S$ et pour tout $\vec{v} \in S$;
- $k\vec{u} \in S$ pour tout $\vec{u} \in S$ et pour tout $k \in \mathbb{R}$.

Preuve

Soit V, un espace vectoriel, et S, un sous-ensemble non vide de V fermé pour l'addition de vecteurs et la multiplication d'un vecteur par un scalaire. Il faut montrer que l'ensemble S est un espace vectoriel, c'est-à-dire qu'il vérifie les dix propriétés d'un tel espace (énoncées à la page 362).

Par hypothèse, les propriétés 1 et 6 sont satisfaites. Quant aux propriétés 2, 3 et 7 à 10, elles sont valables pour tous les éléments de l'espace vectoriel

V et donc, en particulier, pour les éléments de *S* qui sont aussi des éléments de *V*, puisque $S \subseteq V$. Il reste donc à démontrer les propriétés 4 et 5.

Si $\vec{u} \in S$, alors, par hypothèse et en vertu du fait que $k = 0 \in \mathbb{R}$, on a $0\vec{u} \in S$. De plus, la propriété 2 du théorème 10.1 implique que $0\vec{u} = \vec{0}$. Le vecteur nul de *V* appartient donc à *S* et il est aussi le vecteur nul de *S*, puisque $S \subseteq V$. Par conséquent, la propriété 4 est satisfaite.

Si $\vec{u} \in S$, alors, par hypothèse et en vertu du fait que $k = -1 \in \mathbb{R}$, on a $(-1)\vec{u} \in S$. De plus, la propriété 4 du théorème 10.1 implique que $(-1)\vec{u} = -\vec{u}$, d'où $-\vec{u} \in S$. Par conséquent, tout vecteur de *S* a un opposé qui appartient aussi à *S*. La propriété 5 est donc satisfaite.

Les dix propriétés étant vérifiées, *S* est un espace vectoriel, et donc un sous-espace de *V*. ∎

On peut utiliser le théorème 10.2 notamment pour démontrer rapidement qu'un ensemble est un espace vectoriel, en montrant qu'il est un sous-espace d'un espace vectoriel connu.

Exemple

Dans l'exercice 10.3 (p. 368), vous avez sans doute peiné pour montrer que l'ensemble *S* des vecteurs de $\mathbb{R}^4$ dont la quatrième composante est nulle est un espace vectoriel pour les opérations habituelles d'addition et de multiplication par un scalaire. Le théorème 10.2 permet d'en donner une preuve plus simple: il suffit de montrer que l'ensemble *S* est un sous-espace vectoriel de $\mathbb{R}^4$, un espace vectoriel connu.

On veut démontrer que $S = \left\{ \begin{bmatrix} x_1 & x_2 & x_3 & 0 \end{bmatrix} \middle| x_i \in \mathbb{R} \right\}$ est un espace vectoriel.

Preuve

L'ensemble *S* n'est pas vide parce que le vecteur $\begin{bmatrix} 0 & 0 & 0 & 0 \end{bmatrix} \in S$. De plus,

$$S = \left\{ \begin{bmatrix} x_1 & x_2 & x_3 & 0 \end{bmatrix} \middle| x_i \in \mathbb{R} \right\} \subset \left\{ \begin{bmatrix} x_1 & x_2 & x_3 & x_4 \end{bmatrix} \middle| x_i \in \mathbb{R} \right\} = \mathbb{R}^4$$

L'ensemble *S* est donc un sous-ensemble non vide de $\mathbb{R}^4$. Par ailleurs, si

$$\vec{u} = \begin{bmatrix} u_1 & u_2 & u_3 & 0 \end{bmatrix} \in S$$
$$\vec{v} = \begin{bmatrix} v_1 & v_2 & v_3 & 0 \end{bmatrix} \in S \text{ et}$$
$$k \in \mathbb{R}$$

alors

$$\vec{u} + \vec{v} = \begin{bmatrix} u_1 + v_1 & u_2 + v_2 & u_3 + v_3 & 0 \end{bmatrix} \in S$$

et

$$k\vec{u} = \begin{bmatrix} ku_1 & ku_2 & ku_3 & 0 \end{bmatrix} \in S$$

Par conséquent, en vertu du théorème 10.2, l'ensemble S est un sous-espace vectoriel de $\mathbb{R}^4$ et, donc, un espace vectoriel. ∎

EXERCICE 10.6

Montrez que $S = \left\{ a + ax + ax^2 \mid a \in \mathbb{R} \right\}$ est un espace vectoriel.

Tout espace vectoriel V admet un sous-espace. En effet, on peut vérifier que $S = \left\{ \vec{0} \right\}$ et $S = V$ sont des sous-espaces, dits triviaux, de V. Le théorème 10.3 fournit un moyen d'engendrer d'autres sous-espaces d'un espace vectoriel.

Théorème 10.3

Si $\vec{v_1}$, $\vec{v_2}$, ..., $\vec{v_n}$ sont n éléments d'un espace vectoriel V, alors
$$S = \left\{ a_1 \vec{v_1} + a_2 \vec{v_2} + \cdots + a_n \vec{v_n} \mid a_i \in \mathbb{R} \right\}$$
est un sous-espace de V. Ainsi, l'ensemble des combinaisons linéaires d'un sous-ensemble de vecteurs de V constitue un sous-espace de V. On dit que S est l'**espace engendré** par les n vecteurs $\vec{v_1}$, $\vec{v_2}$, ..., $\vec{v_n}$.

ESPACE ENGENDRÉ PAR DES VECTEURS

L'espace vectoriel engendré par les vecteurs $\vec{v_1}$, $\vec{v_2}$, ..., $\vec{v_n}$ d'un espace V est l'ensemble des combinaisons linéaires de ces vecteurs, soit

$$S = \left\{ \sum_{i=1}^{n} a_i \vec{v_i} \;\middle|\; a_i \in \mathbb{R} \right\}$$

Preuve

Si $\vec{v_1}$, $\vec{v_2}$, ..., $\vec{v_n}$ sont n éléments d'un espace vectoriel V et si, de plus, $S = \left\{ a_1 \vec{v_1} + a_2 \vec{v_2} + \cdots + a_n \vec{v_n} \mid a_i \in \mathbb{R} \right\}$, alors S est non vide parce que le vecteur nul appartient à cet ensemble. En effet,

$$0\vec{v_1} + 0\vec{v_2} + \cdots + 0\vec{v_n} = \vec{0} \in S$$

À cause de la fermeture de l'addition et de la multiplication par un scalaire, toute combinaison linéaire de vecteurs de V appartient à V. Par conséquent, tout élément de S appartient à V. L'ensemble S est donc un sous-ensemble de V.

De plus, nous constatons que, si $\vec{s_1} = a_1 \vec{v_1} + a_2 \vec{v_2} + \cdots + a_n \vec{v_n} \in S$, si $\vec{s_2} = b_1 \vec{v_1} + b_2 \vec{v_2} + \cdots + b_n \vec{v_n} \in S$ et si k est un scalaire, alors

$$\vec{s_1} + \vec{s_2} = (a_1 + b_1)\vec{v_1} + (a_2 + b_2)\vec{v_2} + \cdots + (a_n + b_n)\vec{v_n} \in S$$

et

$$k\vec{s_1} = (ka_1)\vec{v_1} + (ka_2)\vec{v_2} + \cdots + (ka_n)\vec{v_n} \in S$$

Par conséquent, en vertu du théorème 10.2, S est un sous-espace de V. ∎

10.2.3 BASE ET DIMENSION D'UN ESPACE VECTORIEL

Le théorème 10.3 laisse entendre qu'on peut exprimer un espace vectoriel V comme un ensemble de combinaisons linéaires de vecteurs. En fait, un ensemble de n vecteurs $\vec{v_1}$, $\vec{v_2}$, ..., $\vec{v_n}$ est un **système générateur d'un espace vectoriel** V si et seulement si tout vecteur de V s'écrit comme une combinaison linéaire de ces n vecteurs.

SYSTÈME GÉNÉRATEUR D'UN ESPACE VECTORIEL

Un système générateur d'un espace vectoriel V est un ensemble de vecteurs tel que tout vecteur de V s'écrit comme une combinaison linéaire des vecteurs du système générateur.

Exemple

Les vecteurs $\begin{bmatrix} 1 & 0 & 0 & 0 \end{bmatrix}$, $\begin{bmatrix} 0 & 1 & 0 & 0 \end{bmatrix}$, $\begin{bmatrix} 0 & 0 & 1 & 0 \end{bmatrix}$ et $\begin{bmatrix} 0 & 0 & 0 & 1 \end{bmatrix}$ forment un système générateur de $\mathbb{R}^4$. En effet, tout vecteur $\begin{bmatrix} a & b & c & d \end{bmatrix}$ de $\mathbb{R}^4$ s'écrit comme une combinaison linéaire de ces quatre vecteurs :

$$\begin{bmatrix} a & b & c & d \end{bmatrix} = a\begin{bmatrix} 1 & 0 & 0 & 0 \end{bmatrix} + b\begin{bmatrix} 0 & 1 & 0 & 0 \end{bmatrix} + c\begin{bmatrix} 0 & 0 & 1 & 0 \end{bmatrix} + d\begin{bmatrix} 0 & 0 & 0 & 1 \end{bmatrix}$$

Un ensemble de n vecteurs $\vec{v_1}$, $\vec{v_2}$, ..., $\vec{v_n}$ constitue une **base d'un espace vectoriel** V si et seulement si ces vecteurs sont linéairement indépendants et qu'ils forment un système générateur de V.

BASE D'UN ESPACE VECTORIEL

Une base d'un espace vectoriel V est un ensemble de vecteurs linéairement indépendants de V qui constituent un système générateur de V.

Exemple

Pour montrer que les vecteurs $\vec{v_1} = \begin{bmatrix} 1 & 0 & 1 & 0 \end{bmatrix}$, $\vec{v_2} = \begin{bmatrix} 1 & 1 & 0 & 1 \end{bmatrix}$, $\vec{v_3} = \begin{bmatrix} 0 & 0 & 1 & 1 \end{bmatrix}$ et $\vec{v_4} = \begin{bmatrix} 0 & 0 & 0 & 1 \end{bmatrix}$ forment une base de $\mathbb{R}^4$, il faut vérifier que ces quatre vecteurs sont linéairement indépendants et qu'ils forment un système générateur de $\mathbb{R}^4$.

De l'équation vectorielle $a_1\vec{v_1} + a_2\vec{v_2} + a_3\vec{v_3} + a_4\vec{v_4} = \vec{0}$, on tire le système d'équations

$$\begin{aligned} a_1 + a_2 \quad\quad\quad &= 0 \\ a_2 \quad\quad &= 0 \\ a_1 \quad\quad + a_3 \quad &= 0 \\ a_2 + a_3 + a_4 &= 0 \end{aligned}$$

Il est facile de vérifier que le déterminant de la matrice des coefficients de ce système vaut 1. Par conséquent, en vertu de la règle de Cramer, ce système d'équations admet une solution unique. Or, $a_1 = 0$, $a_2 = 0$, $a_3 = 0$ et $a_4 = 0$ étant une solution, c'est la seule solution du système. Les vecteurs $\vec{v_1}$, $\vec{v_2}$, $\vec{v_3}$ et $\vec{v_4}$ sont donc linéairement indépendants.

De plus, tout vecteur $\vec{v} = \begin{bmatrix} a & b & c & d \end{bmatrix} \in \mathbb{R}^4$ s'écrit comme une combinaison linéaire des vecteurs $\vec{v_1}$, $\vec{v_2}$, $\vec{v_3}$ et $\vec{v_4}$. En effet, de l'équation vectorielle

$$a_1 \vec{v_1} + a_2 \vec{v_2} + a_3 \vec{v_3} + a_4 \vec{v_4} = \vec{v} = \begin{bmatrix} a & b & c & d \end{bmatrix}$$

on tire le système d'équations linéaires

$$\begin{aligned} a_1 + a_2 \quad\quad\quad &= a \\ a_2 \quad\quad &= b \\ a_1 \quad\quad + a_3 \quad &= c \\ a_2 + a_3 + a_4 &= d \end{aligned}$$

Le déterminant de la matrice des coefficients de ce système vaut 1. Par conséquent, en vertu de la règle de Cramer, ce système d'équations admet une solution (unique). Les vecteurs $\vec{v_1}$, $\vec{v_2}$, $\vec{v_3}$ et $\vec{v_4}$ forment donc un système générateur de $\mathbb{R}^4$.

Puisque les vecteurs $\vec{v_1}$, $\vec{v_2}$, $\vec{v_3}$ et $\vec{v_4}$ sont linéairement indépendants et qu'ils forment un système générateur de $\mathbb{R}^4$, ils forment une base de $\mathbb{R}^4$.

EXERCICE 10.7

Montrez que les vecteurs à n composantes

$$\vec{e_1} = \begin{bmatrix} 1 & 0 & 0 & \cdots & 0 & \cdots & 0 \end{bmatrix}$$
$$\vec{e_2} = \begin{bmatrix} 0 & 1 & 0 & \cdots & 0 & \cdots & 0 \end{bmatrix}$$
$$\vdots$$
$$\vec{e_i} = \begin{bmatrix} 0 & 0 & 0 & \cdots & 1 & \cdots & 0 \end{bmatrix}$$
$$\vdots$$
$$\vec{e_n} = \begin{bmatrix} 0 & 0 & 0 & \cdots & 0 & \cdots & 1 \end{bmatrix}$$

forment une base de $\mathbb{R}^n$. Cette base est appelée **base canonique de $\mathbb{R}^n$**.

BASE CANONIQUE DE $\mathbb{R}^n$

Ensemble de n vecteurs, notés $\vec{e_1}$, $\vec{e_2}$, ..., $\vec{e_n}$, dont les composantes sont toutes nulles, à l'exception de la i-ième composante de $\vec{e_i}$, qui vaut 1.

ESPACE VECTORIEL DE DIMENSION FINIE

Un espace vectoriel de dimension finie est un espace vectoriel dont une base compte un nombre fini d'éléments.

Si une base d'un **espace vectoriel** comporte un nombre fini d'éléments, on dit que cet espace est **de dimension finie**. Dans le présent manuel, nous ne nous intéresserons qu'aux espaces vectoriels de dimension finie. Ceux-ci possèdent des propriétés intéressantes, regroupées dans les théorèmes 10.4 à 10.7.

Théorème 10.4

Si $\vec{v_1}$, $\vec{v_2}$, ..., $\vec{v_n}$ forment une base d'un espace vectoriel V de dimension finie, alors tout vecteur de V s'écrit, de façon unique, comme une combinaison linéaire des n vecteurs de la base.

Preuve

Si $\vec{v_1}$, $\vec{v_2}$, ..., $\vec{v_n}$ forment une base d'un espace vectoriel V, alors ces vecteurs forment un système générateur de V: tout vecteur $\vec{v} \in V$ s'écrit comme une combinaison linéaire des vecteurs de la base.

Mais il y a plus! Il existe une seule façon d'exprimer un vecteur de V sous la forme d'une combinaison linéaire des vecteurs de la base. En effet, si on suppose qu'il existe deux combinaisons linéaires des vecteurs de la base qui soient égales à $\vec{v} \in V$, alors

$$\vec{v} = a_1\vec{v_1} + a_2\vec{v_2} + \cdots + a_n\vec{v_n} = b_1\vec{v_1} + b_2\vec{v_2} + \cdots + b_n\vec{v_n}$$

d'où on tire

$$(a_1 - b_1)\vec{v_1} + (a_2 - b_2)\vec{v_2} + \cdots + (a_n - b_n)\vec{v_n} = \vec{0}$$

Comme les vecteurs $\vec{v_1}$, $\vec{v_2}$, ..., $\vec{v_n}$ sont linéairement indépendants (puisqu'ils forment une base), on a

$$a_1 - b_1 = a_2 - b_2 = \cdots = a_n - b_n = 0$$

d'où

$$a_1 = b_1, \ a_2 = b_2, \ ..., \ a_n = b_n$$

L'expression du vecteur $\vec{v}$ sous la forme d'une combinaison linéaire des vecteurs de la base est donc unique. ∎

Théorème 10.5

Toute base d'un espace vectoriel de dimension finie comporte le même nombre d'éléments.

Preuve

Soit $S_1 = \left\{ \vec{u_1}, \ \vec{u_2}, \ ..., \ \vec{u_m} \right\}$, une base d'un espace vectoriel V et $S_2 = \left\{ \vec{v_1}, \ \vec{v_2}, \ ..., \ \vec{v_n} \right\}$, une autre base du même espace vectoriel. Il faut montrer que ces deux bases comportent le même nombre d'éléments, c'est-à-dire que $m = n$.

On emploie un raisonnement par l'absurde, c'est-à-dire qu'on suppose que les deux bases ne comptent pas le même nombre d'éléments. On peut poser $m > n$, sans perte de généralité. Il suffit alors de montrer que les vecteurs de S_1 sont linéairement dépendants, ce qui contredit l'hypothèse selon laquelle S_1 est une base. On en conclura que $m = n$, et le théorème sera démontré.

Comme S_2 est une base, tout vecteur de V, et en particulier tout vecteur de S_1, s'écrit comme une combinaison linéaire des vecteurs de S_2. Par conséquent, il existe des scalaires a_{ij} tels que

$$
\begin{aligned}
a_{11}\vec{v_1} + a_{12}\vec{v_2} + \cdots + a_{1n}\vec{v_n} &= \vec{u_1} \\
a_{21}\vec{v_1} + a_{22}\vec{v_2} + \cdots + a_{2n}\vec{v_n} &= \vec{u_2} \\
\vdots \qquad\quad \vdots \qquad\qquad \vdots \qquad\quad &\vdots \\
a_{m1}\vec{v_1} + a_{m2}\vec{v_2} + \cdots + a_{mn}\vec{v_n} &= \vec{u_m}
\end{aligned}
$$

En écrivant le vecteur nul comme une combinaison linéaire des vecteurs de S_1, on a

$$
b_1\vec{u_1} + b_2\vec{u_2} + \cdots + b_m\vec{u_m} = \vec{0}
$$

Si on montre qu'il existe plus d'une combinaison linéaire égale au vecteur nul, c'est-à-dire qu'au moins un des b_i est différent de zéro, cela contredit l'hypothèse selon laquelle S_1 constitue une base.

En remplaçant, dans la dernière combinaison linéaire, chaque vecteur de S_1 par son expression en fonction des vecteurs de S_2, on obtient

$$
b_1(a_{11}\vec{v_1} + a_{12}\vec{v_2} + \cdots + a_{1n}\vec{v_n}) + b_2(a_{21}\vec{v_1} + a_{22}\vec{v_2} + \cdots + a_{2n}\vec{v_n})
$$
$$
+ \cdots + b_m(a_{m1}\vec{v_1} + a_{m2}\vec{v_2} + \cdots + a_{mn}\vec{v_n}) = \vec{0}
$$

ce qui s'écrit également sous la forme

$$
(b_1a_{11} + b_2a_{21} + \cdots + b_ma_{m1})\vec{v_1} + (b_1a_{12} + b_2a_{22} + \cdots + b_ma_{m2})\vec{v_2}
$$
$$
+ \cdots + (b_1a_{1n} + b_2a_{2n} + \cdots + b_ma_{mn})\vec{v_n} = \vec{0}
$$

Comme S_2 est une base de V, les n vecteurs $\vec{v_1}$, $\vec{v_2}$, ..., $\vec{v_n}$ sont linéairement indépendants, de sorte que les coefficients de $\vec{v_1}$, $\vec{v_2}$, ..., $\vec{v_n}$ doivent tous être nuls. On en déduit que

$$
\begin{aligned}
b_1a_{11} + b_2a_{21} + \cdots + b_ma_{m1} &= 0 \\
b_1a_{12} + b_2a_{22} + \cdots + b_ma_{m2} &= 0 \\
\vdots \qquad\quad \vdots \qquad\qquad \vdots \qquad\quad &\vdots \\
b_1a_{1n} + b_2a_{2n} + \cdots + b_ma_{mn} &= 0
\end{aligned}
$$

Ce système d'équations, où les b_i sont des inconnues, comporte un nombre d'inconnues (m) supérieur au nombre d'équations (n). De plus, il admet au moins une solution (soit celle où tous les b_i valent 0). Par conséquent, en vertu du théorème 4.2 (p. 141), le système d'équations admet une infinité de solutions. L'équation $b_1\vec{u_1} + b_2\vec{u_2} + \cdots + b_m\vec{u_m} = \vec{0}$ compte donc plus d'une solution, ce qui contredit l'hypothèse selon laquelle S_1 est une base de V. Par conséquent, on a $m = n$: toutes les bases d'un espace vectoriel de dimension finie comptent un même nombre de vecteurs. ∎

DIMENSION D'UN ESPACE
VECTORIEL

La dimension d'un espace vectoriel de dimension finie est le nombre de vecteurs d'une base de cet espace. L'espace vectoriel $V = \left\{ \vec{0} \right\}$ est de dimension zéro. Tout espace vectoriel qui n'est pas de dimension finie est dit de dimension infinie. La dimension d'un espace vectoriel V est notée dim V.

En vertu du théorème 10.5, le nombre d'éléments d'une base d'un espace vectoriel de dimension finie est une constante. La **dimension d'un espace vectoriel** de dimension finie est, par définition, égale au nombre d'éléments d'une base de cet espace. On note dim V la dimension d'un espace V, et on considère que l'espace vectoriel $V = \left\{ \vec{0} \right\}$ est de dimension zéro, puisqu'il ne compte aucun vecteur linéairement indépendant. On dit d'un espace vectoriel qui n'est pas de dimension finie qu'il est de dimension infinie. Nous ne traiterons pas des espaces de dimension infinie dans ce manuel.

La définition de dimension d'un espace vectoriel est tout à fait en accord avec l'appellation $\mathbb{R}^n$, soit espace euclidien de « dimension » n. En effet, à l'exercice 10.7, on a déterminé une base de $\mathbb{R}^n$ contenant n vecteurs.

Théorème 10.6

Si V est un espace vectoriel de dimension n et si $S_1 = \left\{ \vec{u_1}, \vec{u_2}, ..., \vec{u_m} \right\}$ est un ensemble de m vecteurs linéairement indépendants de V, alors $m \leq n$.

Preuve

Si $S_2 = \left\{ \vec{v_1}, \vec{v_2}, ..., \vec{v_n} \right\}$, est une base de V et si $m > n$, alors il existe des constantes b_1, b_2, ..., b_m qui ne sont pas toutes nulles telles que

$$b_1 \vec{u_1} + b_2 \vec{u_2} + \cdots + b_m \vec{u_m} = \vec{0} \text{ (voir la preuve du théorème 10.5)}$$

Mais cela contredit le fait que les vecteurs $\vec{u_1}$, $\vec{u_2}$, ..., $\vec{u_m}$ sont linéairement indépendants. Par conséquent, $m \leq n$. ∎

EXERCICE 10.8

Montrez que la dimension de tout sous-espace W d'un espace vectoriel V de dimension n est plus petit ou égal à n.

Théorème 10.7

Tout ensemble de n vecteurs linéairement indépendants d'un espace vectoriel de dimension n est une base de cet espace.

Preuve

Soit un espace vectoriel V de dimension n et un ensemble de n vecteurs linéairement indépendants, $\vec{v_1}$, $\vec{v_2}$, ..., $\vec{v_n}$, appartenant à V. Il faut montrer que ces n vecteurs forment une base de V.

Comme les n vecteurs sont indépendants, par hypothèse, il reste à montrer qu'ils forment un système générateur de V, ce qu'on fait au moyen d'un raisonnement par l'absurde.

Si on suppose que les n vecteurs ne forment pas un système générateur, cela implique qu'il existe un vecteur $\vec{u} \in V$ qui ne s'écrit pas comme une combinaison linéaire des vecteurs $\vec{v_1}$, $\vec{v_2}$, ..., $\vec{v_n}$. Les vecteurs $\vec{u}$, $\vec{v_1}$, $\vec{v_2}$, ..., $\vec{v_n}$ sont alors linéairement indépendants.

En effet, si $a_1 \vec{v_1} + a_2 \vec{v_2} + \cdots + a_n \vec{v_n} + a_{n+1} \vec{u} = \vec{0}$, où $a_{n+1} \neq 0$, le vecteur $\vec{u}$ s'écrit comme une combinaison linéaire des vecteurs $\vec{v_1}$, $\vec{v_2}$, ..., $\vec{v_n}$; par exemple

$$\vec{u} = \frac{1}{a_{n+1}} (a_1 \vec{v_1} + a_2 \vec{v_2} + \cdots + a_n \vec{v_n})$$

ce qui entraîne une contradiction, d'où $a_{n+1} = 0$. Par conséquent,

$$a_1 \vec{v_1} + a_2 \vec{v_2} + \cdots + a_n \vec{v_n} + a_{n+1} \vec{u} = \vec{0}$$
$$\Rightarrow \quad a_1 \vec{v_1} + a_2 \vec{v_2} + \cdots + a_n \vec{v_n} = \vec{0}$$

Comme les vecteurs $\vec{v_1}$, $\vec{v_2}$, ..., $\vec{v_n}$ sont linéairement indépendants, alors $a_1 = a_2 = \ldots = a_n = 0$.

Tous les coefficients de l'équation $a_1 \vec{v_1} + a_2 \vec{v_2} + \cdots + a_n \vec{v_n} + a_{n+1} \vec{u} = \vec{0}$ valent donc zéro. Les vecteurs $\vec{u}$, $\vec{v_1}$, $\vec{v_2}$, ..., $\vec{v_n}$ forment donc un ensemble de $n + 1$ vecteurs linéairement indépendants qui sont tous des éléments d'un espace vectoriel de dimension n. Mais cela contredit le théorème 10.6.

Par conséquent, tout vecteur $\vec{u} \in V$ s'écrit comme une combinaison linéaire des vecteurs $\vec{v_1}$, $\vec{v_2}$, ..., $\vec{v_n}$. Comme ils sont linéairement indépendants et qu'ils constituent un système générateur de V, les vecteurs $\vec{v_1}$, $\vec{v_2}$, ..., $\vec{v_n}$ forment une base de V.

En conclusion, tout ensemble de n vecteurs linéairement indépendants d'un espace vectoriel de dimension n est une base de cet espace. ∎

En vertu du théorème 10.7, il suffit de démontrer que n vecteurs d'un espace vectoriel de dimension n sont linéairement indépendants pour montrer qu'ils forment une base de cet espace.

EXERCICE 10.9

Montrez, en appliquant le théorème 10.7, que les vecteurs $\vec{u_1} = \begin{bmatrix} 1 & 0 & 0 & 1 \end{bmatrix}$, $\vec{u_2} = \begin{bmatrix} 1 & 1 & 0 & 1 \end{bmatrix}$, $\vec{u_3} = \begin{bmatrix} 0 & 0 & 1 & 0 \end{bmatrix}$ et $\vec{u_4} = \begin{bmatrix} 0 & 1 & 0 & 1 \end{bmatrix}$ forment une base de $\mathbb{R}^4$.

Par ailleurs, le théorème suivant permet de trouver une base du sous-espace de $\mathbb{R}^n$ formé des combinaisons linéaires d'un sous-ensemble de vecteurs de $\mathbb{R}^n$. Nous nous contentons d'énoncer ce théorème, sans le prouver.

Théorème 10.8

Si on considère les lignes d'une matrice comme des vecteurs, alors :

- les espaces vectoriels engendrés par les vecteurs lignes de deux matrices équivalentes sont identiques ;
- Les lignes non nulles d'une matrice échelonnée forment une base de l'espace vectoriel engendré par les vecteurs lignes de cette matrice.

Voici un exemple qui illustre l'application de ce théorème.

Exemple

On veut trouver une base de l'espace vectoriel formé de l'ensemble des combinaisons linéaires des vecteurs $\vec{u_1} = \begin{bmatrix} 1 & 0 & 0 & 1 \end{bmatrix}$, $\vec{u_2} = \begin{bmatrix} 1 & 1 & 1 & 1 \end{bmatrix}$ et $\vec{u_3} = \begin{bmatrix} 0 & 1 & 1 & 0 \end{bmatrix}$, soit l'espace vectoriel engendré par ces trois vecteurs.

On effectue, sur la matrice A dont les lignes correspondent à ces trois vecteurs, des opérations élémentaires de ligne de manière à obtenir une matrice échelonnée équivalente à A :

$$A = \begin{bmatrix} 1 & 0 & 0 & 1 \\ 1 & 1 & 1 & 1 \\ 0 & 1 & 1 & 0 \end{bmatrix} \sim \begin{bmatrix} 1 & 0 & 0 & 1 \\ 0 & 1 & 1 & 0 \\ 0 & 1 & 1 & 0 \end{bmatrix} \begin{matrix} \\ L_2 \to L_2 - L_1 \\ \\ \end{matrix}$$

$$\sim \begin{bmatrix} 1 & 0 & 0 & 1 \\ 0 & 1 & 1 & 0 \\ 0 & 0 & 0 & 0 \end{bmatrix} \begin{matrix} \\ \\ L_3 \to L_3 - L_2 \end{matrix}$$

Par conséquent, l'espace vectoriel S engendré par les vecteurs $\vec{u_1}$, $\vec{u_2}$ et $\vec{u_3}$ est de dimension 2 et il a comme base les vecteurs $\begin{bmatrix} 1 & 0 & 0 & 1 \end{bmatrix}$ et $\begin{bmatrix} 0 & 1 & 1 & 0 \end{bmatrix}$.

RÉSUMÉ

On peut étendre les espaces euclidiens de dimension 2, noté $\mathbb{R}^2$, et de dimension 3, noté $\mathbb{R}^3$, à l'espace euclidien de dimension n, soit $\mathbb{R}^n$.

L'espace $\mathbb{R}^n$ est l'ensemble des vecteurs à n composantes réelles. On définit de façon analogue les relations et les opérations sur cet espace (tableau 10.1) et sur $\mathbb{R}^2$ et $\mathbb{R}^3$. Toutefois, on ne peut donner une interprétation géométrique des vecteurs de $\mathbb{R}^n$ pour $n > 3$.

TABLEAU 10.1 **Relations et opérations sur les vecteurs de $\mathbb{R}^n$**

VECTEURS	$\vec{u} = \begin{bmatrix} u_1 & u_2 & \cdots & u_n \end{bmatrix}$ et $\vec{v} = \begin{bmatrix} v_1 & v_2 & \cdots & v_n \end{bmatrix}$
VECTEUR NUL	$\vec{0} = \begin{bmatrix} 0 & 0 & \cdots & 0 \end{bmatrix}$
ÉGALITÉ	$\vec{u} = \vec{v} \iff u_1 = v_1,\ u_2 = v_2,\ \ldots,\ u_n = v_n$
NORME EUCLIDIENNE	$\|\vec{u}\| = \sqrt{u_1^2 + u_2^2 + \cdots + u_n^2} = \sqrt{\sum_{i=1}^{n} u_i^2}$
ADDITION	$\vec{u} + \vec{v} = \begin{bmatrix} u_1 + v_1 & u_2 + v_2 & \cdots & u_n + v_n \end{bmatrix}$
MULTIPLICATION PAR UN SCALAIRE	$k\vec{u} = \begin{bmatrix} ku_1 & ku_2 & \cdots & ku_n \end{bmatrix}$
PRODUIT SCALAIRE	$\vec{u} \cdot \vec{v} = u_1 v_1 + u_2 v_2 + \cdots + u_n v_n$

Les espaces vectoriels constituent une extension de $\mathbb{R}^n$. Un espace vectoriel sur le corps des réels $\mathbb{R}$ est un ensemble V – dont les éléments sont appelés vecteurs – muni de deux opérations, soit l'addition de deux vecteurs (notée $\vec{u} + \vec{v}$ ou $\vec{u} \oplus \vec{v}$) et la multiplication d'un vecteur par un scalaire (notée $a\vec{u}$ ou $a \odot \vec{u}$), qui vérifient les dix propriétés suivantes.

Soit $\vec{u}$, $\vec{v}$ et $\vec{w} \in V$, et a et $b \in \mathbb{R}$.

1) $\vec{u} + \vec{v} \in V$ (fermeture de l'espace V par rapport à l'addition de vecteurs).

2) $\vec{u} + \vec{v} = \vec{v} + \vec{u}$ (commutativité de l'addition de vecteurs).

3) $(\vec{u} + \vec{v}) + \vec{w} = \vec{u} + (\vec{v} + \vec{w})$ (associativité de l'addition de vecteurs).

4) Il existe un vecteur $\vec{0} \in V$ tel que $\vec{u} + \vec{0} = \vec{u}$ (existence d'un élément neutre pour l'addition, soit un vecteur nul appartenant à V).

5) Il existe un vecteur $-\vec{u} \in V$, tel que $\vec{u} + (-\vec{u}) = \vec{0}$ (existence d'un opposé, noté $-\vec{u}$, appartenant à V pour tout vecteur $\vec{u}$ de V).

6) $a\vec{u} \in V$ (fermeture de l'espace V par rapport à la multiplication d'un vecteur par un scalaire).

7) $(ab)\vec{u} = a(b\vec{u})$ (associativité mixte).

8) $a(\vec{u} + \vec{v}) = a\vec{u} + a\vec{v}$ (distributivité de la multiplication d'un vecteur par un scalaire par rapport à l'addition de vecteurs).

9) $(a + b)\vec{u} = a\vec{u} + b\vec{u}$ (distributivité de la multiplication d'un vecteur par un scalaire par rapport à l'addition de scalaires).

10) $1\vec{u} = \vec{u}$.

Les vecteurs de $\mathbb{R}^n$, les matrices de format $m \times n$ et les polynômes de P_n, munis des opérations habituelles, sont des exemples d'espaces vectoriels.

Tout sous-ensemble S non vide d'un espace vectoriel V qui est fermé pour les opérations d'addition et de multiplication par un scalaire est aussi un espace vectoriel. On dit que S est un sous-espace vectoriel de V. Ainsi, au nombre des sous-espaces d'un espace V, on compte $\{\vec{0}\}$, V et l'ensemble des combinaisons linéaires d'un sous-ensemble de vecteurs $\vec{v_1}$, $\vec{v_2}$, ..., $\vec{v_n}$ de V, soit $S = \{a_1\vec{v_1} + a_2\vec{v_2} + \cdots + a_n\vec{v_n} \mid a_i \in \mathbb{R}\}$, qui s'appelle l'espace engendré par les vecteurs $\vec{v_1}$, $\vec{v_2}$, ..., $\vec{v_n}$.

Une base d'un espace vectoriel V est un ensemble de vecteurs linéairement indépendants de V qui constituent un système générateur de V.

Un espace vectoriel qui admet une base ayant un nombre fini d'éléments est dit de dimension finie. Toute base d'un espace vectoriel de dimension finie compte le même nombre d'éléments. La dimension d'un espace vectoriel V, notée dim V, est donc le nombre d'éléments d'une base de cet espace.

Tout ensemble de n vecteurs linéairement indépendants d'un espace vectoriel de dimension n forme une base de cet espace.

La dimension d'un sous-espace d'un espace vectoriel de dimension n est plus petite ou égale à n.

Le théorème 10.8 (p. 379) indique comment trouver une base de l'espace engendré par un sous-ensemble de vecteurs de $\mathbb{R}^n$.

EXERCICES RÉCAPITULATIFS

1. (I) Soit les vecteurs $\vec{u_1} = \begin{bmatrix} 1 & -2 & 1 & 2 \end{bmatrix}$, $\vec{u_2} = \begin{bmatrix} 1 & 1 & 1 & 0 \end{bmatrix}$, $\vec{u_3} = \begin{bmatrix} 0 & 1 & 1 & 1 \end{bmatrix}$, $\vec{u_4} = \begin{bmatrix} -1 & -1 & 3 & 0 \end{bmatrix}$, $\vec{u_5} = \begin{bmatrix} 0 & 8 & 2 & 2 \end{bmatrix}$, $\vec{u_6} = \begin{bmatrix} 2 & 1 & 2 & -1 \end{bmatrix}$ et $\vec{u_7} = \begin{bmatrix} 2 & -2 & 1 & 1 \end{bmatrix}$.

a) À quel espace appartiennent ces vecteurs?

b) Que vaut $2\vec{u_1} + 3\vec{u_2} - \vec{u_3}$?

c) Que vaut $2\vec{u_3} - 2\vec{u_4} + 3\vec{u_6}$?

d) Quelles sont les composantes du vecteur $\vec{u_8}$ qui vérifie l'équation $3\vec{u_1} - 2\vec{u_8} + \vec{u_3} = \vec{u_5}$?

e) Que vaut $\vec{u_1} \cdot \vec{u_4}$?

f) Que vaut la norme euclidienne de $\vec{u_4}$?

g) Que vaut $\vec{u_4} \cdot \vec{u_4}$?

h) Comparez les résultats obtenus en f et en g, et tirez-en une règle générale pour les vecteurs de $\mathbb{R}^n$, puis prouvez votre affirmation.

i) Que vaut la norme euclidienne de $\dfrac{1}{\|\vec{u_1}\|}\vec{u_1}$?

j) Que vaut la norme euclidienne de $\dfrac{1}{\|\vec{u_2}\|}\vec{u_2}$?

k) Montrez que les vecteurs $\vec{u_1}$ et $\vec{u_2}$ sont orthogonaux.

l) Montrez que les vecteurs $\vec{u_1}$ et $\vec{u_6}$ sont orthogonaux.

m) Montrez que le vecteur $\vec{u_1}$ est orthogonal à toute combinaison linéaire des vecteurs $\vec{u_2}$ et $\vec{u_6}$.

n) Quelle relation existe-t-il entre les paramètres a et b si les vecteurs $\vec{u_9} = \begin{bmatrix} a & 2 & 3 & b \end{bmatrix}$ et $\vec{u_1}$ sont orthogonaux?

o) Montrez que les vecteurs $\vec{u_1}$, $\vec{u_2}$, $\vec{u_3}$ et $\vec{u_4}$ sont linéairement indépendants.

p) Est-ce que les vecteurs $\vec{u_1}$, $\vec{u_2}$, $\vec{u_3}$ et $\vec{u_7}$ sont linéairement indépendants? Justifiez votre réponse.

q) Exprimez le vecteur $\vec{u_5}$ comme une combinaison linéaire des vecteurs $\vec{u_1}$, $\vec{u_2}$, $\vec{u_3}$ et $\vec{u_4}$.

r) Exprimez le vecteur $\vec{u_6}$ comme une combinaison linéaire des vecteurs $\vec{u_1}$, $\vec{u_2}$, $\vec{u_3}$ et $\vec{u_4}$.

s) Peut-on exprimer le vecteur $\vec{u_6}$ comme une combinaison linéaire des vecteurs $\vec{u_1}$, $\vec{u_2}$ et $\vec{u_3}$? Justifiez votre réponse.

2. (I) Montrez que $\left\| \dfrac{1}{\|\vec{u}\|}\vec{u} \right\| = 1$ pour tout vecteur non nul $\vec{u}$ de $\mathbb{R}^n$.

3. (I) Montrez que si $\vec{u}$ est un vecteur de $\mathbb{R}^n$ tel que $\vec{u} \cdot \vec{v} = 0$ pour tout $\vec{v} \in \mathbb{R}^n$ alors $\vec{u} = \vec{0}$.

4. (I) Soit $\vec{u}$, $\vec{v}$ et $\vec{w}$ des vecteurs de $\mathbb{R}^n$. Montrez que:

a) $\vec{u} \cdot \vec{v} = \vec{v} \cdot \vec{u}$;

b) $\vec{u} \cdot (\vec{v} + \vec{w}) = \vec{u} \cdot \vec{v} + \vec{u} \cdot \vec{w}$.

5. (III) Déterminez si l'ensemble donné, muni des opérations indiquées, constitue un espace vectoriel. Justifiez votre réponse en prouvant qu'il s'agit bien d'un espace vectoriel ou en montrant que l'une des propriétés des espaces vectoriels n'est pas satisfaite.

a) L'ensemble des matrices diagonales d'ordre 3, muni des opérations habituelles d'addition et de multiplication par un scalaire.

b) L'ensemble des matrices régulières d'ordre 3, muni des opérations habituelles d'addition et de multiplication par un scalaire.

c) L'ensemble $\mathbb{R}^+ = \{a \in \mathbb{R} \mid a > 0\}$ muni des opérations définies comme suit. Si a et $b \in \mathbb{R}^+$ et si $k \in \mathbb{R}$, alors

$a \oplus b = ab$ (définition de l'addition)

$k \odot a = a^k$ (définition de la multiplication par un scalaire)

d) L'ensemble des matrices de la forme $\begin{bmatrix} 1 & a \\ a & 1 \end{bmatrix}$ où

a est un nombre réel, muni des opérations habituelles d'addition et de multiplication par un scalaire.

e) L'ensemble

$$W = \{[a \quad b \quad c] \mid a, b \text{ et } c \in \mathbb{R}, \text{ et } abc = 0\}$$

muni des opérations habituelles sur les vecteurs de $\mathbb{R}^3$.

6. (I) Exprimez, si possible, la matrice D comme une combinaison linéaire des matrices

$$A = \begin{bmatrix} 2 & 1 \\ 0 & 0 \end{bmatrix},\ B = \begin{bmatrix} 1 & 0 \\ 1 & 0 \end{bmatrix} \text{ et } C = \begin{bmatrix} 1 & 1 \\ 1 & 0 \end{bmatrix}.$$

a) $D = \begin{bmatrix} 3 & 4 \\ 1 & 0 \end{bmatrix}$

b) $D = \begin{bmatrix} 0 & 0 \\ 0 & 0 \end{bmatrix}$

c) $D = \begin{bmatrix} 0 & 2 \\ 0 & 1 \end{bmatrix}$

7. (I) Déterminez si les matrices d'ordre 2 données sont linéairement dépendantes ou indépendantes.

a) $A = \begin{bmatrix} 1 & 0 \\ 0 & 0 \end{bmatrix}$ $B = \begin{bmatrix} 0 & 1 \\ 0 & 0 \end{bmatrix}$ $C = \begin{bmatrix} 0 & 0 \\ 1 & 0 \end{bmatrix}$

$D = \begin{bmatrix} 0 & 0 \\ 0 & 1 \end{bmatrix}$

b) $A = \begin{bmatrix} 3 & -1 \\ -3 & 2 \end{bmatrix}$ $B = \begin{bmatrix} 1 & 3 \\ 2 & -1 \end{bmatrix}$

$C = \begin{bmatrix} 1 & -7 \\ -7 & 4 \end{bmatrix}$

c) $A = \begin{bmatrix} 2 & 1 \\ 0 & 0 \end{bmatrix}$ $B = \begin{bmatrix} 1 & 0 \\ 1 & 0 \end{bmatrix}$

$C = \begin{bmatrix} 1 & 1 \\ 1 & 0 \end{bmatrix}$

8. (II) Prouvez la propriété 4 du théorème 10.1 (p. 369).

9. (II) Déterminez si l'ensemble W est un sous-ensemble vectoriel de l'espace vectoriel V pour les opérations usuelles d'addition et de multiplication par un scalaire. Justifiez votre réponse.

a) $W = \{[x \quad y \quad z] \mid x, y \text{ et } z \in \mathbb{R}, \text{ et } 2x + 3y - z = 0\}$ et $V = \mathbb{R}^3$.

b) $W = \{[a \quad b \quad a \quad b] \mid a \text{ et } b \in \mathbb{R} \text{ et } ab = 0\}$ et $V = \mathbb{R}^4$.

c) $W = \{[a \quad 2a \quad a \quad b] \mid a \text{ et } b \in \mathbb{R}\}$ et $V = \mathbb{R}^4$.

d) $W = \{[a \quad a \quad a \quad a] \mid a \in \mathbb{R} \text{ et } a > 0\}$ et $V = \mathbb{R}^4$.

e) $W = P_3$ et $V = P_5$.

f) L'ensemble W des matrices carrées d'ordre n dont la trace est 0 et l'espace vectoriel V des matrices carrées d'ordre n.

g) $W = \{\vec{0}\}$ où $\vec{0}$ est le vecteur nul d'un espace vectoriel V.

10. (II) Montrez que l'ensemble des vecteurs de $\mathbb{R}^4$ orthogonaux au vecteur $\vec{u} = [1 \quad 2 \quad -3 \quad 2]$ est un espace vectoriel.

11. (II) Montrez que l'intersection de deux sous-espaces vectoriels d'un espace vectoriel V est elle aussi un sous-espace de V.

12. (I) Quelle est la dimension de l'espace vectoriel des matrices carrées d'ordre 2?

13. (I) Soit les vecteurs $\vec{u_1} = [1 \quad 2 \quad 1 \quad 0]$, $\vec{u_2} = [-1 \quad 1 \quad -4 \quad 3]$, $\vec{u_3} = [2 \quad 3 \quad 3 \quad -1]$ et $\vec{u_4} = [0 \quad 1 \quad -1 \quad 1]$.

a) Ces quatre vecteurs forment-ils une base de $\mathbb{R}^4$?

b) Trouvez une base de l'espace vectoriel V engendré par ces vecteurs.

c) Quelle est la dimension de l'espace vectoriel V?

d) Le vecteur $\vec{u_5} = [0 \quad 0 \quad 1 \quad 0]$ appartient-il à l'espace V?

e) Les vecteurs $\vec{u_1}$, $\vec{u_2}$, $\vec{u_3}$ et $\vec{u_5}$ forment-ils une base de $\mathbb{R}^4$?

14. (I) Soit les vecteurs:

$$\vec{u_1} = [1 \quad 0 \quad 1 \quad 0]$$
$$\vec{u_2} = [1 \quad 1 \quad 1 \quad 1]$$
$$\vec{u_3} = [0 \quad 1 \quad 0 \quad 1]$$
$$\vec{u_4} = [3 \quad 2 \quad 3 \quad 2]$$

a) Quelle est la dimension de l'espace vectoriel V engendré par ces quatre vecteurs?

b) Le vecteur $\vec{u_5} = \begin{bmatrix} 1 & 0 & 0 & 0 \end{bmatrix}$ appartient-il à V? Justifiez votre réponse.

c) Le vecteur $\vec{u_6} = \begin{bmatrix} 1 & -1 & 1 & -1 \end{bmatrix}$ appartient-il à V? Justifiez votre réponse.

15. (I) Dites si chaque énoncé est vrai ou faux, et justifiez votre réponse.

a) Si $\vec{u_1}$, $\vec{u_2}$, $\vec{u_3}$ et $\vec{u_4}$ appartiennent à $\mathbb{R}^n$ et si $3\vec{u_1} - 2\vec{u_2} = \vec{u_4}$, alors les vecteurs $\vec{u_1}$, $\vec{u_2}$, $\vec{u_3}$ et $\vec{u_4}$ sont linéairement dépendants.

b) Si $\vec{u_1}$, $\vec{u_2}$, $\vec{u_3}$ et $\vec{u_4}$ appartiennent à $\mathbb{R}^n$ et si $\vec{u_4}$ ne s'écrit pas comme une combinaison linéaire des trois autres vecteurs, alors les vecteurs $\vec{u_1}$, $\vec{u_2}$, $\vec{u_3}$ et $\vec{u_4}$ sont linéairement indépendants.

c) Si $\vec{u_1}$, $\vec{u_2}$, $\vec{u_3}$ et $\vec{u_4}$ sont des vecteurs linéairement indépendants de $\mathbb{R}^n$, alors $\vec{u_1}$, $\vec{u_2}$ et $\vec{u_3}$ sont aussi linéairement indépendants.

d) $\vec{u} \cdot \vec{0} = \vec{0}$.

e) Des vecteurs $\vec{u_1}$, $\vec{u_2}$, $\vec{u_3}$ et $\vec{u_4}$ de $\mathbb{R}^3$ peuvent être linéairement indépendants.

f) Les vecteurs :

$$\vec{u_1} = \begin{bmatrix} 1 & -2 & 1 & 2 \end{bmatrix}$$
$$\vec{u_2} = \begin{bmatrix} 1 & 1 & 1 & 0 \end{bmatrix}$$

$$\vec{u_3} = \begin{bmatrix} 0 & 1 & 1 & 1 \end{bmatrix}$$
$$\vec{u_4} = \begin{bmatrix} -1 & -1 & 3 & 0 \end{bmatrix}$$
$$\vec{u_5} = \begin{bmatrix} 0 & 8 & 2 & 2 \end{bmatrix}$$

forment une base de $\mathbb{R}^4$.

g) Les vecteurs :

$$\vec{u_1} = \begin{bmatrix} 1 & -2 & 1 & 2 \end{bmatrix}$$
$$\vec{u_2} = \begin{bmatrix} 1 & 1 & 1 & 0 \end{bmatrix}$$
$$\vec{u_3} = \begin{bmatrix} 0 & 1 & 1 & 1 \end{bmatrix}$$
$$\vec{u_4} = \begin{bmatrix} -1 & -1 & 3 & 0 \end{bmatrix}$$
$$\vec{u_5} = \begin{bmatrix} 0 & 8 & 2 & 2 \end{bmatrix}$$

forment un système générateur de $\mathbb{R}^4$.

h) Les vecteurs :

$$\vec{u_1} = \begin{bmatrix} 1 & 2 & 3 & -1 & 2 \end{bmatrix}$$
$$\vec{u_2} = \begin{bmatrix} 1 & -2 & 4 & -1 & 1 \end{bmatrix}$$
$$\vec{u_3} = \begin{bmatrix} 1 & 1 & 0 & 0 & 1 \end{bmatrix}$$
$$\vec{u_4} = \begin{bmatrix} 2 & -1 & 3 & 0 & 0 \end{bmatrix}$$

forment une base de $\mathbb{R}^5$.

i) Le vecteur nul peut faire partie d'une base d'un espace vectoriel.

CHAPITRE 1

1. a) $A = \begin{bmatrix} 50 & 45 & 55 \\ 52 & 70 & 30 \end{bmatrix}$

b) Les coûts de transport du deuxième produit pour chacun des clients.

c) Les coûts de transport de chacun des deux produits pour le troisième client.

d) Les coûts de transport (45 $) du premier produit pour le deuxième client.

2. $\begin{bmatrix} 500\,000 & 50\,000 & 2\,500 \\ 200\,000 & 20\,000 & 1\,000 \\ 100\,000 & 10\,000 & 500 \\ 40\,000 & 4\,000 & 200 \end{bmatrix}$

3. a) $i = j$

b) $i > j$

c) $i < j$

4. a)

Matrice	Format	Trace
A	4 × 5	
B	3 × 3	0
C	2 × 2	4
D	3 × 3	0
E	4 × 1	
F	1 × 3	
G	1 × 1	1
H	2 × 6	
K	3 × 3	1
L	4 × 4	21
M	2 × 2	−1
N	2 × 3	
P	3 × 3	6
Q	2 × 2	0

b) a_{53} n'est pas défini; $a_{35} = 10$; $b_{23} = 7$; $b_{11} = 1$; $c_{22} = 2$; $d_{12} = 2$; $e_{31} = 5$; e_{13} n'est pas défini; $h_{16} = 7$

c) B, C, D, G, K, L, M, P et Q

d) F et G

e) E et G

f) N

g) C, G, L et P

h) C, G, K, M et P

i) C, G et P

j) C et G

k) G

l) B, C, G et P

m) D

n) G, H, K et N

o) G et N

5. a) $A = \begin{bmatrix} 2 & 3 & -1 & 1 \\ 5 & 0 & 3 & 1 \\ -3 & 3 & -2 & 5 \\ 0 & 0 & 0 & 4 \end{bmatrix}$

b) $A = \begin{bmatrix} 1 & 1 \\ 2 & 3 \end{bmatrix}$

6. a) $A = \begin{bmatrix} a & 0 & 0 \\ 0 & b & 0 \\ 0 & 0 & c \end{bmatrix}$ où a, b, $c \in \mathbb{R}$

b) $B = \left[b_{ij} \right]_{n \times n}$ où

$$b_{ij} = \begin{cases} 0 & \text{si } i \neq j \\ k_i & \text{si } i = j \ (k_i \in \mathbb{R}) \end{cases}$$

7. $A = \begin{bmatrix} 0 & -a & -b \\ a & 0 & -c \\ b & c & 0 \end{bmatrix}$

8. $\begin{bmatrix} 0 & 1 \\ 0 & 0 \end{bmatrix}$ $\begin{bmatrix} 0 & 0 \\ 0 & 0 \end{bmatrix}$ $\begin{bmatrix} 1 & 0 \\ 0 & 1 \end{bmatrix}$

9. $O_{3 \times 1} = \begin{bmatrix} 0 \\ 0 \\ 0 \end{bmatrix}$ $O_{2 \times 3} = \begin{bmatrix} 0 & 0 & 0 \\ 0 & 0 & 0 \end{bmatrix}$

$I_3 = \begin{bmatrix} 1 & 0 & 0 \\ 0 & 1 & 0 \\ 0 & 0 & 1 \end{bmatrix}$

10. a) Vrai i) Faux
b) Faux j) Vrai
c) Faux k) Vrai
d) Vrai l) Vrai
e) Faux m) Faux
f) Faux n) Vrai
g) Faux o) Vrai
h) Vrai

11. Les deux matrices doivent avoir le même format et leurs éléments correspondants doivent être égaux.

12. $y = -5$ et $x = -1$ ou $x = 3$

13. $O_{n \times n}$

14. $A = \begin{bmatrix} 1 & -4 & 9 \\ -1 & 4 & -9 \end{bmatrix}$ $B = \begin{bmatrix} 3 & 5 & 7 \\ 4 & 6 & 8 \\ 5 & 7 & 9 \end{bmatrix}$

15. $a_{ij} = 2$ $b_{ij} = i$ $c_{ij} = \begin{cases} 0 & \text{si } i \neq j \\ i^2 & \text{si } i = j \end{cases}$ $d_{ij} = (-1)^{i+j}$

16. a)

MIGRATION INTERPROVINCIALE NETTE
ENTRE LES RECENSEMENTS DE 1986 ET DE 1991,
PROVINCES DE L'OUEST CANADIEN

Résidence (1986)	Résidence (1991)		
	Alberta	Manitoba	Saskatchewan
Alberta	0	−7 550	−29 525
Manitoba	7 550	0	−1 855
Saskatchewan	29 525	1 855	0

b) 0

c) L'Alberta

d) La Saskatchewan

17. a) $C = \begin{bmatrix} 1/2 & 1/3 & 1/4 \\ 2/3 & 1/2 & 2/5 \\ 3/4 & 3/5 & 1/2 \end{bmatrix}$

b) La troisième espèce

c) $c_{ij} + c_{ji} = 1$

18. $T = \begin{bmatrix} 0,80 & 0,20 & 0,05 \\ 0,10 & 0,75 & 0,05 \\ 0,10 & 0,05 & 0,90 \end{bmatrix}$

19. a) $\begin{bmatrix} -5 & -2 & -4 & -8 & -9 & -4 & -2 & -5 \\ -1 & -1 & -1 & -1 & -1 & -1 & -1 & -1 \\ 0 & 0 & 0 & 0 & 0 & 0 & 0 & 0 \\ 0 & 0 & 0 & 0 & 0 & 0 & 0 & 0 \\ 0 & 0 & 0 & 0 & 0 & 0 & 0 & 0 \\ 0 & 0 & 0 & 0 & 0 & 0 & 0 & 0 \\ 1 & 1 & 1 & 1 & 1 & 1 & 1 & 1 \\ 5 & 2 & 4 & 8 & 9 & 4 & 2 & 5 \end{bmatrix}$

b) a_{44}

c) Les Blancs possèdent encore cinq pions, un fou, la reine, et le roi.

d) $\begin{bmatrix} 0 & 0 & 0 & 0 & 0 & 0 & 0 & 0 \\ 0 & -8 & 0 & 0 & 0 & 0 & 0 & 0 \\ 0 & -1 & 0 & 0 & 0 & 0 & 0 & -1 \\ -1 & 0 & 0 & -9 & 0 & 0 & -1 & 0 \\ 0 & 0 & -1 & 1 & -4 & 0 & 0 & 0 \\ 0 & 0 & 1 & 0 & 8 & 0 & 1 & 0 \\ 0 & 1 & 0 & 0 & 0 & 1 & 4 & 0 \\ 0 & 0 & 0 & 0 & 0 & 0 & 9 & 0 \end{bmatrix}$

20. a) 5

b) 5×5

c) i) 8×8 ii) $n \times n$

d) Toute matrice d'adjacence est symétrique.

e) $\begin{bmatrix} 0 & 1 & 1 & 0 \\ 1 & 0 & 1 & 1 \\ 1 & 1 & 0 & 1 \\ 0 & 1 & 1 & 0 \end{bmatrix}$

f)

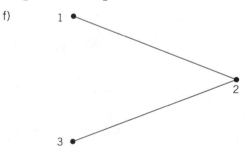

g) La matrice A n'est pas symétrique.

21. a) Hypothèse : A est une matrice nulle carrée. Conclusion : A est une matrice scalaire. On aurait également pu formuler le théorème comme suit : « Si A est une matrice nulle carrée, alors A est une matrice scalaire ».

Une matrice nulle carrée est une matrice scalaire.

Preuve

Si A est une matrice nulle carrée, alors tous ses éléments sont nuls. Tous les éléments de la matrice A non situés sur sa diagonale sont donc nuls. La matrice A est donc diagonale. De plus, tous les éléments de la diagonale principale de A valent zéro et sont donc identiques. Par conséquent, la matrice A est une matrice scalaire. ◼

b) Hypothèse : A est une matrice scalaire dont la trace vaut zéro. Conclusion : A est une matrice nulle. On aurait également pu formuler le théorème comme suit : « Si A est une matrice scalaire dont la trace vaut zéro, alors A est une matrice nulle ».

Une matrice scalaire dont la trace vaut zéro est une matrice nulle.

Preuve

Si A est une matrice scalaire d'ordre n, alors tous les éléments de sa diagonale principale sont égaux et tous les autres éléments de A valent zéro. Si on note a la valeur de chaque élément de la diagonale principale, alors la trace de A vaut na. Comme la trace de A vaut zéro par hypothèse, on a $na = 0$, d'où $a = 0$. Ainsi, tous les éléments de A, qu'ils appartiennent ou non à la diagonale principale, valent zéro. Par conséquent, la matrice A est une matrice nulle. ◼

c) Hypothèse : A est une matrice antisymétrique. Conclusion : La diagonale principale de A ne comporte que des zéros. On aurait également pu formuler le théorème comme suit : « Si A est une matrice antisymétrique, alors la diagonale principale de A ne comporte que des zéros ».

La diagonale principale d'une matrice antisymétrique ne comporte que des zéros.

Preuve

Dans une matrice antisymétrique $A = \left[a_{ij} \right]_{n \times n}$, on a $a_{ij} = -a_{ji}$ pour toutes les valeurs de i et de j. Par conséquent, $a_{ii} = -a_{ii}$, d'où $a_{ii} = 0$. La diagonale principale de A ne comporte donc que des zéros. ◼

22. Deux matrices scalaires de même format sont égales si et seulement si leurs traces sont égales.

Preuve

La preuve se divise en deux parties.

($\Rightarrow$) Distinguons l'hypothèse et la conclusion : si A et B sont des matrices scalaires de même format et que A et B sont égales (hypothèse), alors $\text{Tr}(A) = \text{Tr}(B)$ (conclusion).

Comme A et B sont des matrices égales, leurs éléments correspondants sont égaux. Comme cela est

vrai en particulier pour les éléments des diagonales principales, la somme des éléments de la diagonale principale de A est égale à la somme des éléments de la diagonale principale de B : $\text{Tr}(A) = \text{Tr}(B)$.

($\Leftarrow$) Distinguons l'hypothèse et la conclusion : si A et B sont des matrices scalaires de même format et que leurs traces sont égales (hypothèse), alors $A = B$ (conclusion).

Comme A et B sont des matrices de même format, il suffit de montrer que leurs éléments correspondants sont égaux pour vérifier l'égalité. Or, tous les éléments non situés sur les diagonales principales respectives des matrices valent zéro, car A et B sont des matrices scalaires. De plus, si A et B sont d'ordre n, alors $\text{Tr}(A) = na$ et $\text{Tr}(B) = nb$ où a et b sont les valeurs respectives des éléments de la diagonale principale de A et de la diagonale principale de B. Enfin, également par hypothèse, les traces respectives des deux matrices sont égales ; par conséquent, $na = nb$. On en déduit que $a = b$. Tous les éléments correspondants de A et de B, qu'ils appartiennent ou non à la diagonale principale, sont égaux et les matrices ont le même format. Par conséquent, $A = B$.

CHAPITRE 2

1. a) $A + C = \begin{bmatrix} 4 & -1 & 4 \\ 0 & 1 & 0 \\ 5 & 0 & 8 \end{bmatrix}$

b) $2A - 3C = \begin{bmatrix} -17 & 13 & 3 \\ 0 & -28 & 20 \\ 5 & -10 & -19 \end{bmatrix}$

c) $2 + E$ n'est pas défini.

d) $3F + 0{,}25\,G^t = \begin{bmatrix} 7 & -1{,}5 & 17 & 15 \end{bmatrix}$

e) $2F - G$ n'est pas défini.

f) $B^t - D^t + E = \begin{bmatrix} -4 & -1 & -5 \\ 1 & -5 & 0 \end{bmatrix}$

g) $D + E^t = \begin{bmatrix} 11 & -5 \\ 8 & 1 \\ 15 & 8 \end{bmatrix}$

h) $D^t + E = \begin{bmatrix} 11 & 8 & 15 \\ -5 & 1 & 8 \end{bmatrix}$

i) $A + O_{3 \times 3} = A$

j) $E + O_{3 \times 2}$ n'est pas défini.

2. $C = \begin{bmatrix} 4 & 6 & 8 \\ 8 & 10 & 12 \\ 14 & 16 & 18 \end{bmatrix}$

3. $15A + 32B^t$

4. a) p_{23} = prix du deuxième produit dans le troisième point de vente, en 1996.

r_{43} = prix du quatrième produit dans le troisième point de vente, en 1997.

q_{32} = quantité vendue du troisième produit dans le deuxième point de vente, en 1996.

b) La troisième colonne de la matrice S représente les quantités de chacun des m produits vendues dans le troisième point de vente, en 1997. La quatrième ligne de S représente les quantités du quatrième produit vendues dans chacun des n points de vente, en 1997.

c) Si on considère les matrices P et Q uniquement comme des matrices de nombres, on peut les additionner parce qu'elles ont le même format. Toutefois, il est difficile de trouver un sens à cette opération puisqu'elle consiste à additionner des prix et des quantités de produits.

d) Les matrices P et R étant deux matrices de prix de même format, on peut les additionner. Toutefois, bien malin qui pourrait donner un sens à cette opération.

e) On peut calculer $\frac{1}{2}(P + R)$ et le résultat est la matrice du prix moyen de chaque produit dans chacun des points de vente pour les années 1996 et 1997.

f) On peut calculer $Q + S$ et le résultat est la matrice des quantités totales de chaque produit vendues dans chacun des points de vente pour les années 1996 et 1997.

g) On peut calculer $\frac{1}{2}(Q + S)$ et le résultat est la matrice de la quantité moyenne de chaque produit vendue dans chacun des points de vente pour les années 1996 et 1997.

5. *Propriété 2*

Si A, B et C sont des matrices format $m \times n$, alors $(A + B) + C = A + (B + C)$.

Preuve

Si $A = \begin{bmatrix} a_{ij} \end{bmatrix}_{m \times n}$, $B = \begin{bmatrix} b_{ij} \end{bmatrix}_{m \times n}$ et $C = \begin{bmatrix} c_{ij} \end{bmatrix}_{m \times n}$, alors
$(A + B) + C = \begin{bmatrix} a_{ij} + b_{ij} \end{bmatrix}_{m \times n} + \begin{bmatrix} c_{ij} \end{bmatrix}_{m \times n}$
(définition de l'addition de matrices)

$= \begin{bmatrix} (a_{ij} + b_{ij}) + c_{ij} \end{bmatrix}_{m \times n}$
(définition de l'addition de matrices)

$= \begin{bmatrix} a_{ij} + (b_{ij} + c_{ij}) \end{bmatrix}_{m \times n}$
(associativité de l'addition dans les réels)

$= \begin{bmatrix} a_{ij} \end{bmatrix}_{m \times n} + \begin{bmatrix} b_{ij} + c_{ij} \end{bmatrix}_{m \times n}$
(définition de l'addition de matrices)

$= A + (B + C)$
(définition de l'addition de matrices) ∎

Propriété 4

Si A est une matrice $m \times n$, alors $A + (-A) = O_{m \times n}$.

Preuve

Si $A = \begin{bmatrix} a_{ij} \end{bmatrix}_{m \times n}$, alors
$A + (-A) = \begin{bmatrix} a_{ij} \end{bmatrix}_{m \times n} + \begin{bmatrix} -a_{ij} \end{bmatrix}_{m \times n}$
(définition de la matrice opposée)

$= \begin{bmatrix} a_{ij} + (-a_{ij}) \end{bmatrix}_{m \times n}$
(définition de l'addition de matrices)

$= \begin{bmatrix} 0 \end{bmatrix}_{m \times n}$
(définition de l'opposé dans les réels)

$= O_{m \times n}$
(définition de la matrice nulle) ∎

Propriété 5

Si A et B sont des matrices de format $m \times n$ et si r est un scalaire, alors $r(A + B) = rA + rB$.

Preuve

Si $A = \begin{bmatrix} a_{ij} \end{bmatrix}_{m \times n}$ et $B = \begin{bmatrix} b_{ij} \end{bmatrix}_{m \times n}$, et si r est un scalaire, alors
$r(A + B) = r\begin{bmatrix} a_{ij} + b_{ij} \end{bmatrix}_{m \times n}$
(définition de l'addition de matrices)

$= \begin{bmatrix} r(a_{ij} + b_{ij}) \end{bmatrix}_{m \times n}$
(définition de la multiplication d'une matrice par un scalaire)

$= \begin{bmatrix} ra_{ij} + rb_{ij} \end{bmatrix}_{m \times n}$
(distributivité dans les réels)

$= \begin{bmatrix} ra_{ij} \end{bmatrix}_{m \times n} + \begin{bmatrix} rb_{ij} \end{bmatrix}_{m \times n}$
(définition de l'addition de matrices)

$= r\begin{bmatrix} a_{ij} \end{bmatrix}_{m \times n} + r\begin{bmatrix} b_{ij} \end{bmatrix}_{m \times n}$
(définition de la multiplication d'une matrice par un scalaire)

$= rA + rB$ ∎

Propriété 11

Si A est une matrice de format $m \times n$ et si k est un scalaire, alors $(kA)^t = kA^t$.

Preuve

Si $A = \left[a_{ij}\right]_{m \times n}$ et si k est un scalaire, alors

$(kA)^t = \left(\left[ka_{ij}\right]_{m \times n}\right)^t$

    (définition de la multiplication d'une matrice par un scalaire)

$= \left[ka_{ji}\right]_{n \times m}$

    (définition de la transposée d'une matrice)

$= k\left[a_{ji}\right]_{n \times m}$

    (définition de la multiplication d'une matrice par un scalaire)

$= kA^t$

    (définition de la transposée d'une matrice) ∎

Propriété 12

Si A et B sont des matrices de format $m \times n$, alors $(A + B)^t = A^t + B^t$.

Preuve

Si $A = \left[a_{ij}\right]_{m \times n}$ et $B = \left[b_{ij}\right]_{m \times n}$, alors

$(A + B)^t = \left(\left[a_{ij} + b_{ij}\right]_{m \times n}\right)^t$

    (définition de l'addition de matrices)

$= \left[a_{ji} + b_{ji}\right]_{n \times m}$

    (définition de la transposée d'une matrice)

$= \left[a_{ji}\right]_{n \times m} + \left[b_{ji}\right]_{n \times m}$

    (définition de l'addition de matrices)

$= A^t + B^t$

    (définition de la transposée d'une matrice) ∎

6. Les éléments de la diagonale principale d'une matrice antisymétrique sont tous nuls.

Preuve

Si $A = \left[a_{ij}\right]_{n \times n}$ est une matrice antisymétrique, alors

$A = -A^t$

$a_{ij} = -a_{ji}$ (définition de l'égalité de deux matrices)

$a_{ii} = -a_{ii}$ (lorsque $i = j$)

$a_{ii} = 0$

Par conséquent, tous les éléments de la diagonale principale d'une matrice antisymétrique valent 0. ∎

7. a) Si A est une matrice carrée, alors $S = \frac{1}{2}(A + A^t)$ est une matrice symétrique.

Preuve

Si A est une matrice carrée, alors les matrices A et A^t sont compatibles pour l'addition et

$S^t = \left[\frac{1}{2}(A + A^t)\right]^t$

$= \frac{1}{2}(A + A^t)^t$

$= \frac{1}{2}(A^t + (A^t)^t)$

$= \frac{1}{2}(A^t + A)$

$= \frac{1}{2}(A + A^t)$

$= S$

Par conséquent, S est une matrice symétrique. ∎

b) Si A est une matrice carrée, alors $N = \frac{1}{2}(A - A^t)$ est une matrice antisymétrique.

Preuve

Si A est une matrice carrée, alors les matrices A et A^t sont compatibles pour l'addition et

$N^t = \left[\frac{1}{2}(A - A^t)\right]^t$

$= \frac{1}{2}(A - A^t)^t$

$= \frac{1}{2}(A^t - (A^t)^t)$

$= \frac{1}{2}(A^t - A)$

$= -\frac{1}{2}(A - A^t)$

$= -N$

On en déduit que $N = -N^t$. Par conséquent, N est une matrice antisymétrique. ∎

c) Si A est une matrice carrée, alors $A = S + N$: toute matrice carrée s'écrit comme la somme d'une matrice symétrique (S) et d'une matrice antisymétrique (N).

Preuve

$(S + N) = \left[\frac{1}{2}(A + A^t) + \frac{1}{2}(A - A^t)\right]$

$= \frac{1}{2}(2A)$

$= A$ ∎

8. $X = \begin{bmatrix} -2 & 2 \\ -5{,}5 & -11{,}5 \end{bmatrix}$

9. a) A, B et C sont trois matrices diagonales.

b) $A^2 = \begin{bmatrix} 4 & 0 \\ 0 & 9 \end{bmatrix}$

c) $A^3 = \begin{bmatrix} 8 & 0 \\ 0 & 27 \end{bmatrix}$

d) $B^3 = \begin{bmatrix} -1 & 0 & 0 \\ 0 & 64 & 0 \\ 0 & 0 & 8 \end{bmatrix}$

e) Si $D = \left[d_{ij}\right]_{n \times n} = C^2$, alors $d_{ij} = c_{ij}^2$ pour tout i et tout j.

f) Si $D = \left[d_{ij}\right]_{n \times n} = C^k$, alors $d_{ij} = c_{ij}^k$ pour tout i et tout j.

10. a) $BD = \begin{bmatrix} 1 & 0 \\ 0 & 1 \end{bmatrix}$

b) $O_{3 \times 2}$

c) $FE - 2A$ n'est pas défini.

d) $A^2 = \begin{bmatrix} 13 & -18 & 8 \\ 16 & 17 & -16 \\ 0 & 16 & 5 \end{bmatrix}$

e) E^2 n'est pas défini.

f) $3 + GH$ n'est pas défini.

g) $EF = \begin{bmatrix} 14 & 28 & 58 \\ 3 & 6 & 51 \\ 3 & 6 & 71 \end{bmatrix}$

h) $F^t E^t = \begin{bmatrix} 14 & 3 & 3 \\ 28 & 6 & 6 \\ 58 & 51 & 71 \end{bmatrix}$.

On constate que $F^t E^t = (EF)^t$.

i) $I_3 E = E = \begin{bmatrix} 10 & -4 \\ 6 & 3 \\ 8 & 5 \end{bmatrix}$

j) $CI_3 = C = \begin{bmatrix} 5 & -3 & 1 \\ 0 & 6 & -4 \\ 1 & 2 & 7 \end{bmatrix}$

k) $AEF = \begin{bmatrix} 1 & 2 & 257 \\ -3 & -6 & 29 \\ 53 & 106 & 201 \end{bmatrix}$

11. $n \times m$

12. a) $M^2 = \begin{bmatrix} a^2 & 2a \\ 0 & a^2 \end{bmatrix}$

b) $M^3 = \begin{bmatrix} a^3 & 3a^2 \\ 0 & a^3 \end{bmatrix}$

c) $M^k = \begin{bmatrix} a^k & ka^{k-1} \\ 0 & a^k \end{bmatrix}$

13. a) $5BA^t$

b) $A + 5B^t$

c) $A^2 - A^t A + AA^t - (A^2)^t$

14. Si $AB = A$ et $BA = B$, alors la matrice AB est une matrice idempotente.

Preuve

$$(AB)^2 = (AB)(AB)$$
$$= A(BA)B$$
$$= A(B)B$$
$$= (AB)B$$
$$= (A)B$$
$$= AB$$

Par conséquent, AB est une matrice idempotente. ◼

15. $D^2 = \begin{bmatrix} -36 & -27 & 18 \\ 64 & 48 & -32 \\ 24 & 18 & -12 \end{bmatrix}$ et $D^3 = \begin{bmatrix} 0 & 0 & 0 \\ 0 & 0 & 0 \\ 0 & 0 & 0 \end{bmatrix}$.

Par conséquent, D est une matrice nilpotente d'indice 3.

16. a) Faux   i) Vrai

b) Vrai   j) Vrai

c) Faux   k) Faux

d) Faux   l) Faux

e) Faux   m) Vrai

f) Faux   n) Faux

g) Faux   o) Vrai

h) Vrai

17. Si $ABA = A$, alors BA est une matrice idempotente.

Preuve

$(BA)^2 = (BA)(BA) = B(ABA) = B(A) = BA$. Par conséquent, BA est une matrice idempotente. ◼

18. Si A et B sont deux matrices diagonales de même format, alors le produit AB est aussi une matrice diagonale et $AB = BA$.

Preuve

Si $A = \left[a_{ij}\right]_{n \times n}$ et $B = \left[b_{ij}\right]_{n \times n}$, alors

$$C = AB = \left[c_{ij}\right]_{n \times n} \text{ où } c_{ij} = \sum_{k=1}^{n} a_{ik}b_{kj} \text{ et}$$

$$D = BA = \left[d_{ij}\right]_{n \times n} \text{ où } d_{ij} = \sum_{k=1}^{n} b_{ik}a_{kj}$$

Les matrices AB et BA ont donc le même format ($n \times n$). Puisque les matrices A et B sont diagonales, tous les éléments non situés sur la diagonale principale sont nuls : si $i \neq j$, alors $a_{ij} = 0 = b_{ij}$. Par conséquent, si $i \neq j$, alors $a_{ik}b_{kj} = 0$ et $b_{ik}a_{kj} = 0$, car au moins un des deux facteurs de chacun de ces produits est nul quelle que soit la valeur de k. Donc, si $i \neq j$, alors $c_{ij} = \sum_{k=1}^{n} a_{ik}b_{kj} = 0$ et $d_{ij} = \sum_{k=1}^{n} b_{ik}a_{kj} = 0$ parce que chacun des termes de ces deux sommes vaut 0. Les matrices AB et BA sont donc diagonales et elles ont le même format. Il suffit maintenant de montrer que les éléments correspondants des diagonales principales des matrices AB et BA sont identiques, c'est-à-dire que $c_{ii} = d_{ii}$. Or, $c_{ii} = \sum_{k=1}^{n} a_{ik}b_{ki} = a_{ii}b_{ii}$ puisque tous les autres termes de la somme sont nuls. Pour la même raison, $d_{ii} = \sum_{k=1}^{n} b_{ik}a_{ki} = b_{ii}a_{ii} = a_{ii}b_{ii}$. On en conclut que $c_{ii} = d_{ii}$; ainsi $AB = BA$. ∎

19. Le produit de deux matrices triangulaires supérieures de même ordre est une matrice triangulaire supérieure.

Preuve

Si $A = \left[a_{ij}\right]_{n \times n}$ et $B = \left[b_{ij}\right]_{n \times n}$ sont des matrices triangulaires supérieures, alors $a_{ij} = 0$ et $b_{ij} = 0$ lorsque $i > j$. On note le produit de ces deux matrices $C = AB = \left[c_{ij}\right]_{n \times n}$ où $c_{ij} = \sum_{k=1}^{n} a_{ik}b_{kj}$. Il faut montrer que $c_{ij} = 0$ lorsque $i > j$. Or, si $i > j$, alors $a_{ik} = 0$ pour les valeurs de k allant de 1 à $i - 1$ inclusivement, et $b_{kj} = 0$ pour les valeurs de k allant de i à n. Par conséquent, $a_{ik}b_{kj} = 0$ quelle que soit la valeur de k puisqu'au moins l'un des deux termes de ce produit est nul. On en déduit que si $i > j$, alors $c_{ij} = \sum_{k=1}^{n} a_{ik}b_{kj} = 0$ parce que chacun des termes de cette somme vaut 0. La matrice AB est donc une matrice triangulaire supérieure. ∎

20. Si A est une matrice carrée d'ordre n telle que $A^t A = I_n$, alors $(I_n - A)^t(I_n + A)$ est une matrice antisymétrique.

Preuve

Par hypothèse, $A^t A = I_n$. De plus,

$$(I_n - A)^t(I_n + A) = (I_n - A^t)(I_n + A)$$
$$= I_n - A^t + A - A^t A$$
$$= I_n - A^t + A - I_n$$
$$= -A^t + A$$

et

$$\left[(I_n - A)^t(I_n + A)\right]^t = (I_n + A)^t(I_n - A)$$
$$= (I_n + A^t)(I_n - A)$$
$$= I_n + A^t - A - A^t A$$
$$= A^t - A$$

Par conséquent,

$$\left[(I_n - A)^t(I_n + A)\right]^t = A^t - A$$
$$= -(-A^t + A)$$
$$= -(I_n - A)^t(I_n + A)$$

On en conclut que $(I_n - A)^t(I_n + A)$ est une matrice antisymétrique. ∎

21. a) a_{24} représente la note de Jasmine (89,5) au quatrième examen, a_{32} la note de Julien (87,0) au deuxième examen et a_{13} représente la note de James (80,5) au troisième examen.

b) Cette ligne représente les notes de Jasmine à chacun des examens.

c) Cette colonne représente les notes de James, Jasmine et Julien au quatrième examen.

d) Le produit matriciel AB donne la note finale des trois élèves. Ainsi.

$$AB = \begin{bmatrix} 86,375 & 87,125 & 86,750 \end{bmatrix}^t$$

e) Il faut effectuer le produit AC où

$$C = \begin{bmatrix} 0,2 & 0,2 & 0,3 & 0,3 \end{bmatrix}^t$$

On obtient alors

$$AC = \begin{bmatrix} 86,15 & 87,05 & 87,55 \end{bmatrix}^t$$

22. a) $a_{21} = 80\,000$ \$. En septembre, le montant des ventes de voitures compactes effectuées par M. Dupuis s'est élevé à 80 000 \$.

b) $b_{13} = 90\,000$ \$. En octobre, le montant des ventes de voitures de luxe effectuées par M. Tremblay s'est élevé à 90 000 \$.

c) $A + B$ représente la valeur totale des ventes effectuées par chacun des deux vendeurs, pour chacun des modèles de voitures, au cours des mois de septembre et octobre.

d) $\frac{1}{2}(A + B)$

e) $(0,01)\, B$

f) Le produit $A\begin{bmatrix} 1 & 1 & 1 \end{bmatrix}^t$ représente la valeur totale des ventes effectuées par chaque vendeur au cours du mois de septembre.

g) $B\begin{bmatrix} 0,01 & 0,015 & 0,02 \end{bmatrix}^t$

23. a) $M = \begin{bmatrix} 20 & 5 & 10 \end{bmatrix}$

b) $C = \begin{bmatrix} 0,25 \\ 2,00 \\ 0,90 \end{bmatrix}$

c) $MC = \begin{bmatrix} 24 \end{bmatrix}$. La valeur totale, en dollars canadiens, des devises européennes rapportées par la voyageuse, soit 24 $.

24. a) $AB = \begin{bmatrix} 761,25 & 769,50 & 786,00 & 790,50 & 793,50 \end{bmatrix}$. Cette matrice représente la valeur du portefeuille de l'individu à chaque jour de la semaine en question.

b) Le vendredi.

25. a) $Q = \begin{bmatrix} 1,5 & 5 & 4 \\ 1 & 2 & 2 \end{bmatrix}$

b) $U = \begin{bmatrix} 18 \\ 12 \\ 25 \end{bmatrix}$

c) Il faut multiplier les matrices Q et U:

$$C = QU = \begin{bmatrix} 187 \\ 92 \end{bmatrix}$$

d) $R = \begin{bmatrix} 300 \\ 125 \end{bmatrix}$

e) Il faut soustraire la matrice C de la matrice R. Si P est la matrice des profits, alors

$$P = R - C = \begin{bmatrix} 113 \\ 33 \end{bmatrix}$$

Le profit réalisé sur la vente d'une bague est de 113 $ et le profit réalisé sur la vente d'une paire de boucles d'oreille est de 33 $.

26. a) $QP = \begin{bmatrix} 46 & 91 \\ 19 & 16 \\ 18 & 18 \end{bmatrix}$, où Q = la matrice des quantités et P = la matrice de production.

b) 19 kg

c) 91 kg

27. a) $A = \begin{bmatrix} 1\,000 & 2\,000 & 1\,000 \\ 5\,000 & 1\,000 & 0 \end{bmatrix}$

b) $0,7\,A$

c) $0,7\,A = \begin{bmatrix} 700 & 1\,400 & 700 \\ 3\,500 & 700 & 0 \end{bmatrix}$

d) $V = 0,3\,A = \begin{bmatrix} 300 & 600 & 300 \\ 1\,500 & 300 & 0 \end{bmatrix}$

e) $P = \begin{bmatrix} 20 \\ 25 \\ 30 \end{bmatrix}$

f) La matrice R représente les revenus, par entrepôt, que l'éditeur prévoit tirer de la vente des volumes de l'auteur au cours de l'année.

g) $R = VP$

$$= \begin{bmatrix} 300 & 600 & 300 \\ 1\,500 & 300 & 0 \end{bmatrix} \begin{bmatrix} 20 \\ 25 \\ 30 \end{bmatrix}$$

$$= \begin{bmatrix} 30\,000 \\ 37\,500 \end{bmatrix}$$

28. a) a_{21} représente la quantité (13 g) de fibres alimentaires dans 30 g du premier aliment.

b) b_{13} représente la proportion (0,4) d'aliment 1 dans une portion de 30 g du déjeuner de type 3.

c) La deuxième colonne de la matrice A représente la quantité (en grammes) de protéines, de fibres alimentaires et de matières grasses dans 30 g du deuxième aliment.

d) Le produit matriciel BA n'a pas de sens.

e) Le produit matriciel AB donne les quantités (en grammes) de protéines (ligne 1), de fibres alimentaires (ligne 2) et de matières grasses (ligne 3) contenues dans une portion de 30 g de chacun des déjeuners représentés par une colonne de la matrice AB.

$$AB = \begin{bmatrix} 3,4 & 3,8 & 4,2 \\ 10,6 & 8,2 & 5,8 \\ 1,2 & 1,4 & 1,6 \end{bmatrix}$$

29. a) $P^{(0)} = \begin{bmatrix} 0,50 \\ 0,30 \\ 0,20 \end{bmatrix}$

b) $T = \begin{bmatrix} 0,80 & 0,20 & 0,05 \\ 0,10 & 0,75 & 0,05 \\ 0,10 & 0,05 & 0,90 \end{bmatrix}$

c) Elle vaut 1 ou 100 %. La somme de la part du marché qu'une entreprise a conservée et des parts qu'elle a perdues au profit de ses concurrents est égale à 100 % du marché que l'entreprise détenait au début du mois.

d) Oui, parce que tous les éléments de la matrice sont non négatifs et que la somme des éléments de chaque colonne est 1.

e) $TP^{(0)} = \begin{bmatrix} 0{,}470 \\ 0{,}285 \\ 0{,}245 \end{bmatrix}$. Cette matrice représente la part

du marché détenue par chaque entreprise à la fin du mois. On la note $P^{(1)}$. Ainsi, à la fin du mois, l'entreprise 1 détient 47 % du marché, l'entreprise 2 en détient 28,5 % et l'entreprise 3 en détient 24,5 %. On observe également que la somme des éléments de $TP^{(0)}$ est 1, ou 100 %.

f) $P^{(2)} = TP^{(1)} = T(TP^{(0)}) = T^2 P^{(0)} = \begin{bmatrix} 0{,}44525 \\ 0{,}27300 \\ 0{,}28175 \end{bmatrix}$

g) $P^{(n)} = TP^{(n-1)} = T(TP^{(n-2)}) = \cdots = T^n P^{(0)}$

30. a) $A = \begin{bmatrix} d_1 & d_2 & \cdots & d_i & \cdots & d_{n-1} & d_n \\ s_1 & 0 & \cdots & 0 & \cdots & 0 & 0 \\ 0 & s_2 & \cdots & 0 & \cdots & \cdots & \cdots \\ \vdots & \vdots & \vdots & \vdots & \vdots & \vdots & \vdots \\ 0 & 0 & \cdots & s_i & \cdots & 0 & 0 \\ \vdots & \vdots & \vdots & \vdots & \vdots & \vdots & \vdots \\ 0 & 0 & \cdots & 0 & \cdots & s_{n-1} & 0 \end{bmatrix}$

b) $X^{(2)} = AX^{(1)} = A(AX^{(0)}) = A^2 X^{(0)}$

c) $X^{(k)} = AX^{(k-1)} = A(AX^{(k-2)}) = \cdots = A^k X^{(0)}$

d) Le nombre 0,06 représente le taux de survie des truites durant l'année qui suit leur naissance. Ainsi, seulement 6 % des truites vivent jusqu'à l'âge de 1 an.

e) Les truites de 4 ans donnent naissance, en moyenne, à 82 descendantes par année.

f) Deux ans.

g) Au temps $t = 0$, il y a 600 truites d'un an ou plus mais de moins de deux ans dans le *Hunt Creek*.

h) $X^{(1)} = AX^{(0)} = \begin{bmatrix} 11\,010 \\ 600 \\ 204 \\ 32 \\ 4 \end{bmatrix}$

31. a) Si A et B sont des carrés magiques d'ordre n, alors $A + B$ est aussi un carré magique et
$$S(A + B) = S(A) + S(B)$$

Preuve

Si $A = \begin{bmatrix} a_{ij} \end{bmatrix}_{n \times n}$ et $B = \begin{bmatrix} b_{ij} \end{bmatrix}_{n \times n}$, alors
$$A + B = \begin{bmatrix} a_{ij} + b_{ij} \end{bmatrix}_{n \times n}$$

La somme des éléments de la i-ième ligne de la matrice $A + B$ est
$$\sum_{j=1}^{n} (a_{ij} + b_{ij}) = \sum_{j=1}^{n} a_{ij} + \sum_{j=1}^{n} b_{ij} = S(A) + S(B)$$

On peut montrer de façon analogue que la somme des éléments de la j-ième colonne de $A + B$ vaut aussi $S(A) + S(B)$. Par conséquent, la matrice $A + B$ est un carré magique tel que la somme des éléments de chaque ligne ou de chaque colonne vaut $S(A) + S(B)$, d'où $S(A + B) = S(A) + S(B)$.
∎

b) Si A et B sont des carrés magiques d'ordre n, alors AB est un carré magique et $S(AB) = S(A) \times S(B)$.

Preuve

Si $A = \begin{bmatrix} a_{ij} \end{bmatrix}_{n \times n}$ et $B = \begin{bmatrix} b_{ij} \end{bmatrix}_{n \times n}$, alors
$$C = AB = \begin{bmatrix} c_{ij} \end{bmatrix}_{n \times n} \text{ où } c_{ij} = \sum_{k=1}^{n} a_{ik} b_{kj}$$

Il faut prouver que la somme des éléments de la j-ième colonne de C, soit $\displaystyle\sum_{i=1}^{n} c_{ij}$, et que la somme des éléments de la i-ième ligne de C, soit $\displaystyle\sum_{j=1}^{n} c_{ij}$ valent $S(A) \times S(B)$. Autrement dit, il faut donc montrer que $\displaystyle\sum_{i=1}^{n} c_{ij} = \sum_{j=1}^{n} c_{ij} = S(A) \times S(B)$. Or, la somme des éléments de la j-ième colonne de C est

$$\begin{aligned} \sum_{i=1}^{n} c_{ij} &= \sum_{i=1}^{n} \sum_{k=1}^{n} a_{ik} b_{kj} \\ &= \sum_{k=1}^{n} \sum_{i=1}^{n} a_{ik} b_{kj} \\ &= \sum_{k=1}^{n} \left(b_{kj} \sum_{i=1}^{n} a_{ik} \right) \\ &= \sum_{k=1}^{n} (b_{kj} \times S(A)) \\ &= S(A) \sum_{k=1}^{n} b_{kj} \\ &= S(A) \times S(B) \end{aligned}$$

De façon analogue, $\displaystyle\sum_{j=1}^{n} c_{ij} = S(A) \times S(B)$. Par conséquent, la matrice AB est un carré magique tel que la somme des éléments de chaque ligne ou de chaque colonne vaut $S(A) \times S(B)$, d'où
$$S(AB) = S(A) \times S(B)$$
∎

32. *Propriété 3*

Lorsque les opérations matricielles sont définies, $r(AB) = (rA)B = A(rB)$.

Preuve

Soit $A = \left[a_{ij}\right]_{m \times n}$, $B = \left[b_{ij}\right]_{n \times p}$ et $C = AB = \left[c_{ij}\right]_{m \times p}$

où $c_{ij} = \sum_{k=1}^{n} a_{ik} b_{kj}$. Alors,

$$
\begin{aligned}
r(AB) &= rC \\
&= \left[r \sum_{k=1}^{n} a_{ik} b_{kj}\right]_{m \times p} \\
&= \left[\sum_{k=1}^{n} r(a_{ik} b_{kj})\right]_{m \times p} \\
&= \left[\sum_{k=1}^{n} (ra_{ik}) b_{kj}\right]_{m \times p} \\
&= (rA)B
\end{aligned}
$$

De plus,

$$
\begin{aligned}
r(AB) &= rC \\
&= \left[r \sum_{k=1}^{n} a_{ik} b_{kj}\right]_{m \times p} \\
&= \left[\sum_{k=1}^{n} r(a_{ik} b_{kj})\right]_{m \times p} \\
&= \left[\sum_{k=1}^{n} a_{ik} (rb_{kj})\right]_{m \times p} \\
&= A(rB)
\end{aligned}
$$

Par conséquent, $r(AB) = (rA)B = A(rB)$. ∎

Propriété 5

Lorsque les opérations matricielles sont définies, $A(B + C) = AB + AC$ et $(D + E)F = DF + EF$.

Preuve

Nous n'allons démontrer que la première partie de la propriété, la preuve de la deuxième partie étant analogue.

Soit $A = \left[a_{ij}\right]_{m \times n}$, $B = \left[b_{ij}\right]_{n \times p}$ et $C = \left[c_{ij}\right]_{n \times p}$. Alors,

$$
\begin{aligned}
A(B + C) &= \left[\sum_{k=1}^{n} a_{ik}(b_{kj} + c_{kj})\right]_{m \times p} \\
&= \left[\sum_{k=1}^{n} (a_{ik}b_{kj} + a_{ik}c_{kj})\right]_{m \times p} \\
&= \left[\sum_{k=1}^{n} a_{ik}b_{kj} + \sum_{k=1}^{n} a_{ik}c_{kj}\right]_{m \times p} \\
&= \left[\sum_{k=1}^{n} a_{ik}b_{kj}\right]_{m \times p} + \left[\sum_{k=1}^{n} a_{ik}c_{kj}\right]_{m \times p} \\
&= AB + AC
\end{aligned}
$$
∎

Propriété 7

$$O_{m \times n}\, A_{n \times p} = O_{m \times p} \text{ et } A_{n \times p}\, O_{p \times q} = O_{n \times q}$$

Preuve

Nous n'allons démontrer que la première partie de la propriété, la preuve de la deuxième partie étant analogue.

Si $A = \left[a_{ij}\right]_{n \times p}$, alors

$$O_{m \times n}\, A_{n \times p} = \left[\sum_{k=1}^{n} 0 \times a_{kj}\right]_{m \times p} = \left[0\right]_{m \times p} = O_{m \times p}$$
∎

33. a) $I_n - A^k$

b) En vertu du résultat obtenu en *a*,

$$(I_n - A)S_k = I_n - A^k \Rightarrow S_k = (I_n - A)^{-1}(I_n - A^k)$$

c) $\lim_{k \to \infty} S_k = (I_n - A)^{-1}$

d) $A^2 = \begin{bmatrix} a^2 & 0 \\ 0 & b^2 \end{bmatrix}$, $A^3 = \begin{bmatrix} a^3 & 0 \\ 0 & b^3 \end{bmatrix}$,

$A^k = \begin{bmatrix} a^k & 0 \\ 0 & b^k \end{bmatrix}$, $\lim_{k \to \infty} A^k = \begin{bmatrix} 0 & 0 \\ 0 & 0 \end{bmatrix}$ et

$$\lim_{k \to \infty} S^k = \begin{bmatrix} 1/(1-a) & 0 \\ 0 & 1/(1-b) \end{bmatrix}$$

34. $A^{-1} = \begin{bmatrix} \tfrac{1}{2} & \tfrac{1}{2} \\ -\tfrac{1}{2} & \tfrac{1}{2} \end{bmatrix}$

35. Pour montrer que $B = \dfrac{1}{ad - bc} \begin{bmatrix} d & -b \\ -c & a \end{bmatrix}$ est la matrice inverse de *A*, il faut vérifier que $BA = AB = I_2$. Or,

$$
\begin{aligned}
BA &= \frac{1}{ad - bc} \begin{bmatrix} d & -b \\ -c & a \end{bmatrix} \begin{bmatrix} a & b \\ c & d \end{bmatrix} \\
&= \frac{1}{ad - bc} \begin{bmatrix} ad - bc & 0 \\ 0 & ad - bc \end{bmatrix} \\
&= \begin{bmatrix} 1 & 0 \\ 0 & 1 \end{bmatrix} \\
&= I_2
\end{aligned}
$$

Il est tout aussi facile de vérifier que

$$
\begin{aligned}
AB &= \begin{bmatrix} a & b \\ c & d \end{bmatrix} \left(\frac{1}{ad - bc} \begin{bmatrix} d & -b \\ -c & a \end{bmatrix} \right) \\
&= \begin{bmatrix} 1 & 0 \\ 0 & 1 \end{bmatrix} \\
&= I_2
\end{aligned}
$$

Par conséquent, la matrice B est la matrice inverse de A, ce qu'on écrit $B = A^{-1}$.

36. a) $AB = \begin{bmatrix} 0 & 0 \\ 0 & 0 \end{bmatrix}$

b) Non

c) $AC = \begin{bmatrix} 7 & 11 \\ 0 & 0 \end{bmatrix} = AD$

d) En effet, $C \neq D$ et pourtant $AC = AD$.

37. a) $x = 2$ et $y = 1$

b) $x = 2$ et $y = 5$

c) $x = 1$ et $y = 1$

38. Comme

$$AC = \begin{bmatrix} 1 & 2 & 3 \\ 1 & 3 & 5 \\ 2 & 5 & 9 \end{bmatrix} \begin{bmatrix} 2 & -3 & 1 \\ 1 & 3 & -2 \\ -1 & -1 & 1 \end{bmatrix} = \begin{bmatrix} 1 & 0 & 0 \\ 0 & 1 & 0 \\ 0 & 0 & 1 \end{bmatrix}$$

alors C est l'inverse de A, c'est-à-dire que $C = A^{-1}$. Par conséquent, $x = 25$, $y = -15$ et $z = 5$.

39. Il est toujours possible d'additionner et de multiplier deux nombres réels; par contre, il n'est pas toujours possible d'additionner ou de multiplier deux matrices. La multiplication de nombres réels est commutative, alors qu'en général la multiplication de matrices ne l'est pas. Tous les nombres réels, à l'exception de 0, possèdent un inverse, alors que les matrices carrées non nulles ne possèdent pas toutes un inverse (une matrice inverse). L'expression a^n est définie pour tout nombre réel a et tout entier positif n, tandis que A^n n'est défini que si A est une matrice carrée. Si le produit de deux nombres réels est nul, alors au moins un des deux facteurs est nul; par contre, le produit de deux matrices non nulles peut être une matrice nulle. Enfin, il existe des matrices A, B et C telles que A n'est pas une matrice nulle et $AB = AC$ sans toutefois que $B = C$.

CHAPITRE 3

1. a) -5

b) -22

c) 10

d) 12

e) Le déterminant n'est pas défini.

f) -1

g) 625

h) 0

i) -36

2. Les mineurs et les cofacteurs pour la matrice A sont:
$M_{12} = -11$ et $A_{12} = 11$
$M_{22} = -2$ et $A_{22} = -2$
$M_{23} = -5$ et $A_{23} = 5$

Dans le cas de la matrice B, les mineurs et les cofacteurs sont:
$M_{12} = -1$ et $B_{12} = 1$
$M_{22} = -10$ et $B_{22} = -10$
$M_{23} = 70$ et $B_{23} = -70$

3. a) $A_{32} = (-1)^{3+2} \begin{vmatrix} 0 & -2 & 1 & -3 & 6 \\ 1 & -3 & 0 & 2 & 4 \\ -6 & 7 & 0 & 1 & 6 \\ 2 & 4 & 0 & 8 & 0 \\ 1 & 6 & 0 & 3 & 1 \end{vmatrix}$ et

$A_{53} = (-1)^{5+3} \begin{vmatrix} 0 & 5 & 1 & -3 & 6 \\ 1 & -1 & 0 & 2 & 4 \\ 3 & 9 & 0 & 1 & 1 \\ -6 & 7 & 0 & 1 & 6 \\ 1 & 2 & 0 & 3 & 1 \end{vmatrix}$

b) Les calculs sont beaucoup plus simples si on choisit la ligne ou la colonne qui compte le plus grand nombre de zéros, soit la quatrième colonne.

4. a) 0

b) 0

c) -2

d) Faux

e) Faux

5. a) Vrai

b) Vrai

c) Faux

d) Faux

e) Vrai

f) Faux

g) Vrai

h) Vrai

i) Faux

j) Vrai

6. a) det $B = -$det A

b) det $B = -6$ det A

c) det $B = $ det A

d) det $B = 3^5$ det A

e) det $B = $ det A

7. Une matrice carrée d'ordre n qui compte plus de $n^2 - n$ zéros est singulière.

Preuve

Soit A une matrice carrée d'ordre n qui compte plus de $n^2 - n$ zéros. Il faut montrer que det $A = 0$. Or, la matrice A compte n^2 éléments et au moins une ligne formée entièrement de zéros. En effet, si toutes les lignes comptaient au moins un élément différent de 0, alors la matrice A compterait au moins n éléments non nuls et au plus $n^2 - n$ zéros, ce qui contredit l'hypothèse. Par conséquent, la matrice A comprend au moins une ligne formée entièrement de zéros. En vertu de la propriété 5 (th. 3.1), le déterminant de A vaut 0 et la matrice A est donc singulière. ∎

8. a) Une matrice nilpotente d'ordre n et d'indice k est singulière.

Preuve

Si A est une matrice nilpotente d'ordre n et d'indice k, alors

$$A^k = O_{n \times n} \quad \Rightarrow \quad \det(A^k) = 0 \quad \Rightarrow \quad (\det A)^k = 0$$

Par conséquent, det $A = 0$, et la matrice A est singulière. ∎

b) Si A est une matrice nilpotente d'ordre n d'indice k, alors, pour toute valeur de x

$$(I_n + xA + x^2A^2 + \cdots + x^{k-1}A^{k-1})(I_n - xA) = I_n$$

Preuve

c) $(I_n + xA + x^2A^2 + \cdots + x^{k-1}A^{k-1})(I_n - xA)$
$= (I_n + xA + x^2A^2 + \cdots + x^{k-1}A^{k-1})(I_n)$
$\quad - (I_n + xA + x^2A^2 + \cdots + x^{k-1}A^{k-1})(xA)$
$= I_n + xA + x^2A^2 + \cdots + x^{k-1}A^{k-1}$
$\quad - (xA + x^2A^2 + \cdots + x^{k-1}A^{k-1} + x^kA^k)$
$= I_n - x^kA^k$
$= I_n - x^kO_{n \times n}$
$= I_n$ ∎

9. a) 0

b) −336

c) 0

d) −4

e) Si $n = 1$, le déterminant vaut x_1y_1. Si $n > 1$, le déterminant vaut 0.

f) $(-1)^{n+1}$

10. a) −105

b) 10

11. a) 2^n

b) $1 \times 2 \times 3 \times \cdots \times n = n!$

12. a) −4

b) −4

c) 12

d) −16

13. Si A et B sont deux matrices carrées d'ordre n dont l'une est singulière, alors le produit AB est aussi une matrice singulière.

Preuve

Il s'agit de montrer que det $AB = 0$. Or, comme l'une des matrices A et B est singulière, on a det $A = 0$ ou det $B = 0$. En vertu de la propriété 11 (th. 3.1),

$$\det AB = \det A \times \det B$$

Ainsi, det $AB = 0$ (det B) ou det $AB = ($det A) 0 et, par conséquent, det $AB = 0$. ∎

14. Si on additionne un multiple d'une colonne d'une matrice à une autre colonne, on ne change pas la valeur du déterminant. En ajoutant 10 000 fois la première colonne, 1 000 fois la deuxième colonne, 100 fois la troisième colonne et 10 fois la quatrième colonne de la matrice A à la dernière colonne, on obtient l'égalité

$$|A| = \begin{vmatrix} 1 & 2 & 3 & 8 & 8 \\ 6 & 9 & 4 & 2 & 6 \\ 8 & 2 & 9 & 3 & 5 \\ 4 & 2 & 2 & 1 & 8 \\ 2 & 1 & 3 & 9 & 4 \end{vmatrix}$$

$$= \begin{vmatrix} 1 & 2 & 3 & 8 & 12\,388 \\ 6 & 9 & 4 & 2 & 69\,426 \\ 8 & 2 & 9 & 3 & 82\,935 \\ 4 & 2 & 2 & 1 & 42\,218 \\ 2 & 1 & 3 & 9 & 21\,394 \end{vmatrix}$$

$$= 19 \times \begin{vmatrix} 1 & 2 & 3 & 8 & 652 \\ 6 & 9 & 4 & 2 & 3\,654 \\ 8 & 2 & 9 & 3 & 4\,365 \\ 4 & 2 & 2 & 1 & 2\,222 \\ 2 & 1 & 3 & 9 & 1\,126 \end{vmatrix}$$

Le déterminant de la matrice A est donc un multiple de 19.

15. a) $T = \begin{bmatrix} b & c & c & c & c \\ c & b & c & c & c \\ c & c & b & c & c \\ c & c & c & b & c \\ c & c & c & c & b \end{bmatrix}$

b) det $T = (b - c)^4(b + 4c)$

Preuve

Si on ajoute les deuxième, troisième, quatrième et cinquième colonnes de la matrice T à la première colonne, on ne change pas la valeur du déterminant.

$$\det T = \begin{vmatrix} b & c & c & c & c \\ c & b & c & c & c \\ c & c & b & c & c \\ c & c & c & b & c \\ c & c & c & c & b \end{vmatrix}$$

$$= \begin{vmatrix} b+4c & c & c & c & c \\ b+4c & b & c & c & c \\ b+4c & c & b & c & c \\ b+4c & c & c & b & c \\ b+4c & c & c & c & b \end{vmatrix}$$

De même, on ne change pas la valeur du déterminant en soustrayant la première ligne de chacune des autres lignes.

$$\det T = \begin{vmatrix} b+4c & c & c & c & c \\ b+4c & b & c & c & c \\ b+4c & c & b & c & c \\ b+4c & c & c & b & c \\ b+4c & c & c & c & b \end{vmatrix}$$

$$= \begin{vmatrix} b+4c & c & c & c & c \\ 0 & b-c & 0 & 0 & 0 \\ 0 & 0 & b-c & 0 & 0 \\ 0 & 0 & 0 & b-c & 0 \\ 0 & 0 & 0 & 0 & b-c \end{vmatrix}$$

Or, le déterminant d'une matrice triangulaire est égal au produit des éléments de la diagonale principale : $\det T = (b-c)^4(b+4c)$. ∎

16. $\det A = \det B + \det C$.

Preuve

En développant le déterminant des matrices A, B et C selon la j-ième colonne, on obtient

$$\det A = \sum_{i=1}^{n} (b_{ij} + c_{ij})(A_{ij})$$

$$= \sum_{i=1}^{n} b_{ij}A_{ij} + \sum_{i=1}^{n} c_{ij}A_{ij}$$

$$= \det B + \det C \qquad ∎$$

17. a) 1

b) x^4

c) -1

18. a) $A^{-1} = \begin{bmatrix} 3/7 & 2/7 \\ 2/7 & -1/7 \end{bmatrix}$

b) $B^{-1} = \begin{bmatrix} 1/5 & 1/5 \\ -3/5 & 2/5 \end{bmatrix}$

c) $C^{-1} = \begin{bmatrix} \dfrac{a}{a^2-4} & \dfrac{-2}{a^2-4} \\ \dfrac{-2}{a^2-4} & \dfrac{a}{a^2-4} \end{bmatrix}$. La matrice inverse

existe si et seulement si $a^2 - 4 \neq 0$, c'est-à-dire si et seulement si $a \neq 2$ et $a \neq -2$.

d) D^{-1} n'existe pas.

e) $E^{-1} = \begin{bmatrix} -1/44 & 3/44 & 7/44 \\ 31/44 & 39/44 & 3/44 \\ 19/44 & 31/44 & -1/44 \end{bmatrix}$

f) F^{-1} n'existe pas.

g) $G^{-1} = \begin{bmatrix} -2/21 & 1/3 & 10/21 \\ 1/21 & 1/3 & -5/21 \\ 5/21 & -1/3 & -4/21 \end{bmatrix}$

19. Si A est une matrice régulière d'ordre n, alors $\det(A^{-1}) = \dfrac{1}{\det A}$.

Preuve

Puisque A est une matrice régulière d'ordre n, alors $\det A \neq 0$ et A admet une matrice inverse A^{-1} telle que $AA^{-1} = I_n$. On a donc

$$\det(AA^{-1}) = \det I_n \implies (\det A)\det(A^{-1}) = 1$$

Par conséquent, $\det(A^{-1}) = \dfrac{1}{\det A}$ ∎

20. a) $-7,5$

b) On ne dispose pas de suffisamment d'informations pour évaluer $\det(A - B)$.

c) -27

d) $-0,1\overline{3}$

e) $506,25$

f) $-7,5$

21. a) $x = 3$ et $x = -2$

b) Si $x \neq 3$ et $x \neq -2$,

$$A^{-1} = \frac{1}{-x^2 + x + 6} \begin{bmatrix} x & 3 & -x \\ -2 & 1-x & 2 \\ 6-x^2 & -3 & x \end{bmatrix}$$

c) Il n'existe aucune valeur réelle de x pour laquelle $\det A = 14$.

22. a) $\det A = -1 \neq 0$: la matrice A est toujours inversible.

b) $A^{-1} = \begin{bmatrix} 1 & 2 & -x-2y \\ 0 & -1 & y \\ 0 & 0 & 1 \end{bmatrix}$

c) det $B = -(x - 1)^2(x + 2)$. Par conséquent, det $B \neq 0$ lorsque $x \neq 1$ et $x \neq -2$. La matrice B est donc inversible pour toutes les valeurs de x à l'exception de $x = 1$ et $x = -2$.

d) $\det C = \begin{vmatrix} 1 & a & a^2 \\ 1 & b & b^2 \\ 1 & c & c^2 \end{vmatrix}$

$= \begin{vmatrix} 1 & a & a^2 \\ 0 & b - a & b^2 - a^2 \\ 0 & c - a & c^2 - a^2 \end{vmatrix} \begin{matrix} \\ L_2 \to L_2 - L_1 \\ L_3 \to L_3 - L_1 \end{matrix}$

$= \begin{vmatrix} b - a & (b - a)(b + a) \\ c - a & (c - a)(c + a) \end{vmatrix}$

$= (b - a)(c - a)\begin{vmatrix} 1 & b + a \\ 1 & c + a \end{vmatrix}$

$= (b - a)(c - a)(c - b)$

e) La matrice C est inversible seulement si $a \neq b$, $b \neq c$ et $a \neq c$.

f) $\det D = \begin{vmatrix} 1 & 1 & 1 \\ a & b & c \\ bc & ac & ab \end{vmatrix}$

$= \begin{vmatrix} 0 & 1 & 1 \\ a - b & b & c \\ bc - ac & ac & ab \end{vmatrix}$

$= \begin{vmatrix} 0 & 1 & 1 \\ a - b & b & c \\ -c(a - b) & ac & ab \end{vmatrix}$

$= (a - b)\begin{vmatrix} 0 & 1 & 1 \\ 1 & b & c \\ -c & ac & ab \end{vmatrix}$

g) $\det E = \begin{vmatrix} 1 & 1 & 1 \\ a & b & c \\ b + c & a + c & a + b \end{vmatrix}$

$= \begin{vmatrix} 1 & 1 & 1 \\ a & b & c \\ a + b + c & a + b + c & a + b + c \end{vmatrix}$

$= 0$

parce que la troisième ligne est un multiple de la première ligne. La matrice E n'est donc pas inversible.

h) $\det F = \begin{vmatrix} a & ab \\ b & a^2 + b^2 \end{vmatrix}$

$= a\begin{vmatrix} 1 & b \\ b & a^2 + b^2 \end{vmatrix}$

$= a(a^2 + b^2 - b^2)$

$= a^3$

Donc det $F \neq 0$ seulement si $a \neq 0$, et la matrice F est inversible seulement si $a \neq 0$.

23. La matrice identité est la seule matrice idempotente dont le déterminant est différent de 0.

Preuve

Soit A une matrice idempotente ($A^2 = A$) d'ordre n dont le déterminant est différent de 0. Il faut montrer que $A = I_n$. Or, le déterminant de A étant différent de 0, la matrice A est régulière, et donc inversible. Ainsi,

$$A^2 = A \implies A^{-1}A^2 = A^{-1}A \implies A = I_n \quad \blacksquare$$

24. a) Vrai

b) Vrai

c) Faux

25. a) Une matrice diagonale est inversible seulement si sa diagonale principale ne compte aucun élément nul.

b) Si $A = \begin{bmatrix} a_{ij} \end{bmatrix}_{n \times n}$ est une matrice diagonale inversible, alors A^{-1} est la matrice diagonale dont la diagonale principale est formée des éléments $1/a_{ii}$.

26. Si $AB = O_{n \times n}$ et qu'une des deux matrices, A par exemple, est régulière, et donc inversible, alors

$$AB = O_{n \times n} \implies A^{-1}AB = A^{-1}O_{n \times n} \implies B = O_{n \times n}$$

Cela contredit l'hypothèse selon laquelle aucun des facteurs n'est la matrice nulle.

27. Soit A et B deux matrices carrées de même ordre. Si B est inversible, alors det $(B^{-1}AB) = \det A$.

Preuve

En vertu de la propriété 11 (th. 3.1) et de la propriété 7 (th. 3.4),

$$\det (B^{-1}AB) = \det (B^{-1}) \times \det A \times \det B$$
$$= \frac{1}{\det B} \times \det A \times \det B$$
$$= \det A \quad \blacksquare$$

28. $\begin{bmatrix} 1 & 4 & 1 \\ 12 & 24 & 9 \\ 10 & 16 & 8 \end{bmatrix}$

29. a) L'inverse de la matrice identité est la matrice identité, c'est-à-dire $I_n^{-1} = I_n$, et il en est de même pour la transposée : $I_n^t = I_n$. Par conséquent, la transposée de la matrice identité est égale à l'inverse de cette matrice, et ainsi la matrice identité est orthogonale.

b) $A^{-1} = \dfrac{1}{\det A} \text{ adj } A$

$\quad = \dfrac{1}{\sin^2\theta + \cos^2\theta} \begin{bmatrix} \sin\theta & -\cos\theta \\ \cos\theta & \sin\theta \end{bmatrix}$

$\quad = \dfrac{1}{1} \begin{bmatrix} \sin\theta & -\cos\theta \\ \cos\theta & \sin\theta \end{bmatrix}$

$\quad = A^t$

c) Le déterminant d'une matrice orthogonale vaut 1 ou -1.

Preuve

Si A est une matrice orthogonale, alors $A^{-1} = A^t$ et $\det A^t = \det (A^{-1})$. Or, en vertu des propriétés 4 (th. 3.1) et 7 (th. 3.4), on a $\det A^t = \det A$ et $\det (A^{-1}) = \dfrac{1}{\det A}$. On a donc

$$\det A = \dfrac{1}{\det A} \quad \Rightarrow \quad (\det A)^2 = 1$$

Par conséquent, $\det A = 1$ ou $\det A = -1$ ∎

30. a) Si A et B sont des matrices non singulières telles que $AB = BA$, alors $AB^{-1} = B^{-1}A$.

Preuve

$$AB = BA \quad \Rightarrow \quad B^{-1}ABB^{-1} = B^{-1}BAB^{-1}$$
$$\Rightarrow \quad B^{-1}A = AB^{-1} \quad ∎$$

b) Si A et B sont des matrices non singulières telles que $AB = BA$, alors $A^{-1}B^{-1} = B^{-1}A^{-1}$.

Preuve

$$AB = BA \quad \Rightarrow \quad (AB)^{-1} = (BA)^{-1}$$
$$\Rightarrow \quad B^{-1}A^{-1} = A^{-1}B^{-1} \quad ∎$$

c) Si A et B sont des matrices non singulières telles que $AB = BA$, alors $A^tB^t = B^tA^t$.

Preuve

$$AB = BA \quad \Rightarrow \quad (AB)^t = (BA)^t$$
$$\Rightarrow \quad B^tA^t = A^tB^t \quad ∎$$

31. a) B

b) AB

c) $B = A^{-1}AB$

d) $AB = \begin{bmatrix} 4 & 14 \\ 10 & 17 \\ 1 & -14 \end{bmatrix}$

e) Je t'aime.

f) Une matrice de codage doit être inversible, sinon il est impossible de décoder le message.

g) La matrice C n'est pas inversible.

32. a) $a = 2$, $b = 0$ et $c = 1$

b) On ne peut pas résoudre le système d'équations par la méthode de la matrice inverse.

c) $x = 5$, $y = -3$ et $z = \frac{1}{2}$

d) On ne peut pas résoudre le système d'équations par la méthode de la matrice inverse.

CHAPITRE 4

1. a) $x = {}^{17}\!/_{16}$ $\quad y = -{}^{3}\!/_{16}$

b) $x = -4$ $\quad y = 4$

c) Le système d'équations n'admet aucune solution.

d) $x = -{}^{17}\!/_{29}$ $\quad y = {}^{52}\!/_{29}$ $\quad z = -{}^{1}\!/_{29}$

e) Le système d'équations admet une infinité de solutions.

f) Le système d'équations n'admet aucune solution.

g) $x = \pm\sqrt{2}$ $\quad y = \pm\sqrt{3}$

h) $x = \frac{1}{2}$ $\quad y = -1$ $\quad z = 1$

2. a) *Premier cas*: $k \neq 2$ et $k \neq -6$: $x = 0$ $\quad y = 0$

Deuxième cas: $k = 2$ ou $k = -6$: le système d'équations admet une infinité de solutions pour chacune de ces deux valeurs de k.

b) *Premier cas*: $k \neq 0$: $x = \dfrac{k+1}{k^2}$ $\quad y = \dfrac{2k+1}{k^2}$

Deuxième cas: $k = 0$: le système d'équations n'admet aucune solution.

c) *Premier cas*: $k \neq 6$ et $k \neq -6$: $x = \dfrac{k}{k+6}$

$y = \dfrac{-k-2}{k+6}$

Deuxième cas: $k = -6$: le système d'équations n'admet aucune solution.

Troisième cas: $k = 6$: le système d'équations admet une infinité de solutions.

d) *Premier cas*: $k \neq 1$: $x = \dfrac{2k}{1-k}$ $\quad y = \dfrac{k-3k^2}{1-k}$

Deuxième cas: $k = 1$: le système d'équations n'admet aucune solution.

e) *Premier cas*: $k \neq 1$ et $k \neq -1$: $x = k$ $\quad y = 1$

Deuxième cas: $k = 1$: le système d'équations admet une infinité de solutions.

Troisième cas: $k = -1$: le système d'équations admet une infinité de solutions.

3. $i_1 = -3$ $\quad i_2 = 6$ $\quad i_3 = 9$

4. a)

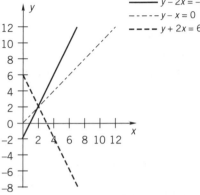

Les droites ne sont pas nécessairement distinctes comme l'indique le graphique suivant.

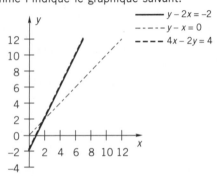

b)

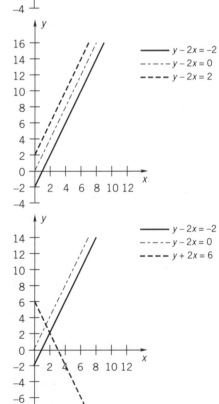

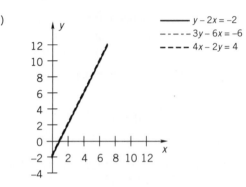

c)

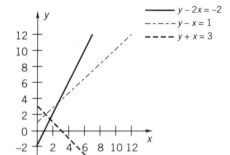

5. Le système formé des trois équations tirées du triangle est

$$b\cos\alpha + a\cos\beta \qquad = c$$
$$c\cos\beta + b\cos\gamma = a$$
$$c\cos\alpha \qquad + a\cos\gamma = b$$

où les inconnues sont $\cos\alpha$, $\cos\beta$ et $\cos\gamma$.

$$\Delta = \begin{vmatrix} b & a & 0 \\ 0 & c & b \\ c & 0 & a \end{vmatrix} = 2abc \quad \text{et}$$

$$\Delta_{\cos\gamma} = \begin{vmatrix} b & a & c \\ 0 & c & a \\ c & 0 & b \end{vmatrix} = c(a^2 + b^2 - c^2), \text{ d'où}$$

$$\cos\gamma = \frac{\Delta_{\cos\gamma}}{\Delta} = \frac{c(a^2 + b^2 - c^2)}{2abc} = \frac{a^2 + b^2 - c^2}{2ab}$$

6. $\det A_{n \times n} = \sum_{\substack{\text{Ensemble des} \\ \text{permutations} \\ \text{des } n \text{ premiers} \\ \text{entiers positifs}}} (-1)^r a_{i_1 1} a_{i_2 2} a_{i_3 3} \cdots a_{i_n n}$ où

r = nombre de « dérangements » observés dans la permutation i_1, i_2, i_3, ..., i_n des n premiers entiers.

7. a) $a \neq -2$

b) $a = -2$ et $b \neq 4$

c) $a = -2$ et $b = 4$

8. a) $S = \left\{ \begin{bmatrix} 4/3 & 0 \end{bmatrix}^t \right\}$ ou $x = 4/3$ et $y = 0$

b) $S = \left\{ \begin{bmatrix} \dfrac{5k-1}{2} & \dfrac{7-5k}{4} & k \end{bmatrix}^t \,\middle|\, k \in \mathbb{R} \right\}$

c) $S = \left\{ \begin{bmatrix} \dfrac{4-6k}{3} & k & 0 \end{bmatrix}^t \,\middle|\, k \in \mathbb{R} \right\}$

d) Le système d'équations n'admet aucune solution.

e) $S = \left\{ \begin{bmatrix} 2 & 0 & 1 \end{bmatrix}^t \right\}$ ou $a = 2$, $b = 0$ et $c = 1$

f) Le système d'équations n'admet aucune solution.

g) $S = \left\{ \begin{bmatrix} 3/2 & -2 & 1 & 7/2 \end{bmatrix}^t \right\}$ ou $x_1 = 3/2$, $x_2 = -2$, $x_3 = 1$ et $x_4 = 7/2$

h) $S = \left\{ \begin{bmatrix} -1 & 1 & -1 & 1 \end{bmatrix}^t \right\}$ ou $x_1 = -1$, $x_2 = 1$, $x_3 = -1$ et $x_4 = 1$

9. Les ensembles solution présentés en *a*, *c* et *d*

10. a) $S = \left\{ \begin{bmatrix} \dfrac{8-3k}{5} & \dfrac{8-3k}{5} & \dfrac{4+k}{5} & k \end{bmatrix}^t \,\middle|\, k \in \mathbb{R} \right\}$

b) Oui

c) Non

d) $x = -2$, $y = -2$ et $z = 2$

11. a) $A = 1/2$ et $B = -1/2$

b) $A = 1/6$, $B = -3/10$ et $C = 2/15$

c) $A = -3/4$, $B = 3/4$ et $C = 1/2$

d) $A = 2$, $B = -1$ et $C = -3$

12. a) $x_i = 0$ pour $i = 1, 2, 3, \ldots, n$

b) Oui. Si le déterminant de la matrice des coefficients du système d'équations vaut zéro, alors celui-ci admet une infinité de solutions.

c) Si $K = \begin{bmatrix} k_1 & k_2 & \cdots & k_n \end{bmatrix}^t$ et $J = \begin{bmatrix} j_1 & j_2 & \cdots & j_n \end{bmatrix}^t$ sont des solutions distinctes du système $AX = O_{n \times 1}$, alors $K + J$ est aussi une solution de ce système.

Preuve

Comme K et J sont des solutions du système $AX = O_{n \times 1}$, alors $AK = O_{n \times 1}$ et $AJ = O_{n \times 1}$. Par conséquent,

$$A(K + J) = AK + AJ = O_{n \times 1} + O_{n \times 1} = O_{n \times 1}$$

c'est-à-dire que $K + J$ est une solution du système $AX = O_{n \times 1}$. ■

d) Si $K = \begin{bmatrix} k_1 & k_2 & k_3 & \cdots & k_n \end{bmatrix}^t$ est une solution du système $AX = O_{n \times 1}$ et si c est une constante, alors cK est aussi une solution de ce système.

Preuve

Comme K est une solution du système $AX = O_{n \times 1}$, alors $AK = O_{n \times 1}$. Par conséquent,

$$A(cK) = c(AK) = cO_{n \times 1} = O_{n \times 1}$$

c'est-à-dire que cK est une solution du système $AX = O_{n \times 1}$. ■

e) Tout système d'équations homogène qui possède plus d'une solution en admet une infinité.

Preuve

Si $K = \begin{bmatrix} k_1 & k_2 & k_3 & \cdots & k_n \end{bmatrix}^t$ est une solution du système $AX = O_{n \times 1}$ différente de la solution $K = O_{n \times 1}$ et si c est une constante, alors cK est aussi une solution de ce système. Or, il existe une infinité de constantes c, qui donnent chacune une solution différente. Par conséquent, si le système d'équations possède plus d'une solution, alors il en admet une infinité. ■

13. Soit X_1 et X_2 deux solutions distinctes du système d'équations linéaires $AX = B$ à m équations et n inconnues.

a) $X_1 - X_2$ est une solution de $AX = O_{m \times 1}$.

Preuve

Si $X = X_1 - X_2$, alors

$AX = A(X_1 - X_2) = AX_1 - AX_2 = B - B = O_{m \times 1}$

Donc, $X_1 - X_2$ est une solution de $AX = O_{m \times 1}$. ■

b) $X_1 + k(X_1 - X_2)$ est une solution de $AX = B$.

Preuve

Si $X = X_1 + k(X_1 - X_2)$, alors

$$\begin{aligned} AX &= A(X_1 + k(X_1 - X_2)) \\ &= AX_1 + kA(X_1 - X_2) \\ &= B + kO_{m \times 1} \\ &= B \end{aligned}$$

Donc, $X_1 + k(X_1 - X_2)$ est une solution de $AX = B$. ■

c) Un système d'équations linéaires qui possède plus d'une solution en admet une infinité.

Preuve

En vertu de l'énoncé démontré en *b*, si un système admet deux solutions distinctes X_1 et X_2, alors $X_1 + k(X_1 - X_2)$ est aussi une solution de ce système. Or, on peut montrer (en raisonnant par l'absurde) que, pour deux valeurs k_1 et k_2 distinctes, $X_1 + k(X_1 - X_2)$ et $X_1 + k_2(X_1 - X_2)$ sont aussi des solutions distinctes du système d'équations. Ce système admet donc au moins autant de solutions qu'il y a de valeurs distinctes de k, soit une infinité. ■

14. a) 0

b) 2

c) 1

15. a) 3

b) 1

c) Oui

d) Oui

e) Non

f) Si $r = {}^k/_2$, alors $2r = k$ et $2r + 5 = k + 5$. Par conséquent,

$$S' = \left\{ \begin{bmatrix} {}^k/_2 & k & k + 5 \end{bmatrix}^t \mid k \in \mathbb{R} \right\}$$

représente également l'ensemble solution du système.

g) Si $r = \dfrac{m - 5}{2}$, alors $2r = m - 5 \neq m + 5$. Par conséquent,

$$S'' = \left\{ \begin{bmatrix} \dfrac{m - 5}{2} & m + 5 & m \end{bmatrix}^t \middle| m \in \mathbb{R} \right\}$$

ne représente pas l'ensemble solution du système.

16. NATURE DES SOLUTIONS D'UN SYSTÈME D'ÉQUATIONS LINÉAIRES $AX = B$

Matrice A	Type de système	Nature des solutions, selon la matrice B	
		$B \neq O_{n \times 1}$	$B = O_{n \times 1}$
$|A| \neq 0$ La matrice A est **12**. Le rang de A est **8**. Le rang de $[A \mid B]$ est **8**.	Le système d'équations est **6**.	1	2
$|A| = 0$ La matrice A n'est pas **12**. Le rang de $[A \mid B]$ est **10**.	Le système d'équations est compatible.	4	3
$|A| = 0$ La matrice A est **11**. Le rang de $[A \mid B]$ est plus grand que celui de A.	Le système d'équations est **7**.	5	Ne s'applique pas.

17. a) $A^{-1} = \begin{bmatrix} 0{,}4 & -0{,}2 \\ 0{,}1 & 0{,}2 \end{bmatrix}$

b) $B^{-1} = \begin{bmatrix} 2 & 1 \\ -3 & -1 \end{bmatrix}$

c) La matrice C n'est pas régulière : elle n'admet pas d'inverse.

d) $D^{-1} = \begin{bmatrix} 0 & -1 & 0 \\ 1 & 2 & 1 \\ 0 & 1 & 1 \end{bmatrix}$

18. a) La quantité offerte de porc augmente.

b) La quantité demandée de porc diminue.

c) La quantité demandée de porc augmente. Le porc et le bœuf sont des substituts l'un de l'autre.

d) $P_b = 3$, $P_p = 4$, $Q_p = 100$ et $Q_b = 200$

e) La quantité offerte de chemises augmente.

f) La quantité demandée de chemises diminue.

g) La quantité demandée de chemises diminue. Les chemises et les cravates sont des biens complémentaires.

h) $P_c = 60$, $P_r = 30$, $Q_c = 120$ et $Q_r = 60$

19. Le mélange doit être composé de ${}^{30}/_7$ litres de lait et de ${}^5/_7$ litre de crème.

20. Le mélange doit être formé de ${}^2/_3$ litre de la solution A et de ${}^1/_3$ litre de la solution B.

21. L'usine doit produire 1 000 unités du modèle A, 800 unités du modèle B et 600 unités du modèle C.

22. Le propriétaire du chenil possède 5 dalmatiens, 10 labradors et 15 bergers anglais.

23. L'entrepreneur a construit 25 maisons comptant une seule salle de bain, 50 maisons en comptant deux et 25 maisons en comptant trois.

24. a) La température est de 10 °C au point x_1, de 8,75 °C au point x_2 et de 11,25 °C au point x_3.

b) La température est de 11,5 °C au point x_1, de 11,5 °C au point x_2, de 6,5 °C au point x_3 et de 6,5 °C au point x_4.

25. L'individu a investi 3 000 $ dans le premier fonds et 2 000 $ dans le deuxième fonds.

26. Le revenu que le club de golf tire des cotisations est de 310 000 $.

27. Le club de golf a vendu 50 cartes donnant accès au terrain dès l'avant-midi, 25 cartes donnant accès au terrain à partir de midi et 20 cartes donnant accès au terrain à compter de 15 heures.

28. a) Il est impossible de déterminer le nombre d'actions de chaque compagnie dans le portefeuille.

b) Le portefeuille est composé de 60 actions de la première compagnie, de 40 actions de la deuxième compagnie et de 80 actions de la troisième compagnie.

c) Il est impossible que le portefeuille comprenne 200 actions de la deuxième compagnie.

29. ${}^1/_3$ kg

30. a) On représente les différentes inconnues comme suit : x = nombre de portions de 100 g de pommes de terre, y = nombre de portions de 100 g de maïs et z = nombre de portions de 100 g de bœuf haché. La solution générale de ce problème est $S = \left\{ \begin{bmatrix} 2 + 3k & 4 - 4k & k \end{bmatrix}^t \mid 0 \leq k \leq 1 \right\}$.

b) Le « pâté chinois » végétarien contient 200 g de pommes de terre (soit 2 portions de 100 g) et 400 g de maïs (soit 4 portions de 100 g).

c) Il est impossible de confectionner un « pâté chinois » ne contenant pas de pommes de terre tout en respectant les contraintes relatives à la quantité de protéines et au nombre de calories.

d) Le « pâté chinois » sans maïs contient 500 g de pommes de terre (soit 5 portions de 100 grammes) et 100 g de bœuf haché.

e) Le « pâté chinois » à 2,20 $ contient 350 g de pommes de terre (soit 3,5 portions de 100 g), 200 g de maïs (soit 2 portions de 100 g) et 50 g de bœuf haché (soit $\frac{1}{2}$ portion de 100 g).

f) Il est impossible de préparer un « pâté chinois » qui coûte 1,50 $ en respectant les contraintes relatives au nombre de calories et à la quantité de protéines.

g) 1,60 $

31. a) Oui

b) Le programme se compose d'une demi-heure de marche rapide, d'une heure de natation et d'une demi-heure de vélo d'appartement.

c) Un tel programme est impossible.

32. a) $x = 0,9$ N et $y = 0,6$ N

b) $x = 1$ cm et $y = 0,2$ N

33. a) $3\,NO_2 + H_2O \rightarrow 2\,HNO_3 + NO$

b) $Cu_2S + O_2 \rightarrow 2\,Cu + SO_2$

c) $Fe_2O_3 + 6\,HCl \rightarrow 2\,FeCl_3 + 3\,H_2O$

34. a) L'équation doit être satisfaite puisque les trois revendeurs détiennent la totalité du marché ; la somme de leurs parts du marché doit être égale à 100 % ou 1.

b)
$$\begin{aligned}
p_1 &= 0,8p_1 + 0,2p_2 + 0,05p_3 \\
p_2 &= 0,1p_1 + 0,75p_2 + 0,05p_3 \\
p_3 &= 0,1p_1 + 0,05p_2 + 0,9p_3 \\
p_1 &+ p_2 + p_3 = 1
\end{aligned}$$

ou, sous la forme habituelle,

$$\begin{aligned}
0,2p_1 &- 0,2p_2 - 0,05p_3 = 0 \\
-0,1p_1 &+ 0,25p_2 - 0,05p_3 = 0 \\
-0,1p_1 &- 0,05p_2 + 0,1p_3 = 0 \\
p_1 &+ p_2 + p_3 = 1
\end{aligned}$$

c) La part du marché détenue par les revendeurs 1, 2 et 3 à l'état d'équilibre est respectivement de $\frac{1}{3}$, $\frac{2}{9}$ et $\frac{4}{9}$.

d) La part du marché de chaque revendeur à l'état d'équilibre n'est pas fonction de la part du marché que chacun d'entre eux détenait initialement.

e) Chaque mois, la nouvelle compagnie 2 perd 10 % de ses clients au profit de la compagnie 1, et la compagnie 1 conserve 80 % de ses clients.

f) La part du marché détenue par les compagnies 1 et 2 à l'état d'équilibre est respectivement de $\frac{1}{3}$ et de $\frac{2}{3}$.

35. a)
$$\begin{aligned}
Y - C &= I_0 + G_0 \\
bY - C &= -a
\end{aligned}$$

b) $Y = \dfrac{I_0 + G_0 + a}{1 - b} \quad C = \dfrac{a + b(I_0 + G_0)}{1 - b}$

c) $Y = 1\,750 \quad C = 1\,450$

d) Le produit intérieur brut double.

36. a)
$$\begin{aligned}
Y - C &= I_0 + G_0 \\
bY - C - bT &= -a \\
tY - T &= -d
\end{aligned}$$

b) $Y = \dfrac{I_0 + G_0 + a - bd}{1 - b(1 - t)}$

$C = \dfrac{a - bd + b(I_0 + G_0)(1 - t)}{1 - b(1 - t)}$

$T = \dfrac{t(a + I_0 + G_0) + d(1 - b)}{1 - b(1 - t)}$

37. a) Vrai   g) Faux

b) Faux   h) Vrai

c) Faux   i) Vrai

d) Faux   j) Faux

e) Faux   k) Faux

f) Faux   l) Faux

38. Un système d'équations qui comporte des paramètres ou qui compte un même nombre, peu élevé, d'équations et d'inconnues.

39. Un système d'équations qui comporte un nombre différent d'équations et d'inconnues ; un système qui

comporte un grand nombre d'équations et d'inconnues; un système d'équations qui admet une infinité
de solutions.

CHAPITRE 5

1.

Vecteur	Norme	Direction
$\vec{u}$	3,4 cm	65°
$\vec{v}$	1,5 cm	160°
$\vec{w}$	2,5 cm	270°
$\vec{t}$	2,6 cm	320°

2.

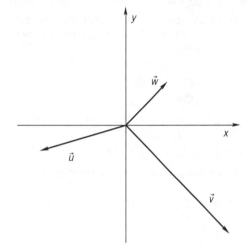

3. a)

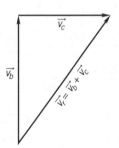

b) $\|\vec{v_r}\| = 10$ kn

4. a) Les vecteurs $\vec{x}$ et $\vec{v}$ sont égaux.

b) Les vecteurs $\vec{r}$ et $\vec{s}$ sont opposés.

c)

d)

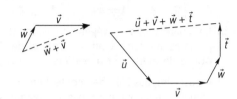

e) $\vec{y} = 2\vec{w}$

f) $\vec{z} = \vec{w} + 2\vec{r}$

g)

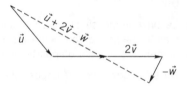

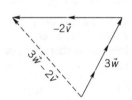

h)

$\vec{w} + \vec{v} = \vec{v} + \vec{w}$

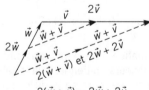

$2(\vec{w} + \vec{v}) = 2\vec{w} + 2\vec{v}$

5.

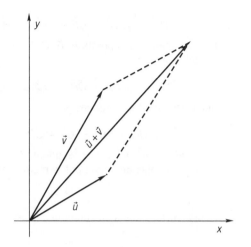

$\|\vec{u} + \vec{v}\| \approx 7{,}7$ et la direction du vecteur $\vec{u} + \vec{v}$ est d'environ $48{,}8°$.

6. La direction du vecteur $-\vec{u}$ est contraire à celle de $\vec{u}$, mais les deux vecteurs ont la même longueur.

7. $\|4\vec{u}\| = 4\|\vec{u}\| = 20$ et $\|-6\vec{u}\| = |-6|\,\|\vec{u}\| = 30$

8. $\overrightarrow{AD} - \overrightarrow{BC} = \vec{0}$

$\overrightarrow{AB} + \overrightarrow{AD} + \overrightarrow{CB} = \overrightarrow{AB}$

$\overrightarrow{AD} + \overrightarrow{DC} - \overrightarrow{AB} = \overrightarrow{BC}$

9. a) $\vec{0}$

b) $2\,\overrightarrow{BA}$

10. a) $\overrightarrow{u_8}$

b) $\overrightarrow{u_3}$

c) $2\,\overrightarrow{u_4}$ (ou $-2\,\overrightarrow{u_8}$ ou $\overrightarrow{DB}$)

d) $\overrightarrow{u_2}$

e) $2\,\overrightarrow{u_7}$

f) $-\overrightarrow{u_8}$ ou $\overrightarrow{u_4}$

11. $\left\|\dfrac{k}{\|\vec{u}\|}\vec{u}\right\| = \left|\dfrac{k}{\|\vec{u}\|}\right|\|\vec{u}\| = \dfrac{|k|}{\|\vec{u}\|}\|\vec{u}\| = |k|$. Le vecteur

$\dfrac{-5}{\|\vec{u}\|}\vec{u}$ est un vecteur de longueur 5 et sa direction est contraire à celle de $\vec{u}$.

12. a) $\overrightarrow{AE} = \frac{1}{2}\overrightarrow{AB} + \overrightarrow{BC}$

b) $\overrightarrow{AF} = \overrightarrow{BC} + x\overrightarrow{AB}$

13.

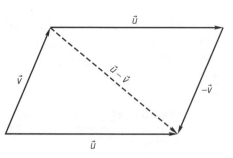

14. Si A, B et C sont trois points non colinéaires, alors $\dfrac{1}{\|\overrightarrow{AB}\|}\overrightarrow{AB} + \dfrac{1}{\|\overrightarrow{AC}\|}\overrightarrow{AC}$ divise l'angle de sommet A en deux angles égaux.

Preuve

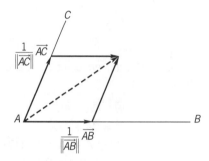

Les vecteurs $\dfrac{1}{\|\overrightarrow{AB}\|}\overrightarrow{AB}$ et $\dfrac{1}{\|\overrightarrow{AC}\|}\overrightarrow{AC}$ sont des vecteurs

unitaires et ils correspondent aux côtés d'un losange.

Le vecteur $\dfrac{1}{\|\overrightarrow{AB}\|}\overrightarrow{AB} + \dfrac{1}{\|\overrightarrow{AC}\|}\overrightarrow{AC}$ correspond à la dia-

gonale de ce losange qui est issue du point A; il est donc porté par la bissectrice de l'angle A. Ainsi, comme la bissectrice, ce vecteur partage l'angle A en deux angles égaux. ∎

15. ABC et CBA

16. Le barycentre P d'un ensemble de n points du plan, P_1, P_2, …, P_n, vérifie l'équation vectorielle $\overrightarrow{OP} = \frac{1}{n}(\overrightarrow{OP_1} + \overrightarrow{OP_2} + \cdots + \overrightarrow{OP_n})$ où O est un point auxiliaire.

Preuve

Si P est le barycentre des points P_1, P_2, …, P_n, alors $\overrightarrow{PP_1} + \overrightarrow{PP_2} + \cdots + \overrightarrow{PP_n} = \vec{0}$. De cette équation, on déduit que

$$\overrightarrow{PO} + \overrightarrow{OP_1} + \overrightarrow{PO} + \overrightarrow{OP_2} + \cdots + \overrightarrow{PO} + \overrightarrow{OP_n} = \vec{0}$$
$$n\overrightarrow{PO} + \overrightarrow{OP_1} + \overrightarrow{OP_2} + \cdots + \overrightarrow{OP_n} = \vec{0}$$
$$n\overrightarrow{OP} = \overrightarrow{OP_1} + \overrightarrow{OP_2} + \cdots + \overrightarrow{OP_n}$$
$$\overrightarrow{OP} = \tfrac{1}{n}(\overrightarrow{OP_1} + \overrightarrow{OP_2} + \cdots + \overrightarrow{OP_n}) \qquad ∎$$

17. a) Le quadrilatère *EFGH* dont les sommets sont les milieux d'un quadrilatère distinct *ABCD* est un parallélogramme.

Preuve

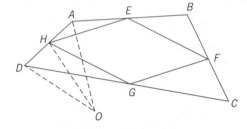

Le point *O* étant un point auxiliaire quelconque, on a

$$\overrightarrow{OH} = \overrightarrow{OA} + \overrightarrow{AH}$$
$$= \overrightarrow{OA} + \tfrac{1}{2}\overrightarrow{AD}$$
$$= \overrightarrow{OA} + \tfrac{1}{2}(\overrightarrow{AO} + \overrightarrow{OD})$$
$$= \tfrac{1}{2}(\overrightarrow{OA} + \overrightarrow{OD})$$

Par un argument similaire, on obtient

$$\overrightarrow{OE} = \tfrac{1}{2}(\overrightarrow{OA} + \overrightarrow{OB})$$
$$\overrightarrow{OF} = \tfrac{1}{2}(\overrightarrow{OB} + \overrightarrow{OC})$$
$$\overrightarrow{OG} = \tfrac{1}{2}(\overrightarrow{OC} + \overrightarrow{OD})$$

De ces différentes égalités, on déduit, d'une part, que

$$\overrightarrow{EF} = -\overrightarrow{OE} + \overrightarrow{OF} = \tfrac{1}{2}(\overrightarrow{OC} - \overrightarrow{OA})$$

et, d'autre part, que

$$\overrightarrow{HG} = -\overrightarrow{OH} + \overrightarrow{OG} = \tfrac{1}{2}(\overrightarrow{OC} - \overrightarrow{OA})$$

de sorte que $\overrightarrow{EF} = \overrightarrow{HG}$. On montre de façon analogue que $\overrightarrow{EH} = \overrightarrow{FG}$. Le quadrilatère *EFGH* a donc des côtés opposés parallèles et de même longueur. Par conséquent, *EFGH* est un parallélogramme. ∎

b) Le barycentre des milieux des côtés d'un quadrilatère est identique au barycentre des sommets de ce quadrilatère.

Preuve

Le barycentre des points *E*, *F*, *G* et *H* est le point P_1 tel que

$$\overrightarrow{OP_1} = \tfrac{1}{4}(\overrightarrow{OE} + \overrightarrow{OF} + \overrightarrow{OG} + \overrightarrow{OH})$$

et le barycentre des points *A*, *B*, *C* et *D* est le point P_2 tel que

$$\overrightarrow{OP_2} = \tfrac{1}{4}(\overrightarrow{OA} + \overrightarrow{OB} + \overrightarrow{OC} + \overrightarrow{OD})$$

Selon les égalités obtenues en *a*,

$$(\overrightarrow{OE} + \overrightarrow{OF} + \overrightarrow{OG} + \overrightarrow{OH}) = (\overrightarrow{OA} + \overrightarrow{OB} + \overrightarrow{OC} + \overrightarrow{OD})$$

d'où $\overrightarrow{OP_1} = \overrightarrow{OP_2}$ et, par conséquent, $P_1 = P_2$: les deux ensembles de points ont le même barycentre. ∎

18. a) L'angle inscrit dans un demi-cercle est un angle droit.

Preuve

Soit *ABC*, un angle inscrit dans un demi-cercle.

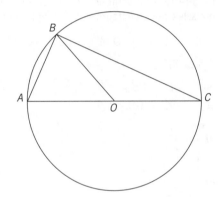

Il est à noter que la longueur des trois vecteurs $\overrightarrow{OA}$, $\overrightarrow{OB}$ et $\overrightarrow{OC}$ est égale au rayon du cercle.

Pour montrer que l'angle *ABC* est un angle droit, il faut montrer que les vecteurs $\overrightarrow{BA}$ et $\overrightarrow{BC}$ sont perpendiculaires ou encore, en vertu de la propriété 6 (th. 5.4), que $\overrightarrow{BA} \cdot \overrightarrow{BC} = 0$. Or,

$$\overrightarrow{BA} \cdot \overrightarrow{BC} = (\overrightarrow{BO} + \overrightarrow{OA}) \cdot (\overrightarrow{BO} + \overrightarrow{OC})$$
$$= (\overrightarrow{BO} + \overrightarrow{OA}) \cdot (\overrightarrow{BO} - \overrightarrow{OA})$$
$$= \overrightarrow{BO} \cdot \overrightarrow{BO} - \overrightarrow{BO} \cdot \overrightarrow{OA} + \overrightarrow{OA} \cdot \overrightarrow{BO} - \overrightarrow{OA} \cdot \overrightarrow{OA}$$
$$= \|\overrightarrow{BO}\|^2 - \|\overrightarrow{OA}\|^2$$
$$= 0$$

Un angle inscrit dans un demi-cercle est donc un angle droit. ∎

b) Les diagonales d'un losange se coupent à angle droit.

Preuve

Soit un losange *ABCD*.

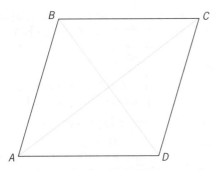

On sait que les quatre côtés d'un losange ont tous la même longueur. Il faut montrer que le produit scalaire des vecteurs correspondant aux diagonales est zéro, c'est-à-dire que $\overrightarrow{AC} \cdot \overrightarrow{BD} = 0$. Or,

$$\begin{aligned}
\overrightarrow{AC} \cdot \overrightarrow{BD} &= (\overrightarrow{AB} + \overrightarrow{BC}) \cdot (\overrightarrow{BC} + \overrightarrow{CD}) \\
&= (\overrightarrow{AB} + \overrightarrow{BC}) \cdot (\overrightarrow{BC} - \overrightarrow{AB}) \\
&= \overrightarrow{AB} \cdot \overrightarrow{BC} - \overrightarrow{AB} \cdot \overrightarrow{AB} + \overrightarrow{BC} \cdot \overrightarrow{BC} - \overrightarrow{BC} \cdot \overrightarrow{AB} \\
&= -\|\overrightarrow{AB}\|^2 + \|\overrightarrow{BC}\|^2 \\
&= 0
\end{aligned}$$

Ainsi, les vecteurs correspondant aux diagonales du losange sont perpendiculaires. Les diagonales d'un losange se coupent donc à angle droit. ∎

19. Trois vecteurs quelconques du plan sont linéairement dépendants.

Preuve

Soit $\vec{u}$, $\vec{v}$ et $\vec{w}$, trois vecteurs du plan. Il faut considérer trois cas.

Premier cas: L'un des trois vecteurs est le vecteur nul.

On peut supposer, sans perte de généralité, que $\vec{u}$ est le vecteur nul. Ainsi,

$$\vec{u} + 0\vec{v} + 0\vec{w} = \vec{0}$$

Il existe donc une combinaison linéaire des trois vecteurs égale au vecteur nul et telle qu'au moins un des coefficients est non nul. Par conséquent, les vecteurs $\vec{u}$, $\vec{v}$ et $\vec{w}$ sont linéairement dépendants.

Deuxième cas: Un des trois vecteurs est parallèle à un des deux autres.

On peut supposer, sans perte de généralité, que $\vec{u}$ est parallèle à $\vec{v}$ et qu'il existe un scalaire $k \neq 0$ tel que $\vec{u} = k\vec{v}$. Ainsi,

$$\vec{u} - k\vec{v} + 0\vec{w} = \vec{0}$$

Il existe donc une combinaison linéaire des trois vecteurs égale au vecteur nul et telle qu'au moins un des coefficients est non nul. Ainsi, les vecteurs $\vec{u}$, $\vec{v}$ et $\vec{w}$ sont linéairement dépendants.

Troisième cas: Les trois vecteurs sont non nuls et aucun n'est parallèle à un des deux autres.

En vertu du théorème 5.3, le vecteur $\vec{w}$ s'écrit comme une combinaison linéaire des deux autres vecteurs: $a\vec{u} + b\vec{v} = \vec{w}$. Ainsi, $a\vec{u} + b\vec{v} - \vec{w} = \vec{0}$. Il existe donc une combinaison linéaire des trois vecteurs égale au vecteur nul et telle qu'au moins un des coefficients est non nul. Par conséquent, les vecteurs $\vec{u}$, $\vec{v}$ et $\vec{w}$ sont linéairement dépendants. ∎

20. $\vec{u} = \vec{i} + 3\vec{j}$, $\vec{v} = -\vec{i} + \vec{j}$ et $\vec{w} = 2\vec{i} + 2,5\vec{j}$

21. $D(1, 0)$

22. a) $\overrightarrow{AB} = \begin{bmatrix} 1 & -2 \end{bmatrix}$; $\overrightarrow{CB} = \begin{bmatrix} 4 & -2 \end{bmatrix}$; $\overrightarrow{CD} = \begin{bmatrix} 3 & 3 \end{bmatrix}$; $\overrightarrow{ED} = \begin{bmatrix} -2 & 4 \end{bmatrix}$; $\overrightarrow{AE} = \begin{bmatrix} 2 & -1 \end{bmatrix}$; $\overrightarrow{AB} - \overrightarrow{CB} + \overrightarrow{CD} - \overrightarrow{ED} = \begin{bmatrix} 2 & -1 \end{bmatrix}$. Les deux dernières expressions sont égales parce que

$$\overrightarrow{AB} - \overrightarrow{CB} + \overrightarrow{CD} - \overrightarrow{ED} = \overrightarrow{AB} + \overrightarrow{BC} + \overrightarrow{CD} + \overrightarrow{DE} = \overrightarrow{AE}$$

b) $\|\overrightarrow{AB}\| = \sqrt{5}$; $\|\overrightarrow{CB}\| = 2\sqrt{5}$; $\|\overrightarrow{ED}\| = 2\sqrt{5}$

23. a)

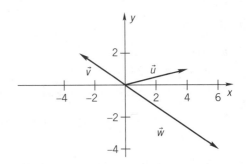

b) $\vec{u} + \vec{v} = \begin{bmatrix} 1 & 3 \end{bmatrix}$

c) $3\vec{u} + 2\vec{v} - 4\vec{w} = \begin{bmatrix} -18 & 23 \end{bmatrix}$

d) $5\vec{u} - 2\vec{v} - \vec{w} = \begin{bmatrix} 20 & 5 \end{bmatrix}$

e) $\|\vec{u} - \vec{v}\| = 5\sqrt{2}$

f) $\theta_{\vec{u}} = \text{arc tg}(\frac{1}{4}) \approx 14,0°$;
$\theta_{\vec{v}} = \text{arc tg}(-\frac{2}{3}) \approx 146,3°$;
$\theta_{\vec{w}} = \text{arc tg}(-\frac{4}{6}) \approx 326,3°$

g) Environ $132,3°$

h) $180°$. Les deux vecteurs $\vec{v}$ et $\vec{w}$ sont donc parallèles et de directions contraires.

24. $\sqrt{13}$ et $\sqrt{41}$.

25. Les composantes du vecteur $\vec{u} = \begin{bmatrix} u_1 & u_2 \end{bmatrix}$ sont $u_1 = 5 \cos 75° \approx 1,3$ et $u_2 = 5 \sin 75° \approx 4,8$.

26. Les composantes du vecteur unitaire $\vec{u} = \begin{bmatrix} u_1 & u_2 \end{bmatrix}$ sont $u_1 = \cos(7\pi/12)$ et $u_2 = \sin(7\pi/12)$.

27. a)

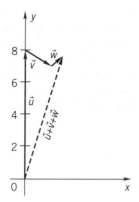

b) Si on représente les trois roulés par $\vec{u} = \begin{bmatrix} u_1 & u_2 \end{bmatrix}$, $\vec{v} = \begin{bmatrix} v_1 & v_2 \end{bmatrix}$ et $\vec{w} = \begin{bmatrix} w_1 & w_2 \end{bmatrix}$, alors $\vec{u} = \begin{bmatrix} 0 & 8 \end{bmatrix}$, $\vec{v} = \begin{bmatrix} \sqrt{2} & -\sqrt{2} \end{bmatrix}$ et $\vec{w} = \begin{bmatrix} \sqrt{2}/2 & \sqrt{2}/2 \end{bmatrix}$.

c) Le vecteur $\vec{u} + \vec{v} + \vec{w}$ représente le roulé que le golfeur aurait dû faire pour que la balle atteigne le trou en un coup.

d) La balle se trouvait initialement à environ 7,6 m du trou.

28. $\|\vec{F_2}\| = 5\sqrt{2}$ N

29. a) Non

b) $\vec{F_4} = \begin{bmatrix} -4 & -2 \end{bmatrix}$

c) $\vec{F_3} = \begin{bmatrix} -5 & -5(\sqrt{3}-1) \end{bmatrix}$, $\|\vec{F_3}\| \approx 6,2$ N et $\theta = 216,2°$

d) $\vec{F_3} = \begin{bmatrix} -\frac{13}{2} & 5-7(\sqrt{3}/2) \end{bmatrix}$, $\|\vec{F_3}\| \approx 6,6$ N et $\theta = 189,3°$

30. a) $\|\vec{T_1}\| = 50\sqrt{2}$ N et $\|\vec{T_2}\| = 50\sqrt{2}$ N

b) $\|\vec{T_2}\| = \dfrac{100}{1+\sqrt{3}}$ N $\approx 36,6$ N

$\|\vec{T_1}\| = \dfrac{50\sqrt{6}}{1+\sqrt{3}}$ N $\approx 44,8$ N

31. a) $\vec{D} = \begin{bmatrix} -2 & -4\sqrt{3} \end{bmatrix}$: l'axe électrique du cœur du sujet est droit.

b) $\vec{D} = \begin{bmatrix} 19 & -21\sqrt{3} \end{bmatrix}$: l'axe électrique du cœur du sujet est normal.

32. $\vec{u} \cdot \vec{u} \geq 0$

Preuve

$\vec{u} \cdot \vec{u} = \|\vec{u}\| \|\vec{u}\| \cos 0°$
(définition du produit scalaire ; l'angle entre $\vec{u}$ et $\vec{u}$ vaut 0°)

$= \|\vec{u}\|^2 \geq 0$
l'égalité étant vérifiée seulement si $\|\vec{u}\| = 0$, c'est-à-dire si $\vec{u} = \vec{0}$. ∎

33. Si $\vec{u}$ et $\vec{v}$ sont des vecteurs non nuls, alors ces deux vecteurs déterminent un angle aigu lorsque leur produit scalaire est positif.

Preuve

$\vec{u} \cdot \vec{v} = \|\vec{u}\| \|\vec{v}\| \cos \theta$ où θ est le plus petit angle ($0 \leq \theta \leq \pi$) déterminé par $\vec{u}$ et $\vec{v}$. Par conséquent,

$\vec{u} \cdot \vec{v} > 0 \Rightarrow \|\vec{u}\| \|\vec{v}\| \cos \theta > 0 \Rightarrow \cos \theta > 0$

parce que $\|\vec{u}\| > 0$ et $\|\vec{v}\| > 0$. Or, $\cos \theta > 0$ et $0 \leq \theta \leq \pi \Rightarrow 0 \leq \theta < \pi/2$. Par conséquent, les deux vecteurs déterminent un angle aigu. ∎

34. $\|\vec{u} + \vec{v}\| \leq \|\vec{u}\| + \|\vec{v}\|$

Preuve

Comme $\|\vec{u} + \vec{v}\| \geq 0$, $\|\vec{u}\| \geq 0$ et $\|\vec{v}\| \geq 0$, il faut montrer que $\|\vec{u} + \vec{v}\|^2 \leq (\|\vec{u}\| + \|\vec{v}\|)^2$. Or,

$$\|\vec{u} + \vec{v}\|^2 = (\vec{u} + \vec{v}) \cdot (\vec{u} + \vec{v})$$
$$= \vec{u} \cdot \vec{u} + \vec{u} \cdot \vec{v} + \vec{v} \cdot \vec{u} + \vec{v} \cdot \vec{v}$$
$$= \vec{u} \cdot \vec{u} + \vec{u} \cdot \vec{v} + \vec{u} \cdot \vec{v} + \vec{v} \cdot \vec{v}$$
$$= \|\vec{u}\|^2 + 2\|\vec{u}\| \|\vec{v}\| \cos \theta + \|\vec{v}\|^2$$

De plus, $\cos \theta \leq 1$. Par conséquent,

$\|\vec{u} + \vec{v}\|^2 \leq \|\vec{u}\|^2 + 2\|\vec{u}\| \|\vec{v}\| + \|\vec{v}\|^2 = (\|\vec{u}\| + \|\vec{v}\|)^2$

Donc, $\|\vec{u} + \vec{v}\| \leq \|\vec{u}\| + \|\vec{v}\|$ ∎

35. Le travail est égal à 3 000 cos 30° ≈ 2 598 N · m.

36. Si $\vec{u}$ et $\vec{v}$ sont des vecteurs non nuls, alors $|\vec{u} \cdot \vec{v}| = \|\vec{u}\| \|\vec{v}\|$ si et seulement si $\vec{u}$ et $\vec{v}$ sont parallèles.

Preuve

Les vecteurs $\vec{u}$ et $\vec{v}$ étant non nuls, on a $\|\vec{u}\| \neq 0$ et $\|\vec{v}\| \neq 0$. De plus,

$|\vec{u} \cdot \vec{v}| = |\|\vec{u}\| \|\vec{v}\| \cos \theta| = \|\vec{u}\| \|\vec{v}\| |\cos \theta|$

où θ est le plus petit angle ($0 \leq \theta \leq \pi$) déterminé par $\vec{u}$ et $\vec{v}$. Par conséquent,

$|\vec{u} \cdot \vec{v}| = \|\vec{u}\| \|\vec{v}\| \Leftrightarrow |\cos \theta| = 1 \Leftrightarrow \theta = 0$ ou $\theta = \pi$

c'est-à-dire si et seulement si les vecteurs $\vec{u}$ et $\vec{v}$ sont parallèles. ∎

37. a) $\vec{u} = \begin{bmatrix} 3\sqrt{3}/2 & \frac{3}{2} \end{bmatrix}$ et $\vec{v} = \begin{bmatrix} \frac{5}{2} & 5\sqrt{3}/2 \end{bmatrix}$

b) $\vec{u} + \vec{v} = \begin{bmatrix} (3\sqrt{3}+5)/2 & (3+5\sqrt{3})/2 \end{bmatrix}$

c) $\|\vec{u} + \vec{v}\| \approx 7,7$ et $\theta_{\vec{u}+\vec{v}} \approx 48,8°$. Ces résultats sont identiques aux solutions du no 5.

38. a) Les vecteurs $\vec{u}$ et $\vec{v}$ sont perpendiculaires parce que $\vec{u} \cdot \vec{v} = 0$.

b) $\vec{r} = \frac{17}{13}\vec{u} - \frac{3}{13}\vec{v}$

c) $\vec{s} = \dfrac{4a+6b}{26}\vec{u} + \dfrac{2b-3a}{26}\vec{v}$

d) Les vecteurs $\vec{u}$ et $\vec{v}$ forment une base orthogonale (mais pas orthonormée) de $\mathbb{R}^2$.

e) Les vecteurs $\vec{w}$ et $\vec{t} = \begin{bmatrix} -\dfrac{1}{2} & -\dfrac{\sqrt{3}}{2} \end{bmatrix}$ (ou $-\vec{t} = \begin{bmatrix} \dfrac{1}{2} & \dfrac{\sqrt{3}}{2} \end{bmatrix}$) forment une base orthonormée de $\mathbb{R}^2$.

39. L'angle ayant son sommet en B est un angle droit. L'angle ayant son sommet en A vaut donc 45°, et il en est de même pour l'angle ayant son sommet en C.

40. a) $a = 6$ ou $a = -6$
b) $a = 0$

41. Les expressions données en b, d, f, g et i n'ont pas de sens.

42. a) Faux   h) Faux
b) Faux   i) Vrai
c) Vrai   j) Faux
d) Faux   k) Faux
e) Vrai   l) Faux
f) Faux   m) Faux
g) Vrai

43. a)

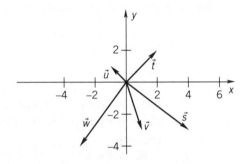

b) $\|\vec{s}\| = 5$, $\|\vec{t}\| = 2\sqrt{2}$, $\|\vec{u}\| = \sqrt{2}$, $\|\vec{v}\| = \sqrt{10}$ et $\|\vec{w}\| = 5$

c) $\theta_{\vec{s}} \approx 323{,}1°$, $\theta_{\vec{t}} = 45°$, $\theta_{\vec{u}} = 135°$, $\theta_{\vec{v}} \approx 288{,}4°$ et $\theta_{\vec{w}} \approx 233{,}1°$

d) $\vec{a} = \vec{s} + \vec{t} = \begin{bmatrix} 6 & -1 \end{bmatrix}$. On aurait également pu choisir $\vec{a} = \vec{s} - \vec{t}$ ou encore $\vec{a} = \vec{t} - \vec{s}$.

e) $\vec{u} + 3\vec{s} = \begin{bmatrix} 11 & -8 \end{bmatrix}$, $-3\vec{u} + 2\vec{w} + \vec{t} = \begin{bmatrix} -1 & -9 \end{bmatrix}$ et $5\vec{s} + 3\vec{t} - 2\vec{u} = \begin{bmatrix} 28 & -11 \end{bmatrix}$

f) $\vec{u} \cdot \vec{v} = -4$, $\vec{s} \cdot \vec{t} = 2$, $\vec{u} \cdot 3\vec{s} = -21$
$2\vec{u} \cdot (3\vec{s} + 4\vec{t}) = -42$

g) L'angle entre $\vec{u}$ et $\vec{v}$ est $\theta_1 \approx 153{,}4°$ et l'angle entre $\vec{s}$ et $\vec{t}$ est $\theta_2 \approx 81{,}9°$.

h) Comme $\vec{s} \cdot \vec{w} = 0$, les vecteurs $\vec{s}$ et $\vec{w}$ sont orthogonaux.

i) Les points $A(0, 3)$ et $B(4, 0)$ appartiennent à la droite, d'où le vecteur $\overrightarrow{AB} = \begin{bmatrix} 4 & -3 \end{bmatrix}$ est parallèle à la droite. De plus, $\overrightarrow{AB} \cdot \vec{w} = 0$. Par conséquent, les vecteurs $\overrightarrow{AB}$ et $\vec{w}$ sont perpendiculaires. Le vecteur $\vec{w}$ est donc perpendiculaire à la droite donnée.

j) $\vec{v} = -9\vec{u} - 2\vec{s}$

k) $\vec{v} = 4\vec{w} + 6{,}5\vec{t}$

l) $\vec{s} = \dfrac{2k - 25}{7}\vec{u} + \dfrac{4k - 1}{7}\vec{w} + k\vec{t}$ où $k \in \mathbb{R}$. Il existe une infinité de façons d'écrire le vecteur $\vec{s}$ comme une combinaison linéaire des vecteurs $\vec{u}$, $\vec{w}$ et $\vec{t}$.

m) Les vecteurs $\vec{u}$, $\vec{w}$ et $\vec{s}$ sont linéairement dépendants.

n) Parce que les vecteurs $\vec{u}$, $\vec{w}$ et $\vec{s}$ ne sont pas linéairement indépendants.

o) Il est impossible d'exprimer le vecteur $\vec{v}$ comme une combinaison linéaire des vecteurs $\vec{u}$ et $\vec{p}$.

p) Les vecteurs $\vec{u}$ et $\vec{p}$ sont linéairement dépendants et ne forment pas un système générateur de $\mathbb{R}^2$.

q) Comme $\vec{r} = (3a + 4b)\vec{u} + (a + b)\vec{s}$, les vecteurs $\vec{u}$ et $\vec{s}$ forment un système générateur de $\mathbb{R}^2$.

r) Pour montrer que les vecteurs $\vec{u}$ et $\vec{s}$ sont linéairement indépendants, il faut montrer que la seule combinaison linéaire de ces vecteurs qui soit égale au vecteur nul est celle dont tous les coefficients valent zéro. Or,

$$\vec{0} = x\vec{u} + y\vec{s}$$
$$\Rightarrow \begin{bmatrix} 0 & 0 \end{bmatrix} = x\begin{bmatrix} -1 & 1 \end{bmatrix} + y\begin{bmatrix} 4 & -3 \end{bmatrix}$$

Il faut résoudre le système d'équations linéaires

$$-x + 4y = 0$$
$$-x - 3y = 0$$

La solution unique de ce système est $x = 0$ et $y = 0$. Par conséquent, les vecteurs $\vec{u}$ et $\vec{s}$ sont linéairement indépendants.

s) Les vecteurs $\vec{u}$ et $\vec{s}$ forment une base de $\mathbb{R}^2$.

t) Les vecteurs $\vec{t}$ et $\vec{s}$ forment une base de $\mathbb{R}^2$ parce qu'ils sont linéairement indépendants et qu'ils constituent un système générateur de $\mathbb{R}^2$.

u) $-4\vec{v} = \begin{bmatrix} -4 & 12 \end{bmatrix}$

v) $\begin{bmatrix} -3/\sqrt{10} & -1/\sqrt{10} \end{bmatrix}$ et $\begin{bmatrix} 3/\sqrt{10} & 1/\sqrt{10} \end{bmatrix}$

w) $\begin{bmatrix} 2\sqrt{5}/5 & -\sqrt{5}/5 \end{bmatrix}$ et $\begin{bmatrix} -\sqrt{5}/5 & -2\sqrt{5}/5 \end{bmatrix}$

x) $\vec{s}_{\vec{t}} = \begin{bmatrix} 1/2 & 1/2 \end{bmatrix}$

y) $\vec{s}_{\vec{w}} = \vec{0}$. Les vecteurs $\vec{s}$ et $\vec{w}$ sont perpendiculaires.

44. a) $\|\vec{u}\| = 1$ et $\|\vec{v}\| = 1$

b)

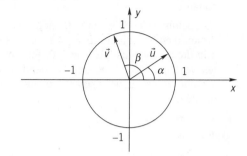

c) $\beta - \alpha$ représente l'angle entre les vecteurs $\vec{u}$ et $\vec{v}$.

d) $\vec{u} \cdot \vec{v} = \cos\alpha\cos\beta + \sin\alpha\sin\beta$

e) $\vec{u} \cdot \vec{v} = \|\vec{u}\| \|\vec{v}\| \cos(\beta - \alpha) = \cos(\beta - \alpha)$. En posant l'égalité entre cette expression de $\vec{u} \cdot \vec{v}$ et celle qu'on a obtenue en d, on a

$$\cos(\beta - \alpha) = \cos\alpha\cos\beta + \sin\alpha\sin\beta$$

45. a) $\begin{bmatrix} 1 & 0 \\ 0 & 0 \end{bmatrix} \begin{bmatrix} a \\ b \end{bmatrix} = \begin{bmatrix} a \\ 0 \end{bmatrix}$

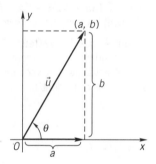

Le produit est la projection du vecteur $\vec{u}$ sur l'axe des abscisses.

b) $\begin{bmatrix} 0 & 0 \\ 0 & 1 \end{bmatrix} \begin{bmatrix} a \\ b \end{bmatrix} = \begin{bmatrix} 0 \\ b \end{bmatrix}$

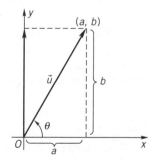

Le produit est la projection du vecteur $\vec{u}$ sur l'axe des ordonnées.

c) Le produit matriciel s'obtient par réflexion du vecteur $\vec{u}$ par rapport à l'axe des ordonnées.

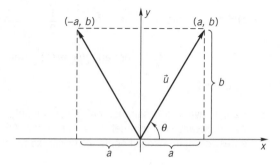

d) $\begin{bmatrix} 1 & 0 \\ 0 & -1 \end{bmatrix}$

e) $\begin{bmatrix} 0 & 1 \\ 1 & 0 \end{bmatrix}$

f) Il s'agit d'une élongation du vecteur $\vec{u}$ par un facteur 2. La longueur du vecteur est doublée, mais sa direction reste inchangée.

g) Il s'agit d'une élongation du vecteur $\vec{u}$ par un facteur $|k|$. La longueur du vecteur est multipliée par un facteur $|k|$. Sa direction reste inchangée si le scalaire k est positif et elle est inversée si k est négatif.

h) On exprime les composantes du vecteur $\vec{w}$ en fonction du module et de la direction de $\vec{u}$:

$$\vec{w} = \begin{bmatrix} \cos\varphi & -\sin\varphi \\ \sin\varphi & \cos\varphi \end{bmatrix} \begin{bmatrix} a \\ b \end{bmatrix}$$
$$= \begin{bmatrix} a\cos\varphi - b\sin\varphi \\ a\sin\varphi + b\cos\varphi \end{bmatrix}$$
$$= \begin{bmatrix} \|\vec{u}\|\cos\theta\cos\varphi - \|\vec{u}\|\sin\theta\sin\varphi \\ \|\vec{u}\|\cos\theta\sin\varphi + \|\vec{u}\|\sin\theta\cos\varphi \end{bmatrix}$$
$$= \begin{bmatrix} \|\vec{u}\|\cos(\theta + \varphi) \\ \|\vec{u}\|\sin(\theta + \varphi) \end{bmatrix}$$

Par conséquent, $\vec{w}$ a la même longueur que $\vec{u}$ et sa direction est $\theta + \varphi$.

CHAPITRE 6

1. a) $y = 2x + 1$

b) $y = -x + 3$

c) $y = -\frac{1}{2}x - 1$

d) $x = 5$

e) $x = 2$

f) $y = 1$

2. $R = 100x + 300$

3. a) $R = 10\,000x + 50\,000$

b) $D = 8\,000x + 150\,000$

c)

Dépenses et revenu, selon le nombre de représentations

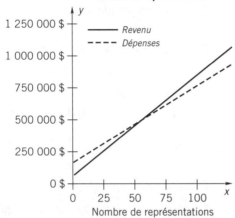

d) $P = 2\,000x - 100\,000$

e) L'abscisse du point d'intersection des deux droites est égale au nombre de représentations de la pièce que la troupe doit donner pour que le revenu soit égal aux dépenses, c'est-à-dire pour que le profit soit nul : c'est le seuil de rentabilité.

f) La troupe subit une perte de 50 000 $.

g) 50

4. a) Environ 63,4°

b) 135°

c) Environ 153,4°

d) 90°

e) 90°

f) 0°

5. a) 15 %

b) $y = 0,1x + k$ où $k \in \mathbb{R}$

c) Environ 5,7°

6. a) $\sqrt{3}/3$

b) 2

c) −3

d) $\frac{5}{3}$

e) $-\frac{2}{3}$

7. $\operatorname{tg}\varphi = \dfrac{m_2 - m_1}{1 + m_1 m_2}$

Preuve

$\theta_2 = \theta_1 + \varphi$

$\operatorname{tg}\theta_2 = \operatorname{tg}(\theta_1 + \varphi) = \dfrac{\operatorname{tg}\theta_1 + \operatorname{tg}\varphi}{1 - \operatorname{tg}\theta_1 \operatorname{tg}\varphi}$

$\operatorname{tg}\theta_2(1 - \operatorname{tg}\theta_1 \operatorname{tg}\varphi) = \operatorname{tg}\theta_1 + \operatorname{tg}\varphi$

$\operatorname{tg}\theta_2 - \operatorname{tg}\theta_1 = \operatorname{tg}\varphi + \operatorname{tg}\theta_1 \operatorname{tg}\theta_2 \operatorname{tg}\varphi$

$\qquad\qquad\quad = \operatorname{tg}\varphi(1 + \operatorname{tg}\theta_1 \operatorname{tg}\theta_2)$

$\operatorname{tg}\varphi = \dfrac{\operatorname{tg}\theta_2 - \operatorname{tg}\theta_1}{1 + \operatorname{tg}\theta_1 \operatorname{tg}\theta_2} = \dfrac{m_2 - m_1}{1 + m_1 m_2}$ ∎

Si $m_1 = -\dfrac{1}{m_2}$, alors $\operatorname{tg}\varphi$ n'est pas défini, d'où $\varphi = 90°$.

Par conséquent, les deux droites sont perpendiculaires.

8. a) $y - 3 = 3(x + 1)$

b) $x = 2$

c) $y + 2 = -\sqrt{3}(x + 1)$

d) $y - 1 = 4(x - 1)$

9. a)

$\begin{vmatrix} 1 & x_1 & y_1 \\ 1 & x_2 & y_2 \\ 1 & x & y \end{vmatrix} = \begin{vmatrix} 1 & x_1 & y_1 \\ 0 & x_2 - x_1 & y_2 - y_1 \\ 0 & x - x_1 & y - y_1 \end{vmatrix} \begin{matrix} \\ L_2 \to L_2 - L_1 \\ L_3 \to L_3 - L_1 \end{matrix}$

$\qquad = (x_2 - x_1)(y - y_1) - (x - x_1)(y_2 - y_1)$

b) $\begin{vmatrix} 1 & x_1 & y_1 \\ 1 & x_2 & y_2 \\ 1 & x & y \end{vmatrix} = 0$

$\Rightarrow \quad (x_2 - x_1)(y - y_1) - (x - x_1)(y_2 - y_1) = 0$

Par conséquent,

$\qquad (x_2 - x_1)(y - y_1) = (x - x_1)(y_2 - y_1)$ et

$\qquad\qquad \dfrac{y - y_1}{x - x_1} = \dfrac{y_2 - y_1}{x_2 - x_1}$

Cette dernière équation (qui donne deux points) décrit la droite qui passe par les points (x_1, y_1) et (x_2, y_2).

10. a) Vecteur directeur : $\vec{d} = \overrightarrow{AB} = \begin{bmatrix} -3 & -6 \end{bmatrix}$

Équation vectorielle :

$\begin{bmatrix} x & y \end{bmatrix} = \begin{bmatrix} 2 & 5 \end{bmatrix} + k\begin{bmatrix} -3 & -6 \end{bmatrix}$ où $k \in \mathbb{R}$

Équations paramétriques : $\begin{cases} x = 2 - 3k \\ y = 5 - 6k \end{cases}$ où $k \in \mathbb{R}$

Équation symétrique : $\dfrac{x - 2}{-3} = \dfrac{y - 5}{-6}$

b) Vecteur directeur : $\vec{d} = \overrightarrow{AB} = \begin{bmatrix} 2 & -2 \end{bmatrix}$

Équation vectorielle :
$\begin{bmatrix} x & y \end{bmatrix} = \begin{bmatrix} 3 & 0 \end{bmatrix} + k\begin{bmatrix} 2 & -2 \end{bmatrix}$ où $k \in \mathbb{R}$

Équations paramétriques : $\begin{cases} x = 3 + 2k \\ y = -2k \end{cases}$ où $k \in \mathbb{R}$

Équation symétrique : $\dfrac{x-3}{2} = \dfrac{y}{-2}$

c) Vecteur directeur : $\vec{d} = \overrightarrow{AB} = \begin{bmatrix} -8 & 4 \end{bmatrix}$

Équation vectorielle :
$\begin{bmatrix} x & y \end{bmatrix} = \begin{bmatrix} 4 & -3 \end{bmatrix} + k\begin{bmatrix} -8 & 4 \end{bmatrix}$ où $k \in \mathbb{R}$

Équations paramétriques : $\begin{cases} x = 4 - 8k \\ y = -3 + 4k \end{cases}$ où $k \in \mathbb{R}$

Équation symétrique : $\dfrac{x-4}{-8} = \dfrac{y+3}{4}$

d) Vecteur directeur : $\vec{d} = \overrightarrow{AB} = \begin{bmatrix} 0 & -2 \end{bmatrix}$

Équation vectorielle :
$\begin{bmatrix} x & y \end{bmatrix} = \begin{bmatrix} 5 & 3 \end{bmatrix} + k\begin{bmatrix} 0 & -2 \end{bmatrix}$ où $k \in \mathbb{R}$

Équations paramétriques : $\begin{cases} x = 5 \\ y = 3 - 2k \end{cases}$ où $k \in \mathbb{R}$

Équation symétrique : $x = 5$ et $\dfrac{y-3}{-2} = k$ où $k \in \mathbb{R}$

e) Vecteur directeur : $\vec{d} = \overrightarrow{AB} = \begin{bmatrix} 0 & 3 \end{bmatrix}$

Équation vectorielle :
$\begin{bmatrix} x & y \end{bmatrix} = \begin{bmatrix} 2 & 1 \end{bmatrix} + k\begin{bmatrix} 0 & 3 \end{bmatrix}$ où $k \in \mathbb{R}$

Équations paramétriques : $\begin{cases} x = 2 \\ y = 1 + 3k \end{cases}$ où $k \in \mathbb{R}$

Équation symétrique : $x = 2$ et $\dfrac{y-1}{3} = k$ où $k \in \mathbb{R}$

f) Vecteur directeur : $\vec{d} = \overrightarrow{AB} = \begin{bmatrix} 3 & 0 \end{bmatrix}$

Équation vectorielle :
$\begin{bmatrix} x & y \end{bmatrix} = \begin{bmatrix} 2 & 1 \end{bmatrix} + k\begin{bmatrix} 3 & 0 \end{bmatrix}$ où $k \in \mathbb{R}$

Équations paramétriques : $\begin{cases} x = 2 + 3k \\ y = 1 \end{cases}$ où $k \in \mathbb{R}$

Équation symétrique : $\dfrac{x-2}{3} = k$ et $y = 1$ où $k \in \mathbb{R}$

11. a) $\begin{bmatrix} x & y \end{bmatrix} = \begin{bmatrix} 0 & 4 \end{bmatrix} + k\begin{bmatrix} 3 & -5 \end{bmatrix}$ où $k \in \mathbb{R}$

b) $\begin{bmatrix} x & y \end{bmatrix} = \begin{bmatrix} 6 & 1 \end{bmatrix} + k\begin{bmatrix} -\sqrt{2}/2 & \sqrt{2}/2 \end{bmatrix}$ où $k \in \mathbb{R}$

c) $\begin{bmatrix} x & y \end{bmatrix} = \begin{bmatrix} 4 & 0 \end{bmatrix} + k\begin{bmatrix} 4 & -10 \end{bmatrix}$ où $k \in \mathbb{R}$ ou
$\begin{bmatrix} x & y \end{bmatrix} = \begin{bmatrix} 4 & 0 \end{bmatrix} + k\begin{bmatrix} 4 & 10 \end{bmatrix}$ où $k \in \mathbb{R}$

d) $\begin{bmatrix} x & y \end{bmatrix} = \begin{bmatrix} 0 & 5 \end{bmatrix} + k\begin{bmatrix} 10 & -5 \end{bmatrix}$ où $k \in \mathbb{R}$ ou
$\begin{bmatrix} x & y \end{bmatrix} = \begin{bmatrix} 0 & -5 \end{bmatrix} + k\begin{bmatrix} -10 & 5 \end{bmatrix}$ où $k \in \mathbb{R}$

12. a) Équation vectorielle :
$\begin{bmatrix} x & y \end{bmatrix} = \begin{bmatrix} 1 & 2 \end{bmatrix} + k\begin{bmatrix} 4 & 2 \end{bmatrix}$ où $k \in \mathbb{R}$

Équations paramétriques : $\begin{cases} x = 1 + 4k \\ y = 2 + 2k \end{cases}$ où $k \in \mathbb{R}$

Équation symétrique : $\dfrac{x-1}{4} = \dfrac{y-2}{2}$
Équation cartésienne : $-2x + 4y = 6$

b) Équation vectorielle :
$\begin{bmatrix} x & y \end{bmatrix} = \begin{bmatrix} -1 & 1 \end{bmatrix} + k\begin{bmatrix} 3 & 0 \end{bmatrix}$ où $k \in \mathbb{R}$

Équations paramétriques : $\begin{cases} x = -1 + 3k \\ y = 1 \end{cases}$ où $k \in \mathbb{R}$

Équation symétrique : $\dfrac{x+1}{3} = k$ et $y = 1$ où $k \in \mathbb{R}$
Équation cartésienne : $3y = 3$ ou, ce qui est équivalent, $y = 1$

c) Équation vectorielle :
$\begin{bmatrix} x & y \end{bmatrix} = \begin{bmatrix} 2 & 4 \end{bmatrix} + k\begin{bmatrix} 3 & 2 \end{bmatrix}$ où $k \in \mathbb{R}$

Équations paramétriques : $\begin{cases} x = 2 + 3k \\ y = 4 + 2k \end{cases}$ où $k \in \mathbb{R}$

Équation symétrique : $\dfrac{x-2}{3} = \dfrac{y-4}{2}$
Équation cartésienne : $-2x + 3y = 8$

d) Équation vectorielle :
$\begin{bmatrix} x & y \end{bmatrix} = \begin{bmatrix} 2 & 3 \end{bmatrix} + k\begin{bmatrix} 1 & 1 \end{bmatrix}$ où $k \in \mathbb{R}$

Équations paramétriques : $\begin{cases} x = 2 + k \\ y = 3 + k \end{cases}$ où $k \in \mathbb{R}$

Équation symétrique : $x - 2 = y - 3$
Équation cartésienne : $-x + y = 1$

e) Équation vectorielle :
$\begin{bmatrix} x & y \end{bmatrix} = \begin{bmatrix} 0 & 4 \end{bmatrix} + k\begin{bmatrix} 1 & 3 \end{bmatrix}$ où $k \in \mathbb{R}$

Équations paramétriques : $\begin{cases} x = k \\ y = 4 + 3k \end{cases}$ où $k \in \mathbb{R}$

Équation symétrique : $x = \dfrac{y-4}{3}$

Équation cartésienne : $-3x + y = 4$

13. Équation vectorielle :

$$\begin{bmatrix} x & y \end{bmatrix} = \begin{bmatrix} p_1 & p_2 \end{bmatrix} + k \begin{bmatrix} d_1 & d_2 \end{bmatrix} \text{ où } k \in \mathbb{R}$$

Équations paramétriques : $\begin{cases} x = p_1 + kd_1 \\ y = p_2 + kd_2 \end{cases}$ où $k \in \mathbb{R}$

Équation symétrique : $\dfrac{x - p_1}{d_1} = \dfrac{y - p_2}{d_2}$ où $d_1 \neq 0$ et $d_2 \neq 0$

Équation cartésienne : $-d_2 x + d_1 y = -p_1 d_2 + p_2 d_1$

14. a) Si $k = 2$, on a le point $(4, 11)$; si $k = 6$, on a le point $(8, 27)$.

b) Il s'agit du segment de droite compris entre les points $(4, 11)$ et $(8, 27)$.

15. a) $\dfrac{16}{\sqrt{13}} \approx 4{,}4$ unités

b) $\Delta_2 : -2x + 3y = 12$

c) $A(-\tfrac{9}{13}, \tfrac{46}{13})$

d) Le point A est le point de la droite Δ_1 le plus proche du point P.

e) Le point A d'une droite Δ_1 le plus proche d'un point P donné, extérieur à la droite, est le point d'intersection de Δ_1 et de la droite Δ_2 perpendiculaire à Δ_1 qui passe par le point P.

16. a) $\tfrac{3}{2}$

b) -9

c) $\tfrac{2}{7}$

d) $-\tfrac{2}{3}$

17. a) $-\tfrac{2}{3}$

b) 1

c) $-\tfrac{7}{2}$

d) $\tfrac{3}{2}$

18. a) $\dfrac{3\sqrt{5}}{5} \approx 1{,}3$ unité

b) 3 unités

c) 0 unité. Le point Q appartient à la droite.

d) $\dfrac{\sqrt{2}}{2} \approx 0{,}7$ unité

e) $\dfrac{3\sqrt{10}}{5} \approx 1{,}9$ unité

19. $\dfrac{30\sqrt{13}}{13} \approx 8{,}3$ unités

20. a)

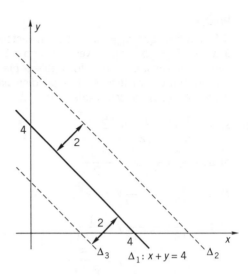

b) $\Delta_2 : x + y = 4 + 2\sqrt{2}$ et $\Delta_3 : x + y = 4 - 2\sqrt{2}$

21. a) $\Delta_3 : -x + y = 0$

b) Si $Q(q_1, q_2)$ est un point de la droite Δ_3, alors $-q_1 + q_2 = 0 \Rightarrow q_1 = q_2$. Par conséquent, tous les points de la droite Δ_3 sont de la forme $Q(q, q)$. La distance du point Q à la droite Δ_1 est égale à

$$\left| \frac{aq_1 + bq_2 - c}{\sqrt{a^2 + b^2}} \right| = \left| \frac{4q - 3q - 1}{5} \right| = \left| \frac{q - 1}{5} \right|$$

et la distance du point Q à la droite Δ_2 est égale à

$$\left| \frac{aq_1 + bq_2 - c}{\sqrt{a^2 + b^2}} \right| = \left| \frac{3q - 4q - (-1)}{5} \right|$$
$$= \left| \frac{-(q - 1)}{5} \right|$$
$$= \left| \frac{q - 1}{5} \right|$$

Donc, la distance de tout point de la droite Δ_3 à la droite Δ_1 est identique à la distance de ce point à la droite Δ_2.

c) arc $\cos \tfrac{24}{25} \approx 16{,}26°$

d) arc $\cos \dfrac{7}{5\sqrt{2}} \approx 8{,}13°$

e) La droite Δ_3 divise l'angle entre les droites Δ_1 et Δ_2 en deux angles égaux. La droite Δ_3 est donc la bissectrice de cet angle.

22. Les droites $\Delta_1 : ax - by = c_1$ et $\Delta_2 : bx + ay = c_2$ sont perpendiculaires.

Preuve

Il faut vérifier que $\overrightarrow{n_1} = \begin{bmatrix} a & -b \end{bmatrix}$, un vecteur normal à Δ_1, et $\overrightarrow{n_2} = \begin{bmatrix} b & a \end{bmatrix}$, un vecteur normal à Δ_2, sont perpendiculaires. On a $\overrightarrow{n_1} \cdot \overrightarrow{n_2} = ab + (-b)a = 0$. Par conséquent, ces vecteurs sont perpendiculaires et les droites Δ_1 et Δ_2 le sont également. ◼

23. a) $\Delta: \dfrac{1}{\sqrt{2}}x + \dfrac{1}{\sqrt{2}}y = \dfrac{5}{\sqrt{2}}$

b) $\Delta: -\dfrac{\sqrt{3}}{2}x + \dfrac{1}{2}y = \dfrac{\sqrt{3}+2}{2}$

c) $\Delta: \dfrac{4}{\sqrt{17}}x - \dfrac{1}{\sqrt{17}}y = -\dfrac{9}{\sqrt{17}}$

d) $\Delta: \dfrac{2}{\sqrt{13}}x - \dfrac{3}{\sqrt{13}}y = \dfrac{14}{\sqrt{13}}$

e) $\Delta: \dfrac{2}{\sqrt{53}}x - \dfrac{7}{\sqrt{53}}y = \dfrac{5}{2\sqrt{53}}$

f) $\Delta: -\dfrac{3}{\sqrt{13}}x + \dfrac{2}{\sqrt{13}}y = -\dfrac{6}{\sqrt{13}}$

24. a) $\begin{bmatrix} \dfrac{1}{\sqrt{5}} & -\dfrac{2}{\sqrt{5}} \end{bmatrix}$ et $\begin{bmatrix} -\dfrac{1}{\sqrt{5}} & \dfrac{2}{\sqrt{5}} \end{bmatrix}$

b) $\begin{bmatrix} \dfrac{2}{\sqrt{5}} & \dfrac{1}{\sqrt{5}} \end{bmatrix}$ et $\begin{bmatrix} -\dfrac{2}{\sqrt{5}} & -\dfrac{1}{\sqrt{5}} \end{bmatrix}$

c) $\begin{bmatrix} \dfrac{3}{\sqrt{13}} & -\dfrac{2}{\sqrt{13}} \end{bmatrix}$ et $\begin{bmatrix} -\dfrac{3}{\sqrt{13}} & \dfrac{2}{\sqrt{13}} \end{bmatrix}$

25. a) Les droites Δ_1 et Δ_2 sont données sous la forme normale.

b) Les droites Δ_1 et Δ_2 sont parallèles parce qu'elles ont un vecteur normal unitaire commun, soit

$$\overrightarrow{n_u} = \begin{bmatrix} \dfrac{a}{\sqrt{a^2 + b^2}} & \dfrac{b}{\sqrt{a^2 + b^2}} \end{bmatrix}$$

c) La distance entre les droites

$$\Delta_1: \frac{a}{\sqrt{a^2 + b^2}}x + \frac{b}{\sqrt{a^2 + b^2}}y = h_1 \quad \text{et}$$

$$\Delta_2: \frac{a}{\sqrt{a^2 + b^2}}x + \frac{b}{\sqrt{a^2 + b^2}}y = h_2$$

est égale à $|h_1 - h_2|$.

Preuve

La distance entre deux droites parallèles est égale à la distance d'un point de la première droite à la deuxième droite. Si $Q(q_1, q_2)$ est un point de la droite Δ_1, alors il vérifie l'équation

$$\frac{a}{\sqrt{a^2 + b^2}}q_1 + \frac{b}{\sqrt{a^2 + b^2}}q_2 = h_1$$

La distance du point $Q(q_1, q_2)$ à la droite Δ_2 est donc égale à

$$\left| \frac{\dfrac{a}{\sqrt{a^2+b^2}}q_1 + \dfrac{b}{\sqrt{a^2+b^2}}q_2 - h_2}{\sqrt{\dfrac{a^2}{a^2+b^2} + \dfrac{b^2}{a^2+b^2}}} \right|$$

$$= \left| \frac{\dfrac{a}{\sqrt{a^2+b^2}}q_1 + \dfrac{b}{\sqrt{a^2+b^2}}q_2 - h_2}{1} \right|$$

$$= \left| \frac{a}{\sqrt{a^2+b^2}}q_1 + \frac{b}{\sqrt{a^2+b^2}}q_2 - h_2 \right|$$

$$= |h_1 - h_2| \qquad ◼$$

26. a)

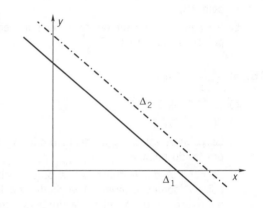

b)

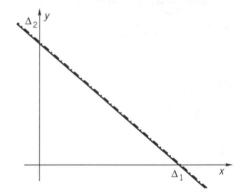

c)

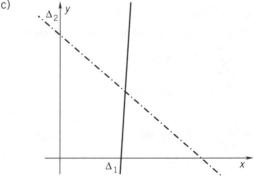

d) Les droites Δ_1 et Δ_2 sont parallèles et distinctes lorsque le système formé des équations cartésiennes de ces deux droites n'admet aucune solution ; Δ_1 et Δ_2 sont confondues lorsque ce système admet une infinité de solutions ; Δ_1 et Δ_2 sont concourantes lorsque ce système admet une solution unique.

27. a) Les droites Δ_1 et Δ_2 sont concourantes, et leur point d'intersection est $(1, {}^5\!/_2)$.

b) Les droites Δ_1 et Δ_2 sont parallèles distinctes, et la distance qui les sépare est égale à $\dfrac{15\sqrt{13}}{26}$, soit environ à 2,1 unités.

c) Les droites Δ_1 et Δ_2 sont parallèles distinctes, et la distance qui les sépare est égale à $\dfrac{11\sqrt{13}}{13}$, soit environ à 3,1 unités.

d) Les droites Δ_1 et Δ_2 sont concourantes, et leur point d'intersection est $({}^{17}\!/_4, -{}^{13}\!/_8)$.

e) Les droites Δ_1 et Δ_2 sont confondues, et la distance qui les sépare est nulle.

f) Les droites Δ_1 et Δ_2 sont concourantes, et leur point d'intersection $(4, 0)$.

g) Les droites Δ_1 et Δ_2 sont confondues, et la distance qui les sépare est nulle.

h) Les droites Δ_1 et Δ_2 sont parallèles distinctes, et la distance qui les sépare est égale à $\dfrac{7\sqrt{2}}{2} \approx 4{,}9$ unités.

i) Les droites Δ_1 et Δ_2 sont parallèles distinctes, et la distance qui les sépare est égale à $\dfrac{\sqrt{5}}{5} \approx 0{,}4$ unité.

28. a) $70°$

b) arc $\cos(0{,}6) \approx 53{,}1°$

c) $45°$

d) arc $\cos \dfrac{11}{\sqrt{17} \times \sqrt{13}} \approx 42{,}3°$

29. a) $A(1, 1)$, $B({}^3\!/_2, -{}^1\!/_2)$ et $C({}^7\!/_3, {}^1\!/_3)$

b)

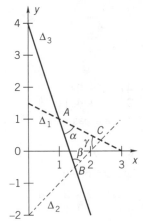

c) $\alpha = 45°$, $\beta \approx 63{,}4°$ et $\gamma \approx 71{,}6°$

d) $\sqrt{5/2} + \sqrt{20/9} + \sqrt{25/18} \approx 4{,}3$ unités

30. a) Les droites Δ_1 et Δ_2 sont parallèles distinctes.

b) Les droites Δ_1 et Δ_2 sont confondues.

c) Les droites Δ_1 et Δ_2 sont concourantes.

31. a)

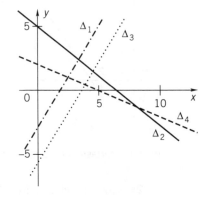

b) $x = {}^{16}\!/_3$ et $y = -{}^{11}\!/_2$

c) $x = 5$ et $y = -1$

d) $({}^{11}\!/_3, 0)$ et $(0, -{}^{11}\!/_2)$

e) Δ_4

f) arc tg$(-{}^1\!/_3) \approx 161{,}6°$

g) $3x - 2y = 8$

h) La pente de la droite Δ_1 est ${}^3\!/_2$ et son angle d'inclinaison est $\theta =$ arc tg$({}^3\!/_2) \approx 56{,}3°$.

i) Les droites Δ_1 et Δ_2 sont concourantes, leur point d'intersection est $({}^{54}\!/_{13}, {}^{29}\!/_{13})$, et l'angle qu'elles déterminent est $90°$.

j) Les droites Δ_1 et Δ_3 sont parallèles distinctes. La distance entre les droites est égale à $\dfrac{3\sqrt{13}}{13}$, soit environ à 0,8 unités.

k) Les droites Δ_1 et Δ_4 sont concourantes, leur point d'intersection est $({}^{34}\!/_{11}, {}^7\!/_{11})$, et l'angle qu'elles déterminent est $\theta =$ arc $\cos \dfrac{3}{\sqrt{13}\sqrt{10}} \approx 74{,}7°$.

l) $\Delta_4 : \dfrac{x - 5}{-3} = \dfrac{y}{1}$

m) $\Delta_3 : \begin{cases} x = 1 + 2k \\ y = -4 + 3k \end{cases}$ où $k \in \mathbb{R}$

n) $\Delta_5 : \begin{bmatrix} x & y \end{bmatrix} = \begin{bmatrix} 1 & 1 \end{bmatrix} + k\begin{bmatrix} -3 & 2 \end{bmatrix}$ où $k \in \mathbb{R}$

o) $\dfrac{3\sqrt{10}}{2} \approx 4{,}7$ unités

p) $(^7/_2, \, ^1/_2)$

q) $(^{30}/_{13}, \, ^{45}/_{13})$

r) $k \in \left[-5, \, 1\right]$

s)

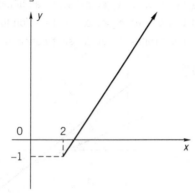

t) Les équations cartésiennes des droites Δ_2 et Δ_3 sont

$$\Delta_2 : 2x + 3y = 15 \text{ et } \Delta_3 : 3x - 2y = 11$$

Le vecteur $\vec{n_2} = \begin{bmatrix} 2 & 3 \end{bmatrix}$ est normal à la droite Δ_2 et $\vec{n_3} = \begin{bmatrix} 3 & -2 \end{bmatrix}$ est normal à la droite Δ_3. Ces deux vecteurs sont perpendiculaires puisque $\vec{n_2} \cdot \vec{n_3} = 0$. Par conséquent, les droites Δ_2 et Δ_3 sont perpendiculaires.

32.
a) Vrai   f) Vrai

b) Vrai   g) Vrai

c) Faux   h) Faux

d) Faux   i) Faux

e) Vrai   j) Vrai

CHAPITRE 7

1. a) $x = \pm 2i$

b) $x = -2 \pm \sqrt{2}\, i$

c) $x = \dfrac{5}{6} \pm \dfrac{\sqrt{23}}{6}\, i$

2. $4 + 2i$ et $4 - 2i$

3. a) $-7 + 16i$

b) $-25 + 5i$

c) $-2 + i$

d) $-250 + 250i$

e) $-i$

f) i

g) -1

h) $\sqrt{305} \approx 17,5$

i) 27

j) 10

k) $3 - 8i$

l) $3 - 8i$. Les deux résultats sont identiques. Il ne s'agit pas d'une coïncidence. En effet, si $z_1 = a + bi$ et $z_2 = c + di$, alors

$$\overline{z_1} + \overline{z_2} = (a - bi) + (c - di)$$
$$= (a + c) - (b + d)i$$
$$= \overline{z_1 + z_2}$$

m) $-25 - 5i$

n) $-25 - 5i$. Les deux résultats sont identiques. Il ne s'agit pas d'une coïncidence. En effet, si

$$z_1 = a + bi \text{ et } z_2 = c + di$$

alors, d'une part,

$$\overline{z_1}\ \overline{z_2} = ac - bd - (ad + bc)i$$

et, d'autre part,

$$z_1 z_2 = (ac - bd) + (ad + bc)i$$
$$\Rightarrow \quad \overline{z_1 z_2} = (ac - bd) - (ad + bc)i$$

Par conséquent, $\overline{z_1}\ \overline{z_2} = \overline{z_1 z_2}$.

o) $^5/_{13} - {}^{25}/_{13}\, i$

p) $^{61}/_{41} - {}^{66}/_{41}\, i$

q) $^1/_{10} - {}^1/_{10}\, i$

4. a) $n = 0$, $n = 1$ ou $n = -1$

5. a) $-^3/_{13} - {}^2/_{13}\, i$

b) $2 + 2i$

6. a) $\begin{bmatrix} 4 & 6 - i \\ 4 - i & 2 \end{bmatrix}$

b) $\begin{bmatrix} 5 + 4i & 2 - 2i \\ 5 - 3i & 1 + 4i \end{bmatrix}$

c) $2A + C$ n'est pas défini.

d) $\begin{bmatrix} 10 - i & 7 \\ 3 - 6i & 17 \end{bmatrix}$

e) CB n'est pas défini.

f) $\begin{bmatrix} 11 - 13i & 7 - 3i & 11 - 9i \\ 1 - i & 3 + 9i & 4 - 4i \end{bmatrix}$

g) $\begin{bmatrix} -1 & 0 \\ 0 & -1 \end{bmatrix}$

h) $\begin{bmatrix} 0 & -i \\ -i & 0 \end{bmatrix}$

i) $\begin{bmatrix} 0 & i \\ i & 0 \end{bmatrix}$

7. a) $\overline{z_1} + \overline{z_2} = \overline{z_1 + z_2}$

Preuve

Si $z_1 = a_1 + b_1 i$ et $z_2 = a_2 + b_2 i$, alors $z_1 + z_2 = (a_1 + a_2) + (b_1 + b_2)i$, de sorte que

$$\overline{z_1 + z_2} = (a_1 + a_2) - (b_1 + b_2)i$$

Par ailleurs, $\overline{z_1} = a_1 - b_1 i$ et $\overline{z_2} = a_2 - b_2 i$, de sorte que

$$\overline{z_1} + \overline{z_2} = (a_1 + a_2) - (b_1 + b_2)i$$

Par conséquent, $\overline{z_1} + \overline{z_2} = \overline{z_1 + z_2}$. ∎

b) $\overline{z_1}\,\overline{z_2} = \overline{z_1 z_2}$

Preuve

Si $z_1 = a_1 + b_1 i$ et $z_2 = a_2 + b_2 i$, alors $z_1 z_2 = (a_1 a_2 - b_1 b_2) + (a_1 b_2 + a_2 b_1)i$, de sorte que

$$\overline{z_1 z_2} = (a_1 a_2 - b_1 b_2) - (a_1 b_2 + a_2 b_1)i$$

Par ailleurs, $\overline{z_1} = a_1 - b_1 i$ et $\overline{z_2} = a_2 - b_2 i$, de sorte que

$$\overline{z_1}\,\overline{z_2} = (a_1 a_2 - b_1 b_2) - (a_1 b_2 + a_2 b_1)i$$

Par conséquent, $\overline{z_1}\,\overline{z_2} = \overline{z_1 z_2}$. ∎

c) $z_1 \in \mathbb{R} \Leftrightarrow z_1 = \overline{z_1}$

Preuve

On pose $z_1 = a_1 + b_1 i$.

($\Rightarrow$) Si $z_1 \in \mathbb{R}$, alors $\text{Im}(z_1) = 0$, de sorte que $z_1 = a_1 + 0i$. Par conséquent,

$$z_1 = a_1 + 0i = a_1 - 0i = \overline{z_1}$$

($\Leftarrow$) Si $z_1 = \overline{z_1}$, alors $a_1 + b_1 i = a_1 - b_1 i$, de sorte que $b_1 = 0$. Par conséquent,

$$z_1 = a_1 + 0i = a_1 \in \mathbb{R}$$

Donc, $z_1 \in \mathbb{R} \Leftrightarrow z_1 = \overline{z_1}$. ∎

8. Si $p(z) = a_0 + a_1 z + a_2 z^2 + \cdots + a_n z^n$ est un polynôme à coefficients réels ($a_k \in \mathbb{R}$) et si z est une racine de ce polynôme, alors $\overline{z}$ en est aussi une racine.

Preuve

Si z est une racine du polynôme, alors

$$p(z) = a_0 + a_1 z + a_2 z^2 + \cdots + a_n z^n = 0$$

d'où

$$\overline{a_0 + a_1 z + a_2 z^2 + \cdots + a_n z^n} = \overline{0} = 0$$

Il faut montrer que

$$p(\overline{z}) = a_0 + a_1 \overline{z} + a_2 \overline{z}^2 + \cdots + a_n \overline{z}^n = 0$$

Or, en employant les égalités démontrées au n° 7 pour transformer l'équation obtenue ci-dessus, on a

$$\overline{a_0 + a_1 z + a_2 z^2 + \cdots + a_n z^n} = \overline{0} = 0$$
$$\overline{a_0} + \overline{a_1 z} + \overline{a_2 z^2} + \cdots + \overline{a_n z^n} = 0$$
$$\overline{a_0} + \overline{a_1}\,\overline{z} + \overline{a_2}\,\overline{z^2} + \cdots + \overline{a_n}\,\overline{z^n} = 0$$
$$\overline{a_0} + \overline{a_1}\,\overline{z} + \overline{a_2}\,\overline{z}^2 + \cdots + \overline{a_n}\,\overline{z}^n = 0$$

De plus, comme $a_k \in \mathbb{R}$, en vertu de la troisième égalité du n° 7, on a $\overline{a_k} = a_k$, de sorte que

$$a_0 + a_1 \overline{z} + a_2 \overline{z}^2 + \cdots + a_n \overline{z}^n = 0$$

Donc, $p(\overline{z}) = a_0 + a_1 \overline{z} + a_2 \overline{z}^2 + \cdots + a_n \overline{z}^n = 0$: l'ensemble des racines d'un polynôme à coefficients réels est formé de paires de nombres conjugués. ∎

9.

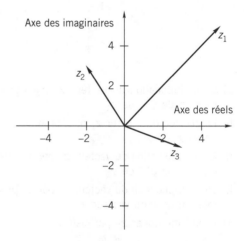

10. a) $z_1 = 5\sqrt{2}\ \text{cis}(3\pi/4)$

b) $z_2 = 2\ \text{cis}(3\pi/2)$

c) $z_3 = 4\ \text{cis}(0)$

d) $z_4 = 6\ \text{cis}(7\pi/6)$

e) $z_5 = 2\ \text{cis}(5\pi/3)$

11. a) $z_1 = 4i$

b) $z_2 = -\dfrac{\sqrt{3}}{2} + \dfrac{1}{2}i$

c) $z_3 = \dfrac{3\sqrt{3}}{2} - \dfrac{3}{2}i$

d) $z_4 = -2$

12. a) $|z_1| = 1$, $|z_2| = 2$, $|z_3| = 1$ et $|z_4| = \sqrt{13} \approx 3{,}6$

b) $\theta_1 = 30°$, $\theta_2 = 45°$, $\theta_3 = \theta$ et

$\theta_4 = \text{arc tg}\left(\dfrac{-3}{2}\right) \approx 303{,}7°$

c) $z_1 z_2 = 2 \text{ cis}(75°)$

d) Les modules des deux nombres complexes sont identiques : $|z_2| = 2 = |z_1 z_2|$.

e) $\text{Arg}(z_2) = 45°$ et $\text{Arg}(z_1 z_2) = 75°$. L'écart entre les arguments des deux nombres complexes est donc de $30°$, soit la valeur de l'argument de z_1.

f)

g) La multiplication du vecteur z_1 par i produit une rotation de 90° de z_1.

h) La division du vecteur z_1 par i produit une rotation de 270° de z_1.

i) La multiplication du vecteur z_2 par z_1 produit une rotation de 30° de z_2.

j) La multiplication du vecteur z_2 par z_3 produit une rotation de θ du vecteur z_2.

k) Il faut multiplier z_2 par $\text{cis}(60°)$.

l) $\dfrac{-2\sqrt{3} + 3}{2} + \dfrac{2 + 3\sqrt{3}}{2} i$

13. a) $10i$

b) $1{,}25 \text{ cis}(275°)$

c) $3^5 \text{ cis}(7\pi/6)$

d) 2^{-6}

e) $2\,187\sqrt{3} - 2\,187 i$

f) -2^{10}

g) $\dfrac{1}{2} - \dfrac{\sqrt{3}}{2} i$

h) 1

14. Lorsque n est un multiple entier positif de 6.

15. En vertu du théorème de Moivre

$$(\cos\theta + i\sin\theta)^2 = \cos(2\theta) + i\sin(2\theta)$$

Si on évalue $(\cos\theta + i\sin\theta)^2$ en multipliant les deux facteurs exprimés sous forme cartésienne, on a $(\cos\theta + i\sin\theta)^2 = (\cos^2\theta - \sin^2\theta) + 2i\sin\theta\cos\theta$. En posant l'égalité entre les parties réelles et les parties imaginaires correspondantes des deux expressions, on obtient $\cos(2\theta) = \cos^2\theta - \sin^2\theta$ et $\sin(2\theta) = 2\sin\theta\cos\theta$.

16. a) 1, i, -1 et $-i$

b) $2^{1/6} \text{ cis}(\pi/12)$, $2^{1/6} \text{ cis}(3\pi/4)$ et $2^{1/6} \text{ cis}(17\pi/12)$

c) $6^{1/6} \text{ cis}(11\pi/36)$, $6^{1/6} \text{ cis}(23\pi/36)$, $6^{1/6} \text{ cis}(35\pi/36)$, $6^{1/6} \text{ cis}(47\pi/36)$, $6^{1/6} \text{ cis}(59\pi/36)$ et $6^{1/6} \text{ cis}(71\pi/36)$

17. a) 3, $3i$, -3 et $-3i$

b) $2 \text{ cis}(\pi/3)$, -2, $2 \text{ cis}(5\pi/3)$, 3, $3 \text{ cis}(2\pi/3)$ et $3 \text{ cis}(4\pi/3)$

18. a) Faux

b) Faux

c) Vrai

d) Vrai

e) Faux

f) Vrai

CHAPITRE 8

1. a) $\overrightarrow{AF} = \overrightarrow{AB} + \overrightarrow{BG} + \overrightarrow{GF}$

b) $\overrightarrow{AF}$

c) Oui

d) $\overrightarrow{BH}$

e) $\sqrt{61} \approx 7{,}8$ cm

f) $\sqrt{77} \approx 8{,}8$ cm

g) $\sqrt{77} \approx 8{,}8$ cm

h) $\overrightarrow{AC} + \overrightarrow{AH} + \overrightarrow{AF} = 2\overrightarrow{AG}$

Preuve

$$\begin{aligned}
\overrightarrow{AC} + \overrightarrow{AH} + \overrightarrow{AF} &= \overrightarrow{AG} + \overrightarrow{GC} + \overrightarrow{AG} + \overrightarrow{GH} + \overrightarrow{DG} \\
&= 2\overrightarrow{AG} + \overrightarrow{GC} + \overrightarrow{GH} + \overrightarrow{DG} \\
&= 2\overrightarrow{AG} + \overrightarrow{GD} + \overrightarrow{DG} \\
&= 2\overrightarrow{AG} + \vec{0} \\
&= 2\overrightarrow{AG} \qquad \blacksquare
\end{aligned}$$

2. a) 1

b) $\sqrt{14} \approx 3{,}7$ unités

c)

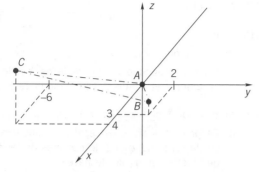

d) $\sqrt{5} \approx 2,2$ unités

e) $\sqrt{74} \approx 8,6$ unités

3. a)

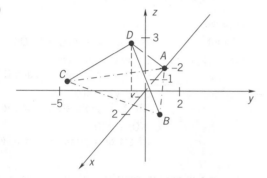

b) 3 unités

4.

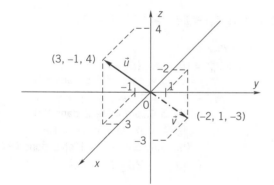

5. a) $\vec{u} = \begin{bmatrix} 2 & 3 & 4 \end{bmatrix}$

b) $\vec{v} = \begin{bmatrix} 1 & 0 & -1 \end{bmatrix}$

c) $\vec{w} = \begin{bmatrix} 0 & 3 & -2 \end{bmatrix}$

d) $\vec{t} = \begin{bmatrix} 0 & 0 & 1 \end{bmatrix}$

6. a) $\vec{u} = \vec{i} + 2\vec{j} + 4\vec{k}$

b) $\vec{v} = -2\vec{i} + \vec{k}$

c) $\vec{w} = -2\vec{j}$

7. a) $\overrightarrow{AB} = \begin{bmatrix} 3 & -4 & 8 \end{bmatrix}$ et $\|\overrightarrow{AB}\| = \sqrt{89} \approx 9,4$ unités;
$\overrightarrow{CD} = \begin{bmatrix} -1 & 0 & -8 \end{bmatrix}$ et $\|\overrightarrow{CD}\| = \sqrt{65} \approx 8,1$ unités;
$\overrightarrow{EF} = \begin{bmatrix} -2 & 3 & 6 \end{bmatrix}$ et $\|\overrightarrow{EF}\| = 7$ unités

b) $\begin{bmatrix} \dfrac{3}{\sqrt{89}} & \dfrac{-4}{\sqrt{89}} & \dfrac{8}{\sqrt{89}} \end{bmatrix}$, $\begin{bmatrix} \dfrac{-1}{\sqrt{65}} & 0 & \dfrac{-8}{\sqrt{65}} \end{bmatrix}$ et $\begin{bmatrix} -\dfrac{2}{7} & \dfrac{3}{7} & \dfrac{6}{7} \end{bmatrix}$

c) Les cosinus directeurs des vecteurs $\overrightarrow{AB}$, $\overrightarrow{CD}$ et $\overrightarrow{EF}$ respectivement.

d) $\alpha_{\overrightarrow{AB}} = \text{arc cos} \dfrac{3}{\sqrt{89}} \approx 71,5°$,

$\beta_{\overrightarrow{AB}} = \text{arc cos} \dfrac{-4}{\sqrt{89}} \approx 115,1°$ et

$\gamma_{\overrightarrow{AB}} = \text{arc cos} \dfrac{8}{\sqrt{89}} \approx 32,0°$;

$\alpha_{\overrightarrow{CD}} = \text{arc cos} \dfrac{-1}{\sqrt{65}} \approx 97,1°$,

$\beta_{\overrightarrow{CD}} = \text{arc cos} 0 \approx 90°$ et

$\gamma_{\overrightarrow{CD}} = \text{arc cos} \dfrac{-8}{\sqrt{65}} \approx 172,9°$;

$\alpha_{\overrightarrow{EF}} = \text{arc cos} \left(-\dfrac{2}{7}\right) \approx 106,6°$,

$\beta_{\overrightarrow{EF}} = \text{arc cos} \dfrac{3}{7} \approx 64,6°$ et

$\gamma_{\overrightarrow{EF}} = \text{arc cos} \dfrac{6}{7} \approx 31,0°$.

e) $\begin{bmatrix} 3 & -8 & -8 \end{bmatrix}$

f) $\begin{bmatrix} 9 & -16 & -32 \end{bmatrix}$

8. a) $D(1, -1, 12)$

b) $D(1, 7, -2)$

c) $D(1, 19, -23)$

9. a) $\begin{bmatrix} -1 & 0 & 8 \end{bmatrix}$

b) $\begin{bmatrix} -14 & 1 & 10 \end{bmatrix}$

c) $\sqrt{513} \approx 22,6$ unités

d) $\sqrt{579} \approx 24,1$ unités

e) 15

f) 13

g) −80

h) −194

i) 90°. Les vecteurs $\vec{u}$ et $\vec{v}$ sont perpendiculaires.

j) 180°. Les vecteurs $\vec{u}$ et $\vec{w}$ sont de directions opposées.

k) $\operatorname{arc\,cos}\dfrac{-3}{\sqrt{5}\,\sqrt{75}} \approx 98{,}9°$

l) $\cos\alpha_{\vec{u}} = \dfrac{1}{\sqrt{21}} \approx 0{,}218$, $\cos\beta_{\vec{u}} = \dfrac{-2}{\sqrt{21}} \approx -0{,}436$

   et $\cos\gamma_{\vec{u}} = \dfrac{4}{\sqrt{21}} \approx 0{,}873$

m) $\alpha_{\vec{v}} = \operatorname{arc\,cos}\dfrac{-2}{\sqrt{6}} \approx 144{,}7°$,

   $\beta_{\vec{v}} = \operatorname{arc\,cos}\dfrac{1}{\sqrt{6}} \approx 65{,}9°$ et

   $\gamma_{\vec{v}} = \operatorname{arc\,cos}\dfrac{1}{\sqrt{6}} \approx 65{,}9°$

n) Non

o) Oui

p) Oui

q) Oui

r) $\vec{w} = -3\vec{u} + 0\vec{v}$

s) Non

t) $\left[\begin{array}{ccc} \dfrac{2}{\sqrt{6}} & -\dfrac{1}{\sqrt{6}} & -\dfrac{1}{\sqrt{6}} \end{array}\right]$

u) $\begin{bmatrix} -4 & 2 & 7 \end{bmatrix}$. Cette solution n'est pas unique.

10. $\alpha_{-\vec{u}} = 180° - \alpha_{\vec{u}}$, $\beta_{-\vec{u}} = 180° - \beta_{\vec{u}}$ et $\gamma_{-\vec{u}} = 180° - \gamma_{\vec{u}}$

11. $\operatorname{arc\,cos}(-\tfrac{1}{3}) \approx 109{,}5°$

12. a) Les angles α, β et γ ne peuvent pas être les angles directeurs d'un vecteur.

   b) Les angles α, β et γ ne peuvent pas être les angles directeurs d'un vecteur.

   c) Les angles α, β et γ sont les angles directeurs du vecteur $\left[\begin{array}{ccc} \dfrac{1}{2} & \dfrac{1}{2} & \dfrac{\sqrt{2}}{2} \end{array}\right]$.

13. a) $\gamma = \beta = \operatorname{arc\,cos}(\pm\sqrt{1/8}) \approx 69{,}3°$ ou $110{,}7°$

   b) $\gamma = \pi/2$

   c) $\beta = \operatorname{arc\,cos}(\pm\sqrt{1/2}) = \pi/4$ ou $3\pi/4$

14. $\left[\begin{array}{ccc} \dfrac{1}{\sqrt{3}} & \dfrac{1}{\sqrt{3}} & \dfrac{1}{\sqrt{3}} \end{array}\right]$ et $\left[\begin{array}{ccc} -\dfrac{1}{\sqrt{3}} & -\dfrac{1}{\sqrt{3}} & -\dfrac{1}{\sqrt{3}} \end{array}\right]$

15. a) $\sqrt{27} + \sqrt{69} + \sqrt{30} \approx 19{,}0$ unités

   b) $\operatorname{arc\,cos}\dfrac{33}{\sqrt{27}\,\sqrt{69}} \approx 40{,}1°$

16. $\|\overrightarrow{AB}\| = 7 = \|\overrightarrow{AC}\|$: il s'agit d'un triangle isocèle. De plus, comme $\overrightarrow{AB} \cdot \overrightarrow{AC} = 0$, les deux vecteurs sont perpendiculaires : il s'agit d'un triangle rectangle dont l'angle droit est en A.

17. $k = 1$ et $k = -2$

18. a) $k = -\tfrac{5}{2}$

   b) $k = -1$ ou $k = 3$

   c) Il n'existe aucune valeur réelle de k telle que les vecteurs $\vec{u}$ et $\vec{v}$ soient perpendiculaires.

19. a) $\vec{q} = \begin{bmatrix} q_1 & q_2 & q_3 \end{bmatrix}$ et $\vec{\pi} = \begin{bmatrix} \pi_1 & \pi_2 & \pi_3 \end{bmatrix}$

   b) Ce produit scalaire est égal au profit total réalisé sur la vente de q_1 kg de pommes de terre, q_2 kg de carottes et q_3 kg de navets.

20. Si le vecteur $\vec{u}$ est orthogonal à chacun des vecteurs $\vec{v}$ et $\vec{w}$, alors il est orthogonal à toute combinaison linéaire des vecteurs $\vec{v}$ et $\vec{w}$.

Preuve

Il faut montrer que $\vec{u} \cdot (a\vec{v} + b\vec{w}) = 0$. Or,

$\vec{u} \cdot (a\vec{v} + b\vec{w}) = \vec{u} \cdot (a\vec{v}) + \vec{u} \cdot (b\vec{w})$
   (th. 5.4, propriété 2 dans $\mathbb{R}^3$)

   $= a(\vec{u} \cdot \vec{v}) + b(\vec{u} \cdot \vec{w})$
   (th. 5.4, propriété 3 dans $\mathbb{R}^3$)

   $= a(0) + b(0)$
   ($\vec{u}$ est orthogonal à $\vec{v}$ et à $\vec{w}$)

   $= 0$

Comme le produit scalaire est nul, les deux vecteurs sont orthogonaux. Par conséquent, $\vec{u}$ est orthogonal à toute combinaison linéaire des vecteurs $\vec{v}$ et $\vec{w}$. ∎

21. $\|\vec{u} + \vec{v}\|^2 = \|\vec{u}\|^2 + 2\vec{u} \cdot \vec{v} + \|\vec{v}\|^2$

Preuve

$\|\vec{u} + \vec{v}\|^2 = (\vec{u} + \vec{v}) \cdot (\vec{u} + \vec{v})$
   (th. 5.4, propriété 5 dans $\mathbb{R}^3$)

   $= \vec{u} \cdot \vec{u} + \vec{u} \cdot \vec{v} + \vec{v} \cdot \vec{u} + \vec{v} \cdot \vec{v}$
   (th. 5.4, propriété 2 dans $\mathbb{R}^3$)

   $= \|\vec{u}\|^2 + \vec{u} \cdot \vec{v} + \vec{u} \cdot \vec{v} + \|\vec{v}\|^2$
   (th. 5.4, propriétés 1 et 5 dans $\mathbb{R}^3$)

   $= \|\vec{u}\|^2 + 2\vec{u} \cdot \vec{v} + \|\vec{v}\|^2$ ∎

22. $\|\vec{u} + \vec{v}\|^2 = \|\vec{u}\|^2 + \|\vec{v}\|^2$ si et seulement si $\vec{u}$ est orthogonal à $\vec{v}$.

Preuve

$(\Rightarrow)$ $\|\vec{u} + \vec{v}\|^2 = \|\vec{u}\|^2 + \|\vec{v}\|^2$
   $\Rightarrow \|\vec{u}\|^2 + 2\vec{u} \cdot \vec{v} + \|\vec{v}\|^2 = \|\vec{u}\|^2 + \|\vec{v}\|^2$
   $\Rightarrow 2\vec{u} \cdot \vec{v} = 0$
   $\Rightarrow \vec{u} \cdot \vec{v} = 0$

Par conséquent, $\vec{u}$ est orthogonal à $\vec{v}$.

$(\Leftarrow)$ Si $\vec{u}$ est orthogonal à $\vec{v}$, alors $\vec{u} \cdot \vec{v} = 0$. Par conséquent,

$$\|\vec{u} + \vec{v}\|^2 = \|\vec{u}\|^2 + 2\vec{u} \cdot \vec{v} + \|\vec{v}\|^2$$
$$= \|\vec{u}\|^2 + 0 + \|\vec{v}\|^2$$
$$= \|\vec{u}\|^2 + \|\vec{v}\|^2 \qquad \blacksquare$$

23. $\|a\vec{u} + b\vec{v}\| = \sqrt{a^2\|\vec{u}\|^2 + b^2\|\vec{v}\|^2}$

24. Déplaçons d'abord le vecteur $\vec{a}$ de façon que son origine coïncide avec celle du vecteur $\vec{b}$.

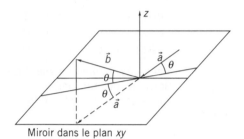

Miroir dans le plan *xy*

Les vecteurs $\vec{a}$ et $\vec{b}$ sont situés dans un même plan perpendiculaire au plan *xy* et ils ont la même longueur ($\|\vec{b}\| = \|\vec{a}\|$). Leurs projections orthogonales dans le plan *xy* sont identiques et il en est donc de même de leurs composantes en *x* et en *y*. La cote de l'extrémité du vecteur $\vec{b}$ (sa distance au plan *xy*) est $\|\vec{b}\|\sin\theta$, alors que la cote du vecteur $\vec{a}$ est $-\|\vec{a}\|\sin\theta$. Les cotes des deux vecteurs sont donc égales en valeur absolue, mais de signes contraires. Par conséquent, les deux premières composantes des vecteurs $\vec{a}$ et $\vec{b}$ sont identiques tandis que leurs troisièmes composantes sont opposées. Donc, puisque $\vec{a} = \begin{bmatrix} a_1 & a_2 & a_3 \end{bmatrix}$, alors $\vec{b} = \begin{bmatrix} a_1 & a_2 & -a_3 \end{bmatrix}$.

25. a) $\|\overrightarrow{AB}\| = \|\overrightarrow{AD}\| = \|\overrightarrow{BD}\| = \sqrt{2}$: le triangle *ABD* est équilatéral. Il en est de même pour les autres triangles formant les faces du tétraèdre.

b) $\|\overrightarrow{CA}\| = \|\overrightarrow{CB}\| = \|\overrightarrow{CD}\| = \|\overrightarrow{CE}\| = \sqrt{3}/2$: l'atome de carbone est situé à égale distance de chacun des atomes de fluor.

c) $\theta = \text{arc } \cos(-\frac{1}{3}) \approx 109,5°$

d) Il faut vérifier que $\overrightarrow{CA} + \overrightarrow{CB} + \overrightarrow{CD} + \overrightarrow{CE} = \vec{0}$. Or,

$$\overrightarrow{CA} + \overrightarrow{CB} + \overrightarrow{CD} + \overrightarrow{CE} = \begin{bmatrix} -\frac{1}{2} & -\frac{1}{2} & -\frac{1}{2} \end{bmatrix}$$
$$+ \begin{bmatrix} \frac{1}{2} & \frac{1}{2} & -\frac{1}{2} \end{bmatrix}$$
$$+ \begin{bmatrix} \frac{1}{2} & -\frac{1}{2} & \frac{1}{2} \end{bmatrix}$$
$$+ \begin{bmatrix} -\frac{1}{2} & \frac{1}{2} & \frac{1}{2} \end{bmatrix}$$
$$= \begin{bmatrix} 0 & 0 & 0 \end{bmatrix}$$
$$= \vec{0}$$

26. a) Les points *A*, *B* et *C* ne sont pas colinéaires.

b) Les points *A*, *B* et *C* sont colinéaires.

c) Les points *A*, *B* et *C* sont colinéaires.

d) Les points *A*, *B* et *C* ne sont pas colinéaires.

27. a) $\begin{bmatrix} 4 & -2 & -7 \end{bmatrix}$

b) $\begin{bmatrix} 0 & 10 & 5 \end{bmatrix}$

c) $\begin{bmatrix} 8 & -14 & -9 \end{bmatrix}$

d) $\begin{bmatrix} -22 & -23 & -6 \end{bmatrix}$

e) $\begin{bmatrix} 15 & 20 & -40 \end{bmatrix}$. Le produit vectoriel n'est pas associatif.

f) L'opération n'est pas définie.

g) -20

28. $\begin{bmatrix} \dfrac{17}{\sqrt{339}} & -\dfrac{7}{\sqrt{339}} & \dfrac{1}{\sqrt{339}} \end{bmatrix}$ ou

$\begin{bmatrix} -\dfrac{17}{\sqrt{339}} & \dfrac{7}{\sqrt{339}} & -\dfrac{1}{\sqrt{339}} \end{bmatrix}$

29. $\begin{bmatrix} -\dfrac{35}{\sqrt{171}} & -\dfrac{5}{\sqrt{171}} & \dfrac{55}{\sqrt{171}} \end{bmatrix}$ ou

$\begin{bmatrix} \dfrac{35}{\sqrt{171}} & \dfrac{5}{\sqrt{171}} & -\dfrac{55}{\sqrt{171}} \end{bmatrix}$

30. $\sqrt{19} \approx 4,4$ unités carrées

31. a) Les coordonnées du point *B* sont
$(30\cos 20°, 30\sin 20°) \approx (28,2 \,;\, 10,3)$
et les coordonnées du point *C* sont
$(50\cos 130°, 50\sin 130°) \approx (-32,1 \,;\, 38,3)$

b) $\|\overrightarrow{AB}\| + \|\overrightarrow{BC}\| + \|\overrightarrow{CA}\| \approx 146,5$ m.

c) Dans l'espace, les coordonnées des sommets du triangle sont *A*(0, 0, 0), *B*(28,2 ; 10,3 ; 0) et *C*(−32,1 ; 38,3 ; 0).

d) L'aire du triangle ≈ 705 m^2.

32. Si $P(x_0, y_0)$, $Q(x_1, y_1)$ et $R(x_2, y_2)$ sont trois points non colinéaires du plan, alors l'aire *A* du triangle *PQR* est donnée par
$$A = \frac{1}{2}\left|(x_1 - x_0)(y_2 - y_0) - (x_2 - x_0)(y_1 - y_0)\right|$$

Preuve

On ajoute une cote 0 aux coordonnées de chacun des trois points pour les transformer en coordonnées de l'espace :
$$P(x_0, y_0, 0), \ Q(x_1, y_1, 0) \text{ et } R(x_2, y_2, 0)$$

Les vecteurs
$\overrightarrow{PQ} = \begin{bmatrix} x_1 - x_0 & y_1 - y_0 & 0 \end{bmatrix}$ et
$\overrightarrow{PR} = \begin{bmatrix} x_2 - x_0 & y_2 - y_0 & 0 \end{bmatrix}$

correspondent à deux côtés du triangle, et l'aire de celui-ci est égale à la moitié de l'aire du parallélogramme qui a en commun ces deux côtés. Par conséquent, l'aire A du triangle est égale à la moitié du module du produit vectoriel de $\overrightarrow{PQ}$ et $\overrightarrow{PR}$, c'est-à-dire que $A = \frac{1}{2} \|\overrightarrow{PQ} \times \overrightarrow{PR}\|$. Or,

$$\overrightarrow{PQ} \times \overrightarrow{PR} = \begin{vmatrix} \vec{i} & \vec{j} & \vec{k} \\ x_1 - x_0 & y_1 - y_0 & 0 \\ x_2 - x_0 & y_2 - y_0 & 0 \end{vmatrix}$$

$$= \left[(x_1 - x_0)(y_2 - y_0) - (x_2 - x_0)(y_1 - y_0) \right] \vec{k}$$

d'où,

$$\|\overrightarrow{PQ} \times \overrightarrow{PR}\| = \sqrt{\left[(x_1 - x_0)(y_2 - y_0) - (x_2 - x_0)(y_1 - y_0) \right]^2}$$
$$= \left| (x_1 - x_0)(y_2 - y_0) - (x_2 - x_0)(y_1 - y_0) \right|$$

Par conséquent,

$$A = \frac{1}{2} \left| (x_1 - x_0)(y_2 - y_0) - (x_2 - x_0)(y_1 - y_0) \right| \quad \blacksquare$$

33. 15 N·m

34. 4 unités cubes

35. Les points A, B, C et D sont coplanaires.

36. Le volume du tétraèdre décrit au n° 3 est égal à 11 unités cubes, et celui du tétraèdre décrit au n° 25 est égal à $\frac{1}{3}$ unité cube.

37.
a) Faux g) Vrai
b) Vrai h) Faux
c) Vrai i) Vrai
d) Faux j) Faux
e) Faux k) Vrai
f) Faux l) Vrai

38. Les vecteurs

$$\vec{u} = \begin{bmatrix} u_1 & u_2 & u_3 \end{bmatrix}$$
$$\vec{v} = \begin{bmatrix} v_1 & v_2 & v_3 \end{bmatrix}$$
$$\vec{w} = \begin{bmatrix} w_1 & w_2 & w_3 \end{bmatrix}$$

forment une base de $\mathbb{R}^3$ si et seulement si

$$\begin{vmatrix} u_1 & v_1 & w_1 \\ u_2 & v_2 & w_2 \\ u_3 & v_3 & w_3 \end{vmatrix} \neq 0$$

Preuve

($\Rightarrow$) Si $\vec{u} = \begin{bmatrix} u_1 & u_2 & u_3 \end{bmatrix}$, $\vec{v} = \begin{bmatrix} v_1 & v_2 & v_3 \end{bmatrix}$ et $\vec{w} = \begin{bmatrix} w_1 & w_2 & w_3 \end{bmatrix}$ forment une base de $\mathbb{R}^3$, alors ces vecteurs sont linéairement indépendants. Par conséquent, l'unique solution de l'équation vectorielle $a\vec{u} + b\vec{v} + c\vec{w} = \vec{0}$ est $a = 0$, $b = 0$ et $c = 0$. Le système d'équations linéaires associé à cette équation vectorielle est

$$u_1(a) + v_1(b) + w_1(c) = 0$$
$$u_2(a) + v_2(b) + w_2(c) = 0$$
$$u_3(a) + v_3(b) + w_3(c) = 0$$

et il admet donc une solution unique. En vertu de la règle de Cramer, le déterminant de la matrice des coefficients du système doit être différent de zéro, c'est-à-dire que

$$\begin{vmatrix} u_1 & v_1 & w_1 \\ u_2 & v_2 & w_2 \\ u_3 & v_3 & w_3 \end{vmatrix} \neq 0$$

($\Leftarrow$) Soit $\vec{u} = \begin{bmatrix} u_1 & u_2 & u_3 \end{bmatrix}$, $\vec{v} = \begin{bmatrix} v_1 & v_2 & v_3 \end{bmatrix}$ et $\vec{w} = \begin{bmatrix} w_1 & w_2 & w_3 \end{bmatrix}$ trois vecteurs de $\mathbb{R}^3$ tels que

$$\begin{vmatrix} u_1 & v_1 & w_1 \\ u_2 & v_2 & w_2 \\ u_3 & v_3 & w_3 \end{vmatrix} \neq 0$$

Si $a\vec{u} + b\vec{v} + c\vec{w} = \vec{0}$, alors

$$u_1(a) + v_1(b) + w_1(c) = 0$$
$$u_2(a) + v_2(b) + w_2(c) = 0$$
$$u_3(a) + v_3(b) + w_3(c) = 0$$

Comme le déterminant de la matrice des coefficients de ce système est différent de zéro, en vertu de la règle de Cramer, le système admet une solution unique. Or, la solution $a = 0$, $b = 0$ et $c = 0$ est cette solution unique. Par conséquent,

$$a\vec{u} + b\vec{v} + c\vec{w} = \vec{0} \Rightarrow a = 0,\ b = 0 \text{ et } c = 0$$

Les vecteurs $\vec{u}$, $\vec{v}$ et $\vec{w}$ sont donc linéairement indépendants.

Il faut également vérifier que les vecteurs $\vec{u}$, $\vec{v}$ et $\vec{w}$ forment un système générateur avant de conclure qu'ils forment une base de $\mathbb{R}^3$. On doit donc montrer que si $\vec{t} = \begin{bmatrix} t_1 & t_2 & t_3 \end{bmatrix}$ est un vecteur quelconque de $\mathbb{R}^3$, alors ce vecteur s'écrit comme une combinaison linéaire des vecteurs $\vec{u}$, $\vec{v}$ et $\vec{w}$. Or, $a\vec{u} + b\vec{v} + c\vec{w} = \vec{t}$ donne le système d'équations linéaires

$$u_1(a) + v_1(b) + w_1(c) = t_1$$
$$u_2(a) + v_2(b) + w_2(c) = t_2$$
$$u_3(a) + v_3(b) + w_3(c) = t_3$$

où les inconnues sont a, b et c. Le déterminant de la matrice des coefficients étant différent de zéro, en vertu de la règle de Cramer, le système admet une solution unique. Par conséquent, tout vecteur $\vec{t} = \begin{bmatrix} t_1 & t_2 & t_3 \end{bmatrix}$ de $\mathbb{R}^3$ s'écrit comme une combinaison linéaire des vecteurs $\vec{u}$, $\vec{v}$ et $\vec{w}$. Ces trois vecteurs forment donc un système générateur de $\mathbb{R}^3$.

Comme les vecteurs $\vec{u}$, $\vec{v}$ et $\vec{w}$ sont linéairement indépendants et qu'ils forment un système générateur de $\mathbb{R}^3$, ils forment une base de $\mathbb{R}^3$. ∎

39. a) $\vec{u} \cdot \vec{v} = 0$: les vecteurs sont orthogonaux.

b) $\vec{w} = \vec{u} \times \vec{v} = \begin{bmatrix} -2 & -8 & 4 \end{bmatrix}$

c) $\begin{bmatrix} \dfrac{2}{\sqrt{14}} & \dfrac{1}{\sqrt{14}} & \dfrac{3}{\sqrt{14}} \end{bmatrix}$, $\begin{bmatrix} -\dfrac{2}{\sqrt{6}} & \dfrac{1}{\sqrt{6}} & \dfrac{1}{\sqrt{6}} \end{bmatrix}$ et $\begin{bmatrix} -\dfrac{1}{\sqrt{21}} & -\dfrac{4}{\sqrt{21}} & \dfrac{2}{\sqrt{21}} \end{bmatrix}$

40. Le produit vectoriel de deux vecteurs $\vec{u}$ et $\vec{v}$ est un vecteur perpendiculaire au plan contenant $\vec{u}$ et $\vec{v}$. Dans le cas de deux vecteurs de $\mathbb{R}^2$, on obtiendrait un vecteur extérieur au plan xy, qu'on ne pourrait pas décrire sans l'aide d'une troisième composante. Or, les vecteurs de $\mathbb{R}^2$ n'ayant que deux composantes, le produit vectoriel n'est pas défini pour ces vecteurs. On peut toutefois ajouter une cote 0 à deux vecteurs quelconques de $\mathbb{R}^2$ pour les transformer en des vecteurs de $\mathbb{R}^3$, et il est alors possible de calculer leur produit vectoriel.

41. a) Scalaire
b) Vecteur
c) Non défini
d) Non défini
e) Scalaire
f) Scalaire
g) Vecteur
h) Scalaire

CHAPITRE 9

1. La formulation de l'équation vectorielle d'une droite n'est pas unique. Vos réponses peuvent différer de celles qui sont proposées.

a) $\Delta_1 : \begin{bmatrix} x & y & z \end{bmatrix} = \begin{bmatrix} -1 & -3 & 2 \end{bmatrix} + k_1 \begin{bmatrix} 5 & 5 & 0 \end{bmatrix}$
où $k_1 \in \mathbb{R}$

b) $\Delta_2 : \begin{bmatrix} x & y & z \end{bmatrix} = \begin{bmatrix} 2 & 4 & 6 \end{bmatrix} + k_2 \begin{bmatrix} 1 & 3 & -1 \end{bmatrix}$
où $k_2 \in \mathbb{R}$

c) $\Delta_3 : \begin{bmatrix} x & y & z \end{bmatrix} = \begin{bmatrix} -1 & -2 & 3 \end{bmatrix} + k_3 \begin{bmatrix} 0 & 1 & 0 \end{bmatrix}$
où $k_3 \in \mathbb{R}$

d) $\Delta_4 : \begin{bmatrix} x & y & z \end{bmatrix} = \begin{bmatrix} 3 & -2 & 1 \end{bmatrix} + k_4 \begin{bmatrix} -8 & -2 & -12 \end{bmatrix}$
où $k_4 \in \mathbb{R}$

e) $\Delta_5 : \begin{bmatrix} x & y & z \end{bmatrix} = k_5 \begin{bmatrix} 2 & -1 & 2 \end{bmatrix}$ où $k_5 \in \mathbb{R}$

2. A et D

3. a) $P_1(3, 1, 2)$ et $\vec{d_1} = \begin{bmatrix} 2 & 4 & -3 \end{bmatrix}$
b) $P_2(0, 0, 0)$ et $\vec{d_2} = \begin{bmatrix} -1 & 2 & -2 \end{bmatrix}$
c) $P_3(4, 2, 0)$ et $\vec{d_3} = \begin{bmatrix} -2 & -1 & 1 \end{bmatrix}$
d) $P_4(3, 0, 2)$ et $\vec{d_4} = \begin{bmatrix} -4 & 1 & 0 \end{bmatrix}$
e) $P_5(1, -1, -4)$ et $\vec{d_5} = \begin{bmatrix} 3 & 2 & -5 \end{bmatrix}$
f) $P_6(0, 4, 6)$ et $\vec{d_6} = \begin{bmatrix} 3 & 2 & 0 \end{bmatrix}$

4. a) $b_1 = 1$ et $c_1 = -9$
b) $a_2 = 7$ et $c_2 = 10$
c) $a_3 = 4$ et $b_3 = -2$

5. La formulation des équations paramétriques ou symétriques d'une droite n'est pas unique. Vos réponses peuvent différer de celles qui sont proposées.

a) $\Delta_1 : \left. \begin{array}{l} x = -1 + 5\,k_1 \\ y = -3 + 5\,k_1 \\ z = 2 \end{array} \right\}$ où $k_1 \in \mathbb{R}$ et

$\Delta_1 : \dfrac{x+1}{5} = \dfrac{y+3}{5} \quad z = 2$

b) $\Delta_2 : \left. \begin{array}{l} x = 2 + k_2 \\ y = 4 + 3\,k_2 \\ z = 6 - k_2 \end{array} \right\}$ où $k_2 \in \mathbb{R}$ et

$\Delta_2 : x - 2 = \dfrac{y-4}{3} = \dfrac{z-6}{-1}$

c) $\Delta_3 : \left. \begin{array}{l} x = -1 \\ y = -2 + k_3 \\ z = 3 \end{array} \right\}$ où $k_3 \in \mathbb{R}$ et

$\Delta_3 : x = -1 \quad z = 3 \quad y \in \mathbb{R}$

d) $\Delta_4 : \left. \begin{array}{l} x = 3 - 8\,k_4 \\ y = -2 - 2\,k_4 \\ z = 1 - 12\,k_4 \end{array} \right\}$ où $k_4 \in \mathbb{R}$ et

$\Delta_4 : \dfrac{x-3}{-8} = \dfrac{y+2}{-2} = \dfrac{z-1}{-12}$

e) $\Delta_5 : \left.\begin{array}{l} x = 2k_5 \\ y = -k_5 \\ z = 2k_5 \end{array}\right\}$ où $k_5 \in \mathbb{R}$ et

$$\Delta_5 : \frac{x}{2} = \frac{y}{-1} = \frac{z}{2}$$

f) $\Delta_6 : \left.\begin{array}{l} x = 4 + 2k_6 \\ y = 1 - k_6 \\ z = 1 + 2k_6 \end{array}\right\}$ où $k_6 \in \mathbb{R}$ et

$$\Delta_6 : \frac{x - 4}{2} = \frac{y - 1}{-1} = \frac{z - 1}{2}$$

6. Si $\vec{d}$ est un vecteur directeur d'une droite Δ, et si $\overrightarrow{OP}$ et $\overrightarrow{OQ}$ sont des vecteurs position respectifs de deux points de la droite Δ, alors $\overrightarrow{OP} \times \vec{d} = \overrightarrow{OQ} \times \vec{d}$.

Preuve

P et Q étant deux points de la droite Δ, le vecteur $\overrightarrow{PQ}$ est parallèle à tout vecteur directeur de cette droite. Par conséquent,

$$\overrightarrow{PQ} \times \vec{d} = \vec{0}$$
$$(\overrightarrow{PO} + \overrightarrow{OQ}) \times \vec{d} = \vec{0}$$
$$\overrightarrow{PO} \times \vec{d} + \overrightarrow{OQ} \times \vec{d} = \vec{0}$$
$$\overrightarrow{OQ} \times \vec{d} = -\overrightarrow{PO} \times \vec{d} = \overrightarrow{OP} \times \vec{d} \qquad \blacksquare$$

7. La formulation de l'équation vectorielle d'une droite n'est pas unique. Vos réponses peuvent différer de celles qui sont proposées.

a) $\Delta_1 : \begin{bmatrix} x & y & z \end{bmatrix} = \begin{bmatrix} 1 & -1 & -4 \end{bmatrix} + k_1\begin{bmatrix} 3 & 2 & -5 \end{bmatrix}$ où $k_1 \in \mathbb{R}$

b) $\Delta_2 : \begin{bmatrix} x & y & z \end{bmatrix} = \begin{bmatrix} 4 & 2 & 0 \end{bmatrix} + k_2\begin{bmatrix} -2 & -1 & 1 \end{bmatrix}$ où $k_2 \in \mathbb{R}$

c) $\Delta_3 : \begin{bmatrix} x & y & z \end{bmatrix} = \begin{bmatrix} 2 & 5 & 2 \end{bmatrix} + k_3\begin{bmatrix} 3 & -8 & 0 \end{bmatrix}$ où $k_3 \in \mathbb{R}$

d) $\Delta_4 : \begin{bmatrix} x & y & z \end{bmatrix} = \begin{bmatrix} 4 & -2 & 5 \end{bmatrix} + k_4\begin{bmatrix} 0 & 3 & -1 \end{bmatrix}$ où $k_4 \in \mathbb{R}$

e) $\Delta_5 : \begin{bmatrix} x & y & z \end{bmatrix} = \begin{bmatrix} 2 & 1 & -1 \end{bmatrix} + k_5\begin{bmatrix} -1 & 1 & -4 \end{bmatrix}$ où $k_5 \in \mathbb{R}$

f) $\Delta_6 : \begin{bmatrix} x & y & z \end{bmatrix} = \begin{bmatrix} 2 & -1 & 3 \end{bmatrix} + k_6\begin{bmatrix} \dfrac{1}{2} & -\dfrac{1}{2} & \dfrac{\sqrt{2}}{2} \end{bmatrix}$ où $k_6 \in \mathbb{R}$

8. a) $\dfrac{\sqrt{224}}{\sqrt{38}} \approx 2{,}4$ unités

b) $\dfrac{\sqrt{502}}{\sqrt{43}} \approx 3{,}4$ unités

c) 0 unité : le point Q_3 appartient à la droite Δ_3.

d) $\dfrac{\sqrt{315}}{\sqrt{14}} \approx 4{,}7$ unités

9. Si P et Q sont des points distincts d'une droite Δ de l'espace et si R est un point extérieur à cette droite, alors la distance du point R à la droite Δ est égale à

$$h = \frac{\|\overrightarrow{RP} \times \overrightarrow{RQ}\|}{\|\overrightarrow{PQ}\|}$$

Preuve

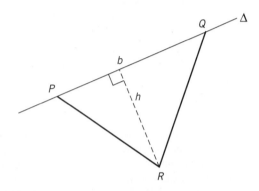

D'une part, l'aire du triangle PQR représenté ci-dessus est égale à

$$\frac{1}{2} bh = \frac{1}{2} \|\overrightarrow{PQ}\| h$$

où h désigne à la fois la hauteur du triangle et la distance entre le point R et la droite qui passe par les points P et Q.

D'autre part, on sait que l'aire du triangle PQR est aussi égale à $\frac{1}{2}\|\overrightarrow{RP} \times \overrightarrow{RQ}\|$. Par conséquent,

$$\|\overrightarrow{RP} \times \overrightarrow{RQ}\| = \|\overrightarrow{PQ}\| h \quad \Rightarrow \quad h = \frac{\|\overrightarrow{RP} \times \overrightarrow{RQ}\|}{\|\overrightarrow{PQ}\|}$$

La distance du point R à la droite Δ est donc égale à

$$\frac{\|\overrightarrow{RP} \times \overrightarrow{RQ}\|}{\|\overrightarrow{PQ}\|} \qquad \blacksquare$$

10. a) Les droites Δ_1 et Δ_2 sont gauches.

b) Les droites Δ_3 et Δ_4 sont parallèles distinctes, et la distance qui les sépare est égale à

$$\frac{\sqrt{173}}{\sqrt{14}} \approx 3{,}5 \text{ unités}$$

c) Les droites Δ_5 et Δ_6 sont parallèles confondues.

d) Les droites Δ_7 et Δ_8 sont concourantes, leur point d'intersection est $(2, -1, 1)$ et l'angle qu'elles déterminent est égal à

$$\arccos \frac{1}{\sqrt{6}\,\sqrt{22}} \approx 85,0°$$

e) Les droites Δ_9 et Δ_{10} sont concourantes, leur point d'intersection est $(-9,\ 10,\ 5)$, et l'angle qu'elles déterminent est égal à

$$\arccos \frac{102}{\sqrt{61}\,\sqrt{236}} \approx 31,8°$$

f) Les droites Δ_{11} et Δ_{12} sont concourantes, leur point d'intersection est $(4,\ 4,\ 4)$, et l'angle qu'elles déterminent est égal à

$$\arccos \frac{11}{\sqrt{3}\,\sqrt{43}} \approx 14,4°$$

g) Les droites Δ_{13} et Δ_{14} sont gauches.

h) Les droites Δ_{15} et Δ_{16} sont parallèles distinctes, et la distance qui les sépare est égale à

$$\frac{\sqrt{168}}{\sqrt{14}} \approx 3,5 \text{ unités}$$

11. a) $\left(\dfrac{5}{3},\ \dfrac{5}{3},\ -\dfrac{5}{3}\right)$

b) $\left(\dfrac{7}{6},\ \dfrac{8}{3},\ -\dfrac{7}{6}\right)$

c) $(3,\ -1,\ -3)$

d) $\left(\dfrac{7}{3},\ \dfrac{1}{3},\ -\dfrac{7}{3}\right)$

12. a) La droite Δ est incluse dans un plan parallèle au plan xz.

b) La droite Δ passe par l'origine.

c) La droite Δ est parallèle à l'axe des ordonnées et perpendiculaire au plan xz.

d) La droite Δ est parallèle à l'axe des abscisses et perpendiculaire au plan yz.

e) La droite Δ est incluse dans un plan parallèle au plan yz.

13. Si $p_2 d_3 = p_3 d_2 \neq 0$, alors la droite donnée par

$$\Delta: x = p_1 + d_1 k \quad y = p_2 + d_2 k \quad z = p_3 + d_3 k$$

où $k \in \mathbb{R}$ coupe l'axe des abscisses.

Preuve

Pour montrer que la droite Δ coupe l'axe des abscisses, il faut montrer qu'elle passe par un point dont l'ordonnée et la cote valent zéro. Or, $d_3 \neq 0$ parce que $p_2 d_3 \neq 0$. Par conséquent,

$$z = 0 \quad \Rightarrow \quad k = -\frac{p_3}{d_3}$$

$$\Rightarrow \quad y = p_2 + d_2\left(-\frac{p_3}{d_3}\right) = \frac{p_2 d_3 - p_3 d_2}{d_3}$$

Comme $p_2 d_3 = p_3 d_2 \Rightarrow p_2 d_3 - p_3 d_2 = 0$, on en déduit que $y = 0$. Par conséquent, la droite Δ passe par un point dont l'ordonnée et la cote valent zéro. La droite Δ coupe donc l'axe des abscisses. ■

14. Si a, b et c sont trois nombres réels non nuls, alors la droite Δ passant par le point $A(a,\ b,\ c)$ et de vecteur directeur $\vec{d} = \begin{bmatrix} a & b & c \end{bmatrix}$ passe par l'origine.

Preuve

Il faut montrer que la droite Δ passe par le point $(0,\ 0,\ 0)$. Les équations paramétriques de cette droite sont données par

$$\Delta: x = a + ak \quad y = b + bk \quad z = c + ck$$

où $k \in \mathbb{R}$.

Si on pose $k = -1$, on obtient $x = 0$, $y = 0$ et $z = 0$. Par conséquent, la droite Δ passe par l'origine. ■

15. Les équations symétriques de la droite qui passe par les points $A(a_1,\ b_1,\ c_1)$ et $B(a_2,\ b_2,\ c_2)$ (dont les coordonnées correspondantes sont distinctes) s'écrivent sous la forme

$$\frac{x - a_1}{a_2 - a_1} = \frac{y - b_1}{b_2 - b_1} = \frac{z - c_1}{c_2 - c_1}$$

Preuve

Le vecteur $\overrightarrow{AB} = \begin{bmatrix} a_2 - a_1 & b_2 - b_1 & c_2 - c_1 \end{bmatrix}$ est un vecteur directeur de la droite dont toutes les composantes sont non nulles parce que les coordonnées correspondantes des points A et B sont distinctes. Si on choisit le point A et qu'on prend $\overrightarrow{AB}$ comme vecteur directeur, les équations symétriques de la droite sont

$$\frac{x - a_1}{a_2 - a_1} = \frac{y - b_1}{b_2 - b_1} = \frac{z - c_1}{c_2 - c_1}$$ ■

16. $k = -\dfrac{\vec{d} \cdot \overrightarrow{OP}}{\|\vec{d}\|^2}$

17. Tous les points $X(x,\ y,\ z)$ de la droite qui passe par les points $P(p_1,\ p_2,\ p_3)$ et $Q(q_1,\ q_2,\ q_3)$ vérifient les équations paramétriques

$$x = (1 - k)p_1 + kq_1$$
$$y = (1 - k)p_2 + kq_2$$
$$z = (1 - k)p_3 + kq_3$$

où $k \in \mathbb{R}$.

Preuve

Le vecteur $\overrightarrow{PQ} = \begin{bmatrix} q_1 - p_1 & q_2 - p_2 & q_3 - p_3 \end{bmatrix}$ est un vecteur directeur de la droite. Si on choisit le point P et qu'on prend $\overrightarrow{PQ}$ comme vecteur directeur, les équations paramétriques de la droite sont

$$x = p_1 + k(q_1 - p_1)$$
$$y = p_2 + k(q_2 - p_2)$$
$$z = p_3 + k(q_3 - p_3)$$

où $k \in \mathbb{R}$.

En regroupant les termes en p_i, on obtient les équations paramétriques

$$x = (1 - k)p_1 + kq_1$$
$$y = (1 - k)p_2 + kq_2$$
$$z = (1 - k)p_3 + kq_3$$

où $k \in \mathbb{R}$. ∎

18. Les plans π_1, π_4 et π_8 sont mutuellement parallèles. Les plans π_2, π_3, π_5 et π_7 sont mutuellement parallèles. Seul le plan π_6 n'est parallèle à aucun autre plan.

19. Les plans π_1 et π_2 sont perpendiculaires; il en est de même pour les plans π_1 et π_4 ainsi que pour les plans π_2 et π_3.

20. Seules les droites Δ_1, Δ_2 et Δ_4 sont parallèles au plan π.

21. Seules les droites Δ_2, Δ_4 et Δ_5 sont perpendiculaires au plan π.

22. La formulation de l'équation cartésienne d'un plan n'est pas unique. Vos réponses peuvent différer de celles qui sont proposées.

a) $\pi_1 : -5x + 5y + 30z = 50$ ou encore
$\pi_1 : -x + y + 6z = 10$

b) $\pi_2 : -x + 4y + 2z = 1$

c) $\pi_3 : 3x + 2y - 5z = 20$

d) $\pi_5 : 3x - 4y + 5z = 20$

e) $\pi_6 : 3x + 4y + 5z = 40$

f) $\pi_7 : 3x - 3y - 3z = 6$ ou $\pi_7 : x - y - z = 2$

g) $\pi_{10} : -x + 6y - 3z = -1$

h) $\pi_{11} : -4y = -8$ ou encore $\pi_{11} : y = 2$

23. a) $b = 9$

b) $a = -10$ et $b = 5$

c) A, C et D

d) $(2, 4, -14)$

24. La formulation de l'équation normale d'un plan n'est pas unique. Vos réponses peuvent différer de celles qui sont proposées.

a) $\pi_1 : \dfrac{6}{7}x + \dfrac{2}{7}y + \dfrac{3}{7}z = -1$

b) $\pi_2 : \dfrac{6}{7}x + \dfrac{2}{7}y + \dfrac{3}{7}z = \dfrac{18}{7}$

c) $\pi_3 :$
$$\dfrac{bc}{\sqrt{b^2c^2 + a^2c^2 + a^2b^2}}x$$
$$+ \dfrac{ac}{\sqrt{b^2c^2 + a^2c^2 + a^2b^2}}y$$
$$+ \dfrac{ab}{\sqrt{b^2c^2 + a^2c^2 + a^2b^2}}z$$
$$= \dfrac{abc}{\sqrt{b^2c^2 + a^2c^2 + a^2b^2}}$$

25. a) La droite Δ_1 est parallèle au plan π_1 quelle que soit la valeur de s.

b) 6

c) $s = -9$ ou $s = 21$

d) $t = 17$. La distance entre la droite Δ_1 et le plan π_2 est égale à $\dfrac{58}{\sqrt{425}} \approx 2,8$ unités.

e) -8

f) $r = 4$. Le point d'intersection des droites Δ_1 et Δ_2 est $(11, 18, 17)$.

26. a) $\dfrac{50}{\sqrt{950}} \approx 1,6$ unité

b) $\dfrac{1}{\sqrt{21}} \approx 0,2$ unité

c) La distance du plan π_3 à l'origine vaut
$$\dfrac{20}{\sqrt{38}} \approx 3,2 \text{ unités}$$
La distance du plan π_4 à l'origine vaut
$$\dfrac{3}{\sqrt{38}} \approx 0,5 \text{ unité}$$

d) $\dfrac{20}{\sqrt{50}} \approx 2,8$ unités

e) $\dfrac{40}{\sqrt{50}} \approx 5,7$ unités

f) La distance du plan π_7 à l'origine vaut
$$\dfrac{6}{\sqrt{27}} \approx 1,2 \text{ unité}$$
La distance du plan π_8 à l'origine vaut
$$\dfrac{3}{\sqrt{6}} \approx 1,2 \text{ unité}$$
La distance du plan π_9 à l'origine vaut
$$\dfrac{2}{\sqrt{6}} \approx 0,8 \text{ unité}$$

g) $\dfrac{1}{\sqrt{46}} \approx 0{,}1$ unité

h) 2 unités

27. a) $\dfrac{10{,}5}{\sqrt{14}} \approx 2{,}8$ unités

b) $\dfrac{4}{\sqrt{11}} \approx 1{,}2$ unité

c) $\dfrac{12}{\sqrt{6}} \approx 4{,}9$ unités

d) 0 unité

e) 0 unité

f) $\dfrac{11}{\sqrt{24}} \approx 2{,}2$ unités

g) 0 unité

h) 0 unité

28. a) Les vecteurs normaux respectifs aux plans π_1 et π_2 ne sont pas parallèles ; les plans π_1 et π_2 ne le sont donc pas non plus. Or, la formule employée s'applique uniquement au calcul de la distance entre deux plans parallèles.

b) La formule employée s'applique uniquement dans le cas où les coefficients des inconnues sont identiques dans les équations respectives des deux plans. Il aurait donc fallu diviser d'abord chaque membre de l'équation du plan π_2 par 2. La distance entre les plans π_1 et π_2 est en réalité égale à

$$\dfrac{1}{\sqrt{14}} \approx 0{,}3 \text{ unité}$$

c) La formule employée est celle de la distance entre une droite et un plan parallèles. Dans ce cas, tout vecteur directeur de la droite est perpendiculaire à un vecteur normal au plan. Or, $\vec{n} \cdot \vec{d} = 9 \neq 0$. par conséquent, le vecteur normal au plan n'est pas perpendiculaire au vecteur directeur de la droite, et la droite n'est donc pas parallèle au plan. En fait, la droite coupe le plan au point $(1, \tfrac{14}{3}, \tfrac{1}{3})$.

29. $(\tfrac{5}{3}, \tfrac{5}{3}, \tfrac{5}{3})$

30. a) $(\tfrac{39}{14}, \tfrac{5}{28}, \tfrac{73}{28})$

b) $(\tfrac{23}{6}, \tfrac{5}{6}, -\tfrac{2}{3})$

c) $(2, -1, 3)$

d) $(\tfrac{5}{2}, 0, \tfrac{1}{2})$

31. a) $\dfrac{5}{\sqrt{90}} \approx 0{,}5$ unité

b) $\dfrac{14}{\sqrt{104}} \approx 1{,}4$ unité

c) $\dfrac{\sqrt{475}}{\sqrt{14}} \approx 5{,}8$ unités

32. a) $(\tfrac{5}{3}, 0, 0)$, $(0, \tfrac{5}{2}, 0)$ et $(0, 0, -5)$

b) L'intersection des plans π_2, π_3 et π_4 est vide : les trois plans n'ont pas de point commun.

c) $(\tfrac{2}{3}, \tfrac{7}{3}, -2)$

d) La droite Δ_2.

e) $(8, -32, -21)$

f) L'intersection de la droite Δ_4 et le plan π_8 est vide : la droite et le plan n'ont aucun point commun ; la droite Δ_4 est parallèle au plan π_8.

33. a) La droite Δ est parallèle au plan π si $\vec{n} \cdot \vec{d} = 0$.

Preuve

Une droite est parallèle à un plan si tout vecteur directeur de la droite est perpendiculaire à un vecteur normal au plan, c'est-à-dire si $\vec{n} \cdot \vec{d} = 0$. ∎

b) Si $\vec{n} \cdot \vec{d} \neq 0$, le vecteur position du point d'intersection R de la droite Δ avec le plan π est égal à

$$\overrightarrow{OP} + \left(\dfrac{\vec{n} \cdot \overrightarrow{PQ}}{\vec{n} \cdot \vec{d}} \right) \vec{d}$$

Preuve

Comme P et R sont deux points de la droite Δ,

$$\overrightarrow{PR} = k\vec{d} \; \Rightarrow \; \overrightarrow{PO} + \overrightarrow{OR} = k\vec{d}$$
$$\Rightarrow \; \overrightarrow{OR} = \overrightarrow{OP} + k\vec{d}$$

Comme Q et R sont deux points du plan π,

$$\vec{n} \cdot \overrightarrow{QR} = 0 \; \Rightarrow \; \vec{n} \cdot (\overrightarrow{QO} + \overrightarrow{OR}) = 0$$
$$\Rightarrow \; \vec{n} \cdot \overrightarrow{OR} = \vec{n} \cdot \overrightarrow{OQ}$$

En remplaçant, dans l'équation du plan π, le vecteur $\overrightarrow{OR}$ par le membre de droite de $\overrightarrow{OR} = \overrightarrow{OP} + k\vec{d}$ puis en isolant la constante k, on obtient

$$\vec{n} \cdot \overrightarrow{OR} = \vec{n} \cdot \overrightarrow{OQ}$$
$$\vec{n} \cdot (\overrightarrow{OP} + k\vec{d}) = \vec{n} \cdot \overrightarrow{OQ}$$
$$k(\vec{n} \cdot \vec{d}) = \vec{n} \cdot \overrightarrow{PO} + \vec{n} \cdot \overrightarrow{OQ}$$
$$k = \dfrac{\vec{n} \cdot \overrightarrow{PQ}}{\vec{n} \cdot \vec{d}}$$

Si on remplace k par sa valeur dans l'équation de la droite Δ, on a

$$\overrightarrow{OR} = \overrightarrow{OP} + k\vec{d} \; \Rightarrow \; \overrightarrow{OR} = \overrightarrow{OP} + \left(\dfrac{\vec{n} \cdot \overrightarrow{PQ}}{\vec{n} \cdot \vec{d}} \right) \vec{d}$$ ∎

c) La distance entre le point P de Δ et le point d'intersection R de la droite Δ avec le plan π est égale à

$$\left| \frac{\vec{n} \cdot \overrightarrow{PQ}}{\vec{n} \cdot \vec{d}} \right| \|\vec{d}\|$$

Preuve

La distance entre les points P et R est égale au module du vecteur $\overrightarrow{PR}$. Or,

$$\overrightarrow{PR} = \overrightarrow{PO} + \overrightarrow{OR}$$

$$= \overrightarrow{PO} + \overrightarrow{OP} + \left(\frac{\vec{n} \cdot \overrightarrow{PQ}}{\vec{n} \cdot \vec{d}} \right) \vec{d}$$

$$= \left(\frac{\vec{n} \cdot \overrightarrow{PQ}}{\vec{n} \cdot \vec{d}} \right) \vec{d}$$

Par conséquent, $\|\overrightarrow{PR}\| = \left| \dfrac{\vec{n} \cdot \overrightarrow{PQ}}{\vec{n} \cdot \vec{d}} \right| \|\vec{d}\|$. $\blacksquare$

34. a) $\text{arc cos} \dfrac{1}{\sqrt{14}\,\sqrt{6}} \approx 83,7°$

b) $\text{arc sin} \dfrac{9}{\sqrt{14}\,\sqrt{9}} \approx 53,3°$

c) $\text{arc cos} \dfrac{5}{\sqrt{101}\,\sqrt{3}} \approx 73,3°$

d) $\text{arc sin} \dfrac{5}{\sqrt{6}\,\sqrt{17}} \approx 29,7°$

35. La formulation de l'équation vectorielle et des équations paramétriques d'un plan n'est pas unique. Vos réponses peuvent différer de celles qui sont proposées.

a) $\pi_1 : \begin{bmatrix} x & y & z \end{bmatrix} = \begin{bmatrix} 7/4 & 0 & 0 \end{bmatrix} + r \begin{bmatrix} -7/4 & 7/6 & 0 \end{bmatrix} + s \begin{bmatrix} -7/4 & 0 & -7/2 \end{bmatrix}$

où r et $s \in \mathbb{R}$ (équation vectorielle)

$\pi_1 : x = (7/4) - (7/4)r - (7/4)s \qquad y = (7/6)r$
$z = (-7/2)s$

où r et $s \in \mathbb{R}$ (équations paramétriques)

b) $\pi_2 : \begin{bmatrix} x & y & z \end{bmatrix} = \begin{bmatrix} 6 & 0 & 0 \end{bmatrix} + r \begin{bmatrix} -6 & 6 & 0 \end{bmatrix} + s \begin{bmatrix} -6 & 0 & -3 \end{bmatrix}$

où r et $s \in \mathbb{R}$ (équation vectorielle)

$\pi_2 : x = 6 - 6r - 6s \qquad y = 6r \qquad z = -3s$

où r et $s \in \mathbb{R}$ (équations paramétriques)

c) $\pi_3 : \begin{bmatrix} x & y & z \end{bmatrix} = \begin{bmatrix} -1 & 2 & -3 \end{bmatrix} + r \begin{bmatrix} -1 & 3 & 2 \end{bmatrix} + s \begin{bmatrix} 4 & 1 & 3 \end{bmatrix}$

où r et $s \in \mathbb{R}$ (équation vectorielle)

$\pi_3 : x = -1 - r + 4s \qquad y = 2 + 3r + s$
$z = -3 + 2r + 3s$

où r et $s \in \mathbb{R}$ (équations paramétriques)

d) $\pi_4 : \begin{bmatrix} x & y & z \end{bmatrix} = \begin{bmatrix} -1 & 3 & 2 \end{bmatrix} + r \begin{bmatrix} 0 & 1 & 0 \end{bmatrix} + s \begin{bmatrix} 0 & 0 & 1 \end{bmatrix}$

où r et $s \in \mathbb{R}$ (équation vectorielle)

$\pi_4 : x = -1 \qquad y = 3 + r \qquad z = 2 + s$

où r et $s \in \mathbb{R}$ (équations paramétriques)

e) $\pi_5 : \begin{bmatrix} x & y & z \end{bmatrix} = \begin{bmatrix} 2 & 4 & -2 \end{bmatrix} + r \begin{bmatrix} 1 & 0 & 0 \end{bmatrix} + s \begin{bmatrix} 0 & 0 & 1 \end{bmatrix}$

où r et $s \in \mathbb{R}$ (équation vectorielle)

$\pi_5 : x = 2 + r \qquad y = 4 \qquad z = -2 + s$

où r et $s \in \mathbb{R}$ (équations paramétriques)

36. La formulation de l'équation d'une droite n'est pas unique. Vos réponses peuvent différer de celles qui sont proposées.

a) $\Delta_1 : \dfrac{x+1}{3} = \dfrac{y+3}{2} = \dfrac{z-2}{-5}$

b) $\Delta_2 : x = 9/2 - k_2 \quad y = 3/2 \quad z = k_2$ où $k_2 \in \mathbb{R}$

c) $\Delta_3 : \begin{bmatrix} x & y & z \end{bmatrix} = \begin{bmatrix} 0 & 3 & 0 \end{bmatrix} + k_3 \begin{bmatrix} 1 & -1 & 1 \end{bmatrix}$
où $k_3 \in \mathbb{R}$

d) $\Delta_4 : \begin{bmatrix} x & y & z \end{bmatrix} = \begin{bmatrix} -4/5 & -29/5 & 0 \end{bmatrix} + k_4 \begin{bmatrix} 13/10 & 3/10 & 1 \end{bmatrix}$

où $k_4 \in \mathbb{R}$

e) $\Delta_5 : \dfrac{x-1}{3} = \dfrac{y-1}{5} = \dfrac{z-1}{6}$

37. Soit A, B, C et D quatre points de l'espace. Ces points sont coplanaires si l'une des conditions suivantes est satisfaite :

- Les vecteurs $\overrightarrow{AB}$, $\overrightarrow{AC}$ et $\overrightarrow{AD}$ sont linéairement dépendants ;

- l'un des quatre points appartient à un plan qui passe par les trois autres points ;

- le produit mixte des vecteurs $\overrightarrow{AB}$, $\overrightarrow{AC}$ et $\overrightarrow{AD}$ est nul.

38. On a

$$\overrightarrow{AB} = \begin{bmatrix} 2 & -3 & 5 \end{bmatrix}$$

$$\overrightarrow{AC} = \begin{bmatrix} -2 & -3 & 13 \end{bmatrix}$$

$$\overrightarrow{AD} = \begin{bmatrix} 1 & -4 & 10 \end{bmatrix}$$

Donc,

$$\overrightarrow{AB} \cdot (\overrightarrow{AC} \times \overrightarrow{AD}) = \begin{vmatrix} 2 & -3 & 5 \\ -2 & -3 & 13 \\ 1 & -4 & 10 \end{vmatrix} = 0$$

Ainsi, le volume du parallélépipède dont trois arêtes correspondent respectivement aux vecteurs $\overrightarrow{AB}$, $\overrightarrow{AC}$ et $\overrightarrow{AD}$ vaut zéro : les points A, B, C et D appartiennent à un même plan. On aurait également pu déterminer l'équation du plan qui passe par les points A, B et C, puis vérifier que le point D appartient aussi à ce plan.

39. $4x - 2y + 2z = 14$

40. Si un plan π, situé à une distance p de l'origine, coupe les axes de coordonnées aux points $A(a, 0, 0)$, $B(0, b, 0)$ et $C(0, 0, c)$ où a, b et c sont des constantes différentes de zéro, alors

$$\frac{1}{p^2} = \frac{1}{a^2} + \frac{1}{b^2} + \frac{1}{c^2}$$

Preuve

Les vecteurs $\overrightarrow{AB} = \begin{bmatrix} -a & b & 0 \end{bmatrix}$ et $\overrightarrow{AC} = \begin{bmatrix} -a & 0 & c \end{bmatrix}$ sont parallèles au plan π. Par conséquent,

$$\overrightarrow{AB} \times \overrightarrow{AC} = \begin{vmatrix} \vec{i} & \vec{j} & \vec{k} \\ -a & b & 0 \\ -a & 0 & c \end{vmatrix} = \begin{bmatrix} bc & ac & ab \end{bmatrix}$$

est un vecteur normal à ce plan. L'équation cartésienne du plan π est donc

$$bcx + acy + abz = abc$$

Comme a, b et c sont des constantes différentes de zéro, on peut diviser chaque membre de cette équation par abc. On obtient ainsi l'équation cartésienne de π

$$\frac{1}{a}x + \frac{1}{b}y + \frac{1}{c}z = 1$$

La distance du plan π à l'origine est donnée par

$$p = \frac{1}{\sqrt{\dfrac{1}{a^2} + \dfrac{1}{b^2} + \dfrac{1}{c^2}}}$$

On en déduit que

$$\frac{1}{p^2} = \frac{1}{a^2} + \frac{1}{b^2} + \frac{1}{c^2} \qquad \blacksquare$$

41. Si $X(x, y, z)$ est un point quelconque du plan qui passe par les points A, B et C, alors le vecteur $\overrightarrow{AX}$ est un vecteur du plan et il est donc perpendiculaire à tout vecteur normal au plan. Comme le vecteur $\overrightarrow{AB} \times \overrightarrow{AC}$ est perpendiculaire à la fois à $\overrightarrow{AB}$ et à $\overrightarrow{AC}$, il est normal au plan qui contient ces deux vecteurs, et donc au plan qui passe par les points A, B et C. Par conséquent, $\overrightarrow{AX}$ est perpendiculaire à $\overrightarrow{AB} \times \overrightarrow{AC}$. On en déduit que $\overrightarrow{AX} \cdot (\overrightarrow{AB} \times \overrightarrow{AC}) = 0$.

On peut également utiliser le raisonnement suivant. Si X est un point quelconque du plan qui passe par les points A, B et C, alors ces quatre points sont coplanaires et le produit mixte $\overrightarrow{AX} \cdot (\overrightarrow{AB} \times \overrightarrow{AC})$ est donc nul. Ainsi, l'équation $\overrightarrow{AX} \cdot (\overrightarrow{AB} \times \overrightarrow{AC}) = 0$ décrit l'ensemble des points $X(x, y, z)$ appartenant au plan qui passe par les points A, B et C.

42. Pour définir l'ensemble des points $X(x, y, z)$ d'un plan de l'espace, il faut déterminer :

- soit trois points non colinéaires du plan ;
- soit un point du plan et un vecteur normal (perpendiculaire) au plan ;
- soit deux vecteurs linéairement indépendants et parallèles au plan et un point du plan.

43. L'équation $\vec{n} \cdot \overrightarrow{PX} = 0$ correspond au fait qu'un plan est complètement déterminé par la donnée d'un point du plan et d'un vecteur perpendiculaire au plan. En effet, un vecteur $\overrightarrow{PX}$ du plan est perpendiculaire à un vecteur normal au plan, de sorte que leur produit scalaire est nul.

L'équation $\overrightarrow{PX} = k_1\vec{u} + k_2\vec{v}$ où k_1 et $k_2 \in \mathbb{R}$ correspond au fait qu'un plan est complètement déterminé par deux vecteurs linéairement indépendants parallèles au plan et un point du plan. En effet, tout vecteur d'un plan s'écrit comme une combinaison linéaire de deux vecteurs linéairement indépendants et parallèles à ce plan.

L'équation $\overrightarrow{AX} \cdot (\overrightarrow{AB} \times \overrightarrow{AC}) = 0$ correspond au fait qu'un plan est complètement déterminé par trois points non colinéaires du plan. En effet, si X est un point quelconque du plan, alors le volume du parallélépipède déterminé par trois vecteurs du plan $\overrightarrow{AX}$, $\overrightarrow{AB}$ et $\overrightarrow{AC}$ est nul.

44.

a) Vrai	j) Vrai
b) Vrai	k) Faux
c) Faux	l) Faux
d) Faux	m) Vrai
e) Vrai	n) Vrai
f) Faux	o) Vrai
g) Vrai	p) Vrai
h) Faux	q) Vrai
i) Vrai	

45. a) $\Delta_1 : \begin{bmatrix} x & y & z \end{bmatrix} = \begin{bmatrix} 2 & 4 & -3 \end{bmatrix} + k_1\begin{bmatrix} 2 & 1 & -3 \end{bmatrix}$
où $k_1 \in \mathbb{R}$

b) Les trois points A, B et C appartiennent à la droite Δ_1.

c) $\overrightarrow{d_2} = \begin{bmatrix} 3 & 2 & -1 \end{bmatrix}$

d) $\Delta_2 : x = 7 + 3k_2 \quad y = 7 + 2k_2 \quad z = -7 - k_2$
   où $k_2 \in \mathbb{R}$

e) $\Delta_3 : \dfrac{x-3}{3} = \dfrac{y-2}{2} = \dfrac{z+3}{-1}$

f) Comme deux vecteurs directeurs des droites Δ_2 et Δ_3 sont parallèles ($\vec{d_2} = \begin{bmatrix} 3 & 2 & -1 \end{bmatrix} = \vec{d_3}$), ces droites sont parallèles. La distance entre les droites Δ_2 et Δ_3 est égale à

$$\dfrac{\sqrt{122}}{\sqrt{14}} \approx 3{,}0 \text{ unités}$$

g) Le point d'intersection des droites Δ_1 et Δ_2 est $(4, 5, -6)$. L'angle déterminé par ces deux droites est

$$\text{arc cos} \dfrac{11}{14} \approx 38{,}2°$$

h) $\dfrac{\sqrt{236}}{\sqrt{14}} \approx 4{,}1 \text{ unités}$

i) $\left(-\dfrac{10}{7}, \dfrac{16}{7}, \dfrac{15}{7} \right)$

j) $\dfrac{19}{\sqrt{75}} \approx 2{,}2 \text{ unités}$

k) $\pi_1 : \begin{bmatrix} x & y & z \end{bmatrix} = \begin{bmatrix} 2 & 4 & -3 \end{bmatrix} + r \begin{bmatrix} 2 & 1 & -3 \end{bmatrix} + s \begin{bmatrix} 3 & 2 & -1 \end{bmatrix}$
   où r et $s \in \mathbb{R}$

l) $\pi_1 : x = 2 + 2r + 3s \quad y = 4 + r + 2s \quad z = -3 - 3r - s$
   où r et $s \in \mathbb{R}$

m) $\pi_1 : 5x - 7y + z = -21$

n) $\dfrac{21}{\sqrt{75}} \approx 2{,}4 \text{ unités}$

o) $\left(-\dfrac{7}{5}, \dfrac{49}{25}, -\dfrac{7}{25} \right)$

p) $\text{arc sin} \dfrac{1}{\sqrt{75}} \approx 6{,}6°$

q) $\Delta_4 : \begin{bmatrix} x & y & z \end{bmatrix} = \begin{bmatrix} ^{7}/_{6} & ^{23}/_{6} & 0 \end{bmatrix} + k_4 \begin{bmatrix} -^{1}/_{12} & ^{1}/_{12} & 1 \end{bmatrix}$
   où $k_4 \in \mathbb{R}$

r) $\text{arc cos} \dfrac{2}{\sqrt{75}\sqrt{2}} \approx 80{,}6°$

s) $\pi_3 : -x + y + 12z = 13$

t) Le point d'intersection est $\left(-^{111}/_{13}, -^{74}/_{13}, ^{11}/_{13} \right)$. L'angle entre le plan et la droite est

$$\text{arc sin} \dfrac{13}{\sqrt{146}\sqrt{14}} \approx 16{,}7°$$

u) Les équations paramétriques de la droite Δ_5 sont
$$x = 4 + 6k_5 \quad y = -7 - 6k_5 \quad z = 2 + k_5$$
où $k_5 \in \mathbb{R}$

Ces valeurs de x, y et z vérifient l'équation du plan π_3 quelle que soit la valeur de k_5. En effet,

$$-x + y + 12z = -(4 + 6k_5) + (-7 - 6k_5) + 12(2 + k_5)$$
$$= 13$$

Par conséquent, la droite Δ_5 appartient au plan π_3.

CHAPITRE 10

1. a) $\mathbb{R}^4$

b) $\begin{bmatrix} 5 & -2 & 4 & 3 \end{bmatrix}$

c) $\begin{bmatrix} 8 & 7 & 2 & -1 \end{bmatrix}$

d) $\begin{bmatrix} ^{3}/_{2} & -^{13}/_{2} & 1 & ^{5}/_{2} \end{bmatrix}$

e) 4

f) $\sqrt{11} \approx 3{,}3 \text{ unités}$

g) 11

h) $\vec{u_4} \cdot \vec{u_4} = 11 = \|\vec{u_4}\|^2$. En général, si $\vec{u} \in \mathbb{R}^n$, alors $\vec{u} \cdot \vec{u} = \|\vec{u}\|^2$.

Preuve

Si $\vec{u} = \begin{bmatrix} u_1 & u_2 & \cdots & u_n \end{bmatrix}$, alors

$$\vec{u} \cdot \vec{u} = (u_1)(u_1) + (u_2)(u_2) + \cdots + (u_n)(u_n)$$
$$= u_1^2 + u_2^2 + \cdots + u_n^2$$
$$= \|\vec{u}\|^2 \qquad \blacksquare$$

i) 1

j) 1

k) $\vec{u_1} \cdot \vec{u_2} = 0$. Par conséquent, les vecteurs $\vec{u_1}$ et $\vec{u_2}$ sont orthogonaux.

l) $\vec{u_1} \cdot \vec{u_6} = 0$. Par conséquent, les vecteurs $\vec{u_1}$ et $\vec{u_6}$ sont orthogonaux.

m) $\vec{u_1} \cdot (a\vec{u_2} + b\vec{u_6}) = a\vec{u_1} \cdot \vec{u_2} + b\vec{u_1} \cdot \vec{u_6}$
$$= a(0) + b(0)$$
$$= 0$$

Par conséquent, le vecteur $\vec{u_1}$ est orthogonal à toute combinaison linéaire des vecteurs $\vec{u_2}$ et $\vec{u_6}$.

n) $a = 1 - 2b$

o) De l'équation vectorielle $a\vec{u_1} + b\vec{u_2} + c\vec{u_3} + d\vec{u_4} = \vec{0}$, on tire le système de quatre équations à quatre inconnues

$$\begin{array}{rcl} a + b \quad - \quad d &=& 0 \\ -2a + b + c - \quad d &=& 0 \\ a + b + c + 3d &=& 0 \\ 2a \quad + c \quad &=& 0 \end{array}$$

Le déterminant de la matrice des coefficients vaut -20. Comme ce nombre est différent de zéro, le système d'équations admet une solution unique, soit $a = 0$, $b = 0$, $c = 0$ et $d = 0$. Par conséquent, les quatre vecteurs sont linéairement indépendants.

p) De l'équation vectorielle $a\overrightarrow{u_1} + b\overrightarrow{u_2} + c\overrightarrow{u_3} + d\overrightarrow{u_7} = \vec{0}$ on tire le système de quatre équations à quatre inconnues.

$$\begin{aligned} a + b \quad\quad + 2d &= 0 \\ -2a + b + c - 2d &= 0 \\ a + b + c + \quad d &= 0 \\ 2a \quad\quad + c + \quad d &= 0 \end{aligned}$$

Ce système admet au moins une solution, soit $a = 0$, $b = 0$, $c = 0$ et $d = 0$. De plus, le déterminant de la matrice des coefficients vaut 0. Par conséquent, en vertu de la règle de Cramer, le système admet une infinité de solutions, ce qui implique que les vecteurs sont linéairement dépendants.

q) $\overrightarrow{u_5} = (-{}^6\!/_5)\,\overrightarrow{u_1} + ({}^3\!/_5)\,\overrightarrow{u_2} + ({}^{22}\!/_5)\,\overrightarrow{u_3} + (-{}^3\!/_5)\,\overrightarrow{u_4}$

r) $\overrightarrow{u_6} = 0\,\overrightarrow{u_1} + ({}^9\!/_4)\,\overrightarrow{u_2} + (-1)\,\overrightarrow{u_3} + ({}^1\!/_4)\,\overrightarrow{u_4}$

s) Il est impossible d'écrire le vecteur $\overrightarrow{u_6}$ comme une combinaison linéaire des vecteurs $\overrightarrow{u_1}$, $\overrightarrow{u_2}$ et $\overrightarrow{u_3}$.

2. $\left\|\dfrac{1}{\|\vec{u}\|}\vec{u}\right\| = 1$ pour tout vecteur non nul $\vec{u}$ de $\mathbb{R}^n$.

Preuve

On a
$$\vec{u} = \begin{bmatrix} u_1 & u_2 & \cdots & u_n \end{bmatrix} \neq \vec{0} \Rightarrow \|\vec{u}\| = \sqrt{\sum_{i=1}^{n} u_i^2} \neq 0$$
d'où

$$\frac{1}{\|\vec{u}\|}\vec{u} = \begin{bmatrix} \dfrac{u_1}{\sqrt{\sum\limits_{i=1}^{n} u_i^2}} & \dfrac{u_2}{\sqrt{\sum\limits_{i=1}^{n} u_i^2}} & \cdots & \dfrac{u_n}{\sqrt{\sum\limits_{i=1}^{n} u_i^2}} \end{bmatrix}$$

Par conséquent,

$$\left\|\frac{1}{\|\vec{u}\|}\vec{u}\right\| = \sqrt{\frac{u_1^2}{\sum\limits_{i=1}^{n} u_i^2} + \frac{u_2^2}{\sum\limits_{i=1}^{n} u_i^2} + \cdots + \frac{u_n^2}{\sum\limits_{i=1}^{n} u_i^2}} = 1 \quad \blacksquare$$

3. Si $\vec{u}$ est un vecteur de $\mathbb{R}^n$ tel que $\vec{u} \cdot \vec{v} = 0$ pour tout $\vec{v} \in \mathbb{R}^n$ alors $\vec{u} = \vec{0}$.

Preuve

Si $\vec{u} = \begin{bmatrix} u_1 & u_2 & \cdots & u_n \end{bmatrix}$ et $\vec{u} \cdot \vec{v} = 0$ pour tout $\vec{v} \in \mathbb{R}^n$ alors, pour $\vec{v} = \vec{u}$, on a $\vec{u} \cdot \vec{u} = 0$, d'où $u_1^2 + u_2^2 + \cdots + u_n^2 = 0$

Une somme de carrés ne vaut zéro que si chacun des termes vaut zéro, d'où $u_i = 0$ pour $i = 1, 2, \ldots, n$. Par conséquent, $\vec{u} = \vec{0}$. $\quad \blacksquare$

4. a) Si $\vec{u}$ et $\vec{v}$ sont des vecteurs de $\mathbb{R}^n$, alors
$$\vec{u} \cdot \vec{v} = \vec{v} \cdot \vec{u}$$

Preuve

Si $\vec{u} = \begin{bmatrix} u_1 & u_2 & \cdots & u_n \end{bmatrix}$ et $\vec{v} = \begin{bmatrix} v_1 & v_2 & \cdots & v_n \end{bmatrix}$ alors, comme la multiplication est commutative dans les réels, on a

$$\vec{u} \cdot \vec{v} = \sum_{i=1}^{n} u_i v_i = \sum_{i=1}^{n} v_i u_i = \vec{v} \cdot \vec{u} \quad \blacksquare$$

b) Si $\vec{u}$, $\vec{v}$ et $\vec{w}$ sont des vecteurs de $\mathbb{R}^n$, alors $\vec{u} \cdot (\vec{v} + \vec{w}) = \vec{u} \cdot \vec{v} + \vec{u} \cdot \vec{w}$.

Preuve

Si $\vec{u} = \begin{bmatrix} u_1 & u_2 & \cdots & u_n \end{bmatrix}$ et $\vec{v} = \begin{bmatrix} v_1 & v_2 & \cdots & v_n \end{bmatrix}$ et $\vec{w} = \begin{bmatrix} w_1 & w_2 & \cdots & w_n \end{bmatrix}$ alors, en raison des propriétés de distributivité et de commutativité dans les réels, on a

$$\begin{aligned} \vec{u} \cdot (\vec{v} + \vec{w}) &= \sum_{i=1}^{n} u_i(v_i + w_i) \\ &= \sum_{i=1}^{n} (u_i v_i + u_i w_i) \\ &= \sum_{i=1}^{n} u_i v_i + \sum_{i=1}^{n} u_i w_i \\ &= \vec{u} \cdot \vec{v} + \vec{v} \cdot \vec{u} \quad \blacksquare \end{aligned}$$

5. a) L'ensemble des matrices diagonales d'ordre 3 muni des opérations habituelles d'addition et de multiplication par un scalaire constitue un espace vectoriel.

b) L'ensemble des matrices régulières d'ordre 3 ne comporte pas d'élément neutre pour l'addition; il ne constitue donc pas un espace vectoriel.

c) L'ensemble $\mathbb{R}^+ = \{ a \in \mathbb{R} \mid a > 0 \}$ constitue un espace vectoriel pour les opérations définies comme suit :

$a \oplus b = ab$ (définition de l'addition)
$k \odot a = a^k$ (définition de la multiplication par un scalaire)

d) L'ensemble des matrices de la forme $\begin{bmatrix} 1 & a \\ a & 1 \end{bmatrix}$ ne constitue pas un espace vectoriel. En effet, même si I_2 appartient à cet ensemble et que 2 est un scalaire réel, $2I_2$ n'appartient pas à l'ensemble. La propriété 6 d'un espace vectoriel n'est donc pas satisfaite.

e) L'ensemble

$$W = \left\{ \begin{bmatrix} a & b & c \end{bmatrix} \mid a \in \mathbb{R},\, b \in \mathbb{R},\, c \in \mathbb{R} \text{ et } abc = 0 \right\}$$

muni des opérations habituelles sur les vecteurs de $\mathbb{R}^3$ ne constitue pas un espace vectoriel. En effet, $\vec{u} = \begin{bmatrix} 1 & 1 & 0 \end{bmatrix} \in W$, $\vec{v} = \begin{bmatrix} 0 & 1 & 1 \end{bmatrix} \in W$, mais $\vec{u} + \vec{v} = \begin{bmatrix} 1 & 2 & 1 \end{bmatrix} \notin W$. La propriété 1 d'un espace vectoriel n'est donc pas satisfaite.

6. a) $D = A + (-2)B + 3C$

b) $D = 0A + 0B + 0C$

c) Il est impossible d'exprimer la matrice D comme une combinaison linéaire des matrices A, B et C.

7. a) Les matrices A, B, C et D sont linéairement indépendantes.

b) Les matrices A, B et C sont linéairement dépendantes.

c) Les matrices A, B et C sont linéairement indépendantes.

8. Si V est un espace vectoriel dont le vecteur nul est noté $\vec{0}$, alors $(-1)\vec{v} = -\vec{v}$ pour tout vecteur $\vec{v} \in V$.

Preuve

Si $\vec{v} \in V$, alors

$$
\begin{aligned}
(-1)\vec{v} &= (-1)\vec{v} + \vec{0} \\
&= (-1)\vec{v} + \left[\vec{v} + (-\vec{v}) \right] \\
&= \left[(-1)\vec{v} + \vec{v} \right] + (-\vec{v}) \\
&= \left[(-1)\vec{v} + 1\vec{v} \right] + (-\vec{v}) \\
&= \left[(-1) + 1 \right]\vec{v} + (-\vec{v}) \\
&= (0)\vec{v} + (-\vec{v}) \\
&= \vec{0} + (-\vec{v}) \\
&= -\vec{v} \qquad \blacksquare
\end{aligned}
$$

9. a) $W = \left\{ \begin{bmatrix} x & y & z \end{bmatrix} \mid x, y \text{ et } z \in \mathbb{R}, \text{ et } 2x + 3y - z = 0 \right\}$ est un sous-espace de $\mathbb{R}^3$.

b) W n'est pas un espace vectoriel parce qu'il n'est pas fermé pour l'addition. En effet,

$$
\begin{aligned}
\vec{u} &= \begin{bmatrix} 1 & 0 & 1 & 0 \end{bmatrix} \in W \text{ et} \\
\vec{v} &= \begin{bmatrix} 0 & 1 & 0 & 1 \end{bmatrix} \in W \text{ mais} \\
\vec{u} + \vec{v} &= \begin{bmatrix} 1 & 1 & 1 & 1 \end{bmatrix} \notin W.
\end{aligned}
$$

Par conséquent, W n'est pas un sous-espace de $\mathbb{R}^4$.

c) $W = \left\{ \begin{bmatrix} a & 2a & a & b \end{bmatrix} \mid a \text{ et } b \in \mathbb{R} \right\}$ est un sous-espace de $\mathbb{R}^4$.

d) W n'est pas un espace vectoriel parce qu'il ne contient pas de vecteur nul.

e) $W = P_3$ est un sous-espace de P_5.

f) L'ensemble W des matrices carrées d'ordre n dont la trace est 0 est un sous-espace de l'espace V des matrices carrées d'ordre n.

g) $W = \left\{ \vec{0} \right\}$ est un sous-espace de n'importe quel espace vectoriel V dont le vecteur nul est $\vec{0}$.

10. L'ensemble V des vecteurs de $\mathbb{R}^4$ orthogonaux au vecteur $\vec{u} = \begin{bmatrix} 1 & 2 & -3 & 2 \end{bmatrix}$ est un espace vectoriel.

Preuve

Il suffit de montrer que V est un sous-espace de $\mathbb{R}^4$, en utilisant le fait que des vecteurs sont orthogonaux si et seulement si leur produit scalaire est zéro. $\vec{0} = \begin{bmatrix} 0 & 0 & 0 & 0 \end{bmatrix} \in V$ parce que $\vec{0} \cdot \vec{u} = 0$. Donc l'ensemble V n'est pas vide, et il est clair que V est un sous-ensemble de $\mathbb{R}^4$. Par conséquent, V est un sous-ensemble non vide de $\mathbb{R}^4$.

Si les vecteurs

$$
\begin{aligned}
\vec{v} &= \begin{bmatrix} v_1 & v_2 & v_3 & v_4 \end{bmatrix} \text{ et} \\
\vec{w} &= \begin{bmatrix} w_1 & w_2 & w_3 & w_4 \end{bmatrix}
\end{aligned}
$$

sont orthogonaux au vecteur $\vec{u} = \begin{bmatrix} 1 & 2 & -3 & 2 \end{bmatrix}$ et si $k \in R$, alors $\vec{u} \cdot \vec{v} = v_1 + 2v_2 - 3v_3 + 2v_4 = 0$ et $\vec{u} \cdot \vec{w} = w_1 + 2w_2 - 3w_3 + 2w_4 = 0$, de sorte que

$$
\begin{aligned}
\vec{u} \cdot (\vec{v} + \vec{w}) &\\
= (v_1 + w_1) + 2(v_2 + w_2) &- 3(v_3 + w_3) + 2(v_4 + w_4) \\
= (v_1 + 2v_2 - 3v_3 + 2v_4) &+ (w_1 + 2w_2 - 3w_3 + 2w_4) \\
= 0 + 0 &\\
= 0 &
\end{aligned}
$$

et

$$
\begin{aligned}
\vec{u} \cdot (k\vec{v}) &= kv_1 + 2kv_2 - 3kv_3 + 2kv_4 \\
&= k(v_1 + 2v_2 - 3v_3 + 2v_4) \\
&= k(0) \\
&= 0
\end{aligned}
$$

Les vecteurs $\vec{v} + \vec{w}$ et $k\vec{v}$ sont donc orthogonaux au vecteur $\vec{u}$. Par conséquent, $\vec{v} + \vec{w} \in V$ et $k\vec{v} \in V$. Selon le théorème 10.2, l'ensemble V est un sous-espace de $\mathbb{R}^4$ et c'est donc aussi un espace vectoriel.

$\blacksquare$

11. L'intersection de deux sous-espaces vectoriels d'un espace vectoriel V est elle aussi un sous-espace de V.

Preuve

Si les ensembles S et W sont des sous-espaces de V, alors ce sont des sous-ensembles de V, de sorte que leur intersection, $S \cap W$, est aussi un sous-ensemble de V. De plus, comme S et W sont des sous-espaces vectoriels de V, ils possèdent tous deux le même vecteur nul $\vec{0}$, de sorte que $\vec{0} \in S \cap W$. Par conséquent, $S \cap W$ est un sous-ensemble non vide de V.

Si $\vec{u}$ et $\vec{v} \in S \cap W$, alors $\vec{u} \in S$, $\vec{u} \in W$, $\vec{v} \in S$ et $\vec{v} \in W$, de sorte que $\vec{u} + \vec{v} \in S$ et $\vec{u} + \vec{v} \in W$ parce que S et W sont des sous-espaces de V. Par conséquent, $\vec{u} + \vec{v} \in S \cap W$.

Si $\vec{u} \in S \cap W$ et si $k \in \mathbb{R}$, alors $k\vec{u} \in S$ et $k\vec{u} \in W$ parce que $\vec{u} \in S$ et $\vec{u} \in W$ et que S et W sont des espaces vectoriels. Par conséquent, $k\vec{u} \in S \cap W$.

Selon le théorème 10.2, l'ensemble $S \cap W$ est donc un sous-espace de V. ∎

12. 4

13. a) Les vecteurs $\vec{u_1}$, $\vec{u_2}$, $\vec{u_3}$ et $\vec{u_4}$ n'engendrent qu'un espace de dimension 2 : ils ne peuvent former une base de $\mathbb{R}^4$.

b) $\vec{u_1} = \begin{bmatrix} 1 & 2 & 1 & 0 \end{bmatrix}$ et $\vec{u_4} = \begin{bmatrix} 0 & 1 & -1 & 1 \end{bmatrix}$ forment une base de V.

c) 2

d) $\vec{u_5} \notin V$

e) Les vecteurs $\vec{u_1}$, $\vec{u_2}$, $\vec{u_3}$ et $\vec{u_5}$ n'engendrent qu'un espace de dimension 3 : ils ne peuvent former une base de $\mathbb{R}^4$.

14. a) 2

b) $\vec{u_5} \notin V$

c) $\vec{u_6} = \vec{u_1} - \vec{u_3} \Rightarrow \vec{u_6} \in V$

15. a) Vrai   f) Faux

b) Faux   g) Vrai

c) Vrai   h) Faux

d) Faux   i) Faux

e) Faux

Glossaire

DIAGONALE PRINCIPALE   p. 8

La diagonale principale d'une matrice carrée $A = \begin{bmatrix} a_{ij} \end{bmatrix}_{n \times n}$ est formée des éléments a_{ii} de A.

DIMENSION D'UN ESPACE VECTORIEL   p. 377

La dimension d'un espace vectoriel de dimension finie est le nombre de vecteurs d'une base de cet espace. L'espace vectoriel $V = \left\{ \vec{0} \right\}$ est de dimension zéro. Tout espace vectoriel qui n'est pas de dimension finie est dit de dimension infinie. La dimension d'un espace vectoriel V est notée dim V.

DIRECTION CONTRAIRE   p. 171

Deux vecteurs ont des directions contraires lorsque l'angle entre ces deux vecteurs vaut π ou 180°. On emploie aussi l'expression *direction opposée*.

DIRECTION D'UN VECTEUR DU PLAN   p. 171

La direction d'un vecteur du plan est l'angle, mesuré dans le sens contraire des aiguilles d'une montre, que fait ce vecteur avec la partie positive de l'axe des abscisses lorsque le vecteur est issu de l'origine.

DROITES CONCOURANTES   p. 225

Deux droites du plan cartésien sont dites concourantes si elles se coupent en un seul point.

DROITES GAUCHES   p. 314

Deux droites de l'espace sont dites gauches si elles ne sont pas parallèles et qu'elles ne se coupent pas.

ÉGALITÉ DE DEUX MATRICES   p. 10

Deux matrices $A = \begin{bmatrix} a_{ij} \end{bmatrix}_{m \times n}$ et $B = \begin{bmatrix} b_{ij} \end{bmatrix}_{p \times q}$ sont égales si et seulement si elles ont le même format ($m = p$ et $n = q$) et que leurs éléments correspondants sont égaux ($a_{ij} = b_{ij}$).

ÉGALITÉ DE DEUX VECTEURS GÉOMÉTRIQUES   p. 169

Deux vecteurs géométriques sont égaux si et seulement s'ils ont le même module et la même direction.

ÉLÉMENT D'UNE MATRICE   p. 7

Un élément d'une matrice est un nombre de cette matrice. L'élément situé à l'intersection de la i-ième ligne et de la j-ième colonne d'une matrice A est notée a_{ij}.

ÉLIMINATION GAUSSIENNE   p. 132

La méthode d'élimination gaussienne, qui sert à résoudre un système d'équations linéaires, consiste à trouver une matrice échelonnée équivalente à la matrice augmentée du système, puis à effectuer, à rebours, une série de substitutions de manière à déterminer l'ensemble solution.

ENSEMBLE SOLUTION   p. 120

L'ensemble solution d'un système d'équations linéaires $AX = B$ est l'ensemble des valeurs des inconnues qui vérifient ce système, c'est-à-dire l'ensemble des matrices X qui vérifient l'équation matricielle $AX = B$ où A représente la matrice des coefficients et B, la matrice des constantes.

ÉQUATION CARTÉSIENNE D'UNE DROITE DU PLAN   p. 233

L'équation cartésienne d'une droite perpendiculaire au vecteur $\vec{n} = \begin{bmatrix} a & b \end{bmatrix}$ et passant par le point $P(p_1, p_2)$ est $ax + by = c$ où $c = ap_1 + bp_2$.

ÉQUATION CARTÉSIENNE D'UN PLAN   p. 323

L'équation cartésienne d'un plan π passant par un point $P(p_1, p_2, p_3)$ et de vecteur normal $\vec{n} = \begin{bmatrix} a & b & c \end{bmatrix}$ est donnée par

$$\pi : ax + by + cz = d$$

où $d = ap_1 + bp_2 + cp_3$.

ÉQUATION NORMALE D'UNE DROITE DU PLAN   p. 234

L'équation normale d'une droite perpendiculaire au vecteur unitaire

$$\vec{n_u} = \begin{bmatrix} \dfrac{a}{\sqrt{a^2 + b^2}} & \dfrac{b}{\sqrt{a^2 + b^2}} \end{bmatrix}$$ et passant

par le point $P(p_1, p_2)$ est

$$\frac{a}{\sqrt{a^2 + b^2}}x + \frac{b}{\sqrt{a^2 + b^2}}y = h$$

ou encore

$$(\cos\varphi)x + (\sin\varphi)y = h$$

où φ représente la direction du vecteur $\vec{n_u}$ et

$$h = \frac{a}{\sqrt{a^2 + b^2}}p_1 + \frac{b}{\sqrt{a^2 + b^2}}p_2$$

ÉQUATION NORMALE D'UN PLAN   p. 324

L'équation normale d'un plan est l'équation cartésienne de ce plan obtenue avec un vecteur unitaire normal à ce plan.

ÉQUATIONS PARAMÉTRIQUES D'UNE DROITE DE L'ESPACE   p. 311

Les équations paramétriques d'une droite Δ qui passe par le point $P(p_1, p_2, p_3)$ et dont $\vec{d} = \begin{bmatrix} d_1 & d_2 & d_3 \end{bmatrix}$ est un vecteur directeur sont

$$x = p_1 + kd_1$$
$$y = p_2 + kd_2$$
$$z = p_3 + kd_3$$

où $k \in \mathbb{R}$.

ÉQUATIONS PARAMÉTRIQUES D'UNE DROITE DU PLAN   p. 229

Les équations paramétriques de la droite Δ dont $\vec{d} = \begin{bmatrix} d_1 & d_2 \end{bmatrix}$ est un vecteur directeur et qui passe par le point $P(p_1, p_2)$ sont

$$\Delta : \begin{cases} x = p_1 + kd_1 \\ y = p_2 + kd_2 \end{cases} \quad \text{où } k \in \mathbb{R}$$

ÉQUATIONS PARAMÉTRIQUES D'UN PLAN   p. 342

Les équations paramétriques d'un plan π qui passe par le point $P(p_1, p_2, p_3)$ et qui est parallèle aux vecteurs linéairement indépendants $\vec{u} = \begin{bmatrix} u_1 & u_2 & u_3 \end{bmatrix}$ et $\vec{v} = \begin{bmatrix} v_1 & v_2 & v_3 \end{bmatrix}$ sont

$$x = p_1 + ru_1 + sv_1$$
$$y = p_2 + ru_2 + sv_2$$
$$z = p_3 + ru_3 + sv_3$$

où r et $s \in \mathbb{R}$.

ÉQUATIONS SYMÉTRIQUES D'UNE DROITE DE L'ESPACE   p. 312

Les équations symétriques d'une droite Δ qui passe par le point $P(p_1, p_2, p_3)$ et dont $\vec{d} = \begin{bmatrix} d_1 & d_2 & d_3 \end{bmatrix}$ est un vecteur directeur sont

$$\frac{x - p_1}{d_1} = \frac{y - p_2}{d_2} = \frac{z - p_3}{d_3}$$

à la condition que les composantes du vecteur directeur soient toutes différentes de zéro.

ÉQUATION SYMÉTRIQUE D'UNE DROITE DU PLAN   p. 231

L'équation symétrique de la droite Δ qui passe par le point $P(p_1, p_2)$ et dont $\vec{d} = \begin{bmatrix} d_1 & d_2 \end{bmatrix}$ est un vecteur directeur tel que $d_1 \neq 0$ et $d_2 \neq 0$ est

$$\Delta : \frac{x - p_1}{d_1} = \frac{y - p_2}{d_2}$$

ÉQUATION VECTORIELLE D'UNE DROITE DE L'ESPACE   p. 309

L'équation vectorielle d'une droite Δ qui passe par le point $P(p_1,\ p_2,\ p_3)$ et dont $\vec{d} = \begin{bmatrix} d_1 & d_2 & d_3 \end{bmatrix}$ est un vecteur directeur est

$$\begin{bmatrix} x & y & z \end{bmatrix} = \begin{bmatrix} p_1 & p_2 & p_3 \end{bmatrix} + k\begin{bmatrix} d_1 & d_2 & d_3 \end{bmatrix}$$

où $k \in \mathbb{R}$.

ÉQUATION VECTORIELLE D'UNE DROITE DU PLAN   p. 228

L'équation vectorielle de la droite dont $\vec{d} = \begin{bmatrix} d_1 & d_2 \end{bmatrix}$ est un vecteur directeur et qui passe par le point $P(p_1,\ p_2)$ est

$$\begin{bmatrix} x & y \end{bmatrix} = \begin{bmatrix} p_1 & p_2 \end{bmatrix} + k\begin{bmatrix} d_1 & d_2 \end{bmatrix}$$

où $k \in \mathbb{R}$.

ÉQUATION VECTORIELLE D'UN PLAN   p. 341

L'équation vectorielle d'un plan π qui passe par le point $P(p_1,\ p_2,\ p_3)$ et qui est parallèle aux vecteurs linéairement indépendants $\vec{u} = \begin{bmatrix} u_1 & u_2 & u_3 \end{bmatrix}$ et $\vec{v} = \begin{bmatrix} v_1 & v_2 & v_3 \end{bmatrix}$ est

$$\begin{bmatrix} x & y & z \end{bmatrix} = \begin{bmatrix} p_1 & p_2 & p_3 \end{bmatrix} + r\begin{bmatrix} u_1 & u_2 & u_3 \end{bmatrix} + s\begin{bmatrix} v_1 & v_2 & v_3 \end{bmatrix}$$

où r et $s \in \mathbb{R}$.

ESPACE ENGENDRÉ PAR DES VECTEURS   p. 372

L'espace vectoriel engendré par les vecteurs $\vec{v_1},\ \vec{v_2},\ ...,\ \vec{v_n}$ d'un espace V est l'ensemble des combinaisons linéaires de ces vecteurs, soit

$$S = \left\{ \sum_{i=1}^{n} a_i \vec{v_i} \,\middle|\, a_i \in \mathbb{R} \right\}$$

ESPACE EUCLIDIEN DE DIMENSION DEUX   p. 195

L'espace euclidien de dimension deux, noté $\mathbb{R}^2$, est l'ensemble de tous les vecteurs algébriques du plan cartésien.

ESPACE EUCLIDIEN DE DIMENSION n p. 357

L'espace euclidien de dimension n, noté $\mathbb{R}^n$, est l'ensemble de tous les vecteurs algébriques à n composantes réelles (ou n-uplets), soit l'ensemble des matrices de format $1 \times n$ dont les éléments sont des nombres réels. En langage symbolique,

$$\mathbb{R}^n = \left\{ \begin{bmatrix} x_1 & x_2 & x_3 & \cdots & x_n \end{bmatrix} \,\middle|\, x_i \in \mathbb{R} \right\}$$

L'espace euclidien de dimension n est un espace vectoriel.

ESPACE EUCLIDIEN DE DIMENSION TROIS   p. 278 et p. 282

L'espace euclidien de dimension trois est l'ensemble des vecteurs de l'espace, soit l'ensemble des vecteurs algébriques comportant trois composantes.

ESPACE VECTORIEL   p. 362

Un espace vectoriel sur le corps des réels $\mathbb{R}$ est un ensemble V – dont les éléments sont appelés vecteurs – muni de deux opérations, soit l'addition de deux vecteurs (notée $\vec{u} + \vec{v}$ ou $\vec{u} \oplus \vec{v}$) et la multiplication d'un vecteur par un scalaire (notée $a\vec{u}$ ou $a \odot \vec{u}$), qui vérifient dix propriétés, dont la fermeture pour les deux opérations, l'associativité, la commutativité, la distributivité, l'existence d'un vecteur nul et de l'opposé de tout vecteur de V.

ESPACE VECTORIEL DE DIMENSION FINIE   p. 374

Un espace vectoriel de dimension finie est un espace vectoriel dont une base compte un nombre fini d'éléments.

FORMAT   p. 7

Le format d'une matrice indique le nombre de ses lignes et de ses colonnes. Une matrice de format $m \times n$ compte m lignes et n colonnes.

FORME CARTÉSIENNE D'UN NOMBRE COMPLEXE   p. 253

La forme cartésienne (ou binomiale ou rectangulaire) d'un nombre complexe z est donnée par $z = a + bi$.

FORME TRIGONOMÉTRIQUE D'UN NOMBRE COMPLEXE   p. 262

La forme trigonométrique (ou polaire) d'un nombre complexe $z = a + bi$ est donnée par l'une des expressions suivantes :

$$z = \rho \cos\theta + i\rho \sin\theta$$
$$= \rho(\cos\theta + i\sin\theta)$$
$$= \rho\operatorname{cis}\theta$$

où $\rho = |z| = \sqrt{a^2 + b^2}$ et $\theta = \operatorname{arc\ tg}\dfrac{b}{a}$.

INCOMPATIBILITÉ POUR L'ADDITION   p. 29

Si deux matrices n'ont pas le même format, on dit qu'elles sont incompatibles pour l'addition.

INCONNUES LIBRES   p. 139

Lorsqu'un système d'équations linéaires admet plus d'une solution, les inconnues paramétrées sont appelées inconnues libres.

INCONNUES LIÉES   p. 139

Lorsqu'un système d'équations linéaires admet plus d'une solution, les inconnues exprimées en fonction des inconnues libres sont appelées inconnues liées.

INDICE DE NILPOTENCE   p. 44

Si A est une matrice nilpotente, alors le plus petit entier positif k tel que $A^k = O_{n \times n}$ est appelé indice de nilpotence.

MATRICE   p. 7

Une matrice $A = \begin{bmatrix} a_{ij} \end{bmatrix}_{m \times n}$ est un tableau de mn nombres disposés sur m lignes et n colonnes.

MATRICE ADJOINTE   p. 98

La matrice adjointe d'une matrice A est la transposée de la matrice des cofacteurs des éléments de A. La matrice adjointe de A est notée adj A.

MATRICE ANTISYMÉTRIQUE   p. 14 et p. 34

Une matrice antisymétrique est une matrice carrée $A = \begin{bmatrix} a_{ij} \end{bmatrix}_{n \times n}$ telle que $a_{ij} = -a_{ji}$ pour toutes les valeurs de i et de j. Une matrice A est une matrice antisymétrique si et seulement si $A = -A^t$ ou, ce qui est équivalent, si et seulement si $A^t = -A$.

MATRICE AUGMENTÉE   p. 131

La matrice augmentée $\begin{bmatrix} A \,\big|\, B \end{bmatrix}$ d'un système d'équations linéaires ($AX = B$) est la matrice des coefficients (A) à laquelle on ajoute la matrice des constantes (B).

MATRICE CARRÉE   p. 8

Une matrice carrée est une matrice qui comporte un même nombre de lignes et de colonnes. On dit d'une matrice carrée qu'elle est d'ordre n lorsqu'elle comporte n lignes et n colonnes ; elle est alors notée $A = \begin{bmatrix} a_{ij} \end{bmatrix}_{n \times n}$.

MATRICE COLONNE   p. 7

Une matrice colonne est une matrice de format $m \times 1$.

MATRICE DIAGONALE   p. 12

Une matrice diagonale est une matrice carrée dont tous les éléments non situés sur la diagonale principale sont nuls.

MATRICE ÉCHELONNÉE   p. 14

Une matrice échelonnée est une matrice dont toutes les lignes nulles sont situées sous les lignes non nulles, où le premier élément non nul de chaque ligne, le pivot, vaut 1 et où le pivot de chaque ligne se trouve à droite du pivot de la ligne précédente.

MATRICE ÉCHELONNÉE RÉDUITE   p. 15

Une matrice échelonnée réduite est une matrice échelonnée telle que, dans une colonne contenant un pivot, tous les éléments valent zéro à l'exception du pivot lui-même.

MATRICE IDEMPOTENTE   p. 44

Une matrice carrée A d'ordre n est idempotente si et seulement si $A^2 = A$.

MATRICE IDENTITÉ   p. 13

Une matrice identité est une matrice scalaire dans laquelle tous les éléments de la diagonale principale valent 1. La matrice identité d'ordre n est notée I_n.

MATRICE INVERSE   p. 55

La matrice inverse d'une matrice carrée A d'ordre n est, si elle existe, la matrice, notée A^{-1}, telle que $AA^{-1} = A^{-1}A = I_n$.

MATRICE INVERSIBLE   p. 101

Une matrice est dite inversible si elle admet une matrice inverse.

MATRICE LIGNE   p. 7

Une matrice ligne est une matrice de format $1 \times n$.

MATRICE NILPOTENTE   p. 44

Une matrice carrée A d'ordre n est nilpotente si et seulement s'il existe un entier positif k tel que $A^k = O_{n \times n}$.

MATRICE NULLE   p. 11

Une matrice nulle est une matrice dont tous les éléments valent zéro. La matrice nulle de format $m \times n$ est notée $O_{m \times n}$.

MATRICE OPPOSÉE   p. 32

La matrice opposée d'une matrice $A = \left[a_{ij} \right]_{m \times n}$ est la matrice $-A = \left[-a_{ij} \right]_{m \times n}$. La somme de deux

matrices opposées est la matrice nulle de format $m \times n$, c'est-à-dire que $A + (-A) = O_{m \times n}$.

MATRICE RÉGULIÈRE   p. 70

Une matrice régulière (ou non singulière) est une matrice carrée dont le déterminant est différent de zéro.

MATRICE SCALAIRE   p. 12

Une matrice scalaire est une matrice diagonale dans laquelle tous les éléments de la diagonale principale sont identiques.

MATRICE SINGULIÈRE   p. 70

Une matrice singulière est une matrice carrée dont le déterminant vaut zéro.

MATRICE SYMÉTRIQUE   p. 14 et
                                                    p. 34

Une matrice symétrique est une matrice carrée $A = \left[a_{ij} \right]_{n \times n}$, telle que $a_{ij} = a_{ji}$ pour toutes les valeurs de i et de j. Une matrice A est une matrice symétrique si et seulement si $A = A^t$.

MATRICE TRIANGULAIRE INFÉRIEURE   p. 12

Une matrice triangulaire inférieure est une matrice carrée dont tous les éléments situés au-dessus de la diagonale principale sont nuls.

MATRICE TRIANGULAIRE SUPÉRIEURE   p. 12

Une matrice triangulaire supérieure est une matrice carrée dont tous les éléments situés sous la diagonale principale sont nuls.

MATRICES ÉQUIVALENTES   p. 132

Deux matrices sont équivalentes si on peut obtenir l'une des matrices en effectuant une série d'opérations élémentaires de ligne sur l'autre.

MÉTHODE DE GAUSS-JORDAN   p. 144

La méthode de Gauss-Jordan, qui sert à résoudre un système d'équations linéaires, est une extension de la méthode d'élimination gaussienne et elle consiste à calculer une matrice échelonnée réduite équivalente à la matrice augmentée du système. La méthode de Gauss-Jordan sert également à trouver l'inverse d'une matrice régulière.

MÉTHODE DU PARALLÉLOGRAMME   p. 173

Méthode employée pour additionner deux vecteurs géométriques non parallèles.

Elle consiste à faire coïncider les origines des deux vecteurs, puis à compléter le parallélogramme dont deux côtés correspondent à ces vecteurs. La somme recherchée est le vecteur correspondant à la diagonale du parallélogramme issue de l'origine des vecteurs à additionner.

MÉTHODE DU TRIANGLE   p. 173

Méthode employée pour additionner deux vecteurs géométriques. Elle consiste, en premier lieu, à faire coïncider l'origine du deuxième vecteur avec l'extrémité du premier. Le vecteur résultant est le vecteur allant de l'origine du premier vecteur à l'extrémité du second.

MINEUR   p. 80

Le mineur, noté M_{ij}, de l'élément a_{ij} d'une matrice carrée A est égal au déterminant de la matrice résiduelle obtenue en supprimant la i-ième ligne et la j-ième colonne de A.

MODULE D'UN NOMBRE COMPLEXE   p. 257

Le module du nombre complexe $z = a + bi$ est noté $|z|$ et il est donné par $|z| = \sqrt{a^2 + b^2}$.

MODULE D'UN VECTEUR   p. 169

Le module d'un vecteur est égal à la longueur de ce vecteur. Les termes *norme*, *intensité* et *grandeur* sont synonymes de module. On note le module d'un vecteur $\vec{u}$ par $\|\vec{u}\|$.

MULTIPLICATION DE DEUX MATRICES   p. 38

La multiplication de deux matrices $A = \left[a_{ij} \right]_{m \times n}$ et $B = \left[b_{ij} \right]_{n \times p}$ est une opération matricielle dont le résultat est la matrice

$$AB = \left[\sum_{k=1}^{n} a_{ik} b_{kj} \right]_{m \times p}$$

MULTIPLICATION D'UNE MATRICE PAR UN SCALAIRE   p. 32

La multiplication d'une matrice $A = \left[a_{ij} \right]_{m \times n}$ par un scalaire (un nombre) k est une opération dont le résultat est la matrice $kA = \left[ka_{ij} \right]_{m \times n}$.

NOMBRES COMPLEXES   p. 253

L'ensemble des nombres complexes, noté $\mathbb{C}$, est

$$\mathbb{C} = \left\{ a + bi \mid a \text{ et } b \in \mathbb{R} \text{ et } i^2 = -1 \right\}$$

Norme euclidienne d'un vecteur de $\mathbb{R}^2$ p. 198

La norme euclidienne d'un vecteur
$$\vec{u} = \begin{bmatrix} u_1 & u_2 \end{bmatrix} \in \mathbb{R}^2$$
est $\|\vec{u}\| = \sqrt{u_1^2 + u_2^2}$.

Norme euclidienne d'un vecteur de $\mathbb{R}^n$ p. 358

La norme euclidienne d'un vecteur
$\vec{u} = \begin{bmatrix} u_1 & u_2 & \cdots & u_n \end{bmatrix} \in \mathbb{R}^n$
est donnée par
$$\|\vec{u}\| = \sqrt{u_1^2 + u_2^2 + \cdots + u_n^2}$$
$$= \sqrt{\sum_{i=1}^{n} u_i^2}$$

Opérations élémentaires de ligne   p. 130

Les opérations élémentaires de ligne sont des opérations effectuées sur les équations d'un système d'équations linéaires ou sur les lignes d'une matrice pour obtenir un système équivalent ou une matrice équivalente. Ces opérations sont au nombre de trois :

- l'interversion de deux lignes $(L_i \leftrightarrow L_j)$,
- la multiplication d'une ligne par une constante différente de zéro $(L_i \rightarrow kL_i)$
- l'addition d'un multiple d'une ligne à une autre ligne $(L_i \rightarrow L_i + kL_j)$.

Ordonnée à l'origine d'une droite   p. 223

L'ordonnée à l'origine d'une droite est l'ordonnée du point d'intersection de la droite avec l'axe des y. Une droite de pente m qui passe par un point (x_1, y_1) a comme ordonnée à l'origine $b = y_1 - mx_1$.

Ordre d'un déterminant   p. 69

L'ordre du déterminant d'une matrice carrée est identique à l'ordre de la matrice.

Ordre d'une matrice carrée   p. 8

L'ordre d'une matrice carrée est le nombre de ses lignes (ou de ses colonnes).

Paramètre   p. 126

Un paramètre désigne, par opposition au terme « inconnue », un coefficient en fonction duquel on cherche à exprimer les solutions d'un système d'équations. Il s'agit donc d'une constante symbolique qu'on pourra fixer librement.

Partie imaginaire d'un nombre complexe   p. 253

La partie imaginaire d'un nombre complexe $z = a + bi$ est égale à b, ce qui s'écrit $\text{Im}(z) = b$.

Partie réelle d'un nombre complexe   p. 253

La partie réelle d'un nombre complexe $z = a + bi$ est égale à a, ce qui s'écrit $\text{Re}(z) = a$.

Pente d'une droite   p. 222

La pente d'une droite du plan est le quotient de la variation des ordonnées sur la variation des abscisses. La pente m de la droite qui passe par deux points (x_1, y_1) et (x_2, y_2) est donnée par
$$m = \frac{y_2 - y_1}{x_2 - x_1}$$

Pivot   p. 14

Le pivot d'une ligne d'une matrice est le premier élément non nul de cette ligne.

Plan d'Argand   p. 259

Un plan d'Argand est un plan cartésien où l'axe horizontal est appelé axe des réels et l'axe vertical est appelé axe des imaginaires. Un tel plan sert à la représentation graphique des nombres complexes interprétés comme des vecteurs.

Plans sécants   p. 334

Deux plans sont dits sécants si leur intersection est une droite.

Preuve   p. 17

Une preuve est un raisonnement servant à établir la vérité d'une proposition à l'aide d'énoncés considérés comme vrais.

Produit d'un vecteur par un scalaire   p. 180

Le produit d'un vecteur $\vec{u}$ par un scalaire k, noté $k\vec{u}$, est un vecteur possédant les propriétés suivantes :

- $\|k\vec{u}\| = |k| \, \|\vec{u}\|$.
- Le vecteur $k\vec{u}$ est parallèle au vecteur $\vec{u}$.
- Les vecteurs $\vec{u}$ et $k\vec{u}$ ont la même direction si $k > 0$ et des directions contraires si $k < 0$. Si $k = 0$, le vecteur $k\vec{u}$ est le vecteur nul, c'est-à-dire que $0\vec{u} = \vec{0}$.

Produit mixte   P. 296

Le produit mixte des vecteurs
$$\vec{u} = \begin{bmatrix} u_1 & u_2 & u_3 \end{bmatrix},$$
$$\vec{v} = \begin{bmatrix} v_1 & v_2 & v_3 \end{bmatrix} \text{ et}$$
$$\vec{w} = \begin{bmatrix} w_1 & w_2 & w_3 \end{bmatrix}$$
est un scalaire noté $\vec{u} \cdot (\vec{v} \times \vec{w})$ et défini par
$$\vec{u} \cdot (\vec{v} \times \vec{w}) = \begin{vmatrix} u_1 & u_2 & u_3 \\ v_1 & v_2 & v_3 \\ w_1 & w_2 & w_3 \end{vmatrix}$$

Produit scalaire   p. 185 et p. 203

Le produit scalaire est une opération sur deux vecteurs, dont le résultat est un scalaire. Le produit scalaire de deux vecteurs $\vec{u}$ et $\vec{v}$ est donné par l'expression
$$\vec{u} \cdot \vec{v} = \|\vec{u}\| \, \|\vec{v}\| \cos\theta$$
où θ représente l'angle déterminé par les vecteurs $\vec{u}$ et $\vec{v}$. Le produit scalaire de deux vecteurs
$\vec{u} = \begin{bmatrix} u_1 & u_2 \end{bmatrix}$ et $\vec{v} = \begin{bmatrix} v_1 & v_2 \end{bmatrix}$
est donné par $\vec{u} \cdot \vec{v} = u_1 v_1 + u_2 v_2$.

Produit scalaire de deux vecteurs de $\mathbb{R}^n$ p. 358

Le produit scalaire, $\vec{u} \cdot \vec{v}$, de deux vecteurs de $\mathbb{R}^n$, $\vec{u} = \begin{bmatrix} u_1 & u_2 & \cdots & u_n \end{bmatrix}$ et $\vec{v} = \begin{bmatrix} v_1 & v_2 & \cdots & v_n \end{bmatrix}$, est un scalaire :
$$\vec{u} \cdot \vec{v} = u_1 v_1 + u_2 v_2 + \cdots + u_n v_n$$

Produit vectoriel   p. 287 et p. 293

Le produit vectoriel des vecteurs
$$\vec{u} = \begin{bmatrix} u_1 & u_2 & u_3 \end{bmatrix} \text{ et}$$
$$\vec{v} = \begin{bmatrix} v_1 & v_2 & v_3 \end{bmatrix}$$
est un vecteur noté $\vec{u} \times \vec{v}$ et défini par
$$\vec{u} \times \vec{v} = \begin{vmatrix} \vec{i} & \vec{j} & \vec{k} \\ u_1 & u_2 & u_3 \\ v_1 & v_2 & v_3 \end{vmatrix}$$
Le produit vectoriel de vecteurs $\vec{u}$ et $\vec{v}$ déterminant un angle θ est
$$\vec{u} \times \vec{v} = (\|\vec{u}\| \, \|\vec{v}\| \sin\theta)\vec{n}$$
où $\vec{n}$ est un vecteur unitaire perpendiculaire à chacun des vecteurs $\vec{u}$ et $\vec{v}$ et dont la direction est donnée par la règle de la main droite.

Projection orthogonale   p. 206

La projection orthogonale de $\vec{u}$ sur $\vec{v}$, notée $\vec{u}_{\vec{v}}$, est le vecteur $\vec{u}_{\vec{v}} = \dfrac{\vec{u} \cdot \vec{v}}{\vec{v} \cdot \vec{v}} \vec{v}$.

On utilise également l'expression *vecteur projection*.

RACINE *N*-IÈME D'UN NOMBRE COMPLEXE   p. 267

On appelle racine n-ième d'un nombre complexe z différent de zéro tout nombre complexe w tel que $w^n = z$, et on écrit $w = z^{1/n}$.

RANG   p. 140

Le rang d'une matrice A est égal au nombre de lignes non nulles (ou au nombre de pivots) d'une matrice échelonnée équivalente à A.

RÈGLE DE CHASLES   p. 176

La règle de Chasles s'énonce comme suit : si A, B et C sont des points du plan ou de l'espace, alors

$$\overrightarrow{AB} + \overrightarrow{BC} = \overrightarrow{AC}$$

La généralisation de cette règle, appliquée à un nombre quelconque de points, est

$$\overrightarrow{AB} + \overrightarrow{BC} + \overrightarrow{CD} + \cdots + \overrightarrow{PQ} + \overrightarrow{QR} = \overrightarrow{AR}$$

RÈGLE DE CRAMER   p. 119

La règle de Cramer est une méthode de résolution d'un système d'équations linéaires comportant autant d'équations que d'inconnues. Elle fait appel au calcul de déterminants et elle fournit une expression symbolique pour les inconnues lorsque le système d'équations linéaires admet une solution unique.

RÈGLE DE LA MAIN DROITE   p. 280 et   p. 291

La règle de la main droite sert à orienter un système d'axes direct de l'espace, c'est-à-dire à déterminer la direction positive de chacun des axes de coordonnées. Dans un système d'axes direct, la direction positive des trois axes est donnée par la direction de l'index (axe des x), du majeur (axe des y) et du pouce (axe des z) de la main droite. La règle de la main droite sert à déterminer la direction du produit vectoriel. Ainsi, la direction de $\vec{u} \times \vec{v}$ est indiquée par le pouce lorsqu'on referme la main droite en parcourant l'angle θ entre les deux vecteurs, depuis $\vec{u}$ jusqu'à $\vec{v}$, le poignet de la main droite étant situé à l'origine commune des deux vecteurs.

RÈGLE DE LA VIS   P. 291

La règle de la vis est équivalente à la règle de la main droite. Elle sert à déterminer la direction du produit vectoriel. Ainsi, la direction du produit vectoriel $\vec{u} \times \vec{v}$

correspond à la direction dans laquelle se déplace une vis placée à l'origine commune des deux vecteurs lorsqu'on la fait tourner de $\vec{u}$ vers $\vec{v}$ en parcourant l'angle entre ces deux vecteurs.

RÈGLE DE SARRUS   p. 73

La règle de Sarrus constitue une méthode pratique pour calculer le déterminant d'une matrice $A = \left[a_{ij} \right]_{3 \times 3}$. Elle consiste à ajouter d'abord les deux premières colonnes du déterminant à évaluer à la droite de celui-ci, puis à calculer la somme des produits des éléments situés sur une même flèche, chaque produit étant affecté du signe indiqué dans le schéma suivant.

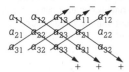

SCALAIRE   p. 166

Pour les physiciens, un scalaire est une quantité physique qui ne comporte qu'une grandeur. Pour les mathématiciens, un scalaire est un nombre.

SOUS-ESPACE VECTORIEL   p. 370

Un sous-espace vectoriel S d'un espace vectoriel V est un sous-ensemble non vide de V qui est aussi un espace vectoriel pour les opérations définies sur V.

SUPPORT D'UN VECTEUR   p. 168

Le support d'un vecteur est la droite qui porte ce vecteur.

SYSTÈME COMPATIBLE   p. 120

Un système d'équations linéaires est dit compatible si son ensemble solution est non vide, c'est-à-dire s'il admet au moins une solution.

SYSTÈME D'AXES DIRECT   p. 279

Un système d'axes direct est un système d'axes orienté selon la règle de la main droite.

SYSTÈME D'AXES RÉTROGRADE   p. 280

Un système d'axes rétrograde est un système d'axes orienté selon la règle de la main gauche au lieu de la règle de la main droite.

SYSTÈME GÉNÉRATEUR   p. 188 et   p. 373

Un ensemble de vecteurs est un système générateur d'un espace vectoriel si tout

vecteur de cet espace s'écrit comme une combinaison linéaire des vecteurs de l'ensemble.

SYSTÈME INCOMPATIBLE   p. 120

Un système d'équations linéaires est dit incompatible si son ensemble solution est vide, c'est-à-dire s'il n'admet aucune solution.

SYSTÈMES D'ÉQUATIONS ÉQUIVALENTS   p. 129

Deux systèmes d'équations linéaires sont équivalents s'ils ont exactement le même ensemble solution.

THÉORÈME   p. 16

Un théorème est une proposition générale qui découle de propositions déjà démontrées, de définitions ou d'axiomes.

TRACE   p. 8

La trace d'une matrice carrée d'ordre n, soit $A = \left[a_{ij} \right]_{n \times n}$, est la somme des éléments de la diagonale principale de A :

$$\text{Tr}(A) = \sum_{i=1}^{n} a_{ii}$$

TRANSLATION   p. 169

Une translation d'un objet géométrique est un déplacement rigide et parallèle de cet objet : chaque point de l'objet est déplacé sur une même distance et dans une même direction.

TRANSPOSÉE D'UNE MATRICE   p. 33

La transposée d'une matrice $A = \left[a_{ij} \right]_{m \times n}$ est la matrice $A^t = \left[a_{ji} \right]_{n \times m}$, obtenue en interchangeant les lignes et les colonnes de la matrice A.

VECTEUR   p. 166

Pour les physiciens, un vecteur est une quantité qui possède une grandeur et une direction.

VECTEUR ALGÉBRIQUE DU PLAN   p. 195

Un vecteur algébrique du plan est un vecteur exprimé sous forme algébrique (une matrice de format 1×2) à l'aide de ses composantes.

VECTEUR DIRECTEUR D'UNE DROITE   p. 227

Un vecteur directeur d'une droite est un vecteur $\vec{d}$ parallèle à cette droite.

VECTEUR GÉOMÉTRIQUE   p. 168

Un vecteur géométrique est un être
mathématique qui possède une grandeur
et une direction et qu'on peut représenter
géométriquement par un segment de droite
orienté (une flèche).

VECTEUR NORMAL   p. 232
À UNE DROITE

Un vecteur normal à une droite est un
vecteur $\vec{n}$ perpendiculaire à cette droite.

VECTEUR NORMAL À UN PLAN   p. 322

Un vecteur normal à un plan est
un vecteur perpendiculaire à ce plan.

VECTEUR NUL   p. 169

Le vecteur nul, noté $\vec{0}$, est un vecteur dont
le module vaut zéro. C'est le seul vecteur
dont la direction est indéterminée.

VECTEUR OPPOSÉ   p. 180

L'opposé d'un vecteur $\vec{u}$, noté $-\vec{u}$, est le
vecteur qui, additionné à $\vec{u}$, donne le
vecteur nul.

VECTEUR POSITION   p. 193

Le vecteur position, ou *rayon vecteur*, d'un
point X est le vecteur $\overrightarrow{OX}$ issu de l'origine
et dont l'extrémité est le point X.

VECTEUR RÉSULTANT   p. 172

Le vecteur résultant, ou la *résultante*, de
deux vecteurs $\vec{u}$ et $\vec{v}$ est la somme de ces
deux vecteurs, soit $\vec{u} + \vec{v}$.

VECTEURS COPLANAIRES   p. 278

Des vecteurs sont dits coplanaires s'ils
appartiennent à un même plan lorsqu'ils
sont issus d'une même origine.

VECTEURS LINÉAIREMENT   p. 184 et
DÉPENDANTS   p. 360

Des vecteurs $\vec{u_1}$, $\vec{u_2}$, ..., $\vec{u_n}$ sont
linéairement dépendants si et seulement
s'il existe une combinaison linéaire de
ces vecteurs égale au vecteur nul et telle
qu'au moins un des coefficients est
différent de zéro, c'est-à-dire s'il existe une
combinaison linéaire égale au vecteur nul
et différente de celle où tous les
coefficients sont nuls.

VECTEURS LINÉAIREMENT   p. 184 et
INDÉPENDANTS   p. 359

Des vecteurs $\vec{u_1}$, $\vec{u_2}$, ..., $\vec{u_n}$ sont dits
linéairement indépendants si et seulement
si *la seule* combinaison linéaire de ces
vecteurs qui soit égale au vecteur nul est
celle où tous les coefficients (ou scalaires)
sont nuls. De manière plus formelle, n
vecteurs $\vec{u_1}$, $\vec{u_2}$, ..., $\vec{u_n}$ sont dits
linéairement indépendants si et
seulement si

$$a_1 \vec{u_1} + a_2 \vec{u_2} + \cdots + a_n \vec{u_n} = \vec{0}$$
$$\Rightarrow \quad a_1 = 0, \ a_2 = 0, \ ..., \ a_n = 0$$

VECTEURS ORTHOGONAUX   p. 188 et
     p. 358

Deux vecteurs sont orthogonaux si
et seulement si leur produit scalaire est
zéro. Dans le plan ou l'espace, des
vecteurs orthogonaux non nuls sont
perpendiculaires.

VECTEUR UNITAIRE   p. 181

Un vecteur unitaire est un vecteur dont le
module (la longueur) vaut 1.

Bibliographie

ALRIC, Guy, *et al. Géométrie vectorielle*, Montréal, McGraw-Hill, 1969, 596 p.

ANTON, Howard et RORRES, Chris. *Elementary Linear Algebra: Applications Version*, 7e éd., New York, John Wiley & Sons, Inc., 1994, 779 p.

ASIMOV, Isaac. *Asimov on Numbers*, New York, Pocket Books, 1977, 286 p.

AUER, John W. *Linear Algebra with Applications*, Scarborough, Prentice-Hall Canada Inc., 1991, 548 p.

BALL, W. W. R. *A Short Account of the History of Mathematics*, New York, Dover Publications, Inc., 1960, 522 p.

BARNETT, Raymond A. et ZIEGLER, Michael R. *Finite Mathematics for Business, Economics, Life Sciences and Social Sciences*, Upper Saddle River, Prentice Hall, 1996, 705 p.

BARUK, Stella. *Dictionnaire de mathématiques élémentaires*, Paris, Éditions du Seuil, 1995, 1345 p.

BELHOSTE, Bruno. *Cauchy: Un mathématicien légitimiste au xixe siècle*, Paris, Belin, 1985, 224 p.

BELL, Eric Temple. *Men of Mathematics*, New York, Simon and Schuster, 1965, 590 p.

BENSON, Harris. *Physique 1: Mécanique*, Saint-Laurent, Éditions du Renouveau Pédagogique Inc., 1993, 428 p.

BLOUIN, Gérard, *et al. Algèbre linéaire et géométrie*, Chicoutimi, Gaëtan Morin, 1982, 371 p.

BOUVERESSE, Jacques, *et al. Histoire des mathématiques*, Paris, Larousse, 1977, 255 p.

BOYER, Carl B. *A History of Mathematics*, New York, John Wiley & Sons, 1968, 717 p.

BÜHLER, W. K. *Gauss: A Biographical Study*, New York, Springer-Verlag, 1981, 208 p.

CAJORI, Florian. *A History of Mathematical Notations*, New York, Dover Publications, Inc., 1993, 820 p.

CALAPRICE, Alice. *The Quotable Einstein*, Princeton, Princeton University Press, 1996, 269 p.

CHAMBADAL, Lucien. *Dictionnaire des mathématiques modernes*, 3e éd., Paris, Librairie Larousse, 1969, 255 p.

CHARRON, Gilles et PARENT, Pierre. *Mathématiques 105: Algèbre linéaire et vectorielle*, édition revue et corrigée, Laval, Éditions Études Vivantes, 1992, 428 p.

COLLETTE, Jean-Paul. *Histoire des mathématiques*, Montréal, Éditions du Renouveau Pédagogique Inc., 1979, 2 vol., 587 p.

CROWE, Michael J. *A History of Vector Analysis: The Evolution of the Idea of a Vectorial System*, New York, Dover Publications, Inc., 1994, 270 p.

CULLEN, Charles G. *Linear Algebra with Applications*, 2e éd., Reading, Addison Wesley Educational Publishers Inc., 1997, 494 p.

CULLEN, Michael R. *Mathematics for the Biosciences*, Boston, PWS-Kent, 1983, 712 p.

DAHAN-DALMEDICO, Amy et PEIFFER, Jeanne. *Une histoire des mathématiques: Routes et dédales*, Paris, Éditions du Seuil, 1986, 309 p.

EDWARDS, C. Henry et PENNEY, David E. *Calculus with Analytic Geometry: Early Transcendentals*, 5e éd., Upper Saddle River, Prentice-Hall, 1998, 1022 p.

Encylopædia Universalis. « Dictionnaire des mathématiques: algèbre, analyse, géométrie », Paris, Albin Michel, 1997, 889 p.

FRALEIGH, John B. et BEAUREGARD, Raymond A. *Linear Algebra*, 3e éd., Reading, Addison-Wesley, 1995, 576 p.

FRIEDBERG, Stephen H. et INSEL, Arnold J. *Introduction to Linear Algebra with Applications*, Englewood Cliffs, Prentice-Hall, 1986, 557 p.

GROSSMAN, Stanley I. *Elementary Linear Algebra*, 4e éd., Philadelphie, Saunders College Publishing, 1991, 503 p.

JAMES, Glenn et JAMES, Robert C. *Mathematics Dictionary*, 4e éd., New York, Van Nostrand Reinhold Company, 1976, 509 p.

JOHNSON, Mildred. *How to Solve Word Problems in Algebra*, édition revue et corrigée, New York, McGraw-Hill, 1992, 166 p.

KATZ, Victor J. *A History of Mathematics: An Introduction*, 2e éd., Reading, Addison-Wesley, 1998, 862 p.

KENSCHAFT, Patricia Clark. *Linear Mathematics: A Practical Approach*, New York, Worth Publishers, Inc., 1978, 392 p.

KLINE, Morris. *Mathematical Thought from Ancient to Modern Times*, New York, Oxford University Press, 1972, 1238 p.

KOLMAN, Bernard. *Introductory Linear Algebra with Applications*, 5e éd., New York, Macmillan Publishing Company, 1993, 619 p.

KREYSZIG, Erwin. *Advanced Engineering Mathematics*, 7e éd., New York, John Wiley & Sons, Inc., 1993, 1271 p.

LACASSE, Raynald et LALIBERTÉ, Jules. *Algèbre linéaire*, Sherbrooke, Loze-Dion éditeur Inc., 1991, 293 p.

LAWSON, Terry. *Linear Algebra*, New York, John Wiley & Sons, Inc., 1996, 408 p.

LAY, David C. *Linear Algebra and its Applications*, Reading, Addison-Wesley, 1996, 445 p.

LE LIONNAIS, François, *et al. Dictionnaire des mathématiques*, Paris, Presses Universitaires de France, 1979, 832 p.

LEROUX, Pierre. *Algèbre linéaire : une approche matricielle*, Outremont, Modulo Éditeur, 1983, 500 p.

LOWMAN, Pauline et STOKES, Joseph. *Introduction to Linear Algebra*, San Diego, Harcourt Brace Jovanovich, 1991, 464 p.

MILLAR, David, *et al. The Cambridge Dictionary of Scientists*, Cambridge, Cambridge University Press, 1996, 387 p.

MORITZ, Robert Edouard. *On Mathematics : A Collection of Witty, Profound, Amusing Passages about Mathematics and Mathematicians*, New York, Dover Publications, Inc., 1942, 410 p.

MUIR, Thomas. *The Theory of Determinants in the Historical Order of Development*, New York, Dover Publications, Inc., vol. 1, 1960, 480 p.

NOBLE, Ben. *Applied Linear Algebra*, Englewood Cliffs, Prentice-Hall Inc., 1969, 523 p.

OSEN, Lynn M. *Women in Mathematics*, Cambridge, MIT Press, 1974, 185 p.

OUELLET, Gilles. *Algèbre linéaire : vecteurs et géométrie*, Sainte-Foy, Les Éditions Le Griffon d'argile, 1994, 476 p.

PAGOULATOS, K., éd. *Petite encyclopédie des mathématiques*, Paris, 1980, 828 p.

PAPILLON, Vincent. *Vecteurs, matrices et nombres complexes*, Mont-Royal, Modulo Éditeur, 1993, 387 p.

PENNEY, Richard C. *Linear Algebra : Ideas and Applications*, New York, John Wiley & Sons, 1998, 382 p.

PORTER, Roy, éd. *The Hutchison Dictionary of Scientific Biography*, Oxford, Helicon, 1994, 891 p.

REBIÈRE, A. *Mathématiques et mathématiciens : pensées et curiosités*, Paris, Librairie Nony & Cie, 1898, 566 p.

REINHARDT, Fritz et SOEDER, Heinrich. *Atlas de mathématiques*, Paris, Le Livre de Poche, 1997, 502 p.

ROBERTS, A. Wayne. *Elementary Linear Algebra*, Menlo Park, The Benjamin/Cummings Publishing Company Inc., 1982, 390 p.

ROMAN, Steven. *An Introduction to Linear Algebra with Applications*, Philadelphia, Saunders College Publishing, 1985, 493 p.

SMITH, David Eugene. *History of Mathematics*, New York, Dover publications, Inc., 1958, 2 vol., 1299 p.

STEWART, James, *et al. Algèbre et géométrie*, Montréal, Guérin, 1993, 503 p.

STRUIK, David. *A Concise History of Mathematics*, New York, Dover Publications, Inc., 1967, 195 p.

SWETZ, F. J., éd. *From Five Fingers to Infinity : A Journey through the History of Mathematics*, Chicago, Open Court, 1994, 770 p.

VENIT, Stewart et BISHOP, Wayne. *Elementary Linear Algebra*, 3e éd., Boston, PWS-Kent, 1989, 462 p.

WANER, Stefan et COSTENOBLE, Steven R. *Finite Mathematics Applied to the Real World*, New York, Harper Collins, 1996, 739 p.

WELLS, David. *The Penguin Book of Curious and Interesting Mathematics*, Londres, Penguin Books, 1997, 319 p.

WILLIAMS, Gareth. *Computational Linear Algebra with Models*, 2e éd., Boston, Allyn and Bacon, Inc., 1978, 480 p.

Index